Lecture Notes in Computer Science   16125

Founding Editors

Gerhard Goos
Juris Hartmanis

Editorial Board Members

Elisa Bertino, *Purdue University, West Lafayette, IN, USA*
Wen Gao, *Peking University, Beijing, China*
Bernhard Steffen, *TU Dortmund University, Dortmund, Germany*
Moti Yung, *Columbia University, New York, NY, USA*

The series Lecture Notes in Computer Science (LNCS), including its subseries Lecture Notes in Artificial Intelligence (LNAI) and Lecture Notes in Bioinformatics (LNBI), has established itself as a medium for the publication of new developments in computer science and information technology research, teaching, and education.

LNCS enjoys close cooperation with the computer science R & D community, the series counts many renowned academics among its volume editors and paper authors, and collaborates with prestigious societies. Its mission is to serve this international community by providing an invaluable service, mainly focused on the publication of conference and workshop proceedings and postproceedings. LNCS commenced publication in 1973.

Margret Keuper · Francesco Locatello
Editors

Pattern Recognition

47th DAGM German Conference, DAGM GCPR 2025
Freiburg, Germany, September 23–26, 2025
Proceedings

 Springer

Editors
Margret Keuper
University of Mannheim
Mannheim, Germany

Francesco Locatello
Institute of Science and Technology Austria
Klosterneuburg, Austria

ISSN 0302-9743   ISSN 1611-3349 (electronic)
Lecture Notes in Computer Science
ISBN 978-3-032-12839-3   ISBN 978-3-032-12840-9 (eBook)
https://doi.org/10.1007/978-3-032-12840-9

This Springer imprint is published by the registered company Springer Nature Switzerland AG
The registered company address is: Gewerbestrasse 11, 6330 Cham, Switzerland

If disposing of this product, please recycle the paper.

Preface

On behalf of the organizers, we are delighted to present the proceedings of DAGM GCPR 2025, the 47th annual conference of the German Association for Pattern Recognition (DAGM). This year's conference took place from September 23 to 26, 2025, at the University of Freiburg, Germany.

As the leading national symposium on pattern recognition, computer vision, machine learning, and data visualization, DAGM GCPR continues to reflect the vibrant research landscape in these fields. The conference featured a broad spectrum of topics, from deep learning applications and autonomous driving to medical imaging. With increasing emphasis on the benefit of foundation models, discussions this year frequently touched upon critical challenges for their use in real-world systems. In this context, explainability, robustness, and performance guarantees in AI have remained central research objectives.

In addition to the core sessions, the conference program offered a tutorial on "AI Agents" organized by Peter Gehler and Matthias Kümmerer (University of Tübingen, Tübingen AI Center), including a hands-on session. An Industry Fair complemented the conference, providing a platform for collaboration between academia and industry.

We were honored to host five distinguished keynote speakers, listed here in the chronological order of the given keynotes: Venkatesh Babu Radhakrishnan (Indian Institute of Science (IISc), Bangalore), Alex Kolesnikov (Meta), Dima Damen (University of Bristol and Google DeepMind), Stefanie Jegelka (MIT EECS and TU Munich), and Efstratios Gavves (University of Amsterdam and Ellogon.AI).

This year, we received **85** paper submissions, out of which **12** were selected for oral presentation and **28** for poster presentations, with a **47%** acceptance rate. We extend our thanks to the program committee members and external reviewers for their thorough and constructive reviews. Additionally, the nectar track provided an opportunity for researchers to present their recently published work to a broader audience, fostering cross-pollination of ideas.

This year's awards were presented as follows:

- **DAGM Best Paper Award**: "CoProU-VO: Combining Projected Uncertainty for End-to-End Unsupervised Monocular Visual Odometry" by Jingchao Xie, Oussema Dhaouadi, Weirong Chen, Johannes Meier, Jacques Kaiser, and Daniel Cremers.
- **Honorable Mentions:**

  - "MCUCoder: Adaptive Bitrate Learned Video Compression for IoT Devices" by Ali Hojjat, Janek Haberer, and Olaf Landsiedel.
  - "Unlocking In-Context Learning for Natural Datasets Beyond Language Modelling" by Jelena Bratulić, Sudhanshu Mittal, David Hoffmann, Samuel Böhm, Robin Schirrmeister, Tonio Ball, Christian Rupprecht, and Thomas Brox.

The **German Pattern Recognition Award** was presented to Jonas Geiping for his outstanding scientific contributions in the area of safety, security, and efficiency in modern pattern recognition, and to Jan-Eric Lenssen for his outstanding scientific contributions in the area of geometric deep learning, graph neural networks, and 3D representation learning.

The **DAGM MVTec Dissertation Award** was awarded to Paul-Edouard Salin (ETH Zürich) for his thesis "On Learning and Geometry for Visual Localization and Mapping", while the **DAGM Best Master's Thesis Award** went to Oleh Kuzyk (ETH Zürich) for his outstanding work on "Visualize Your Recipe".

We would like to express our sincere gratitude to the local organizing team at the University of Freiburg, in particular to the General Chairs Thomas Brox and Abhinav Valada and the numerous volunteers whose efforts were key to making this year's edition a success. A special thank you goes to our sponsors Carl Zeiss AG and Black Forest Labs (Gold Sponsors) and the Tübingen AI Center (Organizer and sponsor of Industry Meetup) for their generous support, which helps foster innovation in machine learning, computer vision, and artificial intelligence.

We look forward to seeing you again at next year's edition of DAGM-GCPR (to be held jointly with VMV).

September 2025

Margret Keuper
Francesco Locatello

Organization

General Chairs

Thomas Brox	University of Freiburg, Germany
Abhinav Valada	University of Freiburg, Germany

Program Chairs

Margret Keuper	University of Mannheim and Max Planck Institute for Informatics, Saarland Informatics Campus, Germany
Francesco Locatello	Institute of Science and Technology Austria, Austria

Special Track Chairs

Pattern Recognition in the Life and Natural Sciences

Joachim Denzler	University of Jena, Germany
Xiaoyi Jiang	University of Münster, Germany

Photogrammetry and Remote Sensing

Helmut Mayer	University of the Bundeswehr Munich, Germany
Uwe Sörgel	University of Stuttgart, Germany
Ribana Roscher	University of Bonn, Germany

Computer Vision Systems and Applications

Bodo Rosenhahn	Leibniz University Hannover, Germany

Contents

Machine Learning Methods

Applications of Foundation Models

Safety and Robustness

3D Perception and Reconstruction

Photogrammetry and Remote Sensing

Computer Vision Systems
and Applications

Box it and Track it: A Weakly Supervised Framework for Cell Tracking

Nabeel Khalid[1,2]([✉])[iD], Mohammadmahdi Koochali[1]([✉])[iD], Khola Naseem[1,2][iD], Gillian Lovell[4][iD], Bianca Migliori[5][iD], Daniel A. Porto[5][iD], Johan Trygg[3,6][iD], Andreas Dengel[1,2][iD], and Sheraz Ahmed[1][iD]

[1] German Research Center for Artificial Intelligence (DFKI) GmbH, Kaiserslautern 67663, Germany
{nabeel.khalid,mohammadmahdi.koochali,khola.naseem,
andreas.dengel,sheraz.ahmed}@dfki.de
[2] RPTU Kaiserslautern–Landau, Kaiserslautern 67663, Germany
[3] Sartorius Corporate Research, Umeå, Sweden
[4] Sartorius, BioAnalytics, Royston, United Kingdom
[5] Sartorius, BioAnalytics, Ann Arbor, United States
{bianca.migliori,daniel.porto}@sartorius.com
[6] Computational Life Science Cluster (CLiC), Umeå University, Umeå, Sweden

Abstract. Accurate cell tracking in microscopy is essential for studying biological dynamics like proliferation and migration. Traditional fully supervised methods demand dense pixel-wise masks for every frame, making them impractical for large-scale use. Recent methods like SAT reduce annotation effort by using sparse point-based supervision, but still require multiple positive and negative points per cell, which remains labor-intensive. BoxTrack offers a lightweight and annotation-efficient alternative, requiring only a single bounding box per cell in the first frame. Without relying on any point-level annotations, it performs end-to-end instance segmentation and tracking over entire sequences. This simplification leads to a substantial reduction in annotation cost while improving performance over SAT. On the CTMC dataset, BoxTrack improves Multiple Object Tracking Accuracy (MOTA) by +**15.96%** over SAT. For the CTC dataset, it yields a +**8.86%** MOTA gain. Code is available at https://github.com/nabeelkhalid92/Box-it-Track-it.

Keywords: Microscopy · Cell Tracking · Segment Anything · Weak Supervision · Temporal Downsampling · Deep Learning

---

N. Khalid and M. Koochali—These authors contributed equally to this work.

M. Keuper and F. Locatello (Eds.): DAGM GCPR 2025, LNCS 16125, pp. 3–17, 2026.
https://doi.org/10.1007/978-3-032-12840-9_1

1   Introduction

Accurate cell tracking in microscopy is essential for understanding dynamic biological processes such as proliferation, migration, and cell-cell interactions [19, 20,28]. It enables researchers to quantify cellular behaviors over time and plays a central role in studying wound healing, cancer metastasis, immune response, and drug screening [5,19]. Traditional cell tracking pipelines are heavily based on fully supervised instance segmentation frameworks [5,12,24,26,28], requiring dense pixel-wise annotations for every frame in a sequence. However, generating such exhaustive labels is prohibitively expensive, especially for high-throughput imaging settings where manual annotation becomes the bottleneck. This has motivated the emergence of weakly supervised approaches [4,10,27] that aim to reduce annotation costs without sacrificing tracking performance.

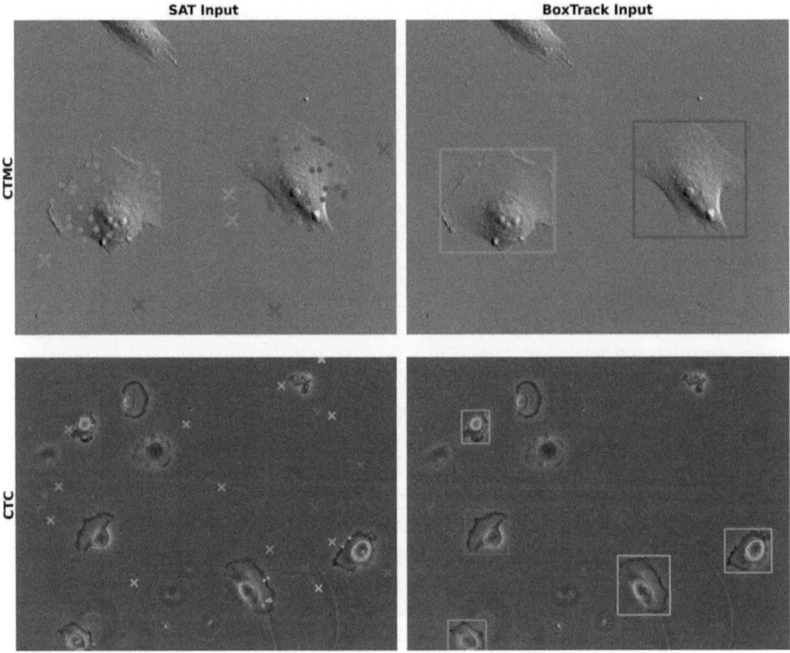

Fig. 1. Comparison of annotation inputs required by SAT and BoxTrack on the first frame of sequences from the CTMC and CTC datasets. SAT relies on dense point-level supervision: 30 positive points (•) and 3 negative points (×) per cell for CTMC, and 6 positive (•) and 3 negative (×) per cell for CTC. In contrast, BoxTrack requires only a single bounding box per cell in the first frame. Despite this drastic reduction in manual effort, BoxTrack achieves **+15.96** MOTA improvement on CTMC and **+8.86** on CTC over SAT.

One such method is SAT (Segment and Track Anything) [10], which proposes an efficient pipeline using sparse point-based supervision in only the first frame.

Specifically, SAT requires annotating both positive points (inside each cell) and negative points (background) to guide segmentation and tracking. Despite its annotation efficiency compared to fully supervised pipelines, SAT still involves considerable manual effort, particularly for dense or large-scale datasets where each cell demands multiple annotated points.

This work introduces **BoxTrack**, a simplified yet highly effective tracking framework that eliminates the need for point-based supervision. BoxTrack relies solely on bounding box annotations in the first frame of each sequence—one box per cell—and leverages modern segmentation and tracking mechanisms to propagate this minimal supervision across the full sequence. This approach significantly reduces annotation overhead, making it highly scalable and well-suited for large microscopy datasets.

Figure 1 compares the annotation burden of SAT and BoxTrack on CTMC [1] and CTC [28]. SAT requires 30 positive ($\bullet$) and 3 negative ($\times$) points per cell for CTMC, and 6 positive plus 3 negative points for CTC. BoxTrack, in contrast, uses only one bounding box per cell in the first frame. Despite this simplification, it achieves a MOTA improvement of **15.96%** on CTMC and **8.86%** on CTC, highlighting box-level supervision as an efficient and scalable alternative for cell tracking in microscopy. Removing the need for point-level labels enables broader applicability in biomedical workflows and large-scale screening. The main contributions of this work are as follows:

- **BoxTrack**: a weakly supervised cell tracking framework using only one bounding box per cell in the first frame.
- Achieves over 6× annotation savings compared to SAT [10], with improved tracking accuracy.
- Outperforms SAT with MOTA gains of **15.96%** (CTMC) and **8.86%** (CTC).
- Generalizes across imaging modalities and cell types (DeepCell results).
- Maintains strong performance under reduced scan frequency, supporting long-term imaging up to 60-minute intervals.

The remainder of the paper is organized as follows: Sect. 2 reviews related work with a focus on weakly supervised cell tracking. Section 3 details the Box-Track framework. Section 4 describes the evaluation datasets (CTMC, CTC, DeepCell), and Sect. 5 outlines the experimental setup. Section 6 reports the results and analysis. Section 7 concludes with key takeaways and future directions for scalable tracking.

2 Related Work

2.1 Cell Tracking and Segmentation

Cell tracking is vital for analyzing proliferation, migration, and interactions [5, 28]. Traditional segmentation-first methods [8,11–13,24,26] require dense labels and struggle to generalize without retraining. Recent models like Trackastra [6], CellTrack R-CNN [3], and SC-Track [17] integrate tracking and segmentation, improving lineage accuracy but still demand high supervision. This highlights the need for scalable, annotation-efficient tracking approaches.

2.2 Weakly Supervised Approaches

Weakly supervised methods have emerged to reduce the annotation burden while preserving accuracy. Point-supervised models [9,14] and box-based techniques [7] offer lighter alternatives to full masks. However, they often depend on pre-trained backbones or complex post-processing, limiting adaptability. Segment and Track Anything (SAT) [10] reduces the labeling per frame by using positive and negative points in the first frame to track cells over time. While efficient, SAT still requires around 30 clicks per cell and can struggle in crowded or noisy settings, where point placement and boundary precision become critical.

2.3 Challenges in Microscopy

Microscopy data presents unique challenges not seen in natural images, including low contrast, diverse modalities (e.g., fluorescence, phase contrast), and densely packed or overlapping cells [25,30,32]. General-purpose models such as YOLO [29] and SAM [15] require significant adaptation to perform reliably in biomedical settings. In addition, long sequences with cell division or morphological changes complicate the tracking. Although domain-specific models such as Trackastra [6] improve performance through customized designs, they still rely on dense supervision and often lack generalizability across modalities.

2.4 Need for BoxTrack

While weak supervision has reduced annotation costs, existing approaches often trade off accuracy or require dense point-level input, which becomes impractical in crowded cell environments. To address this, we introduce *BoxTrack*-a simple yet effective tracking framework that requires only a single bounding box per cell in the first frame. It avoids reliance on point annotations, segmentation masks, or modality-specific tuning, instead leveraging a unified detection-based strategy to track cells across time.

As shown in Fig. 1, BoxTrack drastically lowers annotation effort while outperforming SAT on CTMC and CTC benchmarks, demonstrating that minimal supervision can achieve both accuracy and cross-modal generalizability.

3 BoxTrack: The Proposed Approach

BoxTrack is a zero-shot, inference-only framework for cell segmentation and tracking in microscopy sequences. It requires a single bounding-box prompt per cell in the first frame and generalizes effectively across diverse cell cultures and imaging conditions without retraining. BoxTrack consists of two main modules, as visualized in Fig. 2: the **Segmentation Module** (purple), responsible for generating per-frame mask proposals, and the **Tracking Module** (green), which links these proposals across frames to form consistent trajectories.

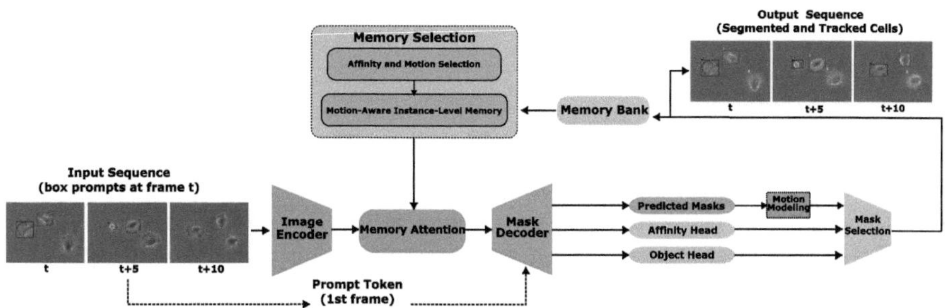

Fig. 2. Overview of the BoxTrack pipeline. Given a video and bounding-box prompts per cell in the first frame only, the **Segmentation Module (purple)** uses a frozen SAM2 backbone [22] to produce object tokens and mask proposals. These feed into the **Tracking Module (green)**, where Motion Modeling with a Kalman filter predicts spatial movement, and a memory-aware scoring mechanism selects the final ID-annotated masks and trajectories [31]. (Color figure online)

3.1   Segmentation Module

The Segmentation Module leverages a frozen backbone derived from SAM2 [22], pretrained on the extensive SA-V dataset. For architectural details of SAM2, including its Image Encoder and prompt fusion design, we refer the reader to the original paper. This module produces object tokens, intermediate masks, and bounding boxes in each frame. As shown in Fig. 2, it comprises the **Prompt Encoder**, **Image Encoder**, **Memory Attention** block, and **Mask Decoder**, which operate sequentially to extract and refine segmentation features.

In the first frame I_1 of a microscopy sequence $V = \{I_1, I_2, \ldots, I_T\}$, bounding boxes $\{b_i^1\}_{i=1}^N$ are annotated to initialize tracking. These provide explicit spatial cues for each cell. A lightweight **Prompt Encoder** converts the bounding boxes into sparse object-specific embeddings $\mathbf{P}_0$:

$$\mathbf{P}_0 = \mathrm{PromptEncoder}(b_1^1, \ldots, b_N^1). \tag{1}$$

These embeddings encapsulate positional and visual context and guide the segmentation process.

Each frame I_t is processed by the frozen **Image Encoder** to extract spatial visual features:

$$\mathbf{F}_t = \mathrm{ImageEncoder}(I_t), \quad \mathbf{F}_t \in \mathbb{R}^{H \times W \times C}, \tag{2}$$

where H and W denote spatial resolution and C the number of feature channels.

The extracted features $\mathbf{F}_t$ are fused with prompt embeddings $\mathbf{P}_0$ and memory tokens from the previous frame, selected by the Tracking Module via the **Memory Attention** block. This fusion incorporates temporal context for refinement. The result is passed to the **Mask Decoder** to generate object tokens $\mathbf{z}_i^t$ and corresponding segmentation masks $\hat{M}_i^t$:

$$\hat{M}_i^t, \mathbf{z}_i^t = \mathrm{MaskDecoder}(\mathbf{P}_0, \mathbf{F}_t, \mathrm{MemoryAttention}). \tag{3}$$

Bounding boxes $\hat{b}_i^t$ are derived from these masks and forwarded to the tracking stage.

3.2   Tracking Module

The Tracking Module links segmentation proposals across frames to ensure temporal consistency, especially in the presence of occlusions and densely packed cells [31]. It consists of two main components: a **Motion Modeling** block, implemented using a **Kalman Filter**, and a **Memory-Aware Mask Selection** block. The **Motion Modeling** block predicts the expected position of each cell in the next frame using the bounding box $\hat{b}_i^{t-1}$ from the previous frame:

$$\tilde{b}_i^t = \text{KalmanPredict}(\hat{b}_i^{t-1}). \tag{4}$$

This prediction serves as a motion prior to reduce association ambiguity by constraining the search space.

Unlike SAM2 [22], which maintains memory internally within the segmentation stream using a fixed-size window (typically 7 frames) and a First-In, First-Out (FIFO) policy that discards the oldest frame regardless of quality, BoxTrack separates memory handling into the Tracking Module. This decoupling enables more flexible and robust memory management. Specifically, when a high-quality candidate is identified, it is added to the memory bank if space is available. If the memory is full, the stored frame with the lowest combined confidence score-recorded at the time of insertion-is evicted and replaced. This score-based replacement strategy actively curates memory content and improves resilience to appearance changes and occlusions, offering a key advantage over FIFO-based approaches.

The memory tokens selected by this process are fed into the Segmentation Module's **Memory Attention** block, enriching it with temporally relevant information for the next frame's prediction.

To determine which mask proposals to retain, the **Memory-Aware Mask Selection** block computes a confidence score s_i^t for each candidate by combining three components:

The **Affinity Score**, measuring token similarity across frames:

$$s_{a,i}^t = \cos(\mathbf{z}_i^t, \mathbf{z}_i^{t-1}), \tag{5}$$

The **Motion Score**, evaluating mask overlap between consecutive frames:

$$s_{m,i}^t = \text{IoU}(\hat{M}_i^t, \hat{M}_i^{t-1}), \tag{6}$$

and the **Objectness Score**, estimated from the current object token via a small multi-layer perceptron (MLP) followed by sigmoid activation:

$$s_{o,i}^t = \sigma(\text{MLP}(\mathbf{z}_i^t)). \tag{7}$$

These are aggregated into a final score:

$$s_i^t = \lambda_a s_{a,i}^t + \lambda_m s_{m,i}^t + \lambda_o s_{o,i}^t, \quad \text{where } \lambda_a + \lambda_m + \lambda_o = 1. \tag{8}$$

The proposal with the highest s_i^t is retained, and its object token is stored in memory for use in the next frame. For each time step, the selected segmentation masks $\hat{M}_i^t$ are assigned persistent track IDs, yielding the **final output** of BoxTrack: a temporally linked sequence of instance segmentation masks across the video.

4   Datasets

BoxTrack builds on a segmentation backbone derived from SAM2 [22], trained on the SA-V dataset comprising 50.9K videos and 35.5M instance masks across 642K masklets.

Evaluation is performed on three microscopy benchmarks. The CTMC dataset [1] includes 86 videos from 14 cell lines; 22 sequences are selected to represent diverse imaging conditions. The CTC dataset [18] provides 2D/3D time-lapse sequences acquired using Bright Field, Phase Contrast, and DIC microscopy. Four 2D sequences are used, totaling 8,017 frames with an average of 33.12 cells per frame. The DeepCell dataset [21] offers 12 test sequences comprising 617 frames and 99,550 annotated cells, enabling evaluation across dense nuclear environments.

In contrast to prior SAM-based methods such as SAT [10], which require supervised training on microscopy data (e.g., LIVECell [5]), BoxTrack operates in a training-free manner using only a single bounding box per cell-demonstrating high generalization with minimal supervision.

5   Experimental Setup

BoxTrack is evaluated under four experimental settings. The *Wide-Ranging Cell Types (CTMC)* setting uses 22 sequences from the CTMC dataset [1] to benchmark BoxTrack against SAT across diverse cell morphologies and motion behaviors. BoxTrack achieves higher tracking accuracy while requiring significantly fewer annotations. The *Multi-Modality Imaging (CTC)* setting includes 2D sequences from the CTC dataset [18], spanning Phase Contrast, Bright Field, and Fluorescent modalities. Here too, BoxTrack consistently outperforms SAT under varying imaging conditions. The *Fluorescent Nuclear Tracking (DeepCell)* setting involves 12 sequences (617 frames, 99,550 annotated cells) from the Deep-Cell test set [21], testing generalization across acquisition protocols and nuclear appearances. The *Temporal Downsampling* setting subsamples CTMC sequences at intervals up to 60 min to evaluate performance with sparse temporal input. Unlike SAT, which is fine-tuned on LIVECell [5], BoxTrack operates without retraining and uses only a single bounding box per cell in the first frame. Performance is evaluated using standard MOT metrics [2,16,23], including MOTA (Multi-Object Tracking Accuracy), IDF1 (ID-based F1 score), IDS (identity switches), MT (mostly tracked), and ML (mostly lost). For MOTA and related formulas, please refer to [2]. For mathematical definitions, including the MOTA formula, we refer readers to the original CLEAR MOT paper [2].

All experiments were carried out with Python 3.10, PyTorch 2.3.1, and TorchVision 0.18.1. The segmentation backbone (SAM2.1-hiera-large) is used in inference-only mode.

5.1   Multi-cell Type Tracking (CTMC)

The CTMC dataset [1] comprises 22 sequences from diverse cell lines exhibiting diverse morphologies, densities, and motion patterns. This setting assesses generalization across varied biological conditions. As shown in Table 1, Box-Track consistently outperforms SAT in both MOTA and IDF1, with substantial gains observed in sequences like `BPAE-run05` (+56.13% MOTA) and `A-10-run05` (+19.74% MOTA). While SAT occasionally reports higher IDF1 (e.g., `CRE-BAG2-run03`), BoxTrack demonstrates more stable overall tracking performance.

5.2   Multi-modality Imaging (CTC)

This setting uses 2D sequences from the CTC dataset [18], spanning Phase Contrast, Bright Field, and Fluorescent microscopy. It evaluates robustness across distinct imaging modalities. Table 2 shows that BoxTrack outperforms SAT across all sequences in MOTA and IDF1. Notable gains are seen in `PhC-C2DH-U373` (01) and `Fluo-N2DH-GOWT1`, with reduced Mostly Lost rates further indicating improved temporal consistency under modality shifts.

5.3   Multi-culture Nuclear Imaging (DeepCell)

The DeepCell DynamicNuclearNet dataset [21] contains fluorescent nuclear images from multiple mammalian cell cultures, introducing variation in nuclear density, shape, and arrangement. This setting tests generalization to unseen visual and biological characteristics. BoxTrack achieves a MOTA of 82.95 and IDF1 of 87.17 without retraining (Table 3), highlighting its robustness in dense nuclear tracking tasks.

5.4   Temporal Resolution Sensitivity (CTMC-Frequency)

This setting evaluates the impact of scan interval length using sub-sampled CTMC sequences. The original acquisition rate of one frame every 30 s is progressively reduced up to one frame every 60 min. As shown in Fig. 3, MOTA gradually declines from 72.01% at 1-min intervals to 55.93% at 60 min. Despite the drop in temporal density, BoxTrack maintains strong performance, demonstrating resilience in low-frequency or long-term imaging conditions.

Table 1. Comparison of BoxTrack and SAT across CTMC dataset. Bold indicates better performance per metric. BoxTrack uses bounding box annotations denoted by ß, while SAT uses point supervision denoted by $P(X)$, where X is the number of annotated points per cell.

Sequence	Supervision		MOTA (%)↑		IDF1 (%) ↑		IDS ↓		MT (%) ↑		ML (%) ↓	
	BoxTrack	SAT	BoxTrack	SAT	BoxTrack	SAT	BoxTrack	SAT	BoxTrack	SAT	BoxTrack	SAT
3T3-run03	ß	$P(18)$	**93.01**	61.49	**88.72**	87.50	2.00	**0.00**	100.00	100.00	0.00	0.00
A-10-run01	ß	$P(23)$	**83.67**	80.78	**91.82**	90.56	0.00	0.00	80.00	80.00	0.00	0.00
A-10-run05	ß	$P(33)$	**99.70**	79.96	**99.85**	95.56	0.00	0.00	100.00	100.00	0.00	0.00
A-10-run07	ß	$P(23)$	**93.87**	77.81	**96.94**	91.25	0.00	0.00	85.71	85.71	0.00	0.00
A-549-run03	ß	$P(28)$	**89.13**	57.51	79.39	**82.00**	2.00	**0.00**	88.89	88.89	0.00	0.00
BPAE-run05	ß	$P(33)$	**82.50**	26.37	**81.16**	77.14	3.00	**0.00**	100.00	100.00	0.00	0.00
CRE-BAG2-run03	ß	$P(23)$	**46.22**	36.62	62.45	**72.41**	1.00	**0.00**	60.00	60.00	6.67	6.67
LLC-MK2-run01	ß	$P(33)$	**76.49**	54.28	68.67	**80.65**	1.00	**0.00**	75.00	75.00	0.00	0.00
LLC-MK2-run02a	ß	$P(33)$	**92.61**	60.06	**95.46**	83.87	1.00	**0.00**	100.00	100.00	0.00	0.00
LLC-MK2-run03	ß	$P(28)$	**96.40**	96.18	**98.20**	98.11	0.00	0.00	100.00	100.00	0.00	0.00
APM-run05	ß	$P(28)$	43.79	**61.85**	69.59	**82.38**	1.00	**0.00**	50.00	**75.00**	0.00	0.00
LLC-MK2-run07	ß	$P(18)$	**77.32**	73.72	**88.66**	88.65	0.00	0.00	77.78	77.78	0.00	0.00
MDBK-run03	ß	$P(28)$	**87.11**	69.76	**93.68**	86.00	0.00	0.00	82.35	82.35	0.00	0.00
MDBK-run09	ß	$P(23)$	**79.77**	53.28	**89.89**	85.88	2.00	**0.00**	80.00	80.00	0.00	0.00
MDOK-run07	ß	$P(18)$	**100.00**	99.80	**100.00**	99.80	0.00	0.00	100.00	100.00	0.00	0.00
OK-run01	ß	$P(18)$	**81.52**	60.94	**90.68**	85.39	0.00	0.00	80.00	80.00	0.00	0.00
OK-run05	ß	$P(33)$	**87.11**	65.11	**93.56**	91.30	0.00	0.00	100.00	100.00	0.00	0.00
OK-run07	ß	$P(18)$	**70.78**	19.52	**85.39**	72.22	0.00	0.00	68.75	68.75	0.00	0.00
PL1Ut-run05	ß	$P(33)$	**99.46**	93.13	**99.73**	96.55	0.00	0.00	100.00	100.00	0.00	0.00
RK-13-run03	ß	$P(33)$	**85.83**	65.11	85.67	85.67	2.00	**0.00**	85.71	85.71	0.00	0.00
U2O-S-run03	ß	$P(28)$	**81.55**	76.58	**90.77**	85.00	0.00	0.00	75.00	75.00	0.00	0.00
U2O-S-run05	ß	$P(33)$	**57.74**	54.44	78.87	**84.62**	0.00	0.00	62.50	62.50	0.00	0.00
Average	–	–	**82.79**	66.83	**87.91**	86.36	0.61	**0.00**	86.28	**86.79**	0.29	0.29

Table 2. Comparison of BoxTrack and SAT across CTC dataset. Bold indicates better performance per metric. BoxTrack uses bounding box annotations denoted by ß, while SAT uses point supervision denoted by $P(X)$, where X is the number of annotated points per cell.

Sequence	Supervision		MOTA (%) ↑		IDF1 (%) ↑		IDS ↓		MT (%) ↑		ML (%) ↓	
	BoxTrack	SAT	BoxTrack	SAT	BoxTrack	SAT	BoxTrack	SAT	BoxTrack	SAT	BoxTrack	SAT
PhC-C2DH-U373 (01)	ß	$P(9)$	**100.00**	79.82	**100.00**	89.00	0.00	0.00	**100.00**	71.43	0.00	0.00
PhC-C2DH-U373 (02)	ß	$P(9)$	**85.71**	82.75	**93.33**	91.94	0.00	0.00	100.00	100.00	0.00	0.00
Fluo-N2DH-GOWT1	ß	$P(6)$	**97.81**	88.24	**98.91**	91.20	0.00	0.00	**91.67**	79.17	**0.00**	8.34
Fluo-N2DH-SIM+	ß	$P(6)$	**85.79**	83.03	**90.44**	88.73	0.00	0.00	**83.84**	83.34	0.00	0.00
Average	–	–	**92.32**	83.46	**95.67**	90.22	**0.00**	0.00	**93.87**	83.45	0.00	2.08

Table 3. Overall performance of BoxTrack-SAT on the DeepCell tracking dataset.

Method	MOTA (%) ↑	IDF1 (%) ↑	IDS ↓	MT (%) ↑	ML (%) ↓
BoxTrack-SAT	82.95	87.17	15.67	68.67	19.13

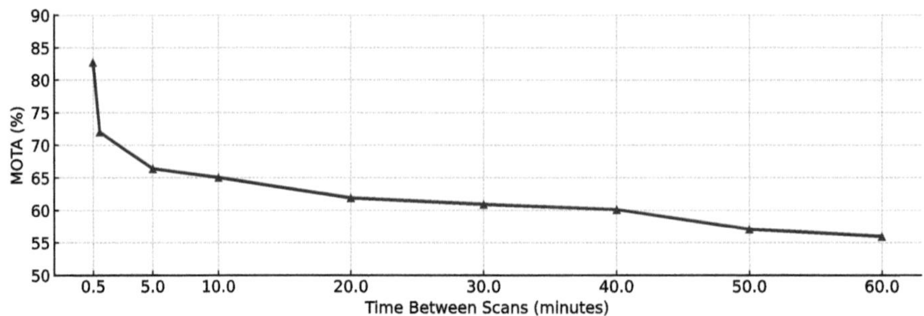

Fig. 3. Tracking performance (MOTA) of BoxTrack across different temporal intervals on CTMC.

6   Analysis and Discussion

This section evaluates the effectiveness of BoxTrack across four experimental settings, each reflecting distinct challenges in microscopy-based cell tracking.

6.1   CTMC: Cell Line Diversity and Tracking Generalization

The Multi-Cell Type Tracking setting used 22 sequences from diverse cell lines in the CTMC dataset. BoxTrack consistently outperformed SAT with an average MOTA improvement of +15.96%. For example, in the OK-run07 sequence (shown in Fig. 4, top), BoxTrack achieved a MOTA of 70.78%, significantly higher than SAT's 19.52. At $t + 790$ minutes, SAT failed to detect and track cell ID 10, which was correctly identified by BoxTrack. By $t + 975$, SAT missed cells 10, 6, 11, 1, and 5-all of which were successfully tracked by BoxTrack. Additional missed detections and less precise boundaries were observed in SAT.

These results highlight BoxTrack's scalability across biologically diverse conditions without the need for retraining or dataset-specific adaptation. Such capabilities are particularly useful in large-scale experiments and high-throughput time-lapse studies, where annotation and tuning overheads are often prohibitive.

6.2   CTC: Robustness Across Imaging Modalities

The *Multi-Modality Imaging* setting assessed performance across Phase Contrast, Bright Field, and Fluorescent microscopy using sequences from the CTC dataset. BoxTrack maintained modality-agnostic performance, achieving average MOTA and IDF1 scores of 92.32% and 95.67% respectively, compared to SAT's 83.46 and 90.22. In the PhC-C2DH-U373 sequence (Fig. 4, bottom), SAT achieved a MOTA of 79.82%, whereas BoxTrack reached 100.00%. At $t + 495$ minutes, SAT inaccurately delineated the boundary of cell ID 4, and this error persisted through $t + 690$. In contrast, BoxTrack preserved precise and consistent tracking throughout the sequence.

The results underline the robustness of BoxTrack under modality shifts and suggest that the approach can be applied across varying acquisition setups without handcrafted modifications. This simplifies its use in multi-institutional studies or labs employing diverse imaging technologies.

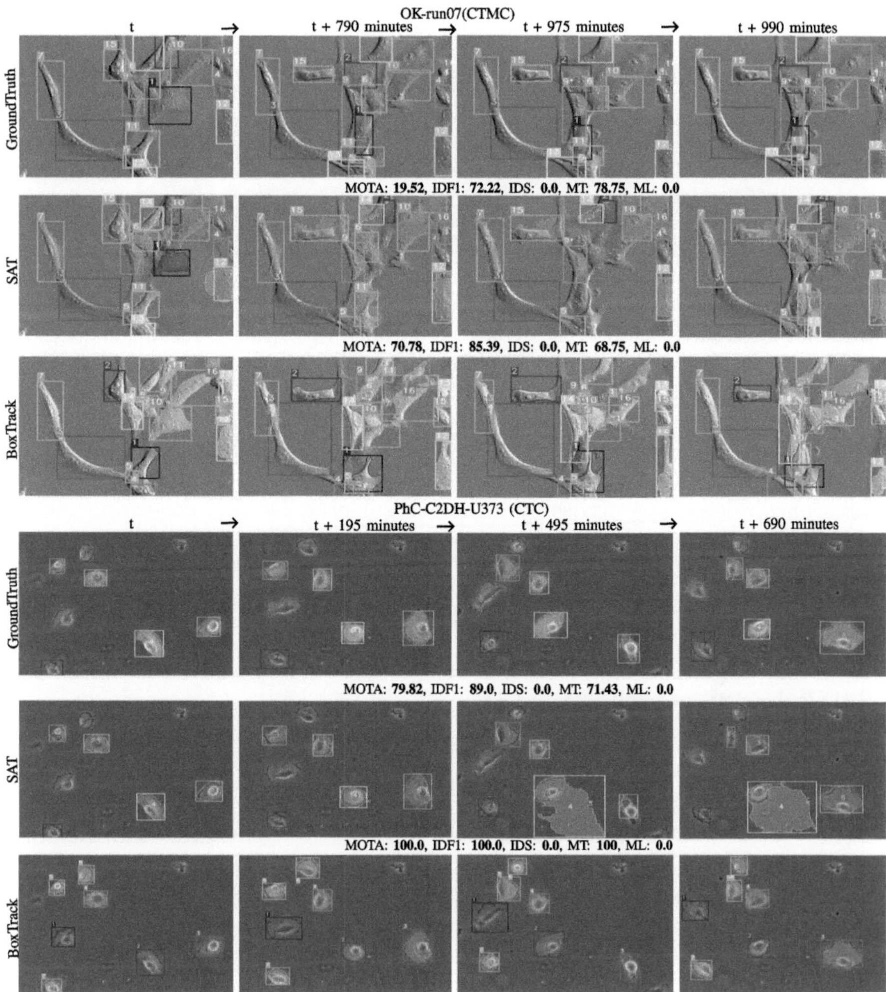

Fig. 4. Qualitative comparison for the first two experimental settings: **CTMC (Top)** and **CTC (Bottom)**. Each row shows Ground Truth, SAT, and BoxTrack predictions over time. Tracking metrics are listed above SAT and BoxTrack rows. BoxTrack consistently outperforms SAT across diverse cell types and imaging modalities.

6.3   DeepCell: Scalability in Dense Nuclear Tracking

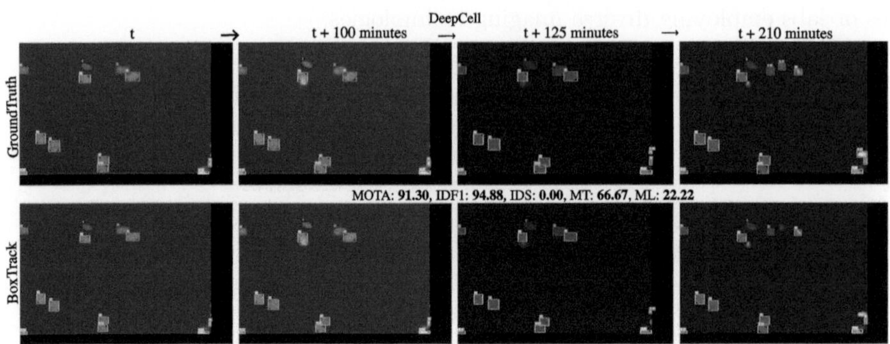

Fig. 5. Qualitative comparison for the third experimental setting: **DeepCell**. Each row shows Ground Truth and BoxTrack predictions over time. Tracking metrics are reported above BoxTrack row. BoxTrack shows strong performance in densely populated, morphologically varied nuclear cultures.

The *Multi-Culture Nuclear Imaging* setting focused on nuclear tracking under fluorescence microscopy across multiple cell cultures. Despite consistent modality, variations in nuclear shape, density, and distribution introduced additional complexity. BoxTrack achieved strong performance with a MOTA of 82.95% and IDF1 of 87.17% across 12 sequences. As shown in Fig. 5, BoxTrack maintained robust accuracy despite contrast changes between $t + 100$ and $t + 125$ minutes. However, at $t + 210$ minutes, the model failed to detect a mitotic event where cell ID 2 divided into cells 17 and 18.

These findings suggest that BoxTrack is well-suited for large-scale nuclear studies in areas such as drug screening or cancer biology, where high-density and morphologically varied samples are common. Future integration of division-aware tracking could enhance its applicability in proliferative assays.

6.4   Temporal Downsampling: Robustness to Reduced Scan Frequency

The *Temporal Resolution Sensitivity* setting tested BoxTrack under lower scan frequencies by subsampling CTMC sequences from 30 s up to 60-minute intervals. As expected, MOTA gradually declined with reduced temporal resolution-from 82.79% at 30 s to 55.93% at 60 min. Despite fewer temporal cues, BoxTrack preserved a MOTA of 60.92% even at 30-minute intervals and remained above 55% at 60 min.

These results indicate that BoxTrack remains effective in temporally sparse conditions, making it suitable for long-term imaging studies where frequent scanning is impractical due to phototoxicity, memory constraints, or biological limitations.

Across all experiments, BoxTrack consistently delivered strong tracking with minimal supervision-only one bounding box per cell-unlike SAT, which requires dense points and backbone tuning. Its zero-shot capability, scalability, and low annotation effort make BoxTrack well-suited for real-world scenarios, including live-cell imaging, large datasets, varied conditions, and low-frequency acquisitions.

7 Conclusion

This work introduced BoxTrack, a training-free, annotation-efficient framework for cell tracking in microscopy images that relies solely on a single bounding box per cell in the first frame. Through extensive experiments across three diverse settings-cell line diversity (CTMC), modality variation (CTC), and nuclear culture dynamics (DeepCell)-BoxTrack consistently outperformed the performance of SAT, a recent state-of-the-art weakly supervised baseline. The results demonstrate that BoxTrack not only reduces manual annotation time by a substantial margin but also generalizes robustly across different cell types, densities, and imaging conditions without retraining or fine-tuning. This highlights the potential of BoxTrack as a universal tracking pipeline for microscopy, bridging the gap between usability and performance. By offering a lightweight yet accurate alternative to heavily supervised or fine-tuned systems, BoxTrack paves the way for broader accessibility in live-cell imaging studies, high-throughput screens, and biomedical applications where resource constraints or annotation budgets are critical bottlenecks. Future work may further explore integration with cell lineage tracing, event detection (e.g., mitosis), and real-time deployment in automated microscopy workflows.

Acknowledgements. This work is partially funded by SAIL (Sartorius AI Lab), a collaboration between the German Research Center for Artificial Intelligence (DFKI) and Sartorius AG.

References

1. Anjum, S., Gurari, D.: CTMC: cell tracking with mitosis detection dataset challenge. In: Proceedings of the IEEE/CVF Conference on Computer Vision and Pattern Recognition Workshops, pp. 982–983 (2020)
2. Bernardin, K., Stiefelhagen, R.: Evaluating multiple object tracking performance: the clear mot metrics. EURASIP J. Image Video Process. (2008)
3. Chen, Y., et al.: Celltrack r-cnn: a novel end-to-end deep neural network for cell segmentation and tracking in microscopy images. In: 2021 IEEE 18th International Symposium on Biomedical Imaging (ISBI), pp. 779–782. IEEE (2021)
4. Cheng, B., Parkhi, O., Kirillov, A.: Pointly-supervised instance segmentation. In: Proceedings of the IEEE/CVF Conference on Computer Vision and Pattern Recognition, pp. 2617–2626 (2022)
5. Edlund, C., et al.: Livecell-a large-scale dataset for label-free live cell segmentation. Nat. Methods (2021)

6. Gallusser, B., Weigert, M.: Trackastra: transformer-based cell tracking for live-cell microscopy. In: European Conference on Computer Vision, pp. 467–484. Springer, Heidelberg (2024). https://doi.org/10.1007/978-3-031-73116-7_27

7. Khalid, N., et al.: Bounding box is all you need: learning to segment cells in 2d microscopic images via box annotations. In: Annual Conference on Medical Image Understanding and Analysis, pp. 314–328. Springer, Heidelberg (2024). https://doi.org/10.1007/978-3-031-66955-2_22

8. Khalid, N., Caroprese, M., Lovell, G., Trygg, J., Dengel, A., Ahmed, S.: Cellspot: deep learning-based efficient cell center detection in microscopic images. In: International Conference on Artificial Neural Networks, pp. 215–229. Springer, Heidelberg (2024). https://doi.org/10.1007/978-3-031-72353-7_16

9. Khalid, N., et al.: Pace: point annotation-based cell segmentation for efficient microscopic image analysis. In: International Conference on Artificial Neural Networks. Springer, Heidelberg (2023). https://doi.org/10.1007/978-3-031-44210-0_44

10. Khalid, N., et al.: Sat: segment and track anything for microscopy. In: Proceedings of the 17th International Conference on Agents and Artificial Intelligence, vol. 2: ICAART, pp. 286–297. INSTICC, SciTePress (2025). https://doi.org/10.5220/0013154200003890

11. Khalid, N., et al.: Deepmucs: a framework for co-culture microscopic image analysis: from generation to segmentation. In: 2022 IEEE-EMBS International Conference on Biomedical and Health Informatics (BHI). IEEE (2022)

12. Khalid, N., et al.: Deepcens: an end-to-end pipeline for cell and nucleus segmentation in microscopic images. In: 2021 International Joint Conference on Neural Networks (IJCNN). IEEE (2021)

13. Khalid, N., et al.: Deepcis: an end-to-end pipeline for cell-type aware instance segmentation in microscopic images. In: 2021 IEEE EMBS International Conference on Biomedical and Health Informatics (BHI). IEEE (2021)

14. Khalid, N., et al.: Point2mask: A weakly supervised approach for cell segmentation using point annotation. In: Medical Image Understanding and Analysis: 26th Annual Conference, MIUA 2022, Cambridge, UK, 27–29 July 2022, Proceedings. Springer, Heidelberg (2022). https://doi.org/10.1007/978-3-031-12053-4_11

15. Kirillov, A., et al.: Segment anything. In: Proceedings of the IEEE/CVF International Conference on Computer Vision (2023)

16. Leal-Taixé, L., Milan, A., Reid, I., Roth, S., Schindler, K.: Motchallenge 2015: towards a benchmark for multi-target tracking. arXiv preprint arXiv:1504.01942 (2015)

17. Li, C., Xie, S.S., Wang, J., Sharvia, S., Chan, K.Y.: Sc-track: a robust cell-tracking algorithm for generating accurate single-cell lineages from diverse cell segmentations. Brief. Bioinf. **25**(3), bbae192 (2024)

18. Maška, M., et al.: The cell tracking challenge: 10 years of objective benchmarking. Nat. Methods **20**(7), 1010–1020 (2023)

19. Masuzzo, P., Van Troys, M., Ampe, C., Martens, L.: Taking aim at moving targets in computational cell migration. Trends Cell Biol. **26**(2), 88–110 (2016)

20. Meijering, E., Dzyubachyk, O., Smal, I., van Cappellen, W.A.: Tracking in cell and developmental biology. In: Seminars in Cell & Developmental Biology, vol. 20, pp. 894–902. Elsevier (2009)

21. Moen, E., et al.: Accurate cell tracking and lineage construction in live-cell imaging experiments with deep learning. In: Biorxiv, p. 803205 (2019)

22. Ravi, N., et al.: Sam 2: segment anything in images and videos. arXiv preprint arXiv:2408.00714 (2024)

23. Ristani, E., Solera, F., Zou, R., Cucchiara, R., Tomasi, C.: Performance measures and a data set for multi-target, multi-camera tracking. In: Hua, G., Jégou, H. (eds.) ECCV 2016. LNCS, vol. 9914, pp. 17–35. Springer, Cham (2016). https://doi.org/10.1007/978-3-319-48881-3_2
24. Scherr, T., et al.: Cell segmentation and tracking using cnn-based distance predictions and a graph-based matching strategy. PLoS ONE **15**(12), e0243219 (2020)
25. Stringer, C., Wang, T., Michaelos, M., Pachitariu, M.: Cellpose: a generalist algorithm for cellular segmentation. Nat. Methods (2020)
26. Stringer, C., et al.: Cellpose: a generalist algorithm for cellular segmentation. Nat. Methods **18**(1), 100–106 (2021)
27. Tian, Z., Shen, C., Wang, X., Chen, H.: Boxinst: high-performance instance segmentation with box annotations. In: Proceedings of the IEEE/CVF Conference on Computer Vision and Pattern Recognition, pp. 5443–5452 (2021)
28. Ulman, V., et al.: An objective comparison of cell-tracking algorithms. Nat. Methods (2017)
29. Wang, C.Y., Bochkovskiy, A., Liao, H.Y.M.: Yolov7: trainable bag-of-freebies sets new state-of-the-art for real-time object detectors. In: Proceedings of the IEEE/CVF Conference on Computer Vision and Pattern Recognition, pp. 7464–7475 (2023)
30. Wang, R., Butt, D., Cross, S., Verkade, P., Achim, A.: Bright-field to fluorescence microscopy image translation for cell nuclei health quantification. Biol. Imaging **3**, e12 (2023)
31. Yang, C.Y., Huang, H.W., Chai, W., Jiang, Z., Hwang, J.N.: Samurai: adapting segment anything model for zero-shot visual tracking with motion-aware memory. arXiv preprint arXiv:2411.11922 (2024)
32. Yazdi, R., Khotanlou, H.: A survey on automated cell tracking: challenges and solutions. Multimedia Tools Appl. (2024)

A Cascaded Dilated Convolution Approach for Mpox Lesion Classification

Ayush Deshmukh$^{(\boxtimes)}$

National Institute of Technology Karnataka, Surathkal, Karnataka 575025, India
aayush.m.deshmukh@gmail.com
https://www.nitk.ac.in

Abstract. The global outbreak of the Mpox virus, classified as a Public Health Emergency of International Concern (PHEIC) by the World Health Organization, presents significant diagnostic challenges due to its visual similarity to other skin lesion diseases. Traditional diagnostic methods for Mpox, which rely on clinical symptoms and laboratory tests, are slow and labor intensive. Deep learning-based approaches for skin lesion classification offer a promising alternative. However, developing a model that balances efficiency with accuracy is crucial to ensure reliable and timely diagnosis without compromising performance. This study introduces the Cascaded Atrous Group Attention (CAGA) module to address these challenges, combining the Cascaded Atrous Attention and the Cascaded Group Attention mechanisms. The Cascaded Atrous Attention module utilizes dilated convolutions and cascades the outputs to enhance multi-scale representation. This is integrated into the Cascaded Group Attention mechanism, which reduces redundancy in Multi-Head Self-Attention. By integrating the Cascaded Atrous Group Attention module with EfficientViT-L1 as the backbone architecture, this approach achieves state-of-the-art performance, reaching an accuracy of 98% on the Mpox Close Skin Image (MCSI) dataset while reducing model parameters by 37.5% compared to the original EfficientViT-L1. The model's robustness is demonstrated through extensive validation on two additional benchmark datasets, where it consistently outperforms existing approaches.

Keywords: Mpox classification · Image Classification · Vision Transformers · Self-attention

1 Introduction

The recent global outbreak of the Mpox virus has presented significant challenges for public health authorities and researchers worldwide. As this zoonotic disease spread beyond endemic regions, it affected multiple non-endemic countries, including the Netherlands [12], Greece [19], Portugal [5], and France [17]. To date, over 100,000 cases have been reported across hundreds of countries,

© The Author(s), under exclusive license to Springer Nature Switzerland AG 2026
M. Keuper and F. Locatello (Eds.): DAGM GCPR 2025, LNCS 16125, pp. 18–27, 2026.
https://doi.org/10.1007/978-3-032-12840-9_2

prompting the World Health Organization (WHO) to declare Mpox a Public Health Emergency of International Concern (PHEIC).

Traditional diagnostic methods relying on clinical symptoms and laboratory testing have proven slow and imprecise, exacerbated by Mpox's clinical resemblance to other skin lesion-based diseases like Chickenpox and Measles [22]. Additionally, reporting delays and difficulties in tracing transmission sources exacerbate the issue [20]. These issues highlight the urgent need for improved diagnostic methods that are both accurate and efficient.

Recent advances in artificial intelligence, particularly Convolutional Neural Networks (CNNs) and Transformers, offer promising solutions to these challenges. Transformers, originally designed for natural language processing, have been adapted for computer vision [10]. However, pure Transformer models often require large datasets and significant computational resources, prompting the development of hybrid architectures that integrate convolutional and attention mechanisms.

CNNs have shown great success in skin lesion classification [11], but their application to Mpox detection remains relatively limited. Notable efforts include Thieme et al. [23] who developed MPXV-CNN, a deep CNN achieving strong diagnostic performance, and introduced PoxApp, a web-based tool for patient management. Similarly, Raha et al. [21] proposed an attention-powered MobileNetV2 architecture emphasizing interpretability through Grad-CAM and LIME techniques. Jaradat et al. [16] showed how data augmentation improved pre-trained model's performance on limited datasets. Asif et al. [3] proposed an ensemble learning approach combining CNN models optimized with Particle Swarm Optimization, achieving improved accuracy.

These studies have primarily concentrated on three key methodologies: adapting pre-trained medical imaging models [7,16], developing specialized neural network structures [21], and implementing advanced feature extraction techniques to capture the unique morphological characteristics of Mpox skin lesions [23].

While these methods show promise, they have limitations. Many studies rely on single-dataset evaluations, limiting their generalizability and reducing reliability for real-world data. Furthermore, comparative studies often inadequately assess performance by comparing attention-based models with a narrow set of alternatives, leading to skewed conclusions about model effectiveness. The lack of large, standardized benchmark datasets further hampers the development of reliable models, slowing their transition from research to clinical use.

A critical gap exists in Mpox classification models that are both rigorously tested and strike a balance between computational efficiency and diagnostic accuracy. While reducing processing times is important, it should never compromise the accuracy of the diagnosis, as reliable diagnosis remains the primary goal in clinical settings.

The main contributions of this paper are thus summarized as follows:

1. I propose a novel Cascaded Atrous Group Attention (CAGA) module, which consists of a novel Cascaded Atrous Attention (CAA) integrated within a

Cascaded Group Attention (CGA) structure. CAGA leverages dilations to capture multi-scale information, self-attention to capture long-range dependencies, and a cascading structure to enhance feature flow across dilations and attention heads.

2. I conducted extensive evaluations on three diverse datasets, demonstrating that the EfficientViT-CAGA model (with EfficientViT-L1 as the backbone for CAGA) achieves the highest accuracy while requiring fewer parameters compared to most other state-of-the-art (SOTA) models.

3. Through comprehensive ablation studies, I validate the effectiveness of CAGA's design choices and further provide visual interpretability through Grad-CAM analysis to demonstrate how the proposed model attends to relevant features.

2   Methodology

This section presents the Cascaded Atrous Group Attention. I first provide a comprehensive overview of the module, followed by detailed explanations of its key components: the Cascaded Atrous Attention (CAA) and the Cascaded Group Attention (CGA) mechanisms.

2.1   Cascaded Atrous Group Attention (CAGA)

I introduce Cascaded Atrous Group Attention (see Fig. 1 (right)) an architecture that builds upon the Cascaded Group Attention (CGA) [18] module. While the CGA directly processes each attention head using standard self-attention, this work replaces this mechanism with the Cascaded Atrous Attention (CAA). By integrating multi-scale dilated convolutions and a sophisticated self-attention mechanism for each dilation, CAA enhances the feature representation capabilities of the CGA approach.

Inspired by DeepLab's Atrous Spatial Pyramid Pooling (ASPP) [8], CAA is a multi-scale feature extraction module that leverages parallel dilated convolutions to effectively capture contextual information at multiple receptive fields. Building upon ASPP's use of varying dilation rates, CAA introduces a cascaded approach that combines dilated inputs with a self-attention mechanism for enhanced feature representation. Figure 2 provides an illustration of the proposed CAA module.

Cascaded Atrous Attention (CAA). I incorporate dilation rates $d \in \{1, 2, 3\}$ applied to convolution operations with kernel size $k \times k$ (typically 3×3) across each attention head $X_i \in \mathbb{R}^{h \times H \times W}$, where (H, W) is the resolution, h denotes the dimensionality of the attention head, and $1 \leq i \leq n$, where n is the total number of heads. Which is followed with a 1×1 convolution to transform the feature map into appropriate dimensionality required for self attention. Let $\tilde{H} = \frac{H - k_{\text{eff}} + s}{s}$ and $\tilde{W} = \frac{W - k_{\text{eff}} + s}{s}$, then the output after dilated convolution is denoted as $X_h^d \in \mathbb{R}^{(3 \times d_{qkv}) \times \tilde{H} \times \tilde{W}}$, where $k_{\text{eff}} = k + (k-1)(d-1)$

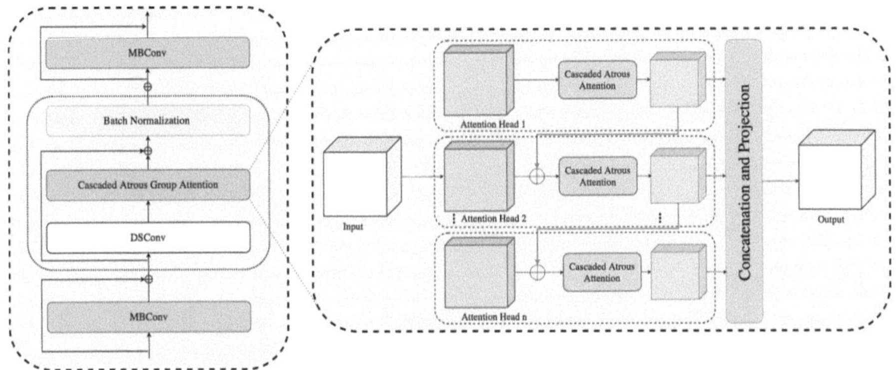

Fig. 1. Integration of CAGA within the Network Architecture (left) and detailed structure of Cascaded Group Attention with Cascaded Atrous Attention (right). *Left:* The MBConv layer represents the Mobile Inverted Bottleneck Convolution, which is part of the EfficientViT-L1 architecture. A Depthwise Separable Convolution is used to reduce computational complexity while preserving spatial and channel-wise feature interactions, converting the input to an $n \times h$ dimension. Batch Normalization is applied to the output of the residual connection.

represents the effective kernel size. Here, d_{qkv} is the dimension of query, key, and value embeddings, and s is the stride. The resulting feature map is split into $Q^d, K^d, V^d \in \mathbb{R}^{d_{qkv} \times (\tilde{H} \times \tilde{W})}$ and passed to the self-attention module. The self-attention then is computed as:

$$Attn_d = \text{Softmax}\left(\frac{Q^d(K^d)^T}{\sqrt{d_{qkv}}}\right) V^d \tag{1}$$

I introduce a hierarchical cascading approach to dilated self-attention maps that progressively aggregates and enhances spatial context. The model incrementally integrates proximal and broader neighborhood features, creating a multi-scale representation that captures nuanced spatial dependencies across different contextual granularities. To address dimensionality disparities between the dilated attention maps and subsequent dilated convolutional inputs, I implement a 1×1 convolution projection layer, thereby ensuring dimensional consistency.

$$\tilde{X}_i^d = X_i^d + \text{Proj}(Attn_{d-1}), \quad 1 < d \leq 3 \tag{2}$$

Each dilated attention map is interpolated to restore the feature representation to its original spatial resolution of (H, W). These maps are then concatenated and subsequently projected back to match the attention head dimensionality.

Cascaded Group Attention (CGA). Multi-Head Self-Attention (MHSA) suffers from attention head redundancy [13,25], resulting in computational inefficiency. To address this limitation [18] propose Cascaded Group Attention, where

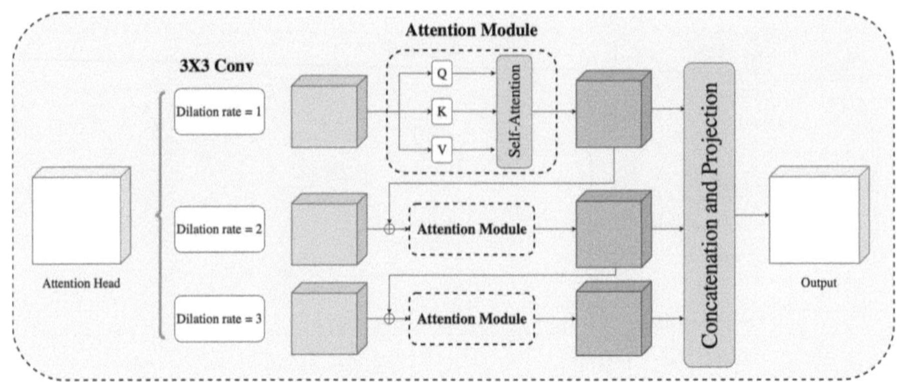

Fig. 2. Cascaded Atrous Attention.

the input $X \in \mathbb{R}^{(n \times h) \times H \times W}$ is split into n distinct heads of dimensionality h. Each attention head is processed independently, with a distinctive feature: for heads beyond the first, the input is augmented by adding the output of the preceding processed head $(\hat{X}_{i-1})$.

$$\tilde{X}_i = X_i + \hat{X}_{i-1}, \quad 1 < i \leq n \tag{3}$$

The processed attention heads are concatenated and projected back to the original input dimensions. A residual connection is then applied, linking the transformed representation with the initial input.

$$\hat{X} = X + \mathrm{Proj}(Concat[\hat{X}_i]_{i=1:n}) \tag{4}$$

This final step ensures that the cascaded attention representation maintains a direct connection to the original input, preserving initial features while incorporating the hierarchically refined representations from the CGA and CAA mechanisms.

3   Experimental Results and Analysis

This section presents the dataset and implementation details, followed by a performance comparison between the proposed method and state-of-the-art architectures. The models compared in this study include ResNet-101 [14], MobileNetV3-Large [15], DeiT3-Medium [24], ViT-Base [10], EfficientViT-L1 [6], and CoAtNet-1 [9]. All models were pre-trained on ImageNet, with the exception of the classifier head, which was randomly initialized in line with common practice. In contrast, for EfficientViT-CAGA, only the EfficientViT-L1 convolutional backbone was pre-trained, while the DSConv and CAGA modules were initialized using the Xavier uniform method.

3.1 Datasets and Implementation Details

To evaluate the performance of the proposed method, I selected three benchmark datasets. All images in the datasets are resized to 224×224.

Table 1. Comparison with SOTA Image Classification Models on MCSI Dataset Results Reported as Mean across 10-Fold Cross-Validation

Architectures	Parameters	Accuracy	Precision	Recall	F1 Score
ResNet-101	47.4M	0.8925	0.8908	0.891	0.884
MobileNetV3-Large	**7.6M**	0.9375	0.9433	0.9473	0.9391
DeiT3-Medium	41.5M	0.9575	0.960	0.958	0.956
ViT-Base	88.7M	0.9575	0.9578	0.9562	0.9542
EfficientViT-L1	58.9M	<u>0.9725</u>	<u>0.9727</u>	<u>0.9744</u>	<u>0.9714</u>
CoAtNet-1	41.7M	0.9675	0.971	0.9671	0.967
EfficientViT-CAGA	<u>36.8M</u>	**0.98**	**0.9789**	**0.9795**	**0.9781**

The **Mpox Close Skin Image Dataset (MCSI)** [7] comprises four classes: Mpox, Chickenpox, Acne, and Normal, with each class containing 100 images.

The **Monkeypox Skin Images Dataset (MSID)** [4] contains 770 total images distributed across four classes: Mpox, Chickenpox, Measles, and Acne.

The **Monkeypox Skin Lesion Dataset (MSLD)** [1,2] is a binary classification dataset with two classes: Mpox and Others (comprising Chickenpox and Measles). The total dataset size is 228 image.

I utilize the ImageNet pre-trained EfficientViT-L1 [6] as the backbone architecture, with the head initialized randomly. The implementation is done using PyTorch and trained on Tesla T4 GPUs. For pre-trained models I use Pytorch Image Models. I employ the AdamW optimizer with a learning rate on the order of 10^{-5}. For the CAA module, I utilize dilation rates $d \in \{1, 2, 3\}$, which are adjusted for each dataset, across a total of 3 attention heads. Each attention head has an embedding dimension of 16, while the dimensions for the query, key, and value embeddings (d_{qkv}) are set to 8. The weights are initialized using the Xavier uniform method with a fixed seed of 82.

3.2 Results

The bolded results for each metric indicate the highest score among all models, while the second-highest scores are underlined. For parameters and FLOPs, the smallest value is bolded, and the second smallest is underlined.

MCSI. The evaluation used 10-fold cross-validation as proposed by [7], with the dataset split into 288 training, 72 validation, and 40 test images per fold. Runtime data augmentation led to a slight performance drop across all models, consistent with [7]. All models used focal loss with class-specific weights (alpha), significantly improving performance even with evenly distributed classes. EfficientViT-CAGA demonstrated high accuracy with only 4.86G FLOPs, 3.5× less than ViT-Base, and reduced parameters by 37.5% compared to EfficientViT-L1 while improving all metrics (Table 1).

MSLD. Containing fewer than 250 images, [2] applied extensive data augmentation (e.g., rotation, translation, brightness jitter, and scaling), expanding the dataset to 1,428 Mpox and 1,764 Others images. The dataset was split into training, validation, and testing sets (70:20:10) with ImageNet normalization. EfficientViT-CAGA outperformed SOTA models across most metrics, using 12% fewer parameters than EfficientViT-L1 and CoAtNet-1 and achieving 100% accuracy on the Mpox class (Table 2).

Table 2. Comparison with SOTA Image Classification Models on MSLD Dataset

Architectures	Parameters	Accuracy	Precision	Recall	F1 Score
ResNet-101	47.1M	0.9593	0.9592	0.9586	0.9589
MobileNetV3-Large	**6.8M**	0.9781	0.9782	0.9776	0.9779
DeiT3-Medium	38.8M	<u>0.9938</u>	<u>0.9937</u>	0.9937	0.9937
ViT-Base	86.5M	<u>0.9938</u>	0.993	<u>0.994</u>	<u>0.994</u>
EfficientViT-L1	42M	0.9875	0.987	0.988	0.987
CoAtNet-1	41.7M	0.9906	0.99	0.99	0.99
EfficientViT-CAGA	<u>36.8M</u>	**0.9969**	**0.997**	**0.997**	**0.997**

MSID. 616 images were used for training and 154 for testing, following an 80-20 split. Data augmentation, similar to MCSI, slightly degraded performance. EfficientViT-CAGA achieved comparable accuracy with 2.2× fewer parameters than ViT-Base and 1.5× fewer than EfficientViT-L1 (Table 3). Across all datasets, EfficientViT-CAGA consistently balanced efficiency and accuracy, making it a robust choice for Mpox detection.

The results show that the proposed architecture, EfficientViT-CAGA, provides reduced computational complexity without compromising accuracy on all three datasets, making it a promising solution for real-world clinical applications.

3.3 Ablation Study

I conducted an ablation study on the MCSI dataset to evaluate the CAA and CGA modules. Models were initialized with random weights to remove pre-training biases. The study used three attention heads with fixed dilation rates ($d \in 1, 2$) and a fixed classifier head for consistency.

Table 3. Comparison with SOTA Image Classification Models on MSID Dataset

Architectures	Parameters	Accuracy	Precision	Recall	F1 Score
ResNet-101	43.5M	0.8961	0.8633	0.8782	0.8686
MobileNetV3-Large	**5.5M**	0.9481	0.94	0.927	0.9327
DeiT3-Medium	38.8M	0.9481	0.9159	0.9308	0.9229
ViT-Base	86.5M	0.9286	0.9097	0.9154	0.9113
EfficientViT-L1	58.9M	0.9481	0.9082	0.9273	0.9165
CoAtNet-1	41.7M	**0.9545**	0.9201	**0.9454**	0.9317
EfficientViT-CAGA	37.8M	**0.9545**	**0.9523**	0.9376	**0.9446**

Table 4. Ablation Study Results

Cascading in CAA	CAA	CGA	Params	Accuracy
✓	✓		36.7M	0.77
	✓	✓	36.8M	0.815
✓	✓	✓	36.8M	0.8175

The study assessed the cascading mechanism in the CAA module by removing cascading between dilations and quantified the CGA module's contribution by excluding it while retaining the CAA module.

Table 4 presents the results, showing average accuracy across 10-fold cross-validation. While parameter counts remained similar, the inclusion of CGA and cascading improved performance slightly.

Furthermore, Grad-CAM heatmaps were generated to interpret the model's focus during classification. These visualizations, applied to MSLD, highlight key input regions influencing predictions, as shown in Fig. 3.

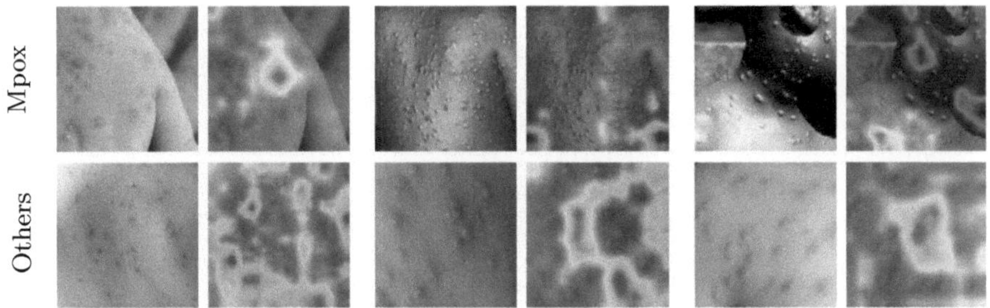

Fig. 3. Original images and their corresponding Grad-CAM visualizations for Mpox and Others from the MSLD.

4   Conclusion

In this work, I proposed the CAGA architecture, which combines the CAA module and the CGA mechanism to improve the efficiency and accuracy for Mpox classification. CAA used dilated convolutions for multi-scale representation and cascaded outputs to enhance spatial and contextual information, encapsulated in a CGA to reduce redundancy in Multi-Head Self-Attention. Experimental results show that the approach highlighted state-of-the-art results on three datasets. In future work, I plan to extend the application of CAGA to broader tasks, such as disease segmentation and object detection, where multi-scale feature representation and efficient attention mechanisms could drive substantial improvements.

References

1. Ali, S.N., et al.: A web-based mpox skin lesion detection system using state-of-the-art deep learning models considering racial diversity. Biomed. Signal Process. Control **98**, 106742 (2024)
2. Ali, S.N., et al.: Monkeypox skin lesion detection using deep learning models: a preliminary feasibility study. arXiv preprint arXiv:2207.03342 (2022)
3. Asif, S., Zhao, M., Tang, F., Zhu, Y., Zhao, B.: Metaheuristics optimization-based ensemble of deep neural networks for mpox disease detection. Neural Netw. **167**, 342–359 (2023). https://doi.org/10.1016/j.neunet.2023.08.035. https://www.sciencedirect.com/science/article/pii/S0893608023004525
4. Bala, D., et al.: Monkeynet: a robust deep convolutional neural network for monkeypox disease detection and classification. Neural Netw. **161**, 757–775 (2023)
5. Borges, V., et al.: Viral genetic clustering and transmission dynamics of the 2022 mpox outbreak in Portugal. Nat. Med. **29**(10), 2509–2517 (2023). https://doi.org/10.1038/s41591-023-02542-x
6. Cai, H., Li, J., Hu, M., Gan, C., Han, S.: Efficientvit: lightweight multi-scale attention for high-resolution dense prediction. In: Proceedings of the IEEE/CVF International Conference on Computer Vision, pp. 17302–17313 (2023)
7. Campana, M.G., Colussi, M., Delmastro, F., Mascetti, S., Pagani, E.: A transfer learning and explainable solution to detect mpox from smartphones images. Perv. Mob. Comput. **98**, 101874 (2024). https://doi.org/10.1016/j.pmcj.2023.101874. https://www.sciencedirect.com/science/article/pii/S1574119223001323
8. Chen, L.C., Papandreou, G., Kokkinos, I., Murphy, K., Yuille, A.L.: Deeplab: semantic image segmentation with deep convolutional nets, atrous convolution, and fully connected crfs. IEEE Trans. Pattern Anal. Mach. Intell. **40**(4), 834–848 (2018). https://doi.org/10.1109/TPAMI.2017.2699184
9. Dai, Z., Liu, H., Le, Q.V., Tan, M.: Coatnet: marrying convolution and attention for all data sizes. Adv. Neural. Inf. Process. Syst. **34**, 3965–3977 (2021)
10. Dosovitskiy, A., et al.: An image is worth 16×16 words: transformers for image recognition at scale (2021). https://arxiv.org/abs/2010.11929
11. Esteva, A., et al.: Dermatologist-level classification of skin cancer with deep neural networks. Nature **542**(7639), 115–118 (2017)
12. van Ewijk, C.E., et al: Mpox outbreak in The Netherlands, 2022: public health response, characteristics of the first 1,000 cases and protection of the first-generation smallpox vaccine. Eurosurveillance **28**(12), 2200772 (2023). https://doi.org/10.2807/1560-7917.ES.2023.28.12.2200772. https://www.eurosurveillance.org/content/10.2807/1560-7917.ES.2023.28.12.2200772

13. Gao, J., He, D., Tan, X., Qin, T., Wang, L., Liu, T.Y.: Representation degeneration problem in training natural language generation models (2019). https://arxiv.org/abs/1907.12009
14. He, K., Zhang, X., Ren, S., Sun, J.: Deep residual learning for image recognition. In: Proceedings of the IEEE Conference on Computer Vision and Pattern Recognition, pp. 770–778 (2016)
15. Howard, A., et al.: Searching for mobilenetv3. In: Proceedings of the IEEE/CVF International Conference on Computer Vision, pp. 1314–1324 (2019)
16. Jaradat, A., et al.: Automated monkeypox skin lesion detection using deep learning and transfer learning techniques. Int. J. Environ. Res. Public Health **20**(5), 4422 (2023). https://doi.org/10.3390/ijerph20054422
17. Krug, C., et al.: Mpox outbreak in France: epidemiological characteristics and sexual behaviour of cases aged 15 years or older, 2022. Eurosurveillance **28**(50), 2200923 (2023). https://doi.org/10.2807/1560-7917.ES.2023.28.50.2200923. https://www.eurosurveillance.org/content/10.2807/1560-7917.ES.2023.28.50.2200923
18. Liu, X., Peng, H., Zheng, N., Yang, Y., Hu, H., Yuan, Y.: Efficientvit: memory efficient vision transformer with cascaded group attention. In: Proceedings of the IEEE/CVF Conference on Computer Vision and Pattern Recognition, pp. 14420–14430 (2023)
19. Mellou, K., et al.: Overview of mpox outbreak in Greece in 2022–2023: is it over? Viruses **15**(6) (2023). https://doi.org/10.3390/v15061384. https://www.mdpi.com/1999-4915/15/6/1384
20. Prasad, S., et al.: A dermatologic assessment of 101 mpox (monkeypox) cases from 13 countries during the 2022 outbreak: Skin lesion morphology, clinical course, and scarring. J. Am. Acad. Dermatol. **88**(5), 1066–1073 (2023). https://doi.org/10.1016/j.jaad.2022.12.035
21. Raha, A.D., et al.: Attention to monkeypox: an interpretable monkeypox detection technique using attention mechanism. IEEE Access **12**, 51942–51965 (2024). https://doi.org/10.1109/ACCESS.2024.3385099
22. Silva, S.J.R.D., Kohl, A., Pena, L., Pardee, K.: Clinical and laboratory diagnosis of monkeypox (mpox): current status and future directions. iScience **26**(6), 106759 (2023). https://doi.org/10.1016/j.isci.2023.106759
23. Thieme, A., Zheng, Y., Machiraju, G., et al.: A deep-learning algorithm to classify skin lesions from mpox virus infection. Nat. Med. **29**, 738–747 (2023). https://doi.org/10.1038/s41591-023-02225-7
24. Touvron, H., Cord, M., Jégou, H.: Deit iii: Revenge of the vit (2022). https://arxiv.org/abs/2204.07118
25. Touvron, H., Cord, M., Sablayrolles, A., Synnaeve, G., Jégou, H.: Going deeper with image transformers. In: Proceedings of the IEEE/CVF International Conference on Computer Vision, pp. 32–42 (2021)

HistDiST: Histopathological Diffusion-Based Stain Transfer

Erik Großkopf, Valay Bundele, Mehran Hosseinzadeh[(✉)],
and Hendrik P.A. Lensch

University of Tübingen, Tübingen, Germany
`erik.grosskopf@student.uni-tuebingen.de`,
`{valay.bundele,mehran.hosseinzadeh,hendrik.lensch}@uni-tuebingen.de`

Abstract. Hematoxylin and Eosin (H&E) staining is the cornerstone of histopathology but lacks molecular specificity. While Immunohistochemistry (IHC) provides molecular insights, it is costly and complex, motivating H&E-to-IHC translation as a cost-effective alternative. Existing translation methods are mainly GAN-based, often struggling with training instability and limited structural fidelity, while diffusion-based approaches remain underexplored. We propose HistDiST, a Latent Diffusion Model (LDM) based framework for high-fidelity H&E-to-IHC translation. HistDiST introduces a dual-conditioning strategy, utilizing Phikon-extracted morphological embeddings alongside VAE-encoded H&E representations to ensure pathology-relevant context and structural consistency. To overcome brightness biases, we incorporate a rescaled noise schedule along with v-prediction, enforcing a zero-SNR condition at the final timestep. During inference, DDIM inversion preserves the morphological structure, while an η-cosine noise schedule introduces controlled stochasticity, balancing structural consistency and molecular fidelity. Moreover, we propose Molecular Retrieval Accuracy (MRA), a novel pathology-aware metric leveraging GigaPath embeddings to assess molecular relevance. Extensive evaluations on MIST and BCI datasets demonstrate that HistDiST significantly outperforms existing methods, achieving a 28% improvement in MRA on the H&E-to-Ki67 translation task, highlighting its effectiveness in capturing true IHC semantics. The code is available at https://github.com/ErikGro/HistDiST.

Keywords: Stain Transfer · Diffusion Models · Digital Pathology

1 Introduction

Histopathology is essential for disease diagnosis, revealing tissue structure and cellular morphology. While Hematoxylin and Eosin (H&E) staining is cost-effective and highlights structural details, it lacks molecular specificity. In contrast, Immunohistochemistry (IHC) provides molecular insights but is expensive

E. Großkopf, V. Bundele and M. Hosseinzadeh—Equal contribution.

and time-consuming. Automated H&E-to-IHC translation offers a scalable solution by inferring molecular details from tissue morphology, reducing costs, and enhancing diagnostic consistency. Deep learning methods, particularly GANs, GANs have shown promise in this task. Li et al. [11] use adaptive supervised PatchNCE loss to preserve structure, while MDCL [23] employs a conditional GAN with multi-domain contrastive learning to enhance cross-domain alignment. Pathology-specific approaches include patch-level feature extraction with multiple instance learning [12] and HER2 scoring enhancement via nuclei density estimation [17]. However, GANs still face mode collapse and require complex loss designs to maintain consistency in pathology screenings.

Recently, diffusion models (DMs) [8] have emerged as a powerful alternative, offering superior stability and synthesis quality. Latent Diffusion Models (LDMs) [19] reduce the computational burden of DMs by operating in the latent space of pretrained autoencoders. LDM-based image editing methods, such as Instruct-Pix2Pix [1] for instruction-based editing and ControlNet [26] for conditional generation, offer structured control. Inference-time optimization techniques using DDIM Inversion [22] and Delta Denoising Score [7] further enhance structural fidelity. Although there has been quite some work on applying LDMs for natural image editing, the application of LDMs for H&E-to-IHC stain translation remains largely unexplored. Existing diffusion-based methods [4, 25] mainly use text prompts or unpaired signal vector conditioning, but often fail to ensure structural and semantic consistency, critical for accurate pathology translation.

To address these limitations, we propose HistDiST, an LDM-based framework for high-fidelity H&E-to-IHC stain translation. Although LDM offers strong generative capabilities, its direct application to stain translation faces three key challenges: (i) lack of explicit morphological conditioning, (ii) brightness bias from conventional diffusion noise schedules, and (iii) insufficient structural preservation at inference. These limitations hinder the model's ability to capture complex morphology-molecular relationships and lead to inaccurate brightness distributions that obscure diagnostically relevant molecular features.

HistDiST overcomes these challenges through three key contributions. First, we employ a dual-conditioning strategy that integrates pathology-specific priors into denoising process. Specifically, Phikon-based embeddings [5] are injected via cross-attention within the U-Net, while VAE-encoded H&E representations are concatenated with latent noise input. This ensures that pathology-relevant context guides denoising for precise molecular reconstruction. Second, to address brightness inconsistencies, we incorporate a rescaled noise schedule and trailing timesteps [13] along with v-prediction [10], enforcing zero terminal SNR. Third, we perform joint training for unconditional H&E generation and H&E-to-IHC translation, a critical step that enables the use of DDIM inversion [21] for structure preservation at inference. However, while inversion effectively anchors structure, the subsequent DDIM denoising—being fully deterministic—restricts generative flexibility. As a result, the model fails to capture subtle but diagnostically relevant molecular variations in the translated IHC image.

To overcome this limitation, we introduce an η-cosine noise schedule that progressively increases stochasticity during DDIM denoising. This modification enables controlled exploration of molecular solution space while preserving morphological consistency. The resulting outputs show improvements in synthesis diversity and fidelity, as reflected by lower FID scores. Moreover, we propose Molecular Retrieval Accuracy (MRA), a novel feature-based metric that quantifies molecular fidelity using cosine similarity. Experiments on MIST and BCI datasets demonstrate that HistDiST outperforms state-of-the-art methods across both qualitative and quantitative benchmarks, achieving superior visual realism, structural preservation, and molecular accuracy. Notably, HistDiST yields 28% improvement in MRA on H&E-to-Ki67 translation, demonstrating highly accurate IHC synthesis.

2   Related Work

2.1   Image Generation Using Diffusion Models

Diffusion models (DMs) have emerged as a powerful alternative to GANs for image generation, offering greater diversity and training stability by learning the data distribution through iterative denoising processes [8]. These models operate either directly in the data space or in a compressed latent space, as in Latent Diffusion Models (LDMs) [19], enabling more efficient computation. Building on their success in generative tasks, conditional diffusion models have been developed to allow guided image synthesis for applications such as image-to-image translation [16] and text-based image editing [1]. Conditioning is typically achieved by injecting external information into the denoising network. For instance, Stable Diffusion [19] and InstructPix2Pix [1] leverage text prompts mapped to a shared embedding space with images, while ControlNet [26] enhances this framework by incorporating spatial guidance, enabling fine-grained structural control. In addition, inference-time optimization techniques—such as DDIM inversion [22] and Delta Denoising Score (DDS) [7]—have been introduced to improve structural fidelity and control in a training-free manner.

2.2   Stain Transfer in Computational Pathology

The generation of virtually stained images given a source staining type image is an active field of research, aiming to alleviate the lack of useful IHC counterparts to H&E images and meanwhile preventing the challenges caused by re-staining or re-sampling tissues. Generative Adversarial Networks (GANs) have been widely employed for H&E-to-IHC translation, with many approaches focusing on preserving structural and pathological integrity. For example, Li et al. [11] introduce an adaptive supervised PatchNCE loss to maintain structure, while Chen et al. [3] improve translation fidelity via a multi-branch discriminator with prototype consistency. Other methods incorporate domain-specific enhancements: Li et al. [12] propose a patch-level pathological feature extractor with multiple-instance learning, and Peng et al. [17] refine HER2 scoring using a nuclei density estimator and auxiliary alignment branch. Wang et al. [23] incorporate Multi-Domain Contrastive Learning (MDCL) within a conditional GAN to enhance cross-domain alignment, and Qu et al. [18] utilize a multi-magnification processing strategy with an attention module to extract fine-grained features while minimizing information loss. Despite their effectiveness, GAN-based methods often struggle with mode collapse and require carefully crafted loss functions to ensure pathological accuracy.

Recently, diffusion models have gained attention for their stability and high-quality synthesis in natural image generation. Their application in virtual staining, however, remains limited. He et al. [6] leverage diffusion models augmented with Schrödinger bridges and structural constraints to achieve stain transfer, though standard evaluation metrics are not reported. Shen et al. [20] employ diffusion solely for style transfer, without addressing cross-stain learning. Text-conditioned diffusion has also been explored: Dubey et al. [4] utilize a latent diffusion model guided by text prompts, but their reliance on pixel-aligned datasets limits practical applicability. Yan et al. [25] propose a unified dual-encoder diffusion framework for multi-stain translation across diverse stain types (H&E, MT, PAS, PASM). Nonetheless, the use of diffusion models for H&E-to-IHC stain translation remains underexplored, with a lack of methods that explicitly target pathological consistency and structural fidelity in this challenging setting.

3   Methodology

3.1   Preliminaries

Diffusion models generate data by learning to reverse a stochastic forward process that gradually corrupts an input sample x_0 with Gaussian noise over T steps, following a variance schedule β_t:

$$q(x_t|x_{t-1}) = \mathcal{N}(x_t; \sqrt{1 - \beta_t}x_{t-1}, \beta_t I). \tag{1}$$

For large T, this process converges to an isotropic Gaussian distribution. The model approximates the reverse process:

$$p_\theta(x_{t-1}|x_t) = \mathcal{N}(x_{t-1}; \mu_\theta(x_t, t), \Sigma_\theta(x_t, t)), \tag{2}$$

where μ_θ and Σ_θ are learnable functions. Training involves predicting the noise component $\epsilon_\theta(x_t, t)$ by minimizing:

$$L = \mathbb{E}_{x_0, t, \epsilon}\left[\|\epsilon - \epsilon_\theta(x_t, t)\|^2\right], \tag{3}$$

where $\epsilon \sim \mathcal{N}(0, I)$ and ϵ_θ is a neural network parameterized by θ. Latent Diffusion Models (LDMs) enhance computational efficiency by operating in a compressed latent space, where an encoder E maps images x_0 to latent representations $z_0 = E(x_0)$.

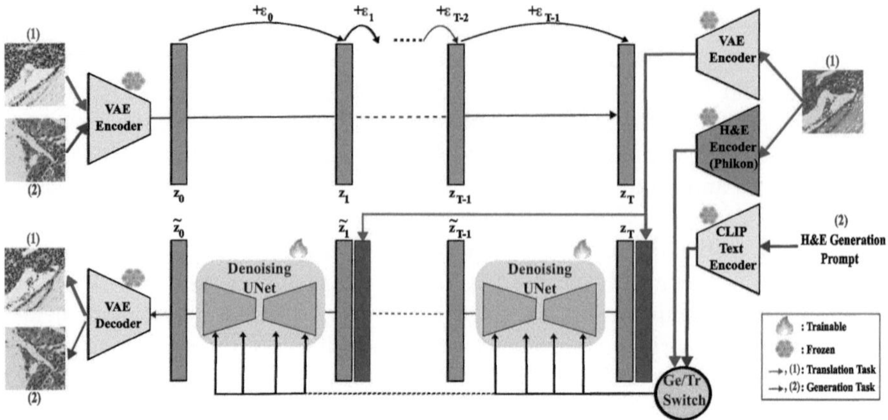

Fig. 1. HistDiST training pipeline, showing H&E generation (red arrows, label (2)) conditioned on CLIP text embeddings, and H&E-to-IHC translation (green arrows, label (1)) guided by Phikon embeddings and VAE-encoded H&E features. The VAE encoder maps images to latent space, where noise is added and later denoised by the U-Net. The Ge/Tr switch selects between generation and translation tasks, with each (numbered input, color-coded pathway) independently followed. (Color figure online)

3.2   HistDiST

We present HistDiST, a novel framework leveraging LDMs for high-fidelity H&E-to-IHC translation. LDMs operate in a variational autoencoder (VAE) latent space and use a U-Net denoising network with residual connections, self-attention, and cross-attention mechanisms. HistDiST achieves superior structural and molecular accuracy through: (1) dual-conditioning (2) v-prediction with rescaled noise schedules, and (3) DDIM inversion followed by DDIM denoising with η-cosine scheduling, balancing determinism with controlled stochasticity.

Dual Conditioning: To capture the intricate relationship between tissue morphology and molecular expression, HistDiST employs a *dual-conditioning* strategy. First, Phikon [5], a self-supervised transformer trained on 40 million histology images, extracts morphological feature embeddings from the input H&E-stained image. These embeddings are injected into the cross-attention layers of the U-Net, enabling the model to integrate pathology-relevant context throughout the denoising process. Second, inspired by InstructPix2Pix [1], we modify the U-Net by applying additional input channels that allow VAE-encoded H&E latents to be concatenated with the latent noise vector at the U-Net input. This modification provides structural guidance from the earliest denoising stages, enabling IHC generation with high structural fidelity and molecular accuracy.

Joint Training: Fig. 1 shows the training pipeline of HistDiST. To enable DDIM inversion for structure preservation at inference, HistDiST is trained jointly on unconditional H&E generation and H&E-to-IHC translation. While the VAE remains frozen, the U-Net is fine-tuned on paired H&E-IHC data. A key limitation in standard diffusion models is that common noise schedules fail to enforce zero SNR at the final timestep, causing residual low-frequency information to be leaked during training [13]. However, at inference, the model starts from pure Gaussian noise, leading to a mismatch between training and inference, resulting in constrained brightness levels. HistDiST addresses this by rescaling the noise schedule under a variance-preserving formulation [13] to enforce zero terminal SNR and enable more accurate brightness distribution in outputs.

Moreover, when SNR is zero, traditional epsilon (ϵ) prediction becomes trivial and does not provide meaningful learning signals. To overcome this, HistDiST adopts a v-prediction and v-loss framework as proposed in [10]. The velocity vector is defined as:

$$v_t = \sqrt{\bar{\alpha}_t}\,\epsilon - \sqrt{1 - \bar{\alpha}_t}\,x_0, \tag{4}$$

where x_0 is the clean latent representation (noise-free image), ϵ is the Gaussian noise added during the forward diffusion process, and $\bar{\alpha}_t$ represents the cumulative product of the noise schedule parameters up to timestep t. The corresponding v-prediction loss function is:

$$\mathcal{L} = \lambda_t \|v_t - \tilde{v}_t\|_2^2, \tag{5}$$

where v_t is the true velocity, $\tilde{v}_t$ is the velocity predicted by the network, and λ_t is a timestep-dependent weighting factor. Finally, HistDiST employs trailing timestep selection, prioritizing later timesteps during training to align with inference, where model starts from pure Gaussian noise. This enables generation of images with diverse brightness levels and helps preserve molecular features.

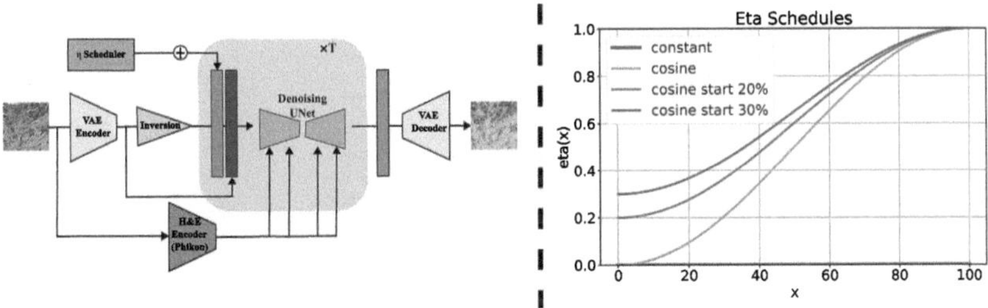

Fig. 2. HistDiST inference pipeline (Left): VAE encoder maps H&E image to latent space, where DDIM inversion derives noise latent and η-noise scheduling injects noise at different timesteps during denoising. The U-Net, conditioned on Phikon embeddings, refines the features, and the VAE decoder generates the final IHC output. (Right) η-schedules, with cosine-start schedules optimizing FID and structural preservation.

Inference: Fig. 2 (Left) shows the inference pipeline. Preserving the *morphological structure* of input images is essential for H&E-to-IHC stain translation. To achieve this, we employ DDIM inversion [21] to map input H&E representation z_0 to its corresponding noise vector z_T. This inversion process effectively "reverses" the generative path, allowing us to find the specific noise that encodes structural elements of the input. By using the inverted noise z_T and then sampling with the trained HistDiST, we obtain translated images that maintain the original morphological features while rendering them in the target IHC modality.

The inversion is performed via deterministic updates:

$$z_{t+1} = \sqrt{\alpha_{t+1}} \left(\frac{z_t - \sqrt{1 - \alpha_t}\, \epsilon_\theta(z_t, t, c_T)}{\sqrt{\alpha_t}} \right) + \sqrt{1 - \alpha_{t+1}}\, \epsilon_\theta(z_t, t, c_T), \qquad (6)$$

where α_t is the cumulative noise schedule, ϵ_θ is the predicted noise, and c_T is the text-based conditioning embedding. While using this inverted noise as the starting point for translation successfully preserved structural features, we observed a increase in FID scores (Table 2 (right), $\eta{=}0$), indicating that deterministic DDIM denoising restricted generative flexibility and hindered the model's ability to capture molecular diversity essential for accurate IHC synthesis.

To address this, we incorporated an η-cosine noise schedule that introduces *controlled stochasticity* during denoising. Unlike standard deterministic DDIM sampling, our schedule progressively increases the noise scale η_t from a non-zero initial value following a cosine schedule:

$$\eta_t(t) = 0.6 - 0.4 \cos \left(\pi \frac{t}{T} \right), \qquad (7)$$

where T is the total number of diffusion steps, and t is the current timestep. The denoising update then becomes:

$$z_{t-1} = \sqrt{\alpha_{t-1}} \left(\frac{z_t - \sqrt{1 - \alpha_t}\epsilon_\theta(z_t, t)}{\sqrt{\alpha_t}} \right) + \sqrt{1 - \alpha_{t-1} - \sigma_t^2} \cdot \epsilon_\theta(z_t, t) + \sigma_t \cdot \eta_t \cdot \epsilon, \qquad (8)$$

where σ_t is diffusion step-size parameter and $\epsilon \sim \mathcal{N}(0, I)$. By progressively increasing η_t from 0.2 to 1.0, the schedule fosters stochastic exploration during translation while maintaining structural coherence. The integration of η-cosine noise schedule lowered FID scores (Table 2 (right), η cosine start 20%), effectively striking a balance between morphological preservation and molecular fidelity.

4   Experiments

Datasets: We evaluate on two public H&E-to-IHC datasets: (1) MIST [11]: Paired H&E patches (1024×1024) with four IHC stains—HER2, Ki67, ER, and PR—using around 4k training pairs per stain and 1000 test pairs each. (2) BCI [14]: H&E–HER2 pairs (1024×1024) with 3896 training and 977 test samples.

Table 1. Evaluations on all translation tasks in the datasets, showing our superlative performance in almost all metrics. For PHV, $T = 0.01$ and KIDs are multiplied by 1K.

Dataset	Method	SSIM↑	PHV_{L1}↓	PHV_{L2}↓	PHV_{L3}↓	PHV_{L4}↓	MRA↑	FID↓	KID↓
MIST_{ER}	CycleGAN	0.1982	0.5175	0.5092	0.3710	0.8672	0.235	125.7	95.1
	Pix2Pix	0.1500	0.5818	0.5282	0.3700	0.8620	–	128.1	79
	PyramidP2P	0.2172	0.4767	0.4538	0.3757	0.8567	–	107.4	84.2
	ASP	0.2061	0.4336	0.4007	0.2649	0.8205	0.248	41.4	5.8
	MDCL	0.2005	0.4533	0.3969	0.2646	0.8238	0.322	34.9	**3.6**
	InstructPix2Pix	0.1536	0.5122	0.4961	0.3601	0.8679	0.210	61.3	38.9
	ControlNet	0.2112	0.4992	0.4479	0.3370	0.8522	0.130	38.0	9.1
	HistDiST	**0.2278**	**0.3645**	**0.3105**	**0.2465**	**0.8226**	**0.552**	**31.3**	**3.6**
MIST_{HER2}	ASP	0.2004	0.4534	0.4150	0.2665	0.8174	0.193	51.4	12.4
	MDCL	0.1810	0.4371	0.3944	0.2518	**0.8171**	0.233	44.4	7.5
	InstructPix2Pix	0.1353	0.5272	0.5045	0.3670	0.8740	0.125	65.6	33.7
	ControlNet	0.1813	0.4437	0.4042	0.3070	0.8415	0.188	**36.9**	6.9
	HistDiST	**0.2059**	**0.3830**	**0.3298**	**0.2512**	0.8245	**0.466**	**36.9**	**3.8**
MIST_{Ki67}	ASP	0.2410	0.4472	0.4001	0.2701	0.8128	0.148	51.0	19.1
	MDCL	0.2236	0.4005	0.3638	0.2465	**0.8064**	0.201	30.8	6.1
	InstructPix2Pix	0.1756	0.5076	0.4894	0.3508	0.8578	0.145	63.0	32.6
	ControlNet	0.2082	0.5205	0.4961	0.3712	0.8663	0.050	85.1	55.7
	HistDiST	**0.2463**	**0.3375**	**0.2893**	**0.2311**	0.8174	**0.484**	**28.05**	**4.4**
MIST_{PR}	ASP	0.2159	0.4484	0.3898	0.2564	0.8080	0.237	44.8	10.2
	MDCL	0.2081	0.4320	0.3768	**0.2499**	**0.8052**	0.317	38.3	7.1
	InstructPix2Pix	0.1339	0.5540	0.5387	0.3909	0.8786	0.126	82.7	60.4
	ControlNet	0.2135	0.4291	0.3866	0.3039	0.8362	0.225	35.6	8.3
	HistDiST	**0.2381**	**0.4001**	**0.3355**	0.2598	0.8265	**0.434**	**33.7**	**4.3**
BCI_{HER2}	ASP	**0.5032**	0.4308	0.3670	0.2235	0.7210	0.058	65.1	9.9
	MDCL	0.5029	0.4962	0.3861	0.2351	0.7344	0.084	51.2	13
	InstructPix2Pix	0.3242	0.5575	0.5142	0.3804	0.8196	0	96.5	50.2
	ControlNet	0.4581	0.5001	0.4233	0.2949	0.7577	0.07	43.5	10.2
	HistDiST	0.4693	**0.3136**	**0.2943**	**0.2165**	**0.7063**	**0.218**	**34.2**	**5.6**

Implementation Details: We fine-tune Stable Diffusion v1.5, training for 500 epochs with a batch size of 16. AdamW optimization is used with a $2e - 4$ learning rate, 1000 warmup steps, and a cosine decay schedule. Training alternates between H&E generation and H&E-to-IHC translation. v-prediction is set to $\gamma = 5$, and noise schedule is rescaled to enforce zero terminal SNR. Lastly, during inference, we use 200 inversion steps and 200 denoising steps.

Evaluation Metrics: We use both unpaired and paired metrics to assess image quality and molecular fidelity. Unpaired metrics include FID and KID for distributional similarity. Paired metrics include SSIM for image quality and PHV [15] for feature-level relevance. To capture pathology-specific semantics, we introduce Molecular Retrieval Accuracy (MRA), a novel metric leveraging GigaPath [24], a pathology foundation model trained on H&E and IHC data. MRA measures molecular fidelity by determining whether predicted IHC embedding best matches its ground-truth counterpart among all IHC embeddings in the test set using cosine similarity.

Results: We compare HistDiST with state-of-the-art stain translation models—CycleGAN [27], Pix2Pix [9], PyramidP2P [14], ASP [11], and MDCL [23]—for H&E-to-ER translation. As there are no specific diffusion-based approaches for H&E-to-IHC stain transfer, we adapt two image translation methods widely used in the natural domain, InstructPix2Pix [1] and ControlNet [26] and make comparisons with them. Specifically, we fine-tune InstructPix2Pix for our task, which is also used as the initialization for ControlNet. We train ControlNet with Canny edge map [2] of the H&E input as the conditioning signal. For stain translation tasks on other staining types, we select the top two GAN-based performers, along with InstructPix2Pix and ControlNet, for comparison. As shown in Table 1, HistDiST achieves consistent performance gains across all key metrics. It achieves the highest MRA scores, surpassing MDCL by 23% on MIST_{ER} and MIST_{HER2}, demonstrating superior molecular fidelity. It also attains the lowest PHV scores, indicating better feature-space alignment, and the best FID/KID scores, confirming that the generated IHC images are more visually realistic and distributionally aligned with real ones.

Table 2. Ablation study (on ER) during training (left) and inference (right). Abbreviations: "SD+IC": Stable Diffusion with input conditioning based on VAE-extracted H&E features (InstructPix2Pix), "v-pred": v-prediction, "Inv": DDIM Inversion followed by DDIM sampling with η-cosine start 20% noise, "xAtt": cross-attention with Phikon-extracted H&E features. The inference strategies involve DDIM inversion for structure preservation, followed by DDIM sampling with different noise schedules (Fig. 2 (right))

Training Strategy	SSIM↑	PHV_{avg} ↓	FID↓
SD+IC	0.154	0.559	61.3
SD+IC, vp	0.198	0.501	37.5
SD+IC, vp, Inv	0.228	0.511	41.3
SD+IC, vp, Inv, xAtt	0.227	0.436	31.3

Inference Strategy	PHV_{avg} ↓	MRA ↑	FID↓
η constant	0.450	0.598	41.7
η cosine	0.443	0.559	34.3
η cosine start 20%	0.436	0.552	31.3
η cosine start 30%	0.433	0.547	30.1

Ablation Studies and Qualitative Results: Table 2 (Left) and Fig. 3 present the quantitative and qualitative impact of different components in our framework. Fine-tuning Stable Diffusion with input conditioning alone on the paired dataset results in poor structural preservation and low molecular fidelity, leading to significant performance degradation across all metrics. Integrating v-prediction improves molecular expression patterns, enhancing FID scores and feature-space alignment. However, structural inconsistencies persist (as can also be seen in Fig. 3), indicating that direct adaptation remains insufficient for accurate stain translation.

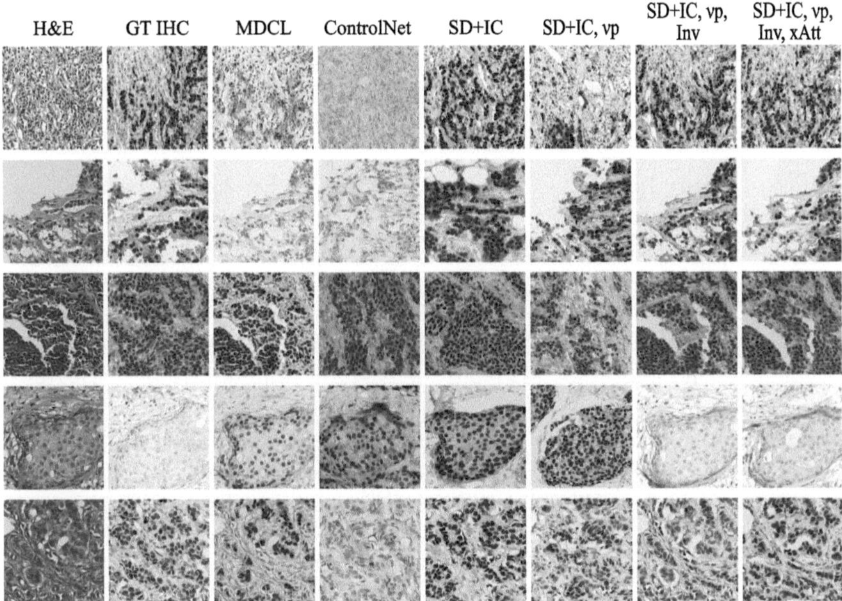

Fig. 3. ER translation outputs across methods (see Table 2 for abbreviations). The first two columns show the H&E input and its corresponding ground-truth ER pair from the dataset, the next two columns (MDCL and ControlNet) show the previous top-performing GAN- and Diffusion-based approaches, and the last four columns are the incremental ablation of the components of our model, with our final model shown as the last column.

To address this, we conduct joint training on H&E generation and H&E-to-IHC translation, and at inference, apply DDIM inversion followed by DDIM sampling with η cosine start 20% noise schedule, which greatly enhances structural preservation. Finally, incorporating Phikon-extracted morphological embeddings into U-Net's cross-attention layers further refines feature-space alignment and enhances structural integrity and molecular fidelity, yielding the best overall performance. This demonstrates that explicit pathology-aware conditioning is critical for accurate molecular reconstruction and high-fidelity stain translation. The qualitative comparison of our method against the best-performing GAN- and Diffusion-based approaches, MDCL and ControlNet, is also shown in Fig. 3. While ControlNet mostly provides improvements over the InstructPix2Pix baseline, it fails to preserve the structure accurately since acquiring Canny edges for low-contrast H&E images is challenging, and also fails to obtain accurate IHC expressions. Furthermore, in most cases, MDCL often introduces artifacts

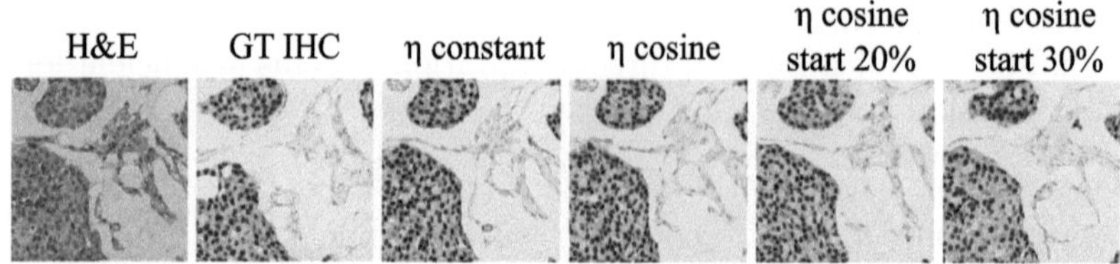

Fig. 4. ER translation outputs across noise schedules (see Table 2 for abbreviations).

or fails to capture fine molecular details. On the other hand, HistDiST better preserves molecular expression patterns and produces more precise IHC intensity distributions, aligning closely with GT IHC. For instance, in the fourth row of Fig. 3, MDCL and ControlNet incorrectly predict the molecular expression pattern (shown with a high expression level) while our method accurately predicts the patterns as low expression levels (last column).

Table 2 (right) and Fig. 4 examine the effect of different η-noise schedules at inference, with Fig. 2 (right) visualizing the tested schedules. Setting $\eta = 0$ yields optimal structural alignment between input H&E and translated IHC but results in high FID scores, indicating a poor match to the real IHC distribution. Introducing a cosine noise schedule starting from zero improves FID scores while preserving structural integrity, suggesting that injecting controlled stochasticity at higher timesteps promotes distributional alignment with real IHC data. Increasing the starting noise level to 0.2 further reduces FID scores with minimal structural loss, while increasing it to 0.3 introduces noticeable structural deviations, despite additional improvements in FID. To balance structural preservation, molecular fidelity, and distributional realism, we adopt the cosine schedule starting at 0.2 as the optimal configuration.

5   Conclusion and Limitations

We present HistDiST, an LDM-based framework for H&E-to-IHC stain translation, integrating pathology-aware conditioning, DDIM inversion, and zero terminal SNR enforcement to enhance structural fidelity and molecular accuracy. Notably, the inversion process helps to preserve the structure; still, we employ controlled stochasticity during denoising as fully-deterministic sampling negatively affects the fidelity of generated images. We also introduce Molecular Retrieval Accuracy (MRA), a novel metric for pathology-aware evaluation based on the alignment of pathological features. Experiments on MIST and BCI datasets demonstrate that HistDiST achieves superior visual fidelity, molecular accuracy and structural preservation compared to the existing approaches. Nevertheless, we emphasize that this method is not clinically applicable at this stage; additional validation and analysis (e.g., expert review or downstream task performance) would be required before considering diagnostic use. Future studies can further explore the potential of stain transfer methods by benchmarking their utility in downstream tasks such as patch-level classification or segmentation.

Acknowledgments. The work described in this paper was conducted in the framework of the Graduate School 2543/1 "Intraoperative Multi-Sensory Tissue Differentiation in Oncology" (project ID 40947457) funded by the German Research Foundation (DFG - Deutsche Forschungsgemeinschaft). This work has been supported by the Deutsche Forschungsgemeinschaft (DFG) âĂŞ EXC number 2064/1 âĂŞ Project number 390727645. The authors thank the International Max Planck Research School for Intelligent Systems (IMPRS-IS) for supporting Valay Bundele and Mehran Hosseinzadeh.

References

1. Brooks, T., Holynski, A., Efros, A.A.: Instructpix2pix: learning to follow image editing instructions. In: Proceedings of the IEEE/CVF Conference on Computer Vision and Pattern Recognition, pp. 18392–18402 (2023)
2. Canny, J.: A computational approach to edge detection. IEEE Trans. Pattern Anal. Mach. Intell. **6**, 679–698 (1986)
3. Chen, F., Zhang, R., Zheng, B., Sun, Y., He, J., Qin, W.: Pathological semantics-preserving learning for h&e-to-ihc virtual staining. In: International Conference on Medical Image Computing and Computer-Assisted Intervention, pp. 384–394. Springer, Heidelberg (2024). https://doi.org/10.1007/978-3-031-72083-3_36
4. Dubey, S., Chong, Y., Knudsen, B., Elhabian, S.Y.: Vims: virtual immunohistochemistry multiplex staining via text-to-stain diffusion trained on uniplex stains. In: International Workshop on Machine Learning in Medical Imaging, pp. 143–155. Springer, Heidelberg (2024). https://doi.org/10.1007/978-3-031-73284-3_15
5. Filiot, A., et al.: Scaling self-supervised learning for histopathology with masked image modeling. medrxiv 2023 (2023)
6. He, Y., et al.: Pst-diff: achieving high-consistency stain transfer by diffusion models with pathological and structural constraints. IEEE Trans. Med. Imaging (2024)
7. Hertz, A., Aberman, K., Cohen-Or, D.: Delta denoising score. In: Proceedings of the IEEE/CVF International Conference on Computer Vision, pp. 2328–2337 (2023)
8. Ho, J., Jain, A., Abbeel, P.: Denoising diffusion probabilistic models. Adv. Neural. Inf. Process. Syst. **33**, 6840–6851 (2020)
9. Isola, P., Zhu, J.Y., Zhou, T., Efros, A.A.: Image-to-image translation with conditional adversarial networks. In: Proceedings of the IEEE Conference on Computer Vision and Pattern Recognition, pp. 1125–1134 (2017)
10. Karras, T., Aittala, M., Aila, T., Laine, S.: Elucidating the design space of diffusion-based generative models. Adv. Neural. Inf. Process. Syst. **35**, 26565–26577 (2022)
11. Li, F., Hu, Z., Chen, W., Kak, A.: Adaptive supervised patchnce loss for learning h&e-to-ihc stain translation with inconsistent groundtruth image pairs. In: International Conference on Medical Image Computing and Computer-Assisted Intervention, pp. 632–641. Springer, Heidelberg (2023). https://doi.org/10.1007/978-3-031-43987-2_61
12. Li, J., et al.: Virtual immunohistochemistry staining for histological images assisted by weakly-supervised learning. In: Proceedings of the IEEE/CVF Conference on Computer Vision and Pattern Recognition, pp. 11259–11268 (2024)

13. Lin, S., Liu, B., Li, J., Yang, X.: Common diffusion noise schedules and sample steps are flawed. In: Proceedings of the IEEE/CVF Winter Conference on Applications of Computer Vision, pp. 5404–5411 (2024)
14. Liu, S., Zhu, C., Xu, F., Jia, X., Shi, Z., Jin, M.: BCI: breast cancer immuno-histochemical image generation through pyramid pix2pix. In: Proceedings of the IEEE/CVF Conference on Computer Vision and Pattern Recognition, pp. 1815–1824 (2022)
15. Liu, S., et al.: Unpaired stain transfer using pathology-consistent constrained generative adversarial networks. IEEE Trans. Med. Imaging **40**(8), 1977–1989 (2021)
16. Nichol, A., et al.: Glide: towards photorealistic image generation and editing with text-guided diffusion models. arXiv preprint arXiv:2112.10741 (2021)
17. Peng, Q., et al.: Advancing h&e-to-ihc virtual staining with task-specific domain knowledge for her2 scoring. In: International Conference on Medical Image Computing and Computer-Assisted Intervention, pp. 3–13. Springer, Heidelberg (2024). https://doi.org/10.1007/978-3-031-72083-3_1
18. Qu, L., Zhang, C., Li, G., Zheng, H., Peng, C., He, W.: Advancing h&e-to-ihc stain translation in breast cancer: a multi-magnification and attention-based approach. In: 2024 IEEE International Conference on Cybernetics and Intelligent Systems (CIS) and IEEE International Conference on Robotics, Automation and Mechatronics (RAM), pp. 441–446. IEEE (2024)
19. Rombach, R., Blattmann, A., Lorenz, D., Esser, P., Ommer, B.: High-resolution image synthesis with latent diffusion models. In: Proceedings of the IEEE/CVF Conference on Computer Vision and Pattern Recognition, pp. 10684–10695 (2022)
20. Shen, Y., Ke, J.: Staindiff: Transfer stain styles of histology images with denoising diffusion probabilistic models and self-ensemble. In: International Conference on Medical Image Computing and Computer-Assisted Intervention, pp. 549–559. Springer, Heidelberg (2023). https://doi.org/10.1007/978-3-031-43987-2_53
21. Song, J., Meng, C., Ermon, S.: Denoising diffusion implicit models. arXiv preprint arXiv:2010.02502 (2020)
22. Tumanyan, N., Geyer, M., Bagon, S., Dekel, T.: Plug-and-play diffusion features for text-driven image-to-image translation. In: Proceedings of the IEEE/CVF Conference on Computer Vision and Pattern Recognition, pp. 1921–1930 (2023)
23. Wang, S., Zhang, Z., Yan, H., Xu, M., Wang, G.: Mix-domain contrastive learning for unpaired h&e-to-ihc stain translation. In: 2024 IEEE International Conference on Image Processing (ICIP), pp. 2982–2988. IEEE (2024)
24. Xu, H., et al.: A whole-slide foundation model for digital pathology from real-world data. Nature **630**(8015), 181–188 (2024)
25. Yan, X., et al.: Versatile stain transfer in histopathology using a unified diffusion framework. In: 2025 IEEE 22nd International Symposium on Biomedical Imaging (ISBI), pp. 1–5. IEEE (2025)
26. Zhang, L., Rao, A., Agrawala, M.: Adding conditional control to text-to-image diffusion models. In: Proceedings of the IEEE/CVF International Conference on Computer Vision, pp. 3836–3847 (2023)
27. Zhu, J.Y., Park, T., Isola, P., Efros, A.A.: Unpaired image-to-image translation using cycle-consistent adversarial networks. In: Proceedings of the IEEE International Conference on Computer Vision, pp. 2223–2232 (2017)

Deep Learning-Assisted Dynamic Mode Decomposition for Non-resonant Background Removal in CARS Spectroscopy

Adithya Ashok Chalain Valapil[1]([✉]) [ID], Carl Messerschmidt[2] [ID],
Maha Shadaydeh[1] [ID], Michael Schmitt[2] [ID], Jürgen Popp[2,3] [ID],
and Joachim Denzler[1] [ID]

[1] Computer Vision Group, Friedrich-Schiller University, 07743 Jena, Germany
{adithya.ashok,maha.shadaydeh,joachim.denzler}@uni-jena.de
[2] Leibniz-Institute of Photonic Technology, 07745 Jena, Germany
{carl.messerschmidt,m.schmitt,juergen.popp}@uni-jena.de
[3] Institute of Physical Chemistry, Friedrich-Schiller University, 07743 Jena, Germany
https://inf-cv.uni-jena.de/

Abstract. Coherent Anti-Stokes Raman Spectroscopy (CARS) provides non-invasive, label-free chemical analysis at high spatial resolution, making it a powerful tool for biomedical and material imaging. However, their effectiveness is hindered by a dominant and unpredictable non-resonant background (NRB) that distorts meaningful spectral features. Existing NRB removal methods often require additional measurements or computationally intensive post-processing. In this work, we present a physics-informed framework that leverages the broadband, low-rank structure of the NRB using Dynamic Mode Decomposition (DMD) for unsupervised separation of resonant Raman modes from non-resonant contributions in the spectral domain. We further introduce **DA-DMD** - a Deep Learning-Assisted DMD approach, that uses an attention mechanism to adaptively weight DMD modes and a CNN with skip connection to enhance Raman signal reconstruction. Trained entirely on synthetic data, DA-DMD eliminates the need for experimental labels or calibration. We validate our methods on synthetic and real CARS measurements, demonstrating superior background suppression, fidelity preservation, and generalization compared to existing approaches. DA-DMD offers fast inference and improves robustness, positioning it as a practical tool for scalable chemical imaging in complex environments.

Keywords: Dynamic Mode Decomposition · Raman Spectroscopy · Channel Attention · Delay Embedding · Unsupervised Learning

Supplementary Information The online version contains supplementary material available at https://doi.org/10.1007/978-3-032-12840-9_4.

1   Introduction

Analyzing molecular composition is fundamental to fields such as biology, materials science, and medicine. Spectroscopy, particularly Raman scattering, enables label-free chemical imaging from spectral measurements by probing vibrational modes of molecules [27,33]. However, traditional Spontaneous Raman (SR) spectroscopy suffers from weak signal intensity, requiring long integration times that limit its use in real-time applications. Coherent Anti-Stokes Raman Spectroscopy (CARS) overcomes this limitation by using nonlinear optical interactions to coherently excite molecular vibrations, boosting signal strength by several orders of magnitude [14]. This makes CARS ideal for high-speed, chemically specific spectral analysis. However, CARS suffers from a critical challenge: the presence of a non-resonant background (NRB) - an intense, broadband signal arising from electronic nonlinearities rather than molecular vibrations. This NRB distorts spectral line shapes and conceals the very information CARS aims to reveal [37].

This study proposes decomposing the CARS spectra into two components, namely the NRB and the Raman signatures, using dynamic mode decomposition (**DMD**). The NRB spectrum is typically broad and featureless [23], implying slow changes over wavenumber or low-frequency dynamics, which can be separated from the Raman spectra that exhibit fast changes over wavenumber or high-frequency dynamics.

DMD is a data-driven method for extracting spatiotemporal patterns in sequential measurements [28]. This is achieved by decomposing these measurements into a set of modes, each of which is associated with a fixed oscillation frequency and a decay/growth rate over time [50]. DMD has been traditionally applied to spatiotemporal dynamic systems in diverse fields such as fluid mechanics [41], robotics [6], ecosystems [42] and neuroscience [8]. For the first time, in this study, we adapt DMD for spectral analysis by reinterpreting wavenumber progression as a pseudo-temporal coordinate. The Raman signature embedded in the CARS spectra causes strong correlation at adjacent wavenumbers of the CARS spectra due to the finite vibrational mode bandwidth, which has a peak centered at a wavenumber and influences the intensity values over a range of adjacent wavenumbers (lineshapes) [14,17]. These correlations manifest as a sequence of local and fast intensity variations across the wavenumber axis, creating a sequential structure that we exploit for NRB removal.

We introduce two approaches using DMD. 1. **Unsupervised DMD**, which clusters the DMD modes into low-frequency (NRB) and high-frequency (Raman) components using spectral priors, while requiring no training data; 2. Deep Learning-Assisted DMD (**DA-DMD**), where we propose to enhance the modes selection by combining the DMD decomposition capability with channel attention [20,46] and further refine the reconstructions via convolutional networks [36].

The efficacy of both approaches is validated through quantitative and qualitative analyses, employing both synthetic and experimental data sets. The results demonstrate that our unsupervised DMD approach not only matches but also surpasses conventional unsupervised methods in suppressing NRB. Additionally,

DA-DMD attains state-of-the-art accuracy with expedited inference while training with considerably fewer samples compared to other deep-learning methods.

2   Related Works

Existing NRB removal strategies face critical trade-offs. There are experimental methods like interferometric CARS [38], frequency modulation CARS [16], and polarization CARS [13] for narrow-band operation, as well as time-resolved CARS [48] and Fourier transform CARS [35] for broadband mode. These methods suppress NRB at the source but require complex instrumentation and sacrifice signal strength.

Alternative approaches focus on the post-processing of measured spectra. There are widely used methods like time domain Kramers-Kronig (TDKK) [11,30] and Maximum Entropy Method (MEM) [45], which are computationally intensive. Therefore, the discrete Hilbert transform used in these methods was later replaced by a learned matrix approach in LeDHT [10]. Another approach uses singular value decomposition (SVD) and transformed basis vectors to establish the "factorized Kramers–Kronig and error correction" (fKK-EC) method [12]. These two methods significantly improved the speed of the phase retrieval task. However, these traditional methods require extra reference spectra, which can be time-consuming and may not always be available [25].

Conversely, deep learning methods offer a promising solution for NRB removal without requiring reference spectra. Methods like SpecNet [24,44], long short-term memory (LSTM) [19], bi-directional LSTM (Bi-LSTM) [25], very deep convolutional autoencoders (VECTOR) [32,49], generative adversarial networks (GAN) [31,47] and convolutional neural networks with gated recurrent units (CNN+GRU) [47] can provide a more efficient and effective way to remove NRB and recover the underlying Raman spectra by training on synthetic spectra. We compare our DA-DMD approach with these methods.

Using multiscale frequency analysis, the wavelet prism signal decomposition technique [39] separates Raman features from NRB. This was recently extended to interpolated inverse discrete wavelet transforms that we refer to as IWT in our work [18]. We also compare our unsupervised DMD setup with this method.

3   Unsupervised Hankelized DMD for NRB Removal

3.1   DMD: Preliminaries

Let $\mathbf{x}_j \in \mathbb{R}^M$ denote sequential data with time index $j = 1, ..., N$, where M and N denote the dimension of each measurement and the number of measurement snapshots, respectively. DMD finds a best-fit linear operator $\mathbf{A} \in \mathbb{R}^{M \times M}$ such that $\mathbf{x}_{j+1} \approx \mathbf{A}\mathbf{x}_j$ holds for all pairs of measurements j [5]. Let $\mathbf{X} = \begin{bmatrix} \mathbf{x}_1 \, \mathbf{x}_2 \cdots \mathbf{x}_{N-1} \end{bmatrix}$ and the time-shifted matrix $\mathbf{X}' = \begin{bmatrix} \mathbf{x}_2 \, \mathbf{x}_3 \ldots \mathbf{x}_N \end{bmatrix}$. This relationship can be described in a matrix form as $\mathbf{X}' \approx \mathbf{A}\mathbf{X}$. The best-fit linear operator is computed as $\mathbf{A} = \mathbf{X}'\mathbf{X}^\dagger$ where † is the Moore-Penrose pseudoinverse, which is computed using the singular value decomposition (SVD) of $\mathbf{X}$.

The eigendecomposition of $\mathbf{A}$ yields the eigenvalues and eigenvectors (modes) that can be used for signal reconstruction. Specifically, let ϕ_i and λ_i be the ith eigenvector-eigenvalue pair of $\mathbf{A}$, $\mathbf{x}_j$ at any time j can be reconstructed as

$$\mathbf{x}_j = \sum_{i=1}^{M} b_i \phi_i \lambda_i^j \tag{1}$$

where b_i denotes the weights of the modes in the initial state $\mathbf{x}_0$.

The eigenvalues λ_i are in general complex numbers that can be defined as $\lambda_i = e^{(\sigma_i + j2\pi f_i)\Delta(t)}$ where σ_i and f_i are respectively the growth/decay rate and the eigenfrequency for the i-the mode, and $\Delta(t)$ is the time interval between two consecutive snapshots of measurement.

3.2 Hankelized DMD of CARS Spectra

Time delay embedding is an established method for the geometric reconstruction of attractors for nonlinear systems [40,43]. As traditional DMD assumes Markovian dynamics, where only the present step matters and lacks memory of past states, we employ delay embedding (Hankelization) [9,51], which captures hidden correlations across wavenumber.

In our study, the dimension of the measurement at each wavenumber of the spectrum equals one. To match the definition of $\mathbf{x}_j$ in Sect. 3.1 and to be able to use DMD to decompose the spectrum into M modes, we use an M dimensional delay embedding vector to represent the wavenumbers. This forms a Hankel matrix $\mathbf{H}$ on input $\mathbf{x}_j$ as in Eq. 2 which embeds pseudo-temporal dynamics into the spectrum, allowing us to analyze the spectral evolution more comprehensively. The Hankel matrix $\mathbf{H}$ is constructed as follows:

$$\mathbf{H} = \begin{bmatrix} x_1 & x_2 & .. & x_L \\ x_2 & x_3 & .. & x_{L+1} \\ . & . & .. & . \\ . & . & .. & . \\ x_M & x_{M+1} & .. & x_N \end{bmatrix}. \tag{2}$$

Here, N refers to the length of original spectrum and $L = N - M + 1$. The embedding delay dimension M is calculated as delay or lag τ that encapsulates maximum information between the spectrum and its delayed version. It can be calculated using autocorrelation function (ACF) metric [7] with Eq. 9 in Appx. A. An example is shown for ethanol spectrum in Fig. 5. Here, the first major dip in the ACF curve at $\tau = 12$ is considered a good value for M in this case.

3.3 Mode Clustering for NRB Removal

After the decomposition of the spectrum into M modes, we separate these modes into two clusters; the first low-frequency cluster is used to reconstruct the NRB, while the second high-frequency cluster is used to reconstruct the Raman signatures. We show this interpretation using ethanol as an example in Appx. B Fig. 6. The first mode resembles NRB spectral contribution, while the combination of the second and third modes shows major similarity with the Raman line shapes. Some of the missing peaks are often present at higher modes. To separate these M modes, we employ 2-class clustering [21] to group the eigenfrequencies of λ_i into two clusters, as illustrated in Fig. 1. The reconstructed cluster, according to Eq. 1, without the first mode, is expected to contain the Raman signatures. To refine results, we iteratively reapply DMD as suggested in [34] to the previous high-frequency cluster to eliminate the very high-frequency modes. Therefore, the cluster with the first mode is retained. The recursive process is terminated when a frequency above a threshold is eliminated [15,29]. We learn this threshold from the Fourier transform of the spectrum. This process ultimately removes very high-frequency noises.

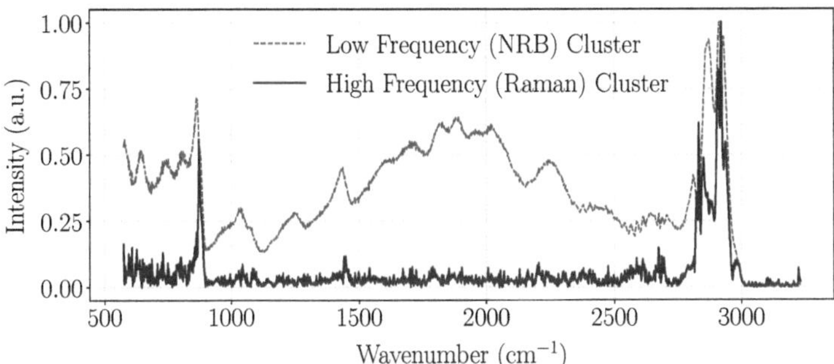

Fig. 1. Clustering example. Reconstruction of clusters for separating the Raman signatures (in blue) and NRB (in red) is shown. A 2-class clustering is applied on the frequencies of the eigenvalues λ_i to extract the Raman modes. Results are shown before the removal of very high-frequency modes in the Raman signature.

4 DA-DMD: Deep Learning-Assisted DMD

The main challenge in the above-discussed DMD method is the selection of relevant modes using clustering. Assuming the ideal selection of clusters, we still need parametrized smoothing functions like a recursive DMD process that sometimes even out relevant peaks. To address these limitations, we propose a deep learning-assisted DMD (DA-DMD) approach as shown in Fig. 2. We introduce an attention mechanism after Hankelized DMD to learn the relevance of each mode using synthetic training data, as each mode contributes differently to the final reconstructed spectrum. Once the importance of each mode is learned, a set of convolutional layers reduces multi-mode input to a single-channel representation corresponding to the clean spectrum.

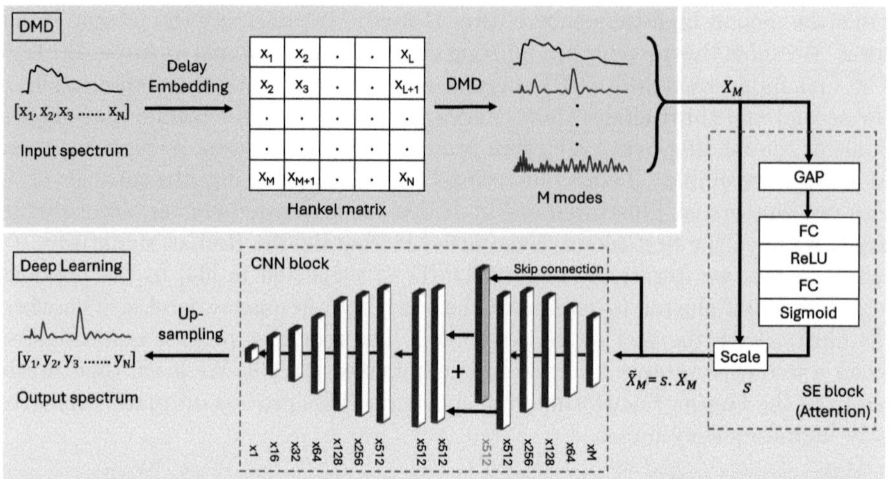

Fig. 2. Flow diagram of DA-DMD. Once the modes are extracted using Hankelized DMD, a Squeeze-and-Excitation (SE) block [20] is used for channel attention to extract the relevance of each mode (Eq. 4). A set of convolutional layers is then used to produce denoised spectra.

A Squeeze-and-Excitation (SE) block is used for attention in our model [20]. It optimizes the feature representation by adaptively reweighing the extracted DMD modes based on the most relevant spectral components, while suppressing less significant ones. The squeeze operation condenses global information from the extracted DMD modes by Global Average Pooling (GAP). For an input $X \in \mathbb{R}^{B \times M \times N}$ with batch size B, number of modes (equal to delay embedding) M and spectral length N, we obtain activation of mode m at spectral point i for batch b as $X_{b,m,i}$. The GAP reduces each mode to a single value as:

$$\bar{X}_m = \frac{1}{N} \sum_{i=1}^{N} X_{m,i}. \tag{3}$$

This reduces X to a compressed feature vector $\bar{X} \in \mathbb{R}^{B \times M}$, which represents the global contribution of mode m across the entire spectrum. Then comes the excitation step, where we pass $\bar{X}_m$ through a fully connected network or gated mechanism to determine the importance of each mode. The excitation mechanism consists of two fully connected layers with ReLU activation, followed by a sigmoid activation to obtain the mode attention vector as:

$$s = \sigma(W_2 \cdot ReLU(W_1 \cdot \bar{X})), \tag{4}$$

where $W_1 \in \mathbb{R}^{(M/k) \times M}$ reduces the dimension by a factor of k and $W_2 \in \mathbb{R}^{M \times (M/k)}$ re-expands it back to match M. The extracted DMD modes are scaled using learned importance weights, i.e., $\tilde{X}_m = s_m.X_m$.

Following the SE block's mode weighting, the architecture employs a CNN block with a set of convolutional layers [36] that expands the multi-channel input (corresponding to DMD modes) to capture fine characteristics, which then collapses into a single feature map (corresponding to Raman spectra). A skip connection is used from the SE block's output to a deeper convolutional layer as shown in Fig. 2. This preserves spatial information by bridging the shallow and deep representations during the forward pass in the network. The deeper layers are used to enhance gradient flow and enable iterative feature refinement. This design choice prevents feature dilution and ensures that the remaining CNN layers reconstruct a clean and accurate Raman spectrum from the learned representations. As the delay embedding step alters the results in reduced spectral length, a linear interpolation-based upsampling layer is added at the end to ensure that the final spectrum $y \in \mathbb{R}^N$ has the same length as the input.

5   Experiments and Results

Experiments are done on synthetic and real samples. We compare the proposed methods with several state-of-the-art techniques, including IWT, TDKK, and other deep learning (DA-DMD, VECTOR, GAN, CNN+GRU, Bi-LSTM, LSTM, SpecNet) methods. Both DMD and IWT are unsupervised methods and require no training. The results of each experiment are discussed mainly in comparison to those of DA-DMD.

We include both qualitative analysis and quantitative metric evaluation. Qualitatively, we discuss the characteristics of a good Raman reconstruction by the visual quality of peak occurrence and intensities. Quantitatively, we compare using two metrics: Mean Square Error (MSE) and Pearson's correlation (r), which are calculated as follows.

$$\text{MSE} = \sum_{i=1}^{K}(\hat{y}_i - y_i)^2, \quad r = \frac{\sum_{i=1}^{K}(\hat{y}_i - \bar{\hat{y}})(y_i - \bar{y})}{\sqrt{\sum_{i=1}^{K}(\hat{y}_i - \bar{\hat{y}})^2}\sqrt{\sum_{i=1}^{K}(y_i - \bar{y})^2}}, \tag{5}$$

where $\hat{y}$ and y are predicted and ground truth respectively. The mean of K spectra is denoted by $\bar{y}$. The MSE is an error metric that is best when close to 0, while r shows the best similarity when close to 1.

5.1   Experiments on Synthetic Spectra

Synthetic Data Generation. We generate synthetic Raman-CARS pairs following [44], modeling Raman spectra as Lorentzian peaks(Eq. 6) with random NRB as noise (Eq. 7) among a fourth-degree polynomial and double sigmoid function. For each spectral pair, the function parameters are also randomly selected as specified below.

$$\text{Resonant: } \chi_r^{(3)}(\omega) = \sum_{p=1}^{P} \frac{E_p}{\Omega_p - \omega - i\gamma_p}, \tag{6}$$

where, $P \sim \mathcal{U}\{1, 25\}$ is number of peaks varied per sample, $E_p \in \mathcal{U}(0.01, 1.0)$ is the amplitude, $\Omega_p \in \mathcal{U}(0, 1)$ is the normalized resonance frequency, $\gamma_p \in \mathcal{U}(0.001, 0.02)$ is the linewidth and ω is the normalized Raman shift ranging 1000 points over $[0, 1]$.

$$\text{Non-resonant: } \chi_{nrb}^{(3)}(\omega) = \begin{cases} \frac{1}{1+e^{-b_1(\omega-c_1)}} \cdot \frac{1}{1+e^{b_2(\omega-c_2)}} & \text{(Sigmoid)} \\ a\omega^4 + b\omega^3 + c\omega^2 + d\omega + e & \text{(Polynomial)} \end{cases}, \tag{7}$$

where, $b_1, b_2 \sim \mathcal{N}(10, 5)$ control the steepness of the rising and falling rates of the sigmoid functions, $c_1 \sim \mathcal{N}(0.2, 0.3)$ and $c_2 \sim \mathcal{N}(0.7, 0.3)$ determine the position of inflection points of the sigmoid function. The coefficients of polynomial function are $a, c \sim \mathcal{U}(-1, 1)$ and $b, d, e \sim \mathcal{U}(-10, 10)$.

$$\text{CARS spectrum: } I_{\text{CARS}}(\omega) \propto \left| \chi_r^{(3)}(\omega) + \chi_{\text{nrb}}^{(3)}(\omega) \right|^2, \tag{8}$$

to which a random noise $\sim \mathcal{U}(0.0005, 0.003)$ is also added to simulate high-frequency disturbances. The total spectrum is normalized to ensure that learning focuses on the spectral shape rather than absolute intensity.

DA-DMD Architecture Selection. Our DA-DMD model is implemented on PyTorch 2.2.1 with CUDA 12.1 and cuDNN 8.9.2. The architecture mainly comprises an SE block for reweighting the modes and a CNN block for supervision and spectral refinement. Ablation studies (Table 1) on synthetic spectra have been conducted to confirm the necessity of both of these blocks. We used 1700 spectra to train our model for each setup and then test our prediction on 300 samples. In the first setup (Without SE block), the SE channel attention block is removed by keeping only the CNN layers. In the second setup (Without CNN block), the result of the attention block is reduced to one prediction result. We see that the performance of our model without either SE or CNN block is worse than the complete DA-DMD model.

Table 1. Ablation Study. Testing the impact of each of the SE and CNN blocks in the deep learning architecture of the DA-DMD model based on MSE and correlation (mean $\pm$ standard deviation) for 300 synthetic spectral predictions.

DA-DMD Model	MSE	Corr
Complete model	0.0005 ± 0.0008	0.9494 ± 0.1607
Without SE block	0.0050 ± 0.0025	0.6026 ± 0.1621
Without CNN block	0.0033 ± 0.0021	0.7664 ± 0.1580

In contrast to our CNN block, other architectures like autoencoders were tested and failed. Various techniques like batch normalization, spatial attention, and multiple skip connections were tested to optimize the architecture, but they did not improve the performance significantly. We, therefore, came up with the architecture detailed in Sect. 4. It is trained for 50 epochs. We used Adam Optimizer with a learning rate of 0.001 during backpropagation [26]. The number of delay embedding is selected as $M = 12$ by estimating using ACF as discussed in Sect. 3.2. The reduction ratio $k = 4$ is optimized among common values used in the original SE block [20]. The Mean Square Error (MSE) is our loss function.

Deep Learning Model Evaluation. All deep learning models are trained on synthetic datasets. We use available pretrained models or training setup for VECTOR [4], GAN [2], CNN+GRU [2], Bi-LSTM [3], LSTM [3] and SpecNet [1].

The time-domain Kramers Kronig (TDKK) algorithm needs reference measurements and requires optimizations for phase and scale retrieval parameters. Another major drawback they have is the high computational time. Deep learning models overcome these limitations. The computational complexity of the deep learning models is compared in Table 2. All experiments were conducted on a workstation equipped with an NVIDIA GeForce RTX 1080 GPU (40 GB VRAM), Intel Core i5-11600 CPU, and 32 GB RAM, running Ubuntu 22.04. It is clear that DA-DMD has a significantly low training time. This is mainly because of the need for a significantly lower number of training data (2000 synthetic samples), as DMD largely supports the network with preprocessed or decomposed modes. The prediction time is also low compared to all other models (except GAN). VECTOR also performs closely well in the computational complexity test. Though all the Recurrent Neural Networks (RNN) based models (LSTM, Bi-LSTM, CNN+GRU) have fewer trainable parameters than DA-DMD, they demand high computational time.

Table 2. Model evaluation. Comparison of computational requirements in terms of the training (per epoch) and prediction time (per spectrum), number of samples, and number of parameters for all deep learning models.

	DA-DMD	VECTOR	GAN	CNN+GRU	Bi-LSTM	LSTM	SpecNet
# Training samples	**2k**	200k	200k	200k	50k	50k	50k
Training time/epoch (s)	**6.6**	18.7	142	6667	1360	240	73
# Parameters	0.5M	111.8M	6.2M	84.0k	5.2k	**3.9k**	6.0M
Prediction time (ms)	6	7	**1**	713	168	103	71

Analysis of Results. A comparison of all models is conducted with 1000 newly simulated spectra to assess the consistency of performance. All models' performance for a synthetic sample is shown in Fig. 3. The unsupervised DMD and IWT produce peaks at the correct location. The results of IWT show good peak recovery, but a slight phase shift often remains in the unsupervised setting. DMD also

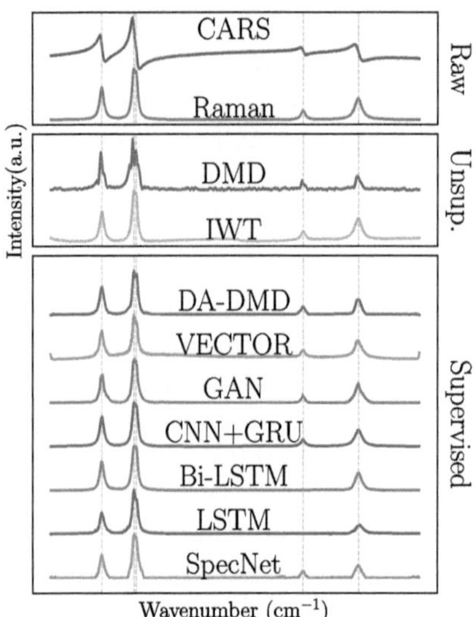

Fig. 3. Qualitative performance of **synthetic spectra** with reconstruction on one sample with all models.

Table 3. Quantitative performance using MSE and correlation is shown on **synthetic data** for the unsupervised DMD, IWT, and the seven supervised deep learning models (DA-DMD, VECTOR, GAN, CNN+GRU, Bi-LSTM, LSTM, SpecNet).

Model	MSE	Corr
DMD	**0.0063** ±0.0132	**0.67** ±0.11
IWT	0.0109 ±0.0062	0.21 ±0.19
DA-DMD	**0.0006** ±0.0006	**0.98** ±0.01
VECTOR	0.0007 ±0.0010	0.97 ±0.02
GAN	0.0033 ±0.0073	0.88 ±0.14
CNN+GRU	0.0031 ±0.0017	0.90 ±0.09
Bi-LSTM	0.0017 ±0.0023	0.90 ±0.13
LSTM	0.0221 ±0.0430	0.78 ±0.31
SpecNet	0.0013 ±0.0016	0.94 ±0.05

produces good performance, predicting peaks that correlate with Raman peaks. From Table 3, we can see that DA-DMD and VECTOR perform best considering all metrics. According to the previous study [47], GAN and CNN+GRU are expected to perform better for synthetic spectra. This performance discrepancy is due to the difference in hyperparameters for synthetic training data generation. Figure 7 in Appx. C shows the results of a second test done using a synthetic data generator provided by [47]. Both GAN and CNN+GRU models perform best in this secondary test. Our DA-DMD and VECTOR show consistently good results across both tests. LSTM shows the worst performance among the deep learning models.

5.2   Experiments on Real CARS Spectra

There are two types of real samples used in our experiments. We use spectra measured using broadband CARS (BCARS) setup. Toluene CARS (3- & 2- color case as in [47]) and Raman spectra, along with the experimental results of existing deep learning models, are provided by Vernuccio et al. [47]. Ethanol CARS and Raman spectra are measured on BCARS, setup as in [22]. The TDKK reconstruction is obtained from the available CARS and NRB spectra. The deep learning models used in the previous section are used for prediction here. Both samples are homogeneous in nature, and the tests on them provide a good understanding of the performance in simple real-world scenarios. Figure 4(a) and Fig. 4(b) show the reconstructed toluene and ethanol spectra, respectively.

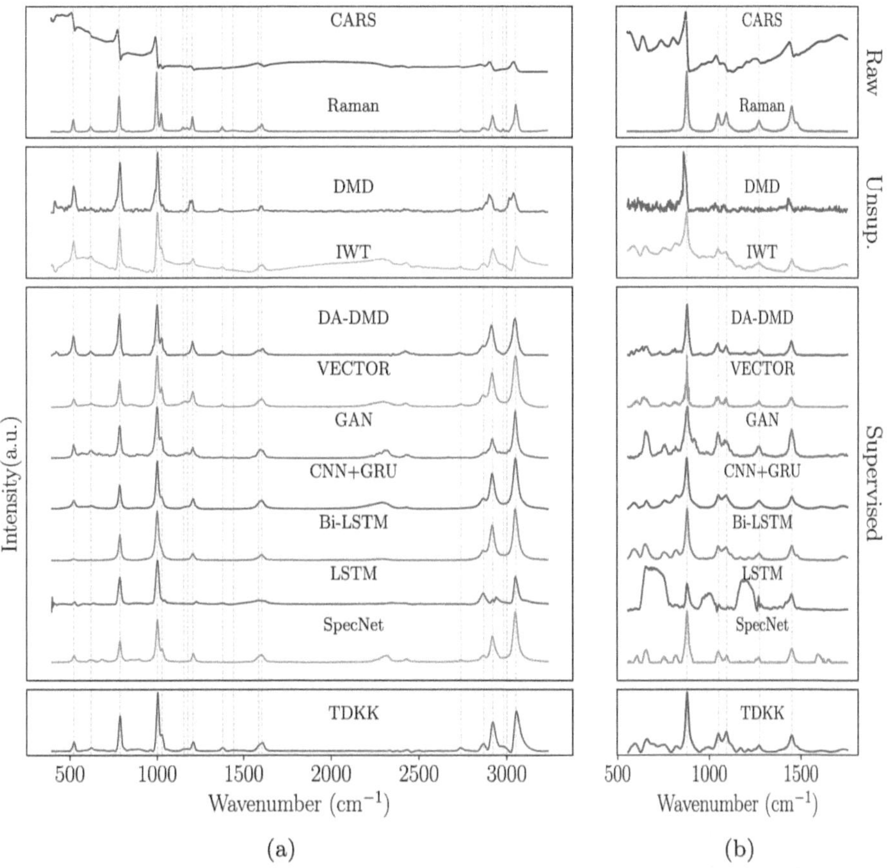

Fig. 4. Qualitative reconstruction performance on **real spectra**: (a) toluene and (b) ethanol fingerprint spectra. Dotted lines mark the original Raman peaks.

Quantitative Analysis. As illustrated in Table 4, our proposed DA-DMD achieves state-of-the-art performance on the fingerprint region of the ethanol spectrum, attaining the lowest MSE (0.0031) and highest correlation (0.8767) among all models, including TDKK, which uses extra reference measurements. Among the deep learning methods, ours shows a clear reduction in MSE and increase in correlation, simply from comparison to the second-best SpecNet model (MSE: 0.0043, correlation: 0.8367). DA-DMD also notably improves upon its unsupervised counterpart DMD (MSE: 0.0151, correlation: 0.3673), demonstrating the effectiveness of our domain adaptation framework. While the GAN and CNN+GRU models show moderate correlation scores (0.7818–0.8113), their MSE values (0.0181–0.0071) remain substantially higher than DA-DMD's. The LSTM model fails completely with a negative correlation (–0.0054), highlighting the challenge of sequential modeling of this task.

Table 4. Quantitative performance on **real spectra** measured using MSE and correlation for all models on toluene (Tol) and ethanol (EtOH) reconstruction, qualitatively shown in Fig. 4.

	DMD	IWT	DA-DMD	VECTOR	GAN	CNN+GRU	Bi-LSTM	LSTM	SpecNet	TDKK
Tol - MSE	**0.0052**	0.0150	<u>0.0060</u>	0.0087	**0.0057**	0.0084	0.0080	0.0244	0.0063	0.0037
Tol - Corr	**0.7359**	0.7288	**0.8746**	0.8332	<u>0.8699</u>	0.8023	0.8017	0.8656	0.8043	0.8970
EtOH - MSE	**0.0151**	0.0502	**0.0031**	0.0047	0.0181	0.0071	0.0064	0.1267	<u>0.0043</u>	0.0050
EtOH - Corr	0.3673	**0.4270**	**0.8767**	0.7978	0.7818	0.8113	0.8245	-0.0054	<u>0.8367</u>	0.8753

For toluene analysis, DA-DMD delivers the highest correlation (0.8746) with competitive MSE (0.0060) just after GAN (0.0057), outperforming all other deep learning approaches, including Bi-LSTM (MSE: 0.0080, correlation: 0.8017) and SpecNet (MSE: 0.0063, correlation: 0.8043). While the TDKK baseline achieves marginally better MSE (0.0037) and correlation (0.8970), DA-DMD's performance remains within 0.0023 MSE units of this benchmark. The GAN model's strong MSE (0.0057) but lower correlation (0.8699) suggests that it captures magnitude variations better than spectral shapes, whereas DA-DMD balances both metrics effectively. Our method shows remarkable improvement over the original DMD implementation, increasing correlation by 18.8% (DMD: 0.7359 $\rightarrow$ DA-DMD: 0.8746) despite slightly higher MSE. LSTM shows the lowest performance among the models when considering MSE. However, it shows a decent correlation of 0.8656 compared to other models. These results show the relevance of including multiple metrics for evaluation and the importance of qualitative analysis.

Qualitative Analysis. For ethanol's fingerprint region (Fig. 4(b)), most deep learning models successfully capture all major spectral features but introduce high-frequency noise due to unsmoothed reconstructions. DA-DMD shows fewer artifacts and detects all peaks. Most methods struggle with minor false positives concentrated below 800 cm^{-1}. VECTOR, Bi-LSTM, and CNN+GRU also reconstruct good peak shapes at the correct positions. Notably, LSTM produces severe distortions, including artificial peaks at 700 cm^{-1} and 1200 cm^{-1} that obscure true spectral content. While unsupervised DMD and IWT avoid these artifacts, their reconstructions lack the sharpness required for precise intensity quantification, particularly in overlapping band regions.

As shown in Fig. 4(a), DA-DMD, Bi-LSTM, and GAN demonstrate superior performance in reconstructing toluene spectra, with both methods accurately resolving peak positions and relative intensities across the characteristic vibrational bands, especially in detecting peak 5. Very small single peaks (2, 9, 12) and double peaks (10, 11) are better detected in DA-DMD. Most of the models (except DMD and VECTOR) predict slight false variations in the silent region (1800–2800 cm^{-1}). The unsupervised DMD and IWT methods show promising baseline agreement but struggle with precise peak localization. DMD introduces positional errors, while IWT suffers from inconsistent phase correction artifacts.

6   Conclusion

In this study, we use DMD to decompose CARS spectra into different modes where low-frequency modes correspond to NRB, and high frequencies show Raman contribution. We then employ an unsupervised two-class clustering approach to remove NRB. Compared to state-of-the-art unsupervised methods such as IWT, DMD matches or outperforms IWT. To enhance the performance further, we then replace this mode clustering step with a supervised deep learning approach, DA-DMD, which improves mode selection. Compared to state-of-the-art deep learning methods, DA-DMD offers several advantages. 1. It provides low-latency prediction (less than 10 ms per spectrum); 2. There is no need for reference measurements, and only minimal training on synthetic data is required, making DA-DMD easily adaptable to new samples and setups with minimal changes; 3. It accurately reconstructs the Raman signatures for both synthetic and real spectra. However, similar to other methods, our DMD-based models are sensitive to NRB magnitudes and peak overlap resolution. Future work will focus on: 1. Optimizing the deep learning architecture (layer depth and DMD mode count), informed by physical constraints in the loss function; 2. Synthesizing training data that better captures real-world spectral complexity; 3. Including comprehensive, comparable data from FT-Raman (ground truth) and BCARS spectra of various samples, to strengthen the broad applicability of the proposed methods.

Acknowledgment. This study was supported by the European Union's Horizon Europe research and innovation program for the project uCAIR with Grant Agreement No. 101135175. This study was also supported by the ERC Synergy Grant: Understanding and Modelling of the Earth System with Machine Learning (USMILE).

Code availability. The DA-DMD model with related code and training data is available in GitHub https://github.com/spectra-analysis/DA_DMD

References

1. Valensise, C., et al.: SpecNet code. https://github.com/Valensicv/SpecNet
2. Vernuccio, F., et al.: GAN and CNN+GRU code. https://github.com/crimson-project-eu/NRB_removal
3. Junjuri, R., et al.: LSTM and Bi-LSTM code. https://github.com/Junjuri/Four-DL-models-comparison-for-evaluating-CARS
4. Wang, Z., et al.: VECTOR code. https://github.com/villawang/VECTOR-CARS
5. Baddoo, P.J., Herrmann, B., McKeon, B.J., Nathan Kutz, J., Brunton, S.L.: Physics-informed dynamic mode decomposition. Proc. R. Soc. A: Math. Phys. Eng. Sci. **479**(2271) (2023). https://doi.org/10.1098/rspa.2022.0576

6. Berger, E., Sastuba, M., Vogt, D., Jung, B., Ben Amor, H.: Estimation of perturbations in robotic behavior using dynamic mode decomposition. Adv. Robot. **29**(5), 331–343 (2015). https://doi.org/10.1080/01691864.2014.981292

7. Box, G.E., Jenkins, G.M.: Time Series Analysis: Forecasting and Control. Holden-Day (1976)

8. Brunton, B.W., Johnson, L.A., Ojemann, J.G., Kutz, J.N.: Extracting spatial-temporal coherent patterns in large-scale neural recordings using dynamic mode decomposition. J. Neurosci. Methods **258**, 1–15 (2016). https://doi.org/10.1016/j.jneumeth.2015.10.010

9. Brunton, S.L., Brunton, B.W., Proctor, J.L., Kaiser, E., Kutz, J.N.: Chaos as an intermittently forced linear system. Nat. Commun. **8**(1) (2017). https://doi.org/10.1038/s41467-017-00030-8

10. Camp, C.H.: Raman signal extraction from cars spectra using a learned-matrix representation of the discrete hilbert transform. Opt. Express **30**(15), 26057 (2022). https://doi.org/10.1364/oe.460543

11. Camp, C.H., Lee, Y.J., Cicerone, M.T.: Quantitative, comparable coherent anti-Stokes Raman scattering (CARS) spectroscopy: correcting errors in phase retrieval. J. Raman Spectrosc. **47**(4), 408–415 (2016). https://doi.org/10.1002/jrs.4824

12. Camp, C.H., Jr., Bender, J.S., Lee, Y.J.: Real-time and high-throughput Raman signal extraction and processing in CARS hyperspectral imaging. Opt. Express **28**(14), 20422–20437 (2020). https://doi.org/10.1364/OE.397606

13. Cheng, J.X., Book, L.D., Xie, X.S.: Polarization coherent anti-stokes Raman scattering microscopy. Opt. Lett. **26**(17), 1341 (2001). https://doi.org/10.1364/ol.26.001341

14. Cheng, J.X., Xie, X.S.: Coherent anti-stokes Raman scattering microscopy: instrumentation, theory, and applications. J. Phys. Chem. B **108**(3), 827–840 (2003). https://doi.org/10.1021/jp035693v

15. Cooley, J.W., Lewis, P.A.W., Welch, P.D.: The fast Fourier transform and its applications. IEEE Trans. Educ. **12**(1), 27–34 (1969). https://doi.org/10.1109/te.1969.4320436

16. Ganikhanov, F., Evans, C.L., Saar, B.G., Xie, X.S.: High-sensitivity vibrational imaging with frequency modulation coherent anti-stokes Raman scattering (fm cars) microscopy. Opt. Lett. **31**(12), 1872 (2006). https://doi.org/10.1364/ol.31.001872

17. Griffiths, P.R.: Introduction to the theory and instrumentation for vibrational spectroscopy (2001). https://doi.org/10.1002/0470027320.s8935

18. Härkönen, T., Vartiainen, E.: Interpolated inverse discrete wavelet transforms in additive and non-additive spectral background corrections. Opt. Continuum **2**(5), 1068 (2023). https://doi.org/10.1364/optcon.488136

19. Houhou, R., Barman, P., Schmitt, M., Meyer, T., Popp, J., Bocklitz, T.: Deep learning as phase retrieval tool for CARS spectra. Opt. Express **28**(14), 21002 (2020). https://doi.org/10.1364/OE.390413

20. Hu, J., Shen, L., Sun, G.: Squeeze-and-excitation networks. In: 2018 IEEE/CVF Conference on Computer Vision and Pattern Recognition, pp. 7132–7141 (2018). https://doi.org/10.1109/CVPR.2018.00745

21. Jin, X., Han, J.: K-means clustering. In: Encyclopedia of Machine Learning, pp. 563–564. Springer, Boston (2011). https://doi.org/10.1007/978-0-387-30164-8_425

22. Junjuri, R., et al.: Estimation of biological variance in coherent Raman microscopy data of two cell lines using chemometrics. Analyst **149**(17), 4395–4406 (2024). https://doi.org/10.1039/d4an00648h

23. Junjuri, R., Meyer-Zedler, T., Popp, J., Bocklitz, T.: Investigating the effect of non-resonant background variation on the CARS data analysis of bacteria samples and classification using machine learning. Opt. Contin. **3**(11), 2244 (2024). https://doi.org/10.1364/OPTCON.528930

24. Junjuri, R., Saghi, A., Lensu, L., Vartiainen, E.M.: Convolutional neural network-based retrieval of Raman signals from CARS spectra. Opt. Continuum **1**(6), 1324 (2022). https://doi.org/10.1364/OPTCON.457365

25. Junjuri, R., Saghi, A., Lensu, L., Vartiainen, E.M.: Evaluating different deep learning models for efficient extraction of Raman signals from cars spectra. Phys. Chem. Chem. Phys. **25**(24), 16340–16353 (2023). https://doi.org/10.1039/d3cp01618h

26. Kingma, D.P., Ba, J.: Adam: a method for stochastic optimization. arXiv preprint (2014). https://doi.org/10.48550/ARXIV.1412.6980

27. Krafft, C., Schie, I.W., Meyer, T., Schmitt, M., Popp, J.: Developments in spontaneous and coherent Raman scattering microscopic imaging for biomedical applications. Chem. Soc. Rev. **45**(7), 1819–1849 (2016). https://doi.org/10.1039/c5cs00564g

28. Kutz, J.N., Brunton, S.L., Brunton, B.W., Proctor, J.L.: Dynamic mode decomposition: data-driven modeling of complex systems. SIAM (2016). https://doi.org/10.1137/1.9781611974508

29. Liu, B., Wang, Y., Wang, W.: Spectrogram enhancement algorithm: a soft thresholding-based approach. Ultrasound Med. Biol. **25**(5), 839–846 (1999). https://doi.org/10.1016/S0301-5629(99)00024-1

30. Liu, Y., Lee, Y.J., Cicerone, M.T.: Broadband CARS spectral phase retrieval using a time-domain Kramers-Kronig transform. Opt. Lett. **34**(9), 1363 (2009). https://doi.org/10.1364/OL.34.001363

31. Luo, Z., Xu, X., Lin, D., Qu, J., Lin, F., Li, J.: Removing non-resonant background of cars signal with generative adversarial network. Appl. Phys. Lett. **124**(26) (2024). https://doi.org/10.1063/5.0201616

32. Muddiman, R., O' Dwyer, K., Camp, C.H., Hennelly, B.: Removing non-resonant background from broadband cars using a physics-informed neural network. Anal. Methods **15**(32), 4032–4043 (2023). https://doi.org/10.1039/d3ay01131c

33. Müller, M., Zumbusch, A.: Coherent anti-stokes Raman scattering microscopy. ChemPhysChem **8**(15), 2156–2170 (2007). https://doi.org/10.1002/cphc.200700202

34. Noack, B.R., Stankiewicz, W., Morzyński, M., Schmid, P.J.: Recursive dynamic mode decomposition of transient and post-transient wake flows. J. Fluid Mech. **809**, 843–872 (2016). https://doi.org/10.1017/jfm.2016.678

35. Ogilvie, J.P., Beaurepaire, E., Alexandrou, A., Joffre, M.: Fourier-transform coherent anti-stokes Raman scattering microscopy. Opt. Lett. **31**(4), 480 (2006). https://doi.org/10.1364/ol.31.000480

36. O'Shea, K., Nash, R.: An introduction to convolutional neural networks. arXiv preprint (2015). https://doi.org/10.48550/ARXIV.1511.08458

37. Polli, D., Kumar, V., Valensise, C.M., Marangoni, M., Cerullo, G.: Broadband coherent Raman scattering microscopy. Laser Photon. Rev. **12**(9), 1800020 (2018). https://doi.org/10.1002/lpor.201800020

38. Potma, E.O., Evans, C.L., Xie, X.S.: Heterodyne coherent anti-stokes Raman scattering (cars) imaging. Opt. Lett. **31**(2), 241 (2006). https://doi.org/10.1364/ol.31.000241

39. Saghi, A., Junjuri, R., Lensu, L., Vartiainen, E.M.: Semi-synthetic data generation to fine-tune a convolutional neural network for retrieving Raman signals from cars

spectra. Optics Continuum **1**(11), 2360 (2022). https://doi.org/10.1364/optcon.469753

40. Sauer, T., Yorke, J.A., Casdagli, M.: Embedology. J. Stat. Phys. **65**(3–4), 579–616 (1991). https://doi.org/10.1007/bf01053745

41. Schmid, P.J., Li, L., Juniper, M.P., Pust, O.: Applications of the dynamic mode decomposition. Theor. Comput. Fluid Dyn. **25**(1–4), 249–259 (2010). https://doi.org/10.1007/s00162-010-0203-9

42. Shadaydeh, M., Denzler, J., Migliavacca, M.: Physics informed modeling of ecosystem respiration via dynamic mode decomposition with control input. In: ICLR Workshop on Machine Learning for Remote Sensing (ICLR-WS) (2024). https://doi.org/10.48550/arXiv.2402.17625

43. Takens, F.: Detecting strange attractors in turbulence. In: Dynamical Systems and Turbulence, Warwick 1980, Pp. 366–381. Springer, Heidelberg (1981). https://doi.org/10.1007/bfb0091924

44. Valensise, C.M., Giuseppi, A., Vernuccio, F., De la Cadena, A., Cerullo, G., Polli, D.: Removing non-resonant background from cars spectra via deep learning. APL Photon. **5**(6), 061305 (2020). https://doi.org/10.1063/5.0007821

45. Vartiainen, E.M., Rinia, H.A., Müller, M., Bonn, M.: Direct extraction of Raman line-shapes from congested CARS spectra. Opt. Express **14**(8), 3622 (2006). https://doi.org/10.1364/OE.14.003622

46. Vaswani, A., et al.: Attention is all you need. In: Guyon, I., et al. (eds.) Advances in Neural Information Processing Systems, vol. 30. Curran Associates, Inc. (2017). https://doi.org/10.48550/arXiv.1706.03762

47. Vernuccio, F., et al.: Non-resonant background removal in broadband cars microscopy using deep-learning algorithms. Sci. Rep. **14**(1) (2024). https://doi.org/10.1038/s41598-024-74912-5

48. Volkmer, A., Book, L.D., Xie, X.S.: Time-resolved coherent anti-stokes Raman scattering microscopy: imaging based on Raman free induction decay. Appl. Phys. Lett. **80**(9), 1505–1507 (2002). https://doi.org/10.1063/1.1456262

49. Wang, Z., O' Dwyer, K., Muddiman, R., Ward, T., Camp, C.H., Hennelly, B.M.: VECTOR: very deep convolutional autoencoders for non-resonant background removal in broadband coherent anti-stokes Raman scattering. J. Raman Spectrosc. **53**(6), 1081–1093 (2022). https://doi.org/10.1002/jrs.6335

50. Wu, Z., Brunton, S.L., Revzen, S.: Challenges in dynamic mode decomposition. J. R. Soc. Interface **18**(185) (2021). https://doi.org/10.1098/rsif.2021.0686

51. Yang, C., Mehouachi, F.B., Menendez, M., Jabari, S.E.: Urban traffic analysis and forecasting through shared koopman eigenmodes. arXiv preprint (2024). https://doi.org/10.48550/ARXIV.2409.04728

γ-QUANT: Towards Learnable Quantization for Low-Bit Pattern Recognition

Mishal Fatima[1]([✉]), Shashank Agnihotri[1], Marius Bock[2],
Kanchana Vaishnavi Gandikota[2], Kristof Van Laerhoven[2], Michael Möller[2],
and Margret Keuper[1,3]

[1] University of Mannheim, Mannheim, Germany
mishal.fatima@uni-mannheim.de
[2] University of Siegen, Siegen, Germany
[3] MPI for Informatics, Saarland Informatics Campus, Saarbrücken, Germany

Abstract. Most pattern recognition models are developed on pre-processed data. In computer vision, for instance, RGB images processed through image signal processing (ISP) pipelines designed to cater to human perception are the most frequent input to image analysis networks. However, many modern vision tasks operate without a human in the loop, raising the question of whether such pre-processing is optimal for automated analysis. Similarly, human activity recognition (HAR) on body-worn sensor data commonly takes normalized floating-point data arising from a high-bit analog-to-digital converter (ADC) as an input, despite such an approach being highly inefficient in terms of data transmission, significantly affecting the battery life of wearable devices. In this work, we target low-bandwidth and energy-constrained settings where sensors are limited to low-bit-depth capture. We propose γ-QUANT, i.e. the task-specific *learning* of a non-linear quantization for pattern recognition. We exemplify our approach on raw-image object detection as well as HAR of wearable data, and demonstrate that raw data with a learnable quantization using as few as 4-bits can perform on par with the use of raw 12-bit data. All code to reproduce our experiments will be released upon acceptance.

Keywords: Efficient Sensing · Object Detection · Human Activity Recognition

1 Introduction

Deep learning techniques have revolutionized the performance of numerous pattern recognition tasks in the last decade by training on large-scale image datasets. Yet, comparably little attention has been paid to the type and quantization of the input data. In computer vision, for instance, most pipelines consider

M. Fatima, S. Agnihotri and M. Bock—Equal contribution.

M. Keuper and F. Locatello (Eds.): DAGM GCPR 2025, LNCS 16125, pp. 57–72, 2026.
https://doi.org/10.1007/978-3-032-12840-9_5

pre-processed sRGB images with a standard bit depth of 8 bits. In the imaging process, cameras usually capture visual information in a higher-bit-depth RAW format which is converted to the standard format by an image signal processor (ISP) using a series of operations including black light subtraction, demosaicking, denoising, white balancing, gamma correction, color manipulation, and tone-mapping to finally obtain a visually pleasing 8-bit sRGB image. As photography-oriented ISP pipelines may not be optimal for vision tasks, recent works [13,30,33,38] have also successfully optimized ISP pipelines together with the downstream vision task. Yet, the idea to explicitly optimize the quantization for a given (automated) machine learning task has not been exploited so far.

Similarly, most studies in human activity recognition (HAR) from body-worn data simply use linearly quantized high-bit (e.g. 12-bit) information from the sensors. While settings of lower bit quantizations have been investigated (see [3,10]), the idea to *learn* an optimal quantization has not been studied.

In both settings, computer vision and HAR, the quantization of the analog data into a digital signal plays a critical role in balancing data quality, memory requirements, and energy consumption at the analog-to-digital converter (ADC), see e.g. [23]. Moreover, significant bandwidth can be saved if the recorded data is sent to the cloud in a low-bit format for further analysis.

In this paper, we demonstrate that a tailored *learned* quantization has significant advantages over a naïve linear quantization. Specifically, we study a learnable non-linear quantization via

$$\mathcal{Q}(\mathcal{X}, \gamma, \mu) = Q_{\hat{N}}(\mathrm{sign}(\mathcal{X} - \mu) \cdot |\mathcal{X} - \mu|^{\gamma}) \tag{1}$$

for (normalized) analog input values $\mathcal{X}$, a linear quantizer $Q_{\hat{N}}$ to a target bit-depth of $\hat{N}$ bit, and learnable parameters γ as well as an offset μ. This learnable non-linear quantization is optimized together with neural networks for specific tasks. We refer to our approach (1) as γ-QUANT.

We demonstrate that γ-QUANT improves the performance of object detection on raw data on diverse vision datasets like the PASCAL-RAW dataset [32] and the RAOD dataset [46] by simulating γ-QUANT on analog signals by using raw (high bit depths) images of the respective datasets. We show generality of the approach by conducting a similar study for a completely different modality, i.e., inertial, body-worn sensor data, using different datasets commonly used in HAR.

In summary, the contributions of this work are as follows:

– We show that naïve low-bit quantization of accelerometer data as well as of images harms model performance.
– We propose γ-QUANT, a learnable non-linear quantization (parameterized similar to a gamma correction), as a solution.
– We demonstrate that our proposed method allows reducing the recorded data to up to 4-bit for object detection and even 2-bit for human activity recognition without significant performance drops in comparison to high-bit data. Moreover, we demonstrate that learning the quantization via γ-QUANT yields systematic improvements over a classical (linear) quantization.

2   Related Work

Work in the direction of jointly optimizing sensor and neural network parameters is limited, though some substantial contributions have been made recently. We summarize them in our two application domains, computer vision and wearable sensor data analysis, separately.

2.1   Quantization of Wearable Sensor Data

Energy efficiency is crucial for wearable human activity recognition on edge devices with limited battery capacity. Transmission of HAR data accounts for significant energy consumption at the wearable device [22] which can be minimized by reducing expensive communications, for instance, by aggregating or compressing data, and doing on-device feature extraction and classification to avoid sending raw signals. Recent work has focused on efficient inference of neural networks for on-device HAR using pruning [24], adaptive inference [35] and quantization [11,12,49]. Unlike the quantization of HAR data, network quantization has been widely studied. Exemplary approaches include sub-byte and mixed-precision quantization with adaptive inference in 1D CNNs [11], full-integer quantization of DeepConv LSTM [49], and binary quantization of weights and activations in neural networks [12]. Orthogonal to these techniques, power savings can also be achieved by turning off the sensors when inactive or lowering their sampling rates [31,48] or adapting sampling rates per activity [9,47]. Further techniques have also been proposed to handle such HAR data captured at variable sampling rates, including modifications to neural network architectures [28], and data augmentation [16]. Unlike these techniques, we address the often-overlooked challenge of reducing energy use during data capture by applying low-bit quantization directly at the inertial sensor, which can provide task-aware data compression immediately at acquisition, complementing the existing energy-saving techniques.

2.2   Codesigning Imaging System and Vision Models

Instead of the traditional approach where imaging hardware and perception models are developed independently, a recent trend in efficient machine learning is to code-sign imaging systems and computer vision models [20], creating tightly integrated solutions that maximize performance while reducing the hardware or computing requirements. [21] formulate imaging building blocks as context-free grammar whose parameters can be optimized through a reinforcement learning framework. [6,7,14] jointly optimize for the downstream computer vision model along with the optical layer to exploit its potential computation capability. [40] proposes a differentiable approach to jointly optimize the size and distribution of pixels on the imaging sensor along with the downstream computer vision model. However, none of these works deal with quantization at the sensor, which is the focus of our work.

RAW images contain more information than standard RGB images (sRGB), which could potentially be beneficial for higher-level vision tasks such as object detection [27,45,46]. In this context, a hardware-in-the-loop method is introduced in [30] to optimize hardware ISP for end-to-end task-specific networks by using zero-order optimization. Diamond *et al.* [13] use Anscombe networks as neural ISPs which are jointly trained with task-specific neural networks. [29] train a minimal neural ISP pipeline for object detection that improves generalization to unseen camera sensors. Robidoux *et al.* [38] optimize HDR ISP hyperparameters together with detector network, whereas [33] train a neural network for automatic exposure selection that is trained jointly with ISP pipeline and a network for HDR object detection. Instead of using the whole ISP, [3,46] identifies the key components of the ISP for downstream vision tasks. Prior works [26,27,46] learn specific parameterized ISP functions such as demosaicking and gamma correction, color correction in an end-to-end fashion along with the object detector. While some of these works [27,46] learn a gamma correction, this is a part of the ISP pipeline after a digital image has been obtained, while we propose to learn this function before quantization at the sensor for the analog input. While [3,10] consider the effect of low bit quantization on vision tasks, they do not optimize this process. Instead of learning fixed ISP parameters, [44] introduces a scene-adaptive ISP to automatically generate an optimal ISP pipeline and the corresponding ISP parameters to maximize the detection performance. Yet, the learned computational steps are applied to the digital (= already quantized) image. To the best of our knowledge the *learning* of a quantization to be applied within the analog-to-digital converter of a camera, has not been considered before.

3 Our Approach γ-QUANT

3.1 Preliminaries

Many sensors use a physical effect to induce a voltage which is converted to a digital measurement by an analog-to-digital converter (ADC). For instance, variable capacitance Micro-Electro-Mechanical Systems (MEMS) accelerometers that are present in many mobile and wearable systems, sense tiny mass' distance changes between two capacitor plates. An in-chip ADC converts the resulting amplified voltages to quantized digital values that are handled in a local processing unit. Similarly, in imaging, a CMOS sensor uses photodiodes (and the photo-electric effect) to induce a charge, which is transferred to a capacitor. The charge is converted to a voltage, amplified and passed to the ADC. For both modalities the ADC typically uses a linear quantization with at least 8, more commonly 12 or even 16 bits per value. Yet, both the energy consumption as well as the readout speed are crucially influenced by the bit-depth, such that a reduction can have significant benefits: According to [43], simply reducing the image bit-depth from 16-bit to 12-bit has shown speedups by a factor of two in industry. It was shown in [5] that – for energy-constrained sensors – ADCs alone contribute up to 50% of the energy consumption in an image sensor. Similarly, in wearable sensorics, transferring the recorded accelerometer data wirelessly has shown to be the by far most energy-consuming operation, such that a reduced bit-depth has an immediate and significant effect on the wearable's battery life.

3.2   A Learnable Quantization Approach

The most straight-forward ADCs produce lower bit-depths via linear quantization, i.e., converting each analog value $\mathcal{X}$ (assumed to be normalized to $[0, 1]$) to a digital value $\mathcal{X}_Q$ via

$$Q_{\hat{N}}(\mathcal{X}) = \left\lfloor \mathcal{X} \cdot (2^{\hat{N}} - 1) \right\rfloor, \tag{2}$$

where $\hat{N}$ is the desired bit depth, and $\lfloor . \rfloor$ is the floor operation.

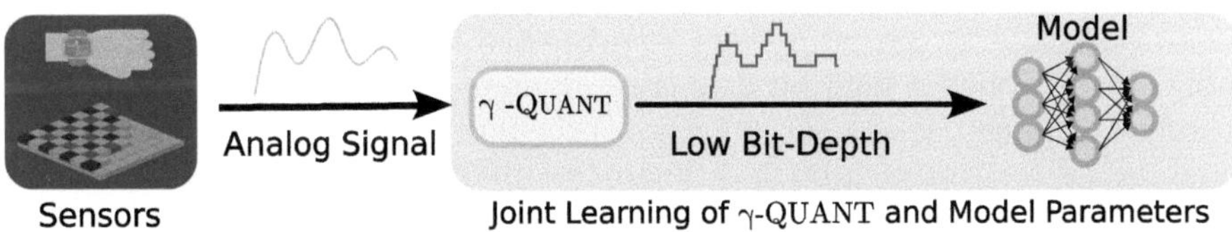

Fig. 1. γ-QUANT learns the quantization of an ADC to convert the analog signal of a sensor to a low bit depth digital signal, which is subsequently sent to the neural network for performing the downstream task. The parameters of the quantization are trained jointly with the parameters of the neural network in a task-specific fashion. γ-QUANT can reduce the energy consumption of the sensor significantly with a minimal loss in performance.

In imaging, the Image Signal Processor (ISP) converts the raw digital values to standard RGB (sRGB) images through a sequence of pre-processing steps including demosaicking, denoising, white-balancing, color conversion, and tonemapping. Yet, low bit-depth raw-images often lead to poor visual quality. As the human visual system rather scales logarithmically, [1,3] proposed to scale the analog signals before quantization via

$$\mathcal{X}_{\log} = \log(\mathcal{X} + \epsilon), \tag{3}$$

where ϵ is required to bound the input to the logarithm from below. [3] use $\epsilon{=}1$ and quantize the resulting signal via

$$\mathcal{X}_Q = \left\lfloor \frac{\mathcal{X}_{\log} - \min(\mathcal{X}_{\log})}{\max(\mathcal{X}_{\log}) - \min(\mathcal{X}_{\log})} \cdot (2^{\hat{N}} - 1) \right\rfloor . \tag{4}$$

Yet, the quantization is ad-hoc, independent of the target bit-depth $\hat{N}$, and the effect of ϵ heavily depends on the dynamic range of the analog signal, such that it might need domain- and downstream-task specific adaption.

For body-worn accelerometer data, values are typically in $[-1, 1]$ (up to a scaling) as accelerations for each axis can happen in two (opposite) directions, reflected by different signs. Thus, a logarithmic quantization is not straightforward. Moreover, accelerometers might constantly yield a non-zero signal in the gravitational field of the earth such that zero might not be a natural candidate for the finest quantization anymore.

For these reasons, we propose γ-QUANT, i.e., an automated approach for *learning* the quantization of sensor signals in an automated and *task-specific* way, see Fig. 1. More precisely, we propose to learn a non-linear low-bit ADC parameterized via (1) along with a neural network for a specific task by optimizing

$$\min_{\theta,\gamma,\mu} \ \mathbb{E}_{(\mathcal{X},\mathrm{y})}\left[\mathcal{L}(\eta(\mathcal{Q}(\mathcal{X},\gamma,\mu);\theta),\mathrm{y})\right], \tag{5}$$

where η is the task-specific neural network with parameters θ, γ and μ are the parameters of the learnable ADC (i.e., the quantizer $\mathcal{Q}$), and $\mathcal{L}$ is a suitable loss function comparing the network output and the ground truth prediction y.

To optimize (5), we propose to *simulate* the learnable ADC $\mathcal{Q}(\mathcal{X},\gamma,\mu)$ by using readily available high-bit data $\hat{\mathcal{X}}$ as an approximation to the analog signal $\mathcal{X}$. Since the quantization operation stops the flow of gradients in the backward pass, we use a straight-through estimator to allow gradient-based optimization of γ and μ.

While a simulation enables the training of (5) with standard first-order methods on large data sets, the resulting learned (non-linear) ADCs can be realized in hardware: For body-worn sensors such as 3D accelerometer MEMS, the in-chip Digital Signal Processor can be re-configured to adjust ADC settings such as the resolution or sensitivity range through internal registers. These subsequently alter the step size or quantization level of the digital output. Custom transfer functions or lookup tables can be implemented in the sensor to apply non-linear scaling. For CMOS image sensors non-linear quantization in the ADC can also be realized as demonstrated in [4,15]. Thus, our learnable quantization framework targets specific application (such as smart watches for human activity recognition or object detection cameras in an autonomous driving setting) where dedicated hardware is built/programmed using the task-specific learned quantization.

3.3 Specifics of γ-QUANT for HAR and Object Detection

When applying γ-QUANT to imaging applications, we built upon findings of priors works (e.g. [3]) that low intensity values are important to resolve in a more fine-grained manner. Therefore fix the offset $\mu = 0$, and simplify γ-QUANT to

$$\mathcal{Q}(\mathcal{X},\gamma) = Q_{\hat{N}}(\mathcal{X}^\gamma) = \left\lfloor \mathcal{X}^\gamma \cdot (2^{\hat{N}-1}) \right\rfloor, \tag{6}$$

where we assume $\mathcal{X}$ to be normalized to $[0,1]$. More specifically, when simulating $\mathcal{X}$ from a high-bit digital signal, we divide the digital signal by $2^N - 1$ for an N-bit signal. For a faithful simulation of an analog signal, N needs to be significantly larger than our target bit depth $\hat{N}$. The resulting γ-QUANT approach can learn to resemble a simple linear quantization ($\gamma = 1$), compress large values more strongly ($\gamma < 1$), or compress small values more strongly ($\gamma > 1$), see Fig. 2, right.

When applying γ-QUANT to body-worn sensors for HAR, we use the full approach (1) as data is typically normalized to $[-1, 1]$ and offsets can be important. Explicitly writing out the linear quantizer for $[-1, 1]$ our approach becomes

$$\mathcal{Q}(\mathcal{X}, \gamma, \mu) = \text{round} \left(\left((\text{sign}(\mathcal{X} - \mu) \cdot |\mathcal{X} - \mu|^{\gamma}) + 1 \right)/2 \cdot (2^N - 1) \right), \qquad (7)$$

resulting in exemplary curves illustrated in Fig. 2 on the left. As the function (7) is non-differentiable at $\mathcal{X} = \mu$ for $\gamma < 1$, we found the replacement of $|\mathcal{X} - \mu|^{\gamma}$ by $(|\mathcal{X} - \mu| + \epsilon)^{\gamma}$ for a small ϵ, e.g. $\epsilon = 10^{-3}$ to stabilize the training process.

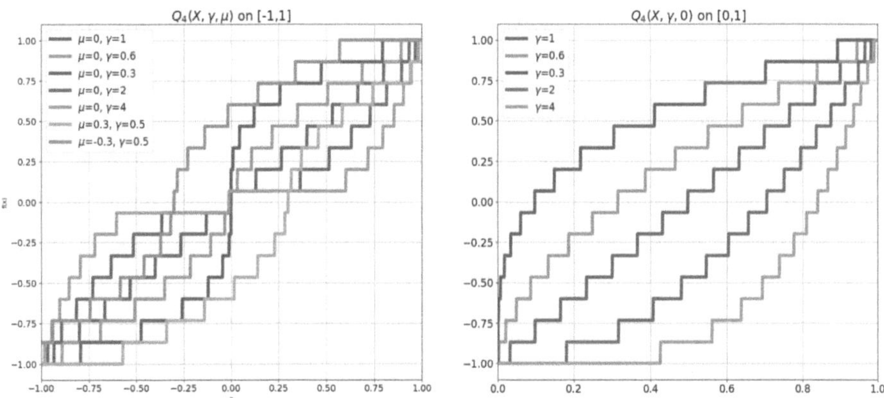

Fig. 2. Exemplifying different γ-QUANT quantization for HAR on $[-1, 1]$ data (left) and object detection on $[0, 1]$ data (right).

4 Experiments on Learnable Quantizations for Accelerometer-Based Human Activity Recognition

As a first use case of our γ-QUANT we focus on inertial sensors, specifically accelerometers used in the context of Human Activity Recognition. The following will outline datasets used as well as experiments conducted. As accelerations measured by wearable sensors can go in both directions, value ranges of the investigated datasets are between $[-1, 1]$. We thus apply the version of γ-QUANT for wearable accelerometer data as shown in (7).

4.1 Datasets

In total, we investigate five wearable accelerometer datasets (see Table 1). The WEAR dataset [2] records participants outdoors, while performing a set of workout-related activities such as running, stretching and strength-based activities. Similarly, the Hang-Time [18] dataset records a team of basketball players during their practice session consisting of a warm-up, drill and game session. Recorded in a biology wet lab, the Wetlab dataset [39] records recurring activities, such as pipetting, occurring during a DNA extraction experiment. Lastly, the RWHAR [42] and SBHAR dataset [37] has participants consists of various of locomotion activities such as walking stairs, with the SBHAR dataset providing annotations of additional transitional activity periods that mark the transition from one to another activity. Note that all but the RWHAR dataset provide continuous recording data, thus providing an additional *NULL*-class which represents times during the recording participants did not perform any of the activities of relevancy.

Table 1. Investigated HAR datasets. Table provides: participant count, activity count (classes), sensor axes count and overall recording scenario. Each sensor axes provides accelerometer data sampled at 50 Hz.

Dataset	participants	classes	axes	scenario
WEAR [2]	18	19	12	body-weight workout
Wetlab [39]	22	9	3	laboratory
Hang-Time [18]	24	6	3	basketball
RWHAR [42]	15	8	21	locomotion
SBHAR [37]	30	13	3	locomotion + transitional

4.2 Experimental Setup and Implementation

During experiments, we follow a Leave-One-Subject-Out (LOSO) cross-validation, where each participant in the dataset is used as the validation set exactly once, while all other participants are used for training. We report the class-averaged macro F1-score averaged across all validation splits (i.e., participants). We further seed-average our experiments repeating each experiment using a set of three different random seeds. For all experiments we employ a sliding window of one second with a 50% overlap, normalize all accelerometer signals between $[-1, 1]$ using min-max normalization applied across the full dataset, a weighted cross-entropy loss and the Adam optimizer, with a learning rate of $1e^{-4}$, weight decay of $1e^{-6}$. We train for 30 epochs with a batch size of 100, using a learning rate schedule that multiplies the learning rate by a factor of 0.9 every 10 epochs. As a model architecture of choice we use the DeepConvLSTM, a widely-adopted HAR model [34]. For each dataset we compare results using linear quantized and γ-QUANT quantized accelerometer signals as input, differing bit depths to be either 2 or 4. We further provide results using the raw accelerometer signal as provided by the datasets. We further compare a dataset-wide versus sensor-axis-specific learnable quantization using γ-QUANT, i.e., learning a (γ, μ)-pair for each sensor axis in the dataset. In all experiments using γ-QUANT we initialize γ with 0.4, as we generally estimate differences accelerations close to 0, i.e., fine-grained movements, to contain more information than the differences in large accelerations, i.e., strong movements.

4.3   Evaluation Results

Table 2 presents the per-dataset results of the experiments described above. It is evident that with 4-bit linear quantization, performance on the WEAR and Wetlab dataset drops significantly compared to using raw data. With 2-bit linear quantization, all five investigated HAR datasets witness a substantial decline in performance. However, across all datasets, γ-QUANT consistently outperforms models trained on linearly quantized data. In particular, for the WEAR and Wetlab datasets, sensor-axis-specific learnable quantizations lead to notable improvements, achieving prediction F1-scores comparable to raw data, even with 2-bit input.

Table 2. Per-dataset HAR results comparing training using raw data with training using linear, dataset-wide γ-QUANT or per-axis γ-QUANT quantized accelerometer signals. We provide results for bit depths $\hat{N} = 2$ and $\hat{N} = 4$.

		WEAR	Wetlab	Hang-Time	RWHAR	SBHAR
	Raw data	*71.01 ± 0.18*	*25.61 ± 0.07*	*33.88 ± 0.09*	*71.21 ± 0.90*	*54.58 ± 0.22*
$\hat{N} = 4$	linear	63.74 ± 0.22	21.72 ± 0.18	33.69 ± 0.22	69.78 ± 0.63	52.14 ± 0.26
	γ-QUANT	70.14 ± 0.51	23.00 ± 0.24	33.63 ± 0.17	69.28 ± 0.46	**52.58 ± 0.20**
	γ-QUANT(per-axis)	**70.17 ± 0.39**	**23.63 ± 0.20**	**33.67 ± 0.17**	**71.16 ± 1.26**	52.52 ± 0.21
$\hat{N} = 2$	linear	58.91 ± 0.13	12.62 ± 0.34	28.01 ± 0.14	64.82 ± 0.62	33.02 ± 0.39
	γ-QUANT	60.45 ± 0.43	12.94 ± 0.18	**30.67 ± 0.12**	**71.41 ± 0.51**	40.18 ± 0.32
	γ-QUANT(per-axis)	**63.95 ± 0.14**	**16.85 ± 0.54**	30.60 ± 0.22	69.21 ± 0.32	**41.88 ± 0.32**

Figure 3 illustrates representative quantization functions learned during HAR experiments. The left subplot shows that different datasets yield distinct global scaling factors γ, while the learnable offset μ remains close to zero across datasets. However, as demonstrated in the right subplot for the Wetlab dataset, if γ-QUANT is learned individually on a per-axis level, both a negative offset ($\mu < 0$) for the x-axis as well as a positive offset ($\mu > 0$) for the z-axis of the sensor are learned. Supported by the overall pattern of improved prediction results of the per-sensor application of γ-QUANT, we hypothesize that the learned offsets allow a better compensation of the static gravitational components captured by fixed accelerometers, where certain axes exhibit constant acceleration depending on their orientation relative to the ground. This compensation works especially well for sensors whose orientation is rather static, e.g., because they are placed at body parts that do not exhibit strong rotations, e.g., the chest or waist of a participant, or capture mostly activities, which do not exhibit strong movements such as sitting. Conversely, one can only expect smaller gains from per-axis quantization on sensors which exhibit frequent changes in orientation due to fast movements of e.g. sport-related activities such as present in the Hang-Time dataset, as gravitational components do not remain static.

5   Experiments on Learnable Quantizations for Object Detection on CMOS Sensor Data

5.1   Datasets

We use the PASCAL RAW dataset [32] having a bit-depth of 12, with three classes, namely 'Car', 'Bicycle', and 'Person'. The training data consists of 2129 images, and the test data is 2130 images. Experiments on a second data set, RAOD [46], can be found in the appendix.

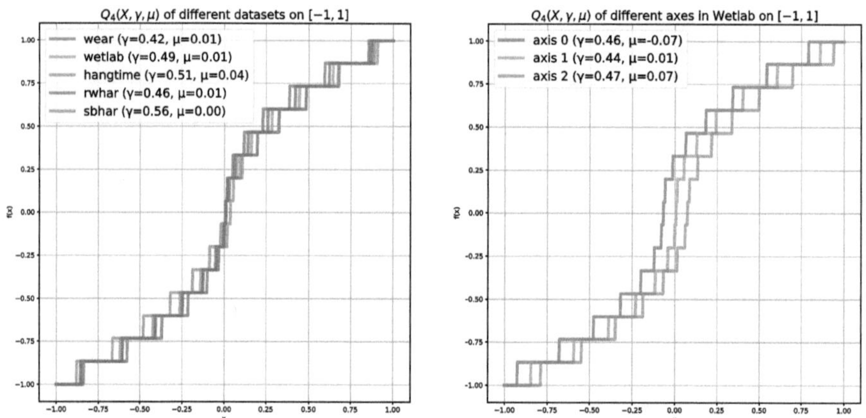

Fig. 3. Visualization of exemplary learned quantization function using γ-QUANT. The left plot shows the per-dataset learned quantization functions. The right plot shows the per-axis quantization functions when predicting the Wetlab dataset. γ and μ values in both plots are averaged across validation splits.

5.2   Experimental Setup and Implementation

We use the mmdetection [8] framework from openmmlab for conducting experiments. Following previous works [32,46] that perform object detection on RAW images, we used Faster-RCNN [36], and PAA [19] models with pre-trained ResNet50 [17] backbone. We conduct experiments by quantizing the Bayer patterned higher bit-depth RAW images to lower bit depths of 4, 6, 8, and 12 using

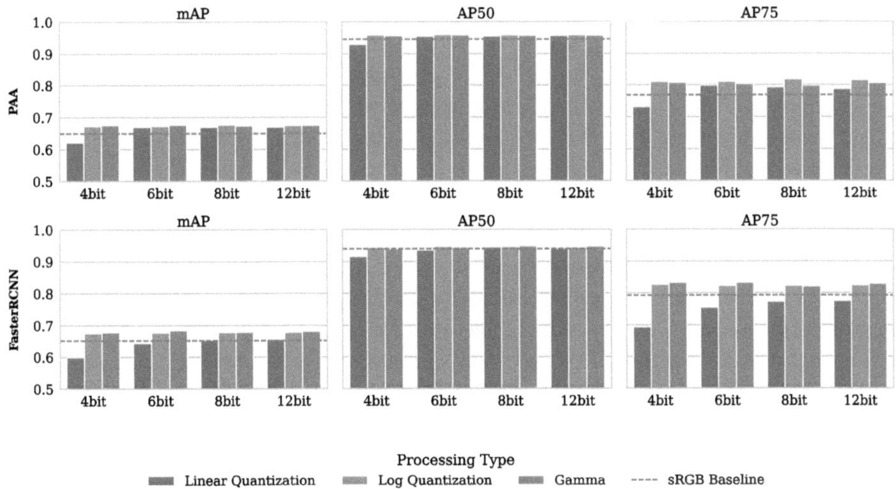

Fig. 4. Results with γ-QUANT, log and linear quantization on PAA and FasterRCNN for different bit depths. The blue dashed lines represented the performance of the model on sRGB input images.

γ-QUANT and compare against Linear quantization (Linear Quant) as well as the logarithmic quantization (4). The Bayer pattern RGGB image is viewed as a four-channel image, subsampled, and converted to a three-channel RGB image by averaging the two green channels. All the images are scaled to a range of [0, 255] before being used as input to the neural network. We report the following quantitative evaluation metrics: mean average precision (mAP) is calculated by averaging the Average Precision (AP) values across the intersection over union (IoU) thresholds ranging from [0.5, 0.95] with a step size of 0.05, resulting in 10 threshold values. We also report performance with IoU-thresholds of 0.5 and 0.75 (AP50 and AP75) for each case.

Following the multi-scale training setup commonly used [25, 36], during training, the shorter image side is scaled to one of the sides randomly selected from a set of sides: [480, 512, 544, 576, 608, 640, 672, 704, 736, 768, 800] using nearest neighbor interpolation and the longer side is scaled to maintain the aspect ratio. At test time, the shorter edge length is kept at 800. We use a batch size of 16 and train the FasterRCNN model for 140 epochs and PAA for 70 epochs. For FasterRCNN, we apply warm-up for the first 1000 iterations, linearly increasing the lr from $1e^{-4}$ to $2.5e^{-3}$ followed by a multi-step learning rate scheduler. We use SGD with Nestrov Momentum [41] as the optimizer with a weight decay of $1e^{-4}$. For PAA, we apply a warmup strategy for the first 4000 iterations, followed by cosine annealing for the learning rate schedule. The base learning rate is set to $1e^{-3}$, with a weight decay of $1e^{-3}$.

5.3   Evaluation Results

To demonstrate the effectiveness of the proposed γ-QUANT, we design a set of experiments across 4 different quantization levels, i.e., 4, 6, 8, 12 bits. For every quantization level, we run three quantization methods, namely, linear quantization, logarithmic quantization as shown in (4), and γ-QUANT. The quantitative results obtained for different bit depths using the three models on PASCAL RAW are presented in Fig. 4.

We observe that performance with *4-bit linear quantization is the worst* across all architectures. Low-bit linear quantization is especially hurting details in lower luminance regions, which account for a majority of the intensity values and therefore result in the lowest performance. Results with γ-QUANT show systematic improvement across both architectures. In particular, there is surprisingly little difference between the different bit depths, indicating that - although a 4-bit image might not be visually pleasing - it is a sufficient bit depth for faithful object detection. Moreover, it is highly encouraging that the performance on standard (ISP processed) RGB images is met or even surpassed: γ-QUANT learns to scale the distribution of pixel values such that low-intensity pixels are amplified, thus providing more contrast in the input. This allows features and details to be better visible, enabling the model to learn more informed feature representations.

Our experiments demonstrate that the log-quantization (4) performs on par with our proposed γ-QUANT. While this might be discouraging at first glance, such results are based on a well chosen value of ϵ, i.e., $\epsilon = 1$ when simulating analog signals with digital 12-bit raw data or, correspondingly, $\epsilon \approx 0.00024414$ for analog signals scaled to $[0, 1]$. More concretely, for an analog signal, there is no natural ϵ, such that it becomes a hyperparameter to be tuned. Our framework can be seen as an automatic (differentiable) way of learning such a hyperparameter. In particular, ϵ in log-quantization could also be learned in the same framework. While this (and further much more flexible) parametrizations of the quantization are an interesting direction for future research, we decided to study γ-QUANT for the sake of simplicity: The range of the output in the log-quantization depends on ϵ such that a rescaling to $[0,1]$ needs to be included in the learning. Our γ-QUANT automatically preserves the $[0, 1]$ range. We thus consider the fact that γ-QUANT reaches the performance of a logarithmic quantization to be encouraging. In particular, for FasterRCNN, the learned values of γ are 0.294, 0.338, 0.354, 0.359 for 4, 6, 8, and 12 bits, respectively. Thus, the logarithmic shape of the curve is learned to be optimal and does not need to be derived from prior assumptions that might be violated in significantly different application scenarios.

6   Conclusion

Our proposed task-specific quantization framework, γ-QUANT offers a significant advancement in optimizing the non-linear quantization of ADCs for pattern recognition with different modalities. By moving beyond traditional high-bit-depth linear quantization and manual choice of a non-linear quantization (e.g., based on human perception), we develop an automatic task-aware quantization framework. This helps achieve substantial improvements in object detection and human activity recognition from body-worn sensors with sensor hardware constraints such as energy consumption and memory usage compared to traditional data processing pipelines. Our results highlight the potential of γ-QUANT to maintain the performance of high-bit data in different tasks while minimizing energy consumption, memory usage, and data transmission costs, ultimately contributing to more efficient and sustainable machine learning workflows. While our current work is focused on hardware constraints at the sensor, in the future, we would expand on this framework to combine efficient network architectures and network quantization for inference, offering further improvements in computational efficiency.

Limitations: It is impossible to have a dataset with truly analog signals. Thus, in our work, high-bit depth RAW images serve as a proxy for analog signals. While this is a valid assumption that stems its roots in signal processing theory, there is still some loss of information between true analog and high-bit depth RAW input. Ideally, we would like to test our proposed γ-QUANT on sensors directly to work on analog signals, with the potential benefit of further gains in accuracy.

Acknowledgments. This work was supported by the German Research Foundation (DFG) as part of the Research Unit FOR 5336 "Learning to Sense".

References

1. Bermak, A., Kitchen, A.: A novel adaptive logarithmic digital pixel sensor. IEEE Photonics Technol. Lett. **18**(20), 2147–2149 (2006). https://doi.org/10.1109/LPT.2006.883893
2. Bock, M., Kuehne, H., Van Laerhoven, K., Moeller, M.: WEAR: an outdoor sports dataset for wearable and egocentric activity recognition. ACM Interact. Mobile Wearable Ubiq. Technol. **8**(4) (2024). https://doi.org/10.1145/3699776
3. Buckler, M., Jayasuriya, S., Sampson, A.: Reconfiguring the imaging pipeline for computer vision. In: Proceedings of the IEEE International Conference on Computer Vision (ICCV) (2017)
4. Cao, Y., Pan, X., Zhao, X., Wu, H.: An analog gamma correction scheme for high dynamic range cmos logarithmic image sensors. Sensors **14**(12), 24132–24145 (2014). https://doi.org/10.3390/s141224132. https://www.mdpi.com/1424-8220/14/12/24132
5. Chae, Y., et al.: A 2.1 m pixels, 120 frame/s cmos image sensor with column-parallel $\delta\sigma$ adc architecture. IEEE J. Solid-State Circ. **46**(1), 236–247 (2010)
6. Chang, J., Sitzmann, V., Dun, X., Heidrich, W., Wetzstein, G.: Hybrid optical-electronic convolutional neural networks with optimized diffractive optics for image classification. Sci. Rep. **8**(1), 1–10 (2018)

7. Chang, J., Wetzstein, G.: Deep optics for monocular depth estimation and 3d object detection. In: Proceedings of the IEEE/CVF International Conference on Computer Vision, pp. 10193–10202 (2019)

8. Chen, K., Wang, J., et al.: Mmdetection: open mmlab detection toolbox and benchmark (2019)

9. Cheng, W., Erfani, S., Zhang, R., Kotagiri, R.: Learning datum-wise sampling frequency for energy-efficient human activity recognition. In: Proceedings of the AAAI Conference on Artificial Intelligence, vol. 32 (2018)

10. Christie, O., Rego, J., Jayasuriya, S.: Analyzing sensor quantization of raw images for visual slam. In: 2020 IEEE International Conference on Image Processing (ICIP), pp. 246–250 (2020). https://doi.org/10.1109/ICIP40778.2020.9191352

11. Daghero, F., et al.: Human activity recognition on microcontrollers with quantized and adaptive deep neural networks. ACM Trans. Embed. Comput. Syst. (TECS) **21**(4), 1–28 (2022)

12. Daghero, F., et al.: Ultra-compact binary neural networks for human activity recognition on risc-v processors. In: Proceedings of the 18th ACM International Conference on Computing Frontiers, pp. 3–11 (2021)

13. Diamond, S., Sitzmann, V., Julca-Aguilar, F., Boyd, S., Wetzstein, G., Heide, F.: Dirty pixels: towards end-to-end image processing and perception. ACM Trans. Graph. (TOG) **40**(3), 1–15 (2021)

14. Fu, Y., et al.: Sacod: sensor algorithm co-design towards efficient cnn-powered intelligent phlatcam. In: Proceedings of the IEEE/CVF International Conference on Computer Vision, pp. 5168–5177 (2021)

15. Ham, S., et al.: Cmos image sensor with analog gamma correction using nonlinear single-slope adc. In: 2006 IEEE International Symposium on Circuits and Systems (ISCAS), pp. 4-pp.-3581 (2006). https://doi.org/10.1109/ISCAS.2006.1693400

16. Hasegawa, T.: Smartphone sensor-based human activity recognition robust to different sampling rates. IEEE Sens. J. **21**(5), 6930–6941 (2021). https://doi.org/10.1109/JSEN.2020.3038281

17. He, K., Zhang, X., Ren, S., Sun, J.: Deep residual learning for image recognition. In: Proceedings of the IEEE Conference on Computer Vision and Pattern Recognition, pp. 770–778 (2016)

18. Hoelzemann, A., Romero, J.L., Bock, M., Laerhoven, K.V., Lv, Q.: Hang-Time HAR: a benchmark dataset for basketball activity recognition using wrist-worn inertial sensors. Sensors **23**(13) (2023). https://doi.org/10.3390/s23135879

19. Kim, K., Lee, H.S.: Probabilistic anchor assignment with IoU prediction for object detection. In: Vedaldi, A., Bischof, H., Brox, T., Frahm, J.-M. (eds.) ECCV 2020. LNCS, vol. 12370, pp. 355–371. Springer, Cham (2020). https://doi.org/10.1007/978-3-030-58595-2_22

20. Klinghoffer, T., Somasundaram, S., Tiwary, K., Raskar, R.: Physics vs. learned priors: rethinking camera and algorithm design for task-specific imaging. In: 2022 IEEE International Conference on Computational Photography (ICCP), pp. 1–12. IEEE (2022)

21. Klinghoffer, T., Tiwary, K., Behari, N., Agrawalla, B., Raskar, R.: Diser: designing imaging systems with reinforcement learning. In: Proceedings of the IEEE/CVF International Conference on Computer Vision, pp. 23632–23642 (2023)

22. Lara, O.D., Labrador, M.A.: A survey on human activity recognition using wearable sensors. IEEE Commun. Surv. Tutor. **15**(3), 1192–1209 (2012)

23. Leñero-Bardallo, J.A., Fernández-Berni, J., Rodríguez-Vázquez, Á.: Review of adcs for imaging. In: Image Sensors and Imaging Systems 2014, vol. 9022, pp. 145–150. SPIE (2014)

24. Liberis, E., Lane, N.D.: Differentiable neural network pruning to enable smart applications on microcontrollers. Proc. ACM Interact. Mob. Wearable Ubiq. Technol. **6**(4), 1–19 (2023)
25. Lin, T.Y., Goyal, P., Girshick, R., He, K., Dollár, P.: Focal loss for dense object detection. In: Proceedings of the IEEE International Conference on Computer Vision, pp. 2980–2988 (2017)
26. Liu, A., Mu, S., Xu, S.: A learnable color correction matrix for raw reconstruction. In: British Machine Vision Conference (2024)
27. Ljungbergh, W., Johnander, J., Petersson, C., Felsberg, M.: Raw or cooked? Object detection on raw images. In: Scandinavian Conference on Image Analysis, pp. 374–385. Springer, Heidelberg (2023). https://doi.org/10.1007/978-3-031-31435-3_25
28. Malekzadeh, M., Clegg, R., Cavallaro, A., Haddadi, H.: Dana: dimension-adaptive neural architecture for multivariate sensor data. Proc. ACM Interact. Mob. Wearable Ubiq. Technol. **5**(3), 1–27 (2021)
29. Morawski, I., Chen, Y.A., Lin, Y.S., Dangi, S., He, K., Hsu, W.H.: Genisp: neural isp for low-light machine cognition. In: Proceedings of the IEEE/CVF Conference on Computer Vision and Pattern Recognition, pp. 630–639 (2022)
30. Mosleh, A., Sharma, A., Onzon, E., Mannan, F., Robidoux, N., Heide, F.: Hardware-in-the-loop end-to-end optimization of camera image processing pipelines. In: Proceedings of the IEEE/CVF Conference on Computer Vision and Pattern Recognition, pp. 7529–7538 (2020)
31. Nakajima, Y., Murao, K., Terada, T., Tsukamoto, M.: A method for energy saving on context-aware system by sampling control and data complement. In: International Symposium on Wearable Computers (ISWC) 2010, pp. 1–4 (2010). https://doi.org/10.1109/ISWC.2010.5665860
32. Omid-Zohoor, A., Ta, D., Murmann, B.: Pascalraw: raw image database for object detection (2014)
33. Onzon, E., Mannan, F., Heide, F.: Neural auto-exposure for high-dynamic range object detection. In: Proceedings of the IEEE/CVF Conference on Computer Vision and Pattern Recognition (CVPR), pp. 7710–7720 (2021)
34. Ordóñez, F.J., Roggen, D.: Deep convolutional and LSTM recurrent neural networks for multimodal wearable activity recognition. MDPI Sensors **16**(1) (2016). https://doi.org/10.3390/s16010115
35. Rashid, N., Demirel, B.U., Abdullah Al Faruque, M.: Ahar: adaptive cnn for energy-efficient human activity recognition in low-power edge devices. IEEE Internet Things J. **9**(15), 13041–13051 (2022). https://doi.org/10.1109/JIOT.2022.3140465
36. Ren, S., He, K., Girshick, R., Sun, J.: Faster r-cnn: towards real-time object detection with region proposal networks. IEEE Trans. Pattern Anal. Mach. Intell. **39**(6), 1137–1149 (2016)
37. Reyes-Ortiz, J.L., Oneto, L., Samà, A., Parra, X., Anguita, D.: Transition-aware human activity recognition using smartphones. Neurocomputing **171** (2016). https://doi.org/10.1016/j.neucom.2015.07.085
38. Robidoux, N., Capel, L.E.G., Seo, D.E., Sharma, A., Ariza, F., Heide, F.: End-to-end high dynamic range camera pipeline optimization. In: Proceedings of the IEEE/CVF Conference on Computer Vision and Pattern Recognition, pp. 6297–6307 (2021)
39. Scholl, P.M., Wille, M., Van Laerhoven, K.: Wearables in the wet lab: a laboratory system for capturing and guiding experiments. In: International Joint Conference on Pervasive and Ubiquitous Computing. ACM (2015). https://doi.org/10.1145/2750858.2807547

40. Sommerhoff, H., Agnihotri, S., Saleh, M., Moeller, M., Keuper, M., Kolb, A.: Differentiable sensor layouts for end-to-end learning of task-specific camera parameters. arXiv preprint arXiv:2304.14736 (2023)
41. Sutskever, I., Martens, J., Dahl, G., Hinton, G.: On the importance of initialization and momentum in deep learning. In: Dasgupta, S., McAllester, D. (eds.) Proceedings of the 30th International Conference on Machine Learning. Proceedings of Machine Learning Research, vol. 28, pp. 1139–1147. PMLR, Atlanta (2013). https://proceedings.mlr.press/v28/sutskever13.html
42. Sztyler, T., Stuckenschmidt, H.: On-body localization of wearable devices: an investigation of position-aware activity recognition. In: International Conference on Pervasive Computing and Communications. IEEE (2016). https://doi.org/10.1109/PERCOM.2016.7456521
43. Teledyne Vision Solutions: Bit depth, full well, and dynamic range (2024). https://www.teledynevisionsolutions.com/en-in/learn/learning-center/imaging-fundamentals/bit-depth-full-well-and-dynamic-range/. Accessed 09 Apr 2025
44. Wang, Y., Xu, T., Fan, Z., Xue, T., Gu, J.: Adaptiveisp: learning an adaptive image signal processor for object detection. In: Globerson, A., et al. (eds.) Advances in Neural Information Processing Systems, vol. 37, pp. 112598–112623. Curran Associates, Inc. (2024). https://proceedings.neurips.cc/paper_files/paper/2024/file/cc596a803bedc7a03a87e98c77a22efe-Paper-Conference.pdf
45. Wu, Z., et al.: Dense object detection methods in raw UAV imagery based on yolov8. Sci. Rep. **14**(1), 18019 (2024)
46. Xu, R., et al.: Toward raw object detection: a new benchmark and a new model. In: Proceedings of the IEEE/CVF Conference on Computer Vision and Pattern Recognition, pp. 13384–13393 (2023)
47. Yan, Z., Subbaraju, V., Chakraborty, D., Misra, A., Aberer, K.: Energy-efficient continuous activity recognition on mobile phones: an activity-adaptive approach. In: 2012 16th International Symposium on Wearable Computers, pp. 17–24 (2012). https://doi.org/10.1109/ISWC.2012.23
48. Zheng, L., et al.: A novel energy-efficient approach for human activity recognition. Sensors **17**(9), 2064 (2017)
49. Zhou, H., Zhang, X., Feng, Y., Zhang, T., Xiong, L.: Efficient human activity recognition on edge devices using deepconv lstm architectures. Sci. Rep. **15**(1), 13830 (2025)

EVCS: A Benchmark for Fine-Grained Electric Vehicle Charging Station Detection

Lin Chen[1(✉)] [iD], Sönke Südbeck[1], Christoph Riggers[2] [iD], Tobias Geib[1] [iD], Kai Cordes[1] [iD], and Hellward Broszio[1]

[1] VISCODA GmbH, 30167 Hanover, Germany
`{chen,suedbeck,geib,cordes,broszio}@viscoda.com`
[2] Institute of Microelectronic Systems (IMS), Leibniz University Hanover, Hanover, Germany
`christoph.riggers@ims.uni-hannover.de`

Abstract. Detecting Electric Vehicle Charging Stations (EVCS) is attracting increasing attention for autonomous and assisted driving of electric vehicles. One of the main challenges is the scarcity of EVCS detection data. Thus, we propose a camera-based EVCS detection dataset. The dataset is composed of two parts: The first part contains images labeled at a fine-grained level of categories with eight classes. The second part contains images of 13 additional EVCS types annotated at a supercategory level as "electric vehicle charging station". The images are annotated with bounding boxes and object masks, together with a visibility level for each EVCS instance. For evaluation, protocols considering both fine-grained and supercategory EVCS detection, including fine-tuning, prompt tuning, and zero-shot detection are proposed. Four baseline methods, including both closed-set and open-set detectors, are evaluated. Our evaluation reveals that with our dataset, closed-set detectors can be trained with a reasonable performance. Also, it shows that tuning the open-set detector to work with EVCS at a fine-grained level while preserving its ability to detect common objects forms an interesting research direction. This dataset is the first dataset for camera-based electric vehicle charging station detection. The dataset is accessible here: https://evcs.viscoda.com.

Keywords: Electric Vehicle Charging Station · Object Detection · Open-set Detection · Close-set Detection

---

Supplementary Information The online version contains supplementary material available at https://doi.org/10.1007/978-3-032-12840-9_6.

1   Introduction

The number of battery and plug-in electric vehicles has grown dramatically since 2016[1]. This surge has been accompanied by a corresponding increase in the number of *Electric Vehicle Charging Stations* (EVCS) being installed. For camera-based autonomous parking at EVCS, the localization of the charging station and the classification of its type from an image is required.

Fig. 1. Data examples with annotated bounding box, object type, object mask (different object types depicted in different colors), and visibility level 0 to 3 (orange numbers). (Color figure online)

For advancing research and development of EVCS detection, a comprehensive EVCS dataset is a prerequisite. To the best of our knowledge, there is currently no publicly available dataset specifically developed for EVCS detection. We address this gap and propose a camera-based EVCS detection benchmark. This benchmark includes 4404 annotated EVCS images, clearly defined EVCS detection tasks, and comprehensive evaluation criteria.

Object detection, the process of localizing and classifying object types within images, typically operates under a closed-set paradigm, where object categories are predefined. Widely used object detection datasets focus either on detecting everyday objects, such as COCO [26], or traffic related objects without addressing EVCS, e.g., KITTI [11] and nuScenes [2]. Our dataset covers the closed-set EVCS detection of eight EVCS types. Detecting the type of an EVCS helps in acquiring information which is highly related to the charging event, such as the cable type and charging power. However, there are many different types of EVCS and incrementally extending a detection algorithm to new classes of charging stations is expensive. Instead, the open-set detection with language

---

[1] https://www.statista.com/outlook/mmo/electric-vehicles/worldwide.

input [24], which allows for the detection of unseen object categories specified by human language, presents a promising approach and deserves further exploration. To facilitate research in this area, we have curated a supplementary subset containing 13 additional, unseen EVCS types that are not included in the aforementioned eight-class set for closed-set EVCS detection. The dataset and evaluation code is published at https://evcs.viscoda.com for further research.

2   Related Work

Object Detection: The R-CNN family of detectors including R-CNN [14], SPP-net [17], Fast R-CNN [13], Faster-RCNN [36], and FPN [25] proposes candidate regions in the first stage and classifies the object and refines the location in the second stage (**two-stage** methods). Pixel-level masks of objects are predicted by Mask-RCNN [16] on top of Faster-RCNN by incorporating a separate object mask prediction branch. Alternatively, YOLO [34] regresses the location of objects and classifies them in one stage (**one-stage** method). It is extended to a large family of methods, such as YOLOv2 [35], YOLOv3 [33], and YOLOv4 [1]. SSD [29] and RetinaNet [37] further optimize the detection performance.

DETR [3] (*DEtection TRansformer*) formulates object detection as a set prediction problem and eliminates the need for non-maximum-suppression and anchor parameters. Thus, it simplifies the design of object detection methods. Based on the original DETR which requires long training schedules, many works propose methods to speed up training, such as DAB-DETR [27] and DN-DETR [23]. Deformable DETR [42] introduces deformable attention and uses multi-scale features. DINO [40] combines and improves upon techniques introduced in DAB-DETR, DN-DETR, and Deformable DETR.

While closed-set methods detect objects belonging to a predefined set of classes, open-set detectors incorporate language input in which the objects to be detected are described. CLIP [32] predicts the similarity between a textual description and an image through contrastive learning of visual and textual features. GLIP [24] further relates images and textual description on a fine-grained level by aligning the image region features to the categories of objects contained in the textual description. Grounding DINO [28] builds upon the transformer-based detector DINO and fuses language and image features at multiple levels, resulting in a notable performance improvement. More recently, YOLO World [7] extends YOLO to open-set detection by including language features, while preserving the compact architecture. An extended version of the object detection review is provided in the supplementary material.

Datasets: Since object detection is a widely studied field, a considerable quantity of datasets is publicly available. Using large datasets containing annotations of diverse sets of everyday objects, such as Pascal VOC [9], COCO [26], Objects365 [38] or LVIS [15], has been the primary way to evaluate general advances in object detection algorithms. Over time, the scale of such datasets has been increasing rapidly from 20 categories and 11.5K images in Pascal VOC to 1000 categories in LVIS or 1.9 million images in Open Images v7 [21], posing additional challenges such as long-tail distributions, where some object categories are significantly more frequent than others. Furthermore, more comprehensive types of annotations are provided using complete sentences, e.g., Flickr30K [31] and Visual Genome Caption [20] or as question-answer pair in GQA [19].

Although these datasets are well suited for general object detection and evaluating algorithmic progress, specific applications require specific datasets. One such application is autonomous driving, where detecting other road users improves safety. To train road user detectors, traffic-related object detection datasets are employed. Mostly used datasets are KITTI [11], Cityscapes [10], ApolloScape [18], nuScenes [2], BDD100K [39], A2D2 [12], and Mapillary Vistas [30]. They typically contain bounding box or instance mask annotations for up to a few dozens of common object categories appearing in driving scenarios, e.g., pedestrian, car, truck, cyclist. However, to the best of our knowledge, none of the existing traffic-related datasets contain annotated EVCS. Although not essential for safety functions, EVCS detection can improve comfort features like assisted parking.

More related to our EVCS dataset are relatively smaller but more task-specific datasets. There are collections of such datasets, e.g., Roboflow 100 [8], which is comprised of 100 task-specific datasets ranging from a few hundreds to a few thousands of images for tasks like detecting different types of chess figures, bottles, or fish. Another such dataset collection consisting of 35 different datasets is provided by the ODinW challenge [22, 24], which aims to evaluate the transfer ability of pre-trained open-set detectors to specific domains.

3   EVCS Dataset

In this section, we delve into the process of planning, collecting, and annotating our EVCS dataset. Subsequently, we will present the distributions of images, numbers of annotations, and visibility levels per EVCS type.

3.1   Dataset Planning, Recording and Annotation

Dataset Planning. We first investigate possible sites for recording EVCS based on representativeness and accessibility. By combining online research, e.g. websites like chargemap[2], chargefinder[3], and Plugshare[4], as well as on-site scouting, we listed 25 recording sites in the range of our mobile data collection platform. In addition, self-recorded sequences using mobile devices such as smartphones or GoPro cameras are recorded at 26 sites to increase the EVCS type variety. The recording sites encompass a representative and diverse range of environments for electric vehicle charging, including urban city centers, motorway service stations, and supermarket parking lots. The numbers of EVCS at these sites range from one to more than 20. Background conditions vary from clean, open spaces with no parked vehicles to cluttered settings featuring a mix of cars, infrastructure, and pedestrians.

---

[2] https://de.chargemap.com/map.
[3] https://chargefinder.com/de.
[4] https://www.plugshare.com/.

Data Recording and Anonymization. Short image sequences in Full HD (1920 × 1080 pixels) were captured at 30 frames per second during two primary maneuvers: passing by and driving into EVCS parking spaces. These maneuvers represent common driving scenarios in which automated charging station detection is useful. Furthermore, they provide application-relevant EVCS perspectives from varying viewing distances and angles. In total, 21 different types of EVCS in 51 recording sites are included in our dataset. Among those 21 types of EVCS, 8 are well represented. They are listed in Table 1.

The collected data is anonymized by blurring the vehicle license plates and human faces. For this task, the tool *Anonymizer*[5] developed by understand.ai is utilized, combined with manual checks and corrections.

Table 1. Example images for each EVCS type of the fine-grained dataset

Type	Image	Type	Image	Type	Image	Type	Image
wallbe ZAS		HYC 300		HYC 150		Tritium PK350	
Compleo DUO IMS		ABB Terra 54		Compleo DUO		Tesla Super-charger	

EVCS Annotation. To avoid repetitive views, every 10th frame of the recorded sequences is selected for annotation. We developed an annotation tool based on MiVOS (*Modular interactive Video Object Segmentation*) [6]. For each sequence, we first annotate EVCS instances with masks using the S2M (*Scribble to Mask*) module in one frame. To be more specific, only the main body of each EVCS is annotated. When charging cables are available, only the cable parts tightly attached to the main body of EVCS are annotated. Then, the annotated labels are propagated to neighboring frames [6], followed by quality checks and manual editing. To avoid gross propagation errors, we restrict the maximum propagation length to 20 frames. For sequences containing densely distributed EVCS, e.g., Tesla Supercharger and Compleo DUO, the automatic propagation of object masks yields unsatisfactory results. This issue occurs at four recording sites. In these cases, the objects are annotated manually with S2M. Finally, masks and bounding boxes around the objects are obtained. Two manual checking and correction rounds were carefully conducted to provide high annotation accuracy.

---

[5] https://github.com/understand-ai/anonymizer.

The visibility level of each annotated EVCS is manually assigned on a scale from 0 to 3, as follows:

0: The main body of the EVCS is visible and well recognizable as EVCS
1: Partially occluded but still well recognizable
2: Largely occluded and barely recognizable as EVCS
3: Largely occluded and not recognizable as EVCS without the video context

Finally, the annotated data is converted to the COCO annotation format[6], a widely used format for object detection tasks. Examples for annotated images including the visibility level for each EVCS are shown in Fig. 1.

3.2   Data Statistics

The dataset is divided into the parts A and B. Part A contains 3645 images with 8 major EVCS types as listed in Table 1. The contained types are well represented, enabling the training of fine-grained EVCS detectors. Part B includes 13 additional EVCS types. These types have fewer samples and recording sites per class compared to part A. This creates a notable domain shift between the two parts. However, the domain gap between EVCS in part A and B is expected to be smaller than that between EVCS and other object categories. Therefore, part B is used to evaluate the generalization ability of EVCS detectors trained to distinguish EVCS and non-EVCS objects.

Part A: Figure 2 illustrates the number of images per class (left) and annotations per visibility level per class (right). The number of annotated objects for each type ranges from 491 to 1118. The number of images containing each EVCS type varies between 208 and 1027, primarily due to differences in EVCS density. Tesla Superchargers, often located next to each other on parking grounds, have 4.38 annotations per image on average, while Tritium PK350 and Compleo DUO have 2 to 3 annotations per image. The remaining classes show 1 to 2 annotations per image. The visibility levels of all annotated EVCS per type are shown in Fig. 2. For most classes, more than half of the annotations have visibility level 0 and a large proportion has visibility level 1. The annotations with visibility 2 and 3 only account for a small portion.

Part B: This part comprises 759 images, annotated across 13 types of EVCS. The details about class and visibility distribution are presented in the supplementary material.

4   Evaluation Setup

This section covers the data split, the evaluation protocol and the selection of baseline methods for detecting EVCS.

---

[6] https://cocodataset.org/#format-data.

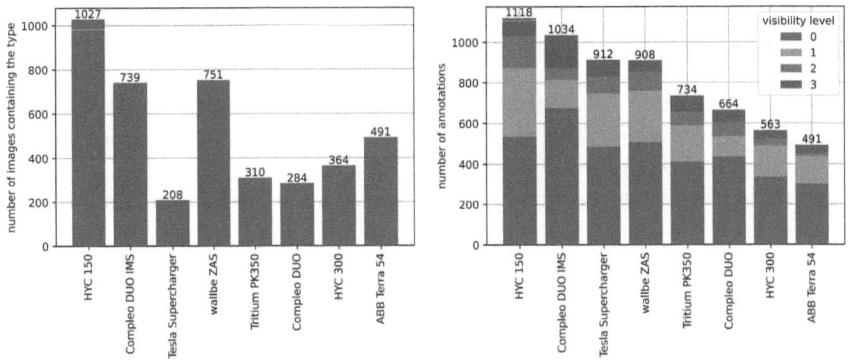

Fig. 2. EVCS dataset part A statistics: Number of images containing each type of EVCS (left) and number of annotations per visibility level per type (right).

4.1   Data Split

Part A: The EVCS dataset part A is divided into a training, a validation, and a test set based on recording sites. Specifically, 25 sites are assigned to the training set, 14 to the validation set, and 11 sites to the test set. In this way, having highly similar images belonging to the same site both in training and evaluation is avoided, contributing to fair validation and test. After splitting, the dataset comprises 2129 training images, 770 validation images, and 746 test images. The corresponding numbers of annotated EVCS are 3903, 1204, and 1263, respectively. A detailed breakdown of the image distribution across different sets for each EVCS type is provided in supplementary material.

Part B: Part B of the EVCS dataset is annotated with a single supercategory ("electric vehicle charging station"), enabling the evaluation of generalization abilities of **one-class** EVCS detectors trained on part A.

4.2   Evaluation Protocol

Annotations with visibility levels 0, 1, and 2 are used for training, validation, and testing. The benchmark considers two detection scenarios:

- Fine grained EVCS (**eight-class**): Detection of EVCS at fine-grained level, classification into the eight categories defined in part A of the dataset. Training, validation, and testing are performed on part A data.
- Supercategory EVCS (**one-class**): Detection of EVCS at supercategory level with the class "electric vehicle charging station", without distinguishing between specific types. Training and validation are conducted on the training and validation set of part A, respectively. Testing is performed on both test sets of part A and part B.

Detection Setup: Three types of object detection setups are considered: fine-tuning, zero-shot, and prompt tuning.

– Fine tuning: Train the **eight-class** and **one-class** detector variant starting from an object detector with pre-trained weights, e.g., pre-trained on COCO [26]. This setup applies to closed-set and open-set detectors.
– Zero-shot: Evaluates how well pre-trained open-set detectors can transfer to detect EVCS, a less common type of object, at supercategory and fine-grained class level. This setup directly applies the pre-trained open-set detectors to **eight-class** and **one-class** EVCS detection. For closed-set detectors, zero-shot is not applicable.
– Prompt tuning: This refers to tuning the input text features of open set detectors while fixing the weights of other network modules to enhance the EVCS detection performance. Both **eight-class** and **one-class** detection are tested for this setup.

Evaluation Criteria: For all three object detection setups, mean average precision (mAP) is used as the primary evaluation criterion. Also, the mean average precision with IoU threshold 75% (mAP_{75})and 50% (mAP_{50}) are reported. After fine-tuning, open-set detectors exhibit improved EVCS detection performance. However, their ability to detect other general object classes, e.g., people or cars may significantly degrade, as the model's parameters are optimized specifically for EVCS detection. The degeneration level Δ is quantified by comparing the detection performance on a common object detection benchmark, e.g., COCO before and after fine-tuning. For the one-class setup, the fine-tuning process utilizes part A data for training, making part B a source of unseen EVCS types. The model's ability to handle this domain shift is assessed by calculating the performance gap δ between the test sets of part A and part B. A smaller δ indicates better generalization ability. The generalization of prompt-tuned one-class models is evaluated using the same metric. A summary table of the evaluation criteria is provided in Sect. 1 of the supplementary material.

4.3   Baseline Selection

We establish a comprehensive baseline by selecting four object detection models: Faster-RCNN [36] representing two-stage detectors, YOLOX [41] for one-stage detectors, DINO [40] showcasing transformer-based approaches, and Grounding-DINO [28] demonstrating open-set detection capabilities. For each baseline, we choose one or two backbones. The MMDetection [4] framework[7] is used for training. Initial experiments show that fine-tuning consistently yields significantly better performance than training from scratch. Consequently, all subsequent model variants use pre-trained weights. A comprehensive overview of all models used in the evaluation is presented in Table 2, including 15 model variants from

---

[7] https://github.com/open-mmlab/mmdetection.

different detectors, backbones, and detection setups for both **eight-class** and **one-class** scenarios.

For both zero-shot and prompt tuning setups, we use Grounding-DINO. The prompt tuning is implemented using the code base of Chen et al. [5]. The language embedding for each class is defined with 10 tunable tokens. The tokens are initialized using the standard normal distribution. While the language embeddings are optimized using EVCS training data, the weights of parameters belonging to other modules in Grounding-DINO are fixed.

Table 2. The selected baseline methods. For the prompt tuning variants, the number of tunable parameters (text embedding) is 6144 for eight-class variant and 768 for one-class variant.

Model	Backbone	Pretraining Data	Setup	# Para.
eight-class				
Faster-RCNN-R50-FT	ResNet50	COCO	Fine-Tune	41.4M
Faster-RCNN-R101-FT	ResNeXt101	COCO	Fine-Tune	60.0M
YOLOX-s-FT	CSPDarkNet	COCO	Fine-Tune	8.9M
YOLOX-l-FT	CSPDarkNet larger	COCO	Fine-Tune	54.2M
DINO-R50-FT	ResNet50	COCO	Fine-Tune	47.6M
DINO-L-FT	Swin-L	COCO	Fine-Tune	218.7M
Grounding-DINO-t-FT	Swin-T	O365, GoldG, Cap4M	Fine-Tune	172.9M
Grounding-DINO-t-PT	Swin-T	O365, GoldG	Prompt tuning	173.5M[†]
Grounding-DINO-t-ZS	Swin-T	O365, GoldG,Cap4M	Zero-Shot	173.5M
one-class				
DINO-1c-L-FT	Swin-L	COCO	Fine-Tune	218.7M
DINO-1c-R50-FT	ResNet50	COCO	Fine-Tune	47.6M
Grounding-DINO-1c-t-FT	Swin-T	O365, GoldG,Cap4M	Fine-Tune	173.0M
Grounding-DINO-1c-R50-FT	Swin-T	COCO	Fine-Tune	172.5M
Grounding-DINO-1c-t-PT	Swin-T	O365, GoldG	Prompt tuning	173.5M[‡]
Grounding-DINO-1c-t-ZS	Swin-T	O365, GoldG,Cap4M	Zero-Shot	173.5M

[†] 6144 text embeddings
[‡] 768 text embeddings

5   Results and Discussion

The results for the mAP and the performance gap δ for different settings are shown in Table 3. Specifically, the results on the test set of part A are reported for all variants and the results on part B are reported only for the **one-class** variants. All experiments that require training are repeated three times and we report the median results. The training details are specified in the model configuration files, available at: https://github.com/VISCODA-git/EVCS_Benchmark_Readme.

Table 3. Results of the selected baseline methods [in %]. The best results for test set of part A mAP (eight- and one-class) and part B mAP^B (one-class) are highlighted.

Model	validation			test			mAP^B	$\delta \downarrow$
	mAP	mAP$_{50}$	mAP$_{75}$	mAP	mAP$_{50}$	mAP$_{75}$		
eight-class								
Faster-RCNN-R50-FT	64.2	83.4	73.3	64.1	81.5	75.0	–	–
Faster-RCNN-R101-FT	64.5	80.7	75.3	65.2	82.2	74.0	–	–
YOLOX-s-FT	51.9	67.6	61.1	52.1	70.6	61.3	–	–
YOLOX-l-FT	63.1	76.8	71.4	63.0	77.2	71.6	–	–
DINO-R50-FT	64.3	80.5	72.0	71.8	84.6	79.4	–	–
DINO-L-FT	72.3	85.7	79.5	69.7	83.4	77.6	–	–
Grounding-DINO-t-FT	67.6	80.8	74.6	**75.0**	87.0	82.5	–	–
Grounding-DINO-t-PT	34.4	46.9	39.4	20.2	32.5	20.2	–	–
Grounding-DINO-t-ZS	–	–	–	0.3	0.6	0.2	–	–
one-class								
DINO-1c-L-FT	81.7	95.7	90.8	**84.3**	97.4	93.3	74.7	9.6
DINO-1c-R50-FT	78.6	94.7	88.4	80.3	95.2	90.5	60.2	20.1
Grounding-DINO-1c-t-FT	83.2	97.2	92.3	83.9	97.1	92.9	**76.0**	7.9
Grounding-DINO-1c-R50-FT	80.4	95.9	88.5	81.5	97.6	92.2	61.1	20.4
Grounding-DINO-1c-t-PT	65.0	90.5	74.7	65.1	93.9	73.6	52.8	12.3
Grounding-DINO-1c-t-ZS	–	–	–	33.1	42.2	36.5	30.4	2.7

5.1   Fine Tuning

For eight-class detection, Grounding-DINO performs the best. It is slightly better than DINO, followed by YOLOX-l-FT and Faster-RCNN variants. For Faster-RCNN, the results with two different backbones are similar. The size of the backbones has more influence on the performance of DINO and YOLOX on the validation set. Surprisingly, the difference in mAP between DINO-R50-FT and DINO-L-FT (71.8% and 69.7%) on the test set is only 2.1%, while this gap is already 8.0% on the validation set. For Grounding-DINO, the eight-class fine-tuning reaches 75.0% on the test set. YOLOX-s shows a notably lower mAP than other variants, probably due to its small parameter size (8.94M).

For one-class detection, the fine-tuning is done only for DINO and Grounding-DINO with two different backbones. All four variants show similar performance with mAP between 80.3% and 84.3%. The δ for DINO-1c-L-FT and Grounding-DINO-1c-t-FT is 9.6% and 7.9%, respectively. The gap δ increases to 20.1% and 20.4% for DINO-1c-R50-FT and Grounding-DINO-1c-R50-FT. Presumably, the larger number of parameters contributes to a better generalization here. Considering the domain shift between part A and part B, the relatively small performance gap achieved here indicates that the one-class detector already learned good common features to differentiate EVCS from other types of objects.

Table 4. Performance (mAP) before and after fine-tuning (FT).

Model	COCO Performance		
	Before FT	After FT	Δ
Grounding-DINO-t-FT	48.5	27.9	20.6
Grounding-DINO-1c-t-FT		46.0	2.5
Grounding-DINO-1c-R50-FT	48.9	14.0	34.9

The degeneration level Δ (explained in Sect. 4.2) for Grounding-DINO-t-FT, Grounding-DINO-1c-t-FT, and Grounding-DINO-1c-R50-FT is listed in Table 4. The one-class detector for Grounding-DINO has a relatively small $\Delta = 2.5\%$. In comparison, the model with **eight-class** shows a significantly larger $\Delta = 20.6\%$. Since Grounding-DINO-1c-R50-FT is pre-trained using only COCO, the parameters of this detector are optimized more specifically for COCO classes. Fine-tuning the network to adapt its parameters specifically to EVCS classes directly changes network parameters originally tuned for COCO class detection. This adversely affects the model's ability of detecting COCO classes, resulting in a much larger $\Delta = 34.9\%$.

5.2   Zero-Shot

Zero-shot detection fails for eight-class detection (cf. Table 3) for two reasons. Firstly, fine-grained EVCS objects, such as HYC 150, are absent from any pre-training dataset for Grounding-DINO, making it difficult to align them within a shared language-vision feature space. Secondly, the fine-grained names such as "wallbe ZAS", "HYC 150" are less common than object types like "people" and "car", leading to less informative language features generated from their textual encoding. In contrast, the one-class detection task employs the type name "electric vehicle charging station", which has clear representations for each word and sub-phrase. This enables effective visual grounding, achieving an mAP of 33.1% on part A and 30.4% on part B of the test set.

A significant performance gap persists between zero-shot and fine-tuned Grounding-DINO variants, particularly for eight-class detection. Consequently, incorporating visual data into the fine-tuning process remains crucial to enable open-set detectors to accurately detect fine-grained object categories.

5.3   Prompt Tuning

The one-class prompt tuning of Grounding-DINO reaches 65.1, showing advantages over the zero-shot one-class detector (Grounding-DINO-1c-t-ZS). However, the difference in mAP between PT and FT for one-class (65.1% vs. 83.9%) is still notably large.

The prompt tuning of eight-class detection for Grounding-DINO does not work properly. Our interpretation is that the learned visual features from pre-training data might only be able to distinguish between EVCS and non-EVCS, rather than differentiating between specific EVCS subtypes. In addition, the limited number of optimizable variables (only 8 sets of text tokens) may be insufficient for learning to differentiate between EVCS subtypes. Thus, prompt tuning fails in fine-grained class detection.

5.4 Discussion

For closed-set EVCS detection, DINO and Grounding-DINO achieve impressive performance, exceeding an mAP of 70% for eight-class detection and 80% for one-class detection. This indicates that only limited potential exists for further improvements for detecting EVCS in a closed-set setting. In contrast, substantial research is required for the open-set EVCS detection. As shown in our experiments, the fine-tuned detectors reach acceptable performance but suffer from losing their ability to detect common objects, often called *catastrophic forgetting*. This phenomenon is even stronger for the fine-grained level of EVCS detection. Enabling the open-set methods to detect fine-grained level EVCS while preserving their detection ability on general object types in a data efficient way forms an interesting research direction. In addition, compressing the EVCS detection models with minimal detection performance drop and, thus, enabling real-time deployment on edge devices is crucial.

6 Conclusions

We introduce the first camera-based EVCS detection dataset. Images contained in this dataset are annotated at both fine-grained (eight-class) and supercategory level (one-class). The annotations are provided in high quality with bounding boxes, accurate object masks, and visibility levels, enabling the training of models for both object detection and instance segmentation.

Representative detection methods belonging to different categories of detectors are evaluated. We employ two-stage Faster-RCNN, one-stage YOLOX, transformer-based DINO for closed-set detection, and Grounding-DINO for open-set detection. Each detector is trained with multiple configurations, spanning a comprehensive range of 15 detector baselines. We fine-tune all detectors and additionally apply zero-shot detection and prompt tuning to the open-set detection variants. All variants are evaluated using the proposed EVCS dataset.

The evaluation results show that our dataset allows for training reasonable closed-set EVCS detectors. However, the performance gaps remain considerably large between fine-tuning versus zero-shot and prompt tuning, respectively. This indicates that achieving fine-grained EVCS detection (comparable to fine-tuned EVCS detection) while preserving the ability of detecting common objects (as in zero-shot and prompt tuning) is an interesting future research direction, for which our dataset is well suited. Gradually, our work contributes to the research and development of EVCS detection. It eases the integration of EVCS detection into autonomous and assisted driving and enhances the overall driving experience.

Acknowledgment. We acknowledge the support by the German Federal Ministry of the Environment, Nature Conservation, Nuclear Safety and Consumer Protection through the GreenAutoML4FAS project (No. 67KI32007A).

References

1. Bochkovskiy, A., Wang, C.Y., Liao, H.Y.M.: YOLOv4: optimal speed and accuracy of object detection. arXiv preprint (2020). https://doi.org/10.48550/arXiv.2004.10934
2. Caesar, H., et al.: nuScenes: A multimodal dataset for autonomous driving. In: Proceedings of IEEE/CVF Conference on Computer Vision and Pattern Recognition (CVPR), pp. 11621–11631 (2020). https://doi.org/10.1109/CVPR42600.2020.01164
3. Carion, N., Massa, F., Synnaeve, G., Usunier, N., Kirillov, A., Zagoruyko, S.: End-to-End object detection with transformers. In: Vedaldi, A., Bischof, H., Brox, T., Frahm, J.-M. (eds.) ECCV 2020. LNCS, vol. 12346, pp. 213–229. Springer, Cham (2020). https://doi.org/10.1007/978-3-030-58452-8_13
4. Chen, K., et al.: MMDetection: open MMLab detection toolbox and benchmark. arXiv preprint (2019). https://doi.org/10.48550/arXiv.1906.07155
5. Chen, Q., et al.: Exploration of visual prompt in grounded pre-trained open-set detection. In: ICASSP 2024-2024 IEEE International Conference on Acoustics, Speech and Signal Processing (ICASSP), pp. 6115–6119. IEEE (2024). https://doi.org/10.1109/ICASSP48485.2024.10447589
6. Cheng, H.K., Tai, Y.W., Tang, C.K.: Modular interactive video object segmentation: Interaction-to-mask, propagation and difference-aware fusion. In: Proceedings of the IEEE/CVF Conference on Computer Vision and Pattern Recognition (CVPR), pp. 5559–5568 (2021). https://doi.org/10.1109/CVPR46437.2021.00551
7. Cheng, T., Song, L., Ge, Y., Liu, W., Wang, X., Shan, Y.: YOLO-world: real-time open-vocabulary object detection. In: Proceedings of IEEE Conference on Computer Vision and Pattern Recognition (CVPR) (2024). https://doi.org/10.1109/CVPR52733.2024.01599
8. Ciaglia, F., Zuppichini, F.S., Guerrie, P., McQuade, M., Solawetz, J.: Roboflow 100: a rich, multi-domain object detection benchmark (2022). https://arxiv.org/abs/2211.13523
9. Everingham, M., Van Gool, L., Williams, C.K., Winn, J., Zisserman, A.: The PASCAL visual object classes (VOC) challenge. Int. J. Comput. Vision **88**, 303–338 (2010). https://doi.org/10.1007/s11263-009-0275-4
10. Gählert, N., Jourdan, N., Cordts, M., Franke, U., Denzler, J.: Cityscapes 3D: dataset and benchmark for 9 DoF vehicle detection. arXiv preprint (2020). https://doi.org/10.48550/arXiv.2006.07864
11. Geiger, A., Lenz, P., Urtasun, R.: Are we ready for autonomous driving? The KITTI vision benchmark suite. In: Proceedings of IEEE/CVF Conference on Computer Vision and Pattern Recognition (CVPR), pp. 3354–3361. IEEE (2012). https://doi.org/10.1109/CVPR.2012.6248074
12. Geyer, J., et al.: A2D2: audi autonomous driving dataset. arXiv preprint (2020). https://doi.org/10.48550/arXiv.2004.06320
13. Girshick, R.: Fast R-CNN. In: Proceedings of the IEEE International Conference on Computer Vision (ICCV), pp. 1440–1448 (2015). https://doi.org/10.1109/ICCV.2015.169

14. Girshick, R., Donahue, J., Darrell, T., Malik, J.: Rich feature hierarchies for accurate object detection and semantic segmentation. In: Proceedings of the IEEE Conference on Computer Vision and Pattern Recognition (CVPR), pp. 580–587 (2014). https://doi.org/10.1109/CVPR.2014.81

15. Gupta, A., Dollar, P., Girshick, R.: LVIS: a dataset for large vocabulary instance segmentation. In: Proceedings of the IEEE/CVF Conference on Computer Vision and Pattern Recognition (CVPR), pp. 5356–5364 (2019). https://doi.org/10.1109/CVPR.2019.00550

16. He, K., Gkioxari, G., Dollár, P., Girshick, R.: Mask R-CNN. In: Proceedings of the IEEE International Conference on Computer Vision (ICCV), pp. 2961–2969 (2017). https://doi.org/10.1109/ICCV.2017.322

17. He, K., Zhang, X., Ren, S., Sun, J.: Spatial pyramid pooling in deep convolutional networks for visual recognition. IEEE Trans. Pattern Anal. Mach. Intell. (TPAMI) **37**(9), 1904–1916 (2015). https://doi.org/10.1109/TPAMI.2015.2389824

18. Huang, X., Wang, P., Cheng, X., Zhou, D., Geng, Q., Yang, R.: The ApolloScape open dataset for autonomous driving and its application. IEEE Trans. Pattern Anal. Mach. Intell. **42**(10), 2702–2719 (2019). https://doi.org/10.1109/TPAMI.2019.2926463

19. Hudson, D.A., Manning, C.D.: GQA: a new dataset for real-world visual reasoning and compositional question answering. In: Proceedings of the IEEE/CVF Conference on Computer Vision and Pattern Recognition (CVPR), pp. 6700–6709 (2019). https://doi.org/10.1109/CVPR.2019.00686

20. Krishna, R., et al.: Visual genome: connecting language and vision using crowd-sourced dense image annotations. Int. J. Comput. Vision **123**(1), 32–73 (2017). https://doi.org/10.1007/s11263-016-0981-7

21. Kuznetsova, A., et al.: The open images dataset V4. Int. J. Comput. Vision **128**(7), 1956–1981 (2020). https://doi.org/10.1007/s11263-020-01316-z

22. Li, C., et al.: ELEVATER: a benchmark and toolkit for evaluating language-augmented visual models. In: Koyejo, S., Mohamed, S., Agarwal, A., Belgrave, D., Cho, K., Oh, A. (eds.) Advances in Neural Information Processing Systems, vol. 35, pp. 9287–9301. Curran Associates, Inc. (2022). https://proceedings.neurips.cc/paper_files/paper/2022/file/3c4688b6a76f25f2311daa0d75a58f1a-Paper-Datasets_and_Benchmarks.pdf

23. Li, F., Zhang, H., Liu, S., Guo, J., Ni, L.M., Zhang, L.: DN-DETR: accelerate DETR training by introducing query denoising. In: Proceedings of the IEEE/CVF Conference on Computer Vision and Pattern Recognition (CVPR), pp. 13619–13627 (2022). https://openaccess.thecvf.com/content/CVPR2022/html/Li_DN-DETR_Accelerate_DETR_Training_by_Introducing_Query_DeNoising_CVPR_2022_paper.html

24. Li, L.H., et al.: Grounded language-image pre-training. In: Proceedings of IEEE/CVF Conference on Computer Vision and Pattern Recognition (CVPR), pp. 10965–10975 (2022). https://doi.org/10.1109/CVPR52688.2022.01069

25. Lin, T.Y., Dollár, P., Girshick, R., He, K., Hariharan, B., Belongie, S.: Feature pyramid networks for object detection. In: Proceedings of the IEEE Conference on Computer Vision and Pattern Recognition (CVPR), pp. 2117–2125 (2017). https://doi.org/10.1109/CVPR.2017.106

26. Lin, T.-Y., et al.: Microsoft COCO: common objects in context. In: Fleet, D., Pajdla, T., Schiele, B., Tuytelaars, T. (eds.) ECCV 2014. LNCS, vol. 8693, pp. 740–755. Springer, Cham (2014). https://doi.org/10.1007/978-3-319-10602-1_48

27. Liu, S., et al.: DAB-DETR: dynamic anchor boxes are better queries for DETR. In: International Conference on Learning Representations (ICLR) (2022). https://iclr.cc/virtual/2022/poster/7150

28. Liu, S., et al.: Grounding DINO: marrying DINO with grounded pre-training for open-set object detection. In: Computer Vision – ECCV 2024, pp. 38–55. Springer, Cham (2025). https://doi.org/10.1007/978-3-031-72970-6_3

29. Liu, W., et al.: SSD: single shot multibox detector. In: Leibe, B., Matas, J., Sebe, N., Welling, M. (eds.) ECCV 2016. LNCS, vol. 9905, pp. 21–37. Springer, Cham (2016). https://doi.org/10.1007/978-3-319-46448-0_2

30. Neuhold, G., Ollmann, T., Rota Bulo, S., Kontschieder, P.: The mapillary vistas dataset for semantic understanding of street scenes. In: Proceedings of the IEEE International Conference on Computer Vision (ICCV), pp. 4990–4999 (2017). https://doi.org/10.1109/ICCV.2017.534

31. Plummer, B.A., Wang, L., Cervantes, C.M., Caicedo, J.C., Hockenmaier, J., Lazebnik, S.: Flickr30k entities: collecting region-to-phrase correspondences for richer image-to-sentence models. In: Proceedings of the IEEE International Conference on Computer Vision (ICCV), pp. 2641–2649 (2015). https://doi.org/10.1109/ICCV.2015.303

32. Radford, A., et al.: Learning transferable visual models from natural language supervision. In: International Conference on Machine Learning, pp. 8748–8763. PMLR (2021). https://proceedings.mlr.press/v139/radford21a.html

33. Redmon, J.: YOLOv3: an incremental improvement. arXiv preprint (2018). https://doi.org/10.48550/arXiv.1804.02767

34. Redmon, J., Divvala, S., Girshick, R., Farhadi, A.: You only look once: unified, real-time object detection. In: Proceedings of the IEEE Conference on Computer Vision and Pattern Recognition (CVPR) (2016). https://doi.org/10.1109/CVPR.2016.91

35. Redmon, J., Farhadi, A.: YOLO9000: better, faster, stronger. In: Proceedings of the IEEE Conference on Computer Vision and Pattern Recognition (CVPR), pp. 7263–7271 (2017). https://doi.org/10.1109/CVPR.2017.690

36. Ren, S., He, K., Girshick, R., Sun, J.: Faster R-CNN: towards real-time object detection with region proposal networks. In: Advances in Neural Information Processing Systems, vol. 28. Curran Associates, Inc. (2015). https://proceedings.neurips.cc/paper_files/paper/2015/file/14bfa6bb14875e45bba028a21ed38046-Paper.pdf

37. Ross, T.Y., Dollár, G.: Focal loss for dense object detection. In: Proceedings of the IEEE Conference on Computer Vision and Pattern Recognition (CVPR), pp. 2980–2988 (2017). https://doi.org/10.1109/ICCV.2017.324

38. Shao, S., et al.: Objects365: a large-scale, high-quality dataset for object detection. In: Proceedings of the IEEE/CVF International Conference on Computer Vision (ICCV), pp. 8430–8439 (2019). https://doi.org/10.1109/ICCV.2019.00852

39. Yu, F., et al.: BDD100K: a diverse driving dataset for heterogeneous multi-task learning. In: Proceedings of the IEEE/CVF Conference on Computer Vision and Pattern Recognition (CVPR), pp. 2636–2645 (2020). https://doi.org/10.1109/CVPR42600.2020.00271

40. Zhang, H., et al.: DINO: DETR with improved denoising anchor boxes for end-to-end object detection. In: International Conference on Learning Representations (ICLR) (2023). https://iclr.cc/virtual/2023/poster/11884

41. Zheng, G., Songtao, L., Feng, W., Zeming, L., Jian, S., et al.: YOLOX: exceeding yolo series in 2021. arXiv preprint (2021). https://doi.org/10.48550/arXiv.2107.08430
42. Zhu, X., Su, W., Lu, L., Li, B., Wang, X., Dai, J.: Deformable DETR: deformable transformers for end-to-end object detection. In: Proceedings of the International Conference on Learning Representations (ICLR) (2021). https://iclr.cc/virtual/2021/oral/3448

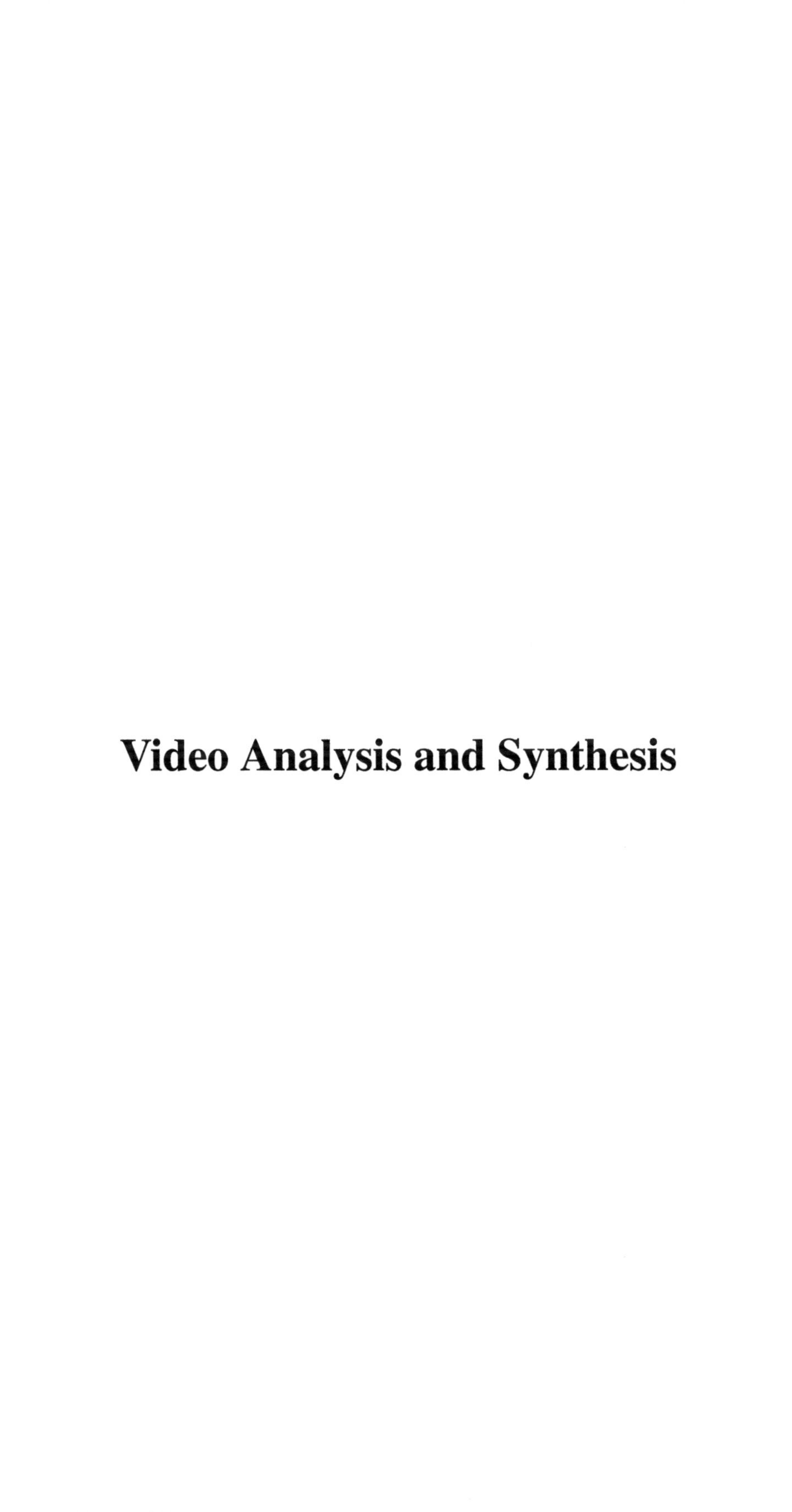

Video Analysis and Synthesis

SegSLR: Promptable Video Segmentation for Isolated Sign Language Recognition

Sven Schreiber[iD], Noha Sarhan[iD], Simone Frintrop[iD],
and Christian Wilms[(✉)][iD]

Computer Vision Group, University of Hamburg, Hamburg, Germany
{sven.schreiber,noha.sarhan,simone.frintrop,
christian.wilms}@uni-hamburg.de

Abstract. Isolated Sign Language Recognition (ISLR) approaches primarily rely on RGB data or signer pose information. However, combining these modalities often results in the loss of crucial details, such as hand shape and orientation, due to imprecise representations like bounding boxes. Therefore, we propose the ISLR system SegSLR, which combines RGB and pose information through promptable zero-shot video segmentation. Given the rough localization of the hands and the signer's body from pose information, we segment the respective parts through the video to maintain all relevant shape information. Subsequently, the segmentations focus the processing of the RGB data on the most relevant body parts for ISLR. This effectively combines RGB and pose information. Our evaluation on the complex ChaLearn249 IsoGD dataset shows that SegSLR outperforms state-of-the-art methods. Furthermore, ablation studies indicate that SegSLR strongly benefits from focusing on the signer's body and hands, justifying our design choices.

Keywords: Sign language recognition · Action recognition · Segmentation

1 Introduction

Sign language is a central way to communicate for the deaf or hard-of-hearing. It transmits information through several visual parameters, most importantly manual parameters like hand shape, orientation, position, or movement, but also non-manual parameters like body posture, facial expressions, or head movements [1]. Outside the deaf or hard-of-hearing community, few people understand sign language, which substantially limits the social interaction of the deaf or hard-of-hearing. To bridge this gap, Isolated Sign Language Recognition (ISLR) systems classify a video sequence of sign language on a gloss-level.

ISLR systems rely on various techniques [25,30]. Several systems explicitly focus on the most relevant image areas like the signer's body, hands, or face to capture the manual and non-manual parameters [4,7,12,13,18,31,32]. This

M. Keuper and F. Locatello (Eds.): DAGM GCPR 2025, LNCS 16125, pp. 91–105, 2026.
https://doi.org/10.1007/978-3-032-12840-9_7

is done by attending to the relevant parts of the RGB video frames (RGB-based) or adding dedicated networks, which encode pose information (pose-based). Pose-based models extract keypoints of the signer and subsequently generate a skeleton-like graph, which is then processed by complex architectures [13,18,22,33]. In contrast, RGB-based models mostly extract crops around the signer's hands or the signer itself. These crops are classified as one part of the system. Note that some RGB-based methods use pose information to locate the relevant parts in the image. Thus, most methods either operate solely on RGB or pose information, or use the pose mostly to guide the extraction of crops, losing critical details about the pose, such as hand shape, hand orientation, or body posture.

Recently, foundation models for promptable segmentation of images and videos revolutionized segmentation in several domains and tasks [3,9,24,35,37]. Promptable segmentation refers to segmenting a coherent part of the image given a suitable prompt, like point coordinates or a bounding box. SAM [16] for images and SAM 2 [26] for videos, address these tasks and generate high-quality segmentations in a zero-shot manner without domain-specific training data. Hence, these models are also well-suited for ISLR.

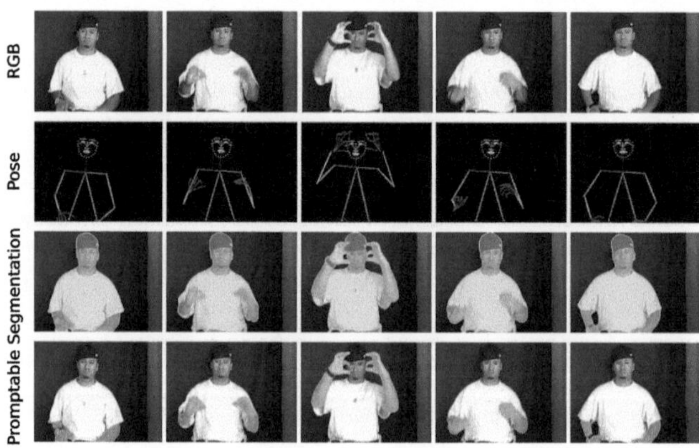

Fig. 1. Idea of the proposed SegSLR system: We combine RGB information (first row) and pose information (second row) through promptable video segmentation. The pose information is used as prompts to segment the RGB frames. This leads to segmentations of the signer's body (third row) and hands (fourth row) to focus processing on the most relevant image areas for ISLR.

In this paper, we combine RGB-based and pose-based ISLR through the innovative use of promptable video segmentation in our novel ISLR system SegSLR, visualized in Fig. 2. SegSLR uses a multi-stream approach. Besides Inflated 3D CNN (I3D CNN) [2] based streams for plain RGB information and optical flow, ensuring a comprehensive understanding of both spatial and temporal dynamics, SegSLR contains segmentation streams, which combine RGB and pose information through promptable video segmentation. The innovative idea of these streams is, first, to utilize pose information to locate the signer's body and hands in the form of point sets. Second, these point sets are utilized by the promptable video segmentation method SAM 2 to generate high-quality segmentations (masklets) of the signer's body and hands through the video in a zero-shot manner to retain rich pose information (see Fig. 1 for an example). Finally, these masklets are used to focus the processing of the RGB frames in the subsequent classifiers based on I3D CNNs to the most important image areas for ISLR. This results in a unified architecture exclusively relying on simple I3D CNNs for classification. Based on this innovative combination of pose and RGB information, SegSLR outperforms state-of-the-art systems on the complex ChaLearn249 IsoGD dataset, as our evaluation shows. Ablation studies also demonstrate the benefit of the key design decisions.

Overall, our contributions are three-fold:

- We introduce SegSLR, a novel ISLR method, leveraging both RGB and pose information.
- We use foundation models for promptable video segmentation in ISLR to combine pose and RGB information, which retains rich pose information through high-quality segmentations.
- SegSLR outperforms the existing state-of-the-art by up to 4.17%, while ablation studies validate the design choices.

2   Related Work

Methods for ISLR evolved from models based on hand-crafted features to learned CNN-, LSTM-, or transformer-based architectures [25, 30]. Here, we will discuss learned methods since they substantially outperform traditional ones. Learned models for ISLR can be divided into three groups: methods that mainly rely on RGB information, on pose information, or hybrid methods.

Methods relying only on RGB input either encode the entire frame or, additionally, crops of relevant areas. [28] encode entire RGB frames of a video in an I3D CNN architecture [2] and add a second stream with optical flow to better capture the temporal dynamics. Subsequently, the streams are fused on score-level. Similarly, [20] apply I3D CNN to the RGB input and add weakly supervised data to improve the feature extraction. [41] combine 3D CNNs for short-term temporal dependencies with a Conv LSTM for long-term ones.

Several RGB-based methods additionally focus on the signer's body parts as important parameters for sign language recognition. [21] apply simple hand detectors based on Haar-like features to extract bounding boxes around the hands and track them through the video, yielding a hand energy image for classification. [29, 31, 32] all extend the two-stream model of [28] by focusing on different aspects. While [32] extract masks of the hands in an individual stream to mask the RGB input, [29] focus the RGB input on the moving areas in an end-to-end learned manner, resulting in attending hands and arms. Finally, [31] utilize pseudo depth as an additional stream, effectively segmenting the signer without combining this information with the RGB stream.

Using only pose information, [22] apply a graph convolutional network (GCN) to the skeleton graph generated by a pose estimation system, while also applying advanced data augmentations, which mix signs. Also utilizing GCNs as their backbone, [36] add text embeddings in a contrastive learning framework, while [33] use GCNs at the frame-level and model the temporal dependency using BERT [5]. [13,40] use BERT for self-supervised pre-training. In [13], masked hand poses are reconstructed for pre-training. In contrast to previous methods, [18] apply transformer-based modules instead of GCNs.

Hybrid methods combine RGB and pose information. [14] propose a multi-stream architecture with 3D CNNs for RGB and optical flow input as well as a GCN for the skeleton graph, combining them through score fusion. Several systems [4,7,8,12] crop parts of the RGB frames or latent representations around the hands, face, or the entire signer for focused processing based on pose information. Yet, only bounding boxes [4,7,12] or rough segmentations [8] are used. Finally, [42] encode the position of specific joints of the signer into heatmaps that can be processed by 3D CNNs, which also capture RGB information [14].

Closest to our proposed SegSLR are the hybrid methods, which use pose information to focus processing of the RGB data on relevant areas like the signer's body or hands. However, [4,7,12] only use bounding boxes, losing information about the hand shape, hand orientation, or the signer's body posture, which are all highly relevant for sign language recognition. [8] generate pixel-precise segmentations, yet they are derived from the pose information through dilation. This results in low-quality segmentation masks. In contrast, SegSLR employs high-quality segmentations of the signer's body and hands using a foundation model, retaining important details about body posture and manual parameters.

3   Revisit Segment Anything Model 2

Original SAM [16] for images is a segmentation system trained on a large-scale dataset, which is applied to various tasks in a zero-shot manner. To guide SAM, prompts (points, boxes, or masks) are used, which indicate what to segment within an image. SAM 2 [26] extends this idea to videos and leverages the temporal information to segment consistent masklets. SAM 2 consists of three major components: encoders, a decoder, and a memory mechanism. The image and prompt encoders consist of a masked autoencoder [10] for images as well as positional and learned embeddings for the prompts. Given these embeddings, the mask decoder predicts a segmentation mask and an IoU score. To ensure temporal consistency across the video, a memory attention mechanism is added. For training SAM 2, [26] proposed a new dataset SA-V, with manually or semi-automatically annotated videos.

4   Method

This section introduces our novel SegSLR system for ISLR, as depicted in Fig. 2. SegSLR follows the general approach of [28], comprising a multi-stream architecture based on Inflated 3D CNNs (I3D CNNs) [2] with streams for processing plain RGB frames and derived optical flow information, as visible in the center and top of Fig. 2. In addition, SegSLR has four segmentation streams (see bottom part in Fig. 2) to effectively combine RGB and pose information. To this end, a promptable video segmentation module as visualized in Fig. 4 first estimates the signer's pose and generates keypoints for the signer's body and hands. A selection of these keypoints is used to prompt SAM 2, yielding high-quality segmentation masks of the signer's body and hands. Subsequently, two streams in SegSLR directly take the logits of the segmentation masks for the body and both hands, respectively. The other two segmentation streams mask the RGB frames, to focus processing on the relevant parts of the RGB input while maintaining rich pose information (hand shape, hand orientation, and body posture) through the high-quality segmentations. Finally, the data of each stream is processed by an I3D CNN per stream, and the results of all I3D CNNs are combined using score-level fusion (see right part in Fig. 2). In the following sections, we discuss each step in more detail.

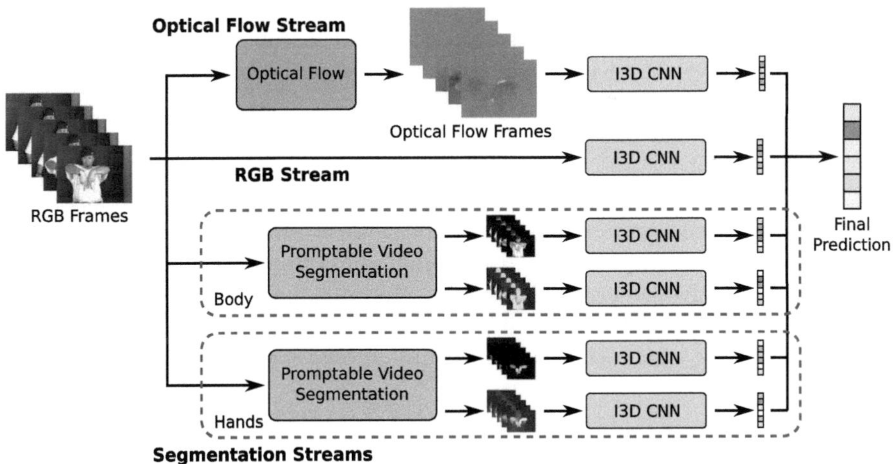

Fig. 2. Overview of our proposed SegSLR system. Based on RGB frames of a video, the first stream (Optical Flow Stream) calculates the optical flow and, subsequently, classifies these optical flow frames using an I3D CNN. The second stream, RGB Stream, directly applies an I3D CNN to the plain RGB frames. As the key novelty of SegSLR, we propose the segmentation streams, which combine RGB and pose information using promptable video segmentation modules (see Fig. 4) to generate four outputs: RGB frames focused on the signer's body and hands as well as the respective segmentation logits. These outputs are processed by I3D CNNs. Finally, score-level fusion is applied to aggregate the results.

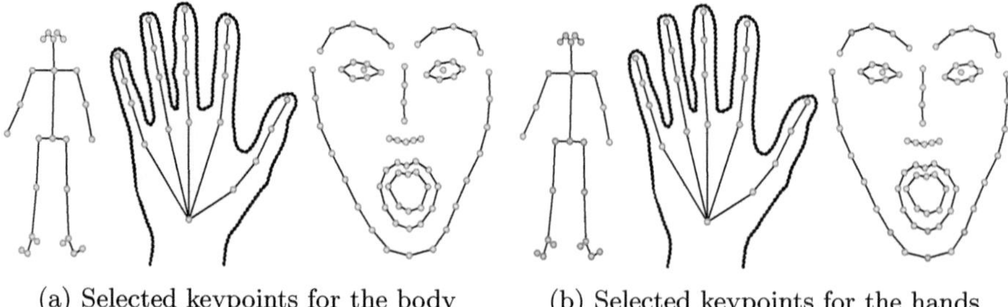

(a) Selected keypoints for the body   (b) Selected keypoints for the hands

Fig. 3. Overview of RTMW [15] keypoints for prompting SAM 2 to segment the signer's body (a) and hands (b). Green keypoints are positive point prompts, red keypoints are negative point prompts, and blue keypoints are ignored.

4.1   Pose Estimation and Prompt Generation

As a first step in all segmentation streams of SegSLR, we derive point prompts based on pose information for prompting SAM 2 in our promptable video segmentation module (see Fig. 4). As outlined in Sect. 1, pose estimation results are used in ISLR to capture the body posture or locate the hands [4,7,8,12]. Therefore, we take the state-of-the-art human pose estimation system RTMW [15] and initially extract 116 keypoints, as visualized in Fig. 3, covering the entire signer's body. Given these keypoints, we create two subsets. The first subset (see Fig. 3a) captures the entire signer's body, therefore, we use all keypoints except for detailed hand and face keypoints, since this level of detail is not necessary. The second subset focuses on the hands and includes the keypoints around the first joint per finger, as visualized in Fig. 3b. We ignore the other hand keypoints since they are frequently outside the hands due to imprecise localization. We also select negative keypoints to discern the hands from the remaining body in SAM-2. As negative keypoints, we select all major body keypoints and important face keypoints. All keypoints in both subsets are the point prompts to guide SAM 2. Note that undetected keypoints are ignored for prompt generation.

4.2   Best Frame Selection

Before applying SAM 2, we select the best frame to start the segmentation through the video in our promptable video segmentation module. Frame selection is important since the first frame might not cover the hands, as the signer's hands are usually at hip level. For instance, this is apparent from the initial frame in Fig. 1. To select the best frame, we assess the quality of the detected keypoints per frame by calculating the average keypoint confidence, the size of the bounding box around all keypoints, and the overlap between hands and face keypoints. The keypoint confidence is a per-keypoint output from RTMW and a surrogate for RTMW's confidence about the keypoint. To calculate a single

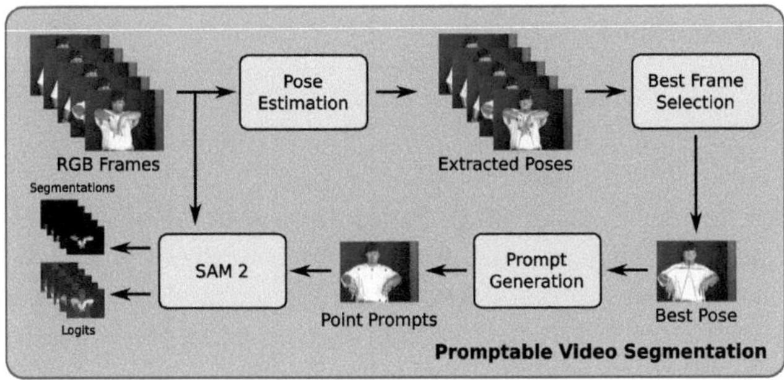

Fig. 4. Detailed view of our promptable video segmentation module for hands segmentation. For segmenting the signer's body, the same pipeline is applied with different point prompts. From the input RGB frames, the signer's pose is estimated, and the best frame to initiate the video segmentation is determined. In this frame, several keypoints are converted to positive or negative point prompts. Using these prompts, SAM 2 is applied to the RGB frames. The results are the RGB frames masked by the SAM 2 segmentations and the segmentations' logits. Note that the estimated poses and the point prompts are overlayed with the RGB frames for visualisation only.

score, we take the average across all detected keypoints. The remaining two measures are used to select a frame, which shows no or only a minimal overlap between the hands and the face. Hands in front of the face frequently occur in sign language. However, due to their similarity in color, it is challenging to discern these regions for a segmentation system when they overlap. Therefore, we first calculate the area of the bounding box covering all keypoints. This helps to measure how sprawled the arms are. To prevent cases where only the upper arms are stretched out and the hands are still close to the face, we determine the maximum overlap between one hand's bounding box and the bounding box around the face. Note that all bounding boxes are created based on the detected RTMW keypoints. To combine the three scores, we first normalize the scores by their respective per-video maximum, subtract the maximum overlap from 1, and multiply them. Hence, the best frame will receive the maximum score. Given this frame, we use the respective sets of point prompts for prompting SAM 2.

4.3   Mask Generation

Given the two sets of point prompts for the signer's body and hands on the best frame of a video sequence, we bidirectionally prompt SAM 2 starting from the best frame in our promptable video segmentation module. Hence, we apply SAM 2 from the best frame forward through the video and backward. This process is conducted for each set. The resulting masklet per set is applied to the RGB frames to focus on either the signer's body or hands. Besides the binary segmentation masks, we also extract the per-frame logits of the segmentations to capture the global scene context through SAM 2's per-pixel confidence.

4.4   ISLR Classification

Our new segmentation streams are integrated into the framework of [28] for ISLR classification. This results in SegSLR, as visible in Fig. 2. SegSLR consists of three main streams, one for the plain RGB data, one for optical flow data extracted from the RGB data using [38], and the aforementioned segmentation streams. As visible from Fig. 2, there exist four segmentation streams working on the outputs of the two promptable video segmentation modules for segmenting the signer's body and hands. The first stream uses masked RGB frames, effectively masking the background and focusing the processing on the signer based on the pose information. In contrast, the second stream processes the logits of the body segmentation. Similarly, for the two hands, the third and fourth streams do the same, processing masked RGB frames and the logits for both hands simultaneously. This focuses processing on the dominant parameter for ISLR, the hands. In case of the logits, the captured global context includes information about the location of the signer, making the relative location of the hands visible (see Fig. 5d). In contrast to most ISLR works focusing on hands, the precise and temporally consistent segmentations by SAM 2 capture the hand shapes, hand orientation, and even details about the fingers as visible in the examples in Fig. 5. We evaluate the design choices regarding the streams in Sect. 5.2.

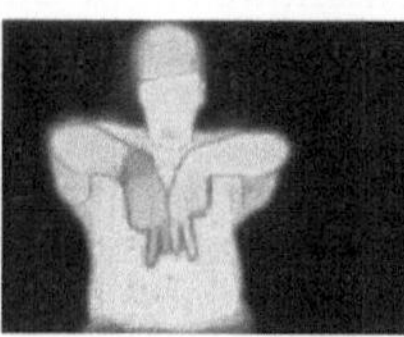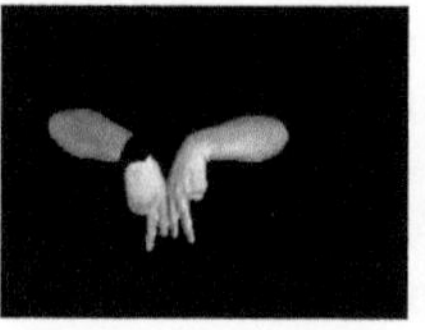

(a) Body segmenta-   (b) Body logits   (c) Hands segmen-   (d) Hands logits
tion   tation

Fig. 5. Examples of the body segmentation, body logits, hands segmentation, and hands logits as intermediate outputs of the segmentation streams in SegSLR.

Finally, each segmentation stream in SegSLR uses an I3D CNN as commonly applied in ISLR literature [12,20,28] to capture spatial and temporal dependencies. The per-stream results are combined using score-level fusion.

4.5   Implementation Details

SegSLR consists of three trainable components: (1) SAM 2, (2) RTMW, and (3) six I3D CNNs. For SAM 2, we apply a model pre-trained on SA-1B [16] and SA-V [26] as proposed by [26] and do not add fine-tuning, since segmentation annotations are unavailable in ISLR datasets. Similarly, we directly apply the pose estimation system RTMW, which is pre-trained on 14 datasets as suggested by [15]. For the I3D CNNs in SegSLR, we follow [28] and pre-train the I3D CNNs on ImageNet [27] and the Kinetics dataset [2]. Subsequently, each I3D CNN is fine-tuned individually with Adam optimizer, a batch size of 4, and early stopping with a patience of 3. We apply standard categorical cross-entropy loss per stream. When training or testing on videos, we uniformly sample 40 frames and extract a central 224×224 crop from each frame. This ensures a constant size and length of the videos for the I3D CNNs. We additionally utilize data augmentation for training the I3D CNNs and shift the extracted crop horizontally or vertically and adjust the brightness [28].

5 Evaluation

We evaluate SegSLR on the commonly used ChaLearn249 IsoGD dataset [34] comprising 249 gestures across 47,933 videos in complex environments and under challenging lighting conditions. For details about the covered gestures, we refer to [34]. We use the training dataset to train SegSLR and report results on the validation and test sets. Note that we train SegSLR five times on the training set and report the result with the median validation accuracy for a fair comparison. This model is also used to generate the test results. We additionally report the mean and standard deviation across the five trainings. We compare SegSLR against several recent ISLR methods utilizing RGB and/or pose information. This includes the baseline system of SegSLR [28], methods that focus on the signer's body [19,31] or hands [19,32], and a method combining RGB and pose information [19]. Note that we do not compare to methods utilizing depth, since this would be unfair, given the strong semantic cues of depth data for ISLR. A comparison to other methods like [7,8,12] is impossible due to missing publicly available implementations. For assessing the quality, we use standard accuracy.

5.1 Results on ChaLearn249 IsoGD Dataset

Table 1 presents the results on the validation and test sets of ChaLearn249 IsoGD. The results clearly show that SegSLR outperforms all other methods on both sets by a substantial margin. This includes outperforming methods, which focus on the signer's hands through bounding boxes [19,32] or the signer's body [19,31]. The earlier explicitly shows the advantage of utilizing hand segmentations preserving hand shape details over simple boxes. Moreover, [19] also combine RGB and pose information by focusing their system on boxes around the hands, elbows, and shoulders of the signer. Comparing SegSLR to its baseline system, I3D-SLR, which only comprises the RGB stream and the optical flow stream, SegSLR shows an improvement of 9.21% and 8.32% in accuracy on validation and test sets. This is the result of adding the segmentation stream, combining RGB and pose information. Compared to the other variations of I3D-SLR, adding pseudo depth [31], focusing on moving areas [29], and focusing on the signer's hands [32], SegSLR shows large improvements of up to 8.80% and 6.56% on the validation and test sets, respectively. Overall, this shows the strong performance of SegSLR based on combining pose and RGB information through promptable video segmentation.

Table 1. Comparison of the proposed SegSLR to state-of-the-art ISLR methods on the ChaLearn249 IsoGD dataset. For SegSLR, we report the median accuracy on the validation set over five trainings, along with the respective mean and standard deviation in parentheses. *: Numbers were not reported by the respective paper.

Method	Accuracy (%)	
	Validation	Test
C3D-LSTM [41]	43.88	-*
SYSU ISEE [19]	50.02	-*
XDETVP [39]	51.31	-*
8-MFFs-3flc (5 crop) [17]	57.40	-*
I3D-SLR [28]	62.09	64.44
I3D-pseudoDepth [31]	62.50	66.20
2SCVN-RGB-Fusion [6]	62.72	-*
Hybrid Attn-I3D-SLR [29]	65.02	68.89
TD-SLR [32]	67.13	70.91
SegSLR (ours)	**71.30**	**72.76**
	($\mu = 71.39$, $\sigma = 0.41$)	

The qualitative segmentation results in Fig. 6 on ChaLearn249 IsoGD support the aforementioned quantitative results of SegSLR. Across all videos in Fig. 6, the segmentations of the signer's body and hands are accurate and suitable to focus the processing of SegSLR on these highly relevant areas. Even despite substantial hand movement or highly-textured backgrounds, the segmentations consistently capture the signer's body and hands. Specifically, in the videos in the first two rows, a waving hand is visible that challenges SAM 2 due to the high velocity of the movement. Yet, the segmentations are consistent. In the second and third rows, the videos show glosses where a hand is moved in front of the face. Despite visual similarity between the hands and the face, SAM 2, prompted with our point prompts derived from pose information, distinguishes between hands and face. This is due to the negative prompts covering the face when generating the hand segmentation. Finally, the last row also shows an example of a sign with a complex finger posture. Still, the hand segmentation in SegSLR captures all fingers in detail, given the pose-based point prompts.

5.2   Ablation Studies

Input Streams. To assess the impact of SegSLR's focus on the signer's body and hands, and the importance of utilizing both the binary segmentation mask and the logits, we present in Table 2 the step-by-step results, from the baseline system [28] to SegSLR. In each step, we add segmentation streams to combine pose and RGB information. Given the baseline, we first add SegSLR's body segmentation by masking the respective RGB frame (Body$_{RGB}$ in Table 2). The improvements of 3.42% and 2.91% clearly indicate the advantage of an additional

Fig. 6. Qualitative body (green masks) and hands (blue masks) segmentation results generated within our SegSLR on videos of the ChaLearn249 IsoGD test dataset. For each video, one sequence of frames is overlayed with the body segmentation and the hands segmentations, respectively. Note that we only show 8 of the 40 frames per video for brevity. (Color figure online)

Table 2. Results of SegSLR on the ChaLearn249 IsoGD dataset with three versions for the segmentation streams. $Body_{RGB}$ denotes the segmentation stream utilizing masked RGB frames. $Body_{Logits}$ is the segmentation stream processing the raw logits of the body segmentation. $Hands_{RGB}$ and $Hands_{Logits}$ are the respective streams segmenting the hands.

Input Streams	Accuracy (%)	
	Validation	Test
Base	62.09	64.42
+ $Body_{RGB}$	65.51	67.33
+ $Body_{RGB}$ + $Body_{Logits}$	67.10	69.78
+ $Body_{RGB}$ + $Body_{Logits}$ + $Hands_{RGB}$ + $Hands_{Logits}$	**71.30**	**72.76**

focus on the signer's body. Adding the logits of the body segmentation in another stream ($Body_{Logits}$ in Table 2) further improves the results by 1.59%/2.45% and shows the additional value of the logits. Finally, adding the same segmentation streams for the hands ($Hands_{RGB}$ and $Hands_{Logits}$ in Table 2), further improves the results by 4.22% and 2.98%, highlighting the importance of hands for ISLR. Overall, the results in Table 2 clearly show the value of all segmentation streams combining RGB and pose information.

Segmentation Method. We present the results of SegSLR with three different segmentation methods: well-known Mask R-CNN [11] trained on the COCO dataset [23] to segment only humans, denoted as Mask R-CNN$_{\text{Person}}$, SAM [16], and SAM 2 [26] as in the proposed SegSLR. Note that we utilize only the segmentation stream for the signer's body in SegSLR to match Mask R-CNN's training on COCO. For SAM and SAM 2, we apply the same keypoints as described in Sect. 4.1 The results in Table 3 show that SegSLR outperforms the baseline with any segmentation stream. Yet, SAM and SAM 2 surpass Mask R-CNN by up to 3.20%, which underlines the strong zero-shot segmentation ability of these foundation models. Comparing SAM and SAM 2 shows that SAM 2 leads to an improvement of 1.37% and 0.87%. A major reason for this is the temporal consistency of the segmentations between the frames. This is also visible in the qualitative results in Fig. 7, where the SAM segmentations (upper row) flicker substantially between the frames, while the SAM 2 segmentations (lower row) consistently cover the entire body.

Table 3. Results of SegSLR with different segmentation methods on the ChaLearn249 IsoGD dataset. Note that SegSLR only includes the body segmentation stream (Body$_{RGB}$) here.

Input Streams	Accuracy (%)	
	Validation	Test
Base	62.09	64.42
Base + Mask R-CNN$_{\text{Person}}$	62.31	65.44
Base + SAM (Body$_{RGB}$ only)	64.14	66.46
Base + SAM 2 (Body$_{RGB}$ only)	65.51	67.33

Fig. 7. Comparison of segmentations of the signer's body with SAM (upper row) and SAM 2 (lower row) in SegSLR on four frames of a video from the ChaLearn249 IsoGD test dataset.

6   Conclusion

Effectively utilizing both RGB and pose information is key for high-quality ISLR. To address this combination of RGB and pose information without losing details important to understand sign language, we proposed the novel ISLR system SegSLR. It innovatively combines RGB and pose information through promptable video segmentation using pose keypoints to prompt SAM 2 and detect the signer's body and hands for a focused processing of the RGB data. The strength of this novel design for ISLR is supported by our experiments on the ChaLearn249 IsoGD dataset, where SegSLR outperforms all competing methods. Our ablation studies also validated the focus of SegSLR on the signer's body and hands as well as the use of SAM 2 based on prompts from pose estimation data. Overall, SegSLR presents another step to bridge the communication gap between people inside and outside the deaf or hard-of-hearing community.

References

1. Baker-Shenk, C.L., Cokely, D.: American Sign Language: A Teacher's Resource Text on Grammar and Culture. Gallaudet University Press (1991)
2. Carreira, J., Zisserman, A.: Quo vadis, action recognition? A new model and the kinetics dataset. In: Conference on Computer Vision and Pattern Recognition (2017)
3. Cheng, H.K., Oh, S.W., Price, B., Schwing, A., Lee, J.Y.: Tracking anything with decoupled video segmentation. In: International Conference on Computer Vision (2023)
4. De Coster, M., Van Herreweghe, M., Dambre, J.: Isolated sign recognition from RGB video using pose flow and self-attention. In: Computer Vision and Pattern Recognition Workshop (2021)
5. Devlin, J.: BERT pre-training of deep bidirectional transformers for language understanding. arXiv preprint arXiv:1810.04805 (2018)
6. Duan, J., Wan, J., Zhou, S., Guo, X., Li, S.Z.: A unified framework for multi-modal isolated gesture recognition. Trans. Multimedia Comput. Commun. Appl. (2018)
7. Gökçe, Ç., Özdemir, O., Kındıroğlu, A.A., Akarun, L.: Score-level multi cue fusion for sign language recognition. In: European Conference on Computer Vision Workshop (2020)
8. Gruber, I., Krnoul, Z., Hrúz, M., Kanis, J., Bohacek, M.: Mutual support of data modalities in the task of sign language recognition. In: Computer Vision and Pattern Recognition Workshop (2021)
9. He, C., et al.: Weakly-supervised concealed object segmentation with SAM-based pseudo labeling and multi-scale feature grouping. In: Advances in Neural Information Processing Systems (2024)
10. He, K., Chen, X., Xie, S., Li, Y., Dollár, P., Girshick, R.: Masked autoencoders are scalable vision learners. In: Conference on Computer Vision and Pattern Recognition (2022)
11. He, K., Gkioxari, G., Dollar, P., Girshick, R.: Mask R-CNN. In: International Conference on Computer Vision (2017)
12. Hosain, A.A., Santhalingam, P.S., Pathak, P., Rangwala, H., Kosecka, J.: Hand pose guided 3D pooling for word-level sign language recognition. In: Winter Conference on Applications of Computer Vision (2021)

13. Hu, H., Zhao, W., Zhou, W., Wang, Y., Li, H.: SignBERT: pre-training of hand-model-aware representation for sign language recognition. In: International Conference on Computer Vision (2021)
14. Jiang, S., Sun, B., Wang, L., Bai, Y., Li, K., Fu, Y.: Skeleton aware multi-modal sign language recognition. In: Computer Vision and Pattern Recognition Workshop (2021)
15. Jiang, T., Xie, X., Li, Y.: RTMW: real-time multi-person 2D and 3D whole-body pose estimation. arXiv preprint arXiv:2407.08634 (2024)
16. Kirillov, A., et al.: Segment anything. In: International Conference on Computer Vision (2023)
17. Kopuklu, O., Kose, N., Rigoll, G.: Motion fused frames: data level fusion strategy for hand gesture recognition. In: Computer Vision and Pattern Recognition Workshop (2018)
18. Lee, T., Oh, Y., Lee, K.M.: Human part-wise 3D motion context learning for sign language recognition. In: International Conference on Computer Vision (2023)
19. Li, B., Li, W., Tang, Y., Hu, J.F., Zheng, W.S.: GL-PAM RGB-D gesture recognition. In: International Conference on Image Processing (2018)
20. Li, D., Yu, X., Xu, C., Petersson, L., Li, H.: Transferring cross-domain knowledge for video sign language recognition. In: Computer Vision and Pattern Recognition (2020)
21. Lim, K.M., Tan, A.W.C., Lee, C.P., Tan, S.C.: Isolated sign language recognition using convolutional neural network hand modelling and hand energy image. Multimedia Tools Appl. **78** (2019)
22. Lin, K., Wang, X., Zhu, L., Zhang, B., Yang, Y.: SKIM: skeleton-based isolated sign language recognition with part mixing. Trans. Multimedia **26** (2024)
23. Lin, T.Y., et al.: Microsoft COCO: common objects in context. In: European Conference on Computer Vision (2014)
24. Ma, J., He, Y., Li, F., Han, L., You, C., Wang, B.: Segment anything in medical images. Nat. Commun. **15**(1) (2024)
25. Rastgoo, R., Kiani, K., Escalera, S.: Sign language recognition: a deep survey. Expert Syst. Appl. (2021)
26. Ravi, N., et al.: Sam 2: segment anything in images and videos. arXiv preprint arXiv:2408.00714 (2024)
27. Russakovsky, O., et al.: Imagenet large scale visual recognition challenge. Int. J. Comput. Vision **115** (2015)
28. Sarhan, N., Frintrop, S.: Transfer learning of videos: from action recognition to sign language recognition. In: International Conference on Image Processing (2020)
29. Sarhan, N., Frintrop, S.: Sign, attend and tell: spatial attention for sign language recognition. In: International Conference on Automatic Face and Gesture Recognition (2021)
30. Sarhan, N., Frintrop, S.: Unraveling a decade: a comprehensive survey on isolated sign language recognition. In: International Conference on Computer Vision Workshop (2023)
31. Sarhan, N., Willruth, J.M., Fritnrop, S.: Pseudodepth-slr: generating depth data for sign language recognition. In: International Conference on Computer Vision Systems (2023)
32. Sarhan, N., Wilms, C., Closius, V., Brefeld, U., Frintrop, S.: Hands in focus: sign language recognition via top-down attention. In: International Conference on Image Processing (2023)

33. Tunga, A., Nuthalapati, S.V., Wachs, J.: Pose-based sign language recognition using GCN and BERT. In: Winter Conference on Applications of Computer Vision (2021)
34. Wan, J., Zhao, Y., Zhou, S., Guyon, I., Escalera, S., Li, S.Z.: Chalearn looking at people RGB-D isolated and continuous datasets for gesture recognition. In: Computer Vision and Pattern Recognition Workshop (2016)
35. Wilms, C., Rolff, T., Hillemann, M., Johanson, R., Frintrop, S.: SOS: segment object system for open-world instance segmentation with object priors. In: European Conference on Computer Vision (2024)
36. Wong, R., Camgoz, N.C., Bowden, R.: Learnt contrastive concept embeddings for sign recognition. In: Computer Vision and Pattern Recognition Workshop, pp. 1945–1954 (2023)
37. Wu, J., et al.: Medical SAM adapter: adapting segment anything model for medical image segmentation. arXiv preprint arXiv:2304.12620 (2023)
38. Zach, C., Pock, T., Bischof, H.: A duality based approach for realtime TV-L1 optical flow. In: German Conference on Pattern Recognition (2007)
39. Zhang, L., Zhu, G., Shen, P., Song, J., Afaq Shah, S., Bennamoun, M.: Learning spatiotemporal features using 3DCNN and convolutional LSTM for gesture recognition. In: International Conference on Computer Vision Workshop (2017)
40. Zhao, W., Hu, H., Zhou, W., Shi, J., Li, H.: BEST: BERT pre-training for sign language recognition with coupling tokenization. In: AAAI Conference on Artificial Intelligence (2023)
41. Zhu, G., Zhang, L., Shen, P., Song, J.: Multimodal gesture recognition using 3-D convolution and convolutional LSTM. IEEE Access **5** (2017)
42. Zuo, R., Wei, F., Mak, B.: Natural language-assisted sign language recognition. In: Computer Vision and Pattern Recognition (2023)

Video Object Segmentation-Aware Audio Generation

Ilpo Viertola[1(✉)] [iD], Vladimir Iashin[2] [iD], and Esa Rahtu[1] [iD]

[1] Tampere University, Tampere, Finland
`ilpo.viertola@tuni.fi`
[2] University of Oxford, Oxford, UK

Abstract. Existing multimodal audio generation models often lack precise user control, which limits their applicability in professional Foley workflows. In particular, these models focus on the entire video and do not provide precise methods for prioritizing a specific object within a scene, generating unnecessary background sounds, or focusing on the wrong objects. To address this gap, we introduce the novel task of video object segmentation-aware audio generation, which explicitly conditions sound synthesis on object-level segmentation maps. We present SAGANet, a new multimodal generative model that enables controllable audio generation by leveraging visual segmentation masks along with video and textual cues. Our model provides users with fine-grained and visually localized control over audio generation. To support this task and further research on segmentation-aware Foley, we propose Segmented Music Solos, a benchmark dataset of musical instrument performance videos with segmentation information. Our method demonstrates substantial improvements over current state-of-the-art methods and sets a new standard for controllable, high-fidelity Foley synthesis. Code, samples, and Segmented Music Solos are available at https://saganet.notion. site/.

Keywords: Artificial Foley · Multimodal · Generative Modeling

1 Introduction

Multimodal audio generation focuses on synthesizing audio, given a conditional video feed, a textual description, or conditions in other modalities. These models can be utilized in *Foley* processing, where the goal is to produce a soundtrack for a video. For the artificial Foley models to thrive, *e.g.*, as a video post-processing tool, the end-user has to have high control over the synthesized result. In addition to controllability, the model has to produce high-quality samples with great semantic and temporal accuracy.

Recent advances in diffusion [29] and conditional flow matching (CFM) [54] models have improved the audio quality of the artificial Foley models [5, 6, 36, 40, 57, 58, 62]. However, existing models still lack precise user guidance and control.

M. Keuper and F. Locatello (Eds.): DAGM GCPR 2025, LNCS 16125, pp. 106–122, 2026.
https://doi.org/10.1007/978-3-032-12840-9_8

Although recent models [5, 6, 36, 40] introduce more modalities to guide the audio generation process, they still lack precision. In complex scenes, describing the target object using *e.g.*, text, quickly becomes unfeasible.

To improve control in Foley generation, we propose a new audio synthesis task: video object segmentation-aware audio generation. This task focuses on nuanced control, highlighting the model's ability to generate audio for a specific object in the video rather than for the full scene. To the best of our knowledge, we are the first to utilise visual segmentation information in the audio generation task.

Existing state-of-the-art methods [5, 6, 40, 56, 58] focus on training the models from scratch, utilizing large uni- and multimodal datasets. It demands significant computational resources and quickly becomes infeasible in academic environments. For example, Movie Gen Audio [40] was pretrained on 384 high-end H100 GPUs for 14 days and later fine-tuned on 64 H100s for 24 h. MMAudio [6] was trained on the same high-end GPU hardware, only utilizing fewer GPU hours per training run.

Alternatively, recent works reduce training costs by using lightweight *aligners* or *adapters* to condition pretrained text-to-audio models on video sequences [19, 36, 57, 61]. While these models are more efficient to train, they often struggle with temporal alignment, as fine-tuning text-to-audio models without built-in temporal control remains challenging.

Our approach draws on recent advances in multimodal audio generation [6] and localized image captioning [27]. To enable segmentation-aware audio generation, we develop a self-supervised control module on top of a pretrained network that enables users to select a specific object in a video to generate sound for. By training our control component on a small yet high-quality dataset, we achieve better controllability, temporal synchronization, and semantic quality compared to the original model, training only a fraction of the parameters. Although our model is trained on videos with a single audio source, it can generalize to scenes with multiple audio sources and generate audio for the target object.

To train the segmentation-aware control module, we propose a high-quality dataset with sounding object segmentation maps and a high audio-video correspondence. The dataset consists of solo acts played on a variety of musical instruments. We curate the dataset based on Solos [37], AVSBench [66, 67], and MUSIC21 [64, 65] datasets. We design a pipeline that generates short video clips given the original videos, ensuring that the target sounding object is present in both the auditory and visual modalities. Additionally, we extract visual segmentation maps of the target (sounding) object. We refer to this dataset as Segmented Music Solos. For testing purposes, we utilize the University of Rochester Multi-Modal Music Performance (URMP) dataset [25].

Our contributions can be summarized as follows: i) a new audio synthesis task, namely video object segmentation-aware audio generation, ii) a video object segmentation-aware control for a state-of-the-art multimodal generative audio model, iii) we show that by training our model with single-source samples it can generate audio for target object in multi-source scenes, and iv) a new benchmark dataset, Segmented Music Solos, with sounding object segmentation information.

2 Related Work

2.1 Video Object Segmentation

Video Object Segmentation (VOS) refers to the task of segmenting and tracking objects at the pixel level across video frames while maintaining temporal consistency [41]. It typically involves distinguishing foreground objects, such as people, animals, or vehicles, from the background.

Different types of VOS tasks include semi-supervised and unsupervised VOS. In semi-supervised VOS, a ground-truth mask is provided for the target object in the first frame, and the goal is to segment the object in the remaining frames [41]. In unsupervised VOS, no initial mask is given. The goal is to discover and segment prominent objects automatically [9].

Recent advancements have introduced promptable VOS models. SAM2 [43] is a widely adopted and powerful semi-supervised video object segmentation model capable of real-time object segmentation with images and videos. The initial mask of the segmented object can be provided manually or based on location coordinates. SAM2 facilitates applications such as video editing, mixed reality experiences, and efficient annotation of visual data for training computer vision systems.

GroundedSAM2 [46] combines SAM2 with grounding models in a single pipeline, enabling grounding and tracking anything in videos. GroundedSAM2 enables segmenting objects based on natural language queries, making it a powerful tool, *e.g.*, in data generation. We utilize GroundedSAM2 with Florence-2 [60] foundation model by prompting it with text labels of target objects and SAM2 by prompting it with location coordinates in our data generation pipeline. The resulting segmentation maps of sounding objects are then used during training.

2.2 Artificial Foley Models

Artificial Foley models have gained considerable popularity. Many published models are built on top of autoregressive transformer architecture [17,35,49,56]. Also, another transformer-based approach is to utilize Masked Generative Image Transformer (MaskGIT) [2] schema for the audio generation task [32,38,51,68]. Another popular approach is to utilize diffusion [3,34,62] or flow-matching methods [6,58]. To avoid resource- and time-exhaustive training from scratch, prior work has explored using pretrained text-to-audio models for video-to-audio generation by training lightweight feature aligners or control modules between the modalities [19,36,57,61]. Although these models achieve good audio quality, they often struggle to generate temporally aligned audio. When the text modality is fixed during training, learning an aligned feature space between modalities becomes challenging.

The current Foley methods lack controllability. For artists to fulfil their needs in applications such as video post-processing, they must have fine-grained control over the model. One way to add control is to introduce conditioning signals from other modalities, *e.g.*, text.

Although early multimodal approaches, *e.g.* text-and-video-to-audio models, did not meet the generation quality compared with dedicated video-to-audio models [21,47,52,53], recent work [5,6,40] has shown that artificial Foley models can benefit from multimodality. For example, Cheng et al. [6] show that training a generative audio network with combined text-audio and text-video-audio data enables high generation quality while preserving temporal and semantic alignment with video and text. However, the user controllability remains limited since describing the target objects with textual prompts in complex scenes can be difficult or infeasible. To tackle this, we develop a novel model that supports audio generation conditioned with text and video, but also allows users to define the sounding object with a semantic mask. In practice, user can click an object from a video frame, and our model generates audio for that specific object.

2.3   Controlled Generation with Pretrained Audio Networks

Adapting large pretrained networks to new conditioning inputs is a widely studied topic. In the diffusion model domain, training a ControlNet [63] is a popular approach [14,19,36,59]. ControlNet enables fine-grained control by injecting conditioning features, such as visual cues, semantic tags, or motion information, into the denoising process of a frozen diffusion model.

However, training a parallel ControlNet [63] to condition MMAudio [6] with video object segmentation information is unnecessary. Lian et al. [27] show that in visual captioning, combining local and global visual features from the same extractor using learnable gated cross-attention [1,26], along with object segmentation masks, improves localized captions. Their large transformer-based [55] captioning model is kept frozen, and only the feature extraction process is modified. Motivated by their findings, we design and implement a localized visual feature extraction model in parallel to MMAudio's [6] Synchformer-based [18] global feature extractor.

Introducing the segmentation information already at the feature extraction stage allows us to use the same control module across all variants of the generative model. Thus, the number of trainable parameters remains the same even though the generative network size increases. In contrast, fusing the segmentation information via a ControlNet-based approach would require training a separate control module per model variant. Our approach integrates visual segmentation masks as a new conditioning modality, without requiring full model fine-tuning or training of variant-specific control modules.

3   Method

We propose a generative audio network that offers fine-grained user control through multiple input modalities: text, video, and video object segmentation masks. To enable this, we introduce a novel video object segmentation-aware audio generation task. Our approach builds on top of the MMAudio model [6], a state-of-the-art audio generation model conditioned on text and video. We extend MMAudio with a segmentation-aware control module, resulting in the proposed model, Segmentation-Aware Generative Audio Network (SAGANet). To the best of our knowledge, we are the first to utilize visual segmentation information in the audio generation task.

MMAudio is a CFM-based [28,31,54,58] model, utilizing Diffusion Transformer (DiT) [39] to approximate the velocity vector field. In addition to the improved usability of the original model, segmentation information enhances the quality and alignment of the synthesized audio. The overall architecture is shown in Fig. 1.

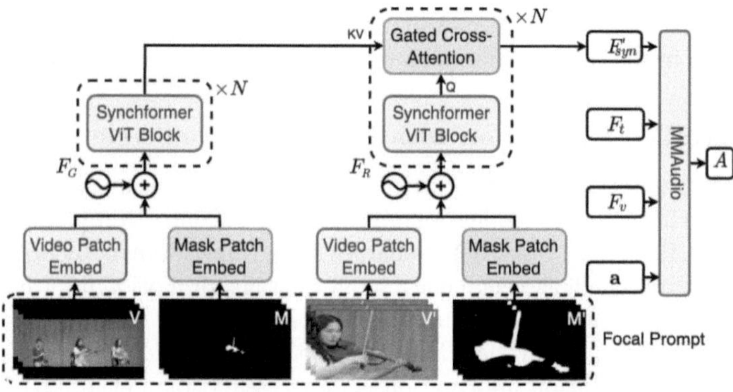

Fig. 1. Overview of SAGANet control module. Given a video and its corresponding segmentation masks, the model combines global and local information streams. Gated Cross-Attention layers [1,26] are used to fuse global and local features extracted by Synchformer [18], with shared weights across both branches. Only the layers highlighted in orange are updated during training. The final audio is generated following the same procedure as in the base MMAudio model. For additional details on MMAudio, refer to [6].

3.1 Video Object Segmentation-Aware Audio Generation Task Formulation

To challenge the precise control in artificial Foley models, we introduce a new audio synthesis task: video object segmentation-aware audio generation. To support the proposed task, we curate a dataset tailored to it (Sect. 4). In VOS-aware audio generation, the goal is to generate audio focused on the specified region within the video. Current artificial Foley models focus on the full scene, lacking fine-grained user controllability. However, focusing only on the small region is not enough, since the overall context is still vital in the generation of credible audio. For example, the perceived sound of a car is different in a parking hall and on an open road.

Formally, given a visual stream $V \in \mathbb{R}^{T_v \times H \times W \times 3}$, ($T_v$ is frame count, H is height, W is width, and 3 is RGB color channels), and corresponding stream of binary masks $M \in \{0,1\}^{T_v \times H \times W \times 1}$, the goal is to produce audio focusing on the specified region in the visual stream $A = G_M(V, M, ...) \in \mathbb{R}^{T_a}$, ($G_M$ is the generative model and T_a is a temporal dimension). Input modalities are model-dependent, and different models might leverage additional ones.

3.2 SAGANet Architecture

Drawing on the success of DAM [27] in localized captioning, we adapt it into audio generation. The video object segmentation-aware control module is fused with the Synchformer's [18] Vision Transformer (ViT) [8] based feature extractor, TimeSformer, that is pretrained contrastively on a sub-clip level with audio.

Focal Prompt. To provide detailed information coupled with the global context and segmentation information for the visual feature extractor, Lian et al. [27] introduce a focal prompt. The focal prompt consists of two different visual stream inputs. A global video V and its focal crop V', along with their corresponding spatial segmentation masks M and M'. These masks highlight the sounding object (*e.g.*, instruments) in the video stream and are used to steer the audio generation. The segmentation mask extraction procedure is detailed in Sect. 4. Unlike Lian et al. [27], who paired vision with language, we use these masks directly with a vision transformer tailored for audio-video synchronization.

The cropping is done based on the mask. We crop the original video so that the masked area is visible throughout the video, but enforce a minimum size of 48×48 pixels [27].

Localized Vision Backbone with Temporal Mask Embedding. Our approach builds on Lian et al. [27], extending it to video-based multimodal generation, where our goal is to extract temporally-aware and localized visual features to control an audio generation process. To process the focal prompt, we first embed visual and mask streams into a shared spatiotemporal representation. Specifically, both video and mask streams are passed through respective 3D patch embedding layers, E_V and E_M. We apply learnable positional encodings P to inject temporal ordering and spatial locality, critical for enabling the transformer to learn meaningful correspondences across frames. The resulting embeddings are:

$$\mathbf{x} = E_V(V) + E_M(M) + P, \quad \mathbf{x}' = E_V(V') + E_M(M') + P. \tag{1}$$

Here, $\mathbf{x}$ and $\mathbf{x}'$ represent the embedded global and focal inputs, respectively. The mask embedding layer E_M is initialized to output zeros, preventing early-stage training instabilities from disrupting the backbone. This design follows the initialization strategy in DAM [27].

Next, we extract visual features at two scales. The global stream $\mathbf{x}$ is processed by a global feature extractor F_G, while the focal stream $\mathbf{x}'$ is passed through a regional feature extractor F_R that shares self-attention weights with F_G. This weight sharing encourages alignment and reuse of representations across global and local views:

$$F_{syn} = F_G(\mathbf{x}), \quad F'_{syn} = F_R(\mathbf{x}', F_{syn}). \tag{2}$$

To allow focal features to condition on the global visual context, we adopt gated cross-attention adapters [1,26]. These modules are inserted after the self-attention and feedforward layers in each Synchformer block, enabling fine-grained integration of focal and global information. Each block in F_R is updated as follows:

$$\mathbf{h}^{(l)'} = \mathbf{h}^{(l)} + \tanh(\gamma^{(l)}) \times \mathrm{CrossAttn}(\mathbf{h}^{(l)}, F_{syn}) \tag{3}$$

$$\mathbf{h}^{(l)}_{\mathrm{Adapter}} = \mathbf{h}^{(l)'} + \tanh(\beta^{(l)}) \times \mathrm{FFN}(\mathbf{h}^{(l)'}). \tag{4}$$

Here, $\mathbf{h}^{(l)}$ is the output of the l-th self-attention block in F_R, $\gamma^{(l)}$ and $\beta^{(l)}$ are learnable scale parameters initialized to zero to suppress noisy gradients at early training stages. $\mathbf{h}^{(l)}_{\mathrm{Adapter}}$ is used in place of $\mathbf{h}^{(l)}$ in the preceding Transformer block. The cross-attention enables focal tokens to selectively attend to relevant global features from F_{syn}, improving localization and temporal consistency in the fused visual representation.

The final fused representation F'_{syn} is used to condition the DiT-based audio generator. By processing video and mask inputs in both global and localized views, we are able to capture fine-grained spatial cues and their temporal dynamics, essential for generating semantically aligned audio.

Audio Generation. Fused visual features are used to condition the audio generation process of MMAudio [6] instead of the Synchformer [18] features. Otherwise, the conditioning is kept similar. Adapting the task formulation described in Sect. 3.1, we get $A = G_M(F'_{syn}, F_v, F_t, \mathbf{a})$, ($G_M$ is the MMAudio model, F'_{syn} is the fused visual features, F_v is the visual CLIP [42] features, F_t is the textual features, and $\mathbf{a}$ is the noisy audio latent). For details of the extraction of F_v and F_t, please refer to [6].

To further enhance SAGANet performance, we experiment with fine-tuning the generative model by using Low-Rank Adaptation (LoRA) [15] during training. Specifically, we add low-rank matrices for query and value projections of the DiT attention blocks associated with the segmentation-aware visual features.

4   Segmented Music Solos Dataset

To facilitate the training of a video object segmentation-aware generative audio model, we propose Segmented Music Solos. We draw inspiration from audio-visual segmentation datasets, where data consists of single and multi-source videos [66,67]. We hypothesize that by training our model using single-source videos, accompanied by the sounding object masks, our model learns to use the segmentation information for the audio generation. When a multi-source scene is introduced during test time, the model is capable of generating sound for the segmented object. Our data pipeline draws inspiration from VGGSound [4] (Fig. 2).

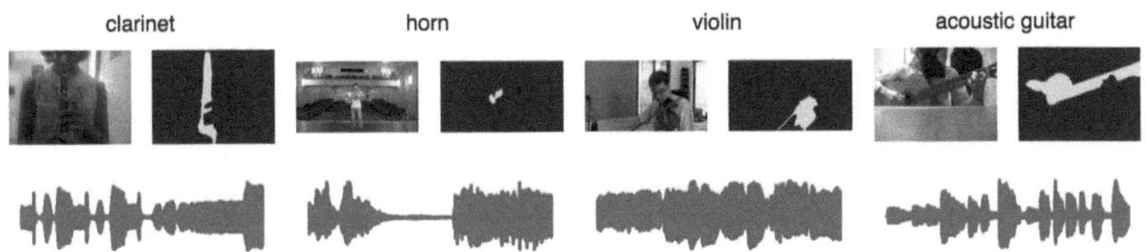

Fig. 2. Samples from Segmented Music Solos. The top row indicates the musical instrument label. The second row displays the first frames of the video and the corresponding mask stream. Last row displays the audio associated with the sample.

Stage 1: Source Videos. The training data consists of video clips of people playing a single instrument and segmentation masks of the instruments. The raw videos are gathered across multiple datasets. For the training and validation data, we combine solo performance videos from MUSIC21 [64,65], AVSBench [66,67], and Solos [37]. For testing, we use the URMP dataset [25]. It comprises several multi-instrument musical pieces assembled from separately recorded performances of individual tracks. Meaning that the final audio is a combination of separate audio recordings. Thus, each instrument in a multi-source scenario has a separately recorded audio, which is used as the ground truth in video object segmentation-aware audio generation.

Stage 2: Visual Verification. We verify that the target instrument is visually present in the video. First, we split the video into scenes based on abrupt changes, then clip each scene to avoid transitions that could confuse the segmentation model. This helps SAM2 [43] maintain consistent tracking of the object across frames. Next, we check for the target object in each scene. We sample frames at 2 FPS and classify them using a pretrained CNN-based model [20] trained on ImageNet [7]. If the target appears in the top 5 predictions for a frame, we mark it as present. Because our target classes don't always match ImageNet labels directly, we use semantic similarity. We embed both our N audio classes (depends on the dataset) and the 1000 ImageNet classes using MPNet [50], then compute cosine similarities to find the top 5 closest ImageNet labels for each audio class. These act as the visual signatures. A sample is accepted if at least one of these matching labels appears in the top 5 predictions with a confidence above 0.2.

Stage 3: Auditory Verification. For each visually verified scene, we window the audio to match the temporal dimension of the visual verification process. For audio classification, we utilize Audio Spectrogram Transformer (AST) [12]. We follow the same procedure as in visual verification to compute the label similarities between the AST classifier and our audio classes. If the target object is present (or silence is detected) in the top 5 predictions for an audio window, we classify the object as present. We include silence to support learning of natural pauses during instrument play.

Stage 4: Clipping Raw Videos. Given the scenes, we use the presence information to clip the raw videos into 5-second sequences. We require that the object be detected within the visual and auditory streams throughout the clip.

Stage 5: Mask Generation. For train data, we utilize the GroundedSAM2 framework [22,43,45] and obtain the initial mask by prompting the Florence-2 [60] foundation model with the instrument label. Florence-2 produces the initial segmentation mask based on a textual prompt, and SAM2 propagates the mask throughout the clip. Florence-2 was chosen based on its performance on a small manually verified data subset compared with GroundingDINO versions 1.5 and 1.6 [30,44]. For test data, we manually provide location coordinates of the target objects to prompt SAM2. Manual prompting yielded more coherent masks compared to using a grounding model, but limited resources prevented us from manually annotating target objects in the training data.

Finally, Segmented Music Solos consists of 5 395 training, 665 validation, and 745 test 5-second samples spanning over 35 different musical instruments. Every video is accompanied by segmentation masks that have the same number of frames as the video and the label of the segmented object. The frame rate of all samples is 25 FPS, and the audio sample rate is 44 100 Hz.

5   Experiments

5.1   Implementation Details

We train and evaluate our method using Segmented Music Solos (Sect. 4). Training data consists of solo musical instrument performance videos, instrument text labels, and segmentation masks. During training, we drop the textual label with probability of 50% to facilitate learning of the segmentation information. Evaluation data consists of multi-instrument performance videos where the audio is from the segmented instrument, instrument text labels, and segmentation masks. Following [6,16], we use H.264 and AAC video and audio encodings, resampled to 25 FPS and 44.1 kHz. The audio length is set to five seconds.

For our pretrained model, we utilize MMAudio [6]. We train the video object segmentation-aware control module on top of the pretrained model and compare our method against the base model. We use a learning rate of 1×10^{-4}, and

AdamW optimizer [33] with $\beta = [0.9, 0.95]$. Other training parameters are initialized following [6]. We train on 4 NVIDIA A100 40GB GPUs for $\sim$40 epochs until convergence. We also experiment with LoRA [15] fine-tuning of the query and value projections of the DiT layers associated with the segmentation-aware features. We use LoRA rank of 16 and set $\alpha = 32$. During testing, we utilize classifier-free guidance [13] with the scale of 7.0. We use a scale of 4.5 for the base model, as it yields the best performance.

5.2   Evaluation Metrics

For fair comparison, we utilize the same evaluation pipeline as described in MMAudio [6]. Quality is evaluated over four different aspects: distribution matching, audio quality, semantic alignment, and temporal alignment.

Distribution Matching. We compute Fréchet Distance (FD) and Kullback-Leibler Distance (KL) between generated and ground truth samples. FD is calculated using VGGish [10] (FD_{VGG}), PANNs (FD_{PANNs}) [23], and PaSST (FD_{PaSST}) [24] embeddings. KL is calculated using PANN (KL_{PANNs}) and PaSST (KL_{PaSST}) embeddings.

Audio Quality. We utilize PANNs to calculate Inception Score (IS) [48]. IS does not compare the generated sample to the ground truth. It is a metric of objective quality and diversity.

Semantic Alignment. Using ImageBind [11] to calculate a similarity score (IB-score) between the video and generated audio [56]. IB-score is the cosine distance between the audio and video embeddings. The ground truth video is cropped to primarily show the segmented instrument and its player.

Temporal Alignment. We use Synchformer [18] to compute the average of absolute offset predictions between audio and video (DeSync) [56]. The ground truth videos are processed similarly to the IB-score (Fig. 3).

5.3   Results

SAGANet shows the benefit of video object segmentation-aware control compared to the base model. Added control is crucial in the scenes where the target object is presented among other sounding instruments. Note that the evaluation data consists of multi-source videos containing multiple instruments. Despite being trained solely on single-source samples, our model demonstrates strong generalization to multi-source scenarios, effectively focusing on the target regardless of multiple instruments in the visual input. Textually describing the target object, accompanied by visual feed, does not provide strong enough guidance for the base model to generate temporally and semantically aligned audio.

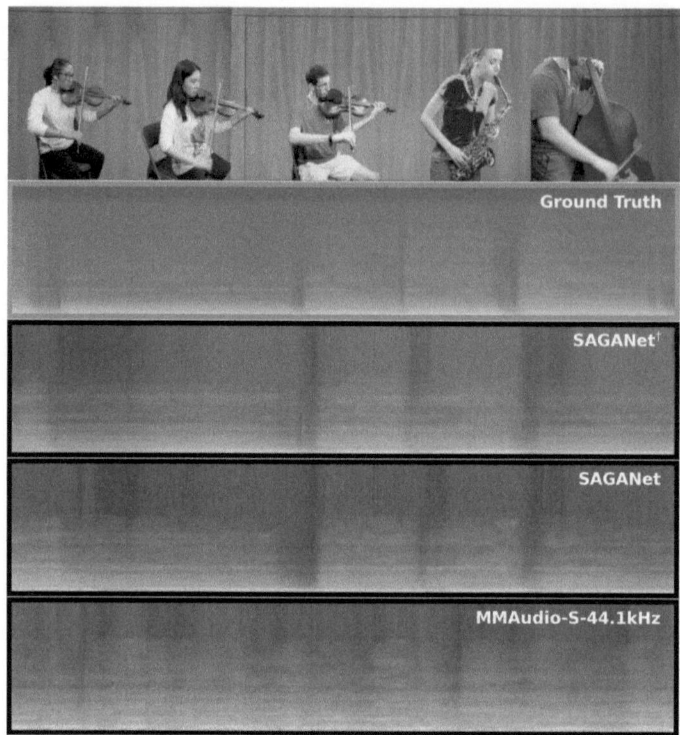

Fig. 3. SAGANet generates accurate audio for the target object (indicated by the red mask). Ground truth is separately recorded audio of the masked object. SAGANet generates matching audio, but MMAudio [6] is unable to focus on the target object conditioned solely on video and target instrument label.

Main Results. We report the results in Table 1. We use Segmented Music Solos evaluation set (Sect. 4) and average over 5 samples. During evaluation, MMAudio [6] is conditioned on the full frames and with the textual label of the target object. Still, MMAudio also focuses on other instruments within the scene. Adding segmentation-aware control guides the model to focus solely on the target object. This is evident from the strong semantic similarity and temporal alignment achieved by our approach. Finetuning the DiT layers related to visual segmentation-aware features using LoRA [15] improves performance by helping the generative model better adapt to these features.

Our method exceeds all the metrics compared to the base model, excluding FD_{VGG} $\downarrow$. The greatest difference is with the temporal synchronization and semantic alignment. Without the segmentation-aware control module, the model fails to attend to the correct object. Thus, even though the overall audio quality is sufficient, the temporal and semantic alignment is missing.

Table 1. SAGANet outperforms the base model. The added video object segmentation-aware control module helps our model to focus on the correct object. MMAudio [6] allows guiding the focus only through the textual condition. Results were averaged over 5 samples of Segmented Music Solos (Sect. 4) evaluation data. We utilize the MMAudio-S-44.1kHz variant in our experiments. †: Fine-tuned DiT-layers associated with visual segmentation-aware features using LoRA [15].

	$\mathrm{FD_{PaSST}}\downarrow$	$\mathrm{FD_{PANNs}}\downarrow$	$\mathrm{FD_{VGG}}\downarrow$	$\mathrm{KL_{PANNs}}\downarrow$	$\mathrm{KL_{PaSST}}\downarrow$	IS↑	IB-score↑	DeSync↓
MMAudio [6]	530.60	23.83	**13.26**	1.17	1.00	2.24	35.94	0.95
SAGANet	364.07	21.31	17.19	0.79	0.59	**3.34**	39.62	0.44
SAGANet†	**330.01**	**17.88**	19.36	**0.69**	**0.56**	3.27	**41.50**	**0.30**

Ablation Study. In Table 2, we analyze the effect of different visual prompts on the generated audio quality. Masks are embedded and fused in a same way as described in Sect. 3.2. Last row indicates the performance of the proposed model that fuses information across both streams. Our study shows that both the global and local information are crucial in generating high-quality and aligned audio.

Using only the global visual stream (V) yields the lowest performance across semantic alignment (IB) and temporal synchronization (DeSync), despite achieving a relatively good inception score (IS). This suggests decent audio quality but poor relevance to the target object. Incorporating segmentation information (V+M) substantially improves performance, particularly in temporal synchronization, highlighting the importance of precise spatial focus in VOS-aware audio generation

Using only local information (V', V'+M') further improves alignment of the audio with the ground truth, with a trade-off in audio quality: tighter localization reduces overall quality. However, using only local information outperforms global-only prompts across distribution matching metrics (FD, KL). The results highlight the value of detailed spatial information for high-fidelity audio generation. Fusing local and global features results in superior temporal performance and audio quality. We hypothesize that the drop in $\mathrm{FD_{PANNs}}$ and $\mathrm{FD_{VGG}}$ metrics is due to the model not fully adapting to the segmentation-aware local and global visual features. Further fine-tuning and additional data might improve performance. However, our method generates semantically (IB-Score) and temporally (DeSync) most relevant audio with highest quality (IS) and relevance (KL), highlighting the importance of combining the global context with detailed local information.

Table 2. Ablation study of different visual prompts. V' and M' refer to using only the detailed crop without global (V, M) visual information. F. Prompt refers to using combined local and global information. Masks (M, M') are embedded and fused with the same strategy as with the proposed method. We utilize the MMAudio-S-44.1kHz [6] variant in our experiments. †: Fine-tuned DiT-layers associated with visual segmentation-aware features using LoRA [15].

	FD_{PaSST} ↓	FD_{PANNs}↓	FD_{VGG} ↓	KL_{PANNs}↓	KL_{PaSST}↓	IS↑	IB-score↑	DeSync↓
V	530.60	23.83	13.26	1.17	1.00	2.24	35.94	0.96
V+M	394.46	19.81	19.89	0.84	0.70	3.11	39.25	0.56
V'	419.30	**17.41**	**11.88**	0.86	0.70	2.56	39.19	0.40
V'+M'	363.86	17.74	17.90	0.74	0.63	3.05	39.96	0.52
F. Prompt†	**330.01**	17.88	19.36	**0.69**	**0.56**	**3.27**	41.50	**0.30**

6 Conclusion

Current generative audio models lack precise controllability, which limits their introduction *e.g.*, in video post-production. To address the gap, we introduced a novel audio synthesis task: Video Object Segmentation-Aware Audio Generation. It enables precise control over audio synthesis by conditioning the audio synthesis on visual segmentation masks. For the task, we proposed SAGANet, a generative audio model conditioned on text, video, and video object segmentation masks. Our method incorporates both global and localized visual information using a dedicated control module, allowing the model to focus on specific objects within a video. Our approach significantly improves semantic relevance and temporal alignment, particularly in complex, multi-source scenes where textual or global visual cues fall short.

Furthermore, we presented Segmented Music Solos, a benchmark dataset that supports the development and evaluation of VOS-aware audio generation models. We show that by training our model with single-source videos, our method can generalize to multi-source samples during test time. This work lays the foundation for the development of more controllable and user-friendly Foley models.

Acknowledgement. The work was supported by the Academy of Finland projects 353139 and 362409. We also acknowledge CSC – IT Center for Science, Finland, for computational resources.

Disclosure of Interests. The authors have no competing interests to declare that are relevant to the content of this article.

References

1. Alayrac, J.B., et al.: Flamingo: a visual language model for few-shot learning. In: Advances in Neural Information Processing Systems (NeurIPS), vol. 35, pp. 23716–23736 (2022)
2. Chang, H., Zhang, H., Jiang, L., Liu, C., Freeman, W.T.: Maskgit: masked generative image transformer. In: Proceedings of the Computer Vision and Pattern Recognition Conference (CVPR), pp. 11315–11325 (2022)
3. Chen, C., et al.: Action2sound: ambient-aware generation of action sounds from egocentric videos. In: European Conference on Computer Vision (ECCV), pp. 277–295 (2024)
4. Chen, H., Xie, W., Vedaldi, A., Zisserman, A.: Vggsound: a large-scale audio-visual dataset. In: Proceedings of International Conference on Acoustics, Speech and Signal Processing (ICASSP), pp. 721–725 (2020)
5. Chen, Z., et al.: Video-guided foley sound generation with multimodal controls. In: Proceedings of the Computer Vision and Pattern Recognition Conference (CVPR), pp. 18770–18781 (2025)
6. Cheng, H.K., Ishii, M., Hayakawa, A., Shibuya, T., Schwing, A., Mitsufuji, Y.: Mmaudio: taming multimodal joint training for high-quality video-to-audio synthesis. In: Proceedings of the Computer Vision and Pattern Recognition Conference (CVPR), pp. 28901–28911 (2025)
7. Deng, J., Dong, W., Socher, R., Li, L.J., Li, K., Fei-Fei, L.: Imagenet: a large-scale hierarchical image database. In: Proceedings of the Computer Vision and Pattern Recognition Conference (CVPR), pp. 248–255 (2009)
8. Dosovitskiy, A., et al.: An image is worth 16x16 words: transformers for image recognition at scale. arXiv preprint arXiv:2010.11929 (2020)
9. Fragkiadaki, K., Arbelaez, P., Felsen, P., Malik, J.: Learning to segment moving objects in videos. In: Proceedings of the International Conference on Computer Vision (CVPR), pp. 4083–4090 (2015)
10. Gemmeke, J.F., et al.: Audio set: an ontology and human-labeled dataset for audio events. In: Proceedings of International Conference on Acoustics, Speech and Signal Processing (ICASSP), pp. 776–780 (2017)
11. Girdhar, R., et al.: Imagebind: one embedding space to bind them all. In: Proceedings of the Computer Vision and Pattern Recognition Conference (CVPR), pp. 15180–15190 (2023)
12. Gong, Y., Chung, Y.A., Glass, J.: AST: audio spectrogram transformer. arXiv preprint arXiv:2104.01778 (2021)
13. Ho, J., Salimans, T.: Classifier-free diffusion guidance. arXiv preprint arXiv:2207.12598 (2022)
14. Hou, S., et al.: Editing music with melody and text: using controlnet for diffusion transformer. In: Proceedings of International Conference on Acoustics, Speech and Signal Processing (ICASSP), pp. 1–5 (2025)
15. Hu, E.J., et al.: Lora: low-rank adaptation of large language models. arxiv 2021. arXiv preprint arXiv:2106.09685 (2021)
16. Iashin, V., Xie, W., Rahtu, E., Zisserman, A.: Sparse in space and time: audio-visual synchronisation with trainable selectors. In: British Machine Vision Conference (BMVC) (2022)
17. Iashin, V., Rahtu, E.: Taming visually guided sound generation. arXiv preprint arXiv:2110.08791 (2021)

18. Iashin, V., Xie, W., Rahtu, E., Zisserman, A.: Synchformer: efficient synchronization from sparse cues. In: Proceedings of International Conference on Acoustics, Speech and Signal Processing (ICASSP), pp. 5325–5329 (2024)
19. Jeong, Y., Kim, Y., Chun, S., Lee, J.: Read, watch and scream! sound generation from text and video. In: AAAI Conference on Artificial Intelligence (AAAI), pp. 17590–17598 (2025)
20. Jocher, G., et al.: ultralytics/yolov5: v7. 0-yolov5 sota realtime instance segmentation. Zenodo (2022)
21. Kim, G., et al.: A versatile diffusion transformer with mixture of noise levels for audiovisual generation. arXiv preprint arXiv:2405.13762 (2024)
22. Kirillov, A., et al.: Segment anything. arXiv preprint arXiv:2304.02643 (2023)
23. Kong, Q., Cao, Y., Iqbal, T., Wang, Y., Wang, W., Plumbley, M.D.: PANNs: large-scale pretrained audio neural networks for audio pattern recognition. Trans. Audio Speech Lang. Process. **28**, 2880–2894 (2020)
24. Koutini, K., Schlüter, J., Eghbal-Zadeh, H., Widmer, G.: Efficient training of audio transformers with patchout. arXiv preprint arXiv:2110.05069 (2021)
25. Li, B., Liu, X., Dinesh, K., Duan, Z., Sharma, G.: Creating a multitrack classical music performance dataset for multimodal music analysis: challenges, insights, and applications. Trans. Multimedia **21**(2), 522–535 (2018)
26. Li, J., Li, D., Xiong, C., Hoi, S.: Blip: bootstrapping language-image pre-training for unified vision-language understanding and generation. In: International Conference on Machine Learning (ICML), pp. 12888–12900 (2022)
27. Lian, L., et al.: Describe anything: detailed localized image and video captioning. arXiv preprint arXiv:2504.16072 (2025)
28. Lipman, Y., Chen, R.T., Ben-Hamu, H., Nickel, M., Le, M.: Flow matching for generative modeling. arXiv preprint arXiv:2210.02747 (2022)
29. Liu, H., et al.: Audioldm: text-to-audio generation with latent diffusion models. arXiv preprint arXiv:2301.12503 (2023)
30. Liu, S., et al.: Grounding dino: marrying dino with grounded pre-training for open-set object detection. In: European Conference on Computer Vision (ECCV), pp. 38–55 (2024)
31. Liu, X., Gong, C., Liu, Q.: Flow straight and fast: learning to generate and transfer data with rectified flow. arXiv preprint arXiv:2209.03003 (2022)
32. Liu, X., Su, K., Shlizerman, E.: Tell what you hear from what you see–video to audio generation through text. arXiv preprint arXiv:2411.05679 (2024)
33. Loshchilov, I., Hutter, F.: Decoupled weight decay regularization. arXiv preprint arXiv:1711.05101 (2017)
34. Luo, S., Yan, C., Hu, C., Zhao, H.: Diff-foley: synchronized video-to-audio synthesis with latent diffusion models. In: Advances in Neural Information Processing Systems (NeurIPS), pp. 48855–48876 (2023)
35. Mei, X., et al.: Foleygen: visually-guided audio generation. In: International Workshop on Machine Learning for Signal Processing (MLSP), pp. 1–6 (2024)
36. Mo, S., Shi, J., Tian, Y.: Text-to-audio generation synchronized with videos. arXiv preprint arXiv:2403.07938 (2024)
37. Montesinos, J.F., Slizovskaia, O., Haro, G.: Solos: a dataset for audio-visual music analysis. In: International Workshop on Multimedia Signal Processing (MMSP), pp. 1–6 (2020)
38. Pascual, S., Yeh, C., Tsiamas, I., Serrà, J.: Masked generative video-to-audio transformers with enhanced synchronicity. In: European Conference on Computer Vision (ECCV), pp. 247–264 (2024)

39. Peebles, W., Xie, S.: Scalable diffusion models with transformers. In: Proceedings of the Computer Vision and Pattern Recognition Conference (CVPR), pp. 4195–4205 (2023)
40. Polyak, A., et al.: Movie gen: a cast of media foundation models. arXiv preprint arXiv:2410.13720 (2024)
41. Pont-Tuset, J., Perazzi, F., Caelles, S., Arbeláez, P., Sorkine-Hornung, A., Van Gool, L.: The 2017 davis challenge on video object segmentation. arXiv preprint arXiv:1704.00675 (2017)
42. Radford, A., et al.: Learning transferable visual models from natural language supervision. In: International Conference on Machine Learning (ICML), pp. 8748–8763 (2021)
43. Ravi, N., et al.: Sam 2: segment anything in images and videos. arXiv preprint arXiv:2408.00714 (2024)
44. Ren, T., et al.: Grounding dino 1.5: advance the "edge" of open-set object detection. arXiv preprint arXiv:2405.10300 (2024)
45. Ren, T., et al.: Grounded SAM: assembling open-world models for diverse visual tasks. arXiv preprint arXiv:2401.14159 (2024)
46. Ren, T., et al.: Grounded SAM: assembling open-world models for diverse visual tasks. arXiv preprint arXiv:2401.14159 (2024)
47. Ruan, L., et al.: Mm-diffusion: learning multi-modal diffusion models for joint audio and video generation. In: Proceedings of the Computer Vision and Pattern Recognition Conference (CVPR), pp. 10219–10228 (2023)
48. Salimans, T., Goodfellow, I., Zaremba, W., Cheung, V., Radford, A., Chen, X.: Improved techniques for training GANs. In: Advances in Neural Information Processing Systems (NeurIPS), vol. 29 (2016)
49. Sheffer, R., Adi, Y.: I hear your true colors: image guided audio generation. In: Proceedings of International Conference on Acoustics, Speech and Signal Processing (ICASSP), pp. 1–5 (2023)
50. Song, K., Tan, X., Qin, T., Lu, J., Liu, T.Y.: Mpnet: masked and permuted pre-training for language understanding. In: Advances in Neural Information Processing Systems (NeurIPS), vol. 33, pp. 16857–16867 (2020)
51. Su, K., Liu, X., Shlizerman, E.: From vision to audio and beyond: a unified model for audio-visual representation and generation. arXiv preprint arXiv:2409.19132 (2024)
52. Tang, Z., Yang, Z., Khademi, M., Liu, Y., Zhu, C., Bansal, M.: Codi-2: in-context interleaved and interactive any-to-any generation. In: Proceedings of the Computer Vision and Pattern Recognition Conference (CVPR), pp. 27425–27434 (2024)
53. Tang, Z., Yang, Z., Zhu, C., Zeng, M., Bansal, M.: Any-to-any generation via composable diffusion. In: Advances in Neural Information Processing Systems (NeurIPS), pp. 16083–16099 (2023)
54. Tong, A., et al.: Improving and generalizing flow-based generative models with minibatch optimal transport. arXiv preprint arXiv:2302.00482 (2023)
55. Vaswani, A., et al.: Attention is all you need. In: Advances in Neural Information Processing Systems (NeurIPS) (2017)
56. Viertola, I., Iashin, V., Rahtu, E.: Temporally aligned audio for video with autoregression. In: Proceedings of International Conference on Acoustics, Speech and Signal Processing (ICASSP), pp. 1–5 (2025)
57. Wang, H., Ma, J., Pascual, S., Cartwright, R., Cai, W.: V2a-mapper: a lightweight solution for vision-to-audio generation by connecting foundation models. In: Proceedings of the AAAI Conference on Artificial Intelligence (AAAI), vol. 38, pp. 15492–15501 (2024)

58. Wang, Y., et al.: Frieren: efficient video-to-audio generation network with rectified flow matching. In: Advances in Neural Information Processing Systems (NeurIPS), vol. 37, pp. 128118–128138 (2024)
59. Wu, S.L., Donahue, C., Watanabe, S., Bryan, N.J.: Music controlnet: multiple time-varying controls for music generation. Trans. Audio Speech Lang. Process. **32**, 2692–2703 (2024)
60. Xiao, B., et al.: Florence-2: advancing a unified representation for a variety of vision tasks. arXiv preprint arXiv:2311.06242 (2023)
61. Xing, Y., He, Y., Tian, Z., Wang, X., Chen, Q.: Seeing and hearing: open-domain visual-audio generation with diffusion latent aligners. In: Proceedings of the Conference on Computer Vision and Pattern Recognition (CVPR), pp. 7151–7161 (2024)
62. Xu, M., et al.: Video-to-audio generation with hidden alignment. arXiv preprint arXiv:2407.07464 (2024)
63. Zhang, L., Rao, A., Agrawala, M.: Adding conditional control to text-to-image diffusion models. In: Proceedings of the Conference on Computer Vision and Pattern Recognition (CVPR), pp. 3836–3847 (2023)
64. Zhao, H., Gan, C., Ma, W.C., Torralba, A.: The sound of motions. In: Proceedings of the International Conference on Computer Vision (CVPR), pp. 1735–1744 (2019)
65. Zhao, H., Gan, C., Rouditchenko, A., Vondrick, C., McDermott, J., Torralba, A.: The sound of pixels. In: Proceedings of the European Conference on Computer Vision (ECCV), pp. 570–586 (2018)
66. Zhou, J., Shen, X.: Audio-visual segmentation with semantics. arXiv preprint arXiv:2301.13190 (2023)
67. Zhou, J., et al.: Audio–visual segmentation. In: European Conference on Computer Vision (ECCV), pp. 386–403 (2022)
68. Ziv, A., et al.: Masked audio generation using a single non-autoregressive transformer. arXiv preprint arXiv:2401.04577 (2024)

MCUCoder: Adaptive Bitrate Learned Video Compression for IoT Devices

Ali Hojjat[1,2]([✉]) [iD], Janek Haberer[1] [iD], and Olaf Landsiedel[1,2] [iD]

[1] Department of Computer Science, Kiel University, Kiel, Germany
`{ali.hojjat,janek.haberer}@cs.uni-kiel.de`
[2] Institute for Networked Cyber-Physical Systems, Hamburg University of Technology (TUHH), Hamburg, Germany
`olaf.landsiedel@tuhh.de`

Abstract. The rapid growth of camera-based Internet of Things (IoT) devices demands the need for efficient video compression, particularly for edge applications where devices face hardware constraints, often with only 1 or 2 MB of RAM and unstable internet connections. Traditional and deep video compression methods are designed for high-end hardware, exceeding the capabilities of these constrained devices. Consequently, video compression in these scenarios is often limited to Motion-JPEG (M-JPEG) due to its high hardware efficiency and low complexity. This paper introduces `MCUCoder`, an open-source adaptive bitrate video compression model tailored for resource-limited IoT settings. `MCUCoder`features an ultra-lightweight encoder with only 10.5K parameters and a minimal 350KB memory footprint, making it well-suited for edge devices and Microcontrollers (MCUs). While `MCUCoder`uses a similar amount of energy as M-JPEG, it reduces bitrate by 55.65% on the MCL-JCV dataset and 55.59% on the UVG dataset, measured in Multi-Scale Structural Similarity (MS-SSIM). Moreover, `MCUCoder`supports adaptive bitrate streaming by generating a latent representation that is sorted by importance, allowing transmission based on available bandwidth. This ensures smooth real-time video transmission even under fluctuating network conditions on low-resource devices. Source code available at https://github.com/ds-kiel/MCUCoder.

Keywords: Deep Video Compression · Internet of Things · Adaptive Bitrate Encoding

1 Introduction

Motivation: The number of camera-based IoTs devices using always-on MCU is growing rapidly, reaching tens of billions [35]. These devices are widely used in applications such as surveillance cameras [21,27,42], wearable cameras [50], robotics [43], wildlife monitoring [24], road monitoring [20], and smart farming [30]. Typically, they capture raw frames through a camera sensor, encode

M. Keuper and F. Locatello (Eds.): DAGM GCPR 2025, LNCS 16125, pp. 123–138, 2026.
https://doi.org/10.1007/978-3-032-12840-9_9

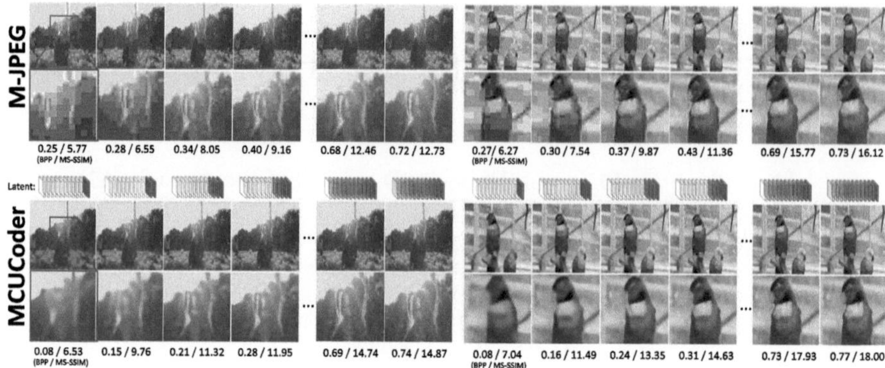

Fig. 1. Qualitative comparison of MCUCoderand M-JPEG across various compression rates on two videos from the MCL-JCV [51] and UVG [40] datasets. As we can see, MCUCoderoffers a significantly better trade-off between MS-SSIM and bpp. For instance, at 0.15 bpp in the left example, with MCUCoderwe can see the person's face whereas with M-JPEG we need at least 0.34 bpp to make out the face. Note that the images in each column do not necessarily have the same bitrate. More examples are reported in Fig. 12.

them, and transmit the compressed version to a server via the Internet for further processing, including human observation or AI tasks such as object detection and classification [20]. Therefore, a video encoder is necessary to efficiently compress the captured frames before transmission. However, in IoT environments, there are two primary limitations: constrained hardware resources and limited communication bandwidth.

1 - Limited Hardware: Although traditional video codecs like H.264 [52], H.265 [47], and the newer H.266 [8] provide excellent performance, they demand significant hardware for extracting the intra and inter-frame correlations. For example, H.265 encoding involves highly computationally intensive tasks such as motion estimation with sub-pixel accuracy, Rate Distortion Optimization (RDO) for choosing optimal intra-prediction modes, and Context Adaptive Binary Arithmetic Coding (CABAC) for entropy coding. Additionally, a single video frame at 224×224

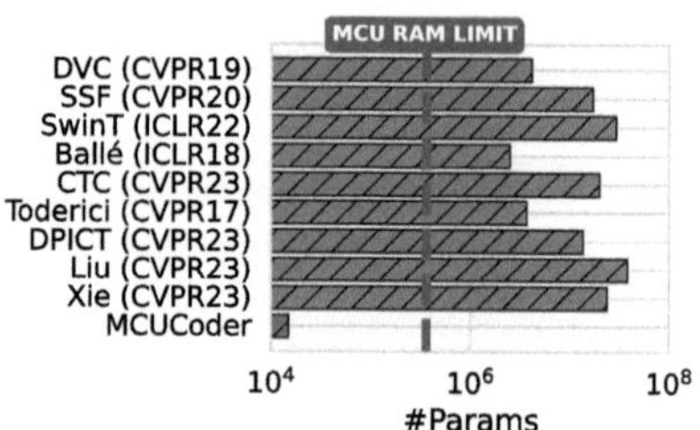

Fig. 2. Number of parameters of MCUCoderand other learned image compression [5, 25, 32, 37, 48, 54, 58] and video compression models [3, 38].

resolution requires about 150 KB of RAM, which is a lot for the low-cost, low-energy MCUs used in IoT devices that typically have only **1–2 MB of RAM**. Consequently, inter-frame compression or any other kind of multi-frame analysis is not practically feasible on such constrained devices. Similarly, while Neural Networks (NNs) and AI-based compression methods outperform traditional models [3,38], they also often require considerable RAM and GPU resources. For instance, just storing a model with 1M parameters requires around 4 MB of RAM; see Fig. 2. As a result, in such settings, devices are typically limited to using Motion-JPEG (M-JPEG) [44], a video compression format where each frame is compressed individually as a JPEG image, which is efficient and hardware-friendly.

2 - Limited Internet: Many IoT devices are located in remote areas where Internet connection is weak and unstable, making it necessary for the encoder to have an **Adaptive Bitrate Encoding** that can generate video streams with varying bitrate. This feature allows the encoder to dynamically adjust its quality according to the available bandwidth, ensuring continuous and smooth playback. This is especially important for real-time applications like live monitoring, where it is crucial to avoid interruptions and maintain a consistent user experience despite fluctuating network conditions. However, implementing an adaptive bitrate encoder adds complexity, as it requires mechanisms to prioritize bit stream information based on its impact on frame quality (e.g., Peak Signal to Noise Ratio (PSNR) or MS-SSIM), which is challenging for constrained devices.

Approach: To address these challenges, we introduce `MCUCoder`, an adaptive bitrate deep video compression codec tailored for resource-limited IoT devices. Our approach focuses on creating an "asymmetric" compression model that features an ultra-lightweight encoder designed to be both computationally efficient and memory-friendly. Moreover, to produce an "adaptive" bitstream, we train the `MCUCoder`'s latent representation with *stochastic channel dropout*, see Fig. 4. This procedure sorts the N latent feature maps by their contribution to reconstruction quality, thereby forcing the model to produce a *progressive bitstream*: early channels in the latent carry the most salient information, and later channels refine the result.

At inference time, the MCU transmits only the first $k \leq N$ channels that fit the instantaneous bandwidth; the decoder then reconstructs the frame from this subset (see Fig. 1). This approach is beneficial for low-power MCUs since it shifts the complexity of identifying important data to the training phase rather than the inference phase. Also, by employing stochastic dropout training, the decoder can reconstruct the frame even with partial data availability, which is essential for maintaining smooth and uninterrupted video transmission in real-time applications, where network conditions can vary. Additionally, `MCUCoder`'s encoder is INT8 quantized, allowing it to utilize Digital Signal Processor (DSP) and CMSIS-NN [4] accelerators for faster processing and reduced power consumption.

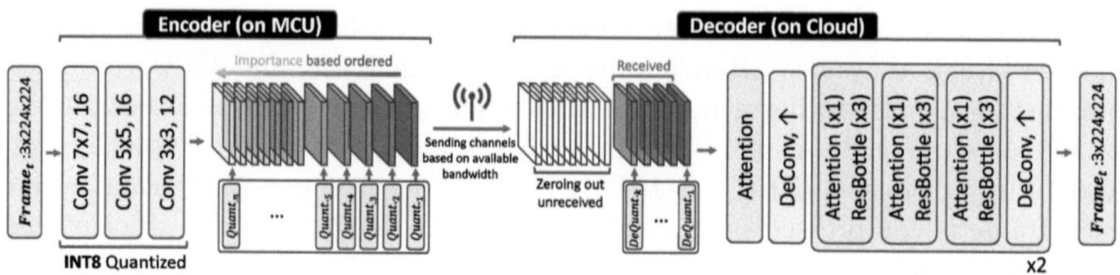

Fig. 3. Overview of MCUCoderarchitecture. The encoder compresses the input frame into a sorted latent space. Afterward, channels are independently quantized and transmitted based on available bandwidth. The decoder reconstructs the frame by zeroing out missing channels.

Contributions:

1. MCUCoderhas an ultra-lightweight encoder with only 10.5K parameters and a minimal memory footprint of roughly 350KB RAM on nRF5340 and STM32F7 MCUs, making it suitable for such low-resource IoT devices.
2. MCUCoderhas an energy-efficient INT8 quantized encoder, which leverages the MCU's DSP and CMSIS-NN accelerators to achieve JPEG-level energy efficiency. Compared to its main baseline, M-JPEG, it saves 55.65% overall bit rate on the MCL-JCV dataset and 55.59% on the UVG dataset, measured in MS-SSIM.
3. MCUCoderproduces a progressive bitstream that enables adaptive bitrate streaming, allowing robust video transmission under varying network conditions.

2   Related Work

Traditional and NN Based Video Compression: Video compression is a field that has been evolving for decades. Beyond traditional codecs like H.264 [52], H.265 [47], and H.266 [8], deep learning-based approaches often replace conventional modules such as motion compensation [3,56], transform coding [13,58], and entropy coding [39,53]. Also, some work has been done regarding the end-to-end optimization of video compression models [17,28,49]. Lu et al. [38] introduce DVC, the first end-to-end deep video compression model. Hu et al. [22,23] extend DVC to operate in both pixel and feature domains. Li et al. [34] and Liu et al. [36] reduce bitrates by modeling probabilities over video frames using conditional coding. Also, in recent years, there has been growing interest in using implicit neural representations for video compression [9,31]. However, due to their substantial hardware requirements, these models are unsuitable for deployment on low-resource IoT devices.

Video Compression for IoT: We can categorize IoT-based video encoders into two parts: hardware-based and software-based. Hardware approaches primarily focus on designing more power-efficient camera sensors [6,26,41] and more efficient MCU circuits and processors [33,45,55]. Due to its simplicity, scalability, low latency, and very low energy consumption, the most common software-based video encoder on IoT devices is M-JPEG [44]. Nevertheless, there have been few works exploring alternative software-based models: Veluri et al. [50] employ M-JPEG on the encoder to capture black-and-white and colorized frames at two different resolutions and uses super-resolution methods to interpolate and colorize frames on the decoder. However, unlike MCUCoder, it is not adaptive and relies on a JPEG encoder on MCUs. Hu et al. [21] propose a deep image encoder model for MCUs, but it is also non-adaptive. Additionally, they patchify the input, which significantly increases encoding time, making it impractical for real-time video compression. MCUCodercombines the advantages of both worlds: it offers the adaptive bitrate feature of more complex encoders, while maintaining the efficiency necessary for low-resource devices, making it an ideal solution for IoT video compression.

3 MCUCoder

In this section, we introduce MCUCoder, an adaptive bitrate asymmetric video compression model, specifically designed for IoT settings. We begin by detailing the asymmetric encoder-decoder architecture of MCUCoder, including the customized quantization processes. Then, we present the stochastic dropout training method, which trains the encoder of MCUCoderto store information in its channels based on importance.

3.1 Asymmetric Compression

MCUs are characterized by highly constrained hardware resources, such as limited RAM, CPU, FLASH, and power availability. Additionally, existing MCU-specific NN frameworks like TFLite Micro support only a limited set of NN layers [21]. To address these constraints, we propose an asymmetric [57] encoder-decoder architecture optimized for constrained devices. Due to hardware constraints, MCUCoderencodes each frame independently, as inter-frame compression is not feasible. The encoder contains only 10.5K parameters, while the decoder utilizes approximately 3M parameters and leverages SOTA image decompression blocks; see Fig. 3. The encoding process begins by passing input frame f_t through three convolutional layers. To maximize the data range for subsequent quantization, no activation function is applied in the final encoder layer, avoiding the negative truncation caused by ReLU. Afterward, each channel of the latent is quantized into INT8 individually, followed by a

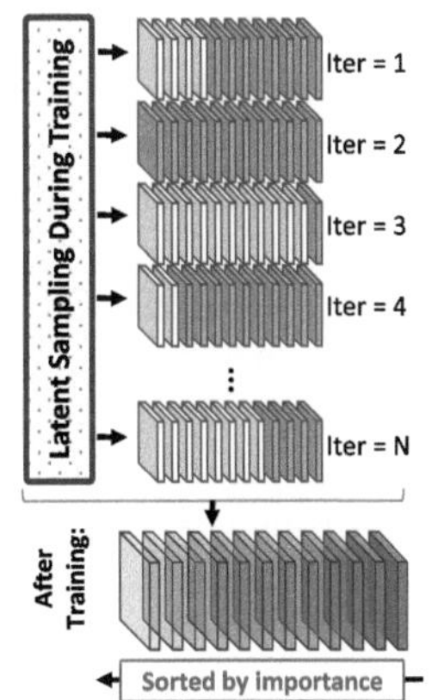

Fig. 4. Stochastic dropout training.

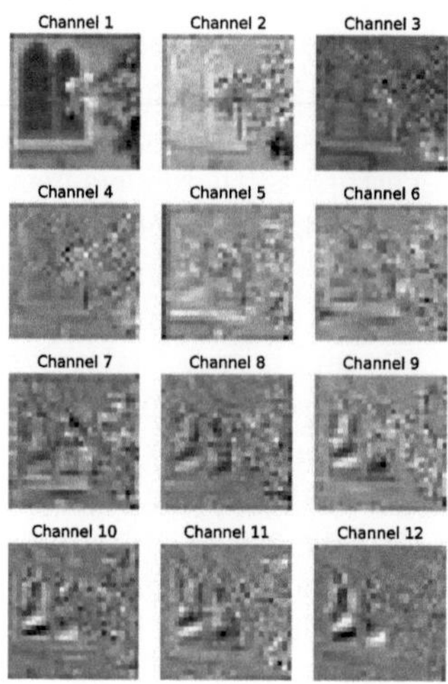

Fig. 5. `MCUCoder` latent channels: Early channels (important ones) capture low-frequency features, while later channels capture high-frequency features, similar to the DCT in JPEG.

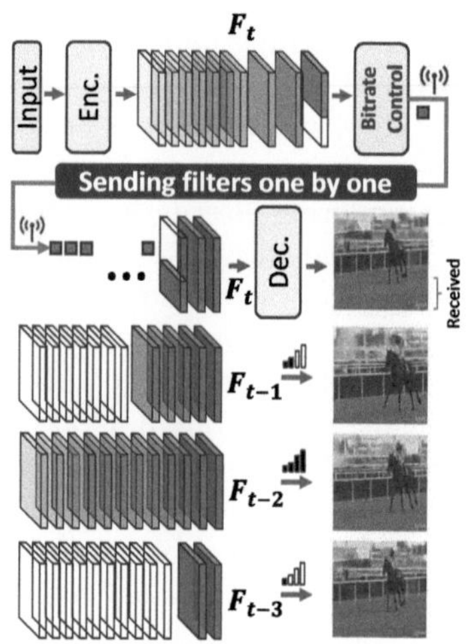

Fig. 6. An example of `MCUCoder` bitrate adaptation under dynamic network bandwidth, where the bitrate control module acts as a gate to determine the number of channels to send.

further reduction to 5-bit precision to enhance compression efficiency. For the decoder, inspired by [15], we integrate a combination of attention blocks [10] and residual bottleneck blocks [18] to reconstruct the frame; see Fig. 3.

3.2 Stochastic Dropout Training

Bitrate adaptation is a feature that typically introduces additional complexity to the encoding process, which can be challenging to implement on MCUs due to resource constraints. In the literature, dropout [46] serves as a powerful tool for enhancing generalization in NNs. Building on this insight, we employ a "biased" version of dropout to train `MCUCoder` in a way that instead of random dropping, it drops from the tail of the latent [14,19]. Specifically, on each iteration, after the encoder E gets the input frame f_t, it generates the latent representation z_N, where N is the number of the channels of the latent. Afterward, from a uniform distribution, denoted as $\mathcal{U}_{(0,1)}$, it generates a number, denoted as k, and drops (zero out) the last $\lfloor k \times N \rfloor$ channels from z_N. As a result, instead of z_N, the decoder D gets $z_{[0:\lfloor k \times N \rfloor]}$, fills the missing channels with zero, and then reconstructs the output.

$$f_t \rightarrow E(f_t) \rightarrow z_N \xrightarrow{k \sim \mathcal{U}_{(0,1)}} z_{[0:\lfloor k \times N \rfloor]} \rightarrow D(z_{[0:\lfloor k \times N \rfloor]}) \rightarrow \hat{f}_t \qquad (1)$$

This tailored version of dropout biases the training to prioritize the earlier channels over the later ones. Consequently, the encoder learns to encode more critical information (low frequency) in the initial feature maps and less important (high frequency) details in the subsequent ones; see Fig. 4. This prioritization enables flexible bitrate adaptation: upon encoding each frame, the encoder starts transmitting the most significant channels first. Depending on the available bandwidth, the bitrate control module determines how many channels need to be sent to the decoder to ensure uninterrupted streaming; see Fig. 6. Importantly, because the latent features are pre-ordered by significance, the bitrate control module basically acts like a simple gate and does not add any extra computational complexity to the encoder.

4   Evaluation

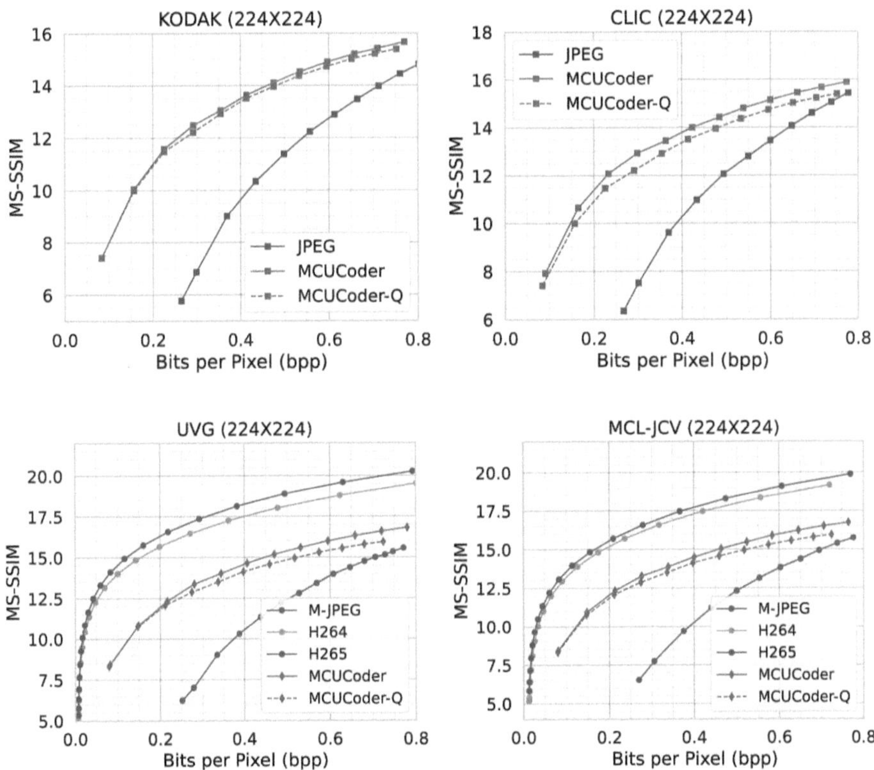

Fig. 7. Comparison of `MCUCoder`(quantized and non-quantized model) and baselines on the image (KODAK [29], CLIC [2]) and video (MCL-JCV [51], UVG [40]) compression datasets. For context, we also compare with H.264 and H.265 on video datasets, despite being impractical for MCUs due to high hardware demands. All datasets are resized to 224 × 224.

We train `MCUCoder`on the 300K largest ImageNet images [11] and apply noise-downsampling preprocessing [5,16]. We use Adam with an initial learning rate

Table 1. BD-rate results (Quantized). The anchor is M-JPEG.

Type	Dataset	MS-SSIM	PSNR
Video	MCL-JCV	−55.65%	−47.39%
	UVG	−55.59%	−35.28%
Image	KODAK	−55.75%	−43.01%
	CLIC	−49.54%	−38.02%

Table 2. Resource demands of MCUCoder on nRF5340 and STM32F7 MCUs.

	nRF5340	STM32F7
Exec (ms)	1,969	237
RAM (KB)	344 (33%)	360 (17%)
Flash (KB)	100 (10%)	107 (5%)

of 10^{-4} and a batch size of 16, and train for 1M iterations, lowering the learning rate to 10^{-5} in the final 50K iterations [15]. To address quantization effects, we add random noise to the latent. Since MCUCoder is specifically designed for IoT environments, where the structure of the output is more critical than fine details, we use MS-SSIM as the loss function. We also quantize inputs, weights, and activations to INT8 for RAM efficiency and to leverage DSP and CMSIS-NN accelerators [4] in MCUs. We use post-training quantization existing in TFLite-Micro [1] to reduce latency, processing power, and model size with minimal degradation in model accuracy. For all comparisons, we report performance metrics for both the FLOAT32 and INT8 models.

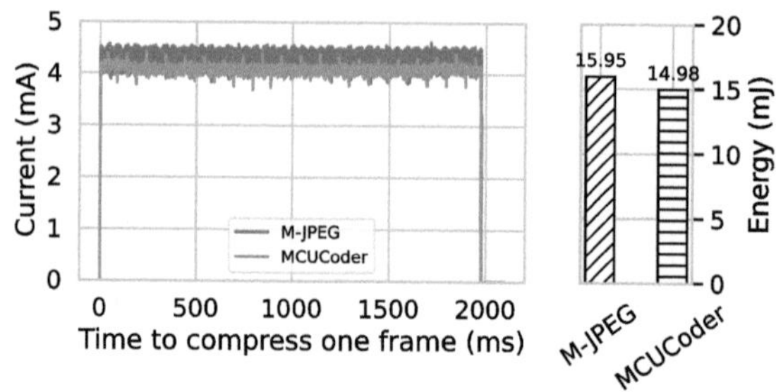

Fig. 8. Energy (Millijoule) and current (Milliampere) consumption of MCUCoder compared to M-JPEG for compressing one frame on the nRF5340. MCUCoder achieves comparable energy efficiency to M-JPEG while exceeding it in BD-rate. However, the nRF5340 exhibits relatively slow processing speeds for both MCUCoder and M-JPEG, suggesting that its energy efficiency is better suited for event-driven applications rather than real-time streaming, where the STM32F7 excels.

4.1 Quantitative Results

Due to the limited hardware resources of MCUs, inter-frame compression is not practically feasible. As a result, in such devices, video compression is limited to M-JPEG where each frame is compressed independently. Therefore, in addition to evaluating MCUCoderand its baselines from the perspective of video compression, we also assess its performance on image compression datasets. Given the lower resolution commonly encountered in IoT scenarios, we resize all the videos and images to 224×224.

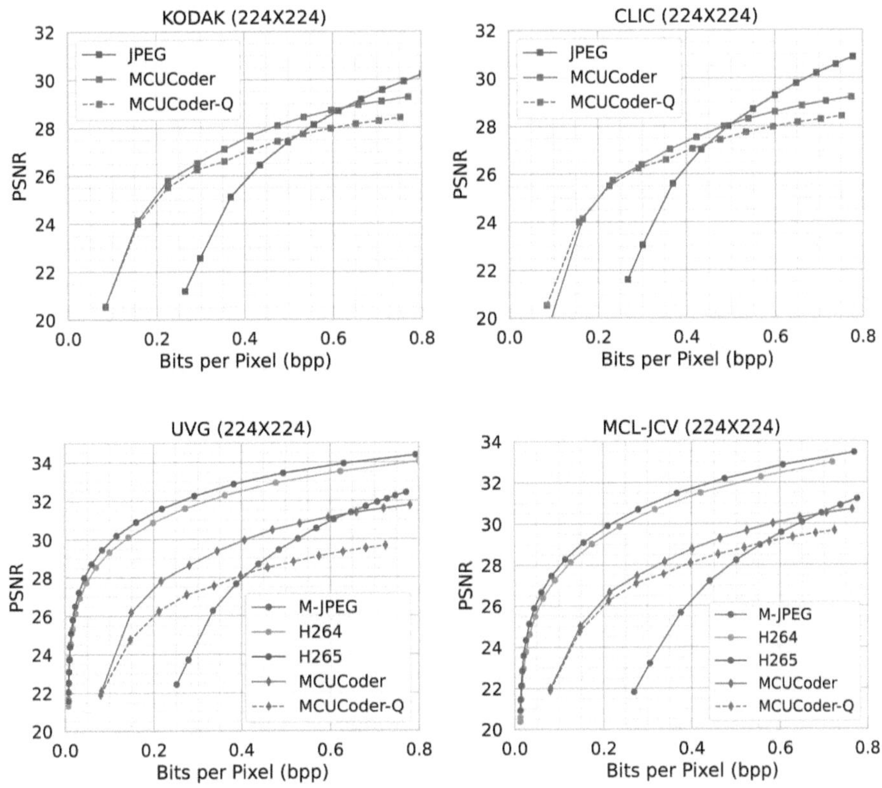

Fig. 9. PSNR comparison of MCUCoderand baselines across image (KODAK [29], CLIC [2]) and video (MCL-JCV [51], UVG [40]) compression datasets.

Video Compression: We evaluate MCUCoderon the UVG [40] and MCL-JCV [51] datasets, comparing its performance to M-JPEG, see Fig. 7. For additional context, we include comparisons with traditional video codecs such as H.264 [52] and H.265 [47], even though these codecs are impractical for deployment on MCUs due to their significant computational and hardware demands. Also, we report the Bjøntegaard Delta (BD) rate [7] for both datasets in Table 1. The results indicate that MCUCoderachieves a significantly higher MS-SSIM per bit compared to M-JPEG, highlighting its ability to deliver better video quality at lower bitrates. This is especially valuable for IoT applications, where achieving high compression rates with minimal computational overhead is crucial due to limited hardware resources. Additionally, `MCUCoder` has 12 "stacked" channels in its latent space, which provides 12 levels of quality that can be dynamically adjusted based on the available network bandwidth. In Fig. 10, we illustrate the bpp and MS-SSIM for each frame in a video from the UVG dataset for all 12 levels of quality. The results show that using more channels for decoding leads to a higher MS-SSIM, which verifies the effectiveness of the proposed stochastic dropout training. The PSNR results are reported in Fig. 9.

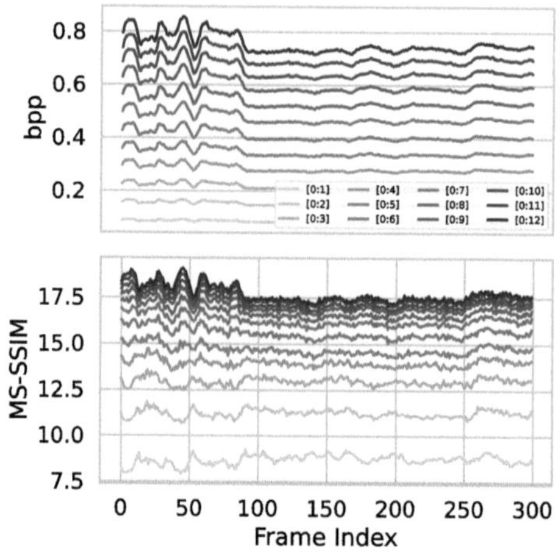

Fig. 10. MS-SSIM and bpp for the SunBath video from UVG [40] dataset. $[0 : k]$ shows the use of the first k channels (out of 12) for decoding.

Image Compression: To assess the image compression capabilities of `MCUCoder`, we conduct experiments on the CLIC [2] and KODAK [12] datasets, see Fig. 7. The results in Table 1 show that `MCUCoder` achieves an impressive average bitrate reduction of 55.75% on the KODAK dataset and 49.54% on the CLIC dataset, compared to JPEG. The PSNR results are reported in Fig. 9.

4.2   Latent Ordering and DCT-JPEG Alignment

Figure 5 illustrates the 12 latent channels derived from training with the stochastic dropout method. These channels display an intriguing hierarchical structure, where the early channels capture broad, low-frequency features, while the later channels progressively focus on finer, high-frequency details. This pattern closely resembles the Discrete Cosine Transform (DCT) basis matrix utilized in JPEG compression. In JPEG, the DCT plays a pivotal role in transforming image data into frequency components, allowing for efficient compression by prioritizing lower frequencies, which tend to carry more significant visual information. Similarly to `MCUCoder`, progressive JPEG leverages this frequency ordering, encoding data in a manner that allows the decoder to initially reconstruct the image using only low-frequency components, and as decoding progresses, higher-frequency details are incrementally added, resulting in a progressively refined image reconstruction.

4.3   Performance on MCUs

We implement MCUCoder on two widely-used MCU platforms, the STM32F7 and nRF5340 MCUs, using TFLite-Micro and Zephyr RTOS. The STM32F7 features 2 MB of Flash memory, 2 MB of RAM, and a Cortex-M7 processor, while the nRF5340 is equipped with 1 MB of Flash, 512 KB of RAM, and a Cortex-M33 processor. Both MCUs support DSP and CMSIS-NN acceleration, making them well-suited for running lightweight deep learning models. As detailed in Table 2, MCUCoder demonstrates a low memory footprint, consuming 360 KB of RAM on the STM32F7 and 344 KB on the nRF5340, which is significantly efficient for such constrained devices. This compact memory usage highlights the suitability of MCUCoder for low-power, resource-constrained IoT applications. To assess the energy efficiency of MCUCoder, we conducted a comparative analysis against M-JPEG. Specifically, we measured the energy consumption of MCUCoder and an optimized JPEG encoder for the Cortex-M series[1] on the nRF5340 platform; see Fig. 8. The results indicate that MCUCoder achieves comparable energy consumption to JPEG, while providing superior performance in terms of BD-rate, as shown in Table 1. However, the nRF5340 exhibits noticeably slower processing performance compared to the STM32F7 for both MCUCoder and M-JPEG. This discrepancy suggests that while the nRF5340 is energy-efficient, its lower computational capabilities make it more appropriate for event-driven applications rather than real-time streaming tasks, where the STM32F7 excels.

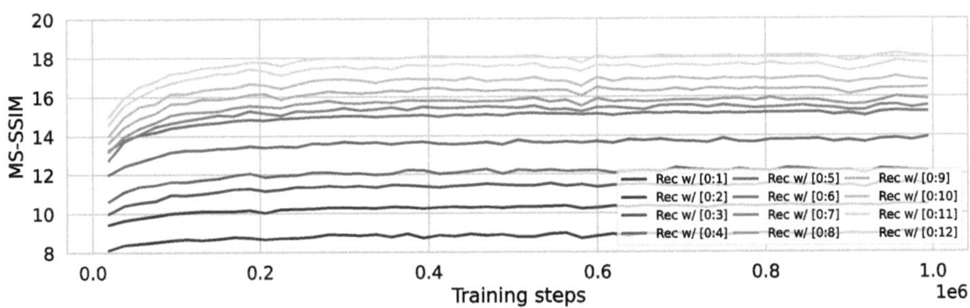

Fig. 11. MS-SSIM values on the KODAK dataset during training. The notation $[0 : k]$ represents the MS-SSIM of the reconstructed image using the first k latent channels out of a total of 12. As shown, with stochastic dropout training, all the sub-latents can be trained simultaneously without overfitting to any particular sub-latent.

---

[1] https://github.com/noritsuna/JPEGEncoder4Cortex-M.

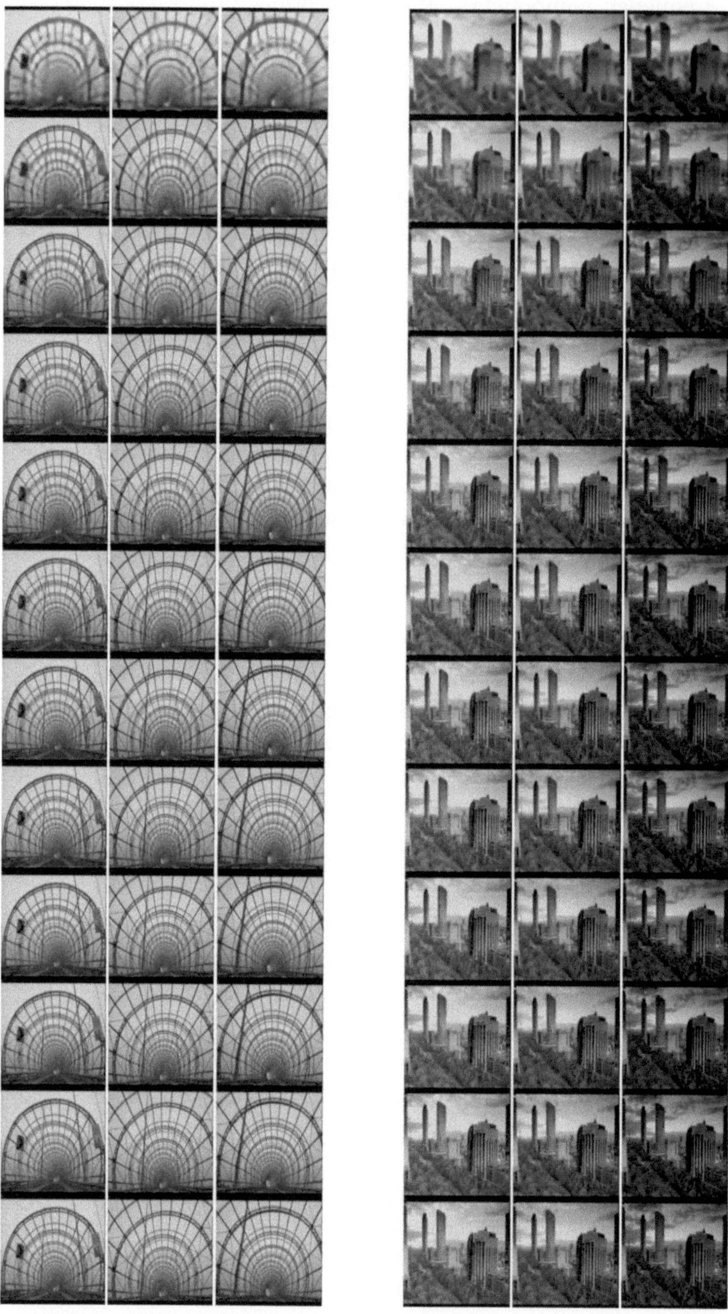

Fig. 12. Some samples from the MCL-JCV [51] dataset. The columns represent different frames, while the rows display progressively improving levels of quality from top to bottom, produced by `MCUCoder`.

4.4 Stochastic Dropout Training Analysis

One potential challenge with stochastic dropout training is the risk of overfitting to specific loss functions when optimizing multiple losses concurrently. To evaluate this, we track the MS-SSIM of `MCUCoder` on the KODAK [12] dataset across varying numbers of active latent channels during training. The training logs, shown in Fig. 11, demonstrate that all the sub-latents are trained in parallel without overfitting to any specific sub-latent, which verifies the effectiveness of the uniform latent sampling strategy employed in the training.

5 Conclusion

We introduced `MCUCoder`, an ultra-lightweight asymmetric video compression model for resource-constrained IoT devices. With just 10.5K parameters and a 350KB memory footprint, compared to M-JPEG, `MCUCoder` reduces bitrate by over 55% on both the MCL-JCV and UVG datasets while matching the efficiency of M-JPEG. Its adaptive bitrate streaming ensures smooth video transmission under fluctuating network conditions, making it ideal for edge applications.

Acknowledgements. This research received funding from the Federal Ministry for Digital and Transport under the CAPTN-Förde 5G project (grant no. 45FGU139H), the German Ministry of Transport and Digital Infrastructure through the CAPTN Förde Areal II project (grant no. 45DTWV08D), and the Federal Ministry for Economic Affairs and Climate Action under the Marispace-X project (grant no. 68GX21002E). It was supported in part by high-performance computing resources provided by the Kiel University Computing Centre and the Hydra computing cluster, funded by the German Research Foundation (grant no. 442268015) and the Petersen Foundation (grant no. 602157).

References

1. TensorFlow Lite Micro. https://www.tensorflow.org/lite/micro. Accessed 2023
2. Workshop and challenge on learned image compression (CLIC) (2020). http://www.compression.cc
3. Agustsson, E., Minnen, D., Johnston, N., Balle, J., Hwang, S.J., Toderici, G.: Scale-space flow for end-to-end optimized video compression. In: Proceedings of the IEEE/CVF Conference on Computer Vision and Pattern Recognition, pp. 8503–8512 (2020)
4. ARM-software: CMSIS-NN: efficient neural network kernels for arm cortex-m CPUs (2024). https://github.com/ARM-software/CMSIS-NN. Accessed 22 Sept 2024
5. Ballé, J., Minnen, D., Singh, S., Hwang, S.J., Johnston, N.: Variational image compression with a scale hyperprior. arXiv preprint arXiv:1802.01436 (2018)
6. Bejarano-Carbo, A., et al.: Millimeter-scale ultra-low-power imaging system for intelligent edge monitoring. arXiv preprint arXiv:2203.04496 (2022)
7. Bjøtegaard, G.: Calculation of average PSNR differences between RD-curves (VCEG-M33). In: VCEG Meeting (ITU-T SG16 Q. 6), Austin, Texas, USA, Technical Report M, vol. 16090 (2001)

8. Bross, B., et al.: Overview of the versatile video coding (VVC) standard and its applications. IEEE Trans. Circuits Syst. Video Technol. **31**(10), 3736–3764 (2021)

9. Chen, H., He, B., Wang, H., Ren, Y., Lim, S.N., Shrivastava, A.: Nerv: neural representations for videos. Adv. Neural. Inf. Process. Syst. **34**, 21557–21568 (2021)

10. Cheng, Z., Sun, H., Takeuchi, M., Katto, J.: Learned image compression with discretized gaussian mixture likelihoods and attention modules. In: Proceedings of the IEEE/CVF Conference on Computer Vision and Pattern Recognition, pp. 7939–7948 (2020)

11. Deng, J., Dong, W., Socher, R., Li, L.J., Li, K., Fei-Fei, L.: Imagenet: a large-scale hierarchical image database. In: 2009 IEEE Conference on Computer Vision and Pattern Recognition, pp. 248–255. IEEE (2009)

12. Eastman Kodak: Kodak lossless true color image suite (photocd pcd0992) (1993). http://r0k.us/graphics/kodak

13. Gao, G., et al.: Neural image compression via attentional multi-scale back projection and frequency decomposition. In: Proceedings of the IEEE/CVF International Conference on Computer Vision, pp. 14677–14686 (2021)

14. Haberer, J., Hojjat, A., Landsiedel, O.: Hydravit: stacking heads for a scalable VIT. arXiv preprint arXiv:2409.17978 (2024)

15. He, D., Yang, Z., Peng, W., Ma, R., Qin, H., Wang, Y.: ELIC: efficient learned image compression with unevenly grouped space-channel contextual adaptive coding. In: Proceedings of the IEEE/CVF Conference on Computer Vision and Pattern Recognition, pp. 5718–5727 (2022)

16. He, D., Zheng, Y., Sun, B., Wang, Y., Qin, H.: Checkerboard context model for efficient learned image compression. In: Proceedings of the IEEE/CVF Conference on Computer Vision and Pattern Recognition, pp. 14771–14780 (2021)

17. He, G., et al.: A video compression framework using an overfitted restoration neural network. In: Proceedings of the IEEE/CVF Conference on Computer Vision and Pattern Recognition Workshops, pp. 148–149 (2020)

18. He, K., Zhang, X., Ren, S., Sun, J.: Deep residual learning for image recognition. In: Proceedings of the IEEE Conference on Computer Vision and Pattern Recognition, pp. 770–778 (2016)

19. Hojjat, A., Haberer, J., Landsiedel, O.: Progdtd: progressive learned image compression with double-tail-drop training. In: Proceedings of the IEEE/CVF Conference on Computer Vision and Pattern Recognition (CVPR) Workshops, pp. 1130–1139 (2023)

20. Hojjat, A., Haberer, J., Zainab, T., Landsiedel, O.: Limitnet: progressive, content-aware image offloading for extremely weak devices & networks. In: Proceedings of the 22nd Annual International Conference on Mobile Systems, Applications and Services, Kodak lossless true color image suite (photocd pcd0992, pp. 519–533. Association for Computing Machinery, New York (2024). https://doi.org/10.1145/3643832.3661856

21. Hu, P., Im, J., Asgar, Z., Katti, S.: Starfish: resilient image compression for AIOT cameras. In: Proceedings of the 18th Conference on Embedded Networked Sensor Systems, pp. 395–408 (2020)

22. Hu, Z., Lu, G., Guo, J., Liu, S., Jiang, W., Xu, D.: Coarse-to-fine deep video coding with hyperprior-guided mode prediction. In: Proceedings of the IEEE/CVF Conference on Computer Vision and Pattern Recognition, pp. 5921–5930 (2022)

23. Hu, Z., Lu, G., Xu, D.: FVC: a new framework towards deep video compression in feature space. In: Proceedings of the IEEE/CVF Conference on Computer Vision and Pattern Recognition, pp. 1502–1511 (2021)

24. Iyer, V., Najafi, A., James, J., Fuller, S., Gollakota, S.: Wireless steerable vision for live insects and insect-scale robots. Sci. Robot. **5**(44), eabb0839 (2020)

25. Jeon, S., Choi, K.P., Park, Y., Kim, C.S.: Context-based trit-plane coding for progressive image compression. In: Proceedings of the IEEE/CVF Conference on Computer Vision and Pattern Recognition, pp. 14348–14357 (2023)

26. Ji, S., Pu, J., Lim, B.C., Horowitz, M.: A 220pj/pixel/frame CMOS image sensor with partial settling readout architecture. In: 2016 IEEE Symposium on VLSI Circuits (VLSI-Circuits), pp. 1–2. IEEE (2016)

27. Josephson, C., Yang, L., Zhang, P., Katti, S.: Wireless computer vision using commodity radios. In: Proceedings of the 18th International Conference on Information Processing in Sensor Networks, pp. 229–240 (2019)

28. Khani, M., Sivaraman, V., Alizadeh, M.: Efficient video compression via content-adaptive super-resolution. In: Proceedings of the IEEE/CVF International Conference on Computer Vision, pp. 4521–4530 (2021)

29. Eastman kodak. kodak lossless true color image suite (photocd pcd0992) (1993). https://r0k.us/graphics/kodak

30. Koh, P.W., et al.: Wilds: a benchmark of in-the-wild distribution shifts. In: International Conference on Machine Learning, pp. 5637–5664. PMLR (2021)

31. Kwan, H.M., Gao, G., Zhang, F., Gower, A., Bull, D.: Hinerv: video compression with hierarchical encoding-based neural representation. In: Advances in Neural Information Processing Systems, vol. 36 (2024)

32. Lee, J.H., Jeon, S., Choi, K.P., Park, Y., Kim, C.S.: DPICT: deep progressive image compression using trit-planes. In: Proceedings of the IEEE/CVF Conference on Computer Vision and Pattern Recognition, pp. 16113–16122 (2022)

33. Lefebvre, M., Moreau, L., Dekimpe, R., Bol, D.: 7.7 a 0.2-TO-3.6 TOPS/W programmable convolutional imager SOC with in-sensor current-domain ternary-weighted mac operations for feature extraction and region-of-interest detection. In: 2021 IEEE International Solid-State Circuits Conference (ISSCC), vol. 64, pp. 118–120. IEEE (2021)

34. Li, J., Li, B., Lu, Y.: Deep contextual video compression. Adv. Neural. Inf. Process. Syst. **34**, 18114–18125 (2021)

35. Lin, J., Chen, W.M., Lin, Y., Gan, C., Han, S., et al.: Mcunet: tiny deep learning on IoT devices. Adv. Neural. Inf. Process. Syst. **33**, 11711–11722 (2020)

36. Liu, J., et al.: Conditional entropy coding for efficient video compression. In: European Conference on Computer Vision, pp. 453–468. Springer (2020)

37. Liu, J., Sun, H., Katto, J.: Learned image compression with mixed transformer-CNN architectures. In: Proceedings of the IEEE/CVF Conference on Computer Vision and Pattern Recognition (CVPR), pp. 14388–14397 (2023)

38. Lu, G., Ouyang, W., Xu, D., Zhang, X., Cai, C., Gao, Z.: DVC: an end-to-end deep video compression framework. In: Proceedings of the IEEE/CVF Conference on Computer Vision and Pattern Recognition, pp. 11006–11015 (2019)

39. Mentzer, F., et al.: VCT: a video compression transformer. arXiv preprint arXiv:2206.07307 (2022)

40. Mercat, A., Viitanen, M., Vanne, J.: UVG dataset: 50/120fps 4k sequences for video codec analysis and development. In: Proceedings of the 11th ACM Multimedia Systems Conference, pp. 297–302 (2020)

41. Morishita, F., et al.: A CMOS image sensor and an AI accelerator for realizing edge-computing-based surveillance camera systems. In: 2021 Symposium on VLSI Circuits, pp. 1–2. IEEE (2021)

42. Naderiparizi, S., Hessar, M., Talla, V., Gollakota, S., Smith, J.R.: Towards {Battery-Free}{HD} video streaming. In: 15th USENIX Symposium on Networked Systems Design and Implementation (NSDI 2018), pp. 233–247 (2018)
43. Nakanoya, M., et al.: Co-design of communication and machine inference for cloud robotics. Auton. Robot. **47**(5), 579–594 (2023)
44. Pennebaker, W.B., Mitchell, J.L.: JPEG: Still Image Data Compression Standard. Springer (1992)
45. Rossi, D., et al.: 4.4 a 1.3 TOPS/W@ 32GOPS fully integrated 10-core SOC for IoT end-nodes with 1.7 μw cognitive wake-up from MRAM-based state-retentive sleep mode. In: 2021 IEEE International Solid-State Circuits Conference (ISSCC), vol. 64, pp. 60–62. IEEE (2021)
46. Srivastava, N., Hinton, G., Krizhevsky, A., Sutskever, I., Salakhutdinov, R.: Dropout: a simple way to prevent neural networks from overfitting. J. Mach. Learn. Res. **15**(1), 1929–1958 (2014)
47. Sullivan, G.J., Ohm, J.R., Han, W.J., Wiegand, T.: Overview of the high efficiency video coding (HEVC) standard. IEEE Trans. Circuits Syst. Video Technol. **22**(12), 1649–1668 (2012)
48. Toderici, G., et al.: Full resolution image compression with recurrent neural networks. In: Proceedings of the IEEE Conference on Computer Vision and Pattern Recognition, pp. 5306–5314 (2017)
49. Van Rozendaal, T., Brehmer, J., Zhang, Y., Pourreza, R., Wiggers, A., Cohen, T.S.: Instance-adaptive video compression: improving neural codecs by training on the test set. arXiv preprint arXiv:2111.10302 (2021)
50. Veluri, B., Pernu, C., Saffari, A., Smith, J., Taylor, M., Gollakota, S.: Neuricam: key-frame video super-resolution and colorization for IoT cameras. In: Proceedings of the 29th Annual International Conference on Mobile Computing and Networking, pp. 1–17 (2023)
51. Wang, H., et al: MCL-JCV: a JND-based H.264/AVC video quality assessment dataset. In: 2016 IEEE International Conference on Image Processing (ICIP), pp. 1509–1513 (2016). https://doi.org/10.1109/ICIP.2016.7532610
52. Wiegand, T., Sullivan, G.J., Bjontegaard, G., Luthra, A.: Overview of the H. 264/AVC video coding standard. IEEE Trans. Circ. Syst. Video Technol. **13**(7), 560–576 (2003)
53. Xiang, J., Tian, K., Zhang, J.: Mimt: masked image modeling transformer for video compression. In: The Eleventh International Conference on Learning Representations (2023)
54. Xie, Y., Cheng, K.L., Chen, Q.: Enhanced invertible encoding for learned image compression. In: Proceedings of the 29th ACM International Conference on Multimedia, pp. 162–170 (2021)
55. Xu, H., et al.: Macsen: a processing-in-sensor architecture integrating mac operations into image sensor for ultra-low-power BNN-based intelligent visual perception. IEEE Trans. Circuits Syst. II Express Briefs **68**(2), 627–631 (2020)
56. Yang, R., Mentzer, F., Gool, L.V., Timofte, R.: Learning for video compression with hierarchical quality and recurrent enhancement. In: Proceedings of the IEEE/CVF Conference on Computer Vision and Pattern Recognition, pp. 6628–6637 (2020)
57. Yao, S., et al.: Deep compressive offloading: Speeding up neural network inference by trading edge computation for network latency. In: Proceedings of the 18th Conference on Embedded Networked Sensor Systems, pp. 476–488 (2020)
58. Zhu, Y., Yang, Y., Cohen, T.: Transformer-based transform coding. In: International Conference on Learning Representations (2022)

VisualChef: Generating Visual Aids in Cooking via Mask Inpainting

Oleh Kuzyk[1(✉)], Li Zuoyue[1], Marc Pollefeys[1,2], and Xi Wang[1,3,4]

[1] ETH Zürich, Rämistrasse 101, 8092 Zürich, Switzerland
okuzyk@ethz.ch, {li.zuoyue,marc.pollefeys,xi.wang}@inf.ethz.ch
[2] Microsoft Spatial AI Lab, Seestrasse 356, 8038 Zürich, Switzerland
[3] Technical University of Munich, Arcisstraße 21, 80333 München, Germany
[4] Munich Center for Machine Learning, Arcisstraße 21, 80333 München, Germany

Abstract. Cooking requires not only following instructions but also understanding, executing, and monitoring each step–a process that can be challenging without visual guidance. Although recipe images and videos offer helpful cues, they often lack consistency in focus, tools, and setup. To better support the cooking process, we introduce VisualChef, a method for generating contextual visual aids tailored to cooking scenarios. Given an initial frame and a specified action, VisualChef generates images depicting both the action's execution and the resulting appearance of the object, while preserving the initial frame's environment. Previous work aims to integrate knowledge extracted from large language models by generating detailed textual descriptions to guide image generation, which requires fine-grained visual-textual alignment and involves additional annotations. In contrast, VisualChef simplifies alignment through mask-based visual grounding. Our key insight is identifying action-relevant objects and classifying them to enable targeted modifications that reflect the intended action and outcome while maintaining a consistent environment. In addition, we propose an automated pipeline to extract high-quality initial, action, and final state frames. We evaluate VisualChef quantitatively and qualitatively on three egocentric video datasets and show its improvements over state-of-the-art methods.

Keywords: Image generation · Visual grounding

1 Introduction

Cooking is a complex task that requires not only following instructions, but also understanding, executing, and monitoring each step. Often, the only resource available is a step-by-step recipe, which can leave important details ambiguous.

Many cooks turn to images or videos for guidance, as visual cues like sauce consistency or vegetable thickness greatly aid cooking [22,31,47]. However, these generic resources often differ in ingredients, tools, or setups, making them less compatible with one's environment and progress. They lack the contextual alignment needed to support a unique situation. Motivated by this, we aim to generate

M. Keuper and F. Locatello (Eds.): DAGM GCPR 2025, LNCS 16125, pp. 139–154, 2026.
https://doi.org/10.1007/978-3-032-12840-9_10

Fig. 1. Generating contextual action and final state frames via mask inpainting. Given an initial frame and an action, VisualChef generates two frames visualizing both the action's execution and the resulting appearance of the object while preserving the environment depicted in the input frame.

visual aids adapted to the cook's environment and progress in the recipe, offering more personalized, contextually relevant guidance. These aids benefit human users and robotic agents designed to perform cooking tasks in the kitchen.

In this paper, we propose VisualChef, a simple yet effective approach to generate visual aids in cooking scenarios. Given an initial frame and a specified action, VisualChef generates two context-preserving images: one showing how the action is executed and the other depicting the state of the resulting object (Fig. 1). Previous methods integrate knowledge extracted from large language models by generating detailed textual descriptions to guide image generation [4, 12,23,43,48]. However, they require fine-grained visual-textual alignment and extra data annotations. In contrast, VisualChef simplifies alignment through mask-based visual grounding and focuses on object-centric inpainting.

Our central idea is to identify action-relevant objects and develop tailored strategies based on their roles to guide the inpainting process. Specifically, we classify objects into three categories: *core objects*, central to the action (e.g., ingredients); *location objects*, which define spatial context (e.g., cutting boards); and *functional objects*, which assist the action without being essential to the final state (e.g., knives). This categorization enables selective editing. We use masked inpainting [21,30,40,46,52] to generate realistic, context-aware images aligned with the cooking action and final state. To train effectively, we introduce a data curation pipeline that extracts triplets of initial, action, and final frames from egocentric videos using hand detection, object presence, and relevance filtering.

We evaluate VisualChef against state-of-the-art approaches on three egocentric video datasets: Ego4D [23], EGTEA Gaze+ [27] and EPIC-KITCHENS-100 (EK-100) [7]. VisualChef achieves higher fidelity in depicting the action and final state frames compared to previous generation models [4,23,40,43], especially outperforming the state-of-the-art methods [23,43], highlighting the effectiveness of selective inpainting. Our code, data, and models will be available for research purposes. In summary, our contributions are as follows.

- We propose VisualChef, a mask-based image inpainting model that generates visual aids in cooking scenarios, given an initial frame and a specified action.
- We introduce an automatic data curation pipeline that extracts initial-action-final frame triplets from egocentric videos with action annotations.
- We evaluate VisualChef on 3 egocentric video datasets with qualitative and quantitative results that show improvements over state-of-the-art methods.

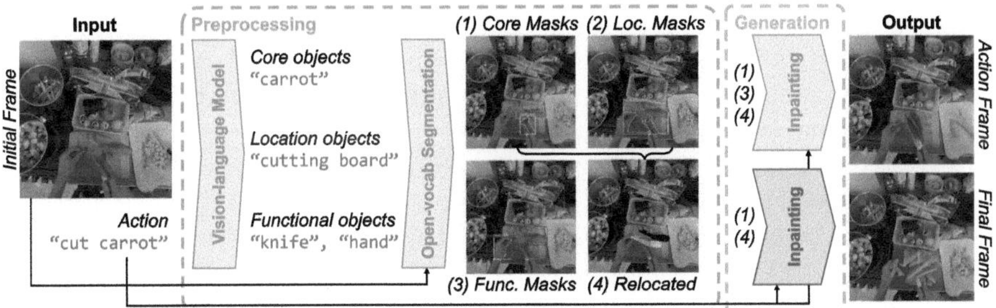

Fig. 2. The VisualChef pipeline for context-aware inpainting within a cooking scenario. It starts with an *Initial Frame* (f_{in}) as input, paired with an *Action* description (e.g., "cut carrot"). The vision-language model LLaVA [28] is employed to identify relevant objects and classify them into three categories: Core objects (e.g., "carrot"), Location objects (e.g., "cutting board"), and Functional objects (e.g., "knife" and "hand"). Using the open-vocabulary segmentation model Grounding DINO [29], the masks for these objects are generated: (1) *Core Masks*, (2) *Location Masks*, and (3) *Functional Masks*. Core objects are *Relocated* in an additional step (4) as needed. The generation phase involves two different inpainting modules based on Stable Diffusion [40], conditioned on different combinations of the masks for creating the *Action Frame* (f_{action}) that reflects the step being performed and the *Final Frame* (f_{final}) showing the status upon action completion. The output thus visualizes the progression of the cooking scenario in a realistic manner.

2 Related Work

Our work is at the cross section of image editing, conditional image generation, and egocentric vision. We discuss related works according to the underlying categories in the following.

Conditional image generation has evolved from traditional GANs [34] to modern diffusion models [14], enabling high-resolution generation based on given condition signals. While GANs were used for text- and image-conditioned synthesis [17,35], diffusion models [8,14,51,53] offer stronger performance by better modeling complex data distributions. Unlike general-purpose methods targeting broad use cases, our approach is tailored to cooking, enabling targeted, context-aware image updates that preserve visual consistency.

Image editing has advanced significantly with generative models, particularly diffusion models that excel in text-conditioned image generation. Notable methods include Imagic [20], which enables precise edits without disrupting the global structure, and Prompt-to-Prompt [12], which allows fine-grained visual control through text. InstructPix2Pix [4] supports detailed user-driven edits, while SDEdit [33] uses a stochastic process for realistic, context-aware alterations. ProxEdit [10] and InstructEdit [48] further enhance controlled editing via text-driven modifications. Recent advancements have integrated multimodal and action-guided generation, such as GenHowTo [43], LEGO [23], and Instruct-Imagen [16], which synthesize visual content from combined image-text inputs. GenHowTo and LEGO rely on vision-language models to caption input frames and generate output prompts. LEGO also uses in-context learning to extract fine-grained action descriptions with hand and object bounding boxes. Although many of these models are built on Stable Diffusion [40], alternatives such as Text2LIVE [3] offer text-guided, real-time edits. These developments reflect the field's shift toward interactive, user-friendly visual content creation.

For mask-based editing, models like DiffEdit [5] and Locate and Forget [24] allow for high-precision mask-guided modifications. LAR-Gen [36] improves inpainting control via textual guidance, and BrushNet [18] advances plug-and-play editing with a dual-branch diffusion setup. Further contributions such as Point&Instruct [11], MAG-Edit [32], and CoVLM [26] focus on localized and contextual editing, while FoI [9] employs attention mechanisms for multi-instruction editing. Collectively, these works drive precise mask-based image editing, broadening the scope and flexibility of visual content manipulation. Our work relies on the principles of mask-based inpainting to selectively alter relevant parts of the frame. However, our key novelty lies in categorizing objects (core, location, functional) to guide which regions to inpaint, aligning visual modifications with specific actions in cooking sequences. Our method goes beyond the capabilities of the state-of-the-art by emphasizing object relevance and context retention during editing.

Egocentric vision research has prospered with the emergence of rich multimodal datasets capturing real-world activities. EGTEA Gaze+ [27] focuses on cooking, providing fine-grained annotations such as hand masks and gaze tracking. EPIC-KITCHENS [6,7] expands on this with unscripted, culturally diverse kitchen videos and detailed action labels, making it one of the largest egocentric cooking datasets for kitchen tasks. Ego4D [1] and EgoExo4D [2] also offer diverse daily activities, including cooking, captured with multimodal data such as 3D scans and gaze. Our work leverages such egocentric kitchen data to extract high-quality triplets (initial, action, final) for training. This enables our model to learn task-specific edits aligned with real-world practice, setting our approach apart from general vision-language models that lack this cooking-specific focus.

3   Method

We first describe the task of generating action-conditioned images and the empirical observations that motivated our approach. These are followed by vision-language model prompting and diffusion-based inpainting.

3.1   Overview

Given an input frame f_{in} representing the current cooking state and the next action a from a recipe, we aim to generate images illustrating how this action is performed in f_{action} and how relevant object(s) appear afterward in f_{final}. Here, f_{in} is the *initial* frame, f_{action} depicts the action execution, and f_{final} represents the post-action state. Both f_{action} and f_{final} build on f_{in} as the starting environment. See Fig. 2 for an example.

Unlike previous approaches [23,43] that rely on vision-language models to generate detailed captions, our method VisualChef distinguishes between different types of objects and applies tailored strategies for each (see Fig. 2).

3.2   Selecting Image Triplets

While most egocentric video datasets provide action labels with start/end timestamps, few annotate critical frames. To obtain image triplets from these videos, we develop a selection strategy. We define t_s and t_f as the start and end times of the action, respectively. We select the frame at the beginning of each action as the *initial frame*, i.e. $f_{\text{in}} = f_{t_s}$. Similar to previous work [23], the action frame is chosen from the midpoint of the action, i.e. $f_{\text{action}} = f_{\frac{1}{2}(t_s+t_f)}$, under the assumption that this frame captures the core of the activity. Although multiple frames could serve as the action frame, our empirical results show that selecting the middle frame yields more qualitative results (see Sect. 4.2 for details). For the *final frame*, we opt for the frame at 90% of duration, i.e., $f_{\text{final}} = f_{\frac{1}{10}t_s+\frac{9}{10}t_f}$ to ensure that relevant objects remain visible before cleanup or transition begins.

Filtering. We then filter out image triplets that do not contain action-relevant objects through the following steps.

1. **Object Identification:** We use LLaVA [28] to identify visible objects relevant to the action (see Sect. 3.3). The input to the model consists of the action a and the initial frame f_{in}. The output is a list of objects $[o_i]$ present in f_{in} and associated with a.

2. **Object Detection:** An open-vocabulary object detector [29] processes f_{in} and $[o_i]$. The output includes detection scores $[s_i]$. Detection for f_{final} is omitted to avoid excluding informative triplets, as objects may change shape or disappear at the end of the action. Any detection with $s_i < 0.3$ is discarded.

3. **Hand Detection:** We observe that all quality frames tend to include hands in f_{in}, as the person is likely preparing to perform an action, often with their hands already in contact with objects. Additionally, the hand may partly cover an object, making it challenging for the model to accurately identify the object. We use the model to detect hands in both f_{in} and f_{action}. Detection is omitted in f_{final} because it usually shows the completed action without hands.

4. **Frame Filtering:** Based on the detection results, we filter the image triplets $(f_{\text{in}}, f_{\text{action}}, f_{\text{final}})$ where f_{in} does not include at least hands or any of the identified relevant objects, or where f_{action} lacks visible hands.

These criteria are input requirements for using the model in real-world cases.

3.3   Classifying Relevant Objects

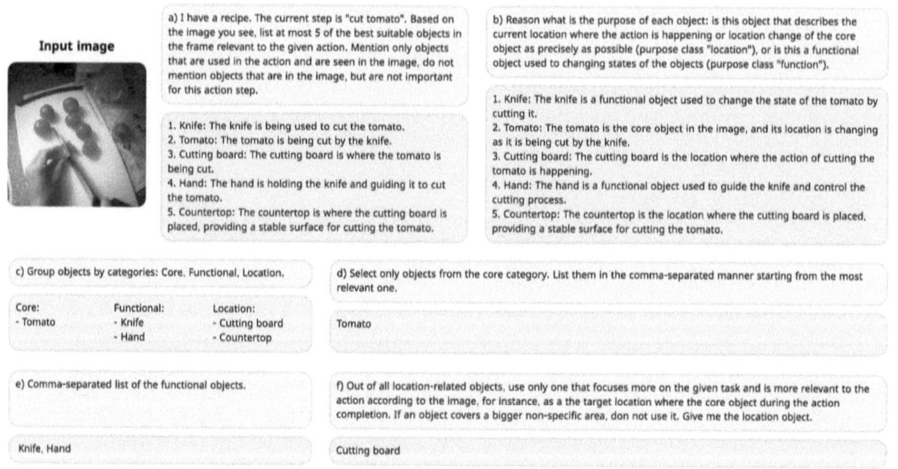

Fig. 3. Chain-of-thoughts reasoning for relevant object identification. Given an input image, we use the chain-of-thoughts strategy to prompt LLaVA [28] to get a categorized list of objects relevant to the given action.

VisualChef first identifies the key objects relevant to a given action; for example, a knife is generally required for cutting. We ground the requirements in the scene, adapting based on the available objects in case an alternative way is feasible; e.g., if a cutting board is absent, the action may still proceed on a plate.

Real-world scenes are often cluttered with many objects, yet not all are relevant to the action. Conversely, we observe that relying solely on the objects explicitly mentioned in the action is insufficient (see supp. mat. for details). VisualChef, therefore, identifies action-relevant objects and categorizes them based on specific roles. Specifically, we consider the following three object categories:

1. *Core objects* that are essential to the action itself (e.g., the tomato in a "Cut tomato" action).
2. *Location objects* that describe the initial or final locations of the objects involved (e.g., a cutting board, pan, or stove).
3. *Functional objects*: These serve a purpose in the action but do not move other objects, nor is their location important (e.g., hands or a knife when cutting a tomato).

We follow the chain-of-thoughts strategy [50] to prompt the open-source vision language model, LLaVA [28], for object relevance and categorization. The model is first asked to identify action-relevant objects and then categorize them by type (see Fig. 3 for prompt examples).

Often, multiple *location objects* refer to the same spatial area. For example, in the action of placing cheese (see supp. mat.), LLaVA may return the burger, pan, and stove. Although all of them are valid, the burger defines the target location the most precisely. To address this, we add a reasoning step prompting LLaVA to filter and retain only the most specific location object for the action.

3.4   Masking Relevant Objects

If we apply a diffusion pipeline to the entire image, we risk generating an image that looks completely different. While the target action may be depicted, the environment, tools, and core objects can change drastically. Our goal, instead, is to preserve the original setting, modifying only elements that require change.

To achieve this, we use existing visual grounding methods [29, 39] to segment the relevant objects. Their bounding boxes form a mask used for inpainting to generate the target frames. Empirical results show that bounding boxes are an effective, compact representation that provides object-related information while being coarse enough to allow shape and pose changes.

We always mask all *core objects*, as they are central to the action, and use their locations for generating both f_{action} and f_{final}. The bounding box of the *location object* is used to move the *core object* to its final location in both frames. *Functional objects* are used only for generating f_{action}, where they support the depiction of the action, but are not involved in f_{final} generation.

3.5   Diffusion-Based Inpainting

The final stage of our pipeline uses Stable Diffusion [40] for inpainting. In this stage, we provide the initial image f_{in}, a natural language description of the action a, and the masks generated earlier. The stage output includes the generated target frames f_{action} and f_{final}. To generate f_{action}, we use a two-step inpainting procedure. First, we inpaint *functional objects* to put them into position for performing a. Then we inpaint this intermediate result using *core object* masks. When generating f_{final}, we skip the first step and directly inpaint the f_{in}. For optimization, we use a loss function based on the negative log CLIP score:

$$\mathcal{L}(f_{\text{in}}, \hat{f}_{\text{out}}) = -\log \mathbf{CLIP}(f_{\text{in}}, \hat{f}_{\text{out}}), \tag{1}$$

where **CLIP** measures cosine similarity between the CLIP embeddings [37] of f_{in} and the target frame $\hat{f}_{\text{out}}$ (f_{action} or f_{final}). Similar to negative log-likelihood, this approach ensures that the generated image remains semantically consistent with the given action description while achieving high-quality inpainting results.

Implementation Details. We use the version of Stable Diffusion specifically designed for masked inpainting tasks [40]. The model is fine-tuned separately on our datasets for two target frames over 5 epochs.

4   Experiments

We introduce the experimental setup in Sect. 4.1, compare to previous SOTA methods in Sect. 4.3, and discuss the ablation studies in Sect. 4.5.

4.1   Experimental Setup

Datasets. To ensure a fair and dataset-specific evaluation, the model was trained and evaluated separately on each of the three datasets. Specifically, for each experiment, the model was trained using only the training split of a single dataset and evaluated on its corresponding test split.

- **Ego4D** [1]. We extract cooking activities from the Ego4D dataset for the *Forecasting + Hands & Objects* task, yielding 80 videos with 11K actions and annotations for three key frames per action. These are the pre-condition (*PRE*), point-of-no-return (*PNR*), and post-condition (*POST*) frames, which correspond to f_{in}, f_{action} and f_{final}. Following a setup similar to LEGO and GenHowTo, we split 80% of the data for training and 20% for testing.
- **EGTEA Gaze+** [27] is a multimodal egocentric cooking video dataset. It contains 28 h of video content, with frame-level action annotations, pixel-level hand masks, and gaze-tracking data. Using our strategy, we select 3K image triplets, allocating 80% for training and 20% for testing.
- **EK-100** [7] is the largest egocentric cooking dataset with 100 h of unscripted daily routine cooking videos with automatically annotated hand-object bounding boxes and object masks. We select 3K triplets, splitting them into 80% for training and 20% for testing.

Baselines. We compare our method with state-of-the-art methods for action-conditioned image generation, including Stable Diffusion [40], Instruct-Pix2Pix [4], GenHowTo [43], and LEGO [23].

- **Stable Diffusion** [40] is included in its original form to demonstrate the improvement achieved for this task compared to the standard model.

- **InstructPix2Pix** [4] is a model based on Stable Diffusion, trained for editing images according to instructions.
- **GenHowTo** [43] shares the same task setting and focuses on action and final state frames. It builds on Stable Diffusion, using U-Net and ControlNet.
- **LEGO** [23] is a model for action image generation in egocentric videos that utilizes VLM to enrich narrations.

GenHowTo and LEGO are two closest baselines; however, VisualChef offers a simpler, more efficient alternative with improved alignment and lower overhead (full details in the supp. material).

For the SOTA baselines, we used the official implementations and pretrained weights from the original authors. When dataset-specific weights were available (e.g., LEGO), we used those. For models that were designed to be general-purpose, we relied on publicly available weights without additional finetuning.

Evaluation Metrics. Following standard evaluation protocols for generative models [14,19,38,41,42], we report FID [13], PSNR [15] and SSIM [49] scores. Recognizing the limitations of these metrics [44], we additionally introduce a set of novel evaluation metrics based on CLIP similarity between pairs of images.

- **CLIP** [37] cosine similarity.
- **M-CLIP** compares only the masked areas where changes are applied.
- **D-CLIP** considers the similarity between f_{in} and $f_{\mathrm{out}}^{\mathrm{GT}}$. When similarity is high, the metric penalizes major changes to preserve the initial frame. When low, it allows and even encourages greater deviations in the generated output.

$$\text{D-CLIP}(f_{\mathrm{in}}, \hat{f}_{\mathrm{out}}) = \frac{\text{CLIP}(f_{\mathrm{in}}, f_{\mathrm{out}}^{\mathrm{GT}}) - \text{CLIP}(f_{\mathrm{in}}, \hat{f}_{\mathrm{out}})}{\text{CLIP}(f_{\mathrm{in}}, f_{\mathrm{out}}^{\mathrm{GT}})}$$

4.2   Evaluation of Dataset Curation Strategy

To evaluate our data curation strategy, we manually select 50 triplets from EGTEA Gaze+ that best represent the initial, action, and final states of each action, creating a benchmark evaluation set. We then measured the similarity between these and the automatically selected frames using CLIP scores.

The quantitative results in Table 1 demonstrate the effectiveness of the strategy, with 80 empirically set as the threshold for strong similarity. On average, the automatically selected frames align well with the manual evaluation set. The action frames f_{action} show a high degree of similarity,

Table 1. Data curation evaluation. We assess our strategy on a manually selected set and show the impact of filtering.

Frame	Before filtering		After filtering	
	CLIP	Quantile $\geq$ 80	CLIP	Quantile $\geq$ 80
f_{in}	83.53	70.8%	85.56	81.5%
f_{action}	90.87	91.7%	91.14	92.6%
f_{final}	82.11	62.5%	85.71	74.1%

as evidenced by the defined quantile. This can be attributed to the repetitive nature of many actions; e.g., during a tomato cutting, most frames are nearly identical, differing only in incremental progress. The initial frames f_{in} also perform well, while the final frames f_{final} score the lowest, reflecting the common tendency in cooking videos to move quickly to the next step after completing an action without stopping to show the result. This challenge has been observed consistently throughout the project and explains why other models (e.g., [23]) prioritize f_{action} over f_{final}. After selection, we apply filtering to exclude low quality or insufficient frames which significantly improve CLIP scores (see Table 1; more on the supp. mat).

Table 2. Comparison with the state-of-the-art. Our method VisualChef outperforms state-of-the-art methods by a large margin in terms of content relevance, indicated by CLIP and D-CLIP.

Dataset	Target	Method	CLIP ↑	M-CLIP ↑	D-CLIP ↓	FID ↓	PSNR ↑	SSIM ↑
Ego4D	f_{action}	StableDiffusion [40]	53.75	64.84	41.57	162.47	28.33	37.03
		InstructPix2Pix [4]	56.95	64.72	38.11	137.57	28.20	38.12
		GenHowTo [43]	69.36	**70.85**	24.70	67.47	28.43	38.19
		LEGO [23]	73.39	70.48	20.32	87.71	28.09	36.33
		VisualChef	**82.87**	68.69	**10.11**	**55.14**	**29.08**	**43.07**
	f_{final}	StableDiffusion [40]	51.17	62.96	41.33	162.84	28.20	32.59
		InstructPix2Pix [4]	52.71	61.70	39.55	151.10	28.03	33.26
		GenHowTo [43]	59.36	64.94	32.07	85.44	28.07	31.01
		VisualChef	**79.99**	**68.15**	**8.69**	**57.98**	**28.50**	**36.71**
EGTEA Gaze+	f_{action}	StableDiffusion [40]	46.32	63.94	40.89	139.50	28.03	36.53
		InstructPix2Pix [4]	50.07	64.35	35.21	144.01	28.00	**42.71**
		GenHowTo [43]	61.89	71.86	22.13	82.53	28.14	39.22
		VisualChef	**69.62**	66.34	**12.44**	**78.78**	28.26	40.48
	f_{final}	StableDiffusion [40]	42.61	63.10	44.05	151.00	28.01	35.80
		InstructPix2Pix [4]	47.20	63.20	38.09	153.49	27.96	**43.14**
		GenHowTo [43]	48.95	64.49	36.09	109.08	27.98	37.57
		VisualChef	**68.44**	**65.91**	**11.60**	**79.26**	**28.19**	40.37
EPIC-KITCHENS	f_{action}	StableDiffusion [40]	27.49	49.49	67.08	389.27	27.91	7.32
		InstructPix2Pix [4]	49.14	63.81	42.17	125.94	28.03	**28.73**
		GenHowTo [43]	62.51	70.90	26.61	**72.66**	28.19	27.46
		LEGO [23]	66.33	**72.65**	21.81	98.59	28.02	25.83
		VisualChef	**69.97**	65.02	**18.08**	94.33	**28.36**	28.52
	f_{final}	StableDiffusion [40]	27.96	49.69	65.34	387.22	27.90	6.71
		InstructPix2Pix [4]	47.39	62.75	41.87	132.13	27.97	**27.48**
		GenHowTo [43]	51.37	63.63	36.65	**95.02**	27.99	23.87
		VisualChef	**70.06**	**66.39**	14.72	99.12	**28.25**	27.36

4.3 Comparison with State-of-the-Art

Table 2 compares baseline models and our method on Ego4D, EGTEA Gaze+, and EK-100 datasets, evaluating their ability to generate accurate *action* and *final frames*. LEGO [23]'s goal is to generate action frames only, we report its results only for that. We do not report LEGO results on EGTEA Gaze+, because it only provides pre-trained weights for Ego4D and EK-100.

CLIP and M-CLIP scores reflect semantic similarity to reference images, with higher values indicating closer alignment. D-CLIP captures semantic discrepancy between images (lower is better). The evaluation is performed on the test sets: 1,000 triplets from Ego4D, 650 from EGTEA Gaze+, and 750 from EK-100.

First of all, the results exhibit consistent behavior across all datasets, especially EGTEA Gaze+ and EK-100, indicating that VisualChef generalizes well to egocentric cooking data and consistently produces high-quality results.

VisualChef consistently achieves the highest CLIP and lowest D-CLIP scores, indicating strong semantic and contextual alignment. Occasionally, it achieves a higher CLIP score, but a lower M-CLIP score compared to LEGO or GenHowTo, suggesting they may better refine masked regions but introduce unwanted changes elsewhere. VisualChef's SSIM values are lower than other models like InstructPix2Pix, indicating that while it is semantically accurate, its structural quality could be marginally improved. StableDiffusion and InstructPix2Pix show competitive SSIM values but are generally outperformed by VisualChef and GenHowTo in content relevance. At the same time, VisualChef achieves the highest PSNR scores and among the best FID results. Overall, VisualChef emerges as the top-performing model across semantic metrics.

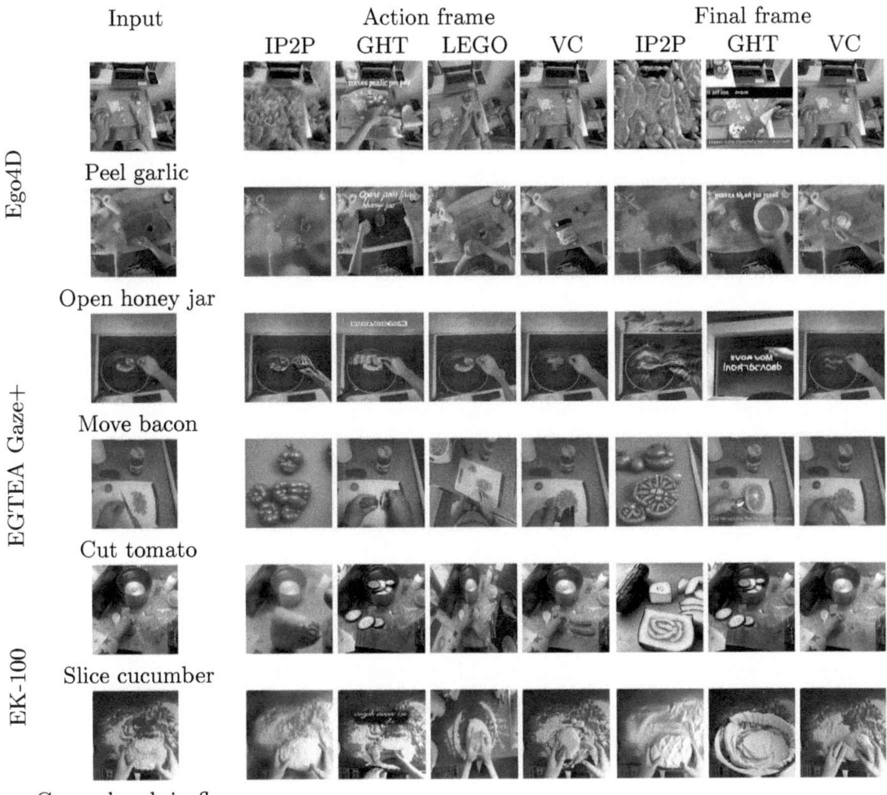

Fig. 4. Qualitative comparison with related work. VisualChef has the best performance in aligning generated images to the input action and preserving the environment compared to state-of-the-art methods.

Table 3. Ablation study. (a) We analyze the effect of fine-tuning the diffusion pipeline. Higher scores for the fine-tuned model indicate a positive training impact. (b) We evaluate cross-dataset generalization by applying Ego4D-trained weights of VisualChef and LEGO to the EGTEA Gaze+ test set. VisualChef consistently outperforms LEGO.

(a) Effect of fine-tuning

Method	Action		Final	
	CLIP ↑	D-CLIP ↓	CLIP ↑	D-CLIP ↓
Inpainting	70.65	16.58	71.00	13.80
VisualChef	**71.33**	**15.72**	**71.07**	**13.75**

(b) Cross-dataset generalization

Method	CLIP ↑	M-CLIP ↑	D-CLIP ↓
LEGO	68.93	**68.24**	18.57
VisualChef	**71.22**	63.66	**15.96**

Figure 4 shows the generation results from VisualChef and SOTA methods across three datasets. InstructPix2Pix and GenHowTo often fail to maintain scene consistency. LEGO exhibits a stronger capability for preserving scene consistency, but it occasionally introduces deformations. LEGO does not generate f_{final}, which positions our model as the most complete and effective approach.

Since automatic evaluation of egocentric video generation is not a mature field, we conducted a binary comparison study with 30 users. Each participant viewed 25 image pairs (one generated by VisualChef and the other by either LEGO or GenHowTo) with the action and initial image. The users selected the best image that depicts the action or its result in terms of accuracy, quality, and clarity. Figure 5 shows that VisualChef was preferred in 70% of action frames and 80% of final frames. While LEGO often depicts the action well, object deformations reduce visual appeal. GenHowTo shows more variable quality ranging from high to poor, which led to higher average preference over LEGO.

4.4   Generation of Various Actions

Figure 6 shows an example where the same initial frame is used to generate different actions. To qualitatively assess generalization, we used a custom image as the input. The resulting final frames accurately reflect the intended actions while preserving the scene, highlighting VisualChef's practical applicability.

4.5   Ablations

Effect of Fine-Tuning. Table 3a shows that fine-tuning the inpainting model on a randomly selected subset of EGTEA Gaze+ improves the quality of generated frames compared to using the pretrained model.

Cross-Dataset Generalization. Both VisualChef and LEGO [23] use dataset-specific weights. To test generalization, we generated images on the EGTEA Gaze+ evaluation set using weights trained on Ego4D. As shown in Table 3b, VisualChef generalizes better than LEGO.

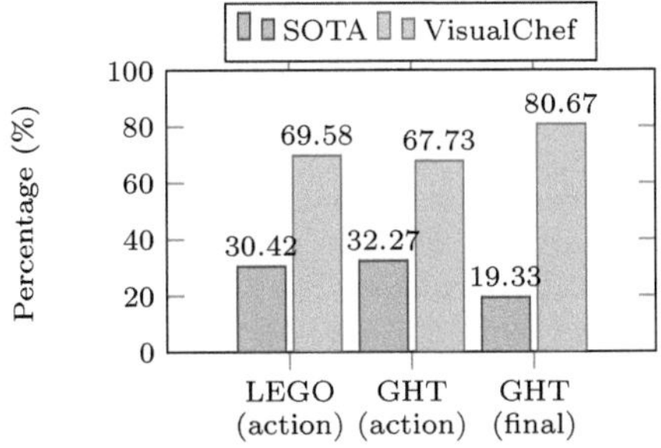

Fig. 5. Human comparison of SOTA models and VisualChef. The users tend to select images generated by VisualChef more often.

Fig. 6. Different actions with the same input. VisualChef generalizes across actions while retaining context.

5   Conclusion

In this work, we present a novel approach for improving cooking instructions with automated visual aids that addresses the limitations of text-based recipes. Leveraging egocentric datasets like Ego4D, EGTEA Gaze+, and EK-100, our model effectively selects and generates frames that depict key stages of cooking actions. By using a diffusion-based pipeline with masked inpainting, we ensure precise edits that preserve scene consistency while focusing on core elements.

Limitations. In some cases, we observe a slight drop in the quality of generated action frames due to the difficulty of synthesizing plausible hand poses. To account for shape changes, we use bounding boxes for inpainting and to handle location changes, the relocation procedure; however, to handle complex shape changes, one might refer to a more complex model (e.g., [45]).

Most actions in the datasets are atomic—for instance, instead of a single action like "put a tomato from the fridge onto the table," we typically see a sequence of smaller steps: "open fridge," "take tomato," "put tomato on table," and "close fridge." As a result, cases where objects disappear due to viewpoint changes are rare. However, when they do occur, our model cannot handle them.

References

1. Grauman, K., et al.: Ego4d: around the world in 3,000 hours of egocentric video (2022)
2. Grauman, K., et al.: Ego-exo4d: understanding skilled human activity from first- and third-person perspectives (2023)
3. Bar-Tal, O., Ofri-Amar, D., Fridman, R., Kasten, Y., Dekel, T.: Text2live: text-driven layered image and video editing (2022)
4. Brooks, T., Holynski, A., Efros, A.A.: Instructpix2pix: learning to follow image editing instructions (2023)
5. Couairon, G., Verbeek, J., Schwenk, H., Cord, M.: Diffedit: diffusion-based semantic image editing with mask guidance (2022). https://arxiv.org/abs/2210.11427
6. Damen, D., et al.: Scaling egocentric vision: the epic-kitchens dataset. In: European Conference on Computer Vision (ECCV) (2018)
7. Damen, D., et al.: Rescaling egocentric vision: collection, pipeline and challenges for epic-kitchens-100. Int. J. Comput. Vision (IJCV) **130**, 33–55 (2022). https://doi.org/10.1007/s11263-021-01531-2
8. Dhariwal, P., Nichol, A.: Diffusion models beat GANs on image synthesis (2021). https://arxiv.org/abs/2105.05233
9. Guo, Q., Lin, T.: Focus on your instruction: fine-grained and multi-instruction image editing by attention modulation (2023). https://arxiv.org/abs/2312.10113
10. Han, L., et al.: Improving tuning-free real image editing with proximal guidance (2023)
11. Helbling, A., Lee, S., Chau, P.: Point and instruct: enabling precise image editing by unifying direct manipulation and text instructions (2024). https://arxiv.org/abs/2402.07925
12. Hertz, A., Mokady, R., Tenenbaum, J., Aberman, K., Pritch, Y., Cohen-Or, D.: Prompt-to-prompt image editing with cross attention control (2022)
13. Heusel, M., Ramsauer, H., Unterthiner, T., Nessler, B., Hochreiter, S.: GANs trained by a two time-scale update rule converge to a local nash equilibrium. In: Advances in Neural Information Processing Systems, vol. 30 (2017)
14. Ho, J., Jain, A., Abbeel, P.: Denoising diffusion probabilistic models (2020). https://arxiv.org/abs/2006.11239
15. Horé, A., Ziou, D.: Image quality metrics: PSNR vs. SSIM. In: 2010 20th International Conference on Pattern Recognition, pp. 2366–2369 (2010). https://doi.org/10.1109/ICPR.2010.579
16. Hu, H., et al.: Instruct-imagen: image generation with multi-modal instruction (2024)
17. Huang, X., Mallya, A., Wang, T.C., Liu, M.Y.: Multimodal conditional image synthesis with product-of-experts GANs (2021). https://arxiv.org/abs/2112.05130
18. Ju, X., Liu, X., Wang, X., Bian, Y., Shan, Y., Xu, Q.: Brushnet: a plug-and-play image inpainting model with decomposed dual-branch diffusion (2024). https://arxiv.org/abs/2403.06976
19. Kasem, H.M., Hung, K.W., Jiang, J.: Spatial transformer generative adversarial network for robust image super-resolution. IEEE Access **7**, 182993–183009 (2019). https://doi.org/10.1109/ACCESS.2019.2959940
20. Kawar, B., et al.: Imagic: text-based real image editing with diffusion models (2023)
21. Köhler, R., Schuler, C., Schölkopf, B., Harmeling, S.: Mask-specific inpainting with deep neural networks. In: Jiang, X., Hornegger, J., Koch, R. (eds.) GCPR 2014. LNCS, vol. 8753, pp. 523–534. Springer, Cham (2014). https://doi.org/10.1007/978-3-319-11752-2_43

22. Kuoppamäki, S., Tuncer, S., Eriksson, S., McMillan, D.: Designing kitchen technologies for ageing in place: a video study of older adults' cooking at home. Proc. ACM Interact. Mob. Wearable Ubiquitous Technol. **5**(2), 1–19 (2021)
23. Lai, B., Dai, X., Chen, L., Pang, G., Rehg, J.M., Liu, M.: Lego: learning egocentric action frame generation via visual instruction tuning (2024)
24. Li, J., Hu, L., He, Z., Zhang, J., Zheng, T., Wang, D.: Text guided image editing with automatic concept locating and forgetting (2024). https://arxiv.org/abs/2405.19708
25. Li, J., Li, D., Xiong, C., Hoi, S.: Blip: bootstrapping language-image pre-training for unified vision-language understanding and generation (2022)
26. Li, J., et al.: Covlm: composing visual entities and relationships in large language models via communicative decoding (2023). https://arxiv.org/abs/2311.03354
27. Li, Y., Liu, M., Rehg, J.M.: In the eye of the beholder: gaze and actions in first person video (2020)
28. Liu, H., Li, C., Wu, Q., Lee, Y.J.: Visual instruction tuning (2023). https://arxiv.org/abs/2304.08485
29. Liu, S., et al.: Grounding dino: marrying dino with grounded pre-training for open-set object detection (2024). https://arxiv.org/abs/2303.05499
30. Lugmayr, A., Danelljan, M., Romero, A., Yu, F., Timofte, R., Van Gool, L.: Repaint: inpainting using denoising diffusion probabilistic models. In: Proceedings of the IEEE/CVF Conference on Computer Vision and Pattern Recognition, pp. 11461–11471 (2022)
31. Madera, J.M., Dawson, M., Neal, J.A., Busch, K.: Breaking a communication barrier: the effect of visual aids in food preparation on job attitudes and performance. J. Hospitality Tourism Res. **37**(2), 262–280 (2013)
32. Mao, Q., Chen, L., Gu, Y., Fang, Z., Shou, M.Z.: Mag-edit: localized image editing in complex scenarios via mask-based attention-adjusted guidance (2023). https://arxiv.org/abs/2312.11396
33. Meng, C., et al.: Sdedit: guided image synthesis and editing with stochastic differential equations (2022)
34. Mirza, M., Osindero, S.: Conditional generative adversarial nets (2014). https://arxiv.org/abs/1411.1784
35. Odena, A., Olah, C., Shlens, J.: Conditional image synthesis with auxiliary classifier GANs (2017). https://arxiv.org/abs/1610.09585
36. Pan, Y., Mao, C., Jiang, Z., Han, Z., Zhang, J.: Locate, assign, refine: taming customized image inpainting with text-subject guidance (2024). https://arxiv.org/abs/2403.19534
37. Radford, A., et al.: Learning transferable visual models from natural language supervision (2021)
38. Ramesh, A., et al.: Zero-shot text-to-image generation (2021). https://arxiv.org/abs/2102.12092
39. Ren, T., et al.: Grounded SAM: assembling open-world models for diverse visual tasks (2024)
40. Rombach, R., Blattmann, A., Lorenz, D., Esser, P., Ommer, B.: High-resolution image synthesis with latent diffusion models (2022). https://arxiv.org/abs/2112.10752
41. Saharia, C., et al.: Photorealistic text-to-image diffusion models with deep language understanding (2022). https://arxiv.org/abs/2205.11487
42. Song, T.A., Chowdhury, S.R., Yang, F., Dutta, J.: Pet image super-resolution using generative adversarial networks. Neural Netw. **125**, 83–91 (2020). https://doi.org/

10.1016/j.neunet.2020.01.029. https://www.sciencedirect.com/science/article/pii/S0893608020300393

43. Souček, T., Damen, D., Wray, M., Laptev, I., Sivic, J.: Genhowto: learning to generate actions and state transformations from instructional videos (2024)

44. Stein, G., et al.: Exposing flaws of generative model evaluation metrics and their unfair treatment of diffusion models. In: Advances in Neural Information Processing Systems, vol. 36 (2024)

45. Sudhakar, S., Liu, R., Hoorick, B.V., Vondrick, C., Zemel, R.: Controlling the world by sleight of hand (2024). https://arxiv.org/abs/2408.07147

46. Suvorov, R., et al.: Resolution-robust large mask inpainting with fourier convolutions. In: Proceedings of the IEEE/CVF Winter Conference on Applications of Computer Vision, pp. 2149–2159 (2022)

47. Tran, Q.T., Calcaterra, G., Mynatt, E.D.: COOK'S collage. In: Sloane, A. (ed.) Home-Oriented Informatics and Telematics. IIFIP, vol. 178, pp. 15–32. Springer, Boston (2005). https://doi.org/10.1007/11402985_2

48. Wang, Q., Zhang, B., Birsak, M., Wonka, P.: Instructedit: improving automatic masks for diffusion-based image editing with user instructions (2023)

49. Wang, Z., Bovik, A., Sheikh, H., Simoncelli, E.: Image quality assessment: from error visibility to structural similarity. IEEE Trans. Image Process. **13**(4), 600–612 (2004). https://doi.org/10.1109/TIP.2003.819861

50. Wei, J., et al.: Chain-of-thought prompting elicits reasoning in large language models (2023). https://arxiv.org/abs/2201.11903

51. Zhang, L., Rao, A., Agrawala, M.: Adding conditional control to text-to-image diffusion models (2023). https://arxiv.org/abs/2302.05543

52. Zhu, M., et al.: Image inpainting by end-to-end cascaded refinement with mask awareness. IEEE Trans. Image Process. **30**, 4855–4866 (2021)

53. Zhu, Y., Li, Z., Wang, T., He, M., Yao, C.: Conditional text image generation with diffusion models (2023). https://arxiv.org/abs/2306.10804

StorySync: Training-Free Subject Consistency via Region Harmonization

Gopalji Gaur[1]([envelope]) [iD], Mohammadreza Zolfaghari[2] [iD], and Thomas Brox[1] [iD]

[1] Albert-Ludwigs-Universität Freiburg, University of Freiburg, 79098 Freiburg, Germany
gopaljigaur@gmail.com
[2] Zebracat AI, Berlin, Germany
info@zebracat.ai
https://www.zebracat.ai/

Abstract. Generating a coherent sequence of images that tells a visual story, using text-to-image diffusion models, often faces the critical challenge of maintaining subject consistency across all story scenes. Existing approaches, which typically rely on fine-tuning or retraining models, are computationally expensive, time-consuming, and often interfere with the model's pre-existing capabilities. In this paper, we follow a training-free approach and propose an efficient consistent-subject-generation method. This approach works seamlessly with pre-trained diffusion models by introducing *masked cross-image attention sharing* to dynamically align subject features across a batch of images, and *Regional Feature Harmonization* to refine visually similar details for improved subject consistency. Experimental results demonstrate that our approach successfully generates visually consistent subjects across a variety of scenarios while maintaining the creative abilities of the diffusion model.

Keywords: Subject Consistency · Visual Storytelling · Diffusion models

1 Introduction

Current text-to-image diffusion models [2,28,31] struggle with maintaining subject consistency when generating multiple images. The lack of subject consistency in visual story generation extends beyond storytelling applications. In fields, such as animation, game design, video creation, and synthetic data creation, consistent character representations are crucial for achieving coherence and realism.

Most methods follow the idea of checkpoint personalization [3,6,15,19,22,33, 41,50], where the model is finetuned to generate a consistent subject. However, these approaches typically require extensive subject-specific training and struggle with incorporating multiple subjects in the same image [33]. In contrast, training-free methods [1,11,20,45], use an image-conditioned diffusion process that takes a reference image as input and generates similar output images. However, these

M. Keuper and F. Locatello (Eds.): DAGM GCPR 2025, LNCS 16125, pp. 155–170, 2026.
https://doi.org/10.1007/978-3-032-12840-9_11

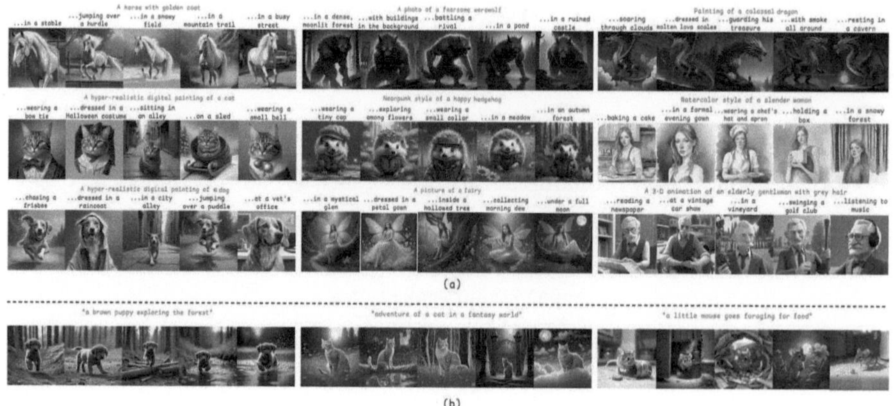

Fig. 1. Demonstrating *StorySync*'s consistency capabilities. (a) Subject consistency maintained across various subject categories including humans, animals, and fictional characters. (b) Visual story generation showing StorySync's ability to maintain subject identity throughout multi-scene visual story sequences.

methods restrict the model's creative potential and produce images that do not closely follow the input prompts.

Existing training-free consistent subject generation approaches [38, 49] share visual knowledge about the subject among all images through attention sharing. Instead of relying on personalization or reference-based alignment, they leverage cross-image feature sharing to enforce zero-shot subject consistency in a batch of generated images. Other methods [3, 23] implement additional modifications to the input embeddings. Despite achieving impressive subject consistency, these methods either fail to adhere to the conditioning prompts, or they lack alignment of finer details of the consistent subjects.

In this work, we introduce *StorySync*, which is built on **three technical innovations**. **(1)** We introduce masked cross-image attention sharing, a dense interaction of attention features localized to subject regions in the images. **(2)** To improve on the consistency of subtle subject details, we introduce Regional Feature Harmonization. **(3)** We present Base Layout Interpolation to enable sufficient diversity in the generated images, despite the consistency constraints. As a result, *StorySync* is able to generate story scenes with a high level of visual consistency of the story characters and surpasses existing training-free approaches, as shown in Fig. 1.

Furthermore, we demonstrate the plug-and-play capability of this approach on different text-to-image diffusion models. We test the approach with *SDXL* [28] and *Kandinsky 3* [2], both of which build on U-Net [32], as well as with the time-distilled *FLUX.1-schnell* model based on a transformer model.

2   Related Work

Encoder-Based Approaches. There have been multiple approaches [12,18,25, 35,48] to solve the challenge of generating visual stories using Diffusion Models [16]. These approaches collectively address critical challenges such as maintaining coherence across scenes and ensuring character consistency. Ye et al. [45] introduced *IP-Adapter*, while Wei et al. [42] proposed *ELITE*, both of which encode visual concepts into textual embeddings for customized T2I generation. Jeong et al. [18] introduced a zero-shot framework leveraging Latent Diffusion Models and textual inversion to generate coherent storybooks directly from textual inputs. Building on this work, other approaches [25,35] introduced frameworks for disentanglement of character and scene generation to produce cohesive visual narratives. These contributions, although successful in generating cohesive storyboards, depend largely on input reference images to influence the generation.

Model Finetuning. Subsequent works have focused on model personalization for consistent subject generation in diffusion models [6,9,11,17,30,47,51]. Multiple approaches [1,10,19,30,33] embed novel subjects into a model's knowledge space, enabling consistent concept generation through reconstruction. Finetuning T2I models on storyboard datasets has also shown promise for visual storytelling [7,21]. Wu et al. [43] extended this approach to video generation, achieving temporal consistency with personalized T2I models. Decentralized methods [13,27] utilize ensemble models to generate multi-subject consistent scenes. Wang et al. [39] further advanced this by sampling latent noise from localized regions of the latent space. However, these approaches require computationally expensive finetuning of model checkpoints.

In addition to addressing coherence, multi-modal frameworks such as *SEED-Story* by Yang et al. [44], *TaleCrafter* by Gong et al. [12] and Liu et al.'s *Intelligent Grimm* [22] push the boundaries of interactive and multi-modal storytelling using Latent Diffusion Models [31]. Together, these works offer robust solutions for generating visually similar subjects, but often require finetuning the diffusion models to generate visually consistent subjects.

Training-free Consistency. Achieving one-shot consistency in generated images is crucial for enabling visually coherent stories or images without the overhead of finetuning or additional computational resources [38,49]. Shi et al. [34] introduced *InstantBooth*, offering near-instant model personalization without test-time finetuning. In image editing, Cao et al. [5] proposed *MasaCtrl*, which employs mutual self-attention to share information between input and generated images. Wang et al. [40] introduced *RISA* and *SFCA* mechanisms to enforce layout-defined subject consistency.

Training-free approaches such as *ConsiStory* [38] and *StoryDiffusion* [49] introduce self-attention modifications to enforce subject consistency. He et al. [14] proposed *DreamStory*, focusing on open-domain story visualization with attention sharing among images. ConsiStory enforces strong cross-frame context and query blending, which suppresses pose diversity. StoryDiffusion propagates context beyond subject regions, resulting in repeated visual patches. In contrast, our method injects pose cues via an independent branch and constrains attention using subject masks, improving both consistency and diversity. We take inspiration from such techniques and devise our Cross-Image Attention Sharing, Regional Feature Harmonization and Base Layout Interpolation to generate compelling visual stories with consistent subjects.

3   StorySync

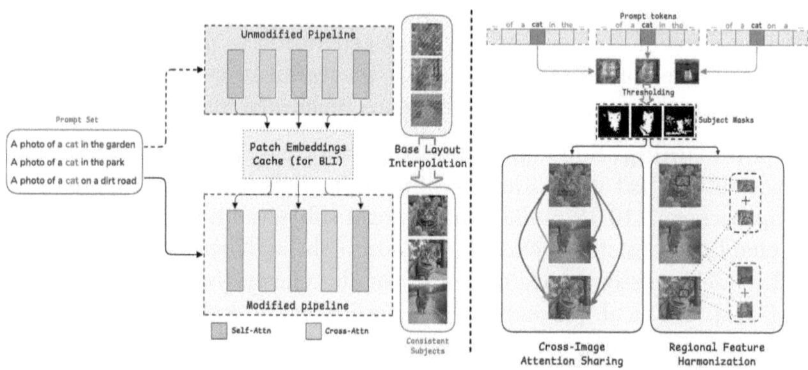

Fig. 2. Proposed Architecture: (1) We cache queries generated by the base model during image generation, (2) We modify the image generation pipeline's attention processors with our own implementations, (3) We generate images with consistent subjects using the modified pipeline. *In modified Cross Attention layers*: we extract attention maps to generate subject masks. *In modified Self-Attention layers*: We implement Cross-Image Attention Sharing and Regional Feature Harmonization to enforce subject consistency in generated images.

In this section, we present our approach *StorySync* for achieving subject consistency in Text-to-Image generation pipelines. As shown in Fig. 2, StorySync enhances subject consistency through three primary mechanisms: (1) Cross-Image Attention Sharing restricted to subject regions, (2) Regional Feature Harmonization to strengthen fine-grained visual similarity of subject across generated images, and (3) Base Layout Interpolation to boost prompt adherence. Together, these mechanisms enforce subject consistency while preserving scene diversity.

3.1   Preliminaries

Extracting Subject Masks. We begin with standard QKV computation (see Appendix A). To ensure consistency only in subject regions, we extract cross-attention maps associated with the subject token in Cross-Attention layers of the de-noising network.

For a given subject token s in the textual input, the attention map for an image i is computed as:

$$\mathcal{A}_{s,i} = \text{softmax}\left(\frac{Q_{s,i}K_i^T}{\sqrt{d_k}}\right), \tag{1}$$

where $Q_{s,i}$ represents the query vector corresponding to the subject token, and K_i are the key vectors derived from the patch embeddings of image i.

The resulting attention map $\mathcal{A}_{s,i}$ is averaged over cross-attention layers in the model, and then summed for all subjects S in an image i to create a robust representation of the influence of the subjects in image patches:

$$\bar{\mathcal{A}}_{s,i} = \frac{1}{L}\sum_{l=1}^{L}\mathcal{A}_{s,i}^{(l)}, \tag{2}$$

$$\bar{\mathcal{A}}_i = \sum_{s=1}^{S}\bar{\mathcal{A}}_{s,i} \tag{3}$$

where L is the total number of layers from which the maps were extracted, and $\bar{\mathcal{A}}_i$ is the aggregated map.

Finally, thresholding with Otsu's method [24] converts the attention maps $\bar{\mathcal{A}}_i$ into binary subject masks $\mathcal{M}_i$ for each image i. We found Otsu's method to be the most effective at isolating subjects in cross-image attention maps compared to other thresholding schemes such as Sauvola, Niblack and Adaptive thresholding.

3.2 Boosting Subject Consistency

To prevent unwanted consistency in background patches across images, we use subject masks [38], obtained in Eq. 2. Unlike ConsiStory [37], we aggregate cross-attention maps only from the current generation timestep to prevent overhead of storing the cross-attention maps from previous generation timesteps. This temporal optimization enables *StorySync* to achieve superior subject consistency with less computational cost while it's more responsive to the evolving state of the generation process.

Cross-Image Attention Sharing. We enable controlled interaction between patches in the current image and those sampled from subject regions across other images in the batch of size N (Fig. 3). By utilizing the subject masks $\mathcal{M}_i$ (see Eq. 2), we constrain attention calculation to ensure information flows exclusively between subject-specific regions across different images while preserving standard self-attention within each individual image. This feature of StorySync also consequently allows character transfer across stories without any model retraining, (please see more details in Appendix A) via shared extracted attention features.

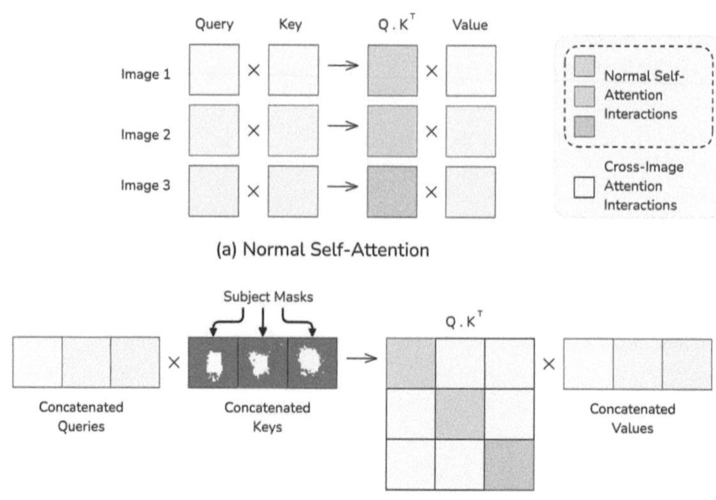

(a) Normal Self-Attention

(b) Cross-Image Attention Sharing

Fig. 3. Cross-Image Attention Sharing. Contrary to normal Attention Calculation (a), we enable interaction among the Query, Key, and Value tensors from subject regions across images (b).

To enforce these constraints, we define a propagation mask Γ_i, which determines which regions in other images can attend to the current image:

$$\Gamma_i = \bigoplus_{j=1}^{N} \delta_{ij} \mathcal{M}_j, \quad \text{where} \quad \delta_{ij} = \begin{cases} \mathbf{1}, & j = i \\ \mathcal{M}_j, & j \neq i \end{cases}. \tag{4}$$

Here, δ_{ij} ensures that the propagation masks includes both self and cross-image subject masks to preventing background interference while preserving self-image features during attention calculation.

Once the Query, Key, and Value tensors are obtained for each image in the batch (see Appendix A, for QKV extraction), we stack the obtained matrices:

$$Q_{\text{all}} = \bigcup_{j=1}^{N} Q_j, \quad K_{\text{all}} = \bigcup_{j=1}^{N} K_j, \quad V_{\text{all}} = \bigcup_{j=1}^{N} V_j \tag{5}$$

Here, $\bigcup$ denotes a set-like stacking operation that preserves individual image structures but allows joint computations across images.

The attention mechanism then becomes:

$$\mathcal{A}_i = \text{softmax}\left(\frac{Q_i(K_{\text{all}})^T}{\sqrt{d_k}} + \log \Gamma_i\right), \tag{6}$$

$$h_i = \mathcal{A}_i \cdot V_{\text{all}}. \tag{7}$$

where $\mathcal{A}_i$ represents the attention matrix, where regions with $\Gamma_i = 0$ are assigned $-\infty$ before applying softmax, ensuring restricted interactions and h_i is the output activation incorporating information from relevant subject regions across all images in the batch.

Regional Feature Harmonization. We propose Regional Feature Harmonization (RFH) based on the principle that semantically equivalent regions across generated images should maintain visual coherence while preserving their contextual uniqueness. We use a distribution-based correspondence approach that identifies and aligns similar regions across the image batch. Unlike static feature injection approaches [38] that rely on pre-computed DIFT embeddings [36], our method calculates feature alignments in real-time during de-noising iterations, as visualized in Fig. 2-right.

RFH utilizes intermediary region representations $\mathcal{R}_i$ from self-attention block, which capture rich textural and structural information. To identify optimal region correspondences between images i (I_i) and j (I_j), we formulate a region-wise compatibility function:

$$\mathcal{H}_{i,j}(r,\omega) = \frac{\exp(\langle \mathcal{R}_i(r), \mathcal{R}j(\omega)\rangle/\tau)}{\sum_{\omega' \in \Omega_j} \exp(\langle \mathcal{R}_i(r), \mathcal{R}_j(\omega')\rangle/\tau)} \tag{8}$$

where $\langle \cdot, \cdot \rangle$ denotes normalized inner product, and Ω_j is defined as the index set of foreground patches belonging to an image I_j, and τ is a temperature parameter. The optimal region mapping function $\mathcal{C}_i(r, I_j)$ for the region r of I_i and all regions of I_j is then obtained:

$$\mathcal{C}_i(r, I_j) = \omega^* \quad \text{where} \quad \omega^* = \underset{\omega \in \Omega_j}{\mathrm{argmax}}, \mathcal{H}_{i,j}(r,\omega), j \neq i \tag{9}$$

The corresponding regions are then harmonized through an adaptive regional fusion mechanism:

$$\hat{\mathcal{R}}_i(r) = \mathcal{R}_i(r) + \gamma \cdot \mathcal{M}_i(r) \cdot (\mathcal{R}_j(\mathcal{C}_i(r, I_j)) - \mathcal{R}_i(r)) \tag{10}$$

where γ represents the harmonization coefficient. The term $(\mathcal{R}_j(\mathcal{C}_i(r, I_j)) - \mathcal{R}_i(r))$ represents the feature adaptation vector needed to transform region r's features to more closely match its correspondence in image I_j. By adding a scaled version of this difference vector to the original region features, we're effectively pushing the region's representation toward its correspondence in feature space. With subject mask $\mathcal{M}_i(r)$, we restrict harmonization to subject regions to keep background features unaffected. Additionally, Otsu's Thresholding [24] limits harmonization only to regions with sufficiently high correspondence. RFH adaptively aligns overlapping visual regions by modulating intermediate features. This is more than subregion alignment: it allows consistent fusion of subject and scene. Its quantitative impact and the role of the strength parameter γ are evaluated in the Quantitative ablation table in Appendix A.

3.3 Boosting Prompt Adherence

Since early generation steps heavily influence layout formation [4, 26], some works disable consistent subject generation during these steps to allow pose variation at the cost of subject similarity. ConsiStory [38] performs vanilla query blending to incorporate vanilla subject poses, however, the pose diversity is diluted due to the integration of query blending steps directly in image generation timesteps. We introduce a Base Layout Interpolation (BLI) method to incorporate the pose information from the images generated by the base model into our generated images.

BLI is implemented in two steps and it helps *StorySync* achieve high level of prompt adherence. Initially, we start image generation using the vanilla base model and at each timestep t, and in each self-attention layer l of the model, we cache the intermediate patch embeddings $X^l_{t,cached}$. These embeddings capture rich compositional information from the prompt-driven, unconstrained generation process. Next, we start the consistency-enhanced image generation process, and during each timestep t, the patch embeddings in each self-attention layer $X^l_{t,consist}$ are adaptively integrated with the compositional guidance from the cached embeddings:

$$
\begin{aligned}
&\text{Step 1:}\quad \text{Vanilla denoising and cache embeddings}\\
&\qquad X^l_{t,\text{cached}} \leftarrow \text{Denoise}_{\text{vanilla}}(z_t, l)\quad \forall t \in T, \forall l \in L\\
&\text{Step 2:}\quad \text{Cosistency-enhanced denoising with alignment}\\
&\qquad X^l_{t,\text{consist}} \leftarrow \text{Denoise}_{\text{consistent}}(z_t, l)\\
&\qquad X^l_{t,\text{final}} \leftarrow (1 - \lambda) \cdot X^l_{t,\text{consist}} + \lambda \cdot X^l_{t,\text{cached}}
\end{aligned}
\tag{11}
$$

where λ controls the degree of interpolation, and T is the number of timesteps we perform BLI for.

As shown in Fig. 2, we are able adapt the poses and layouts of the subjects to their layouts as generated by the base model. By decoupling the embedding caching step from the consistency-enhanced generation step, we incorporate diverse compositional information that might otherwise be homogenized by consistency mechanisms. To further enhance prompt adherence, we introduce dropouts in the different sections of our approach that boost subject consistency: 1) Cross-Image Attention Sharing, 2) Regional Feature Harmonization, and 3) in the subject masks.

4 Experiments

4.1 Qualitative Analysis

In Fig. 4, we present qualitative comparisons of our approach with state-of-the-art training-free approaches [38, 49]. For comparison, for each prompt p, we generate the output image using ConsiStory [38], StoryDiffusion [49], and *StorySync* on a pre-trained SDXL model. From the Fig. 4, we can observe that our approach achieves a high degree of subject consistency while maintaining strong adherence to the input text prompts. While ConsiStory [38] is able to generate visually similar subjects, the alignment of the generated images is low, and, in the case of StoryDiffusion [49], the subjects follow the input prompts but sometimes lack visual subject consistency. Our approach achieves the best balance between subject consistency and prompt adherence.

Fig. 4. Qualitative Results. While ConsiStory [38] achieves subject consistency, it sometimes has problems adhering to subject prompts (e.g. in *girl* and *person* examples, it generates same poses irrespective of prompt), StoryDiffusion [49] struggles with subject consistency (e.g. in *dragon* example) in some cases because it does not use subject masking. Our approach achieves overall excellent subject consistency while also following the instructions provided by the input prompts.

4.2   Quantitative Analysis

We evaluate *StorySync* using quantitative metrics to compare the prompt relevance and the visual similarity of generated subjects. We utilize the ConsiStory benchmark [38] for evaluations. To quantify both prompt adherence and subject similarity across the generated images, we employ *CLIP-score* [29] as our primary evaluation metric. We denote the score for prompt adherence using CLIP embeddings as CLIP-T and for subject similarity as CLIP-I as used in previous similar works [23]. We use Learned Perceptual Image Patch Similarity (LPIPS)

Table 1. Quantitative Analysis. We compare the performance of our approach against Consistory [38] and StoryDiffusion [49] on *SDXL* model. The best score in each column is highlighted in **bold**. Our approach achieves best scores on perceptual similarity metrics (CLIP-I, and DreamSim) and also competitive scores in prompt alignment metric (CLIP-T). Additionally, we present the scores of our approach on *Kandinsky 3*, and *FLUX.1* models. Base model scores are for reference only.

Method	Base Model	CLIP-T↑	CLIP-I↑	LPIPS↑	DreamSim↓
Base SDXL	-	0.8749	0.7819	0.3497	0.5263
Base Kandinsky 3	-	0.8758	0.7944	0.3239	0.4929
Base FLUX.1	-	0.8968	0.8026	0.3320	0.4806
ConsiStory	SDXL	0.8071	0.8289	0.3996	0.3440
StoryDiffusion	SDXL	**0.8126**	0.8572	**0.4198**	0.3589
StorySync (Ours)	SDXL	0.8108	**0.8735**	0.4143	**0.2869**
StorySync (Ours)	Kandinsky 3	0.8075	0.8763	0.4091	0.2804
StorySync (Ours)	FLUX.1-schnell	0.8244	0.8765	0.4039	0.2883

[46] and DreamSim [8] to measure the similarity of generated subjects in the images. Background of the images is removed using Carvekit to measure the perceptual similarity of only the subjects. It is to be noted that during evaluation *DreamSim* scores should be given more preference, as they better align with human perceptual assessment of image similarity [8]. In contrast, LPIPS [46] primarily quantifies visual similarity based on spatial layout.

In Table 1, we report the quantitative comparison of our approach *StorySync*, against SOTA consistent subject generation approaches such as ConsiStory [38] and StoryDiffusion [49]. From the Table 1, we can see that *StorySync* achieves the best scores CLIP-I and DreamSim metrics, compared to ConsiStory [38], and StoryDiffusion [49] when evaluated on SDXL model. StoryDiffusion [49] shows marginally higher on LPIPS scores mainly due to its random masking approach during attention sharing, which induces feature averaging across subjects. However, this metric advantage does not necessarily translate to better visual coherence in generated subjects, as emphasized by Tewel et al. [38].

4.3   Ablation

For this study, we disable a component of our approach one at a time, while keeping all the other components enabled. We generate 5 images of a simple subject (*cat*), with rudimentary prompts to prevent any interference in the experiment due to prompt complexity. In Fig. 5, we can observe that without any of the components of our approach enabled, the subject *cat* is visually dissimilar in all 5 generated images. When we disable the subject masks, the visual appearance and layout of the subject, as well as the backgrounds are identical in images. We also observe deformation of some subject regions due to uncontrolled RFH in

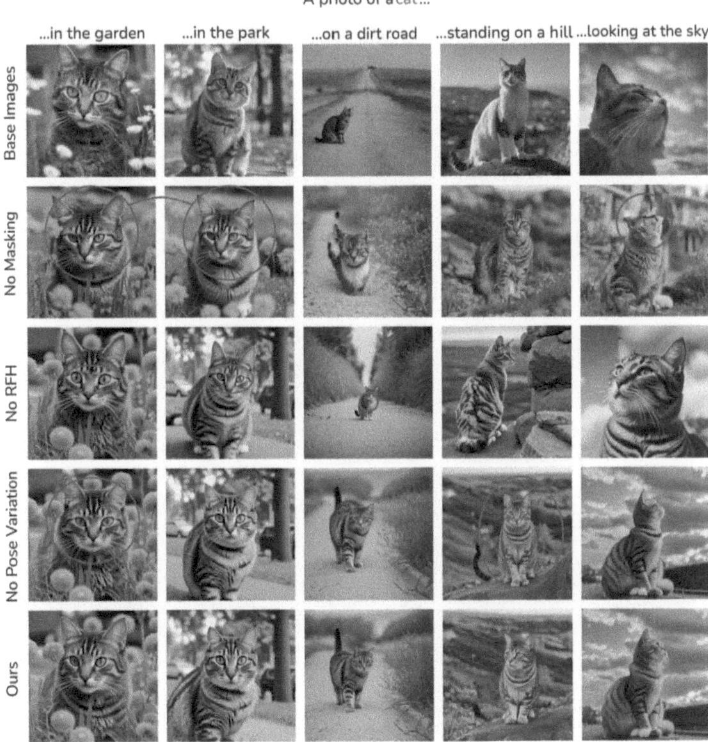

Fig. 5. Ablation Study. Without using subject masks, we observe similarity in subject poses and some deformation (red circle in second row); Without RFH, smaller details of subject such as the eyes and coat pattern are less similar; Images without Pose variation techniques (BLI and Dropouts) have a cat that faces only forward in all images. (Color figure online)

background regions. Hence, subject masks play an important role in generating visually appealing subjects in a visual story with consistent subjects.

Without RFH, there is some deterioration in subject similarity (Fig. 5). Especially the image for the prompt *"a photo of a cat on a dirt road"*, in which the subject no longer resembles other subjects. When disabling pose variation techniques, we observe increased similarity in subject poses across the images, highlighting the importance of BLI and Dropouts in enforcing prompt adherence and layout diversity. Please find further ablation results with the quantitative effects of our approach's components in Appendix A.

4.4   Limitations

One limitation of *StorySync* is its dependence on subject masks from cross-attention maps. If these masks fail to align with subject regions, it can cause

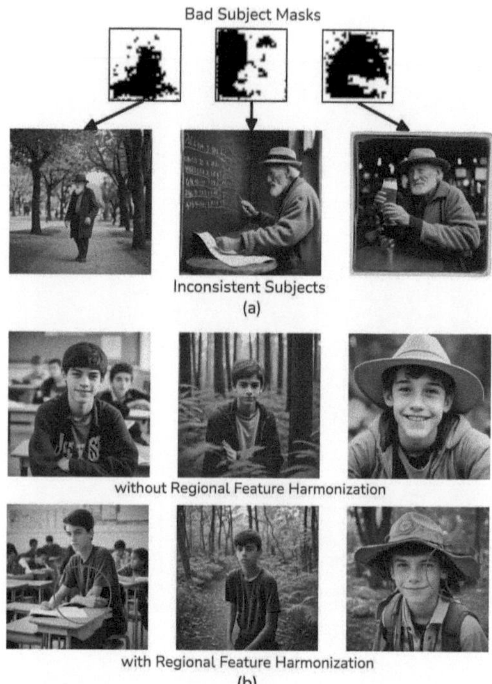

Fig. 6. Limitations: (a) Incorrect subject masks can block attention sharing and therefore lead to inconsistency; (b) Subject deformation (red circle) may occur when unrelated regions are fused with the subject regions. (Color figure online)

inconsistencies in the rendered subject across different images (Fig. 6a). Additionally, Regional Feature Harmonization can occasionally misidentify corresponding regions based on color, texture, or pattern similarity. Such misalignment can deform the generated subject or introduce inconsistencies in fine details, as seen in Fig. 6b. However, these issues occur in only a small fraction of cases.

5   Conclusion

We introduced *StorySync*, an approach for subject consistency in text-to-image diffusion models, a critical aspect for applications like visual storytelling, animation, and content creation. Building upon previous training-free consistency approaches, we developed a comprehensive pipeline that integrates three key components: Masked cross-Image Attention Sharing, Regional Feature Harmonization, and Base Layout Interpolation. Our extensive experiments demonstrate that *StorySync* achieves superior performance in comparison to SOTA training-free consistent subject generation approaches in both subject consistency and prompt adherence. Notably, *StorySync* is model-agnostic and can be integrated with any state-of-the-art diffusion model without additional training. Our evaluations with SDXL, Kandinsky 3, and FLUX.1-schnell, demonstrate superior quality with these models. *StorySync* enhances consistency of the generated subjects while also ensuring sufficient creative diversity.

References

1. Arar, M., et al.: Domain-agnostic tuning-encoder for fast personalization of text-to-image models. In: SIGGRAPH Asia 2023 Conference Papers (2023). https://api.semanticscholar.org/CorpusID:259847716
2. Arkhipkin, V., et al.: Kandinsky 3.0 technical report (2024). https://arxiv.org/abs/2312.03511
3. Avrahami, O., et al.: The chosen one: consistent characters in text-to-image diffusion models. In: Special Interest Group on Computer Graphics and Interactive Techniques Conference Conference Papers 2024, SIGGRAPH 2024, pp. 1–12. ACM (2024). https://doi.org/10.1145/3641519.3657430
4. Balaji, Y., et al.: eDiff-I: text-to-image diffusion models with an ensemble of expert denoisers. arXiv abs/2211.01324 (2022). https://api.semanticscholar.org/CorpusID:253254800
5. Cao, M., Wang, X., Qi, Z., Shan, Y., Qie, X., Zheng, Y.: Masactrl: tuning-free mutual self-attention control for consistent image synthesis and editing. In: 2023 IEEE/CVF International Conference on Computer Vision (ICCV), pp. 22503–22513 (2023). https://api.semanticscholar.org/CorpusID:258179432
6. Dong, Z., Wei, P., Lin, L.: DreamArtist: Towards Controllable One-Shot Text-to-Image Generation via Positive-Negative Prompt-Tuning (2023). http://arxiv.org/abs/2211.11337, arXiv:2211.11337
7. Feng, Z., et al.: Improved visual story generation with adaptive context modeling. arXiv preprint arXiv:2305.16811 (2023)
8. Fu, S., et al.: Dreamsim: learning new dimensions of human visual similarity using synthetic data. arXiv preprint arXiv:2306.09344 (2023)
9. Gal, R., et al.: An image is worth one word: personalizing text-to-image generation using textual inversion. arXiv abs/2208.01618 (2022). https://api.semanticscholar.org/CorpusID:251253049
10. Gal, R., et al.: An Image is Worth One Word: Personalizing Text-to-Image Generation using Textual Inversion (2022). http://arxiv.org/abs/2208.01618. arXiv:2208.01618
11. Gal, R., Arar, M., Atzmon, Y., Bermano, A.H., Chechik, G., Cohen-Or, D.: Encoder-based Domain Tuning for Fast Personalization of Text-to-Image Models (2023). http://arxiv.org/abs/2302.12228. arXiv:2302.12228
12. Gong, Y., et al.: Talecrafter: interactive story visualization with multiple characters. arXiv preprint arXiv:2305.18247 (2023)
13. Gu, Y., et al.: Mix-of-show: decentralized low-rank adaptation for multi-concept customization of diffusion models. arXiv abs/2305.18292 (2023). https://api.semanticscholar.org/CorpusID:258960192
14. He, H., et al.: Dreamstory: open-domain story visualization by LLM-guided multi-subject consistent diffusion. arXiv preprint arXiv:2407.12899 (2024)
15. He, J., Tuo, Y., Chen, B., Zhong, C., Geng, Y., Bo, L.: Anystory: towards unified single and multiple subject personalization in text-to-image generation. arXiv preprint arXiv:2501.09503 (2025)

16. Ho, J., Jain, A., Abbeel, P.: Denoising diffusion probabilistic models. arXiv preprint arxiv:2006.11239 (2020)
17. Huang, Z., Wu, T., Jiang, Y., Chan, K.C.K., Liu, Z.: ReVersion: Diffusion-Based Relation Inversion from Images (2023). http://arxiv.org/abs/2303.13495. arXiv:2303.13495
18. Jeong, H., Kwon, G., Ye, J.C.: Zero-shot generation of coherent storybook from plain text story using diffusion models. arXiv preprint arXiv:2302.03900 (2023)
19. Kumari, N., Zhang, B., Zhang, R., Shechtman, E., Zhu, J.Y.: Multi-concept customization of text-to-image diffusion. In: 2023 IEEE/CVF Conference on Computer Vision and Pattern Recognition (CVPR), pp. 1931–1941. IEEE, Vancouver, BC, Canada (2023). https://doi.org/10.1109/CVPR52729.2023.00192. https://ieeexplore.ieee.org/document/10203856/
20. Li, D., Li, J., Hoi, S.C.H.: Blip-diffusion: pre-trained subject representation for controllable text-to-image generation and editing. arXiv abs/2305.14720 (2023). https://api.semanticscholar.org/CorpusID:258865473
21. Liu, C., Wu, H., Zhong, Y., Zhang, X., Xie, W.: Intelligent grimm - open-ended visual storytelling via latent diffusion models. In: 2024 IEEE/CVF Conference on Computer Vision and Pattern Recognition (CVPR), pp. 6190–6200 (2023). https://api.semanticscholar.org/CorpusID:258999141
22. Liu, C., Wu, H., Zhong, Y., Zhang, X., Wang, Y., Xie, W.: Intelligent grimm-open-ended visual storytelling via latent diffusion models. In: Proceedings of the IEEE/CVF Conference on Computer Vision and Pattern Recognition, pp. 6190–6200 (2024)
23. Liu, T., et al.: One-prompt-one-story: Free-lunch consistent text-to-image generation using a single prompt. arXiv preprint arXiv:2501.13554 (2025)
24. Otsu, N.: A threshold selection method from gray-level histograms. IEEE Trans. Syst. Man Cybern. **9**, 62–66 (1979). https://api.semanticscholar.org/CorpusID:15326934
25. Pan, X., Qin, P., Li, Y., Xue, H., Chen, W.: Synthesizing coherent story with auto-regressive latent diffusion models. In: 2024 IEEE/CVF Winter Conference on Applications of Computer Vision (WACV), pp. 2908–2918 (2022). https://api.semanticscholar.org/CorpusID:253734226
26. Patashnik, O., Garibi, D., Azuri, I., Averbuch-Elor, H., Cohen-Or, D.: Localizing object-level shape variations with text-to-image diffusion models. In: 2023 IEEE/CVF International Conference on Computer Vision (ICCV), pp. 22994–23004 (2023). https://api.semanticscholar.org/CorpusID:257632209
27. Po, R., Yang, G., Aberman, K., Wetzstein, G.: Orthogonal adaptation for modular customization of diffusion models. In: 2024 IEEE/CVF Conference on Computer Vision and Pattern Recognition (CVPR), pp. 7964–7973 (2023). https://api.semanticscholar.org/CorpusID:265659333
28. Podell, D., et al.: SDXL: improving latent diffusion models for high-resolution image synthesis. arXiv preprint arXiv:2307.01952 (2023)
29. Radford, A., et al.: Learning transferable visual models from natural language supervision. In: International Conference on Machine Learning, pp. 8748–8763. PmLR (2021)
30. Richardson, E., Goldberg, K., Alaluf, Y., Cohen-Or, D.: Conceptlab: creative generation using diffusion prior constraints. arXiv abs/2308.02669 (2023). https://api.semanticscholar.org/CorpusID:260683062
31. Rombach, R., Blattmann, A., Lorenz, D., Esser, P., Ommer, B.: High-resolution image synthesis with latent diffusion models. CoRR abs/2112.10752 (2021). https://arxiv.org/abs/2112.10752

32. Ronneberger, O., Fischer, P., Brox, T.: U-net: convolutional networks for biomedical image segmentation. CoRR abs/1505.04597 (2015). http://arxiv.org/abs/1505.04597

33. Ruiz, N., Li, Y., Jampani, V., Pritch, Y., Rubinstein, M., Aberman, K.: Dreambooth: fine tuning text-to-image diffusion models for subject-driven generation. In: 2023 IEEE/CVF Conference on Computer Vision and Pattern Recognition (CVPR), pp. 22500–22510 (2022). https://api.semanticscholar.org/CorpusID:251800180

34. Shi, J., Xiong, W., Lin, Z., Jung, H.J.: Instantbooth: personalized text-to-image generation without test-time finetuning. In: 2024 IEEE/CVF Conference on Computer Vision and Pattern Recognition (CVPR), pp. 8543–8552 (2023). https://api.semanticscholar.org/CorpusID:258041269

35. Su, S., Guo, L., Gao, L., Shen, H., Song, J.: Make-a-storyboard: a general framework for storyboard with disentangled and merged control. arXiv abs/2312.07549 (2023). https://api.semanticscholar.org/CorpusID:266191147

36. Tang, L., Jia, M., Wang, Q., Phoo, C.P., Hariharan, B.: Emergent correspondence from image diffusion. arXiv abs/2306.03881 (2023). https://api.semanticscholar.org/CorpusID:259089017

37. Tewel, Y., Gal, R., Samuel, D., Atzmon, Y., Wolf, L., Chechik, G.: Add-it: training-free object insertion in images with pretrained diffusion models. arXiv preprint arXiv:2411.07232 (2024)

38. Tewel, Y., et al.: Training-free consistent text-to-image generation. ACM Trans. Graph. (TOG) **43**(4), 1–18 (2024)

39. Wang, J., et al.: Oneactor: consistent character generation via cluster-conditioned guidance. arXiv preprint arXiv:2404.10267 (2024)

40. Wang, J., et al.: Spotactor: training-free layout-controlled consistent image generation. arXiv preprint arXiv:2409.04801 (2024)

41. Wang, Q., et al.: Characterfactory: sampling consistent characters with GANs for diffusion models. arXiv preprint arXiv:2404.15677 (2024)

42. Wei, Y., Zhang, Y., Ji, Z., Bai, J., Zhang, L., Zuo, W.: Elite: encoding visual concepts into textual embeddings for customized text-to-image generation. In: 2023 IEEE/CVF International Conference on Computer Vision (ICCV), pp. 15897–15907 (2023). https://api.semanticscholar.org/CorpusID:257219968

43. Wu, J.Z., et al.: Tune-a-video: one-shot tuning of image diffusion models for text-to-video generation. In: Proceedings of the IEEE/CVF International Conference on Computer Vision, pp. 7623–7633 (2023)

44. Yang, S., et al.: Seed-story: multimodal long story generation with large language model. arXiv preprint arXiv:2407.08683 (2024)

45. Ye, H., Zhang, J., Liu, S., Han, X., Yang, W.: IP-adapter: text compatible image prompt adapter for text-to-image diffusion models. arXiv preprint arXiv:2308.06721 (2023)

46. Zhang, R., Isola, P., Efros, A.A., Shechtman, E., Wang, O.: The unreasonable effectiveness of deep features as a perceptual metric. In: Proceedings of the IEEE Conference on Computer Vision and Pattern Recognition, pp. 586–595 (2018)

47. Zhang, Y., et al.: Inversion-based style transfer with diffusion models. In: 2023 IEEE/CVF Conference on Computer Vision and Pattern Recognition (CVPR), pp. 10146–10156. IEEE, Vancouver, BC, Canada (2023). https://doi.org/10.1109/CVPR52729.2023.00978. https://ieeexplore.ieee.org/document/10203866/

48. Zheng, S., Fu, Y.: Contextualstory: consistent visual storytelling with spatially-enhanced and storyline context. arXiv preprint arXiv:2407.09774 (2024)

49. Zhou, Y., Zhou, D., Cheng, M.M., Feng, J., Hou, Q.: Storydiffusion: consistent self-attention for long-range image and video generation. Adv. Neural. Inf. Process. Syst. **37**, 110315–110340 (2024)
50. Zhou, Z., Li, J., Li, H., Chen, N., Tang, X.: Storymaker: towards holistic consistent characters in text-to-image generation. arXiv preprint arXiv:2409.12576 (2024)
51. Zhu, J., Ma, H., Chen, J., Yuan, J.: DomainStudio: Fine-Tuning Diffusion Models for Domain-Driven Image Generation using Limited Data (2023). http://arxiv.org/abs/2306.14153. arXiv:2306.14153

Structured Universal Adversarial Attacks on Object Detection for Video Sequences

Sven Jacob[1,2(✉)], Weijia Shao[1], and Gjergji Kasneci[2,3]

[1] Federal Institute for Occupational Safety and Health (BAuA), Dresden, Germany
`{jacob.sven,shao.weijia}@baua.bund.de`
[2] School of Computation, Information and Technology, Technical University of Munich, Munich, Germany
[3] School of Social Sciences and Technology, Technical University of Munich, Munich, Germany

Abstract. Video-based object detection plays a vital role in safety-critical applications. While deep learning-based object detectors have achieved impressive performance, they remain vulnerable to adversarial attacks, particularly those involving universal perturbations. In this work, we propose a minimally distorted universal adversarial attack tailored for video object detection, which leverages nuclear norm regularization to promote structured perturbations concentrated in the background. To optimize this formulation efficiently, we employ an adaptive, optimistic exponentiated gradient method that enhances both scalability and convergence. Our results demonstrate that the proposed attack outperforms both low-rank projected gradient descent and Frank-Wolfe-based attacks in effectiveness while maintaining high stealthiness. All code and data are publicly available at https://github.com/jsve96/AO-Exp-Attack.

Keywords: Adversarial Attacks · Object Detection · AI Safety · Robustness

1 Introduction

Video-based object detection plays an increasingly important role in safety monitoring systems for machine and occupational environments, enabling the localization of human workers, tools, and obstacles to identify potential hazards before they escalate into accidents [1,8,24]. As a core task in computer vision, object detection involves identifying and localizing semantic objects within images or videos. Recent advances in deep learning have significantly improved object detection performance, enabling its deployment in a range of safety-critical domains, ranging from autonomous driving [7,12], real-time surveillance [2,19], and industrial applications [27,41]. In these contexts, object detection not only contributes to operational efficiency but also serves as a first line of defense in preventing unsafe interactions between humans and machines.

© The Author(s), under exclusive license to Springer Nature Switzerland AG 2026
M. Keuper and F. Locatello (Eds.): DAGM GCPR 2025, LNCS 16125, pp. 171–185, 2026.
https://doi.org/10.1007/978-3-032-12840-9_12

Most state-of-the-art object detection methods rely on Deep Learning (DL) techniques [40]. Despite their substantial advancements over the past decade, DL models are vulnerable to adversarial attacks (AT) [15,35], which craft perturbations to the inputs to mislead the model into making incorrect predictions. While research on adversarial attacks in image classification has been extensively studied [10], such attacks on object detection systems, especially in the context of video data, have received considerably less attention [26]. At first glance, adversarial attacks on video object detection may appear straightforward, as they seem to require applying existing techniques for attacking static object detectors to each frame of the video clip [18,36,37]. In [23], the authors have empirically proved the existence of universal adversarial perturbations against all frames, which cause object detectors to fail on most of the frames [23,38]. Effective universal attacks pose a more significant threat as they are transferable across frames without further accessing the target model, and are more convenient to be applied in the real physical world [23,26].

Although prior studies have aimed to generate adversarial examples posing greater threats, they have predominantly focused on perturbations bounded by ℓ_2 and ℓ_∞ norms [26]. In image-based attacks, ℓ_1-bounded perturbations can be especially threatening due to their ability to introduce sparse yet imperceptible changes [9]. However, in video-based settings, the direct application of ℓ_1 attacks often results in visible patches on moving objects across frames. This not only reduces the sparsity but also challenges stealthiness in dynamic scenes. As adversarial defense mechanisms continue to evolve, identifying a broader range of attack strategies is essential for robust evaluation and understanding of their limitations.

Building on robust principal component analysis for segmentation [4] and structured adversarial perturbation methods for image classification [20], this work introduces a novel strategy that leverages structured but non-suspicious background modifications for object vanishing attacks. To this end, we propose a minimally distorted attack method based on nuclear norm regularization. Figure 1 provides a preliminary visual comparison illustrating the difference between ℓ_1 attacks, which tend to produce sparse patches on moving objects, and our nuclear norm-based attack, which generates more structured perturbations primarily in the background. While nuclear norm regularization provides a powerful tool for promoting low-rank structure in background perturbations, it poses significant optimization challenges. To address this, we employ optimistic exponentiated gradient descent [31], which enables efficient and scalable optimization under nuclear norm regularization. We evaluate our proposed object vanishing attack on public video datasets and video object detection models. The results demonstrate that our method effectively generates structured background perturbations that consistently remove the bounding boxes predicted by these models. Compared to existing nuclear norm-based attack approaches, our method achieves superior attack success while being significantly more computationally efficient.

Our main contributions are summarized as follows:

Fig. 1. The ℓ_1 attack introduces flickering noise that trails moving objects and spreads across the street in subsequent frames, whereas the nuclear norm-based attack perturbs orthogonal spatial patterns of the video frames, resulting in more structured and spatially coherent perturbations.

- We introduce a minimally distorted universal attack formulation based on nuclear norm regularization, which promotes structured perturbations of the orthogonal spatial patterns across video frames (Equation (1)).
- To efficiently solve the associated optimization problem, we adapt an adaptive optimistic exponentiated gradient descent method, enabling scalable optimization under nuclear norm constraints (Algorithm 1).
- We conduct comprehensive evaluations on public video datasets and a state-of-the-art video object detection model, demonstrating that our method consistently suppresses bounding boxes through subtle background changes (Fig. 4, Fig. 5a).
- Our method achieves superior attack success and computational efficiency compared to existing nuclear norm-based adversarial attacks (Table 2).

The rest of the paper is organized as follows. Section 2 reviews related work, and Sect. 3 introduces the notation used throughout the paper. In Sect. 4, we present our attack algorithm, which is evaluated on real-world video object detection datasets and the popular object detection model Mask-RCNN in Sect. 5. Finally, Sect. 6 concludes the paper by discussing the limitations of our approach and outlining future research directions.

2   Related Work

While the literature on adversarial attacks in image classification is extensive, research on adversarial attacks targeting object detection, especially in video settings, remains relatively limited. We refer to recent surveys [3, 26] for an overview of existing techniques and challenges in this area. This work focuses on object vanishing attacks, which aim to make the model fail to detect certain objects in the input frames. Several works have explored object vanishing attacks on images by manipulating bounding box outputs using adversarial perturbations, either constrained within ℓ_2 or ℓ_∞ norm balls or applied as localized patches on foreground objects [18,23,36–39].

The methods listed above can be directly applied to each frame of a video independently. However, applying attacks separately to each frame ignores the temporal coherence of video data, often resulting in flickering perturbations across frames that reduce stealth. Universal adversarial perturbations [25], which are input-agnostic and applied uniformly across inputs, offer a more natural fit for object detection in video settings [23,38]. Yet, the existing universal attacks [23,38] apply noise uniformly over the entire image without leveraging the spatial structure unique to videos.

The investigation of low-rank structures for high-dimensional problems has a long history following the manifold hypothesis, which states that high-dimensional data tend to live near a lower-dimensional manifold [11]. This assumption led to many dimensionality reduction methods in general but was also utilized in crafting adversarial perturbations using Autoencoder [13,33], PCA [21,22], or UMAP [34]. More recently, researchers have also focused on low-rank representation for adversarial attacks induced by nuclear norm regularization [20]. Moreover, a combination of nuclear norm regularization and optimizing adversarial perturbation using projected gradient descent (PGD) was introduced in [30]. In [29], a group-wise sparse attack is generated, which only perturbs a few semantically meaningful areas of an image.

3   Notation

Throughout the paper, we write $x \in [0,1]^{H \times W \times C}$ for an image with height H, width W, and C channels. Suppose an object detection model $f : [0,1]^{H \times W \times C} \to \mathcal{S}$ that takes an input image and outputs a set $\mathcal{S}$. The minimal output set is a collection of bounding boxes and labels for each detected object within an image. The output depends on the choice of f, e.g., Mask R-CNN [17] additionally outputs confidence scores $\xi_i \in (0,1]$ and masks $m_i \in [0,1]^{H \times W}$ where i is the index of the corresponding bounding box in $\mathcal{S}$. For vector-valued inputs $x \in \mathbb{R}^n$, the ℓ_p-norm is given by $||x||_p = (\sum_{i=1}^n |x_i|^p)^{\frac{1}{p}}$ for $p \geq 1$.

Recall, for a matrix $A \in \mathbb{R}^{H \times W}$ its singular value decomposition (SVD) is $A = U\Sigma V^T$, where $U \in \mathbb{R}^{H \times H}$ and $V \in \mathbb{R}^{W \times W}$ are orthonormal matrices whose columns are the orthonormal basis for the column and row space of A, and $\Sigma \in \mathbb{R}^{H \times W}$ is a rectangular diagonal matrix storing the singular values $\sigma_i \geq 0$ for $i = 1, \ldots, r$ where $r = \min\{H, W\}$ is the rank of A. Define the function

$$\text{diag} : \mathbb{R}^r \to \mathbb{R}^{H \times W}, \sigma \mapsto \Sigma \text{ with } \Sigma_{ij} = \begin{cases} \sigma_i, & \text{if } i = j \\ 0 & \text{otherwise.} \end{cases}$$

The SVD decomposition can be equivalently written as $A = U \text{diag}(\sigma)V^T$.

The Schatten p-norm of a matrix A is the ℓ_p-norm of the vector of its singular values $||A||_p = (\sum_{i=1}^r (\sigma_i)^p)^{\frac{1}{p}}$. The matrix norm for $p = 2$ is also called Frobenius norm, notated as $||A||_F$. The nuclear norm ($p = 1$) of a matrix A is the ℓ_1-norm of its singular values $||A||_* = \sum_{i=1}^{r} \sigma_i$.

For $p = \infty$, we have the spectral norm of a matrix, which is the largest singular value, $||A||_\infty = \max_{1 \le i \le r} \sigma_i$.

4   Adversarial Attack Formulation

The goal of an adversarial attack is to determine some minimal perturbation δ which maximizes some loss function $\mathcal{L} : \mathcal{S} \mapsto \mathbb{R}_+$ of the object detector f, when added to x. A non-targeted adversarial attack can be formulated as,

$$\min_{\delta \in \mathbb{R}^{H \times W \times C}} \quad - \mathcal{L}(f(x + \delta), f(x)) + \lambda \mathcal{R}(\delta)$$

$$\text{s.t.} \quad x + \delta \in [0, 1]^{H \times W \times C}$$

where $\mathcal{R}$ denotes some regularization of the perturbation and $\lambda > 0$ is the regularization parameter. In the following, we propose to split the loss function into background and foreground loss, $\mathcal{L} = \mathcal{L}_{\text{fg}} + \mathcal{L}_{\text{bg}}$. Consider the set of clean masks $\mathcal{M} = \{m_i | \xi_i > \tau; i \in [S]\}$ obtained with $f(x)$, with a confidence score above τ. We combine all clean masks in $\mathcal{M}$ to obtain a unified mask $m = \sum_{i \in \mathcal{M}} m_i$ for all confident detections and derive a binary mask

$$y_{ij} = \begin{cases} 1 & \text{if } m_{ij} > 0 \\ 0 & \text{otherwise} \end{cases}$$

which we use as the ground-truth segmentation for the clean image. We separate the mask into foreground pixels $\mathcal{F}$ and background pixels $\mathcal{B}$ and calculate the average cross-entropy loss between y and the predicted masks which are the output of $f(x + \delta)$,

$$\mathcal{L}_{\text{fg}} = \frac{1}{|\mathcal{F}|} \sum_{i \in \mathcal{F}} \text{CE}(p_i, y_i), \quad \mathcal{L}_{\text{bg}} = \frac{1}{|\mathcal{B}|} \sum_{i \in \mathcal{B}} \text{CE}(p_i, y_i).$$

Additionally, we seek to guide the model into less confident predictions of bounding boxes, therefore we introduce the confidence loss

$$\mathcal{L}_{\text{conf}} = \sum_{i \in [S]} \xi_i \cdot \mathbf{1}_{(\xi_i > \tau)}$$

which penalizes any predictions above threshold τ - affecting the foreground. In summary, we use a combination of

$$\mathcal{L}_{\text{total}} = \underbrace{\alpha \mathcal{L}_{\text{fg}} + \gamma \mathcal{L}_{\text{conf}}}_{\text{Foreground}} + \underbrace{\beta \mathcal{L}_{\text{bg}}}_{\text{Background}}.$$

Usually, regularization is introduced to ensure a sparse perturbation. For vector-valued inputs, common choices are ℓ_p-norms or the Frobenius ℓ_1-norm, which suppresses the perturbation to have few non-zero values. The nuclear norm is related to the rank of the matrix where the minimization of it leads to sparsity in singular values, resulting in a low-rank matrix. Nuclear norm regularization is popular among image denoising [16] and low-rank matrix approximation. It has also shown promising results in domain generalization [32].

We introduce a combination of Frobenius norm and nuclear norm as the regularizer

$$\mathcal{R}(\delta) = \lambda_1 ||\delta||_* + \lambda_2 ||\delta||_F,$$

which balances sparsity and low-rank of the universal adversarial perturbation.

4.1   Universal Attack

The objective of this work is to generate an adversarial perturbation that is applied uniformly across all frames of a video and degrades the performance of a target model f. Let $\{x_b | 1 \leq b \leq B\}$ be the set of frames in a video clip, where B is the number of frames. We formalize the attack as the following regularized optimization problem

$$\min_{\delta \in \mathbb{R}^{H \times W \times C}} -\frac{1}{B} \sum_{b=1}^{B} \mathcal{L}_{\text{total}}(f(x_b + \delta), f(x_b)) + \sum_{c=1}^{C} (\lambda_1 ||\delta^c||_* + \frac{\lambda_2}{2} ||\delta^c||_F^2). \quad (1)$$

Denote the gradient information

$$\nabla \mathcal{G}(\delta^c) = \frac{1}{B} \sum_{b=1}^{B} \nabla_{\delta^c} \mathcal{L}_{\text{total}}(f(x_b + \delta^c), f(x_b)),$$

which is the loss gradient averaged over all frames concerning a perturbation channel δ^c. Given the access to $\nabla \mathcal{G}(\delta^c)$, we iteratively update each perturbation channel δ^c by applying the adaptive optimistic exponentiated method (AO-Exp) proposed in [31]. The algorithm is described in Algorithm 1.

At each iteration t, in addition to the perturbation δ_t^c, we maintain a decision variable in the form of factors of an SVD decomposition

$$\delta_t^c = U_{c,t} \operatorname{diag}(z_t^c) V_{c,t}^\top$$

for each channel, where $z_t^c \in \mathbb{R}_{\geq 0}^{\min\{W,H\}}$ is the vector of singular values and $U_{c,t} \in \mathbb{R}^{W \times W}, V_{c,t} \in \mathbb{R}^{H \times H}$ are the orthogonal bases. To obtain the intermediate perturbation, we apply the following procedure:

(1) OPTIMISTIC UPDATE: We first perform an optimistic update using the gradient information at iterations t and $t - 1$

$$\eta_t^c \leftarrow \eta_{t-1}^c + t^2 ||\nabla \mathcal{G}(\delta_t^c) - \nabla \mathcal{G}(\delta_{t-1}^c)||_\infty^2$$
$$\bar{z}_{t,i}^c \leftarrow \log(z_{t,i}^c + 1) \text{ for all } i \in \{1, \ldots, \min\{W, H\}\} \quad (2)$$
$$U_{c,t+1} \operatorname{diag}(\theta_t^c) V_{c,t+1}^\top \leftarrow \eta_t^c \cdot U_{c,t} \operatorname{diag}(\bar{z}_t^c) V_{c,t}^\top + (2t + 1) \nabla \mathcal{G}(\delta_t^c) - t \nabla \mathcal{G}(\delta_{t-1}^c)$$

to obtain the orthogonal bases of iteration $t+1$.

(2) SINGULAR VALUES OF DECISION VARIABLE: Then, we find the singular values of the decision variable at iteration $t+1$ by calculating the principal branch of the Lambert function

$$z_{t+1,i}^c = \frac{\eta_t^c}{\lambda_2} W_0 \left(\frac{\lambda_2}{\eta_t^c} \exp \left(\frac{\lambda_2 + \max\{\theta_{t,i}^c - \lambda_1, 0\}}{\eta_t} \right) \right) - 1. \tag{3}$$

(3) CONSTRUCT PERTURBATION: Finally, we obtain the perturbation δ_{t+1}^c by taking the weighted average of $z_1^c, \ldots, z_{t+1}^c$. We propose to use the top k values of the decision variable z_t^c in the reconstruction of δ_{t+1}^c which further compresses the information in δ, thus promoting low-rank with. Let $z_{t,1:k}^c = (z_{t,1}^c, \ldots, z_{t,k}^c, 0, \ldots, 0)$, then the low-rank perturbation is obtained with

$$\delta_{t+1}^c = \frac{2}{t(t+1)} \sum_{s=1}^{t} s \cdot U_{c,t} \operatorname{diag}(z_{s,1:k}^c) V_{c,t}^\top. \tag{4}$$

The per-iteration complexity of the algorithms depends on the complexity of performing the SVD-decomposition and solving the principal branch of the Lambert function.

Algorithm 1. AO-Exp Update

Input: Gradient: $\nabla \mathcal{G}(\delta_t)$, Regularization parameter: $\boldsymbol{\lambda_1, \lambda_2}$.
 1: Initialize δ_0^c, η_0^c, $U_{c,0}$, $V_{c,0}$, z_0^c for all channels $c = 1, \ldots, C$
 2: **for** $t = 1$ to T **do**
 3:     **for** each channel $c = 1$ to C **do**
 4:         (1) OPTIMISTIC UPDATE: Update $U_{c,t+1}$, $V_{c,t+1}$, and θ_t^c ▷ Eq. (2)
 5:         (2) SINGULAR VALUE UPDATE: Compute $z_{t+1,1:k}^c$ ▷ Eq. (3)
 6:         (3) PERTURBATION UPDATE: Compute δ_{t+1}^c ▷ Eq. (4)
 7:     **end for**
 8: **end for**
Output: $\boldsymbol{\delta_{T+1}}$

---

5 Experiments and Evaluation

This section details the empirical evaluation of the proposed algorithms. We first describe the experimental setup, including the baseline attack, metrics, datasets, and models used within this experimental scope. We then present and analyze the results. All code and data used in our experiments are publicly available online[1].

---

[1] https://github.com/jsve96/AO-Exp-Attack.

5.1   Baseline Attack

LoRa-PGD: The low-rank PGD attack is a variation of the projected gradient descent (PGD) that directly searches for a low-rank structured perturbation [30]. The k-th iteration of a PGD attack is the following perturbation

$$\delta_k = \mathcal{P}\left(\delta_{k-1} + \epsilon \frac{\nabla_\delta \mathcal{L}}{||\nabla_\delta \mathcal{L}||}\right),$$

where $\mathcal{P}$ denotes the projection on some feasible set of perturbations. For the LoRa-PGD attack, the perturbation is decomposed into two lower-rank matrices $U \in \mathbb{R}^{H \times r \times C}$ and $V \in \mathbb{R}^{r \times W \times C}$ where $r \leq \min\{H, W\}$, such that each entry of the perturbation for each channel $c \in C$ is given by

$$\delta_{ijc} = (U \otimes V)_{ijc} = \sum_{k=1}^{r} U_{ikc} V_{kjc}.$$

The update rule is applied independently on U and V such that

$$U_k = U_{k-1} + \frac{\nabla_U \mathcal{L}}{||\nabla_U \mathcal{L}||} \qquad V_k = V_{k-1} + \frac{\nabla_V \mathcal{L}}{||\nabla_V \mathcal{L}||}$$

and the updated perturbation is $\delta_{k+1} = (U_{k+1} \otimes V_{k+1})$. Putting this together, in our universal framework, the LoRa-PGD attack has the following formulation:

$$(U_*, V_*) = \begin{cases} \underset{U,V}{\arg\max} & \dfrac{1}{B}\sum_{b=1}^{B} \mathcal{L}_{\text{total}}(f(x_b + \delta), f(x_b)) \\ \text{s.t.} & U \in \mathbb{R}^{H \times r \times C}, V \in \mathbb{R}^{r \times W \times C} \\ & r \leq \min\{H, W\} \quad \text{(rank constraint)} \\ & ||U \otimes V||_* \leq \tau \quad \text{(nuclear norm constraint)} \end{cases}$$

FW-Nucl: The Frank-Wolfe nuclear norm group attack (FW-Nucl) obtains structured adversarial examples by constraining perturbations using nuclear group norm regularization [20]. It iteratively applies the Frank-Wolfe algorithm to construct a sparse adversarial perturbation. In our universal attack formulation, FW-Nucl has the following form:

$$\delta^* = \begin{cases} \underset{\delta \in \mathbb{R}^{H \times W \times C}}{\arg\min} & \dfrac{1}{B}\sum_{b=1}^{B} \mathcal{L}_{\text{total}}(f(x_b + \delta), f(x_b)) \\ \text{s.t.} & ||\delta||_{\mathcal{G},1,p} \leq \epsilon \end{cases}$$

5.2   Metrics

Intersection over Union (IoU), also known as the Jaccardi Index, is a well-known measure for the similarity of two shapes or sets $A, A' \in \mathbb{R}^n$,

$$\text{IoU}(A, A') = \frac{|A \cap A'|}{|A \cup A'|},$$

which is often used as a loss function for bounding box regression [28], where A denotes the predicted bounding box of the vision model and A' is a ground truth location of the bounding box. Suppose there are a total of n ground truth bounding boxes of the vision model using the clean frame x_t, and the adversarial example $x_t + \delta$ leads to m predicted bounding boxes, then the IoU for frame x_t is

$$\mathrm{IoU}_t = \sum_{i=1}^{n} \sum_{j=1}^{m} \mathrm{IoU}(A_i, A'_j).$$

We evaluate the average IoU score over all frames and report the accumulated IoU

$$\mathrm{IoU}_{acc} = \frac{1}{T} \sum_{t=1}^{T} \mathrm{IoU}_t$$

to assess the impact of the adversarial attack on the whole sequence. Moreover, we report the ratio of the sum of bounding boxes of the adversarial video clip and the sum of ground truth bounding boxes for the clean video clip (advBR). The Box Ratio indicates whether all ground truth bounding boxes are removed (advBR $= 0$) or the object detector is fooled when additional bounding boxes appear for the adversarial video frames (advBR > 1). Additionally, we report perceptibility, which we measure based on the mean absolute perturbation (MAP)

$$\mathrm{MAP} = \frac{1}{H \cdot W} \sum_{i,j=1}^{H,W} \sum_{c=1}^{C} |\delta_{ij}^c|.$$

Table 1. Overview of datasets used and key attributes.

Name	Resolution	Scenes	Frames per second	Avg. frames per scene
PETS 2009 S2L1 [14]	768×576	7	7	795
EPFL-RLC [6]	1920×1080	3	60	5000
CW4C	1920×880	15	60	7200

5.3   Datasets

PETS 2009 S2L1 [14]: The PETS 2009 dataset is a benchmark video surveillance dataset designed to evaluate algorithms for multi-camera tracking, crowd analysis, and event detection. It features synchronized footage from multiple camera views capturing various real-world scenarios, such as people walking, meeting, splitting up, or leaving objects behind (Fig. 2 and Table 1). It is widely used in academic research for tasks like people tracking, group activity recognition, and anomaly detection.

Fig. 2. Shows frame number 55 of the PETS 2009 dataset for three different camera views.

EPFL-RLC [6]: The EPFL-RLC dataset is a multi-camera video dataset captured at the Rolex Learning Center of EPFL using three synchronized HD cameras with overlapping fields of view. Each camera records at a resolution of 1920×1080 at 60 frames per second, with the dataset comprising 8,000 frames per view. This dataset is particularly valuable for developing and evaluating multi-view pedestrian detection and tracking algorithms [5].

CW4C[2] (Coldwater 4 corners): This dataset contains 15 video clips from the publicly available CW4C data[3]. The data captures 4 Corners Park, located at the intersection of Chicago St and Marshall St, in Coldwater (Michigan). In order to limit and save computational cost, we applied downsampling and modified the resolution to 960×440 (Fig. 3).

Fig. 3. Shows three frames from the first video clip of the camera capturing the crossroad intersection in Coldwater (CW4C).

5.4   Evaluation

For LoRa-PGD attacks and full AO-Exp attacks, we use 100 iterations to obtain a universal perturbation. We set the regularization parameter λ_1 for Algorithm 1 to $\lambda_1 = 0.1$ for PETS datasets, and set $\lambda_2 = \lambda_1/500$ (CW4C), $\lambda_2 = \lambda_1/10$ (PETS2009). We set $\lambda_1 = 0.75$ and $\lambda_2 = 0.005$ (EPFL-RLC). For FW-Nucl, we set $\epsilon = 40$ for comparable results using the same perturbation budget as for AO-Exp.

Moreover, we set the number of iterations to 30 and use five updates for each line search. For the PGD-LoRa attacks, we report three variants with $r = 10\%, 50\%, 100\%$ of the full rank and set the nuclear norm budget to 60. For the low-rank adaption of AO-Exp, we only use the top value ($k = 1$) in (4) and consider 50 iterations.

---

[2] https://www.coldwater.org/676/Coldwater-Area-Webcams.

[3] https://tinyurl.com/CW4C-Data.

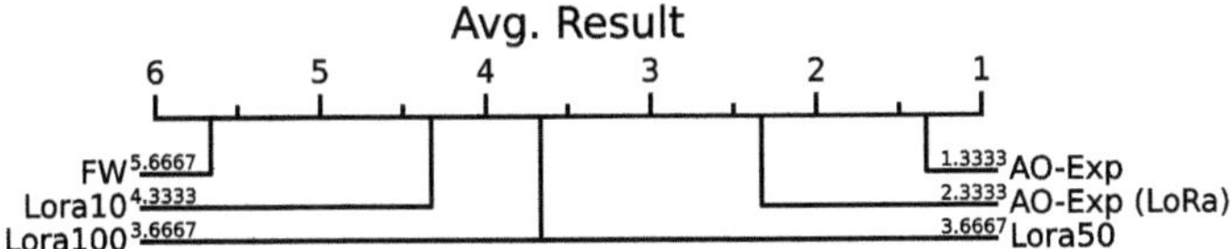

Fig. 4. Shows the critical difference diagram of the average result, obtained based on the scores of IoU_{acc}, advBR, and $||\delta||_*$ (Table 2), across all datasets for each attack method.

We observe that our proposed method, AO-Exp, achieves the best adversarial box ratio across all datasets while minimizing the accumulated IoU and notably minimal nuclear norm, as shown in Table 2. This also holds for the MAP, indicating stealth attacks in general. Notably, our low-rank adaption not only yields comparable results in the average adversarial box ratio but also drastically minimizes the nuclear norm of the perturbation compared to AO-Exp, as shown in Fig. 5a. Our proposed attack method, AO-Exp, and its low-rank adaption surpass the considered baseline attacks across all datasets, averaged over three main metrics, see Fig. 4. Moreover, we observe that different values of k in the update rule of Algorithm 1 yield similar advBR for each camera angle of the EPFL dataset, Fig. 5b. Increasing the number of singular values for the construction of the structured adversarial perturbation enhances the effectiveness of the adversarial attack, as expected.

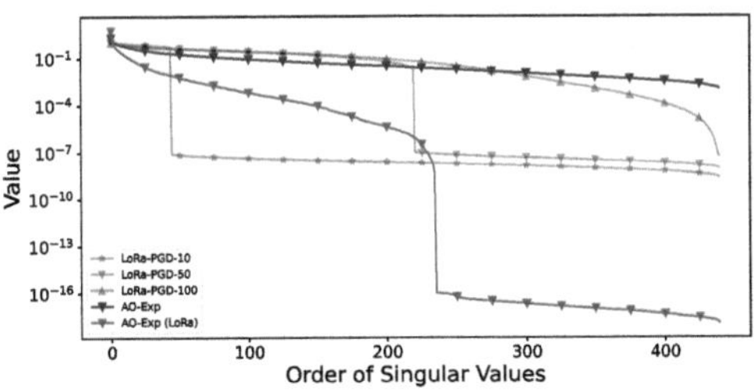

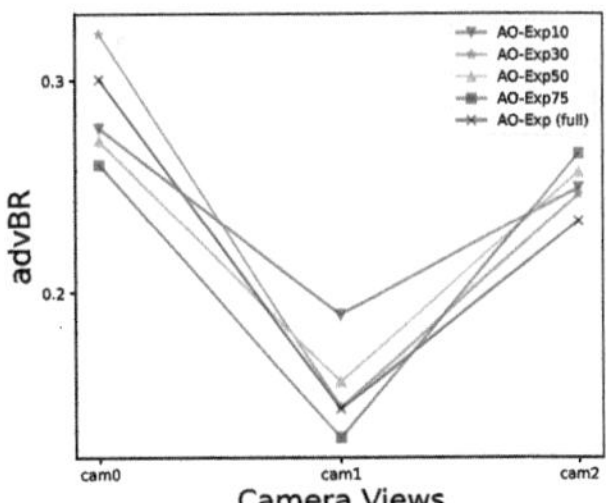

(a) Median singular values of LoRa-PGD attacks, AO-Exp attack, and low-rank adaption (AO-Exp LoRa) for CW4C dataset. AO-Exp (LoRa) uses only the top singular value in Equation (4).

(b) Shows adversarial box ratio of five variants of AO-Exp with different values of k in Equation (4) for each camera view of the EPFL dataset.

Fig. 5. Additional results for CW4C and EPFL datasets considering low-rank adaptions of AO-Exp.

Table 2. Results of baseline attack methods and our proposed minimally structured universal attack method AO-Exp over three real-world datasets. For each method, we report the mean value and standard deviation across all scenes of the corresponding dataset. Bold values indicate best result, underlined values second best result.

Dataset	Attack Method	IoU$_{acc}$($\downarrow$)	advBR ($\downarrow$)	MAP ($\downarrow$)	$\|\delta\|_*$ ($\downarrow$)
PETS2009	FW-Nucl	4.77 ± 1.09	1.04 ± 0.25	$\mathbf{1.2 \pm 0.3}$	$\underline{36.5} \pm 5.84$
	LoRa-PGD-10	1.98 ± 1.31	0.94 ± 0.68	4.0 ± 0.4	39.6 ± 1.73
	LoRa-PGD-50	1.48 ± 1.05	0.67 ± 0.41	4.0 ± 0.5	60.9 ± 10.3
	LoRa-PGD-100	$\underline{1.22} \pm 0.91$	0.63 ± 0.42	4.0 ± 0.3	60.3 ± 10.3
	AO-Exp	$\mathbf{0.29 \pm 0.27}$	$\mathbf{0.06 \pm 0.04}$	$\underline{2.9} \pm 0.1$	41.3 ± 16.6
	AO-Exp (LoRa)	1.88 ± 1.38	$\underline{0.45} \pm 0.33$	6.0 ± 0.2	$\mathbf{17.7 \pm 4.3}$
EPFL-RLC	FW-Nucl	4.83 ± 0.96	0.86 ± 0.14	$\mathbf{5.4 \pm 2.0}$	37.54 ± 1.53
	LoRa-PGD-10	0.25 ± 0.15	0.31 ± 0.05	14.6 ± 3.0	31.59 ± 1.38
	LoRa-PGD-50	$\mathbf{0.17 \pm 0.03}$	$\underline{0.29} \pm 0.14$	14.0 ± 2.7	42.84 ± 2.95
	LoRa-PGD-100	$\underline{0.20} \pm 0.06$	0.37 ± 0.11	14.0 ± 3.0	43.5 ± 4.3
	AO-Exp	0.9 ± 0.37	$\mathbf{0.22 \pm 0.07}$	$\underline{6.0} \pm 4.0$	$\underline{27.52} \pm 15.8$
	AO-Exp (LoRa)	1.39 ± 0.60	0.33 ± 0.1	7.0 ± 3.0	$\mathbf{4.7 \pm 0.93}$
CW4C	FW-Nucl	4.64 ± 3.69	0.82 ± 0.16	$\mathbf{1.3 \pm 0.2}$	39.4 ± 0.5
	LoRa-PGD-10	2.72 ± 2.61	0.48 ± 0.25	5.0 ± 0.4	$\underline{36.1} \pm 1.1$
	LoRa-PGD-50	2.32 ± 2.24	0.41 ± 0.22	4.0 ± 0.2	65.2 ± 6.7
	LoRa-PGD-100	$\underline{1.95} \pm 1.91$	$\underline{0.34} \pm 0.2$	5.0 ± 0.2	67.9 ± 10
	AO-Exp	$\mathbf{0.88 \pm 0.45}$	$\mathbf{0.19 \pm 0.06}$	$\underline{3.8} \pm 1.0$	37.9 ± 8.9
	AO-Exp (LoRa)	2.12 ± 1.18	0.42 ± 0.17	5.0 ± 4.0	$\mathbf{14.3 \pm 7.6}$

6   Limits and Conclusion

In this work, we proposed a novel minimally distorted universal adversarial attack designed for video-based object detection systems. By leveraging nuclear norm regularization, our method promotes structured perturbations that primarily target the background, enabling stealthier and more natural-looking adversarial examples. To tackle the associated computational complexity, we leverage an adaptive optimistic exponentiated gradient descent approach, which improves both scalability and convergence.

Despite these promising results, our approach has some limitations. First, the current formulation assumes a static camera setup, limiting its applicability to dynamic camera scenarios. Second, the attack's performance is sensitive to the choice of hyperparameters, such as the nuclear norm weight and Frobenius regularization, which may require task-specific tuning.

Future work may explore extending this approach to dynamic camera settings, extending the work to object tracking, developing adaptive or learned hyperparameter strategies, and integrating semantic or temporal consistency constraints to improve generalizability and stealth in more complex real-world scenarios. Additionally, one may explore countermeasures and defenses tailored specifically to structured and temporally consistent adversarial attacks.

Acknowledgement. This research was funded by the German Federal Ministry of Labour and Social Affairs through the establishment of a Junior Research Group on Artificial Intelligence at the Federal Institute of Occupational Safety and Health (BAuA). The presented results contribute to the development and evaluation of reliable and safe AI for industrial applications, with the overarching aim of laying the scientific foundations necessary to meet the requirements of the European Machinery Directive (2023) and the European AI Act (2024).

References

1. Alkaabi, S., AlAzri, A., AlZakwani, S., Altamimi, F.: A methodology to evaluate video analytics for drilling safety operation using machine learning. In: Middle East Oil, Gas and Geosciences Show. OnePetro (2023)
2. Almujally, N.A., et al.: A novel framework for vehicle detection and tracking in night ware surveillance systems. IEEE Access (2024)
3. Amirkhani, A., Karimi, M.P., Banitalebi-Dehkordi, A.: A survey on adversarial attacks and defenses for object detection and their applications in autonomous vehicles. Vis. Comput. **39**(11), 5293–5307 (2023)
4. Bouwmans, T., Javed, S., Zhang, H., Lin, Z., Otazo, R.: On the applications of robust PCA in image and video processing. Proc. IEEE **106**(8), 1427–1457 (2018). https://doi.org/10.1109/JPROC.2018.2853589
5. Chavdarova, T., et al.: Wildtrack: a multi-camera HD dataset for dense unscripted pedestrian detection. In: Proceedings of the IEEE Conference on Computer Vision and Pattern Recognition, pp. 5030–5039 (2018)
6. Chavdarova, T., Fleuret, F.: Deep multi-camera people detection. In: 2017 16th IEEE International Conference on Machine Learning and Applications (ICMLA), pp. 848–853. IEEE (2017)
7. Chen, X., Kundu, K., Zhang, Z., Ma, H., Fidler, S., Urtasun, R.: Monocular 3D object detection for autonomous driving. In: Proceedings of the IEEE Conference on Computer Vision and Pattern Recognition (CVPR) (2016)
8. Cocca, P., Marciano, F., Alberti, M.: Video surveillance systems to enhance occupational safety: a case study. Saf. Sci. **84**, 140–148 (2016)
9. Croce, F., Hein, M.: Mind the box: l_1-APGD for sparse adversarial attacks on image classifiers. In: International Conference on Machine Learning, pp. 2201–2211. PMLR (2021)
10. Ding, J., Xu, Z.: Adversarial attacks on deep learning models of computer vision: a survey. In: Qiu, M. (ed.) ICA3PP 2020. LNCS, vol. 12454, pp. 396–408. Springer, Cham (2020). https://doi.org/10.1007/978-3-030-60248-2_27
11. Fefferman, C., Mitter, S., Narayanan, H.: Testing the manifold hypothesis. J. Am. Math. Soc. **29**(4), 983–1049 (2016)
12. Feng, D., et al.: Deep multi-modal object detection and semantic segmentation for autonomous driving: datasets, methods, and challenges. IEEE Trans. Intell. Transp. Syst. **22**(3), 1341–1360 (2020)
13. Feng, J., Cai, Q.Z., Zhou, Z.H.: Learning to confuse: generating training time adversarial data with auto-encoder. In: Advances in Neural Information Processing Systems, vol. 32 (2019)

14. Ferryman, J., Shahrokni, A.: Pets2009: dataset and challenge. In: 2009 Twelfth IEEE International Workshop on Performance Evaluation of Tracking and Surveillance, pp. 1–6. IEEE (2009)
15. Goodfellow, I.J., Shlens, J., Szegedy, C.: Explaining and harnessing adversarial examples. arXiv preprint arXiv:1412.6572 (2014)
16. Gu, S., Zhang, L., Zuo, W., Feng, X.: Weighted nuclear norm minimization with application to image denoising. In: Proceedings of the IEEE Conference on Computer Vision and Pattern Recognition, pp. 2862–2869 (2014)
17. He, K., Gkioxari, G., Dollár, P., Girshick, R.: Mask R-CNN. In: Proceedings of the IEEE International Conference on Computer Vision, pp. 2961–2969 (2017)
18. Huang, H., Wang, Y., Chen, Z., Tang, Z., Zhang, W., Ma, K.K.: Rpattack: refined patch attack on general object detectors. In: 2021 IEEE International Conference on Multimedia and Expo (ICME), pp. 1–6 (2021). https://doi.org/10.1109/ICME51207.2021.9428443
19. Jha, S., Seo, C., Yang, E., Joshi, G.P.: Real time object detection and trackingsystem for video surveillance system. Multimedia Tools Appl. **80**(3), 3981–3996 (2021)
20. Kazemi, E., Kerdreux, T., Wang, L.: Minimally distorted structured adversarial attacks. Int. J. Comput. Vision **131**(1), 160–176 (2023)
21. Kim, B., Sagduyu, Y.E., Davaslioglu, K., Erpek, T., Ulukus, S.: Channel-aware adversarial attacks against deep learning-based wireless signal classifiers. IEEE Trans. Wireless Commun. **21**(6), 3868–3880 (2021)
22. Kravchik, M., Shabtai, A.: Efficient cyber attack detection in industrial control systems using lightweight neural networks and PCA. IEEE Trans. Dependable Secure Comput. **19**(4), 2179–2197 (2021)
23. Li, D., Zhang, J., Huang, K.: Universal adversarial perturbations against object detection. Pattern Recogn. **110**, 107584 (2021)
24. Malburg, L., Rieder, M.P., Seiger, R., Klein, P., Bergmann, R.: Object detection for smart factory processes by machine learning. Procedia Comput. Sci. **184**, 581–588 (2021)
25. Moosavi-Dezfooli, S.M., Fawzi, A., Fawzi, O., Frossard, P.: Universal adversarial perturbations. In: Proceedings of the IEEE Conference on Computer Vision and Pattern Recognition, pp. 1765–1773 (2017)
26. Nguyen, K.N.T., et al.: A survey and evaluation of adversarial attacks in object detection. IEEE Trans. Neural Netw. Learn. Syst. (2025)
27. Pérez, L., Rodríguez, Í., Rodríguez, N., Usamentiaga, R., García, D.F.: Robot guidance using machine vision techniques in industrial environments: a comparative review. Sensors **16**(3), 335 (2016)
28. Rezatofighi, H., Tsoi, N., Gwak, J., Sadeghian, A., Reid, I., Savarese, S.: Generalized intersection over union: a metric and a loss for bounding box regression. In: Proceedings of the IEEE/CVF Conference on Computer Vision and Pattern Recognition, pp. 658–666 (2019)
29. Sadiku, S., Wagner, M., Pokutta, S.: GSE: group-wise sparse and explainable adversarial attacks. arXiv preprint arXiv:2311.17434 (2023)
30. Savostianova, D., Zangrando, E., Tudisco, F.: Low-rank adversarial PGD attack. arXiv preprint arXiv:2410.12607 (2024)
31. Shao, W., Sivrikaya, F., Albayrak, S.: Optimistic optimisation of composite objective with exponentiated update. Mach. Learn. (2022). https://doi.org/10.1007/s10994-022-06229-1
32. Shi, Z., Ming, Y., Fan, Y., Sala, F., Liang, Y.: Domain generalization via nuclear norm regularization. In: Conference on Parsimony and Learning, pp. 179–201. PMLR (2024)

33. Shukla, N., Banerjee, S.: Generating adversarial attacks in the latent space. In: Proceedings of the IEEE/CVF Conference on Computer Vision and Pattern Recognition, pp. 730–739 (2023)
34. Subhash, V., Bialas, A., Pan, W., Doshi-Velez, F.: Why do universal adversarial attacks work on large language models?: geometry might be the answer. In: The Second Workshop on New Frontiers in Adversarial Machine Learning (2023)
35. Szegedy, C., et al.: Intriguing properties of neural networks. arXiv preprint arXiv:1312.6199 (2013)
36. Thys, S., Van Ranst, W., Goedemé, T.: Fooling automated surveillance cameras: adversarial patches to attack person detection. In: Proceedings of the IEEE/CVF Conference on Computer Vision and Pattern Recognition Workshops (2019)
37. Wang, Y., an Tan, Y., Zhang, W., Zhao, Y., Kuang, X.: An adversarial attack on DNN-based black-box object detectors. J. Netw. Comput. Appl. **161**, 102634 (2020). https://doi.org/10.1016/j.jnca.2020.102634. https://www.sciencedirect.com/science/article/pii/S1084804520301089
38. Wu, X., Huang, L., Gao, C.: G-UAP: generic universal adversarial perturbation that fools RPN-based detectors. In: Lee, W.S., Suzuki, T. (eds.) Proceedings of The Eleventh Asian Conference on Machine Learning. Proceedings of Machine Learning Research, vol. 101, pp. 1204–1217. PMLR (2019). https://proceedings.mlr.press/v101/wu19a.html
39. Zhang, H., Zhou, W., Li, H.: Contextual adversarial attacks for object detection. In: 2020 IEEE International Conference on Multimedia and Expo (ICME), pp. 1–6 (2020). https://doi.org/10.1109/ICME46284.2020.9102805
40. Zhao, Z.Q., Zheng, P., Xu, S.T., Wu, X.: Object detection with deep learning: a review. IEEE Trans. Neural Netw. Learn. Syst. **30**(11), 3212–3232 (2019). https://doi.org/10.1109/TNNLS.2018.2876865
41. Zhou, X., et al.: Intelligent small object detection for digital twin in smart manufacturing with industrial cyber-physical systems. IEEE Trans. Industr. Inf. **18**(2), 1377–1386 (2021)

Road Obstacle Video Segmentation

Shyam Nandan Rai[1(✉)], Shyamgopal Karthik[2,3,4],
Mariana-Iuliana Georgescu[3,4], Barbara Caputo[1], Carlo Masone[1],
and Zeynep Akata[3,4]

[1] Politecnico di Torino, Turin, Italy
shyam.rai@polito.it
[2] University of Tübingen, Tübingen, Germany
[3] Technical University of Munich and Helmholtz Munich, Munich, Germany
[4] Munich Center for Machine Learning and Munich Data Science Institute,
Munich, Germany

Abstract. With the growing deployment of autonomous driving agents,
the detection and segmentation of road obstacles have become critical
to ensure safe autonomous navigation. However, existing road-obstacle
segmentation methods are applied on individual frames, overlooking the
temporal nature of the problem, leading to inconsistent prediction maps
between consecutive frames. In this work, we demonstrate that the road-
obstacle segmentation task is inherently temporal, since the segmentation maps for consecutive frames are strongly correlated. To address
this, we curate and adapt four evaluation benchmarks for road-obstacle
video segmentation and evaluate 11 state-of-the-art image- and video-
based segmentation methods on these benchmarks. Moreover, we introduce two strong baseline methods based on vision foundation models.
Our approach establishes a new state-of-the-art in road-obstacle video
segmentation for long-range video sequences, providing valuable insights
and direction for future research.

Keywords: Obstacle detection · Video Segmentation

1 Introduction

Semantic segmentation, *i.e.*, the task of delineating objects in visual scenes
with pixel-level granularity, is an essential component of the perception stack
in autonomous cars [11]. However, semantic segmentation models learn to identify and segment only objects that are contained in the training set. Such models, when deployed in the real world, could encounter a road-obstacle[1] (novel
object class absent during training), and incorrectly classify it as one of its
known classes, potentially leading to unsafe behaviors. To address this safety-
critical challenge, image-based segmentation methods [1,15,16,32,34] have been
extended to detect road obstacles (anomalies) in driving scenes. Currently, these

---

[1] Also referred to as *anomaly segmentation* in the road-scene segmentation literature.

M. Keuper and F. Locatello (Eds.): DAGM GCPR 2025, LNCS 16125, pp. 186–201, 2026.
https://doi.org/10.1007/978-3-032-12840-9_13

models are evaluated on various benchmarks [4,5,25,33] consisting solely of static images, thus completely disregarding the inherent temporal consistency of the task. Consequently, existing image-based road-obstacle segmentation methods [1,15,16,32,34] have inherent limitations, since they rely solely on individual frames (as shown in Fig. 1), despite the fact that driving applications utilize sensors that capture continuous data streams. Hence, incorporating temporal information is advantageous, as dependencies between consecutive frames enable models to leverage contextual cues from neighboring frames, leading to more accurate obstacle segmentation results.

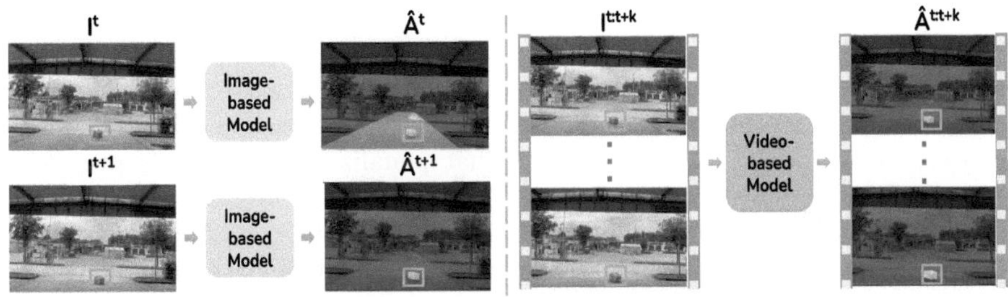

Fig. 1. Image- vs Video-based road-obstacle segmentation: We illustrate the key difference between road-obstacle segmentation performance at image- and video-level on a set of consecutive image frames. Due to overlooking the temporal information, the image-level framework (left) fails to consistently predict the road-obstacle map across consecutive frames. However, the video-level framework (right) effectively leverages the temporal information, resulting in consistent maps. The box in blue encloses a road obstacle. (Color figure online)

Taking into account the limitations mentioned above, we propose using video-based methods to enhance the quality of road obstacle segmentation. Hence, we introduce a new task of **road-obstacle video segmentation**. This enables us to leverage temporal information, improving both the accuracy and consistency of road-obstacle segmentation models. To evaluate our proposed task, we establish benchmarks, evaluation metrics, and baseline methods. We collect relevant evaluation datasets for the task using the existing datasets, including Lidar-SOD [40], SOS [29], and Lost&Found [33]. However, these datasets lack long-term temporal sequences and are small in scale for the video road-obstacle segmentation task. To fill this gap, we create Apolloscape Road-Obstacle (AsRO), a large-scale road-obstacle dataset with long-range image sequences. We utilize the Apolloscape [21] dataset to create AsRO. We employ existing evaluation metrics, such as AuROC and AuPRC, to assess the performance of image- and video-based methods. In particular, to evaluate the temporal consistency of the models, we employ the Video Consistency (VC) [30] metric. However, we notice that VC does not penalize false positive pixels as it only takes into account the intersection of the predicted mask and the ground-truth mask. Therefore, we introduce VC^*, a harmonic mean of video consistency for the road-obstacle and background classes that mitigates the aforementioned bias.

We benchmark these curated datasets on a set of 11 image- and video-based road-obstacle segmentation methods, reporting the performance in terms of image- and video-level metrics. Our key finding states that ignoring the temporal dimension leads to inconsistent road-obstacle predictions, as illustrated in Fig. 1. Furthermore, we introduce two strong road-obstacle segmentation baselines built on Mask2Former-Video [7] and SAM 2 [37], which achieve state-of-the-art results on the proposed benchmarks.

In summary, our contributions are the following.

- We propose the road-obstacle (anomaly) video segmentation task, along with four novel benchmarks.
- We evaluate, adapt, and retrain 11 state-of-the-art image- and video-based segmentation methods for the new setting on the proposed benchmarks. Moreover, we introduce the VC^* metric that penalizes the methods producing many false positive pixels.
- We introduce two new baselines for road-obstacle video segmentation, leveraging foundation models. Our experiments indicate that these models originally developed for video segmentation can be effectively adapted for the similar-yet-distinct task of road-obstacle segmentation.

2   Related Work

Semantic Segmentation. Traditionally, semantic segmentation methods have been based on fully convolutional encoder-decoder architectures [6,24,28,46]. However, there has been a paradigm shift towards transformer-based architectures [41], especially relying on the Swin transformer backbone [27]. These methods [8,10] introduce a mask transformer architecture and a per-pixel decoder to predict the segmentation output. More recently, there has also been the introduction of foundation segmentation models [23,37] which tackle the segmentation task in a promptable manner.

Anomaly Segmentation. Semantic segmentation models perform well on known classes but struggle to segment anomalies or unknown objects. Anomaly segmentation is the task of per-pixel labeling of image anomaly detection. This problem was first tackled by repurposing image-level methods to utilize soft-max scores to predict anomalies [4,19,20,26]. Afterwards, uncertainty quantification solutions have also been used for this task, including deep ensembles [13], Bayesian deep learning [14,31] and class-logits reasoning [18,22]. An alternative line of research has explored the usage of generative models trained on anomaly-free data to detect anomalies at testing times by their generation discrepancy [12,25,42,43]. Recently, a common practice has been to add supervision during training with outlier exposure to improve performance [3,12,44]. However, all these methods have typically been proposed to work on individual frames, without using the full temporal context provided in videos. Differently, we propose comprehensive video anomaly (road obstacles in our setup) segmentation benchmarks, and introduce novel methods based on the efficient adaptation of foundation segmentation models.

Video Anomaly Detection. A different line of research focuses on video abnormal events detection [2,36,38]. In this scenario, an anomaly could be anything that diverges from the normal data through appearance or motion, even though the anomalous objects are included in the training data. Our work is different from this distantly related task, as our goal is to identify *unseen* objects (obstacles) on the road.

Anomaly Segmentation Benchmarks. Several benchmarks have been proposed for anomaly segmentation in road scenes, such as FishyScapes [4], Road Anomaly [25], Lost&Found [33] and Segment Me If You Can [5]. However, most of these datasets have been geared towards using static images. In this work, we establish video road-obstacle segmentation benchmarks from the Lidar SOD [40], Lost & Found [33], Apolloscape [21], and SOS [29] datasets.

3   Road-Obstacle Video Segmentation

The task of anomaly segmentation in urban road scenes as a video task is more suitable to achieve accurate and consistent anomaly segmentation. This is because an anomalous region detected in one frame is likely to appear in the following frames as well. Foundation models have become the standard approach for many computer vision tasks, suggesting their potential applicability to anomaly segmentation.

However, anomaly segmentation is not a conventional task, since it is highly dependent on the context and requires additional information. We investigate how a segmentation foundation model can be employed to segment anomalies in road scenes. Therefore, we propose two techniques based on foundation models. The first strategy is to fine-tune the decoder of SAM 2 to achieve anomaly segmentation. The second technique is to employ a state-of-the-art segmentation model, namely M2FVideo [7] and substitute its encoder with the powerful encoder of SAM 2 [37].

3.1   Problem Setting

Given a segmentation model Ψ, our objective is to accurately segment road obstacles at the pixel level **throughout the video**. We train Ψ using a set of video snippets and their corresponding *semantic segmentation* ground-truth labels. It is important to note that during training, the video snippets do not contain any instances of road obstacles (anomalies). Consider a *test* video sequence containing T frames with road obstacles and a set temporal window that spans for k frames. The k-span snippet from a random time stamp t, $I^{t:t+k} = \{I^t, I^{t+1}, \ldots, I^{t+k}\}$, has the corresponding ground-truth road-obstacle snippet given as $A^{t:t+k} = \{A^t, A^{t+1}, \ldots, A^{t+k}\}$. A^t is a binary image map where 1 denotes road obstacles and 0 indicates background regions. During *inference*, Ψ functions as a road-obstacle video segmentation model by applying a simple approach of maximum softmax probability [20], predicting road-obstacle masks as $\hat{A}^{t:t+k} = \{\hat{A}^t, \hat{A}^{t+1}, \ldots, \hat{A}^{t+k}\}$.

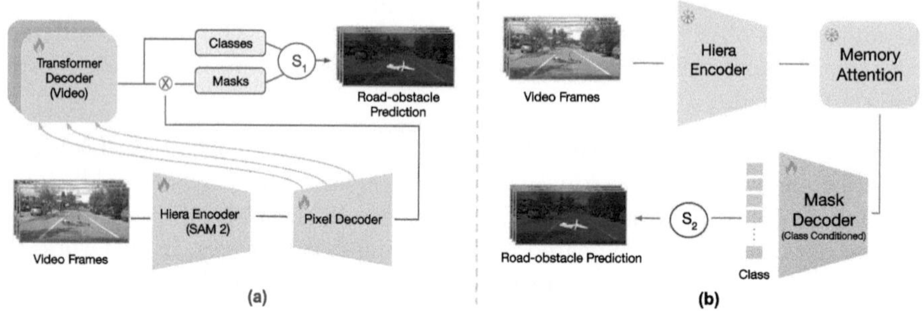

Fig. 2. (a) We present the **HM2F-Video** architecture. It consists of the Hiera backbone with the Mask2Former-video decoder. S_1 represents the road-obstacle scores calculated in Eq. (1). (b) The **Class-Conditioned SAM 2** framework. We inject class information in SAM 2 by introducing a class-conditioned mask-decoder. S_2 represents the road-obstacle scores calculated in Eq. (2)

3.2 Background

We provide an overview of the Segment Anything Model 2 (SAM 2) [37] and Mask2Former-Video [9] models, which serves as the basis for our methods.

SAM 2 [37] is a recent state-of-the-art model that extends SAM [23]. SAM 2 is equipped with video processing, obtaining impressive results on multiple segmentation benchmarks [37]. Its architecture enabled large-scale training, resulting in the generation of high-quality class-agnostic segmentation masks during inference. SAM 2 architecture consists of: a) An *image encoder* based on Hiera [39] that was pre-trained using the MAE [17] technique. The Hiera architecture provides hierarchical features enabling decoding at multi-scale. b) A *memory attention* that condition the image embeddings on the previous predictions and new prompts. c) A *prompt encoder* which guides the model to discover potential objects in the input image, capable of processing points, bounding boxes, or masks. d) A *memory encoder* that generates a memory by downsampling the output mask received from the mask decoder. e) A *memory bank* that retains information about past predictions for the target objects in the video. f) A *mask decoder* that outputs the final predictions that are class-agnostic.

Mask2Former-Video's [7] meta-architecture consists of three parts: a) a *backbone* that acts as feature extractor for a set of video frames, b) a *pixel-decoder* that upsamples the low-resolution features extracted from the backbone to get high-resolution *per-pixel embeddings* of the frames, and c) a *video transformer decoder* based on Mask2Former [9] with an additional joint spatio-temporal masked attention and a temporal positional encoding.

3.3   HM2F-Video

SAM 2 [37] is trained on millions of masks, providing an effective image encoder with generalized features. Therefore, we utilize the Hiera backbone [39] together with the Mask2Former-video [7] decoder. We name this method HM2F-Video and illustrate it in Fig. 2(a). During inference, the model predicts a set of *class masks* $M \in \mathbb{R}^{N \times \tau \times (H \times W)}$ and their associated *class scores* $C \in \mathbb{R}^{N \times K}$, where N is the number of queries, K is the number of training classes, τ is the number of frames, and H and W are the spatial dimensions. The road-obstacle segmentation score for an input video I is computed as:

$$S_1(I) = 1 - \max_{k=1}^{K} \left(C^T \times M \right). \tag{1}$$

3.4   Class Conditioned SAM2

We introduce Class-Conditioned SAM 2 (CC-SAM2) that injects class information into SAM 2, by adding a class-conditioned mask decoder into the SAM 2 architecture, as illustrated in Fig. 2(b). The class-conditioned mask decoder architecture is similar to the SAM 2 class-agnostic mask decoder, but differs in the number of output masks, which depends on the number of classes contained in the training dataset. During training, the SAM 2 model is frozen, while only the class-conditioned mask decoder is updated. During inference, the road-obstacle segmentation score of an input video I is computed as:

$$S_2(I) = - \max_{k=1}^{K} \Upsilon(I), \tag{2}$$

where S_2 and Υ are the scoring function and the CC-SAM2 model, respectively.

Table 1. Dataset Statistics. We compare our proposed Apolloscape-Road-Obstacle (AsRO) with SOS [29], Lost&Found [33], and LidarSOD [40]. Highest value in each column is bold.

Dataset	Resolution	#Frames	Average Length	Location
SOS [29]	1920 × 1080	1004	56.4	Germany
Lost&Found [33]	2048 × 1024	1779	149.2	Germany
LidarSOD [40]	1280 × 720	2421	194.6	India
AsRO (Ours)	**3384 × 2710**	**12480**	**1192.7**	China

4   Road-Obstacle Video Segmentation Benchmark

There are several benchmarks for image-based road-obstacle (anomaly) segmentation [4,5][2]. However, these benchmarks are not suitable for the road-obstacle video segmentation task, because they lack temporal consistency and evaluation protocols to assess model performance for videos. Therefore, we adapt the existing road-scene segmentation datasets, namely SOS [29], LidarSOD [40], and Lost&Found [33] to road-obstacle segmentation. To create the datasets, we only select the obstacles that are located on the road. However, the aforementioned datasets do not have long-range temporal sequences or the scale to assess this task effectively. Therefore, we propose Apolloscape-Road-Obstacle (AsRO), a large-scale road-obstacle video dataset consisting of long-range videos (Fig. 3).

Fig. 3.   Apolloscape-Road-Obstacle: *Top:* Sample images of each anomaly type. *Bottom:* Average location per anomaly type. Please zoom in for clarity.

4.1   Apolloscape-Road-Obstacle (AsRO):

We curate the Apolloscape dataset [21], which consists of 143K video frames. Among all frames, 51,865 frames contain obstacles on the road labeled as: Traffic cone, Road pole, Tricycle, Tricycle group and Dustbin. However, we observe that some images have obstacles outside the road. Therefore, we remove all obstacles that do not have their center on the road. After this step, we obtain 12,480 images in 12 video sequences, with an average sequence length of 1192 frames. Table 1 presents the comparison between AsRO and the other datasets. We notice that our AsRO dataset has the highest number of frames and the highest average sequence length among the compared datasets.

4.2   Evaluation Metrics

We provide a holistic evaluation of the road-obstacle video segmentation methods by employing the following metrics.

---

[2] Also refer to as anomaly segmentation in the road-scene segmentation literature.

Pixel-Level. We consider the Area under the Receiver Operating Curve (AuROC), the Area under the Precision-Recall Curve (AuPRC), and the False Positive Rate at a True Positive Rate of 95% (FPR_{95}).

Component-Level. We employ component-level metrics, as they are not affected by the size of the object, unlike pixel-level metrics, which are biased toward object size. We use an adjusted version of the component-wise intersection over union (sIoU) that excludes pixels that correctly intersect with another ground-truth component, positive predictive value (PPV component-wise precision), and component-wise F1-score (F1_1^*).

Video-Level. We employ Video Consistency [30], a video evaluation metric that is widely used to assess the consistency of segmentation predictions. Given a ground-truth binary mask $\{A_i\}_{i=1}^{T}$ and a predicted binary mask $\{\hat{A}_i\}_{i=1}^{T}$, where T is the number of frames, the video consistency is computed as:

$$VC_T = \frac{(\hat{A}_1 \cap \ldots \cap \hat{A}_T) \cap (A_1 \cap \ldots \cap A_T)}{(A_1 \cap \ldots \cap A_T)}. \tag{3}$$

Calculating the VC score only for the road-obstacle class gives an advantage to methods that have a higher false positive rate since the intersection between the ground truth maps and the prediction maps would be higher. To alleviate this problem, we introduce VC^*, a harmonic mean of video consistency for road-obstacle VC^{RO}, and background (non-road obstacle area) VC^{BG} given as:

$$VC^* = 2\frac{VC^{RO} \cdot VC^{BG}}{VC^{RO} + VC^{BG}}. \tag{4}$$

We select the harmonic mean because it achieves a trade-off between the true positive and the false negative rates, similar to the well-known F1-score. For example, a perfect video segmentation model would obtain a maximum score for VC^{RO} and VC^{BG} equal to 1, therefore the value of VC^* would be 1. On the other hand, this metric effectively penalizes methods that predict many false positives, which also have high VC^{RO} scores (many false positive obstacles lead to a higher probability of matching the ground truth maps), but the VC^{BG} score would be low, because the background would not be segmented correctly, leading to a lower VC^* score.

4.3   Baselines

We establish two baseline categories: (a) **Image-based** obstacle segmentation methods: Entropy [20], Max Softmax [20], Energy [26], Max Logit [19], Void Classifier [4], Mask2Anomaly [35], EAM [16], AEM [16], and RbA [32]; (b) **Video-based** semantic segmentation methods: M2F-Video [7] and DVIS [45], adapted to our task by Max Softmax [20]. We evaluate all baselines using the metrics and datasets and compare them with our proposed methods in the following sections.

5   Experiments

5.1   Implementation Details

Implementation details about the baselines are in the supplementary.

HM2F-Video: The image encoder is the pre-trained Hiera-B+ from SAM 2 and the decoder architecture is adopted from Mask2Former-Video. During training, two consecutive frames were processed setting the batch size to 4. We trained the model for 32,000 iterations while keeping the learning rate equal to $1e-4$. The number of mask-decoder layers was set to 9, while the number of output queries is equal to 100.

Table 2. Quantitative results on **Lost&Found** [33]. We compare our proposed baselines, CC-SAM2 and HM2F-Video, to various state-of-the-art methods [4,7,16,19,20, 26,32,35,45]. Best results are in **bold** and second best are underlined.

	Methods	Pixel-Level Metrics			Component-Level Metrics			Video Metrics
		AuROC↑	AuPRC↑	FPR_{95} ↓	sIoU↑	PPV↑	$F1_i^*$ ↑	VC^* ↑
Image Level	Random	50.00	0.73	94.99	0.53	1.33	0.00	0.00
	Entropy [20]	86.72	5.65	72.32	28.83	26.63	26.70	22.87
	Energy [26]	85.88	6.22	78.69	28.59	25.92	25.70	0.00
	Max Softmax [20]	89.03	7.31	56.08	37.55	35.48	35.57	22.84
	Max Logit [19]	90.53	10.39	36.08	**46.10**	42.73	44.34	<u>52.11</u>
	Void Classifier [4]	54.43	11.28	99.99	0.54	1.80	0.05	23.34
	Mask2Anomaly [35]	92.95	14.99	<u>22.81</u>	39.34	47.03	41.29	48.86
	EAM [16]	84.20	7.33	93.27	41.11	<u>53.42</u>	**46.67**	49.33
	AEM [16]	83.89	7.15	92.80	41.02	**53.48**	<u>46.57</u>	49.22
	RbA [32]	87.31	43.01	94.40	7.54	9.32	7.53	36.54
Video Level	M2F-Video [7]	<u>95.11</u>	**60.51**	27.31	38.33	50.59	37.25	35.06
	DVIS [45]	93.33	<u>59.91</u>	57.59	<u>43.51</u>	29.66	30.78	25.24
	CC-SAM2 (Ours)	**98.44**	57.83	**6.22**	15.13	38.90	14.70	**54.15**
	HM2F-Video (Ours)	93.87	54.00	53.59	31.74	50.92	34.67	32.43

CC-SAM2: In CC-SAM2, we utilized SAM 2 with Hiera-B+ as image encoder. The model was trained for 40 epochs with a batch size of 1. The base learning rate is set to $1e-4$, and the input image resolution is 1024×1024 pixels. The number of consecutive input video frames is set to 2.

Fig. 4. Qualitative Results. Road-obstacle prediction maps from RbA [32], Mask2Anomaly [34], HM2F-Video and CC-SAM2 on the SOS dataset [29]. HM2F-Video accurately segments road-obstacles across temporal frames.

Table 3. Quantitative results on **SOS** [29]. We compare our proposed baselines, CC-SAM2 and HM2F-Video, to various state-of-the-art methods [4,7,16,19,20,26,32,35, 45]. Best results are in **bold** and second best are underlined.

	Methods	Pixel-Level Metrics			Component-Level Metrics			Video Metrics
		AuROC↑	AuPRC↑	FPR$_{95}$ ↓	sIoU↑	PPV↑	F1$_1^*$ ↑	VC* ↑
Image Level	Random	50.00	0.89	95.00	0.73	1.76	0.00	0.00
	Entropy [20]	96.43	39.16	20.50	31.24	12.91	17.47	13.31
	Energy [26]	95.20	65.85	24.72	27.53	11.46	15.57	0.00
	Max Softmax [20]	96.99	72.24	20.05	44.23	20.26	25.90	13.32
	Max Logit [19]	96.94	74.44	20.99	**53.42**	24.14	<u>31.35</u>	**60.21**
	Void Classifier [4]	68.39	41.81	99.96	0.65	3.17	0.01	21.33
	Mask2Anomaly [35]	96.10	64.81	25.11	<u>45.35</u>	<u>30.24</u>	**31.97**	<u>52.42</u>
	EAM [16]	90.32	71.76	64.41	41.95	24.44	28.76	43.75
	AEM [16]	90.22	71.35	64.03	41.96	23.64	28.08	43.79
	RbA [32]	97.09	**86.19**	<u>7.67</u>	8.20	9.31	7.47	44.70
Video Level	M2F-Video [7]	<u>97.41</u>	57.23	15.61	48.71	19.43	21.05	43.13
	DVIS [45]	94.34	14.22	28.65	45.17	9.50	10.89	26.85
	CC-SAM2 (Ours)	**99.24**	<u>79.24</u>	**3.69**	31.14	**47.00**	28.14	43.27
	HM2F-Video (Ours)	83.62	1.23	46.03	8.35	6.96	4.67	7.93

5.2   Results

Pixel-Level. We report the pixel-level evaluation details on the SOS [29], Lidar-SOD [40], Lost&Found [33] and AsRO datasets in Tables 2, 3, 4 and 5. We observe the FPR$_{95}$ performance obtained by CC-SAM2 of 3.69% (SOS), 25.56% (LidarSOD), 3.90% (AsRO), and 6.22% (Lost&Found), is the lowest among all

Table 4. Quantitative results on **Lidar SOD** [40]. We compare our proposed baselines, CC-SAM2 and HM2F-Video, to various state-of-the-art methods [4,7,16,19,20,26,32, 35,45]. Best results are in **bold** and second best are underlined.

	Methods	Pixel-Level Metrics			Component-Level Metrics			Video Metrics
		AuROC↑	AuPRC↑	FPR_{95} ↓	sIoU↑	PPV↑	$F1_i^*$ ↑	VC* ↑
Image Level	Random	50.00	0.39	94.99	0.14	0.64	0.01	0.00
	Entropy [20]	87.21	2.03	55.60	18.17	11.93	13.99	3.66
	Energy [26]	85.15	1.77	75.17	14.92	10.47	12.01	0.00
	Max Softmax [20]	88.29	1.84	27.06	21.86	11.99	14.02	3.65
	Max Logit [19]	88.67	1.80	_26.14_	**23.97**	12.82	14.56	37.53
	Void Classifier [4]	50.45	0.71	99.80	0.12	0.69	0.02	10.53
	Mask2Anomaly [35]	84.39	2.55	46.42	14.69	9.06	7.63	26.36
	EAM [16]	_91.40_	_5.10_	30.91	_22.60_	_14.02_	**14.90**	_37.81_
	AEM [16]	91.17	4.89	31.36	22.42	**14.06**	_14.82_	37.61
	RbA [32]	86.74	2.05	86.42	0.89	1.80	0.95	23.99
Video Level	M2F-Video [7]	81.43	1.09	54.09	9.63	10.39	6.08	20.37
	DVIS [45]	79.58	1.00	61.82	12.84	8.63	6.53	15.84
	CC-SAM2 (Ours)	**92.52**	**14.00**	**25.56**	9.11	4.96	3.25	**40.48**
	HM2F-Video (Ours)	83.62	1.23	46.03	8.35	6.96	4.67	13.80

Table 5. Quantitative results on Apolloscape-Road-Obstacle. Best results are in **bold** and second best are underlined. † are video-based road obstacle segmentation methods.

Methods	Pixel-Level Metrics			Component-Level Metrics			Video Metrics
	AuROC↑	AuPRC↑	FPR_{95} ↓	sIoU↑	PPV↑	$F1_i^*$ ↑	VC* ↑
Random	49.92	0.02	95.09	4.1	0.23	0.04	0.00
Mask2Anomaly [35]	89.94	0.44	64.62	10.01	0.35	0.38	0.02
EAM [16]	64.67	_0.72_	99.71	5.43	**0.73**	_0.47_	1.62
M2F-Video [7] †	92.66	0.50	29.81	8.91	_0.59_	0.44	1.85
DVIS [45] †	_94.07_	0.68	_21.69_	_11.41_	0.52	_0.47_	1.03
CC-SAM2 (Ours) †	**98.83**	**2.13**	**3.90**	**16.79**	0.48	**0.48**	**8.28**

compared methods. This demonstrates that leveraging temporal information in video-level methods significantly reduces false positives. Moreover, video-level methods also show strong performance on other pixel-level evaluation metrics.

Component-Level. Tables 2, 3, 4 and 5 present the results obtained on the road-obstacle video segmentation datasets in terms of component-level metrics. Notably, the image-based models reach the highest performance, for instance EAM obtains an $F1_1^*$ value of 46.67% (Lost&Found), AEM reaches a PPV score of 14.06% (Lidar SOD), and MaxLogit attains an sIoU value of 53.42% (SOS). In contrast, on the AsRO benchmark, CC-SAM2 stands out as one of the best performing methods, achieving a score of 16.79% in terms of sIoU and an $F1_1^*$ value of 0.48%. These results reinforce the observation that image-level methods are strong baselines. However, for the road-obstacle video segmentation task, video-based methods perform better longer video sequence dataset i.e. AsRO.

Video-Level. In Tables 2, 3, 4 and 5, we report the evaluation in terms of video-level metrics on the road-obstacle video segmentation datasets. CC-SAM2 achieves strong performance in terms of VC* across all datasets. In particular, on the AsRO dataset, CC-SAM2 attains a VC* score of 8.28, which is significantly better than the baseline methods (the second-best score of 1.85 is reached by M2F-Video). This highlights the effectiveness of video-based approaches for road-obstacle video segmentation.

Qualitative Results. Figure 4 presents a qualitative comparison between the baselines, RbA [32] and Mask2Anomaly [34], and our proposed HM2F-Video and CC-SAM2. We notice that CC-SAM2 provides coherent and accurate road-obstacle segmentation maps, outperforming the image-based methods. In contrast, Mask2Anomaly [34] and RbA [32] predict many false positives, indicating the importance of temporal consistency.

5.3   Discussion

Image-based vs Video-based methods: We observe from Tables 2, 3 and 4, that the performance of image-based methods are close to the video-based ones, in terms of pixel-level metrics (EAM [16] obtains the second-best score on Lidar-SOS [40], Table 3). In terms of output consistency (VC), most image-based methods obtain low scores (RbA [32] attains 36.54% on Lost&Found [33], Table 2), showing limited correlation between the output of consecutive frames. However, as shown in Table 5, CC-SAM2 achieves the best performance on almost all evaluation metrics. In summary, our empirical experiments indicate that image-based methods perform better on short video sequences, whereas for longer sequences i.e. AsRO dataset, video-based methods like CC-SAM2 show better results.

CC-SAM2 and HM2F-Video Performance: From Tables 2, 3 and 4, we observe a significant performance gap between CC-SAM2 and HM2F-Video, which is attributed to differences in their architectural designs. CC-SAM2 is based on SAM2, a foundation model architecture showing strong generalizability, whereas HM2F-Video is based on M2F-Video architecture [7].

5.4   Ablation Results

We utilize SOS [29] as the evaluation dataset for ablations.

Freeze vs Unfreeze Hiera encoder in HM2F-Video: We investigate the performance obtained by the HM2F-Video framework while keeping its backbone frozen or fine-tuned, as shown in Table 6a. Keeping the Hiera encoder frozen results in an AuROC score of 77.79%. However, fine-tuning the encoder during HM2F-Video training substantially improves performance, achieving an AuROC value of 93.44% and an AuPRC value of 53.89%.

Table 6. Ablation results performance obtained on the SOS dataset [29]. Top results are highlighted in **bold**.

(a) Performance of the HM2F-Video method when the encoder is frozen or finetuned.

Encoder	Pixel-Level Metrics					Component-Level Metrics
	AuROC↑	AuPRC↑	FPR_{95} ↓	sIoU↑	PPV↑	$F1_i^*$ ↑
Freeze	77.79	3.30	77.60	33.00	2.28	3.10
Unfreeze	**93.44**	**53.89**	**43.38**	**46.96**	**7.15**	**8.87**

(b) CC-SAM2 performance when varying the number of input frames.

#Frames	Pixel-Level Metrics					Component-Level Metrics
	AuROC↑	AuPRC↑	FPR_{95} ↓	sIoU↑	PPV↑	$F1_i^*$ ↑
2	**99.16**	**65.29**	3.48	**31.92**	47.44	**26.26**
4	99.15	42.63	**2.71**	22.44	**59.63**	25.64
8	97.71	16.92	6.13	3.89	26.47	2.71

Number of Frames: We analyze the effect of varying the number of input frames in the CC-SAM2 method, as shown in Table 6b. We observe that the best performance is obtained when the number of frames is set to 2, while the performance decreases drastically when the number of input frames increases to 8. However, it is important to note that the frames are taken at 3 FPS (25 FPS original video annotated every 8th frame), resulting in weak correlation between consecutive frames. We hypothesize that a dataset with higher FPS would benefit from an increased number of input frames.

6 Conclusion

In this work, we introduced the road-obstacle video segmentation task. To evaluate the task: a) we curated four video road-segmentation datasets, b) evaluated nine image-based road-obstacle segmentation methods and two video semantic segmentation methods, along with our proposed baselines (CC-SAM2, and HM2F-Video), and c) selected evaluation metrics that assess model performance at pixel-, component-, and video-level. In addition, we conducted extensive evaluations to provide critical insight and discussion. We believe that road-obstacle video segmentation could pave the way for new tasks, such as few-shot road-obstacle video segmentation.

Acknowledgements. This work is financially supported by the ELLIS Turin Unit. This work was partially funded by the ERC (853489 - DEXIM) and the Alfried Krupp von Bohlen und Halbach Foundation, which we thank for their generous support. The authors gratefully acknowledge the Gauss Centre for Supercomputing e.V. (https://www.gauss-centre.eu) for funding this project by providing computing time on the GCS Supercomputer JUWELS at Jülich Supercomputing Centre (JSC).

References

1. Ackermann, J., Sakaridis, C., Yu, F.: Maskomaly: zero-shot mask anomaly segmentation. In: British Machine Vision Conference (2023)
2. Ahn, S., Jo, Y., Lee, K., Park, S.: Videopatchcore: an effective method to memorize normality for video anomaly detection. In: Proceedings of the Asian Conference on Computer Vision (ACCV), pp. 2179–2195 (2024)
3. Bevandić, P., Krešo, I., Oršić, M., Šegvić, S.: Discriminative out-of-distribution detection for semantic segmentation. CoRR abs/1808.07703 (2018)
4. Blum, H., Sarlin, P.E., Nieto, J., Siegwart, R., Cadena, C.: The Fishyscapes benchmark: measuring blind spots in semantic segmentation. Int. J. Comput. Vis. **129**(11), 3119–3135 (2021)
5. Chan, R., et al.: SegmentMeIfYouCan: a benchmark for anomaly segmentation. In: Advances in Neural Information Processing Systems (2021)
6. Chen, L.C., Zhu, Y., Papandreou, G., Schroff, F., Adam, H.: Encoder-decoder with atrous separable convolution for semantic image segmentation. In: European Conference on Computer Vision, pp. 833–851 (2018)
7. Cheng, B., Choudhuri, A., Misra, I., Kirillov, A., Girdhar, R., Schwing, A.G.: Mask2former for video instance segmentation. CoRR abs/2112.10764 (2021). https://arxiv.org/abs/2112.10764
8. Cheng, B., Misra, I., Schwing, A.G., Kirillov, A., Girdhar, R.: Masked-attention mask transformer for universal image segmentation. In: IEEE Conference on Computer Vision and Pattern Recognition, pp. 1280–1289 (2022)
9. Cheng, B., Misra, I., Schwing, A.G., Kirillov, A., Girdhar, R.: Masked-attention mask transformer for universal image segmentation. In: CVPR (2022)
10. Cheng, B., Schwing, A., Kirillov, A.: Per-pixel classification is not all you need for semantic segmentation. In: Advances in Neural Information Processing Systems (2021)
11. Cordts, M., et al.: The Cityscapes dataset for semantic urban scene understanding. In: IEEE Conference on Computer Vision and Pattern Recognition, pp. 3213–3223 (2016)
12. Di Biase, G., Blum, H., Siegwart, R., Cadena, C.: Pixel-wise anomaly detection in complex driving scenes. In: IEEE Conference on Computer Vision and Pattern Recognition, pp. 16913–16922 (2021)
13. Fort, S., Hu, H., Lakshminarayanan, B.: Deep ensembles: a loss landscape perspective. arXiv preprint arXiv:1912.02757 (2019)
14. Gal, Y., Ghahramani, Z.: Dropout as a Bayesian approximation: representing model uncertainty in deep learning. In: International Conference on Machine Learning (2016)
15. Grcić, M., Bevandić, P., Šegvić, S.: Dense open-set recognition with synthetic outliers generated by real NVP. In: International Joint Conference on Computer Vision, Imaging and Computer Graphics Theory and Applications (2021)
16. Grcic, M., Saric, J., Segvic, S.: On advantages of mask-level recognition for outlier-aware segmentation. In: IEEE Conference on Computer Vision and Pattern Recognition Workshop, pp. 2937–2947 (2023)
17. He, K., Chen, X., Xie, S., Li, Y., Dollár, P., Girshick, R.B.: Masked autoencoders are scalable vision learners. In: IEEE/CVF Conference on Computer Vision and Pattern Recognition, CVPR 2022, New Orleans, LA, USA, 18–24 June 2022, pp. 15979–15988. IEEE (2022). https://doi.org/10.1109/CVPR52688.2022.01553

18. Hendrycks, D., et al.: Improving and assessing anomaly detectors for large-scale settings (2022)
19. Hendrycks, D., et al.: Scaling out-of-distribution detection for real-world settings. In: Chaudhuri, K., Jegelka, S., Song, L., Szepesvári, C., Niu, G., Sabato, S. (eds.) International Conference on Machine Learning, ICML 2022, 17–23 July 2022, Baltimore, Maryland, USA. Proceedings of Machine Learning Research, vol. 162, pp. 8759–8773. PMLR (2022). https://proceedings.mlr.press/v162/hendrycks22a.html
20. Hendrycks, D., Gimpel, K.: A baseline for detecting misclassified and out-of-distribution examples in neural networks. In: International Conference on Learning Representations (2017)
21. Huang, X., Wang, P., Cheng, X., Zhou, D., Geng, Q., Yang, R.: The apolloscape open dataset for autonomous driving and its application. IEEE Trans. Pattern Anal. Mach. Intell. **42**(10), 2702–2719 (2020). https://doi.org/10.1109/TPAMI.2019.2926463
22. Jung, S., Lee, J., Gwak, D., Choi, S., Choo, J.: Standardized max logits: a simple yet effective approach for identifying unexpected road obstacles in urban-scene segmentation. In: International Conference on Computer Vision, pp. 15405–15414 (2021)
23. Kirillov, A., et al.: Segment anything. In: ICCV (2023)
24. Lin, G., Milan, A., Shen, C., Reid, I.: RefineNet: multi-path refinement networks for high-resolution semantic segmentation. In: IEEE Conference on Computer Vision and Pattern Recognition, pp. 5168–5177 (2017)
25. Lis, K., Nakka, K., Fua, P., Salzmann, M.: Detecting the unexpected via image resynthesis. In: International Conference on Computer Vision, pp. 2152–2161 (2019)
26. Liu, W., Wang, X., Owens, J., Li, Y.: Energy-based out-of-distribution detection. In: Advances in Neural Information Processing Systems (2020)
27. Liu, Z., et al.: Swin transformer: hierarchical vision transformer using shifted windows. In: ICCV (2021)
28. Long, J., Shelhamer, E., Darrell, T.: Fully convolutional networks for semantic segmentation. In: IEEE Conference on Computer Vision and Pattern Recognition, pp. 3431–3440 (2015)
29. Maag, K., Chan, R., Uhlemeyer, S., Kowol, K., Gottschalk, H.: Two video data sets for tracking and retrieval of out of distribution objects. In: Wang, L., Gall, J., Chin, T., Sato, I., Chellappa, R. (eds.) ACCV 2022, Part V. LNCS, vol. 13845, pp. 476–494. Springer, Cham (2022). https://doi.org/10.1007/978-3-031-26348-4_28
30. Miao, J., Wei, Y., Wu, Y., Liang, C., Li, G., Yang, Y.: VSPW: a large-scale dataset for video scene parsing in the wild. In: IEEE Conference on Computer Vision and Pattern Recognition, CVPR 2021, virtual, 19–25 June 2021, pp. 4133–4143. Computer Vision Foundation/IEEE (2021). https://doi.org/10.1109/CVPR46437.2021.00412. https://openaccess.thecvf.com/content/CVPR2021/html/Miao_VSPW_A_Large-scale_Dataset_for_Video_Scene_Parsing_in_the_CVPR_2021_paper.html
31. Mukhoti, J., Gal, Y.: Evaluating Bayesian deep learning methods for semantic segmentation. CoRR abs/1811.12709 (2018)
32. Nayal, N., Yavuz, M., Henriques, J.F., Güney, F.: RbA: segmenting unknown regions rejected by all. In: International Conference on Computer Vision, pp. 711–722 (2023)
33. Pinggera, P., Ramos, S., Gehrig, S., Franke, U., Rother, C., Mester, R.: Lost and found: detecting small road hazards for self-driving vehicles. In: 2016 IEEE/RSJ

International Conference on Intelligent Robots and Systems, IROS 2016, Daejeon, South Korea, 9–14 October 2016, pp. 1099–1106. IEEE (2016). https://doi.org/10.1109/IROS.2016.7759186

34. Rai, S.N., Cermelli, F., Caputo, B., Masone, C.: Mask2anomaly: mask transformer for universal open-set segmentation. T-PAMI (2024)

35. Rai, S.N., Cermelli, F., Fontanel, D., Masone, C., Caputo, B.: Unmasking anomalies in road-scene segmentation. In: International Conference on Computer Vision, pp. 4014–4023 (2023)

36. Ramachandra, B., Jones, M.J.: Street scene: a new dataset and evaluation protocol for video anomaly detection. In: 2020 IEEE Winter Conference on Applications of Computer Vision (WACV), pp. 2558–2567 (2020)

37. Ravi, N., et al.: Sam 2: segment anything in images and videos. arXiv preprint arXiv:2408.00714 (2024). https://arxiv.org/abs/2408.00714

38. Ristea, N.C., Croitoru, F.A., Ionescu, R.T., Popescu, M., Khan, F.S., Shah, M.: Self-distilled masked auto-encoders are efficient video anomaly detectors. In: 2024 IEEE/CVF Conference on Computer Vision and Pattern Recognition (CVPR), pp. 15984–15995 (2024)

39. Ryali, C., et al.: Hiera: a hierarchical vision transformer without the bells-and-whistles. In: Krause, A., Brunskill, E., Cho, K., Engelhardt, B., Sabato, S., Scarlett, J. (eds.) International Conference on Machine Learning, ICML 2023, 23–29 July 2023, Honolulu, Hawaii, USA. Proceedings of Machine Learning Research, vol. 202, pp. 29441–29454. PMLR (2023). https://proceedings.mlr.press/v202/ryali23a.html

40. Singh, A., Kamireddypalli, A., Gandhi, V., Krishna, K.M.: Lidar guided small obstacle segmentation. In: IEEE/RSJ International Conference on Intelligent Robots and Systems, IROS 2020, Las Vegas, NV, USA, 24 October 2020–24 January 2021, pp. 8513–8520. IEEE (2020). https://doi.org/10.1109/IROS45743.2020.9341465

41. Vaswani, A., et al.: Attention is all you need. In: Advances in Neural Information Processing Systems (2017)

42. Vojir, T., Šipka, T., Aljundi, R., Chumerin, N., Reino, D.O., Matas, J.: Road anomaly detection by partial image reconstruction with segmentation coupling. In: International Conference on Computer Vision, pp. 15631–15640 (2021)

43. Xia, Y., Zhang, Y., Liu, F., Shen, W., Yuille, A.: Synthesize then compare: detecting failures and anomalies for semantic segmentation. In: European Conference on Computer Vision, pp. 145–161 (2020)

44. Zhang, D., Sakmann, K., Beluch, W., Hutmacher, R., Li, Y.: Anomaly-aware semantic segmentation via style-aligned OoD augmentation. In: International Conference on Computer Vision Workshop, pp. 4067–4075 (2023)

45. Zhang, T., et al.: DVIS: decoupled video instance segmentation framework. In: International Conference on Computer Vision, pp. 1282–1291 (2023)

46. Zhang, Z., Zhang, X., Peng, C., Xue, X., Sun, J.: ExFuse: enhancing feature fusion for semantic segmentation. In: European Conference on Computer Vision, pp. 273–288 (2018)

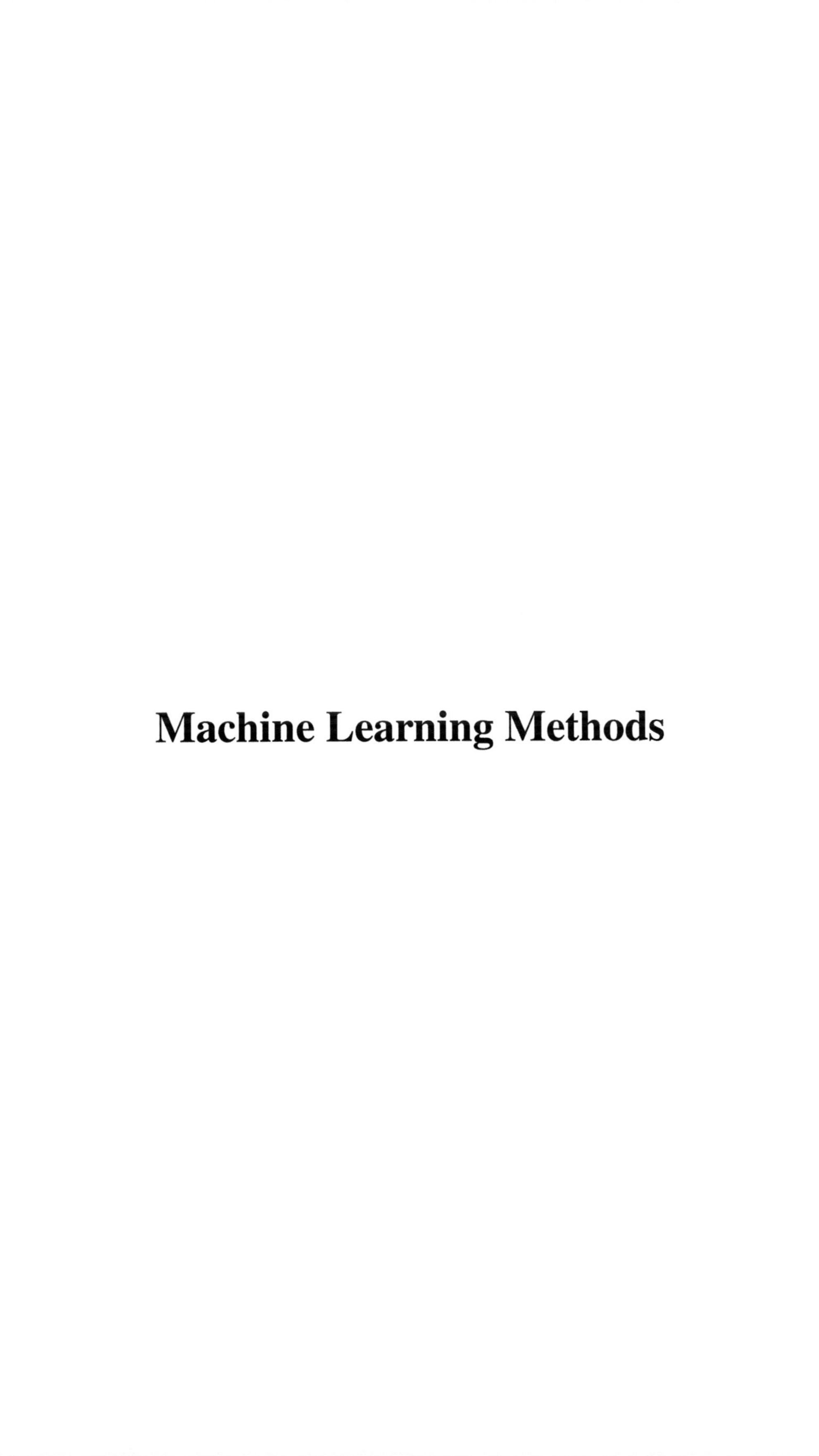

Machine Learning Methods

Don't Miss Out on Novelty: Importance of Novel Features for Deep Anomaly Detection

Sarath Sivaprasad[(✉)] and Mario Fritz

CISPA Helmholtz Center for Information Security, Saarbrücken, Germany
{sarath.sivaprasad,fritz}@cispa.de

Abstract. Anomaly Detection (AD) is the task of identifying samples that do not conform to a learned model of normality. Prior work in deep AD is predominantly based on a *familiarity hypothesis*, where *familiar* features serve as reference in a pre-trained *embedding space*. While this strategy has proven highly successful, it turns out that it results in consistent false negatives when anomalies are caused by truly *novel* features that are not well captured by the pre-trained encoding – similar to a "blind spot". We propose a new approach to AD using explainability to capture such novel features as unexplained observations in the *input space*. Hereby, we achieve state-of-the-art performance across various AD benchmarks by combining familiarity and novelty in a hybrid approach. Our approach has additional benefits such as eliminating the need for an outlier models. Inline with our motivation, we show that taking novel features into account reduces false negative anomalies by up to 40% on challenging benchmarks compared to methods relying solely on familiarity and provide visually inspectable explanations for pixel-level anomalies.

Keywords: Familiarity hypothesis · anomaly detection · novelty

1 Introduction

Anomaly detection (AD) is the task of identifying test samples that deviate significantly from the normal training distribution. Detecting anomaly samples is critical across a wide range of applications such as identifying rare diseases in medical imaging [16], flagging manufacturing defects on assembly lines [55] and enhancing security surveillance [6]. Beyond its applications in specific domains, AD helps identify and address potential aberrations in a system, reducing the likelihood of problems escalating into catastrophic outcomes [19]. Neural networks (NNs), learning expressive representations of image data, have driven the development of a broad family of deep image AD methods that identify anomalies as outliers in the feature space [40].

These methods predominantly rely on the familiarity hypothesis, which detects anomalies by their lack of familiar features [15]. Familiar features are the

M. Keuper and F. Locatello (Eds.): DAGM GCPR 2025, LNCS 16125, pp. 205–220, 2026.
https://doi.org/10.1007/978-3-032-12840-9_14

input features that the trained neural encoder has learned to represent meaningfully in the feature space. At inference, these approaches assume that normal data and all potential anomaly samples are distinguishable in the learned feature space, based on the familiar features.

Though prior methods have achieved significant success in learning such feature representations, relying solely on familiar features leads to two major issues in deep AD. Relying solely on familiar features leads to two major issues in deep AD. Firstly, neural networks owe much of their success to their ability to generalize well beyond the training data [52], often showing representation invariance even for Out-Of-Distribution (OOD) samples [21]. This means that the encoder may assign similar representations to both normal and OOD samples. Since anomalies are a specific case of OOD, such invariance often results in false negatives in deep AD.

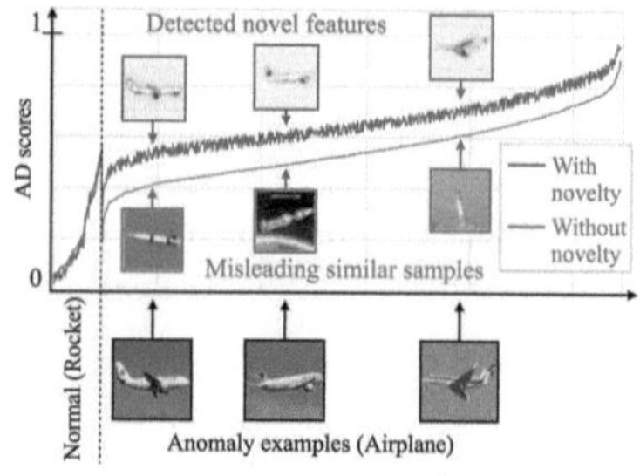

Fig. 1. 'rocket' = normal; 'airplane' = anomalies. Some aircraft images share cues with rocket images. We need to look for novel features like wings and turbines, to spot them as anomlaies.

Secondly, this paradigm fails to detect anomalies caused by features that are truly novel, not solely characterized by the absence of familiar features. AD methods that fail to account for novel features result in false negatives when input features causing anomalies are poorly represented or entirely absent from the feature space.

Excessive representation invariance is often addressed by modeling complex outlier distributions, encouraging separation between the representations of samples from normal distribution and those of outlier samples. Competitive performance has been demonstrated by methods that learn the representations by fine-tuning encoders on binary classification tasks using normal samples and synthetic data generated near the 'boundaries' of the normal distribution [25,28,33,53,54]. While these approaches make significant strides in addressing excessive representation invariance, they do not account for the challenge of detecting anomalies caused by novel features. These AD systems give false negatives when anomalies are characterized by novel features unseen in training. This is especially important since an encoder trained without assumptions on potential anomalies, however expressive, will not be sensitive to some novel features [31], and the set of possible anomalies is an open set.

We propose a hybrid approach for AD that addresses both these key issues by jointly modeling the lack of familiar features and the presence of novel features in an input sample. We use the features extracted by the encoder to quantify familiarity and capture novel features as unexplained observations in the input space. In our experiments, we evaluate the performance of the joint model and show that accounting for novel features in AD reduces false negatives and the reliance on a complex outlier distribution to control excessive representation invariance. We show that accounting for novel features helps detect anomalies that share features with some of the normal samples and would otherwise go undetected or get a low AD score (Figure 1).

We evaluate our method across multiple benchmarks establishing new state-of-the-art performance in most cases especially on semantic anomaly benchmarks. In particular, we show that taking account of novel features reduces false negative in AD by up to 40% across different challenging settings. Our experiments demonstrate that the joint modeling removes the need for modeling expensive outlier samples for training the encoder. Furthermore, for pixel-level anomalies, our method gives visually inspectable results along with the detection. In short, we make the following contributions:

- We introduce the concept of familiar and novel features in anomaly detection (AD). Specifically, we define novel features as those that remain unexplained when analyzed using a pixel-level explanation method.
- We propose a joint model for AD that accounts for the lack of *familiarity* and the presence of *novelty* in an input sample, achieving state-of-the-art results across multiple AD benchmarks.
- We show that the proposed method, by accounting for novel features, reduces false negatives and minimizes reliance on the complexity of outlier samples used to train the encoder.

2   Related Work

Most deep AD methods train an encoder to learn a representation of normal samples and then compare representations of test samples to those of normal training samples to compute the anomaly score [18,20]. Since anomaly samples are not available in the training phase, proxy tasks are employed to shape the encoder's representation with the assumption that potential anomaly samples will appear sufficiently different from normal samples in the learned feature space. Though no proxy task has given guarantees on the representation of anomalies, discriminating normal samples from 'outlier' samples as a proxy task has shown promising results [2,25,28,30,33,36,53,54]. Various inventive methods have been proposed to design effective outlier samples. A more comprehensive discussion of these approaches is in Appendix 10. However, this encoding might yield a lower anomaly score to a test sample with novel features alongside familiar ones [15]. AD, though often used interchangeably with novelty detection, is frequently approached by detecting the absence of familiar features.

AD and OOD Detection: AD is a specific case of OOD detection where all the In-Distribution(ID) samples are treated as a single distribution. This means that regardless of the number of classes (or statistical modalities) in ID data, AD task does not require differentiation in the ID samples. This feature is an important distinction between AD and other sub-topics such as open-set recognition and OOD detection [49]. Within the AD framework, based on the different distribution shifts that cause them, anomalies are divided into pixel-level anomalies and semantic anomalies (Appendix 1). [22,48].

Pixel-level anomalies like MVTec [1]–which contain dense familiar features, and only pixel level anomalies–are challenging to detect via familiar features alone. Most methods use locally sensitive dense feature extractors such that a novelty in input can come only at the cost of lost familiarity [5,12,34,47]. With the increasing number of normal samples, the memory bank becomes exceedingly large, with it both the inference time and memory required [34]. Other prominent methods for detecting pixel-level anomalies include (a) flow-based methods, such as CFlow [17] and PyramidFlow [26]; (b) distillation-based methods, including RD [13], RD++ [43], and DSR [50], (c) selective amplification of patterns in anomalous regions, including DifferNet [35] and AttentDifferNet [39] and (d) for detection and localization [7–9]. Accounting for novelty is a simple and intuitive way of improving pixel-level AD performance without using spatial annotation of anomalies for training.

Familiarity Hypothesis: For a regular NN, activation in the last layer for an OOD sample is typically lower than samples from training distribution. This difference alone can model a good open-set-detector [44]. Furthermore, this final layer representation provides denser activations when familiar features are present in the input compared to samples without them [41]. Dietterich *et al.* describe the methods that leverage this property under the'familiarity hypothesis', arguing that familiarity-based detection is an inevitable consequence of using encoder feature for AD, potentially leading to false negatives [15].

Earlier novelty detection methods use the reconstruction errors from GANs or auto-encoders to quantify novel features. These approaches depend on the reliability of the decoder with the assumption that poor reconstruction signifies that the sample lies outside the training distribution [45,51]. Measuring reconstruction error on features further improves over image level reconstruction approaches for semantic anomalies [37]. Methods that integrate feature and reconstruction error based AD typically use two encoders: one for prediction, and the other for reconstruction error [42]. Our method improves capturing novelty without the need to train two different branches or rely on decoders, improving the faithfulness in capturing novel features.

3   Joint Model for Familiarity and Novelty-Based Anomaly Detection

As discussed earlier, relying solely on the familiarity hypothesis can lead to false negatives in anomaly detection due to a 'blind spot' effect, where novel features may remain undetected. To address this limitation, we propose a joint approach that combines familiarity-based detection with a mechanism to capture novel features as illustrated in Fig. 2. For an input sample x_{test}, the anomaly score is computed taking into account (a) the absence of familiar features and (b) the presence of novel features in the sample. The joint anomaly score, $\mathcal{A}_s(x_{\text{test}})$, is derived as a combination of the familiarity and novelty scores for the sample.

$$\mathcal{A}_s(x_{\text{test}}) = \mathcal{F}_s(x_{\text{test}}) + \mathcal{G}_s(x_{\text{test}}) \tag{1}$$

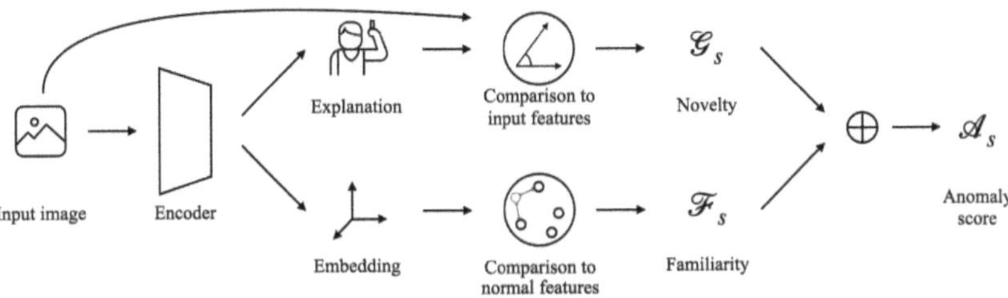

Fig. 2. The figure shows the proposed pipeline. The top portion computes Explanation-based Novelty Score (ENS), and the bottom branch computes Familiar Feature based anomaly Score (FFS). The final score, novelty accounted anomaly score, is a combination of both.

Here, $\mathcal{F}_s$ represents the Familiar Feature Score (FFS), and $\mathcal{G}_s$ represents the Explanation-based Novelty Score (ENS). For a given test sample, the FFS is computed based on the features of normal training samples and the ENS is computed using the encoder explanation.

We first train an encoder F to discriminate normal training samples n from generated 'outlier' samples b to obtain parameters θ. Outliers are generated by approximating the normal training distribution. The error in approximating the normal distribution distinguishes the generated samples from the original normal distribution. Note that, these outliers are generated without specific assumptions on the potential test time anomalies and used to learn a compact representation of the normal distribution.

We define 'familiar features' in an AD as the input features the trained encoder (F_θ) has learned to represent meaningfully in its feature space. However, a test sample can contain features outside this set. We define 'novel features' as the features in a test sample that are not familiar features. In other words, these are features in the test input that the encoder does not represent meaningfully in the feature space. Glossary in Appendix 13 gives formal definitions for important terms used in the work. We quantify familiar features by comparing $F_\theta(x_{\text{test}})$ to the features of normal training data. In contrast, we quantify novel features by comparing x_{test} to the explanation of F_θ given (x_{test}).

3.1 Familiar Feature Score (FFS)

To detect anomalies arising from the absence of familiar features in test samples, we employ a mechanism analogous to those used in previous studies. A state-of-the-art method to generate b employs a diffusion model that is prematurely early-stopped while approximating the normal training distribution [28]. An ablation study on the mechanisms for generating b demonstrates our method's robustness to this choice 4.3. We use a two-class classification head to train the encoder for discriminating normal samples n from generated outliers b using categorical loss.

Using F_θ as the encoder, we compute the distance between the features of the test sample and its K-Nearest normal training samples. The FFS score, $\mathcal{F}_s$, is the sum of distances of $(F_\theta(x_{\text{test}}))$ to its K-nearest samples in the set $F_\theta(n_i), \forall n_i \in n$. Following prior work [28], we use $K = 2$. The method's robustness to K is in Appendix 3.

In practice, $F(\theta, n_i), \forall n_i \in n$ is computed and stored in a matrix M in the training phase and given a test sample the 2 nearest neighbors M_0 and M_1 are retrieved based on L_2 distance from $(F_\theta(x_{\text{test}}))$. The FFS score, is computed as

$$\mathcal{F}_s(x_{\text{test}}) = \|F_\theta(x_{\text{test}}) - M_0\| + \|F_\theta(x_{\text{test}}) - M_1\| \tag{2}$$

Adapting to Anomaly Types: As discussed in Sect. 2, familiarity based methods use dense feature matching for detecting pixel-level anomalies. To improve FFS on such anomalies, we employ dense feature extraction and matching similar to [34]. Specifically, rather than relying on a single global representation per normal training sample $F_\theta(n_i), \forall n_i \in n$, we extract patch-level feature representations across spatial locations for each training sample. These patch-level features are stored as individual rows in the matrix M, a collection of nominal patch features. Each spatial position (h, w) in a sample n_i corresponds to a patch-level feature $F_\theta(n_i)_{h,w}$, which captures localized information. During inference, we calculate the Familiar Feature Score (FFS) $\mathcal{F}_s$ by measuring the distance between each test patch feature $F_\theta(x_{\text{test}})_{h,w}$ and its nearest neighbor in M. The FFS is then defined as the cumulative distance between each patch feature in the test sample and its closest match in M.

3.2   Explanation-Based Novelty Score (ENS)

Novel features refer to features in the input sample that are not adequately represented in the encoding. To inspect the encoder computation we use it's explanation and quantify the novel features as the parts of the input image that is not explained. To get a such an inspectable pixel accurate, faithful explanation of the encoder we build on a B-cos style network [4]. The strong localization of the explanation enables quantification of novel features as the difference between the input and the explanation of the encoder. As the number of unexplained features in the input increases, the measured difference also increases. ENS score $(\mathcal{G}_s(x_{\text{test}}))$ is measured as by $1 - \text{cosine distance}(x_{\text{test}}, \text{explanation}(F))$.

B-Cos for Localized Explanations: A B-cos encoder generates a faithful explanation of its computation. B-cos networks are neural networks in which all the linear layers (along with activations) are replaced by B-cos layers. For more details on the formulation and training of these networks, we refer the reader to [3,4]. We choose the B-cos network for two reasons. Firstly, we need to compare the input sample to the encoder explanation and B-cos has an input dependent non-linearity that collapses encoder computations into a linear transformation with the same dimension as test sample. Secondly, the resulting linear operation aligns with input features that contribute to a high output. This alignment can be used to quantify how much each feature activates the output. The operation of a B-cos layer at a node, for an input x and weights w leading to the node, is given by

$$\text{B-cos}(x; w) = \|x\| \cdot \|w\| \cdot |\cos(\angle(x, w))|^B \cdot \text{sign}\left(\cos(\angle(x, w))\right) \tag{3}$$

where B is a hyper-parameter that influences the extent to which alignment between x and w contributes to the magnitude of the output. Given an input x, the B-cos layer becomes a linear layer followed by a scalar multiplication (the cosine score, Eq. 3). As each layer becomes a linear operation, the network collapses into a single linear transform that faithfully summarizes the entire model computations. Moreover, the B-cos layers introduce alignment pressure on their weights during optimization. For the output of a node to be high, the input must align well with the node's incoming parameters, indicated by a high $\cos(\angle(x, w))$. Thus, the linear operation into which the B-cos encoder collapses enable the inspection of input features that contribute to the output. More details on the construction of B-cos for our experiments are provided in Appendix 4.

Detecting Novelty by a Lack of Explanation: We use the lack of this explanation from a B-cos network as evidence for the presence of novel features. We quantify the novel features as the cosine distance (alignment) between x_{test} and the encoder explanation. We call this measure as the novelty score (ENS). The B-cos network provides a faithful summarization of the encoder computation (not an approximate explanation), enabling the identification of novel features in the input.

Following notation in [3], for an input x, the explanation of an L layer network with parameter θ is given by $\theta_{1 \to L}(x)$. We compute the Explanation-based Novelty Score (ENS), denoted by $\mathcal{G}_s$, for a test input x_{test} and an encoder with parameters θ as

$$\mathcal{G}_s(x_{\text{test}}) = 1 - \cos(\angle(\theta_{1 \to L}(x_{\text{test}}), x_{\text{test}})) \tag{4}$$

Adapting to Anomaly Types: We use a B-cos network pre-trained on ImageNet [14] as the encoder, keeping the initial layers frozen during training to discriminate between n (normal data) and b (outliers). It is therefore meaningful to check for novel features in the later layers of the network, especially when the anomaly involves semantic features, as these layers capture a higher semantic hierarchy. For a test sample, Böhle *et al.* use $\theta_{1 \to L}(x_{\text{test}})$ to visualize the decision explanation. We modify this to compute $\theta_{l \to L}$ where l is the layer at which we evaluate the novelty and L is the final layer. Novelty at layer i is computed as

$$\mathcal{G}_s{}^i(x_{\text{test}}) = 1 - \cos(\angle(\theta_{(i+1) \to L}(f_i), f_i)) \tag{5}$$

where f_i is the feature representation at layer i. For pixel-level anomalies, we look for novel features in the input; setting $i = 1$ and Eq. 5 becomes similar to the formulation in [4]. Here, the choice of layer is a hyper-parameter to adapt to anomalies at different semantic levels (details in Appendix 1). This enables the method to scale to different anomaly types.

Finally, we compute the joint anomaly score as the sum of the familiarity and novelty scores, Eq. 1. This combination can be further improved by using a weighted addition of the two scores. We avoid using validation data for each class to find the optimal weight value. To enable comparison with other methods on the same benchmarks, we use a simple addition for the combination in the benchmark experiments. Ablations using varying weights are presented in Appendix 5.

4   Experiments and Results

In this section, we present three sets of experiments to evaluate the effectiveness of accounting for novel features in computing anomaly scores. In the first set, we demonstrate the efficacy of the proposed joint model across eight different AD benchmarks in semantic anomaly and three pixel-level anomaly benchmarks. The second set of experiments shows ablations to demonstrate that accounting for novelty indeed improves AD performance, specifically reducing false negatives. In the final experiment, we present results showing how our method reduces the reliance on the complexity of outlier samples used in training the encoder.

4.1   Benchmarking Across Different AD Tasks

Across anomaly types, we benchmark the efficacy of accounting for novel features for AD. We add novelty to familiarity computed by (a) global feature representation and (b) dense feature computation, for a sample.

Adding ENS to FFS by Global Representation: For benchmarking on semantic anomalies, we choose eight different datasets across the three anomaly types following [28], namely: CIFAR-10 [24], CIFAR-100 [24], Flowers [29], Birds [46], FGVC [27], Stanford-Cars [23], and CIFAR-10 vs CIFAR-100 [28]. The effective number of benchmarks evaluated is in fact 734 as we perform evaluations with each class within these datasets as the normal class. For each dataset, we report the mean AUROC of the test anomaly samples across all classes. CIFAR-10 vs CIFAR-100 (C10-100) [28] is a challenging new near-semantic benchmark, where most prior AD methods struggle to retain good performance. For creating this benchmark, each category in CIFAR-10 is paired with its semantically nearest category from CIFAR-100 (more details on the formulation of this benchmark can be found in Appendix 1).

For each normal class, we fine-tune an ImageNet [14] pretrained B-cos ViT backbone as F, and get a single global feature per sample. The encoder is fine-tuned with a dual classification head for the normal and outlier class. We use the same training procedure as in [28] (exact hyper-parameters of training in Appendix 11). Furthermore, our method introduces a hyper-parameter to control the semantic level at which the anomalies are detected (denoted as i in Sect. 3.2). We do not tune this parameter to optimize the performance on each dataset for a fair comparison, as our aim is not just to establish state-of-the-art results but to show the importance of accounting for novelty in AD. To adapt to anomaly types, we set $i = 0$ for pixel-level anomalies (explanation of input) and $i = L - 1$ for semantic anomalies (more details in Appendix 1).

Table 1. The performance of the proposed method (% AUROC) in AD setting on different datasets. For each dataset, the performance of the best-performing model is bold, and the performance of the second-best method is underlined.

Method	Datasets								
	Semantic near AD				Semantic far AD			Pixel-level AD	
	CIFAR-10	CIFAR-100	Flowers	Birds	FGVC	Cars	C10-100	MVTec	Average
CSI [41]	94.3	89.6	60.8	52.4	64.6	66.5	76.1	63.6	71.0
MSAD(ViT) [32]	94.1	93.0	98.6	93.3	81.3	85.7	79.5	85.5	88.8
Transformaly [11]	98.3	97.3	99.9	97.8	84.0	86.7	82.5	87.9	91.8
PANDA [30]	96.2	94.1	94.1	95.3	77.7	87.6	76.8	86.5	88.5
FITYMI [28]	99.1	98.1	99.9	98.5	88.7	90.8	89.4	86.4	93.8
Our method	99.3	98.5	99.9	98.8	89.3	90.5	91.8	92.6	95.1

Table 1 shows the % AUROC performance of the proposed method compared with prior methods that use global features. The performance on some datasets, such as CIFAR-10 and Flowers, has reached saturation (above 99%). Hence, following [28], we also use C10-100 for comparing model performances. Our method establishes a new state-of-the-art on this benchmark, outperforming the next best model by 2.4%. On average across benchmarks, our model outperforms the next best model by about 1.3%.

Jiang *et al.* surveys methods for pixel-level anomalies and notes that most methods tuned for semantic anomalies perform poorly in detecting pixel-level anomalies and vice-versa [22]. This is verified by the relative lower performance of previous methods on MVTec in Table 1. These anomalies have dense familiar features and aberrations only in a few input pixels. Accounting for novelty gives about 5% improvement over the next best global feature based method.

Visualization: For pixel-level AD, the global explanation for an input x_{test} is computed as $(\theta_{1 \to L}(x_{\text{test}}))$ (Sect. 3.2). Figure 3 shows the explanation in the input generated by the B-cos model for the anomaly branch of the classification head. In other words, the explanation is computed for the decision that the input sample is an anomaly. This demonstrates how the method can not only detect but also explain the anomaly. Note that these visualizations are generated by projecting the $\theta_{1 \to L}(x_{\text{test}})$ value into color space using non-linear projections, following [3]. The anomaly score is computed using the raw value.

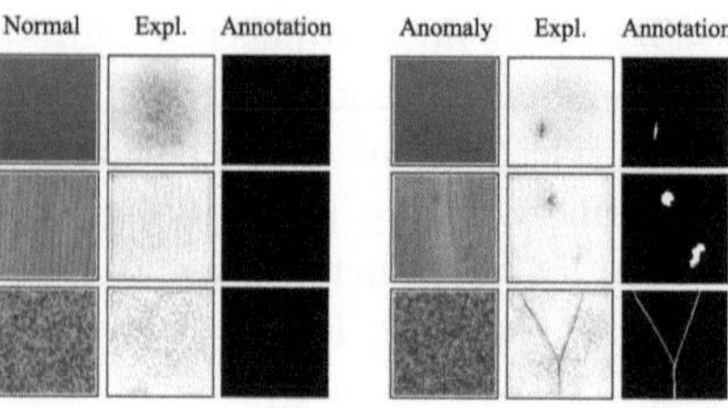

Fig. 3. Figure shows examples of test samples from MVTecAD dataset, and their explanation. ENS score is computed as the distance between the two.

Dense Feature Matching: We also add the ENS score to the FFS score computed by dense feature matching. For benchmarking on pixel-level anomaly using dense matching we use InsPLAD [38], MVTec [1] and RAD [10]. We use a B-cos ResNet101 backbone for dense feature extraction similar to prior work [34]). More details and results in Appendix 11. By explicitly capturing novel features, our method achieves near-perfect performance on texture classes in the MVTec dataset, setting a new state-of-the-art. As shown in Fig. 3, novel features that cause anomalies in texture classes

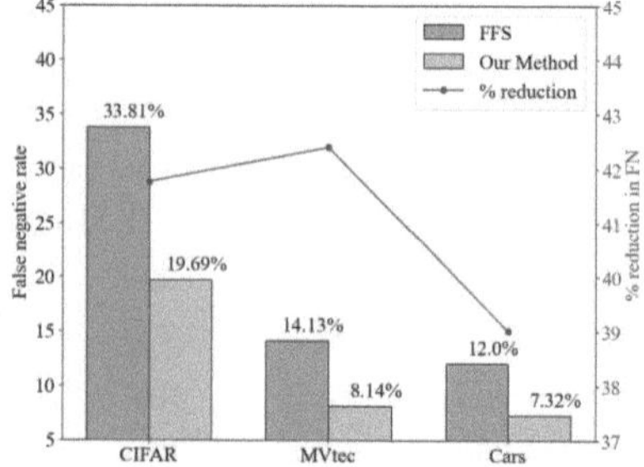

Fig. 4. False-negative comparison. Left axis: raw FN rate. Right axis: percentage reduction after accounting for novelty.

often appear alongside familiar features. The performance improvement aligns with our intuition that accounting for novel features should improve performance on such benchmarks. Overall, our method achieves the best or second-best performance in nine of the eleven evaluations. On the RAD dataset [10], our method achieves state-of-the-art performance with an improvement of up to 1.5% over competitive methods such as [34]. The full results for this high-resolution dataset are in Appendix 7.

4.2   Effect of Accounting for Novelty

Reducing False Negatives. Methods that rely solely on familiar features struggle to detect anomalies caused by *truly novel* cues, which leads to false-negative predictions [15]. In this experiment we study how explicitly modelling novelty affects the FN rate on three benchmarks: Stanford-Cars (semantic far AD), C10-100 (semantic near AD) and MVTec (pixel-level AD). We binarise the anomaly score and use an oracle threshold that maximises the F_1 score for every class. We first evaluate FFS computed with a global representation and then re-evaluate with added ENS.

The results (in Figure 4) show that incorporating novelty reduces false negatives by about 40% across different anomaly types. This strengthens the hypothesis in [15]: AD relying solely on familiar features may miss anomalies caused by novel features. The false positive rates remain almost unchanged (absolute differences of 0.6%, 0.8%, and 0.3% for C10-100, MVTec, and Cars data, respectively), indicating that the improvement in AUROC resulted from correcting false negatives. The teaser figure (Figure 1) illustrates this effect on a modified C10-100 configuration, where 'rocket' is the normal class, and all test samples of C10 along with a few samples from FGVC are used as anomalies.

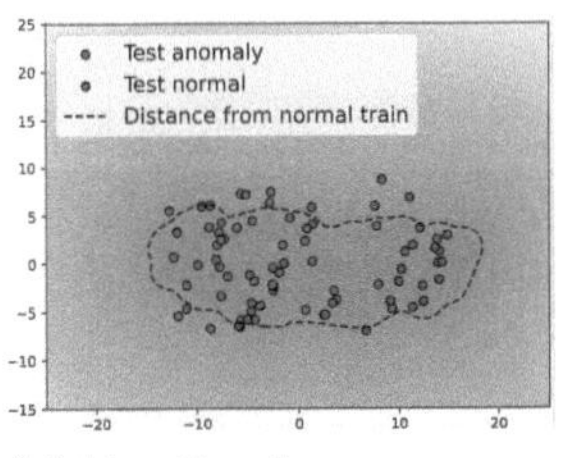

(a) Familiar features space

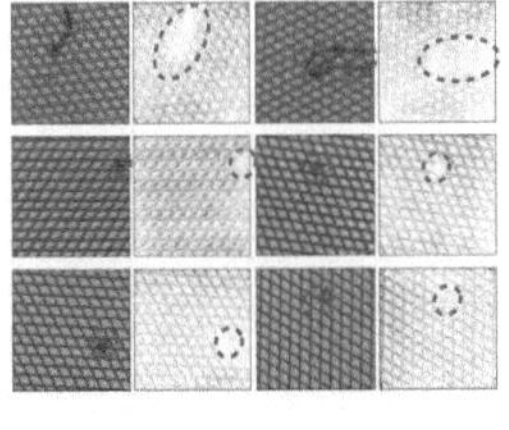

(b) Novelty as lack of explanation

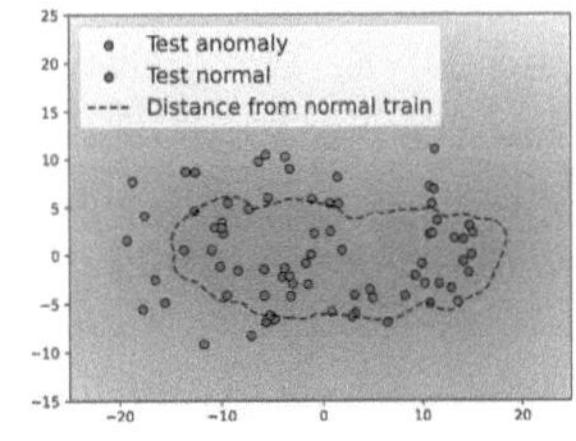

(c) Novelty accounted familiar features

Fig. 5. The PCA plots (a and b) shows the normal test and anomaly test samples plotted on the two principal components. The first plot (a) is the PCA plot of familiar features, nd the second plot (b) is with a novelty score added to the features. The contour shows the sum of distances to the two nearest train normal samples. The samples shown in the middle (c) are the ones that give maximum deviation from the normal train samples when adding novelty scores (with corresponding explanations of being normal).

Qualitative Analysis: To study the reduction of false negatives by accounting for novel features, we select a random class of MVTec AD dataset: 'Grid'. Figure 5 shows the features of normal test samples and test anomalies projected onto their two principal component space. The color of the contour at each point represents the sum of the distances to the two nearest normal training samples (FFS). The third plot in the figure shows the same points but with the sign-corrected novelty score added to the feature representation. Accounting for unexplained novel features shifts the anomaly samples further from the normal training data compared to normal test samples, explaining the reduction in false negatives. The figure also shows the samples with the highest novelty score, along with their explanations. We can see how the network (for normal classification) fails to explain the novel features in the input. ENS is computed as the distance between the image and the explanation, which increases with an increase in unexplained regions.

Table 2. Ablation showing the performance of prior art, FFS, ENS and the proposed joint model on C10-100 Dataset. Reported numbers are AUROC (range 0–1) of the evaluated score and label.

Class	Plane	Auto	Bird	Cat	Deer	Dog	Frog	Horse	Ship	Truck	Avg
Anomaly	Rocket	Truck	Shrew	Leopard	Cattle	Rabbit	Lizard	Cattle	Bridge	Bus	-
FITYMI	0.95	0.83	0.92	0.86	0.92	0.85	0.94	0.97	0.93	0.77	0.894
FFS Acc	0.94	0.83	0.87	0.9	0.89	0.78	0.92	0.96	0.92	0.83	0.884
ENS Acc	0.91	0.8	0.81	0.86	0.87	0.77	0.91	0.95	0.9	0.81	0.859
Joint model	**0.95**	**0.85**	**0.96**	**0.90**	**0.93**	**0.91**	**0.94**	**0.97**	**0.94**	**0.83**	**0.918**

Ablation Showing the Effect of FFS and ENS: We present additional ablation studies to demonstrate the contribution of ENS in computing the joint anomaly score using the classes of the C10-100 dataset. Table 2 illustrates the impact of incorporating novel features when computing the anomaly scores. For instance, when class 'Dog' is the normal class and class 'Rabbit' is the anomaly, the improvement from adding ENS is greater than 10% (absolute difference). Compared to [28], the FFS is slightly lower due to the lower generalization of B-cos, but the joint score is greater than both FFS and prior state-of-the-art method.

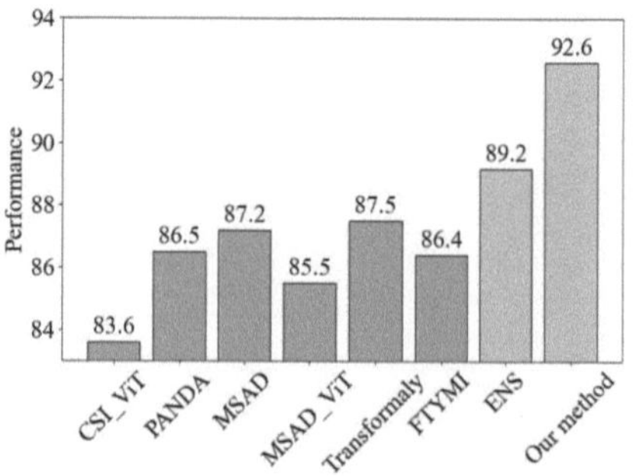

Fig. 6. Comparison of ENS and proposed method with previous familiarity based AD methods on MVTec dataset.

Bar plots showing the FFS and ENS for all test anomalies are provided in Appendix 5. It is interesting to note that ENS and FFS somewhat complement each other. This indicates that the novel features not accounted for in the FFS computation are captured by the ENS.

Ablation: Benchmarking ENS for AD: In this experiment, we evaluate the efficacy of using ENS for AD. For this analysis, we use the MVTec dataset [1], which contains pixel-level anomalies. As discussed earlier, previous feature-based methods that do not use dense matching have demonstrated lower performance on this task relative to other benchmarks (Table 1). We compare the performance of ENS (not the joint model) with other familiarity based methods on MVTec (Fig. 6). The ENS alone outperforms the SOTA familiarity based method. This improvement comes without storing features of normal training samples for inference. Accounting for novelty improves performance by about 5%.

4.3   Reducing the Role of Modelling Outlier Samples

Reducing reliance on training outlier classes is desirable for improving the robustness of an AD method (Appendix 6). This helps the method scale to the diverse anomalies encountered in the real world. However, most current AD methods use features learned from discriminating generated outliers from normal samples. Mirzaei *et al.* [28] generate outliers with a diffusion model and report gains over GAN- or VAE-generated outliers.

To demonstrate the reduced reliance on training outliers, we use a simple Gaussian approximation of the normal class to generate training outliers on the C10-100 dataset. We compute the mean and covariance of the normal dataset and sample from a Gaussian distribution with these parameters to generate training outliers. The true distribution of images of each class follow a complex distribution, and a normal approximation cannot capture this complexity. This error in approximation makes the normal samples n different from outliers b. The encoder is then trained with a classifier to discriminate n from b. We compare the performance of our method with diffusion model generated outliers with Gaussian approximation based outliers in Fig. 7. While prior method drops by 3% with this simple outlier model, the performance of our method with the two outliers is comparable.

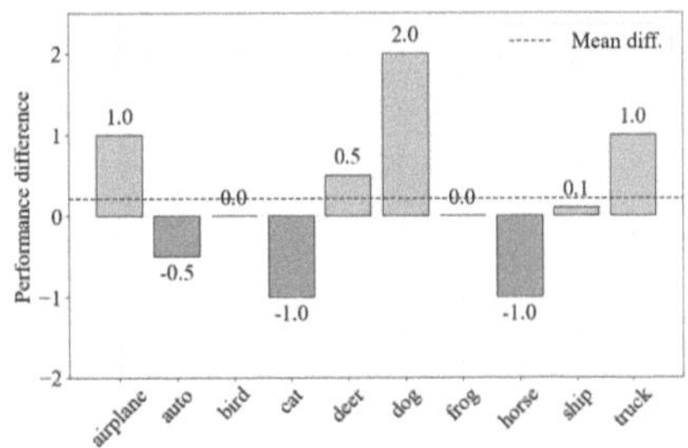

Fig. 7. AUROC differences when training the encoder with (a) Gaussian outliers (b) diffusion-generated outliers. Green bars = improvement of (a) over (b), blue = drop.

5   Conclusion

This paper highlights the need for Anomaly Detection (AD) to go beyond *familiar* features and account for *novel* features. We propose a method to capture novel features as unexplained observations and show that accounting for them reduces false negatives in AD, establishing state-of-the-art on multiple benchmarks across anomaly types. We believe this idea can be scaled to related tasks like open-set recognition, one-class-classification (Appendix 8) and OOD detection. This idea can also be scaled by adding a mechanism to decide if the detected novel features are indeed making the sample anomalous or not (discussion in Appendix 9,12).

Acknowledgements. This work was partially funded by ELSA – European Lighthouse on Secure and Safe AI funded by the European Union under grant agreement No.101070617. Views and opinions expressed are, however, those of the authors only and do not necessarily reflect those of the European Union or European Commission. Neither the European Union nor the European Commission can be held responsible for them. The project on which this report is based was funded by the Federal Ministry of Education and Research under the funding code 16KIS2012. The responsibility for the content of this publication lies with the authors.

References

1. Bergmann, P., Fauser, M., Sattlegger, D., Steger, C.: Mvtec ad-a comprehensive real-world dataset for unsupervised anomaly detection. In: Proceedings of the IEEE/CVF Conference on Computer Vision and Pattern Recognition, pp. 9592–9600 (2019)
2. Bergmann, P., Fauser, M., Sattlegger, D., Steger, C.: Uninformed students: Student-teacher anomaly detection with discriminative latent embeddings. In: Proceedings of the IEEE/CVF Conference on Computer Vision and Pattern Recognition, pp. 4183–4192 (2020)
3. Böhle, M., Fritz, M., Schiele, B.: Holistically explainable vision transformers. arXiv preprint arXiv:2301.08669 (2023)
4. Böhle, M., Fritz, M., Schiele, B.: B-cos networks: Alignment is all we need for interpretability. In: CVPR (2022)
5. Cao, Y., Xu, X., Liu, Z., Shen, W.: Collaborative discrepancy optimization for reliable image anomaly localization. IEEE Trans. Industr. Inf. **19**(11), 10674–10683 (2023)
6. Chandrakala, S., Deepak, K., Revathy, G.: Anomaly detection in surveillance videos: a thematic taxonomy of deep models, review and performance analysis. Artif. Intell. Rev. **56**(4), 3319–3368 (2023)
7. Chen, Q., Luo, H., Gao, H., Lv, C., Zhang, Z.: Progressive boundary guided anomaly synthesis for industrial anomaly detection. IEEE Trans. Circ. Syst. Video Technol. (2024)
8. Chen, Q., Luo, H., Lv, C., Zhang, Z.: A unified anomaly synthesis strategy with gradient ascent for industrial anomaly detection and localization. In: European Conference on Computer Vision, pp. 37–54. Springer (2024)
9. Chen, Z., Xie, X., Yang, L., Lai, J.H.: Hard-normal example-aware template mutual matching for industrial anomaly detection. Int. J. Comput. Vision, 1–23 (2024)
10. Cheng, Y., Cao, Y., Chen, R., Shen, W.: Rad: A comprehensive dataset for benchmarking the robustness of image anomaly detection. arXiv preprint arXiv:2406.07176 (2024)
11. Cohen, M.J., Avidan, S.: Transformaly-two (feature spaces) are better than one. In: CVPR (2022)
12. Cohen, N., Hoshen, Y.: Sub-image anomaly detection with deep pyramid correspondences. arXiv preprint arXiv:2005.02357 (2020)
13. Deng, H., Li, X.: Anomaly detection via reverse distillation from one-class embedding. In: Proceedings of the IEEE/CVF Conference on Computer Vision and Pattern Recognition, pp. 9737–9746 (2022)
14. Deng, J., Dong, W., Socher, R., Li, L.J., Li, K., Fei-Fei, L.: Imagenet: A large-scale hierarchical image database. In: 2009 IEEE Conference on Computer Vision and Pattern Recognition, pp. 248–255. IEEE (2009)
15. Dietterich, T.G., Guyer, A.: The familiarity hypothesis: explaining the behavior of deep open set methods. Pattern Recogn. **132**, 108931 (2022)
16. Fernando, T., Gammulle, H., Denman, S., Sridharan, S., Fookes, C.: Deep learning for medical anomaly detection-a survey. ACM Comput. Surv. (CSUR) **54**(7), 1–37 (2021)
17. Gudovskiy, D., Ishizaka, S., Kozuka, K.: Cflow-ad: Real-time unsupervised anomaly detection with localization via conditional normalizing flows. In: Proceedings of the IEEE/CVF Winter Conference on Applications of Computer Vision, pp. 98–107 (2022)

18. Han, S., Hu, X., Huang, H., Jiang, M., Zhao, Y.: Adbench: Anomaly detection benchmark. NeurIPS (2022)
19. Hendrycks, D., Mazeika, M., Woodside, T.: An overview of catastrophic AI risks. arXiv preprint arXiv:2306.12001 (2023)
20. Hojjati, H., Ho, T.K.K., Armanfard, N.: Self-supervised anomaly detection: A survey and outlook. arXiv preprint arXiv:2205.05173 (2022)
21. Jacobsen, J.H., Behrmann, J., Zemel, R., Bethge, M.: Excessive invariance causes adversarial vulnerability. arXiv preprint arXiv:1811.00401 (2018)
22. Jiang, X., et al.: A survey of visual sensory anomaly detection. arXiv preprint arXiv:2202.07006 (2022)
23. Krause, J., Stark, M., Deng, J., Fei-Fei, L.: 3D object representations for fine-grained categorization. In: Proceedings of the IEEE International Conference on Computer Vision Workshops, pp. 554–561 (2013)
24. Krizhevsky, A., Hinton, G., et al.: Learning multiple layers of features from tiny images (2009)
25. Kwon, G., Kim, J., Choi, H.J., Yoon, B.M., Choi, S., Jung, K.H.: Improving out-of-distribution detection performance using synthetic outlier exposure generated by visual foundation models. In: BMVC, pp. 10–11 (2023)
26. Lei, J., Hu, X., Wang, Y., Liu, D.: Pyramidflow: High-resolution defect contrastive localization using pyramid normalizing flow. In: Proceedings of the IEEE/CVF Conference on Computer Vision and Pattern Recognition, pp. 14143–14152 (2023)
27. Maji, S., Rahtu, E., Kannala, J., Blaschko, M., Vedaldi, A.: Fine-grained visual classification of aircraft. arXiv preprint arXiv:1306.5151 (2013)
28. Mirzaei, H., et al.: Fake it until you make it : Towards accurate near-distribution novelty detection. In: ICLR (2023)
29. Nilsback, M.E., Zisserman, A.: Automated flower classification over a large number of classes. In: 2008 Sixth Indian Conference on Computer Vision, Graphics & Image Processing, pp. 722–729. IEEE (2008)
30. Reiss, T., Cohen, N., Bergman, L., Hoshen, Y.: Panda: Adapting pretrained features for anomaly detection and segmentation. In: CVPR (2021)
31. Reiss, T., Cohen, N., Hoshen, Y.: No free lunch: The hazards of over-expressive representations in anomaly detection. arXiv preprint arXiv:2306.07284 (2023)
32. Reiss, T., Hoshen, Y.: Mean-shifted contrastive loss for anomaly detection. In: AAAI (2023)
33. Rivera, A.R., Khan, A., Bekkouch, I.E.I., Sheikh, T.S.: Anomaly detection based on zero-shot outlier synthesis and hierarchical feature distillation. IEEE Trans. Neural Netw. Learn. Syst. **33**(1), 281–291 (2020)
34. Roth, K., Pemula, L., Zepeda, J., Schölkopf, B., Brox, T., Gehler, P.: Towards total recall in industrial anomaly detection (2021)
35. Rudolph, M., Wandt, B., Rosenhahn, B.: Same same but differnet: Semi-supervised defect detection with normalizing flows. In: Proceedings of the IEEE/CVF Winter Conference on Applications of Computer Vision, pp. 1907–1916 (2021)
36. Salehi, M., Sadjadi, N., Baselizadeh, S., Rohban, M.H., Rabiee, H.R.: Multiresolution knowledge distillation for anomaly detection. In: Proceedings of the IEEE/CVF Conference on Computer Vision and Pattern Recognition, pp. 14902–14912 (2021)
37. Shi, Y., Yang, J., Qi, Z.: Unsupervised anomaly segmentation via deep feature reconstruction. Neurocomputing **424**, 9–22 (2021)
38. Vieira e Silva, A.L.B., et al.: Insplad: A dataset and benchmark for power line asset inspection in UAV images. Int. J. Rem. Sens. **44**(23), 7294–7320 (2023)

39. Simões, F., Kowerko, D., Schlosser, T., Battisti, F., Teichrieb, V., et al.: Attention modules improve image-level anomaly detection for industrial inspection: A differnet case study. In: Proceedings of the IEEE/CVF Winter Conference on Applications of Computer Vision, pp. 8246–8255 (2024)

40. Sodemann, A.A., Ross, M.P., Borghetti, B.J.: A review of anomaly detection in automated surveillance. IEEE Trans. Syst. Man Cybern. Part C (Applications and Reviews) **42**(6), 1257–1272 (2012)

41. Tack, J., Mo, S., Jeong, J., Shin, J.: Csi: Novelty detection via contrastive learning on distributionally shifted instances. NeurIPS (2020)

42. Tang, Y., Zhao, L., Zhang, S., Gong, C., Li, G., Yang, J.: Integrating prediction and reconstruction for anomaly detection. Pattern Recogn. Lett. **129**, 123–130 (2020)

43. Tien, T.D., et al.: Revisiting reverse distillation for anomaly detection. In: Proceedings of the IEEE/CVF Conference on Computer Vision and Pattern Recognition, pp. 24511–24520 (2023)

44. Vaze, S., Han, K., Vedaldi, A., Zisserman, A.: Open-set recognition: a good closed-set classifier is all you need? In: ICLR (2022)

45. Vojir, T., Šipka, T., Aljundi, R., Chumerin, N., Reino, D.O., Matas, J.: Road anomaly detection by partial image reconstruction with segmentation coupling. In: Proceedings of the IEEE/CVF International Conference on Computer Vision, pp. 15651–15660 (2021)

46. Wah, C., Branson, S., Welinder, P., Perona, P., Belongie, S.: The caltech-ucsd birds-200-2011 dataset (2011)

47. Wan, Q., Gao, L., Li, X., Wen, L.: Industrial image anomaly localization based on gaussian clustering of pretrained feature. IEEE Trans. Industr. Electron. **69**(6), 6182–6192 (2021)

48. Yang, J., et al.: Openood: Benchmarking generalized out-of-distribution detection. In: NeurIPS (2022)

49. Yang, Z., Sinnott, R.O., Bailey, J., Ke, Q.: A survey of automated data augmentation algorithms for deep learning-based image classification tasks. Knowl. Inf. Syst. 1–57 (2023)

50. Zavrtanik, V., Kristan, M., Skočaj, D.: Dsr-a dual subspace re-projection network for surface anomaly detection. In: European Conference on Computer Vision, pp. 539–554. Springer (2022)

51. Zenati, H., Romain, M., Foo, C.S., Lecouat, B., Chandrasekhar, V.: Adversarially learned anomaly detection. In: 2018 IEEE International Conference on Data Mining (ICDM), pp. 727–736. IEEE (2018)

52. Zhang, C., Bengio, S., Hardt, M., Recht, B., Vinyals, O.: Understanding deep learning (still) requires rethinking generalization. Commun. ACM **64**(3), 107–115 (2021)

53. Zhang, J., Inkawhich, N., Linderman, R., Luley, R., Chen, Y., Li, H.: Sio: Synthetic in-distribution data benefits out-of-distribution detection. arXiv preprint arXiv:2303.14531 (2023)

54. Zhang, X., Xu, M., Zhou, X.: Realnet: A feature selection network with realistic synthetic anomaly for anomaly detection. In: Proceedings of the IEEE/CVF Conference on Computer Vision and Pattern Recognition, pp. 16699–16708 (2024)

55. Zipfel, J., Verworner, F., Fischer, M., Wieland, U., Kraus, M., Zschech, P.: Anomaly detection for industrial quality assurance: a comparative evaluation of unsupervised deep learning models. Comput. Indus. Eng. **177**, 109045 (2023)

LADB: Latent Aligned Diffusion Bridges for Semi-Supervised Domain Translation

Xuqin Wang[1,2], Tao Wu[1], Yanfeng Zhang[1], Lu Liu[1], Dong Wang[1],
Mingwei Sun[1], Yongliang Wang[1], Niclas Zeller[3], and Daniel Cremers[2(✉)]

[1] Huawei Technologies Deutschland, Munich, Germany
[2] Technical University of Munich, Munich, Germany
{xuqin.wang,cremers}@tum.de
[3] Karlsruhe University of Applied Sciences, Karlsruhe, Germany

Abstract. Diffusion models excel at generating high-quality outputs but face challenges in data-scarce domains, where exhaustive retraining or costly paired data are often required. To address these limitations, we propose Latent Aligned Diffusion Bridges (LADB), a semi-supervised framework for sample-to-sample translation that effectively bridges domain gaps using partially paired data. By aligning source and target distributions within a shared latent space, LADB seamlessly integrates pretrained source-domain diffusion models with a target-domain Latent Aligned Diffusion Model (LADM), trained on partially paired latent representations. This approach enables deterministic domain mapping without the need for full supervision. Compared to unpaired methods, which often lack controllability, and fully paired approaches that require large, domain-specific datasets, LADB strikes a balance between fidelity and diversity by leveraging a mixture of paired and unpaired latent-target couplings. Our experimental results demonstrate superior performance in depth-to-image translation under partial supervision. Furthermore, we extend LADB to handle multi-source translation (from depth maps and segmentation masks) and multi-target translation in a class-conditioned style transfer task, showcasing its versatility in handling diverse and heterogeneous use cases. Ultimately, we present LADB as a scalable and versatile solution for real-world domain translation, particularly in scenarios where data annotation is costly or incomplete.

Keywords: Diffusion Model · Domain Translation · Semi-Supervised Learning · Optimal Transport · Image-to-Image Translation

1 Introduction

Diffusion models excel at modeling complex data distributions by gradually denoising random noises into structured outputs. They have achieved remarkable successes in image generation, producing outputs with high perceptual quality

[15,32,38]. Moreover, various works have advanced their capabilities for controllable generation, incorporating text, masks, geometric priors, and other conditions [32,50]. Research has also expanded into more complex domains, such as novel view synthesis and 3D generation [9,12,28].

While diffusion models excel in domains with abundant data, their performance degrades in data-scarce settings. In 3D generation for instance, photometric data collection requires dense multi-view data which are labor-intensive to collect and process [19]. Other approaches rely on in-domain expertise to create assets [11,44]. In addtion, training of 3D diffusion models in [40,47] requires human annotations and expert-crafted rules for precise scene graph construction.

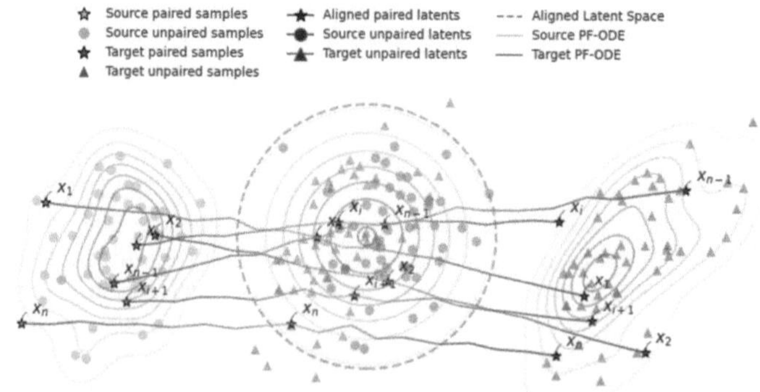

Fig. 1. Latent Aligned Diffusion Bridges. LADB achieves a cycle-consistent translation from source to target domain with partially available source-target couplings (marked by ★), through a semi-supervised learning framework. The source and target samples are aligned in a common latent space, supervised by (limited) source-to-target annotations. An LADB trajectory is formed by concatenation of the source and target PF-ODEs, thus preserving cycle consistency in the training data.

In this context, transferring knowledge from one or multiple source domains to a target domain has strong potentials to leverage the strengths of existing generative models for new scenarios. Ideally, any sample from known domains could be translated to the target domain with the assistance of generative models. However, major challenges persist. Firstly, aligning distributions across domains is non-trivial [6,30,52]. Also, translation must retain structural consistency to ensure meaningful cross-domain mappings, yet existing diffusion-based methods struggle to preserve fine-grained details across diverse scenarios [27,34,43]. Besides, generalization across domains is tedious and often requires fully paired data or domain-specific tuning [26,48].

Sample-to-sample translation emerges as a promising solution for generative model-based translation to new domains. Since generative models are designed to sample from fitted data distributions, translation naturally occurs if the sample distributions are aligned. However, existing approaches face trade-offs. Unpaired translation methods [7,39,52] require no supervision but lack controllability in translation. Fully paired translation methods, such as bridge models [21,23,51], define bidirectional diffusion processes between domains but require per-domain training. Conditional diffusion models [32,48,50] incorporate various priors for translation but necessitate architectural changes for new conditions, thus limiting their extensibility. Crucially, none of these works commits to efficient utilization of partially paired data to balance controllability and generality.

To this end, we propose Latent Aligned Diffusion Bridges (LADB), a semi-supervised learning framework that leverages partially paired data for content-consistent domain translation; see Fig. 1 for a schematic overview. More concretely, we utilize a pretrained source-domain latent diffusion model to translate limited source-to-target paired correspondences deterministically into latent-to-target alignments. This is followed by semi-supervised learning of a latent aligned diffusion model (LADM) from a mixture of paired and unpaired latent-target couples. The concatenation of source and target diffusions forms a Latent Aligned Diffusion Bridge (LADB) for sample-to-sample translation during inference. This framework is seamlessly extensible to multi-source and multi-target settings, opening up possibilities for a wide scope of downstream tasks (Fig. 2).

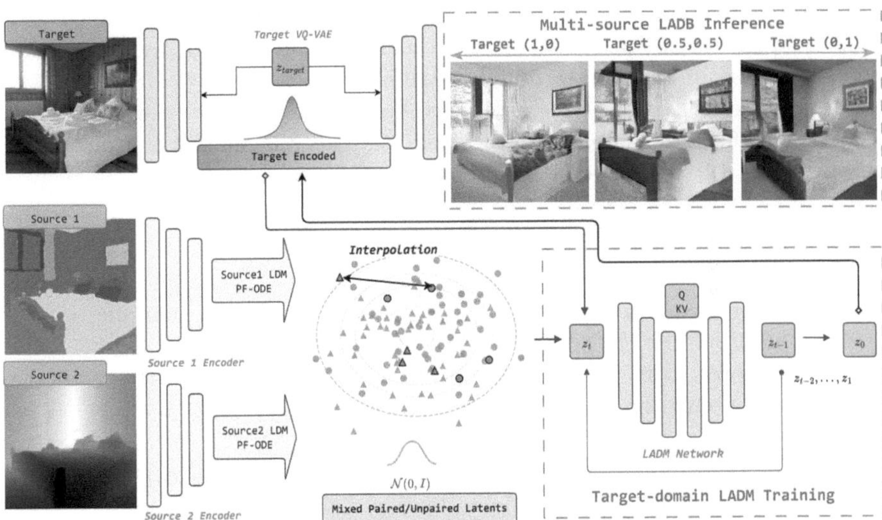

Fig. 2. Model architecture (training and inference). **LADM training**: (1) Infer latents from source(s) using pretrained source LDM(s), then construct paired latent-to-target correspondences. (2) Couple paired and unpaired (random) latents with target samples into a mixture distribution. (3) Train target-domain LADM with the mixture distribution via score matching. **LADB inference**: (1) Source-to-latent translation with pretrained source LDM. In case of multi-source inputs, additionally perform interpolation on translated latents. (2) Latent-to-target translation with trained target-domain LADM.

In the experiments, we first present our LADB on depth-to-image translation compared favorably against other approaches on a suite of metrics and show our superiority under partial supervision. Our experiments continue with image translation from cross-modal sources (depth maps and semantic segmentation masks), highlighting smooth source interpolation achieved by LADB.

2   Preliminaries

We recap prior works on score-based diffusion and bridge models, based on which our Latent Aligned Diffusion Bridge (LADB) is proposed.

2.1   Score-Based Diffusion Models

Given a d-dimensional data distribution $q_0(x_0)$, the diffusion model [14,38], initiated with a sample $x_0 \sim q_0$, follows a stochastic differential equation (SDE):

$$dx_t = f(x_t, t)dt + g(t)dw_t, \tag{1}$$

with $t \in [0,1]$ the time variable, $f : \mathbb{R}^d \times [0,1] \to \mathbb{R}^d$ the vector-valued drift, $g : [0,1] \to \mathbb{R}_+$ the scalar-valued diffusion coefficient, and $(w_t)_{0 \leq t \leq 1}$ the standard Wiener process in $\mathbb{R}^d$. The terminal distribution $q_1(x_1)$ at $t = 1$ is an easy-to-sample prior distribution, e.g., a standard Gaussian.

To generate data samples from a noise $x_1 \sim q_1$, one simulates a probability flow ordinary differential equation (PF-ODE) [37] from $t = 1$ to 0:

$$dx_t = \left[f(x_t, t) - \frac{1}{2}g^2(t)\nabla_{x_t} \log q_t(x_t) \right] dt, \tag{2}$$

with the score function $\nabla_{x_t} \log q_t(x_t)$ of the time-dependent marginal q_t. The reverse-time PF-ODE (2) preserves the marginals $(q_t)_{0 \leq t \leq 1}$ from (1).

The unknown score function is typically parameterized as a neural network s_θ and trained with the denoising score matching loss [42]:

$$\min_\theta \mathbb{E}_{\substack{t \sim \mathcal{U}(0,1),\, x_0 \sim q_0, \\ x_1 \sim q_1,\, x_t = \alpha_t x_0 + \sigma_t x_1}} \left[\omega(t) \big\| s_\theta(x_t, t) - \nabla_{x_t} \log q(x_t|x_0) \big\|^2 \right]. \tag{3}$$

The transition kernel admits an analytical form such as $q(x_t|x_0) = \mathcal{N}(\alpha_t x_0, \sigma_t^2 I)$, which renders the score matching loss in (3) tractable.

2.2   Dual Diffusion Implicit Bridges

The PF-ODE (2), with learned score s_θ, enables uniquely identifiable encoding [38] through the drift:

$$v[s_\theta](x_t, t) = f(x_t, t) - \frac{1}{2}g^2(t)s_\theta(x_t, t), \tag{4}$$

via the first-order integrator:

$$\text{ODESolve}(x(t_0), s_\theta, t_0, t_1) = x(t_0) + \int_{t_0}^{t_1} v[s_\theta](x_t, t)dt. \tag{5}$$

The dual diffusion implicit bridge (DDIB) [39] consists of two concatenated ODE solves for translating a source-domain sample $x_0^{(s)}$ to a target-domain sample $x_0^{(t)}$:

$$x_1^{(t)} = x_1^{(s)} = \text{ODESolve}(x_0^{(s)}, s_\theta^{(s)}, 0, 1), \tag{6}$$

$$x_0^{(t)} = \text{ODESolve}(x_1^{(t)}, s_\theta^{(t)}, 1, 0). \tag{7}$$

Each ODESolve is carried out by an independently trained score on source (resp. target) domain. The translation is cycle-consistent [52] but *unpaired*, since no explicit control via any predefined correspondences $(x_0^{(s)}, x_0^{(t)})$ is enforced.

2.3   Denoising Diffusion Bridge Models

The denoising diffusion bridge model (DDBM) [51] considers the same diffusion process in (1), but pinned to a fixed endpoint $y \in \mathbb{R}^d$ almost surely via Doob's h-transform:

$$dx_t = \left[f(x_t, t) + g^2(t)\nabla_{x_t} \log q(x_1 = y|x_t) \right] dt + g(t)dw_t. \tag{8}$$

A conditional generator $q(x_t|x_1 = y)$ can be obtained from the reverse SDE:

$$dx_t = \left[f(x_t, t) - g^2(t)\left(\nabla_{x_t} \log q(x_t|x_1 = y) - \nabla_{x_t} \log q(x_1 = y|x_t) \right) \right] dt + g(t)d\bar{w}_t. \tag{9}$$

The endpoint x_1 is not restricted to follow a Gaussian prior, only the transition kernel $q(x_t|x_0, x_1)$ needs to be analytically tractable. DDBM trains the conditional score $s_\theta(x_t, t, x_1)$ on *fully paired* data $(x_0, x_1) \sim q_{01}$ with the denoising bridge score matching loss [51]:

$$\min_\theta \; \mathbb{E}_{\substack{t\sim\mathcal{U}(0,1),\,(x_0,x_1)\sim q_{01},\\ x_t\sim q(x_t|x_0,x_1)}} \left[\omega(t) \big\| s_\theta(x_t, t, x_1) - \nabla_{x_t} \log q(x_t|x_0, x_1) \big\|^2 \right]. \tag{10}$$

2.4   Latent Diffusion Models

The latent diffusion model (LDM) [32] enhances pixel-level diffusion models by incorporting an autoencoder over a latent space of reduced dimensionality. A pair of encoder $\mathcal{E}_\phi$ and decoder $\mathcal{D}_\psi$ are trained with a sum of a reconstruction loss, a perceptual loss, and a patch-based adversarial loss. In a follow-up stage, a diffusion network[1] s_θ is trained on the latents of the original data samples $z = \mathcal{E}_\phi(x)$. For imagery data, a typical architectural choice for diffusion networks comes with U-Net [33], coupled with cross-attention channels in the presence of conditioning [32].

---

[1] The official LDM implementation follows DDPM's parameterization [14] with a noise predictor ϵ_θ, which relates to the score function s_θ by $s_\theta(x_t, t) = \epsilon_\theta(x_t, t)/\sigma_t$.

3   Methodology

3.1   Latent Aligned Diffusion Bridges

Partially Paired Correspondences. Our task concerns translating a sample from the source domain $x_0^{(s)}$ to a sample in the target domain $x_0^{(t)}$, given paired source-target correspondences $(\hat{x}_{0,k}^{(s)}, \hat{x}_{0,k}^{(t)})_{k \in \mathcal{K}}$ and unpaired target-domain data $(\tilde{x}_{0,l}^{(t)})_{l \in \mathcal{L}}$. The paired correspondences are possibly sourced from neural predictors, human labelers, or a hybrid of both. Considering that high-quality labeling on cross-domain data are costly and scarce particularly if human efforts are involved, the partially paired setup is of high practical relevance.

Algorithm 1. LADM training

Require: paired source-target samples $(\hat{x}_{0,k}^{(s)}, \hat{x}_{0,k}^{(t)})_{k \in \mathcal{K}}$, unpaired target-domain samples $(\tilde{x}_{0,l}^{(t)})_{l \in \mathcal{L}}$, pretrained source-domain LDM $(\mathcal{E}_{\phi'}^{(s)}, \mathcal{D}_{\psi'}^{(s)}, s_{\theta'}^{(s)})$, pretrained target-domain autoencoder $(\mathcal{E}_\phi^{(t)}, \mathcal{D}_\psi^{(t)})$.
  1: Infer source-to-latent correspondences via (11).
  2: Construct the coupling distribution $q_{01}^{(t)}(x_0^{(t)}, x_1^{(t)})$ in (12).
  3: Train the LADM score $s_\theta^{(t)}$ via (13).
  4: **return** the LADM tuple $(\mathcal{E}_\phi^{(t)}, \mathcal{D}_\psi^{(t)}, s_\theta^{(t)})$.

Algorithm 2. LADB sampling

Require: source-domain sample $x_0^{(s)}$, source-domain LDM $(\mathcal{E}_{\phi'}^{(s)}, \mathcal{D}_{\psi'}^{(s)}, s_{\theta'}^{(s)})$, target-domain LDAM $(\mathcal{E}_\phi^{(t)}, \mathcal{D}_\psi^{(t)}, s_\theta^{(t)})$.
  1: Perform source-to-latent translation: $x_1^{(t)} = \text{ODESolve}(\mathcal{E}_{\phi'}^{(s)}(x_0^{(s)}), s_{\theta'}^{(s)}, 0, 1)$.
  2: Perform latent-to-target translation: $x_0^{(t)} = \text{ODESolve}(x_1^{(t)}, s_\theta^{(t)}, 1, 0)$.
  3: **return** the decoded target sample $\mathcal{D}_\psi(x_0^{(t)})$.

Transferring Correspondences on Source Domain. If not available beforehand, a latent diffusion model (LDM) on the source domain need be trained following the standard pipeline from the LDM repository[2]. Given the encoder-decoder $(\mathcal{E}_{\phi'}^{(s)}, \mathcal{D}_{\psi'}^{(s)})$ and the score $s_{\theta'}^{(s)}$ on the latent domain, one can infer a matched latent $\hat{x}_{1,k}^{(t)}$ from an encoded source sample $\mathcal{E}_{\phi'}^{(s)}(\hat{x}_{0,k}^{(s)})$ via the ODESolve in (5):

$$\hat{x}_{1,k}^{(t)} = \hat{x}_{1,k}^{(s)} = \text{ODESolve}(\mathcal{E}_{\phi'}^{(s)}(\hat{x}_{0,k}^{(s)}), s_{\theta'}^{(s)}, 0, 1). \tag{11}$$

Thus, the original source-to-target correspondences $(\hat{x}_{0,k}^{(s)}, \hat{x}_{0,k}^{(t)})_{k \in \mathcal{K}}$ are translated into paired latent-to-target correspondences $(\hat{x}_{1,k}^{(t)}, \hat{x}_{0,k}^{(t)})_{k \in \mathcal{K}}$, provided that the source and target LDMs share a common latent space.

---

[2] https://github.com/CompVis/latent-diffusion.

Semi-supervised Learning on Target Domain. With available latent-to-target correspondences in hand, we formulate the training of target-domain latent diffusion models as *semi-supervised learning* [18]. That is, we have both paired samples $(\hat{x}_{0,k}^{(t)}, \hat{x}_{1,k}^{(t)})_{k\in\mathcal{K}}$ and unpaired samples $(\tilde{x}_{0,l}^{(t)})_{l\in\mathcal{L}}$ as training data and, therefore, the coupling distribution $q_{01}^{(t)}(x_0^{(t)}, x_1^{(t)})$ as a mixture distribution:

$$q_{01}^{(t)}(x_0^{(t)}, x_1^{(t)}) = \frac{1}{|\mathcal{K}| + |\mathcal{L}|} \cdot \left(\sum_{k\in\mathcal{K}} \delta_{(\hat{x}_{0,k}^{(t)}, \hat{x}_{1,k}^{(t)})}(x_0^{(t)}, x_1^{(t)}) + \sum_{l\in\mathcal{L}} \delta_{\tilde{x}_{0,l}^{(t)}}(x_0^{(t)}) \otimes q_1(x_1^{(t)}) \right). \tag{12}$$

With the (pretrained) autoencoder $(\mathcal{E}_\phi^{(t)}, \mathcal{D}_\psi^{(t)})$ on the target domain, the latent aligned diffusion model (LADM) is trained with the score matching loss sampled from the coupling distribution $q_{01}^{(t)}$:

$$\min_\theta \mathbb{E}_{\substack{t\sim\mathcal{U}(0,1),\, (x_0^{(t)}, x_1^{(t)})\sim q_{01}^{(t)}, \\ x_t = \alpha_t \mathcal{E}_\phi^{(t)}(x_0^{(t)}) + \sigma_t x_1^{(t)}}} \left[\omega(t) \big\| s_\theta^{(t)}(x_t, t) - \nabla_{x_t} \log q(x_t | \mathcal{E}_\phi^{(t)}(x_0^{(t)})) \big\|^2 \right]. \tag{13}$$

The LADM training pipeline is depicted in Algorithm 1.

Sampling with Latent Aligned Diffusion Bridges. A source-domain LDM and a target-domain LADM together form a latent aligned diffusion bridge (LADB), depicted in Algorithm 2, for source-to-target translation. The source-to-latent (resp. latent-to-target) translation is carried out by an ODESolve (5) involving the source LDM (resp. the target LADM). On par with DDIB [39], cycle consistency is guaranteed in LADB (on the latent level).

Incorporating Conditioning. Our LADB framework is flexible to handle *conditioning*, that is, each target sample $x_{0,i}^{(t)}$ is attached with a condition variable $\xi_i^{(t)}$ being a class label or a continuous embedding of some text caption. In the presence of conditioning, we parameterize the score network $s_\theta^{(t)}(x_t, t, \xi)$ with condition ξ, through either concatenation or cross-attention [32]. A class-conditioned LADB for neural style transfer will be demonstrated in the supplementary.

3.2   Extension to Multi-source Translation

The LADB framework admits a natural extension to *multi-source domain translation*, depicted in Algorithms 3 and 4. In the setup of multi-source LADM training, we are given paired and unpaired samples from J source domains in total, i.e., $(\hat{x}_{0,k_j}^{(s_j)}, \hat{x}_{0,k_j}^{(t)})_{k_j\in\mathcal{K}_j,\, j\in[J]}$ for paired and $(\tilde{x}_{0,l_j}^{(s_j)})_{l_j\in\mathcal{L}_j,\, j\in[J]}$ for unpaired. The source domains can be as diversified as cross-modal [36], but required to have pretrained LDMs $(\mathcal{E}_{\phi_j'}^{(s_j)}, \mathcal{D}_{\psi_j'}^{(s_j)}, s_{\theta_j'}^{(s_j)})_{j\in[J]}$ over a common latent domain. For each source, the paired samples are encoded to their latent correspondences via

$$\hat{x}_{1,k_j}^{(t)} = \hat{x}_{1,k_j}^{(s_j)} = \text{ODESolve}(\mathcal{E}_{\phi_j'}^{(s_j)}(\hat{x}_{0,k_j}^{(s_j)}), s_{\theta_j'}^{(s_j)}, 0, 1). \tag{14}$$

Algorithm 3. Multi-source LADM training

Require: paired samples $(\hat{x}_{0,k_j}^{(s_j)}, \hat{x}_{0,k_j}^{(t)})_{k_j \in \mathcal{K}_j, j \in [J]}$, unpaired samples $(\tilde{x}_{0,l_j}^{(s_j)})_{l_j \in \mathcal{L}_j, j \in [J]}$,
    pretrained source-domain LDMs $(\mathcal{E}_{\phi_j'}^{(s_j)}, \mathcal{D}_{\psi_j'}^{(s_j)}, s_{\theta_j'}^{(s_j)})_{j \in [J]}$, pretrained target-domain
    autoencoder $(\mathcal{E}_\phi^{(t)}, \mathcal{D}_\psi^{(t)})$.
1: Infer source-to-latent correspondences via (14).
2: Construct the coupling distribution $q_{01}^{(t)}(x_0^{(t)}, x_1^{(t)})$ in (15).
3: Train the LADM score $s_\theta^{(t)}$ via (13).
4: **return** the LADM tuple $(\mathcal{E}_\phi^{(t)}, \mathcal{D}_\psi^{(t)}, s_\theta^{(t)})$.

Algorithm 4. Multi-source LADB sampling

Require: weighted source-domain samples $(x_{0,i}^{(s_i)}, \rho_i)_{i \in \mathcal{I}}$, source-domain LDMs
    $(\mathcal{E}_{\phi_i'}^{(s_i)}, \mathcal{D}_{\psi_i'}^{(s_i)}, s_{\theta_i'}^{(s_i)})_{i \in \mathcal{I}}$, target-domain LADM $(\mathcal{E}_\phi^{(t)}, \mathcal{D}_\psi^{(t)}, s_\theta^{(t)})$.
Ensure: $\mathcal{I}$ is a multiset supported on $(s_j)_{j \in [J]}$; $\rho_i > 0 \ \forall i \in \mathcal{I}$ and $\sum_{i \in \mathcal{I}} \rho_i = 1$.
1: **for** $i \in \mathcal{I}$ **do**
2:    Perform source-to-latent translation: $x_{1,i}^{(s_i)} = \mathrm{ODESolve}(\mathcal{E}_{\phi_i'}^{(i)}(x_0^{(s_i)}), s_{\theta_i'}^{(s_i)}, 0, 1)$.
3: **end for**
4: Compute a weighted average of latent correspondences: $x_1^{(t)} = \sum_{i \in \mathcal{I}} \rho_i x_{1,i}^{(s_i)}$.
5: Perform latent-to-target translation: $x_0^{(t)} = \mathrm{ODESolve}(x_1^{(t)}, s_\theta^{(t)}, 1, 0)$.
6: **return** the decoded target sample $\mathcal{D}_\psi(x_0^{(t)})$.

The mixture coupling distribution $q_{01}^{(t)}(x_0^{(t)}, x_1^{(t)})$ combines paired and unpaired samples from all sources:

$$
q_{01}^{(t)}(x_0^{(t)}, x_1^{(t)}) = \frac{1}{\sum_{j=1}^J (|\mathcal{K}_j| + |\mathcal{L}_j|)} \cdot \sum_{j=1}^J \Big(\sum_{k_j \in \mathcal{K}_j} \delta_{(\hat{x}_{0,k_j}^{(t)}, \hat{x}_{1,k_j}^{(t)})}(x_0^{(t)}, x_1^{(t)})
$$
$$
+ \sum_{l_j \in \mathcal{L}_j} \delta_{\tilde{x}_{0,l_j}^{(t)}}(x_0^{(t)}) \otimes q_1(x_1^{(t)}) \Big), \tag{15}
$$

from which a multi-source LADM can be trained with (13).

    Sampling with multi-source LADB is highly versatile, compared to fully paired methods [51] and conditional models [32, 48, 50]. The user is free to translate a single source sample or an arbitrarily weighted combination of multiple source samples. In particular, the underlying weighted average among multiple sources is the Fréchet mean [10] over the shared latent space in the same spirit of latent interpolation [17, 31].

4   Related Work

Classic denoising diffusion and score matching methods [8, 14, 38] achieve an expressive generative model by gradually transforming a Gaussian noise to a data sample through a PF-ODE or an SDE. A series of unpaired translation methods, which were rooted in the Schrödinger bridge problem and dynamical optimal transport [20], have recently been proposed for transferring data between arbitrary pairs of empirical distributions, including rectified flow [25], flow matching [22,41], bridge matching [29,35], and stochastic interpolants [1,2]. When the empirical distributions arise with known couplings (typical in inverse problems such as image restoration [16]), paired translation methods are better suited, among which bridge methods [21,23,51] are prominent examples of using pinned diffusion processes to incorporate data couplings. While being more general-purpose, conditional diffusion [32,48,50] or conditional flow matching [22] counts as another viable option for paired translation.

It is well understood that score/flow/bridge matching methods typically preserve time-dependent marginals but *not* the coupling distribution of endpoints [3,22,24]. Our proposed LADB framework is strongly inspired by rectification [25] and iterative Markovian projection [29,35]. Different from these prior works which directly rectify correspondences between source and target distributions, in this work we leverage partially available source-target pairs to circuitously forge latent-target correspondences through pre-trained source-domain LDMs.

5   Experiments

5.1   Experimental Setup

Datasets. We evaluate our method using the LSUN-Bedroom and LSUN-Churches datasets [46]. For depth-to-image translation and multi-source-to-image translation, we utilize depth images and segmentation masks from the LSUN-Bedroom dataset. Specifically, we randomly select 100,000 training images and obtain their paired correspondences using the open-source annotators: LeRes [45] and DDPM-segmentation [4].

Task Coverage. We validate the proposed LADB through three experimental paradigms. First, we testify LADB in Algorithms 1 and 2 on depth-to-image translation in Sect. 5.2, demonstrating its robustness to partially paired settings while balancing translation quality and fidelity. Building upon this, in Sect. 5.3 we instantiate Algorithms 3 and 4 to image translation from two source modalities, namely depth maps and semantic segmentation masks. Finally, we showcase LADB's extensibility to multi-target translation with class-conditioned style transfer task (results in supplementary). These tasks collectively demonstrate LADB's core strengths: (1) semi-supervised latent alignment for data-efficient translation; (2) unified latent modeling for multi-source interpolation; (3) extensible conditioning mechanisms for multi-target generation. Additionally, we apply the same workflow of 5.2 to HED-to-image, canny-to-image, and sketch-to-image translation and refer to the supplementary for exemplary results.

Evaluation Methods. We compare our method with representative state-of-the-art approaches: (unpaired) DDIB [39], (fully paired) DDBM [51], conditional LDM (CondLDM) [32], ControlNet [48] and (multi-conditioned) Uni-ControlNet

[50]. For quantitative evaluation, we use a validation dataset of 1,000 samples at resolution 256×256 from LSUN-Bedroom, containing paired correspondences for translating from depth images to RGB images and from segmentation masks to RGB images. We evaluate translation quality using FrÃĺchet Inception Distance (FID) [13] and Inception Scores (IS) [5], and measure perceptual similarity and translation faithfulness using LPIPS [49] and MSE (in $[0, 1]$ scale).

5.2 Depth-To-Image Translation

Table 1. Depth-to-Image Translation: (pixel) and (latent) stand for pixel- and latent-space variants. The best (resp. runner-up) metrics under 50% paired are marked red (resp. blue). Best metrics under 10%/25% paired are marked green.

Method	#Paired	FID ↓	IS ↑	LPIPS ↓	MSE ↓
DDIB (pixel)	0	309.55	3.65	0.7491	0.3104
DDIB (latent)	0	123.95	3.86	0.7331	0.2237
DDBM (pixel)	50%	51.96	2.05	0.6320	0.1223
	100%	46.94	2.26	0.6348	0.1705
DDBM (latent)	10%	39.39	2.15	0.6145	0.1147
	25%	35.69	2.21	0.6585	0.1117
	50%	34.23	2.23	0.5947	0.1118
	100%	33.72	2.38	0.6030	0.1206
CondLDM	50%	52.51	2.59	0.7728	0.1372
	100%	44.65	2.72	0.6384	0.1303
ControlNet	50%	43.05	2.66	0.7327	0.1709
	100%	41.50	2.46	0.6660	0.1614
LADB (ours)	10%	33.29	2.23	0.6499	0.1191
	25%	33.44	2.29	0.6375	0.1195
	50%	33.78	2.35	0.6335	0.1125
	100%	34.78	2.43	0.6387	0.1052

Setup. We evaluate our method against DDIB [39], DDBM [51], Conditional LDM (CondLDM) [32] and ControlNet [48] under varying percentages of paired correspondences during training. Both pixel-space and latent-space variants of DDIB and DDBM are implemented for fair comparisons. Conditional LDM is adapted by concatenating depth as a control signal. We conduct thorough comparisons with DDBM (latent) across multiple partially paired settings (10%,

25%, 50%), as it performs the closest to our method. Additionally, we experiment with a DDBM (latent) variant augmented by randomly pairing unpaired images from the full dataset with depth images (results in supplementary). Further details are provided in the supplementary materials.

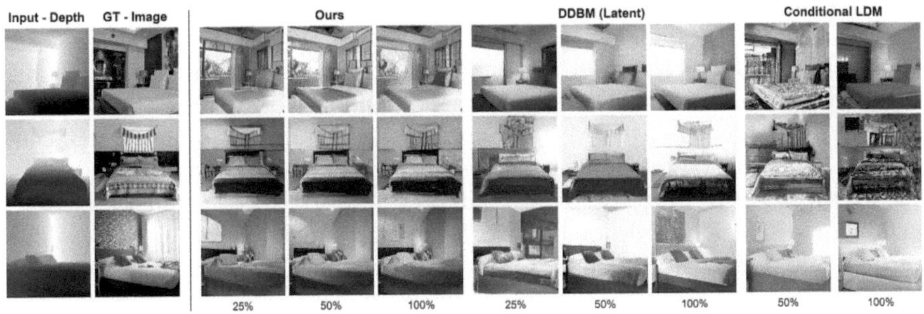

Fig. 3. Qualitative comparisons. Our method produces translations that are visually coherent to the source. It preserves fine-grained details (e.g., sheets and curtain) and avoids artifacts observed in CondLDM and DDBM.

Results. As shown in Table 1, our method achieves superior performances in generation quality (FID, IS) under partially paired settings, and is on par with baselines in translation fidelity (LPIPS, MSE). Notably, LADB suffers less performance degradation compared to other baselines, as the percentage of paired data drops from 100% to 10%. Qualitative results in Fig. 3 further illustrate our method's ability to preserve fine-grained details.

DDBM (latent) achieves high translation faithfulness (LPIPS, MSE) but lacks in generation quality (FID, IS). Conditional LDM and ControlNet prioritizes diversity (IS) at the cost of generation quality and fidelity (FID, LIPIS, MSE), while DDIB falls behind in all metrics except for IS.

Discussion. Our method's success stems from its semi-supervised latent alignment, which learns to encapsulate domain-invariant latent features consistent to both paired and unpaired samples. DDBM's reliance on fully paired training causes overfitting, degrading fidelity (LPIPS, MSE) as the amount of paired data increases. Conditional LDM's dependence on dense supervision leads to catastrophic failure when dealing with partial pairing (FID, IS), as it cannot extrapolate to unseen configurations. In addition, Conditional LDM and ControlNet struggles to achieve high-quality and faithful translations (FID, LPIPS). Furthermore, DDIB fails to produce coherent translations, likely due to significant distributional shift between the source and target domains.

Besides, it is observed that latent-space methods, such as our approach, DDBM (latent), Conditional LDM and ControlNet, outperform pixel-space counterparts. This is attributed to their superior ability to capture essential features and translate them faithfully across domains.

The results suggest that LADB behaves highly robust to lack of paired data, in a way to strike a balance between diversity and fidelity and preserve cross-domain consistency through latent-space alignment. This makes LADB a solution particularly competitive in data scarce translation tasks.

5.3 Multi-source-To-Image Translation

Setup. We evaluate our method against UniControlNet (UniCtrl) [50] and DDBM [51] for multi-source-to-image translation under the 25% partially paired setting. We implement DDBM in latent space and, similar to our LADB, combine paired latent-target samples inferred from all source domains during training. We utilize UniControlNet's local adapter network to condition a pretrained LDM image diffusion model on both segmentation and depth inputs. We evaluate all methods under two settings: single-source input (depths or segmentations) and multi-source input $((\text{depth}, 0.5), (\text{segm}, 0.5))$. Note that UniControlNet only accepts both sources as input but not an interpolant of the two. For more implementation details we refer to the y materials.

Table 2. Multi-Source Translation results: Scores are grouped by method and input source. The best score for each metric in the multi-source setting is bolded.

Metric	DDBM			UniCtrl			LADB		
	depth	segm	interp	depth	segm	both	depth	segm	interp
FID ↓	36.03	38.65	55.43	41.55	41.96	37.03	34.10	38.67	**34.72**
IS ↑	2.21	2.35	2.66	3.02	3.06	**2.92**	2.30	2.33	2.38
LPIPS ↓	0.6181	0.5923	**0.6403**	0.6699	0.6728	0.6478	0.6494	0.6689	0.6798
MSE ↓	0.1108	0.0885	0.1451	0.1399	0.1360	0.1350	0.1191	0.1080	**0.1275**

Results. The quantitative results in Table 2 show our method outperforms both baselines given multi-source inputs (FID: 34.72). Under single-source settings, LADB achieves superior fidelity over UniControlNet (FID, SSIM) and better generalization than DDBM (FID), in spite of DDBM's marginally higher SSIM.

The qualitative results in Fig. 4 highlight LADB's flexibility. Interpolation between depth- and segmentation-derived latents yields coherent blends of styles (such as illumination and colorization) and contents (such layouts and textures), a capability absent in rigidly conditioned baselines. In contrast, UniControlNet exhibits perceivable artifacts when plugged in with multiple modalities, and DDBM produces inconsistent structures across the interpolants.

Discussion. Our unified latent space enables adaptive fusion of cross-modal priors, addressing two key limitations of existing methods: UniControlNet's reliance on fixed per-modality adapters and DDBMâĂŹs brittle pixel-level alignment.

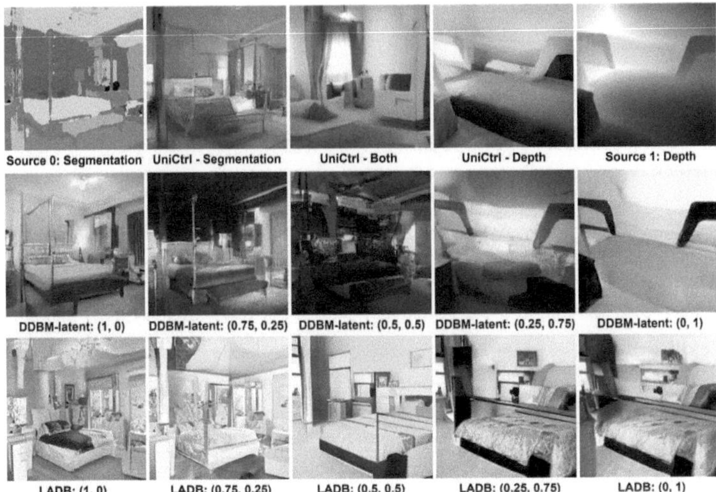

Fig. 4. Multi-Source Translation visualization. Source 0 is a segmentation mask and Source 1 a depth map, with differing GT targets. Interpolated multi-source translations by UniControlNet, DDBM (latent), and LADB are displayed.

While UniControlNet improves with multi-source inputs, it remains inferior to LADB due to its inability to interpolate modalities or generalize to unseen combinations. DDBM suffers larger performance drops during interpolation, as its strict pairing fails to generalize across interpolation between multiple sources. In contrast, our semi-supervised alignment demonstrates highly smooth transitions in generation along interpolation (FID, SSIM), thanks to distribution-level couplings through an aligned latent space. The slight SSIM gap compared with DDBM (latent) in single-source segmentation translation may arise from inherent ambiguities in mask-to-image translation, where sparse semantic cues challenge latent alignment.

By projecting source data onto a unified latent space, our framework generalizes to unseen combinations without retraining (Fig. 4), offering a scalable solution for real-world domain translation with incomplete or heterogeneous data.

References

1. Albergo, M.S., Boffi, N.M., Vanden-Eijnden, E.: Stochastic interpolants: a unifying framework for flows and diffusions. arXiv:2303.08797 (2023)
2. Albergo, M.S., Vanden-Eijnden, E.: Building normalizing flows with stochastic interpolants. In: ICLR (2023)
3. Albergo, M.S., Goldstein, M., Boffi, N.M., Ranganath, R., Vanden-Eijnden, E.: Stochastic interpolants with data-dependent couplings. In: ICML, pp. 921–937 (2024)
4. Baranchuk, D., Rubachev, I., Voynov, A., Khrulkov, V., Babenko, A.: Label-efficient semantic segmentation with diffusion models (2021)

5. Barratt, S., Sharma, R.: A note on the inception score (2018). https://arxiv.org/abs/1801.01973

6. Choi, Y., Choi, M., Kim, M., Ha, J.W., Kim, S., Choo, J.: StarGAN: unified generative adversarial networks for multi-domain image-to-image translation (2018). https://arxiv.org/abs/1711.09020

7. De Bortoli, V., Korshunova, I., Mnih, A., Doucet, A.: Schrödinger bridge flow for unpaired data translation. In: NeurIPS (2024)

8. De Bortoli, V., Thornton, J., Heng, J., Doucet, A.: Diffusion Schrödinger bridge with applications to score-based generative modeling. In: NeurIPS, pp. 17695–17709 (2021)

9. Elata, N., Kawar, B., Ostrovsky-Berman, Y., Farber, M., Sokolovsky, R.: Novel view synthesis with pixel-space diffusion models (2024). https://arxiv.org/abs/2411.07765

10. Fréchet, M.: Les éléments aléatoires de nature quelconque dans un espace distancié. Annales de l'institut Henri Poincaré **10**(4), 215–310 (1948)

11. Fu, H., et al.: 3d-front: 3d furnished rooms with layouts and semantics (2021). https://arxiv.org/abs/2011.09127

12. Gupta, A., Xiong, W., Nie, Y., Jones, I., Oğuz, B.: 3dgen: triplane latent diffusion for textured mesh generation (2023). https://arxiv.org/abs/2303.05371

13. Heusel, M., Ramsauer, H., Unterthiner, T., Nessler, B., Hochreiter, S.: Gans trained by a two time-scale update rule converge to a local nash equilibrium (2018). https://arxiv.org/abs/1706.08500

14. Ho, J., Jain, A., Abbeel, P.: Denoising diffusion probabilistic models. In: NeurIPS, pp. 6840–6851 (2020)

15. Karras, T., Aittala, M., Aila, T., Laine, S.: Elucidating the design space of diffusion-based generative models. In: NeurIPS, pp. 26565–26577 (2022)

16. Kawar, B., Elad, M., Ermon, S., Song, J.: Denoising diffusion restoration models. In: NeurIPS, pp. 23593–23606 (2022)

17. Kingma, D.P., Welling, M.: Auto-encoding variational Bayes. arXiv:1312.6114 (2013)

18. Kingma, D.P., Mohamed, S., Jimenez Rezende, D., Welling, M.: Semi-supervised learning with deep generative models. In: NeurIPS, pp. 3581–3589 (2014)

19. Lee, J., Lee, S., Jo, C., Im, W., Seon, J., Yoon, S.E.: Semcity: semantic scene generation with triplane diffusion (2024). https://arxiv.org/abs/2403.07773

20. Léonard, C.: A survey of the Schrödinger problem and some of its connections with optimal transport. Discrete Contin. Dyn. Syst., Ser. A **34**, 1533–1574 (2014)

21. Li, B., Xue, K., Liu, B., Lai, Y.K.: BBDM: image-to-image translation with Brownian bridge diffusion models. In: CVPR, pp. 1952–1961 (2023)

22. Lipman, Y., Chen, R.T., Ben-Hamu, H., Nickel, M., Le, M.: Flow matching for generative modeling. In: ICLR (2023)

23. Liu, G.H., Vahdat, A., Huang, D.A., Theodorou, E., Nie, W., Anandkumar, A.: I^{2}SB: image-to-image Schrödinger bridge. In: ICML, pp. 22042–22062 (2023)

24. Liu, Q.: Rectified flow: a marginal preserving approach to optimal transport. arXiv:2209.14577 (2022)

25. Liu, X., Gong, C., Liu, Q.: Flow straight and fast: learning to generate and transfer data with rectified flow. In: ICLR (2023)

26. Liu, Z., Dai, P., Li, R., Qi, X., Fu, C.W.: ISS: image as stepping stone for text-guided 3D shape generation. arXiv:2209.04145 (2022)

27. Meng, C., et al.: SDEdit: guided image synthesis and editing with stochastic differential equations (2022). https://arxiv.org/abs/2108.01073

28. Nichol, A., Jun, H., Dhariwal, P., Mishkin, P., Chen, M.: Point-e: a system for generating 3d point clouds from complex prompts (2022). https://arxiv.org/abs/2212.08751
29. Peluchetti, S.: Non-denoising forward-time diffusions. arXiv:2312.14589 (2023)
30. Radford, A., et al.: Learning transferable visual models from natural language supervision. In: ICML, pp. 8748–8763 (2021)
31. Radford, A., Metz, L., Chintala, S.: Unsupervised representation learning with deep convolutional generative adversarial networks. In: ICLR (2016)
32. Rombach, R., Blattmann, A., Lorenz, D., Esser, P., Ommer, B.: High-resolution image synthesis with latent diffusion models. In: CVPR, pp. 10684–10695 (2022)
33. Ronneberger, O., Fischer, P., Brox, T.: U-Net: convolutional networks for biomedical image segmentation. In: Navab, N., Hornegger, J., Wells, W.M., Frangi, A.F. (eds.) MICCAI 2015. LNCS, vol. 9351, pp. 234–241. Springer, Cham (2015). https://doi.org/10.1007/978-3-319-24574-4_28
34. Saharia, C., et al.: Palette: image-to-image diffusion models. In: ACM SIGGRAPH, pp. 1–10 (2022)
35. Shi, Y., De Bortoli, V., Campbell, A., Doucet, A.: Diffusion Schrödinger bridge matching. In: NeurIPS, pp. 62183–62223 (2023)
36. Socher, R., Ganjoo, M., Manning, C.D., Ng, A.: Zero-shot learning through cross-modal transfer. In: NeurIPS, pp. 935–943 (2013)
37. Song, J., Meng, C., Ermon, S.: Denoising diffusion implicit models. In: ICLR (2021)
38. Song, Y., Sohl-Dickstein, J., Kingma, D.P., Kumar, A., Ermon, S., Poole, B.: Score-based generative modeling through stochastic differential equations. In: ICLR (2021)
39. Su, X., Song, J., Meng, C., Ermon, S.: Dual diffusion implicit bridges for image-to-image translation. In: ICLR (2023)
40. Tang, J., Nie, Y., Markhasin, L., Dai, A., Thies, J., Nießner, M.: DiffuScene: denoising diffusion models for generative indoor scene synthesis. In: CVPR, pp. 20507–20518 (2024)
41. Tong, A., et al.: Improving and generalizing flow-based generative models with minibatch optimal transport. arXiv:2302.00482 (2023)
42. Vincent, P.: A connection between score matching and denoising autoencoders. Neural Comput. **23**(7), 1661–1674 (2011)
43. Wang, Y., Yu, J., Zhang, J.: Zero-shot image restoration using denoising diffusion null-space model (2022). https://arxiv.org/abs/2212.00490
44. Wu, Z., et al.: Blockfusion: expandable 3d scene generation using latent tri-plane extrapolation (2024). https://arxiv.org/abs/2401.17053
45. Yin, W., et al.: Learning to recover 3d scene shape from a single image. In: CVPR (2021)
46. Yu, F., Seff, A., Zhang, Y., Song, S., Funkhouser, T., Xiao, J.: Lsun: construction of a large-scale image dataset using deep learning with humans in the loop (2016). https://arxiv.org/abs/1506.03365
47. Zhai, G., et al.: Commonscenes: generating commonsense 3d indoor scenes with scene graph diffusion (2023), https://arxiv.org/abs/2305.16283
48. Zhang, L., Rao, A., Agrawala, M.: Adding conditional control to text-to-image diffusion models. In: ICCV, pp. 3836–3847 (2023)
49. Zhang, R., Isola, P., Efros, A.A., Shechtman, E., Wang, O.: The unreasonable effectiveness of deep features as a perceptual metric. In: CVPR (2018)

50. Zhao, S., et al.: Uni-controlnet: all-in-one control to text-to-image diffusion models. In: NeurIPS (2023)
51. Zhou, L., Lou, A., Khanna, S., Ermon, S.: Denoising diffusion bridge models. In: ICLR (2024)
52. Zhu, J.Y., Park, T., Isola, P., Efros, A.A.: Unpaired image-to-image translation using cycle-consistent adversarial networks. In: ICCV, pp. 2223–2232 (2017)

On the Dangers of Bootstrapping Generation for Continual Learning and Beyond

Daniil Zverev[1]([✉]), A. Sophia Koepke[1,2], and Joao F. Henriques[3]

[1] Technical University of Munich, MCML, Munich, Germany
ewriji@gmail.com
[2] University of Tübingen, Tübingen AI Center, Tübingen, Germany
[3] University of Oxford, Oxford, UK

Abstract. The use of synthetically generated data for training models is becoming a common practice. While generated data can augment the training data, repeated training on synthetic data raises concerns about distribution drift and degradation of performance due to contamination of the dataset. We investigate the consequences of this bootstrapping process through the lens of continual learning, drawing a connection to Generative Experience Replay (GER) methods. We present a statistical analysis showing that synthetic data introduces significant bias and variance into training objectives, weakening the reliability of maximum likelihood estimation. We provide empirical evidence showing that popular generative models collapse under repeated training with synthetic data. We quantify this degradation and show that state-of-the-art GER methods fail to maintain alignment in the latent space. Our findings raise critical concerns about the use of synthetic data in continual learning.

Keywords: Continual Learning · Generative Replay · Generative Collaps

1 Introduction

Generative models have become essential for modern machine learning, being used in various tasks ranging from text generation to image synthesis. These models, such as GPT-based large language models [1] and diffusion-based image generators like Midjourney, are now key components in consumer and industrial applications. A natural consequence of their proliferation is the growing presence of synthetic data in the publicly available data corpus [9]. As this trend continues, future models are likely to be trained on data that was itself generated by other models. This growing reliance on synthetic data raises questions about the consequences of repeatedly training models on data generated by earlier models. While synthetic data can temporarily enrich datasets, incorporating generated samples into future training regimes risks long-term degradation of model performance due to distributional drift and statistical contamination.

M. Keuper and F. Locatello (Eds.): DAGM GCPR 2025, LNCS 16125, pp. 237–250, 2026.
https://doi.org/10.1007/978-3-032-12840-9_16

This phenomenon is closely related to continual learning (CL), specifically in the form of Generative Experience Replay [11,41]. In GER, a model is exposed to a stream of non-i.i.d. tasks and maintains performance across them by using a generative model to replay synthetic samples from past tasks. This setup reflects broader trends in machine learning, where synthetic data is reused across training cycles.

In this paper, we study the statistical and empirical consequences of this synthetic bootstrapping loop. We begin by formalising the continual learning setup and examining the statistical errors introduced by synthetic data. In particular, we consider bias and variance in maximum likelihood estimators when real data is replaced by generated samples. We then analyse GER continual learning algorithms, identifying how these statistical errors manifest in state-of-the-art methods. Our experiments highlight that generative models exhibit instability when repeatedly trained on synthetic samples. We provide empirical evidence that, over time, synthetic datasets diverge from their original distributions, leading to a degradation in downstream performance and increased divergence in latent space representations.

To summarise, our contributions are as follows:

1. We provide a theoretical analysis demonstrating how repeated training on synthetic data introduces bias and variance into standard training objectives, weakening the statistical guarantees of generative model learning.
2. We perform controlled experiments on GANs and diffusion models, empirically showing that repeatedly training on generated data leads to distributional drift and downstream performance degradation, even under ideal conditions.
3. We quantify the divergence of synthetic and real data and show that state-of-the-art GER methods fail to prevent latent space separation between the two domains.

Our findings provide a cautionary perspective on synthetic data usage, along with theoretical grounding for understanding the limitations of GER in continual learning.

2   Related Work

Continual Learning and Generative Replay. CL addresses the challenge of training models on non-stationary data distributions without the important problem of catastrophic forgetting [13,25,34,36,41]. This is commonly addressed by revisiting old data through experience replay methods [7,28,36,38]. A prominent subfamily of methods, Generative Experience Replay (GER) [21,37,41,48], mitigates forgetting by using generative models to recreate past task data [41]. GAN Memory [8] and DDGR [11] further scale GER to more complex datasets using GANs and diffusion models respectively. Our work complements these efforts by showing that even state-of-the-art GER systems suffer from systematic degradation when synthetic data is bootstrapped over time. We quantify this with both statistical analysis and empirical metrics, revealing that synthetic data contamination in GER setups leads to increasing domain shift, classifier collapse, and misalignment in latent space.

Synthetic Data for Training. The rise of generative models has led to an increasing amount of synthetic content in public datasets. For instance, [29] estimated that 0.2% of Reddit posts are AI-generated, while [9] found that annotators can distinguish synthetic from real online data with 96.5% accuracy, revealing a measurable domain shift. According to [49], we may soon exhaust high-quality human-generated data, necessitating reliance on synthetic data to train future models. Several recent works have observed performance degradation when synthetic data is introduced into training [3,14,42,43]. Specifically, [14] investigated the use of synthetic samples for ImageNet [10] and COCO [26] categories, showing notable drops in classification performance. However, these works make strong theoretical assumption about generative models, modeling them as a Gaussian distributions, our work, in contrast, analyses how replacing real data with synthetic samples impacts the statistical assumptions underlying maximum likelihood training, offering a principled explanation for the observed empirical failures, applicable to any generative model.

Measuring Domain Shift. The broader problem of domain shift [23] and out-of-distribution generalisation [52] is well-studied, particularly in transfer learning and robustness contexts. Metrics such as FID [16], OTDD [4], have been proposed to measure divergence between datasets. We adopt and extend these tools to measure how synthetic data diverges from real distributions over time in a continual training loop. We evaluate synthetic collapse not just as a static phenomenon but as a gradual process, showing how recursive training causes statistical instability and undermines the training objectives.

3   Continual Learning

In offline continual learning, a model is trained sequentially on a stream of domains $\mathbf{S} = \{\mathbf{D}_i\}_{i=1}^{T}$. The entire training process is composed of multiple training and evaluation phases which are commonly referred to as domains in the Domain Adaptation literature [51] and as tasks in Continual Learning. In this work, each task contains one domain. Thus, the terms become interchangeable. During each task, we only have access to one domain $\mathbf{D}_t$ for training, and we evaluate on the union of all previous domains $\mathbf{D_{val}} = \bigcup_{i=1}^{t-1} \mathbf{D}_i$. In the following, we define key terminology for the continual learning process. In particular, we define domain and memory, used for retaining information across tasks.

Definition 1. (Domain). *A domain $\boldsymbol{D}_i$ consists of input-label pairs $\{x_j, y_j\}_{j=1}^{N_i}$. If the training objective uses unlabelled data, $y_j = \emptyset$. Each sample within a domain is distributed according to the domain distribution $p_{\mathbf{D_i}}$.*

Definition 2. (Memory). *The memory contains information that is preserved between tasks. We denote it as $\mathcal{M}_{t-1}$. It can contain any parameters θ necessary for training and inference, such as model weights, regularisation parameters, or samples from the previous domain.*

Definition 3. (Continual Learning Process). *The continual learning process consists of an operator P sequentially applied T times on the initial memory M_0, as $\mathcal{M}_t = P(\boldsymbol{D}_t, \mathcal{M}_{t-1})$ for $t = 1, \ldots, T$.*

A connection between continual learning and the standard training of large models (e.g. those in the GPT family [35]) can be established by considering assumptions about data distribution shifts across domains.

When training large models, domains are non-disjoint, i.e. the same data instance x_k can appear in multiple tasks and their related domains. As shown in Table 1, a task corresponds to the time between two public checkpoint releases for GPT-4o. The task domain is the data used for training the corresponding model weights checkpoint. Furthermore, the memory $\mathcal{M}_t$ keeps only parameters necessary for training/inference and the process P at each task consists of SGD training over the corresponding domain $\mathbf{D}_t$.

Table 1. GPT-4o release cycle. S denotes the subset of a domain used to train.

Release date	Task	Domain
2024-05-13	1	$\mathbf{D}_1$ = Initial domain
2024-08-06	2	$\mathbf{D}_2$ = New data + $S(\mathbf{D}_1)$
2024-09-03	3	$\mathbf{D}_3$ = New data + $S(\mathbf{D}_2)$

3.1 Synthetic Data Error

When training neural networks, unavoidable errors occur. The most fundamental is the model family limitation $\mathbf{ERROR}_{\text{model}}$, in statistical learning theory [6] commonly referred to as "approximation error". Every architecture is parametrised by a set of parameters θ and has inherent expressiveness limitations. Over time, the performance of models increases [19], with new architectures like Transformers [45] overthrowing LSTMs [18], and Diffusion models [39] surpassing GANs [12] on benchmarks, thereby reducing $\mathbf{ERROR}_{\text{model}}$.

In addition to model limitations, another statistical error, $\mathbf{ERROR}_{\text{synth}}$, arises when parts of the data stream $\mathbf{S}$ are replaced with synthetic, artificially generated domains $\hat{\mathbf{D}}$. The distributional differences between $\hat{\mathbf{D}}$ and the original domain $\mathbf{D}$ can adversely affect the validation loss when training on one domain and validating on another. This issue is particularly significant when there is no way of knowing whether a dataset was contaminated. For instance, publicly available internet data used to train models like GPT-4 [1] now contains substantial generated content, a trend expected to continue [49].

Synthetic domains may differ from real domains for several reasons. We argue that the primary cause is the inevitable $\mathbf{ERROR}_{\text{model}}$ of the generative model used to produce the synthetic domain. Another reason could be undersampling, where $|\hat{\mathbf{D}}| \ll |\mathbf{D}|$, leading to a loss of information. Both are of great importance. This work provides theoretical proofs and practical examples demonstrating why $\mathbf{ERROR}_{\text{synth}}$ must be addressed.

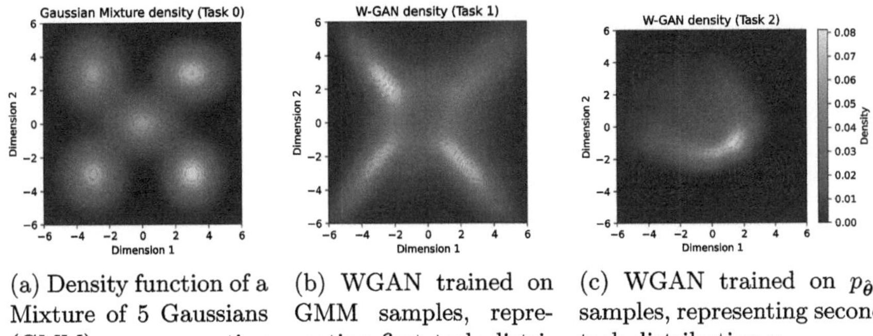

(a) Density function of a Mixture of 5 Gaussians (GMM), representing p_θ.

(b) WGAN trained on GMM samples, representing first task distribution $p_{\hat\theta_1}$.

(c) WGAN trained on $p_{\hat\theta_1}$ samples, representing second task distribution $p_{\hat\theta_2}$.

Fig. 1. Illustration of three training phases of a WGAN [5]. Datasets are undersampled as described in Sect. 3.1, resulting in a domain shift between synthetic and real data. Densities are estimated using kernel density estimation (KDE) [40].

3.2   Training Objective

For large generative models such as LLMS [31], GANS, and Diffusion models, the training objective is commonly based on the Maximum Likelihood Estimator (MLE):

$$\max_\theta L(\mathbf{S}, \theta) = \ln p_\theta(\mathbf{D}_1, ..., \mathbf{D}_t) = \sum_{i=1}^{t} \sum_{j=1}^{N_i} \ln p_\theta(x_{ij}), \tag{1}$$

with the training data stream up to phase t. The term $p_\theta(\mathbf{D}_1, \ldots, \mathbf{D}_t)$ denotes the likelihood of the data given the model parameters θ.

To understand the impact of synthetic data on the estimation process and model performance, we analyse the variance and bias of the MLE under a constantly changing distribution $\mathbf{D}_t$. Each change corresponds to the introduction of synthetic data.

Without loss of generality and for notational simplicity, we consider in the following the case where the entire domain $\mathbf{D}_1$ is replaced by a synthetic domain $\hat{\mathbf{D}}_1$.

Bias. The generative model is trained on a mix of synthetic and non-synthetic domains with the objective of maximising the MLE:

$$\max_{\hat\theta} L(\hat{\mathbf{S}}, \hat\theta) = \ln p_{\hat\theta}(\hat{\mathbf{D}}_1, \mathbf{D}_2..., \mathbf{D}_t). \tag{2}$$

Here, $\hat\theta$ corresponds to the set of weights obtained after optimising Eq. 2, and θ are the weights obtained from Eq. 1. In practice, the learned distribution $p_{\hat\theta}$ assigns non-zero probabilities to samples from $\hat{\mathbf{S}}$ and near-zero probabilities to samples not covered by $\hat{\mathbf{S}}$.

For synthetic data, if $\mathbf{D}_1$ and $\hat{\mathbf{D}}_1$ differ, $p_{\hat\theta}$ will assign low probabilities to samples from $\mathbf{D}_1$ and high probabilities to samples from $\hat{\mathbf{D}}_1$. This discrepancy creates a significant statistical problem, making the MLE estimator biased with respect to the original optimisation maximum, since the validation loss is evaluated as an expectation over the real distribution $p_{\mathbf{D}}$. Using the properties of ln, we can write the bias between the estimators as:

$$\mathbf{bias}(L(\mathbf{S}, \hat{\boldsymbol{\theta}}), L(\mathbf{S}, \boldsymbol{\theta})) = \mathbb{E}_{p_{\mathbf{D}}}\left[L(\mathbf{S}, \hat{\boldsymbol{\theta}}) - L(\mathbf{S}, \boldsymbol{\theta}) \right] = \mathbb{E}_{p_{\mathbf{D}}}\left[\ln \frac{p_{\hat{\boldsymbol{\theta}}}(\mathbf{D}_1)}{p_{\boldsymbol{\theta}}(\mathbf{D}_1)} \right].$$

This shows that as the synthetic domain $\hat{\mathbf{D}}_1$ shifts further from the original domain $\mathbf{D}_1$, the value of $p_{\hat{\boldsymbol{\theta}}}$ on $\mathbf{D}_1$ decreases relative to the fixed $p_{\boldsymbol{\theta}}$, and the bias increases.

We demonstrate this empirically in Fig. 1, showing the difference between density values in the case of 5 Gaussians distributed over a 2-dimensional space (see Supplementary for more details). The distribution learned by a Wasserstein GAN (WGAN) [5] deviates from the target distribution $p_{\boldsymbol{\theta}}$, which increases the bias as described in Eq. 3.

The bias between the two MLEs reduces the statistical reliability of the obtained model and undermines the alignment between the training and validation objectives. By inserting synthetic data, we weaken the statistical guarantees for the validation scores on real domains.

Variance. We compute the variance over the real domain distribution $p_{\mathbf{D}}$ as

$$\mathrm{Var}_{p_{\mathbf{D}}}\left[L(\mathbf{S}, \hat{\boldsymbol{\theta}}) \right] = \mathrm{Var}_{p_{\mathbf{D}}}\left[\sum_{i=1}^{t} \ln p_{\hat{\boldsymbol{\theta}}}(\mathbf{D}_i) \right]. \tag{3}$$

Similar to the bias, the problem with the variance arises on the replaced domain $\mathbf{D}_1$ where $p_{\hat{\boldsymbol{\theta}}}$ returns low values. The variance can be expanded as:

$$\mathrm{Var}_{p_{\mathbf{D}}}\left[L(\mathbf{S}, \hat{\boldsymbol{\theta}}) \right] = \mathbb{E}_{p_{\mathbf{D}}}\left[\ln p_{\hat{\boldsymbol{\theta}}}(\mathbf{D}_1)^2 \right] - \mathbb{E}_{p_{\mathbf{D}}}\left[\ln p_{\hat{\boldsymbol{\theta}}}(\mathbf{D}_1) \right]^2 + \nu, \tag{4}$$

where ν is the variance of the MLE on non-replaced domains.

Smaller $p_{\hat{\boldsymbol{\theta}}}$ on $\mathbf{D}_1$ leads to higher estimator variance as the first term in Eq. 4 is larger than the second.

As illustrated in Fig. 2, the variance is high in subdomains where $p_{\hat{\boldsymbol{\theta}}}$ is low but $p_{\boldsymbol{\theta}}$ is high (see Fig. 1), and lower where both distributions intersect. This demonstrates an additional statistical challenge: in regions where the domains $\mathbf{D}_1$ and $\hat{\mathbf{D}}_1$ diverge, the MLE becomes not only biased but also exhibits high variance. This further undermines the reliability of the

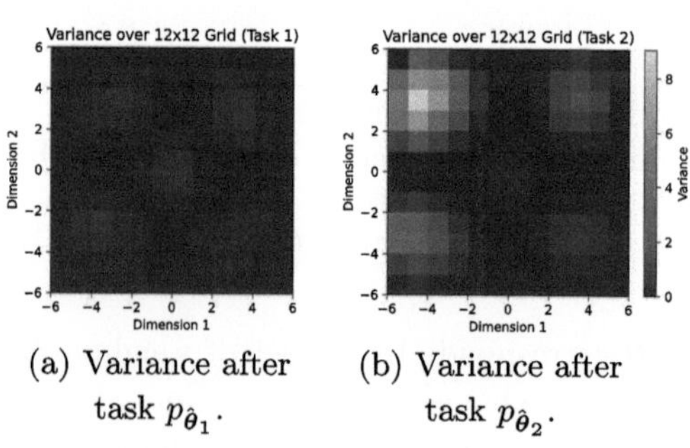

(a) Variance after task $p_{\hat{\boldsymbol{\theta}}_1}$.

(b) Variance after task $p_{\hat{\boldsymbol{\theta}}_2}$.

Fig. 2. Comparison of variances.

obtained weights $\hat{\boldsymbol{\theta}}$ when validated on real domains. The presence of non-zero bias and high variance undermines the core optimisation assumptions of generative models.

4   Continual Learning Methods and Synthetic Data Error

In continual learning, we have a non-i.i.d. setup where we have access only to the current domain $\mathbf{D}_t$. The previous domains $\{\mathbf{D}_i\}_{i=1}^{t-1}$ are commonly replaced with a memory buffer [50]. However, we still validate our model on the entire data stream $\mathbf{S}$. This leads to two objective functions: the training objective $L_t(\mathbf{D}_t, \mathcal{M}_{t-1})$, and the validation objective $L_{\mathrm{val}}(\mathbf{D}_1, \ldots, \mathbf{D}_t)$.

The discrepancy between the memory $\mathcal{M}_{t-1}$ and the past domains $\{\mathbf{D}_i\}_{i=1}^{t-1}$ increases the difference between the minima of the two objectives. Over the past years, the continual learning community has proposed numerous architectures to address this discrepancy [7,28,36,50]. In the following sections, we will show that even state-of-the-art models in generative continual learning cannot mitigate $\mathbf{ERROR}_{\mathrm{synth}}$.

4.1   Generative Experience Replay

Following our notation from Sect. 3, Generative Experience Replay (GER) methods [41] are trained with the MLE objective in the Continual Learning process as follows:

$$\max_{\theta} L(\hat{\mathbf{S}}, \theta) = \ln p_\theta(\hat{\mathbf{D}}_1, \cdots, \hat{\mathbf{D}}_{t-1}, \mathbf{D}_t), \tag{5}$$

$$\mathcal{M}_1 = P(\mathbf{D}_1), \cdots, \mathcal{M}_T = P(\mathbf{D}_T, \hat{\mathbf{D}}_{T-1}, \cdots, \hat{\mathbf{D}}_1). \tag{6}$$

GER methods use a generative model to approximate samples from past domains. They offer an efficient trade-off between the number of generated samples and the memory required to store model parameters. However, they are harder to train as catastrophic forgetting can occur in both the downstream and generative models. GER methods can be divided into two categories: those that train the generative model simultaneously with the downstream model, and those that train them separately (visualised in the Supplementary).

Joint Training. For joint training the generative and downstream models are trained simultaneously and can be separate models [11,22] or one model [47]. In this case, the losses are calculated on the same batch for both models, and weights are updated synchronously. At the end of task t, we utilise the generator to sample past domains $\{\hat{\mathbf{D}}_i\}_{i=1}^{t}$, following Eq. 5.

Separate Training. For separate training [8,41], the downstream model is decoupled from the generative model. First, the generative model is trained on the real domain $\mathbf{D}_t$. Then, a generated synthetic training dataset $\hat{\mathbf{D}}_t = (x_i, y_i)$ is used for the downstream models. In a subsequent task, the next generative model is trained using both the new task's $\mathbf{D}_{t+1}$ training samples and the synthetically generated dataset $\hat{\mathbf{D}}_t$ from previous tasks. This leads to decorrelated gradients, as the loss is calculated on different batches.

4.2   Quantitative Analysis of the Stability of Generative Models

In both GER training setups, the model is exposed to both real and synthetic domains, with the synthetic data $\hat{\mathbf{D}}$ only containing information about past domains. Eqs. 3 and 4 demonstrate the relevance of the statistical difference between the real and synthetic domains $\mathbf{D}$ and $\hat{\mathbf{D}}$, respectively. We quantify this using the following metrics.

Fréchet Inception Distance. (FID) [16] measures the Frãĺchet distance d_F between two feature distributions extracted from images using the InceptionNet model [44]. We compute two scores. For class-unconditional generative models, we compute the standard FID score. For class-conditioned models, we introduce a Conditional FID which computes the distance for each class separately (see Supplementary):

$$\mathbb{E}_Y\left[d_F(X_1|Y, X_2|Y)^2\right] = \frac{1}{k}\sum_{i=1}^{k} d_F(X_1|Y=i, X_2|Y=i)^2. \tag{7}$$

Lower FID scores indicate that the generated images are closer to the real image distribution, making it a suitable metric for assessing divergence between $\mathbf{D}_{\text{dataset}}$ and $\hat{\mathbf{D}}_{\text{dataset}}$.

Optimal Transport Dataset Distance. (OTDD) [4] is a model-agnostic metric introduced to measure the distance between datasets, in our case real and synthetic, in a way that does not depend on training a model or having matching label sets. OTDD computes distances between feature-label pairs across domains by combining geometric awareness with Wasserstein distances, which aligns datasets based on both features and labels.

Classification Degradation. measures the stability of the generative model by considering the classification accuracy. For every class-conditioned generative model and each task t, a ResNet18 classifier [15] is trained on the synthetic dataset $\hat{\mathbf{D}}_t$ with labels $\hat{y}$. The classifier is then validated on the real dataset $\mathbf{D}_{\text{dataset}}$, and the best validation score per task is reported.

While FID and OTDD are proxy metrics that measure the divergence of the synthetic data $\hat{x}$ from the real domain, the classification score provides a direct measure of how accurately the synthetic classes $\hat{y}$ represent the real distribution. A drop in classification performance suggests that the synthetic data $\hat{y}$ is diverging from the real data distribution. These metrics quantify the domain shift [23], which as we showed undermines statistical guarantees of MLE objective.

Experimental Setup. For GER methods, degradation in $\hat{\mathbf{D}}$ directly correlates with downstream performance evaluated on $\mathbf{D}$.

To find an upper bound on model stability and quantify domain drift, we consider a scenario where the model is never exposed to the real domain.

The training consists of T stages shown in Fig. 3. In the first stage, the generative model is trained on the entire real dataset $\mathbf{D}_{\text{dataset}} = \bigcup_{i=1}^{T} \mathbf{D}_i$. Subsequently, the real domains are replaced with synthetic domains $\hat{\mathbf{D}}_{\text{dataset}} = \bigcup_{i=1}^{T} \hat{\mathbf{D}}_i$, and the model is retrained on this synthetic data. To assess the stability of the generator we compute FID, OTDD, and classification scores.

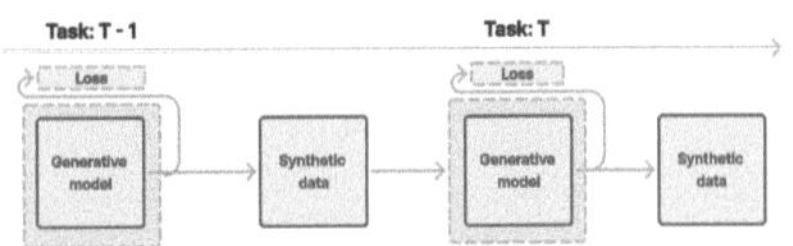

Fig. 3. The generative model is sequentially trained on synthetic data sampled from the weights obtained in the previous task.

In our experiments, we use Flower102 [32] as our initial real dataset $\mathbf{D}_{\text{dataset}}$ and train two class-unconditional generative models: Denoising Diffusion Probabilistic Model (DDPM) [17] and StyleGANv2 [20]. Furthermore, we train a class-conditioned variant of DDPM where, at every denoising step, we concatenate a learnable class embedding to the time embedding. For the conditioned StyleGANv2, we follow [33], concatenating a learnable class embedding with the latent input for the mapping network. We train each model for several stages. At the end of each stage t, we generate synthetic samples $\{\hat{\mathbf{D}}_i^t\}_{i=1}^{N_t}$ equal in size to Flower102. These samples are used to compute our evaluation metrics and serve as the training input for the next stage.

Experimental Findings. We observe that over time FID and CFID scores increase (Figs. 4aand 4b), indicating that the generated images increasingly differ from the original dataset in the image and latent space. We include the FID score between Flower102 and CIFAR-10 as a baseline (blue line) to flag that the synthetic samples eventually are as different from the initial dataset as CIFAR-10 is. We provide visual examples in the Supplementary.

Figure 4cshows similar trends for OTDD. Interestingly, over the course of the training process, the sampled datasets from the StyleGAN family remain stable, suggesting that the latent distribution of the GAN model does not change significantly, even if the sample quality decreases. Figure 4dshows that the domain drift between the distribution of original labels y and synthetic labels $\hat{y}$ occurs faster than that between x and $\hat{x}$. The classification performance almost collapses to the lower boundary of a random classifier within a few steps, implying that both model families are unstable in modelling the distribution of labels. The results confirm that the statistical reliability of the weights decreases significantly over time.

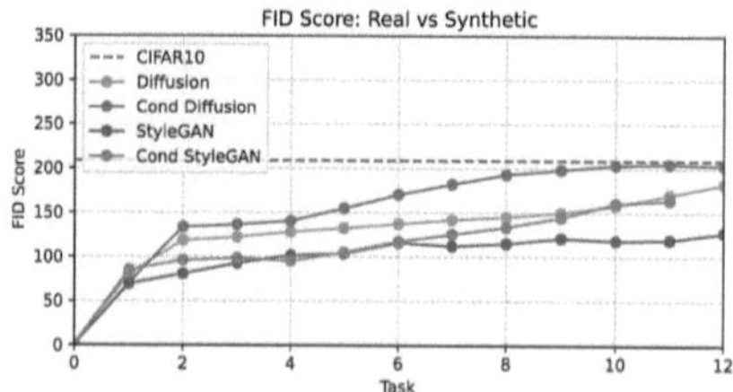

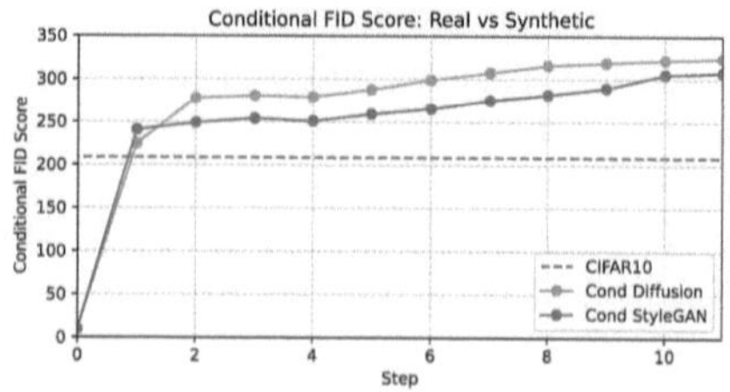

(a) FID score between the generated dataset and the Flower102 dataset.

(b) CFID score between the conditional synthetic dataset and the Flower102 dataset.

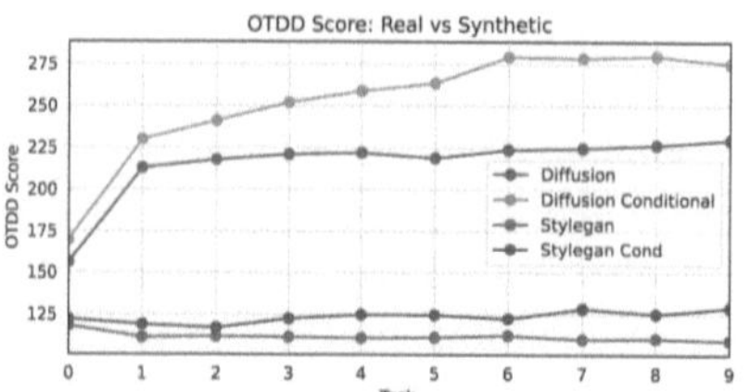

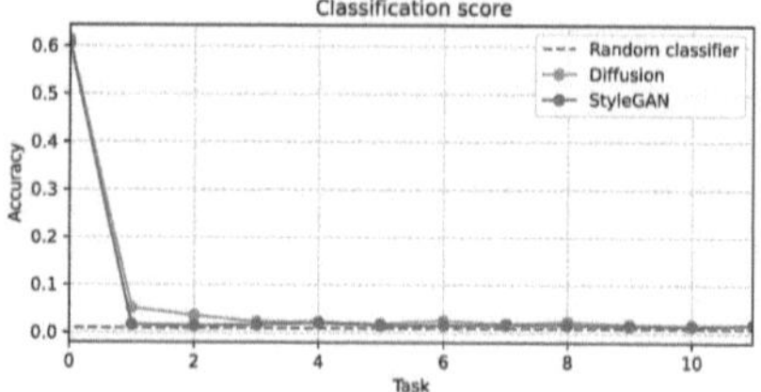

(c) OTDD score between the generated synthetic dataset and the Flower102 dataset.

(d) Classification accuracy of ResNet18 trained on synthetic data and validated on Flower102.

Fig. 4. Comparison of FID, CFID, OTDD, and classification accuracy between synthetic data and the original Flower102 dataset [32] measured at the end of each task. The baseline line in (a) and (b) in blue shows the FID / CFID score between Flower102 and CIFAR10.

4.3   GER Model Stability Qualitative Analysis of the Latent Space

In this section, we analyse the latent spaces of two GER methods: GAN-Memory [8] and DDGR [11]. These methods represent distinct training procedures. GAN-Memory adopts a separate training strategy, whereas DDGR follows a joint training approach. We selected these methods because they are among the few capable of operating on large-scale datasets, including ImageNet [10], CelebA [27], and Flower102 [32]. We show that even though these methods were specifically designed to work with synthetic data, the latent discrepancy between the real domain $\mathbf{D}$ and the synthetic domain $\hat{\mathbf{D}}$ remains significant.

Deep Diffusion-based Generative Replay. Following the procedure from the original paper, we train DDGR on CIFAR-100 [24] split into five tasks, and generate a set of images at the end of each training phase. We then fit a UMAP [30] model to the concatenation of classifier embeddings for real task data and generated synthetic samples. Fig. 5 aillustrates the embedding space of the classifier, where one can observe that starting from the first phase, embeddings for real and synthetic data are separated on the embedding manifold. Additionally, we linearly probe [2] the embeddings to distinguish real from synthetic data. We achieve

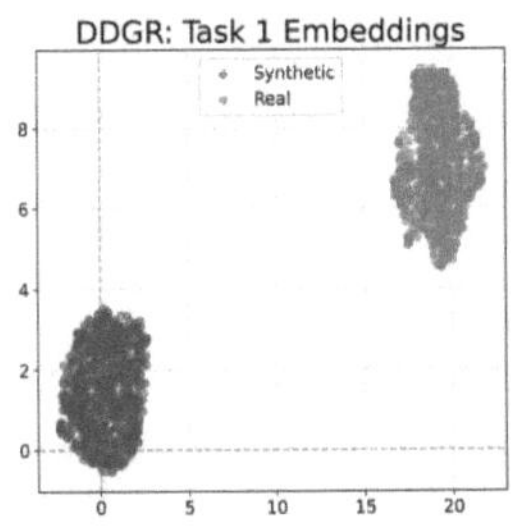
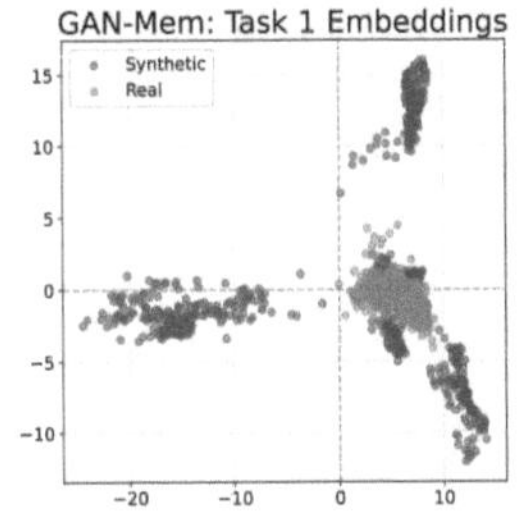
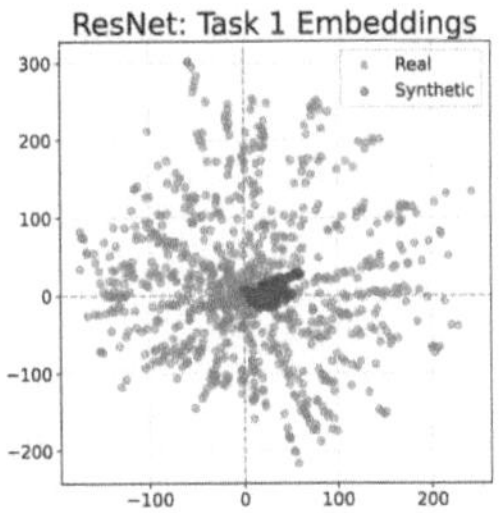

(a) DDGR classifier embeddings projected with UMAP.

(b) GAN memory classifier trained on synthetic data $\hat{\mathbf{D}}$.

(c) GAN memory classifier trained on real data $\mathbf{D}$.

Fig. 5. Visualisation of embeddings for DDGR and GAN memory classifiers for real (orange) and synthetic domains (blue). See the Supplementary for additional tasks. (Color figure online)

perfect or near-perfect accuracy at each task ($\geq$ 99.9%). This provides further strong evidence that the model separates the domains.

Generative Memory Buffer. GAN Memory [8] uses a GAN [12] whose outputs supervise the classifier. We use their training procedure, separating the Flower102 dataset into 6 tasks, each containing 17 classes. We train GAN Memory to reproduce samples from tasks. To investigate the latent structure of the learned model, we train classifiers (Resnet18) for each task on GAN-generated samples. GAN Memory uses a conditional GAN, the synthetic domains $\hat{\mathbf{D}}_i$ are obtained with data samples $\hat{x}$ and their respective labels $\hat{y}$. For visualisation, we use the dimensionality bottleneck from [46] (details in) which projects the latent space into two dimensions. We observe in Fig. 5b that the real domain is projected close to the origin, indicating that it is out of distribution for this model.

We also consider the reversed scenario, where the classifier (ResNet50) is trained on the original dataset $\mathbf{D}_{\text{dataset}}$ (Fig. 5c). We observe the same behaviour: the synthetic domains not only differ significantly in latent space shape from the real domain but are also generally closer to the centre of coordinates than any part of the real star-shaped latent space.

5   Conclusion

In this work, we analysed statistical properties of generative models in the context of continual learning methods, such as Generative Experience Replay. We found that collapse is an inevitable property, both with mild theoretical assumptions and verified it empirically in standard CL benchmarks. This points to fundamental issues with GER as a tool for CL, which must be resolved to achieve the goal of maintaining performance through repeated training and generation iterations. Furthermore, our findings point towards a necessary critical reevaluation of the growing proportion of synthetic data in the internet data corpus used for the continual training of models.

References

1. Achiam, J., et al.: Gpt-4 technical report. arXiv preprint arXiv:2303.08774 (2023)
2. Alain, G., Bengio, Y.: Understanding intermediate layers using linear classifier probes. arXiv preprint arXiv:1610.01644 (2016)
3. Alemohammad, S., et al.: Self-consuming generative models go mad. In: ICLR (2024)
4. Alvarez-Melis, D., Fusi, N.: Geometric dataset distances via optimal transport (2020)
5. Arjovsky, M., Chintala, S., Bottou, L.: Wasserstein generative adversarial networks. In: ICML (2017)
6. Bousquet, O., Boucheron, S., Lugosi, G.: Introduction to statistical learning theory. In: Summer School on Machine Learning, pp. 169–207. Springer (2003)
7. Chaudhry, A., et al.: On tiny episodic memories in continual learning. arXiv preprint arXiv:1902.10486 (2019)
8. Cong, Y., Zhao, M., Li, J., Wang, S., Carin, L.: Gan memory with no forgetting. In: NeurIPS (2020)
9. Cui, W., Zhang, L., Wang, Q., Cai, S.: Who said that? benchmarking social media ai detection. arXiv preprint arXiv:2310.08240 (2023)
10. Deng, J., Dong, W., Socher, R., Li, L.J., Li, K., Fei-Fei, L.: Imagenet: a large-scale hierarchical image database. In: CVPR (2009)
11. Gao, R., Liu, W.: Ddgr: continual learning with deep diffusion-based generative replay. In: ICML (2023)
12. Goodfellow, I.J., et al.: Generative adversarial nets. In: NeurIPS (2014)
13. Grossberg, S., Grossberg, S.: How does a brain build a cognitive code? neural principles of learning, perception, development, cognition, and motor control, studies of mind and brain (1982)
14. Hataya, R., Bao, H., Arai, H.: Will large-scale generative models corrupt future datasets? In: ICCV (2023)
15. He, K., Zhang, X., Ren, S., Sun, J.: Deep residual learning for image recognition. In: CVPR (2016)
16. Heusel, M., Ramsauer, H., Unterthiner, T., Nessler, B., Hochreiter, S.: GANs trained by a two time-scale update rule converge to a local nash equilibrium (2017)
17. Ho, J., Jain, A., Abbeel, P.: Denoising diffusion probabilistic models. In: NeurIPS (2020)
18. Hochreiter, S.: Long short-term memory. Neural Computation MIT-Press (1997)
19. Kaplan, J., et al.: Scaling laws for neural language models. arXiv preprint arXiv:2001.08361 (2020)
20. Karras, T., Laine, S., Aittala, M., Hellsten, J., Lehtinen, J., Aila, T.: Analyzing and improving the image quality of stylegan. In: CVPR (2020)
21. Kemker, R., Kanan, C.: Fearnet: brain-inspired model for incremental learning. CoRR abs/1711.10563 (2017). http://arxiv.org/abs/1711.10563
22. Kemker, R., Kanan, C.: Fearnet: brain-inspired model for incremental learning. arXiv preprint arXiv:1711.10563 (2017)

23. Kouw, W.M., Loog, M.: An introduction to domain adaptation and transfer learning. arXiv preprint arXiv:1812.11806 (2018)
24. Krizhevsky, A., Hinton, G., et al.: Learning multiple layers of features from tiny images (2009)
25. Lesort, T., Lomonaco, V., Stoian, A., Maltoni, D., Filliat, D., Díaz-Rodríguez, N.: Continual learning for robotics: definition, framework, learning strategies, opportunities and challenges (2019)
26. Lin, T.Y., et al.: Microsoft coco: common objects in context. In: ECCV (2014)
27. Liu, Z., Luo, P., Wang, X., Tang, X.: Deep learning face attributes in the wild. In: ICCV (2015)
28. Lopez-Paz, D., Ranzato, M.: Gradient episodic memory for continual learning. Adv. Neural Inf. Process. Syst. **30** (2017)
29. Matatov, H., Quéré, M.A.L., Amir, O., Naaman, M.: Examining the prevalence and dynamics of AI-generated media in art subreddits. arXiv preprint arXiv:2410.07302 (2024)
30. McInnes, L., Healy, J., Melville, J.: Umap: uniform manifold approximation and projection for dimension reduction. arXiv preprint arXiv:1802.03426 (2018)
31. Naveed, H., et al.: A comprehensive overview of large language models. arXiv preprint arXiv:2307.06435 (2023)
32. Nilsback, M.E., Zisserman, A.: Automated flower classification over a large number of classes. In: Indian Conference on Computer Vision, Graphics and Image Processing (2008)
33. Oeldorf, C., Spanakis, G.: Loganv2: conditional style-based logo generation with generative adversarial networks. In: IEEE International Conference on Machine Learning and Applications (2019)
34. Prabhu, A., Torr, P.H.S., Dokania, P.K.: GDumb: a simple approach that questions our progress in continual learning. In: Vedaldi, A., Bischof, H., Brox, T., Frahm, J.-M. (eds.) ECCV 2020. LNCS, vol. 12347, pp. 524–540. Springer, Cham (2020). https://doi.org/10.1007/978-3-030-58536-5_31
35. Radford, A., Narasimhan, K., Salimans, T., Sutskever, I.: Improving language understanding by generative pre-training (2018)
36. Rebuffi, S.A., Kolesnikov, A., Sperl, G., Lampert, C.H.: iCaRL: Incremental Classifier and Representation Learning (2017)
37. Robins, A.: Catastrophic forgetting, rehearsal and pseudorehearsal. Connect. Sci. **7**(2), 123–146 (1995)
38. Rolnick, D., Ahuja, A., Schwarz, J., Lillicrap, T., Wayne, G.: Experience replay for continual learning. NeurIPS (2019)
39. Rombach, R., Blattmann, A., Lorenz, D., Esser, P., Ommer, B.: High-resolution image synthesis with latent diffusion models. In: CVPR (2022)
40. Scott, D.W.: Multivariate density estimation: theory, practice, and visualization. John Wiley & Sons (2015)
41. Shin, H., Lee, J.K., Kim, J., Kim, J.: Continual learning with deep generative replay. In: NeurIPS (2017)
42. Shumailov, I., Shumaylov, Z., Zhao, Y., Gal, Y., Papernot, N., Anderson, R.J.: The curse of recursion: training on generated data makes models forget. arXiv preprint arXiv:2305.17493 (2023)
43. Shumailov, I., Shumaylov, Z., Zhao, Y., Papernot, N., Anderson, R., Gal, Y.: AI models collapse when trained on recursively generated data. Nature (2024)
44. Szegedy, C., Vanhoucke, V., Ioffe, S., Shlens, J., Wojna, Z.: Rethinking the inception architecture for computer vision. In: CVPR (2016)

45. Vaswani, A., et al.: Attention is all you need. In: NeurIPS (2017)
46. Vaze, S., Han, K., Vedaldi, A., Zisserman, A.: Open-set recognition: a good closed-set classifier is all you need? In: ICLR (2022)
47. Van de Ven, G.M., Tolias, A.S.: Generative replay with feedback connections as a general strategy for continual learning. arXiv preprint arXiv:1809.10635 (2018)
48. van der Ven, M., Tolias, A.S.: Generative replay with feedback connections as a general strategy for continual learning. CoRR abs/1809.10635 (2018). http://arxiv.org/abs/1809.10635
49. Villalobos, P., Sevilla, J., Heim, L., Besiroglu, T., Hobbhahn, M., Ho, A.: Will we run out of data? an analysis of the limits of scaling datasets in machine learning. arXiv preprint arXiv:2211.04325 (2022)
50. Wang, L., Zhang, X., Su, H., Zhu, J.: A comprehensive survey of continual learning: theory, method and application. IEEE TPAMI (2024)
51. Wang, M., Deng, W.: Deep visual domain adaptation: a survey. Neurocomputing (2018)
52. Yang, J., Zhou, K., Li, Y., Liu, Z.: Generalized out-of-distribution detection: a survey. IJCV (2024)

Combined Image Data Augmentations Diminish the Benefits of Adaptive Label Smoothing

Georg Siedel[1,2(✉)] [ID], Ekagra Gupta[2], Weijia Shao[1], Silvia Vock[1],
and Andrey Morozov[2]

[1] Federal Institute for Occupational Safety and Health (BAuA), Dresden, Germany
`{siedel.georg,shao.weijia,vock.silvia}@baua.bund.de`
[2] University of Stuttgart, Stuttgart, Germany

Abstract. Soft augmentation regularizes the supervised learning process of image classifiers by reducing label confidence of a training sample based on the magnitude of a Random Crop augmentation applied to it. This paper extends this adaptive label smoothing framework to other types of aggressive augmentations beyond Random Crop. Specifically, we demonstrate the effectiveness of the method for random erasing and noise injection data augmentation. Adaptive label smoothing permits stronger regularization via higher-intensity Random Erasing. However, its benefits vanish when applied with a diverse range of image transformations as in the state-of-the-art TrivialAugment method, and excessive label smoothing harms robustness to common corruptions. Our findings suggest that adaptive label smoothing should only be applied when the training data distribution is dominated by a limited, homogeneous set of image transformation types.

Keywords: image classification · data augmentation · label smoothing

1 Introduction

Vision models have long surpassed human accuracy on tasks such as image classification [14]. A key success factor to their ability to learn general and robust representations of data is data augmentation, which enriches training data diversity by applying controlled transformations to images or labels [24]. Among image data augmentations, very aggressive transformations have proved effective in methods such as TrivialAugment [20]. However, excessively transforming images can lead to information loss in the image (see Fig. 1). In this case, a model will learn confident labels from uncertain information, which could lead to its miscalibration [16]. Soft augmentation [16] addresses this issue by combining image augmentation with adaptive label smoothing. The method scales down label confidences the higher the magnitude of image transformations become. Specifically applied to Random Cropping augmentations, this enabled more aggressive crops during training without overfitting or model miscalibration.

M. Keuper and F. Locatello (Eds.): DAGM GCPR 2025, LNCS 16125, pp. 251–266, 2026.
https://doi.org/10.1007/978-3-032-12840-9_17

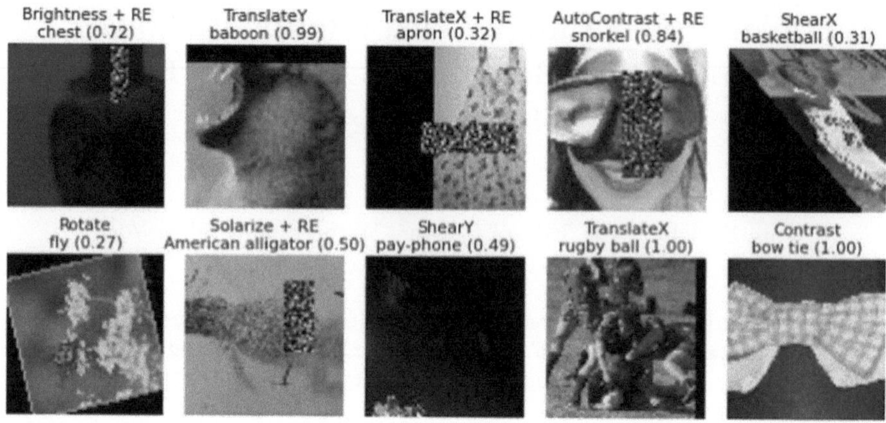

Fig. 1. TinyImageNet images transformed with soft TrivialAugment and soft Random Erasing (RE) data augmentation. The titles display the TrivialAugment transformation type and whether RE is applied, as well as the label and its softened confidence. The confidence is calculated as a function of the augmentation severity for every transformation type individually. Here, the functions are derived from a proxy model's average accuracy on that transformation type and severity, as can be seen from Fig. 3.

In this work, we extend adaptive label smoothing to well-established, aggressive image augmentation strategies like TrivialAugment and Random Erasing to further enhance their efficacy, as demonstrated by the image examples in Fig. 1. Our contributions can be summarized as follows:[1]

- We integrate adaptive label smoothing with TrivialAugment. We model magnitude-confidence mapping functions for its various transformation types from human vision studies, proxy networks, and image similarity metrics.
- Through image classification experiments, we show that adaptive label smoothing enables more aggressive parameter settings for Random Erasing and can improve the performance of noise injection data augmentation.
- We demonstrate that the benefit of adaptive label smoothing vanishes when applied across a heterogeneous set of augmentations as in TrivialAugment, which constrains its practical applicability.

2   Related Work

2.1   Image Augmentation

Early geometric image augmentations such as random flips and Random Crops (RC) [14,36] are now standard in training pipelines. Occlusion methods such as Cutout [6] and Random Erasing (RE) [39] eliminate image regions to force reliance on global context. Noise injections, ranging from Gaussian Noise [22]

---

[1] Code available at https://github.com/georgsiedel/soft_label_random_augmentation.

over general p-norm noise [25] to Patch Gaussian noise [17], randomizes pixel-level statistics and induces robustness against high-frequency corruptions.

AutoAugment and RandAugment [4,5] were pioneering approaches for more advanced combination policies over a set of fourteen transformations types. The latest TrivialAugment (TA) [20] simplified this approach using the same transformation types: it randomly selects one transform and a more aggressive magnitude compare to its predecessors. TA is tuning-free and matches or outperforms AutoAugment and RandAugment.

These input-only augmentation schemes are state-of-the-art in classification accuracy and robustness to common corruptions [8,28]. They presume that important image content, in particular the class labels, remain invariant under all transformations, but aggressive distortions as in TA can violate this, as displayed in Fig. 1, yielding overconfident or miscalibrated predictions [16]. This shortcoming motivates a complementary line of research: augmenting the labels themselves to better represent the actual transformed image data.

2.2 Label Augmentation

Label augmentation alters ground-truth targets in the training data. Early methods include randomly flipping labels [32], and Label Smoothing, which redistributes a fraction α of the probability mass uniformly across non-target classes [26]. While effective at regularizing, these approaches apply to every sample in an identical way.

Adaptive label augmentation tailors the label smoothing to the image data. Online Label Smoothing derives targets from the model's own predicted class confidences at each iteration [37]. Label Refinery employs a teacher network to generate softer labels that better reflect each image's content [2]. Meta-learning–based schemes estimate optimal labels per sample via an auxiliary objective [29].

Other methods jointly augment inputs and labels. Mixup and Cutmix interpolate paired images and their labels, enforcing linear behavior between classes and improving accuracy, robustness and model calibration [35,38]. However, neither deploy image transformations to add additional diversity to the training process.

2.3 Soft Augmentation

Co-designing input and label perturbations lets a model learn diverse distortions while calibrating its confidence to their severity. In *soft augmentation* [16], each image-label-pair (x_i, y_i) is transformed as

$$\underbrace{\left(x_i, y_i\right)}_{\text{Training data tuple}} \mapsto \left(\underbrace{t_{\phi \sim S}(x_i)}_{\text{Image augmentation}}, \underbrace{g_\alpha(\phi)(y_i)}_{\text{Adaptive label smoothing}}\right) \tag{1}$$

where $\phi \sim S$ denotes the transformation type and magnitude sampled from a set S, which informs the factor α of the label smoothing function $g_\alpha(y_i)$. Intuitively, stronger augmentations yield lower target confidence. An additional reweighting [21] of the loss with the reduced confidence further amplifies the smoothing regularization. Liu et al. [16] show that this adaptive scheme enables more aggressive image augmentation without overfitting, improving both accuracy and calibration. Their work, however, is limited to Random Cropping (RC).

2.4   Human Vision Studies

The soft RC augmentation is inspired by human visual perception, long the gold standard for vision models [23,40]. Liu et al. [16] map the reduction in label confidence to the magnitude of RC on an image by adapting data from a human vision study (HVS). The study measures classification accuracy on occluded image and finds that human performance remains high under mild to moderate occlusion but degrades nonlinearly toward chance level as occlusion intensifies [27].

Comparable HVS for other image transformations are available for noise and blur [7], contrast variation [1], and rotation [11,12]. Note, however, that many psychophysical experiments report response time rather than classification accuracy [9,19], making them unsuitable proxies for mapping label confidence.

3   Adaptive Label Smoothing for Aggressive Image Data Augmentation

In this paper, we extend the soft augmentation from Eq. 1 from Random Cropping (RC) to other, aggressive image augmentation schemes in order to find out if the method transfers. However, for every new transformation type in an image augmentation scheme, we need to model functions that map transformation magnitude to smoothed label confidence in a reasonable way. To this end, several approaches can be used to estimate how much information is lost in the image due to transformation of this type with certain magnitude.

3.1   Mapping Label Confidence to Image Transformation Magnitude

This section describes such approaches used in this study. Figure 2 shows the mapping functions for those approaches exemplarily for the rotation transformation.

HVS. Wherever available, we adopt HVS data to set label confidence to average human classification accuracy under a given distortion level, as in [16]. If the HVS covers only parts of the magnitude range, we linearly interpolate between measured points. Transformations lacking any HVS accuracy data get no smoothing under what we denote the HVS scheme in the following.

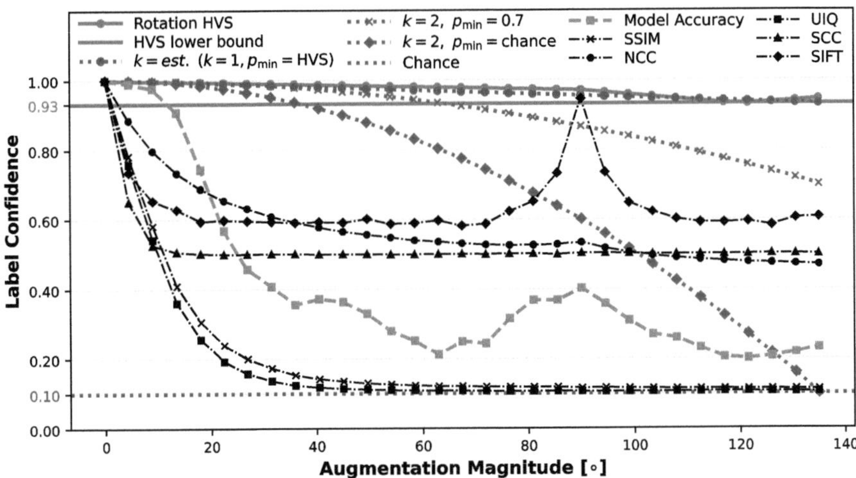

Fig. 2. This diagram displays the functions defining how an images label is adjusted based on the magnitude of the image transformation. For the "Rotate" transformation in TrivialAugment, the functions map label confidence to image rotation in degrees. The functions are based on human vision studies (blue), on a proxy model's outputs (green), on custom polynomial functions (red) and on image similarity metrics (black). Here, functions differ significantly between all approaches, emphasizing the potential differences in modeling approaches for adaptive label smoothing. The polynomial function $k = est.$ mimics HVS data if that is available like in for image rotations, otherwise it mimics model accuracy. (Color figure online)

Model-accuracy Inspired by [2, 29, 37], we derive what we denote a model-accuracy mapping from a classifier's accuracy on CIFAR-10 images. The model has been pretrained with Mixup and noise injections, but with no transformations contained in TA or RE. We measure the average model accuracy on training images subjected to the transformations to be mapped. This setup corresponds to a model that knows all images, but is confronted with unknown transformations. Starting from 100 %, accuracy falls depending on transformation magnitude, which we use as a fixed label confidence mapping.

Image similarity metrics Alternatively, we explored image similarity metrics to quantify distortion severity. We applied Structural Similarity Index Measure (SSIM) [31], (Fast) Normalized Cross Correlation (NCC) [34], Spatial Correlation Coefficient (SCC) [3], Universal Image Quality (UIQ) [30] and Scale-Invariant Feature Transform (SIFT) [18] to 500 image pairs at each transformation magnitude. All metrics except SIFT yield scores in $[-1, 1]$, which we naively rescaled to $[chance, 1]$. For SIFT, which is used only on geometric transforms, we measured the fraction of tracked keypoints retained through a transformation. As shown in Figs. 2 and 3 for the transformation types contained in TA, NCC and SIFT align with HVS and model-accuracy data on geometric transformations, whereas SSIM, UIQ, and SCC better reflect color transformations.

However, no single metric consistently behaves intuitively and comparably to HVS or model accuracy across the transformation types. Since it appeared far-fetched to assemble a mapping based on a manually crafted mixture of metrics, we omitted the image similarity approach from our training experiments.

Polynomial estimate As a parametric fallback, we also tested a simple polynomial mapping:

$$\alpha(\phi) = \phi^k \left(1 - p_{\min}\right),$$

where $\phi \in [0, 1]$ is the transformation magnitude (e.g. occluded image ratio, rotation angle with maximum rotation normalized to 1), $p_{\min}$ is the minimum confidence and k controls the functions curvature.

We evaluate four polynomial variants:

1. $k = 2$, $p_{\min} = chance$: Baseline as in [16]. $chance = 1/classes$, so that $p_{\min}$ floors label smoothing at random-guessing level.
2. $k = 2$, $p_{\min} = 0.7$: Yields an average label smoothing factor of 0.1 as is standard [26], given uniformly distributed ϕ.
3. $k = est.$: k and $p_{\min}$ individually approximate the HVS curve (or the model-accuracy mapping when HVS is unavailable).
4. $k = 2$, $p_{\min} = 0.3$: Only for noise, based on HVS in [7].

3.2 Soft TrivialAugment

Next, we select data augmentation candidates to which adaptive label smoothing should be extended. TA is a natural candidate for softening due to its remarkable performance and the aggressive image transformations it employs. This method randomly selects from 14 transformation types and 31 discrete magnitudes, uniformly distributed over predefined intervals specific to each type. Table 1 summarizes all transformation types in TA, their respective data sources for the HVS mapping (where available), and the data used for the $k = est.$ mapping.

Figure 3 summarizes all available mapping functions as described in detail earlier, for those 11 transformations in TA that have variable magnitudes.

3.3 Soft Random Erasing

We extend adaptive label smoothing to RE [39], an occlusion-based augmentation method, hence it may benefit from adaptive label smoothing similarly to RC. Following the methodology in Liu et al. [16] and occlusion-based HVS data in [27], we adopt the polynomial mapping function $k = 2$, $p_{\min} = chance$, where the transformation magnitude is the occluded area ratio of the image.

3.4 Soft Noise

Last, we apply adaptive label smoothing to two noise injection variants: Gaussian noise is drawn from $N(0, 0.1)$ and applied across the entire image. Patch

Table 1. All TrivialAugment transformations and the human vision study data used for mapping the label confidence to the transformation magnitude for this transformations. We transfer human vision study data from Rotation to Shear and from Contrast to Brightness, because we found the proxy models behaviour and several image similarity metrics to behave similarly on these transformations, in the same manner as [16] use Occlusion studies for Translation transformations. Four transformations have no human vision study data available that fits this transformation. The last column shows whether the $k = est.$ mapping mimics the human vision study data or model accuracy. The last three TrivialAugment transformations have no mapping for adaptive label smoothing at all, as they are no transformation (Identity) or non-variable in magnitude (Equalize and AutoContrast).

TrivialAugment Transformation	Human Vision Study mapping	$k = est.$ mapping
Rotate	Rotation [11,12]	HVS
ShearX	Rotation [11,12]	HVS
ShearY	Rotation [11,12]	HVS
TranslateX	Occlusion [27]	HVS
TranslateY	Occlusion [27]	HVS
Brightness	Contrast [1]	HVS
Contrast	Contrast [1]	HVS
Sharpness	-	Model Accuracy
Color	-	Model Accuracy
Posterize	-	Model Accuracy
Solarize	-	Model Accuracy
Equalize, AutoContrast, Identity	-	

Gaussian noise is drawn from $N(0, 1.0)$ and applied to a fixed square region (25 pixels, 50 for TinyImageNet) centered randomly on the image as in [17].

In both cases, noise is scaled by a random factor drawn uniformly from $[0, 1.0]$ per image. The transformation magnitude is defined as the product of the Gaussian standard deviation, the scaling factor, and the relative area affected by the noise. Label confidence is then computed using the polynomial mapping function $k = 2$, $p_{\min} = 0.3$, as estimated from the HVS study in [7].

4   Experiments

We test our approach on the image classification datasets CIFAR-10 (C10), CIFAR-100 (C100) [13], and TinyImageNet (TIN) [15], primarily using a WideResNet-28-4 backbone [36] or a ResNeXt-29-32x4d [33] for validation. Training hyperparameters are detailed in Appendix A.

Beyond test accuracy, we evaluate the corruption robustness of models. The corruption robustness of a classifier $f : X \to Y$ according to [10] is:

$$\mathbb{E}_{c \sim C} \left[P_{(x,y) \sim D} \big(f(c(x)) = y \big) \right] \qquad (2)$$

where x, y are data samples from the data distribution D. C is a set of corruptions which perturb x. Here, C is the corruption robustness benchmark from [10] that contains 19 real-world corruptions in 5 severities. Robustness denotes the average accuracy across all corruptions of this benchmark dataset on all test images.

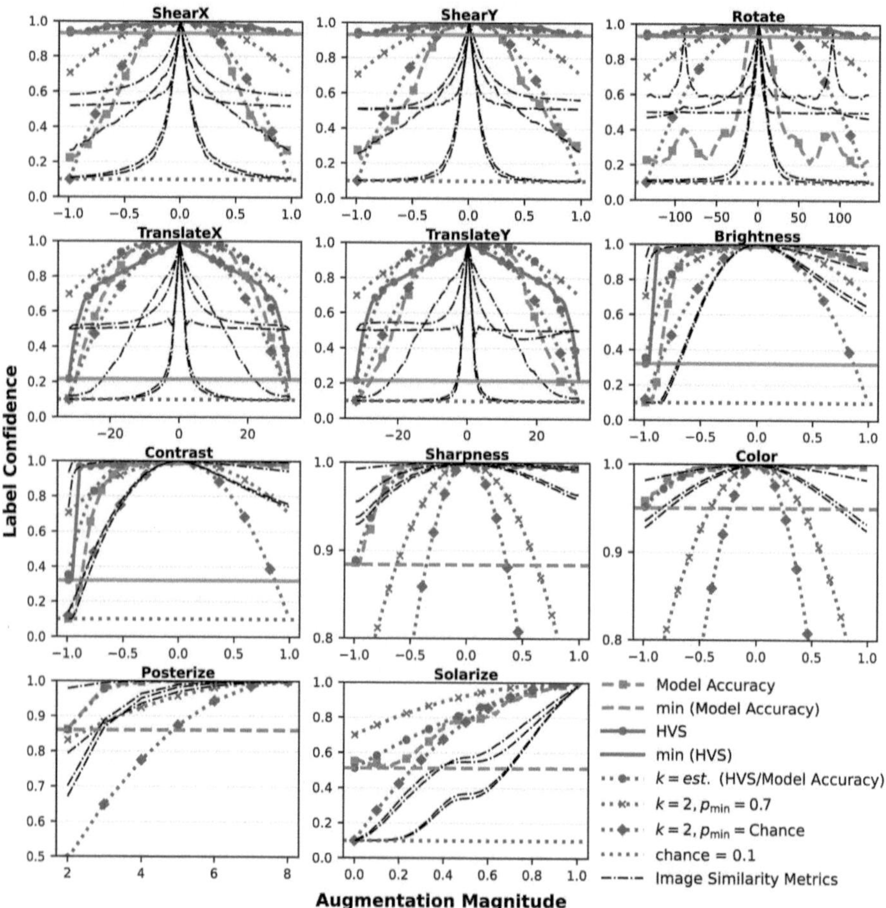

Fig. 3. A summary of the functions defining how an images label is adjusted based on the magnitude of the image transformation, for all transformation types used in TrivialAugment (find a closer view for one transformation type in Fig. 2. The functions are based on a proxy models outputs (green, dashed), on human vision studies (HVS) (blue, solid), on custom polynomial functions (red, dotted) and on image similarity metrics (black, dash-dotted). The polynomial function $k = est.$ mimics HVS data if available and model accuracy otherwise - the respective minimum confidence value is displayed as a horizontal line. (Color figure online)

Table 2. Mean accuracy and robustness with standard deviations over 5 runs for different soft TrivialAugment mapping approaches compared to hard label TrivialAugment and TrivialAugment with standard label smoothing (with 0.1 label weight redistributed). (w) denotes a reweighted variant of the most promising mapping $k = 2, p_{min} = 0.7$, while the second block validates this mappings slight advantage on CIFAR datasets on the ResNeXt model architecture. Note that no improvement over the baseline is larger than the combined standard deviations, indicating little statistical significance.

Mapping	CIFAR-10		CIFAR-100		TinyImageNet	
	Acc.	Rob.	Acc.	Rob.	Acc.	Rob.
WRN-28-4						
Hard Labels	96.62 ±0.16	87.12 ±0.43	80.20 ±0.25	62.55 ±0.64	65.44 ±0.28	31.02 ±0.94
Label Smoothing	96.66 ±0.07	86.91 ±0.56	80.30 ±0.14	**63.31** ±0.46	**65.52** ±0.18	**32.56** ±0.82
Model Accuracy	96.50 ±0.17	**87.48** ±0.35	79.70 ±0.39	62.73 ±0.61	64.02 ±0.48	30.64 ±0.86
HVS	96.55 ±0.12	87.22 ±0.31	80.16 ±0.31	62.74 ±0.51	64.90 ±0.69	30.20 ±1.06
$k = est.$	96.58 ±0.20	87.20 ±0.44	80.26 ±0.23	62.38 ±0.43	64.88 ±0.20	30.85 ±1.80
$k = 2, p_{min} = chance$	96.42 ±0.15	85.37 ±0.89	79.66 ±0.17	60.01 ±0.65	63.95 ±0.53	26.42 ±2.05
$k = 2, p_{min} = 0.7$	**96.78** ±0.08	86.93 ±0.32	**80.37** ±0.12	62.35 ±0.36	65.08 ±0.37	30.38 ±1.99
$k = 2, p_{min} = 0.7$ (w)	96.60 ±0.15	86.83 ±0.18	80.08 ±0.32	61.60 ±0.75	65.25 ±0.39	27.95 ±1.84
ResNeXt-29-32x4d						
Hard Labels	96.43±0.06	86.50±0.39	80.12±0.19	61.44±0.86	**67.13**±0.18	**32.05**±0.72
$k = 2, p_{min} = 0.7$	**96.61**±0.15	**86.78**±0.54	**80.64**±0.52	**61.76**±0.50	67.06±0.65	29.83±0.83

4.1 Analysis of Different Mappings Approaches and Transformation Types in Soft TrivialAugment

Table 2 compares different soft TA mapping functions to TA and TA with fixed label smoothing. The conservative $k = 2, p \geq 0.7$ mapping yields a small gain over TA and fixed label smoothing on CIFAR, but not on TIN. All aggressive mappings ($k = 2, p \geq chance$, model accuracy, weighted) degrade performance. Any observed improvements lie within the standard deviations across 5 runs, indicating little statistical significance.

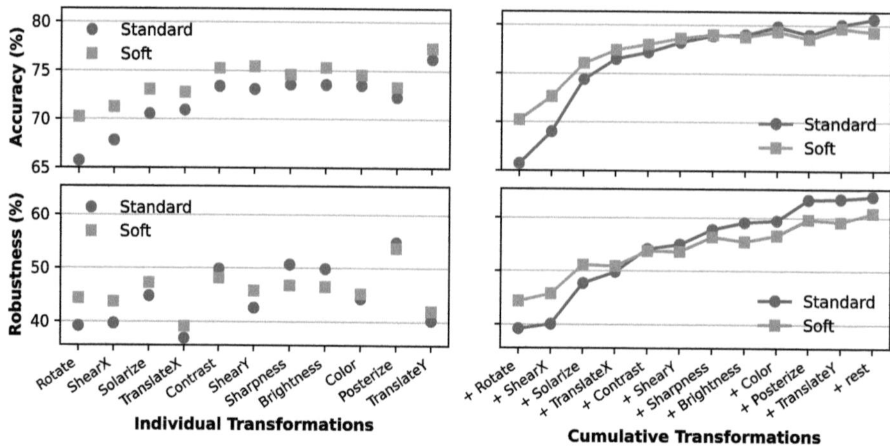

Fig. 4. Standard TrivialAugment and TrivialAugment with adaptive label smoothing (soft) are compared for individual transformation types from its set (left) and when incrementally adding transformations (right), evaluating accuracy (top) and robustness (bottom). The transformations are ordered along the x-axis by decreasing incremental benefit of adaptive label smoothing. The $k = 2, p_{min} \geq chance$ mapping is used.

To diagnose the limited overall benefit of soft TA, we isolate each transformation type in TA and retrain with adaptive label smoothing. Figure 4 shows that adaptive label smoothing does boosts accuracy on individual augmentations. However, as transformations are incrementally accumulated, the gains vanish and eventually reverse, particularly deteriorating robustness to common corruptions. Even when we use all transformations, but apply adaptive label smoothing only to the 3 transformation types that benefit the most from it, the model accuracy is no better than for standard TA.

4.2 More Aggressive Parametrization of Soft Random Erasing

Inspired by soft RC's tolerance for stronger distortions in [16], we perform a grid sweep for standard and soft RE over its two key hyperparameters - application probability and maximum area ratio, which is the upper bound to the randomly drawn occluded image proportion. As shown in Fig. 5, soft RE consistently outperforms its hard-label counterpart. At a low application probability of 0.25, the improvement is modest. However, it increases substantially as both the probability and the size of the occlusion grow, confirming the effectiveness of adaptive label smoothing in allowing for stronger image distortions. In all following experiments, we use the optimal parameters found for both methods.

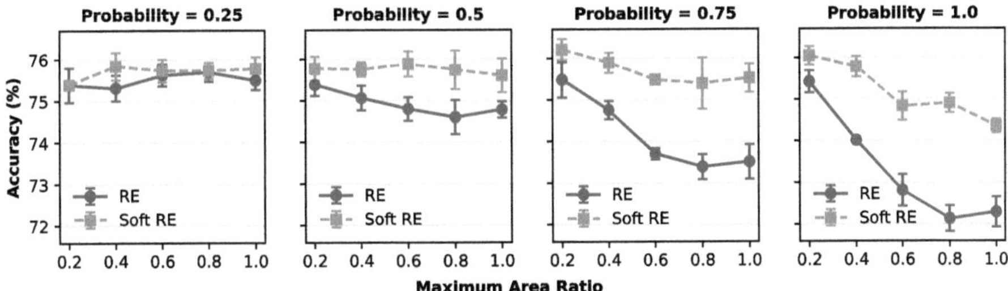

Fig. 5. Grid search over the two main hyperparameters of Random Erasing, probability and maximum area ratio, compared for standard and soft Random Erasing. Displayed are means and standard deviations over 5 runs on CIFAR-100, no reweighting or other augmentations are applied. Softening allows for more aggressive hyperparameters.

Table 3. Single-transform augmentations vs. their soft versions, applied individually and on top of TrivialAugment. Standard deviations are reported over 5 runs - notice that not all improvements can be considered statistically significant. P.-Gaussian means Patch Gaussian, (w) highlight experiments with reweighted labels. Only soft Random Crop boosts accuracy by significant margins consistently across datasets. Soft Random Erasing and soft Patch Gaussian work well on CIFAR, but less so on TinyImageNet.

Method	CIFAR-10		CIFAR-100		TinyImageNet	
	Acc.	Rob.	Acc.	Rob.	Acc.	Rob.
Baseline	93.92 ±0.11	72.98 ±0.24	73.87 ±0.33	45.52 ±0.61	58.83 ±0.34	22.29 ±0.69
P.-Gaussian	94.32 ±0.08	81.37 ±0.56	73.71 ±0.28	55.33 ±0.40	58.34 ±0.33	23.17 ±0.63
P.-Gaussian (Soft)	94.84 ±0.12	82.70 ±0.76	73.50 ±0.31	55.74 ±0.45	58.26 ±0.21	23.29 ±0.55
Gaussian	91.66 ±0.21	83.29 ±0.41	68.85 ±0.17	**57.19** ±0.32	57.71 ±0.35	23.86 ±0.82
Gaussian (Soft)	91.84 ±0.15	**83.32** ±0.22	68.70 ±0.44	57.06 ±0.29	56.87 ±0.55	**23.97** ±0.68
RE	94.86 ±0.13	74.19 ±0.29	75.69 ±0.25	47.77 ±0.48	60.52 ±0.29	20.83 ±0.73
RE (Soft)	94.98 ±0.11	74.32 ±0.99	76.21 ±0.28	47.96 ±0.60	60.05 ±0.26	21.15 ±0.53
RE (Soft) (w)	94.95 ±0.06	74.71 ±0.56	75.98 ±0.44	48.30 ±0.64	60.16 ±0.24	21.69 ±0.38
RC	95.09 ±0.11	73.40 ±0.39	76.58 ±0.21	46.10 ±0.55	60.62 ±0.18	21.95 ±0.81
RC (Soft)	**95.99** ±0.11	71.94 ±0.59	**78.01** ±0.33	43.49 ±0.58	**62.06** ±0.57	19.96 ±0.91
RC (Soft) (w)	95.92 ±0.22	70.98 ±0.40	77.43 ±0.32	43.33 ±0.62	61.70 ±0.71	20.52 ±0.84
TrivialAugment	96.42 ±0.07	86.78 ±0.14	80.41 ±0.14	63.97 ±0.46	65.35 ±0.42	31.68 ±1.33
+P.-Gaussian	96.32 ±0.02	90.96 ±0.17	79.56 ±0.37	68.79 ±0.36	65.56 ±0.39	32.21 ±0.93
+P.-Gaussian (Soft)	96.44 ±0.14	**91.36** ±0.21	79.86 ±0.14	**68.97** ±0.27	65.43 ±0.53	33.53 ±2.11
+Gaussian	95.52 ±0.08	90.97 ±0.16	77.30 ±0.33	68.09 ±0.19	64.85 ±0.34	**34.91** ±1.90
+Gaussian (Soft)	95.65 ±0.14	91.09 ±0.08	77.24 ±0.10	68.16 ±0.23	64.93 ±0.50	34.35 ±1.24
+RE	96.56 ±0.19	87.48 ±0.43	80.68 ±0.14	64.39 ±0.61	66.25 ±0.47	31.40 ±1.70
+RE (Soft)	96.70 ±0.21	87.59 ±0.41	**80.74** ±0.20	64.58 ±0.60	66.05 ±0.40	31.67 ±1.78
+Soft RE (w)	96.71 ±0.11	87.69 ±0.57	80.45 ±0.26	63.62 ±0.37	66.22 ±0.36	31.68 ±1.67
+RC	96.64 ±0.18	87.21 ±0.42	80.20 ±0.25	62.55 ±0.64	65.44 ±0.28	31.02 ±0.94
+RC (Soft)	**96.76** ±0.11	86.04 ±0.62	80.50 ±0.28	61.89 ±0.92	**66.54** ±0.44	31.56 ±1.02
+RC (Soft) (w)	96.63 ±0.19	85.54 ±0.65	80.65 ±0.21	61.52 ±0.94	66.39 ±0.32	30.86 ±1.31

4.3 Soft Random Erasing and Noise Injections

Following our soft TA analysis, we expect the single-transform augmentations RE, Gaussian and Patch Gaussian to benefit from adaptive label smoothing much like RC. Table 3 confirms that models trained with soft RE or soft noise generally outperform their hard-label counterparts, both alone and on top of TA. Soft RE on TIN is a lone exception - the reason likely is that we did not parametrize RE on TIN, but reused the parameters for C100 from Sect. 4.2, which may not transfer optimally. Noise injections show an overall tendency to improve with soft labels, though not uniformly across experiments and not by large margins. Soft RC stands out as the most effective method for improving accuracy, but it consistently hurts robustness. Patch Gaussian (in most cases soft) offers the best tradeoff between accuracy and robustness. Contrary to findings by Liu et al. [16], reweighting does not benefit training in any experiment.

In Table 4 we show ablation studies where augmentations are incrementally applied, with and without adaptive label smoothing, on top of TA. The results show that RC and RE can be combined and, on TIN, still benefit from softening, even when applied on top of TA. For Gaussian and Patch Gaussian noise injections, softening is unfavorable, likely due to the fact that in this ablation study, noise is the third consecutive augmentation. Here, the reduced confidence is multiplied for all soft augmentations, so the label smoothing extend may become excessive. With respect to robustness, softening is unfavorable almost across the board. Patch Gaussian offers a more favorable tradeoff between accuracy and robustness on CIFAR, but its parametrization appears less applicable for TIN.

Table 4. Ablation study applying various (soft) augmentations incrementally on top of standard, not softened TrivialAugment. All entries except TA show mean $\Delta \pm$ standard deviation of Δ (relative to TrivialAugment). When multiple soft augmentations are applied, the reduced confidence is multiplied, which combines the adaptive label smoothing of all soft augmentations. P.-Gaussian means Patch Gaussian. Overall, the best augmentation combination varies from dataset to dataset and does not always involve adaptive label smoothing at all.

Method	CIFAR-10		CIFAR-100		TinyImageNet	
	Acc.	Rob.	Acc.	Rob.	Acc.	Rob.
TrivialAugment	96.42 ±0.07	86.78 ±0.14	80.41 ±0.14	63.97 ±0.46	65.35 ±0.42	31.68 ±1.33
+RC	+0.23 ±0.21	+0.42 ±0.39	−0.21 ±0.24	−1.41 ±0.79	+0.09 ±0.49	−0.66 ±1.97
+RC (Soft)	+0.35 ±0.13	−0.74 ±0.60	+0.08 ±0.35	−2.08 ±0.53	+1.19 ±0.12	−0.12 ±2.01
+RC+RE	**+0.44** ±0.08	+0.88 ±0.44	+0.22 ±0.16	−0.34 ±0.50	+0.85 ±0.41	+0.66 ±2.29
+RC+RE (Soft)	+0.33 ±0.10	−0.14 ±0.97	**+0.42** ±0.35	−1.09 ±0.69	**+1.54** ±0.40	+0.59 ±1.65
+RC+RE+P.-Gaussian	+0.15 ±0.09	+4.18 ±0.33	−0.51 ±0.17	+4.49 ±0.46	+0.83 ±0.49	+0.10 ±1.94
+RC+RE+P.-Gaussian (Soft)	−0.31 ±0.14	+3.73 ±0.17	−1.12 ±0.23	+4.30 ±0.46	−0.14 ±0.44	+1.78 ±2.45
+RC+RE+Gaussian	−0.43 ±0.16	**+4.39** ±0.22	−2.43 ±0.19	**+4.86** ±0.51	+0.93 ±0.54	**+3.47** ±1.78
+RC+RE+Gaussian (Soft)	−0.44 ±0.13	+4.09 ±0.22	−1.98 ±0.17	+4.50 ±0.34	+1.15 ±0.58	+2.13 ±2.07

5   Discussion

Our results confirm that adaptive label smoothing tied to a single-transform augmentation other than RC can enable more aggressive parameter settings and improve training with that augmentation. While we could show these benefits for RE, it was less significant for noise injections. In many cases, extensive search is needed to find the optimal parametrization that yields an advantage for adaptive label smoothing. Overall, our results suggest that practitioners that predominantly work with a single type of augmentation, like RE for occlusion-sensitive applications, should consider adaptive label smoothing.

By contrast, when multiple transformations are applied together (e.g. in TrivialAugment or mixed schemes), the diversity of distortions alone suffices to regularize the model, and adaptive smoothing yields only marginal or no additional benefit. In fact, overly aggressive smoothing generally appears to reduce robustness to corruptions, as is also true of the generally beneficial soft Random Crop method. A reason could be that excessive label smoothing on strong transformations hinders learning strict label invariance for these transformations.

We note several simplifying assumptions in our current framework. Even though the label smoothing is adaptive, we treat every transformation type and magnitude as inducing a uniform drop in label confidence, irrespective of the specific image, class, or dataset context. Future work could refine this by conditioning smoothing factors on image content or class, or by integrating auxiliary label confidence estimators.

6   Conclusion

This study proposed multiple approaches to extend adaptive label smoothing beyond Random Cropping to work with other aggressive, state-of-the-art augmentations. It leveraged human-vision data and proxy-model accuracy to map transformation magnitude to adaptive label confidence. This approach enhances the efficacy of data augmentation schemes building on individual transformations such as Random Erasing, allowing a more aggressive parametrization without miscalibrating the model. However, the advantage vanishes when a heterogeneous set of transformations is deployed on the image data. Our findings narrow down the regime in which adaptive label smoothing is valuable: namely, when a singular transformation dominates the augmentation distribution.

Acknowledgements. This research was funded by the German Federal Ministry of Labour and Social Affairs through the establishment of a Junior Research Group on Artificial Intelligence at the Federal Institute of Occupational Safety and Health (BAuA). The presented results contribute to the development and evaluation of reliable and safe AI for industrial applications, with the overarching aim of laying the scientific foundations necessary to meet the requirements of the European Machinery Directive (2023) and the European AI Act (2024).

References

1. Avidan, G., Harel, M., Hendler, T., Ben-Bashat, D., Zohary, E., Malach, R.: Contrast sensitivity in human visual areas and its relationship to object recognition. J. Neurophysiol. **87**(6), 3102–3116 (2002)
2. Bagherinezhad, H., Horton, M., Rastegari, M., Farhadi, A.: Label refinery: improving imagenet classification through label progression. arXiv preprint arXiv:1805.02641 (2018)
3. Brown, M., Lowe, D.: Invariant features from interest point groups. In: 13th British Machine Vision Conference, vol. 4, pp. 398–410 (2002)
4. Cubuk, E.D., Zoph, B., Mane, D., Vasudevan, V., Le, Q.V.: Autoaugment: learning augmentation strategies from data. In: Proceedings of the IEEE/CVF Conference on Computer Vision and Pattern Recognition, pp. 113–123 (2019)
5. Cubuk, E.D., Zoph, B., Shlens, J., Le, Q.V.: Randaugment: practical automated data augmentation with a reduced search space. In: Proceedings of the IEEE/CVF Conference on Computer Vision and Pattern Recognition Workshops, pp. 702–703 (2020)
6. DeVries, T., Taylor, G.W.: Improved regularization of convolutional neural networks with cutout. arXiv preprint arXiv:1708.04552 (2017)
7. Dodge, S., Karam, L.: Human and DNN classification performance on images with quality distortions: a comparative study. ACM Trans. Appl. Perception (TAP) **16**(2), 1–17 (2019)
8. Erichson, B., Lim, S.H., Xu, W., Utrera, F., Cao, Z., Mahoney, M.: NoisyMix: boosting model robustness to common corruptions. In: Proceedings of the 27th International Conference on Artificial Intelligence and Statistics. Proceedings of Machine Learning Research, vol. 238, pp. 4033–4041. PMLR (2024)
9. Gardner, J.L., Sun, P., Waggoner, R.A., Ueno, K., Tanaka, K., Cheng, K.: Contrast adaptation and representation in human early visual cortex. Neuron **47**(4), 607–620 (2005)
10. Hendrycks, D., Dietterich, T.: Benchmarking neural network robustness to common corruptions and perturbations. In: International Conference on Learning Representations, p. 16 (28032019) (2019)
11. Hollard, V.D., Delius, J.D.: Rotational invariance in visual pattern recognition by pigeons and humans. Science **218**(4574), 804–806 (1982)
12. Kail, R.: Development of mental rotation: a speed-accuracy study. J. Exp. Child Psychol. **40**(1), 181–192 (1985)
13. Krizhevsky, A., Hinton, G., et al.: Learning multiple layers of features from tiny images (2009)
14. Krizhevsky, A., Sutskever, I., Hinton, G.E.: Imagenet classification with deep convolutional neural networks. In; Advances in Neural Information Processing Systems **25** (2012)
15. Le, Y., Yang, X.: Tiny imagenet visual recognition challenge. CS 231N, 2015 (2015)
16. Liu, Y., Yan, S., Leal-Taixé, L., Hays, J., Ramanan, D.: Soft augmentation for image classification. In: Proceedings of the IEEE/CVF Conference on Computer Vision and Pattern Recognition, pp. 16241–16250 (2023)
17. Lopes, R.G., Yin, D., Poole, B., Gilmer, J., Cubuk, E.D.: Improving robustness without sacrificing accuracy with patch gaussian augmentation. arXiv preprint arXiv:1906.02611 (2019)
18. Lowe, D.G.: Distinctive image features from scale-invariant keypoints. Int. J. Comput. Vis. **60**, 91–110 (2004)

19. Mazade, R., Jin, J., Rahimi-Nasrabadi, H., Najafian, S., Pons, C., Alonso, J.M.: Cortical mechanisms of visual brightness. Cell Rep. **40**(13) (2022)
20. Müller, S.G., Hutter, F.: Trivialaugment: tuning-free yet state-of-the-art data augmentation. In: Proceedings of the IEEE/CVF International Conference on Computer Vision, pp. 774–782 (2021)
21. Ren, M., Zeng, W., Yang, B., Urtasun, R.: Learning to reweight examples for robust deep learning. In: International Conference on Machine Learning, pp. 4334–4343. PMLR (2018)
22. Rusak, E., et al.: A simple way to make neural networks robust against diverse image corruptions. In: Vedaldi, A., Bischof, H., Brox, T., Frahm, J.-M. (eds.) ECCV 2020. LNCS, vol. 12348, pp. 53–69. Springer, Cham (2020). https://doi.org/10.1007/978-3-030-58580-8_4
23. Serre, T., Oliva, A., Poggio, T.: A feedforward architecture accounts for rapid categorization. Proc. Natl. Acad. Sci. **104**(15), 6424–6429 (2007)
24. Shorten, C., Khoshgoftaar, T.M.: A survey on image data augmentation for deep learning. J. Big Data **6**(1), 1–48 (2019)
25. Siedel, G., Shao, W., Vock, S., Morozov, A.: Investigating the corruption robustness of image classifiers with random p-norm corruptions. In: Proceedings of the 19th International Joint Conference on Computer Vision, Imaging and Computer Graphics Theory and Applications - Volume 2: VISAPP, pp. 171–181 (2024)
26. Szegedy, C., Vanhoucke, V., Ioffe, S., Shlens, J., Wojna, Z.: Rethinking the inception architecture for computer vision. In: Proceedings of the IEEE Conference on Computer Vision and Pattern Recognition, pp. 2818–2826 (2016)
27. Tang, H., et al.: Recurrent computations for visual pattern completion. Proc. Natl. Acad. Sci. **115**(35), 8835–8840 (2018)
28. Vryniotis, V.: How to train state-of-the-art models using Torchvision's latest primitives (2021). https://pytorch.org/blog/how-to-train-state-of-the-art-models-using-torchvision-latest-primitives/. Accessed 18 Nov 2021
29. Vyas, N., Saxena, S., Voice, T.: Learning soft labels via meta learning. arXiv preprint arXiv:2009.09496 (2020)
30. Wang, Z., Bovik, A.C.: A universal image quality index. IEEE Signal Process. Lett. **9**(3), 81–84 (2002)
31. Wang, Z., Bovik, A.C., Sheikh, H.R., Simoncelli, E.P.: Image quality assessment: from error visibility to structural similarity. IEEE Trans. Image Process. **13**(4), 600–612 (2004)
32. Xie, L., Wang, J., Wei, Z., Wang, M., Tian, Q.: Disturblabel: regularizing CNN on the loss layer. In: Proceedings of the IEEE Conference on Computer Vision and Pattern Recognition, pp. 4753–4762 (2016)
33. Xie, S., Girshick, R., Dollár, P., Tu, Z., He, K.: Aggregated residual transformations for deep neural networks. In: Proceedings of the IEEE Conference on Computer Vision and Pattern Recognition, pp. 1492–1500 (2017)
34. Yoo, J.C., Han, T.H.: Fast normalized cross-correlation. Circuits Syst. Signal Process. **28**, 819–843 (2009)
35. Yun, S., Han, D., Oh, S.J., Chun, S., Choe, J., Yoo, Y.: Cutmix: regularization strategy to train strong classifiers with localizable features. In: Proceedings of the IEEE/CVF International Conference on Computer Vision, pp. 6023–6032 (2019)
36. Zagoruyko, S., Komodakis, N.: Wide residual networks. In: British Machine Vision Conference 2016. British Machine Vision Association (2016)
37. Zhang, C.B., et al.: Delving deep into label smoothing. IEEE Trans. Image Process. **30**, 5984–5996 (2021)

38. Zhang, H., Cisse, M., Dauphin, Y.N., Lopez-Paz, D.: mixup: beyond empirical risk minimization. In: International Conference on Learning Representations (2018)
39. Zhong, Z., Zheng, L., Kang, G., Li, S., Yang, Y.: Random erasing data augmentation. In: Proceedings of the AAAI Conference on Artificial Intelligence, vol. 34, pp. 13001–13008 (2020)
40. Zhu, H., Tang, P., Park, J., Park, S., Yuille, A.: Robustness of object recognition under extreme occlusion in humans and computational models. In: Proceedings of the Annual Meeting of the Cognitive Science Society, vol. 41 (2019)

Efficient Masked Attention Transformer
for Few-Shot Classification
and Segmentation

Dustin Carrión-Ojeda[1,2]([✉])(iD), Stefan Roth[1,2](iD), and Simone Schaub-Meyer[1,2](iD)

[1] Department of Computer Science, Technical University of Darmstadt, Darmstadt,
Germany
`dustin.carrion@visinf.tu-darmstadt.de,`
`{stefan.roth,simone.schaub}@visinf.tu-darmstadt.de`
[2] Hessian Center for AI (hessian.AI), Darmstadt, Germany
`https://visinf.github.io/emat`

Abstract. Few-shot classification and segmentation (FS-CS) focuses on jointly performing multi-label classification and multi-class segmentation using few annotated examples. Although the current state of the art (SOTA) achieves high accuracy in both tasks, it struggles with small objects. To overcome this, we propose the **E**fficient **M**asked **A**ttention **T**ransformer (EMAT), which improves classification and segmentation accuracy, especially for small objects. EMAT introduces three modifications: a novel memory-efficient masked attention mechanism, a learnable downscaling strategy, and parameter-efficiency enhancements. EMAT outperforms all FS-CS methods on the PASCAL-5^i and COCO-20^i datasets, using at least four times fewer trainable parameters. Moreover, as the current FS-CS evaluation setting discards available annotations, despite their costly collection, we introduce two novel evaluation settings that consider these annotations to better reflect practical scenarios.

Keywords: Few-shot learning · Efficiency · Segmentation · Classification

1 Introduction

Recently, data-intensive methods have been introduced for various deep learning applications [5,8,23,25,32,34,41]. These methods rely on large training datasets, making them impractical in fields where collecting extensive datasets is challenging or costly [13,14,65]. Consequently, few-shot learning (FSL) methods have gained significant attention for their ability to learn from just a few examples and quickly adapt to new classes [1,44,52,56]. In computer vision, FSL has

---

Supplementary Information The online version contains supplementary material available at https://doi.org/10.1007/978-3-032-12840-9_18.

M. Keuper and F. Locatello (Eds.): DAGM GCPR 2025, LNCS 16125, pp. 267–283, 2026.
https://doi.org/10.1007/978-3-032-12840-9_18

been mostly applied to image classification (FS-C) [3,18,40,43] and segmentation (FS-S) [11,30,55,62,63].

FS-C and FS-S often co-occur in real-world applications, *e.g.*, in agriculture, where crops must be segmented and classified by type or health status. Hence, recent works [19,20] integrate multi-label classification and multi-class segmentation into a single few-shot classification and segmentation (FS-CS) task. While FS-CS addresses some limitations of FS-C (*e.g.*, assuming the query image contains only one class) and FS-S (*e.g.*, assuming the target class is always present in the query image), it also increases the task difficulty by simultaneously tackling classification and segmentation. Moreover, some applications, *e.g.*, medical imaging, rely on precise small-object analysis [13,16,65]. Thus, achieving high accuracy on small objects is a desired property for FS-CS methods. Yet, as shown in Fig. 1, the current state-of-the-art (SOTA) FS-CS method [20] struggles with small objects, a limitation we address in this work.

Fig. 1. Qualitative comparison of small objects (*i.e.*, objects that occupy less than 15 % of the image) between the current SOTA FS-CS method (CST) [20] and our proposed EMAT. CST* uses the same backbone as EMAT (*i.e.*, DINOv2 [32]). By processing high-resolution correlation tokens, EMAT preserves finer details, yielding more accurate segmentation masks.

To better align the evaluation of FS-CS models with practical scenarios, FS-CS uses the N-way K-shot configuration, where the model learns N classes from $N \times K$ examples (K per class). However, the current evaluation setting [19, 20] discards available annotations, which is not ideal given the cost of data annotation. To address this, we introduce two new evaluation settings.

Contributions. *(1)* Building on the current SOTA FS-CS method [20], we propose an efficient masked attention transformer (EMAT), which enhances classification and segmentation accuracy, particularly for small objects, while using approximately four times fewer trainable parameters. *(2)* Our EMAT outperforms all FS-CS methods on the PASCAL-5^i and COCO-20^i datasets, supports the N-way K-shot configuration, and can generate empty segmentation masks when no target objects are present. *(3)* Finally, we introduce two new FS-CS evaluation settings that better utilize available annotations during inference.

2   Related Work

Few-Shot Classification (FS-C) methods can be categorized into three groups based on what the model learns. *Representation-based* approaches learn class-agnostic, discriminative embeddings [3,17,21,39,46,48,60]. *Optimization-based* approaches learn the optimal set of weights that allow the model to adapt to new classes in just a few optimization steps [4,15,35,40]. *Transfer-based* approaches adapt large pre-trained [6,10,24,28,43] or foundation models [18,37,64]. A major limitation of most FS-C methods is the assumption of a single label per image [2,38], limiting them in multi-label settings.

Few-Shot Segmentation (FS-S) methods can also be categorized into three groups: *prototype matching*, which aligns support embeddings with query features [11,26,45,50,51,58]; *dense correlation*, which constructs support-query correlation tensors [7,29,30,33,53,54]; and *model-adaptation*, which fine-tunes large pre-trained models [27,49,57,61,62]. Despite the advancements in FS-S, most methods have two main limitations: *(1)* they target only the 1-way K-shot configuration and *(2)* they assume the query image contains the target class, preventing the models from predicting empty segmentation masks. Only a few recent works [42,59] address the more general N-way K-shot configuration.

Few-Shot Classification and Segmentation (FS-CS) focuses on jointly predicting the multi-label classification vector and multi-class segmentation mask without assuming support classes are present in the query image [19]. The current SOTA FS-CS method, the classification-segmentation transformer (CST) [20], uses a memory-intensive masked-attention mechanism that requires significant downsampling of the correlation features, reducing its accuracy on small objects. In this work, we enhance CST by proposing an efficient masked-attention formulation and adding further refinements, resulting in a more memory- and parameter-efficient method with improved accuracy, especially for small objects.

3   Problem Definition

This work focuses on the few-shot classification and segmentation (FS-CS) task [19], formulated as an N-way K-shot learning problem [48]. We assume two disjoint class sets: $\mathcal{C}_{\text{train}}$ for training and $\mathcal{C}_{\text{test}}$ for testing. Accordingly, training tasks are sampled from $\mathcal{C}_{\text{train}}$, and testing tasks from $\mathcal{C}_{\text{test}}$. Each task consists of a support set $\mathcal{S}$ and a query image $\mathbf{I}_q$, where $\mathcal{S}$ contains N classes $\mathcal{C}_{\text{s}}$ ($\mathcal{C}_{\text{s}} \subseteq \mathcal{C}_{\text{train}}$ or $\mathcal{C}_{\text{s}} \subseteq \mathcal{C}_{\text{test}}$), each represented by K examples:

$$\mathcal{S} = \left\{ \left\{ (\mathbf{I}_j^i, \mathbf{M}_j^i, y_j^i) \mid y_j^i \in \mathcal{C}_{\text{s}} \right\}_j^K \right\}_i^N , \tag{1}$$

where $\mathbf{I}_j^i$, $\mathbf{M}_j^i$, and y_j^i denote the support image, segmentation mask, and class label for the jth example of the ith class. Although $y_j^i = i \ \forall j$ in Eq. (1), we use this notation for compatibility with multi-label settings where $\mathbf{y}_j^i$ can vary.

The goal of FS-CS is to learn from $\mathcal{S}$ such that, given $\mathbf{I}_q$, the model can *(i)* identify which support classes are present (multi-label classification), and *(ii)* segment those classes (multi-class segmentation). Moreover, FS-CS allows $\mathbf{I}_q$ to contain a subset of the support classes. Thus, when $N > 1$, $\mathbf{I}_q$ can contain: *(1)* none of the support classes ($\mathcal{C}_q = \varnothing$), *(2)* a subset of them ($\mathcal{C}_q \subset \mathcal{C}_s$), or *(3)* all support classes ($\mathcal{C}_q = \mathcal{C}_s$). Note that case *(1)* is important in real-world applications where query images may not contain relevant classes, requiring models to predict empty segmentation masks when necessary.

The drawback of the current FS-CS setting is that each support image $\mathbf{I}_j^i$ is assumed to contain only one annotated class (y_j^i). If $\mathbf{I}_j^i$ includes multiple support classes ($\mathbf{y}_j^i \subseteq \mathcal{C}_s$), its label vector and segmentation mask need to be adjusted before constructing $\mathcal{S}$. This adjustment discards available annotations, as illustrated in Fig. 2, where $\mathbf{I}_1^1$ contains both support classes (person, bike). However, since it is an example of the 1st class (person), the annotations of the 2nd class (bike) are removed in the original setting.

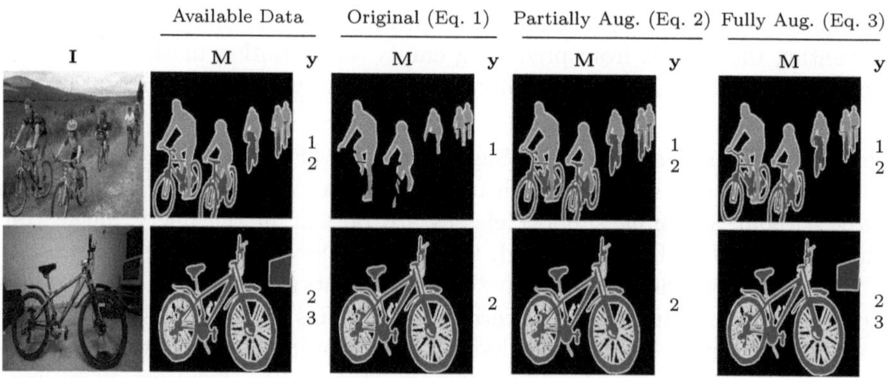

Fig. 2. Example of a 2-way 1-shot (base configuration) support set across different few-shot evaluation settings. I, M, and **y** represent the images, segmentation masks, and labels, respectively.

3.1 Proposed Evaluation Settings

To better utilize available annotations and reflect more realistic evaluation scenarios, we introduce two novel FS-CS evaluation settings.

Partially Augmented Setting. This setting keeps all annotations from the support classes:

$$\mathcal{S} = \left\{ \left\{ (\mathbf{I}_j^i, \mathbf{M}_j^i, \mathbf{y}_j^i) \mid \mathbf{y}_j^i \subseteq \mathcal{C}_s \right\}_j^K \right\}_i^N . \tag{2}$$

Note that when $N=1$, this setting is equivalent to Eq. (1). Figure 2 shows an example for this setting, where $\mathbf{M}_1^1$ and $\mathbf{y}_1^1$ keep the annotations of the 2nd class (bike), even though the image is selected as an example of the 1st class (person).

Fully Augmented Setting. This setting keeps all available annotations for each support image, regardless of whether the corresponding classes are part of the support classes:

$$\mathcal{S} = \left\{ \left\{ (\mathbf{I}_j^i, \mathbf{M}_j^i, \mathbf{y}_j^i) \mid \mathbf{y}_j^i \subseteq \mathcal{C}_{\text{train}} \cup \mathcal{C}_{\text{test}} \right\}_j^K \right\}_i^N. \tag{3}$$

For example, in Fig. 2, $\mathbf{M}_1^1$ and $\mathbf{y}_1^1$ include annotations for both support classes (person, bike), while $\mathbf{M}_1^2$ and $\mathbf{y}_1^2$ are augmented with annotations of a non-support class (TV), which can belong to either $\mathcal{C}_{\text{train}}$ or $\mathcal{C}_{\text{test}}$. In this setting, the model is expected to classify and segment all support and augmented classes present in $\mathbf{I}_q$. Additionally, this setting aligns closely with the generalized few-shot setting (GFSL) [44], which also evaluates on base classes. However, unlike standard GFSL, which evaluates on all base classes seen during training, our setting restricts evaluation to only those classes present in the support set.

4   Efficient Masked Attention Transformer

Figure 3 illustrates the pipeline used by our proposed efficient masked attention transformer (EMAT), which builds upon the classification-segmentation transformer (CST) [20]. Both methods share the same feature extraction process: support and query images $\mathbf{I}_j^i, \mathbf{I}_q \in \mathbb{R}^{H \times W \times 3}$ are processed by a frozen, pre-trained ViT [12] with patch size p, producing support and query image tokens $\mathbf{T}_{s_i}, \mathbf{T}_{q_i} \in \mathbb{R}^{h \times w \times d}$, and a support class token $\mathbf{T}_{s_c} \in \mathbb{R}^{1 \times d}$, where $h = H/p$, $w = W/p$, and d is the token dimension of a single ViT head. The support tokens $\mathbf{T}_{s_i}$ are downsampled via bilinear interpolation and reshaped to $\mathbf{T}_{s_i}^f \in \mathbb{R}^{(h' \cdot w') \times d}$. Similarly, query image tokens $\mathbf{T}_{q_i}$ are reshaped to $\mathbf{T}_{q_i}^f \in \mathbb{R}^{(h \cdot w) \times d}$. Next, $\mathbf{T}_{s_i}^f$ and $\mathbf{T}_{s_c}$ are concatenated to form $\mathbf{T}_s^c$. Finally, cosine similarity between $\mathbf{T}_s^c$ and $\mathbf{T}_{q_i}^f$ is computed across all ViT layers l and attention heads g, resulting in the correlation tokens $\mathbf{C} \in \mathbb{R}^{t_s \times t_q \times (l \cdot g)}$, where $t_s = h' \cdot w' + 1$ and $t_q = h \cdot w$.

EMAT differs from CST in the two-layer transformer (purple blocks in Fig. 3) that processes the correlation tokens $\mathbf{C}$ and feeds task-specific heads for multi-label classification and multi-class segmentation. EMAT enhances this transformer with three key improvements: *(1)* a novel memory-efficient masked attention formulation (see Sect. 4.1) that allows using higher-resolution correlation tokens, *(2)* a learnable downscaling strategy (see Sect. 4.2) that avoids reliance on large pooling kernels, and *(3)* additional modifications for improved parameter efficiency (see Sect. 4.3), which can help to reduce overfitting a small support set.

Following CST, EMAT is trained using the 1-way 1-shot configuration. Since EMAT uses task-specific heads, it is trained with two losses:

$$\mathcal{L}_{\text{clf}} = -y \log \widehat{y}, \tag{4}$$

$$\mathcal{L}_{\text{seg}} = -\frac{1}{HW} \sum_{i=1}^{H} \sum_{j=1}^{W} \mathbf{M}_{ij} \log \widehat{\mathbf{M}}_{ij}, \tag{5}$$

where $y \in \{0,1\}$ and $\mathbf{M}_{ij} \in \{0,1\}$ are the ground-truth classification and segmentation labels, and $\widehat{y}$, $\widehat{\mathbf{M}}_{ij}$ are the corresponding predictions. The final loss function jointly optimizes both losses using a balancing hyperparameter λ:

$$\mathcal{L} = \lambda \mathcal{L}_{\mathrm{clf}} + \mathcal{L}_{\mathrm{seg}}. \tag{6}$$

Inference on N-way K-shot task is performed as in CST [20], by treating each class as an independent 1-way K-shot task: class-wise logits and segmentation masks are averaged over the K examples, producing N predictions. Logits above a threshold $\delta = 0.5$ form the multi-label vector, and each pixel $\widehat{\mathbf{M}}_{ij}$ is assigned to the class with the highest score, or to background if all scores fall below δ, thereby allowing empty masks.

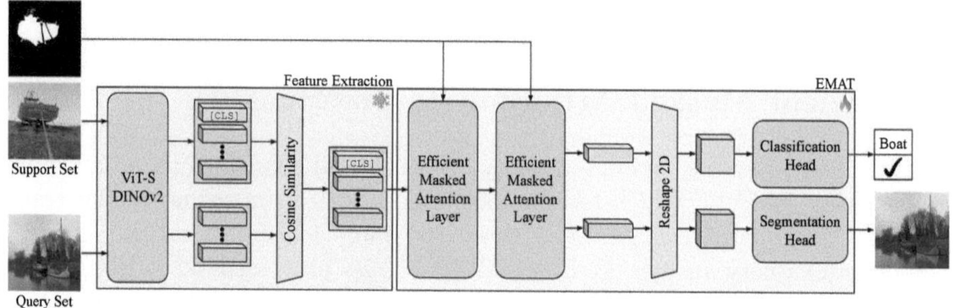

Fig. 3. FS-CS pipeline used by our EMAT. A frozen, pre-trained ViT [12] extracts image and class tokens from support and query images, which are correlated via cosine similarity. The resulting correlation tokens are processed by a two-layer transformer equipped with our masked attention mechanism, learnable downscaling, and parameter-efficient design (see Sects. 4.1 to 4.3). Task-specific heads then predict the multi-label classification vector and multi-class segmentation mask.

4.1 Memory-Efficient Masked Attention

The SOTA FS-CS method, CST [20], uses a masked attention mechanism based on self-attention [12,47] to process the correlation tokens $\mathbf{C} \in \mathbb{R}^{t_s \times t_q \times (l \cdot g)}$. Due to the high memory cost of self-attention, CST significantly downsamples the support tokens $\mathbf{T}_{s_i}$ when computing $\mathbf{C}$, sacrificing fine-grained spatial details (see Fig. 5). To address this, we propose a novel memory-efficient masked attention formulation that allows EMAT to use high-resolution correlation tokens.

Given $\mathbf{C}$, let $\mathbf{Q}^d \in \mathbb{R}^{t_d \times t_q \times e}$, $\mathbf{K}, \mathbf{V} \in \mathbb{R}^{t_s \times t_q \times e}$ denote the query, key, and value matrices, where e is the embedding size. The dimensions of $\mathbf{Q}^d$ differ from those of $\mathbf{K}$ and $\mathbf{V}$ because the query matrix is progressively downscaled (see Sect. 4.2). Additionally, as shown in Fig. 3, the segmentation mask $\mathbf{M} \in \mathbb{R}^{H \times W}$ enters directly into the attention mechanism without being processed by the feature extractor. Thus, it is resized, flattened, and then append a trailing "1" to obtain $\mathbf{M}^f \in \mathbb{R}^{h' \cdot w' + 1}$. This appended "1" ensures that the support class token is never masked in Eqs. (7) and (8).

For one attention head, CST computes:

$$\mathbf{O}_{ijk} = \sum_p \left[\text{softmax} \left((\mathbf{Q}_{ijk}^d \cdot \mathbf{K}_{:jk}) \odot \mathbf{M}_:^f \right) \right]_p \odot \mathbf{V}_{pjk}, \tag{7}$$

where $i \in \{1, \ldots, t_d\}$, $j \in \{1, \ldots, t_q\}$, $k \in \{1, \ldots, e\}$, and $p \in \{1, \ldots, t_s\}$. Here $t_d = h'' \cdot w'' + 1$, $t_q = h \cdot w$, and $t_s = h' \cdot w' + 1$, the "+1" accounts for the support class token, and $(\cdot)'$ denotes a downscaled value. The operator $\odot$ represents element-wise multiplication.

In CST, the support dimension t_s is 145 ($h' = w' = 12$) in the first attention layer and 10 ($h' = w' = 3$) in the second. Consequently, in the second layer most values of $\mathbf{M}^f$ are zero (see Fig. 5). As a result, Eq. (7) zeros out most attention values, but they are still processed in all intermediate computations, leading to a memory-inefficient formulation. To overcome this, we introduce a memory-efficient reformulation that excludes the masked-out entries:

$$\mathbf{O}_{ijk} = \sum_{p^\oslash} \left[\text{softmax} \left(\mathbf{Q}_{ijk}^d \cdot (\mathbf{K}_{:jk} \oslash \mathbf{M}_:^f) \right) \right]_{p^\oslash} \odot \left(\mathbf{V}_{:jk} \oslash \mathbf{M}_:^f \right)_{p^\oslash}, \tag{8}$$

where $\oslash$ is our element-wise masking operator:

$$(\mathbf{Z}_{pjk} \oslash \mathbf{M}_p^f) = \begin{cases} \mathbf{Z}_{pjk} & \text{if } \mathbf{M}_p^f = 1, \\ \varnothing & \text{otherwise,} \end{cases} \quad \forall p \in \{1, \ldots, t_s\}, \tag{9}$$

with $\mathbf{Z} \in \mathbb{R}^{t_s \times t_q \times e}$ and $\varnothing$ indicating that the corresponding entry is excluded. This exclusion of elements results in the reduced set of indices $p^\oslash \subseteq p$ used in Eq. (8), where $p^\oslash = p$ only if $\mathbf{M}^f$ contains no zeros. Excluding masked-out tokens reduces memory usage allowing EMAT to increase the support dimension t_s to 401 ($h' = w' = 20$) in the first attention layer (≈ 2.7 times more than CST) and 101 ($h' = w' = 10$) in the second (≈ 11 times more than CST). Note that the index set $p^\oslash$ varies across images in a batch; thus, Eq. (8) is computed sequentially for each image. However, batch processing is still used both before and after this step because the input and output tensors ($\mathbf{C}$ and $\mathbf{O}$) have the same dimensions for every image. By computing attention only over unmasked entries, EMAT still achieves a runtime comparable to CST.

4.2 Learnable Downscaling

As mentioned in Sect. 4.1, the query matrix $\mathbf{Q} \in \mathbb{R}^{t_s \times t_q \times e}$ is progressively downscaled. This downscaling occurs before computing the masked-attention in each layer and it keeps t_q and e fixed, while shrinking the support spatial dimensions h' and w', which reduces the support dimension ($t_s = h' \cdot w' + 1$). Unlike CST, which uses only average pooling, EMAT introduces a lightweight, learnable strategy that combines small convolutions with pooling. This hybrid design removes the need for the large pooling kernels that would otherwise be required to handle the higher-resolution correlation tokens used by EMAT.

In the first attention layer, EMAT splits $\mathbf{Q}$ into support image tokens $\mathbf{Q}_i$ and a single class token $\mathbf{Q}_c$. After reshaping $\mathbf{Q}_i$ to its $h' \times w'$ support spatial layout, a 3D convolution followed by another reshape produces $\mathbf{Q}_i^r \in \mathbb{R}^{(h'' \cdot w'') \times t_q \times e}$. Simultaneously, a 2D convolution transforms $\mathbf{Q}_c$ into $\mathbf{Q}_c^r \in \mathbb{R}^{1 \times t_q \times e}$. These outputs are concatenated to form the downscaled query matrix $\mathbf{Q}^d \in \mathbb{R}^{t_d \times t_q \times e}$ used in Eq. (8), where $t_d = h'' \cdot w'' + 1$.

The second attention layer repeats the process, but before the concatenation $\mathbf{Q}_i^r$ is collapsed to a single spatial token by a 3D average pool, producing $\mathbf{Q}_i^p \in \mathbb{R}^{1 \times t_q \times e}$. Concatenating $\mathbf{Q}_i^p$ with $\mathbf{Q}_c^r$ gives the downscaled query matrix $\mathbf{Q}^d \in \mathbb{R}^{2 \times t_q \times e}$ used during the attention computation.

4.3   Modifications for Parameter Efficiency

Few-shot models with too many parameters risk overfitting the small support set, thereby reducing their ability to adapt to new classes. Therefore, EMAT reduces the number of channels across all operations: its two attention layers use 64 and 32 channels, versus 32 and 128 in CST, and its two task-specific heads use 32 and 16 channels, versus 128 and 64 in CST. These channel reductions significantly decrease the number of trainable parameters in EMAT.

5   Experiments

Datasets. We evaluated our EMAT on the widely used PASCAL-5^i [36] and COCO-20^i [31] datasets. Although they were designed for few-shot segmentation, both can also be used for few-shot classification and segmentation [19]. PASCAL-5^i comprises 20 classes and COCO-20^i 80 classes, each partitioned into four non-overlapping folds.

Implementation Details. EMAT uses a frozen ViT-S encoder [12] pre-trained with DINOv2 [32]. The two-layer transformer uses our memory-efficient masked attention with 8 heads. We train for 80 epochs with a batch size of 9 using the Adam optimizer [22] with learning rate 10^{-3}. Following [20], we use 1-way 1-shot tasks with the original setting (see Eq. 1) and set the loss weight λ in Eq. (6) to 0.1. Moreover, we re-train CST [20] with the same DINOv2 backbone used by EMAT and denote it as CST*. All training was conducted on three NVIDIA RTX A6000 GPUs, with evaluation performed on a single GPU.

5.1   Comparison to SOTA FS-CS

To evaluate the effectiveness of our EMAT, we compare it with CST [20] and other state-of-the-art few-shot classification and segmentation (FS-CS) methods. Table 1 shows the mean classification accuracy (Acc.) and mean Intersection over

Union (mIoU) over the four folds of PASCAL-5^i [36] and COCO-20^i [31], for 2-way 1-shot tasks across all evaluation settings (see Sect. 3). Although DINOv2 pre-training [32] already significantly improves CST* over its original version, EMAT consistently outperforms all methods across all settings. These results validate the benefit of processing higher-resolution correlation tokens enabled by our memory-efficient masked attention (see Sect. 4.1). Moreover, EMAT requires at least four times fewer parameters than CST, making it the most parameter-efficient method among SOTA FS-CS models. The supplementary material provides per-fold results for Table 1 and additional results on $\{1, \ldots, 5\}$-way 5-shot tasks, demonstrating the scalability of our method.

The results in Table 1 also show that our partially augmented setting slightly improves accuracy and mIoU for most methods, confirming the benefit of better exploiting the available annotations. However, the improvement is marginal, likely because only 242 and 106 out of 4000 tasks are augmented for PASCAL-5^i and COCO-20^i, respectively. In contrast, our fully augmented setting lowers accuracy and mIoU for every method, although less significantly for mIoU. As discussed in Sect. 3.1, this setting augments not only the support examples but also includes every class present in the support images, making the tasks harder. This setting augments 1243 and 1515 out of the 4000 tasks for PASCAL-5^i and COCO-20^i, respectively. The augmentations in both of our proposed settings highlight that the original evaluation setting fails to use available annotations.

5.2   Qualitative Results

As explained in Sect. 3, when handling N-way K-shot tasks with $N > 1$, the query image can contain *(1)* none, *(2)* some, or *(3)* all of the support classes. The top part of Fig. 4 shows that EMAT produces more accurate segmentation masks than CST* in these three scenarios, confirming that EMAT can predict empty masks and masks with one or multiple classes. The bottom part of Fig. 4 illustrates the same task across all few-shot evaluation settings. In the original setting, both models segment the 1st class (orange) correctly but make errors on the 2nd class (glass), mistakenly segmenting visually similar objects (salt shaker). In the partially augmented setting, the additional annotations for the 2nd class degrade CST, while EMAT maintains a precise segmentation, though both still incorrectly segment non-target objects. In the fully augmented setting, both methods correctly segment the additional class (book).

Support ($\mathbf{I}_1^1$)   Support ($\mathbf{I}_1^2$)   Query ($\mathbf{I}_q$)   GT Mask   CST* [20]   EMAT

Fig. 4. Qualitative comparison of CST* *vs.* our EMAT on COCO-20^i [31] using 2-way 1-shot tasks. **(Top)** *Row 1:* Query w/o support classes, *Row 2:* Query w/ subset of support classes, *Row 3:* Query w/ all support classes. **(Bottom)** *Row 1:* Original setting, *Row 2:* Partially augmented setting, *Row 3:* Fully augmented setting.

To illustrate the effect of higher-resolution tokens, Fig. 5 compares the segmentation masks used in the masked-attention layers of CST and EMAT. Thanks to our memory-efficient formulation (see Sect. 4.1), EMAT preserves more details across layers. The difference is most visible in the second layer, where the mask used by CST barely contains any information since it has a resolution of 3×3, whereas EMAT, with a 10×10 resolution, retains meaningful details and structure. For instance, the person in the bottom-right corner of the last row of Fig. 5

Table 1. Comparison of FS-CS methods on PASCAL-5^i and COCO-20^i across all evaluation settings: original, partially augmented, and fully augmented, using 2-way 1-shot tasks (base configuration). CST* and EMAT were trained and evaluated, while other methods were only evaluated using the checkpoints from [19]. CST* uses the same backbone as EMAT (*i.e.*, DINOv2 [32]). All values, except the number of trainable parameters (in millions), are percentages (higher is better). Highlight indicates our proposed method. **Bold** and <u>underlined</u> values indicate the best and second best results.

Dataset	Method	Train. Params.	Original		Partially Augmented		Fully Augmented	
			Acc.	mIoU	Acc.	mIoU	Acc.	mIoU
PASCAL-5^i	PANet [50]	23.51	56.53	37.20	56.93	37.49	55.75	37.25
	PFENet [45]	31.96	39.35	35.57	39.48	35.61	36.88	35.08
	HSNet [29]	2.57	67.27	44.85	67.75	44.72	65.92	44.40
	ASNet [19]	1.32	68.30	47.87	68.62	47.78	66.40	47.58
	CST [20]	<u>0.37</u>	70.37	53.78	70.60	53.81	68.45	53.76
	CST*	<u>0.37</u>	<u>80.58</u>	<u>63.28</u>	<u>80.60</u>	<u>63.23</u>	<u>78.57</u>	<u>63.08</u>
	EMAT	**0.09**	**82.70**	**63.38**	**82.92**	**63.32**	**81.23**	**63.24**
COCO-20^i	PANet [50]	23.51	51.30	23.64	51.32	23.78	45.07	23.17
	PFENet [45]	31.96	36.45	23.37	36.50	23.39	29.33	21.61
	HSNet [29]	2.57	62.43	30.58	62.40	30.66	55.15	29.44
	ASNet [19]	1.32	63.05	31.62	63.03	31.64	55.47	30.47
	CST [20]	<u>0.37</u>	64.02	36.23	64.10	36.20	56.30	35.60
	CST*	<u>0.37</u>	<u>78.70</u>	<u>51.47</u>	<u>78.87</u>	<u>51.53</u>	<u>71.18</u>	<u>50.76</u>
	EMAT	**0.09**	**80.07**	**52.81**	**80.25**	**52.82**	**73.00**	**51.99**

remains visible in both layers of EMAT but vanishes in the second layer of CST. This ability to preserve fine details explains why EMAT produces more accurate masks especially for small objects, *e.g.*, the dog in the last row of the top part of Fig. 4, the handle of the beer glass in the bottom part of Fig. 4, and the boat and person in Fig. 1.

Full Res. 700×700	Max Res. 50×50	$CST_{l=1}$ 12×12	$CST_{l=2}$ 3×3	$EMAT_{l=1}$ 20×20	$EMAT_{l=2}$ 10×10

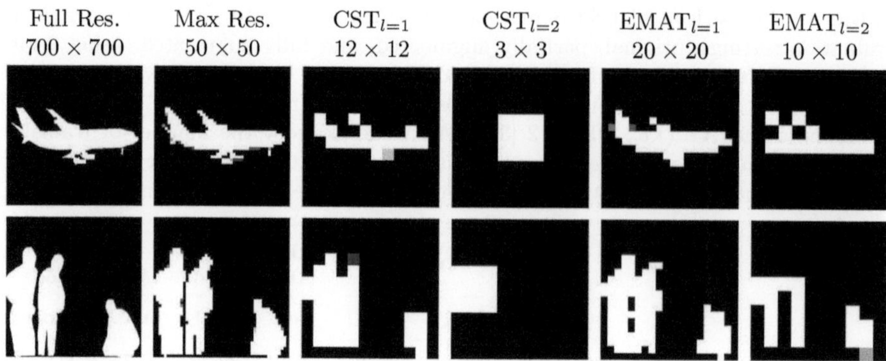

Fig. 5. Segmentation masks used by CST [20] and EMAT. "Full Res." shows the mask at full resolution, while "Max Res." is to the highest resolution compatible with the masked-attention layers of both methods. "$CST_{l=(.)}$" and "$EMAT_{l=(.)}$" indicate the mask resolution used in layer $l \in \{1, 2\}$ of CST and EMAT, respectively.

5.3   Analysis of Small Objects

To further analyze the impact of higher-resolution correlation tokens on small objects, we filter each fold of PASCAL-5^i [36] and COCO-20^i [31] based on object size, creating three splits: objects occupying 0–5 %, 5–10 %, and 10–15 % of the image (see the supplementary material for details on how these splits were defined). Figure 6 shows the average accuracy and mIoU of CST* and the corresponding improvement achieved by EMAT across the three splits for both datasets. The results indicate that accuracy and mIoU increase with object size, and EMAT provides the largest improvement over CST* for the smallest objects, gradually decreasing as object size increases. The enhanced classification and segmentation accuracy of EMAT is likely due to better localization enabled by its higher-resolution correlation tokens (see Fig. 5).

5.4   Ablation Study

Table 2 first reports the results of CST* with its original support dimension per layer t_s^l. For fair comparison, we increased the t_s^l of CST* to use the same as EMAT, but it required about 63 GB of GPU memory, which exceeded the 48 GB capacity of our GPUs, so we instead use the largest t_s^l that fits in our memory. For EMAT we progressively integrated: *(1)* memory-efficient masked attention (see Sect. 4.1), *(2)* learnable downscaling of the query matrix (see Sect. 4.2), and *(3)* parameter-efficiency modifications (see Sect. 4.3). Although Table 2 includes results on the full PASCAL-5^i test set, the discussion below focuses on the small-object subset to highlight the effect of each modification introduced by EMAT.

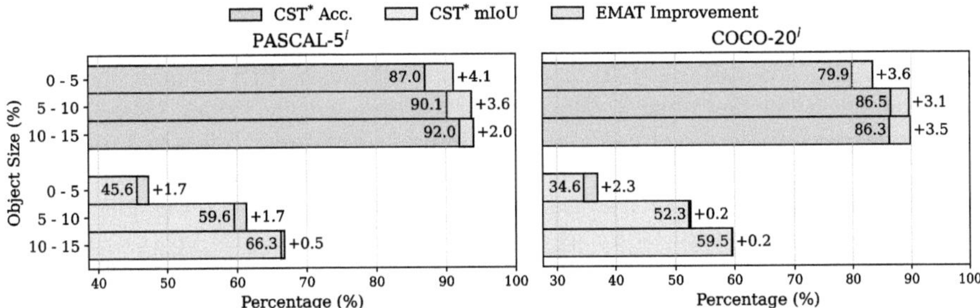

Fig. 6. Analysis of small objects on PASCAL-5^i [36] and COCO-20^i [31]. Each bar represents the average across the four folds of each dataset, filtered by object size, using 1-way 1-shot tasks. To enable a more controlled analysis, we modified the original setting (see Sect. 3) to ensure that the query image always contain the class of the support image. CST* uses the same backbone as EMAT (*i.e.*, DINOv2 [32]).

Adding our memory-efficient masked attention alone lowers memory usage by 26 GB ($\approx 41\,\%$) but does not improve accuracy or mIoU compared to either variant of CST*, likely because the model relies on large pooling windows for processing the higher-resolution correlation tokens. Incorporating our learnable downscaling removes those large windows and yields absolute accuracy gains of $+1.53\,\%$ over the original CST* and of $+0.84\,\%$ over the variant with the larger t_s^l. It also achieves an absolute mIoU gain of $+0.57\,\%$ compared with the original CST*, while matching the mIoU of the variant with larger t_s^l.

Because our learnable downscaling increases the number of trainable parameters, we next apply our parameter-efficiency modifications that remove 318 K parameters ($\approx 79\,\%$), while still saving about $39\,\%$ of the memory CST* would need for using the same t_s^l as EMAT. These modifications result in absolute accuracy gains of $+2.78\,\%$ over the original CST* and $+2.09\,\%$ over the variant with the larger t_s^l; mIoU improves by $+1.01\,\%$ and $+0.42\,\%$, respectively. EMAT also slightly improves accuracy and mIoU on the full test set, but its largest gains appear on images containing small objects.

6   Limitations

While the results of Table 2 validate that our proposed EMAT is memory and parameter efficient for high-resolution correlation tokens, its memory efficiency is constrained to datasets where the segmentation masks contain unlabeled areas. This limitation arises because our memory-efficient masked attention mechanism is equivalent to self-attention [12,47] when applied to dense semantic-segmentation datasets like Cityscapes [9], where each pixel in the segmentation mask corresponds directly to one of the semantic classes in the image.

Table 2. Ablation study of EMAT on PASCAL-5^i [36] under the original evaluation setting. "t_s^l" indicates the value of t_s for each layer $l \in \{1, 2\}$. The memory efficiency (ME), learnable downscaling (LD), and parameter efficiency (PE) columns correspond to the modifications described in Sects. 4.1 to 4.3, respectively. "Mem. Usage" reports the average per-GPU memory used during training. "All Dataset" refers to 2-way 1-shot evaluation on the full test set, while "Small Objects" restricts evaluation to objects occupying less than 15 % of the image, using 1-way 1-shot tasks in which the query always contains the support class. CST* uses the same backbone as EMAT (*i.e.*, DINOv2 [32]). **(Top)** CST* with its original support dimension per layer t_s^l. **(Middle)** CST* with the largest t_s^l that fits in our 48 GB GPUs. **(Bottom)** successive modifications introduced by EMAT. Highlight indicates our complete model. **Bold** and <u>underlined</u> values indicate the best and second best results.

t_s^l per Layer	Method	ME	LD	PE	Mem. Usage	Train. Params.	All Dataset		Small Objects	
							Acc.	mIoU	Acc.	mIoU
t_s^1=145 t_s^2=10	CST*	–	–	–	**8.68**	<u>366.00</u>	80.58	63.28	88.96	58.16
t_s^1=325 t_s^2=37	CST*	–	–	–	39.22	<u>366.00</u>	<u>82.23</u>	63.31	89.65	<u>58.75</u>
	CST*	–	–	–	≈ 63	<u>366.00</u>	N/A	N/A	N/A	N/A
t_s^1=401 t_s^2=101	EMAT	✓	–	–	36.92	<u>366.00</u>	81.95	62.97	87.99	58.06
	EMAT	✓	✓	–	<u>36.53</u>	404.48	82.17	<u>63.36</u>	<u>90.49</u>	58.73
	EMAT	✓	✓	✓	38.31	**86.02**	**82.70**	**63.38**	**91.74**	**59.17**

7   Conclusion

In this work, we propose EMAT, an enhancement over CST, the state-of-the-art method for few-shot classification and segmentation (FS-CS). EMAT incorporates our novel memory-efficient masked attention mechanism that allows our model to process high-resolution correlation tokens while maintaining memory and parameter efficiency. Our results demonstrate that EMAT consistently outperforms all FS-CS methods across all evaluation settings while requiring at least four times fewer trainable parameters. Moreover, our qualitative results highlight that EMAT is capable of correctly generating empty segmentation masks when necessary and capturing finer details more accurately, which improves accuracy when dealing with small objects. Additionally, we introduce two novel few-shot evaluation settings designed to maximize the use of the available annotations during inference, reflecting practical few-shot scenarios.

Acknowledgments. This work was funded by the Hessian Ministry of Science and Research, Arts and Culture (HMWK) through the project "The Third Wave of Artificial Intelligence – 3AI". The work was further supported by the Deutsche Forschungsgemeinschaft (German Research Foundation, DFG) under Germany's Excellence Strategy (EXC 3057/1 "Reasonable Artificial Intelligence", Project No. 533677015). Stefan Roth acknowledges support by the European Research Council (ERC) under the European Union's Horizon 2020 research and innovation programme (grant agreement No. 866008).

References

1. Aggarwal, P., Deshpande, A., Narasimhan, K.R.: SemSup-XC: semantic supervision for zero and few-shot extreme classification. In: ICML, vol. 202, pp. 228–247 (2023)
2. Alfassy, A., et al.: LaSO: label-set operations networks for multi-label few-shot learning. In: CVPR, pp. 6548–6557 (2019)
3. Allen, K.R., Shelhamer, E., Shin, H., Tenenbaum, J.B.: Infinite mixture prototypes for few-shot learning. In: ICML, vol. 97, pp. 232–241 (2019)
4. Antoniou, A., Edwards, H., Storkey, A.J.: How to train your MAML. In: ICLR (2019)
5. Caron, M., et al.: Emerging properties in self-supervised vision transformers. In: ICCV, pp. 9650–9660 (2021)
6. Carrión-Ojeda, D., Alam, M., Escalera, S., et al.: NeurIPS'22 cross-domain MetaDL challenge: results and lessons learned. In: NeurIPS Competition Track, vol. 220, pp. 50–72 (2022)
7. Chen, H., Dong, Y., Lu, Z., Yu, Y., Han, J.: Pixel matching network for cross-domain few-shot segmentation. In: WACV, pp. 978–987 (2024)
8. Chen, Z., et al.: InternVL: scaling up vision foundation models and aligning for generic visual-linguistic tasks. In: CVPR, pp. 24185–24198 (2024)
9. Cordts, M., et al.: The Cityscapes dataset for semantic urban scene understanding. In: CVPR, pp. 3213–3223 (2016)
10. Dhillon, G.S., Chaudhari, P., Ravichandran, A., Soatto, S.: A baseline for few-shot image classification. In: ICLR (2020)
11. Dong, N., Xing, E.P.: Few-shot semantic segmentation with prototype learning. In: BMVC (2018)
12. Dosovitskiy, A., et al.: An image is worth 16×16 words: transformers for image recognition at scale. In: ICLR (2021)
13. Fan, X., Wang, X., Gao, J., Wang, J., Luo, Z., Liu, R.: Bi-level learning of task-specific decoders for joint registration and one-shot medical image segmentation. In: CVPR, pp. 11726–11735 (2024)
14. Fang, Z., Wang, X., Li, H., Liu, J., Hu, Q., Xiao, J.: FastRecon: few-shot industrial anomaly detection via fast feature reconstruction. In: ICCV, pp. 17481–17490 (2023)
15. Finn, C., Abbeel, P., Levine, S.: Model-agnostic meta-learning for fast adaptation of deep networks. In: ICML, vol. 70, pp. 1126–1135 (2017)
16. Gong, X., Xia, X., Zhu, W., Zhang, B., Doermann, D., Zhuo, L.: Deformable Gabor feature networks for biomedical image classification. In: WACV, pp. 4004–4012 (2021)
17. Hao, F., He, F., Liu, L., Wu, F., Tao, D., Cheng, J.: Class-aware patch embedding adaptation for few-shot image classification. In: ICCV, pp. 18905–18915 (2023)
18. Herzog, J.: Adapt before comparison: a new perspective on cross-domain few-shot segmentation. In: CVPR, pp. 23605–23615 (2024)
19. Kang, D., Cho, M.: Integrative few-shot learning for classification and segmentation. In: CVPR, pp. 9979–9990 (2022)

20. Kang, D., Koniusz, P., Cho, M., Murray, N.: Distilling self-supervised vision transformers for weakly-supervised few-shot classification & segmentation. In: CVPR, pp. 19627–19638 (2023)
21. Kang, D., Kwon, H., Min, J., Cho, M.: Relational embedding for few-shot classification. In: ICCV, pp. 8822–8833 (2021)
22. Kingma, D.P., Ba, J.: Adam: a method for stochastic optimization. In: ICLR (2015)
23. Kirillov, A., et al.: Segment anything. In: ICCV, pp. 4015–4026 (2023)
24. Li, W.H., Liu, X., Bilen, H.: Cross-domain few-shot learning with task-specific adapters. In: CVPR, pp. 7161–7170 (2022)
25. Liu, H., Li, C., Wu, Q., Lee, Y.J.: Visual instruction tuning. In: NeurIPS (2023)
26. Liu, J., Bao, Y., Xie, G.S., Xiong, H., Sonke, J.J., Gavves, E.: Dynamic prototype convolution network for few-shot semantic segmentation. In: CVPR, pp. 11553–11562 (2022)
27. Liu, Y., Zhu, M., Li, H., Chen, H., Wang, X., Shen, C.: Matcher: segment anything with one shot using all-purpose feature matching. In: ICLR (2024)
28. Ma, T., Sun, Y., Yang, Z., Yang, Y.: ProD: prompting-to-disentangle domain knowledge for cross-domain few-shot image classification. In: CVPR, pp. 19754–19763 (2023)
29. Min, J., Kang, D., Cho, M.: Hypercorrelation squeeze for few-shot segmentation. In: ICCV, pp. 6941–6952 (2021)
30. Moon, S., et al.: MSI: maximize support-set information for few-shot segmentation. In: ICCV, pp. 19266–19276 (2023)
31. Nguyen, K., Todorovic, S.: Feature weighting and boosting for few-shot segmentation. In: ICCV, pp. 622–631 (2019)
32. Oquab, M., Darcet, T., Moutakanni, T., et al.: DINOv2: learning robust visual features without supervision. Trans. Mach. Learn. Res. (2024)
33. Peng, B., et al.: Hierarchical dense correlation distillation for few-shot segmentation. In: CVPR, pp. 23641–23651 (2023)
34. Radford, A., et al.: Learning transferable visual models from natural language supervision. In: ICML, vol. 139, pp. 8748–8763 (2021)
35. Raghu, A., Raghu, M., Bengio, S., Vinyals, O.: Rapid learning or feature reuse? Towards understanding the effectiveness of MAML. In: ICLR (2020)
36. Shaban, A., Bansal, S., Liu, Z., Essa, I., Boots, B.: One-shot learning for semantic segmentation. In: BMVC (2017)
37. Silva-Rodríguez, J., Hajimiri, S., Ben Ayed, I., Dolz, J.: A closer look at the few-shot adaptation of large vision-language models. In: CVPR, pp. 23681–23690 (2024)
38. Simon, C., Koniusz, P., Harandi, M.: Meta-learning for multi-label few-shot classification. In: WACV, pp. 346–355 (2022)
39. Snell, J., Swersky, K., Zemel, R.S.: Prototypical networks for few-shot learning. In: NIPS, pp. 4077–4087 (2017)
40. Sun, Q., Liu, Y., Chua, T.S., Schiele, B.: Meta-transfer learning for few-shot learning. In: CVPR, pp. 403–412 (2019)
41. Team, G.G.: Gemini: a family of highly capable multimodal models. arXiv:2312.11805 [cs.CL] (2023)
42. Tian, P., Wu, Z., Qi, L., Wang, L., Shi, Y., Gao, Y.: Differentiable meta-learning model for few-shot semantic segmentation. In: AAAI, pp. 12087–12094 (2020)
43. Tian, Y., Wang, Y., Krishnan, D., Tenenbaum, J.B., Isola, P.: Rethinking few-shot image classification: a good embedding is all you need? In: ECCV, vol. 12359, pp. 266–282 (2020)

44. Tian, Z., et al.: Generalized few-shot semantic segmentation. In: CVPR, pp. 11563–11572 (2022)
45. Tian, Z., Zhao, H., Shu, M., Yang, Z., Li, R., Jia, J.: Prior guided feature enrichment network for few-shot segmentation. IEEE T. Pattern Anal. Mach. Intell. **44**(2), 1050–1065 (2022)
46. Ullah, I., et al.: Meta-album: multi-domain meta-dataset for few-shot image classification. In: NeurIPS, vol. 35, pp. 3232–3247 (2022)
47. Vaswani, A., et al.: Attention is all you need. In: NIPS, pp. 5998–6008 (2017)
48. Vinyals, O., Blundell, C., Lillicrap, T., Kavukcuoglu, K., Wierstra, D.: Matching networks for one shot learning. In: NIPS, pp. 3630–3638 (2016)
49. Wang, J., Zhang, B., Pang, J., Chen, H., Liu, W.: Rethinking prior information generation with CLIP for few-shot segmentation. In: CVPR, pp. 3941–3951 (2024)
50. Wang, K., Liew, J.H., Zou, Y., Zhou, D., Feng, J.: PANet: few-shot image semantic segmentation with prototype alignment. In: ICCV, pp. 9196–9205 (2019)
51. Wang, Y., Luo, N., Zhang, T.: Focus on query: adversarial mining transformer for few-shot segmentation. In: NeurIPS, vol. 36, pp. 31524–31542 (2023)
52. Wu, A., Han, Y., Zhu, L., Yang, Y.: Universal-prototype enhancing for few-shot object detection. In: ICCV, pp. 9567–9576 (2021)
53. Xie, G.S., Xiong, H., Liu, J., Yao, Y., Shao, L.: Few-shot semantic segmentation with cyclic memory network. In: ICCV, pp. 7293–7302 (2021)
54. Xu, Q., Zhao, W., Lin, G., Long, C.: Self-calibrated cross attention network for few-shot segmentation. In: ICCV, pp. 655–665 (2023)
55. Yang, Y., Chen, Q., Feng, Y., Huang, T.: MIANet: aggregating unbiased instance and general information for few-shot semantic segmentation. In: CVPR, pp. 7131–7140 (2023)
56. Ye, C., Zhu, H., Liao, Y., Zhang, Y., Chen, T., Fan, J.: What makes for effective few-shot point cloud classification? In: WACV, pp. 1829–1838 (2022)
57. Zhang, A., Gao, G., Jiao, J., Liu, C., Wei, Y.: Bridge the points: graph-based few-shot segment anything semantically. In: NeurIPS (2024)
58. Zhang, B., Xiao, J., Qin, T.: Self-guided and cross-guided learning for few-shot segmentation. In: CVPR, pp. 8312–8321 (2021)
59. Zhang, M., Shi, M., Li, L.: MFNet: multiclass few-shot segmentation network with pixel-wise metric learning. IEEE T. Circuits Syst. Video Tech. **32**(12), 8586–8598 (2022)
60. Zhou, F., Wang, P., Zhang, L., Wei, W., Zhang, Y.: Revisiting prototypical network for cross domain few-shot learning. In: CVPR, pp. 20061–20070 (2023)
61. Zhou, Z., Xu, H.M., Shu, Y., Liu, L.: Unlocking the potential of pre-trained vision transformers for few-shot semantic segmentation through relationship descriptors. In: CVPR, pp. 3817–3827 (2024)
62. Zhu, L., Chen, T., Ji, D., Ye, J., Liu, J.: LLaFS: when large language models meet few-shot segmentation. In: CVPR, pp. 3065–3075 (2024)
63. Zhu, L., Chen, T., Yin, J., See, S., Liu, J.: Addressing background context bias in few-shot segmentation through iterative modulation. In: CVPR, pp. 3370–3379 (2024)
64. Zhu, X., et al.: Not all features matter: enhancing few-shot clip with adaptive prior refinement. In: ICCV, pp. 2605–2615 (2023)
65. Zhu, Y., Wang, S., Xin, T., Zhang, H.: Few-shot medical image segmentation via a region-enhanced prototypical transformer. In: MICCAI, pp. 271–280 (2023)

Applications of Foundation Models

Using Knowledge Graphs to Harvest Datasets for Efficient CLIP Model Training

Simon Ging(✉) [iD], Sebastian Walter [iD], Jelena Bratulić, Johannes Dienert [iD], Hannah Bast [iD], and Thomas Brox

University of Freiburg, Freiburg im Breisgau, Germany
{gings,swalter,bratulic,dienertj,bast,brox}@cs.uni-freiburg.de
https://entity-net.github.io

Abstract. Training high-quality CLIP models typically requires enormous datasets, which limits the development of domain-specific models – especially in areas that even the largest CLIP models do not cover well – and drives up training costs. This poses challenges for scientific research that needs fine-grained control over the training procedure of CLIP models. In this work, we show that by employing smart web search strategies enhanced with knowledge graphs, a robust CLIP model can be trained from scratch with considerably less data. Specifically, we demonstrate that an expert foundation model for living organisms can be built using just 10M images. Moreover, we introduce EntityNet, a dataset comprising 33M images paired with 46M text descriptions, which enables the training of a generic CLIP model in significantly reduced time.

1 Introduction

Contrastive Language-Image Pretraining (CLIP) [1] has become a cornerstone for training Vision-Language Models (VLMs). CLIP models learn high-quality visual embeddings and establish a link to the semantic level of brief text descriptions by training on pairs of images and their corresponding text descriptions collected from the web. The features and the link between images and text have been used directly for, e.g., zero-shot classification or text-to-image retrieval, and enable dialogues with visual input, such as in the LLaVA family of models [2–4]. The link can also be exploited in the opposite direction to enable text-conditional image generation, e.g., Stable Diffusion [5].

Training state-of-the-art CLIP models is computationally expensive. The original CLIP model has seen 12.8B image-text pairs, and later works have scaled this further [6,7]. This need for scale has limited most of the research to fine-tuning, which comes with reduced architectural flexibility and control over the data selection. It is particularly problematic for analytic research that demands full control over training to find causes of emergent behavior.

Supplementary Information The online version contains supplementary material available at https://doi.org/10.1007/978-3-032-12840-9_19.

M. Keuper and F. Locatello (Eds.): DAGM GCPR 2025, LNCS 16125, pp. 287–302, 2026.
https://doi.org/10.1007/978-3-032-12840-9_19

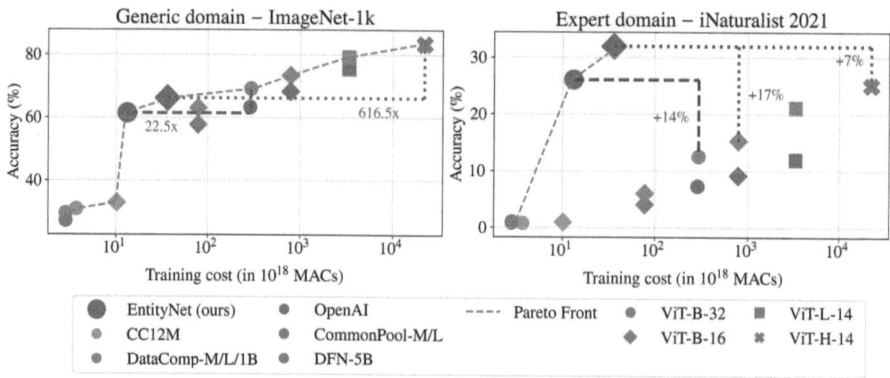

Fig. 1. We demonstrate how to harvest datasets for training CLIP models with an improved quality-cost trade-off, for a generic (left) or an expert domain (right).

The effort to collect vast datasets is also a key bottleneck for building foundation models for expert domains. Although CLIP models are supposed to be generic and cover most of the world, they are not good enough for use in specific expert domains such as medicine or biology. Building foundation models for expert domains requires an efficient data collection process, taking into account the availability of fewer data samples in these domains.

Our goal is to tackle these challenges from the dataset side while keeping the CLIP algorithm fixed. This strategy is backed by recent literature. For example, Li et al. [8] explored CLIP "along three dimensions: data, architecture, and training strategies" and they stress the "significance of high-quality training data". For Large Language Models (LLMs), data curation was shown to reduce training time and model size, achieved through heavily filtered publicly available web data and synthetic data [9]. With the dataset creation process, we aim (1) for improved performance in the expert domain of living organisms, in order to demonstrate the creation of expert foundation models; and (2) we aim for a good trade-off between training efficiency and model performance on the broad domain of the visual world, in order to enable compute-efficient from-scratch analysis of fully functional CLIP models.

We built a dataset we call *EntityNet*, where we leveraged knowledge graphs and targeted web image search. Specifically, from the knowledge graphs Wikidata and WordNet, we collected 135k entities (e.g. *eagle*) as well as their aliases and descriptions. We extracted entity attributes from Wikidata related to color, partonomy, behavior, and other aspects, and used them to guide an LLM in generating entity-attribute queries for image search. For example, from the entity *plastic* and the attribute *small* we generated the query *small plastic item*.

The resulting EntityNet consists of 33M images paired with 45M alt texts and 613k text labels from the knowledge graphs. The dataset is partitioned into a subset of 10M images of living organisms, capturing high-quality visual and semantic information about the taxonomy of animals, plants, and funghi, as well as a subset of 23M images covering a wide range of categories, such as tools, geographical features, materials, and buildings. Notably, from this process we obtain not only alt texts, but also a link back to the knowledge graph information that was used to create the search query for a given image. We show that this information can be used during training to achieve better performance than by training on alt texts alone. The method of creating our dataset is largely generic and can be applied to other knowledge graphs.

Training on this dataset, we obtain a foundation model that is both specialized on the target expert domain and is also able to understand the overall visual world. In our domain-specific evaluations on iNaturalist and RareSpecies, the model demonstrates robust generalization and clearly surpasses CLIP models trained on much more data (Fig. 1). On ImageNet, we demonstrate our dataset to be highly compute efficient and to achieve a performance comparable to models trained 20x longer (Fig. 1).

- We propose a method to automatically create a vision-language dataset based on a given knowledge graph and an image search engine.
- We apply this method to create the *EntityNet* dataset, consisting of 33M images paired with 45M alt texts and supplementary text information from the knowledge graphs.
- We train an expert CLIP model for living organisms on a single 8xL40S machine from scratch in 55 h. This *EntityNet-CLIP* is highly specialized in the target expert domain of living organisms, *and* comparably strong on ImageNet.
- We evaluate our model and a suite of other CLIP models for object classification, image retrieval, and domain shift robustness. In the expert domain of animals and plants, our model achieves higher performance than models with orders of magnitude more parameters or training data. It is also much stronger than CLIP models that specialize only for this domain. In the generic domain, our model performs remarkably well given the low amount of compute required to train it.

2   Related Work

Datasets. Many recent studies have investigated methods for building large-scale datasets for multimodal training. Radford et al. [1] trained the original CLIP model on a private dataset of 400M images using image-text pairs with text derived from Wikipedia and WordNet terms. Schuhmann et al. [10] further built the publicly available LAION-400M dataset by filtering HTML data from Common Crawl [11] based on the similarity estimated by the CLIP model. In a follow-up work, they [12] scaled their approach one order of magnitude with the multilingual LAION-5B dataset. Xu et al. [13] sought to replicate the original CLIP's data curation approach. Gadre et al. [6] proposed DataComp, a filtering challenge containing up to 13B image-text pairs from CommonCrawl, and

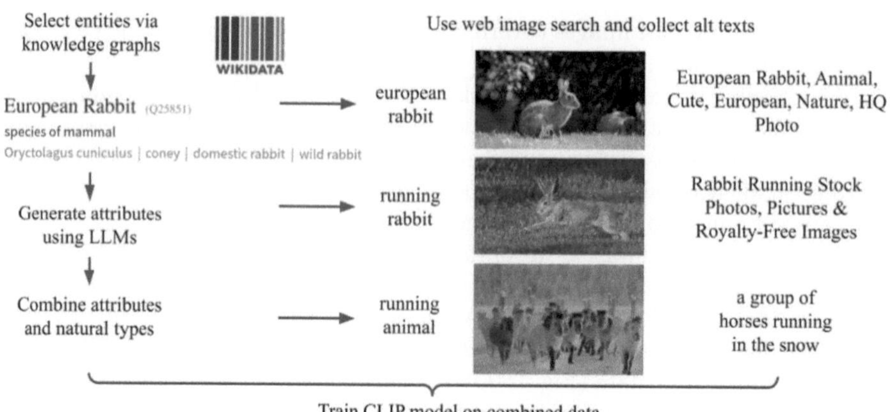

Fig. 2. We create a dataset for vision-language pretraining: First, we extract entities from knowledge graphs, then generate attributes and natural types for them. We search for different combinations of entities, attributes, and types in image search engines, and collect alt texts for each image. Finally, we train our model on the combined data.

a baseline DataComp-1B dataset. It contains 1.4B pairs filtered with a combination of CLIP score and clustering to match ImageNet [14] training examples. Fang et al. [7] trained a Data Filtering Network on 357M human-verified image-text pairs, which they used to filter 42B candidates into the DFN-5B dataset and use that dataset to train the current top model of the OpenCLIP leaderboard [15]. These large datasets have largely supplanted smaller ones like ConceptualCaptions12M (CC12M) [16], relying on unimodal heuristics, and Yahoo Flickr Creative Commons 15M (YFCC15M), a derived subset of 15M image-text pairs from Flickr [17]. While many prior works have focused on scaling up multimodal datasets and models, we aim to improve research on high-quality CLIP models when data and compute efficiency is essential, such as setting up a CLIP model for an expert domain or for scientific analysis of CLIP training.

Stevens et al. [18] curated the TreeOfLife-10M dataset from biological sources [19–21] to train BioCLIP, a model for organismal biology. They evaluated it on RareSpecies, a benchmark of 400 species not seen during training. While BioCLIP leverages domain-specific biological knowledge, we propose a dataset construction method that generalizes to arbitrary domains using knowledge graphs.

Training Algorithms. Several works have investigated algorithmic improvements to CLIP. Li et al. [22] simply train and fine-tune with different image resolutions, while Li et al. [23] suggests masking parts of the image to reduce computation. Zhai et al. [24] propose a sigmoid loss which reduces the computational load especially in big distributed settings. They follow up [25] by extending the training objective using multiple previously developed techniques, including captioning-based pretraining [26], self-distillation [27] and online data curation [28] into a unified training strategy. Vasu et al. [29] improve learning efficiency with synthetic captions created by an image captioning model and an ensemble of CLIP teachers to train their model. Chen et al. [30] evaluate vision encoder choices and design a hybrid architecture that improves over vanilla vision transformers (ViT) based CLIP models. These algorithmic improvements are orthogonal to our contribution. In this work, we fix the algorithm and architecture to enable a fair comparison with ViT-based CLIP baselines.

Li et al. [8] analyze scaling effects across data, architecture, and training strategies, showing that huge models require larger datasets, and data quality plays a crucial role. They create improved datasets by filtering the 3.4B WebLI dataset [31] with CLIP, while we pursue a different dataset collection process.

3 Dataset Creation

Our dataset creation process consists of four steps: entity extraction, attribute generation, query building, and image search. This process is generally applicable to all visual domains covered by the underlying knowledge graph. We construct a dataset covering most visual entities in our world, additionally focusing on animals and plants, referred to as the *organism* subset. See Fig. 2 for the dataset creation process and Table 1 for examples of entities and attributes.

3.1 Entity Extraction

A high-quality list of visual entities forms the basis for our dataset, built from the Wikidata knowledge graph [32] and utilizing the hierarchical structure provided by the subclass of relation within Wikidata. For example, the entity dog is a subclass of the pet entity, which in turn is a subclass of domesticated animal. This hierarchy enables easy collection of entities related to a super-entity. First, we manually build a list of 21 super-entities that cover most physical and visual entities in Wikidata. For the *organism* subset, the super-entities are just animal and plant. Examples of *non-organism* super-entities include food, building, or physical tool, with all super-entities listed in the supplementary material. Next, we extract all entities from Wikidata linked to at least one of the super-entities through the *subclass of* relation. For animals and plants, Wikidata also models their biological taxon hierarchy via the parent taxon relation. Because the taxon hierarchy substantially increases the coverage of our *organism* subset, we use it together with the regular *subclass* hierarchy to extract entities. We exclude named entities (e.g., specific persons), as Wikidata models these via the *instance of* relation; we focus solely on the *subclass of* and *parent taxon* relations. For every entity, we also download its name, description, aliases, and its number of Wikimedia sitelinks[1] as additional information. Finally, we apply two filtering steps: First, we remove all entities with a sitelink count below a predefined threshold, eliminating very rare or low-quality entities unlikely to produce strong search results. We then use a LLM to filter out any remaining non-visual entities.

---

[1] The number of Wikimedia sitelinks is a commonly used and high-quality proxy for the popularity of an entity [33].

Table 1. Top: Examples of entities and additional information as extracted from the Wikidata knowledge graph. **Bottom:** Examples of attributes and corresponding search queries for different entities as generated by the LLM.

Entity	Description	Sitelinks	Aliases
tiger	species of big cat	216	tigress, tigers, Panthera tigris
chest	box-shaped type of furniture	51	coffer, kist
muscle car	type of high-performance car	30	high performance car

Entity	Category	Attribute	Search query
rock	Pattern and texture	porous	porous rock
wolf	Environment	snow	wolf in the snow
residence	Parts	arches	arches in residence architecture
garlic	Shape and size	big	big garlic bulb
farm	Other	tourist	tourists visiting a farm
boot	Color	multicolor	multicolored boots

For our expert domain, the *organism* subset, we also add all nouns from WordNet [34] that are a subclass of the *living thing* node, excluding humans, named entities and entities that cannot be seen with the bare eye, e.g., microorganisms. Finally, we employ heuristic methods to detect and remove potentially offensive entities via a profanity filter.

3.2   Attribute Generation

Besides searching for the entities directly, we also aim to search for variations of them in different contexts, by combining them with attributes. We manually define 6 visual attribute categories we want to search for: *Color, Pattern and texture, Parts, Shape and size, Environment,* and *Other.* We extract potential attributes for each entity from the Wikidata knowledge graph and prompt an LLM[2] with this entity and attribute information to generate a list of visual attributes. We first considered generating attributes without categories, however, the results lacked diversity, and adding categories improves the variety of attributes. For each attribute we also generate a search query combining the attribute itself with the corresponding entity. We generate between 1 and 10 attributes per category and generate them for the most popular entities only, as image search engines fail to respect attributes in search queries for rare entities, where they often even struggle to return good results for the entity alone.

3.3   Query Building

For the entities themselves, we use their names and aliases as search queries. We search entity-attribute combinations using the search queries generated by

---

[2] We use three LLMs and merge their generated attributes: Qwen2.5 7B [35], OpenAI GPT-4o, and OpenAI GPT-4o mini (both accessed via API at platform.openai.com).

Table 2. Details of our EntityNet dataset. We show the number of unique elements for each column, e.g. the number of images after deduplication or all unique entity aliases in the respective sets.

Query set	Images	Queries	Entities	Aliases	Attributes	Alt texts	Example query
World entity	23M	158k	74k	101k	-	23M	ship
+ attribute	19M	139k	6k	16k	20k	16M	small handbag
Living entity	9M	72k	63k	51k	-	8M	kohlrabi
+ attribute	9M	53k	1k	3k	5k	6M	tropical plant
All	33M	416k	135k	149k	23k	45M	-

the LLM. We then create additional queries based on the attributes: First, we determine the entity's natural type – the super-entity a human would most likely associate with it, e.g., *bird* for *eagle*, or *clothing* for *hat*. It is neither too general nor too specific, and can typically help disambiguate entities sharing the same name. We use an LLM to select the most fitting super-entity from an entity's super-class hierarchy as its natural type and generate a brief description explaining why this type is appropriate. The description is used during training as a potential text label. We then replace entity mentions in the attribute search queries with their natural types. For example, the attribute query *eagle in its nest* may turn into *bird in its nest*, or *black BMW M4* into *black car*.

3.4   Image Search and Filtering

We execute our search queries using the image search APIs of Bing and Google. Initial tests on the *organism* subset revealed Bing's search results to be of much higher quality at a lower cost, so we rely solely on the Bing API for all other queries. The image search APIs also provide the URL for the website hosting the image, which we use to collect alt texts from the HTML image tag. After downloading images and alt texts, we perform the following postprocessing steps.

Similar to Changpinyo et al. [16], we apply *relaxed filtering heuristics*. We do not use multimodal filtering, but rely on search engines to provide image-text correspondences. We remove JSON-like and too long text. We also remove images with an aspect ratio of more than 4 or covering less than 4096 pixels.

We deduplicate all downloaded images using the Self-Supervised Descriptor for Image Copy Detection method (SSCD) [36]. For duplicates, we retain the largest image and collect all unique alt texts and related entities from the duplicates. Deduplication increases the dataset diversity per sample, since the domain coverage stays the same, while the number of samples decreases. We also remove images that appear in any evaluation dataset using the same SSCD method.

Our final dataset comprises approximately 33M images and 45M alt texts, obtained from 416k queries. This amounts to 79 images per query and 1.4 alt texts per image on average. The total cost for all image search API calls was around 10,000$. See Table 2 for an overview over our dataset.

4   Experimental Setup

4.1   Training

We trained all models with the standard CLIP loss [1], using a batch size of 8,192 for pretraining and 32,768 during finetuning, along with random resized crop augmentation. We sampled text labels from both the image alt texts and the knowledge graph. For each image, 50% of the time, we chose a random alt text, and 50% of the time, we chose randomly between search queries, aliases, or descriptions of the corresponding entity. We trained all models for 18 epochs. Training on 33M images takes ~55 h on 8 L40s GPUs (48GB VRAM per GPU). Our training code is based on OpenCLIP [15]. Further training details and text sampling examples are in the supplementary material.

4.2   Evaluated Models

On our EntityNet dataset, we trained ViT CLIP models of size B-32 and B-16 from random initialization. For a comparison with a similarly sized dataset, we also trained models on CC12M by downloading all available URLs, and then detecting and removing duplicates relative to the evaluation datasets using the same procedure as detailed in Sect. 3.4, obtaining 9.3M images. We finetuned B-32 and B-16 CLIP models trained on DataComp-1B on our dataset to compare finetuning and pretraining performance. We also evaluate the original *OpenAI CLIP* [1], models pretrained on *DataComp-M/L/1B*, *CommonPool-M/L* [6], and DFN-5B [7], as well as the biological domain expert model BioCLIP [18], a ViT-B-16 CLIP model finetuned from OpenAI-CLIP on the TreeOfLife-10M dataset.

4.3   Object Classification Evaluation

To test the VLMs on object classification, we use the same procedure as CLIP [1], see the supplementary material for a detailed description. We evaluate all models on just encoding the class name, and on using the average embedding of the 80 context prompts that the CLIP authors used for ImageNet, and report the higher top-1 accuracy. For zero-shot object classification, we require models not to have been trained on the training set of the benchmark, to test "generalization to unseen datasets" [1]

Benchmarks in the Generic Domain. We evaluate on ImageNet [14], a popular image classification benchmark [37]. We use the ILSVRC2012 validation set, which contains 50,000 images from 1,000 classes. The classes include simple objects, such as *park bench*, as well as more fine-grained labels like 23 types of terrier dogs, e.g., *Staffordshire Bull Terrier*. We further evaluate the robustness under distribution shifts on ImageNet-A [38], ImageNet-R [39], ImageNet-Sketch [40], ImageNet-V2 [41], and ObjectNet [42] as proposed by Taori et al. [43]. ImageNet-A contains 7500 samples of 200 ImageNet classes. The samples were adversarially filtered to make ResNet-50s misclassify them, providing a more challenging test. ImageNet-R contains 30000 renditions, such as paintings or embroidery, of 200 ImageNet object classes. ImageNet-Sketch contains 50000 sketches, covering 200 ImageNet classes. ImageNet-V2 replicates the original ImageNet generation process, providing an additional 10000 test images. The object-centered ObjectNet contains 18574 images from 113 ImageNet classes with control over background, rotation and viewpoint.

Benchmarks in the Expert Domain. We evaluate our models on iNaturalist 2021 [20], a fine-grained species classification benchmark that contains 100k images in the validation set of 10k different species. Similar to Parashar et al. [44], we report the best results after testing on both the English common name and the Latin taxon name. We further test on the Caltech-UCSD Birds (CUB) [45] dataset, which contains 5,794 images of birds in the original author's test set, each annotated as one of 200 fine-grained bird species, e.g., *grasshopper sparrow*. Additionally, we evaluate on the Rare Species benchmark proposed by Stevens et al. [18], comprising 400 species with 30 images each, specifically tailored to assess generalization to unseen taxa. To comply with the benchmark requirements of not seeing the testing 400 species during training, we exclude all entities and queries from our dataset that appear in RareSpecies, using substring matching. As class names, we evaluate all text types proposed by Stevens et al. [18]: combinations of the Latin taxonomy and the English common name. Same as in Sect. 4.3 we evaluate on both the CLIP ImageNet prompt and no prompt, and report the better of both accuracies.

4.4   Retrieval Evaluation

We evaluate the COCO Karpathy test split [46], a subset of 5000 samples from the MS-COCO [47] dataset paired with 5 texts each. We also evaluate the 1000 samples in the Karpathy test split of Flickr30k [48] annotated with 5 texts per image, as well as on the 3600 image-text pairs in XM3600 [49]. We report the average of image-to-text and text-to-image recall@1 over all datasets.

5   Results

We evaluate CLIP **pretrained from scratch** on our EntityNet dataset and CLIP models trained on other datasets. In Figs. 1 and 3 we contrast the effectiveness of models with their training cost. We show the results in detail in Table 3. In the generic domain, our models surpass others trained on similarly sized datasets while achieving comparable performance on object classification with models trained 20x longer. On image-text retrieval, our model performs similarly to models trained on the same amount of compute. While our pipeline creates a dataset efficient for understanding objects and their properties, understanding complex scenes still requires learning mainly from the alt texts more than from objects and attributes. In the expert domain, we outperform even the largest CLIP models on the challenging iNaturalist 2021 dataset, which requires classifying images among 10k fine-grained species. Our model also excels on CUB by distinguishing 200 bird species better than all other CLIP models of

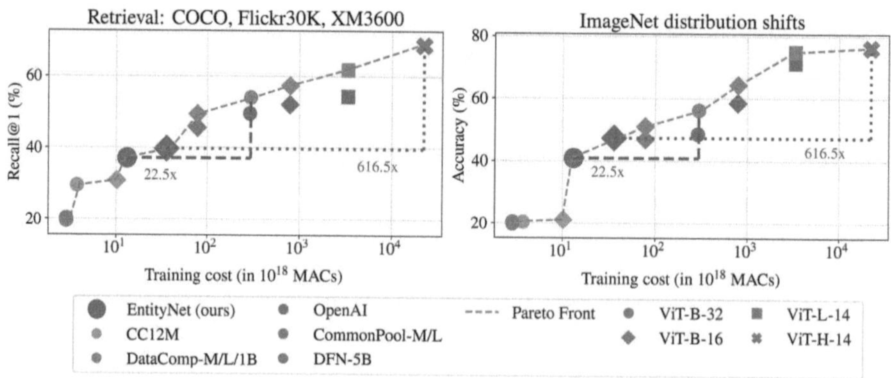

Fig. 3. Results on image retrieval and distribution shift robustness on ImageNet.

the same size. Further, when compared to the expert model *BioCLIP*, explicitly trained for organismal biology at a similar training cost, our model demonstrates superior performance. On the Rare Species benchmark, our model outperforms *BioCLIP* on unseen species, showing the effectiveness of our dataset collection method over a manually designed living organism training set.

We investigate improving existing CLIP models via **finetuning** in Table 4. The results show that our dataset can be leveraged to create expert CLIP models that outperform both the base model and our model pretrained from scratch on the expert domain. This improvement comes at the cost of trading off some capabilities in the other domains. When finetuning only on the expert domain, we trade off more capabilities, yet obtain even stronger experts.

We further validate and verify our design choices through a **component analysis** in Table 5. Training separately on the generic and the domain expert part of our dataset reveals that, while the best generic model emerges from training on everything, a slightly better expert model is the result of training only on the expert domain (first table segment). However, generalization to unseen species slightly benefits when training on the full dataset, showing that our generic domain data can enhance generalization capabilities within the expert domain. We also observe that generating and downloading attribute queries contributes to improved performance of the pretrained model.

In the second segment of the table, we evaluate the mixture of alt text and knowledge graph labels used during training. Notably, both training only on alt texts or only on knowledge graph labels mostly performs worse than our 50-50 mix. The exception is image-text retrieval, where training fully on alt text performs slightly better. Potentially, the knowledge graph labels are less useful for learning the matching between longer text queries and images, and more useful for learning fine-grained object classification.

Finally, we reduce the scale of our dataset by powers of two. While the model performance expectedly drops with reduced dataset size, the efficiency of

Table 3. Results for training CLIP B-32 and B-16 on our EntityNet dataset from scratch.

Arch.	Dataset	MACs (1e18)	Images in dataset (M)	Image-Net	Retrie- val	Distr. shift	iNat. 2021	CUB	Rare Species
B-32	CC12M	3.7	9.3	28.6	25.6	18.3	0.7	9.2	–
B-32	CommonPool-M	2.9	128.0	27.2	20.2	19.8	0.8	10.1	–
B-32	DataComp-M	2.9	14.0	29.7	19.5	20.5	1.0	16.8	–
B-32	OpenAI	288.6	400.0	63.4	49.6	48.7	7.4	51.8	–
B-32	DataComp-1B	295.4	1400.0	**69.2**	**54.0**	**56.3**	12.6	73.8	–
B-32	EntityNet (ours)	13.1	32.7	61.5	37.2	41.0	**26.1**	**79.5**	**42.7**
B-16	BioCLIP	61.3	10.4	18.6	0.8	15.4	–	78.1	38.1
B-16	CommonPool-L	78.2	1280.0	57.8	45.6	47.0	4.1	35.1	–
B-16	DataComp-L	78.2	140.0	63.1	49.4	51.1	6.1	48.1	–
B-16	DataComp-1B	791.4	1400.0	**73.5**	**57.4**	**64.4**	15.3	79.0	–
B-16	OpenAI	784.6	400.0	68.3	52.1	58.6	9.2	56.1	–
B-16	EntityNet (ours)	36.0	32.7	66.2	39.8	47.4	**32.0**	**85.3**	**47.1**
L-14	OpenAI	3328.4	400.0	75.5	54.3	71.4	12.0	62.9	–
L-14	DataComp-1B	3338.6	1400.0	79.2	61.8	74.9	21.1	85.5	–
L-14	DFN-2B	3338.6	2000.0	81.4	64.2	74.8	21.6	86.5	–
H-14	DFN-5B	22164.0	5000.0	**83.4**	**68.7**	**76.3**	25.1	**88.1**	–

our dataset per datapoint stays high, with the model still reaching 33% accuracy on ImageNet with only 4M images.

6 Limitations

The proposed data harvesting approach assumes that there is a knowledge graph for the target domain and that there is a searchable database with noisy pairing of images and text. However, knowledge graphs exist in many domains, e.g., *UniProt* [50] with 246M protein sequence records or *AgriKG* [51] with 150k agricultural entities. Also, if no image search engine is available for the given domain, but a large amount of image-text data exists, pairs can be found by searching for the queries via substring matching in the image-text pairs.

Another limitation is the small, but significant drop in performance on image-text retrieval and classifying ImageNet distribution shifts in the generic domain, when finetuning a large model with EntityNet. First, our dataset by design has a strong focus on the expert domain and trades off some performance in the generic domain during finetuning. Second, our search pipeline finds many clean object-centric images and annotates them with entity information, which tremendously helps understanding object semantics, but to improve efficiency on image-text retrieval in a similar way, one needs to tackle the quality of alt texts and their alignment to the images [52]. Finally, we focused on searching photos, which explains slightly lower accuracy when classifying paintings and sketches – the

Table 4. Results for finetuning the DataComp-1B CLIP model on EntityNet. .

Arch.	Dataset	MACs (1e18)	Images in dataset (M)	Image-Net	Retrie- val	Distr. shift	iNat 2021	CUB
B-32	DataComp-1B	295.4	1400.0	69.2	**54.0**	**56.3**	12.6	73.8
B-32	EntityNet	13.3	32.7	**69.5**	50.8	53.3	29.5	83.3
B-32	Only organisms	4.2	10.2	48.2	31.2	33.3	**37.0**	**87.0**
B-16	DataComp-1B	791.4	1400.0	**73.5**	**57.4**	**64.4**	15.3	79.0
B-16	EntityNet	36.1	32.7	**73.5**	52.2	61.0	34.9	86.5
B-16	Only organisms	11.3	10.2	51.4	34.8	39.2	**42.7**	**90.3**

Table 5. Analysis of performance when varying dataset composition, text sampling and dataset size.

Arch.	Dataset	MACs (1e18)	Images in dataset (M)	Image-Net	Retrie- val	Distr. shift	iNat. 2021	CUB	Rare Species
B-32	Everything	13.1	32.7	**61.5**	**37.2**	**41.0**	26.1	79.5	**42.7**
B-32	No organisms	9.0	22.5	39.2	32.1	28.0	0.8	6.2	6.9
B-32	Only organisms	4.1	10.2	36.0	16.5	21.0	**28.6**	**83.2**	42.0
B-32	No attributes	8.7	21.8	54.8	28.6	33.8	25.6	79.7	39.2
B-32	50% alt text	13.1	32.7	**61.5**	37.2	**41.0**	**26.1**	**79.5**	**42.7**
B-32	100% alt text	13.1	32.7	59.1	**38.3**	38.1	22.9	78.8	39.7
B-32	0% alt text	13.1	32.7	55.7	13.5	35.5	24.2	78.1	29.7
B-32	Full size	13.1	32.7	**61.5**	**37.2**	**41.0**	**26.1**	**79.5**	**42.7**
B-32	1/2 size	6.6	16.4	54.1	30.3	33.6	20.1	74.1	36.6
B-32	1/4 size	3.3	8.2	45.2	23.5	25.7	13.2	64.9	28.0
B-32	1/8 size	1.6	4.1	33.3	16.6	17.7	7.3	47.8	19.4
B-32	1/16 size	0.8	2.0	19.9	9.4	10.0	2.8	27.4	11.8

EntityNet dataset simply contains a lower percentage of such types of images than datasets like CommonPool.

7 Conclusions

We demonstrated how to use knowledge graphs to harvest datasets that are efficient for training CLIP models. Our strategy allows to create an expert domain dataset with little manual effort, enabling the development of CLIP models that significantly outperform standard models in the expert domain. The expert domain dataset can be used for training a model from scratch or for finetuning an existing vanilla model. The substantial size and diversity of the expert domain dataset ensures that the good generalization properties of CLIP exist also in the expert domain, in contrast to training with an over-specialized expert dataset.

Furthermore, we demonstrated that the proposed harvesting strategy is also viable to create a common domain dataset, which allows us to achieve a better quality-compute trade-off than training with previous datasets. Future work can use our EntityNet dataset to train CLIP models with all emergent properties much more efficiently, thus allowing for experiments, where training can be controlled. So far, this has been possible only with models of lacking quality.

Acknowledgements. This work was funded by the Deutsche Forschungsgemeinschaft (DFG, German Research Foundation) âĂŞ Project-ID 499552394 âĂŞ SFB 1597 âĂŞ Project-ID 417962828 âĂŞ Project-ID 539134284. The authors acknowledge support from the state of Baden-Württemberg through bwHPC.

References

1. Radford, A., et al.: Learning transferable visual models from natural language supervision. In: Meila, M., Zhang, T. (eds.) Proceedings of the 38th International Conference on Machine Learning. Proceedings of Machine Learning Research, vol. 139, pp. 8748–8763. PMLR (2021). https://proceedings.mlr.press/v139/radford21a.html
2. Liu, H., Li, C., Wu, Q., Lee, Y.J.: Visual instruction tuning. In: Oh, A., Naumann, T., Globerson, A., Saenko, K., Hardt, M., Levine, S. (eds.) Advances in Neural Information Processing Systems, vol. 36, pp. 34892–34916. Curran Associates, Inc. (2023). https://proceedings.neurips.cc/paper_files/paper/2023/file/6dcf277ea32ce3288914faf369fe6de0-Paper-Conference.pdf
3. Liu, H., Li, C., Li, Y., Lee, Y.J.: Improved Baselines with Visual Instruction Tuning (2023)
4. Liu, H., et al.: LLaVA-NeXT: improved reasoning, OCR, and world knowledge (2024). https://llava-vl.github.io/blog/2024-01-30-llava-next/
5. Podell, D., et al.: SDXL: improving latent diffusion models for high-resolution image synthesis (2023). https://arxiv.org/abs/2307.01952
6. Gadre, S.Y., et al.: DataComp: in search of the next generation of multimodal datasets. In: Oh, A., Naumann, T., Globerson, A., Saenko, K., Hardt, M., Levine, S. (eds.) Advances in Neural Information Processing Systems, vol. 36, pp. 27092–27112. Curran Associates, Inc. (2023). https://proceedings.neurips.cc/paper_files/paper/2023/file/56332d41d55ad7ad8024aac625881be7-Paper-Datasets_and_Benchmarks.pdf
7. Fang, A., Jose, A.M., Jain, A., Schmidt, L., Toshev, A.T., Shankar, V.: Data filtering networks. In: The Twelfth International Conference on Learning Representations (2024). https://openreview.net/forum?id=KAk6ngZ09F
8. Li, Z., Xie, C., Cubuk, E.D.: Scaling (Down) CLIP: a comprehensive analysis of data, architecture, and training strategies. arXiv preprint arXiv:2404.08197 (2024)
9. Abdin, M., et al.: Phi-3 technical report: a highly capable language model locally on your phone (2024). https://arxiv.org/abs/2404.14219
10. Schuhmann, C., et al.: LAION-400M: open dataset of clip-filtered 400 million image-text pairs. arXiv preprint arXiv:2111.02114 (2021)
11. Rana, A.: Common crawl – building an open web-scale crawl using hadoop (2010). https://www.slideshare.net/hadoopusergroup/common-crawlpresentation
12. Schuhmann, C., et al.: LAION-5B: an open large-scale dataset for training next generation image-text models. In: Koyejo, S., Mohamed, S., Agarwal, A., Belgrave, D., Cho, K., Oh, A. (eds.) Advances in Neural

Information Processing Systems, vol. 35, pp. 25278–25294. Curran Associates, Inc. (2022). https://proceedings.neurips.cc/paper_files/paper/2022/file/a1859debfb3b59d094f3504d5ebb6c25-Paper-Datasets_and_Benchmarks.pdf

13. Xu, H., et al.: Demystifying CLIP data. In: The Twelfth International Conference on Learning Representations (2024). https://openreview.net/forum?id=5BCFlnfE1g

14. Deng, J., Dong, W., Socher, R., Li, L.J., Li, K., Fei-Fei, L.: ImageNet: a large-scale hierarchical image database. In: IEEE Conference on Computer Vision and Pattern Recognition (2009)

15. Ilharco, G., et al.: OpenCLIP (2021). https://doi.org/10.5281/zenodo.5143773

16. Changpinyo, S., Sharma, P., Ding, N., Soricut, R.: Conceptual 12M: pushing web-scale image-text pre-training to recognize long-tail visual concepts. In: 2021 IEEE/CVF Conference on Computer Vision and Pattern Recognition (CVPR). IEEE (2021). https://doi.org/10.1109/cvpr46437.2021.00356

17. Thomee, B., et al.: YFCC100M: the new data in multimedia research. Commun. ACM **59**(2), 64–73 (2016). https://doi.org/10.1145/2812802

18. Stevens, S., et al.: BioCLIP: a vision foundation model for the tree of life. In: Proceedings of the IEEE/CVF Conference on Computer Vision and Pattern Recognition (CVPR), pp. 19412–19424 (2024)

19. Encyclopedia of Life (2018). http://eol.org

20. Van Horn, G., et al.: The iNaturalist species classification and detection dataset. In: Proceedings of the IEEE Conference on Computer Vision and Pattern Recognition (CVPR) (2018)

21. Gharaee, Z., et al.: A step towards worldwide biodiversity assessment: The BIOSCAN-1M insect dataset. In: Oh, A., Neumann, T., Globerson, A., Saenko, K., Hardt, M., Levine, S. (eds.) Advances in Neural Information Processing Systems, vol. 36, pp. 43593–43619. Curran Associates, Inc. (2023). https://proceedings.neurips.cc/paper_files/paper/2023/file/87dbbdc3a685a97ad28489a1d57c45c1-Paper-Datasets_and_Benchmarks.pdf

22. Li, R., Kim, D., Bhanu, B., Kuo, W.: RECLIP: Resource-efficient CLIP by Training with Small Images (2023)

23. Li, X., Wang, Z., Xie, C.: CLIPA-v2: scaling CLIP training with 81.1% zero-shot imagenet accuracy within a $10,000 budget; an extra$4,000 unlocks 81.8% accuracy. arXiv preprint arXiv:2306.15658 (2023)

24. Zhai, X., Mustafa, B., Kolesnikov, A., Beyer, L.: Sigmoid loss for language image pre-training. In: 2023 IEEE/CVF International Conference on Computer Vision (ICCV). IEEE (2023). https://doi.org/10.1109/iccv51070.2023.01100

25. Tschannen, M., et al.: Siglip 2: multilingual vision-language encoders with improved semantic understanding, localization, and dense features. arXiv preprint arXiv:2502.14786 (2025)

26. Wan, B., et al.: Locca: visual pretraining with location-aware captioners. Adv. Neural. Inf. Process. Syst. **37**, 116355–116387 (2024)

27. Naeem, M.F., Xian, Y., Zhai, X., Hoyer, L., Van Gool, L., Tombari, F.: Silc: improving vision language pretraining with self-distillation. In: European Conference on Computer Vision, pp. 38–55. Springer, Cham (2024)

28. Udandarao, V., et al.: Active data curation effectively distills large-scale multimodal models. arXiv preprint arXiv:2411.18674 (2024)

29. Vasu, P.K.A., Pouransari, H., Faghri, F., Vemulapalli, R., Tuzel, O.: MobileCLIP: fast image-text models through multi-modal reinforced training. In: Proceedings of the IEEE/CVF Conference on Computer Vision and Pattern Recognition (CVPR) (2024)

30. Chen, J., Yu, Q., Shen, X., Yuille, A., Chen, L.C.: Design scalable vision models in the vision-language era. In: Proceedings of the IEEE/CVF Conference on Computer Vision and Pattern Recognition (2024)
31. Chen, X., et al.: PaLI: a jointly-scaled multilingual language-image model. In: The Eleventh International Conference on Learning Representations (2023). https://openreview.net/forum?id=mWVoBz4W0u
32. Vrandečić, D., Krötzsch, M.: Wikidata: a free collaborative knowledge base. Commun. ACM **57**, 78–85 (2014). http://cacm.acm.org/magazines/2014/10/178785-wikidata/fulltext
33. Peshterliev, S., Dupuy, C., Kiss, I.: Self-attention gazetteer embeddings for named-entity recognition. arXiv preprint arXiv:2004.04060 (2020)
34. Fellbaum, C.: WordNet: An Electronic Lexical Database. Language, Speech and Communication. MIT Press (1998). http://books.google.at/books?id=Rehu8OOzMIMC
35. Yang, A., et al.: Qwen2.5 technical report. arXiv preprint arXiv:2412.15115 (2024)
36. Pizzi, E., Roy, S.D., Ravindra, S.N., Goyal, P., Douze, M.: A self-supervised descriptor for image copy detection. In: 2022 IEEE/CVF Conference on Computer Vision and Pattern Recognition (CVPR). IEEE (2022). https://doi.org/10.1109/cvpr52688.2022.01413
37. Russakovsky, O., et al.: ImageNet large scale visual recognition challenge. Int. J. Comput. Vis. (2015). https://doi.org/10.1007/s11263-015-0816-y
38. Hendrycks, D., Zhao, K., Basart, S., Steinhardt, J., Song, D.: Natural adversarial examples. In: Proceedings of the IEEE/CVF Conference on Computer Vision and Pattern Recognition, pp. 15262–15271 (2021)
39. Hendrycks, D., et al.: The many faces of robustness: a critical analysis of out-of-distribution generalization. In: Proceedings of the IEEE/CVF International Conference on Computer Vision, pp. 8340–8349 (2021)
40. Wang, H., Ge, S., Lipton, Z., Xing, E.P.: Learning robust global representations by penalizing local predictive power. In: Advances in Neural Information Processing Systems, vol. 32 (2019)
41. Recht, B., Roelofs, R., Schmidt, L., Shankar, V.: Do imagenet classifiers generalize to imagenet? In: International Conference on Machine Learning, pp. 5389–5400. PMLR (2019)
42. Barbu, A., et al.: Objectnet: a large-scale bias-controlled dataset for pushing the limits of object recognition models. In: Advances in Neural Information Processing Systems, vol. 32 (2019)
43. Taori, R., Dave, A., Shankar, V., Carlini, N., Recht, B., Schmidt, L.: Measuring robustness to natural distribution shifts in image classification. In: Advances in Neural Information Processing Systems, vol. 33, pp. 18583–18599 (2020)
44. Parashar, S., Lin, Z., Li, Y., Kong, S.: Prompting scientific names for zero-shot species recognition. In: The 2023 Conference on Empirical Methods in Natural Language Processing (2023). https://openreview.net/forum?id=OgK0kMz5Va
45. Wah, C., Branson, S., Welinder, P., Perona, P., Belongie, S.: The Caltech-UCSD Birds-200-2011 Dataset. Technical Report. CNS-TR-2011-001, California Institute of Technology (2011)
46. Karpathy, A., Fei-Fei, L.: Deep visual-semantic alignments for generating image descriptions. In: Proceedings of the IEEE Conference on Computer Vision and Pattern Recognition, pp. 3128–3137 (2015)
47. Lin, T.-Y., et al.: Microsoft COCO: common objects in context. In: Fleet, D., Pajdla, T., Schiele, B., Tuytelaars, T. (eds.) ECCV 2014. LNCS, vol. 8693, pp. 740–755. Springer, Cham (2014). https://doi.org/10.1007/978-3-319-10602-1_48

48. Young, P., Lai, A., Hodosh, M., Hockenmaier, J.: From image descriptions to visual denotations: New similarity metrics for semantic inference over event descriptions. Trans. Assoc. Comput. Linguist. **2**, 67–78 (2014)
49. Thapliyal, A.V., Pont-Tuset, J., Chen, X., Soricut, R.: Crossmodal-3600: a massively multilingual multimodal evaluation dataset. arXiv preprint arXiv:2205.12522 (2022)
50. Consortium, T.U.: Uniprot: the universal protein knowledgebase in 2025. Nucleic Acids Res. **53**(D1), D609–D617 (2024). https://doi.org/10.1093/nar/gkae1010
51. Chen, Y., Kuang, J., Cheng, D., Zheng, J., Gao, M., Zhou, A.: Agrikg: an agricultural knowledge graph and its applications. In: Li, G., Yang, J., Gama, J., Natwichai, J., Tong, Y. (eds.) Database Systems for Advanced Applications, pp. 533–537. Springer, Cham (2019)
52. Xu, H., et al.: Altogether: image captioning via re-aligning alt-text. In: Conference on Empirical Methods in Natural Language Processing (2024)

Unlocking In-Context Learning for Natural Datasets Beyond Language Modelling

Jelena Bratulić[1]([⊠]), Sudhanshu Mittal[1], David T. Hoffmann[1], Samuel Böhm[2], Robin Tibor Schirrmeister[3], Tonio Ball[2], Christian Rupprecht[4], and Thomas Brox[1]

[1] Computer Vision Group, University of Freiburg, Freiburg im Breisgau, Germany
`bratulic@cs.uni-freiburg.de`
[2] Neuromedical A.I. Lab, Medical Center – University of Freiburg, Freiburg im Breisgau, Germany
[3] Medical Physics, Medical Center – University of Freiburg, Freiburg im Breisgau, Germany
[4] Visual Geometry Group, University of Oxford, Oxford, UK

Abstract. Large Language Models (LLMs) exhibit In-Context Learning (ICL), which enables the model to perform new tasks conditioning only on the examples provided in the context without updating the model's weights. While ICL offers fast adaptation across natural language tasks and domains, its emergence is less straightforward for modalities beyond text. In this work, we systematically uncover properties present in LLMs that support the emergence of ICL for autoregressive models and various modalities by promoting the learning of the needed mechanisms for ICL. We identify exact token repetitions in the training data sequences as an important factor for ICL. Such repetitions further improve stability and reduce transiency in ICL performance. Moreover, we emphasise the significance of training task difficulty for the emergence of ICL. Finally, by applying our novel insights on ICL emergence, we unlock ICL capabilities for various visual datasets and a more challenging EEG classification task. Code is available at https://github.com/jelenab98/unlocking_icl.

Keywords: In-Context Learning · Training dynamics · Generalization · EEG · Image classification

1 Introduction

In-context learning (ICL) is a notable emerging feature observed primarily in transformer models, such as Large Language Models (LLMs) [9,43]. ICL presents the ability to gather information to solve tasks that were not seen during training, such as looking up class labels or learning an algorithm (mapping rule), by solely

---

Supplementary Information The online version contains supplementary material available at https://doi.org/10.1007/978-3-032-12840-9_20.

M. Keuper and F. Locatello (Eds.): DAGM GCPR 2025, LNCS 16125, pp. 303–319, 2026.
https://doi.org/10.1007/978-3-032-12840-9_20

conditioning on the examples provided in the context. To achieve this, no weight updates or fine-tuning is required; instead, examples are used to define a task within the context during inference. ICL contrasts with the "classical" in-weight learning (IWL), where the knowledge required for inference tasks is embedded within the model weights during training. The performance and generalization of the IWL depend on the pretraining task, and it is less flexible, as it does not allow for fast adaptation to new tasks without weight updates via gradient descent.

In-context learning was first described as few-shot learning in LLMs [9, 43]. Given its rapid adaptation capabilities, it has become a standard way for humans to interact with language models for everyday use and has found various applications in different domains [1, 34, 36, 39, 44]. Furthermore, ICL has been proven helpful for vision-language models (VLMs) [4, 27, 53], and even for tabular data [22, 23] as it enables fast online adaptation, online algorithm learning, adaptation to novel datasets and novel label mappings [3, 5, 19, 23]. Overall, ICL promises to be a fast and reliable method for new tasks with limited training data. For instance, applications that require few-shot adaptation to novel users or novel sensor/input data sets, like EEG-based brain-computer interfaces, could greatly benefit from high-quality adaptation methods that do not rely on retraining or fine-tuning the model.

Despite its promising capabilities, the emergence of ICL within models is non-trivial; it only emerges under specific training conditions. For instance, training on natural language often elicits strong ICL performance. Chan et al. [10] attribute this to particular data distributional properties inherent to natural language, namely 1) burstiness: an increased likelihood to observe a token again, after it was seen recently, and 2) skewness: a sharply declining distribution over token frequencies with a long tail data distribution. Chan et al. further demonstrate the effectiveness of these training properties on Omniglot [26], resulting in the emergence of ICL. However, as we show here, this does not generalize to more complex vision datasets like CIFAR [8], Caltech-101 [18] and DTD [12], nor does it transfer to other modalities such as EEG. Thus, we ask ourselves: **What do we need to unlock ICL for more general and arguably noisy datasets and modalities?**

Answering this question requires a deeper understanding of ICL; specifically, we need to understand what a model needs to learn for ICL. In general, ICL requires: 1) a knowledge aggregation function, which extracts algorithms, rules or information from the context and aggregates this knowledge in specific tokens of the context and 2) a look-up mechanism that allows retrieving this aggregated information that is relevant to the current last token in a sequence (the so-called query) [37, 46, 51]. Different ICL tasks will have slight differences in these two functions. In our classification setup, shown on Fig. 1A, where the sequence contains paired signal-label tokens, the aggregation function gathers information from the previous signal token into the corresponding label token, forming a previous-token head, and the lookup mechanism is a simple similarity function that identifies similar tokens, relevant to the query signal.

Learning from a previous token-attending head does not contribute to ICL unless the similarity (look-up) mechanism is also learned, as there is no learn-

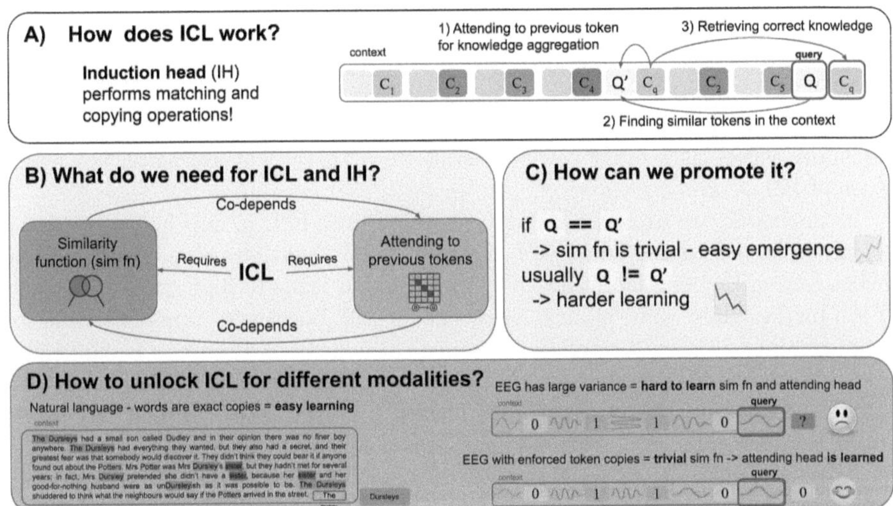

Fig. 1. A) ICL requires two operations: a similarity function and a head that attends to the previous token for knowledge aggregation; together, they present an induction head. B) A similarity function needs to be established for the previous-token heads to form. Still, the similarity function has no purpose if it can not be associated with relevant knowledge. C) The formation of a previous-token head should be promoted by simplifying the similarity function – by including exact token copies in the sequence. D) Enforcing exact copies in the sequences enables ICL for noisy and complex data beyond text, such as images and EEG.

ing signal from the loss. Conversely, learning the look-up function (similarity function) between query and similar tokens is not helpful unless useful information has already been aggregated in those tokens. In essence, the learning of each component is interdependent: the similarity function requires that the previous token head has already been learned and learning the previous token head requires the similarity function to be learned (see Fig. 1B).

These mechanistic insights compel us to investigate why ICL succeeds on language tasks, and Omniglot [10] but fails to generalize effectively to broader datasets and domains. We believe that the answers lie in the learning interplay of the two components: 1) We show in the supplementary material that language naturally contains many exact copies of tokens and n-grams as well as synonyms in a continuous sequence of tokens. Moreover, prior work has shown that synonyms tend to be clustered or represented closely [13, 17, 30, 35, 41, 49, 56]. We hypothesise that this simplifies the learning of the similarity function, as the required function is close to the identity and, by doing so, it breaks the interdependence between the aggregation and similarity components necessary for ICL to emerge. Thus, we argue that introducing exact token repetitions into training sequences – when they are not naturally present – can facilitate the learning of ICL (see Fig. 1CD). We further suggest that 2) the relative difficulty (and expected accuracy) of the ICL and the IWL solution influence whether the model prioritizes ICL or not. When the IWL task is overly simple, the model may exhibit a simplicity bias, prioritising IWL learning and bypassing in-context learning. We suspect this phenomenon extends to LLMs as well, where language modelling serves as a fairly complex IWL task, thereby encouraging the emergence of ICL.

In this work, we examine the details of learning ICL in depth, investigating the circumstances under which ICL emerges. 1) We find that using exact copies of tokens during training facilitates ICL learning and leads to higher ICL accuracy. 2) We further show that, against prior beliefs [10], burstiness is not essential for the emergence of ICL. A single exact token copy in the context can be sufficient. 3) We present evidence that exact token copies simplify the ICL learning task by reducing the complexity of the similarity function to be learned, giving an initial boost to the ICL learning mechanisms. 4) We further show that ICL vs. IWL task difficulty is a significant driver of ICL emergence, i.e. if, the IWL task is difficult and complex, the model is more likely to learn ICL. 5) Finally, we demonstrate that our novel insight unlocks ICL for multiple standard vision datasets and even enables ICL for noisy continuous data, such as EEG, where ICL allows few-shot transfer to novel datasets.

2   Related Work

In-Context Learning (ICL). In-context learning, initially observed as an emerging ability in LLMs [19], enables fast adaptation to various new tasks without gradient updates [4,6,7,23,61,63]. Plenty of research has been dedicated to understanding how to obtain the best ICL performance by analyzing the importance of pretraining data [10,20,21,28,31,36,59], demonstration selection and prompt design [47,54,58,60,61] or framing ICL as in-context vectors [24,32,40]. On the other hand, some works [2,14,57] provided insights into the ICL working mechanisms by studying ICL on a simple regression task, showing how transformers act as meta-optimisers performing gradient descent.

Numerous works indicate that the training data distribution plays a role in the emergence of ICL, where challenging examples and long-tail tokens, and a large number of rarely occurring classes have been demonstrated to promote ICL [10,21], while Razeghi et al. [45] found a correlation between the input data term frequency and the ICL performance. Furthermore, Chan et al. [10] demonstrate how certain data distributional properties, such as skewed token distribution and burstiness, benefit the ICL in a small synthetic scenario, while Singh et al. [50] subsequently showed that the ICL in this setup can become transient, highlighting the conflict between the ICL and IWL circuits. Similarly, Chen et al. [11] argued that parallel structures, which follow similar semantic or syntactic templates in the pretraining textual data facilitate ICL in language models. Our work builds upon previous studies on the importance of data distributional properties [10,50] and provides additional insights into unlocking ICL for various modalities and complex data.

Understanding ICL Mechanisms. Mechanistic studies on the emergence of ICL have identified a specialized attention pattern, i.e. an induction head, that conducts matching and copying operations as a key mechanism for ICL [37]. Recent works have been studying the formation of the induction heads and their role for ICL in a simplistic scenario [16,46,51], where Reddy [46] demonstrates with a simple two-parameter model that ICL is driven by the formation of an induction head, which emerges due to nested non-linearities in a multi-layer attention network. Our work builds on this interpretability framework to trace the dynamics of the induction heads during training. We explain how certain data distributional properties influence the formation of induction heads and the performance of ICL.

Generalization in EEG for Motor Imagery. Due to individual variability, cross-dataset generalization in EEG-based motor imagery (MI), although highly desirable, remains a challenge. While zero-shot EEG methods are increasing, they typically perform multi-modal alignment with EEG and enable classification to unseen classes from the same datasets only [29,33,52]. For MI-decoding, pre-trained EEG transformer models show promise but lack zero-shot capabilities [25,38]. To our knowledge, only [15] have explored zero-shot learning for MI-EEG using outlier detection for base and novel classes. Our work demonstrates how enabling ICL for EEG provides a promising new direction for cross-dataset EEG generalization without any fine-tuning.

3   Experimental Setup

We investigate how ICL emerges by training a causal GPT-2 model [43] on sequences of image-label pairs from standard few-shot learning datasets: Omniglot [26], CIFAR-100 [8], Caltech-101 [18], and DTD [12].

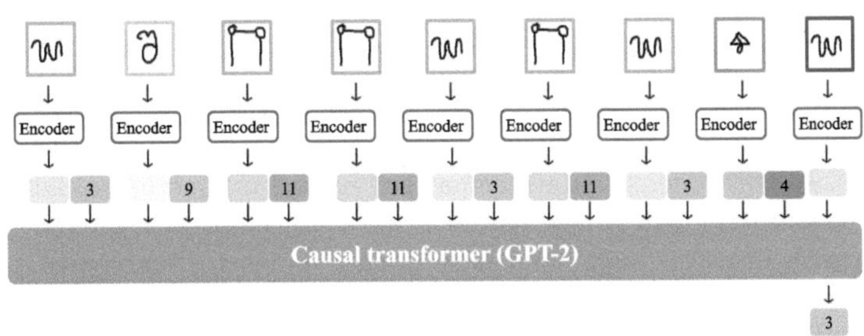

Fig. 2. We train GPT-2 as a next-token prediction from scratch with image-label pairs forming a sequence with control of the training sequence distribution.

The autoregressive model in this work is trained with a sequence length of $2L + 1$ with L image-label pairs in the context followed by a query image, as shown in Fig. 2. The in-weight learning objective is to predict the label of the last image, which is the $(2L + 1)$-th token, given a sequence of L interleaved image-label pairs. Each image-label pair is converted into token embeddings separately. The model is trained to maximize the likelihood of the next token, with the loss applied to the final query output, thus using last-token prediction as the IWL training objective.

Training Sequences. We employ a mixture of (1) **standard sequences**, in which sample-label pairs are uniform randomly selected from the training dataset without any repetitions in the sequence, and (2) **in-context (bursty) sequences**, where the query image-label information is enforced to be present in the sequence by using a pair similar to the query image-label pair. Using in-context sequences, the model can solve the task without relying solely on the model weights. The proportion of each sequence type in the total amount of training sequences is treated as a hyper-parameter. Following the setup from [10] we use 10% of standard and 90% of in-context sequences.

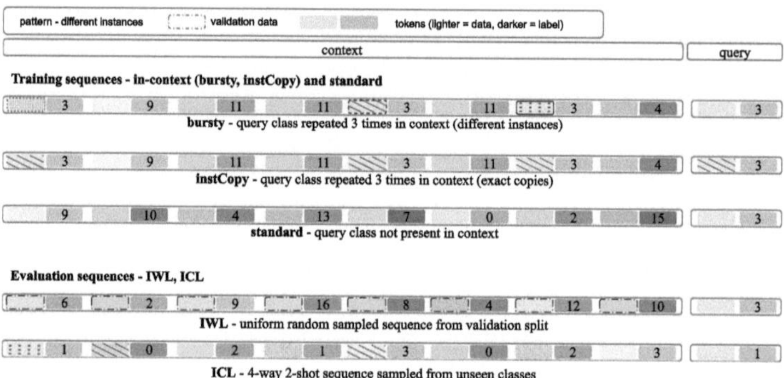

Fig. 3. Different training and evaluation sequences with the main difference being the number of repetitions and the use of identical copies in the context.

We illustrate the difference between the sequences leveraged in our experimental setup on Fig. 3. We employ a sequence of length $L = 8$ with eight image-label pairs. In this case, standard sequences have 8 unique image-label pairs in the context, and the 9th image comes from a 9th class. For bursty sequences, we distinguish between high burstiness in the sequence (referred to as **bursty sequence**) with three instances from the query class in the sequence and low burstiness (referred to as **bursty (low) sequence**) with one example from the query class in the sequence. We further introduce bursty sequence **instCopy**, which follows the same logic as bursty sequence, but instead of having three instances from the query class in the sequence, it has the same example as the query image repeated (copy-pasted) three times in the sequence (see the same pattern in query-class instances on Fig. 3). We introduce this type of sequence motivated by the frequent repetitions in natural language.

Evaluation Sequences. During the evaluation, we leverage 2 different types – IWL and ICL evaluation sequences, following a similar evaluation protocol as in [10]. IWL is evaluated for the multi-class classification task on the held-out samples from the training classes. The standard sequences, with an uniformly sampled format, are used for IWL evaluation (see Fig. 3). ICL is evaluated in a few-shot classification setting for 2-way 4-shot and 4-way 2-shot tasks. We present results in the main paper for the more challenging 4-way 2-shot setting, while 2-way 4-shot results are included in the supplementary material. This evaluation is performed on held-out novel classes. The trained classifier output is used for the few-shot evaluation, utilising label mappings from 0–1 or 0–3, to 2-way 4-shot and 4-way 2-shot evaluation, respectively.

Dataset Construction. We conduct our controlled experiments and analysis on the Omniglot dataset [26] and scale to the more realistic visual dataset, often used in few-shot learning evaluation: CIFAR-100 [8], Caltech-101 [18], and DTD texture datasets [12]. Omniglot contains 1623 classes with 20 images each, following previous work [10], we use 1600 classes for training and the remaining 23 as novel classes for ICL evaluation. For CIFAR-100, Caltech-101 and DTD datasets we perform ICL evaluation using 20, 10, and 10 novel classes, respectively. More experimental details are included in the supplementary material.

4 How to Enable ICL?

Prior work has identified specific circuits in transformer models as the working mechanism of ICL – induction heads [37, 46, 51]. The induction head embodies the core concept of in-context learning: examining the context to identify the most similar or relevant token and then retrieving the associated, already aggregated knowledge. ICL require two underlying components to be established: a similarity or look-up function and a head attending to the previous token. These two components are mutually dependent – the similarity function is ineffective without meaningful aggregated information by the previous-token head, and the previous-token cannot be optimized without a similarity mechanism to retrieve and apply the stored information.

4.1 Why Is ICL Learned and Non-Transient on Text but Not on Visual Data?

The presence of ICL capabilities in LLMs is well established. However, prior work has struggled to obtain stable ICL in other domains, such as vision. Chen et al. [10] demonstrated that burstiness in the training sequences and skewness in data – both inherently present in natural language – show the emergence of ICL in simple visual tasks using the Omniglot dataset [26]. However, despite these changes, the vision model still suffers from diminished IWL performance along with a decline in ICL performance as training progresses.

Besides burstiness and skewness, we argue that natural language typically contains many exact token copies and n-grams (as shown in the supplementary Material), which, we believe, is an important factor for stable and non-transient

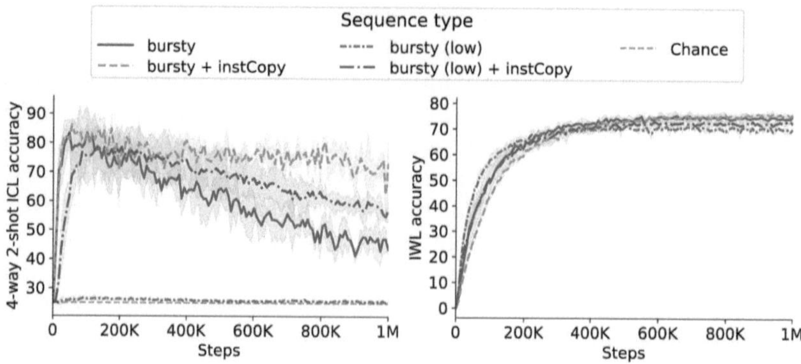

Fig. 4. Exact copies in the context (instCopy) promote ICL performance and reduce transiency. Only a single copy ensures ICL emergence (bursty (low) case).

ICL in LLMs. We train the model conforming to the bursty sequences introduced by Chan et al. [10] and propose a new type of bursty sequence with exact instance copies in the context (instCopy) to test this hypothesis. The difference between the sequences is illustrated and explained in Fig. 3.

From Fig. 4, we observe that including bursty sequences in the training data indeed leads to the emergence of the ICL, which supports previous works [10,50,51]. However, the model achieves strong and more stable (less transient) ICL performance while using exact copies in the bursty sequences (instCopy). Furthermore, we can see that high burstiness is not essential for ICL – a single exact copy in the context (bursty (low) + instCopy) is sufficient to obtain ICL. Finally, we observe that applying exact copies in the context does not harm the IWL performance of the model, and at the same time, it encourages the emergence of ICL. **This confirms that exact copies are a stronger driving factor for ICL, even surpassing the burstiness, as previously reported** [10].

4.2   Why Do Exact Copies Help?

In Fig. 4, we show that exact copies facilitate strong and stable ICL performance. We argue that this is due to the simplified similarity function, which breaks its interdependence with previous-token head learning and ensures that the model prioritizes the formation of the previous-token head.

To confirm this argument, we compare the QK attention scores of the model trained with bursty sequences and the model trained with combined burstiness and exact copies (instCopy) as in-context sequences. We calculate the average attention score on the diagonal with an offset of 1, as this pattern represents the previous-token head. In the supplementary material, we provide additional information about the attention-based metrics, similar to those proposed in [46], used for tracking and explaining the emergence of ICL.

During training, we observe higher scores for tokens corresponding to the query label and formation of previous-token heads only for the model with inst-

Copy sequences. In Fig. 5 (top), we trace the formation of previous-token heads during training by computing the averaged QK values off the diagonal (expected positions for previous-token head) over the training process. The previous token heads indicate aggregation of knowledge from the image to the label token. Since the similarity function is now trivial, the model learns to attend query to previous tokens and successfully perform the needed ICL operations.

We observe the same patterns during inference for 2-way 4-shot classification on novel classes, as illustrated in Fig. 5 (bottom). We observe ICL performance only for the model trained with bursty sequences and exact copies (bursty + instCopy). For the same model, we observe more attention between similar tokens in the sequence and a visible previous-token head. This confirms that **including exact copies in the context indeed simplifies the learning of the similarity function and promotes the formation of a previous-token head, which is then utilised during inference to make a correct ICL prediction.**

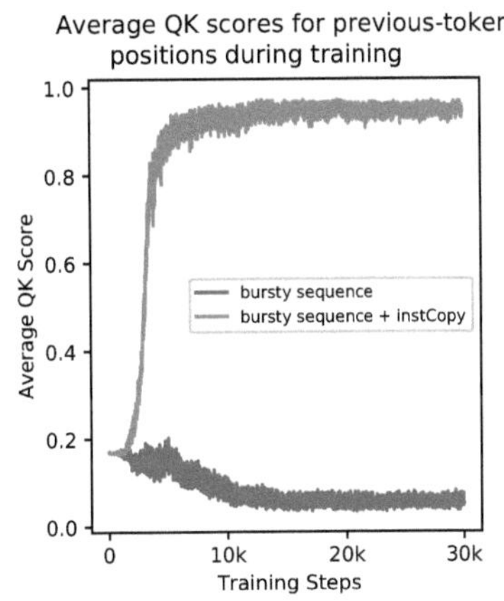

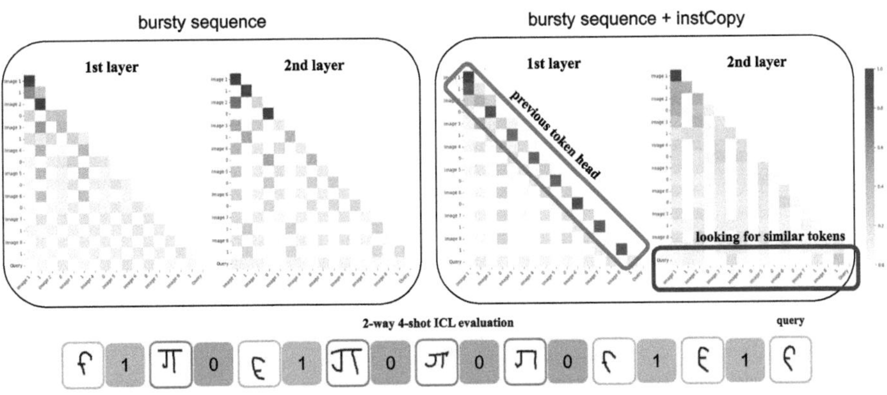

Fig. 5. Top: Average QK scores over the previous-token head positions during training for models trained with burstiness and with exact copies (bursty + instCopy). High attention scores for instCopy sequences confirm the formation of a previous-token head. **Bottom:** QK attention space during inference of a 2-way 4-shot sequence (classes 0 and 1). We observe a clear induction head and ICL emergence during inference only for the model trained with burstiness and exact copies (bursty + InstCopy). Attention patterns in the QK space reveal a previous-token head in layer one (diagonal with offset 1) and a query token attending to the most similar label tokens in layer two.

4.3   What Unlocks ICL for Various Visual Datasets?

Previously, we confirmed that bursty sequences (without exact copies) unlock in-context learning on vision datasets like Omniglot. However, we find that the same setup fails to obtain any ICL for more complex vision datasets like DTD [12], CIFAR-100 [8], and Caltech-101 [18], as shown in Fig. 6.

We hypothesize that burstiness alone does not provide a sufficient signal to learn the similarity function, which is also much harder for complex images. Here, we include exact instance copies (instCopy) in the bursty sequences. We observe that **instCopy enables strong ICL performance for all three visual datasets**, as shown in Fig. 6. We also observe that the IWL performance remains largely unaffected.

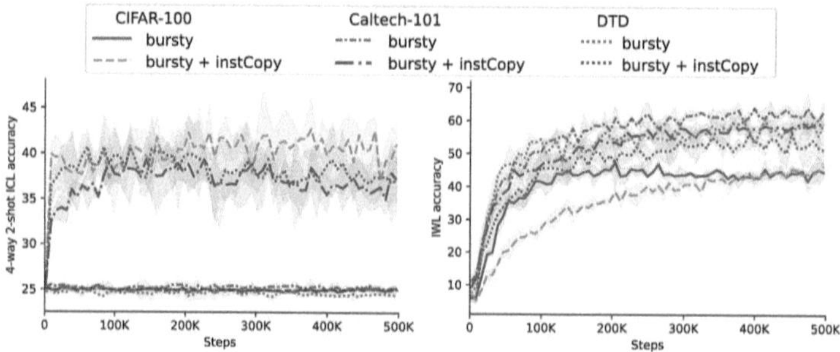

Fig. 6. Only when employing exact copies in the context (bursty + instCopy), we ensure ICL emergence on the image classification datasets CIFAR-100, Caltech-101 and DTD.

4.4   Does in-Weight Learning (IWL) Task Influence ICL?

Language modelling is a significantly harder task than Omniglot classification, yet we naturally observe strong ICL performance in LLMs, but not in Omniglot. Does the IWL task influence ICL? If yes, then how?

The emergence of ICL requires the formation of induction heads. However, when the IWL task is overly simple, the model can exhibit simplicity bias and prioritizes IWL learning over learning of induction heads. Even highly bursty in-context sequences may fail to enable ICL in such cases. Following this, we argue that an in-weight task must have a minimum level of complexity to encourage the emergence of ICL.

To test this hypothesis, we make IWL tasks more challenging in two ways – increasing the number of classes and adding label noise by label swapping. Please see the supplementary material, where we demonstrate two more ways.

Number of Training Classes vs. ICL. We create IWL tasks on Omniglot dataset with an increasing number of classes varying from 200 to 1600 classes.

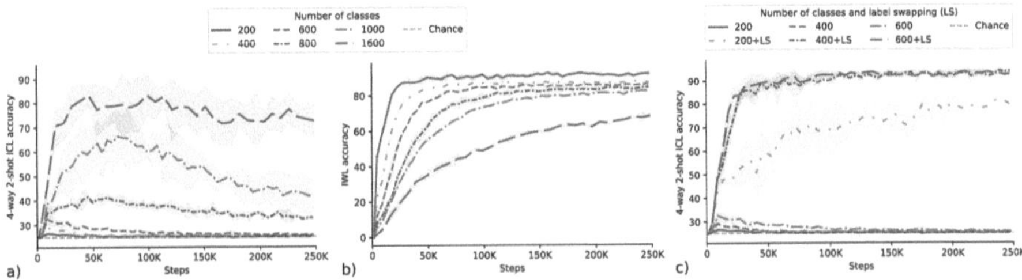

Fig. 7. When increasing the number of classes monotonically (a, b) or applying label swapping (c), ICL performance improves as the IWL objective gets harder.

Using the training setup with bursty in-context sequences (without instCopy), we evaluate ICL and IWL performance. In Fig. 7ab, we observe that IWL converges more slowly as the number of classes increases, indicating that IWL task becomes more challenging with a larger class set. In contrast, ICL performance improves when the number of classes increase. This trend suggests a competition between IWL and ICL circuits in the early phase of training. If the IWL task is too simple, it may fulfil the IWL objective without learning the ICL mechanism. Prior work [10, 46] indicate similar findings. However, they attribute this improvement to the presence of many rarely occurring classes, which can be interpreted as another way to make the IWL task harder. This shows that **increasing the number of classes makes IWL harder and improves ICL**.

Label Noise vs. ICL. Here, we create different training setups with label noise using Omniglot [26]. We perform random label swapping, where labels of the query items are randomly assigned to another training class in 20% of all sequences. For the case of a bursty sequence, we change the label mappings to all repetitions in sequences belonging to the query class. We train models with 200, 400, and 600 classes, where no ICL was observed without noise, shown in Fig. 7ab, possibly due to the overly simple IWL. In Fig. 7c, we observe that label swapping significantly improves ICL performance while for IWL, we observe similar trend of slower convergence as in Fig. 7b (additional results available in the supplementary material). Label swapping makes the IWL task challenging due to the introduced label noise in the standard sequences. In contrast, label swapping promotes in-context mechanisms in bursty sequences since the model cannot rely on in-weight class embeddings to minimize the loss. We observe strong ICL performance even for the simple IWL case of 200 classes with added label swapping. This further confirms that **hard IWL task with label noise via label swapping leads to ICL**.

5 Enabling ICL for EEG Classification

ICL ensures fast adaptation to new tasks, algorithms, and unseen scenarios – a desirable feature for many applications. Enabling ICL can be challenging for real-world datasets, which are often noisy or exhibit significant variance between instances – a common problem in EEG data. On the other hand, EEG tasks would greatly benefit from ICL ability, as it would enable fast adaptation to novel datasets and setups without the need for retraining, which is currently not the case [15,38]. Thus, we aim to enable ICL for EEG data, a modality more challenging and noisy than text or images.

We modify our initial setup from image classification to EEG classification (experimental details in the supplementary material) and attempt to enable ICL by relying solely on burstiness following [10]. However, similar to image classification results in Sect. 4.3 – we observe no ICL emergence. This suggests that enabling ICL for EEG classification requires further interventions to help the model overcome the learning of the similarity function and form the previous-token head, inline with the insights we have provided in Sect. 4.

Enabling ICL for EEG. We build on our insights from Sect. 4.2 and Sect. 4.3 about the importance of the similarity function and previous-token head for ICL. Given the high noise and variability in EEG data, we posit that using exact copies can help the model to initially bypass the complex similarity function and more effectively learn the previous-token head. We further investigate the relationship between the difficulty of IWL task and ICL emergence. Our EEG setup doesn't allow us many base classes for IWL task, therefore, we only employ label swapping to make IWL task harder to promote ICL. Details about the training setup and sequence construction are provided in the supplementary material.

Results. In Table 1, we present the results for ICL performance on three novel datasets: BNCI [55], HGD [48], and Zhou [62] while using a mixture of datasets for training (details provided in the supplementary material). We compare three models: 1) a baseline bursty model trained with a combination of bursty in-context and standard sequences only, 2) a model with burstiness and label swapping method, and finally, 3) a model employing burstiness with exact copies and label swapping.

Table 1. ICL generalization results across different novel datasets with random chance of 33%. We observe the best ICL emergence when exact copies are present in the context (instCopy), and label swapping has made the IWL task harder.

burstiness	label swapping	instCopy	BNCI [55]	HGD [48]	Zhou [62]
✓			33.49	33.24	33.82
✓	✓		35.15	34.75	38.82
✓	✓	✓	**37.56**	**39.65**	**47.66**

Consistent with the image classification results, we observe no ICL performance when using only a combination of bursty in-context and standard sequences. Utilizing burstiness with label swapping yields little to no ICL. However, **ICL reliably emerges for EEG data when both bursty sequences**

with exact token copies and label swapping are applied, as this provides a balance that supports both ICL and IWL learning. This further supports our insights into the training dynamics for ICL emergence; they not only apply to diverse image datasets but also in more real-world domains such as EEG.

6 Discussion

Key Insights. In this work, we demonstrate how to unlock ICL for various modalities beyond text, providing novel insights into the training dynamics of ICL. Specifically, we demonstrate that ICL can be learned more easily by breaking the interdependence between the two operations necessary for ICL: a similarity function that matches the relevant tokens with the query and a previous-token head for knowledge aggregation.

We confirm earlier works [10, 46, 50] on the importance of data distributional properties coming from natural language for ICL emergence. However, we find that using exact token copies during training facilitates stronger in-context learning, leading to higher accuracy and more stable results. We further show that, against prior beliefs [10], burstiness is not essential for the emergence of ICL – a single token copy in the context can be sufficient for ICL emergence. We provide an explanation and evidence of why exact token copies could facilitate ICL emergence: they simplify the similarity function to be learned, breaking the interdependence of ICL learning mechanisms and allowing the formation of previous-token heads.

We further identify another strong driver for ICL emergence – the relationship between ICL and IWL task difficulty. When the IWL task is more challenging, the model is more likely to rely on context and learn ICL. Finally, we confirm our novel insights by demonstrating that exact token copies and increased task difficulty unlock ICL performance across various visual datasets, where previous findings failed to do so [10]. We even enable ICL on much more complex and noisy continuous data, such as EEG, where ICL now, for the first time, allows few-shot transfer to novel datasets.

Limitations and Future Work. ICL performance exhibits high variance when trained with simple IWL tasks, probably due to its sensitivity to training sequences [42]. Furthermore, we observe a significant impact on ICL stability due to certain model design choices. Promising future research directions include improving robustness and expanding our training insights to additional applications beyond image and EEG classification.

Acknowledgments. This research was funded by the German Research Foundation (DFG) 417962828, 539134284 and 499552394 (SFB 1597 - Small Data), and by the German Ministry for Economy and Climate Protection via a decision by the German parliament (19A23014R).

References

1. Agarwal, R., et al.: Many-shot in-context learning. In: The Thirty-eighth Annual Conference on Neural Information Processing Systems (2024). https://openreview.net/forum?id=AB6XpMzvqH
2. Akyürek, E., Schuurmans, D., Andreas, J., Ma, T., Zhou, D.: What learning algorithm is in-context learning? Investigations with linear models. In: The Eleventh International Conference on Learning Representations (2023). https://openreview.net/forum?id=0g0X4H8yN4I
3. Akyürek, E., Wang, B., Kim, Y., Andreas, J.: In-context language learning: architectures and algorithms (2024)
4. Alayrac, J.B., et al.: Flamingo: a visual language model for few-shot learning. In: Advances in Neural Information Processing Systems (2022). https://openreview.net/forum?id=EbMuimAbPbs
5. Bai, Y., Chen, F., Wang, H., Xiong, C., Mei, S.: Transformers as statisticians: provable in-context learning with in-context algorithm selection. In: Advances in Neural Information Processing Systems (2023)
6. Bai, Y., et al.: Sequential modeling enables scalable learning for large vision models. In: 2024 IEEE/CVF Conference on Computer Vision and Pattern Recognition (CVPR) (2024)
7. Bar, A., Gandelsman, Y., Darrell, T., Globerson, A., Efros, A.A.: Visual prompting via image inpainting. In: Advances in Neural Information Processing Systems (2022). https://openreview.net/forum?id=o4uFFg9_TpV
8. Bertinetto, L., Henriques, J.F., Torr, P., Vedaldi, A.: Meta-learning with differentiable closed-form solvers. In: International Conference on Learning Representations (2019). https://openreview.net/forum?id=HyxnZh0ct7
9. Brown, T., et al.: Language models are few-shot learners. In: Advances in Neural Information Processing Systems (2020)
10. Chan, S., et al.: Data distributional properties drive emergent in-context learning in transformers. In: Advances in Neural Information Processing Systems (2022)
11. Chen, Y., Zhao, C., Yu, Z., McKeown, K., He, H.: Parallel structures in pre-training data yield in-context learning (2024). https://arxiv.org/abs/2402.12530
12. Cimpoi, M., Maji, S., Kokkinos, I., Mohamed, S., Vedaldi, A.: Describing textures in the wild. In: Proceedings of the IEEE Conference on Computer Vision and Pattern Recognition (CVPR) (2014)
13. Clark, K., Khandelwal, U., Levy, O., Manning, C.D.: What does BERT look at? An analysis of BERT's attention. In: Proceedings of the 2019 ACL Workshop BlackboxNLP: Analyzing and Interpreting Neural Networks for NLP (2019). https://aclanthology.org/W19-4828/
14. Dai, D., et al.: Why can GPT learn in-context? language models secretly perform gradient descent as meta-optimizers. In: Findings of the Association for Computational Linguistics: ACL 2023 (2023)
15. Duan, L., et al.: Zero-shot learning for EEG classification in motor imagery-based BCI system. IEEE Trans. Neural Syst. Rehabil. Eng. **28**(11), 2411–2419 (2020)
16. Edelman, E., Tsilivis, N., Edelman, B.L., Malach, E., Goel, S.: The evolution of statistical induction heads: in-context learning Markov chains. In: Advances in Neural Information Processing Systems (2024)
17. Elhelo, A., Geva, M.: Inferring functionality of attention heads from their parameters (2025). https://arxiv.org/abs/2412.11965

18. Fei-Fei, L., Fergus, R., Perona, P.: Learning generative visual models from few training examples: an incremental Bayesian approach tested on 101 object categories. In: 2004 Conference on Computer Vision and Pattern Recognition Workshop (2004)
19. Garg, S., Tsipras, D., Liang, P.S., Valiant, G.: What can transformers learn in-context? A case study of simple function classes. In: Advances in Neural Information Processing Systems (2022)
20. Gu, Y., Dong, L., Wei, F., Huang, M.: Pre-training to learn in context (2023). https://arxiv.org/abs/2305.09137
21. Han, X., Simig, D., Mihaylov, T., Tsvetkov, Y., Celikyilmaz, A., Wang, T.: Understanding in-context learning via supportive pretraining data. In: Proceedings of the 61st Annual Meeting of the Association for Computational Linguistics (Volume 1: Long Papers) (2023)
22. Hollmann, N., Müller, S., Eggensperger, K., Hutter, F.: Tabpfn: a transformer that solves small tabular classification problems in a second. In: International Conference on Learning Representations 2023 (2023)
23. Hollmann, N., et al.: Accurate predictions on small data with a tabular foundation model. Nature (2025). https://doi.org/10.1038/s41586-024-08328-6. https://www.nature.com/articles/s41586-024-08328-6
24. Huang, B., Mitra, C., Arbelle, A., Karlinsky, L., Darrell, T., Herzig, R.: Multimodal task vectors enable many-shot multimodal in-context learning (2024). https://arxiv.org/abs/2406.15334
25. Jiang, W.B., Zhao, L.M., Lu, B.L.: Large brain model for learning generic representations with tremendous EEG data in BCI. arXiv preprint arXiv:2405.18765 (2024)
26. Lake, B.M., Salakhutdinov, R., Tenenbaum, J.B.: Human-level concept learning through probabilistic program induction. Science **350**(6266), 1332–1338 (2015)
27. Laurençon, H., et al.: Obelics: an open web-scale filtered dataset of interleaved image-text documents (2023). https://arxiv.org/abs/2306.16527
28. Levine, Y., Wies, N., Jannai, D., Navon, D., Hoshen, Y., Shashua, A.: The inductive bias of in-context learning: rethinking pretraining example design. In: International Conference on Learning Representations (2022). https://openreview.net/forum?id=lnEaqbTJIRz
29. Li, L., Wei, B.: A two-stage EEG zero-shot classification algorithm guided by class reconstruction. Available at SSRN 5177120 (2025)
30. Lindsey, J., et al.: On the biology of a large language model. Transformer Circuits Thread (2025). https://transformer-circuits.pub/2025/attribution-graphs/biology.html
31. Liu, J., Shen, D., Zhang, Y., Dolan, B., Carin, L., Chen, W.: What makes good in-context examples for GPT-3? In: Proceedings of Deep Learning Inside Out (DeeLIO 2022): The 3rd Workshop on Knowledge Extraction and Integration for Deep Learning Architectures (2022)
32. Liu, S., Ye, H., Xing, L., Zou, J.: In-context vectors: Making in context learning more effective and controllable through latent space steering (2024). https://arxiv.org/abs/2311.06668
33. Liu, Y., Ma, Y., Zhou, W., Zhu, G., Zheng, N.: Brainclip: bridging brain and visual-linguistic representation via clip for generic natural visual stimulus decoding. arxiv 2023. arXiv preprint arXiv:2302.12971 (2023)
34. Long, Q., Wang, W., Pan, S.: Adapt in contexts: retrieval-augmented domain adaptation via in-context learning. In: Proceedings of the 2023 Conference on Empirical Methods in Natural Language Processing (2023)

35. Mikolov, T., Sutskever, I., Chen, K., Corrado, G.S., Dean, J.: Distributed representations of words and phrases and their compositionality. In: Advances in Neural Information Processing Systems (2013). https://proceedings.neurips.cc/paper_files/paper/2013/file/9aa42b31882ec039965f3c4923ce901b-Paper.pdf
36. Min, S., Lewis, M., Zettlemoyer, L., Hajishirzi, H.: MetaICL: learning to learn in context. In: Proceedings of the 2022 Conference of the North American Chapter of the Association for Computational Linguistics: Human Language Technologies (2022)
37. Olsson, C., et al.: In-context learning and induction heads. Transformer Circuits Thread (2022). https://transformer-circuits.pub/2022/in-context-learning-and-induction-heads/index.html
38. Patil, S., Schirrmeister, R.T., Hutter, F., Ball, T.: Coordconformer: heterogenous EEG datasets decoding using transformers. In: ICML 2024 Workshop on Geometry-Grounded Representation Learning and Generative Modeling (2024)
39. Pawelczyk, M., Neel, S., Lakkaraju, H.: In-context unlearning: Language models as few shot unlearners (2024). https://arxiv.org/abs/2310.07579
40. Peng, Y., Hao, C., Yang, X., Peng, J., Hu, X., Geng, X.: Live: learnable in-context vector for visual question answering (2024). https://arxiv.org/abs/2406.13185
41. Pennington, J., Socher, R., Manning, C.: GloVe: global vectors for word representation. In: Proceedings of the 2014 Conference on Empirical Methods in Natural Language Processing (EMNLP) (2014). https://aclanthology.org/D14-1162/
42. Press, O., Zhang, M., Min, S., Schmidt, L., Smith, N., Lewis, M.: Measuring and narrowing the compositionality gap in language models. In: Findings of the Association for Computational Linguistics: EMNLP 2023 (2023)
43. Radford, A., et al.: Language models are unsupervised multitask learners. OpenAI blog (2019)
44. Ram, O., et al.: In-context retrieval-augmented language models. Trans. Assoc. Comput. Linguist. (2023)
45. Razeghi, Y., Logan, R.L., IV., Gardner, M., Singh, S.: Impact of pretraining term frequencies on few-shot numerical reasoning. In: Findings of the Association for Computational Linguistics: EMNLP 2022 (2022)
46. Reddy, G.: The mechanistic basis of data dependence and abrupt learning in an in-context classification task. In: The Twelfth International Conference on Learning Representations (2024). https://openreview.net/forum?id=aN4Jf6Cx69
47. Rubin, O., Herzig, J., Berant, J.: Learning to retrieve prompts for in-context learning. In: Proceedings of the 2022 Conference of the North American Chapter of the Association for Computational Linguistics: Human Language Technologies (2022)
48. Schirrmeister, R.T., et al.: Deep learning with convolutional neural networks for EEG decoding and visualization. Hum. Brain Mapp. **38**(11), 5391–5420 (2017)
49. Serina, L., Putelli, L., Gerevini, A.E., Serina, I.: Synonyms, antonyms and factual knowledge in bert heads. Future Internet **15**(7) (2023). https://doi.org/10.3390/fi15070230. https://www.mdpi.com/1999-5903/15/7/230
50. Singh, A.K., Chan, S.C., Moskovitz, T., Grant, E., Saxe, A.M., Hill, F.: The transient nature of emergent in-context learning in transformers. In: Thirty-seventh Conference on Neural Information Processing Systems (2023). https://openreview.net/forum?id=Of0GBzow8P
51. Singh, A.K., Moskovitz, T., Hill, F., Chan, S.C., Saxe, A.M.: What needs to go right for an induction head? A mechanistic study of in-context learning circuits and their formation. arXiv preprint arXiv:2404.07129 (2024)
52. Song, Y., Liu, B., Li, X., Shi, N., Wang, Y., Gao, X.: Decoding natural images from EEG for object recognition. arXiv preprint arXiv:2308.13234 (2023)

53. Sun, Q., et al.: Generative multimodal models are in-context learners (2023)
54. Suo, W., Lai, L., Sun, M., Zhang, H., Wang, P., Zhang, Y.: Visual prompt selection for in-context learning segmentation (2024). https://api.semanticscholar.org/CorpusID:271213205
55. Tangermann, M., et al.: Review of the BCI competition IV. Fronti. Neurosci. **6** (2012). https://doi.org/10.3389/fnins.2012.00055. https://www.frontiersin.org/journals/neuroscience/articles/10.3389/fnins.2012.00055
56. Thießen, F., D'Souza, J., Stocker, M.: Probing large language models for scientific synonyms. In: SEMANTICS Workshops (2023). https://api.semanticscholar.org/CorpusID:265068593
57. Von Oswald, J., et al.: Transformers learn in-context by gradient descent. In: International Conference on Machine Learning (2023)
58. Voronov, A., Wolf, L., Ryabinin, M.: Mind your format: towards consistent evaluation of in-context learning improvements. arXiv [cs.CL] (2024)
59. Wies, N., Levine, Y., Shashua, A.: The learnability of in-context learning. In: Advances in Neural Information Processing Systems (2023)
60. Yang, J., Ma, S., Wei, F.: Auto-ICL: in-context learning without human supervision. arXiv preprint arXiv:2311.09263 (2023)
61. Zhang, Y., Zhou, K., Liu, Z.: What makes good examples for visual in-context learning? In: Advances in Neural Information Processing Systems (2023). https://proceedings.neurips.cc/paper_files/paper/2023/file/398ae57ed4fda79d0781c65c926d667b-Paper-Conference.pdf
62. Zhou, B., Wu, X., Lv, Z., Zhang, L., Guo, X.: A fully automated trial selection method for optimization of motor imagery based brain-computer interface. PLOS ONE **11**(9), 1–20 (2016). https://doi.org/10.1371/journal.pone.0162657
63. Zhu, J.Y., Cano, C.G., Bermudez, D.V., Drozdzal, M.: Incoro: in-context learning for robotics control with feedback loops (2024). https://arxiv.org/abs/2402.05188

Investigating Structural Pruning and Recovery Techniques for Compressing Multimodal Large Language Models: An Empirical Study

Yiran Huang[1,2]([envelope]), Lukas Thede[2,3], Massimiliano Mancini[4], Wenjia Xu[5], and Zeynep Akata[1,2]

[1] Technical University of Munich, Munich, Germany
{yiran.huang,zeynep.akata}@tum.de
[2] Helmholtz Munich, Munich Center for Machine Learning, Munich, Germany
Lukas.Thede@t-online.de
[3] University of Tübingen, Tübingen AI Center, Tübingen, Germany
[4] University of Trento, Trento, Italy
massimiliano.mancini@unitn.it
[5] Beijing University of Posts and Telecommunications, Beijing, China
xuwenjia@bupt.edu.cn

Abstract. While Multimodal Large Language Models (MLLMs) demonstrate impressive capabilities, their substantial computational and memory requirements pose significant barriers to practical deployment. Current parameter reduction techniques primarily involve training MLLMs from Small Language Models (SLMs), but these methods offer limited flexibility and remain computationally intensive. To address this gap, we propose to directly compress existing MLLMs through structural pruning combined with efficient recovery training. Specifically, we investigate two structural pruning paradigms—layerwise and widthwise pruning—applied to the language model backbone of MLLMs, alongside supervised finetuning and knowledge distillation. Additionally, we assess the feasibility of conducting recovery training with only a small fraction of the available data. Our results show that widthwise pruning generally maintains better performance in low-resource scenarios with limited computational resources or insufficient finetuning data. As for the recovery training, finetuning only the multimodal projector is sufficient at small compression levels (<20%). Furthermore, a combination of supervised finetuning and hidden-state distillation yields optimal recovery across various pruning levels. Notably, effective recovery can be achieved with as little as 5% of the original training data, while retaining over 95% of original performance. Through empirical study on two representative MLLMs, i.e., LLaVA-v1.5-7B and Bunny-v1.0-3B, this study offers actionable insights for practitioners aiming to compress MLLMs effectively without extensive computation resources or sufficient data.

Keywords: Multimodal LLMs · Model Compression · Pruning

M. Keuper and F. Locatello (Eds.): DAGM GCPR 2025, LNCS 16125, pp. 320–336, 2026.
https://doi.org/10.1007/978-3-032-12840-9_21

1   Introduction

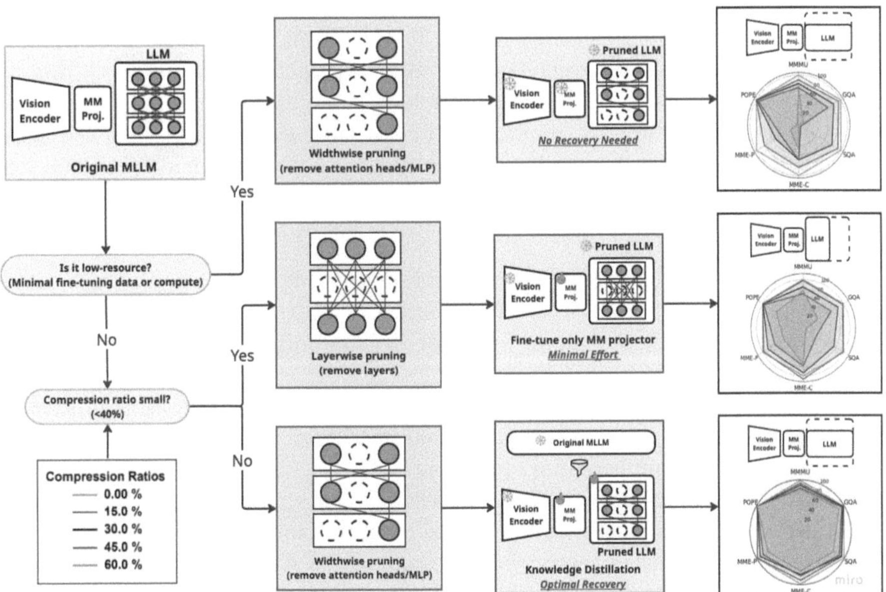

Fig. 1. Compression decision flow for MLLMs. The left panel presents a decision flowchart that guides the choice of pruning and recovery based on resource availability and compression ratio requirements.(i) widthwise pruning only (no recovery) in *extremely low-resource settings*; (ii) layerwise pruning with MM-projector fine-tuning for *moderate compression* ($\leq 40\%$); and (iii) widthwise pruning + knowledge distillation for *high compression* ($\geq 40\%$). The right panel shows spider plots of the retained performance across six multimodal benchmarks at 0–60 % compression, demonstrating each strategy's effectiveness at various compression levels.

State-of-the-art MLLMs [4,5,32] based on Large Language Models (LLMs) [23,45] require substantial resources. For instance, models in the LLaVA [32] family commonly range from 7 billion up to 34 billion parameters, and even compact models like Bunny-v1.0 (3 billion parameters) present significant deployment challenges in resource-constrained environments. Reducing the size of these models without compromising performance is crucial for adapting them to diverse deployment scenarios with varying resource constraints.

Existing approaches to this challenge focus mainly on building MLLMs from Small Language Models (SLMs) [5,17,56]. However, these methods suffer from fundamental limitations: they are constrained by the fixed size of the underlying SLM and require expensive training from scratch to meet target specifications.

We investigate an orthogonal and more flexible approach: structurally compressing the language components in MLLMs. Specifically, we apply two pruning paradigms originally developed for LLMs to the MLLM setting. The first, layerwise pruning, removes entire transformer blocks, leveraging evidence that many layers are redundant [10,41]. The second, widthwise pruning, drops unimportant attention heads and MLP neurons, reflecting observations that only a subset of these sub-components is essential [22,36,38,46]. Crucially, we pair these pruning strategies with various recovery training methods, including supervised finetuning and knowledge distillation on both logits and hidden states. Finally, we vary the pruning ratio and the amount of available data to map out the accuracy/efficiency frontier. Our systematic empirical analysis provides insights into how pruning and recovery techniques impact MLLM performance under various compression levels and data availability scenarios. Specifically, we found:

- Widthwise pruning is more effective in low-resource scenarios, i.e., when computational resources or sufficient finetuning data are unavailable. With recovery training, layerwise pruning is better for small ratios while widthwise pruning usually outperforms it at larger ones ($>40\%$).
- Finetuning only the multimodal projector is sufficient at small compression levels ($<20\%$), as pruning has a minimal impact on the language model itself, but damages the multimodal alignment.
- Supervised finetuning with hidden-state distillation consistently provides the highest performance recovery across all compression ratios.
- Higher pruning ratios require larger amounts of data for effective recovery, while minimal data (5%) can suffice at moderate compression levels($<30\%$).

We highlight our key findings in Fig. 1. Our findings enable practitioners to efficiently compress MLLMs, allowing researchers to build upon empirically supported strategies without undertaking extensive experimentation themselves.

2   Related Work

Pruning. *Unstructured pruning* [9,12,13,27,39,43] removes individual weights or neurons. While such approaches can achieve strong compression rates with minimal accuracy trade-offs, they usually require specialized hardware or software for effective acceleration. In contrast, *structured pruning* [8,28,33,53] eliminates entire groups of parameters to reduce both the model size and its computational overhead. Within LLMs, recent work demonstrates that structured pruning can remove full layers or attention heads with modest performance drop [11,35,48]. Dynamic schemes that adapt the pruning pattern during training have also been explored [6]. Our study builds on these advances, concentrating on structured pruning for the language-model backbone of MLLMs and systematically pairing them with recovery training.

Other Compression Methods. *Quantization* [2,51,55] reduces parameter precision to shrink memory, while *low-rank factorization* [1,20,21,26] approximates large weight matrices with low-rank products. These methods are complementary to pruning while do not directly address architectural redundancy. We focus on pruning to permit fine-grained control over model structure.

Knowledge Distillation (KD) transfers knowledge from a large teacher model to a smaller student model [14,18,42]. For language models KD has been applied to classification [30,42] and generation [49], with extensions to hidden-state mimicry [24,44], attention alignment [47], and reverse-KL objectives [15]. We adopt KD as a recovery mechanism after aggressive pruning and empirically compare its benefits with those of lighter finetuning schemes.

Efficient MLLMs. Current efforts to build lightweight multimodal systems rely on SLMs such as Phi-2 in LLaVA-Phi [57], specialized projector designs in MobileVLM [5], or careful data curation in Bunny-v1.0 [17]. While effective, these approaches inherit the fixed size of the underlying SLM. Our study specifically addresses methods for customizing the size of existing MLLMs through structured pruning and recovery strategies.

3 Methodology

Notation. Given a triplet $\mathbf{X} = \{\mathbf{x}_v, \mathbf{x}_p, \mathbf{x}_r\}$, the objective of an MLLM m_θ, parameterized by $\theta = \{\psi, \phi, \mathbf{W}\}$, is to generate a response $\mathbf{x}_r$ based on an input image $\mathbf{x}_v$ and a text prompt $\mathbf{x}_p$, such that $m_\theta(\mathbf{x}_v, \mathbf{x}_p) = \mathbf{x}_r$. The MLLM typically consists of a vision encoder $g_\psi(\cdot)$, an LLM $f_\phi(\cdot)$, and a multimodal projector $\mathbf{W}$ aligning the two modalities. The prompt $\mathbf{x}_p$ is tokenized into $\mathbf{T}_p$, while the vision encoder processes the image $\mathbf{x}_v$ to extract visual features, which are then converted into language embedding tokens $\mathbf{T}_v$ via the multimodal projector:

$$\mathbf{T}_v = \mathbf{W} \cdot g_\psi(\mathbf{x}_v) \quad \text{and} \quad f_\phi(\mathbf{T}_v \odot \mathbf{T}_p) = \mathbf{x}_r. \tag{1}$$

The concatenated visual tokens $\mathbf{T}_v$ and prompt tokens $\mathbf{T}_p$ are fed into the LLM's M layers, producing hidden states $\{\mathbf{H}_i \in \mathbb{R}^{T \times d}\}_{i=1}^M$, where T is the number of tokens and d is the hidden dimension. Finally, the probabilities $p_{m_\theta}(\mathbf{x}_r | \mathbf{x}_v, \mathbf{x}_p, \tau)$ are computed by passing the final hidden state through the classification head with softmax temperature τ.

3.1 Pruning

Large Transformers are largely over-parameterized, as whole layers can be dropped with little accuracy loss [10,41], and only a few attention heads or MLP units per layer truly matter [22,36,38,46]. Motivated by these findings, we explore two pruning paradigms specifically targeting the language model backbone within MLLMs: layerwise pruning, which removes entire transformer layers, and widthwise pruning, which eliminates the least important components within each layer. To determine which layers or components to prune, we draw a small subset of n samples from the original visual instruct-tuning dataset as the calibration dataset $\mathcal{D} = \{\mathbf{x}_v^j, \mathbf{x}_p^j, \mathbf{x}_r^j\}_{j=1}^n$. The importance of each layer or component is assessed, and those with the lowest importance are pruned.

Layerwise Pruning. To identify the redundant layers, we use the Block Influence (BI) score [37], which quantifies the importance of layer i through the cosine distance between input $\mathbf{H}_i$ and output hidden states $\mathbf{H}_{i+1}$. The key assumption is that layers that cause larger changes in hidden states have a greater influence on model performance. The BI score of layer i is then calculated by

$$\mathrm{BI}_i(\mathcal{D}) = 1 - \mathbb{E}_{\mathbf{X}\sim\mathcal{D},t}\left[\frac{\mathbf{H}_{i,t}^{\mathsf{T}}\mathbf{H}_{i+1,t}}{\|\mathbf{H}_{i,t}\|_2\|\mathbf{H}_{i+1,t}\|_2}\right],\tag{2}$$

where $\mathbf{H}_{i,t}$ represents the tth row of $\mathbf{H}_i$. After calculating the BI scores, the layers are ranked by importance, and those with the lowest scores are pruned.

Widthwise Pruning. To address the widthwise redundancy, we apply dependency-based structural pruning. Following [11] and [35], we build a dependency graph inside each LLM layer. Let N_i and N_j represent two neurons in the layer, where $\mathrm{In}(N_i)$ and $\mathrm{Out}(N_i)$ represent the neurons connected to N_i as inputs and outputs, respectively. Neuron N_j is dependent on on N_i if

$$N_j \in \mathrm{Out}(N_i) \cap \mathrm{Num}_{\mathrm{In}(N_j)} = 1, \text{ or } N_j \in \mathrm{In}(N_i) \cap \mathrm{Num}_{\mathrm{Out}(N_j)} = 1,\tag{3}$$

where $\mathrm{Num}_{\mathrm{In}(N_j)}$ refers to the number of input neurons of N_j and $\mathrm{Num}_{\mathrm{Out}(N_j)}$ is the number of the output neurons of N_j. In words, N_i is the only downstream or upstream node of N_j. If neuron N_i is pruned, all its dependent neurons N_j must also be pruned. This process results in a set of dependency graphs $G = \{w_i^k\}_{i=1}^M$, where M is the number of structures in the graph and w_i^k represents the kth weight parameter within a structure. We assess their importance at the group level since all weights within a graph must be pruned together. Group importance is evaluated by comparing the loss of vision language modeling $\mathcal{L}_{CE}(m_\theta(\mathbf{x}_v, \mathbf{x}_q), \mathbf{x}_r)$ in the calibration data set, with and without weight. To efficiently approximate the importance, we apply a Taylor expansion using gradient information:

$$I_{w_i^k}(\mathbf{X}) = |\mathcal{L}_{CE}(\mathbf{X}, m_\theta) - \mathcal{L}_{CE}(\mathbf{X}, m_\theta^{w_i^k=0})| \approx \left|\frac{\partial\mathcal{L}_{CE}(\mathbf{X}, m_\theta)}{\partial w_i^k}w_i^k\right|.\tag{4}$$

We then prune the graphs with the lowest group importance I_G:

$$I_G(\mathcal{D}) = \mathbb{E}_{\mathbf{X}\sim\mathcal{D}}\left[\sum_i^M \sum_k I_{w_i^k}(\mathbf{X})\right].\tag{5}$$

3.2 Recovery Training

Pruning a large multimodal language model results in performance degradation, affecting both language modeling and cross-modality alignment. To mitigate this, we investigate two recovery training methods: supervised finetuning (Sect. 3.2) and knowledge distillation (Sect. 3.2). We consider the original teacher model m_θ^{T}, the pruned student model $m_{\theta'}^{\mathsf{S}}$, and a recovery dataset $\mathcal{D}$.

Recovery Training with Supervised Finetuning (FT). We first focus on training only the multimodal projector to realign the vision and language spaces. Second, we jointly finetune the projector and the pruned language model while keeping the vision encoder fixed, as finetuning the vision encoder does not improve performance [25]. We use the cross-entropy loss for supervised finetuning:

$$\mathcal{L}_{sft}(m_{\theta'}^{\mathrm{S}}, \mathcal{D}) = \mathbb{E}_{\mathbf{X} \sim \mathcal{D}}[\mathcal{L}_{CE}(m_{\theta'}^{\mathrm{S}}(\mathbf{x}_v, \mathbf{x}_p), \mathbf{x}_r)]. \tag{6}$$

Recovery Training with Knowledge Distillation. KD allows the pruned model to regain lost performance by mimicking the decision-making process of the more capable teacher (original model). We explore two main strategies, logits-based KD and hidden state based KD.

Logits-based KD aligns the output probability distributions of the pruned model with those of the teacher model. The logits-based KD loss is defined as

$$\mathcal{L}_{logits}(m_{\theta'}^{\mathrm{S}}, m_{\theta}^{\mathrm{T}}, \mathcal{D}) = \mathbb{E}_{\mathbf{X} \sim \mathcal{D}} \left[\mathcal{L}_{KD}(p_{m_{\theta}^{\mathrm{T}}}(\mathbf{x}_r | \mathbf{x}_v, \mathbf{x}_p, \tau), p_{m_{\theta'}^{\mathrm{S}}}(\mathbf{x}_r | \mathbf{x}_v, \mathbf{x}_p, \tau)) \right]. \tag{7}$$

We explore two losses to evaluate the differences between the logit distributions of the student p_θ and the teacher $q_{\theta'}$: Kullback–Leibler divergence (KL), denoted as $\mathbf{KL}(p_\theta \| q_{\theta'})$ and its reversed form (RKL), denoted as $\mathbf{KL}(q_{\theta'} \| p_\theta)$. The standard KD objective, minimizing the approximated forward KL, encourages the student distribution to match all modes of the teacher distribution. In contrast, using RKL encourages $q_{\theta'}$ to focus on the major modes of p_θ while assigning low probabilities to its less significant regions. This helps the student model avoid learning unnecessary long-tail variations of the teacher distribution and instead focus on generating more accurate responses [15,19].

Hidden State Matching involves aligning the pruned model's intermediate representations (hidden states) $\mathbf{H}_i^{m_{\theta'}^{\mathrm{S}}}$ with the teacher model's $\mathbf{H}_i^{m_{\theta}^{\mathrm{T}}}$. The corresponding loss for a layer i can be defined as

$$\mathcal{L}_{match}(m_{\theta'}^{\mathrm{S}}, m_{\theta}^{\mathrm{T}}, \mathcal{D}) = \mathbb{E}_{\mathbf{X} \sim \mathcal{D}} \left[\mathcal{L}_{feat}(\mathbf{H}_i^{m_{\theta'}^{\mathrm{S}}}, \mathbf{H}_i^{m_{\theta}^{\mathrm{T}}}) \right], \tag{8}$$

where $\mathcal{L}_{feat}$ refers to a feature matching loss. Both [50] and [40] suggest that applying a feature-based L2 distillation loss improves the student model's performance, particularly for pre-trained vision-language models. Consequently, we employ L2 loss as the feature matching loss $\mathcal{L}_{feat} = \| \cdot - \cdot \|_2^2$. The total loss for recovery training is computed as:

$$\mathcal{L}(m_{\theta}^{\mathrm{S}}, m_{\theta}^{\mathrm{T}}, \mathcal{D}) = \alpha \mathcal{L}_{sft}(m_{\theta'}^{\mathrm{S}}, \mathcal{D}) + \beta \mathcal{L}_{logits}(m_{\theta'}^{\mathrm{S}}, m_{\theta}^{\mathrm{T}}, \mathcal{D}) + \gamma \mathcal{L}_{match}(m_{\theta'}^{\mathrm{S}}, m_{\theta}^{\mathrm{T}}, \mathcal{D})$$

where α, β, and γ are the coefficients that balance three loss components.

4   Experiments

Experimental Setup. We evaluate pruning and recovery methods on both a large-scale MLLM model (LLaVA-v1.5-7B (LLaVA) [31]) and a smaller-scale MLLM model (Bunny-v1.0-3B (Bunny) [17]). For both models, we exclusively use their visual instruction tuning datasets: LLaVA-v1-5-mix665k [31] for LLaVA and Bunny-695K [17] for Bunny. During pruning, we randomly select 10 samples from the training dataset as the calibration dataset to compute the importance. For recovery training, we experiment with various portions of the original dataset (5%, 10%, 20%, and 100%) for recovery. We set the distillation temperature to 2.0 for logits-based distillation and use the final layer representation for hidden state matching. We evaluate the pruned and recovery-trained models on visual question-answering tasks using GQA [22] and SQA-I [34], as well as instruction-following tasks with POPE [29], MME-Cognition, MME-Perception [52], and MMMU [54]. To ensure consistency, we use the lmms-eval suite [3] for all evaluations. For clearer comparisons, we calculate the relative performance as a percentage of the original (uncompressed) model's performance on each benchmark.

Table 1. Pruning results for LLaVA-v1.5-7B and Bunny-v1-3B. Size is the number of total parameters of the model, while the compression ratio (Ratio) indicates the proportion of remaining language model parameters compared to the pre-pruning state. For both models, width-wise pruning results in better performance without finetuning compared to depth-wise pruning.

Method	Size	PruneRatio	MMMU	GQA	SQA	MME-C	MME-P	POPE	AVG	AVG-%
LLaVA-v1.5-7B	7.0B		35.10	61.98	68.67	363.21	1511.33	86.99	62.28	100.00%
Width-wise	6.3B	15%	32.40	59.34	63.21	268.93	1432.47	86.57	57.79	92.79%
	5.5B	30%	31.00	52.59	54.29	253.21	1174.93	86.29	52.43	84.17%
	4.8B	45%	27.60	20.86	12.10	70.00	347.45	45.96	22.11	35.49%
	4.0B	60%	23.30	0.43	0.40	2.14	19.24	3.94	4.88	7.84%
Depth-wise	6.3B	15%	31.80	42.77	55.23	202.14	701.83	86.38	46.09	74.00%
	5.5B	30%	32.70	42.18	59.64	210.71	921.88	78.69	47.61	76.43%
	4.8B	45%	26.90	14.39	3.82	132.86	616.63	51.69	24.04	38.60%
	4.0B	60%	25.80	0.00	0.00	0.00	0.00	0.00	4.30	6.90%
Bunny-v10-3B	3.2B		34.10	54.72	70.70	289.30	1487.71	87.82	59.65	100.00%
Width-wise	2.8B	15%	30.90	51.83	65.64	242.50	1207.85	87.94	54.50	95.48%
	2.5B	30%	28.40	45.65	55.73	199.64	807.95	87.13	47.04	87.57%
	2.0B	45%	25.70	37.92	3.42	200.00	618.25	83.12	34.35	60.66%
	1.6B	60%	24.80	6.12	0.00	141.07	293.23	2.34	10.93	13.52%
Depth-wise	2.8B	15%	33.80	29.42	69.66	271.43	1456.41	87.91	54.59	91.52%
	2.5B	30%	29.00	24.77	28.76	272.86	1273.34	86.50	44.47	74.55%
	2.0B	45%	23.90	16.85	3.47	191.43	867.37	80.09	31.94	53.54%
	1.6B	60%	26.60	0.02	17.15	0.71	55.92	0.02	7.78	13.04%

4.1 The Effect of Pruning on the Model Performance and Resources Usage

Comparison of Pruning Techniques. We detail the complete results in Table 1 and contrast layerwise and widthwise pruning across Bunny and LLaVA in Fig. 2. Without any recovery training (blue curves), widthwise pruning consistently preserves more accuracy, retaining 95% of baseline performance on Bunny and 93% on LLaVA at a modest 15% compression, making it a practical choice when compute or data for recovery are scarce and only light pruning ($<20\%$) is required. As compression deepens, performance for both methods declines sharply. Overall, widthwise pruning better preserves the model's structure and information flow, allowing it to keep performance with minimal adjustments, especially at lower compression ratios. Adding recovery training reshapes the landscape (represented by the green lines). For smaller compression ratios ($<40\%$), layerwise pruning offers a slight advantage, while widthwise pruning delivers better overall performance for larger compression ratios ($>40\%$). This suggests that finetuning plays a crucial role in reconstructing inter-layer connections and reoptimizing layer components.

Takeaway. A widthwise pruned model can often be deployed without recovery training with a small compression ratio ($<20\%$). With recovery training, layerwise pruning shows a slight advantage at compression ratios below 30%, while widthwise pruning performs better at higher compression ratios.

From Compression Ratio to Resource Usage. Table 2 provides an overview of how different compression ratios impact memory usage and FLOPS for both the models compressed via widthwise pruning. Memory consumption refers to the allocated GPU memory, while FLOPS are measured using the Calflops codebase[1] The results demonstrate that higher compression ratios consistently lead to both memory and compute reductions. For example, at a 30% compression ratio, we observe a memory reduction of 25% for Bunny and 28% for LLaVA, with a corresponding decrease in FLOPS of 27% for both models. These reductions continue to scale with larger compression ratios; at a 60% compression ratio, memory usage and FLOPS decrease by 50–60%. We observe similar results for layerwise pruning. This indicates that the compressions directly translate into improvements in memory efficiency and computational cost.

Table 2. Memory requirements (Mem.) and FLOPS for the Bunny and LLaVA models at various compression ratios. The models are pruned widthwise. Memory and compute reduction is significant with higher compression ratios.

Ratio	Bunny		LLaVA	
	Mem. (MiB)	FLOPS (T)	Mem. (MiB)	FLOPS (T)
0%	6,167	4.77	13,546	9.57
15%	5,380	4.14	11,530	8.21
30%	4,597	3.50	9,548	6.89
45%	3,770	2.84	7,470	5.49
60%	2,992	2.20	5,435	4.17

---

[1] Calflops codebase: https://github.com/MrYxJ/calculate-flops.pytorch.

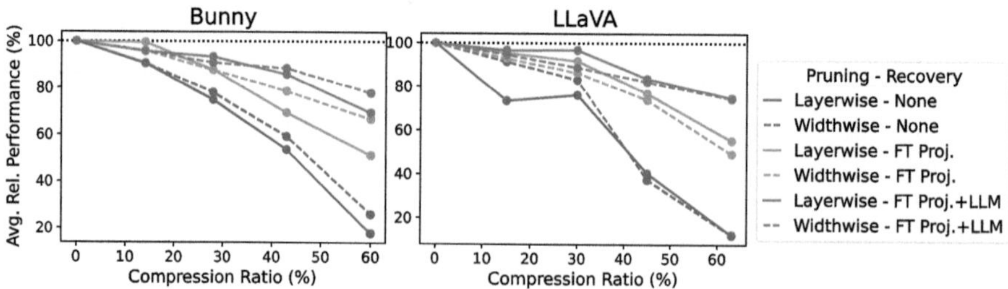

Fig. 2. Comparison of pruning and finetuning strategies on two MLLMs. The plot shows the average relative performance under three scenarios: pruning only, pruning followed by finetuning the projector, and pruning followed by finetuning both the projector and the LLM. For smaller compression ratios (<20%), finetuning only the projector effectively recovers performance. For larger compression ratios, jointly finetuning the projector and the LLM is needed for a better recovery.

4.2   Supervised Finetuning for Performance Recovery

Compressing LLMs can degrade their language modeling capabilities. More critically, the impact of pruning LLM decoders (within MLLMs) on visual understanding and the alignment between vision and language remains largely unexplored. To investigate these effects, we experiment with two approaches: (1) finetuning only the multimodal projector and (2) jointly finetuning both the projector and the LLM. This enables us to pinpoint the source of performance degradation and assess the extent to which each component contributes to the model's overall effectiveness. Following the previous research [25], which shows that training the vision encoder may degrade overall model performance, we keep the vision encoder frozen in both setups. To facilitate fast recovery, we employ the low-rank approximation, LoRA [21], while finetuning the LLM.

Finetuning the Multimodal Projector. As shown in Fig. 2 (orange lines), finetuning the multimodal projector significantly restores performance. At lower compression ratios (<20%), finetuning only the projector achieves results comparable to jointly finetuning the LLM. For both Bunny and LLaVA, finetuning the projector retains at least 95% of the performance at a compression ratio of 15%. As the compression ratio increases, the loss of language modeling ability becomes more pronounced, making projector-only finetuning insufficient to fully recover the model's performance. Nevertheless, even at a compression ratio of 60%, finetuning the multimodal projector can still recover 60 to 80% of the performance by realigning the vision and language inputs. This indicates that pruning specific LLM structures in the MLLM can both impair the language modeling ability and introduce modality misalignment, thereby hindering the model's ability to comprehend visual inputs.

Finetuning Both the Projector and the LLM. While a significant portion of the recovered performance is attributed to realigning the visual and textual inputs, we observe consistent gains from additionally finetuning the pruned

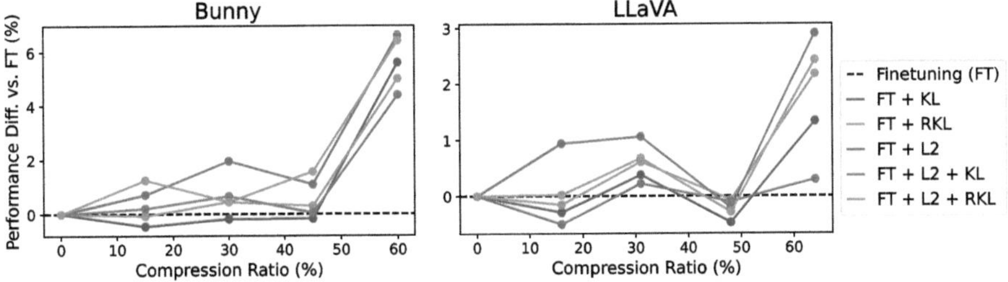

Fig. 3. Comparison of different distillation recovery strategies (KL loss, RKL loss, L2 loss, and their combinations) for Bunny and LlaVA models pruned with widthwise pruning. The plot shows the relative performance improvement of each strategy over standard finetuning across various compression ratios. The results demonstrate that distillation helps recover more performance than finetuning alone, with the L2 loss component consistently leading to the largest performance gains.

LLM (green lines in Fig. 2), especially at higher compression ratios (>40%). This indicates that the pruned model not only suffers from modality misalignment but also experiences a decline in its language modeling capabilities. We can partly restore these lost capabilities by finetuning the LLM. At a compression ratio of 40%, finetuning both the projector and the LLM restores more than 80% of the original model's performance. Even at a compression ratio of 60%, finetuning recovers close to 80% of the model's original performance.

Takeaway. When a small compression ratio of around 15% is required, finetuning the multimodal projector alone is typically sufficient to recover most of the model's performance. For higher compression ratios (>40%), incorporating finetuning of the LLM yields additional performance improvements.

4.3 Knowledge Distillation for Performance Recovery After Pruning

To compare and analyze the effectiveness of FT and KD, we present the recovered results for the layerwise pruned Bunny model. We compare a logit-based approach (RKL) and a hidden state matching strategy (L2), with and without a finetuning loss component in Table 3. At a light 15 % compression, pure distillation already recovers 95 % of the baseline accuracy, with FT alone performing similarly (96.3%). However, as the compression ratio increases, these KD-only variants become unstable: at 60 % compression, L2 degrades to 47.6 % and RKL to just 12.6 %. Crucially, coupling FT with KD not only prevents this collapse but delivers the best results across the board, providing consistent gains of 3 to 23% points.

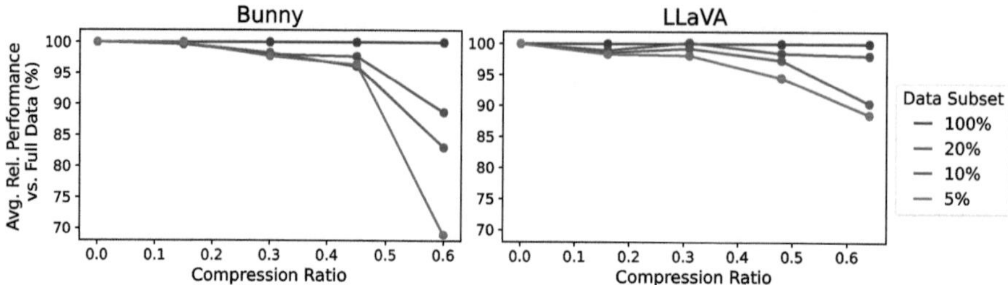

Fig. 4. Comparison of recovery performance using different percentages of training data (100%, 20%, 10%, and 5%) for finetuning and distillation after pruning across Bunny and Llava models. For smaller compression ratios, even a small percentage of the training data (as low as 5%) is sufficient to recover most of the original performance. However, as the compression ratio increases, more training data is required to achieve higher recovery performance.

The pattern underscores a clear message: while KD can partially restore performance after pruning, its reliability declines at high compression; adding FT supplies the hard-label anchor that stabilizes learning, while the soft guidance of distillation offers complementary structural cues, making the FT + KD combination the most dependable strategy across the entire compression spectrum.

Figure 3 compares various distillation strategies based on their relative improvement over finetuning alone when widthwise pruning is applied.

Table 3. Comparison of distillation strategies with and without finetuning for the Bunny model compressed via layerwise pruning. We show the performance ratio between the compressed model and the original model. Finetuning helps stabilize performance and prevents *model collapse*, especially at higher compression ratios.

Ratio	Bunny				
	FT	L2	L2+FT	RKL	RKL+FT
15%	96.30%	95.51%	**99.59%**	96.88%	**98.70%**
30%	94.33%	88.13%	**95.03%**	92.21%	**93.81%**
45%	86.70%	*56.96%*	**90.19%**	82.57%	**88.50%**
60%	69.38%	*47.61%*	**72.62%**	*12.61%*	**69.85%**

Our results indicate that applying the L2 loss to align the hidden states of the student and teacher in the final layer yields the best performance, or at least matches other methods. Unlike logit-based approaches, which require the student to replicate the teacher's output distribution, the L2 loss method enables the student to directly capture the teacher's feature representations, leading to enhanced performance. Additionally, we observe that RKL generally outperforms KL across most compression ratios, a result consistent with the findings of [16].

Takeaway. Knowledge distillation, particularly when combined with finetuning and using L2 loss to map the intermediate states, delivers the most effective performance recovery after pruning across all compression ratios.

4.4   Data Efficient Recovery

Figure 4 shows the models' performance after recovery training with different portions of the original dataset relative to training with the full 100%. Both models undergo widthwise pruning and recovery training, incorporating RKL and L2 loss functions. Remarkably, for compression ratios below 50%, using just 5% of the original data is sufficient to achieve over 95% of the performance compared to using the full dataset. However, as the compression ratio increases, the amount of data required for effective recovery training also grows. For a compression ratio of 60%, the relative performance drops below 90% for LLaVA, and further diminishes to below 70% for Bunny. Nevertheless, using only a small portion of the training data appears to be a valid option, significantly lowering the required time and cost for compressing and finetuning MLLMs.

Takeaway. With a compression ratio smaller than 50%, using just 5% of the dataset is enough to achieve performance comparable to full data training. However, for compression ratios greater than 50%, full data training becomes necessary to recover performance effectively.

4.5 Key Insights for Model Compression

Based on the empirical results from the previous section, we outline the following suggested practices for compressing MLLMs:

- **Widthwise pruning is more effective in low-resource settings**, yielding an efficient model even without the need for recovery training.
- **With recovery training**, layerwise pruning excels for smaller compression ratios (<40%), while widthwise pruning performs better at higher ratios (>40%).
- **For small compression ratios (<20%)**, finetuning just the multi-modal projector is often sufficient to restore performance, with minimal impact from pruning.
- **For recovery training**, combining finetuning with knowledge distillation of the intermediate representations using L2 loss consistently achieves the highest performance across all compression ratios.
- **Data efficiency** can be significantly boosted, requiring only 5% of the original data to match full-data training results, though full datasets are still needed for high compression ratios.

5 Discussion

5.1 How Does Pruning LLM Impact Multi-modal Capability?

Since LLMs comprise the majority of parameters in MLLMs, reducing their size can substantially reduce the overall model's size. However, pruning an LLM presents a dual challenge: it only degrades language modeling capabilities but also disrupts the alignment between modalities, impairing the model's ability to interpret and reason about visual inputs effectively. Our analysis shows that for pruning ratios below 10%, the model retains most of its multimodal functionality. With moderate pruning (up to 15%), modality alignment can still be restored

Table 4. This table compares pruning and quantization applied to LLaVA-v1.5-7b, evaluating their effect on memory usage, average performance across benchmarks, and inference latency. Quantization significantly reduces memory consumption but increases latency, while pruning with recovery maintains a balance between efficiency and performance. Combining both techniques mitigates quantization overhead while preserving compression benefits.

Model	Quantization	Mem (GiB)	Ratio	Avg	Latency (ms)
LLaVA-7B	-	13.5	0%	62.28	105 ± 1.5
LLaVA–7B	✓	7.5	0%	61.85	398 ± 1.3
LLaVA-6B	-	11.6	15%	61.22	95 ± 8.1
LLaVA-6B	✓	6.5	15%	60.82	125 ± 0.9
LLaVA-5B	-	9.5	30%	60.96	80.7 ± 0.6
LLaVA-5B	✓	5.4	30%	59.63	108 ± 5.85

by post-training the multimodal projector. However, beyond this threshold, the degradation of language modeling becomes more pronounced. At higher compression levels, finetuning the projector alone is insufficient to recover performance, making joint training of the LLM necessary to maintain functionality.

5.2 Comparison and Combination with Quantization

Integrating quantization into our framework can further optimize inference time and memory efficiency. In this section, we provide a comparative analysis of structured pruning and quantization, highlighting their complementary strengths. As a representative quantization method, we employ LLM.int8() [7]. As shown in Table 4, LLM.int8() reduces memory usage by 44.5% in the original uncompressed model, while incurring only a minor performance loss of 0.43% points. However, this comes at the cost of a fourfold increase in latency. For LLaVA-6B and LLaVA-5B, combining pruning with quantization offers a well-balanced trade-off between memory efficiency and computational latency.

5.3 Limitation and Future Work

Our experiments demonstrate the effectiveness of structural pruning with recovery training at moderate compression ratios (up to 30%). However, beyond this threshold, performance loss becomes increasingly difficult to recover, suggesting that for applications requiring more aggressive compression, the extreme pruning of a large model is not a viable approach. Due to computational constraints, this work focuses on two pruning techniques applied to three different models. Future work could extend these findings to include a broader range of pruning techniques and models, further refining these strategies.

6   Conclusion

We systematically evaluated two structural pruning schemes - widthwise and layerwise - on LLaVA-7B, Bunny-3B, and InternVL, and paired them with lightweight recovery through supervised finetuning and knowledge distillation. From these experiments, we distilled a decision chart that guides practitioners in choosing the pruning route and recovery budget for different target compression ratios. Our findings provide a concrete path to fit MLLMs within strict memory, compute, or energy budgets without surrendering performance.

Acknowledgements. This work was partially funded by the ERC (853489 - DEXIM) and the Alfried Krupp von Bohlen und Halbach Foundation, which we thank for their generous support. The authors gratefully acknowledge the Gauss Centre for Supercomputing e.V. (www.gauss-centre.eu) for funding this project by providing computing time on the GCS Supercomputer JUWELS at Julich Supercomputing Centre (JSC).

References

1. Ashkboos, S., Croci, M.L., Nascimento, M.G.d., Hoefler, T., Hensman, J.: Slicegpt: compress large language models by deleting rows and columns. arXiv preprint arXiv:2401.15024 (2024)
2. Bai, H., et al.: Binarybert: pushing the limit of bert quantization (2021). https://arxiv.org/abs/2012.15701
3. Bo, L., et al.: Lmms-eval: accelerating the development of large multimoal models (2024). https://github.com/EvolvingLMMs-Lab/lmms-eval
4. Chen, Z., et al.: Internvl: scaling up vision foundation models and aligning for generic visual-linguistic tasks. In: Proceedings of the IEEE/CVF Conference on Computer Vision and Pattern Recognition, pp. 24185–24198 (2024)
5. Chu, X., et al.: Mobilevlm: a fast, reproducible and strong vision language assistant for mobile devices. arXiv preprint arXiv:2312.16886 (2023)
6. Dery, L., Kolawole, S., Kagy, J.F., Smith, V., Neubig, G., Talwalkar, A.: Everybody prune now: structured pruning of LLMs with only forward passes (2024). https://arxiv.org/abs/2402.05406
7. Dettmers, T., Lewis, M., Belkada, Y., Zettlemoyer, L.: Gpt3. int8 (): 8-bit matrix multiplication for transformers at scale. In: Advances in Neural Information Processing Systems, vol. 35, pp. 30318–30332 (2022)
8. Ding, X., Ding, G., Guo, Y., Han, J.: Centripetal SGD for pruning very deep convolutional networks with complicated structure (2019). https://arxiv.org/abs/1904.03837
9. Dong, X., Chen, S., Pan, S.J.: Learning to prune deep neural networks via layerwise optimal brain surgeon (2017). https://arxiv.org/abs/1705.07565
10. Fan, A., Grave, E., Joulin, A.: Reducing transformer depth on demand with structured dropout. arXiv preprint arXiv:1909.11556 (2019)
11. Fang, G., Ma, X., Song, M., Mi, M.B., Wang, X.: Depgraph: towards any structural pruning. In: Proceedings of the IEEE/CVF Conference on Computer Vision and Pattern Recognition, pp. 16091–16101 (2023)

12. Farina, M., Mancini, M., Cunegatti, E., Liu, G., Iacca, G., Ricci, E.: Multiflow: shifting towards task-agnostic vision-language pruning. In: Proceedings of the IEEE/CVF Conference on Computer Vision and Pattern Recognition, pp. 16185–16195 (2024)
13. Frankle, J., Carbin, M.: The lottery ticket hypothesis: finding sparse, trainable neural networks (2019). https://arxiv.org/abs/1803.03635
14. Gou, J., Yu, B., Maybank, S.J., Tao, D.: Knowledge distillation: a survey. Int. J. Comput. Vis. **129**(6), 1789–1819 (2021). https://doi.org/10.1007/s11263-021-01453-z
15. Gu, Y., Dong, L., Wei, F., Huang, M.: Knowledge distillation of large language models. arXiv preprint arXiv:2306.08543 (2023)
16. Gu, Y., Dong, L., Wei, F., Huang, M.: Minillm: knowledge distillation of large language models (2024). https://arxiv.org/abs/2306.08543
17. He, M., et al.: Efficient multimodal learning from data-centric perspective. arXiv preprint arXiv:2402.11530 (2024)
18. Hinton, G., Vinyals, O., Dean, J.: Distilling the knowledge in a neural network (2015). https://arxiv.org/abs/1503.02531
19. Holtzman, A., Buys, J., Du, L., Forbes, M., Choi, Y.: The curious case of neural text degeneration. arXiv preprint arXiv:1904.09751 (2019)
20. Hsu, Y.C., Hua, T., Chang, S., Lou, Q., Shen, Y., Jin, H.: Language model compression with weighted low-rank factorization (2022). https://arxiv.org/abs/2207.00112
21. Hu, E.J., et al.: Lora: low-rank adaptation of large language models (2021). https://arxiv.org/abs/2106.09685
22. Hudson, D.A., Manning, C.D.: GQA: a new dataset for real-world visual reasoning and compositional question answering. In: Proceedings of the IEEE/CVF Conference on Computer Vision and Pattern Recognition, pp. 6700–6709 (2019)
23. Jiang, F.: Identifying and mitigating vulnerabilities in LLM-integrated applications. Master's thesis, University of Washington (2024)
24. Jiao, X., et al.: Tinybert: distilling BERT for natural language understanding (2020). https://arxiv.org/abs/1909.10351
25. Karamcheti, S., Nair, S., Balakrishna, A., Liang, P., Kollar, T., Sadigh, D.: Prismatic vlms: investigating the design space of visually-conditioned language models. arXiv preprint arXiv:2402.07865 (2024)
26. Lan, Z., Chen, M., Goodman, S., Gimpel, K., Sharma, P., Soricut, R.: Albert: a lite bert for self-supervised learning of language representations (2020). https://arxiv.org/abs/1909.11942
27. Lee, N., Ajanthan, T., Gould, S., Torr, P.H.S.: A signal propagation perspective for pruning neural networks at initialization (2020). https://arxiv.org/abs/1906.06307
28. Li, H., Kadav, A., Durdanovic, I., Samet, H., Graf, H.P.: Pruning filters for efficient convnets (2017). https://arxiv.org/abs/1608.08710
29. Li, Y., Du, Y., Zhou, K., Wang, J., Zhao, W.X., Wen, J.R.: Evaluating object hallucination in large vision-language models. arXiv preprint arXiv:2305.10355 (2023)
30. Liang, K.J., et al.: Mixkd: towards efficient distillation of large-scale language models (2021). https://arxiv.org/abs/2011.00593
31. Liu, H., Li, C., Li, Y., Lee, Y.J.: Improved baselines with visual instruction tuning. In: Proceedings of the IEEE/CVF Conference on Computer Vision and Pattern Recognition, pp. 26296–26306 (2024)
32. Liu, H., Li, C., Wu, Q., Lee, Y.J.: Visual instruction tuning (2023). https://arxiv.org/abs/2304.08485

33. Liu, L., et al.: Group fisher pruning for practical network compression (2021). https://arxiv.org/abs/2108.00708
34. Lu, P., et al.: Learn to explain: multimodal reasoning via thought chains for science question answering. Adv. Neural. Inf. Process. Syst. **35**, 2507–2521 (2022)
35. Ma, X., Fang, G., Wang, X.: Llm-pruner: on the structural pruning of large language models. Adv. Neural. Inf. Process. Syst. **36**, 21702–21720 (2023)
36. McCarley, J., Chakravarti, R., Sil, A.: Structured pruning of a bert-based question answering model. arXiv preprint arXiv:1910.06360 (2019)
37. Men, X., et al.: Shortgpt: layers in large language models are more redundant than you expect. arXiv preprint arXiv:2403.03853 (2024)
38. Michel, P., Levy, O., Neubig, G.: Are sixteen heads really better than one? In: Advances in Neural Information Processing Systems, vol. 32 (2019)
39. Park, S., Lee, J., Mo, S., Shin, J.: Lookahead: a far-sighted alternative of magnitude-based pruning (2020). https://arxiv.org/abs/2002.04809
40. Popp, N., Metzen, J.H., Hein, M.: Zero-shot distillation for image encoders: how to make effective use of synthetic data. arXiv preprint arXiv:2404.16637 (2024)
41. Sajjad, H., Dalvi, F., Durrani, N., Nakov, P.: On the effect of dropping layers of pre-trained transformer models. Comput. Speech Lang. **77**, 101429 (2023)
42. Sanh, V., Debut, L., Chaumond, J., Wolf, T.: Distilbert, a distilled version of bert: smaller, faster, cheaper and lighter (2020). https://arxiv.org/abs/1910.01108
43. Sanh, V., Wolf, T., Rush, A.M.: Movement pruning: adaptive sparsity by fine-tuning (2020). https://arxiv.org/abs/2005.07683
44. Sun, S., Cheng, Y., Gan, Z., Liu, J.: Patient knowledge distillation for bert model compression (2019). https://arxiv.org/abs/1908.09355
45. Touvron, H., et al.: Llama: open and efficient foundation language models. arXiv preprint arXiv:2302.13971 (2023)
46. Voita, E., Talbot, D., Moiseev, F., Sennrich, R., Titov, I.: Analyzing multi-head self-attention: specialized heads do the heavy lifting, the rest can be pruned. arXiv preprint arXiv:1905.09418 (2019)
47. Wang, W., Wei, F., Dong, L., Bao, H., Yang, N., Zhou, M.: Minilm: deep self-attention distillation for task-agnostic compression of pre-trained transformers (2020). https://arxiv.org/abs/2002.10957
48. Xia, M., Gao, T., Zeng, Z., Chen, D.: Sheared llama: accelerating language model pre-training via structured pruning (2024). https://arxiv.org/abs/2310.06694
49. Xu, X., et al.: A survey on knowledge distillation of large language models (2024). https://arxiv.org/abs/2402.13116
50. Yang, C., et al.: Clip-kd: an empirical study of clip model distillation. In: Proceedings of the IEEE/CVF Conference on Computer Vision and Pattern Recognition, pp. 15952–15962 (2024)
51. Yao, Z., Aminabadi, R.Y., Zhang, M., Wu, X., Li, C., He, Y.: Zeroquant: efficient and affordable post-training quantization for large-scale transformers (2022). https://arxiv.org/abs/2206.01861
52. Yin, S., et al.: A survey on multimodal large language models. arXiv preprint arXiv:2306.13549 (2023)
53. You, Z., Yan, K., Ye, J., Ma, M., Wang, P.: Gate decorator: global filter pruning method for accelerating deep convolutional neural networks (2019). https://arxiv.org/abs/1909.08174
54. Yue, X., et al.: Mmmu: a massive multi-discipline multimodal understanding and reasoning benchmark for expert AGI. In: Proceedings of CVPR (2024)

55. Zafrir, O., Boudoukh, G., Izsak, P., Wasserblat, M.: Q8bert: quantized 8bit bert. In: 2019 Fifth Workshop on Energy Efficient Machine Learning and Cognitive Computing - NeurIPS Edition (EMC2-NIPS). IEEE (2019). https://doi.org/10.1109/emc2-nips53020.2019.00016
56. Zhu, M., et al.: A comprehensive overhaul of multimodal assistant with small language models. arXiv preprint arXiv:2403.06199 (2024)
57. Zhu, Y., Zhu, M., Liu, N., Xu, Z., Peng, Y.: Llava-phi: efficient multi-modal assistant with small language model. In: Proceedings of the 1st International Workshop on Efficient Multimedia Computing under Limited, pp. 18–22 (2024)

Assessing Foundation Models for Mold Colony Detection with Limited Training Data

Henrik Pichler[1,2]([✉]) [ID], Janis Keuper[1] [ID], and Matthew Copping[2] [ID]

[1] Offenburg University of Applied Sciences, Offenburg, Germany
`h.pichler@biostates.de` , `janis.keuper@hs-offenburg.de`
[2] BioStates GmbH, Baden-Baden, Germany

Abstract. The process of quantifying mold colonies on Petri dish samples is of critical importance for the assessment of indoor air quality, as high colony counts can indicate potential health risks and deficiencies in ventilation systems. Conventionally the automation of such a labor-intensive process, as well as other tasks in microbiology, relies on the manual annotation of large datasets and the subsequent extensive training of models like YoloV9. To demonstrate that exhaustive annotation is not a prerequisite anymore when tackling a new vision task, we compile a representative dataset of 5000 Petri dish images annotated with bounding boxes, simulating both a traditional data collection approach as well as few-shot and low-shot scenarios with well curated subsets with instance-level masks. We benchmark three vision foundation models against traditional baselines on task specific metrics, reflecting realistic real-world requirements. Notably, MaskDINO attains near-parity with an extensively trained YoloV9 model while finetuned only on 150 images, retaining competitive performance with as few as 25 images, still being reliable on $\approx 70\%$ of the samples. Our results show, that data-efficient foundation models can match traditional approaches with only a fraction of the required data, enabling earlier development and faster iterative improvement of automated microbiological systems with a superior upper-bound performance than traditional models would achieve.

Keywords: Vision foundation models · Few-shot learning · instance segmentation · Air quality monitoring · Mold Colony detection

1 Introduction

1.1 Problem Definition

Maintaining clean air in office and production environments is of critical importance to ensure the health and well-being of employees. In accordance with VDI Guideline 6022 [28], the quality of air entering premises via ventilation must be maintained, as poor air quality results in health issues such as respiratory problems. Mold spores represent a significant source of indoor air pollution, which

M. Keuper and F. Locatello (Eds.): DAGM GCPR 2025, LNCS 16125, pp. 337–352, 2026.
https://doi.org/10.1007/978-3-032-12840-9_22

underscores the need for regular monitoring and assessment of air quality. This is particularly important in settings with sensitive environmental conditions, such as hospitals and laboratories [11, 27].

Conventionally air quality assessment involves the collection of air or surface samples on Petri dishes, subsequent incubation for several days to permit the growth of mold colonies, and the enumeration of these colonies. Although the counting process is relatively straightforward, it is inherently labor-intensive due to the manual effort required. In addition, the air quality assessment often requires the differentiation of the colonies as well. This complicates the task, as often a microscopic evaluation is required in this case. In consideration of the growing demand for efficient air quality monitoring [1], there is a pressing need for automated solutions that can reduce manual workload and save time without compromising accuracy.

1.2   Training from Scratch on New Tasks

When training a machine learning model on a new task, a standard approach would often be to first collect large amounts of the data needed for solving the task. In the past, this was necessary, as models like AlexNet, VGG and ResNet needed a lot of data to perform at an acceptable level [10, 13, 23]. This resulted in the development of large datasets for different tasks, including the ImageNet dataset [5] for image classification (1.2–14 million images) and the MS-COCO dataset [16] for object detection (over 200 thousand labeled images), for which the annotation was especially labor-intensive. Even with these datasets, models were dataset-centric, needing a lot more data to potentially adapt to new tasks while still being biased and error-prone to changes in the data [2, 6, 7, 18]. So even though there is an abundance of large annotated datasets, adapting to new tasks takes time and annotation effort.

1.3   Foundation Models in Computer Vision

Recently foundation models have emerged as a prominent topic of interest in both the natural language processing and computer vision domains. These models employ extensively trained backbones, allowing them to capture general, robust and transferable representations of concepts within images. This enables them to perform well on a variety of tasks with minimal or no additional training, known as zero-shot or few-shot learning [31]. While a foundation model is often described as a model trained in an unsupervised or self-supervised manner [4], studies show that backbones trained with a supervised objective are on par with self-supervised backbones. Often they even excel their counterpart, e.g. when the supervised dataset is larger than the unsupervised [8] or when unsupervised pretraining objectives are combined with supervised ones [15].

Despite their wide-ranging applicability, the use of foundation models in niche domains, such as the automated enumeration of mold colonies, remains underexplored. The majority of existing research and applications concentrate on general-purpose datasets such as ImageNet [5], COCO [16] or similar ones, which feature everyday objects and scenes and lack the specific characteristics present in specialized domains. This gap in knowledge makes it unclear whether foundation models can generalize effectively to such tasks. [3] shows how varying the viewpoint of everyday objects poses a significant challenge for many models that previously performed well on datasets like ImageNet. This is to some degree still the case, even when looking at the leading foundation model for image classification, CoCa. Though it has a 91% accuracy on the ImageNet dataset, its performance drops by almost 10% on the ObjectNet dataset [3,33]. This effect might be intensified when switching to a completely new domain. Nevertheless, given their inherent strengths in vision tasks, foundation models present a promising base for adapting to new domains with relatively small amounts of data. This study aims to bridge this gap by evaluating the performance of foundation models in the novel domain of automated mold colony counting, thereby providing insights into their capabilities and limitations when applied to specialized tasks with limited training data, as is the case for many microbiological applications.

1.4 Goal

In this study, we aim to demonstrate that extensive data collection is not a prerequisite for effective model training and utilization. We seek to illustrate that foundation models can rapidly learn and accurately perform the task of mold colony counting, significantly reducing the time and resources required to deploy automated solutions. The contributions of this study can be summarized as follows. **(i)** We conduct the first systematic benchmark of microbiological colony counting with vision foundation models, namely MaskDINO [14], SAM-2 [20], and RF-DETR [21], under carefully annotated high-, few- and low-shot data regimes (see Sect. 4.2). **(ii)** We introduce task-oriented counting metrics, aligning with realistic laboratory reporting requirements and complement average precision (see Sect. 3.3). **(iii)** We compile a 5,000-image Petri dish dataset with bounding box and instance segmentation mask annotations, including stratified subsets for few-shot studies (see Sect. 3.1). We therefore aim to provide practical guidelines for early-stage model deployment in specialized computer vision domains, where data is scarce (see Sect. 5). The study could enhance the efficiency of air quality monitoring without the need for large, annotated datasets typically required by traditional methods. In return, the automation of the task could lead to reduced sample evaluation costs, enabling customers to submit more samples or submit samples more frequently, resulting in cleaner air. Furthermore, the insights derived from this study can be applied to other microbiological tasks, underscoring the potential of foundation models to propel specialized research areas despite limited data availability. To our knowledge, this is the first work assessing the low data performance of foundation models in the domain of microbiological colony detection.

2   Related Work

2.1   Deep Learning Applications in Microbiology

The field of microbiology has seen a growing reliance on deep learning for tasks such as species identification, colony enumeration, and early-stage detection of pathogens. However, the acquisition of large, annotated datasets remains a significant challenge in many microbiological applications. Lab-based image collection involves the culturing and precise imaging of samples, while the heterogeneity of data, including different species, growth phases, and plate types, further complicates model training. [30] developed a CNN-based system that could classify three bacterial types on agar plates, correctly identifying approximately 80% of colonies 12 h earlier than standard protocols. However, their approach required high-quality images and was limited to one plate at a time, highlighting scalability issues for high-throughput laboratories. [26] employed a CNN to classify Aspergillus species, achieving F1-scores above 95%, but only after training on thousands of carefully prepared images, primarily featuring a single, unmistakable colony. Such data requirements can be prohibitive in real-world scenarios where multiple overlapping colonies often appear. In contrast, [35] reported a 97% accuracy in bacterial classification, but their training set contained only 10 images per species. This limitation highlights the risk of overfitting, which can be difficult to detect in limited data sets. [19] attempted an expanded classification of 89 different fungi species. However, the model's accuracy was modest, with approximately 65% when presented with average-quality microscopic images, underscoring the potential for performance decline in less controlled settings.

Recent studies have emerged to advocate for the adoption of advanced architectures such as ConvNeXt [17], which effectively handle increased variability and smaller datasets with greater efficacy than their predecessors. For instance, [32] report accuracy gains of up to 10–15% when comparing ConvNeXt to conventional CNNs in the context of the classification of macular degeneration, suggesting that contemporary models may offer enhanced scalability and robustness, even in scenarios where data is limited.

[12] suggests that research in microbiological machine learning tasks remains dependent on legacy CNN backbones such as InceptionNet-v3 [24] and ResNet-50 [10], yet achieves competitive outcomes through transfer learning rather than through training from scratch. A systematic review of 121 medical-imaging papers reveals that InceptionNet-V3 was the most prevalent model, while fine-tuned feature-extractor regimes exhibited superiority over fully re-trained networks, thereby substantiating the viability of older architectures when strong priors are imported from ImageNet or analogous sources. In consideration of the microbiology-specific studies previously outlined, these observations indicate that architectures explicitly designed for adaptation, i.e., modern foundation models, should exhibit an even better capacity to manage small, heterogeneous datasets and rapidly generalize to novel tasks.

These studies underscore the pressing need to apply deep learning to a broader range of microbiological tasks and reveal how limited, specialized datasets often constrain generalization, with scalability issues becoming more evident when image conditions degrade or when more diverse samples are introduced. Motivated by these insights, this study investigates whether modern model architectures, especially foundation models, can achieve a strong performance in mold colony counting without requiring large-scale datasets.

2.2 Object Detection and Segmentation Architectures

Classical object detection and segmentation models, such as Yolo [25, 29] for object detection and Mask R-CNN [9] for segmentation, have long served as robust baselines in computer vision tasks. These approaches typically rely on training with large amounts of annotated data and benefit from pretrained backbones on large-scale datasets like ImageNet [5] or MS COCO [16]. This extensive supervised pretraining often enables them to achieve strong performance in well-studied domains.

3 Methodology

3.1 Dataset Creation

To evaluate the capability of foundation models in the task of mold colony counting, a dataset that represented the complexity of the problem while accounting for different data availability scenarios was essential. Consequently, a dataset comprising three scenarios was developed: one intended for traditional object detection models trained with a substantial amount of data, and two others designed for testing the low-data capabilities of foundation models. To ensure a valid and reliable comparison of the models, a validation and a test dataset were constructed.

Data Collection. High resolution images (1400×1400 pixels) of Petri dishes with mold colonies were gathered after an incubation period. The surface samples were obtained from a variety of locations throughout Germany and cultivated in DG18-Agar based Petri dishes, enabling only the growth of mold colonies. Most samples showed the growth of at least one colony. A standardized setup with a high-resolution camera and consistent lighting from the side was used to capture images from the obtained and incubated samples. This setup reflected realistic conditions relevant to mold colony counting.

Annotation. The data collection resulted in 5,000 manually annotated images, each containing at least one mold colony. The dataset was divided into three subsets for the training, validation, and testing. The ratio of images in the subsets was 4,000:500:500. To simulate low-data scenarios, a subset of 150 training images was selected from the large 4,000-images dataset. To simulate scenarios with even less data, e.g. when data collection is generally difficult or was just started, 6 additional 25-image subsets were sampled from the 150-image subset,

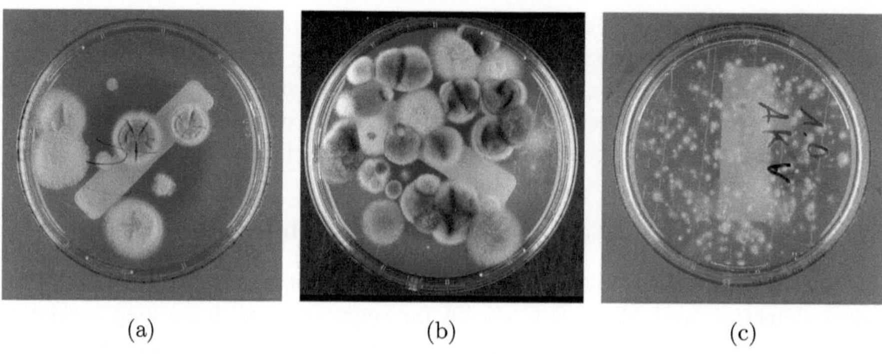

(a)   (b)   (c)

Fig. 1. Comparison between different mold colony growth patterns. (a) A typical sample with well-distinguishable colonies, (b) well-distinguishable but overlapping colonies on a darker background (caused by a changed backdrop throughout the capturing process), and (c) many small colonies, presenting a more challenging scenario.

using the Stratified K-Fold method based on the number of instances per image [22]. The usage of multiple 25-image subsets ensured that the results were not a random success or failure, but could be reliably evaluated. The resulting images as well as the validation and test set were further annotated with instance segmentation masks, ensuring a proper comparison between instance segmentation and object detection methods.

3.2 Experimental Setup

The goal was to provide insights into modern segmentation/foundation model capabilities by comparing them to more traditional methods. Since accurate colony counts were important and colonies often overlap (see Fig. 1b), an object detection and instance segmentation approach was chosen for this study, allowing for a more precise determination of colony boundaries than e.g. a semantic segmentation approach would be able to do. The models were selected for their predefined training scripts, which simplified adaptation to the task. The objective was to understand each approach's strengths, limitations, and capabilities under various data conditions, rather than developing a novel model. Practically, minimal model adaptation with limited fine-tuning is desirable for effective real-world applications.

The comparison covered two conventional architectures (YoloV9 [29] and Mask-RCNN [9]) and four foundation model variants with diverse backbones. Because annotating pixel-accurate masks for the entire 4,000-image dataset is prohibitively time-consuming, only YoloV9 and RF-DETR [21] were trained on the full dataset with bounding-box annotations to additionally enable a comparison of foundation models for the task of object detection. Mask-RCNN, MaskDINO and its variants [14], and SAM2 [20] were instead trained on smaller subsets that included instance segmentation masks, capturing pixel-level boundaries and separating overlapping colonies more reliably than boxes alone. All models were evaluated on the same 500-image test set, either using bounding boxes or segmentation masks, based on their training regime. A detailed summarization of the models can be found in Table 1. An in-depth overview of the training parameters can be found in the supplementary material, but it can be generally said that all models were trained mostly with their standard training parameters until no further improvements could be seen.

SAM2 is a prompt-based segmentation model which can be used to automatically generate masks with a grid of points as input and postprocessing the output with quality filtering methods and de-duplication using non-maxima suppression. The models' results depend on the parameters used for the automatic mask generation, so an optimization of the parameters was conducted, including a custom grid to guide the model towards better predictions. See supplementary material for additional information.

Table 1. Overview of all models evaluated in this study.

Model	Backbone	Pre-training	Fine-tuning data	# Params
YoloV9-E	–	MS COCO	4k/150/25 bbs	57.3 M
RF-DETR-L	DinoV2-b	ImageNet-21k	4k/150/25 bbs	135 M
Mask R-CNN	R50	MS COCO	150/25 masks	45.9 M
MaskDINO	R50	MS COCO	150/25 masks	52 M
MaskDINO	Swin-L	ImageNet-21k	150/25 masks	223 M
SAM2-base	Hiera	SA-1B +SA-V	150/25 masks	80.8 M

3.3   Evaluation Metrics

In order to assess the performance of the models under varying data regimes, a set of metrics was employed for the purpose of evaluating both the precision of the segmentation and the accuracy of the quantification of mold colonies.

Segmentation and Detection Metrics. The evaluation considered the outputs of each model. YoloV9 and RF-DETR were evaluated based on the bounding boxes they produced, and all other models were evaluated on the segmentation masks they provided. These outputs were assessed using standard metrics:

- **Mask Average Precision** (AP_{mask})**:** Evaluates overlap between predicted and ground-truth masks across multiple IoU thresholds.
- **Box Average Precision** (AP_{box})**:** Measures the precision of bounding box predictions at varying IoU thresholds.

Quantification Accuracy Metrics. Since the primary goal is accurate mold colony quantification, a metric was used to assess the models' ability to predict the number of colonies.This metric, Counting Accuracy (CA), describes the percentage of test images with the exact quantity of mold colonies correctly identified:

$$CA = \frac{\text{Number of Images with Correct Count}}{\text{Total Number of Images}} \times 100 \qquad (1)$$

Manual enumeration of mold colonies is subject to small discrepancies. An exact-match metric like counting accuracy can be overly strict for practical purposes. The "Counting Accuracy at 10% tolerance" (CA@10) extension to counting accuracy considers a prediction "correct" if its absolute relative error with respect to the ground-truth count is at most 10%, and therefore 90% correct. Formally,

$$CA@10 = \frac{1}{N} \sum_{i=1}^{N} \mathbb{1}\left(\frac{|c_i - \hat{c}_i|}{c_i} \leq 0.10 \right) \times 100 \qquad (2)$$

where N is the number of samples, c_i is the ground-truth colony count for sample i, $\hat{c}_i$ is the model's predicted count, and $\mathbb{1}(\cdot)$ is the indicator function that returns 1 when the condition is satisfied and 0 otherwise.

CA@10 therefore measures the percentage of plates for which the model's estimate deviates by no more than 10% from the reference count. In routine microbiological quality control, such an error band is acceptable because most of the time it doesn't change the qualitative assessment of contamination level. Therefore, this metric is the most impactful for the study.

To assess the relative counting error of the models, the Mean Absolute Percentage Error (MAPE) in colony count per image (Eq. 3) was additionally computed.

$$MAPE = \frac{1}{N} \sum_{i=1}^{N} \frac{|c_i - \hat{c}_i|}{c_i} \times 100 \qquad (3)$$

4   Results

4.1   Dataset Statistics

A total of 5,000 images of Petri dishes containing 109,636 mold colonies were captured. The dataset was split into three parts: a 4,000-image training set and two 500-image validation and test sets. From the 4,000-image training set, a 150-image subset was sampled, from which six subsets of 25 images each were sampled. A detailed analysis of the distribution of mold colony instances across these dataset partitions reveals a consistent pattern, with median values ranging from five to eight colonies per image and a 90th percentile of around 58 colonies per image. In extreme cases, the number of colonies on a single sample ranged from 327 colonies in the 150-image subset to 424 in the full 4,000-image training set. The smaller 25-image subsets exhibited greater variability, with an average maximum of approximately 166 colonies per image and substantial deviation (± 89.53), thereby underscoring the inherent randomness of sampling. With respect to the relative size of mold colonies, the median colony sizes were consistently small, approximately 0.19% of the total image area, across most subsets. The majority of colonies did not exceed approximately 1.5% of the image area, as indicated by the 90th percentile values (ranging from 0.88% to 1.57%). It is noteworthy that remarkably larger colonies were uncommon. Nevertheless, when present in an image, they could account for up to 70.1% of the image area in the complete dataset.

Additional details about the dataset can be found in the supplementary material.

4.2 Model Training

44 model trainings were carried out. Additionally to their regular trainings, each model was trained on all 6 25-image subsets (see Table 1), for which the results were aggregated. All models were tested on the same test set with 500 images using the metrics denoted in Sect. 3.3.

Table 2. Model results, where the results for the models trained on the 25-image splits are shown as the mean $\pm$ standard deviation. The CA@10 metric (highlighted in gray) is the most insightful metric here, showing how well the model performs in quantification, while still being reliable.

Train Size	Model	CA@10 $\uparrow$	AP $\uparrow$	MAPE $\downarrow$	CA $\uparrow$
4000	YoloV9-E	73	**59.89**	8	57.6
	RF-DETR-L	**84.4**	51.74	**5.95**	**65.8**
150	SAM2-base	15	22.1	62.4	14.2
	Mask R-CNN	37	46.9	45.7	23.8
	YoloV9-E	38.4	39.44	28.2	31.8
	RF-DETR-L	69	40.65	10.89	54.2
	MaskDINO-R50	69	50.06	13	51.4
	MaskDINO-Swin	**72.6**	**51.59**	**8**	**56.2**
25	SAM2-base	10.23 ± 1.53	16.13 ± 1.46	108.68 ± 9.87	7.47 ± 2.11
	YoloV9-E	25.67 ± 6.81	31.95 ± 1.26	41.06 ± 4.31	21.37 ± 3.87
	Mask R-CNN	35.97 ± 8.84	39.18 ± 1.77	41.43 ± 17.69	24.63 ± 2.22
	RF-DETR-L	51.63 ± 5.74	33.10 ± 2.39	19.53 ± 5.71	41.97 ± 3.12
	MaskDINO-R50	58.90 ± 2.29	44.17 ± 0.71	20.32 ± 5.58	44.77 ± 1.17
	MaskDINO-Swin	$\mathbf{67.30 \pm 1.88}$	$\mathbf{46.89 \pm 0.67}$	$\mathbf{10.85 \pm 0.52}$	$\mathbf{50.13 \pm 0.73}$

YoloV9 achieves the highest overall AP performance with 59.8%, although the RF-DETR model outperforms the model in actual quantification of mold colonies with the highest overall CA @ 10 with 84.4%, establishing a solid foundation for the rest of the results.

The findings show that the AP cannot be taken as a definitive indicator here and that actual performance is strongly dependent on the task at hand. This shows in the results of the MaskRCNN model, having a comparable AP_{mask} to the MaskDINO models. However, its quantification performance falls far behind these models and YoloV9. The counterpart to this is the RF-DETR model, which remains behind YoloV9 by 8.15% in AP performance, when trained on 4,000 images, but outperforms it by 11.4% in CA@10 performance. Hence, dense colony enumeration is best evaluated using several metrics, including the presented CA@10, showing what the maximum quantification performance while still being reliable can be.

At 150 training images, MaskDINO-Swin achieves the highest overall performance with a CA@10 of 72.6% (see Table 2). This performance is notable compared to the YoloV9 model trained on 4,000 images, which only exceeds the achieved CA@10 performance by approximately 0.4% while MaskDINO requires $\approx 4\%$ of the training data. The baseline foundation model, RF-DETR, outperforms this MaskDINO-Swin model by 11.8% regarding the CA@10, while showing a similar AP performance. When trained on 150 images, RF-DETR is outperformed by MaskDINO-Swin in all metrics while showing on-par performance with MaskDINO-R50.

At 25 training images, MaskDINO-Swin loses $\approx 5\%$ in CA@10, from 72.6% to 67.3 %. Still, it is only $\approx 5\%$ behind the YoloV9 performance when trained on 4,000 images, while needing just 0.6% of the training data. Noteworthy, the models performance is roughly three times as high as the YoloV9 performance here. A qualitative investigation shows that YoloV9, even when trained on 4,000 images, misses obvious mold colonies and predicts false positives in background regions. With less data, YoloV9 misses more colonies and makes vague suggestions. MaskDINO clearly separates mold colonies, even overlapping ones, with as few as 25 training images, improving in finer mask predictions with additional training data. RF-DETR also shows strong performance here, with only missing a few colonies when trained on 25 images, improving these mistakes when additional data is added (see Fig. 2).

SAM2 exhibits a significant performance deficit compared to other models. The model exhibits a performance of 22% AP_{mask}, 14% CA, and 15% CA@10 with 150 training images, which are less than one-third of the performance metrics achieved by MaskDINO-Swin in the same regime. A reduction to 25 images results in a significant decline of SAM2 to approximately 16% AP_{mask} and 10% CA@10.

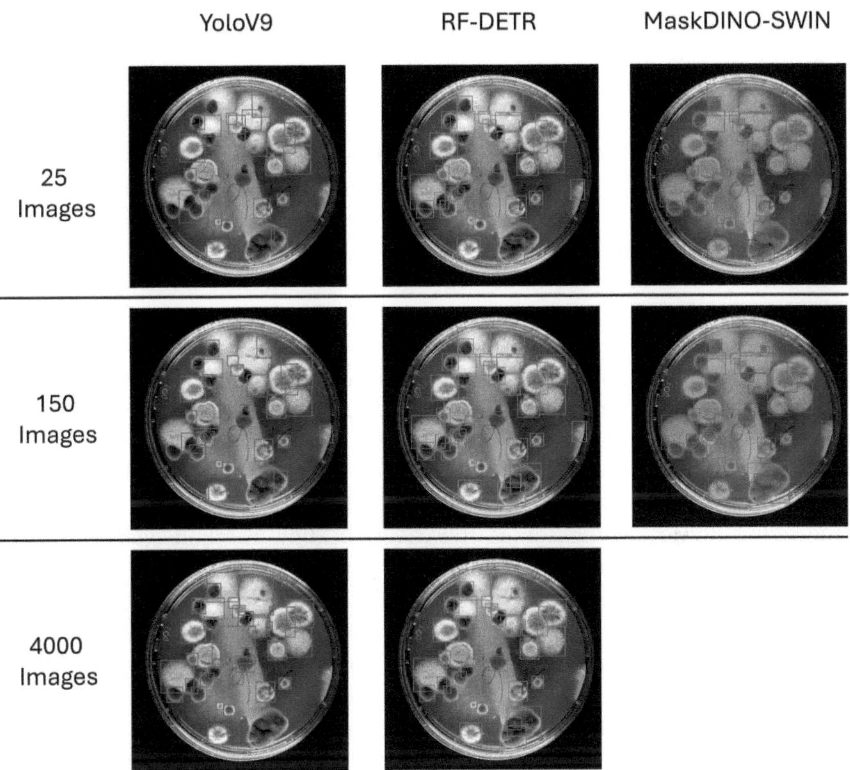

Fig. 2. Comparison of predictions made by YoloV9 (left), RF-DETR (middle) and MaskDINO-SWIN (right) trained on different amounts of data. The images show a typical sample with overlapping and small colonies. Additional comparison images can be found in the material. Images best viewed in color.

5   Discussion

Though the MaskDINO-SWIN model achieved inferior results when trained on just 25 images, it still achieves a CA@10 result of 67%, which already is within 6% of what YoloV9 trained on the full dataset achieved, showing how reliable results can be achieved with just a few carefully annotated samples. This enables a utilization in early stages of projects, while still being reliable for most samples, with an extensive investigation only needed for the most complex samples. The modest accuracy gap between the 25- and 150-image datasets likely stems from the number of samples rather than a shift in data distribution, given the similar statistics of the two datasets. Hence, more samples help the model capture intra-plate variability, but not because they introduce previously unseen colony phenotypes. Therefore, deploying the model in an early stage can help with rapidly increasing the amount of training data, enabling fast improvements.

Although creating and refining bounding box annotations is faster, using mask annotations might be the ideal method to deploy, especially in low-shot scenarios. This is evident in the comparative performance of the MaskDINO and RF-DETR models. RF-DETR exhibits a 15% performance deficit when trained on 25 images, indicating it struggles more in extreme low-data conditions than MaskDINO. However, with the full 4,000-image training set, RF-DETR actually surpasses YoloV9 by a large margin, showcasing the benefit of its foundation model backbone at scale. This suggests that a foundation model like MaskDINO might surpass YoloV9 by an even larger gap if more data were available, further enhancing the results.

A steady, monotonic gain is observed across all architectures when the training set increases from 25 to 150 images, signifying that a project may be initiated with a minimal initial sample set and several model candidates to identify a clear leader at start. Subsequent efforts can then be concentrated on this model alone. In the present study, the initial performance of SAM2 indicated that additional training would not be financially viable. MaskDINO and RF-DETR exhibited encouraging upward trends. This iterative workflow method ensures that the initial investment is minimized, ensuring that labeling resources are spent on models that scale effectively with additional data.

In practice, this suggests deploying a comparable application in a new, likely biomedical, computer vision task can be done with a minimal initial effort, when leveraging foundation models, with only a small initial sample set. This initial sample set must be annotated according to the task at hand (e.g., instance segmentation masks instead of bounding boxes for separating overlapping objects). The use of task-specific metrics aligning with real-world scenarios is essential. With regular usage more data can be easily collected, enabling effective scaling with more accurate results. The ability of foundation models to perform well on less complex samples with little training data, allows for concentrated annotation efforts on more challenging samples, for which the model is likely to struggle with, resulting in a gradual decrease in manual effort and a reduction in the need of supervision.

Overall, foundation models provide two simultaneous benefits when starting a new computer vision project: rapid cold-start performance in few-shot settings and superior upper-bound performance once data accumulates. This makes them the most cost-effective choice across the project life-cycle.

Limitations. SAM2 struggles to segment out negative regions. The prompt generator only provides positive prompts during training, so the model rarely encounters negative regions, never learning to suppress them. This leads to the model misidentifying brown, circular artifacts as colonies. Here, negative samples during training might help, as opposed to merely adding more data.

MaskDINO outperforms RF-DETR in low-shot and few-shot training, though this cannot be reasoned clearly and might be due to the number of parameters, though MaskDINO-R50 has less than half of RF-DETR's, or the annotations. It is clear, that masks capture finer details than bounding boxes, especially for irregularly shaped mold colonies, but further investigation is needed to determine if this gives them an advantage. For this, a model leveraging the same backbone could be trained on bounding boxes and instance segmentation masks, showing the value of investing in pixel-level mask annotation.

Although a standardized imaging setup was employed, the employed side illumination often introduced glare and shadows across mold colonies, complicating the visual separation of adjacent colonies. All reference annotations were produced by a single expert working solely from the captured images without the actual samples at hand, which can increase the risk of wrong labeling. These effects are most pronounced for heavily overgrown samples, where dense colony clusters are hard to properly separate. Future work will therefore incorporate direct plate-level verification and improved lighting to mitigate these sources of error.

6   Conclusion

This study shows that foundation models match or exceed classical detectors in low-data scenarios, demonstrating that data quantity matters not as much than it does with classical approaches when it comes to mold colony counting. These findings suggest an effective workflow: first, focus on annotating a few samples, then refine iteratively to deploy rapidly and grow subsequent datasets. In a subsequent project, insights from this study will expand to address colony differentiation, a complex but valuable task for automated air quality monitoring. Foundation models may be crucial for rapid system development, especially with the BiomedParse [34] foundation model, which uses text prompt-based mask generation.

Data Availibility Statement. The dataset that supports the findings of this study is available from the corresponding authors upon request.

References

1. 360iResearch: Indoor air quality monitors market size & forecast to 2030. Market Research Report Report ID 5889448, 360iResearch (2025). https://www.researchandmarkets.com/report/indoor-air-quality-monitoring. Accessed 10 June 2025
2. Alcorn, M.A., Li, Q., Gong, Z., Wang, C., Mai, L., Ku, W.S., Nguyen, A.: Strike (with) a pose: Neural networks are easily fooled by strange poses of familiar objects. In: Proceedings of the IEEE/CVF Conference on Computer Vision and Pattern Recognition (CVPR). pp. 4845–4854. IEEE, Long Beach, CA, USA (Jun 2019). https://doi.org/10.48550/arXiv.1811.11553, https://openaccess.thecvf.com/content_CVPR_2019/html/Alcorn_Strike_With_a_Pose_Neural_Networks_Are_Easily_Fooled_by_CVPR_2019_paper.html
3. Barbu, A., et al.: ObjectNet: a large-scale bias-controlled dataset for pushing the limits of object recognition models. In: Advances in Neural Information Processing Systems 32 (NeurIPS 2019), pp. 9448–9458. Advances in Neural Information Processing Systems, Curran Associates, Inc. (2019). https://proceedings.neurips.cc/paper_files/paper/2019/file/97af07a14cacba681feacf3012730892-Paper.pdf

4. Bommasani, R., Hudson, D.A., et al.: On the opportunities and risks of foundation models. arXiv (2021). https://doi.org/10.48550/arXiv.2108.07258, https://arxiv.org/abs/2108.07258

5. Deng, J., Dong, W., Socher, R., Li, L.J., Li, K., Li, F.F.: ImageNet: a large-scale hierarchical image database. In: Proceedings of the 2009 IEEE Conference on Computer Vision and Pattern Recognition (CVPR), pp. 248–255. IEEE (2009). https://doi.org/10.1109/CVPR.2009.5206848

6. Dodge, S., Karam, L.: A study and comparison of human and deep learning recognition performance under visual distortions. In: Proceedings of the 26th International Conference on Computer Communications and Networks (ICCCN), pp. 1–7. IEEE (2017). https://doi.org/10.1109/ICCCN.2017.8038465

7. Geirhos, R., Rubisch, P., Michaelis, C., Bethge, M., Wichmann, F.A., Brendel, W.: Imagenet-trained CNNs are biased towards texture; increasing shape bias improves accuracy and robustness. In: Proceedings of the 7th International Conference on Learning Representations (ICLR) (2019). https://doi.org/10.48550/arXiv.1811.12231, https://openreview.net/forum?id=Bygh9j09KX

8. Goldblum, M., et al.: Battle of the backbones: a large-scale comparison of pretrained models across computer vision tasks. In: Advances in Neural Information Processing Systems 36 (NeurIPS 2023), Datasets and Benchmarks Track. Proceedings of the Neural Information Processing Systems, vol. 36, pp. 1–29. Neural Information Processing Systems Foundation (2023). https://proceedings.neurips.cc/paper_files/paper/2023/file/5d9571470bb750f0e2325a030016f63f-Paper-Datasets_and_Benchmarks.pdf

9. He, K., Gkioxari, G., Dollár, P., Girshick, R.: Mask R–CNN. In: Proceedings of the 2017 IEEE International Conference on Computer Vision (ICCV), pp. 2980–2988. IEEE (2017). https://doi.org/10.1109/ICCV.2017.322

10. He, K., Zhang, X., Ren, S., Sun, J.: Deep residual learning for image recognition. In: Proceedings of the IEEE/CVF Conference on Computer Vision and Pattern Recognition (CVPR), pp. 770–778. IEEE (2016). https://doi.org/10.1109/CVPR.2016.90

11. Kelman, B., Stock, A., Robbins, C.: Indoor air quality: health effects of airborne mold & how mold is measured. White paper, J.S. Held LLC, Jericho (2022). https://www.jsheld.com/insights/articles/indoor-air-quality-health-effects-of-airborne-mold-how-mold-is-measured-indoors. Accessed 10 June 2025

12. Kim, H.E., Cosa-Linan, A., Santhanam, N., Jannesari, M., Maros, M.E., Ganslandt, T.: Transfer learning for medical image classification: a literature review. BMC Med. Imaging **22**, 69 (2022). https://doi.org/10.1186/s12880-022-00793-7

13. Krizhevsky, A., Sutskever, I., Hinton, G.E.: ImageNet classification with deep convolutional neural networks. In: Pereira, F., Burges, C.J.C., Bottou, L., Weinberger, K.Q. (eds.) Advances in Neural Information Processing Systems 25 (NeurIPS 2012). Advances in Neural Information Processing Systems, vol. 25, pp. 1097–1105. Curran Associates, Inc., Lake Tahoe (2012). https://proceedings.neurips.cc/paper_files/paper/2012/file/c399862d3b9d6b76c8436e924a68c45b-Paper.pdf

14. Li, F., Zhang, H., Xu, H., Liu, S., Zhang, L., Ni, L.M., Shum, H.Y.: Mask DINO: towards a unified transformer-based framework for object detection and segmentation. In: Proceedings of the IEEE/CVF Conference on Computer Vision and Pattern Recognition (CVPR), pp. 3041–3050. IEEE (2023). https://doi.org/10.1109/CVPR52729.2023.00297

15. Liang, F., Li, Y., Marculescu, D.: SupMAE: supervised masked autoencoders are efficient vision learners. arXiv (2022). https://doi.org/10.48550/arXiv.2205.14540,

https://arxiv.org/abs/2205.14540. Edge Intelligence Workshop, AAAI 2024; version 3, Accessed 21 Jan 2024

16. Lin, T.-Y., et al.: Microsoft COCO: common objects in context. In: Fleet, D., Pajdla, T., Schiele, B., Tuytelaars, T. (eds.) ECCV 2014. LNCS, vol. 8693, pp. 740–755. Springer, Cham (2014). https://doi.org/10.1007/978-3-319-10602-1_48

17. Liu, Z., Mao, H., Wu, C., Feichtenhofer, C., Darrell, T., Xie, S.: A convnet for the 2020s. In: Proceedings of the IEEE/CVF Conference on Computer Vision and Pattern Recognition (CVPR), pp. 11976–11986. IEEE (2022). https://doi.org/10.1109/CVPR52688.2022.01167

18. Radford, A., Kim, J.W., Sutskever, I., Krueger, G., Agarwal, S.: CLIP: connecting text and images (2021). https://openai.com/index/clip/. OpenAI Research blog post

19. Rahman, M.A., et al.: Classification of fungal genera from microscopic images using artificial intelligence. J. Pathol. Inform. **14**, 100314 (2023). https://doi.org/10.1016/j.jpi.2023.100314

20. Ravi, N., et al.: SAM 2: segment anything in images and videos. arXiv (2024). https://doi.org/10.48550/arXiv.2408.00714, https://arxiv.org/abs/2408.00714

21. Robinson, I., Robicheaux, P., Popov, M., et al.: RF-DETR: a real-time transformer-based object detection model. https://github.com/roboflow/rf-detr

22. scikit-learn developers: sklearn.model_selection.stratifiedkfold—scikit-learn 1.7.0 documentation (2025). https://scikit-learn.org/stable/modules/generated/sklearn.model_selection.StratifiedKFold.html

23. Simonyan, K., Zisserman, A.: Very deep convolutional networks for large-scale image recognition. In: Proceedings of the 3rd International Conference on Learning Representations (ICLR) (2015). https://doi.org/10.48550/arXiv.1409.1556, https://arxiv.org/abs/1409.1556

24. Szegedy, C., Vanhoucke, V., Ioffe, S., Shlens, J., Wojna, Z.: Rethinking the inception architecture for computer vision. In: Proceedings of the IEEE/CVF Conference on Computer Vision and Pattern Recognition (CVPR), pp. 2818–2826. IEEE (2016). https://doi.org/10.1109/CVPR.2016.308

25. Terven, J., Córdova-Esparza, D., Romero-González, J.: A comprehensive review of YOLO architectures in computer vision: from YOLOv1 to YOLOv8 and YOLO-NAS. Mach. Learn. Knowl. Extract. **5**(4), 1680–1716 (2023). https://doi.org/10.3390/make5040083

26. Tsang, C.C., et al.: Automatic identification of clinically important *Aspergillus* species by artificial intelligence-based image recognition: proof-of-concept study. Emerg. Microbes Infect. **14**(1), 2434573 (2025). https://doi.org/10.1080/22221751.2024.2434573

27. United States Environmental Protection Agency: Care for your air: A guide to indoor air quality. Technical report, U.S. Environmental Protection Agency (2008). https://www.epa.gov/indoor-air-quality-iaq/care-your-air-guide-indoor-air-quality. Accessed 10 June 2025

28. Verein Deutscher Ingenieure: VDI 6022 Blatt 1: Raumlufttechnik, Raumluftqualität – Hygieneanforderungen an raumlufttechnische Anlagen und Geräte (VDI-Lüftungsregeln). VDI Guideline VDI 6022-1, Verein Deutscher Ingenieure e. V. (2018). https://www.vdi.de/en/home/vdi-standards/details/vdi-6022-blatt-1-ventilation-and-indoor-air-quality-hygiene-requirements-for-ventilation-and-air-conditioning-systems-and-units-vdi-ventilation-code-of-practice-1

29. Wang, C., Yeh, I., Liao, H.M.: YOLOv9: learning what you want to learn using programmable gradient information. In: Computer Vision – ECCV 2024. Lecture

Notes in Computer Science, vol. 15089, pp. 1–21. Springer (2024). https://doi.org/10.1007/978-3-031-72751-1_1

30. Wang, H., et al.: Early detection and classification of live bacteria using time-lapse coherent imaging and deep learning. Light: Sci. Appl. **9**, 118 (2020). https://doi.org/10.1038/s41377-020-00358-9

31. Wang, W., Zheng, V.W., Yu, H., Miao, C.: A survey of zero-shot learning: settings, methods, and applications. ACM Trans. Intell. Syst. Technol. **10**(2), 13:1–13:37 (2019). https://doi.org/10.1145/3293318

32. Wu, M., et al.: Classification of dry and wet macular degeneration based on the ConvNeXT model. Front. Comput. Neurosci. **16**, 1079155 (2022). https://doi.org/10.3389/fncom.2022.1079155

33. Yu, J., Wang, Z., Vasudevan, V., Yeung, L., Seyedhosseini, M., Wu, Y.: CoCa: contrastive captioners are image-text foundation models. arxiv abs/2205.01917 (2022). https://doi.org/10.48550/arXiv.2205.01917, https://arxiv.org/abs/2205.01917

34. Zhao, T., et al.: A foundation model for joint segmentation, detection and recognition of biomedical objects across nine modalities. Nature Methods **22**(1), 166–176 (2025). https://doi.org/10.1038/s41592-024-02499-w

35. Zieliński, B., Plichta, A., Misztal, K., Spurek, P., Brzychczy-Włoch, M., Ochońska, D.: Deep learning approach to bacterial colony classification. PLOS ONE **12**(9), e0184554 (2017). https://doi.org/10.1371/journal.pone.0184554

Common Data Properties Limit Object-Attribute Binding in CLIP

Bijay Gurung[1,2(✉)], David T. Hoffmann[1], and Thomas Brox[1]

[1] University of Freiburg, Freiburg im Breisgau, Germany
[2] deepset, Berlin, Germany
gurungb@cs.uni-freiburg.de

Abstract. Contrastive vision-language models like CLIP are used for a large variety of applications, such as zero-shot classification or as vision encoder for multi-modal models. Despite their popularity, their representations show major limitations. For instance, CLIP models learn bag-of-words representations and, as a consequence, fail to distinguish whether an image is of "a yellow submarine and a blue bus" or "a blue submarine and a yellow bus". Previous attempts to fix this issue added hard negatives during training or modified the architecture, but failed to resolve the problem in its entirety. We suspect that the missing insights to solve the binding problem for CLIP are hidden in arguably the most important part of learning algorithms: the data. In this work, we fill this gap by rigorously identifying the influence of data properties on CLIP's ability to learn binding using a synthetic dataset. We find that common properties of natural data such as low attribute density, incomplete captions, and the saliency bias, a tendency of human captioners to describe the object that is "most salient" to them, have a detrimental effect on binding performance. In contrast to common belief, we find that neither scaling the batch size, i.e., implicitly adding more hard negatives, nor explicitly creating hard negatives enables CLIP to learn reliable binding. Only when the data expresses our identified data properties does CLIP learn almost perfect binding.

Keywords: CLIP · Attribute-Binding CLIP · Vision-Language Models

1 Introduction

Contrastive Vision-Language models like CLIP [21] are a cornerstone of computer vision. CLIP-like models are used for various applications, ranging from

---

D. T. Hoffmann and T. Brox—Shared last authorship.
Code available at: https://github.com/bglearning/data-properties-clip-binding.

Supplementary Information The online version contains supplementary material available at https://doi.org/10.1007/978-3-032-12840-9_23.

zero-shot classification to text-to-image and image-to-text retrieval. The image encoders of CLIP-like models are a standard choice for the vision encoder in multi-modal language models [2,8] and the text encoders have been used to guide image generation [19,22,23]. To mitigate deficiencies of CLIP, a whole family of variants with minor architectural differences or modifications of the loss function have been proposed [1,9,17,27,29,30], which we will refer to as CLIP-like models.

Despite the great success and broad applicability of CLIP-like models, they unfortunately fail at the fundamental task of object-attribute binding [16,25,28]. For instance, as shown in Fig. 1a CLIP can't distinguish the "yellow submarine and blue bus" and the incorrect caption in which the color is swapped. This is linked to the finding by Yuksekgonul et al. [28] that CLIP models represent images and text in a bag-of-words (BOW) representation, i.e., CLIP appears to extract a set of concepts from an image and represents an image by an unordered set of these concepts. Naturally, a BOW representation is, for many tasks, insufficient, can result in unexpected results, and can even cause security risks. For example, a self-driving car using BOW representation might fail to bind *red* to the traffic light and confuse a *green*-shirted pedestrian with a green traffic light.

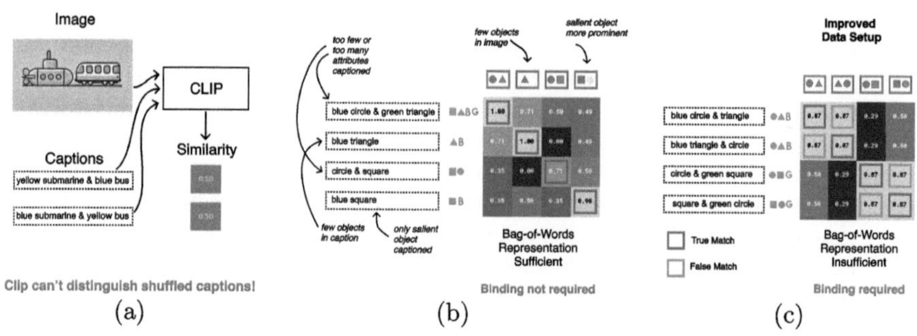

Fig. 1. **(a)** The object-attribute binding problem: CLIP can't distinguish between two captions with swapped attributes. **(b)** We identify data properties that contribute to poor object-attribute binding. If 1) too few or too many attributes per object are in the caption, or 2) too few images with multiple objects or 3) caption mentions too few objects, 4) captioners focus more on salient objects, a bag-of-words (BOW) representation is sufficient to find the correct sample within a batch. Here we study how these data properties influence object-attribute binding of CLIP models and find **(c)** setups that lead to robust binding accuracy of CLIP models, suggesting the binding problem of CLIP is a data problem.

Multiple previous works tried to resolve CLIP's inability to learn reliable object-attribute binding. For instance, Yuksekgonul et al. [28] claim that CLIP fails to learn binding because a BOW representation is sufficient to associate each caption to the correct image. As a remedy, they propose to mine hard negatives. However, as revealed later in Hsieh et al. [13], CLIP's binding ability increases only marginally on a more general test set. Others assume that CLIP's architecture limits its ability to learn object-attribute binding and try to fix the problem by adding an object-centric learning inspired cross-modal interaction layer [1]. But these changes are also insufficient to solve the problem entirely.

This leads to the central question: What prevents CLIP from learning binding? Is it the poor scaling properties of contrastive losses in a large combinatorial space, as indicated by Yuksekgonul et al. [28], or architectural limitations as proposed by Assouel et al. [1]? We suspect that neither fully explains it. Previous works focused on the loss and architecture, but missed arguably the most important component of each learning algorithm: the data. Indeed, as shown in Fig. 1b, we find various data properties common in image-caption datasets to promote BOW representations, as they make the learning of binding obsolete. Could properties of the data itself limit the binding of CLIP models? Could better filtering or re-captioning help? And what would ideal data look like?

Unfortunately, studying the influence of data properties is nontrivial for web-scraped data: the properties are unknown and annotating them is too expensive. Without this annotation it is impossible to run clean data interventions. Even with these annotations, it is necessary to train many CLIP models on different settings, which quickly becomes too expensive. As a remedy, we define a synthetic data generating process that gives us full control over the data properties. To ensure the data properties of our synthetic dataset are representative of real data we annotate the data properties for 100 images from CC12M [7] and pick our default setup close to those observed on real data. Diverging from this "realistic" setup, we can study the influence of individual properties.

But can we be sure that relationships found on synthetic data transfer to real data? Note that studying learning algorithms in a controlled setup reveals basic properties and relations of this learning algorithm. We do not expect that the learning algorithm changes its behavior fundamentally in larger scale training on more complex data. A remaining caveat is that the relations found in our setup could be overshadowed by other factors on real data. Even then this work still contributes to a better understanding of CLIP models.

In summary, our contributions are the following: 1) We design a clean synthetic dataset which allows us to study object-attribute binding of CLIP models in a controllable full-information setup. In particular, we analyze the influence of the **ratio of multi-object to single-object images**, the influence of **number of objects described in the caption**, the **number of attributes per object in the caption**, and the influence of **saliency bias** of annotators on object-attribute binding of CLIP models. 2) We find that the number of objects in the image and in the caption have a significant influence on binding. We find an inverse u-shaped relation between attributes in the caption and binding accuracy, i.e., too few and too many attributes in the caption both hurt binding. We further find that the saliency bias of annotators might be a key factor limiting object-attribute binding. 3) We confirm that our findings are not due to flaws in the experimental design by scaling up the batch size and model complexity. Furthermore, we observe that the trends persist out-of-distribution, ruling out that our models learned a shortcut. 4) Finally, we show that hard negatives alone are insufficient to learn strong binding, and that the data affects the binding accuracy more.

2   Related Works

Yuksekgonul et al. [28] show that CLIP learns a bag-of-words (BOW) representation and hypothesize this is due to batches lacking hard negatives. Without them, the contrastive loss can be minimized with a BOW representation which CLIP learns (following a simplicity bias). Similarly, Tang et al. [25] identify Concept Association Bias (CAB), where CLIP learns strong associations between highly correlated factors (e.g. "purple" and "eggplant") also leading to binding failures.

Several approaches aimed to improve CLIP's binding performance [1,10,28]. Yuksekgonul et al. [28] propose NegCLIP, which is fine-tuned on hard negatives constructed by swapping attributes, object, and relations in the caption. However, later works revealed that the success was overestimated, due to overfitting to specific types of binding used for testing [13]. Assouel et al. [1] propose cross-modal interactions, inspired by object-centric learning, and LLM-based caption decomposition. Despite outsourcing most of the binding to an LLM their approach only partially solves the binding problem, as can be seen by the reported binding-accuracy on Sugarcrepe [13]. Enriching the captions with LLMs also leads to some improvements [10,11], as does generating hard negatives via in-context learning [20], however, these methods also do not solve the binding problem entirely. Koishigarina et al. [15] argue that the binding information is present unimodally and is lost during the cosine similarity computation and propose a contrastively-trained transformation matrix for alignment, showing partial improvements. However, their study centers on overly simplistic datasets.

The datasets used to study object-attribute binding in a controlled setting are based on CLEVR [14] in [16] and PUG:SPAR [3] in [15]. However, they are limited by their low complexity. Note, that both datasets are rendered images, however, complexity for the object-attribute binding does not arise from image quality and realism. Instead, the number of attributes and their combinations with objects is the key driver of the binding task complexity. For instance, PUG:SPAR only has one attribute type (color/material). CLEVR [14] only has 3 object types with 3 attributes, 2 of which have only 2 possible values. As such, these datasets are not sufficiently complex and do not allow for enough control over their data properties to systematically study the influence of training data on CLIP's binding performance. For evaluation of models trained on large scale image-caption datasets benchmarks from the Crepe family [12,13,18] are commonly used. Unfortunately, they do not provide the required control for a systematic analysis of the influence of data properties on binding performance.

In contrast to prior work, we take a data-centric approach to study CLIP's binding problem in detail and develop a synthetic dataset that enables systematic investigation of how common properties of web-scraped image-caption data influence CLIP binding performance. We demonstrate that these data properties of the training data significantly impact binding, and that CLIP trained under favorable data conditions achieves high binding performance.

3   Experimental Setup

To systematically study the influence of training data properties on object-attribute binding we require precise control over data characteristics, which natural datasets cannot provide. As a remedy, we create a synthetic dataset that enables explicit manipulation of these data properties.

3.1   MADMAN: Fully Controllable Synthetic Dataset

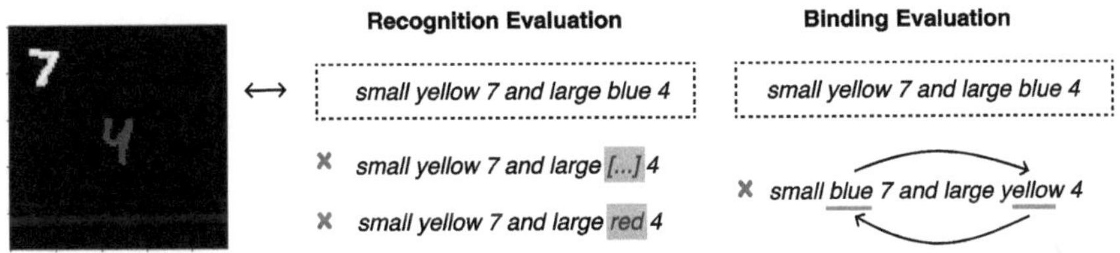

Fig. 2. MADMAN example and evaluation protocols. To evaluate **recognition**, we create zero-shot classification prompts by changing the target attribute. To evaluate **binding**, we swap the target attribute to create a negative and perform zero-shot classification with the true and negative caption. In practice, we evaluate on captions with 3 and 4 attributes per object.

We show an example of our dataset Multi-Attribute and Digit for Multi-Attribute biNding (MADMAN) in Fig. 2 and in the Appendix, Sect. 5.1. It is designed to study object-attribute binding in a controlled way. A dataset for this purpose needs to entail images with multiple objects, each with a set of attributes, all of which are described in a caption. We use the MAD [24] dataset (based on Morpho-MNIST citech23castro2019morpho) as the starting point, add support for multiple objects per image, and extend it with *rotation*. For multi-object images, we create a 3×3 black grid, and fill 2 random cells with images. **Captions** are created by chaining object classes with their attributes, using "and" to separate the objects (see Appendix, Sect. 5.1 for a complete list of augmentations and examples from our dataset).

Data Properties Studied with MADMAN. To study the influence of data properties on binding, we create different versions of MADMAN controlling: **1)** *Two-object-in-image-probability* p(two-obj-img), which controls the probability of a sample to contain 2 objects, **2)** *Two-object-in-caption-probability* p(two-obj-cap|two-obj-img = True), which controls the probability that both objects are described in the caption. Note that this is a conditional probability (given the image is a two-object image) and not the prior probability. However, for most experiments it is identical, as we use p(multi-obj-img) = 1 in our base setup. We also study **3)** the influence of the number of *Attributes-per-object-in-caption*. We observe that humans mention only a few attributes per object in a caption (see Appendix, Sect. 5.2). To model this, we change the probability of an attribute being included in the caption. To avoid overfitting to a specific caption length we define probability distributions over the number of attributes per object, and use the expected value to distinguish them (see Appendix, Fig. 7 to see the underlying distributions). Finally, we are interested in the effect of **4) *Saliency bias*.** Saliency describes the properties of "parts popping out" to human attention. Images commonly contain a number of salient objects, which are more likely to be described in the caption. We model it via a center bias, i.e., we define an object to be salient if it is in the center of the image. Furthermore, salient objects in our setup are always mentioned in the caption and are mentioned first. We control p(saliency) which refers to the probability of an image to contain a salient object.

Determining Realistic Parameters for the Data Properties. To draw conclusions about natural data from synthetic data, we need a MADMAN version that has similar data properties as natural data. To this end, we annotate the four data properties defined above for 100 images from CC12M [7]. For details on the annotation, Appendix 5.2. We refer to this MADMAN variant as "Realistic".

Defining Out-of-Distribution. To evaluate whether our model learns a compositional representation we need an out-of-distribution (OOD) test set. We define the following combinations as OOD:

color: $\{green, red\} \times \{0, 3\}$, $\{blue, magenta\} \times \{4, 5\}$
scaling: $\{large\} \times \{3, 7\}$, $\{small\} \times \{4, 9\}$

Here, $\times$ denotes the Cartesian product. These combinations are included **only** in our OOD testset (only Sect. 4.4). The remaining combinations are used for training and our standard test-set.

3.2   Evaluation and Training Setup

The evaluation images always show two objects and both are described in the caption. The evaluation captions have 3 attributes per object in 50% of samples and 4 for the remaining samples. This ensures a fair comparison across different *Attributes-per-object-in-caption* settings, as all of them have the same probability mass for 3 and 4 attributes (see Fig. 7). We provide an overview of our recognition and binding evaluation in Fig. 2.

Recognition. Our final goal is to evaluate object-attribute binding, however, a prerequisite for binding is that the attribute in question can be recognized. We evaluate recognition accuracy per object and attribute. For each object o and attribute a, we use the evaluation captions and vary only a (or o) over all possible values to create false captions. Recognition is evaluated as zero-shot accuracy over the set of these false captions and the ground-truth caption.

Object-Attribute Binding Accuracy. To measure object-attribute binding accuracy for an attribute a of the set of attributes A we:

1. Filter out **attributes** a for which recognition is close to or below p_{chance}
2. Filter out all **samples** for which attribute a is not recognized for both objects
3. Evaluate *binding-accuracy* for the remaining samples

Criterion 1) is necessary, as the attribute binding metric has no meaning if the attribute is not even recognized. To filter out cases where performance is slightly above chance, we use a slightly stricter threshold: $1.1 \times p_{\text{chance}}$. Criterion 2) factors out failures of binding that are caused by a failed recognition. Finally, for the remaining samples we compute *binding-accuracy* [13,28]:

$$\text{binding-accuracy}(a) = \frac{1}{N} \sum_{n=1}^{N} p(c_n^{\text{gt}}) > p(c_n^{\text{swap}_i}), \tag{1}$$

where c_n^{gt} is the ground truth caption c of sample n, c_n^{swap} is derived from c_n^{gt} by swapping attribute a between the objects and $p(c)$ indicates the probability the model assigns to caption c belonging to the image. As this is a two-alternative forced choice task, the chance level is 0.5.

Model Training Setup. For all results reported in Sect. 4, we train small CLIP models from scratch. We train each model with three random seeds and report/plot the mean and the 95% confidence interval. We vary the data properties of MADMAN as detailed for each experiment.

Compared to natural datasets, MADMAN exhibits only a few factors of variation. Both the number of object classes and attributes are limited. Accordingly, we adjust our model and batch size to match this smaller scale. Text and image encoders are small transformers with 6 layers and 4 attention heads, each. We use a batch size of 16 and an embedding size of 32. In particular the choice of the batch size plays a critical role in contrastive learning models, as it directly affects the likelihood of sampling hard negatives within a batch. This, in turn, influences the number of distinct features (like binding) the model must learn to minimize the loss. We validate our choices in Sect. 4.3, demonstrating that the observed trends are robust to variations in the specific configuration.

4 Results

4.1 CLIP Only Learns Object-Attribute Binding with Ideal Data

Can CLIP even learn object-attribute binding? Does the architecture and loss prevent CLIP from learning a non Bag-of-words (BOW) representation? Is maybe a large enough batch size sufficient to encourage CLIP to learn binding via hard negatives? We can explore these questions using MADMAN with relatively small batch sizes since the number of factors of variation is low.

As can be seen in the top part of Table 1, neither training with very large batch size, nor training a large model, nor their combination enables binding. We

Table 1. Object-Attribute binding in realistic and ideal setup. Here, Realistic Data refers to a setup with properties determined from real data. Ideal Data refers to the best performing dataset properties as found in Sect. 4.2. We ablate the Realistic and Ideal data setting with small and Ideal (large) batch size and model size. It can be seen that ideal data is more important for high binding . Thus, data properties limit binding, not model size or batch size.

Setup			Binding Accuracy					
Data	Batch	Embed	Color	Scaling	Fracture	Rotation	Swelling	Thickness
Realistic	16	32	50.47	54.47	52.34	50.86	53.26	50.05
Realistic	16	256	50.64	59.72	50.81	51.71	52.23	53.50
Realistic	256	32	51.06	50.47	50.91	53.55	54.69	52.44
Realistic	256	256	54.74	65.47	50.13	73.96	54.61	55.36
Ideal	16	32	94.66	91.28	61.93	92.44	66.43	90.02
Ideal	16	256	88.03	96.99	60.17	98.42	69.36	95.72
Ideal	256	256	100.0	98.48	98.18	99.93	98.64	99.43

conclude that CLIP models are unlikely to learn binding when training on data that exhibits realistic values for the four data properties (defined in Sect. 3.1). So either CLIP models can not learn binding, or properties of the data inhibit it. To find out which of these two explanations is true, we optimize the training data setup by changing the four data properties. As detailed in Sect. 4.2, we find that changing the data setup has a significant influence on binding accuracy, leading to almost perfect binding (see Table 1). We conclude that CLIP models are able to learn object-attribute binding but properties of the data inhibit this.

4.2   What Limits the Object-Attribute Binding in CLIP Models?

The previous section shows that CLIP models can learn object-attribute binding under optimal data conditions. But which properties of the data are important? How do they individually influence the binding? Can we find factors that we could change on real data? To answer these questions, we individually investigate the influence of the four data properties defined in Sect. 3.1 on the binding performance. Unless otherwise mentioned, we set *Two-object-in-image-probability* to 1.0, *Two-object-in-caption-probability* to 1.0, the expected number of *Attributes-per-object-in-caption* to 1.8 and *Saliency bias* to 0. For all experiments below, we vary one data property and keep the others constant. By varying one property we create different variants of MADMAN. For each of these versions we train 3 CLIP models from scratch and report the average binding accuracy.

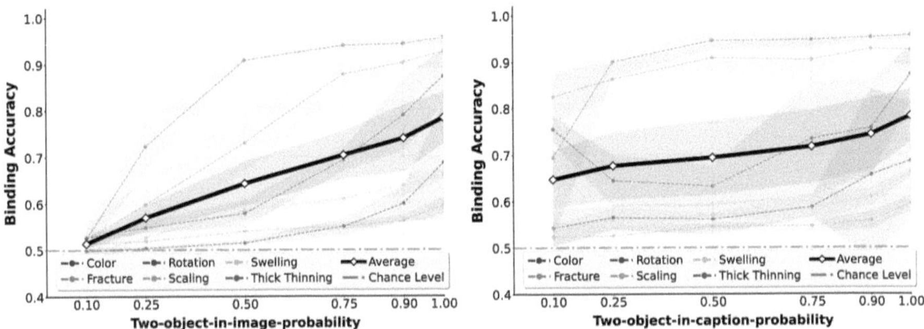

(a) *Two-object-in-image-probability*   (b) *Two-object-in-caption-probability*

Fig. 3. Influence of (a) *Two-object-in-image-probability* and (b) *Two-object-in-caption-probability* on binding accuracy on **MADMAN.** Having more images and captions containing multiple objects improves binding.

What's the Influence of the Ratio of Multi-object Images on Binding? To answer this we vary *Two-object-in-image-probability*. As can be seen in Fig. 3a, object-attribute binding increases steadily for all attributes.

What's the Influence of the Ratio of Two-Object Captions on Binding? Similarly, the number of objects mentioned in the caption likely influences binding. Figure 3b reveals that a small ratio of captions containing two objects are already sufficient to learn binding for a few attributes. Increasing the number of captions containing two objects leads to consistent improvements of binding.

How Does the *Number of Attributes per Object in the Caption* Influence Binding? As can be seen in Fig. 4a, the *Attributes-per-object-in-caption* have a strong influence on binding. Interestingly, for *Attributes-per-object-in-caption* larger than 3.5 the binding accuracy starts to decrease again. We suspect that this is due to the larger discriminativeness of a BOW representation with many concepts due to the combinatorial explosion: If enough attributes are present, a BOW representation is sufficient to discriminate between all samples in a batch (compare Fig. 1b) and thus the model does not need to learn binding. In the other extreme, low *Attributes-per-object-in-caption* prevents binding from being learned, as cases with two attributes where binding is necessary, are too rare.

What's the Influence of the Saliency Bias of Captioners on Binding? Humans typically agree on which object(s) are the most important (or salient) in an image [4,5]. Saliency might hamper binding as it provides shortcut-opportunities to minimize the loss, e.g., by representing primarily the attributes of the salient object without binding them.[1] Indeed we find that already small

---

[1] Note that the text encoder also has information on which object is likely the salient one, as the salient object is always mentioned first in the caption.

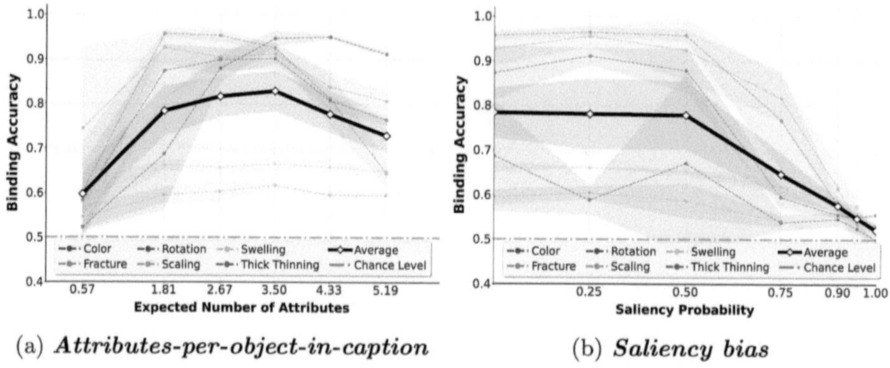

(a) *Attributes-per-object-in-caption*   (b) *Saliency bias*

Fig. 4. Influence of (a) *Attributes-per-object-in-caption* and (b) *Saliency bias* on binding accuracy on MADMAN. (a) Too few and too many *Attributes-per-object-in-caption* hamper the binding accuracy. For large *Attributes-per-object-in-caption* binding is not necessary anymore, as BOW is sufficient to discriminate images due to combinatorial explosion. **(b)** Saliency bias hinders binding, especially at higher values, which is the case for natural data. This is likely because it provides a shortcut for the model to minimize contrastive loss by simply representing the salient object(s) without binding them.

levels of saliency have a negative effect, while levels above 0.75 are detrimental (Fig. 4b).

But can we really expect more than 75% of image-caption pairs to express saliency bias? We expect this to be the case as humans tend to take pictures of objects instead of random images and tend to describe the salient objects with higher probability. To verify this, we use our manually labeled images of CC12M. Indeed, we identified at least one salient object for more than 90% of the images (see Appendix, Sect. 5.2). In our experiments we observe very low binding for these saliency levels (Fig. 4b), suggesting that saliency is likely one of the main limiting factors for CLIP models to learn binding. We even find that the influence of other factors diminishes when saliency is at a natural level (see Table 6). Thus saliency might be a key limiting factor also on real data.

***Color* Often Behaves Differently.** Interestingly, we observe that the attribute *color* binds poorly for most values of *Two-object-in-image-probability* (Fig. 3a) and *Two-object-in-caption-probability* (Fig. 3b), despite being easy to recognize (see Appendix, Sect. 5.5). But why does it bind so poorly? Note that the color attribute can take 7 different values, while all other attributes have fewer possible values. As a result, color has most discriminative power among the attributes, e.g., knowing that there is a *green 6* in the image distinguishes it from more images than knowing there is a *small 6*. Thus, if color(s) and object(s) are in the caption, representing these two factors is often sufficient to distinguish this image/caption from all other captions/images in a batch, making binding unnecessary. Only when colors of more than one object are frequently in the caption, learning the color-object binding reduces the loss (relatively) enough s.t. the model eventually learns binding.

The Ideal Data Setting. Finally, we use the previous experiments to select the best data setup for each of the properties. We end up with: no saliency bias, p(multi-obj-img) = 1, p(multi-obj-cap) = 1 and expected number of *Attributes-per-object-in-caption* = 3.5. As shown in Table 1, combining the optimal setups for all our data properties indeed leads to high binding and combining the best setups for each parameter leads to best binding performance (see Appendix, Sect. 5.3). Table 1 reveals that ideal data alone leads to high object-attribute binding for 4 out of 6 attributes. Using ideal data, a large model and a large batch size results in almost perfect binding for all attributes.

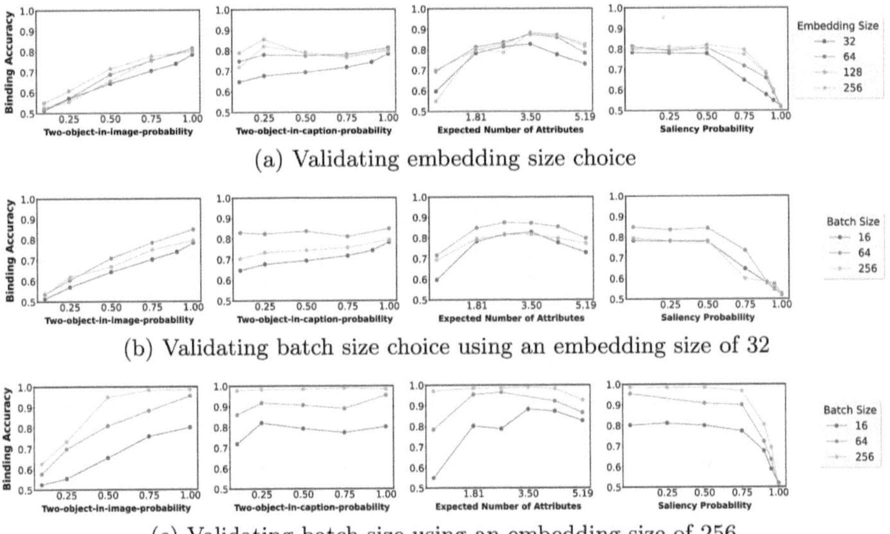

(a) Validating embedding size choice

(b) Validating batch size choice using an embedding size of 32

(c) Validating batch size using an embedding size of 256

Fig. 5. Experimental results are independent of most important hyper-parameters of the experimental setup on MADMAN. We test various combinations of the embedding size and batch size. We observe the same trends for all data properties as found in our main setting, showing that our results are not an artifact of a specific experimental setup.

4.3   Validating Our Experimental Setup

The results presented above could be an artifact of an unlucky choice of the batch size or model size. To rule out that our findings are just an artifact of poor choices for the batch size and model size, we repeat the experiments and vary the batch size and the embedding size of the models. As detailed above, the batch size directly controls the number of hard negatives in the loss, thus testing different batch sizes can be interpreted as changing the hard negative ratio in a batch. By changing the embedding size we test whether the model size limited binding in our experiments. Figure 5a shows that our results are not an artifact of the embedding size. We observe small differences, however, the trends remain the same. Similarly, Figs. 5b and 5c reveal that our findings are independent of the batch size. Changing the batch size leads to small differences, but the trends remain consistent. Combined, these results validate our experimental setting and findings as not being an artifact of the base setup. The only exception of this is the *Two-object-in-caption-probability*, where the effect partially diminishes with increasing embedding size and increasing batch size (Figs. 5a to 5c).

4.4   We Find the Same Relationships Out-of-Distribution

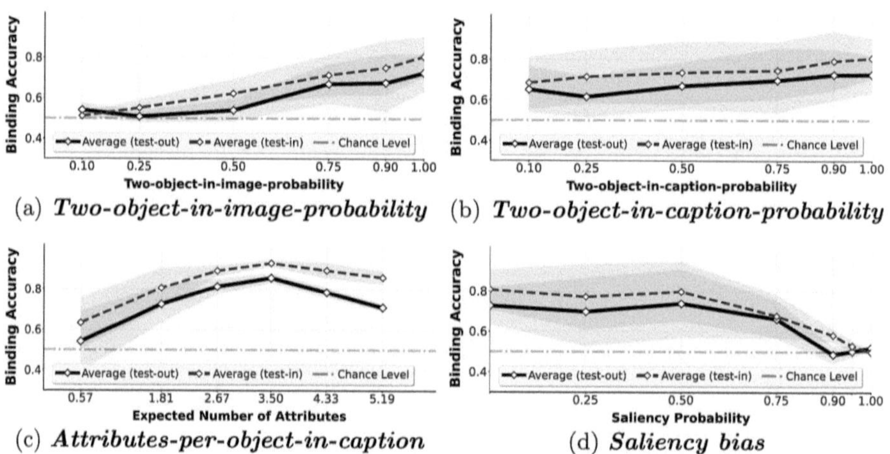

(a) ***Two-object-in-image-probability***   (b) ***Two-object-in-caption-probability***

(c) ***Attributes-per-object-in-caption***   (d) ***Saliency bias***

Fig. 6. Impact of the data properties on the binding for out-of-distribution combinations on MADMAN-OOD. It follows similar trends as in-distribution (denoted by the dashed line).

CLIP models have been shown to learn object-attribute compositional representations [26], meaning that the concept "yellow submarine" is encoded roughly by the sum of the "yellow" vector and the "submarine" vector. However, in a synthetic setting with few factors of variation a model can just treat each object-attribute combination as an individual class, instead of learning such a compositional representation. If our models learn non-compositional representations we can not expect our results to transfer to large scale CLIP training. To test this, we test our models on our OOD test set with unseen object-attribute combinations. A compositional representation can generalize to unseen object-attribute combinations, while a non-compositional representation can not. We also find the same trends for OOD (see Fig. 6). Thus, our model learns a similar compositional representation as CLIP models trained on real data, which confirms the validity of our study.

4.5 Are Hard Negatives Enough to Solve the Binding Problem?

Table 2. Attribute binding Performance of NegCLIP with realistic data. The base CLIP when provided with an ideal data setup learns the binding much better, highlighting the importance of getting the right data properties.

Model	Color	Scaling	Fracture	Rotation	Swelling	Thickness
CLIP	50.47	54.47	52.34	50.86	53.26	50.05
CLIP (+Ideal data)	94.66	91.28	61.93	92.44	66.43	90.02
NegCLIP (Text)	77.10	75.65	54.84	74.83	56.44	62.39
NegCLIP (Text+Image)	72.84	76.85	56.14	86.74	58.18	63.93

Previous works tried to resolve binding by changing the training process, for instance by training on hard negatives [28]. The previous sections show that data properties of the training data have a large influence on the binding performance of CLIP models. Naturally, the question arises whether a hard negative training regime, as proposed for NegCLIP [28], can be used to resolve the problems induced by the data properties. To this end, we explore how well NegCLIP performs on the variant of MADMAN following realistic data properties. As Table 2 reveals, NegCLIP indeed improves binding over CLIP, but does not get close to CLIP trained in the ideal data setup. Thus, NegCLIP alone is not enough to resolve the issues caused by the data properties and thus is unlikely to resolve the issue on real data. Our results indicate that better training data might be necessary to resolve the binding problem of CLIP.

5 Conclusion

In this work, we showed that CLIP struggles to learn object-attribute binding even when training under favorable conditions. Via a rigorous analysis using our synthetically generated dataset we showed that specific data properties common in web-scraped image-caption datasets are limiting CLIP's object-attribute binding. In particular, we found that having too few images showing, and too few captions describing multiple objects limits binding. More importantly, we showed that too few *and* too many attributes mentioned in the caption per object hurt binding. Most interestingly, we found that the saliency bias plays a critical role and, at levels common on real data, has a detrimental effect on the binding performance. Furthermore, we found that when the saliency bias is too high, the influence of the other properties diminishes. We verified our experiments thoroughly, by changing model parameters and testing in an OOD setup, where we found the same trends. In summary, our controlled experiments on synthetic data provide evidence that the data properties common for natural image-caption datasets have a negative influence on CLIP's binding performance. To obtain high binding performance of CLIP models on natural data it might be necessary to change some of the data properties of the training data.

Limitations. This work shows the relationship of the aforementioned data properties to binding accuracy of CLIP models; however, our studies are limited to a synthetic setup. We expect to find the same relationship on real data but obtaining the required information to perform these experiments on real data is prohibitively expensive.

Future Work. should use the insights provided by this work to guide filtering or re-captioning approaches. A promising re-captioning approach is to occasionally drop the salient object from the caption. Another promising direction is to explore the optimal number of attributes per object in the caption on real data.

Acknowledgments. We would like to thank Simon Schrodi for helpful comments on the draft. Funded by the German Federal Ministry for Economic Affairs and Energy within the project "NXT GEN AI METHODS" (19A23014R), by the German Research Foundation (DFG) - 417962828, 539134284 and âĂŞ SFB 1597 âĂŞ 499552394.

References

1. Assouel, R., Astolfi, P., Bordes, F., Drozdzal, M., Romero-Soriano, A.: Object-centric binding in contrastive language-image pretraining. arXiv preprint arXiv:2502.14113 (2025)
2. Beyer, L., et al.: PaliGemma: a versatile 3B VLM for transfer. arXiv preprint arXiv:2407.07726 (2024)
3. Bordes, F., Shekhar, S., Ibrahim, M., Bouchacourt, D., Vincent, P., Morcos, A.: PUG: photorealistic and semantically controllable synthetic data for representation learning. Adv. Neural. Inf. Process. Syst. **36**, 45020–45054 (2023)
4. Borji, A., Sihite, D.N., Itti, L.: Quantitative analysis of human-model agreement in visual saliency modeling: a comparative study. IEEE Trans. Image Process. **22**(1), 55–69 (2012)
5. Borji, A., Sihite, D.N., Itti, L.: What stands out in a scene? A study of human explicit saliency judgment. Vision. Res. **91**, 62–77 (2013)
6. Castro, D.C., Tan, J., Kainz, B., Konukoglu, E., Glocker, B.: Morpho-MNIST: quantitative assessment and diagnostics for representation learning. J. Mach. Learn. Res. **20**(178), 1–29 (2019)
7. Changpinyo, S., Sharma, P., Ding, N., Soricut, R.: Conceptual 12M: pushing web-scale image-text pre-training to recognize long-tail visual concepts. In: CVPR (2021)
8. Chen, X., et al.: PaLI: a jointly-scaled multilingual language-image model. In: The Eleventh International Conference on Learning Representations (2023). https://openreview.net/forum?id=mWVoBz4W0u

9. Cherti, M., et al.: Reproducible scaling laws for contrastive language-image learning. In: Proceedings of the IEEE/CVF Conference on Computer Vision and Pattern Recognition, pp. 2818–2829 (2023)
10. Doveh, S., et al.: Dense and aligned captions (DAC) promote compositional reasoning in VL models. Adv. Neural. Inf. Process. Syst. **36**, 76137–76150 (2023)
11. Doveh, S., et al.: Teaching structured vision & language concepts to vision & language models. In: Proceedings of the IEEE/CVF Conference on Computer Vision and Pattern Recognition, pp. 2657–2668 (2023)
12. Dumpala, S.H., Jaiswal, A., Shama Sastry, C., Milios, E., Oore, S., Sajjad, H.: SUGARCREPE++ dataset: vision-language model sensitivity to semantic and lexical alterations. Adv. Neural. Inf. Process. Syst. **37**, 17972–18018 (2024)
13. Hsieh, C.Y., Zhang, J., Ma, Z., Kembhavi, A., Krishna, R.: SUGARCREPE: fixing hackable benchmarks for vision-language compositionality. Adv. Neural. Inf. Process. Syst. **36**, 31096–31116 (2023)
14. Johnson, J., Hariharan, B., Van Der Maaten, L., Fei-Fei, L., Zitnick, C.L., Girshick, R.: CLEVR: a diagnostic dataset for compositional language and elementary visual reasoning. In: 2017 IEEE Conference on Computer Vision and Pattern Recognition (CVPR), pp. 1988–1997. IEEE, Honolulu (2017). https://doi.org/10.1109/CVPR.2017.215, https://ieeexplore.ieee.org/document/8099698/
15. Koishigarina, D., Uselis, A., Oh, S.J.: CLIP behaves like a bag-of-words model cross-modally but not uni-modally. arXiv preprint arXiv:2502.03566 (2025)
16. Lewis, M., et al.: Does CLIP bind concepts? Probing compositionality in large image models. In: Graham, Y., Purver, M. (eds.) Findings of the Association for Computational Linguistics: EACL 2024, pp. 1487–1500. Association for Computational Linguistics, St. Julian's (2024). https://aclanthology.org/2024.findings-eacl.101/
17. Li, Y., et al.: Supervision exists everywhere: a data efficient contrastive language-image pre-training paradigm. In: International Conference on Learning Representations (2022). https://openreview.net/forum?id=zq1iJkNk3uN
18. Ma, Z., Hong, J., Gul, M.O., Gandhi, M., Gao, I., Krishna, R.: CREPE: can vision-language foundation models reason compositionally? In: Proceedings of the IEEE/CVF Conference on Computer Vision and Pattern Recognition, pp. 10910–10921 (2023)
19. Nichol, A., et al.: GLIDE: towards photorealistic image generation and editing with text-guided diffusion models. arXiv preprint arXiv:2112.10741 (2021)
20. Patel, M., et al.: TripletCLIP: improving compositional reasoning of clip via synthetic vision-language negatives. Adv. Neural. Inf. Process. Syst. **37**, 32731–32760 (2024)
21. Radford, A., et al.: Learning transferable visual models from natural language supervision. In: International Conference on Machine Learning, pp. 8748–8763. PmLR (2021)
22. Ramesh, A., Dhariwal, P., Nichol, A., Chu, C., Chen, M.: Hierarchical text-conditional image generation with CLIP latents. arXiv preprint arXiv:2204.06125, vol. 1, no. 2, p. 3 (2022)
23. Rombach, R., Blattmann, A., Lorenz, D., Esser, P., Ommer, B.: High-resolution image synthesis with latent diffusion models. In: Proceedings of the IEEE/CVF Conference on Computer Vision and Pattern Recognition, pp. 10684–10695 (2022)
24. Schrodi, S., Hoffmann, D.T., Argus, M., Fischer, V., Brox, T.: Two effects, one trigger: on the modality gap, object bias, and information imbalance in contrastive vision-language model. In: International Conference on Learning Representations (ICLR) (2025)

25. Tang, Y., Yamada, Y., Zhang, Y., Yildirim, I.: When are lemons purple? The concept association bias of vision-language models. In: Proceedings of the 2023 Conference on Empirical Methods in Natural Language Processing, pp. 14333–14348 (2023)
26. Trager, M., Perera, P., Zancato, L., Achille, A., Bhatia, P., Soatto, S.: Linear spaces of meanings: compositional structures in vision-language models. In: Proceedings of the IEEE/CVF International Conference on Computer Vision, pp. 15395–15404 (2023)
27. Xu, H., et al.: Demystifying CLIP data. In: The Twelfth International Conference on Learning Representations (2024). https://openreview.net/forum?id=5BCFlnfE1g
28. Yuksekgonul, M., Bianchi, F., Kalluri, P., Jurafsky, D., Zou, J.: When and why vision-language models behave like bags-of-words, and what to do about it? In: International Conference on Learning Representations (2023). https://openreview.net/forum?id=KRLUvxh8uaX
29. Zhai, X., Mustafa, B., Kolesnikov, A., Beyer, L.: Sigmoid loss for language image pre-training. In: Proceedings of the IEEE/CVF International Conference on Computer Vision, pp. 11975–11986 (2023)
30. Zhong, Y., et al.: RegionCLIP: region-based language-image pretraining. In: Proceedings of the IEEE/CVF Conference on Computer Vision and Pattern Recognition, pp. 16793–16803 (2022)

SubCellSAM: Zero-Shot (Sub-)Cellular Segmentation for Hit Validation in Drug Discovery

Jacob Hanimann[1], Daniel Siegismund[2], Mario Wieser[2], and Stephan Steigele[2(✉)]

[1] University of Bern, Bern, Switzerland
[2] Genedata AG, Basel, Switzerland
`stephan.steigele@genedata.com`

Abstract. High-throughput screening using automated microscopes is a key driver in biopharma drug discovery, enabling the parallel evaluation of thousands of drug candidates for diseases such as cancer. Traditional image analysis and deep learning approaches have been employed to analyze these complex, large-scale datasets, with cell segmentation serving as a critical step for extracting relevant structures. However, both strategies typically require extensive manual parameter tuning or domain-specific model fine-tuning. We present a novel method that applies a segmentation foundation model in a zero-shot setting (i.e., without fine-tuning), guided by an in-context learning strategy. Our approach employs a three-step process for nuclei, cell, and subcellular segmentation, introducing a self-prompting mechanism that encodes morphological and topological priors using growing masks and strategically placed foreground/background points. We validate our method on both standard cell segmentation benchmarks and industry-relevant hit validation assays, demonstrating that it accurately segments biologically relevant structures without the need for dataset-specific tuning.

Keywords: Biomedical Imaging · In-context Learning · Cell Segmentation · Zero-shot Learning · Drug Discovery

1 Introduction

The development of a new drug is a prolonged and costly process that takes more than ten years with up to four billion dollars of investment [23]. Consequently, the discovery of new drug candidates is a key driving factor in the process of

---

J. Hanimann and D. Siegismund—These authors contributed equally to this work.
J. Hanimann: Work done during an internship at Genedata AG.

Supplementary Information The online version contains supplementary material available at https://doi.org/10.1007/978-3-032-12840-9_24.

developing sophisticated treatment strategies such as cancer immunotherapies [16].

In early drug discovery, high-content screening (HCS) has become a key technology to assess the effects of chemical compounds on cellular systems [36]. By integrating automated microscopy with advanced image analysis, HCS enables the collection of high-dimensional data from individual cells, and as it is run on 384-1536 microtiter plates it allows for the parallel testing of tens of thousands of compounds per experiment. This approach provides detailed spatial and temporal insights into cellular responses, supporting the identification of biologically relevant mechanisms. Among the various HCS methodologies, multiplexed imaging assays such as cell painting have been developed to capture diverse morphological features [4], though many other assay formats are also employed depending on the biological context and research objectives.

A major challenge in HCS assays is the need to analyze both large-volume and biologically complex datasets. Traditionally, such datasets have been analyzed by employing handcrafted features with classical image analysis software such as CellProfiler [7] which is highly time-consuming and biased as the analysis pipeline has to be set up manually by a domain expert for each screening dataset [6]. Hence, deep learning based approaches have been developed to speed up the process by learning image-based representations without requiring the manual set up of image analysis pipelines [8, 24–26, 34, 35]. A crucial step in performing this analysis includes the segmentation of cells and their corresponding compartments from high-content images to extract all relevant structures. This step is particularly important as errors will propagate through the analysis and may influence the downstream result calculations and decision processes. While early approaches relied on classical image segmentation techniques [7], more sophisticated methods specifically targeted at cells have since been introduced in recent years [12, 28, 30, 33]. However, all of the above mentioned methods either require extensive manual parameter tuning (CellProfiler) or specific training or fine-tuning for cell-segmentation tasks.

To address this challenge, we propose an approach that leverages a pre-trained segmentation foundation model without any task-specific fine-tuning, guided by an in-context learning strategy. This strategy is designed to embed key morphological and topological priors characteristic of cell images into the prompting process. Specifically, we first perform nuclei segmentation, followed by an iterative segmentation of the cell body using a loop prompting mechanism that enforces these priors and incorporates both positive and negative anchor points, along with low-resolution masks from previous iterations.

Our contributions can be summarized as follows:

- We propose a novel in-context learning approach for (sub)cellular segmentation based on iterative self-prompting.
- We introduce a prompt sampling strategy that encodes key morphological and topological priors, including cell-to-nucleus relationships and instance separation, to enhance pipeline robustness and generalizability.

- We evaluate our method for cell body segmentation across three diverse datasets, where it shows performance competitive with or exceeding specialized methods.
- We validate the applicability of our method on two hit-validation datasets relevant to drug discovery, where it outperforms the consensus baseline.

2   Related Work

In-Context Learning. In contrast to model training approaches, in-context learning aims to solve specific tasks by conditioning on a certain amount of demonstrations without updating the model weights. Depending on the number of demonstrations which are required to solve a certain task, in-context learning can be further divided into sub-groups: Few-shot learning aims to solve a specific task by providing a number of examples to the model. Especially, large-language models have demonstrated to perform well in such tasks [5]. Moreover, few-shot learning in the context of foundation models has been utilized in various tasks such as object detection [11]. In addition, zero-shot learning aims to solve tasks without providing any demonstrations to the model. Here, large language models have been used to perform zero-shot captioning of images [31], gaze following [10] or on lesion detection [9].

Vision-Language Models. In recent years, large language models have been combined with vision models to reason across multiple modalities. CLIP learns visual concepts from natural language supervision to solve vision tasks across multiple domains [21]. In addition, [1] introduced a vision-language model to solve tasks like visual question-answering in a few-shot fashion. In addition to the previously mentioned tasks, segmentation of objects plays a crucial role in various application areas. Kirillov et al. [15] introduced SAM, a segmentation approach to allow for zero-shot segmentation of new imaging tasks. This approach has subsequently been extended in multiple directions: [14] introduced improvements to segment objects in higher quality while [37] have proposed a CNN backbone instead of a transformer architecture to speed up the segmentation process. More recently, SAM was extended to segment video sequences [22].

Cell-Based Segmentation Models. Building on their success in natural image analysis, vision-language segmentation models have recently been extended to cell segmentation. [19] proposed an extension of SAM to enable nuclei segmentation while [2] introduced a foundation model to segment any kind of microscopy images. Additionally, [28] demonstrated a method for improved cellular segmentation for images which suffer from noise, blurring or undersampling, a common issue in cell microscopy. [12] suggested a method for cell segmentation which trains an object detector for cell detection in combination with a prompt engineering approach to generate segmentations. In contrast to the previous approaches, [33] developed a segmentation method based on convolutional networks for live-cell imaging experiments. These approaches require at least partial retraining of certain parameters.

3   Setup and Preliminaries

Consider a dataset $D = \{x_i\}_{i=1}^N$ which consists of N data samples. Here, $x_i \in \mathbb{R}^{C \times W \times H}$ represents a microscopy image with C channels and dimensions W and H. More specifically, we base our approach on the Segment Anything Model (SAM) [15], an image segmentation model which can be guided by prompts consisting of either text, masks, bounding boxes or points in an image. SAM consists of three main components: An image encoder which maps an image x into a latent representation z. A flexible prompt encoder to guide the segmentation process depending on the prompt input. In our approach, we employ image mask and point prompts which are mapped via an encoder into a latent representation p with equal size of z which is subsequently combined with z [29]. Finally, a segmentation mask decoder is employed which generates an output mask based on the image embedding z and a set of prompt embeddings p. For more detailed information please refer to [15]. In the remaining part of this paper, we assume that our method adheres to the following three assumptions: **Assumption 1: Nuclei marker channel** *We assume that each image contains a nuclei marker channel (e.g., DAPI, Hoechst) as prior information for cell segmentation.* **Assumption 2: Cell shape marker channel** *In order to perform cell segmentation, we require at least one corresponding cell marker channel (e.g., membrane or cytoplasmic stain) which marks the cell boundaries.* **Optional Assumption 3: Subcellular structures channel** *In case we aim to segment subcellular structures, we assume to have a dedicated subcellular marker channel.*

4   Method

We propose subCellSAM, an in-context learning approach for zero-shot segmentation of single cells and their subcellular compartments from multi-channel fluorescence microscopy images. A detailed description of the method may be found in Fig. 1 and an algorithmic explanation is illustrated in Algorithm 1. More specifically, our method is divided into three distinct parts. First, we perform nuclei segmentation to obtain segmentation masks as a starting point for cell segmentation. Subsequently, we enable an in-context learning strategy to perform cell and subcellular entity segmentation as step two and three, respectively.

4.1   Nuclei Segmentation

Nuclei segmentation is performed by employing segmentation followed by mask filtering. For each microscopy image $x \in \mathbb{R}^{C \times W \times H}$, we perform nuclei segmentation on the defined nuclei marker channel (see Fig. 1, Step 1). To do so, we feed the nuclei channel $nm \in \mathbb{R}^{1 \times W \times H}$ into a pretrained segmentation model f (e.g. FastSAM [37]) in order to obtain an initial list of candidate nuclei masks $\{y\}_{i=1}^m$ where y denotes the mask and m the number of candidate masks per image. Note that m may vary for different images. This process is leveraged by SAM's automatic mask generation module. Subsequently, these candidate masks are filtered

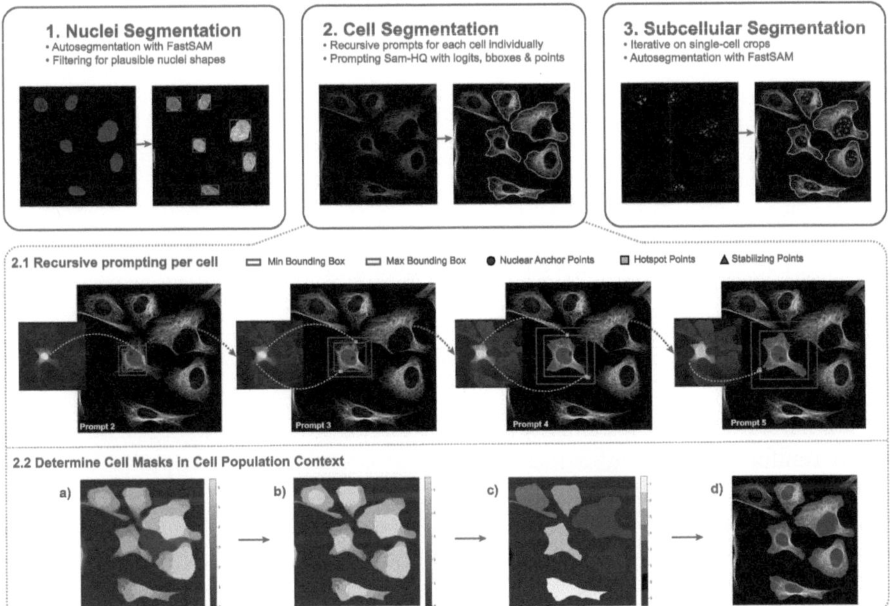

Fig. 1. subCellSAM Workflow Overview. Human Protein Atlas [32] example: UTP6 (green; nucleolus, small-subunit processome), microtubules (red), and nucleus (blue). Modules: (1) *Nuclei*, (2) *Cell*, and (3) *Subcellular Segmentation*. Panel 2.1: Recursive prompting per cell; iterations refine segmentation. Prompts: *Hotspot Points*; sampled within *Min/Max Bbox* using the mean logits map from the two previous masks as a probability map, *Stabilizing Points*, and *Nucleus Anchor Points*. Panel 2.2: Cell mask integration: low coverage regions are removed (a-b), pixels assigned to cell ID/background (c), resulting in final boundaries (d).

to isolate valid nuclei from imaging artifacts, debris, or multi-nucleus conglomerates. This is achieved through statistical outlier detection. For each mask, we compute its area, aspect ratio, and circularity. We then discard any masks whose properties fall significantly outside the population's norm (e.g., more than two standard deviations from the median area), a process that effectively removes implausible objects. The validated nucleus masks are further used as seeds for cell segmentation step. The algorithm is described in the Appendix 1.

4.2 Cell Segmentation Guided by Morphological and Topological Priors

Based on the predicted nucleus bounding boxes (see Sect. 4.1), we segment the corresponding cells by employing the nuclei masks $\{y\}_{i=1}^{m}$ and the corresponding cell marker channel t of image x (see Fig. 1, Step 2). In case that multiple cell marker channels are provided, we perform the cell segmentation process independently per channel. Subsequently, the resulting segmentation maps for each cell

---

Algorithm 1. Zero-Shot Subcellular Segmentation

Require: Microscopy Image $x \in \mathbb{R}^{c \times w \times h}$, max iterations I_{max}
1: $\{y\}, \{y_{\text{center}}\} \leftarrow$ getNucleusMaskandCenter(x)   ▷ Refer to Sect. 4.1
2: cellSeg $\leftarrow$ []
3: subcellSeg $\leftarrow$ []
4: **for** mask in $\{y\}$ **do**
5:     cell $\leftarrow$ segmentCell(x, mask)   ▷ Refer to Sect. 4.2
6:     subcell $\leftarrow$ segmentSubCell(x, mask)   ▷ Refer to Sect. 4.3
7:     cellSeg.append(cell), subcellSeg.append(subcell)
8: **end for**
9: **return** cellSeg, subcellSeg

---

are combined by the confidence-weighted average of the channel-specific weights which reinforces high-confidence regions. An overview of our approach can be found in Algorithm 2. First, we define an initial search region for the cell segmentation using the nuclei mask y_i where i denotes the ith nuclei mask. An initial segmentation is then performed by sampling foreground points within a region 1.25 times the size of the nucleus bounding box and using them as prompts to a pretrained segmentation model $f(x, p)$.

Recursive-Prompting Guided by Cellular Priors. The initial mask is refined over a fixed number of iterations (see Fig. 1, Step 2.1). This iterative process is designed to incorporate morphological and topological priors characteristic of cell images, promoting biologically plausible segmentations. The process is initiated from and anchored to the nucleus, which supports cell integrity by guiding the mask to grow as a single, contiguous object. To incorporate the topological prior of instance separation, the centers of neighboring nuclei are used as background (repulsive) points. This provides spatial context that helps delineate boundaries between adjacent cells and mitigates mask merging. New foreground points are sampled according to multiple criteria:

- *Nucleus Anchor Points:* Points sampled randomly within the nucleus mask. These reinforce the primary anchor, ensuring the growing segmentation remains tethered to the correct cell and its identity.
- *Hotspot Points:* Points sampled from high-confidence regions (high logits) just outside the current mask boundary. These points guide the mask's expansion into plausible new areas of the cytoplasm, promoting the capture of the complete cell while respecting the cell integrity prior.
- *Stabilizing Points:* Points selected from regions where the current prediction diverges from the previous iteration. These help to stabilize boundary refinement by discouraging oscillations and ensuring smoother convergence across iterations.

In each iteration, the prompt p is constructed from these foreground points, the background points derived from neighboring nuclei, and a mean logit mask from the previous two iterations, which serves as a stabilizing spatial prior. This composite prompt is supplied to the segmentation model $f(x, p)$, which progressively refines the segmentation towards a converged state.

Algorithm 2. Cell Segmentation

1: **procedure** SEGMENTCELL(t, y_i)
2:     background, foreground $\leftarrow$ sampleInitialPoints(y_i, t)
3:     segmentation, logits_t $\leftarrow$ f(x, {foreground, background})
4:     logits_t_minus_1 $\leftarrow$ logits_t
5:     **for** iter 1 ... I **do**
6:         prompt_mask $\leftarrow$ (logits_t + logits_t_minus_1) / 2
7:         foreground $\leftarrow$ sampleGuidedForegroundPoints(y_i, segmentation)
8:         background $\leftarrow$ sampleBackgroundFromNeighbors(y_i)
9:         p $\leftarrow$ {foreground, background, prompt_mask}
10:         logits_t_minus_1 $\leftarrow$ logits_t
11:         segmentation, logits_t $\leftarrow$ f(x, p)
12:     **end for**
13:     **return** segmentation
14: **end procedure**

Cell Mask Determination in Cell Population Context. Iterative prompting per cell (Step 2.1) yields a binary mask per iteration (e.g., 7 iterations produce 7 binary masks for that cell). These masks are aggregated into a coverage map, where each pixel value reflects how often it was included across the iterations for a given cell. These per-cell coverage maps are then integrated into a global instance segmentation map (Fig. 1, Step 2.2). Overlapping pixels are assigned to the cell with the highest coverage value. Pixels with low coverage in any cell's map (e.g., appearing in fewer than three of the seven masks, as depicted in Fig. 1 2.2a-b) are discarded and assigned to the background. Finally, cells touching the image borders are excluded. This practice in HCS analysis is to prevent skewed feature measurements that would result from analyzing incomplete cells.

4.3   Subcellular Entity Segmentation

To segment subcellular entities, we use the previously generated cell masks (Sect. 4.2) and the dedicated subcellular marker channel, *ssm*. For each cell, its mask is used to crop the *ssm* channel, isolating the search area. We then apply the automatic mask generation function of FastSAM to this cropped image to detect internal structures. The resulting masks are then re-projected to the full image's coordinates (see Appendix Algorithm 2).

5 Experiments

We conducted two different experiments: (1) evaluating the cell segmentation performance of subCellSAM, and (2) calculating downstream results for drug candidate validation in early drug discovery. To evaluate robustness, the parameters for subCellSAM were held constant across all experiments. Further performance improvements could likely be achieved through dataset-specific tuning. The parameters used are detailed in the Supplementary Material. Each task required a distinct dataset due to their differing objectives and data requirements.

Table 1. Overview of the image datasets to evaluate the performance of subCellSAM.

Dataset	# Images	Biology	Ground truth
Datasets for cell segmentation evaluation			Masks
BBBC008 [17]	12	Human HT29 colon-cancer cells	CellProfiler
Synthetic Benchmark [30]	1502	TREX/NXF1-Mediated RNA Localization in the Nucleus [38]	Synthetically generated
BBBC020 [17]	25	Murine bone-marrow derived macrophages	CellProfiler
Datasets for hit validation in drug discovery			Drug Potency
BBBC013 [17]	96	Human U2OS cells cytoplasm–nucleus translocation	CellProfiler, CNN
BBBC016 [17]	72	Transfluor assay with GFP-tagged β-arrestin to track GPCR activity	CellProfiler, CNN

5.1 Cell Segmentation

Datasets. Table 1 shows an overview of all datasets used in the study. The first three lines in the table denote the datasets used for the analysis of cell segmentation performance. These datasets have a ground truth segmentation mask as provided by producers of the data, but lack information for hit validation, therefore we included a second set of data (see Sect. 5.2). Further information about the biology and imaging procedures are in the Supplement (Sect. 2.1). The

Baseline Methods. We compare subCellSAM against a diverse set of baseline methods specifically developed for cell segmentation tasks: (1) CellPose 3 [28], (2) DeepCell [33], (3) CellSAM [12] and (4) CellProfiler [27]. Notably, the first three methods are trained on cellular images, whereas subCellSAM is applied directly without any fine-tuning or additional training. For more information, see Sect. 2.3 in the Supplement.

Evaluation Metrics. To assess the performance and usability of subCellSAM for cell segmentation we employ two different metrics: the Dice Score (DSC) and the Intersection over Union (IoU). For more information about both metrics please see Sect. 2.4 in the Supplement.

5.2   Hit Validation in Drug Discovery

In drug discovery, hit validation verifies the biological activity of initial "hits" and assesses their suitability as drug candidates. High-content screening (HCS) supports this process through automated imaging: segmentation detects structures such as cells, and feature extraction quantifies attributes like shape, texture, and intensity. These features are essential for identifying cellular responses to treatment. Quantitative metrics such as the Z'-factor and EC_{50}, derived from these features, are used to evaluate assay quality and compound potency (see Sect. 3.3) [3,20].

Feature Generation. Following segmentation, morphological and intensity-based features are extracted from the binary masks at three hierarchical levels: cell, nucleus, and subcellular entity. For further information please see Sect. 3.4 in the Supplement.

Datasets. The bottom part of Table 1 denotes the datasets for the analysis of hit validation in drug discovery. These datasets provide a ground truth where known hit compounds are evaluated in a titration series to validate them. Biological information and imaging procedures are in the Supplement (Sect. 3.1).

Baseline Methods. We evaluate the downstream performance of subCell-SAM in comparison to a diverse set of established baseline methods commonly employed in hit validation assay analysis: (1) Genedata Imagence [26], (2) Cell-Profiler [7,18] and (3) Multiscale CNN [8]. Details can be found in Sect. 3.2 of the Supplement.

Evaluation Metrics. To assess the performance and usability of subCellSAM for Downstream analysis we employ two different metrics: Z'-factor and EC_{50} which are the predominant result read-outs in the biopharma industry for hit validation use cases. Please see Sect. 3.3 in the Supplement for further detail.

6   Results and Discussion

We evaluate subCellSAM's performance on diverse datasets, focusing on cell segmentation and hit validation for early drug discovery. Comparisons with baseline models demonstrate its effectiveness and downstream impact.

6.1   Cell Segmentation

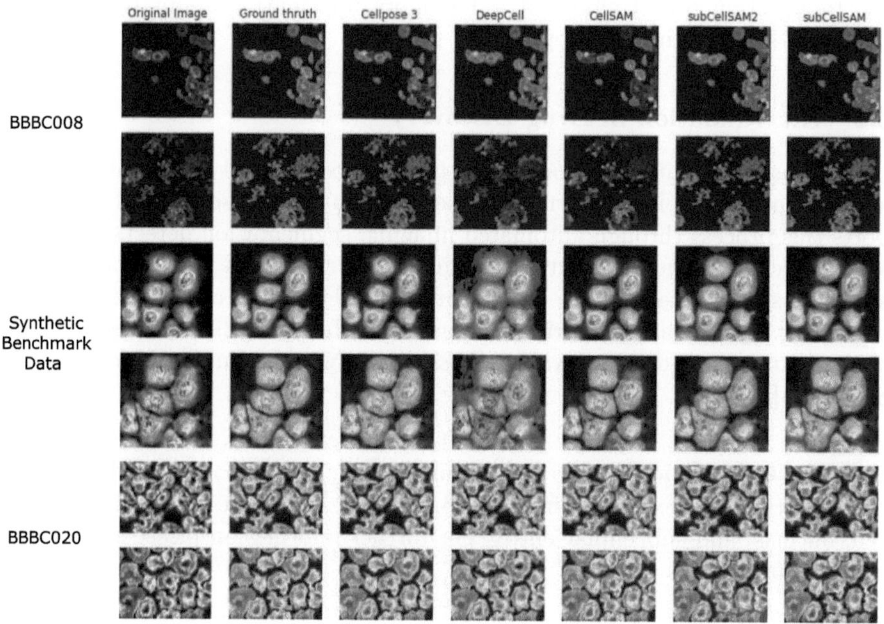

Fig. 2. Overview of cell segmentation performance across three datasets. The first two columns show the original microscopy images (grayscale) and the corresponding ground truth masks (yellow). The remaining columns display segmentation masks from various methods (yellow), overlaid on the original images. Cellpose 3 (column 3), subCellSAM, and subCellSAM2 (columns 6 and 7) demonstrate consistently strong performance across all datasets. In contrast, DeepCell (column 4) and CellSAM (column 5) exhibit notable undersegmentation, particularly in the BBBC008 dataset (first two rows). (Color figure online)

Table 2 presents the mean Dice Score (DSC) and mean Intersection over Union (IoU) for subCellSAM and all baseline models across three datasets. Overall, subCellSAM demonstrates superior segmentation performance, outperforming all baselines on the BBBC008 dataset by 1.5% in DSC and 3.9% in IoU. On the Synthetic and BBBC020 datasets, subCellSAM maintains competitive performance, consistently surpassing both DeepCell and CellSAM. Interestingly,

Table 2. Comparison of the segmentation performance achieved by the different methods. Higher is better. Please note that mean DSC and IoU are computed over the entire mask, as the ground truth for BBBC008 and the Synthetic Benchmark contains non-separable cell masks, which precludes a per-instance metric calculation.

Method	BBBC008 [17]		Synthetic Benchmark [30]		BBBC020 [17]	
	mean DSC	mean IoU	mean DSC	mean IoU	mean DSC	mean IoU
CellPose 3 [28]	0.887	0.801	0.899	0.827	**0.898**	**0.819**
DeepCell [33]	0.737	0.618	0.635	0.470	0.812	0.690
CellSAM [12]	0.602	0.484	0.837	0.739	0.817	0.694
CellProfiler (from [30])	–	–	**0.922**	**0.856**	–	–
subCellSAM (ours)	**0.901**	**0.832**	0.892	0.807	0.868	0.772
subCellSAM2 (ours)	0.900	0.821	0.828	0.714	0.851	0.745

CellProfiler achieves the best results on the Synthetic dataset, likely due to the use of CellProfiler-generated masks as training input for StyleGAN2 [13,38].

Figure 2 illustrates two example images per dataset alongside segmentation outputs from all evaluated methods. Notably, DeepCell and CellSAM tend to under-segment, particularly on the Synthetic and BBBC008 datasets (Fig. 2).

It is important to note that all deep learning-based methods (i.e., all except CellProfiler) in Table 2 and Fig. 2 were trained or fine-tuned using cell segmentation data. In contrast, subCellSAM operates in a zero-shot setting, relying on an in-context learning strategy that incorporates pre-defined morphological and topological priors through its prompting mechanism.

The modular design of subCellSAM (see Sect. 4) allows for flexible integration of different models. We evaluated both SAM-HQ [14] and SAM2 [22] for cell and subcellular segmentation, denoted as subCellSAM and subCellSAM2, respectively, in Table 2 and Fig. 2. Additional model details are provided in the Supplement (Sect. 2.2). Interestingly, SAM-HQ consistently outperforms SAM2, despite the latter generally surpassing the original SAM model [22]. This may be attributed to SAM-HQ's learnable HQ-Output token and global-local feature fusion mechanism [14], which enhance the segmentation of fine structures, an essential aspect of cell segmentation (see Fig. 2). Consequently, we use SAM-HQ for downstream hit validation analysis due to its slightly superior performance.

Remarkably, the same parameter set was used across all datasets for subCellSAM segmentation (see Table 1 in the Supplement for details). An ablation study on the BBBC008 dataset reveals that the parameters with the greatest impact are the "number of prompts per cell" and the "percent coverage across prompts". A qualitative analysis of these parameters is presented in the Supplement (Fig. 2). Fewer prompts result in smaller masks that may miss parts of the cell, while higher coverage thresholds yield more conservative masks by including only the most confidently predicted pixels. While dataset-specific tuning may improve performance, subCellSAM is designed for minimal adjustment, which is especially important given the frequent lack of ground truth data in real-world datasets.

For assays where a heterogeneous morphological cell response is expected, including variations in cell size, particularly in assays involving induced pluripotent stem cells (iPSCs) or primary cells, some parameter presets of subCellSAM may need to be adjusted, potentially on a per-cell basis. However, this is typically not necessary for hit validation assays.

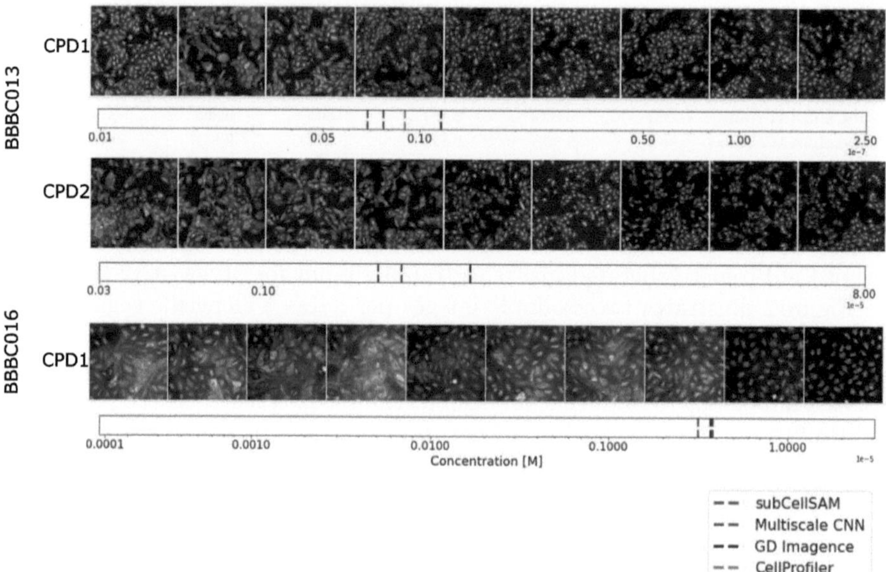

Fig. 3. Overview of dosing behavior of the different compounds for both datasets with the calculated EC_{50} values of the methods (see Supplement). The EC_{50} values are shown in the bar under the respective images that show the nucleus (blue) and protein of interest (green). Note that not all values are available for all baseline methods (see Table 2 in the Supplement)

6.2   Application to Hit Validation in Drug Discovery

Hit validation in drug discovery confirms that a compound truly affects the intended biological target and exhibits reproducible biological activity, rather than being a false positive [3]. To evaluate the performance of subCellSAM for hit validation, conventional image features were extracted from the generated masks of the cell, nucleus, and subcellular structures (see Sect. 5.2). The calculated metrics, the Z'-factor and EC_{50} values, play a critical role in hit analysis and in preparing compounds for further filtering.

Table 2 in the Supplementary Information presents both the maximum Z'-factor and the calculated EC_{50} values for subCellSAM, compared to those obtained using baseline methods (see Sect. 5.2). The features extracted from the subCellSAM masks are on par with the baseline methods in terms of Z'-factor, indicating good assay quality and robustness.

Notably, for the transfluor assay (BBBC016), subCellSAM demonstrates effective performance. Without any parameter tuning, subcellular structures are segmented effectively, resulting in improved signal-to-background ratios and, consequently, a high Z'-factor. The feature used in this case is the number of subcellular entities per cell (see Sect. 3.4 in the Supplementary Information). Regarding EC_{50} values, the results obtained using subCellSAM are in agreement with all baseline methods (see Table 2 in the Supplement). This is illustrated in Fig. 3, which shows the EC_{50} values from both baseline methods and subCell-SAM, alongside representative images depicting cellular responses to compound dosing. All methods are in agreement and are able to detect the switch between start and endpoint cellular phenotypes (see Fig. 3).

7   Conclusion

We introduce subCellSAM, a method for (sub)cellular segmentation in high-content screening that applies a foundation model in a zero-shot setting. The method's core is an in-context learning strategy that incorporates morphological and topological priors of cells to guide the segmentation process. Our experiments demonstrated that this approach yields segmentations that are competitive with specialized methods on three benchmark datasets. When applied to two industry-relevant hit validation tasks, the method produced high-quality downstream results without requiring dataset-specific parameter tuning. This suggests that leveraging structured, domain-specific priors within a general foundation model is a viable strategy for reducing manual configuration in automated HCS analysis pipelines, a conclusion supported by our use of a single hyperparameter set across all experiments.

Limitations. Our approach has two main limitations: First, the recursive prompting strategy leads to a significantly slower inference time compared to fine-tuned models. Second, subCellSAM requires a dedicated nucleus channel to initiate segmentation. Future work will aim to extend subCellSAM's applicability from cell culture systems to more complex tissue samples.

References

1. Alayrac, et al.: Flamingo: a visual language model for few-shot learning. In: Advances in Neural Information Processing Systems (2022)
2. Archit, A., et al.: Segment anything for microscopy. Nat. Methods **22**, 579–591 (2025). https://doi.org/10.1038/s41592-024-02580-4
3. Barcelos, M.P., et al.: Lead optimization in drug discovery. In: Taft, C.A., de Lazaro, S.R. (eds) Research Topics in Bioactivity, Environment and Energy. Engineering Materials, pp. 481–500. Springer, Cham (2022). https://doi.org/10.1007/978-3-031-07622-0_19

4. Bray, M.A., et al.: Cell painting, a high-content image-based assay for morphological profiling using multiplexed fluorescent dyes. Nat. Protoc. **11**(9), 1757–1774 (2016). https://doi.org/10.1038/nprot.2016.105
5. Brown, T., et al.: Language models are few-shot learners. In: Advances in Neural Information Processing Systems (2020)
6. Caicedo, J.C., et al.: Data-analysis strategies for image-based cell profiling. Nat. Methods **14**, 849–863 (2017). https://doi.org/10.1038/nmeth.4397
7. Carpenter, A.E., et al.: Cellprofiler: image analysis software for identifying and quantifying cell phenotypes. Genome Biol. **7**, 1–11 (2006). https://doi.org/10.1186/gb-2006-7-10-r100
8. Godinez, W.J., Hossain, I., Lazic, S.E., Davies, J.W., Zhang, X.: A multi-scale convolutional neural network for phenotyping high-content cellular images. Bioinformatics **33**(13), 2010–2019 (2017). https://doi.org/10.1093/bioinformatics/btx069
9. Guo, M., Yi, H., Qin, Z., Wang, H., Men, A., Lao, Q.: Multiple prompt fusion for zero-shot lesion detection using vision-language models. In: 26th International Conference on Medical Image Computing and Computer Assisted Intervention (2023)
10. Gupta, A., Vuillecard, P., Farkhondeh, A., Odobez, J.M.: Exploring the zero-shot capabilities of vision-language models for improving gaze following. In: IEEE/CVF Conference on Computer Vision and Pattern Recognition (CVPR) Workshops (2024)
11. Han, G., Lim, S.N.: Few-shot object detection with foundation models. In: IEEE/CVF Conference on Computer Vision and Pattern Recognition (CVPR) (2024)
12. Israel, U., et al.: A foundation model for cell segmentation (2023). https://arxiv.org/abs/2311.11004
13. Karras, T., Laine, S., Aittala, M., Hellsten, J., Lehtinen, J., Aila, T.: Analyzing and improving the image quality of styleGAN. In: IEEE/CVF Conference on Computer Vision and Pattern Recognition (CVPR) (2020)
14. Ke, L., et al.: Segment anything in high quality. In: Advances in Neural Information Processing Systems (2023)
15. Kirillov, A., et al.: Segment anything. In: IEEE/CVF International Conference on Computer Vision (ICCV) (2023)
16. Kruger, S., et al.: Advances in cancer immunotherapy 2019 - latest trends. J. Exp. Clin. Cancer Res. **38** (2019). https://doi.org/10.1186/s13046-019-1266-0
17. Ljosa, V., Sokolnicki, K.L., Carpenter, A.E.: Annotated high-throughput microscopy image sets for validation. Nat. Methods **9**(7), 637–637 (2012). https://doi.org/10.1038/nmeth.2083
18. Logan, D.J., Carpenter, A.E.: Screening cellular feature measurements for image-based assay development. J. Biomol. Screen. **15**(7), 840–846 (2010). https://doi.org/10.1177/1087057110370895
19. Na, S., Guo, Y., Jiang, F., Ma, H., Huang, J.: Segment any cell: a SAM-based auto-prompting fine-tuning framework for nuclei segmentation (2024). https://arxiv.org/abs/2401.13220
20. Nichols, A.: High Content Screening as a Screening Tool in Drug Discovery, pp. 379–387. Humana Press, Totowa (2006). https://doi.org/10.1385/1-59745-217-3:379
21. Radford, A., et al.: Learning transferable visual models from natural language supervision. In: International Conference on Machine Learning (2021)
22. Ravi, N., et al.: SAM 2: Segment anything in images and videos. In: International Conference on Learning Representations (2025)

23. Sertkaya, A., Beleche, T., Jessup, A., Sommers, B.D.: Costs of drug development and research and development intensity in the us, 2000–2018. JAMA Netw. Open **7**(6), e2415445–e2415445 (2024). https://doi.org/10.1001/jamanetworkopen.2024.15445

24. Siegismund, D., Wieser, M., Heyse, S., Steigele, S.: Self-supervised representation learning for high-content screening. In: International Conference on Medical Imaging with Deep Learning (2022)

25. Siegismund, D., Wieser, M., Heyse, S., Steigele, S.: Learning channel importance for high content imaging with interpretable deep input channel mixing. In: German Conference on Pattern Recognition (2023)

26. Steigele, S., et al.: Deep learning-based HCS image analysis for the enterprise. SLAS Discov. **25**(7), 812–821 (2020). https://doi.org/10.1177/2472555220918837

27. Stirling, D.R., Swain-Bowden, M.J., Lucas, A.M., Carpenter, A.E., Cimini, B.A., Goodman, A.: CellProfiler 4: improvements in speed, utility and usability. BMC Bioinform. **22**(1), 433 (2021). https://doi.org/10.1186/s12859-021-04344-9

28. Stringer, C., Pachitariu, M.: Cellpose3: one-click image restoration for improved cellular segmentation. Nat. Methods **22**, 295–599 (2025). https://doi.org/10.1038/s41592-025-02595-5

29. Tancik, M., et al.: Fourier features let networks learn high frequency functions in low dimensional domains. In: Advances in Neural Information Processing Systems (2020)

30. Tang, J., Du, W., Shu, Z., Cao, Z.: A generative benchmark for evaluating the performance of fluorescent cell image segmentation. Synthetic Syst. Biotechnol. **9**(4), 627–637 (2024). https://doi.org/10.1016/j.synbio.2024.05.005

31. Tewel, Y., Shalev, Y., Schwartz, I., Wolf, L.: Zero-shot image-to-text generation for visual-semantic arithmetic. In: IEEE/CVF Conference on Computer Vision and Pattern Recognition (2022)

32. Uhlén, M., et al.: Tissue-based map of the human proteome. Science **347**(6220), 1260419 (2015). https://doi.org/10.1126/science.1260419

33. Van Valen, D.A., et al.: Deep learning automates the quantitative analysis of individual cells in live-cell imaging experiments. PLoS Comput. Biol. **12**(11), e1005177 (2016). https://doi.org/10.1371/journal.pcbi.1005177

34. Wieser, M., Siegismund, D., Heyse, S., Steigele, S.: Vision transformers show improved robustness in high-content image analysis. In: Swiss Conference on Data Science (SDS) (2022)

35. Wieser, M., Siegismund, D., Steigele, S.: Revisiting deep archetypal analysis for phenotype discovery in high content imaging. In: IEEE/CVF Winter Conference on Applications of Computer Vision (WACV) (2025)

36. Zanella, F., Lorens, J.B., Link, W.: High content screening: seeing is believing. Trends Biotechnol. **28**(5), 237–245 (2010). https://doi.org/10.1016/j.tibtech.2010.02.005

37. Zhao, X., et al.: Fast segment anything (2023). https://arxiv.org/abs/2306.12156

38. Zuckerman, B., Ron, M., Mikl, M., Segal, E., Ulitsky, I.: Gene architecture and sequence composition underpin selective dependency of nuclear export of long RNAs on NXF1 and the TREX complex. Mol. Cell **79**(2), 251–267 (2020). https://doi.org/10.1016/j.molcel.2020.05.013

Safety and Robustness

synth-dacl: Does Synthetic Defect Data Enhance Segmentation Accuracy and Robustness for Real-World Bridge Inspections?

Johannes Flotzinger[1]([envelope])[ID], Fabian Deuser[1][ID], Achref Jaziri[2][ID], Heiko Neumann[3][ID], Norbert Oswald[1][ID], Visvanathan Ramesh[2][ID], and Thomas Braml[1][ID]

[1] University of the Bundeswehr Munich, Munich, Germany
Johannes.flotzinger@unibw.de
[2] Goethe University Frankfurt am Main, Frankfurt am Main, Germany
[3] University of Ulm, Ulm, Germany

Abstract. Adequate bridge inspection is increasingly challenging in many countries due to growing ailing stocks, compounded with a lack of staff and financial resources. Automating the key task of visual bridge inspection – classification of defects and building components on pixel level – improves efficiency, increases accuracy and enhances safety in the inspection process and resulting building assessment. Models overtaking this task must cope with an assortment of real-world conditions. They must be robust to variations in image quality, as well as background texture, as defects often appear on surfaces of diverse texture and degree of weathering. dacl10k [17] is the largest and most diverse dataset for real-world concrete bridge inspections. However, the dataset exhibits class imbalance, which leads to notably poor model performance particularly when segmenting fine-grained classes such as cracks and cavities. This work introduces "*synth-dacl*" [15], a compilation of three novel dataset extensions based on synthetic concrete textures. These extensions are designed to balance class distribution in dacl10k and enhance model performance, especially for crack and cavity segmentation. When incorporating the *synth-dacl* extensions, we observe substantial improvements in model robustness across 15 perturbed test sets. Notably, on the perturbed test set, a model trained on dacl10k combined with all synthetic extensions achieves a 2% increase in mean IoU, F1 score, Recall, and Precision compared to the same model trained solely on dacl10k.

Keywords: Automated Damage Recognition · Bridge Inspection · Synthetic Data · Semantic Segmentation

1 Introduction

Worldwide, many bridges are exposed to high traffic loads, extreme weather events, sea salt, and de-icing chemicals, leading to defects. At the same time,

M. Keuper and F. Locatello (Eds.): DAGM GCPR 2025, LNCS 16125, pp. 387–402, 2026.
https://doi.org/10.1007/978-3-032-12840-9_25

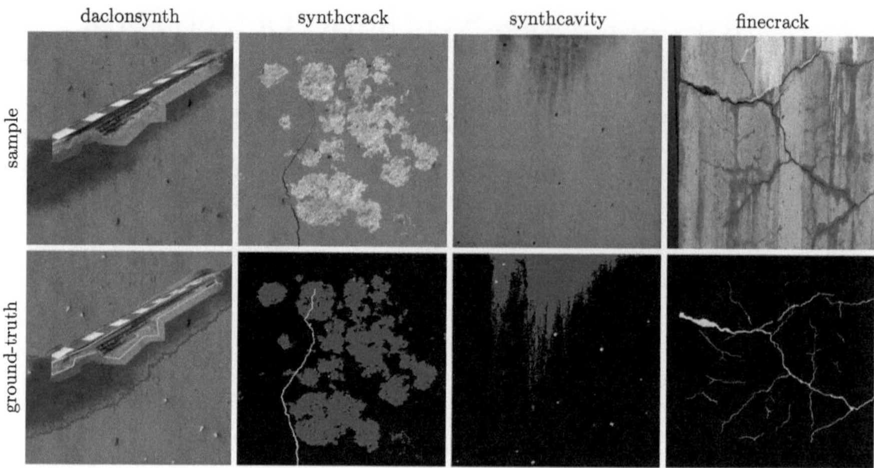

Fig. 1. Left column/daclonsynth: Cropped defect shape from dacl10k pasted on synthetic concrete background and ground-truth below showing polygonal annotations of real-world (*Spalling* with corroded *Exposed Rebars*) and synthetic defects which are namely *Cavity* (pale purple) and *Weathering* (green); Middle-left Column/synthcrack: synthetic concrete surface with synthetic defects and ground-truth showing: *Crack* (rose), *Cavity*, *Weathering*; Middle-right column/synthcavity: synthcavity sample and ground-truth showing three combined masks, *Cavity* from both rendered concrete texture and the cavity generative model, and synthetic *Weathering*; Right column/finecrack: Test sample from dacl10k and fine-resolution crack masks. (Color figure online)

most industrialized countries face a growing stock of old infrastructure [5,8]. To determine rehabilitation measurements and immediate actions, such as traffic restrictions or bridge closures, defects are identified and assessed during inspections. However, the current inspection process is often inefficient and prone to error [1,26,32], highlighting the significant potential of automated inspection methods to improve accuracy and reliability. Within an automated inspection workflow semantic segmentation plays a central role as it classifies, measures and localizes damage at pixel level [9,17,19].

The largest and most diverse dataset for the segmentation of bridge defects and components is dacl10k [17] due to its variety of buildings and classes. However, a major challenge of dacl10k is the strong class imbalance, affecting not only the number of images but also the pixel-level and instance-level distributions. E.g, the dataset contains approximately ten times more images labeled with *Spalling* than with *Rockpocket*, and about ten times more pixels annotated as *Protective Equipment* than as *Crack*. This imbalance is evident in the dacl10k challenge [16], where participants consistently reported significantly poor performance for two concrete defects, *crack* and *cavity*. Addressing this imbalance is critical to improving model robustness, particularly for real-world bridge inspections, where models must be resilient to variations in image quality, camera pose, concrete texture, and the degree of weathering. Real-world applications require models to perform reliably under varying conditions, but despite the wide range of image acquisition scenarios encountered in civil engineering, no study has rigorously investigated the robustness of multi-class or multi-label computer vision models for damage detection in this domain.

In our work, we address these challenges by introducing three synthetic dataset extensions, collectively referred to as *"synth-dacl"*, each designed with 5,000 samples. The first extension addresses the issue of class imbalance. This enhancement superimposes real-world damage polygons on synthetic concrete backgrounds to maintain realistic defect shapes while balancing the representation of underrepresented defect classes. The second and third extension focus on improving model performance for challenging single defect types in practice. We simulate concrete surfaces with one primary synthetic defect – either a crack or a cavity – per set to directly target the detection of these classes. We systematically evaluate how synth-dacl extensions affect average performance, individual class performance, and overall model robustness. Robustness is assessed by applying 15 image perturbations to real-world test data from the dacl10k dataset, simulating conditions such as changes in illumination, noise, and contrast. This step ensures that our models are not only accurate, but also resilient to the unpredictable conditions found in real-world bridge inspections. All datasets introduced in this work are publicly available to facilitate reproducibility and further research [15, 18].

2   Related Work

2.1   Bridge Inspection Datasets

The S2DS dataset [9], which comprises 743 samples, is the first real-world semantic segmentation dataset for bridge inspection with pixel-wise labels for six classes relevant for concrete bridge inspections. In the field of binary crack segmentation both OmniCrack30k [10] and CrackSeg9k [22] are dataset collections for cracked and uncracked surfaces of various materials.

On the other hand, synthetic data has become widely used to enhance performance on real-world tasks, particularly when there is a shortage of well-labeled images [33]. For example, Dwibedi et al. [13] generate synthetic images by cutting and pasting object instances into diverse environments. Other studies explore the role of synthetic data in improving robustness in medical imaging. For instance, Al Khalil et al. [4] examine the usability of synthesized short-axis Cardiac Magnetic Resonance (CMR) images generated using Generative Adversarial Networks to ameliorate the robustness of heart cavity segmentation models across various conditions. A comprehensive review of such applications can be found in [29].

In civil engineering, synthetic data starts to become a resource to mitigate the limited availability of pixel-accurate annotated datasets. Much of the research in this field focuses on crack segmentation [21, 37, 43]. For instance, [21] developed a simulation model in Blender for generating additional synthetic crack data for concrete surfaces. The synthetic cracks in this dataset are modeled using irregular fractals. Another synthetic crack dataset is the Supervisely Synthetic Crack Segmentation dataset [37] which consists of 1,558 synthetic images for road surface crack detection. This dataset employs various generative algorithms, such as random walk, rapidly exploring random trees, and L-systems, to produce a diverse array of crack patterns. [43] introduced a synthetic dataset specifically for dam crack detection. This dataset integrates crack patterns extracted from real-world, open-source datasets with a 3D mesh model of an actual dam, creating realistic training data suited to the unique structural context of dams.

While these datasets have advanced research in the field of automated bridge inspections, each faces limitations when applied to practical scenarios. They typically focus on a single defect class (*Crack*), offer limited diversity in image quality, concrete texture, and environmental conditions, and lack multi-label annotations which is due to the overlapping character of concrete defects crucial. Moreover, existing studies on the robustness of semantic damage segmentation models [6,23] are, again, restricted to binary crack detection and assess only a narrow set of perturbations, which fall short of representing the wide range of real-world challenges encountered during bridge inspections.

3   Datasets

In the following, detailed information on the investigated real-world dataset dacl10k and its finecrack masks (Sect. 3.1) as well as the synthetic extensions (Sect. 3.2) are provided.

3.1   Dacl10k

dacl10k [17] is the first large-scale dataset for automated bridge inspections, containing 9,920 polygon-annotated images across 19 classes, grouped into defects and structural components. It features multi-label semantic segmentation with coarse pixel-level annotations, which stem from real bridge inspections. The dataset includes common defect combinations, as shown in the top-left tile of Fig. 1. For the underlying work a new version v3 of this dataset (referred to as dacl10k) was developed [18]. During transition class ambiguities were resolved: *Spalling* and *Rockpocket* were often confused in v2 due to their visual similarity, even though they arise from different causes: corroding reinforcement versus poor concrete deaeration. The same applied for *Joint Tape* vs. *Restformwork*, and *Weathering* vs. *Wetspot*.

Finecrack Masks. Most open-source datasets for crack or defect segmentation [12,22,27,30,42,45] focus solely on cracks on plain concrete surfaces. These datasets lack important real-world variations, such as wet cracks, efflorescence, graffiti, and weathered backgrounds. Consequently, models trained on these datasets [24,38] tend to generate numerous false positives, as evidenced by the low precision scores in Table 2.

From a civil engineer's perspective, cracks are not necessarily severe. In concrete structures, they occur where the tensile strength of the concrete is exceeded. Depending on the exposure of the building part, cracks with a width up to 0.4 mm (0.016 in) on non-prestressed building parts may be irrelevant regarding structural integrity and durability. However, on pre-stressed bridges, a crack width of 0.1 mm (0.004 in) can indicate tendon failure and be critical [3,36]. According to many inspection guidelines, the required measurement accuracy for crack width is 0.1 mm [2,7,35]. This emphasizes that, for practical use, the crack defect class requires pixel-accurate segmentation.

To address this issue, we created fine-resolution crack masks for the 496 dacl10k test images that contain *Crack* and *ACrack*. First, the polygon is cropped and contrast-enhanced. Then, it is segmented. For Crack instances, we apply Multi-Otsu thresholding to grayscale images. For *ACracks*, we use a pre-trained crack segmentation model [24] to generate approximations of fine crack masks. The results are fused into a binary mask and manually refined by a civil engineer to ensure pixel-level accuracy. Thus, the defect classes *Crack* and *ACrack* from dacl10k are fused within one binary *Crack* mask.

3.2   Synthetic Dataset Extensions

Due to the significant class imbalance and low performance on specific classes in the dacl10k dataset, as well as the high costs associated with data collection and labeling, we explore synthetic data generation methods in the following sections. Details on the class distribution in the original dacl10k-v3 dataset are provided in our supplementary material.

Synthetic Concrete Surfaces. To increase robustness in defect segmentation and overcome class imbalance, we introduce three new dataset extensions based on synthetic concrete surfaces: **daclonsynth**, **synthcrack** and **synthcavity**. To generate these surfaces an extended version of the physics-based rendering (PBR) introduced in Jaziri et al. [21] was used. The rendering pipeline consists of two main stages: (1) scene generation, and (2) defect injection. In the first stage, various texture maps are applied to produce diverse concrete surfaces using Blender's Cycles PBR engine. Optional overlays such as moss or dirt simulate *Weathering* effects (see Fig. 1). In the second stage, up to two defects are added per scene (see Sect. 3.2 and 3.2), and semantic ground-truths including depth, surface normals, and class masks, are generated automatically, including a dedicated map for *Weathering*.

Daclonsynth. Building on these synthetic scenes, we generate the **daclonsynth** extension with the specific goal of mitigating class imbalance in the dacl10k training set. As shown in Fig. 2, several classes, particularly *Rockpocket*, *Exposed Rebars*, *Hollowareas*, and *Wetspot*, are heavily underrepresented in both pixel count and shape count. For instance, *Rockpocket* is annotated only 354 times and accounts for merely 4.5 million pixels, while the average across classes is around 45 million pixels.

To generate new training samples, we first filter the dacl10k training images to include only those containing at least one instance of a targeted underrepresented class. Then, each annotated shape is cropped from the image along with its corresponding polygonal annotation. This cropped region is then randomly rotated and pasted onto a synthetic concrete surface that is also randomly selected. For each class, half of the synthetic samples include *Weathering* overlays, while the other half remain clean to promote better generalization to both conditions.

In cases where the target defect typically co-occurs with a larger structural issue, as is common for *Exposed Rebars* appearing within *Spalling* or *Rockpocket*, the crop is extended to include the full area of the co-located host defect. Furthermore, to prevent models from exploiting the artificial distinction between real annotations and synthetic backgrounds, the shapes of *Spalling*, *Rockpocket*, *Wetspot*, *Hollowareas*, and *Efflorescence* are dilated using a 30×30 kernel prior to compositing.

To determine the number of synthetic samples needed per class, we calculate the number of instances required to bring the pixel and shape counts closer to the averages of all underrepresented classes. We then use the mean of these two estimates to define a target sample count per class. The final distribution of the 5,000 synthetic samples in **daclonsynth** is determined proportionally based on these classwise demands while accounting for the average number of pixels and shapes per sample for each defect. Although complete balance is not possible due to defect co-occurrence and overlaps, the resulting dataset significantly shifts the class distribution towards uniformity. Non-underrepresented classes may also be reproduced due to overlaps, which further contributes to a more diverse and realistic training dataset.

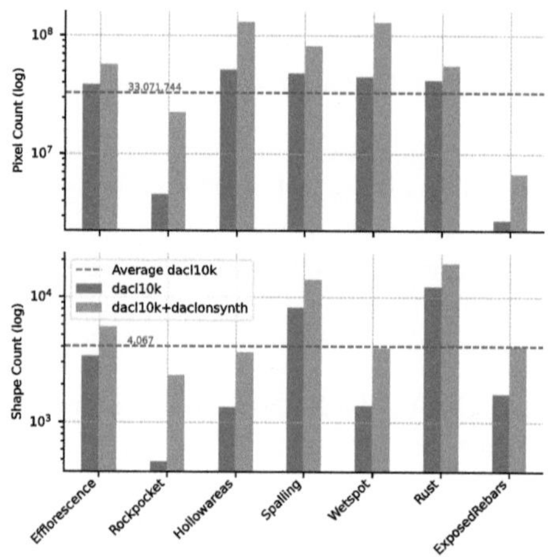

Fig. 2. Comparison of classwise pixel count (left) and shape count (right) of dacl10k train set (blue) and the combination of dacl10k and daclonsynth (orange). The red dashed line marks the average pixel, or rather shape count, over the displayed classes from dacl10k. All stats based on the resized data (512×512). (Color figure online)

Synthcrack. Crack patterns are generated using a fractal model based on [21] and rendered onto synthetic concrete surfaces with corresponding semantic masks. The resulting extension, **synthcrack** matches dacl10k in terms of crack pixel and shape counts. It also contains some incidental *Cavity* shapes, originating from fine-grained surface geometry embedded in the rendering pipeline, but these are not generated explicitly.

Synthcavity. To generate cavities, we introduce a dedicated simulation approach based on Perlin noise. Multiple noise layers with varying octaves (2–32), persistence (0.6–0.9), and lacunarity (1.5 or 2) are combined to create irregular cavity maps. After thresholding and filtering out small regions, the resulting masks are used to build geometry-aware PBR textures. These are rendered and overlaid onto synthetic concrete surfaces to form the synthcavity dataset. Compared to dacl10k, synthcavity contains more cavity shapes, but with smaller area per instance, leading to a lower overall pixel count.

All synthetic datasets also contribute additional background and *Weathering* annotations. Overlaps in **daclonsynth** further introduce crack and cavity shapes, which are reflected in the distributions shown in Fig. 3.

4   Experiments

In this section, we evaluate the effectiveness of our synthetic dataset extensions by testing eight differently trained models on the dacl10k test set. To assess the contribution of synthetic data to model robustness, the same models are also evaluated on a perturbed version of the test set. Additionally, we conduct two ablation studies: one focusing on the segmentation performance for finely annotated cracks, and another analyzing cross-domain generalization from synthetic to real-world data.

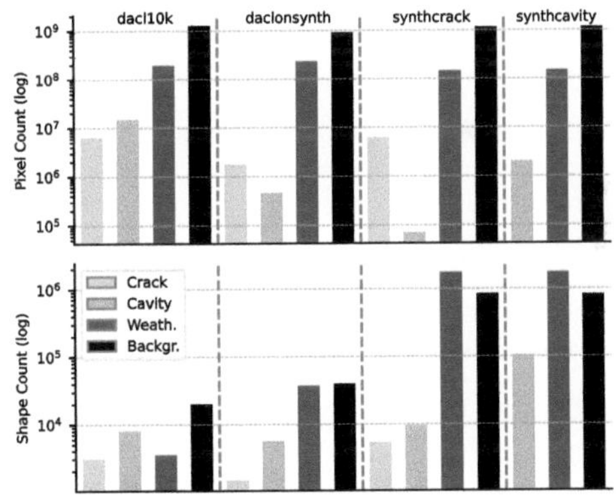

Fig. 3. Pixel (left) and shape (right) counts for *Crack, Cavity, Weathering*, and background in dacl10k and synthetic datasets.

All experiments employ a Feature Pyramid Network (FPN) [25] with a MaxViT-Base Vision Transformer backbone [40]. The primary evaluation metric is Intersection over Union (IoU) as previous work [11,14,44] where IoU is set to 1 when the union is zero. This is complemented by F1 score, Precision, and Recall the analysis of the fine-grained classes and the perturbed testing. In general, the metrics are computed per class at the image level and averaged across the dataset. Mean values are reported by averaging the class-level scores. Further details, such as split size and class imbalance, can be found in the supplementary material.

4.1   Results on Dacl10k

As shown in Table 1, the inclusion of synthetic data improves overall performance, with the six highest mIoU results being achieved when synthetic data is used during training. At class level, extending dacl10k with the semi-synthetic daclonsynth improves IoU in average for the daclonsynth classes by 1.3%, with *Rockpocket* experiencing a notable +4% increase (see Table 1). This boost likely stems from the fivefold increase in representation of this class provided by daclonsynth. Notably, the top three configurations for crack IoU in Table 1 do not include synthcrack, which might seem contradictory at first. This outcome is explained by the fact that synthcrack employs much finer and more detailed crack annotations than those in dacl10k. As a result, the model learns to predict cracks at a finer resolution than what the dacl10k ground-truth can capture. This hypothesis is supported by the result of the model trained only on synthcrack, presented in Table 4, which confirms best performance on the finecrack masks. The results on the finecrack masks, and on *Cavity* are analyzed in the following Sect. 4.2.

Table 1. mIoU and classwise IoU on the dacl10k test split. A check mark in the Training Data column indicates the synthetic data used during training. Bold numbers indicate the highest value in each column, while underlined numbers represent the lowest.

| Train data | | | | | classwise IoU | | | | | | | | | | | | | | | | | | |
dacl10k	daclonsynth	synthcrack	synthcavity	mIoU	Crack	ACrack	Effloresc.	Rockpocket	WConccor	Hollowareas	Cavity	Spalling	Restformw.	Wetspot	Rust	Graffiti	Weathering	ExposedR.	Bearing	EJoint	Drainage	PEquipment	JTape
✓	–	–	–	42.71	31.40	49.81	42.97	21.26	_9.79_	54.88	20.07	_44.83_	31.69	23.52	_47.03_	66.09	**37.26**	39.89	59.16	56.44	60.17	73.61	41.64
✓	✓	–	–	42.93	**31.42**	**51.76**	**43.53**	**25.26**	10.13	56.07	22.02	45.19	31.68	24.22	48.53	66.01	_27.11_	40.61	59.47	55.12	**61.62**	_73.00_	42.85
✓	✓	✓	–	43.12	30.16	49.76	42.73	22.64	**14.25**	55.62	_17.58_	45.50	32.46	_18.43_	48.04	66.00	36.89	_39.59_	**60.98**	**59.96**	60.55	73.20	**44.97**
✓	✓	–	✓	42.85	30.62	47.05	42.58	22.84	13.01	56.41	20.95	45.68	32.28	22.91	48.20	_63.63_	34.82	40.39	58.44	56.22	61.26	74.23	42.58
✓	✓	✓	✓	**43.37**	29.48	50.55	43.25	21.11	11.99	**56.90**	17.89	45.65	**32.60**	23.87	**49.70**	65.65	35.87	**41.73**	60.92	58.56	60.73	74.10	43.51
✓	–	✓	–	42.76	_27.25_	48.55	43.23	22.47	11.14	55.18	23.14	**46.08**	_31.34_	24.62	48.45	66.18	32.17	40.96	60.50	_54.86_	59.47	**74.70**	42.14
✓	–	–	✓	42.88	29.18	47.93	43.15	22.86	11.49	55.02	**24.63**	45.44	31.74	**24.77**	48.57	**66.51**	33.26	40.03	60.28	55.77	58.58	74.00	41.46
✓	–	✓	✓	_41.86_	30.68	_46.82_	_42.41_	_20.21_	11.55	_54.50_	19.06	45.08	32.00	22.61	48.30	64.46	36.98	39.61	_54.38_	56.30	_56.50_	73.05	_40.84_

4.2   Ablation: Results on Fine-Grained Classes

For both fine-grained classes, *Crack* in the form of finecrack masks and *Cavity*, we provide additional metrics in Table 2. All models incorporating synthcrack report better results on finecrack masks than the baseline trained on dacl10k only. The best finecrack IoU is achieved by the model utilizing dacl10k, daclonsynth and synthcrack, 1.3 percent points higher than dacl10k. Regarding *Cavity* the highest IoU (24.63%) and F1 score (39.53%) is reported for the model trained on the combination of dacl10k and synthcavity.

Table 2. IoU, F1 Score, Recall and Precision on the finecrack and cavity masks. Bold numbers indicate the highest value in each column, while underlined numbers represent the lowest. We compare with two open-source baseline methods for crack segmentation (two bottom rows). The train data are: (1) dacl10k, (2) daclonsynth, (3) synthcrack, (4) synthcavity.

Train data				Metrics Finecrack				Metrics Cavity			
(1)	(2)	(3)	(4)	IoU	F1	Rec.	Prec.	IoU	F1	Rec.	Prec.
✓	–	–	–	11.54	20.69	28.87	16.13	20.07	33.43	31.06	<u>36.20</u>
✓	✓	–	–	12.09	21.57	31.19	16.48	22.02	36.09	33.68	38.87
✓	✓	✓	–	**12.88**	**22.82**	26.64	19.96	<u>17.58</u>	<u>29.91</u>	22.34	45.23
✓	✓	–	✓	11.74	21.02	31.99	15.65	20.95	34.65	26.85	48.83
✓	✓	✓	✓	11.97	21.38	23.86	19.37	17.89	30.35	<u>21.46</u>	**51.82**
✓	–	✓	–	12.12	21.38	<u>22.17</u>	**21.11**	23.14	37.59	**36.11**	39.20
✓	–	–	✓	<u>11.34</u>	<u>20.37</u>	**34.11**	<u>14.52</u>	**24.63**	**39.53**	33.86	47.48
✓	–	✓	✓	12.33	21.95	26.50	18.73	19.06	32.02	23.20	51.66
HrSegNet-B64 [24]				3.34	6.47	19.26	3.89	–	–	–	–
CT-CrackSeg [38]				0.59	1.18	84.25	0.60	–	–	–	–

4.3 Results on Perturbed Dacl10k

In real-world bridge inspection applications, factors such as different camera models, varying image acquisition settings and environmental conditions introduce noise that negatively affect model performance. To investigate how this affects our differently trained models, we follow the methodology of Wang et al. [41] and apply 15 different perturbations to the test images. These include different noise functions, blur, brightness changes, and weather effects, which are demonstrated in the supplementary material. The results, averaged over all perturbations, are presented in Table 3.

Apart from the model trained on dacl10k, synthcrack and synthcavity (see Sect. 5) all models trained on both original and synthetically generated data consistently show the "most robust" to these perturbations. The highest IoU, F1 score, and Precision is reported for the model trained on dacl10k combined with all *synth-dacl* extensions. Furthermore, this model shows 1.89% less relative performance loss in mean IoU and 2.54% in mean F1 score (see Table 3).

Table 3. Comparison of IoU, F1, Recall, and Precision on the test split between raw and perturbed (Pert.) images. The *Change* column represents the relative performance difference between testing on raw images and perturbed images, highlighting the degradation in performance caused by the perturbations. Bold numbers indicate the highest value in each column, while underlined numbers represent the lowest. The train data are: (1) dacl10k, (2) daclonsynth, (3) synthcrack, (4) synthcavity.

(1)	(2)	(3)	(4)	mIoU Raw	mIoU Pert.	mIoU Change	mF1 Raw	mF1 Pert.	mF1 Change	mRecall Raw	mRecall Pert.	mRecall Change	mPrecision Raw	mPrecision Pert.	mPrecision Change
✓	–	–	–	42.71	30.87	−27.73	57.89	43.34	−25.13	56.02	38.63	−31.04	60.38	60.79	0.67
✓	✓	–	–	42.93	31.03	−27.72	58.12	43.50	−25.16	55.90	39.30	−29.69	62.18	61.56	−0.99
✓	✓	✓	–	43.12	30.89	−28.36	58.23	43.34	−25.57	55.42	38.76	−30.07	63.01	61.95	−1.69
✓	✓	–	✓	42.85	30.87	−27.95	58.16	43.51	−25.19	56.83	39.84	−29.90	60.96	<u>60.61</u>	−0.58
✓	✓	✓	✓	**43.37**	**32.16**	−25.84	**58.47**	**45.26**	−22.59	<u>54.98</u>	40.11	**−27.05**	**64.20**	**63.05**	−1.79
✓	–	✓	–	42.76	31.14	−27.18	57.98	43.84	−24.39	56.00	38.90	−30.52	61.35	61.88	0.86
✓	–	–	✓	42.88	32.00	**−25.36**	58.20	45.06	**−22.58**	**57.79**	**41.35**	−28.45	<u>59.79</u>	60.81	**1.70**
✓	–	✓	✓	<u>41.86</u>	<u>29.96</u>	−28.43	<u>57.16</u>	<u>42.42</u>	−25.80	55.59	<u>38.07</u>	−31.52	60.26	60.71	0.75

4.4 Ablation: Domain-Partitioned Evaluation

To evaluate cross-domain generalization from synthetic to real-world data, we perform a domain-partitioned ablation in which models are trained exclusively on synthetic datasets and evaluated on the dacl10k test split, thereby isolating the transferability of synthetic feature representations (see Table 4). Our findings indicate that, with the exception of synthcavity, the *synth-dacl* extensions are representative and consistent to generalize to real-world defect types. This is highlighted by the highest IoU on finecrack masks (13.11%) reported for the model trained on dacl10k and synthcrack. Utilizing synthcavity leads, according to Table 4, to 0% IoU on Cavity from dacl10k test set which is further discussed in Chap. 5.

Table 4. Synthetic-only training on three datasets; evaluated on real-world dacl10k test split and finecrack masks.

daclonsynth	synthcrack	synthcavity	mIoU	Crack	Finecrack	Effloresc.	Rockpocket	Hollowareas	Cavity	Spalling	Wetspot	Rust	ExposedR.
✓	–	–	**27.42**	–	–	**29.54**	20.37	35.34	–	**31.81**	**3.29**	**37.15**	34.42
✓	✓	–	26.53	21.04	**13.11**	26.82	**21.77**	**38.34**	–	31.22	3.22	35.35	**34.47**
✓	✓	✓	22.59	**21.76**	12.64	27.72	14.03	34.85	0.00	34.71	3.09	34.14	32.99
–	✓	–	–	6.60	8.29	–	–	–	–	–	–	–	–
–	–	✓	–	–	–	–	–	–	0.15	–	–	–	–

4.5   Qualitative Evaluation

In some cases, the labels in the dacl10k dataset are overly coarse and not precise, which limits the effectiveness of quantitative evaluation metrics like IoU in reflecting the model's performance. Therefore, we complement our evaluation with qualitative results in Fig. 4, providing a clearer assessment of the model's capability in handling the task. The predictions in the second row originate from the baseline trained on "dacl10k" (blue). The predictions in the "dacl10k+synth" row originate from the model trained on dacl10k plus the synthetic split that specifically includes the according class. In this row the three most left columns show predictions by the model trained on dacl10k+daclonsynth (green), followed by the models trained on dacl10k+synthcrack (pink) and dacl10k+synthcavity (turquoise) respectively. The bottom row displays predictions from the network that used all data (grey), or rather the most robust model according to Table 3.

The qualitative examples mostly underline the metrics reported in aforementioned Tables. The predictions on *Wetspot* by the most robust model show no false positives compared to the baseline dacl10k. On *Rockpocket* the prediction gets from top to bottom more accurate indicating that the additional synthetic

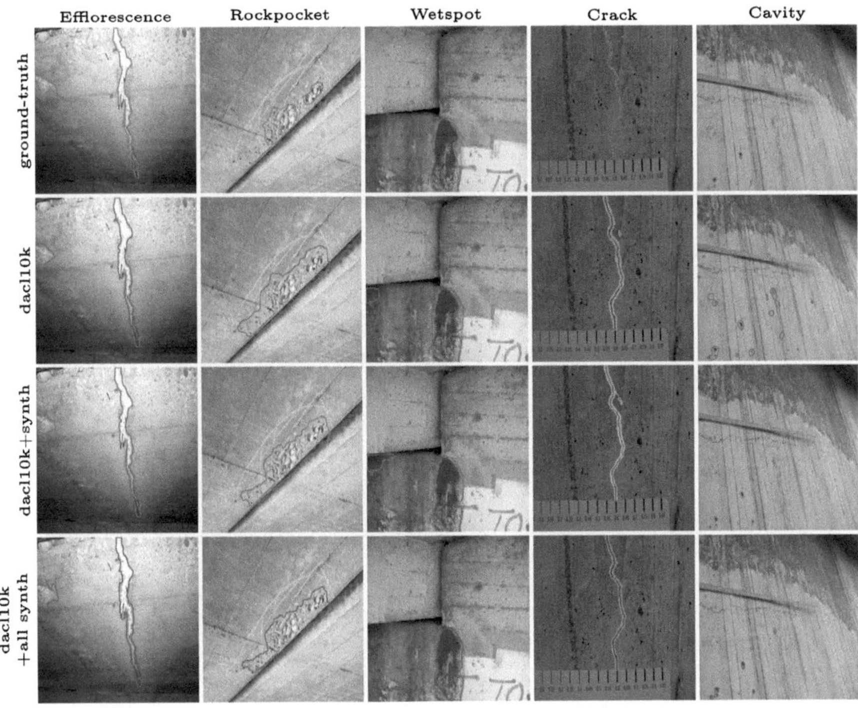

Fig. 4. Qualitative results on dacl10k test samples for different damage classes (columns) across different training data setups (rows), where the row dacl10k+synth shows the predictions of the model achieving highest IoU on the given class. (Color figure online)

data raises Precision. The *Crack* prediction proves that the segmentation gets narrower, thus closer to the crack edges but still leaves room for improvement. Regarding the *Cavity* sample, we observe that only the relevant cavities are marked, indicating higher accuracy.

5   Discussion

According to Table 1, introducing synthetic data specific to certain defects, such as *Cracks* (synthcrack) or *Cavities* (synthcavity), in isolation, the model performs better than without additional extensions. However, when both synthetic *Crack* and *Cavity* data are combined, it results in the lowest scores with respect to accuracy and robustness if trained without the balancing from daclonsynth (see Table 1 and 3). This suggests that while synthetic data can effectively address individual class imbalances, combining certain synthetic datasets can create conflicts that negatively impact model performance by introducing imbalances again. This is illustrated in Fig. 2 and 3. E.g, the number of pixels and shapes showing *Efflorescence* in dacl10k is 40 million pixels and 3,350 polygons, while synthcrack introduces 147 million pixels and 1.7 million polygons showing *Weathering*.

The best performance on *Weathering* in Table 1 is reported for the model trained exclusively on dacl10k, suggesting that synthetic *Weathering* features may not fully capture the characteristics of its real-world counterpart, which strongly rely on the subjacent concrete. Style transfer techniques may help to bridge this domain gap by enhancing the realism of synthetic textures [28].

Although the model's predictions on finecrack masks appear promising (Fig. 4), the achieved IoU of 13% indicates substantial room for improvement in terms of practical applicability. A closer inspection of the predictions by the model trained only on synthcrack (see Supplementary Material) reveals that crack segments are often disrupted when objects such as shadows, Wetspots, or Efflorescence are located adjacent to the crack edges. To improve realism and robustness, future work should focus on augmenting the synthetic pipeline with additional examples of such crack-bordering artifacts.

The isolated use of synthcavity proves insufficient for real-world Cavity detection, as shown in Table 2. Nonetheless, its combination with real-world data improves performance (Table 1), supporting its role as a supplementary rather than standalone training asset. Qualitative analysis of predictions made by the model trained only on synthcavity (see Supplementary Material) reveals common false positives arising, like in the case of synthcrack, from visually alien elements such as bolts, soil patches, or drainage components. Moreover, while the model successfully identifies small cavities, it consistently misses large ones – especially those with sharp, irregular geometries. This limitation stems from the underrepresentation such *Cavity* features in the synthcavity dataset. In order to generate more realistic synthetic *Cavity* images, future work should focus on incorporating methods such as texture-sensitive preprocessing [20], style transfer methods [31,34] or domain randomization strategies [39].

6   Conclusion

In this work, we introduce *synth-dacl*, a new set of three synthetic dataset extensions designed to support automated damage recognition in real-world bridge inspections. Alongside these extensions, we provide a cleaned version of the dacl10k dataset and introduce fine-resolution crack masks for the test set, enabling more precise evaluation. Through a series of experiments, we analyze the impact of synthetic data on segmentation performance and model robustness by combining the original dacl10k dataset with our synthetic extensions.

Our findings show that synthetic data can significantly improve performance, though its effectiveness depends on how it is integrated. Training exclusively on the *synthcrack* dataset yields the best performance on fine-resolution crack prediction, as demonstrated in Table 2. We also found that the *synthcavity* extension improves accuracy only when combined with real-world data, particularly in the dacl10k+*synthcavity* setup. Using all three synthetic extensions (*daclonsynth*, *synthcrack*, and *synthcavity*) leads to the most robust models, especially under challenging conditions.

Beyond these empirical results, our study reveals an important insight: although synthetic data is a powerful tool for augmenting training sets and improving model performance, it is not always ready for seamless integration into real-world applications. Further research is necessary to develop methods for generating synthetic data that more accurately capture the visual complexity, texture diversity, and environmental variability present in real-world bridge inspection scenarios. Our work lays a foundation for this future exploration of synthetic data in structural inspection tasks and the development of robust damage recognition systems.

Acknowledgements. This work was conducted within the research project Risk.twin, supported by dtec.bw – the Digitalization and Technology Research Center of the Bundeswehr – and funded through NextGenerationEU. We thank the German Ministry of Transportation for funding Goethe University's development of infrastructure simulation tools under the KIBA Project (Ref. 45KI16E051). We gratefully acknowledge the Institute for Distributed Intelligent Systems at the University of the Bundeswehr Munich for providing computational resources via the MonacumOne cluster.

References

1. Abdallah, A.M.: A study on bridge inspections: identifying barriers to new practices and providing strategies for change. Phd dissertation, Colorado State University (2021). https://mountainscholar.org/items/ea3087ee-73a2-4beb-8b62-d7b5a3941b46/full
2. ACI Committee 201: 201.1r-08: Guide for conducting a visual inspection of concrete in service. Technical Documents (2008)
3. ACI Committee 224: Control of cracking in concrete structures. American Concrete Institute, Farmington Hills (2001)

4. Al Khalil, Y., Amirrajab, S., Lorenz, C., Weese, J., Pluim, J., Breeuwer, M.: On the usability of synthetic data for improving the robustness of deep learning-based segmentation of cardiac magnetic resonance images. Med. Image Anal. **84**, 102688 (2023)

5. American Road & Transportation Builders Association (ARTBA): ARTBA bridge report (2024). https://artbabridgereport.org/. Accessed 17 Oct 2024

6. Asadi Shamsabadi, E., Xu, C., da Costa, D.D.: Robust crack detection in masonry structures with transformers. Measurement **200**, 111590 (2022). https://doi.org/10.1016/j.measurement.2022.111590, https://www.sciencedirect.com/science/article/pii/S026322412200803X

7. (BaSt), F.H.R.I.: Guideline for the uniform acquisition, assessment, recording and evaluation of results of structural inspections (RI-EBW-PRÜF) (2017)

8. (BaSt), F.H.R.I.: Brückenstatistik (2025). https://www.bast.de/DE/Statistik/Bruecken/Brueckenstatistik.pdf. Accessed 15 May 2025

9. Benz, C., Rodehorst, V.: Image-based detection of structural defects using hierarchical multi-scale attention. In: Andres, B., Bernard, F., Cremers, D., Frintrop, S., Goldlücke, B., Ihrke, I. (eds.) DAGM GCPR 2022. LNCS, vol. 13485, pp. 337–353. Springer, Cham (2022). https://doi.org/10.1007/978-3-031-16788-1_21

10. Benz, C., Rodehorst, V.: Omnicrack30k: a benchmark for crack segmentation and the reasonable effectiveness of transfer learning. In: Proceedings of the IEEE/CVF Conference on Computer Vision and Pattern Recognition (CVPR) Workshops, pp. 3876–3886 (2024)

11. Cordts, M., et al.: The cityscapes dataset for semantic urban scene understanding . In: 2016 IEEE Conference on Computer Vision and Pattern Recognition (CVPR), pp. 3213–3223. IEEE Computer Society, Los Alamitos (2016). https://doi.org/10.1109/CVPR.2016.350, https://doi.ieeecomputersociety.org/10.1109/CVPR.2016.350

12. Dorafshan, S., Thomas, R.J., Maguire, M.: SDNET2018: an annotated image dataset for non-contact concrete crack detection using deep convolutional neural networks. Data Brief **21**, 1664–1668 (2018). https://doi.org/10.1016/j.dib.2018.11.015

13. Dwibedi, D., Misra, I., Hebert, M.: Cut, paste and learn: surprisingly easy synthesis for instance detection. In: Proceedings of the IEEE International Conference on Computer Vision, pp. 1301–1310 (2017)

14. Everingham, M., Eslami, S.M.A., Gool, L.V., Williams, C.K.I., Winn, J.M., Zisserman, A.: The pascal visual object classes challenge: a retrospective. Int. J. Comput. Vision **111**, 98–136 (2014). https://api.semanticscholar.org/CorpusID:207252270

15. Flotzinger, J., Deuser, F., Jaziri, A.: synth-dacl: synthetic extensions for dacl10k Dataset (2025). https://doi.org/10.60776/9D6E4M, https://doi.org/10.60776/9D6E4M

16. Flotzinger, J., et al.: Dacl-challenge: Semantic segmentation during visual bridge inspections. In: Proceedings of the IEEE/CVF Winter Conference on Applications of Computer Vision (WACV) Workshops, pp. 716–725 (2024)

17. Flotzinger, J., Rösch, P.J., Braml, T.: dacl10k: benchmark for semantic bridge damage segmentation. In: Proceedings of the IEEE/CVF Winter Conference on Applications of Computer Vision (WACV), pp. 8626–8635 (2024)

18. Flotzinger, J., Rösch, P.J., Braml, T.: dacl10k (2025). https://doi.org/10.60776/RQUOYN

19. He, Z., Su, C., Deng, Y.: A novel MO-YOLOv4 for segmentation of multi-class bridge damages. Adv. Eng. Inform. **62**, 102586 (2024). https://doi.org/

10.1016/j.aei.2024.102586, https://www.sciencedirect.com/science/article/pii/S1474034624002349

20. Hess, T., Mundt, M., Pliushch, I., Ramesh, V.: A procedural world generation framework for systematic evaluation of continual learning (2021). https://arxiv.org/abs/2106.02585

21. Jaziri, A., Mundt, M., Fernandez, A., Ramesh, V.: Designing a hybrid neural system to learn real-world crack segmentation from fractal-based simulation. In: Proceedings of the IEEE/CVF Winter Conference on Applications of Computer Vision (WACV), pp. 8636–8646 (2024)

22. Kulkarni, S., Singh, S., Balakrishnan, D., Sharma, S., Devunuri, S., Korlapati, S.C.R.: CrackSeg9k: a collection and benchmark for crack segmentation datasets and frameworks. In: Karlinsky, L., Michaeli, T., Nishino, K. (eds.) ECCV 2022. LNCS, vol. 13807, pp. 179–195. Springer, Cham (2022). https://doi.org/10.1007/978-3-031-25082-8_12

23. Lee, D., Kim, J., Lee, D.: Robust concrete crack detection using deep learning-based semantic segmentation. Int. J. Aeronaut. Space Sci. **20**(1), 287–299 (2019). https://doi.org/10.1007/s42405-018-0120-5

24. Li, Y., Ma, R., Liu, H., Cheng, G.: Real-time high-resolution neural network with semantic guidance for crack segmentation. Autom. Constr. **156**, 105112 (2023). https://doi.org/10.1016/j.autcon.2023.105112

25. Lin, T.Y., Dollar, P., Girshick, R., He, K., Hariharan, B., Belongie, S.: Feature pyramid networks for object detection. In: Proceedings of the IEEE Conference on Computer Vision and Pattern Recognition (CVPR) (2017)

26. Liu, P., Shi, Y., Xiong, R., Tang, P.: Quantifying the reliability of defects located by bridge inspectors through human observation behavioral analysis. Dev. Built Environ. **14**, 100167 (2023). https://doi.org/10.1016/j.dibe.2023.100167, https://www.sciencedirect.com/science/article/pii/S2666165923000492

27. Liu, Y., Yao, J., Lu, X., Xie, R., Li, L.: DeepCrack: a deep hierarchical feature learning architecture for crack segmentation. Neurocomputing **338**, 139–153 (2019). https://doi.org/10.1016/j.neucom.2019.01.036, https://www.sciencedirect.com/science/article/pii/S0925231219300566

28. Luan, F., Paris, S., Shechtman, E., Bala, K.: Deep photo style transfer (2017). https://arxiv.org/abs/1703.07511

29. Man, K., Chahl, J.: A review of synthetic image data and its use in computer vision. J. Imaging **8**(11), 310 (2022)

30. Pak, M., Kim, S.: Crack detection using fully convolutional network in wall-climbing robot. In: Park, J.J., Fong, S.J., Pan, Y., Sung, Y. (eds.) Advances in Computer Science and Ubiquitous Computing. LNEE, vol. 715, pp. 267–272. Springer, Singapore (2021). https://doi.org/10.1007/978-981-15-9343-7_36

31. Park, T., Efros, A.A., Zhang, R., Zhu, J.Y.: Contrastive learning for unpaired image-to-image translation (2020). https://arxiv.org/abs/2007.15651

32. Phares, B.M., Washer, G.A., Rolander, D.D., Graybeal, B.A., Moore, M.: Routine highway bridge inspection condition documentation accuracy and reliability. J. Bridg. Eng. **9**(4), 403–413 (2004). https://doi.org/10.1061/(asce)1084-0702(2004)9:4(403), https://doi.org/10.1061/(asce)1084-0702(2004)9:4(403)

33. Poucin, F., Kraus, A., Simon, M.: Boosting instance segmentation with synthetic data: a study to overcome the limits of real world data sets. In: Proceedings of the IEEE/CVF International Conference on Computer Vision, pp. 945–953 (2021)

34. Prabhu, V., et al.: Bridging the sim2real gap with care: supervised detection adaptation with conditional alignment and reweighting (2023). https://arxiv.org/abs/2302.04832

35. for Standardization Registered Association (DIN), G.I.: Engineering structures in connection with roads - inspection and test. Standard DIN 1076:1999-11, DIN German Institute for Standardization, Berlin, Germany (1999). https://www.beuth.de/de/norm/din-1076/23474630

36. for Standardization Registered Association (DIN), G.I.: Eurocode 2: Design of reinforced and prestressed concrete structures - Part 1-1: General design rules and rules for buildings. Standard, DIN German Institute for Standardization, Berlin, Germany (2013)

37. Supervisely: Supervisely synthetic crack segmentation (2023). https://supervisely.com/blog/introducing-supervisely-synthetic-crack-segmentation-dataset/

38. Tao, H., Liu, B., Cui, J., Zhang, H.: A convolutional-transformer network for crack segmentation with boundary awareness. In: 2023 IEEE International Conference on Image Processing (ICIP), pp. 86–90 (2023). https://doi.org/10.1109/ICIP49359.2023.10222276

39. Tobin, J., Fong, R., Ray, A., Schneider, J., Zaremba, W., Abbeel, P.: Domain randomization for transferring deep neural networks from simulation to the real world (2017). https://arxiv.org/abs/1703.06907

40. Tu, Z., Talebi, H., Zhang, H., Yang, F., Milanfar, P., Bovik, A., Li, Y.: MaxViT: Multi-axis vision transformer. In: Avidan, S., Brostow, G., Cissé, M., Farinella, G.M., Hassner, T. (eds.) ECCV 2022. LNCS, vol. 13684, pp. 459–479. Springer Nature Switzerland, Cham (2022). https://doi.org/10.1007/978-3-031-20053-3_27

41. Wang, Y., Zhao, Y., Petzold, L.: An empirical study on the robustness of the segment anything model (SAM). Pattern Recogn. **155**, 110685 (2024). https://doi.org/10.1016/j.patcog.2024.110685, https://www.sciencedirect.com/science/article/pii/S0031320324004369

42. Xu, H., Su, X., Wang, Y., Cai, H., Cui, K., Chen, X.: Automatic bridge crack detection using a convolutional neural network. Appl. Sci. **9**(14) (2019). https://doi.org/10.3390/app9142867, https://www.mdpi.com/2076-3417/9/14/2867

43. Xu, J., Yuan, C., Gu, J., Liu, J., An, J., Kong, Q.: Innovative synthetic data augmentation for dam crack detection, segmentation, and quantification. Struct. Health Monit. **22**(4), 2402–2426 (2023)

44. Zhou, B., Zhao, H., Puig, X., Fidler, S., Barriuso, A., Torralba, A.: Scene parsing through ade20k dataset. In: 2017 IEEE Conference on Computer Vision and Pattern Recognition (CVPR), pp. 5122–5130 (2017). https://doi.org/10.1109/CVPR.2017.544

45. Zou, Q., Cao, Y., Li, Q., Mao, Q., Wang, S.: CrackTree: automatic crack detection from pavement images. Pattern Recogn. Lett. **33**(3), 227–238 (2012). https://doi.org/10.1016/j.patrec.2011.11.004, https://www.sciencedirect.com/science/article/pii/S0167865511003795

FedPCE: Federated Personalized Client Embeddings for Post-training Knowledge Distillation

Soma Hansel[1,2(✉)], Erich Kobler[3], and Alexander Effland[1,2]

[1] Institute of Applied Mathematics, University of Bonn, Bonn, Germany
s6sohans@uni-bonn.de
[2] Imaging Lab, Clinic for Diagnostic and Interventional Neuroradiology and Pediatric Neuroradiology, University Hospital of Bonn, Bonn, Germany
[3] Institute for Machine Learning, LIT AI Lab, Institute for Virtual Morphology, Johannes Kepler University Linz, Linz, Austria

Abstract. Among other drawbacks, models trained via federated learning (FL) often struggle to generalize to new, unseen clients – a challenge that becomes more severe in low-data regimes. Most existing solutions address this issue using hypernetworks, which do not scale well with the size of the underlying model. To overcome these limitations, we introduce Federated Personalized Client Embeddings (FedPCE) – a method that uses embeddings to distill personalized knowledge from existing FL approaches. Our results show that FedPCE performs comparably to popular FL algorithms during both training and personalization. Notably, it outperforms competing methods when only limited data is available for personalization—even with as few as 25 labeled samples (Code available at https://github.com/somcogo/fedpce).

Keywords: Federated Learning · Personalization · Distillation

1 Introduction

Training machine learning models on personal or medical data is limited by privacy regulations that restrict data sharing. Federated learning (FL) has emerged as a promising approach to leverage decentralized data while preserving privacy [31]. Sometimes clients (e.g., medical centers) are unwilling or unable to participate in an FL framework. In such cases, their data can only be used for local model adaptation and evaluation, further complicating the learning process by requiring the model to be easily adaptable to unseen data that may have different

---

S. Hansel and E. Kobler—Equal contribution.

Supplementary Information The online version contains supplementary material available at https://doi.org/10.1007/978-3-032-12840-9_26.

M. Keuper and F. Locatello (Eds.): DAGM GCPR 2025, LNCS 16125, pp. 403–418, 2026.
https://doi.org/10.1007/978-3-032-12840-9_26

characteristics from the data seen during training. As a result, FL frameworks must be able to handle non-independent and non-identically distributed (non-IID) data [23,34] as non-IID data significantly degrades FL performance [43].

Moreover, in many practical applications – particularly in the medical domain – only limited data is available across various sites. For example, in hospitals serving as FL clients, there may be only a small number of patients receiving treatment for specific diseases.

To address these challenges, we introduce a novel approach that enhances model personalization while significantly reducing the dimensionality of the personalization space. Our method draws inspiration from the effectiveness of recent FL approaches [2,27] that personalize different model parts. In particular, we use an FL trained model and distill the knowledge encoded in the personalized clients into a low-dimensional semantic embedding space. We collaboratively train affine maps, implemented as a simple linear layer, to generate the parameters of the personalized model parts from client-specific embedding vectors. Then, the distilled federated model can be adapted to new clients by fine-tuning only the local embedding vector. This novel approach offers several advantages:

- *Parameter efficiency:* Our method increases the overall model size by only 3% while requiring the fine-tuning of only 32 parameters per client, making it highly scalable for real-world applications. In comparison, recent hypernetwork-based approaches can require more than 100 times more parameters than the client model [1,38].
- *Efficient knowledge distillation:* Training the linear layers that generate normalization parameters is computationally inexpensive, as it only involves optimizing a small subset of model parameters and does not require additional networks to generate client embeddings.
- *Label-efficient personalization:* Our method significantly reduces the need for labeled data. Personalizing with just 1% of labeled training data results in only a 2–5% accuracy drop on the evaluated datasets.

2   Related Work

The foundational work [31] introduced the federated averaging (FedAvg) algorithm, which trains models locally on clients and aggregates updates on a central server. However, FedAvg struggles with heterogeneous, non-IID data distributions [11,26,43]. To address this challenge, *personalized* federated learning (PFL) strategies have emerged. Recent advances in PFL can be broadly classified into the following categories.

Optimization-Based. These approaches modify learning objectives or procedures to accommodate client-specific needs. FedProx [25] extends FedAvg by introducing a proximal term to stabilize training on heterogeneous data. Further examples include SCAFFOLD [17], FedMA [41], MOON [24], FedBS [14], FedDNA [5], FedDistill [40], and MetaVers [28]. In particular, FedAS [42] aligns global parameters with local knowledge, and modifies the aggregation weights.

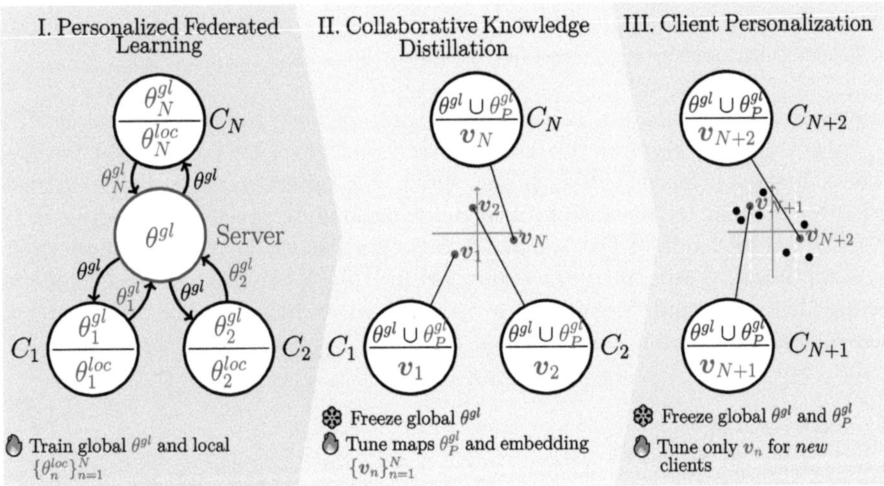

Fig. 1. Illustration of the 3 FedPCE steps. I) Initially, the global parameters θ^{gl} are jointly learned by all clients $\{C_n\}_{n=1}^N$, while the local parameters $\{\theta_n^{loc}\}_{n=1}^N$ are personalized locally. II) Then, we equip every client with a local embedding vector $\{v_n\}_{n=1}^N$ and introduce an affine map $P\colon \mathbb{R}^E \to \mathbb{R}^{|\theta^{loc}|}$ to distill the personalized knowledge into a semantic embedding and thereby approximate the local parameters, i.e., $\theta_n^{loc} \approx P(v_n)$. III) Finally, the personalized knowledge is transferred to new clients $(n > N)$ by just tuning v_n.

Architecture-Based. These methods balance global and local components within model architectures, often personalizing specific neural network layers while sharing others globally. FedPer [2] personalizes only the final linear classifier layer. FedBABU [33] extends this idea by first training the network body collaboratively with random classifier weights and then fine-tuning the classifier weights per client. Meanwhile, FedBN [27] personalizes just the scale and shift parameters of normalization layers to handle non-IID feature shifts effectively.

Clustering-Based. These approaches enhance personalization by grouping clients with similar data distributions and training specialized models within each cluster. Clients are typically assigned to clusters based on loss function evaluations [7,29] or gradient similarities [36]. Each cluster then collaboratively updates its shared model. However, knowledge is not transferred across clusters.

Hypernetwork-Based. Hypernetworks involve training a separate network that generates the weights of the target model, a concept originally proposed in early work [9,37]. In personalized FL, a centralized hypernetwork predicts personalized model parameters for each client based on a descriptor [39]. Recent works in this direction [1,3,38] have explored communication-efficient designs and extensions for future client personalization. However, hypernetworks are difficult to scale due to their high parameter overhead, often limiting personalization to a subset of model parameters (e.g., classifier weights) [3].

Personalization for Future Clients. Several recent ideas focus on extending PFL to future clients. Hypernetwork-based methods generate parameters for new clients based on learned descriptors, which can be extracted from client data using an encoder [1,38] or fine-tuned in an embedding space [39]. Alternatively, Per-FedAvg [6] modifies FedAvg by adding a client-specific training step for better adaptation. A similar idea was pursued in [16]. [4] proposed to freeze a global feature extractor and fine-tune only a classification head. Lastly, [30] used a k-nearest-neighbor-based memorization technique for personalization.

3   Methods

We introduce federated personalized client embeddings (FedPCE) comprising three steps (see Fig. 1). *Personalized federated learning:* We leverage existing federated learning (FL) approaches to train personalized models for all clients available during FL. *Collaborative knowledge distillation:* Using the same clients, we collaboratively distill the knowledge encoded in the personalized parameters into a semantic embedding. *Client personalization:* The collective knowledge is easily transferred to new clients by adapting an associated embedding vector.

3.1   Personalized Federated Learning

Let us briefly recall the concept of architecture-based PFL and introduce the relevant notation. Assume there are N clients $C_1, \ldots, C_N$, each with an associated dataset $X_n = \{(x_n^\ell, y_n^\ell)\}_{\ell=1,\ldots,\ell_n}$, where each pair (x_n^ℓ, y_n^ℓ) consists of an input and a corresponding ground truth. In contrast to standard FL, architecture-based PFL approaches such as FedPer [2] or FedBN [27] divide the model parameters θ_n into global θ_n^{gl} and local $\{\theta_n^{\mathrm{loc}}\}_{n=1}^N$ parts. This split is the same for each client. In PFL, we aim to minimize the objective function

$$\hat{\theta}^{\mathrm{gl}}, \{\hat{\theta}_n^{\mathrm{loc}}\}_{n=1}^N \in \underset{\theta^{\mathrm{gl}}, \{\theta_n^{\mathrm{loc}}\}_{n=1}^N}{\operatorname{argmin}} \sum_{n=1}^N |X_n| \cdot L(X_n; \theta^{\mathrm{gl}}, \theta_n^{\mathrm{loc}}),$$

where L represents the loss function – typically the cross-entropy – and $|X_n|$ is the number of data points at client C_n. Specifically, the parameters are computed by an alternating optimization approach. In several rounds, typically a fixed number of local gradient descent steps are performed locally by clients followed by aggregating the global parameters $\theta^{\mathrm{gl}} = \frac{1}{N}\sum_{n=1}^N \theta_n^{\mathrm{gl}}$. At the beginning of each round, every client fetches the aggregated global parameters θ^{gl} from the server. The local parameters θ_n^{loc} are neither sent to the server nor updated during model aggregation. This process is repeated until a termination condition is met (e.g., aggregating the global parameters for a specified number of times).

3.2   Collaborative Knowledge Distillation

The core idea of FedPCE is to distill the personalization knowledge encoded in the local parameters of each client into a semantic embedding. In detail, we extend PFL approaches in a way that reduces the number of local parameters while still maintaining the ability of the local parameters to impact the features in personalized parts of a trained model. In other words, we aim to avoid transforming local parameters into global ones. Instead, we introduce a low-dimensional embedding space and an affine map to generate the parameters that previously were local. Then, only the embedding vectors are local. Thus we reduce the dimensionality of the local parameter space without sacrificing the ability of the local parameters to impact the features in personalized parts of the model.

To implement this method, we first select an embedding dimension E and define the embedding space as $\mathbb{R}^E$. Then, the local parameters are reparametrized by a mapping of a low-dimensional, client-specific embedding vector $\boldsymbol{v}_n \in \mathbb{R}^E$. These functions, described in detail below, are shared globally across all clients.

Consider a setup with K local layers. Recall that $\hat{\theta}_n^{loc}$ are the local parameters of the nth client, estimated in the PFL step. We denote the number of parameters in the kth layer by d_k. To reduce the number of local parameters without decreasing functionality, we replace the direct parametrization of the elements of $\hat{\theta}_n^{loc}$ with an affine map $P_k : \mathbb{R}^E \to \mathbb{R}^{d_k}$ for all $1 \leq k \leq K$. This is implemented as a linear layer, that is $P_k(\boldsymbol{v}_n) = \boldsymbol{W}_k \boldsymbol{v}_n + \boldsymbol{b}_k$, with weight $\boldsymbol{W}_k \in \mathbb{R}^{d_k \times E}$ and bias $\boldsymbol{b}_k \in \mathbb{R}^{d_k}$. Therefore, the global model parameters extend to $\theta^{\mathrm{gl}} = \hat{\theta}^{gl} \cup \theta_P^{\mathrm{gl}}$, where $\hat{\theta}^{\mathrm{gl}}$ denotes the estimated parameters of the previous PFL step and $\theta_P^{\mathrm{gl}} = \{\boldsymbol{W}_k, \boldsymbol{b}_k\}_{k=1}^K$ subsumes all parameters of the affine maps. In contrast, the local parameters of all clients simplify to $\{\boldsymbol{v}_n\}_{n=1}^N \subset \mathbb{R}^E$. Then, the personalized knowledge is distilled by collaboratively solving the problem

$$\hat{\theta}_P^{\mathrm{gl}}, \{\hat{\boldsymbol{v}}_n\}_{n=1}^N \in \underset{\theta_P^{\mathrm{gl}}, \{\boldsymbol{v}_n\}_{n=1}^N}{\operatorname{argmin}} \sum_{n=1}^N |X_n| \cdot L(X_n; \hat{\theta}^{\mathrm{gl}}, \theta_P^{\mathrm{gl}}, \boldsymbol{v}_n).$$

Note that the already estimated global parameters $\hat{\theta}^{\mathrm{gl}}$ are frozen in this formulation, which simplifies distillation. By choosing E to be sufficiently small, this approach significantly reduces the number of local parameters from $d = \sum_{k=1}^K d_k$ to E. For example, as detailed in Subsect. 4.3, this reduction achieves a 332-fold decrease in the number of local parameters in our experiments. As a trade-off, the introduction of the maps P_k increases the total number of global parameters in the model by only $(1 + \sum_{k=1}^K d_k)E$.

3.3   Client Personalization

The final stage focuses on adapting the model for new clients that were not part of the initial PFL and are available only for local training. In this stage, all global parameters are frozen, and only the embedding vector v_{N+1} is fine-tuned (see Fig. 1). Thus, new clients are incorporated by minimizing the local loss

$$\hat{v}_{N+1} \in \underset{v \in \mathbb{R}^E}{\operatorname{argmin}} L(X_{N+1}; \hat{\theta}^{\mathrm{gl}}, \hat{\theta}^{\mathrm{gl}}_P, v).$$

Due to the low dimensionality of the embedding, only a small fraction of the model parameters need to be optimized, helping to reduce overfitting in the low-data regime. Nevertheless, FedPCE retains the ability to personalize the model effectively. This is because the low-dimensional embedding vector influences all layers of the model which were previously personalized, allowing personalization to be achieved by just learning v.

4   Experimental Design and Datasets

We simulate a scenario where data centralization is infeasible, and certain clients' data cannot be utilized for training. Instead, it is reserved for local adaptation. Thus, we generate clients with artificially non-IID data distributions, use a subset of them for federated training (federated clients), and personalize the model on the remaining clients during personalization. The model personalization is repeated in an artificially created low-data regime where the training set at each personalization client is restricted to contain only a given number of images.

4.1   Datasets

We demonstrate FedPCE's versatility using four datasets:

CIFAR-10 and *CIFAR-100* [19] are classification datasets, each consisting of 50K training and 10K validation images. Each of these RGB images is of size 32×32 and belongs to one of 10 or 100 classes, respectively.

TinyImageNet [20] is a classification dataset consisting of 100K training and 10K validation images of 200 classes. Each image is colored and of size 64×64.

The fourth dataset, which we denote as *Digits*, is the union of four datasets, all containing images of digits (0–9). These are the *MNIST* [22], *USPS* [13], *SVHN* [32], and *SYN* [35] datasets. They contain 60,000, 7,291, 73,257, and 10,000 training images, and 10,000, 2,007, 26,032, and 2,000 validation images, respectively. The SVHN and SYN datasets consist of colored images, while MNIST and USPS were converted to color images from grayscale images. All images were resized to 32×32 using bilinear interpolation.

4.2   Simulating Non-IID Data

For each experiment, we simulate a scenario involving multiple clients with non-IID data. We achieve such a distribution of data using two approaches: attribute skew and label skew [8]. Attribute skew is achieved by applying a data degradation transform to artificially alter the data distribution. Label skew is simulated by partitioning the data points non-uniformly with respect to labels.

In the case of the Digits dataset, we have a "natural" way to achieve attribute skew among the clients. We set the total number of clients to $4K$, a multiple of 4. For each subdataset in Digits, we split the images uniformly into K subsets. This setup yields $4K$ clients, simulating 4 modalities with K clients each.

We synthesize the different data distributions for CIFAR-10, CIFAR-100, and TinyImageNet. We consider the following degradation methods:

- *Attribute skew*: We apply pixel-wise additive Gaussian noise to the images. For each client, the variance of the Gaussian noise is fixed, but the noise instance is randomly sampled every time. If there are M total clients, the variances are M points chosen linearly between 0.005 and 1.
- *Label skew*: When generating the clients corresponding to this degradation, the distribution of class labels is not uniform. This is achieved by using the Dirichlet distribution with parameter $\alpha = 1$.

For each experiment, we fix a dataset and a type of non-IIDness (i.e. attribute or label skew) and generate 20 clients using the aforementioned methods. Training and validation images are partitioned separately but follow the same distribution. Gaussian noise is applied to both the training and the validation images when used to generate attribute skew. The data partitioning process, random selection of *attribute skew* parameters, Gaussian noise application, and data loading are performed in a reproducible manner.

4.3   Architecture

We conduct all of our experiments using *ResNet-18* [10]. The models are implemented as described in [10], with the following modifications. We use the 'CIFAR' version of ResNet, meaning the first convolution layer has a kernel size of 3, and a stride and padding of 1. In our experiments, we take FedBN [27] as a baseline. Thus, all parameters of every normalization layer are personalized. The output of the kth batch norm [15] layer becomes

$$y = \hat{y} \cdot P_k(v_n)_1 + P_k(v_n)_2, \quad \hat{y} = \frac{x - \mathbb{E}[x]}{\sqrt{\mathrm{Var}(x)}}.$$

P_k is initialized using Kaiming uniform distribution, centered around the standard scale and shift parameters of batch norm layers. The embedding vectors are initialized such that $v_n = e^{(n)}$ for $n \leq E$, and $\mathbf{0}$ for $n > E$. We also experimented with various initialization strategies, but observed no significant impact on performance (Subsect. 5.5). This indicates that the method is robust to the choice of initialization. Since the majority of parameters in widely used models are concentrated in convolutional layers or linear layers, the increase in the number of parameters coming from the introduction of the P_k is relatively minor – approximately 3% in our experiments.

We insert an additional batch normalization layer into the classification head, right before the final fully connected layer. This allows the personalization to

Table 1. Validation accuracy after personalization on new clients using either the whole training dataset or only 25 training images. We compare seven personalization approaches applied to CIFAR-10 (C-10), CIFAR-100 (C-100), TinyImageNet (TIm) and Digits (Dig) datasets using either attribute or label skew. Accuracies in **bold** and in *italics* are the best and second best results in each column, respectively.

Dataset	Attribute skew				Label skew		
	C-10	C-100	TIm	Dig	C-10	C-100	TIm
Personalization							
FedAvg FT	47.9±0.6	17.9±0.5	17.3±0.7	90.5±1.1	86.1±0.5	48.5±1.3	39.9±0.9
LoRA FT	*56.4*±0.7	**25.2**±0.5	**24.7**±0.6	86.3±4.3	**90.0**±0.8	**56.1**±0.9	**49.9**±0.8
FedBABU	55.0±0.8	24.1±0.8	22.8±0.7	**91.9**±0.5	89.4±0.7	*55.6*±0.6	47.8±0.6
FedBN	55.3±1.1	23.4±0.2	*24.2*±0.7	90.1±1.2	88.9±1.1	54.0±0.4	47.3±0.7
FedAS	55.4±0.7	15.4±0.9	2.4±0.6	79.5±3.6	88.6±1.0	24.9±1.0	6.2±0.5
FedPCE (ours)	55.4±1.1	*24.2*±0.9	23.5±1.1	89.5±1.2	87.4±0.5	49.1±0.5	42.8±0.9
FedPCE+head (ours)	**56.5**±1.6	**25.2**±0.5	**24.7**±0.8	*91.7*±1.1	*89.7*±0.5	*55.6*±0.3	*48.3*±1.0
Low-Data Personalization (25 training images)							
FedAvg FT	30.8±1.4	9.5±0.8	11.8±0.5	34.9±2.3	80.3±0.6	40.6±1.4	33.9±1.1
LoRA FT	*51.8*±1.9	*21.3*±0.8	**22.1**±0.7	61.8±5.6	*84.4*±1.2	*44.2*±0.3	*38.0*±0.8
FedBABU	49.8±1.1	21.1±0.6	20.5±0.6	52.0±2.0	82.7±0.9	41.4±0.2	32.7±0.8
FedBN	46.2±1.3	19.0±0.7	19.4±0.3	58.3±1.1	81.6±0.9	42.6±0.5	35.5±0.6
FedAS	51.2±1.4	8.4±1.5	1.8±0.7	61.1±6.7	83.2±1.6	17.5±1.7	5.3±1.0
FedPCE (ours)	**53.3**±1.1	**21.4**±1.6	21.1±1.2	**76.3**±2.0	**85.7**±0.6	**44.8**±0.7	**38.7**±1.2
FedPCE+head (ours)	50.4±1.2	21.2±0.5	*21.3*±0.8	*73.2*±2.2	83.6±1.3	42.4±0.7	34.4±1.1

more directly influence the class predictions through the shift and scale vectors of the normalization layer, which is particularly helpful in the case of label skew.

We also present a variation of FedPCE where the classifier head is locally trained during distillation and personalization. We denote it by FedPCE+head.

We compare the collaborative training and personalization of our models with four FL methods: *FedAvg* [31], *FedBABU* [33], *FedBN* [27], and *FedAS* [42]. We personalize FedAvg in two ways. First, we fine-tune the full model on personalization datasets as in [16], referring to this as FedAvg FT. Second, we apply LoRA [12], a low-rank fine-tuning method, and refer to this as LoRA FT. To our knowledge, this approach has not been used for model personalization in the federated setting. FedPCE uses rank $E = 32$, so we use the same rank for LoRA for consistency. For FedBN, the normalization layer parameters remain local during FL, and we only fine-tune them during personalization. For FedBABU and FedAS, models are trained per [33] and [42], respectively, and personalized by fine-tuning only the model head. All other implementation details remain consistent across methods, as described in Sect. 5. We do not compare FedPCE to the hypernetwork-based methods as benchmarks [1,38] as these methods increase the number of parameters at least 100-fold—exceeding

Table 2. Performance of FL trained FedBN model compared to FedPCE and Fed-PCE+head models distilled from FedBN showing validation accuracy on CIFAR-10 (C-10), CIFAR-100 (C-100), TinyImageNet (TIm) and Digits (Dig) datasets using either attribute or label skew. Accuracies in **bold** and in *italics* are the best and second best results in each column, respectively.

Dataset	Attribute skew				Label skew		
	C-10	C-100	TIm	Dig	C-10	C-100	TIm
FedBN	$50.7_{\pm0.5}$	$20.6_{\pm0.2}$	$20.8_{\pm0.2}$	$87.2_{\pm1.0}$	*$84.9_{\pm0.3}$*	**$54.3_{\pm0.6}$**	**$49.5_{\pm0.3}$**
FedPCE (ours)	**$52.4_{\pm0.8}$**	**$23.6_{\pm0.2}$**	**$22.5_{\pm0.3}$**	**$89.4_{\pm0.9}$**	**$85.2_{\pm0.3}$**	$53.7_{\pm0.5}$	*$48.4_{\pm0.3}$*
FedPCE+head (ours)	*$51.5_{\pm1.0}$*	*$22.3_{\pm0.7}$*	*$21.3_{\pm0.3}$*	*$89.2_{\pm1.7}$*	$84.8_{\pm0.2}$	*$54.0_{\pm0.5}$*	**$49.5_{\pm0.3}$**

1 billion parameters for ResNet-18, which is beyond the scope of this paper. For a comparison, see Subsect. 5.4. Source code will be available upon acceptance.

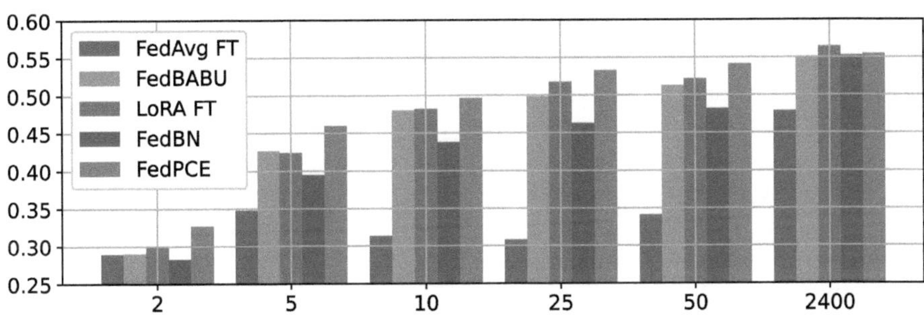

Fig. 2. Validation accuracy after personalization on new clients on CIFAR-10 using attribute skew, plotted against the number of training images available at each client. The size of the whole training set at new clients is 2400.

5 Numerical Results

5.1 Training Details

We conduct experiments using 20 clients under both attribute and label skew settings, except for the Digits dataset. 80% of the clients are used for collaborative training and distillation, and the remaining 20% for client personalization. The experiments are conducted using 5-fold cross-validation. When results are presented, the standard deviation among the cross-validation folds is presented. We split the dataset 80%-20% between the training and validation set. Training is conducted using Adam optimizer [18] and cross-entropy loss. When the number of training images is restricted for a client, we limit the training set; the validation set remains unaffected, ensuring comparability of results. For details we refer to the supplementary material.

5.2 Distillation

Table 2 shows the results of training FedBN models on federated clients and using the same clients to distill knowledge into FedPCE and FedPCE+head. FedPCE only loses performance during distillation in the label skew case, which is recovered by fine-tuning the model head (FedPCE+head). In the attribute skew case, FedPCE even outperforms FedBN, suggesting that the underlying problem can be captured in the 32-dimensional embedding space. Figure 3 depicts 2D visualizations of learned embeddings. The visualizations indicate that the noise level (proportional to the areas of dots) is encoded in the embeddings.

5.3 Personalization

In the personalization experiments, we compare FedPCE and FedPCE+head with five personalization approaches: FL trained FedAvg models with two different personalization strategies, FedBABU, FedAS, and FedBN. The FL trained models were personalized and evaluated on new clients. The results are shown in Table 1. In the upper part, the models had access to the entire training dataset at each new client, while in the lower part, each new client's training dataset was restricted to only 25 images.

FedPCE achieves superior performance in almost all cases in the low-data regime. With the exception of the Digits dataset, the decrease in Fed-PCE performance going from using the full training data to only 25 images ($<1.1\%$ of all images) is between 2–5%. *FedPCE achieves these results by training only 32 parameters instead of 6K to 12M used by competing methods, see Table* 3. Further results focusing on low-data personalization are shown in Fig. 2. FedPCE achieves the best performance for CIFAR-10 and attribute skew.

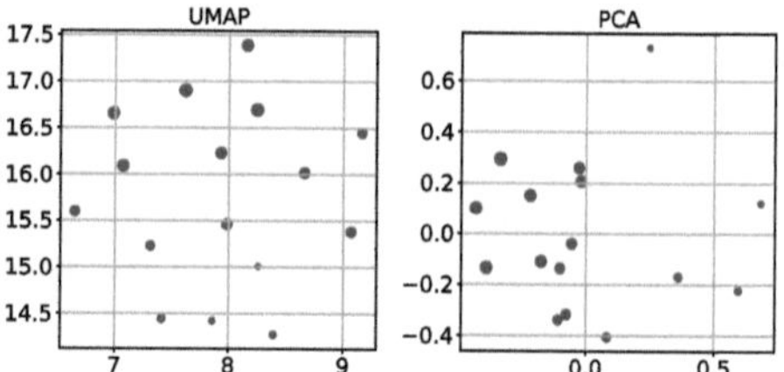

Fig. 3. Embedding vectors obtained after distillation of FedPCE on 16 CIFAR-10 clients with attribute skew. The size of a dot is proportional to the variance of the noise applied at the client. The embedding vectors are visualized using UMAP and the first 2 dimensions of PCA.

In full-data personalization, FedPCE does not achieve outstanding results, particularly in the label skew case, where the personalization of the model head plays a more significant role. As shown in Table 1, fine-tuning the model head – as done in FedPCE+head – addresses this limitation, resulting in the best or second-best accuracy in all cases. FedPCE+head accomplishes this while fine-tuning the same number of parameters as FedBABU and FedAS. Thus, the variations of FedPCE are well-suited for model personalization in both high- and low-data regimes.

Table 3. Number of parameters trained during the personalization of a model.

# classes	FedPCE	FedPCE+head	FedBABU	FedAS	FedBN	FedAvg FT	LoRA FT
10	32	6K	6K	6K	11K	11M	12M
100	32	52K	52K	52K	11K	11M	12M
200	32	104K	104K	104K	11K	11M	12M

Table 4. Comparison of FedPCE and PeFLL using CIFAR-10. FedPCE is personalized using either all the available training images or only 25. Also shown is the total number of learnable parameters in the setting described in Subsect. 5.4.

	# param	Attribute skew			Label skew		
		Trn.	Pers. (all)	Pers. (25)	Trn.	Pers. (all)	Pers. (25)
PeFLL	12M	48.0 ± 0.6	43.7 ± 3.3	43.7 ± 3.3	76.2 ± 0.7	43.5 ± 3.7	43.5 ± 3.7
FedPCE	121K	44.5 ± 0.5	46.6 ± 0.7	45.0 ± 0.8	71.6 ± 0.6	77.5 ± 1.5	76.2 ± 1.3

5.4   Comparison to Hypernetwork Based Methods

We compare FedPCE to a hypernetwork-based framework, PeFLL [38]. In PeFLL, each client generates an embedding using an embedding network. The server uses a hypernetwork to produce the weights for a target model. Finally, the client uses a target network with the generated weights on local data.

In our experiments, we use a LeNet-style model [21], identical to the architecture used in [38], with Batch Normalization layers inserted after each convolutional and fully connected layer. This ensures that normalization layers are present for FedPCE to influence. Because PeFLL includes both an embedding network and a hypernetwork, it utilizes over 100 times more parameters than FedPCE, though the majority of these reside in the server-side hypernetwork.

Table 4 presents the experimental results on CIFAR-10, evaluated under both attribute and label skew. The results indicate that FedPCE only slightly underperforms PeFLL during training, despite using a fraction of the parameters. Moreover, FedPCE requires only 25 labeled training images per client to match or exceed PeFLL's performance during personalization. When the full training set is available, FedPCE outperforms PeFLL in personalization.

In summary, while PeFLL enables zero-shot personalization and strong training performance, it relies on a large hypernetwork and significantly more parameters. FedPCE, by contrast, achieves competitive or superior personalization with over 100 times fewer parameters and only a few labeled samples, making it a more efficient and practical choice in resource-constrained settings.

5.5   Ablation Studies

To better understand the behavior of embeddings, we conduct a series of ablation studies concerning the embedding dimension, the number of clients, the structure

Table 5. Results of the ablation studies regarding the type of mapping from the embedding to the normalization layers, E, and N. Personalization is done either with all available training images or only 25.

	Mapping type			Embedding dimension			
	1 layer	2 layer	3 layer	E=2	E=8	E=32	E=128
Distillation	$52.4{\pm}0.8$	$52.6{\pm}0.6$	$52.4{\pm}0.9$	$53.2{\pm}0.7$	$52.9{\pm}0.6$	$52.4{\pm}0.8$	$53.3{\pm}0.6$
Pers. (all)	$55.5{\pm}1.1$	$56.1{\pm}1.7$	$55.5{\pm}1.4$	$55.6{\pm}1.4$	$56.4{\pm}1.4$	$55.5{\pm}1.1$	$56.5{\pm}1.5$
Pers. (25)	$53.3{\pm}1.1$	$54.2{\pm}1.3$	$53.7{\pm}1.3$	$53.9{\pm}1.2$	$54.6{\pm}1.1$	$53.3{\pm}1.1$	$54.3{\pm}1.4$

	N=50		N=75		N=100	
	FedPCE	FedBN	FedPCE	FedBN	FedPCE	FedBN
Distillation	$49.3{\pm}0.2$	$44.8{\pm}0.3$	$47.4{\pm}0.4$	$42.1{\pm}0.6$	$45.9{\pm}0.5$	$39.8{\pm}0.3$
Pers. (all)	$51.0{\pm}0.5$	$49.7{\pm}1.3$	$45.5{\pm}1.1$	$43.7{\pm}1.2$	$45.9{\pm}1.7$	$42.9{\pm}1.3$
Pers. (25)	$48.1{\pm}0.5$	$42.8{\pm}0.4$	$43.5{\pm}1.3$	$39.8{\pm}1.1$	$43.5{\pm}1.4$	$38.9{\pm}1.3$

of the maps P_k, and the initialization of the embedding vectors. All the ablation experiments were conducted on CIFAR-10 with attribute skew applied, using the training setup in Subsect. 5.1 unless specified otherwise.

The top-left section of Table 5 examines the effect of the structure of the maps P_k on the performance of FedPCE. We compare different versions of FedPCE where the maps P_k are either unchanged or replaced by a 2- or 3-layer Multi-layer Perceptron (MLP) with hidden dimensions of 64. We can view a linear layer as a 1-layer MLP and thus this ablation study is equivalent to studying the effect of the depth of MLPs on the performance of FedPCE. While increasing the depth results in slight performance gains, the improvements are not substantial and significantly increase the number of parameters.

The top-right section of Table 5 presents the results of the embedding dimension (E) ablation experiments, using dimensions ranging from 2 to 128. The performance of FedPCE is not significantly impacted by the embedding dimension. Strong results were achieved even with smaller embedding sizes.

The bottom part of Table 5 shows the results of experiments conducted across 50, 75 and 100 clients. As anticipated in FL, accuracy declines as the number of clients increases due to increased data heterogeneity. However, personalization accuracy declines more slowly for FedPCE than for FedBN as the number of clients increases. This suggests that FedPCE is better at negating the effect of the increased heterogeneity in the training setup than FedBN.

Finally, we examine the effect of embedding vector initialization on the performance of FedPCE during personalization using the full training set at each client.

Table 6. Personalization accuracy with different embedding vector initialization strategies.

FedPCE	zero	one	random
55.4 $\pm_{1.1}$	56.4 $\pm_{1.2}$	55.2 $\pm_{0.9}$	55.7 $\pm_{1.1}$

In Table 6, FedPCE denotes the initialization strategy described in Subsect. 4.3, "zero" and "one" mean that each coordinate of the embedding vectors is initially 0 and 1, respectively. The column 'random' contains the result of choosing each coordinate of the vector uniformly randomly from the interval $[0, 1)$. The random vector was the same for all 5 cross-validation folds. The results demonstrate that the initialization of the embedding vector does not significantly affect the performance of FedPCE.

6   Conclusion

In this work, we proposed FedPCE, a method to distill the implicit representations encoded in the parameters of personalized layers in FL using embeddings. These embeddings are learned from multiple clients through collaborative knowledge distillation. Once trained, the model can be easily extended to new clients with different data distributions by fine-tuning only the client's embedding vector. Extensive numerical experiments show that the proposed FedPCE approach outperforms established personalization methods in the low-data regime while achieving comparable results in collaborative learning and full-data personalization. This suggests that the adaptation problem is inherently low-dimensional. Moreover, fine-tuning fewer parameters not only enhances computational efficiency but also reduces the labeled data required for effective adaptation – an essential advantage in healthcare, where labeled data is scarce and costly.

Acknowledgement. A. Effland is funded by the German Research Foundation under Germany's Excellence Strategy – EXC-2047/1 – 390685813 and – EXC2151 – 390873048. E. Kobler acknowledges funding from the German Research Foundation (DFG) KO 7162/1-1 project number 543939932, and Austrian Science Fund (FWF) [10.55776/COE12].

Disclosure of Interests. The authors have no competing interests to declare that are relevant to the content of this article.

References

1. Amosy, O., Eyal, G., Chechik, G.: Late to the party? On-demand unlabeled personalized federated learning. In: IEEE Winter Conference on Applications of Computer Vision (2024). https://doi.org/10.1109/WACV57701.2024.00218
2. Arivazhagan, M.G., Aggarwal, V., Singh, A.K., Choudhary, S.: Federated learning with personalization layers. arXiv (2019). https://arxiv.org/abs/1912.00818
3. Chen, X., Huang, Y., Xie, Z., Pang, J.: HyperFedNet: communication-efficient personalized federated learning via hypernetwork. arXiv (2024). https://arxiv.org/abs/2402.18445

4. Collins, L., Hassani, H., Mokhtari, A., Shakkottai, S.: Exploiting shared representations for personalized federated learning. In: International Conference on Machine Learning (2021). https://proceedings.mlr.press/v139/collins21a.html

5. Duan, J.-H., Li, W., Lu, S.: FedDNA: federated learning with decoupled normalization-layer aggregation for non-IID data. In: Oliver, N., Pérez-Cruz, F., Kramer, S., Read, J., Lozano, J.A. (eds.) ECML PKDD 2021. LNCS (LNAI), vol. 12975, pp. 722–737. Springer, Cham (2021). https://doi.org/10.1007/978-3-030-86486-6_44

6. Fallah, A., Mokhtari, A., Ozdaglar, A.: Personalized federated learning with theoretical guarantees: a model-agnostic meta-learning approach. In: Advances in Neural Information Processing Systems (2020). https://proceedings.neurips.cc/paper_files/paper/2020/file/24389bfe4fe2eba8bf9aa9203a44cdad-Paper.pdf

7. Ghosh, A., Chung, J., Yin, D., Ramchandran, K.: An efficient framework for clustered federated learning. In: Advances in Neural Information Processing Systems (2020)

8. Gutierrez, D.M.J., et al.: Non-IID data in federated learning: a survey with taxonomy, metrics, methods, frameworks and future directions. arXiv (2024). https://arxiv.org/abs/2411.12377

9. Ha, D., Dai, A.M., Le, Q.V.: HyperNetworks. In: International Conference on Learning Representations (2017). https://openreview.net/forum?id=rkpACe1lx

10. He, K., Zhang, X., Ren, S., Sun, J.: Deep residual learning for image recognition. In: IEEE Conference on Computer Vision and Pattern Recognition (2016). https://doi.org/10.1109/CVPR.2016.90

11. Hsieh, K., Phanishayee, A., Mutlu, O., Gibbons, P.: The non-IID data quagmire of decentralized machine learning. In: International Conference on Machine Learning (2020). https://proceedings.mlr.press/v119/hsieh20a.html

12. Hu, E.J., et al.: LoRA: low-rank adaptation of large language models. In: International Conference on Learning Representations (2022). https://openreview.net/forum?id=nZeVKeeFYf9

13. Hull, J.: A database for handwritten text recognition research. IEEE Trans. Pattern Anal. Mach. Intell. (1994). https://doi.org/10.1109/34.291440

14. Idrissi, M.J., Berrada, I., Noubir, G.: FEDBS: learning on non-IID data in federated learning using batch normalization. In: IEEE Conference on Tools with Artificial Intelligence (2021). https://doi.org/10.1109/ictai52525.2021.00138

15. Ioffe, S., Szegedy, C.: Batch normalization: accelerating deep network training by reducing internal covariate shift. In: International Conference on Machine Learning (2015)

16. Jiang, Y., Konečný, J., Rush, K., Kannan, S.: Improving federated learning personalization via model agnostic meta learning. arXiv (2023). https://arxiv.org/abs/1909.12488

17. Karimireddy, S.P., Kale, S., Mohri, M., Reddi, S., Stich, S., Suresh, A.T.: SCAFFOLD: stochastic controlled averaging for federated learning. In: International Conference on Machine Learning (2020). https://proceedings.mlr.press/v119/karimireddy20a.html

18. Kingma, D.P., Ba, J.: Adam: a method for stochastic optimization. In: International Conference on Learning Representations (2015). http://arxiv.org/abs/1412.6980

19. Krizhevsky, A., Hinton, G., et al.: Learning multiple layers of features from tiny images (2009)

20. Le, Y., Yang, X.: Tiny ImageNet visual recognition challenge. CS 231N **7** (2015)

21. LeCun, Y., Bottou, L., Bengio, Y., Haffner, P.: Gradient-based learning applied to document recognition. Proc. IEEE (1998). https://doi.org/10.1109/5.726791
22. LeCun, Y.: The MNIST database of handwritten digits (1998). http://yann.lecun.com/exdb/mnist/
23. Li, Q., Diao, Y., Chen, Q., He, B.: Federated learning on non-IID data silos: an experimental study. In: IEEE International Conference on Data Engineering (2022). https://doi.org/10.1109/ICDE53745.2022.00077
24. Li, Q., He, B., Song, D.: Model-contrastive federated learning. arXiv (2021). https://arxiv.org/abs/2103.16257
25. Li, T., Sahu, A.K., Zaheer, M., Sanjabi, M., Talwalkar, A., Smith, V.: Federated optimization in heterogeneous networks. Mach. Learn. Syst. (2020)
26. Li, X., Huang, K., Yang, W., Wang, S., Zhang, Z.: On the convergence of FedAvg on non-IID data. arXiv (2020). https://arxiv.org/abs/1907.02189
27. Li, X., Jiang, M., Zhang, X., Kamp, M., Dou, Q.: FedBN: federated learning on non-IID features via local batch normalization. In: International Conference on Learning Representations (2021). https://openreview.net/pdf?id=6YEQUn0QICG
28. Lim, J.H., Ha, S., Yoon, S.W.: MetaVers: meta-learned versatile representations for personalized federated learning. In: IEEE Winter Conference on Applications of Computer Vision, pp. 2587–2596 (2024). https://doi.org/10.1109/WACV57701.2024.00257
29. Mansour, Y., Mohri, M., Ro, J., Suresh, A.T.: Three approaches for personalization with applications to federated learning. arXiv (2020). https://arxiv.org/abs/2002.10619
30. Marfoq, O., Neglia, G., Bellet, A., Kameni, L., Vidal, R.: Federated multi-task learning under a mixture of distributions. In: Advances in Neural Information Processing Systems (2021)
31. McMahan, B., Moore, E., Ramage, D., Hampson, S., y Arcas, B.A.: Communication-efficient learning of deep networks from decentralized data. In: International Conference on Artificial Intelligence and Statistics. PMLR (2017). https://proceedings.mlr.press/v54/mcmahan17a.html
32. Netzer, Y., Wang, T., Coates, A., Bissacco, A., Wu, B., Ng, A.Y.: Reading digits in natural images with unsupervised feature learning. In: NIPS Workshop on Deep Learning and Unsupervised Feature Learning (2011). http://ufldl.stanford.edu/housenumbers/nips2011_housenumbers.pdf
33. Oh, J., Kim, S., Yun, S.Y.: FedBABU: toward enhanced representation for federated image classification. In: International Conference on Learning Representations (2022). https://openreview.net/forum?id=HuaYQfggn5u
34. Rieke, N., et al.: The future of digital health with federated learning. NPJ Digit. Med. (2020). https://doi.org/10.1038/s41746-020-00323-1
35. Roy, P., Ghosh, S., Bhattacharya, S., Pal, U.: Effects of degradations on deep neural network architectures. arXiv (2018). http://arxiv.org/abs/1807.10108
36. Sattler, F., Müller, K.R., Samek, W.: Clustered federated learning: model-agnostic distributed multitask optimization under privacy constraints. IEEE Trans. Neural Netw. Learn. Syst. (2021). https://doi.org/10.1109/TNNLS.2020.3015958
37. Schmidhuber, J.: Learning to control fast-weight memories: an alternative to dynamic recurrent networks. Neural Comput. (1992). https://doi.org/10.1162/neco.1992.4.1.131
38. Scott, J., Zakerinia, H., Lampert, C.H.: PeFLL: personalized federated learning by learning to learn. In: International Conference on Learning Representations (2024)
39. Shamsian, A., Navon, A., Fetaya, E., Chechik, G.: Personalized federated learning using hypernetworks. In: International Conference on Machine Learning (2021)

40. Song, C., Saxena, D., Cao, J., Zhao, Y.: FedDistill: global model distillation for local model de-biasing in non-IID federated learning. arXiv (2024). https://arxiv.org/abs/2404.09210
41. Wang, H., Yurochkin, M., Sun, Y., Papailiopoulos, D., Khazaeni, Y.: Federated learning with matched averaging. arXiv (2020). https://arxiv.org/abs/2002.06440
42. Yang, X., Huang, W., Ye, M.: FedAS: bridging inconsistency in personalized federated learning. In: IEEE Conference on Computer Vision and Pattern Recognition (CVPR), pp. 11986–11995 (2024). https://doi.org/10.1109/cvpr52733.2024.01139
43. Zhao, Y., Li, M., Lai, L., Suda, N., Civin, D., Chandra, V.: Federated learning with non-IID Data. arXiv (2018). https://arxiv.org/abs/1806.00582

Object Risk Estimation for Autonomous Driving Safety

Abdul Hannan Khan[1,2]($\boxtimes$) iD, Syed Shafiq[1] iD, Ludger van Elst[2] iD,
and Andreas Dengel[1,2] iD

[1] Department of Computer Science, RPTU Kaiserslautern-Landau, Kaiserslautern
67663, Germany
[2] German Research Center for Artificial Intelligence (DFKI GmbH), Kaiserslautern
67663, Germany
`hannan.khan@dfki.de`

Abstract. Road traffic accidents claim millions of lives annually, majorly involving vulnerable road users such as pedestrians and cyclists. Proactive traffic scene risk assessment with priority to vulnerable traffic actors can drastically reduce the chances of collision and save lives. To improve the safety of advanced driver-assistance systems (ADAS), we propose Object Risk Estimation (ORE), a novel framework that combines motion, lane-position, and class labels to enable context-aware and ethically prioritized risk assessment. It uses a multitask framework that integrates object detection, Time-to-Contact (TTC) estimation, and semantic segmentation in a single deep neural network. Further, it uses post-processing to combine these outputs to estimate risk per object and overall scene risk. Leveraging a shared backbone, ORE achieves a 27% reduction in inference time while delivering superior performance, with 1.5 higher mAP % and 11% lower oMiD loss on the Waymo dataset. Its modular design ensures transparency, with intermediate outputs directly explaining risk scores, eliminating the need for post-hoc analysis. By facilitating timely transfer of control and protecting vulnerable road users, ORE offers a practical, interpretable, and efficient solution for ADAS and autonomous driving safety, scalable to diverse traffic scenarios and higher autonomy levels.

Keywords: Autonomous Driving Safety · Object Risk Estimation · Time-to-Contact · Lane Segmentation · Scene Risk Assessment

1 Introduction

Road traffic injuries claim approximately 1.19 million lives annually, with over half of the fatalities involving vulnerable road users such as pedestrians, cyclists, and motorcyclists [33]. The goal of autonomous driving is to develop vehicles that navigate roads autonomously, enhancing safety by mitigating human errors, improving traffic efficiency, and providing accessible mobility [29]. However, achieving safe and reliable autonomous driving in dynamic traffic scenes, where

© The Author(s), under exclusive license to Springer Nature Switzerland AG 2026
M. Keuper and F. Locatello (Eds.): DAGM GCPR 2025, LNCS 16125, pp. 419–433, 2026.
https://doi.org/10.1007/978-3-032-12840-9_27

vehicles, pedestrians, and static objects interact across complex lane geometries, remains challenging. Current perception and prediction pipelines often rely on black-box deep learning models, such as Multimodal Large Language Models [38] or a combination of multiple single-task models [15][35]. These models prioritize accuracy but lack interpretability, computational efficiency, or comprehensive risk context, compromising their suitability for safety-critical Advanced Driver Assistance Systems (ADAS).

Scene risk estimation is pivotal for ensuring safe and efficient autonomous driving by providing high-level scene understanding to guide maneuvers and trigger Transfer of Control in ADAS [22]. Accurate risk estimates, informed by object dynamics, lane context, and category-specific priorities (e.g., pedestrians over static objects), can enable vehicles to navigate safely while minimizing resource costs. Despite extensive research on trajectory planning and scene occupancy estimation, research in scene risk estimation remains limited, with existing methods often restricted to specific scenarios, such as occlusions [31], or lacking lane-aware and interpretable risk assessment [30]. This gap underscores the need of a unified, efficient, and transparent risk estimation framework to enhance ADAS safety across diverse traffic environments.

To address these challenges, we propose Object Risk Estimation (ORE), a unified multitask framework for efficient scene and object risk assessment in ADAS. ORE integrates object detection, Time-to-Contact (TTC) estimation, and semantic segmentation of drivable areas (i.e., safe road regions) and lane line markings, computing per-object risk based on class, TTC, and lane position. Moreover, it aggregates these risks to estimate overall scene risk. This transparent design leverages intermediate outputs (e.g., bounding boxes, TTC values, lane maps) for interpretable risk scores, while a shared HRNet backbone [32] reduces computational overhead. Furthermore, ORE can predict risks for planned maneuvers by simulating object or ego-vehicle positions and updating lane-based risks using predicted lane types (e.g., dashed or solid) to enable proactive and safer planning.

The key contributions of this work are;

1. A unified multitask framework integrating object detection, TTC estimation, and semantic segmentation, reducing inference time by 27% compared to sequential models.
2. A novel lane-, motion-, and category-aware risk estimation approach prioritizing vulnerable road users (e.g., pedestrians), enhancing safety across urban and highway scenarios.
3. Transparent risk scoring using intermediate outputs to explain decisions without post-hoc analysis, meeting safety-critical interpretability needs.
4. Predictive risk assessment for planned maneuvers by simulating object positions, enabling proactive safety planning.
5. Superior performance, with 1.5 higher mAP (%) and 11% lower object Motion-in-Depth (oMiD) error on Waymo dataset[27].

2   Related Work

2.1   Object Detection

Object detection has progressed from two-stage detectors like Faster R-CNN [24], which rely on region proposal networks, to single-stage detectors such as YOLO [23] and SSD [17], which prioritize speed for real-time applications. These methods are foundational for traffic scene analysis, detecting vehicles and pedestrians in dynamic environments.

Recent advances include anchor-free detectors like FCOS [28] and RTOD [14], which enhance flexibility, and transformer-based models like DETR [5], Swin Transformer [18] and DyHead [7], which leverage global context for improved accuracy. In traffic safety, [9] employ YOLOv5 for vehicle and pedestrian detection in street view images to assess safety perception, demonstrating the relevance of robust detection in urban traffic scenes. ORE adopts an anchor-free approach to balance accuracy and efficiency in autonomous driving.

2.2   Lane and Driveable Area Segmentation

Semantic segmentation has evolved from hand-crafted features to deep learning models like Fully Convolutional Networks (FCNs) [19], U-Net [25], and HRNet [32], which excel at pixel-level labeling. Transformer-based models, such as Seg-Former [35], capture long-range dependencies for complex scenes. These methods are critical for segmenting driveable areas and lanes in traffic analysis.

In autonomous driving, segmentation is used to delineate road boundaries and lane markings. For instance, [9] apply LM-DeeplabV3+ [10] based segmentation to street view images to quantify safety elements like lanes and traffic lights, supporting risk assessment in urban environments. Similarly, [22] review segmentation techniques for extracting lane and road features from traffic videos, emphasizing their role in safety analysis. ORE leverages HRNet [32] backbone with MLP-Mixer based decoder head [13] for driveable area and lane segmentation, integrated with detection and risk estimation.

2.3   Time-to-Contact and Risk Estimation

Time-to-Contact (TTC) estimation, a key metric for collision risk, originated with geometric methods [36] and optical flow [4], which were computationally intensive. Deep learning approaches, such as oTTC [15], model TTC as an object attribute, reducing false alarms compared to pixel-level methods like Binary TTC [3] and OSF [21]. These methods focus on motion-based risk but often lack spatial context.

Recent works extend risk estimation beyond TTC. [31] propose a Dynamic Bayesian Network to assess risks from occluded objects in autonomous driving, integrating probabilistic modeling for real-time decision-making. [30] develop a Work-Zone Crash Risk Field (WCRF) model using vehicle trajectories from surveillance videos, employing XGBoost and SHAP [20] to identify risk factors. [11] present a deep learning system for real-time accident prevention, using

OpenCV to estimate object distances and categorize collision risks (e.g., T-bone, rear-end). These approaches highlight the importance of contextual risk assessment in traffic scenes.

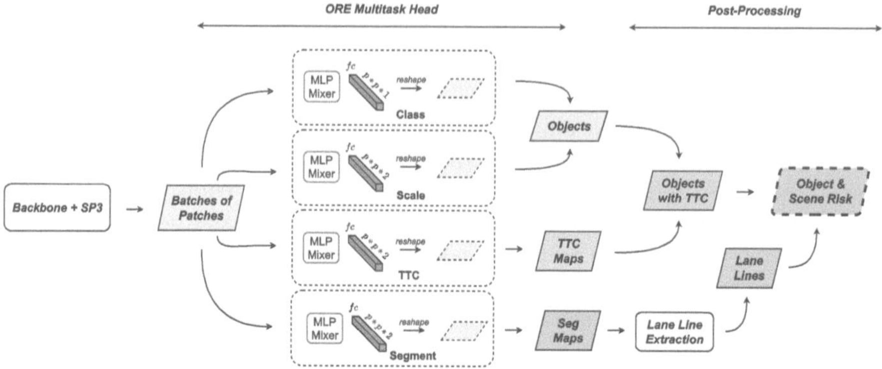

Fig. 1. Abstract architecture of our proposed ORE. It uses HRNetW32 [32] as backbone to extract features and creates local feature pyramids using SP3 [13] to generate high-level semantic features, which are then passed to ORE multitask head in batches of patches fashion.

Multi-task frameworks combine detection, segmentation, and risk estimation to provide holistic scene understanding. [38] introduce SeeUnsafe, a Multi-modal Large Language Model (MLLM) framework for video-based traffic accident analysis, detecting and categorizing incidents (e.g., collisions, near-misses) from surveillance and dashcam videos. [1] use ensemble machine learning (e.g., Random Forest, XGBoost) with SHAP [20] to predict accident severity, identifying risk factors like road category. [22] review multi-task pipelines for traffic safety, integrating segmentation, detection, and trajectory analysis. Unlike these works, ORE unifies object detection, TTC estimation, and lane segmentation into a single deep learning model, achieving efficient risk estimation.

3 Methodology

This section details the architecture and design of the proposed Object Risk Estimation (ORE) framework for real-time risk assessment in autonomous driving. The detailed architecture of ORE is shown in Fig. 1.

3.1 Multi-task Framework

The ORE framework extends the oTTC architecture [15] to perform object detection, Time-to-Contact (TTC) estimation, and semantic segmentation simultaneously, enabling efficient and transparent risk estimation for autonomous driving systems. ORE processes RGB images using a shared HRNet backbone [32], followed by a multitask head with separate branches for detection, TTC estimation, and segmentation.

HRNet Backbone. HRNet backbone maintains high-resolution feature maps across multiple scales, preserving localization information while capturing high-level semantic features [13]. This makes HRNet effective for object detection [8, 12] and semantic segmentation [26, 34, 37]. In oTTC [15], HRNet extracts features for TTC estimation and object detection. ORE uses HRNet as backbone to provide rich, high-resolution features for all tasks, ensuring precise localization of small objects (e.g., pedestrians) and detailed segmentation of drivable areas and lane markings.

Multitask Head. The multitask head, inspired by the Dense Focal Detection Network (DFDN) [15], decodes HRNet features into object detection, TTC estimation, and semantic segmentation outputs. DFDN splits feature maps into patches and processes them in parallel using MLPMixer blocks [13], to efficiently predict bounding boxes, class probabilities, and TTC values. ORE extends DFDN by adding a segmentation branch alongside detection and TTC branches, leveraging HRNetâĂŹs broad spatial context [32]. The detection branch predicts object classes (e.g., vehicles, pedestrians, traffic signs), bounding box scales (height, width), and offsets. The TTC branch estimates motion-in-depth, and the segmentation branch segments drivable areas and lane lines.

The multitask head is optimized using a weighted combination of task losses:

$$\mathcal{L} = \begin{bmatrix} 0.01 & 0.05 & 0.10 & 0.20 & 0.05 \end{bmatrix} \times \begin{bmatrix} \mathcal{L}_{cls} \\ \mathcal{L}_{scl} \\ \mathcal{L}_{off} \\ \mathcal{L}_{ttc} \\ \mathcal{L}_{seg} \end{bmatrix} \tag{1}$$

where the classification loss $\mathcal{L}_{cls}$ uses Focal Loss with Gaussian-based penalty reduction [16]. The scale loss $\mathcal{L}_{scale}$ and offset loss $\mathcal{L}_{offset}$ are Vanilla L1 and Smooth L1 losses, respectively. The *TTC* loss $\mathcal{L}_{ttc}$ uses MiD-loss [15] and the segmentation loss $\mathcal{L}_{seg}$ is cross-entropy loss.

Segmentation Branch. To calculate position-based risk, lane boundary lines need to be identified. These lines can be used to differentiate between the objects in the ego lane and objects separated by a solid or dashed lane line from the ego vehicle. It is also important to further distinguish between objects separated by a dashed line or a solid line, as these objects pose different risks. However, there is limited data available with separate ground truth for solid and dashed lane lines [2]. To deal with this issue, we only employ two segmentation classes, i.e., drivable area and lane lines, and use them to differentiate between solid and dashed lane lines using post-processing.

3.2 Object and Scene Risk Estimation

ORE computes transparent per-object and scene risks to enable safe, interpretable, and proactive decision-making. The following section details the process of estimating risk per object, leveraging multiple network outputs, and using it to estimate an overall scene risk.

Algorithm 1. Lane Boundary Lines Extraction and Classification

---

Require:
1: $D \leftarrow$ drivable area $\qquad\qquad\qquad\qquad$ ▷ Segmentation map, Sec. 3.1
2: $M \leftarrow$ lane marking $\qquad\qquad\qquad\qquad$ ▷ Segmentation map, Sec. 3.1
3: $\delta \leftarrow \sqrt{w^2 + h^2}$ $\qquad\qquad\qquad\qquad\qquad\qquad$ ▷ Image diagonal size
4: $o \leftarrow (w/2, h)$ $\qquad\qquad\qquad\qquad$ ▷ Bottom-center point of image
Ensure: Extracted lines $L = \{l_1, l_2, \dots\}, T(l) \in \{\text{solid}, \text{dashed}\}$
5: $R \leftarrow \triangle$ ROI in D using left-bottom, right-bottom, center-top points
6: $E \leftarrow$ CannyEdgeDetector$(M \cap \triangle R)$ $\qquad\qquad\qquad\qquad$ ▷ Extract edges
7: $S \leftarrow$ HoughTransform(E) $\qquad$ ▷ Extract segments with angle θ, position p
8: $S \leftarrow \{s \in S \mid \|s\| > \tau\}$ $\qquad\qquad$ ▷ Filter small segments, $\tau \ll \delta$
9: $S \leftarrow \{s \in S \mid (p_x < o_x \wedge 15° < \theta < 75°) \vee (p_x > o_x \wedge 105° < \theta < 165°)\}$
10: $\qquad\qquad\qquad\qquad\qquad\qquad\qquad\qquad\qquad\qquad$ ▷ Filter by θ, p
11: $C \leftarrow$ cluster S by angular difference within a threshold $\qquad$ ▷ Empirically tuned
12: $L \leftarrow \emptyset$
13: **for** each $c \in C$ **do**
14: $\quad$ **if** $|c| = 1$ **then** $\qquad\qquad\qquad\qquad\qquad$ ▷ Single line in cluster
15: $\qquad$ $l \leftarrow c$, with $T(l) = $ solid $\qquad\qquad\qquad\qquad$ ▷ Solid line
16: $\quad$ **else if** $|c| > 1$ **then** $\qquad\qquad\qquad$ ▷ Multiple lines in cluster
17: $\qquad$ $l \leftarrow$ FitLineToEndpoints(c), with $T(l) = $ dashed $\qquad$ ▷ Fit dashed line
18: $\quad$ **end if**
19: $\quad$ $L \leftarrow L \cup \{l\}$
20: **end for**
21: **if** $\nexists l \in L \mid p_x < o_x$ **then** $\qquad\qquad\qquad\qquad\qquad$ ▷ No left line
22: $\quad$ $l \leftarrow$ LeftSide$(\triangle R)$, with $T(l) = $ solid
23: $\quad$ $L \leftarrow L \cup \{l\}$ $\qquad\qquad\qquad\qquad\qquad$ ▷ Add left solid line
24: **end if**
25: **if** $\nexists l \in L \mid p_x > o_x$ **then** $\qquad\qquad\qquad\qquad\qquad$ ▷ No right line
26: $\quad$ $r \leftarrow$ RightSide$(\triangle R)$, with $T(r) = $ solid
27: $\quad$ $L \leftarrow L \cup \{r\}$ $\qquad\qquad\qquad\qquad\qquad$ ▷ Add right solid line
28: **end if**
29: **return** L

Per-Object Risk. The ORE network outputs object-bounding boxes with class labels and TTC, and lane markings and drivable area segmentation maps. Our goal is to use the object's lane position, TTC, and class to predict risk. The TTC and class for each object can be obtained from the immediate output of the network without any post-processing. However, for the lane positioning, we post-process the drivable area and lane marking segmentations masks to extract lane boundaries and the boundary of drivable area. The algorithm 1 details the process to extract and classify lane boundary lines. The ego lane can be found by finding the lane in which the closest drivable area pixel to the bottom-center of the image lies. The lane in which this point lies is the ego lane, since we use the images of the camera mounted on the front of the ego vehicle.

Further, the lane-based risk of the traffic objects is obtained by finding the type of lane marking which separates the lane of that traffic object from ego lane. Here, the lane of the traffic object is obtained using the bottom-center of the bounding box. Further, if there are multiple lane markings separating the ego vehicle and the object, lane marking with minimum risk is selected. Following are the lane positioning-based risk values ϕ_{lane} for the traffic objects:

$$\phi_{lane} = \begin{cases} 1.0 & \text{if the object is in the ego lane} \\ 0.5 & \text{if the object is separated by dashed lane} \\ 0.25 & \text{if the object is separated by solid lane,} \end{cases} \tag{2}$$

where the objects which are outside the drivable area are also considered separated by solid lane and assigned least risk. The class- or priority-based risk ϕ_{cls} is defined as follows:

$$\phi_{cls} = \begin{cases} 1.0 & \text{if pedestrian} \\ 0.5 & \text{if vehicle} \\ 0.25 & \text{if static object} \end{cases} . \tag{3}$$

For the TTC-based risk ϕ_{ttc}, the ORE network outputs TTC in the form of ratio of depths (η), which lies in the range $(0.5, 1.3)$. We use the following equation to calculate the TTC-based risk ϕ_{ttc}:

$$\phi_{ttc} = 1 - \frac{\eta - 0.5}{0.8} . \tag{4}$$

The final risk ϕ for each traffic object is calculated by taking the geometric mean of all risks:

$$\phi = \sqrt[3]{\phi_{cls} \times \phi_{lane} \times \phi_{ttc}} . \tag{5}$$

Scene Risk Estimation. The traffic scene is composed of multiple traffic objects, ideally moving predictably. However, all the objects are not given equal importance, i.e., objects that are moving towards the ego vehicle are more important than the ones moving away, objects which are in the same lane are more important than the ones in a different lane, and vulnerable traffic objects like pedestrians and cyclists are more important than cars and static traffic objects. These precedences are already captured by per-object risk estimation, detailed in Sec. 3.2. Now, the overall risk for a traffic scene should consider all traffic objects present in the scene and should weigh the most risky object more. Therefore, we use the following equation to estimate the overall scene risk:

$$\gamma = \frac{\overline{\Phi} + max(\Phi)}{2} \quad , \tag{6}$$

where $\Phi = \{\phi_1, \phi_2, ...\}$ is a set of risks for objects present in the scene and $\overline{\Phi}$ is the mean of these risks. This additive formulation ensures transparency, as γ is traceable to individual object risks (ϕ_i) and ultimately to the intermediate outputs (bounding boxes, TTC values, segmentation maps), eliminating the need for post-hoc analysis. The high γ values can be used to trigger ADAS interventions, such as Transfer of Control to the human driver.

Forward Risk Projections. Proactive maneuver planning requires risk projections in advance for possible next moves. These risk projections can help ADAS identify risky maneuvers and improve safety. Assuming relatively negligible lateral movement, which is valid for scenarios like highways, ORE estimates forward risks by simply updating the positioning-based risks ϕ_{lane} of traffic objects in the scene. Although, limited to the lateral projections, forward risks help in multiple scenarios. For ego vehicles, it can grade the possible lanes by risk. These risks estimates are valid as ego lane change only reflects on change in ϕ_{lane} of traffic objects while keeping ϕ_{cls} and ϕ_{ttc} constant. This capability enables the selection of low-risk trajectories, enhancing safety across highways.

4   Experimental Setup

4.1   Datasets and Preparation

We utilize the Waymo Perception Dataset [27] for training and evaluation, selected for its rich annotations supporting multitask learning in autonomous driving. The Waymo dataset provides 3D bounding boxes, 2D-3D correspondences, pixel-level segmentation masks, and temporal annotations for objects such as vehicles, pedestrians, and cyclists, enabling fine-grained perception tasks [27].

The Waymo Perception Dataset [27] supports object detection, TTC estimation, and semantic segmentation. For object detection and TTC, we use central camera data with LiDAR-projected 2D boxes, while ignoring boxes which are occluded more than 65%. TTC values are calculated using the ratio of depths, yielding $145,094$ training and $35,583$ validation images. Semantic segmentation involves decoding panoptic labels into drivable area and lane markers, from the central camera only. A combined dataset is created including $10,000$ training and $2,000$ validation images with bounding boxes, TTC, and segmentation labels, for joint multitask training.

4.2   Evaluation Metrics

We assess the performance of our multitask framework using task-specific metrics tailored to object detection, lane segmentation, and time-to-contact estimation, as detailed below.

Object Detection. We evaluate object detection using mean average precision (mAP) at multiple IoU thresholds from $(0.5-0.95)$, a standard metric to quantify object detection performance. The mAP is given by:

$$mAP = \frac{1}{|M|} \sum_{M} AP_n, \tag{7}$$

where AP_n is the average precision for class n over recall levels, and M is the set of object labels.

Drivable area and Lane Line Segmentation. The mean Intersection over Union ($mIoU$) is a widely accepted measure to access pixel-level accuracy of segmentation performance. Lane segmentation performance is measured using Intersection over Union (IoU) for drivable area and lane markings, assessing pixel-level accuracy. The $mIoU$ is given by:

$$mIoU = \frac{1}{Q} \sum_{Q} IoU(\omega, \omega_{GT}), \tag{8}$$

where ω is predicted segmentation, ω_{GT} is ground truth, and Q is the set of segmentation labels.

Time-to-Contact Estimation. We evaluate TTC estimation using MiD-Loss [15] to measure its precision. The MiD-Loss is given by:

$$MiD\,Loss = \|\log(\eta) - \log(\eta_{GT})\|_1 \times 10^4, \tag{9}$$

where η is predicted motion-in-depth and η_{GT} is ground truth, calculated using Euclidean distances of the respective objects from the LIDAR center.

4.3   Training and Inference

ORE is implemented using MMDetection [6] and PyTorch, trained on a 4 A100 GPUs for 30 epochs using Adam optimizer with a learning rate of 2×10^{-4}. Horizontal flips and rotation data augmentation are employed to mitigate overfitting. For inference, a single A100 GPU is used with 1 sample per batch. Inference time is measured by taking the mean of the inference time across the validation set, excluding the image loading time to the GPU and post-processing.

5   Experiments and Results

To test the performance of our proposed ORE framework, we conduct a series of experiments. The ORE framework is compared with task-specific models on segmentation, TTC prediction and object detection tasks, where it is evaluated based on performance and inference time. Also, we present qualitative results, showing per-object and overall scene risks.

5.1 Comparison with Task-Specific Models

ORE combines segmentation, object detection, and TTC estimation in a single network, using a shared backbone and feature pyramid network. This way, ORE achieves better efficiency, reducing the overhead of a separate backbone for each task. We compare our multitask model with task-specific models to estimate performance and efficiency gains. For this experiment, we use the combined Waymo dataset [27] explained in Sec. 4.1, to train our proposed ORE multitask framework as well as task-specific models to establish a fair comparison. Table 1 shows the detailed results of this experiment. It is evident that ORE outperforms oTTC in object detection by 1.5 $mAP(\%)$ with a 11% reduction in $oMiD$. Moreover, it achieves slightly better $mIoU$ compared to SegFormer [35]. These improvements are achieved with a 27% reduction in inference time compared to the combined SegFormer [35] and oTTC [15] solution for segmentation, object detection, and TTC estimation. This proves that the ORE framework, successfully performs multiple autonomous driving tasks with shorter inference time compared to separate task-specific models stacked, without compromising accuracy.

5.2 Object Risk Estimation

ORE combines position, motion, and category priority of traffic objects to estimate their risk. Fig. 2 shows the final output of object risk estimation, where detections are shown along with their risk, ranging from $(0, 1)$. It can be seen that, the framework assigns high risk to pedestrians and vehicles in front of ego vehicle. Moreover, vehicles moving toward get higher risks compared to stationary objects and objects that are moving away.

Table 1. Comparison of the multitask framework with task-specific models. ORE demonstrates significantly better mAP and $oMiD$ with slightly better $mIoU$. D. Area and L. Line represent the drivable area and the Lane Line segmentation classes.

Model	mAP (%)	oMiD	mIoU (%)			Inference Time (ms)
			D. Area	L. Line	All	
SegFormer [35]	-	-	94.9	41.0	77.9	42
oTTC [15]	41.8	124	-	-	-	112
ORE (ours)	43.3	110	94.9	41.3	78.1	112

5.3 Scene Risk Estimation

Traffic scene risk is a crucial metric that incorporates risk levels of each object in the scene to give an overall risk estimate for the scene. This metric can be directly used to recommend safe speed ranges and generate transfer on control requests.

Fig. 2. Object risk estimation results. The bounding box color indicates the risk-level assigned to that object, where the redder shade indicates higher risk levels.

Fig. 3. Scene risk estimation results. The objects with the highest risk are highlighted, and annotated with total risk and its components. R represents total risk ϕ while T, C, and L represents ϕ_{ttc}, ϕ_{cls}, and ϕ_{lane} respectively.

Fig. 3 shows the scene risk estimation results. Risk assigned to each scene is given at their respective top-left corners, with color indicating the intensity as well. In addition, the most risky object in the scene is also highlighted with their respective risks in color-coded form. Furthermore, the traffic scenes are arranged in ascending order of scene risk, with the first row indicating low risk objects either out of drivable area or separated by a solid lane line. The second row shows slightly higher risks with inside city scenes at low relative speeds. The third row shows higher risk scenes, including highways and high-risk objects, i.e., pedestrians. This proves that our transparent ORE framework can traceback the scene risk to the risk components of the most risky object, enabling reasoning and interpretations.

6   Conclusion and Future Work

This work proposes a novel, transparent, and comprehensive risk estimation for traffic objects and scenes, namely ORE. It employs a multitask framework to detect objects, segment drivable area and lane line markings and estimate TTC per-object, using a single network. This approach is highly efficient compared to multiple task-specific models. ORE achieves superior performance while having significantly reduced inference time. This performance boost is achieved by the shared, task-agnostic, and strong, semantic features, learned as a result of multi-task training. Moreover, ORE combines position, motion, and priority attributes of detected objects into a single risk metric for each object, using post-processing. Ultimately, these per-object risks are combined to grade the traffic scene by risk level. The transparent nature of the post-processing for risk calculation allows tracing back risk to each individual object and respective attribute causing it, i.e., lane position, Time-to-Contact or category of the object. Furthermore, ORE enables forward risk projections to proactively estimate risk levels of possible traffic maneuvers by simulating traffic scenes. Altogether, ORE provides a light-weight, transparent, multitask framework to estimate comprehensive scene and per-object risks which could be used to plan safe maneuvers and trigger transfer of control.

6.1   Limitations and Future Work

The current approach only works for easily visible straight lane lines, and fails to detect curved, multiple and poorly visible lane lines. Although object risks in these cases, where no lane line is detected, is estimated based on TTC and category alone, which is practical but, extension to handle curved lane lines and establishing virtual lane lines when none is visible can improve the reliability of the approach. Moreover, the risk weights assigned to different cases and categories are empirical and work for a given experimental setup, as the goal is to provide a basic framework which could be built on rather than a concrete solution. Furthermore, the current approach only handles pedestrians, traffic signs and general vehicle category, an extension to more traffic actors and subcategories is desired for richer risk estimates. Additionally, inclusion of out-of-distribution objects can improve the overall safety and efficacy of the approach.

References

1. Ahmed, S., Hossain, M.A., Ray, S.K., Bhuiyan, M.M.I., Sabuj, S.R.: A study on road accident prediction and contributing factors using explainable machine learning models: analysis and performance. Trans. Res. Interdisc. Perspect. **19**, 100814 (2023)
2. Alibeigi, M., et al.: Zenseact open dataset: a large-scale and diverse multimodal dataset for autonomous driving. In: Proceedings of the IEEE/CVF International Conference on Computer Vision, pp. 20178–20188 (2023)
3. Badki, A., Gallo, O., Kautz, J., Sen, P.: Binary TTC: a temporal geofence for autonomous navigation. In: Proceedings of the IEEE/CVF Conference on Computer Vision and Pattern Recognition, pp. 12946–12955 (2021)
4. Brox, T., Bruhn, A., Papenberg, N., Weickert, J.: High Accuracy Optical Flow Estimation Based on a Theory for Warping. In: Pajdla, T., Matas, J. (eds.) ECCV 2004. LNCS, vol. 3024, pp. 25–36. Springer, Heidelberg (2004). https://doi.org/10.1007/978-3-540-24673-2_3
5. Carion, N., Massa, F., Synnaeve, G., Usunier, N., Kirillov, A., Zagoruyko, S.: End-to-end object detection with transformers. In: European conference on computer vision, pp. 213–229. Springer (2020)
6. Chen, K., et al.: Mmdetection: open MMLAB detection toolbox and benchmark. arXiv preprint arXiv:1906.07155 (2019)
7. Dai, X., et al.: Dynamic head: unifying object detection heads with attentions. In: Proceedings of the IEEE/CVF conference on computer vision and pattern recognition, pp. 7373–7382 (2021)
8. Hasan, I., Liao, S., Li, J., Akram, S.U., Shao, L.: Generalizable pedestrian detection: the elephant in the room. In: Proceedings of the IEEE/CVF Conference on Computer Vision and Pattern Recognition, pp. 11328–11337 (2021)
9. Hou, X., Chen, P.: Analysis of road safety perception and influencing factors in a complex urban environment—taking chaoyang district, beijing, as an example. ISPRS Int. J. Geo Inf. **13**(8), 272 (2024)
10. Hou, X., Chen, P., Gu, H.: LM-deeplabv3+: a lightweight image segmentation algorithm based on multi-scale feature interaction. Appl. Sci. **14**(4), 1558 (2024)
11. Kabir, M.F., Roy, S.: Real-time vehicular accident prevention system using deep learning architecture. Expert Syst. Appl. **206**, 117837 (2022)
12. Khan, A.H., Munir, M., van Elst, L., Dengel, A.: F2dnet: fast focal detection network for pedestrian detection. In: 2022 26th International Conference on Pattern Recognition (ICPR), pp. 4658–4664. IEEE (2022)
13. Khan, A.H., Nawaz, M.S., Dengel, A.: Localized semantic feature mixers for efficient pedestrian detection in autonomous driving. In: Proceedings of the IEEE/CVF conference on computer vision and pattern recognition, pp. 5476–5485 (2023)
14. Khan, A.H., Rizvi, S.T.R., Dengel, A.: Real-time traffic object detection for autonomous driving. arXiv preprint arXiv:2402.00128 (2024)
15. Khan, A.H., Rizvi, S.T.R., Macharavtu, D.V.C., Dengel, A.: OTTC: object time-to-contact for motion estimation in autonomous driving. In: 2024 International Conference on Digital Image Computing: Techniques and Applications (DICTA), pp. 343–350. IEEE (2024)

16. Lin, T.Y., Goyal, P., Girshick, R., He, K., Dollár, P.: Focal loss for dense object detection. In: Proceedings of the IEEE international conference on computer vision, pp. 2980–2988 (2017)

17. Liu, W., et al.: SSD: Single Shot MultiBox Detector. In: Leibe, B., Matas, J., Sebe, N., Welling, M. (eds.) ECCV 2016. LNCS, vol. 9905, pp. 21–37. Springer, Cham (2016). https://doi.org/10.1007/978-3-319-46448-0_2

18. Liu, Z., et al.: SWIN transformer: hierarchical vision transformer using shifted windows. In: Proceedings of the IEEE/CVF international conference on computer vision, pp. 10012–10022 (2021)

19. Long, J., Shelhamer, E., Darrell, T.: Fully convolutional networks for semantic segmentation. In: Proceedings of the IEEE conference on computer vision and pattern recognition, pp. 3431–3440 (2015)

20. Lundberg, S.M., Lee, S.I.: A unified approach to interpreting model predictions. Adv. Neural Inf. Proc. Syst. **30** (2017)

21. Menze, M., Geiger, A.: Object scene flow for autonomous vehicles. In: Proceedings of the IEEE conference on computer vision and pattern recognition, pp. 3061–3070 (2015)

22. Razi, A., et al.: Deep learning serves traffic safety analysis: a forward-looking review. IET Intel. Transport Syst. **17**(1), 22–71 (2023)

23. Redmon, J., Divvala, S., Girshick, R., Farhadi, A.: You only look once: unified, real-time object detection. In: Proceedings of the IEEE conference on computer vision and pattern recognition, pp. 779–788 (2016)

24. Ren, S., He, K., Girshick, R., Sun, J.: Faster r-CNN: towards real-time object detection with region proposal networks. IEEE Trans. Pattern Anal. Mach. Intell. **39**(6), 1137–1149 (2016)

25. Ronneberger, O., Fischer, P., Brox, T.: U-Net: Convolutional Networks for Biomedical Image Segmentation. In: Navab, N., Hornegger, J., Wells, W.M., Frangi, A.F. (eds.) MICCAI 2015. LNCS, vol. 9351, pp. 234–241. Springer, Cham (2015). https://doi.org/10.1007/978-3-319-24574-4_28

26. Seong, S., Choi, J.: Semantic segmentation of urban buildings using a high-resolution network (HRNET) with channel and spatial attention gates. Remote Sens. **13**(16), 3087 (2021)

27. Sun, P., et al.: Scalability in perception for autonomous driving: waymo open dataset. In: Proceedings of the IEEE/CVF conference on computer vision and pattern recognition, pp. 2446–2454 (2020)

28. Tian, Z., Shen, C., Chen, H., He, T.: Fcos: a simple and strong anchor-free object detector. IEEE Trans. Pattern Anal. Mach. Intell. **44**(4), 1922–1933 (2020)

29. Urmson, C., et al.: Autonomous driving in urban environments: boss and the urban challenge. J. field Robot. **25**(8), 425–466 (2008)

30. Wang, B., Chen, T., Zhang, C., Wong, Y.D., Zhang, H., Zhou, Y.: Toward safer highway work zones: an empirical analysis of crash risks using improved safety potential field and machine learning techniques. Accident Anal. Prev. **194**, 107361 (2024)

31. Wang, D., Fu, W., Song, Q., Zhou, J.: Potential risk assessment for safe driving of autonomous vehicles under occluded vision. Sci. Rep. **12**(1), 4981 (2022)

32. Wang, J., et al.: Deep high-resolution representation learning for visual recognition. IEEE Trans. Pattern Anal. Mach. Intell. **43**(10), 3349–3364 (2020)

33. World Health Organization: road traffic injuries. Fact sheet (2023). https://www.who.int/news-room/fact-sheets/detail/road-traffic-injuries. Accessed 24 Apr 2025

34. Wu, H., Liang, C., Liu, M., Wen, Z.: Optimized HRNET for image semantic segmentation. Expert Syst. Appl. **174**, 114532 (2021)

35. Xie, E., Wang, W., Yu, Z., Anandkumar, A., Alvarez, J.M., Luo, P.: Segformer: simple and efficient design for semantic segmentation with transformers. Adv. Neural. Inf. Process. Syst. **34**, 12077–12090 (2021)
36. Yang, G., Ramanan, D.: Upgrading optical flow to 3d scene flow through optical expansion. In: Proceedings of the IEEE/CVF Conference on Computer Vision and Pattern Recognition, pp. 1334–1343 (2020)
37. Yu, C., et al.: Lite-HRNET: a lightweight high-resolution network. In: Proceedings of the IEEE/CVF conference on computer vision and pattern recognition, pp. 10440–10450 (2021)
38. Zhang, R., Wang, B., Zhang, J., Bian, Z., Feng, C., Ozbay, K.: When language and vision meet road safety: leveraging multimodal large language models for video-based traffic accident analysis. arXiv preprint arXiv:2501.10604 (2025)

Rethinking Semi-supervised Segmentation Beyond Accuracy: Reliability and Robustness

Steven Landgraf[(✉)] [ID], Markus Hillemann [ID], and Markus Ulrich [ID]

Institute of Photogrammetry and Remote Sensing (IPF), Karlsruhe Institute of Technology (KIT), Karlsruhe, Germany
`{steven.landgraf,markus.hillemann,markus.ulrich}@kit.edu`

Abstract. Semantic segmentation is critical for scene understanding but demands costly pixel-wise annotations, attracting increasing attention to semi-supervised approaches to leverage abundant unlabeled data. While semi-supervised segmentation is often promoted as a path toward scalable, real-world deployment, it is astonishing that current evaluation protocols exclusively focus on segmentation accuracy, entirely overlooking reliability and robustness. These qualities, which ensure consistent performance under diverse conditions (robustness) and well-calibrated model confidences as well as meaningful uncertainties (reliability), are essential for safety-critical applications like autonomous driving, where models must handle unpredictable environments and avoid sudden failures at all costs. To address this gap, we introduce the Reliable Segmentation Score (RSS), a novel metric that combines predictive accuracy, calibration, and uncertainty quality measures via a harmonic mean. RSS penalizes deficiencies in any of its components, providing an easy and intuitive way of holistically judging segmentation models. Comprehensive evaluations of UniMatchV2 against its predecessor and a supervised baseline show that semi-supervised methods often trade reliability for accuracy. While out-of-domain evaluations demonstrate UniMatchV2's robustness, they further expose persistent reliability shortcomings. We advocate for a shift in evaluation protocols toward more holistic metrics like RSS to better align semi-supervised learning research with real-world deployment needs.

Keywords: Semi-supervised Segmentation · Reliability · Robustness

1 Introduction

Semantic segmentation is a fundamental tasks in scene understanding through pixel-wise classifications [4,53,57,102]. However, fully leveraging modern neural networks requires large amounts of dense annotations, which are extremely costly. On Cityscapes [11], for instance, a single image with just 19 classes takes around 1.5 h to label – posing a major obstacle to real-world deployment.

M. Keuper and F. Locatello (Eds.): DAGM GCPR 2025, LNCS 16125, pp. 434–452, 2026.
https://doi.org/10.1007/978-3-032-12840-9_28

For this reason, semi-supervised semantic segmentation has garnered increasing attention [70]. The general idea lies in leveraging large amounts of unlabeled images, accompanied by a handful of manually labeled images to alleviate the massive labeling cost of fully supervised learning [67,98]. Recent works [27,28,34,47,48,51,54,79,85,86,88,94–97,103,104] have managed to steadily improve segmentation quality on various benchmarks datasets [11,16,49,105]. Interestingly, in the most recent state-of-the-art approach, "UniMatchV2: Pushing the Limit of Semi-Supervised Semantic Segmentation", Yang et al. [96] accurately identify that semi-supervised segmentation methods are becoming increasingly sophisticated, and yet performance gains are very marginal. Based on this observation, they argue that it is necessary to switch to more modern Vision Transformer-based model architectures (e.g., DINOv2) [65] and focus on more challenging benchmark datasets.

While we strongly agree with this notion, we argue to consider reliability as a complementary concept in semi-supervised segmentation, i.e., whether a model's confidence reflects the true likelihood of correctness and its uncertainty estimates align with predictive ambiguities and errors. In addition, we emphasize robustness, which refers to a model's ability to maintain high performance under perturbations, noise, or distribution shifts. Although these have already been introduced as an integral component in evaluating semantic segmentation models [12,13,52,63,99,107], astonishingly, they have been overlooked entirely in semi-supervised segmentation. This is, perhaps, a bit surprising since semi-supervised learning builds upon the premise of making deep learning accessible for real-world deployment, where a model's prediction need not just be accurate, but more importantly, also reliable and robust.

Therefore, we advocate rethinking semi-supervised evaluation protocols to prioritize reliability and robustness alongside accuracy. To this end, we propose a novel evaluation metric and evaluate the current state-of-the-art method to guide future research toward real-world deployment needs. More precisely, our contributions can be summarized as follows:

1. We introduce the Reliable Segmentation Score (RSS), a novel metric combining accuracy, calibration, and uncertainty quality via a harmonic mean to penalize deficiencies, enabling holistic assessment of segmentation models' reliability and robustness.
2. Additionally, we provide the first comprehensive evaluation of the current state-of-the-art UniMatchV2 [96] in terms of reliability on two in-domain scenarios, comparing it against UniMatchV1 [95] and a supervised baseline. Thereby, we reveal that semi-supervised methods often sacrifice calibration and uncertainty quality for accuracy.
3. Finally, we perform extensive out-of-domain evaluations on Rainy Cityscapes [29] and Foggy Cityscapes [74], showcasing that UniMatchV2 may be more robust but exhibits persistent reliability shortcomings.

We firmly believe that taking reliability and robustness into account is crucial to understand whether semi-supervised segmentation research is moving in the originally intended direction or just incrementally improving the accuracy on selected benchmark datasets.

2   Related Work

2.1   Semi-supervised Semantic Segmentation

While all semi-supervised semantic segmentation methods try to leverage unlabeled images in addition to a handful of manually labeled images, they can be divided into five categories based on the taxonomy proposed by Peláez et al. [70]. The first category comprises adversarial methods, which either exploit generative models to create synthetic images to incorporate them into the segmentation task [44,78], or GAN-like structures [19], where the segmentation model itself acts as the generator, and a discriminator discerns predicted segmentation maps and the real ground truth labels [31,33,37,56,58,101]. The second category includes consistency regularization techniques that apply perturbations to unlabeled data and train models to remain invariant to these changes, typically achieved through the introduction of an additional regularization term in the loss function [7,9,18,51,64,71,80,92,95,104]. In the third category, pseudo-labeling methods generate pseudo-labels of unlabeled images by utilizing a model pre-trained on labeled data. These approaches either follow a self-training protocol based on high-confidence predictions of a single model [10,23,79,81,85,97,100,109], or involve multiple models through mutual-training [17,45,46,61,108]. The fourth category applies contrastive learning to structure the feature space by clustering similar samples and separating dissimilar ones. Leveraging the success of self-supervised contrastive learning techniques, such as SimCLR [5,6], several semi-supervised segmentation methods have been developed to enhance feature representations [2,8,50]. Finally, the last category describes hybrid methods that combine elements from the previous four categories, particularly pseudo-labeling and consistency regularization [30,48,54,55,72,83,86,87,89,95].

2.2   Reliability and Robustness

Reliability. As mentioned above, reliability encompasses both model calibration, i.e., how well predicted probabilities reflect the true likelihood of correctness, and uncertainty quality, which describes a model's ability to align its confidences with predictive ambiguities and errors. We will go over the importance of distinguishing between both of these in Sect. 3. Even though deep neural networks can have impressive predictive performance, they are known to be overconfident [21,84,90]. In this context, Guo et al. [21] proposed temperature scaling as a simple post-hoc calibration technique, which has remained a widely used baseline due to its simplicity and non-invasiveness compared to alternative approaches [15,32,38,62,68]. While most calibration methods offer an effective way of enhancing reliability in in-domain settings, Ovadia et al. [66] observed that calibration deteriorates significantly under domain shifts. This lack of robustness poses a significant risk in safety-critical contexts like autonomous driving [59], where models must maintain their reliability despite unexpected scenarios.

Robustness. A model's robustness is defined by the ability to remain effective under perturbations, noise, or distribution shifts. Importantly, robustness encompasses not only accuracy but also reliable confidence and uncertainty estimates, as outlined previously. Prior work distinguishes between robustness to perturbations (Gaussian noise, blur, occlusions), adversarial attacks (imperceptible perturbations crafted to induce failure) [20,24,35,36], and natural domain shifts (variations in weather, lighting, or geographic contexts) [25,29,69,73–75,82].

Research Gap. While there are plenty of previous analyses on reliability and robustness in semantic segmentation [3,13,35,36,52,93,106,107] – highlighting the importance of this topic – none of these considered semi-supervised learning. Instead of proposing yet another semi-supervised segmentation method with marginal gains in segmentation accuracy, we investigate the reliability and robustness of the current state of the art to answer the following, crucial question:

"Should we rethink semi-supervised segmentation evaluation protocols to prioritize reliability and robustness alongside accuracy?"

3   Reliable Segmentation Score

Current semi-supervised semantic segmentation methods evaluate their models almost exclusively with the mean Intersection over Union (mIoU) [43]

$$\mathrm{mIoU} = \frac{1}{C} \sum_{c=1}^{C} \frac{TP_c}{FP_c + FN_c + TP_c} \ , \tag{1}$$

where C is the number of classes, TP is the number of true positives, FP is the number of false positives, and FN is the number of false negatives. As depicted, the intersection over union is computed on a per-class basis and then averaged, providing a straightforward metric to quantify the segmentation quality of a model.

The Expected Calibration Error (ECE) [21] is foundational to evaluate the calibration of semantic segmentation models, measuring the average mismatch between a model's confidence and its empirical accuracy across M probability bins:

$$\mathrm{ECE} = \sum_{m=1}^{M} \frac{|B_m|}{N} \left| \mathrm{acc}(B_m) - \mathrm{conf}(B_m) \right| \ , \tag{2}$$

where $|B_m|$ is the number of pixels in the m-th bin, N is the total number of pixels, $\mathrm{acc}(B_m)$ is the accuracy of predictions in the m-th bin, and $\mathrm{conf}(B_m)$ is the average confidence of predictions in the corresponding bin. ECE is vital in safety-critical applications like autonomous driving, where a lack of reliability, e.g., through overconfidence [84,90], can have disastrous consequences.

Recent research has also emphasized the importance of quantifying the uncertainty inherent to a model's prediction to enhance the reliability, robustness, and explainability [1,39,41,42]. To evaluate uncertainty quality, Mukhoti et al. [60] propose the following two simple and intuitive metrics:

1. **p(accurate|certain):** The probability that the model is accurate given that the uncertainty is below a specified threshold.
2. **p(uncertain|inaccurate):** The probability that the uncertainty of the model exceeds a specified threshold given that the prediction is inaccurate.

These conditional probabilities can be calculated as

$$p(\text{acc}|\text{cer}) = \frac{n_{ac}}{(n_{ac} + n_{ic})} \; ,$$
$$p(\text{unc}|\text{inacc}) = \frac{n_{iu}}{(n_{iu} + n_{ic})} \; , \tag{3}$$

where n_{ac} represents the number of pixels that are accurate and certain, n_{ic} the number of pixels that are inaccurate and certain, and n_{iu} the number of pixels that are inaccurate and uncertain. Undoubtedly, the choice of the threshold is significant, with prior work suggesting the median uncertainty of an image as a suitable default [40].

To provide an easy, intuitive, and holistic assessment of semantic segmentation models, the Reliable Segmentation Score (RSS) combines the previous metrics using the harmonic mean:

$$\text{RSS} = \frac{\sum \omega_i}{\frac{\omega_1}{\text{mIoU}} + \frac{\omega_2}{(1-\text{ECE})} + \frac{\omega_3}{p(\text{acc}|\text{cer})} + \frac{\omega_3}{p(\text{unc}|\text{inacc})}} \; , \tag{4}$$

where ω_i are application-specific weights, e.g. $\omega_1 = 1.0, \omega_2 = \omega_3 = \omega_4 = \frac{1}{3}$. To avoid any assumptions about application priorities, we propose to use equal weighting to appropriately reflect the importance of reliability metrics in safety-critical applications, where calibration and uncertainty quality may outweigh raw accuracy.

RSS integrates accuracy (mIoU), calibration (ECE), and uncertainty quality (p(acc|cer) and p(unc|inacc)) into a single metric, leveraging the harmonic mean to penalize poor performance in any component. This approach ensures that a model cannot achieve a high RSS unless it excels in all aspects – accurate predictions, well-calibrated confidences, and reliable uncertainty estimates – providing a strict yet comprehensive measure to evaluate reliability and robustness.

A key question is whether mIoU, ECE, p(acc|cer), and p(unc|inacc) evaluate distinct aspects of model performance, justifying their combination in RSS. We argue that these metrics are largely orthogonal, each capturing complementary properties:

– **mIoU:** Measures pixel-wise accuracy, reflecting the model's ability to correctly classify pixels across all classes. It does not consider any reliability-related aspects.

- **ECE:** Assesses calibration, ensuring confidence aligns with accuracy. A model can achieve high mIoU but poor ECE if it is overconfident or underconfident, highlighting their independence.
- **p(acc|cer):** Evaluates whether low-uncertainty predictions are correct, focusing on the utility of certainty in decision-making.
- **p(unc|inacc):** Assesses whether incorrect predictions are flagged with high uncertainty, enabling error detection or mitigation.

Moreover, mIoU and ECE are fundamentally tied to the confidence of a prediction, i.e., the maximum softmax probability. Both mIoU – through its reliance on hard class decisions – and ECE – which only bins max-softmax values – therefore evaluate only the single highest probability output. This constrained view, which misses whether a model's output is narrowly peaked or spread across multiple classes, is clearly insufficient and was already shown to lead to inconsistencies between different calibration measures [91]. In contrast, the conditional uncertainty probabilities p(acc|cer) and p(unc|inacc) rely on an uncertainty estimate derived from the entire softmax distribution, like the Shannon entropy [76]. This distribution-wide view captures the valuable information about ambiguity between top predictions, which is neglected by mIoU and ECE. Consequently, a model can be well-calibrated (low ECE) yet still fail to flag its inaccuracies as uncertain (low p(unc|inacc)), or conversely be accurate when certain (high p(acc|cer)) but suffer from being overly certain on its errors (low p(unc|inacc)). Hence, by pairing max-softmax-based metrics (mIoU, ECE) – which ensure high accuracy and guard against overconfidence or underconfidence in the predicted class – with conditional uncertainty metrics that require low entropy for correct predictions (p(acc|cer)) and high entropy for errors (p(unc|inacc)), RSS ensures a model is both confident when it should be and uncertain whenever it is inaccurate, yielding a balanced, holistic reliability score.

4   Experimental Setup

4.1   Methodological Background

UniMatchV1 [95] and UniMatchV2 [96] are recent and representative approaches in semi-supervised semantic segmentation that build on consistency regularization, leveraging unlabeled data by enforcing prediction consistency under image- and feature-level perturbations.

UniMatchV1, introduced in 2023, extends FixMatch [77] by generating a weakly perturbed image to produce pseudo-labels, which supervise predictions on a strongly perturbed version of the same image. In addition, UniMatchV1 incorporates an auxiliary feature perturbation stream, using dropout [26], and a dual-stream technique, where two strong views learn from one weak view.

UniMatchV2, presented in 2025, advances its predecessor by adopting Vision Transformer-based architectures (e.g., DINOv2 [65]), pre-trained on large datasets, instead of less potent ResNet encoders [22]. While it maintains the weak-to-strong consistency framework, it unifies the image-level and feature-level augmentations of UniMatchV1 into a single stream and introduces Complementary Dropout, which applies different dropout masks across the two strongly augmented views to encourage feature diversity. This new design reduces training cost and achieves state-of-the-art results on several benchmarks.

Together, UniMatchV1 and UniMatchV2 provide a comprehensive evaluation framework. V1 represents a robust and widely adopted approach, while V2 pushes the boundaries of semi-supervised learning with cutting-edge architectures. Their shared weak-to-strong consistency framework allows for direct comparisons of how architectural advancements, i.e., Convolutional Neural Networks vs. Vision Transformers, impact reliability and robustness. Overall, they form a complementary baseline for answering the critical research question if current semi-supervised segmentation methods are not only accurate but also robust and reliable.

4.2   Datasets

We use Cityscapes [11] and Pascal VOC2012 [16] for in-domain semi-supervised segmentation experiments. For out-of-domain evaluations, we use the validation sets of Foggy Cityscapes [74] and Rainy Cityscapes [29], which introduce increasingly challenging perturbations to the original urban scenes to simulate adverse weather conditions. Foggy Cityscapes offers three different versions, which are defined by the attenuation coefficient β. Higher β values result in thicker fog. Similarly, Rainy Cityscapes offers several options with varying amounts of rain and fog. We evaluate on three sets of parameters, where Rainy_1 uses [0.01, 0.005, 0.01], Rainy_2 uses [0.02, 0.01, 0.005], and Rainy_3 uses [0.03, 0.015, 0.002] as attenuation coefficients α and β and the raindrop radius a. α and β determine the degree of simulated rain and fog in the images.

4.3   Implementation Details

All training procedures adhere to the original configurations proposed in the respective UniMatch versions [95,96], including model architectures, hyperparameters, and dataset splits. The supervised baseline is implemented using the same configuration as UniMatchV2.

For evaluation, we follow the UniMatchV2 protocol for computing the mean Intersection-over-Union (mIoU) [96]. Calibration is assessed using the Expected Calibration Error (ECE), implemented via the torchmetrics package [14] with the default 15-bin discretization.

To quantify the uncertainty, we compute the Shannon entropy [76]

$$H(x) = -\sum_{c=1}^{C} p(\hat{y}_c(x)) \log p(\hat{y}_c(x)) \ , \tag{5}$$

where $p(\hat{y}_c(x))$ denotes the predicted probability for class c for a given input image x. These pixel-wise uncertainty estimates are used to compute the uncertainty metrics, p(acc|cer) and p(unc|inacc), based on the thresholding strategy suggested by Landgraf et al. [40], categorizing pixels as certain or uncertain based on the median uncertainty within each image.

5   Experiments

In the following, we conduct a comprehensive set of experiments for in-domain reliability and out-of-domain robustness. Moreover, we provide qualitative examples for both scenarios to highlight the importance of not only considering segmentation accuracy but also reliability. Due to space constraints, some evaluation results are included in the supplementary material.

5.1   In-Domain Evaluation

Quantitative Analysis. Table 1 summarizes in-domain results on Cityscapes and Pascal VOC2012 across different label regimes. As expected, UniMatchV2 consistently outperforms both the supervised baseline and UniMatchV1 in mIoU, especially with fewer available labels, and segmentation quality generally improves with the larger encoder and more labeled images. However, the supervised baseline excels in terms of reliability, outperforming both semi-supervised approaches concerning ECE, p(acc|cer), and p(unc|inacc) in most cases, particularly on Cityscapes. This is highlighted by our proposed RSS metric, where the supervised ViT-B baseline achieves the highest results across all splits on Cityscapes. Interestingly, even UniMatchV1 attains a higher RSS in 4 out of the 5 splits compared to UniMatchV2, primarily due to the inability of UniMatchV2 to assign high uncertainties to incorrect predictions, as measured by p(unc|inacc). Nonetheless, UniMatchV2 still offers the highest RSS across all label regimes on Pascal VOC2012 due to its remarkable improvements over the supervised baseline and UniMatchV1 concerning segmentation quality as well as staying competitive in terms of the three reliability metrics.

Table 1. In-domain results of a supervised baseline, UniMatchV1 [95], and UniMatchV2 [96] on Cityscapes [11] and Pascal VOC2012 [16] across different training splits. The quantitative comparison includes two DINOv2 encoders [65] – ViT-S and ViT-B – as well as the conventional ResNet-101 (RN-101) backbone [22]. Best results are marked in **bold**.

	Encoder	Cityscapes (Label Fraction)					Pascal VOC2012 (Labeled Images)				
		1/30	1/16	1/8	1/4	1/2	92	183	366	732	1464
mIoU ↑											
Supervised	ViT-S	0.736	0.782	0.803	0.819	0.824	0.661	0.757	0.812	0.832	0.859
UniMatchV2	ViT-S	0.793	0.809	0.814	0.823	0.825	0.758	0.849	0.860	0.871	0.876
Supervised	ViT-B	0.788	0.811	0.829	0.840	0.846	0.765	0.824	0.854	0.876	0.886
UniMatchV1	RN-101	0.727	0.762	0.782	0.793	0.797	0.746	0.777	0.788	0.800	0.803
UniMatchV2	ViT-B	**0.807**	**0.839**	**0.840**	**0.847**	**0.848**	**0.862**	**0.873**	**0.892**	**0.900**	**0.903**
ECE ↓											
Supervised	ViT-S	**0.016**	**0.023**	**0.016**	**0.013**	0.036	0.054	0.035	0.026	0.024	0.019
UniMatchV2	ViT-S	0.029	0.027	0.022	0.018	**0.011**	0.053	0.028	0.025	0.021	0.019
Supervised	ViT-B	0.020	0.025	0.018	0.015	**0.011**	0.038	0.026	**0.019**	**0.018**	0.017
UniMatchV1	RN-101	0.049	0.042	0.041	0.037	0.029	0.051	0.040	0.036	0.032	0.029
UniMatchV2	ViT-B	0.019	0.025	0.022	0.015	**0.011**	**0.030**	**0.022**	0.020	**0.018**	**0.016**
p(acc|cer) ↑											
Supervised	ViT-S	0.880	0.900	0.876	0.880	**0.907**	0.969	0.979	0.985	0.986	0.988
UniMatchV2	ViT-S	0.872	0.871	0.862	0.865	0.854	0.960	0.982	0.985	0.988	**0.989**
Supervised	ViT-B	**0.926**	**0.942**	**0.942**	**0.908**	0.905	0.979	**0.984**	**0.989**	**0.989**	**0.989**
UniMatchV1	RN-101	0.882	0.883	0.923	0.900	0.889	0.958	0.964	0.970	0.974	0.977
UniMatchV2	ViT-B	0.890	0.870	0.873	0.857	0.852	**0.980**	0.981	0.987	0.988	**0.989**
p(unc|inacc) ↑											
Supervised	ViT-S	0.663	0.720	0.641	0.648	**0.713**	0.953	0.964	0.972	0.976	0.979
UniMatchV2	ViT-S	0.606	0.606	0.565	0.576	0.530	0.914	0.960	0.968	0.977	0.978
Supervised	ViT-B	**0.794**	**0.842**	**0.835**	**0.709**	0.698	**0.959**	**0.973**	**0.979**	**0.981**	**0.983**
UniMatchV1	RN-101	0.667	0.666	0.778	0.703	0.675	0.899	0.904	0.913	0.928	0.941
UniMatchV2	ViT-B	0.673	0.586	0.586	0.533	0.515	0.954	0.945	0.961	0.972	0.977
RSS ↑											
Supervised	ViT-S	0.797	0.833	0.806	0.814	0.841	0.860	0.906	0.930	0.938	0.949
UniMatchV2	ViT-S	0.786	0.790	0.772	0.780	0.758	0.887	0.938	0.944	0.951	0.953
Supervised	ViT-B	**0.864**	**0.888**	**0.892**	**0.848**	**0.845**	0.907	0.934	0.947	0.954	0.958
UniMatchV1	RN-101	0.791	0.802	0.853	0.828	0.818	0.879	0.894	0.902	0.912	0.917
UniMatchV2	ViT-B	0.822	0.789	0.790	0.763	0.754	**0.939**	**0.942**	**0.953**	**0.959**	**0.962**

Qualitative Analysis. Figure 1 presents a qualitative comparison between the supervised baseline and the UniMatchV2 model on the Cityscapes and Pascal VOC2012 datasets. Models were trained on Cityscapes using only 1/8th of the labeled data, and on Pascal VOC2012 with just 92 labeled images. On Cityscapes, both models yield similar segmentation predictions overall. However, in a central image region lacking ground truth labels – indicated by black pixels – the supervised model produces noisy predictions but simultaneously yields high uncertainty, reflecting appropriate caution. In contrast, the UniMatchV2 model predicts multiple humans in this region with low uncertainty, raising concerns about overconfidence despite accurate-looking predictions.

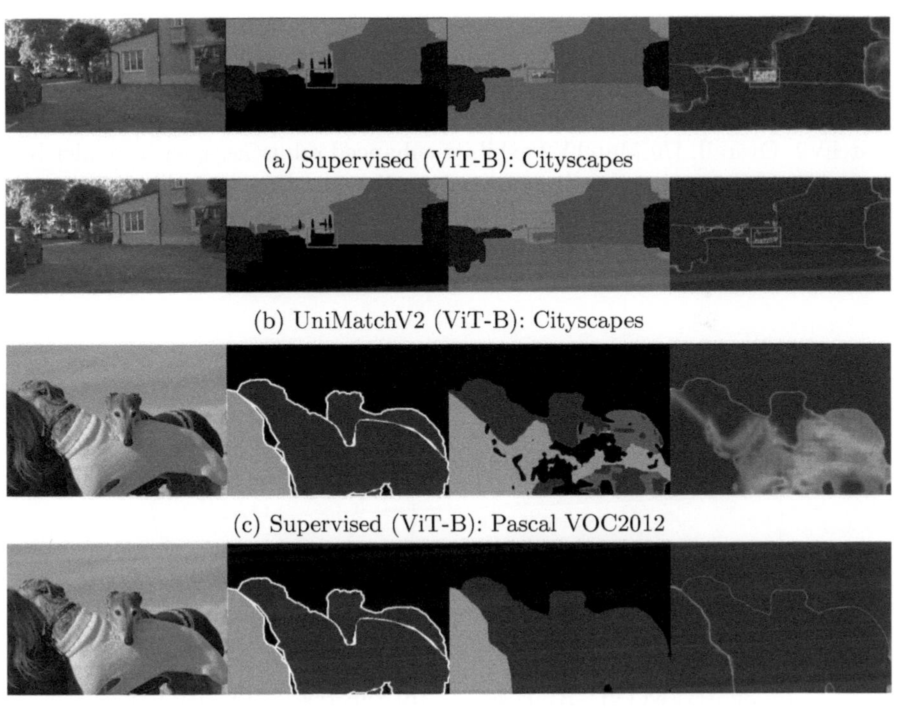

(a) Supervised (ViT-B): Cityscapes

(b) UniMatchV2 (ViT-B): Cityscapes

(c) Supervised (ViT-B): Pascal VOC2012

(d) UniMatchV2 (ViT-B): Pascal VOC2012

Fig. 1. Qualitative comparison between the supervised and UniMatchV2 models on Cityscapes (top) and Pascal VOC2012 (bottom). Each row shows from left to right: Input image, ground truth, prediction, and the corresponding uncertainty, computed using Shannon entropy (see Eq. 5).

For Pascal VOC2012, the supervised model fails to distinguish two dogs in the scene, while the UniMatchV2 model correctly segments both dogs with high confidence. Despite its errors, the supervised model flags the misclassified areas with high uncertainty, offering a valuable trade-off. Overall, this example highlights that while predictive accuracy is important, model reliability remains crucial for safe and trustworthy deployment, especially if we consider the impossibility of perfect segmentation performance – especially in the case of out-of-domain scenarios, which we will examine next.

5.2   Out-of-Domain Evaluation

Quantitative Analysis. Figure 2 compares the robustness of the supervised baseline and UniMatchV2 on Foggy and Rainy Cityscapes datasets, using radar charts. Both models, trained on 1/8th of Cityscapes' labeled data, were evaluated in out-of-domain robustness without fine-tuning. As expected, segmentation performance degrades with increasing perturbation severity, but UniMatchV2 maintains higher mIoU values. Calibration similarly deteriorates under fog, albeit less than segmentation performance, especially for UniMatchV2, and remains comparatively stable under rainy conditions. Interestingly, uncertainty quality shows minimal change under fog and even improves under rain, particularly for UniMatchV2. Overall, UniMatchV2 exhibits enhanced robustness, with smaller RSS degradation due to improved uncertainty estimates despite declining accuracy. However, UniMatchV2 is ultimately still significantly less reliable due to its poor performance in terms of p(unc|inacc), barely exceeding 0.6 whereas the supervised baseline achieves values of approx. 0.85.

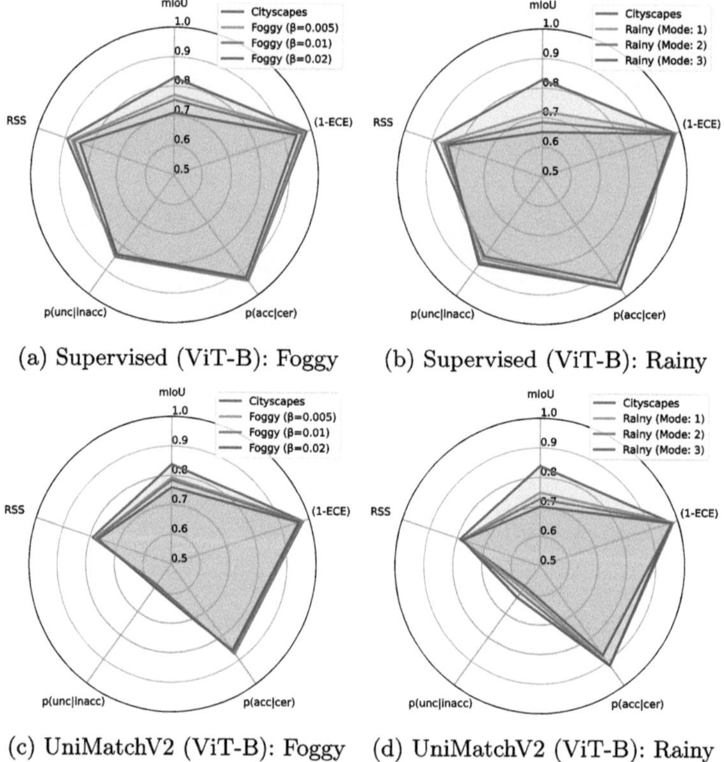

(a) Supervised (ViT-B): Foggy   (b) Supervised (ViT-B): Rainy

(c) UniMatchV2 (ViT-B): Foggy   (d) UniMatchV2 (ViT-B): Rainy

Fig. 2. Quantitative comparison of the predictive performance (mIoU), calibration (ECE), and uncertainty (p(acc|cer), p(unc|inacc)) of the supervised baseline and UniMatchV2 under increasing levels of fog and rain on the Foggy and Rainy Cityscapes datasets.

Qualitative Analysis. Figure 1d compares the supervised baseline and Uni-MatchV2 on the most perturbed versions of Foggy and Rainy Cityscapes. Both models were trained on 1/8 of the labeled data from the original Cityscapes dataset and not fine-tuned for this out-of-domain evaluation. In Foggy Cityscapes, both models misclassify the left region of the image as a building. However, while UniMatchV2 assigns low uncertainty to this incorrect prediction, the supervised model expresses high uncertainty, indicating an awareness of its error. In the Rainy Cityscapes example, UniMatchV2 yields slightly improved segmentation results, particularly in correctly identifying a bus in the background where the supervised model fails. Nonetheless, the supervised baseline assigns high uncertainty to the misclassified bus, in contrast to UniMatchV2's lower uncertainty. These examples highlight a trade-off between reliability and robustness, with UniMatchV2 achieving stronger performance but occasionally failing to reflect uncertainty when errors occur.

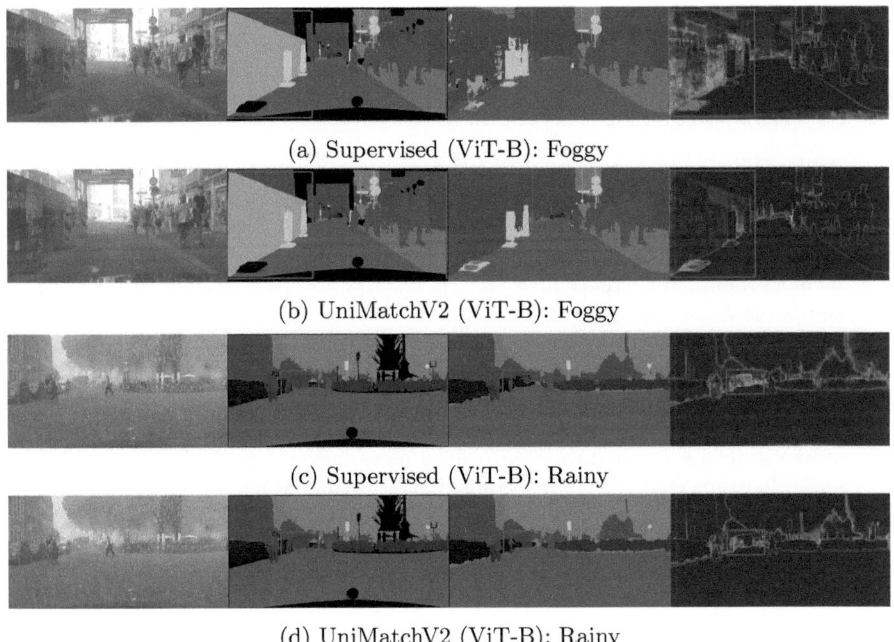

(a) Supervised (ViT-B): Foggy

(b) UniMatchV2 (ViT-B): Foggy

(c) Supervised (ViT-B): Rainy

(d) UniMatchV2 (ViT-B): Rainy

Fig. 3. Qualitative comparison between the supervised and UniMatchV2 models on the strongest perturbed versions of Foggy (top) and Rainy Cityscapes (bottom). Each row shows from left to right: Input image, ground truth, prediction, and the corresponding uncertainty, computed using Shannon entropy (see Eq. 5).

6   Conclusion

In this work, we addressed a critical blind spot in semi-supervised semantic segmentation: The lack of attention to model reliability and robustness. To fill this gap, we introduced the Reliable Segmentation Score (RSS), which holistically integrates accuracy, calibration, and uncertainty quality into a single metric through the harmonic mean, penalizing poor performance in any component. Through comprehensive evaluations on both in-domain and out-of-domain scenarios, we revealed that the current state-of-the-art UniMatchV2 achieves superior predictive performance and robustness but is often less calibrated and produces less reliable uncertainty estimates than its supervised counterpart. These findings raise legitimate questions about whether incremental gains in segmentation accuracy reflect meaningful progress toward reliable and robust deployment. We hope that our investigation and the proposed RSS metric serve as a stepping stone toward more principled evaluation protocols that better align research objectives with real-world requirements, focusing not only on performance but also on reliability and robustness.

References

1. Abdar, M., et al.: A review of uncertainty quantification in deep learning: techniques, applications and challenges. Inf. fusion **76**, 243–297 (2021)
2. Alonso, I., Sabater, A., Ferstl, D., Montesano, L., Murillo, A.C.: Semi-supervised semantic segmentation with pixel-level contrastive learning from a class-wise memory bank. In: Proceedings of the IEEE/CVF international conference on computer vision, pp. 8219–8228 (2021)
3. Arnab, A., Miksik, O., Torr, P.H.: On the robustness of semantic segmentation models to adversarial attacks. In: Proceedings of the IEEE conference on computer vision and pattern recognition, pp. 888–897 (2018)
4. Chen, L.C., Papandreou, G., Kokkinos, I., Murphy, K., Yuille, A.L.: Deeplab: semantic image segmentation with deep convolutional nets, atrous convolution, and fully connected crfs. IEEE Trans. Pattern Anal. Mach. Intell. **40**(4), 834–848 (2017)
5. Chen, T., Kornblith, S., Norouzi, M., Hinton, G.: A simple framework for contrastive learning of visual representations. In: International conference on machine learning, pp. 1597–1607. PMLR (2020)
6. Chen, T., Kornblith, S., Swersky, K., Norouzi, M., Hinton, G.E.: Big self-supervised models are strong semi-supervised learners. Adv. Neural. Inf. Process. Syst. **33**, 22243–22255 (2020)
7. Chen, X., Yuan, Y., Zeng, G., Wang, J.: Semi-supervised semantic segmentation with cross pseudo supervision. In: Proceedings of the IEEE/CVF conference on computer vision and pattern recognition, pp. 2613–2622 (2021)
8. Chen, X., He, K.: Exploring simple siamese representation learning. In: Proceedings of the IEEE/CVF conference on computer vision and pattern recognition, pp. 15750–15758 (2021)
9. Chen, Y., Ouyang, X., Zhu, K., Agam, G.: Complexmix: semi-supervised semantic segmentation via mask-based data augmentation. In: 2021 IEEE International Conference on Image Processing (ICIP), pp. 2264–2268. IEEE (2021)

10. Chen, Z., Zhang, R., Zhang, G., Ma, Z., Lei, T.: Digging into pseudo label: a low-budget approach for semi-supervised semantic segmentation. IEEE Access **8**, 41830–41837 (2020)
11. Cordts, M., et al.: The cityscapes dataset for semantic urban scene understanding. In: Proceedings of the IEEE conference on computer vision and pattern recognition, pp. 3213–3223 (2016)
12. Croce, F., Singh, N.D., Hein, M.: Towards reliable evaluation and fast training of robust semantic segmentation models. In: European Conference on Computer Vision, pp. 180–197. Springer (2024)
13. De Jorge, P., Volpi, R., Torr, P.H., Rogez, G.: Reliability in semantic segmentation: are we on the right track? In: Proceedings of the IEEE/CVF Conference on Computer Vision and Pattern Recognition, pp. 7173–7182 (2023)
14. Detlefsen, N.S., et al.: Torchmetrics-measuring reproducibility in pytorch. J. Open Source Softw. **7**(70), 4101 (2022)
15. Ding, Z., Han, X., Liu, P., Niethammer, M.: Local temperature scaling for probability calibration. In: Proceedings of the IEEE/CVF International Conference on Computer Vision, pp. 6889–6899 (2021)
16. Everingham, M., Eslami, S.A., Van Gool, L., Williams, C.K., Winn, J., Zisserman, A.: The pascal visual object classes challenge: A retrospective. Int. J. Comput. Vision **111**, 98–136 (2015)
17. Feng, Z., et al.: DMT: dynamic mutual training for semi-supervised learning. Pattern Recogn. **130**, 108777 (2022)
18. French, G., Laine, S., Aila, T., Mackiewicz, M., Finlayson, G.: Semi-supervised semantic segmentation needs strong, varied perturbations. arXiv preprint arXiv:1906.01916 (2019)
19. Goodfellow, I.J., et al.: Generative adversarial nets. Adv. neural inf. proc. syst. **27** (2014)
20. Goodfellow, I.J., Shlens, J., Szegedy, C.: Explaining and harnessing adversarial examples. arXiv preprint arXiv:1412.6572 (2014)
21. Guo, C., Pleiss, G., Sun, Y., Weinberger, K.Q.: On calibration of modern neural networks. In: International Conference on Machine Learning, pp. 1321–1330. PMLR (2017)
22. He, K., Zhang, X., Ren, S., Sun, J.: Deep residual learning for image recognition. In: Proceedings of the IEEE conference on computer vision and pattern recognition, pp. 770–778 (2016)
23. He, R., Yang, J., Qi, X.: Re-distributing biased pseudo labels for semi-supervised semantic segmentation: a baseline investigation. In: Proceedings of the IEEE/CVF International Conference on Computer Vision, pp. 6930–6940 (2021)
24. Hendrycks, D., Dietterich, T.: Benchmarking neural network robustness to common corruptions and perturbations. arXiv preprint arXiv:1903.12261 (2019)
25. Hendrycks, D., Zhao, K., Basart, S., Steinhardt, J., Song, D.: Natural adversarial examples. In: Proceedings of the IEEE/CVF conference on computer vision and pattern recognition, pp. 15262–15271 (2021)
26. Hinton, G.E., Srivastava, N., Krizhevsky, A., Sutskever, I., Salakhutdinov, R.R.: Improving neural networks by preventing co-adaptation of feature detectors. arXiv preprint arXiv:1207.0580 (2012)
27. Howlader, P., Das, S., Le, H., Samaras, D.: Beyond pixels: semi-supervised semantic segmentation with a multi-scale patch-based multi-label classifier. In: European Conference on Computer Vision, pp. 342–360. Springer (2024)

28. Hoyer, L., Tan, D.J., Naeem, M.F., Van Gool, L., Tombari, F.: Semivl: semi-supervised semantic segmentation with vision-language guidance. In: European Conference on Computer Vision, pp. 257–275. Springer (2024)

29. Hu, X., Fu, C.W., Zhu, L., Heng, P.A.: Depth-attentional features for single-image rain removal. In: Proceedings of the IEEE/CVF Conference on computer vision and pattern recognition, pp. 8022–8031 (2019)

30. Hu, X., Jiang, L., Schiele, B.: Training vision transformers for semi-supervised semantic segmentation. In: Proceedings of the IEEE/CVF Conference on Computer Vision and Pattern Recognition, pp. 4007–4017 (2024)

31. Hung, W.C., Tsai, Y.H., Liou, Y.T., Lin, Y.Y., Yang, M.H.: Adversarial learning for semi-supervised semantic segmentation. arXiv preprint arXiv:1802.07934 (2018)

32. Ji, B., et al.: Bin-wise temperature scaling (BTS): improvement in confidence calibration performance through simple scaling techniques. In: 2019 IEEE/CVF International Conference on Computer Vision Workshop (ICCVW), pp. 4190–4196. IEEE (2019)

33. Jin, G., Liu, C., Chen, X.: Adversarial network integrating dual attention and sparse representation for semi-supervised semantic segmentation. Inf. Proc. Manag. **58**(5), 102680 (2021)

34. Jin, Y., Wang, J., Lin, D.: Semi-supervised semantic segmentation via gentle teaching assistant. Adv. Neural. Inf. Process. Syst. **35**, 2803–2816 (2022)

35. Kamann, C., Rother, C.: Benchmarking the robustness of semantic segmentation models. In: Proceedings of the IEEE/CVF conference on computer vision and pattern recognition, pp. 8828–8838 (2020)

36. Kamann, C., Rother, C.: Benchmarking the robustness of semantic segmentation models with respect to common corruptions. Int. J. Comput. Vision **129**(2), 462–483 (2021)

37. Ke, Z., Qiu, D., Li, K., Yan, Q., Lau, R.W.H.: Guided Collaborative Training for Pixel-Wise Semi-Supervised Learning. In: Vedaldi, A., Bischof, H., Brox, T., Frahm, J.-M. (eds.) ECCV 2020. LNCS, vol. 12358, pp. 429–445. Springer, Cham (2020). https://doi.org/10.1007/978-3-030-58601-0_26

38. Kull, M., Perello Nieto, M., Kängsepp, M., Silva Filho, T., Song, H., Flach, P.: Beyond temperature scaling: Obtaining well-calibrated multi-class probabilities with dirichlet calibration. Adv. Neural Inf. Proc. Syst. **32** (2019)

39. Landgraf, S., Hillemann, M., Kapler, T., Ulrich, M.: Efficient multi-task uncertainties for joint semantic segmentation and monocular depth estimation. In: DAGM German Conference on Pattern Recognition, pp. 348–364. Springer (2024)

40. Landgraf, S., Hillemann, M., Kapler, T., Ulrich, M.: A comparative study on multi-task uncertainty quantification in semantic segmentation and monocular depth estimation. tm-Technisches Messen (2025)

41. Landgraf, S., Qin, R., Ulrich, M.: A critical synthesis of uncertainty quantification and foundation models in monocular depth estimation. arXiv preprint arXiv:2501.08188 (2025)

42. Landgraf, S., Wursthorn, K., Hillemann, M., Ulrich, M.: Dudes: Deep uncertainty distillation using ensembles for semantic segmentation. PFG-J. Photogrammetry, Remote Sens. Geoinformation Sci. **92**(2), 101–114 (2024)

43. Lateef, F., Ruichek, Y.: Survey on semantic segmentation using deep learning techniques. Neurocomputing **338**, 321–348 (2019)

44. Li, D., Yang, J., Kreis, K., Torralba, A., Fidler, S.: Semantic segmentation with generative models: semi-supervised learning and strong out-of-domain general-

ization. In: Proceedings of the IEEE/CVF Conference on Computer Vision and Pattern Recognition, pp. 8300–8311 (2021)

45. Li, P., et al.: Semi-supervised semantic segmentation under label noise via diverse learning groups. In: Proceedings of the IEEE/CVF International Conference on Computer Vision, pp. 1229–1238 (2023)

46. Li, S., et al.: CFCG: semi-supervised semantic segmentation via cross-fusion and contour guidance supervision. In: Proceedings of the IEEE/CVF International Conference on Computer Vision, pp. 16348–16358 (2023)

47. Li, Y., Wang, X., Yang, L., Feng, L., Zhang, W., Gao, Y.: Diverse cotraining makes strong semi-supervised segmentor. arXiv preprint arXiv:2308.09281 (2023)

48. Liang, C., Wang, W., Miao, J., Yang, Y.: Logic-induced diagnostic reasoning for semi-supervised semantic segmentation. In: Proceedings of the IEEE/CVF International Conference on Computer Vision, pp. 16197–16208 (2023)

49. Lin, T.-Y., et al.: Microsoft COCO: Common Objects in Context. In: Fleet, D., Pajdla, T., Schiele, B., Tuytelaars, T. (eds.) ECCV 2014. LNCS, vol. 8693, pp. 740–755. Springer, Cham (2014). https://doi.org/10.1007/978-3-319-10602-1_48

50. Liu, S., Zhi, S., Johns, E., Davison, A.J.: Bootstrapping semantic segmentation with regional contrast. arXiv preprint arXiv:2104.04465 (2021)

51. Liu, Y., Tian, Y., Chen, Y., Liu, F., Belagiannis, V., Carneiro, G.: Perturbed and strict mean teachers for semi-supervised semantic segmentation. In: Proceedings of the IEEE/CVF conference on computer vision and pattern recognition, pp. 4258–4267 (2022)

52. Loiseau, T., Vu, T.H., Chen, M., Pérez, P., Cord, M.: Reliability in semantic segmentation: can we use synthetic data? In: European Conference on Computer Vision, pp. 442–459. Springer (2024)

53. Long, J., Shelhamer, E., Darrell, T.: Fully convolutional networks for semantic segmentation. In: Proceedings of the IEEE conference on computer vision and pattern recognition, pp. 3431–3440 (2015)

54. Ma, J., Wang, C., Liu, Y., Lin, L., Li, G.: Enhanced soft label for semi-supervised semantic segmentation. In: Proceedings of the IEEE/CVF International Conference on Computer Vision, pp. 1185–1195 (2023)

55. Mai, H., Sun, R., Zhang, T., Wu, F.: Rankmatch: exploring the better consistency regularization for semi-supervised semantic segmentation. In: Proceedings of the IEEE/CVF Conference on Computer Vision and Pattern Recognition, pp. 3391–3401 (2024)

56. Mendel, R., de Souza, L.A., Rauber, D., Papa, J.P., Palm, C.: Semi-supervised Segmentation Based on Error-Correcting Supervision. In: Vedaldi, A., Bischof, H., Brox, T., Frahm, J.-M. (eds.) ECCV 2020. LNCS, vol. 12374, pp. 141–157. Springer, Cham (2020). https://doi.org/10.1007/978-3-030-58526-6_9

57. Minaee, S., Boykov, Y., Porikli, F., Plaza, A., Kehtarnavaz, N., Terzopoulos, D.: Image segmentation using deep learning: a survey. IEEE Trans. Pattern Anal. Mach. Intell. **44**(7), 3523–3542 (2021)

58. Mittal, S., Tatarchenko, M., Brox, T.: Semi-supervised semantic segmentation with high-and low-level consistency. IEEE Trans. Pattern Anal. Mach. Intell. **43**(4), 1369–1379 (2019)

59. Muhammad, K., Ullah, A., Lloret, J., Del Ser, J., De Albuquerque, V.H.C.: Deep learning for safe autonomous driving: current challenges and future directions. IEEE Trans. Intell. Transp. Syst. **22**(7), 4316–4336 (2020)

60. Mukhoti, J., Gal, Y.: Evaluating bayesian deep learning methods for semantic segmentation. arXiv preprint arXiv:1811.12709 (2018)

61. Na, J., Ha, J.W., Chang, H.J., Han, D., Hwang, W.: Switching temporary teachers for semi-supervised semantic segmentation. Adv. Neural Inf. Proc. Syst. **36** (2024)
62. Naeini, M.P., Cooper, G., Hauskrecht, M.: Obtaining well calibrated probabilities using bayesian binning. In: Proceedings of the AAAI conference on artificial intelligence. vol. 29 (2015)
63. Oliveira, G.L., Bollen, C., Burgard, W., Brox, T.: Efficient and robust deep networks for semantic segmentation. Int. J. Robot. Res. **37**(4–5), 472–491 (2018)
64. Olsson, V., Tranheden, W., Pinto, J., Svensson, L.: Classmix: segmentation-based data augmentation for semi-supervised learning. In: Proceedings of the IEEE/CVF winter conference on applications of computer vision, pp. 1369–1378 (2021)
65. Oquab, M., et al.: Dinov2: learning robust visual features without supervision. Transactions on Machine Learning Research Journal, pp. 1–31 (2024)
66. Ovadia, Y., et al.: Can you trust your model's uncertainty? evaluating predictive uncertainty under dataset shift. Adv. Neural Inf. Proc. Syst. **32** (2019)
67. Papandreou, G., Chen, L.C., Murphy, K.P., Yuille, A.L.: Weakly-and semi-supervised learning of a deep convolutional network for semantic image segmentation. In: Proceedings of the IEEE international conference on computer vision, pp. 1742–1750 (2015)
68. Patra, R., Hebbalaguppe, R., Dash, T., Shroff, G., Vig, L.: Calibrating deep neural networks using explicit regularisation and dynamic data pruning. In: Proceedings of the IEEE/CVF Winter Conference on Applications of Computer Vision, pp. 1541–1549 (2023)
69. Pedraza, A., Deniz, O., Bueno, G.: Really natural adversarial examples. Int. J. Mach. Learn. Cybern. **13**(4), 1065–1077 (2022)
70. Peláez-Vegas, A., Mesejo, P., Luengo, J.: A survey on semi-supervised semantic segmentation. arXiv preprint arXiv:2302.09899 (2023)
71. Peng, J., Estrada, G., Pedersoli, M., Desrosiers, C.: Deep co-training for semi-supervised image segmentation. Pattern Recogn. **107**, 107269 (2020)
72. Qiao, P., et al.: Fuzzy positive learning for semi-supervised semantic segmentation. In: Proceedings of the IEEE/CVF Conference on Computer Vision and Pattern Recognition, pp. 15465–15474 (2023)
73. Recht, B., Roelofs, R., Schmidt, L., Shankar, V.: Do imagenet classifiers generalize to imagenet? In: International conference on machine learning, pp. 5389–5400. PMLR (2019)
74. Sakaridis, C., Dai, D., Van Gool, L.: Semantic foggy scene understanding with synthetic data. Int. J. Comput. Vision **126**, 973–992 (2018)
75. Sakaridis, C., Dai, D., Van Gool, L.: ACDC: the adverse conditions dataset with correspondences for semantic driving scene understanding. In: Proceedings of the IEEE/CVF international conference on computer vision, pp. 10765–10775 (2021)
76. Shannon, C.E.: A mathematical theory of communication. The Bell Syst. Tech. J. **27**(3), 379–423 (1948)
77. Sohn, K., et al.: Fixmatch: simplifying semi-supervised learning with consistency and confidence. Adv. Neural. Inf. Process. Syst. **33**, 596–608 (2020)
78. Souly, N., Spampinato, C., Shah, M.: Semi supervised semantic segmentation using generative adversarial network. In: Proceedings of the IEEE international conference on computer vision, pp. 5688–5696 (2017)
79. Sun, B., Yang, Y., Zhang, L., Cheng, M.M., Hou, Q.: Corrmatch: label propagation via correlation matching for semi-supervised semantic segmentation. In: Proceedings of the IEEE/CVF Conference on Computer Vision and Pattern Recognition, pp. 3097–3107 (2024)

80. Tarvainen, A., Valpola, H.: Mean teachers are better role models: weight-averaged consistency targets improve semi-supervised deep learning results. Adv. Neural Inf. Proc. Syst. **30** (2017)
81. Teh, E.W., DeVries, T., Duke, B., Jiang, R., Aarabi, P., Taylor, G.W.: The gist and rist of iterative self-training for semi-supervised segmentation. In: 2022 19th Conference on Robots and Vision (CRV), pp. 58–66. IEEE (2022)
82. Varma, G., Subramanian, A., Namboodiri, A., Chandraker, M., Jawahar, C.: IDD: a dataset for exploring problems of autonomous navigation in unconstrained environments. In: 2019 IEEE winter conference on applications of computer vision (WACV), pp. 1743–1751. IEEE (2019)
83. Wang, C., Xie, H., Yuan, Y., Fu, C., Yue, X.: Space engage: collaborative space supervision for contrastive-based semi-supervised semantic segmentation. In: Proceedings of the IEEE/CVF International Conference on Computer Vision, pp. 931–942 (2023)
84. Wang, D.B., Feng, L., Zhang, M.L.: Rethinking calibration of deep neural networks: do not be afraid of overconfidence. Adv. Neural. Inf. Process. Syst. **34**, 11809–11820 (2021)
85. Wang, H., Zhang, Q., Li, Y., Li, X.: Allspark: Reborn labeled features from unlabeled in transformer for semi-supervised semantic segmentation. In: Proceedings of the IEEE/CVF Conference on Computer Vision and Pattern Recognition, pp. 3627–3636 (2024)
86. Wang, X., Bai, H., Yu, L., Zhao, Y., Xiao, J.: Towards the uncharted: density-descending feature perturbation for semi-supervised semantic segmentation. In: Proceedings of the IEEE/CVF Conference on Computer Vision and Pattern Recognition, pp. 3303–3312 (2024)
87. Wang, X., Zhang, B., Yu, L., Xiao, J.: Hunting sparsity: density-guided contrastive learning for semi-supervised semantic segmentation. In: Proceedings of the IEEE/CVF Conference on Computer Vision and Pattern Recognition, pp. 3114–3123 (2023)
88. Wang, Y., et al.: Semi-supervised semantic segmentation using unreliable pseudo-labels. In: Proceedings of the IEEE/CVF conference on computer vision and pattern recognition, pp. 4248–4257 (2022)
89. Wang, Z., Zhao, Z., Xing, X., Xu, D., Kong, X., Zhou, L.: Conflict-based cross-view consistency for semi-supervised semantic segmentation. In: Proceedings of the IEEE/CVF conference on computer vision and pattern recognition, pp. 19585–19595 (2023)
90. Wilson, A.G., Izmailov, P.: Bayesian deep learning and a probabilistic perspective of generalization. Adv. Neural. Inf. Process. Syst. **33**, 4697–4708 (2020)
91. Wolf, D.W., Balaji, P., Braun, A., Ulrich, M.: Decoupling of neural network calibration measures. In: DAGM German Conference on Pattern Recognition, pp. 117–130. Springer (2024)
92. Wu, Y., Liu, C., Chen, L., Zhao, D., Zheng, Q., Zhou, H.: Perturbation consistency and mutual information regularization for semi-supervised semantic segmentation. Multimedia Syst. **29**(2), 511–523 (2023)
93. Xie, E., Wang, W., Yu, Z., Anandkumar, A., Alvarez, J.M., Luo, P.: Segformer: simple and efficient design for semantic segmentation with transformers. Adv. Neural. Inf. Process. Syst. **34**, 12077–12090 (2021)
94. Xu, H., Liu, L., Bian, Q., Yang, Z.: Semi-supervised semantic segmentation with prototype-based consistency regularization. Adv. Neural. Inf. Process. Syst. **35**, 26007–26020 (2022)

95. Yang, L., Qi, L., Feng, L., Zhang, W., Shi, Y.: Revisiting weak-to-strong consistency in semi-supervised semantic segmentation. In: Proceedings of the IEEE/CVF conference on computer vision and pattern recognition, pp. 7236–7246 (2023)
96. Yang, L., Zhao, Z., Zhao, H.: Unimatch v2: pushing the limit of semi-supervised semantic segmentation. IEEE Transactions on Pattern Analysis and Machine Intelligence (2025)
97. Yang, L., Zhuo, W., Qi, L., Shi, Y., Gao, Y.: St++: make self-training work better for semi-supervised semantic segmentation. In: Proceedings of the IEEE/CVF conference on computer vision and pattern recognition, pp. 4268–4277 (2022)
98. Yang, X., Song, Z., King, I., Xu, Z.: A survey on deep semi-supervised learning. IEEE Trans. Knowl. Data Eng. **35**(9), 8934–8954 (2022)
99. Yu, X., et al.: The robust semantic segmentation uncv2023 challenge results. In: Proceedings of the IEEE/CVF International Conference on Computer Vision, pp. 4618–4628 (2023)
100. Yuan, J., Liu, Y., Shen, C., Wang, Z., Li, H.: A simple baseline for semi-supervised semantic segmentation with strong data augmentation. In: Proceedings of the IEEE/CVF International Conference on Computer Vision, pp. 8229–8238 (2021)
101. Zhang, J., Li, Z., Zhang, C., Ma, H.: Stable self-attention adversarial learning for semi-supervised semantic image segmentation. J. Vis. Commun. Image Represent. **78**, 103170 (2021)
102. Zhao, H., Shi, J., Qi, X., Wang, X., Jia, J.: Pyramid scene parsing network. In: Proceedings of the IEEE conference on computer vision and pattern recognition, pp. 2881–2890 (2017)
103. Zhao, Z., Long, S., Pi, J., Wang, J., Zhou, L.: Instance-specific and model-adaptive supervision for semi-supervised semantic segmentation. In: Proceedings of the IEEE/CVF conference on computer vision and pattern recognition, pp. 23705–23714 (2023)
104. Zhao, Z., Yang, L., Long, S., Pi, J., Zhou, L., Wang, J.: Augmentation matters: a simple-yet-effective approach to semi-supervised semantic segmentation. In: Proceedings of the IEEE/CVF conference on computer vision and pattern recognition, pp. 11350–11359 (2023)
105. Zhou, B., Zhao, H., Puig, X., Fidler, S., Barriuso, A., Torralba, A.: Scene parsing through ade20k dataset. In: Proceedings of the IEEE conference on computer vision and pattern recognition, pp. 633–641 (2017)
106. Zhou, D., et al.: Understanding the robustness in vision transformers. In: International conference on machine learning, pp. 27378–27394. PMLR (2022)
107. Zhou, W., Berrio, J.S., Worrall, S., Nebot, E.: Automated evaluation of semantic segmentation robustness for autonomous driving. IEEE Trans. Intell. Transp. Syst. **21**(5), 1951–1963 (2019)
108. Zhou, Y., Jiao, R., Wang, D., Mu, J., Li, J.: Catastrophic forgetting problem in semi-supervised semantic segmentation. IEEE Access **10**, 48855–48864 (2022)
109. Zhu, Y., et al.: Improving semantic segmentation via efficient self-training. IEEE Trans. Pattern Anal. Mach. Intell. **46**(3), 1589–1602 (2021)

Detection of Synthetic Face Images: Accuracy, Robustness, Generalization

Nela Petrželková and Jan Čech[(✉)]

Faculty of Electrical Engineering, Czech Technical University in Prague,
Prague, Czech Republic
`cechj@fel.cvut.cz`

Abstract. An experimental study on synthetic face image detection is presented. We introduce FF5, a dataset of five fake face generators, including recent diffusion models. A baseline model trained on a specific generator achieves near-perfect accuracy in distinguishing synthetic from real images and handles common distortions (e.g., compression) via data augmentation. Additionally, partial manipulations, where synthetic content is blended into real images, can be detected and localized using a YOLO-based model. However, the model is vulnerable to adversarial attacks and fails to generalize to unseen generators – a limitation shared by state-of-the-art methods. Testing on Realistic Vision, a fine-tuned version of Stable Diffusion, confirms these challenges. Our study provides a quantitative evaluation of key properties and empirical evidence that deepfake detectors primarily learn generator fingerprints embedded in the signal.

Keywords: Deepfake · face · generated images · detection · localization

1 Introduction

Image synthesis has made remarkable progress in recent years, thanks to the advances of generative models such as Generative Adversarial Networks (GANs) [24] and Diffusion Models [41]. Synthesized images are becoming increasingly realistic and hardly distinguishable from real ones to the naked eye of an average human and even of an expert, see Fig. 1. However, this progress also poses serious threats to individuals and society [18,25], as synthesized images, also known as 'deep fakes' [33], can be used for malicious purposes, such as fake porn [29], fake video calls [2,48], fake news [52], or fake videos in election campaigns [31,39]. Therefore, it is important to develop effective and robust methods to detect and expose fake images, especially in the domain of faces, which are often the target of the attacks.

In this paper, we present a comprehensive experimental study that uncovers key properties of neural fake-face detectors. Rather than solely optimizing accuracy on standard datasets, we take a broader approach, using models with standard architectures to explore fundamental challenges in synthetic image detection. Specifically, we investigate the generalization ability of detectors when faced with unseen generators, their robustness to various image degradations and input sizes, their vulnerability to adversarial attacks, and their effectiveness in localizing manipulated regions within partially altered real images.

M. Keuper and F. Locatello (Eds.): DAGM GCPR 2025, LNCS 16125, pp. 453–468, 2026.
https://doi.org/10.1007/978-3-032-12840-9_29

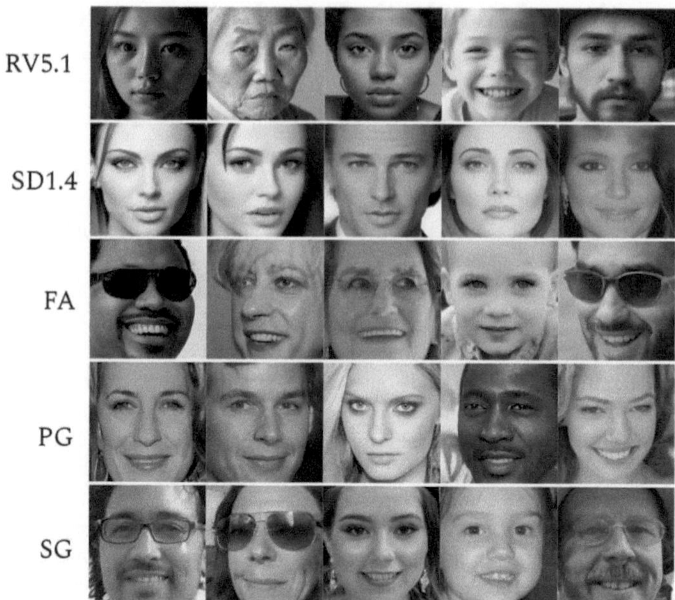

Fig. 1. Samples of our FF5 dataset produced by five generators: two diffusion models – Realistic Vision 5.1 [6] (RV5.1) and Stable Diffusion 1.4 [41] (SD1.4), one commercial app – FaceApp [14] (FA), two GANs – Progressive GAN [22] (PG) and StyleGAN [23] (SG).

In addition to detectors which are accurate in spotting recent generator images (namely, the Stable diffusion [41]—Realistic Vision [6]), our main contribution is a thorough analysis of forgery detectors that revealed many intriguing properties. To the best of our knowledge, no existing work offers a similar in-depth analysis within a compact and easily reproducible setup. Our contributions are summarized below.

1. **Novel FF5 dataset.** We collected a dataset of five fake face image generators. We extended DFFD corpus [10] by images produced by two recent diffusion model generators.
2. **Cross-generator-detector testing.** We show that while it is surprisingly easy to train a detector for a specific synthetic image generator, its accuracy drops dramatically when tested on images produced by a different generator, which was not trained for. This effect is not much reduced by training the detector on images generated by multiple different generators. We quantify this effect and show learning curves that demonstrate the accuracy as a function of a number of training images.
3. **Robustness to input size and degradations analysis.** We tested the detector against blur (reflecting input resolution), JPEG compression, and input patch size reduction via masking. It demonstrated strong robustness, further improving when degradations were included as data augmentation. Notably, our detector spots synthetic images from a 25×25 px patch with about 70% accuracy.
4. **Adversarial attacks vulnerability investigation.** We demonstrate that adversarial images can easily be found to deceive the detector to classify synthetic image as real.

Moreover, we show that residuals found for a particular detector model can also fool other models of a very different architecture. We tested both convolutional networks and a vision transformer.

5. **Localizing partial manipulations.** A likely scenario of a fraudulent act is to blend synthetic images into real photos. Therefore, we prepared a set of partially manipulated images using state-of-the-art inpainting models replacing key regions of the face (eyes, nose, mouth, etc.). We show that such images are easily spotted despite the manipulated area being small. Moreover, the manipulated area is localized within the image with high accuracy.

The rest of the paper is organized as follows. The related work is summarized in Sect. 2, the proposed methodology and results of the experimental analysis are presented in Sect. 3, and finally, Sect. 4 gives conclusions.

2   Related Work

In conjunction with the rapid development of high-quality synthetic image generators, research on the detection of fake images has become very active. For a comprehensive review, we refer to recent surveys [21,30,55] or a handbook [37]. In this section, we review some of the existing methods and challenges for this problem.

Historically, before the boom of deep learning, fake image detection focused on detecting "doctored images" that were manually edited or manipulated from images captured by cameras. These methods relied on various clues, such as steganographic features, compression artifacts, or inconsistencies in lighting or shadows [15,40]. However, these methods are not effective against synthetic images that are generated from scratch or with minimal human intervention.

Forensic low-level signal detectors are another class of methods. They exploit the spectral signatures of synthetic images. Inspiration probably came from the recognition of a camera device [4]. More recently, researchers discovered that the residual spectra of synthetic images contain typical anomalies, which creates a spectral fingerprint of a synthetic generator [7,8,53]. A frequency domain method is presented in [12].

In a similar spirit, other methods suggested that the information for fake image detection is deeply embedded in the image signals and can be detected independently of the image content. Chai et al. [3] used a CNN with a narrow receptive field to detect fake images from signal patches, highlighting hair as a key discriminative region. Tan et al. [46] proposed to spot upsampling artifacts by modeling neighboring pixel relationships. Shiohara et al. [43] proposed detecting blending artifacts in deepfake images.

Wang et al. [53] showed that GAN-generated images have distinctive features, making detection easy with a CNN classifier. Their model generalized well to unseen generators but was tested only on GAN-based images. Very promising approach to detect AI-generated images is by using CLIP [36], as a powerful image encoder, followed by a lightweight classifier head [9,34,56]. The authors report promising generalization abilities.

In this paper, we demonstrate that, in the leave-one-out setup, the generalization of detectors to unseen generators is poor. We show that even recent state-of-the-art synthetic image detectors either fail completely or perform low when tested on images produced by novel unseen generators. A recent work related to ours [35] tested generalization by learning on samples from large scale dataset comprising 4.8k distinct synthetic generator models.

Besides detection, some recent works have also addressed the localization of fake images, which aims to segment the manipulated areas of the real images. The problem is challenging considering possibly a small area of manipulation. Some methods do not use any special architecture for localization, but rely on post-processing techniques. Recent paper [47] compares a popular Grad-CAM [42] to highlight the regions that contribute to the classification decision and the scanning technique of [3] to localize synthetic regions in partially manipulated images. Other methods use more complex architectures, such as multi-branch network [17], or dense self-attention network [19], to explicitly learn the localization maps. Paper [28] fine-tunes a large segmentation model (SAM) [27] to adapt it to the fake image domain. We show that precise localization results are achieved for relatively small regions using a simple YOLO-based architecture [38], namely YOLOv8 [51], as long as the fake images are composed of images produced by the same generator model that was trained on.

Deep neural networks are known to be vulnerable to adversarial attacks [45], which are small imperceptible perturbations of the input that cause a network to make a wrong prediction. This problem has been extensively studied in various domains, such as image classification [16], object detection [54], or face recognition [11]. In this paper, we show that this vulnerability also applies to the fake image detection domain and that a common way of generating adversarial examples can fool the detectors into classifying fake images as real.

3 Methodology and Experimental Results

Our FF5 dataset consists of face images produced by five generators; see Fig. 1. We use two diffusion models: Realistic Vision V5.1 [6] (RV5.1), which is fine-tuned Stable Diffusion sharing the same architecture, and official StabilityAI's Stable Diffusion V1.4 [41] (SD1.4). Then three synthetic sets that are part of the DFFD corpus [10]: FaceApp [14] (FA), which are images produced by a popular commercial mobile phone application with undisclosed technology, and GANs PG-GAN2 [22] (PG), and Style-GAN [23] (SG).

For the diffusion models, we used dynamic prompting [13] which enables us to automatically alter a prompt with terms from predefined options. Our base prompt was "RAW photo" and we randomly altered it with attributes influencing the gender, age, accessories, and the environment. See Sect. 3.5 for more details. That enabled us to quickly generate diverse images. With different random seeds, we generated almost 1.7k images for each diffusion model. The other generators consist of 2k images for each of FA, PG, and SG.

For the negative class of real images, we use images from the FFHQ dataset [23]. All synthetic and real images underwent the same preprocessing procedure, aligning using facial landmarks, cropping with the same margin, and resampling to 224×224 px.

Table 1. Cross-generator testing. Each cell (row, col) shows test accuracy in percent of the models trained (a) on generator row/(b) all without generator row, tested on generator col.

<table>
<tr><td rowspan="2"></td><td rowspan="2"></td><td colspan="5">Test set</td></tr>
<tr><td>RV5.1</td><td>SD1.4</td><td>FA</td><td>PG</td><td>SG</td></tr>
<tr><td rowspan="5">Training set</td><td>RV5.1</td><td>**100**</td><td>58</td><td>49</td><td>50</td><td>50</td></tr>
<tr><td>SD1.4</td><td>51</td><td>**100**</td><td>50</td><td>54</td><td>49</td></tr>
<tr><td>FA</td><td>53</td><td>50</td><td>**80**</td><td>87</td><td>60</td></tr>
<tr><td>PG</td><td>49</td><td>61</td><td>54</td><td>**100**</td><td>50</td></tr>
<tr><td>SG</td><td>48</td><td>48</td><td>54</td><td>66</td><td>**94**</td></tr>
</table>

(a) Training on a single generator

<table>
<tr><td rowspan="2"></td><td rowspan="2"></td><td colspan="5">Test set</td></tr>
<tr><td>RV5.1</td><td>SD1.4</td><td>FA</td><td>PG</td><td>SG</td></tr>
<tr><td rowspan="5">Training set</td><td>-RV5.1</td><td>**58**</td><td>92</td><td>80</td><td>94</td><td>91</td></tr>
<tr><td>-SD1.4</td><td>91</td><td>**84**</td><td>85</td><td>91</td><td>91</td></tr>
<tr><td>-FA</td><td>95</td><td>94</td><td>**55**</td><td>94</td><td>89</td></tr>
<tr><td>-PG</td><td>93</td><td>92</td><td>77</td><td>**79**</td><td>85</td></tr>
<tr><td>-SG</td><td>95</td><td>95</td><td>80</td><td>94</td><td>**52**</td></tr>
</table>

(b) Leave-one-out training

3.1 Cross-Generator Testing

In this experiment, we trained the ResNET-50 backbone binary classifiers [20] between synthetic and real samples. This is the same architecture used by [53]. The dataset was always split to 80-10-10% for disjoint training-validation-test sets, respectively. The ratio between synthetic and real classes was always 50-50%. We used Adam optimizer with default settings and horizontal flipping as data augmentation. We always selected the model that achieved the best accuracy on the validation set.

We performed the following cross-generator experiment. We first trained on single-generator images and tested on all in the set, see Table 1a. Then, the other way around, we trained on all generators with one left out and tested again on all, see Tab. 1b.

We can see in Table 1a that if the detector is trained on the same model as it is tested (diagonal of the table), the accuracy is perfect for RV5.1, SD 1.4, PG, and very high for SG. The accuracy is only 80% for FA. FA, FaceApp [14], a commercial app with unknown technology behind, probably blends the real face with some manipulations, making it harder to identify. However, we can clearly see (off the diagonal) that accuracy drops close to chance when we test on images produced by models for which the detector was not trained on. Interestingly, this is not the case of FA, which achieves even higher accuracy on PG, which might indicate similar technology, but the converse is not true. The generalization does not occur for even very similar models, the diffusion models RV5.1 and SD 1.4 share the same architecture.

In Table 1b, when the detector is trained on multiple models, a certain level of generalization to unseen generators is achieved for some models, as seen in the diagonal now. SD1.4 seems to generalize well while it was not trained on it. However, RV5.1 is fine-tuned version of SD1.4, but the generalization is not reciprocal. PG seems to generalize partially as it is another GAN as SG. The rest is close to chance.

Note that the cross-dataset experiment includes several generators representing the fake class, while the real class is represented by a single source, the FFHQ dataset. This is a limitation, as real-world face images exhibit significantly more diversity than what is captured by this dataset. Therefore, these results should be interpreted as an

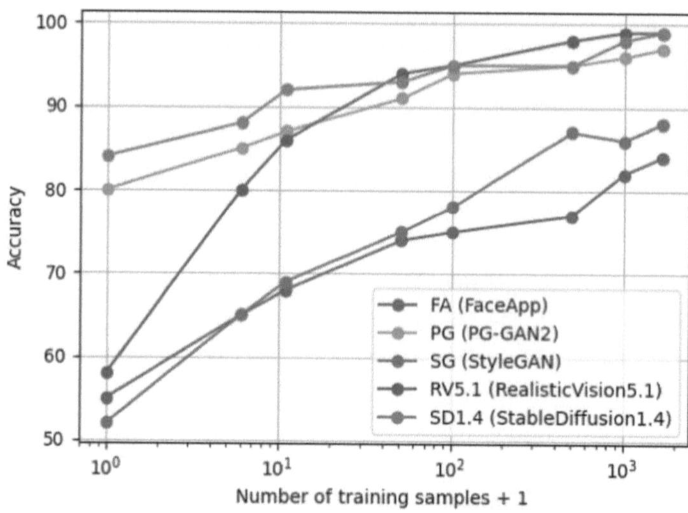

Fig. 2. Learning curves for training a detector to spot images produced by a new generator. Test accuracy as a function of the number of training samples. Horizontal axis is logarithmic.

optimistic upper bound; accuracy is expected to decline when a more diverse and previously unseen real dataset is used.

We see that the detector generalization to an unseen model is a problem. Therefore, in the following experiment, we measure how many samples of the new generator are needed for fine-tuning. We always start from the model that is trained on all the generators of our set except one (i.e., the rows of Table 1b), so its initial accuracy is on the diagonal of Table 1b. Then we gradually add training samples of the new model (0, 5, 10, 50, 100, 500, 1000, 1666) samples and measure the accuracy on the test set. The results are shown as learning curves in Fig. 2. Note that the plot has a logarithmic horizontal axis.

Interestingly, the learning curves are steep. For some generators, only a few units or small tens of training samples are sufficient to significantly improve detection accuracy, indicating that the model quickly captures the fingerprint of the new generator.

Comparison with the State of the Art. We evaluate recent fake image detectors on our test set produced by the RV5.1 generator, see Table 2. The first four methods [9, 17, 46, 53] provide pre-trained models, while the last two models, Durall [12] and our ResNET-50, were trained on an independent training split of the RV5.1 dataset.

Wang [53] claims to generalize to unseen generators, but this does not hold for novel diffusion models such as RV5.1. The model achieved accuracy close to chance, likely because it was trained on GAN-based generators, which do not generalize to the recent diffusion-based RV5.1 generator. HiFi [17] failed despite being trained on diffusion models. Tan [46] performed slightly above chance level, even though the paper reports a generalization to unseen generators by spotting upsampling artifacts. Cozzolino [9] achieves better, but still low, accuracy despite being trained on Stable Diffusion and reporting generalization abilities via CLIP [36].

Table 2. Comparison with the state of the art. Accuracy on test set produced by RV5.1 generator. Last two models were trained on independent split of RV5.1 dataset.

Model	Wang [53] CVPR'20	HiFi [17] CVPR'23	Tan [46] CVPR'24	Cozzolino [9] CVPRw'24	Durall [12] CVPR'20	ResNET-50 ours
Accuracy	48.3	44.2	64.1	70.0	87.7	99.5

Our simple ResNET-50, when trained on the RV5.1 training split, achieved near-perfect recognition. In contrast, Durall [12] resulted in inferior accuracy, likely due to its reliance on very simple features – magnitude spectrum radius and logistic regression.

This experiment demonstrates that generalization to unseen generators remains an unsolved problem in practice. A trivial classifier, when trained on examples from the target generator, outperforms more sophisticated methods. The likely reason is that detectors overfit to known generator fingerprint and are unable to identify more universal traces that separate synthetic and real samples.

The remaining experiments are conducted using our models trained within the dataset, since the competing methods do not generalize well and some perform at chance level, as seen in Table 2.

3.2 Detector Accuracy for Input Degradation

Since the image may be distorted, e.g., resized, compressed, cropped, prior to the distribution, we measured detector accuracy for the distortion. Gaussian blur simulates shrinking the resolution, and JPEG a lossy compression. The size of the input was simulated by masking the input image – a square patch of a given size at random position is kept, while all other pixels are replaced with zeros in all three RGB channels. See Fig. 4 for some examples.

We evaluated two scenarios. First, we tested the original model, which was trained on undistorted images from the RV5.1 set. Second, we re-trained the detector with the image degradation as data augmentation.

The results are shown in Fig. 3. We can see that the detector proves a good robustness to the degradations, especially for the second scenario with re-training. For instance, the detector achieves accuracy about 80% for Gaussian blur $\sigma = 17$ px, 90% for JPEG quality 10, and 70% for a patch as small as 25×25 px.

These findings corroborate that the fingerprint is strong, survives severe image degradations, and can be identified through discriminative learning. The small-patch experiment proves that the fingerprint exists at a low (signal) rather than a high (semantic) level.

3.3 Adversarial Attacks

In this section, we study the vulnerability of our detector to adversarial attacks. An adversarial attack means performing a hardly perceptible modification of an image (residue) that causes a change in classification of the detector, i.e., a synthetic image

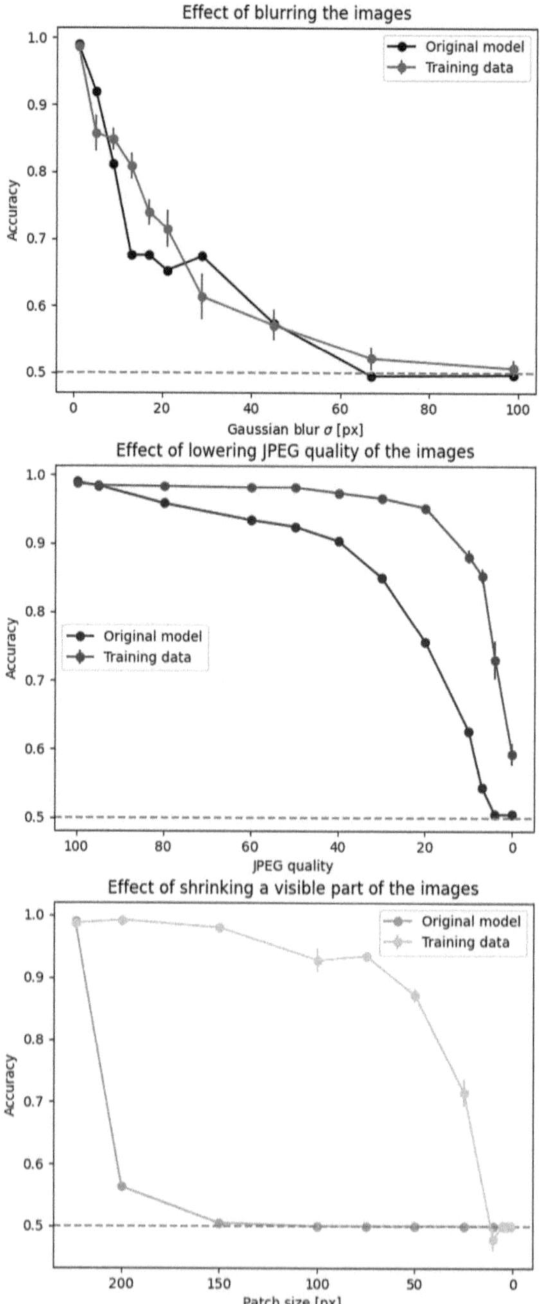

Fig. 3. Detector accuracy for input degradation. From top to bottom: Gaussian blur, JPEG compression, input patch size. Two scenarios are tested: (1) the detector is trained on undistorted images only, (2) the detector is trained on images including the degradations. Plots have error bars of standard deviation across 10 training trials.

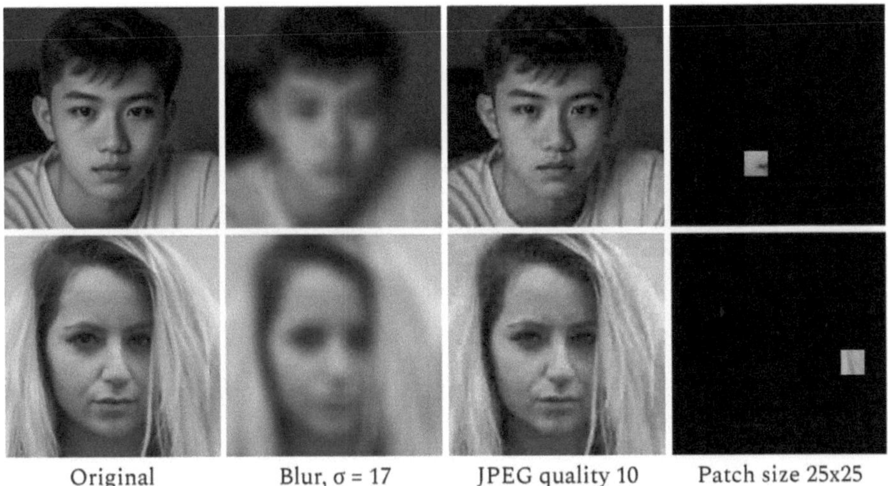

Original   Blur, σ = 17   JPEG quality 10   Patch size 25x25

Fig. 4. Examples of distorted images.

is classified as real. First, we find the adversarial residua for a given image. We use the fast gradient sign method (FGSM) [16]. The adversarial residuum is then an image of the same size as the input receptive field of the model that contains signs of the gradient of the output class score with respect to the input pixel intensities in each channel. This is easily calculated by backpropagation without any optimization.

We tested the attacks on three different architectures of detectors: ResNET-50 [20], Xception [5], ViT-tiny [49], which we trained on our training set RV5.1. All models achieved a perfect 100% accuracy on the test set.

The resulting residua are shown in Fig. 5. The residua are scaled up multiple times in the figures, otherwise the pattern would not be visible. All these residua scaled by strength ϵ if summed with the original images will switch the classification of the corresponding detector to "real". Residua for different models appear different and the pattern is visibly influenced by the structure of the original image, as seen in Fig. 5.

We measured the success of attacks by the *confusion rate*, which depicts a percentage of test cases when the model switched the classification due to the attack from "fake" to "real" over the number of "fake" decisions prior to the attack.

We tested the cross-model scenario, where the adversarial residua are found for a given image and a given model, and are tested also on other models of different architectures. The results for increasing strengths of the residua, ϵ, are summarized in the tables in Fig. 5.

We see that for a small strength $\epsilon = 0.01$, in-model attacks (in the diagonal) are successful for ResNET-50 and Xception. However, for higher strength, cross-model attacks, where a model of *different architecture unknown by the attacker* works also, as seen off the diagonal. For strength $\epsilon = 0.05$ a residue found for ViT-tiny confuses ResNET-50 and Xception too.

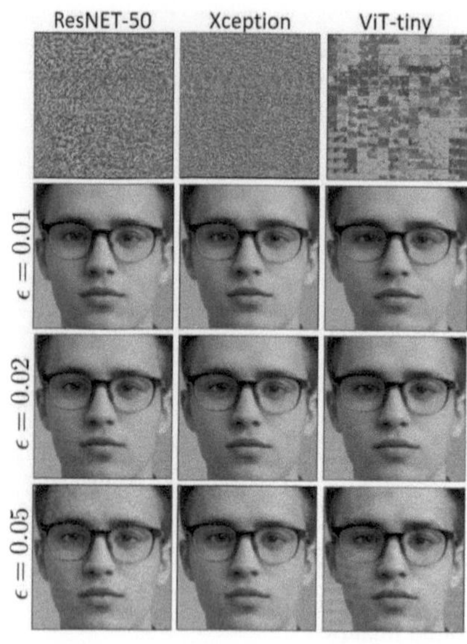

FGSM $\epsilon = 0.01$	ResNET-50	Xception	ViT-tiny
ResNET-50	**100.00**	67.15	7.30
Xception	2.55	**100.00**	6.93
ViT-tiny	0.39	6.64	**59.77**

FGSM $\epsilon = 0.02$	ResNET-50	Xception	ViT-tiny
ResNET-50	**100.00**	100.00	8.76
Xception	48.54	**100.00**	8.39
ViT-tiny	16.80	89.06	**92.97**

FGSM $\epsilon = 0.05$	ResNET-50	Xception	ViT-tiny
ResNET-50	**100.00**	100.0	15.69
Xception	100.00	**100.0**	10.22
ViT-tiny	100.00	100.0	**100.0**

Fig. 5. Cross-architecture adversarial attacks for increasing strength of the residua ϵ. Left: Examples of adversarial residua for specific models created with FGSM method. Right: Results showing confusion rate in percent for each cell (row, col). The attack was targeted against model of architecture in row and tested against the model of architecture in col.

A defense against adversarial attacks on deepfake detectors should be implemented in practice. It has been reported, e.g., in [32], that image compression or low-pass filtering can mitigate adversarial effects. However, as we have shown in this paper, such techniques also weaken the deepfake generator fingerprint. Another option is to use adversarial training [57] or detectors for adversarial patterns, though this remains a non-trivial problem [50], similar in spirit to deepfake detection. Therefore, we believe these problems should be studied together in future research.

3.4 Localizing Partial Manipulations

A likely scenario for constructing a fake image is that a synthetic image is seamlessly blended into a real face image. In this experiment, we will show that these partial manipulations are easy to identify together with localizing the area of the manipulations.

We first prepared a dataset of partially manipulated face images. We randomly sampled real faces (from the FFHQ dataset) and, for each image, uniformly changed either of the eyes, eyebrows, nose, or mouth. These regions were detected using facial landmarks [26], and the change of content within the region was carried out by Stable Diffusion inpainting [41]. This way we produced a dataset of 3.2k partially manipulated images that were mixed with 540 real images.

The data set was divided into training, validation, and test subsets with proportions of 80%, 16%, and 4%, respectively. Then, we trained YOLOv8 [51], which is a YOLO-based architecture [38] with a segmentation head.

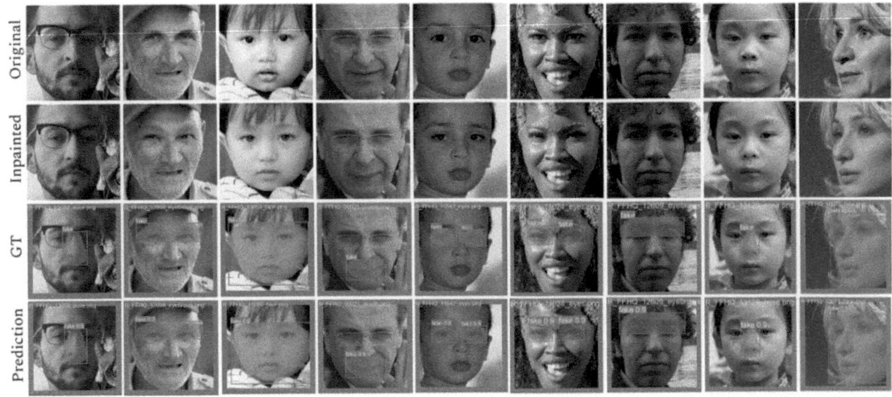

Fig. 6. Localizing partial image manipulations perpetrated by inpainting of the ground-truth (GT) regions for examples of the test set. Localization predictions were found by our YOLOv8-based model.

Qualitative results on the test set are shown in Fig. 6. It is seen that detected regions are found precisely, despite the fact that the manipulated (synthetic region) is sometimes fairly small with respect to the entire (real) image and no obvious artifacts are visible in the images.

Quantitatively, the detector achieved mAP50 98% (mean average precision for 50% prediction/ground-truth detection overlap by intersection over the union). Pixelwise recall and precision were 95% and 91%, respectively.

We compared the detector with HiFi [17] which is supposed to provide localization of the manipulation. However, this detector failed completely and always recognized all our partially manipulated images as real. This again confirms, similarly to our findings in Sect. 3.1, that generalization to localize partial manipulations when using unseen models is very challenging.

On the other hand, we attribute the success of the detector trained for this particular manipulation technique to its sensitivity in identifying small patches of the synthetic signal, as discussed in Sect. 3.2, and possibly to its ability to detect subtle boundary artifacts. The first reason is likely stronger, as the localization accuracy depends on the size of the manipulated area, which is quantified below.

Localization Accuracy as a Function of Manipulated Area Size. In this experiment, we quantify how the size of the manipulated area impacts the localization accuracy of our YOLOv8s-seg segmentation model. We created a dataset consisting of 4.5k of partially manipulated images with various sizes of the manipulated area. In particular, we randomly sampled real (FFHQ dataset) images, then for each image, we generated the manipulated area by a randomly placed, rotated, and cropped ellipse of random size. Finally, as in the previous experiment, we used Stable Diffusion's inpainting to modify the images in these areas. Several examples can be seen in Fig. 7a. The model was trained on 2.7k of the 4.5k images, 1.8k were used for validation and testing.

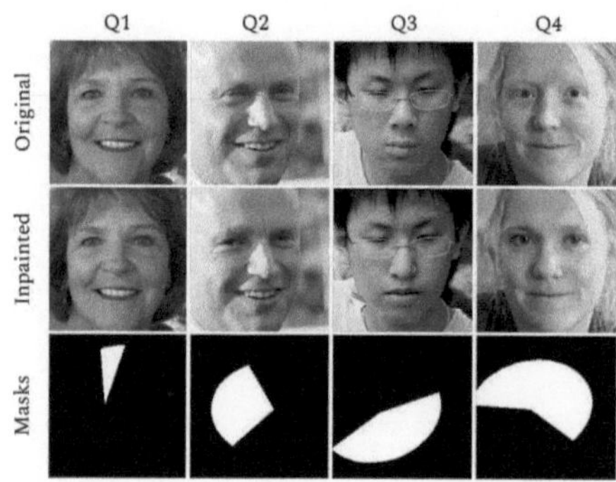

	Q1	Q2	Q3	Q4
Area size [%]	0–8	8–16	16–25	25–36
mAP50 [%]	24	74	90	97

(b) Results – mAP50 on the test images. Area size is the percentage of the manipulated area over the entire area of the face image.

(a) Examples of partial image manipulations by inpainting with random masks.

Fig. 7. Localization accuracy as a function of manipulated area size.

The test set was split into equally sized bins Q1–Q4 according to the size of the manipulated areas: 'Q1': (0, 0.08), 'Q2': (0.08, 0.16), 'Q3': (0.16, 0.25), 'Q4': (0.25, 0.36), where the numbers denote a ratio of the area of the generated parts with respect to the total area. The results are shown in Fig. 7b, where mAP50 is evaluated for each test set bin. We can see that it is obviously easier to localize larger areas for the model. Unlike in previous experiments, where we modified facial features (face, eyes, eyebrows, nose, mouth), here we chose the unpainted regions completely randomly. It happens that especially small regions are located in flat areas without texture. These regions do not manifest much of a usable signal for identification as do larger areas. This can be the reason why the smaller modified areas are more challenging to localize by the model.

3.5 Implementation Details

We used AUTOMATIC1111's Stable Diffusion Web UI [1] for our experiments. Besides graphical interface with many plugins, it also provides a convenient batch processing.

To generate our dataset (RV5.1 and SD1.4), we used dynamic prompt [13]. This is the Web UI extension that implements an expressive template language for the generation of random or combinatorial prompts. In particular, we used the following prompt to get diversity in our datasat: "RAW photo, {older | younger} {man | woman | lady | girl | boy} { {smiling | staring} | with glasses | with hat | with {brown | blonde | dark} {straight | curly | short} hair }, high quality portrait taken with Nikon camera, in {nature | a city | a room | an office | a park | a street | a forest }".

All models were trained with PyTorch framework.

4 Conclusion

In this paper, we conducted several experiments on the detection of synthetic face images. Our results allow us to draw the following conclusions.

The *good news* is that it is possible (if the generator of synthetic images is available) to train a simple model with an off-the-shelf architecture, which has almost perfect accuracy in distinguishing between synthetic and real images. The accuracy achieved far outperforms human abilities [44]. Another positive aspect is that the detector can be trained with data augmentation, to make it robust to common image distortions (reduced resolution, compression), and it can achieve good accuracy with only a small input patch from the face. Moreover, it is easy to detect the case of partial manipulations, where a collage of real and synthetic images is made. The manipulated area is automatically localized by training a standard model [51].

However, there are also *bad news*. It is simple to prepare an adversarial attack. It turns out that the residua found for a target model act adversarially, even on other models of very different architectures. We showed that adversarial images found for vision transformers often confuse convolutional networks. The worst news is that the detectors do not generalize well to generators they were not trained on. This is not just the case of our simple detector, but we showed that many tested state-of-the-art detectors could not reliably detect synthetic images generated by a newer generator, which they were not trained on.

This study presents multiple insights from targeted experiments and provides quantitative evidence on the challenges of synthetic image detection. In summary, current detectors trained discriminatively in a supervised manner learn to identify signal fingerprints of specific generators. Future research will focus on novel learning strategies to mitigate such overfitting and enhance generalization.

Acknowledgement. This work was supported by the national recovery plan projects CEDMO NPO (1.4 CEDMO 1 – Z220312000000) and CEDMO 2.0 NPO (MPO 60273/24/21300/21000) provided by the ministry of industry and trade, and by the CTU student grant SGS23/173/OHK3/3T/13. We thank to Patricie Petriľáková for evaluating the recent detectors on our dataset.

References

1. AUTOMATIC1111: Stable Diffusion Web User Interface. GitHub repository (2023). https://github.com/AUTOMATIC1111/stable-diffusion-webui
2. Bloomberg news: The next wave of scams could be deepfake video calls from your boss (2023). https://www.linkedin.com/pulse/next-wave-scams-could-deepfake-video-calls-from-your-boss/
3. Chai, L., Bau, D., Lim, S.N., Isola, P.: What makes fake images detectable? understanding properties that generalize. In: Proceedings of the ECCV (2020)
4. Chen, M., Fridrich, J., Goljan, M., Lukás, J.: Determining image origin and integrity using sensor noise. IEEE Trans. Inf. Forensics Secur. **3**(1), 74–90 (2008)

5. Chollet, F.: Xception: deep learning with depthwise separable convolutions. In: Proceedings of the CVPR (2017)
6. CivitAI: Realistic vision, v5.1 (2023). https://civitai.com/models/4201/realistic-vision
7. Corvi, R., Cozzolino, D., Zingarini, G., Poggi, G., Nagano, K., Verdoliva, L.: On the detection of synthetic images generated by diffusion models. In: Proceedings of the ICASSP (2023)
8. Corvi, R., Cozzolino, D., Poggi, G., Nagano, K., Verdoliva, L.: Intriguing properties of synthetic images: from generative adversarial networks to diffusion models. In: Proceedings of the CVPR (2023)
9. Cozzolino, D., Poggi, G., Corvi, R., Nießner, M., Verdoliva, L.: Raising the bar of AI-generated image detection with CLIP. In: Proceedings of the CVPR workshops (2024)
10. Dang, H., Liu, F., Stehouwer, J., Liu, X., Jain, A.: On the detection of digital face manipulation. In: Proceedings of the CVPR (2020)
11. Dong, Y., et al.: Efficient decision-based black-box adversarial attacks on face recognition. In: Proceedings of the CVPR (2019)
12. Durall, R., Keuper, M., Keuper, J.: Watch your up-convolution: CNN based generative deep neural networks are failing to reproduce spectral distributions. In: Proceedings of the CVPR (2020)
13. Eyal, A.: Stable Diffusion Dynamic Prompts extension. GitHub repository (2023). https://github.com/adieyal/sd-dynamic-prompts
14. FaceApp Technology Limited: Faceapp (2023). https://www.faceapp.com/
15. Farid, H.: Image forgery detection. IEEE Signal Process. Mag. **26**(2), 16–25 (2009)
16. Goodfellow, I.J., Shlens, J., Szegedy, C.: Explaining and harnessing adversarial examples. In: Proceedings of the ICLR (2015)
17. Guo, X., Liu, X., Ren, Z., Grosz, S., Masi, I., Liu, X.: Hierarchical fine-grained image forgery detection and localization. In: Proceedings of the CVPR (2023)
18. Hancock, J.T., Bailenson, J.N.: The social impact of deepfakes. Cyberpsychol. Behav. Soc. Netw. **24**(3), 149–152 (2021)
19. Hao, J., Zhang, Z., Yang, S., Xie, D., Pu, S.: TransForensics: image forgery localization with dense self-attention. In: Proceedings of the ICCV (2021)
20. He, K., Zhang, X., Ren, S., Sun, J.: Deep residual learning for image recognition. In: Proceedings of the CVPR (2016)
21. Heidari, A., Jafari Navimipour, N., Dag, H., Unal, M.: Deepfake detection using deep learning methods: a systematic and comprehensive review. Wiley Interdisc. Rev.: Data Min. Knowl. Discov. **14**(2), e1520 (2024)
22. Karras, T., Aila, T., Laine, S., Lehtinen, J.: Progressive growing of GANs for improved quality, stability, and variation. In: Proceedings of the ICLR (2018)
23. Karras, T., Laine, S., Aila, T.: A style-based generator architecture for generative adversarial networks. In: Proceedings of the CVPR (2019)
24. Karras, T., Laine, S., Aittala, M., Hellsten, J., Lehtinen, J., Aila, T.: Analyzing and improving the image quality of StyleGAN. In: Proceedings of the CVPR (2020)
25. Kietzmann, J., Lee, L.W., McCarthy, I.P., Kietzmann, T.C.: Deepfakes: trick or treat? Bus. Horiz. **63**(2), 135–146 (2020)
26. King, D.E.: Dlib-ml: a machine learning toolkit. J. Mach. Learn. Res. **10**, 1755–1758 (2009)
27. Kirillov, A., et al.: Segment anything. arXiv preprint arXiv:2304.02643 (2023)
28. Lai, Y., Luo, Z., Yu, Z.: Detect any DeepFakes: segment anything meets face forgery detection and localization. In: Proceedings of the CCBR (2023)
29. Lee, D.: Deepfakes porn has serious consequences. BBC News (2018). https://www.bbc.com/news/technology-42912529
30. Liu, B., Liu, B., Zhu, T., Ding, M.: A review of deepfake and its detection: from generative adversarial networks to diffusion models. Int. J. Intell. Syst. **2025**(1), 9987535 (2025)

31. Meaker, M.: Slovakia's election deepfakes show AI is a danger to democracy. Wired (2023). https://www.wired.co.uk/article/slovakia-election-deepfakes
32. Mumcu, F., Yilmaz, Y.: Detecting adversarial examples. arXiv preprint arXiv:2410.17442 (2024)
33. Nguyen, T.T., et al.: Deep learning for deepfakes creation and detection: a survey. Comput. Vis. Image Underst. **223**, 103525 (2022)
34. Ojha, U., Li, Y., Lee, Y.J.: Towards universal fake image detectors that generalize across generative models. In: Proceedings of the CVPR (2023)
35. Park, J., Owens, A.: Community forensics: using thousands of generators to train fake image detectors. In: Proceedings of the CVPR (2025)
36. Radford, A., et al.: Learning transferable visual models from natural language supervision. In: Proceedings of the ICML. PmLR (2021)
37. Rathgeb, C., Tolosana, R., Vera-Rodriguez, R., Busch, C.: Handbook of Digital Face Manipulation and Detection: From DeepFakes to Morphing Attacks. Springer, Cham (2022)
38. Redmon, J., Divvala, S., Girshick, R., Farhadi, A.: You only look once: unified, real-time object detection. In: Proceedings of the CVPR (2016)
39. Reuters: Erdogan rival accuses Russia of 'deep fake' campaign ahead of presidential vote (2023). https://www.reuters.com/world/middle-east/erdogan-rival-accuses-russia-deep-fake-campaign-ahead-presidential-vote-2023-05-12/
40. Rocha, A., Scheirer, W., Boult, T., Goldenstein, S.: Vision of the unseen: current trends and challenges in digital image and video forensics. ACM Comput. Surv. (CSUR) **43**(4), 1–42 (2011)
41. Rombach, R., Blattmann, A., Lorenz, D., Esser, P., Ommer, B.: High-resolution image synthesis with latent diffusion models. In: Proceedings of the CVPR (2022)
42. Selvaraju, R.R., Cogswell, M., Das, A., Vedantam, R., Parikh, D., Batra, D.: Grad-CAM: visual explanations from deep networks via gradient-based localization. In: Proceedings of the ICCV (2017)
43. Shiohara, K., Yamasaki, T.: Detecting deepfakes with self-blended images. In: Proceedings of the CVPR, pp. 18720–18729 (2022)
44. Somoray, K., Miller, D.J.: Providing detection strategies to improve human detection of deepfakes: an experimental study. Comput. Hum. Behav. **149**, 107917 (2023)
45. Szegedy, C., et al.: Intriguing properties of neural networks (2014)
46. Tan, C., Zhao, Y., Wei, S., Gu, G., Liu, P., Wei, Y.: Rethinking the up-sampling operations in CNN-based generative network for generalizable deepfake detection. In: Proceedings of the CVPR (2024)
47. Tantaru, D., Oneata, E., Oneata, D.: Weakly-supervised deepfake localization in diffusion-generated images. In: Proceedings of the WACV (2024)
48. The Guardian: European politicians duped into deepfake video calls with mayor of Kyiv (2022). https://www.theguardian.com/world/2022/jun/25/european-leaders-deepfake-video-calls-mayor-of-kyiv-vitali-klitschko
49. Touvron, H., Cord, M., Douze, M., Massa, F., Sablayrolles, A., Jégou, H.: Training data-efficient image transformers & distillation through attention. arXiv preprint arXiv:2012.12877 (2020)
50. Tramer, F.: Detecting adversarial examples is (nearly) as hard as classifying them. In: Proceedings of the ICML. PMLR (2022)
51. Ultralytics: YOLO v8. GitHub repository (2023). https://github.com/ultralytics/ultralytics
52. Wakefield, J.: Deepfake presidents used in Russia-Ukraine war. BBC News (2022). https://www.bbc.com/news/technology-60780142
53. Wang, S.Y., Wang, O., Zhang, R., Owens, A., Efros, A.A.: CNN-generated images are surprisingly easy to spot...for now. In: Proceedings of the CVPR (2020)

54. Wei, X., Liang, S., Chen, N., Cao, X.: Transferable adversarial attacks for image and video object detection. In: Proceedings of the International Joint Conference on Artificial Intelligence. AAAI Press (2019)
55. Yan, Z., et al.: DF40: toward next-generation deepfake detection. In: Advances in Neural Information Processing Systems, vol. 37, pp. 29387–29434 (2024)
56. Yermakov, A., Cech, J., Matas, J.: Unlocking the hidden potential of CLIP in generalizable deepfake detection. arXiv preprint arXiv:2503.19683 (2025)
57. Zhao, M., Zhang, L., Ye, J., Lu, H., Yin, B., Wang, X.: Adversarial training: a survey. arXiv preprint arXiv:2410.15042 (2024)

3D Perception and Reconstruction

MT-Occ: Single-View 3D Occupancy Prediction via Multi-task Distillation

Zhi Li[1,2]([✉]), Rahaf Aljundi[3], Daniel Olmeda Reino[3], and Bernt Schiele[1]

[1] Max Planck Institute for Informatics, Saarbrücken, Germany
[2] Saarland Informatics Campus, Saarbrücken, Germany
zhili@mpi-inf.mpg.de
[3] Toyota Motor Europe, Brussels, Belgium

Abstract. 3D occupancy prediction is gaining traction in autonomous driving for its ability to jointly model environment geometry and semantics. Weakly supervised methods learn 3D representations solely from multi-view 2D labels, making them ideal for data-scarce scenarios. However, distilling 2D knowledge into 3D is challenging due to limited information and noisy pseudo labels. To tackle the above challenges, we introduce MT-Occ, a single-view self-supervised 3D occupancy prediction method that enhances 2D-to-3D distillation by leveraging pretrained multi-task features and modelling task interactions. Our approach includes three effective and flexible components: 1) an effective fusion technique utilising pretrained features of multiple relevant tasks, 2) a spatial cross-task attention module for geometric-semantic distillation and 3) a view-consistent label refinement strategy to improve 2D pseudo labels. MT-Occ achieves state-of-the-art results on autonomous driving benchmarks, outperforming prior work with +16.04% relative mIoU on SSCBench-KITTI-360 and +33.33% on SSCBench-nuScenes, particularly excelling on safety-critical small classes. Extensive experiments validate the effectiveness and flexibility of our design choices.

Keywords: Single-view Reconstruction · 3D Scene Understanding · Autonomous Driving

1 Introduction

Accurate 3D scene understanding is crucial for building reliable autonomous driving systems. The task of 3D occupancy prediction [42,54,55,57] proposed in recent years leverages 2D images to capture rich 3D spatial and semantic information, providing critical scene context for autonomous driving perception and planning while reducing the reliance on costly LiDAR sensors. However, training fully supervised 3D occupancy prediction networks requires accurate 3D ground truth (e.g., dense LiDAR data with semantic labels), which is costly and error-prone to collect at scale. Additionally, many existing methods require multi-view or multi-frame images as inputs during inference, which limits flexibility and increases system costs by necessitating specific camera setups and

© The Author(s), under exclusive license to Springer Nature Switzerland AG 2026
M. Keuper and F. Locatello (Eds.): DAGM GCPR 2025, LNCS 16125, pp. 471–487, 2026.
https://doi.org/10.1007/978-3-032-12840-9_30

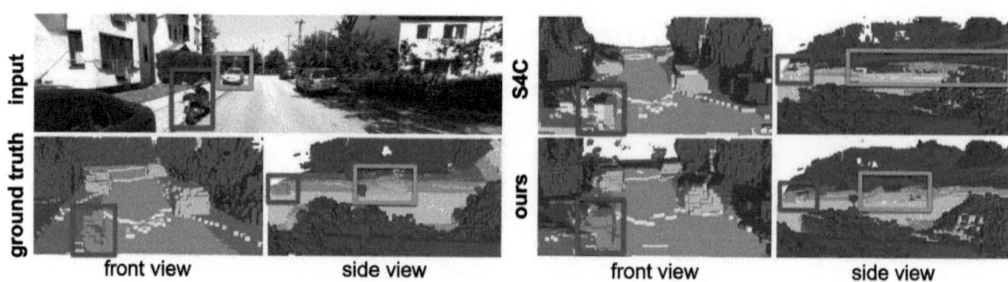

Fig. 1. Single-view 3D occupancy prediction results. Given a single-view image as input (top), we show the 3D occupancy results of the existing method S4C [18] and our MT-Occ, from a front viewpoint (left) and a side viewpoint (right). Our method can capture objects of challenging classes such as motorcycle (highlighted in red boxes), and reconstructs more faithful geometry with semantics especially on self-occluded areas (shown in green boxes).

multi-camera calibration processes [35,36,44,55,57,73]. To develop more adaptable and affordable systems, it is advantageous to use approaches that can be trained with only 2D labels and require only single-view inputs for inference. However, this setup amplifies the inherent difficulty of 3D occupancy estimation, as it demands robust self-supervised methods to compensate for the lack of explicit 3D information and to address the ill-posed nature of the single-view task.

Existing approaches [18,21,44,72] generally achieve self-supervision of 3D occupancy prediction by distilling multi-view 2D information into 3D with neural rendering [41,70], in which continuous neural density fields together with semantic fields are learned from posed images and 2D semantic (pseudo) labels, avoiding the need for 3D groundtruth. However, transferring knowledge from 2D to 3D can be constrained by an information bottleneck, as 2D representations have limited capacity to fully express 3D structures, and the noise in 2D pseudo labels further adds to the challenge. As shown in Fig. 1, existing methods, whose distillation relies on simple learning from limited and noisy 2D pseudo labels, often fail to capture some certain small "thing" classes (e.g. bicycle, motorcycle, person) which are safety-critical but challenging and appear rarer in the training set, and demonstrate unfaithful geometry reconstruction on the side view (termed in previous works [18,32,60] as "trailing artifacts" as the objects tend to "trail" towards the camera ray direction in self-occluded areas).

To address the 2D to 3D data distillation challenge, we argue that the following 3 aspects are essential: enriching 2D feature representation, improving information transfer during network training, and reducing noise in 2D pseudo labels. Recent vision foundation models [27,43,47,67,68] trained on massive datasets offer informative general feature representations that enhance 2D tasks. Although not designed for 3D tasks, these pretrained models can help improve 3D occupancy prediction by refining feature representations and pseudo-labels for tasks like semantic segmentation and depth estimation. Additionally, geometry and semantics in 3D occupancy prediction are tightly coupled, where one can aid the other [56,63,64], which can be utilised for both network training and pseudo-label regularisation.

Here, we propose MT-Occ, a new method to improve single-view, self-supervised 3D occupancy prediction by distilling information from relevant 2D pretraining and multi-task interactions. Our key contributions includes:

- An effective feature fusion technique for single-view 3D occupancy prediction that leverages pretraining from relevant 2D tasks.
- A spatial cross-task attention mechanism in the decoding phase enhancing geometry-semantics interaction.
- A novel label refinement strategy, using relative depth estimation as a proxy to guide 3D occupancy training and refine noisy pseudo-labels.
- Extensive experiments on SSCBench-KITTI-360 and SSCBench-nuScenes benchmarks demonstrate the effectiveness and flexibility of all proposed components

2   Related Works

Semantic Scene Completion and 3D Occupancy Prediction. Semantic Scene Completion (SSC) [33,50,53] integrates 3D geometry and semantic labelling in a voxelised 3D space, using either images together with partial geometry [9,29–31] [39,48,49,61,65] or solely from RGB images [5,6,18,69]. Recently, "3D occupancy prediction" has gained attention in autonomous driving to refer specifically to SSC methods using vision-only inputs [55,57]. While some methods use multi-view, multi-frame inputs [20,23,44,55,57,59], others focus on single-view (monocular, single-frame) input [6,18], which simplifies setup but increases reconstruction difficulty. We target this challenging single-view 3D occupancy prediction, proposing effective strategies for 2D-to-3D inference.

Self-supervised 3D Occupancy Prediction. Methods trained only with 2D (pseudo) labels [18,21,44,72] are dubbed in the literature as self-supervised methods. They typically learn a density-semantic NeRF [41] from posed multi-view images and 2D semantic labels through neural rendering. Most methods [21,44,72] convert multi-view inputs into BEV (bird eye view) features, requiring specific multi-camera setups. Some recent methods [3,7,16,76] leverage Gaussian representation [24] to build multi-view occupancy frameworks. A recent approach [18] tackles single-view, monocular input for practical 3D occupancy, requiring multi-view data only during training. We build on this setup, introducing a single-frame framework that improves performance via multi-task distillation.

Depth and Semantic Priors for NeRFs. Several works demonstrate that leveraging depth estimation or semantic information improves NeRF training. Depth estimation is used in various designs to guide or supervise neural rendering for accuracy or efficiency improvements [10,46,62,66,71]. Additionally, 2D semantic segmentation or panoptic segmentation distills semantic information into NeRF [15,28,75], and vision-language features similarly enhance scene understanding [13,25,32,45]. While these works focus on generating novel views, segmenting objects, or scene reconstruction, we develop techniques specifically for 3D occupancy prediction by distilling multi-task priors.

Multi-task Learning. Jointly predicting multiple 2D tasks from input images is a problem setup addressed by the concept of multi-task learning [14,38,56,63] [1,2,40,64], in which the multi-task interactions, including depth estimation and semantic segmentation, are modelled by various distillation designs enhance one or more tasks in the frameworks. While these approaches focus on 2D tasks, we extend multi-task interaction to 3D occupancy prediction, aiming to improve joint 3D scene reconstruction and semantic prediction.

3   MT-Occ Framework

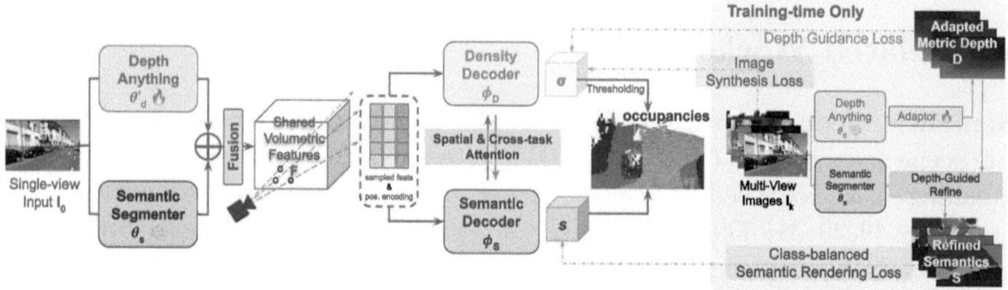

Fig. 2. MT-Occ framework. We extract pixel-aligned implicit features from pre-trained depth and semantic networks to represent density and semantics along image rays. Combined with 3D positional encodings, these features are decoded via spatial cross-task attention into per-point predictions, then aggregated for 3D occupancy. During training, depth-refined multi-view 2D semantics supervise rendering consistency, while adapted depth maps guide density learning.

Our method focuses on the challenging setting of 3D occupancy prediction from a single RGB image without 3D supervision. We illustrate the proposed MT-Occ framework in Fig. 2. In this section, we first introduce our base framework that achieves single-view 2D-supervised 3D occupancy prediction (Sect. 3.1), then detail our proposed components for multi-task feature fusion (Sect. 3.2), spatial cross-task attention (Sect. 3.3) and view-consistent label refinement (Sect. 3.4).

3.1   Framework Overview

MT-Occ reconstructs the full 3D scene from single-view inputs through a generalisable NeRF [70] based encoder-decoder network. Given a single RGB image $I_0 \in \mathbb{R}^{3 \times H \times W}$, along with its corresponding camera intrinsics $K_0 \in \mathbb{R}^{3 \times 4}$ and extrinsics $T_0 \in \mathbb{R}^{4\times4}$, the network encodes the full 3D scene into a dense, pixel-aligned, implicit, and continuous feature field $\mathbf{F} \in \mathbb{R}^{C\times H\times W}$. This feature field represents the density and semantic distributions along the rays cast from the optical centre through the pixels. Given a 3D point $\mathbf{x} \in \mathbb{R}^3$ in the world coordinate system, the density-semantic field $\mathbf{F}$ can be queried at the point's projected location $\mathbf{u} = \pi_0(\mathbf{x})$ on the 2D pixel plane, determined by the projection operation $\pi_0(\mathbf{x}) = K_0 T_0 \mathbf{x}$. The extracted feature $f_{\mathbf{u}}$ is then concatenated with the positional encoding $\gamma(\mathbf{x})$ and decoded by a density decoder $\phi_D(\cdot)$ and a semantic decoder $\phi_S(\cdot)$ to obtain the density value $\sigma \in [0, 1]$ and the semantic class $s \in \{0, ..., c-1\}$, where c is the total number of classes. A threshold τ is applied to σ to obtain a binary occupancy representation. Throughout the encoding-decoding process, MT-Occ enhances feature extraction in $\mathbf{F}$ through multi-task feature fusion (Sect. 3.2) and improves density and semantic decoding using a spatial cross-task attention module in the decoders $\phi_D(\cdot)$ and $\phi_S(\cdot)$ (Sect. 3.3).

During training, multi-view images and their corresponding (pseudo) semantic maps supervise the NeRF-rendered RGB images and semantics, eliminating the need for ground truth 3D labels. To render a viewpoint from the semantic-density field, rays are cast from the camera through each pixel. The rendered color or semantic value of a pixel is computed as the weighted integral of the color or semantic values of 3D points $\mathbf{x}$ along the ray, using the points' probabilities T of not being occluded. In practice, the integral is approximated by the weighted sum of points $\{\mathbf{x}_i | i \in \{0, ..., m\}\}$ at m discrete steps along the ray. Specifically, for the step i, the probability T_i of $\mathbf{x}_i$ being not occluded is given by

$$\alpha_i = exp(1 - \sigma_{\mathbf{x}_i}\delta_i), \quad T_i = \prod_{j=1}^{i-1}(1 - \alpha_j), \tag{1}$$

where δ_i denotes the distance between adjacent sampled points $\mathbf{x}_i$ and $\mathbf{x}_{i+1}$, and $\sigma_{\mathbf{x}_i}$ the density prediction at $\mathbf{x}_i$.

To render the colour values $\hat{c}$, we aggregate the colour values sampled from other view images $\mathbf{I}_k$ by projecting the 3D points $\mathbf{x}$ along the ray onto these views, yielding $c_{\mathbf{x},k} = \mathbf{I}_k(\pi_k(\mathbf{x}))$. The rendered colour of the pixel (w.r.t. the source view k) is then given by

$$\hat{c}_k = \sum_{i=1}^{m} T_i \alpha_i c_{\mathbf{x}_i,k}. \tag{2}$$

Similarly, the semantic class s of the pixel is rendered by aggregating all predicted semantic logits s of the 3D points along the ray:

$$\hat{s} = \arg\max \sum_{i=1}^{m} T_i \alpha_i \cdot \mathrm{softmax}(s_{\mathbf{x}_i}). \tag{3}$$

Additionally, we can render the depth value of the pixel by retrieving the expected ray termination depth $\hat{d}$:

$$\hat{d} = \sum_{i=1}^{m} T_i \alpha_i d_i \tag{4}$$

The network training can then be supervised by calculating the losses between the rendered colour, semantics and depth and the corresponding (pseudo) ground truth 2D labels. At training stage, MT-Occ models multi-task interactions, proposes strategies for view consistent pseudo-label refinement and enables more robust training (Sect. 3.4).

3.2 Multi-task Feature Fusion

At the feature extraction stage, similar to [70], the occupancy network converts single-view RGB inputs into pixel-aligned volumetric features, encoding scene density and semantics within the camera frustum. Prior methods [6,18] achieve feature extraction by training standard architectures (e.g., ResNets [19], UNets [51]) only within the scope of the limited training data. However, this approach is less effective for complex tasks like 3D occupancy prediction, where targeted features are crucial and extensive data is often needed for effective learning.

In NeRF based frameworks, extracted features describe density and semantic distributions along rays extending from the camera centre through each pixel. Intuitively, dense 2D perception tasks like depth estimation and semantic segmentation can aid this learning. To leverage depth priors, we initialise our feature extractor with pretrained weights θ_d from DepthAnythingv2 [68], a foundation model trained on large-scale synthetic data. We modify θ_d by removing its final convolutional layer, yielding θ'_d, which retains its last-layer feature map but excludes direct depth predictions. Since depth estimation encodes only partial geometry (i.e., surfaces), we update θ'_d during training to transform depth information into a density distribution along a ray, capturing full 3D geometry, including occluded regions. Given an input image $\mathbf{I}_0$, we then generate the feature representation of density distribution $\mathbf{F}_d$ by

$$\mathbf{F}_d = f(\mathbf{I}_0, \theta'_d). \tag{5}$$

We enhance the feature representation with semantic information using predictions from a frozen off-the-shelf semantic segmentation network θ_s. To ensure flexibility across architectures, we use its one-hot encoded output $\mathbf{F}_s$:

$$\mathbf{F}_s = f(\mathbf{I}_0, \theta_s)^{onehot}. \tag{6}$$

Next, we concatenate $\mathbf{F}_d$ and $\mathbf{F}_s$, then apply a convolutional layer for fusion, yielding $\mathbf{F}$, a feature representation enriched with both geometry and semantics information:

$$\mathbf{F} = \text{conv}(\text{concat}(\mathbf{F}_d, \mathbf{F}_s)). \tag{7}$$

The fused feature $\mathbf{F}$ describes a density-semantic field of the scene, and can then go through the decoding process to predict density and semantic values of 3D points.

3.3 Spatial Cross-Task Attention

During decoding, sampled features from $\mathbf{F}$ are concatenated with positional embeddings and fed into task decoders ϕ_d and ϕ_s for density and semantic predictions. Unlike prior methods [18,21,44,72] that use separate MLP heads per 3D point, we follow [32] to aggregate features from neighbouring points, enhancing geometry learning. Additionally, we introduce a cross-task attention module to facilitate interaction between geometry and semantics.

Given sampled and positionally embedded features $\mathbf{F}'$, task-specific features $\mathbf{F}'_d$ and $\mathbf{F}'_s$ are computed via fully connected layers. We then apply an efficient linear attention mechanism [32,52], using features from the same task as query $\mathbf{Q}$ and value $\mathbf{V}$, while the other task serves as key $\mathbf{K}$. The global context score G is computed by attending to $\mathbf{K}$ and $\mathbf{V}$, then correlated with $\mathbf{Q}$ to obtain the final attended features $\mathbf{F}_d^{\mathrm{attn}}$ and $\mathbf{F}_s^{\mathrm{attn}}$. Specifically, for density, we have

$$
\begin{aligned}
G_d &= \mathrm{softmax}(\mathbf{K}_s/\sqrt{D})^\top \cdot \mathbf{V}_d, \\
\mathbf{F}_d^{\mathrm{attn}} &= \mathrm{softmax}(\mathbf{Q}_d/\sqrt{D}) \cdot G_d,
\end{aligned}
\tag{8}
$$

and similarly for semantics

$$
\begin{aligned}
G_s &= \mathrm{softmax}(\mathbf{K}_d/\sqrt{D})^\top \cdot \mathbf{V}_s, \\
\mathbf{F}_s^{\mathrm{attn}} &= \mathrm{softmax}(\mathbf{Q}_s/\sqrt{D}) \cdot G_s,
\end{aligned}
\tag{9}
$$

with D being the scaling factor. The spatially and cross-task aggregated features $\mathbf{F}_d^{\mathrm{attn}}$ and $\mathbf{F}_s^{\mathrm{attn}}$ is then fed into the last layers for the final density and semantic prediction.

3.4 View-Consistent Label Refinement

The self-supervised 3D occupancy prediction network is trained using only 2D supervisory signals. During training, it extracts a feature map $\mathbf{F}$ from a single-view input $\mathbf{I}_0$, while multi-view images $\mathbf{I}_k$ (aggregated from the main, stereo, and side-view cameras over multiple video frames, as in [18]) provide supervision. Prior work [18] employs a photometric discrepancy loss $\mathcal{L}_{\mathrm{ph}}$, combining L1 and structural similarity (SSIM [58]), computed between randomly sampled patches $\mathbf{P}$ (from $\mathbf{I}_0$) and reconstructed patches $\hat{\mathbf{P}}_k$ (rendered from $\mathbf{I}_k$) using Eq. 2,

$$
\mathcal{L}_{\mathrm{ph}} = \min_{k \in N_{\mathrm{render}}} (\mathrm{L1}(\mathbf{P}, \hat{\mathbf{P}}_k) + \lambda \mathrm{SSIM}(\mathbf{P}, \hat{\mathbf{P}}_k)),
\tag{10}
$$

and a regularisation loss, dubbed as edge-aware smoothness loss, applied on inverse, mean-normalised reconstructed depths $\mathbf{d}^* = \hat{\mathbf{d}}/\bar{\hat{\mathbf{d}}}$ ($\hat{\mathbf{d}}$ are reconstructed depths from Eq. 4) proposed by [17],

$$
\mathcal{L}_{\mathrm{eas}} = |\partial_x \mathbf{d}^*| e^{-|\partial_x \mathbf{P}|} + |\partial_y \mathbf{d}^*| e^{-|\partial_y \mathbf{P}|},
\tag{11}
$$

where $\partial_x(\cdot)$, $\partial_y(\cdot)$ are partial derivatives along the x, y axis.

For semantics, a binary cross-entropy loss $\mathcal{L}_{sem}$ is applied between sampled patches of 2D pseudo-semantic labels $\mathbf{S}$ (predicted by off-the-shelf semantic networks) and reconstructed semantic patches $\hat{\mathbf{S}}$ (computed via Eq. 3):

$$\mathcal{L}_{\text{sem}} = \text{BCE}(\mathbf{S}, \hat{\mathbf{S}}). \tag{12}$$

However, direct predictions $\mathbf{S}$ from off-the-shelf semantic networks are often noisy. To refine the semantic pseudo-labels $\mathbf{S}$ during training, we leverage multi-view consistency with the aid of depth estimation. Specifically, given a relative depth estimate from DepthAnythingv2 [68] for a target image $\mathbf{I}_{\text{target}}$, we first apply two small convolutional layers as an adaptor to convert the relative depth into absolute-scale depth $\mathbf{D}_{\text{target}}$. These adaptors are trained in a self-supervised manner using the photometric reprojection loss from [17], which measures the discrepancy between $\mathbf{I}_{\text{target}}$ and its reconstructed version $\hat{\mathbf{I}}_{\text{target}}$. The reconstruction is achieved by warping pixels from source images $\mathbf{I}_{\text{source}}$ to the target view using $\mathbf{D}_{\text{target}}$ and camera parameters, following the formulation in [17]. With the learned absolute-scale depth map $\mathbf{D}_{\text{target}}$, we apply the same reconstruction process to refine the semantic pseudo-labels. Specifically, we reconstruct $\hat{\mathbf{S}}_{\text{target}}$ from $\mathbf{S}_{\text{source}}$ and consider only the pixels $\mathbf{u}'$ whose reconstructed labels match the original pseudo-labels as reliable, filtering out the rest, given by

$$\mathbf{u}' = [u|\mathbf{S}_{\text{target}}(u) = \hat{\mathbf{S}}_{\text{target}}(u)]. \tag{13}$$

In addition, we propose semantic-guided class-balanced patch sampling to stabilise training on class-imbalanced datasets. Unlike previous random sampling methods, which bias toward larger or more frequent classes, we enforce equal sampling probability for all classes in $\mathbf{S}_{\text{target}}$, yielding class-balanced patches $\mathbf{S}'$. Thus, Eq. 12 becomes

$$\mathcal{L}_{\text{sem\_refine}} = \text{BCE}(\mathbf{S}'(\mathbf{u}'), \hat{\mathbf{S}}'(\mathbf{u}')). \tag{14}$$

We further apply a depth supervision loss using our refined depth map $\mathbf{D}$ on the rendered depth map $\hat{\mathbf{D}}$ (via Eq. 4). We adopt the scale-invariant SILog loss proposed by [12]. Let n be the number of pixels in $\mathbf{D}$ and $d_j, \hat{d}_j$ the depth value of a pixel j in $\mathbf{D}, \hat{\mathbf{D}}$

$$\mathcal{L}_{\text{depth}} = \frac{1}{n}\sum_i a_j^2 - \frac{1}{n^2}(\sum_i a_j)^2, a_j = \log\hat{d}_j - \log d_j. \tag{15}$$

Our final loss function $\mathcal{L}$ is given by

$$\mathcal{L} = \mathcal{L}_{\text{ph}} + \lambda_e\mathcal{L}_{\text{eas}} + \lambda_s\mathcal{L}_{\text{sem\_refine}} + \lambda_d\mathcal{L}_{\text{depth}}. \tag{16}$$

4   Experiments

4.1   Experimental Setup

Datasets. We evaluate our method on SSCBench-KITTI-360 and SSCBench-nuScenes datasets [33]. **SSCBench-KITTI-360** is a subset of KITTI-360 [37], containing 80% of the data with multi-view sequences from forward-facing stereo and fisheye side cameras. Following [18], we sample 2 frames per view within 4 s (8 views per sample) for training. Ground-truth semantic occupancy is derived from aggregated LiDAR annotations every 5 frames, with the dataset comprising 42k training frames (7 sequences), 15k validation frames (1 sequence), and 13k test frames (1 sequence), totaling 2566 test frames. **SSCBench-nuScenes** is derived from nuScenes [4], providing similar 3D occupancy ground truth but aligned to single-view front-facing sequences. The original nuScenes dataset includes six synchronized surround-view cameras, enabling multi-view training. We sample 4 frames from the front camera and 4 from randomly chosen front/back left/right cameras. The dataset consists of 850 20-second scenes, split into 500 scenes ($\sim$20k frames) for training, 200 ($\sim$8k) for validation, and 150 ($\sim$6k) for testing, with ground-truth voxels available for all frames.

Evaluation. We evaluate scenes of size $51.2m \times 51.2m \times 6.4m$ at a $0.2m$ voxel resolution, which follows the standard setup [33,48,55,57] [6,34,74] [18,22]. Using the threshold $\tau = 0.1$ from [18] we convert predicted densities to binary occupancy. We report IoU (intersection over union) against the 3D voxel groundtruth to assess geometric reconstruction quality and mIoU (mean intersection over union) together with per-class IoUs for semantic reconstruction quality. We further report mIoU and per-class IoU for rendered 2D semantic maps against 2D groundtruth provided for the front views in SSCBench-KITTI-360, to access the front view rendering quality.

Implementation details. We implement our method in PyTorch and train on two Tesla A40 GPUs. For pseudo semantic labels and fusion, we follow [18], using ResNet101 Panoptic-Deeplab [8] trained on Cityscapes [11] as our frozen semantic segmenter θ_s. Our geometry branch θ_d' and depth estimator θ_d use the ViT-B version of DepthAnythingv2 [68]. We train with Adam [26] optimiser using a learning rate of 10^{-4} for decoders and 10^{-6} for θ_d' to preserve pretraining. On SSCBench-KITTI-360, we train for 60 epochs, reducing the learning rate 10x after 120k iterations [18]. For cross-dataset fine-tuning, we initialise with SSCBench-KITTI-360 models and fine-tune on SSCBench-nuScenes for 10 epochs.

4.2 3D Occupancy Prediction Results

We show quantitative 3D occupancy prediction results of our method compared with state-of-the-art single-view methods on SSCBench-KITTI-360 in Table 1. All the methods feature single-view RGB input, with [6,20,22,23,34,74] trained with groundtruth 3D supervision while [18] and MT-Occ with 2D supervision. Our method shows improved performance, for both geometry reconstruction and semantic segmentation, especially on challenging small objects such as "motocyle", "bicycle", "person".

To evaluate whether large-scale cross-domain data improves accuracy, we initialise both the competing method [18] and our MT-Occ with models pretrained on SSCBench-KITTI-360 and report their cross-dataset performance as well as fine-tuned results in Table 2. Results show that cross-domain models

Table 1. Single-view 3D occupancy prediction results on SSCBench-KITTI-360. Our method achieves state-of-art performance against existing 2D pseudo-supervised single-view method (indicated as **2d-psu**), and even surpassing 3D groundtruth supervised methods (**3d-gt-sup**) on some rare "thing" classes. (%) indicates each class label ratio. Best numbers in **bold**.

	Method	IoU (%)	mIoU (%)	car (2.85%)	bicycle (0.01%)	motocycle (0.01%)	truck (0.16%)	other-veh. (5.75%)	person (0.02%)	road (14.98%)	sidewalk (6.43%)	building (15.67%)	fence (0.96%)	vegetation (41.99%)	terrain (7.10%)	pole (0.22%)	traf.-sign (0.06%)	other-obj. (0.28%)
3d-gt-sup	MonoScene[6]	37.87	13.52	19.3	0.4	0.6	8.0	2.0	0.9	48.4	28.1	32.9	3.5	26.2	16.8	6.9	5.7	3.1
	VoxFormer[34]	38.76	13.20	17.8	1.2	0.9	4.6	2.1	1.6	47.0	27.2	31.2	5.0	29.0	14.7	6.5	6.9	2.4
	TPVFormer[22]	40.22	14.95	21.6	1.1	1.4	8.1	2.6	2.4	53.0	31.1	34.8	4.8	30.1	17.5	7.5	5.9	2.7
	OccFormer[74]	40.27	14.97	**22.6**	0.7	0.3	9.9	3.8	2.8	**54.3**	31.5	**36.4**	4.8	**31.0**	**19.5**	7.8	**8.5**	4.6
	GSFormer[23]	35.38	13.79	18.9	1.0	**4.6**	**18.1**	**7.6**	**3.4**	45.5	25.0	28.4	**5.7**	29.5	8.6	3.0	2.3	**5.1**
	GSFormer2[20]	38.37	15.33	21.1	**2.6**	4.2	12.4	5.7	1.6	54.1	**32.3**	32.0	5.0	28.9	17.3	3.6	5.5	3.5
2d-psu	S4C[18]	38.84	10.10	10.3	0.0	0.0	2.2	0.2	**0.4**	48.6	26.4	21.0	2.8	22.3	16.5	0.4	**0.5**	0.0
	MT-Occ	**40.44**	**11.72**	**12.8**	**2.5**	4.2	6.9	2.7	0.3	52.3	26.8	22.8	3.6	23.2	16.5	**0.5**	0.3	**0.1**

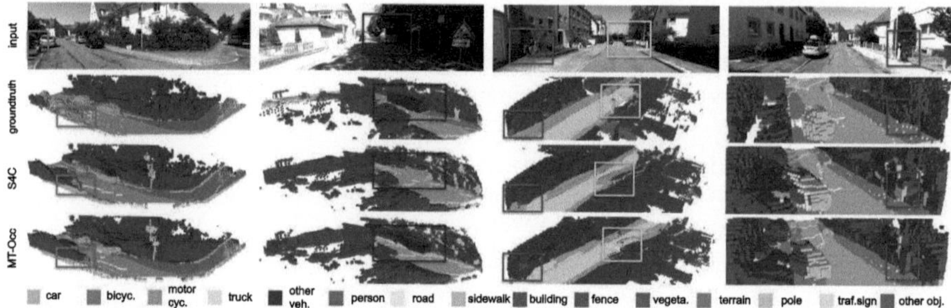

Fig. 3. Qualitative results on SSCBench-KITTI-360. Compared to S4C [18], our MT-Occ captures more accurate geometry and semantics, especially on challenging small classes or rare classes.

achieve better semantic understanding (mIoU) due to increased training data but struggle with geometry reconstruction (IoU) due to domain gaps, such as differing camera parameters. Fine-tuning improves both metrics. Notably, our method outperforms the competing approach in both cross-dataset testing and fine-tuning, demonstrating superior generalisability.

We present qualitative results in Fig. 3. Our method achieves more accurate scene geometry reconstruction, particularly in unseen areas where existing methods often produce "trailing artifacts" – objects (e.g., cars) appearing stretched along the camera's viewing direction in self-occluded regions. This improvement is due to our spatial cross-attention design. Additionally, our approach better captures small or rare objects.

Table 2. Single-view 3D occupancy prediction results on SSCBench-nuScenes. We initialise both methods with SSCBench-KITTI-360 trained models, and report both cross-dataset testing of SSCBench-KITTI-360 trained models ("-kt360") and results of fine-tuned models on SSCBench-nuScenes ("-ft"). Our method achieves state-of-art performance against the existing self-supervised single-view method by a large margin on both settings. (%) indicates each class label ratio. Best numbers in **bold**.

	Method	IoU (%)	mIoU (%)	car (2.47%)	bicycle (0.16%)	motocycle (0.02%)	truck (0.96%)	other-veh. (7.87%)	person (0.24%)	road (36.97%)	sidewalk (8.30%)	building (21.17%)	vegetation (20.97%)	other-obj. (0.11%)
3d-gt-sup	MonoScene[6]	**29.63**	9.34	10.2	1.7	3.8	8.4	8.7	3.7	**38.8**	14.7	7.2	5.5	0.0
	Voxformer[34]	25.16	5.04	5.0	0.3	1.2	2.7	2.5	1.1	23.9	10.1	4.0	4.6	0.1
	OccFormer[74]	28.23	11.24	14.6	2.3	8.0	11.9	9.8	5.9	37.6	18.6	9.1	5.9	0.0
2d-psu	S4C[18]-kt360	12.44	3.37	1.8	0.0	0.0	0.0	0.0	0.7	23.4	5.0	2.5	3.7	0.1
	MT-Occ-kt360	15.79	4.63	2.1	0.6	1.2	0.0	0.0	1.3	32.6	5.3	3.0	5.0	0.1
	S4C[18]-ft	18.24	5.07	7.0	0.0	0.0	0.0	0.0	1.8	26.1	10.0	5.1	5.8	0.1
	MT-Occ-ft	**24.50**	**6.76**	**7.4**	**1.7**	**2.5**	0.0	0.0	**2.0**	36.6	**10.3**	5.9	**7.9**	0.1

Table 3. Rendered 2D semantic segmentation results on SSCBench-KITTI-360. Our method outperforms the existing method by a large margin especially on challenging small classes, and yields even comparative results to the 2D pseudo labels both methods use to train (PanopticDeeplab [8]). (%) indicates each class label ratio. Best numbers in **bold**.

Method	mIoU (%)	car (2.85%)	bicycle (0.01%)	motocycle (0.01%)	truck (0.16%)	other-veh. (5.75%)	person (0.02%)	road (14.98%)	sidewalk (6.43%)	building (15.67%)	fence (0.96%)	vegetation (41.99%)	terrian (7.10%)	pole (0.22%)	traf.-sign (0.06%)	other-obj. (0.28%)
Deeplab[8]	46.55	86.5	21.6	35.1	37.0	10.9	28.4	83.6	57.6	83.5	44.0	85.0	55.2	32.8	37.1	0.2
S4C[18]	39.04	82.7	0.0	0.0	23.8	0.3	9.9	**87.0**	60.3	**84.4**	41.1	**85.0**	**60.6**	24.5	26.0	0.0
MT-Occ	**46.50**	**84.9**	**21.6**	**35.2**	**36.8**	**11.2**	**26.6**	86.4	**62.4**	84.0	**44.2**	85.0	56.8	**29.5**	**32.8**	0.2

4.3   2D Semantic Rendering Results

We further evaluate the quality of 2D rendered semantics against ground-truth 2D semantic maps of front views from SSCBench-KITTI-360. In Table 3, we compare the quality of the semantic pseudo-labels used for training and the rendered semantics of each method. Our approach significantly outperforms the existing method, achieving results close to the pseudo ground truth, especially for challenging small classes like "motorcycle", "bicycle", and "person". Notably, due to SSCBench-KITTI-360's sparse LiDAR aggregation, some small-class voxels (e.g., "person") may be missing in the 3D ground truth. However, 2D rendering results show that our method greatly improves the capture of these classes. The

Table 4. Ablation results on SSCBench-KITTI-360. θ'_d: pretrained encoder; θ_s: semantic fusion; $\mathcal{L}_{\text{depth}}$: depth guidance loss; S': pseudo label refinement; u': semantic-guided sampling; "attn": spatial cross-task attention. Best numbers in **bold**.

| feature fusion | | semantic refine | | | attn | IoU | mIoU |
θ'_d	θ_s	$\mathcal{L}_{\text{depth}}$	S'	u'			
S4C [18]						38.84	10.10
dino _v2 [43]						38.20	9.77
da_v2 [68]						39.99	10.66
da_v2 [68]	✓					40.09	11.03
da_v2 [68]		✓				39.89	10.73
da_v2 [68]		✓	✓			40.03	10.90
da_v2 [68]		✓	✓	✓		40.15	11.06
da_v2 [68]					✓	**40.55**	11.07
da_v2 [68]		✓	✓	✓	✓	40.50	11.30
da_v2 [68]	✓	✓	✓	✓	✓	40.44	**11.72**

substantial improvement in 2D rendered semantics suggests that our method more effectively distils 2D information.

4.4   Ablation Study

We conduct an ablation study on our proposed components for feature fusion, semantic refinement, and spatial cross-task attention in Table 4. The results confirm that each component contributes to performance gains on joint geometric-semantic reconstruction (mIoU), with the full model achieving the best. Pure geometric reconstruction (IoU) is improved effectively by the cross-attention mechanism, and the minor drops on IoU after adding the other two components can be out weighted by the significant improvement on mIoU, as the core of this task is to achieve the best joint geometric-semantic reconstruction. The robust performance gain of each combination of the components also indicates that the proposed components are also flexible to work stand alone, as plug-and-play to similar architectures or frameworks for single-view 3D occupancy prediction.

Additionally, Table 4 also compares the use of the DepthAnythingv2 encoder (da_v2 [68]) against the DINOv2 encoder (dino_v2 [43]). As shown, DepthAnythingv2 brings significant improvements, whereas DINOv2 does not. This highlights the importance of depth pretraining for this task, rather than just architectural changes.

5   Conclusion

In this paper, we address the challenging task of jointly reconstructing scene geometry and semantics from a single view and introduce MT-Occ, a novel approach for single-view 3D occupancy prediction with effective multi-task distillation. By incorporating components for multi-task feature fusion, spatial cross-task attention, and view-consistent pseudo-label refinement, MT-Occ significantly outperforms existing methods. It excels in capturing challenging small objects that are underrepresented in the training set and achieves more realistic, semantic-aware geometry reconstruction, particularly in self-occluded regions. Additionally, MT-Occ demonstrates enhanced cross-dataset generalisation, paving the way for a versatile 3D occupancy prediction framework that can be learned from large-scale unlabelled 2D data.

While MT-Occ provides a valuable approach for developing annotation-free, low-cost systems, it still has limitations that suggest promising directions for future research. Though improved by our proposed components, the accuracy of 2D-supervised methods remains lower than that of methods relying on 3D occupancy annotations. While avoiding the need for 3D ground truth is a significant advantage, further exploration of how large-scale unannotated data, such as aggregating datasets from different domains, could further improve accuracy is worth investigating.

References

1. Bachmann, R., Mizrahi, D., Atanov, A., Zamir, A.: MultiMAE: multi-modal multi-task masked autoencoders. In: Avidan, S., Brostow, G., Cissé, M., Farinella, G.M., Hassner, T. (eds.) Computer Vision – ECCV 2022. ECCV 2022. LNCS, vol. 13697, pp. 348–367. Springer, Cham (2022). https://doi.org/10.1007/978-3-031-19836-6_20
2. Bhattacharjee, D., Zhang, T., Süsstrunk, S., Salzmann, M.: Mult: an end-to-end multitask learning transformer. In: Proceedings of the IEEE/CVF Conference on Computer Vision and Pattern Recognition, pp. 12031–12041 (2022)
3. Boeder, S., Gigengack, F., Risse, B.: Gaussianflowocc: sparse and weakly supervised occupancy estimation using gaussian splatting and temporal flow. arXiv preprint arXiv:2502.17288 (2025)
4. Caesar, H., et al.: nuScenes: a multimodal dataset for autonomous driving. In: CVPR (2020)
5. Cao, A.Q., Dai, A., de Charette, R.: Pasco: urban 3d panoptic scene completion with uncertainty awareness. In: Proceedings of the IEEE/CVF Conference on Computer Vision and Pattern Recognition, pp. 14554–14564 (2024)
6. Cao, A.Q., De Charette, R.: Monoscene: monocular 3d semantic scene completion. In: Proceedings of the IEEE/CVF Conference on Computer Vision and Pattern Recognition, pp. 3991–4001 (2022)
7. Chambon, L., Zablocki, E., Boulch, A., Chen, M., Cord, M.: Gaussrender: learning 3d occupancy with gaussian rendering. arXiv preprint arXiv:2502.05040 (2025)
8. Cheng, B., et al.: Panoptic-deeplab: a simple, strong, and fast baseline for bottom-up panoptic segmentation. In: Proceedings of the IEEE/CVF Conference on Computer Vision and Pattern Recognition, pp. 12475–12485 (2020)
9. Cheng, R., Agia, C., Ren, Y., Li, X., Bingbing, L.: S3cnet: a sparse semantic scene completion network for lidar point clouds. In: Conference on Robot Learning, pp. 2148–2161. PMLR (2021)
10. Chou, Z.T., Huang, S.Y., Liu, I., Wang, Y.C.F., et al.: Gsnerf: generalizable semantic neural radiance fields with enhanced 3d scene understanding. In: Proceedings of the IEEE/CVF Conference on Computer Vision and Pattern Recognition, pp. 20806–20815 (2024)

11. Cordts, M., et al.: The cityscapes dataset for semantic urban scene understanding. In: Proceedings of the IEEE Conference on Computer Vision and Pattern Recognition, pp. 3213–3223 (2016)

12. Eigen, D., Puhrsch, C., Fergus, R.: Depth map prediction from a single image using a multi-scale deep network. Adv. Neural Inf. Process. Syst. **27** (2014)

13. Feng, Z., Yang, L., Jing, L., Wang, H., Tian, Y., Li, B.: Disentangling object motion and occlusion for unsupervised multi-frame monocular depth. In: Avidan, S., Brostow, G., Cissé, M., Farinella, G.M., Hassner, T. (eds.) Computer Vision – ECCV 2022. ECCV 2022. LNCS, vol. 13692, pp. 228–244. Springer, Cham (2022). https://doi.org/10.1007/978-3-031-19824-3_14

14. Fifty, C., Amid, E., Zhao, Z., Yu, T., Anil, R., Finn, C.: Efficiently identifying task groupings for multi-task learning. Adv. Neural Inf. Process. Syst. **34**, 27503–27516 (2021)

15. Fu, X., et al.: Panoptic nerf: 3d-to-2d label transfer for panoptic urban scene segmentation. In: 2022 International Conference on 3D Vision (3DV), pp. 1–11. IEEE (2022)

16. Gan, W., Liu, F., Xu, H., Mo, N., Yokoya, N.: Gaussianocc: fully self-supervised and efficient 3d occupancy estimation with gaussian splatting. arXiv preprint arXiv:2408.11447 (2024)

17. Godard, C., Mac Aodha, O., Firman, M., Brostow, G.J.: Digging into self-supervised monocular depth estimation. In: Proceedings of the IEEE/CVF International Conference on Computer Vision, pp. 3828–3838 (2019)

18. Hayler, A., Wimbauer, F., Muhle, D., Rupprecht, C., Cremers, D.: S4c: self-supervised semantic scene completion with neural fields. In: International Conference on 3D Vision (3DV) (2024)

19. He, K., Zhang, X., Ren, S., Sun, J.: Deep residual learning for image recognition. In: Proceedings of the IEEE Conference on Computer Vision and Pattern Recognition, pp. 770–778 (2016)

20. Huang, Y., Thammatadatrakoon, A., Zheng, W., Zhang, Y., Du, D., Lu, J.: Probabilistic gaussian superposition for efficient 3d occupancy prediction. arXiv preprint arXiv:2412.04384 (2024)

21. Huang, Y., Zheng, W., Zhang, B., Zhou, J., Lu, J.: Selfocc: self-supervised vision-based 3D occupancy prediction. In: Proceedings of the IEEE/CVF Conference on Computer Vision and Pattern Recognition, pp. 19946–19956 (2024)

22. Huang, Y., Zheng, W., Zhang, Y., Zhou, J., Lu, J.: Tri-perspective view for vision-based 3D semantic occupancy prediction. In: Proceedings of the IEEE/CVF Conference on Computer Vision and Pattern Recognition, pp. 9223–9232 (2023)

23. Huang, Y., Zheng, W., Zhang, Y., Zhou, J., Lu, J.: GaussianFormer: scene as gaussians for vision-based 3D semantic occupancy prediction. In: Leonardis, A., Ricci, E., Roth, S., Russakovsky, O., Sattler, T., Varol, G. (eds.) Computer Vision – ECCV 2024. ECCV 2024. LNCS, vol. 15085, pp. 376–393. Springer, Cham (2025). https://doi.org/10.1007/978-3-031-73383-3_22

24. Kerbl, B., Kopanas, G., Leimkühler, T., Drettakis, G.: 3D gaussian splatting for real-time radiance field rendering. ACM Trans. Graph. **42**(4), 139–1 (2023)

25. Kerr, J., Kim, C.M., Goldberg, K., Kanazawa, A., Tancik, M.: Lerf: language embedded radiance fields. In: Proceedings of the IEEE/CVF International Conference on Computer Vision, pp. 19729–19739 (2023)

26. Kingma, D.P., Ba, J.: Adam: a method for stochastic optimization. In: 3rd International Conference on Learning Representations (ICLR) (2015). https://arxiv.org/abs/1412.6980

27. Kirillov, A., et al.: Segment anything. In: Proceedings of the IEEE/CVF International Conference on Computer Vision, pp. 4015–4026 (2023)
28. Kundu, A., et al.: Panoptic neural fields: a semantic object-aware neural scene representation. In: Proceedings of the IEEE/CVF Conference on Computer Vision and Pattern Recognition, pp. 12871–12881 (2022)
29. Li, J., Han, K., Wang, P., Liu, Y., Yuan, X.: Anisotropic convolutional networks for 3d semantic scene completion. In: Proceedings of the IEEE/CVF Conference on Computer Vision and Pattern Recognition, pp. 3351–3359 (2020)
30. Li, J., et al.: Rgbd based dimensional decomposition residual network for 3D semantic scene completion. In: Proceedings of the IEEE/CVF Conference on Computer Vision and Pattern Recognition, pp. 7693–7702 (2019)
31. Li, J., Liu, Y., Yuan, X., Zhao, C., Siegwart, R., Reid, I., Cadena, C.: Depth based semantic scene completion with position importance aware loss. IEEE Robot. Autom. Lett. 5(1), 219–226 (2019)
32. Li, R., Fischer, T., Segu, M., Pollefeys, M., Van Gool, L., Tombari, F.: Know your neighbors: improving single-view reconstruction via spatial vision-language reasoning. In: Proceedings of the IEEE/CVF Conference on Computer Vision and Pattern Recognition, pp. 9848–9858 (2024)
33. Li, Y., et al.: Sscbench: a large-scale 3d semantic scene completion benchmark for autonomous driving. In: 2024 IEEE/RSJ International Conference on Intelligent Robots and Systems (IROS), pp. 13333–13340. IEEE (2024)
34. Li, Y., et al.: Voxformer: sparse voxel transformer for camera-based 3D semantic scene completion. In: Proceedings of the IEEE/CVF Conference on Computer Vision and Pattern Recognition, pp. 9087–9098 (2023)
35. Li, Z., et al.: BEVFormer: learning bird's-eye-view representation from multi-camera images via spatiotemporal transformers. In: Avidan, S., Brostow, G., Cissé, M., Farinella, G.M., Hassner, T. (eds.) Computer Vision – ECCV 2022. ECCV 2022. LNCS, vol. 13669, pp. 1–18. Springer, Cham (2022). https://doi.org/10.1007/978-3-031-20077-9_1
36. Li, Z., Yu, Z., Wang, W., Anandkumar, A., Lu, T., Alvarez, J.M.: Fb-bev: bev representation from forward-backward view transformations. In: Proceedings of the IEEE/CVF International Conference on Computer Vision, pp. 6919–6928 (2023)
37. Liao, Y., Xie, J., Geiger, A.: KITTI-360: a novel dataset and benchmarks for urban scene understanding in 2d and 3d. Pattern Anal. Mach. Intell. (PAMI) (2022)
38. Liu, B., Liu, X., Jin, X., Stone, P., Liu, Q.: Conflict-averse gradient descent for multi-task learning. Adv. Neural Inf. Process. Syst. 34, 18878–18890 (2021)
39. Liu, S., et al.: See and think: disentangling semantic scene completion. Adv. Neural Inf. Process. Syst. 31 (2018)
40. Lopes, I., Vu, T.H., de Charette, R.: Cross-task attention mechanism for dense multi-task learning. In: Proceedings of the IEEE/CVF Winter Conference on Applications of Computer Vision, pp. 2329–2338 (2023)
41. Mildenhall, B., Srinivasan, P.P., Tancik, M., Barron, J.T., Ramamoorthi, R., Ng, R.: Nerf: representing scenes as neural radiance fields for view synthesis. Commun. ACM 65(1), 99–106 (2021)
42. Mobileye: Mobileye ces 2020 presentation (2020). https://youtu.be/HPWGFzqd7pI. Accessed 06 Mar 2025
43. Oquab, M., et al.: DINOv2: learning robust visual features without supervision. In: Proceedings of the International Conference on Learning Representations (ICLR) (2025). https://arxiv.org/abs/2304.07193

44. Pan, M., et al.: Renderocc: vision-centric 3d occupancy prediction with 2d rendering supervision. In: 2024 IEEE International Conference on Robotics and Automation (ICRA), pp. 12404–12411. IEEE (2024)
45. Peng, S., Genova, K., Jiang, C., Tagliasacchi, A., Pollefeys, M., Funkhouser, T., et al.: Openscene: 3d scene understanding with open vocabularies. In: Proceedings of the IEEE/CVF Conference on Computer Vision and Pattern Recognition, pp. 815–824 (2023)
46. Prinzler, M., Hilliges, O., Thies, J.: Diner: depth-aware image-based neural radiance fields. In: Proceedings of the IEEE/CVF Conference on Computer Vision and Pattern Recognition, pp. 12449–12459 (2023)
47. Radford, A., et al.: Learning transferable visual models from natural language supervision. In: International Conference on Machine Learning, pp. 8748–8763. PMLR (2021)
48. Rist, C.B., Emmerichs, D., Enzweiler, M., Gavrila, D.M.: Semantic scene completion using local deep implicit functions on lidar data. IEEE Trans. Pattern Anal. Mach. Intell. **44**(10), 7205–7218 (2021)
49. Roldao, L., de Charette, R., Verroust-Blondet, A.: LMSCNet: lightweight multiscale 3D semantic completion. In: 2020 International Conference on 3D Vision (3DV), pp. 111–119. IEEE (2020)
50. Roldao, L., De Charette, R., Verroust-Blondet, A.: 3D semantic scene completion: a survey. Int. J. Comput. Vis. **130**(8), 1978–2005 (2022)
51. Ronneberger, O., Fischer, P., Brox, T.: U-Net: convolutional networks for biomedical image segmentation. In: Navab, N., Hornegger, J., Wells, W., Frangi, A. (eds.) Medical Image Computing and Computer-Assisted Intervention – MICCAI 2015. MICCAI 2015. LNCS, vol. 9351, pp. 234–241. Springer, Cham (2015). https://doi.org/10.1007/978-3-319-24574-4_28
52. Shen, Z., Zhang, M., Zhao, H., Yi, S., Li, H.: Efficient attention: attention with linear complexities. In: Proceedings of the IEEE/CVF Winter Conference on Applications of Computer Vision, pp. 3531–3539 (2021)
53. Song, S., Yu, F., Zeng, A., Chang, A.X., Savva, M., Funkhouser, T.: Semantic scene completion from a single depth image. In: Proceedings of the IEEE Conference on Computer Vision and Pattern Recognition, pp. 1746–1754 (2017)
54. Tesla: Tesla ai day 2021 (2021). https://www.youtube.com/watch?v=j0z4FweCy4M. Accessed 6 Mar 2025
55. Tong, W., et al.: Scene as occupancy. In: Proceedings of the IEEE/CVF International Conference on Computer Vision, pp. 8406–8415 (2023)
56. Vandenhende, S., Georgoulis, S., Van Gool, L.: MTI-Net: multi-scale task interaction networks for multi-task learning. In: Vedaldi, A., Bischof, H., Brox, T., Frahm, J.-M. (eds.) ECCV 2020. LNCS, vol. 12349, pp. 527–543. Springer, Cham (2020). https://doi.org/10.1007/978-3-030-58548-8_31
57. Wang, X., et al.: Openoccupancy: a large scale benchmark for surrounding semantic occupancy perception. In: Proceedings of the IEEE/CVF International Conference on Computer Vision, pp. 17850–17859 (2023)
58. Wang, Z., Bovik, A.C., Sheikh, H.R., Simoncelli, E.P.: Image quality assessment: from error visibility to structural similarity. IEEE Trans. Image Process. **13**(4), 600–612 (2004)
59. Wei, Y., Zhao, L., Zheng, W., Zhu, Z., Zhou, J., Lu, J.: Surroundocc: multi-camera 3d occupancy prediction for autonomous driving. In: Proceedings of the IEEE/CVF International Conference on Computer Vision, pp. 21729–21740 (2023)

60. Wimbauer, F., Yang, N., Rupprecht, C., Cremers, D.: Behind the scenes: density fields for single view reconstruction. In: Proceedings of the IEEE/CVF Conference on Computer Vision and Pattern Recognition, pp. 9076–9086 (2023)
61. Wu, S.C., Tateno, K., Navab, N., Tombari, F.: Scfusion: real-time incremental scene reconstruction with semantic completion. In: 2020 International Conference on 3D Vision (3DV), pp. 801–810. IEEE (2020)
62. Wu, Y., Lee, J.Y., Zou, C., Wang, S., Hoiem, D.: Monopatchnerf: improving neural radiance fields with patch-based monocular guidance. arXiv preprint arXiv:2404.08252 (2024)
63. Xu, D., Ouyang, W., Wang, X., Sebe, N.: Pad-net: multi-tasks guided prediction-and-distillation network for simultaneous depth estimation and scene parsing. In: Proceedings of the IEEE Conference on Computer Vision and Pattern Recognition, pp. 675–684 (2018)
64. Xu, X., Zhao, H., Vineet, V., Lim, S.N., Torralba, A.: Mtformer: multi-task learning via transformer and cross-task reasoning. In: Avidan, S., Brostow, G., Cissé, M., Farinella, G.M., Hassner, T. (eds.) Computer Vision – ECCV 2022. ECCV 2022. LNCS, vol. 13687, pp. 304–321. Springer, Cham (2022). https://doi.org/10.1007/978-3-031-19812-0_18
65. Yan, X., et al.: Sparse single sweep lidar point cloud segmentation via learning contextual shape priors from scene completion. In: Proceedings of the AAAI Conference on Artificial Intelligence, vol. 35, pp. 3101–3109 (2021)
66. Yang, H., et al.: Contranerf: generalizable neural radiance fields for synthetic-to-real novel view synthesis via contrastive learning. In: Proceedings of the IEEE/CVF Conference on Computer Vision and Pattern Recognition, pp. 16508–16517 (2023)
67. Yang, L., Kang, B., Huang, Z., Xu, X., Feng, J., Zhao, H.: Depth anything: unleashing the power of large-scale unlabeled data. In: Proceedings of the IEEE/CVF Conference on Computer Vision and Pattern Recognition (2024)
68. Yang, L., et al.: Depth anything v2. arXiv preprint arXiv:2406.09414 (2024)
69. Yao, J., et al.: Ndc-scene: boost monocular 3d semantic scene completion in normalized device coordinates space. In: Proceedings of IEEE/CVF International Conference on Computer Vision (ICCV), pp. 9421–9431. IEEE Computer Society (2023)
70. Yu, A., Ye, V., Tancik, M., Kanazawa, A.: pixelNeRF: neural radiance fields from one or few images. In: Proceedings of the IEEE/CVF Conference on Computer Vision and Pattern Recognition, pp. 4578–4587 (2021)
71. Yu, Z., Peng, S., Niemeyer, M., Sattler, T., Geiger, A.: Monosdf: exploring monocular geometric cues for neural implicit surface reconstruction. Adv. Neural Inf. Process. Syst. 35, 25018–25032 (2022)
72. Zhang, C., et al.: Occnerf: self-supervised multi-camera occupancy prediction with neural radiance fields. arXiv preprint arXiv:2312.09243 (2023)
73. Zhang, J., Dong, R., Ma, K.: Clip-fo3d: learning free open-world 3D scene representations from 2d dense clip. In: Proceedings of the IEEE/CVF International Conference on Computer Vision, pp. 2048–2059 (2023)
74. Zhang, Y., Zhu, Z., Du, D.: Occformer: dual-path transformer for vision-based 3d semantic occupancy prediction. In: Proceedings of the IEEE/CVF International Conference on Computer Vision, pp. 9433–9443 (2023)
75. Zhi, S., Laidlow, T., Leutenegger, S., Davison, A.J.: In-place scene labelling and understanding with implicit scene representation. In: Proceedings of the IEEE/CVF International Conference on Computer Vision, pp. 15838–15847 (2021)
76. Zhou, X., Wang, J., Wang, Y., Wei, Y., Dong, N., Yang, M.H.: Occgs: zero-shot 3d occupancy reconstruction with semantic and geometric-aware gaussian splatting. arXiv preprint arXiv:2502.04981 (2025)

Hierarchical Insights: Exploiting Structural Similarities for Reliable 3D Semantic Segmentation

Mariella Dreissig[1]([✉]) [ID], Simon Ruehle[2] [ID], Florian Piewak[2] [ID], and Joschka Boedecker[1] [ID]

[1] University of Freiburg, Neurorobotics Lab, Freiburg, Germany
`mariella.dreissig@email.uni-freiburg.de,`
`jboedeck@informatik.uni-freiburg.de`
[2] Mercedes-Benz AG, Research & Development, Sindelfingen, Germany
`{simon.ruehle,florian.piewak}@mercedes-benz.com`

Abstract. Safety-critical applications such as autonomous driving require robust 3D environment perception algorithms capable of handling diverse and ambiguous surroundings. The predictive performance of classification models is heavily influenced by the dataset and the prior knowledge provided by the annotated labels. While labels guide the learning process, they often fail to capture the inherent relationships between classes that are naturally understood by humans. We propose a training strategy for a 3D LiDAR semantic segmentation model that learns structural relationships between classes through abstraction. This is achieved by implicitly modeling these relationships using a learning rule for hierarchical multi-label classification (HMC). Our detailed analysis demonstrates that this training strategy not only improves the model's confidence calibration but also retains additional information useful for downstream tasks such as fusion, prediction, and planning.

Keywords: 3D Environment Perception · Robustness · Autonomous Driving

1 Introduction

Accurate 3D semantic segmentation is crucial for autonomous vehicles to achieve comprehensive scene understanding, supporting tasks like sensor fusion and prediction for detailed environmental modeling. However, these algorithms face challenges in ambiguous environments and noise. Recognizing and adapting to these

Part of this publication was compiled as part of the research project "KI Delta Learning" (project number: 19A19013A) funded by the Federal Ministry for Economic Affairs and Energy (BMWi) based on a resolution of the German Bundestag.

Supplementary Information The online version contains supplementary material available at https://doi.org/10.1007/978-3-032-12840-9_31.

limitations is essential. Low-confidence classifications, though potentially informative, may be disregarded during sensor fusion, resulting in critical data loss for subsequent tasks. This information is vital for planning algorithms to accurately identify and assess planning-relevant instances, such as vulnerable road users (VRUs). Failure to recognize VRUs as dynamic objects can lead to hazardous situations, particularly concerning VRU protection [33].

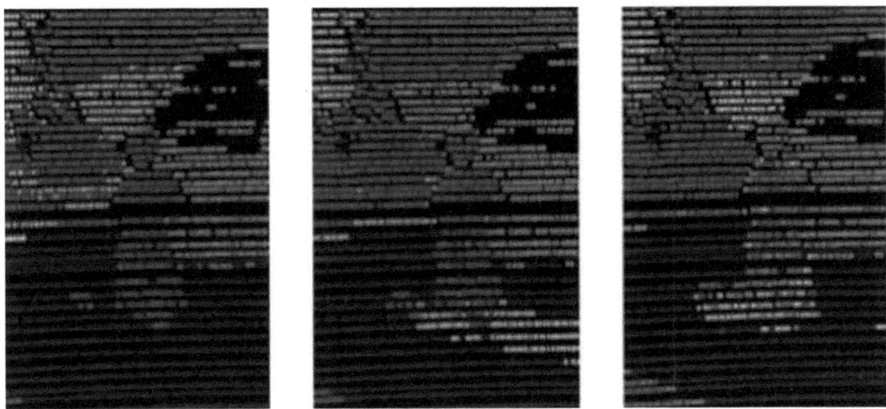

sidewalk, vegetation, terrain, car, building,
bicycle, person, trunk, road, dynamic, static, any

Fig. 1. The point cloud visualization of a nearby kid with a scooter (left: ground truth) from the SemanticKITTI [2] dataset shows a stark difference between the models. A hierarchy-agnostic model (mid) misclassifies it as *vegetation*, whereas our hierarchy-aware model (right) correctly identifies it as *dynamic*.

In this study, we propose a method to provide confident and well-calibrated estimates of instance types at a point-wise level for downstream tasks. We emphasize the importance of high-confidence, detail-agnostic information – such as identifying static or dynamic objects, VRUs, traffic signs, and drivable spaces. To achieve this, we employ a hierarchical multi-label classification (HMC) training strategy for 3D semantic segmentation models, considering structural similarities between semantically related classes. This approach explicitly models relationships to inform the model about alternative class representations and abstractions, as depicted in Fig. 1. Providing high-level information, including abstract attributes like *dynamic*, mitigates the risk of overlooking critical factors in tasks such as vehicle trajectory planning.

We propose a learning rule enabling classification models to provide detailed classifications in clear situations while predicting superclasses in ambiguous circumstances. This approach enhances overall predictive confidence and preserves critical information for downstream tasks. Additionally, we introduce a method to extract implicit model uncertainties from hierarchical classifications. Our analysis quantitatively and qualitatively explores how semantic label definitions and inter-class structural relationships impact model training. We evaluate the model's confidence calibration and abstraction capabilities under a domain shift. Our goal is to optimize the balance between detail level and predictive confidence to maximize information utility in autonomous driving applications. Our contributions can be summarized as follows:

- Introduction a novel approach tailored for 3D semantic segmentation models, enhancing their ability to capture hierarchical relationships between classes.
- Proposal of a technique to derive reliable confidence scores from hierarchical classifications, improving the model's certainty in complex environments.
- Presentation of an evaluation metric to measure the HMC model's ability to generalize across semantic relationships.

2   Related Literature

Extensive research efforts have focused on advancing semantic segmentation algorithms for point clouds, categorized by their underlying data representation. These methods include projection-based approaches, such as range view [4,21] and bird's eye view [38]; point-based methods, such as unordered point clouds [26] and point pillars [6]; and voxel-based methods, including volumetric 3D convolutions [40] and sparse convolutions [30,36].

Semantic segmentation poses a unique challenge due to class imbalances. The widely used mean Intersection over Union (IoU) metric addresses this by ensuring equitable consideration of underrepresented classes. To mitigate imbalance in model classifications, common approaches include loss weighting to favor underrepresented classes [21,23] or designing architectures capable of handling challenges posed by smaller instances [3,24,36]. However, these methods typically do not exploit structural similarities between classes to effectively alleviate class imbalance inherent in semantic segmentation tasks.

Moreover, in the context of autonomous driving, not all class confusions hold equal significance. The authors of [20] and [39] delve into assessing the severity of class confusions in semantic segmentation. They respectively propose a method and a metric that evaluate the criticality of these confusions.

2.1   Uncertainty Estimation in Classification Tasks

Recent advancements in uncertainty estimation have distinguished between two types: epistemic (model) uncertainty and aleatoric (data) uncertainty [1,12]. Aleatoric uncertainty arises from data variability and can be learned during training, as demonstrated by methods like sampling from logits before applying softmax [15]. Addressing epistemic uncertainty remains challenging, with Monte-Carlo Dropout (MCD, [7]) and deep ensembles (DE, [17]) being established approaches.

These techniques, though computationally intensive, improve softmax calibration by approximating posterior distributions across classes [10]. Recent research has focused on deterministic methods for estimating epistemic uncertainty [22,25]. Unlike sampling-based methods, deterministic approaches avoid additional computational complexity but are constrained by the model's inherent limitations. However, these insights are often underutilized, contributing to the information loss highlighted in Sect. 1.

2.2 Hierarchical Multi-label Classification

Hierarchical multi-label classification (HMC), in contrast to hierarchy-agnostic approaches, leverages structural relationships between class labels to enhance the performance and robustness of classification models [3,18,37]. Instead of treating class labels as independent entities, HMC arranges them in a hierarchical tree structure. This approach allows data points to potentially belong to multiple classes simultaneously. This has been applied in biomedical applications and image and text classification [8,27,32,35].

Some studies leverage the structural relationships between classes during training, focusing exclusively on leaf classes [19,31]. Others, such as [9] and [14], harness the hierarchical semantic relationships to address complex tasks like novelty detection and unsupervised semantic segmentation. While these methods utilize learned relational connections to enhance classification performance, they often do not fully exploit these relationships for abstract class classification in uncertain scenarios. We aim to achieve that with our proposed hierarchical multi-label classification (HMC) approach.

3 Methods

The following section outlines our proposed modifications designed to transform any architecture from a hierarchy-agnostic model to a hierarchy-aware model.

3.1 Data and Label Hierarchy

The label hierarchy serves to group semantically similar classes together. Our proposed label hierarchy for the SemanticKITTI dataset is illustrated in Fig. 2. Each original label is associated with multiple superclasses $\mathcal{S}$ on a level l. The dataset's original ground truth labels y_s represent the leaf nodes ($l = 0$). Superclasses are structured as follows: the second level aligns with SemanticKITTI's suggestion ($l = 1$), and the third level introduces binary classes, namely *static* and *dynamic* ($l = 2$). The root node encompasses only the *any* class ($l = 3$). Therefore, the height of this label hierarchy tree is $h = 4$.

The ground truth η_c for HMC training is derived from this hierarchy. We define it such that more than one label can be correct, but never more than one per hierarchy level l. Therefore, the HMC learning rule incorporates multiple correct labels that are learned jointly. The entirety of all classes is denoted as λ, and λ_l represents the set of classes at hierarchy level l. To prevent the model from exclusively predicting the *any* class, we assign weights to the superclasses

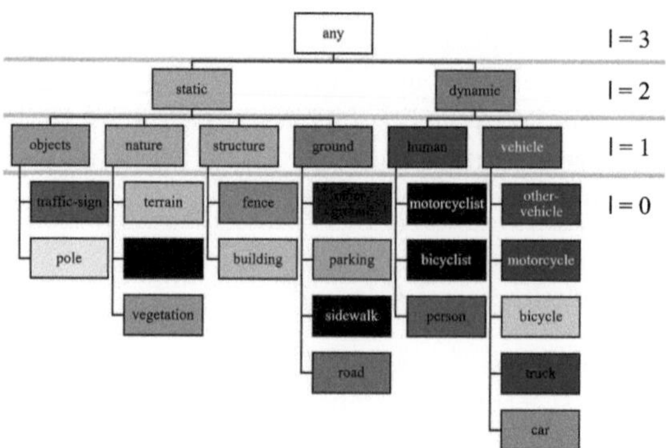

Fig. 2. Label hierarchy for the SemanticKITTI dataset: the original labels are leaf nodes, meta and binary classes are added accordingly. The colors denote the label colors as used in the dataset (except for the *bicyclist* class, whose color is adjusted for improved visibility).

$\mathcal{S}(y_s)$ of each labeled class y_s based on its hierarchy level l. Specifically, labels in the leaf nodes λ_0 are assigned the highest weights, while superclasses λ_1 receive lower weights, and so forth. We propose the following formula to weight the new ground truth:

$$\eta_c = \begin{cases} \frac{1+l(c)}{h}, & \text{if } c \in y_s \cup \mathcal{S}(y_s) \\ 0, & \text{otherwise} \end{cases} \tag{1}$$

The altered ground truth η_c is computed from the original subclass y_s and its superclasses $\mathcal{S}(y_s)$. For all other classes it is assigned 0. According to this ground truth definition, multiple labels assigned to a single measurement trace a path through the hierarchy, reflecting their structural similarity. This implicit relationship modeling enables the model to leverage these relationships for enhanced leaf-node classification as well as meaningful superclass classifications.

3.2   Hierarchical Multi-label Classification

The HMC loss function incorporates the weighted label encoding as presented in Eq. 1. We propose a learning rule that integrates the label hierarchy into the model training process:

$$\mathcal{L}_{HCE} = -\sum_{c \in \lambda} e^{\eta_c} \log \hat{y}_c \tag{2}$$

with c being a given class in λ, and η_c and $\hat{y}_c$ being the hierarchically altered ground truth and the model classifications for that class, respectively.

To benchmark our proposed model against hierarchy-agnostic models, we applied a heuristic hierarchy construction to baseline models using their confidence outputs. Predictions ascend to a higher hierarchy level when accompanied by low confidence. Thresholds are evenly distributed across the hierarchy, defined as $\delta = \frac{l}{h}$: predictions remain at level 0 above 0.75, move to level 2 at 0.5, level 1 at 0.25, and below 0.25 ascend to level 3. This equidistant spacing considers the model's calibration, ensuring that better-calibrated models reflect a consistent confidence structure.

3.3 Hierarchical Classification and Confidence Estimation

Our objective with the proposed HMC training strategy is twofold: **(a)** Enhance classification quality by leveraging the hierarchical structure, where the model yields high confidences corresponding to the level of detail achievable based on the data. For that, high-level classification information is provided and can be confidently utilized by downstream tasks. **(b)** Capture uncertainty through the hierarchical predictions, enabling the model to express confidences specifically for classifications at the finest detail level (leaf classes). Here, the model delivers well-calibrated results specifically at the finest detail level (leaf classes), which is advantageous when superclass classifications are undesired. We propose reporting distinct confidence measures based on the HMC classifications to address this dual objective.

To achieve the first objective, we employ the softmax function over the entire hierarchy λ. This function transforms the model's output logits into class-specific probabilities:

$$p_\sigma = \frac{e^x}{\sum_{c=1}^{\lambda} e^c} \tag{3}$$

with x representing the logit vector, and c denoting all classes in the hierarchy λ, we utilize the softmax function. We calculate $\arg\max(p_\sigma(\lambda))$ to ensure consistent high-confidence classifications across all levels of the label hierarchy.

To capture model uncertainty based on the classification level in the hierarchy, we compute entropy over the softmax probabilities of the original leaf classes, denoted as $p^l = p_\sigma \in p_\sigma(\lambda_0)$. When the model predicts a leaf class in straightforward scenarios, $\arg\max(p_\sigma(\lambda))$ corresponds to the lowest hierarchy level. In uncertain situations, where the model predicts a superclass, softmax values are more evenly distributed among the leaf classes of the predicted superclasses, resulting in higher entropy among the leaf nodes. Thus, predictive uncertainty is quantified by the entropy of these leaf classes:

$$p_\mathcal{H} = -p^l \cdot \log(p^l) \tag{4}$$

Since entropy $\mathcal{H}$ is not a probabilistic measure, we normalize it using the theoretical maximum entropy value $\log(n)$ with n being the number of classes.

The relationship between these measures is demonstrated in Fig. 3, depicting the label hierarchy from Fig. 2. Classes are color-coded based on their average predictive probabilities using p_σ. Instances where the model confidently predicts leaf classes yield low uncertainty (e.g., $\mathcal{H} \sim 0.3$ for *motorcyclist*), whereas high uncertainty (e.g., $\mathcal{H} \sim 1.0$ for *any*) arises when softmax probabilities are evenly distributed across leaf classes due to superclass predictions.

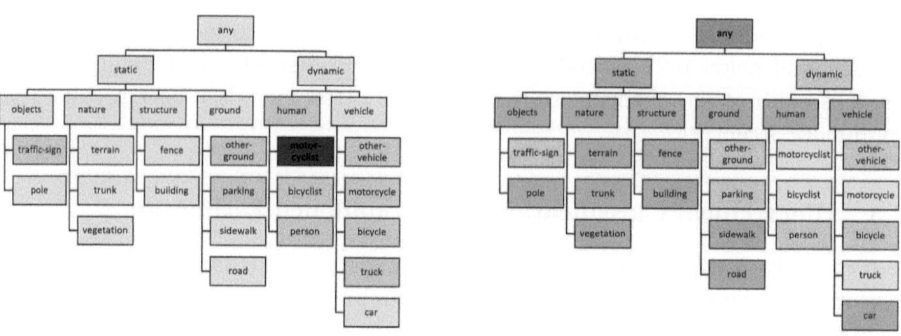

(a) Averaged softmax probabilities for the class *motorcyclist*.

(b) Averaged softmax probabilities for the class *any*.

predictive probabilities:

0.0   1.0

Fig. 3. Softmax probabilities $\sigma(\lambda)$ for classifications of classes *motorcyclist* (3a) and *any* (3b). The colorscale is given below.

3.4   Calibration Metrics for Semantic Segmentation

Since the HMC model can predict abstract superclasses, evaluation metrics for semantic segmentation models need adjustment to ensure fair comparison with hierarchy-agnostic baseline models. The commonly used mIoU metric evaluates True Positives (TP), False Positives (FP), and False Negatives (FN). The Critical Error Rate (CER, [39]) metric evaluates misclassifications within specific class categories. It identifies critical errors by assessing FP and FN within expected categories. To comprehensively evaluate hierarchical classification, we propose the hierarchical IoU (hIoU). During training, superclass classifications are treated as partially correct (cf. Eq. 2). For evaluation, we extend the regular class-wise IoU by incorporating superclass predictions in a similar manner. By default, superclass predictions are considered incorrect, as they are not included in the actual ground truth. We introduce a modulation factor $\alpha \in [0.0..1.0]$ to adjust the weight of correct superclass classifications in the final metric value, referred to as partial True Positives (pTP). Thus, at $\alpha = 0.0$, all superclass predictions are deemed incorrect, while at $alpha = 1.0$, superclasses are considered as correct as the original leaf classes. The $hIoU_s$ for subclass $s \in \lambda_0$ is defined as:

$$hIoU_s = \frac{TP_s + pTP_s}{TP_s + FP_s + FN_s} = \frac{TP_s + \sum_{l=1}^{h-1} \alpha^l \cdot TS_s(l)}{TP_s + FP_s + FN_s} \tag{5}$$

where $TS(l)$ denotes the True Superclasses at each level $\lambda_{1..3}$. All superclass predictions FS, whether true or false, are included in FNs. The overall hIoU is the mean over all original leaf classes: $hIoU = \frac{1}{\lambda_0} \sum_0^{\lambda_0} hIoU_s$.

4   Experimental Results

In the following section, we present experimental results demonstrating the HMC model's proficiency in learning class abstractions and conveying uncertainty through superclass classifications. For all models, including the HMC, we evaluate $\arg\max(p_\sigma)$ for classification and p_H for confidence performances.

Metrics. In addition to quantitative analyses using metrics detailed in Sect. 3.4 (mIoU, hIoU, and CER), we evaluate the model's calibration. Calibration metrics, such as Expected Calibration Error (ECE [10]), Area Under the Sparsification Error Curve (AUSE [13]), and uncertainty-aware mIoU (uIoU [28]), assess the alignment between predicted confidences and actual performance. ECE quantifies accuracy through binning, while AUSE progressively filters low-confidence predictions to evaluate model performance on more confident outputs, adaptable to metrics like Brier Score [11] or semantic segmentation mIoU [5]. uIoU extends mIoU by considering invalid masks, distinguishing True Invalids (TI) and False Invalids (FI) based on a confidence threshold θ, with the final uIoU computed by averaging over thresholds $\theta \in [0.0, 1.0]$.

Training Details. All trainings were conducted on the training sequences of SemanticKITTI dataset [2] on the voxelized point clouds. All models are trained for maximum $e = 100$ epochs with a batch size of $bs = 8$. The early stopping condition is set to a $\delta = 0.001$ on the validation mIoU for 10 epochs. As optimizer we chose Adam [16] with an initial learning rate of 10^{-4} and a cosine scheduler.

Baseline Models. To benchmark our proposed model, we compared it against established uncertainty estimation methods. In addition to a plain cross-entropy loss-trained model (vanilla), we evaluated performance using sampling-based approaches with varying sample numbers to illustrate performance dependency. We selected logit sampling [15] with 10 and 15 samples (logit10, logit15) and Monte Carlo Dropout [7] with 10 and 15 samples (MCD10, MCD15). Given that sampling-based methods require more computational power and inference time, we also included a deterministic baseline, Evidential Deep Learning (EDL) [29]. Furthermore, we compared our HMC model with another hierarchy-based method (TM) [19]. The results presented here use the SPVCNN backbone [30]; additional results on other 3D semantic segmentation backbones are provided in the supplemental material.

4.1   Predictive Performance

To gain initial insights into the HMC model's performance compared to baseline models, we evaluate metrics such as mIoU, CER, and hIoU@$\alpha = 1.0$ (hIoU1.0), along with relative runtime. The results, presented in Table 1, include relative performance gains and losses of our method compared to the best-performing baseline.

The HMC model significantly outperforms all baselines, with only a 6.33% increase in runtime. Runtime is calculated as the average time for one complete

Table 1. Segmentation performance of the HMC and baseline models on the SemanticKITTI [2] validation set. The best performances are marked in bold.

method	mIoU ↑	CER ↓	hIoU1.0 ↑	runtime ↓
vanilla	55.47	18.46	58.78	+0.0%
logits10 [15]	56.32	19.14	59.60	+2.53%
logits15 [15]	55.99	18.83	59.25	+2.53%
MCD10 [7]	56.72	18.34	62.57	+68.35%
MCD15 [7]	56.11	18.25	63.32	+373.42%
EDL [29]	53.15	20.25	54.20	+8.86%
TM [19]	57.41	17.13	62.05	**+0.0%**
HMC (ours)	**58.04 (+1.10%)**	**16.62 (-3.07%)**	**68.69 (+8.91%)**	+6.33%

forward pass across the validation set, with the MCD15 model having a notably higher runtime due to increased memory demands.

The mIoU is calculated from leaf-only predictions in hierarchy-aware models $(p_\sigma(\lambda_0))$. Complementary, the model can predict superclass classifications by placing the softmax over the full tree hierarchy. An exemplary confusion matrix is given in the supplemental material. To understand the role of superclass predictions, we evaluate the hIoU metric at different α values in Table 2. Hierarchy-agnostic models are evaluated with a heuristic hierarchical rule as presented in Sect. 3.2.

Table 2. hIoU values for HMC and baseline models at different α values. The best performances per level are marked in bold.

method	hIoU@α ↑										
	0.0	0.1	0.2	0.3	0.4	0.5	0.6	0.7	0.8	0.9	1.0
vanilla	54.79	55.16	55.54	55.92	56.31	56.71	57.11	57.52	57.93	58.35	58.78
logits10 [15]	**55.59**	**55.96**	55.96	56.35	56.74	57.14	57.55	57.97	58.39	58.82	59.25
logits15 [15]	55.21	55.58	56.34	56.72	57.11	57.51	57.91	58.32	58.74	59.17	59.60
MCD10 [7]	53.93	54.71	55.50	56.32	57.15	58.00	58.88	59.77	60.68	61.62	62.57
MCD15 [7]	54.61	55.42	56.24	57.08	57.94	58.82	59.72	60.64	61.58	62.54	63.52
EDL [29]	53.36	53.44	53.52	53.61	53.69	53.77	53.86	53.94	54.03	54.11	54.20
TM [19]	55.28	55.82	**56.39**	56.99	57.63	58.29	58.98	59.70	60.45	61.24	62.05
HMC (ours)	53.43	54.64	55.89	**57.21**	**58.59**	**60.05**	**61.59**	**63.21**	**64.93**	**66.76**	**68.69**

Starting with a lower mIoU at $\alpha = 0.0$, the HMC model quickly surpasses baseline models at an α as low as 0.3. This suggests that the HMC model effectively predicts superclasses in uncertain situations. Sampling-based approaches with more samples also outperform those with fewer samples at similar levels, likely due to improved calibration leading to increased number of superclass predictions, which are considered *FP*s at lower α values. We propose that the α parameter can be tuned according to specific requirements for autonomous vehicles. For example, one requirement could be ensuring that VRUs are classified as dynamic objects in at least 90% of cases.

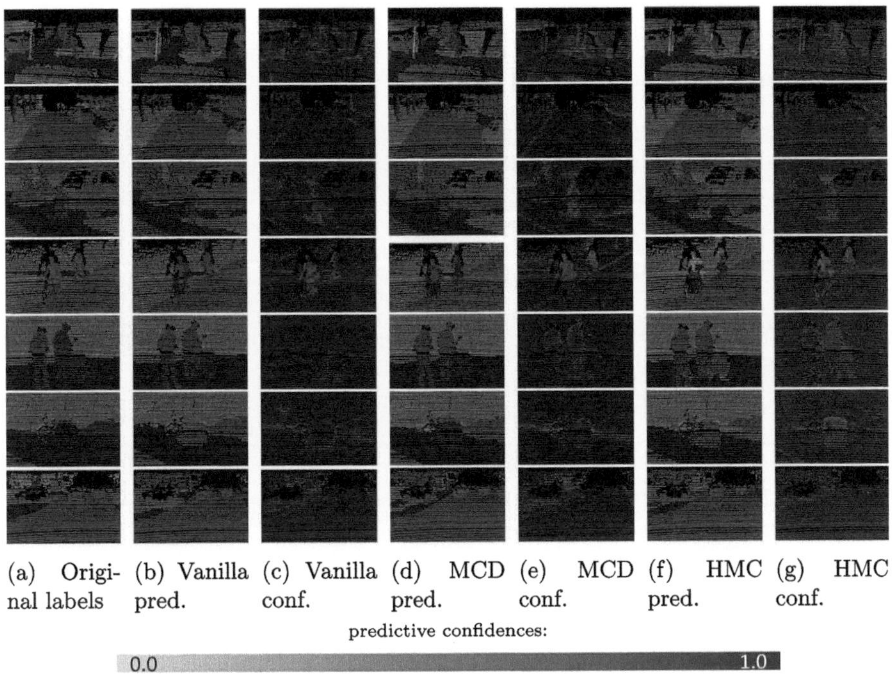

(a) Original labels (b) Vanilla pred. (c) Vanilla conf. (d) MCD pred. (e) MCD conf. (f) HMC pred. (g) HMC conf.

predictive confidences:

Fig. 4. Qualitative samples from the SemanticKITTI [2] dataset, showing the labels 4a and the predictions and confidences of the vanilla [30] (4b & 4c), MCD [7] (4d & 4e) and HMC model (4f & 4g, p_H is used as confidence measure). The semantic class colors are depicted as in 2, the confidence colorscale is given below.

As discussed in Sect. 1, reliably reporting high-level information is crucial for fusion, prediction, and planning, particularly in autonomous driving where VRU protection is paramount. VRU classes are often underrepresented and exhibit high variance in semantic segmentation training data, making them difficult to learn. To illustrate the benefits of the HMC training strategy in safety-critical scenarios, Fig. 4 presents examples featuring various VRU scenarios:

1. The HMC model accurately detects a *human* missed by baseline models.
2. Early detection of a distant bicyclist classified as *dynamic* by the HMC model, missed by baseline models.
3. Detection of a nearby child, similar to previous VRU examples.

4. Addressing challenges in classifying bicyclists, with the HMC model expressing uncertainty through superclass predictions.
5. Similar difficulty in classifying a *motorcyclist*.
6. Correct classification of a bicycle trailer (*other-vehicle*) as *dynamic* by the HMC model, with baseline models misclassifying it.
7. Baseline models struggle to classify the transition from road to parking area accurately, crucial for planning drivable space.

4.2   Calibration and Out of Distribution Robustness

To evaluate the HMC model's calibration, we use the entropy-based confidence scoring rule Eq. 4 and compare it with the entropy over the softmax for all baseline models. Calibration results are detailed in Table 3, with relative performance gains and losses of the HMC model shown as percentages compared to the best baseline model.

Table 3. Calibration performances using entropy-based calibration measures. Best performances are marked in bold.

method	ECE $\downarrow$	AUSE$_{\mathrm{BS}}$ $\downarrow$	AUSE$_{\mathrm{mIoU}}$ $\downarrow$	uIoU $\uparrow$
vanilla	17.24	1.93	12.82	84.56
logits10 [15]	18.24	2.01	12.92	84.12
logits15 [15]	16.55	2.07	13.05	84.52
MCD10 [7]	09.54	1.78	11.82	84.83
MCD15 [7]	10.68	1.85	12.58	**85.66**
EDL [29]	06.34	4.62	15.40	84.12
TM [19]	09.34	2.14	**9.33**	84.55
HMC (ours)	**05.72 (−11.01%)**	**1.60 (−11.25%)**	09.71 (+4.07%)	85.41 (−0.29%)

The results underscore the challenging nature of assessing the calibration of point-wise classification models. The metrics do not indicate a single best model, as each metric evaluates different aspects of calibration. For instance, ECE, AUSE$_{\mathrm{BS}}$, and AUSE$_{\mathrm{mIoU}}$ partially depend on binning and thresholding strategies, while uIoU is heavily influenced by base segmentation performance. Despite minor deviations, our HMC model demonstrates stable performance across all metrics and outperforms most baseline models. Interestingly, the hierarchy-aware TM model exhibits similar capabilities, likely due to its tree-structure training strategy. This approach, which considers the minimum confidence along the path from root to leaf nodes, results in better-calibrated softmax, and thus entropy, values.

To stress-test our HMC approach, we examine its generalization abilities under a domain shift. All models are trained on the SemanticKITTI dataset [2]

Table 4. Domain generalization results on the SemanticSTF [34] dataset, trained on SemanticKITTI data [2]. Best performances are marked in bold.

method	mIoU ↑	CER ↓	hIoU1.0 ↑	ECE ↓	AUSE$_{BS}$ ↓	AUSE$_{mIoU}$ ↓	uIoU ↑
vanilla	19.43	59.18	29.30	34.14	19.03	13.16	40.58
logits10 [15]	22.66	54.19	33.38	34.20	18.98	15.31	42.42
logits15 [15]	20.43	59.77	30.83	34.61	17.46	14.56	40.61
MCD10 [7]	20.46	59.05	36.67	**27.74**	14.69	15.03	40.39
MCD15 [7]	20.44	58.78	38.06	28.55	16.83	16.39	42.73
EDL [29]	17.34	58.58	19.13	45.68	21.62	15.59	36.97
TM [19]	21.49	56.76	31.47	34.81	13.50	10.84	42.88
HMC (ours)	**22.77**	**54.58**	**39.75**	36.06	**10.32**	**10.28**	**43.73**

and evaluated on the adverse weather SemanticSTF dataset [34]. Results are presented in Table 4, covering both segmentation and calibration performances.

Our HMC model demonstrates strong performance across most metrics, except for ECE. This underscores the potential of hierarchy-aware semantic classification models in open-world settings, effectively handling ambiguous and previously unseen scenes and objects. The challenging nature of the domain shift dataset, with adverse weather and unfamiliar surroundings, further emphasizes the robustness and adaptability of the HMC model.

5 Conclusion

This study employed a hierarchical multi-label classification approach for 3D semantic segmentation of LiDAR point clouds in autonomous driving. By organizing class labels hierarchically, our model learns abstract class representations using inherent structural information and defaults to superclass classifications in ambiguous scenarios. This strategy not only reduces overall uncertainty but also preserves valuable information.

Through detailed analysis we demonstrated the efficacy of our approach in identifying safety-critical classes that are challenging to learn from 3D LiDAR data representations. We argue that confidently predicting high-level details, while sacrificing some information granularity, is crucial for downstream tasks in autonomous systems such as prediction and planning. Quantitative evaluation using various performance and calibration metrics showed that our proposed HMC learning rule achieved not only improved classification performances but also surpassed the baselines in terms of calibration and robustness against out-of-distribution data, all while demanding relatively few computational resources.

Future research should explore whether imposing more structured prior knowledge derived from human scene understanding enhances model performance, or allowing the model to autonomously learn flexible structures to abstract representations. This exploration could provide valuable insights into domain generalization, as well as semi- or unsupervised 3D semantic segmentation.

References

1. Arnez, F., et al.: A comparison of uncertainty estimation approaches in deep learning components for autonomous vehicle applications. In: IJCAI - Workshop (2020)
2. Behley, J., et al.: SemanticKITTI: a dataset for semantic scene understanding of LiDAR sequences. In: IEEE ICCV (2019)
3. Chen, C., et al.: HAPGN: hierarchical attentive pooling graph network for point cloud segmentation. IEEE Trans. Multimed. (2021)
4. Cortinhal, T., Tzelepis, G.S., Aksoy, E.E.: SalsaNext: Fast Semantic Segmentation of LiDAR Point Clouds for Autonomous Driving. arXiv (2020)
5. Dreissig, M., Piewak, F., Boedecker, J.: On the calibration of uncertainty estimation in lidar-based semantic segmentation. In: IEEE ITSC (2023)
6. Fei, J., et al.: PillarSegNet: pillar-based semantic grid map estimation using sparse LiDAR data. In: IEEE IV (2021)
7. Gal, Y., Ghahramani, Z.: Dropout as a Bayesian approximation: representing model uncertainty in deep learning. In: ICML (2016)
8. Giunchiglia, E., Lukasiewicz, T.: Coherent hierarchical multi-label classification networks. In: NeurIPS (2020)
9. de Graaff, T., Ribeiro de Menezes, A.: Capsule networks for hierarchical novelty detection in object classification. In: IEEE IV (2022)
10. Guo, C., et al.: On calibration of modern neural networks. In: ICML (2017)
11. Gustafsson, F.K., Danelljan, M., Schon, T.B.: Evaluating scalable Bayesian deep learning methods for robust computer vision. In: IEEE CVPR - Workshops (2020)
12. Hüllermeier, E., Waegeman, W.: Aleatoric and epistemic uncertainty in machine learning: an introduction to concepts and methods. Springer Machine Learning (2021)
13. Ilg, E., et al.: Uncertainty estimates and multi-hypotheses networks for optical flow. In: IEEE ECCV (2018)
14. Ke, T.W., et al.: Unsupervised hierarchical semantic segmentation with multiview cosegmentation and clustering transformers. In: IEEE CVPR (2022)
15. Kendall, A., Gal, Y.: What uncertainties do we need in Bayesian deep learning for computer vision? In: NeurIPS (2017)
16. Kingma, D.P., Ba, J.: Adam: a method for stochastic optimization. CoRR (2014)
17. Lakshminarayanan, B., Pritzel, A., Blundell, C.: Simple and scalable predictive uncertainty estimation using deep ensembles. In: NeurIPS (2017)
18. Levatić, J., Kocev, D., Džeroski, S.: The importance of the label hierarchy in hierarchical multi-label classification. J. Intell. Inf. Syst. **45**(2), 247–271 (2014). https://doi.org/10.1007/s10844-014-0347-y
19. Li, L., et al.: Deep hierarchical semantic segmentation. In: IEEE CVPR (2022)
20. Liu, J., et al.: Simple and principled uncertainty estimation with deterministic deep learning via distance awareness. In: NeurIPS (2020)
21. Milioto, A., et al.: RangeNet ++: fast and accurate LiDAR semantic segmentation. In: IEEE IROS (2019)
22. Mukhoti, J., et al.: Deep deterministic uncertainty: a new simple baseline. In: IEEE CVPR (2023)

23. Paszke, A., et al.: ENet: a deep neural network architecture for real-time semantic segmentation. arXiv (2016)
24. Piewak, F., et al.: Boosting lidar-based semantic labeling by cross-modal training data generation. In: IEEE ECCV - Workshops (2018)
25. Postels, J., et al.: On the practicality of deterministic epistemic uncertainty. In: ICML (2022)
26. Qi, C.R., et al.: PointNet++: deep hierarchical feature learning on point sets in a metric space. In: NeurIPS (2017)
27. Romero, M., Finke, J., Rocha, C.: A top-down supervised learning approach to hierarchical multi-label classification in networks. Appl. Netw. Sci. (2022)
28. Sakaridis, C., Dai, D., Van Gool, L.: Map-Guided Curriculum Domain Adaptation and Uncertainty-Aware Evaluation for Semantic Nighttime Image Segmentation. PAMI (2022)
29. Sensoy, M., Kaplan, L., Kandemir, M.: Evidential deep learning to quantify classification uncertainty. In: NeurIPS (2018)
30. Tang, H., et al.: Searching efficient 3D architectures with sparse point-voxel convolution. In: IEEE ECCV (2020)
31. Vaswani, A., Aggarwal, G., Netrapalli, P., Hegde, N.: All Mistakes Are Not Equal: Comprehensive Hierarchy Aware Multi-label Predictions (CHAMP). arXiv (2022)
32. Wehrmann, J., Cerri, R., Barros, R.: Hierarchical multi-label classification networks. In: ICML (2018)
33. Wikipedia: Death of Elaine Herzberg — Wikipedia, the free encyclopedia (2023). https://en.wikipedia.org/wiki/Death_of_Elaine_Herzberg. Accessed 27 July 2023
34. Xiao, A., et al.: 3D semantic segmentation in the wild: learning generalized models for adverse-condition point clouds. In: IEEE/CVF CVPR (2023)
35. Xu, C., Geng, X.: Hierarchical classification based on label distribution learning. In: AAAI (2019)
36. Xu, J., et al.: RPVNet: a deep and efficient range-point-voxel fusion network for LiDAR point cloud segmentation. In: IEEE ICCV (2021)
37. Zhang, L., Shah, S., Kakadiaris, I.: Hierarchical multi-label classification using fully associative ensemble learning. Pattern Recognit. (2017)
38. Zhang, Y., et al.: PolarNet: an improved grid representation for online LiDAR point clouds semantic segmentation. In: IEEE CVPR (2020)
39. Zhou, J., Beyerer, J.: Category differences matter: a broad analysis of inter-category error in semantic segmentation. In: IEEE CVPR - Workshops (2023)
40. Zhu, X., et al.: Cylindrical and asymmetrical 3D convolution networks for LiDAR segmentation. In: IEEE CVPR (2021)

CoProU-VO: Combining Projected Uncertainty for End-to-End Unsupervised Monocular Visual Odometry

Jingchao Xie[1,3], Oussema Dhaouadi[1,2,3(✉)], Weirong Chen[1,3],
Johannes Meier[1,2,3], Jacques Kaiser[2], and Daniel Cremers[1,3]

[1] TU Munich, Munich, Germany
`{oussema.dhaouadi,jingchao.xie,weirong.chen,j.meier,`
`Daniel.Cremers}@tum.de`
[2] DeepScenario, Munich, Germany
`Jacques.Kaiser@deepscenario.com`
[3] Munich Center for Machine Learning, Munich, Germany
`https://www.deepscenario.com, https://mcml.ai`

Abstract. Visual Odometry (VO) is fundamental to autonomous navigation, robotics, and augmented reality, with unsupervised approaches eliminating the need for expensive ground-truth labels. However, these methods struggle when dynamic objects violate the static scene assumption, leading to erroneous pose estimations. We tackle this problem by uncertainty modeling, which is a commonly used technique that creates robust masks to filter out dynamic objects and occlusions without requiring explicit motion segmentation. Traditional uncertainty modeling considers only single-frame information, overlooking the uncertainties across consecutive frames. Our key insight is that uncertainty must be propagated and combined across temporal frames to effectively identify unreliable regions, particularly in dynamic scenes. To address this challenge, we introduce Combined Projected Uncertainty VO (CoProU-VO), a novel end-to-end approach that combines target frame uncertainty with projected reference frame uncertainty using a principled probabilistic formulation. Built upon vision transformer backbones, our model simultaneously learns depth, uncertainty estimation, and camera poses. Consequently, experiments on the KITTI and nuScenes datasets demonstrate significant improvements over previous unsupervised monocular end-to-end two-frame-based methods and exhibit strong performance in challenging highway scenes where other approaches often fail. Additionally, comprehensive ablation studies validate the effectiveness of cross-frame uncertainty propagation. The code is publicly available at jchao-xie.github.io/CoProU.

Keywords: Visual Odometry · Unsupervised Learning · Uncertainty Estimation · Dynamic Scenarios · Relative Pose Estimation

---

J. Xie and O. Dhaouadi—Shared first authorship.

Supplementary Information The online version contains supplementary material available at https://doi.org/10.1007/978-3-032-12840-9_32.

1   Introduction

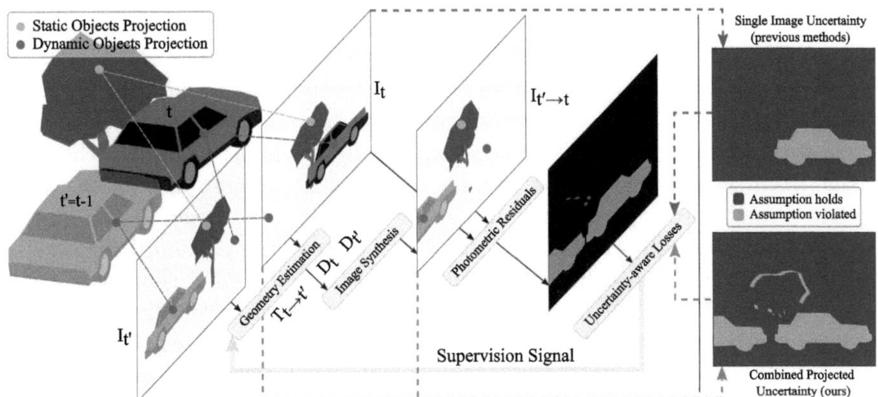

Fig. 1. Our Proposed Combined Projected Uncertainty. Unsupervised monocular VO typically synthesizes a target image I_t from its reference image $I_{t'}$ using the relative pose $T_{t\to t'}$ and depth D_t. The error between the target image I_t and the synthesized image $I_{t'\to t}$ can serve as a supervision signal for geometry estimation, based on the static scene assumption. However, this assumption is violated by dynamic objects and occlusions. Previous methods (red flow) attempt to mask out these elements by predicting uncertainty solely from the target image, which overlooks the uncertainty arising from the reference image. In contrast, our proposed combined projected uncertainty (green flow) considers the uncertainty from both the target and reference images, and robustly masks out all areas violating the static scene assumption. (Color figure online)

Visual Odometry (VO) has emerged as a fundamental component in numerous applications including autonomous driving [13], augmented reality [6], and robotics [41] due to its ability to estimate camera motion using only visual inputs. Despite significant advances, state-of-the-art VO methods still face one or more of the following limitations: the requirement for labeled real-world data, poor real-time performance, and inaccurate motion estimation in dynamic scenes.

While supervised approaches [22, 32, 33, 44] have demonstrated impressive performance in multi-view 3D scene reconstruction and camera pose recovery, with Monst3r [44] and VGGT [32] showing strong results even in dynamic scenes, their reliance on ground-truth annotations inherently limits scalability and generalization to diverse environments. Similarly, although unsupervised methods with supervised pretraining, such as CasualSAM [46] and AnyCAM [35], demonstrate promising results, they depend heavily on predictions from pre-trained optical flow and metric depth foundation models, which are themselves trained on labeled real-world data, thereby constraining the generalization of these methods, particularly in long-tail scenarios.

Fully unsupervised VO, which eliminates the need for annotated real-world data, can be broadly categorized into three categories: classical geometry-based methods [4,25,26], end-to-end methods [2,15,48], and hybrid methods [1,7,31, 38], which combine elements of the first two. Classical methods often fail in highly dynamic scenes, while hybrid methods typically involve computationally intensive optimization, limiting their real-time applicability and scalability to large-scale data. Therefore, in this work, we focus on fully end-to-end approaches.

SC-Depth [2] is a representative fully end-to-end, two-frame-based unsupervised monocular VO approach and serves as our baseline. As illustrated in Fig. 1, given a target image and a reference image, the method synthesizes the target image from the reference image. Under the static scene assumption, the photometric error between the target and synthesized image is used as the supervisory signal. It employs DepthNet and PoseNet to estimate depth and relative camera poses between consecutive frames, and introduces a geometric consistency loss to penalize depth inconsistencies, along with a self-discovered mask to filter out moving objects. However, the method overlooks other violations of the static scene assumption, such as non-Lambertian surfaces. Furthermore, the mask based solely on depth error lacks robustness in complex scenes.

To improve robustness in VO systems, uncertainty modeling has emerged as a powerful technique. Recent works like D3VO [38] demonstrate that modeling heteroscedastic aleatoric uncertainty [20] as a Laplacian probability distribution effectively filters out problematic regions including object boundaries, moving objects, and highly reflective surfaces. Similarly, AnyCAM [35] and KPDepth-VO [31] incorporate uncertainty to enhance robustness against inconsistencies. However, all the unsupervised methods have a fundamental limitation by incorporating uncertainty solely from the target image when filtering unreliable regions.

To overcome this limitation, we present Combined Projected Uncertainty VO (CoProU-VO), a novel visual odometry approach that robustly handles regions violating the static scene assumption. Our method incorporates a lightweight PoseNet trained through robust geometric constraints to maintain real-time performance and independently used at test time. We leverage pre-trained features from DepthAnything [36,37], which is pre-trained without labeled real-world data, for joint depth and uncertainty prediction from a single image. To address violations of the static scene assumption, we project the uncertainty of the reference frame into the target frame and merge it with the native uncertainty of the target frame, which proves more robust than single-image uncertainty estimation, as demonstrated in Fig. 1. This cross-frame uncertainty propagation establishes robust gradient flow between uncertainty and pose estimation, enhancing projection awareness and significantly improving robustness to dynamic objects and other consistency violations.

Our contributions are twofold: (1) we propose a novel projection-aware uncertainty mechanism called *Combined Projected Uncertainty (CoProU)*, which integrates uncertainties from both the target and reference frames to robustly mask regions that violate the static scene assumption; and (2) based on this mechanism, we build *CoProU-VO*, which incorporates pre-trained features from depth foundation models in an end-to-end unsupervised framework, while maintaining real-time performance via a lightweight PoseNet during inference.

2 Related Work

2.1 Unsupervised Monocular Visual Odometry

SfMLearner [48] was the first method to achieve fully unsupervised learning of depth and ego-motion in an end-to-end manner using only monocular video sequences. Despite this advancement, SfMLearner [48] faces two significant limitations: inability to provide pose estimation with consistent global scale and lack of robustness in dynamic scenarios.

Numerous methods have since built upon this foundation to address these shortcomings. SC-Depth [2] introduced a geometric consistency loss to enforce alignment between predicted and synthesized depths, encouraging scale consistent depth predictions. MonoDepth2 [15] employed a minimum reprojection loss to handle occlusions more effectively.

DynamicDepth [12] proposed occlusion-aware training via self-supervised cycle-consistent learning, relying on semantic segmentation to detect dynamic objects. In contrast, our method effectively masks dynamic objects and occluded regions using a principled probabilistic formulation, without external segmentation.

Hybrid methods [7,31,38,43] achieve promising results by combining end-to-end learning with classical geometric algorithms. D3VO [38] integrates predicted depth, pose, and uncertainty into a windowed sparse photometric bundle adjustment framework based on Direct Sparse Odometry (DSO) [11]. AnyCam [35] demonstrates camera tracking using pre-trained foundation models without prior knowledge of camera intrinsics. However, these methods often rely on computationally intensive non-linear optimization at inference, limiting their practical applicability. In contrast, CoProU-VO uses a straightforward single-pass inference approach that maintains accuracy while being computationally efficient.

2.2 3D Vision Foundation Models

The adoption of Vision Transformers [10] in 2D vision has led to the development of several foundation models for 3D vision [22,32,33,36,37]. DUSt3R [33] and MASt3R [22] directly estimate aligned dense point clouds from image pairs without requiring camera parameters, enabling multi-view geometry reasoning.

VGGT [32], a Visual Geometry Grounded Transformer inspired by CLIP [29] and DINO [5,8,27], has shown promising results for 3D scene prediction through training on large-scale annotated data. While these supervised approaches achieve good performance, they remain limited by their dependence on labeled data.

DepthAnythingV2 [37], a foundation model for monocular depth estimation, addresses this limitation through semi-supervised training. Its teacher model is initially trained on synthetic depth maps, followed by a student model trained on unlabeled real-world data using knowledge distillation [17]. This eliminates the need for labeled real-world data while maintaining performance. Given its capabilities in monocular depth estimation, we adopt the DINOv2 [27]-based encoder from DepthAnythingV2 [37] as the backbone for CoProU-VO, enabling depth and uncertainty estimation without labeled real-world data.

2.3   Uncertainty Estimation

Uncertainty in unsupervised VO can be categorized into two primary types: photometric and depth uncertainties. Photometric uncertainty emerges from violations of the static scene assumption, particularly due to non-Lambertian surfaces, moving objects, and occlusions that break the brightness constancy assumption. Depth uncertainty primarily manifests itself in low-texture regions or at large distances, where significant depth estimation errors produce negligible changes in the photometric reconstruction loss, making these areas inherently difficult to constrain through photometric supervision alone.

Klodt et al. [21] extended SfMLearner [48], using a probabilistic model to estimate photometric, depth, and pose uncertainty. D3VO [38] addresses heteroscedastic aleatoric uncertainty [20] by modeling photometric loss as a Laplacian distribution, identifying unreliable regions during training.

For depth uncertainty, recent works [9,24,28,31] show significant progress.

VDN [9] proposed modeling depth uncertainty with a Variational Depth Network, while KPDepth-VO [31] introduced photometric-sensitive depth uncertainty to improve scale recovery.

In this work, we focus on photometric uncertainty. Existing unsupervised VO methods use only the uncertainty of the target image to filter unreliable regions. However, photometric loss stems from target and reference images. We tackle this by introducing the CoProU-VO that integrates uncertainty information from both frames to better identify regions that violate the assumption of static scene in dynamic environments.

3   Method

Following [48], given a target image I_t at time t and a reference image $I_{t'}$ at time $t' \in \{t-1, t+1\}$, our goal is to synthesize the target image from the reference image using geometry estimation in the form of depth and relative camera pose. The photometric error between I_t and the synthesized image $I_{t' \to t}$ serves as the unsupervised training signal in our framework, illustrated in Fig. 2. We describe the image synthesis process in Sect. 3.1 and formulate our novel combined projected uncertainty in Sect. 3.2, which is the key innovation enabling robust handling of dynamic objects and occlusions. Finally, we detail how this uncertainty is integrated into our overall training objective in Sect. 3.3.

3.1   Image Synthesis

Depth and Pose Estimation. We independently pass both target and reference images through a frozen, pre-trained vision transformer to extract image features. These features are decoded by a randomly initialized DPT layer [30] to estimate target depth D_t, reference depth $D_{t'}$, target photometric uncertainty Σ_t, and reference photometric uncertainty $\Sigma_{t'}$. To estimate the relative pose $T_{t \to t'} \in SE(3)$ from the target view to the reference view, we concatenate the target and reference images and process them through a modified ResNet-18 PoseNet [16].

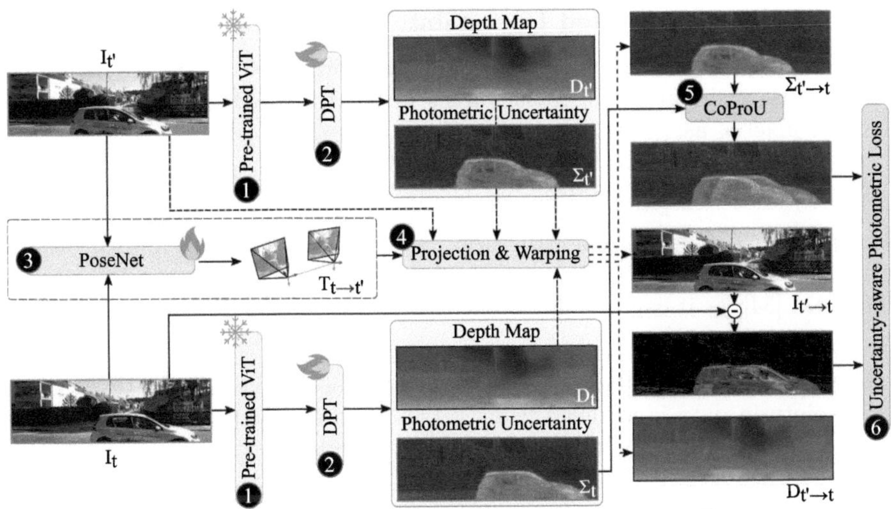

Fig. 2. Overview of Our CoProU-VO Approach. Given two consecutive frames (target I_t and reference $I_{t'}$), (1) features are extracted using a pre-trained vision transformer backbone, (2) depth maps and uncertainty estimates are produced through a decoder network for both frames, (3) relative camera pose is predicted by a PoseNet module, (4) projection and warping operations synthesize views between frames, and (5) our novel CoProU module integrates uncertainty information from both target and reference frames, which is used to (6) compute the uncertainty-aware loss.

Projection and Warping. Let $p_t \in \mathbb{R}^3$ denote homogeneous pixel coordinates in the target view and $K \in \mathbb{R}^{3 \times 3}$ be the camera intrinsics matrix. The projected coordinates of p_t onto the reference view are:

$$p_{t→t'} \sim K\, T_{t→t'}\, D_t(p_t)\, K^{-1}\, p_t \,. \tag{1}$$

For brevity, the conversion from/to homogeneous coordinates is omitted in the remainder of this paper. We employ differentiable bilinear sampling [19,48] to obtain the synthesized image $I_{t'→t}$, the synthesized depth $D_{t'→t}$, and the synthesized uncertainty $\Sigma_{t'→t}$. The synthesized image intensity at a pixel p_t is computed as:

$$I_{t'→t}(p_t) = \sum_{i \in \{tl,tr,bl,br\}} w^i I_{t'}(p^i_{t→t'}) \,. \tag{2}$$

Here, $p^i_{t→t'}$ with $i \in \{tl, tr, bl, br\}$ denotes the four neighboring pixels of the continuous projected coordinate $p_{t→t'}$, and w^i are spatial weights summing to 1. Similarly, $D_{t'→t}$ and $\Sigma_{t'→t}$ are derived from $D_{t'}$ and $\Sigma_{t'}$, respectively.

3.2 Combined Projected Uncertainty

Photometric Residual. Following previous work [2,15,31,38], we define the photometric residual between the target image I_t and the synthesized image $I_{t' \to t}$ at pixel p_t as:

$$r\big(I_t(p_t), I_{t' \to t}(p_t)\big) = \frac{\alpha}{2}\Big(1 - \mathrm{SSIM}\big(I_t(p_t), I_{t' \to t}(p_t)\big)\Big) + (1 - \alpha)\big\|I_t(p_t) - I_{t' \to t}(p_t)\big\|_1, \quad (3)$$

where $\alpha \in [0,1]$ balances the Structural Similarity Index (SSIM) and L_1 components. To handle illumination changes and other noise sources, we incorporate the SSIM [34], as it captures luminance, contrast, and structural similarity.

Uncertainty Formulation. In supervised methods, heteroscedastic aleatoric uncertainty in data is modeled using a Laplacian distribution, while assuming no uncertainty in the prediction according to [20]. Existing unsupervised VO methods, such as D3VO [38], naively adopt this single uncertainty mechanism into unsupervised VO.

However, in unsupervised VO, the prediction (synthesized image $I_{t' \to t}$) also contains noise from the reference image $I_{t'}$. To capture this, we model each pixel intensity as an independent Laplace random variable: $I_t(p_t) \sim$ Laplace$\big(\mu_1, \Sigma_t(p_t)\big)$ and $I_{t' \to t}(p_t) \sim$ Laplace$\big(\mu_2, \Sigma_{t' \to t}(p_t)\big)$, where μ_1 and μ_2 represent the underlying true pixel intensities.

We approximate the likelihood of the photometric residual by accounting for both uncertainty sources:

$$p\Big(r\big(I_t(p_t), I_{t' \to t}(p_t)\big) \,\Big|\, \Sigma_t(p_t), \Sigma_{t' \to t}(p_t)\Big) = \frac{1}{2\sigma_{\mathrm{eff}}(p_t)} \exp\left(-\frac{r\big(I_t(p_t), I_{t' \to t}(p_t)\big)}{\sigma_{\mathrm{eff}}(p_t)}\right), \quad (4)$$

with negative log-likelihood:

$$-\log p\Big(r\big(I_t(p_t), I_{t' \to t}(p_t)\big) \,\Big|\, \Sigma_t(p_t), \Sigma_{t' \to t}(p_t)\Big) = \frac{r\big(I_t(p_t), I_{t' \to t}(p_t)\big)}{\sigma_{\mathrm{eff}}(p_t)} + \log \sigma_{\mathrm{eff}}(p_t) + \mathrm{const}. \quad (5)$$

We integrate the uncertainties in our CoProU formulation as follows:

$$\sigma_{\mathrm{eff}}(p_t) = \sqrt{\Sigma_t(p_t)^2 + \Sigma_{t' \to t}(p_t)^2}. \quad (6)$$

This principled combination better identifies regions that violate the static scene assumption in dynamic environments by integrating uncertainty from both frames. We provide details on the proposed CoProU formulation in the supplementary materials.

3.3 Training Losses

Uncertainty-Aware Photometric Loss. Using our combined projected uncertainty, we define:

$$\mathcal{L}_P = \frac{1}{|\mathcal{V}|} \sum_{p \in \mathcal{V}} \left(\frac{r\big(I_t(p), I_{t' \to t}(p)\big)}{\sigma_{\mathrm{eff}}(p)} + \log \sigma_{\mathrm{eff}}(p)\right), \quad (7)$$

where $\mathcal{V}$ denotes the set of valid points successfully projected from target to reference image.

Geometry Consistency Loss. We adopt the geometry consistency loss from SC-Depth [2], which penalizes inconsistency between projected depth of p_t from target view to reference view, denoted as $D_t^{t'}(p_t)$, and synthesized depth $D_{t' \to t}(p_t)$:

$$D_t^{t'}(p_t) = [T_{t \to t'} \, D_t(p_t) \, K^{-1} \, p_t]_z \,, \tag{8}$$

$$\mathcal{L}_{\text{Geo}} = \frac{1}{|\mathcal{V}|} \sum_{p \in \mathcal{V}} \frac{\left| D_{t' \to t}(p) - D_t^{t'}(p) \right|}{D_{t' \to t}(p) + D_t^{t'}(p)} \,, \tag{9}$$

where $[\cdot]_z$ denotes the z-coordinate extraction operator.

Smoothness Loss. To address depth discontinuities in low-texture regions, we employ an edge-aware smoothness term on all points on target image and reference image:

$$\mathcal{L}_S = \sum_p \left(e^{-\nabla I_t(p)} \cdot \nabla D_t(p) \right)^2 \,. \tag{10}$$

Auto-Mask. Following Monodepth2 [15], we apply an auto-mask to filter out relative static points moving with the camera:

$$M_a(p) = \begin{cases} 1 & \text{if } \|I_t(p) - I_{t' \to t}(p)\|_1 < \|I_t(p) - I_{t'}(p)\|_1 \\ 0 & \text{otherwise} \end{cases} \,. \tag{11}$$

Training Objective. Our final objective combines all losses:

$$\mathcal{L} = M_a \cdot (w_p \mathcal{L}_P + w_g \mathcal{L}_{\text{Geo}}) + w_s \mathcal{L}_S \,, \tag{12}$$

where w_p, w_g, and w_s are weighting factors for each loss term.

4 Experiments

In this section, we evaluate our CoProU-VO framework on the KITTI odometry benchmark [14] and the nuScenes dataset [3]. We first present both quantitative and qualitative results for visual odometry, followed by ablation studies to validate the effectiveness of the proposed CoProU. For implementation details and additional results, please refer to the supplementary material.

4.1   Visual Odometry on KITTI

Evaluation Metrics. We adopt the relative translation error t_{err} (%), and the relative rotation error r_{err} ($°/100\,$m), following the KITTI odometry benchmark [14]. We also report the commonly used Absolute Trajectory Error (ATE). Since our method is monocular-based, we perform a 7-DoF alignment to recover a global scale that best aligns the predicted trajectory with the ground-truth for metric computation, following [2].

Quantitative Results. We compare our CoProU-VO against state-of-the-art fully end-to-end unsupervised methods for monocular visual odometry on the KITTI benchmark.

As shown in Table 1, Zou et al. [49] achieve the best performance by learning long-term dependencies from video sequences. Our method, CoProU-VO, despite using only two consecutive frames, achieves comparable performance to Zou's video-based method and even outperforms it on the ATE metric. Notably, in challenging scenarios like Seq. 01 (highway sequence), where most methods struggle, CoProU-VO produces best results, primarily due to our robust CoProU approach for handling dynamic objects. For a quantitative comparison with methods from other VO categories, including classical approaches and hybrid approaches (combination of classical and ene-to-end algorithms), please refer to the supplementary materials.

Table 1. End-to-End Visual Odometry Results on KITTI [13]. All methods use monocular training with two consecutive frames, except where † denotes stereo training, and ‡ indicates video input. "–" signifies unreported values. The best result is shown in **bold**, and the second-best is underlined. We adopt ATE [m], t_{err} [%], and r_{err} [$°/100\,$m] as evaluation metrics.

Methods	Seq. 01			Seq. 09			Seq. 10		
	ATE	t_{err}	r_{err}	ATE	t_{err}	r_{err}	ATE	t_{err}	r_{err}
SfMLearner [48]	109.61	22.41	2.79	77.79	19.15	6.82	67.34	40.40	17.69
Depth-VO-Feat† [42]	203.44	23.78	1.75	52.12	11.89	3.60	24.70	12.82	3.41
MonoDepth2 [15]	–	–	–	76.22	17.17	3.85	20.35	11.68	5.31
Zou et al.‡ [49]	–	–	–	_11.30_	**3.49**	**1.00**	_11.80_	**5.81**	**1.80**
SC-Depth (Baseline) [2]	313.86	87.04	**1.17**	26.86	7.80	3.13	13.00	7.70	4.90
Manydepth2 [47]	–	–	–	–	7.01	_1.76_	–	_7.29_	_2.65_
CoProU-VO + DINOv2	**63.73**	**19.61**	_1.54_	14.01	4.70	1.89	13.46	7.64	3.67
CoProU-VO + DepthAnythingV2	_75.27_	_22.08_	1.99	**9.84**	_4.56_	2.02	**11.28**	7.76	3.58

Qualitative Results. Visualization of the trajectory results for sequences 01, 09, and 10 are presented in Fig. 3. In sequence 01, the hybrid method DF-VO [43] completely fails, while SC-Depth [2] exhibits larger deviations compared to our

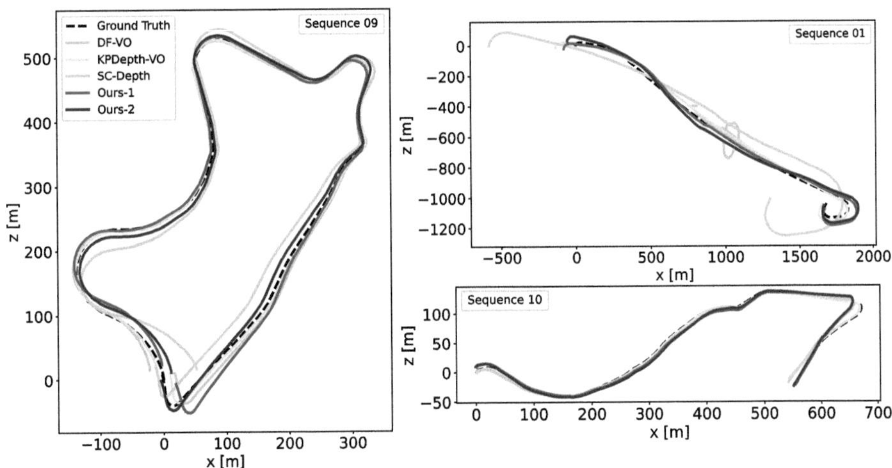

Fig. 3. Visualization of Trajectories on KITTI [13]. In the legend, *Ours-1* represents CoProU-VO + DINOv2, and *Ours-2* represents CoProU-VO + DepthAnythingV2.

method, which achieves significantly more accurate trajectories. In sequence 09, CoProU-VO with DepthAnythingV2 [37] demonstrates performance comparable to established hybrid methods, including DF-VO [43] and KP-Depth-VO [31], demonstrating that our approach achieves comparable accuracy to hybrid methods without the computational overhead of their multi-stage processing pipelines.

4.2   Visual Odometry on NuScenes

Evaluation Metrics. On the nuScenes dataset [3], we adopt the same ATE metric used in previous experiments on KITTI. However, due to the shorter sequence lengths in nuScenes, we report the frame-to-frame Relative Pose Error (RPE) for translation RPE_{trans} (m) and rotation RPE_{rot} (°) to reflect local accuracy instead of relative translation error.

Qualitative Results. As shown in Fig. 4, our method predicts more accurate trajectories than the baseline under challenging conditions, such as dynamic scenes and rainy weather. In Fig. 5, we observe that the proposed CoProU is able to mask out regions that violate the static scene assumption in dynamic scenes robustly.

Quantitative Results. Table 2 presents the results on the nuScenes dataset. When the interval between the reference and target images is small, CoProU-VO only slightly outperforms the baseline. This is because the nuScenes dataset has a high sampling frequency of 12 Hz, and the vehicle moves at relatively low speeds compared to the KITTI dataset, which leads to limited motion between

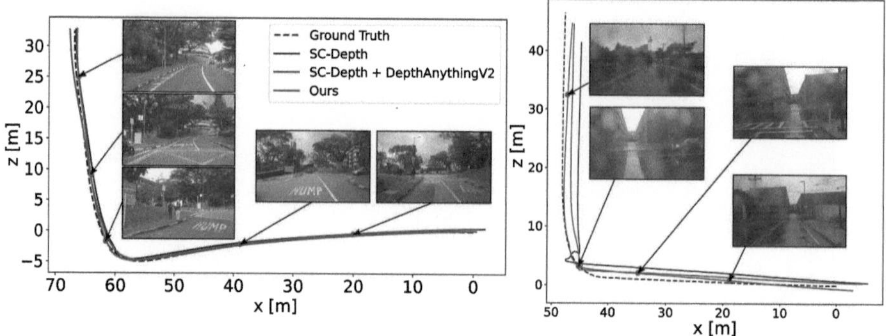

Fig. 4. Visualization of Trajectories on nuScenes [3]. The left and right plots correspond to scene-0928 and scene-0636, respectively. In the legend, *Ours* represents CoProU-VO + DepthAnythingV2.

Fig. 5. Uncertainty Visualization on nuScenes [3]. Gray areas in the images indicate invalid regions excluded from loss calculation. Photometric residual brightness represents error magnitude, while CoProU brightness reflects uncertainty. Dynamic objects may appear distorted due to the static scene assumption. Our method robustly masks high-uncertainty regions, distinguishes parked cars (e.g. green box) from moving cars (e.g. red boxes), and detects occluded parts of parked vehicles (e.g. yellow box). (Color figure online)

consecutive frames. To make the scenes more dynamic and better highlight the advantages of our method, we reduce the sampling frequency by increasing the interval between frames. As the interval increases, our method outperforms the baseline by a significantly larger margins.

Table 2. Visual Odometry Results on nuScenes [3]. We report ATE [m], RPE_{trans} [m], and RPE_{rot} [°]. Our method proves robust and increasingly outperforms the baseline as training and inference intervals increase.

Methods	Training interval	Inference interval	Validation set			Test set		
			ATE	RPE_{trans}	RPE_{rot}	ATE	RPE_{trans}	RPE_{rot}
SC-Depth [2]	1	1	0.906	0.035	0.051	0.984	0.041	0.054
SC-Depth [2] + DepthAnythingV2	1	1	0.839	0.032	**0.048**	0.910	0.039	0.052
CoProU + DepthAnythingV2	1	1	**0.826**	**0.031**	0.049	**0.883**	**0.037**	**0.052**
SC-Depth [2]	2	1	0.932	0.039	0.052	1.132	0.048	0.056
SC-Depth [2] + DepthAnythingV2	2	1	0.833	0.033	**0.046**	0.877	0.037	0.051
CoProU + DepthAnythingV2	2	1	**0.771**	**0.029**	0.047	**0.814**	**0.033**	**0.050**
SC-Depth [2]	2	2	0.874	0.080	0.074	1.110	0.097	0.084
SC-Depth [2] + DepthAnythingV2	2	2	0.697	0.060	0.070	0.810	0.071	0.079
CoProU + DepthAnythingV2	2	2	**0.629**	**0.054**	**0.068**	**0.744**	**0.065**	**0.077**

4.3   Ablation Study

Uncertainty. We validate the advantages of our proposed CoProU in two aspects. First, we show in Table 3 that PoseNet trained with CoProU more efficiently masks out dynamic objects, leading to better pose estimation and outperforming PoseNet trained with single uncertainty. We verify this by training our model under a single uncertainty setting. For the single uncertainty baseline, following [7, 31, 35, 38], we use only the predicted uncertainty Σ_t from the target image I_t as the effective uncertainty in Eq. (7). Second, as illustrated in Fig. 6, training with CoProU results in lower training and validation losses by filtering out more regions that violate the static scene assumption, thereby improving accuracy.

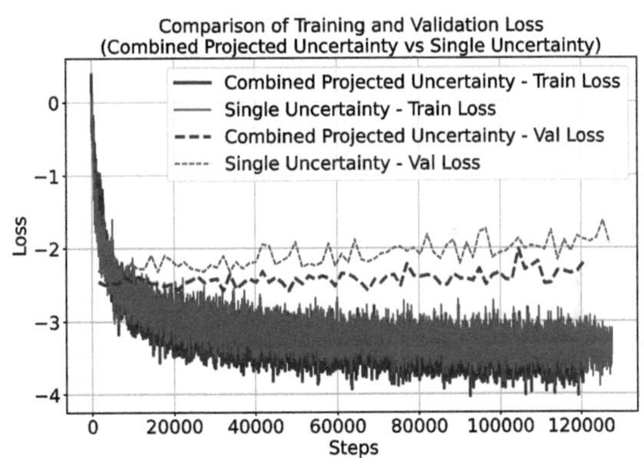

Fig. 6. Training and Validation Curves. Overfitting comparison between CoProU and single uncertainty settings.

DepthNet Backbone. Unlike previous end-to-end works [15, 48] and our baseline SC-Depth [2] that use ResNet [16] for depth prediction, we employ the Vision Transformer Small (ViT-S) from either DINOv2 [27] or DepthAnythingV2 [37]. To isolate the effect of our CoProU from backbone improvements, we conduct an ablation study with results presented in Table 4.

Table 3. Ablation Study of the Proposed CoProU on the KITTI Dataset [13]. Comparison of CoProU and single uncertainty baseline. We adopt ATE [m], t_{err} [%], and r_{err} [°/100 m] as evaluation metrics.

Methods	Seq. 09			Seq. 10		
	ATE	t_{err}	r_{err}	ATE	t_{err}	r_{err}
Single uncertainty + DepthAnythingV2	17.06	8.35	3.16	15.62	10.54	4.05
CoProU + DepthAnythingV2	**9.84**	**4.56**	**2.02**	**11.28**	**7.76**	**3.58**

Table 4. Ablation Study on the Effect of the DepthNet Backbone on the KITTI Dataset [13]. The ViT-S is from DepthAnythingV2 [37]. The self-discovered mask refers to the dynamic mask proposed in SC-Depth [2]. We report ATE [m], t_{err} [%], and r_{err} [°/100 m].

Methods	Backbone	Frozen	How to mask dynamic objects?	Seq. 09			Seq. 10		
				ATE	t_{err}	r_{err}	ATE	t_{err}	r_{err}
SC-Depth [2]	ResNet-50	no	self-discovered mask	26.86	7.80	3.13	13.00	7.70	4.90
SC-Depth [2]	ViT-S	yes	self-discovered mask	10.75	5.47	**1.87**	13.74	8.84	**3.44**
CoProU-VO (ours)	ViT-S	yes	CoProU	**9.84**	**4.56**	2.02	**11.28**	**7.76**	3.58

When replacing ResNet-50 in SC-Depth [2] with ViT-S from DepthAnythingV2 [37], performance on Seq. 09 improves significantly. Applying CoProU leads to further improvements, confirming that our uncertainty approach contributes substantially to the overall performance gains. A similar performance improvement is observed in Table 2 for the nuScenes [3] dataset.

5   Conclusion

In this paper, we presented CoProU-VO, a robust visual odometry system introducing a novel combined projected uncertainty approach. Our method effectively masks out regions that violate the static scene assumption from both target and reference images, significantly outperforming existing two-frame-based end-to-end VO methods on the KITTI odometry benchmark and nuScenes dataset, particularly in challenging scenarios like highway driving and dynamic scenes.

Limitations and Future Work. While effective, CoProU-VO has limitations. The ResNet-18 backbone in PoseNet restricts representation capacity, suggesting the need for more advanced architectures. Frame-independent uncertainty prediction would benefit from better inter-frame modeling, especially in dynamic scenes. While our method shows significant improvement in relative translation error, the gains in absolute trajectory error are more modest. Future work will address these challenges, utilize larger datasets, refine our occlusion handling approach, and employ unfrozen backbones to further enhance monocular visual odometry.

References

1. Bangunharcana, A., Magd, A., Kim, K.S.: Dualrefine: self-supervised depth and pose estimation through iterative epipolar sampling and refinement toward equilibrium. In: Proceedings of the IEEE/CVF Conference on Computer Vision and Pattern Recognition, pp. 726–738 (2023)
2. Bian, J.W., et al.: Unsupervised scale-consistent depth learning from video. Int. J. Comput. Vis. (IJCV) (2021)
3. Caesar, H., et al.: Nuscenes: a multimodal dataset for autonomous driving. In: CVPR (2020)
4. Campos, C., Elvira, R., Rodríguez, J.J.G., Montiel, J.M., Tardós, J.D.: Orb-slam3: an accurate open-source library for visual, visual-inertial, and multimap slam. IEEE Trans. Rob. **37**(6), 1874–1890 (2021)
5. Caron, M., et al.: Emerging properties in self-supervised vision transformers. In: Proceedings of the IEEE/CVF International Conference on Computer Vision, pp. 9650–9660 (2021)
6. Chen, C., Wang, B., Lu, C.X., Trigoni, N., Markham, A.: Deep learning for visual localization and mapping: a survey. IEEE Trans. Neural Netw. Learn. Syst. (2023)
7. Dai, J., Gong, X., Li, Y., Wang, J., Wei, M.: Self-supervised deep visual odometry based on geometric attention model. IEEE Trans. Intell. Transp. Syst. **24**(3), 3157–3166 (2022)
8. Darcet, T., Oquab, M., Mairal, J., Bojanowski, P.: Vision transformers need registers. arXiv preprint arXiv:2309.16588 (2023)
9. Dikov, G., Van Vugt, J.: Variational depth networks: uncertainty-aware monocular self-supervised depth estimation. In: Karlinsky, L., Michaeli, T., Nishino, K. (eds.) Computer Vision – ECCV 2022 Workshops. ECCV 2022. LNCS, vol. 13808, pp. 43–60. Springer, Cham (2023). https://doi.org/10.1007/978-3-031-25085-9_3
10. Dosovitskiy, A., et al.: An image is worth 16 × 16 words: transformers for image recognition at scale. arXiv preprint arXiv:2010.11929 (2020)
11. Engel, J., Koltun, V., Cremers, D.: Direct sparse odometry. IEEE Trans. Pattern Anal. Mach. Intell. **40**(3), 611–625 (2017)
12. Feng, Z., Yang, L., Jing, L., Wang, H., Tian, Y., Li, B.: Disentangling object motion and occlusion for unsupervised multi-frame monocular depth. In: Avidan, S., Brostow, G., Cissé, M., Farinella, G.M., Hassner, T. (eds.) Computer Vision – ECCV 2022. ECCV 2022. LNCS, vol. 13692, pp. 228–244. Springer, Cham (2022). https://doi.org/10.1007/978-3-031-19824-3_14
13. Geiger, A., Lenz, P., Stiller, C., Urtasun, R.: Vision meets robotics: the kitti dataset. Int. J. Robot. Res. **32**(11), 1231–1237 (2013)
14. Geiger, A., Lenz, P., Urtasun, R.: Are we ready for autonomous driving? The kitti vision benchmark suite. In: Conference on Computer Vision and Pattern Recognition (CVPR) (2012)
15. Godard, C., Mac Aodha, O., Firman, M., Brostow, G.J.: Digging into self-supervised monocular depth estimation. In: Proceedings of the IEEE/CVF International Conference on Computer Vision, pp. 3828–3838 (2019)
16. He, K., Zhang, X., Ren, S., Sun, J.: Deep residual learning for image recognition. In: Proceedings of the IEEE Conference on Computer Vision and Pattern Recognition, pp. 770–778 (2016)
17. Hinton, G., Vinyals, O., Dean, J.: Distilling the knowledge in a neural network. arXiv preprint arXiv:1503.02531 (2015)

18. Ilg, E., et al.: Uncertainty estimates and multi-hypotheses networks for optical flow. In: Proceedings of the European Conference on Computer Vision (ECCV), pp. 652–667 (2018)

19. Jaderberg, M., Simonyan, K., Zisserman, A., et al.: Spatial transformer networks. Adv. Neural Inf. Process. Syst. **28** (2015)

20. Kendall, A., Gal, Y.: What uncertainties do we need in bayesian deep learning for computer vision? Adv. Neural Inf. Process. Syst. **30** (2017)

21. Klodt, M., Vedaldi, A.: Supervising the new with the old: learning sfm from sfm. In: Proceedings of the European Conference on Computer Vision (ECCV), pp. 698–713 (2018)

22. Leroy, V., Cabon, Y., Revaud, J.: Grounding image matching in 3D with MASt3R. In: Leonardis, A., Ricci, E., Roth, S., Russakovsky, O., Sattler, T., Varol, G. (eds.) Computer Vision – ECCV 2024. ECCV 2024. LNCS, vol. 15130, pp. 71–91. Springer, Cham (2025). https://doi.org/10.1007/978-3-031-73220-1_5

23. Loshchilov, I., Hutter, F.: Decoupled weight decay regularization. arXiv preprint arXiv:1711.05101 (2017)

24. Marsal, R., Chabot, F., Loesch, A., Grolleau, W., Sahbi, H.: Monoprob: self-supervised monocular depth estimation with interpretable uncertainty. In: Proceedings of the IEEE/CVF Winter Conference on Applications of Computer Vision, pp. 3637–3646 (2024)

25. Mur-Artal, R., Montiel, J.M.M., Tardos, J.D.: Orb-slam: a versatile and accurate monocular slam system. IEEE Trans. Rob. **31**(5), 1147–1163 (2015)

26. Mur-Artal, R., Tardós, J.D.: Orb-slam2: an open-source slam system for monocular, stereo, and rgb-d cameras. IEEE Trans. Rob. **33**(5), 1255–1262 (2017)

27. Oquab, M., et al.: Dinov2: learning robust visual features without supervision. Trans. Mach. Learn. Res. J. 1–31 (2024)

28. Poggi, M., Aleotti, F., Tosi, F., Mattoccia, S.: On the uncertainty of self-supervised monocular depth estimation. In: Proceedings of the IEEE/CVF Conference on Computer Vision and Pattern Recognition, pp. 3227–3237 (2020)

29. Radford, A., et al.: Learning transferable visual models from natural language supervision. In: International Conference on Machine Learning, pp. 8748–8763. PmLR (2021)

30. Ranftl, R., Bochkovskiy, A., Koltun, V.: Vision transformers for dense prediction. In: Proceedings of the IEEE/CVF International Conference on Computer Vision, pp. 12179–12188 (2021)

31. Wang, C., Zhang, G., Zhou, W.: Self-supervised learning of monocular visual odometry and depth with uncertainty-aware scale consistency. In: 2024 IEEE International Conference on Robotics and Automation (ICRA), pp. 3984–3990. IEEE (2024)

32. Wang, J., Chen, M., Karaev, N., Vedaldi, A., Rupprecht, C., Novotny, D.: Vggt: visual geometry grounded transformer. In: Proceedings of the IEEE/CVF Conference on Computer Vision and Pattern Recognition (2025)

33. Wang, S., Leroy, V., Cabon, Y., Chidlovskii, B., Revaud, J.: Dust3r: geometric 3d vision made easy. In: Proceedings of the IEEE/CVF Conference on Computer Vision and Pattern Recognition, pp. 20697–20709 (2024)

34. Wang, Z., Bovik, A.C., Sheikh, H.R., Simoncelli, E.P.: Image quality assessment: from error visibility to structural similarity. IEEE Trans. Image Process. **13**(4), 600–612 (2004)

35. Wimbauer, F., Chen, W., Muhle, D., Rupprecht, C., Cremers, D.: Anycam: learning to recover camera poses and intrinsics from casual videos. In: Proceedings of the Computer Vision and Pattern Recognition Conference (CVPR), pp. 16717–16727 (2025)

36. Yang, L., Kang, B., Huang, Z., Xu, X., Feng, J., Zhao, H.: Depth anything: unleashing the power of large-scale unlabeled data. In: Proceedings of the IEEE/CVF Conference on Computer Vision and Pattern Recognition, pp. 10371–10381 (2024)

37. Yang, L., et al.: Depth anything v2. Adv. Neural Inf. Process. Syst. **37**, 21875–21911 (2024)

38. Yang, N., Stumberg, L.V., Wang, R., Cremers, D.: D3VO: deep depth, deep pose and deep uncertainty for monocular visual odometry. In: Proceedings of the IEEE/CVF Conference on Computer Vision and Pattern Recognition, pp. 1281–1292 (2020)

39. Yang, N., Wang, R., Stuckler, J., Cremers, D.: Deep virtual stereo odometry: leveraging deep depth prediction for monocular direct sparse odometry. In: Proceedings of the European Conference on Computer Vision (ECCV), pp. 817–833 (2018)

40. Yin, Z., Shi, J.: Geonet: unsupervised learning of dense depth, optical flow and camera pose. In: Proceedings of the IEEE Conference on Computer Vision and Pattern Recognition, pp. 1983–1992 (2018)

41. Yousif, K., Bab-Hadiashar, A., Hoseinnezhad, R.: An overview to visual odometry and visual slam: applications to mobile robotics. Intell. Ind. Syst. **1**(4), 289–311 (2015)

42. Zhan, H., Garg, R., Weerasekera, C.S., Li, K., Agarwal, H., Reid, I.: Unsupervised learning of monocular depth estimation and visual odometry with deep feature reconstruction. In: Proceedings of the IEEE Conference on Computer Vision and Pattern Recognition, pp. 340–349 (2018)

43. Zhan, H., Weerasekera, C.S., Bian, J.W., Reid, I.: Visual odometry revisited: what should be learnt? In: 2020 IEEE International Conference on Robotics and Automation (ICRA), pp. 4203–4210. IEEE (2020)

44. Zhang, J., et al.: Monst3r: a simple approach for estimating geometry in the presence of motion. arXiv preprint arxiv:2410.03825 (2024)

45. Zhang, S., Zhang, J., Tao, D.: Towards scale consistent monocular visual odometry by learning from the virtual world. In: 2022 International Conference on Robotics and Automation (ICRA), pp. 5601–5607. IEEE (2022)

46. Zhang, Z., Cole, F., Li, Z., Rubinstein, M., Snavely, N., Freeman, W.T.: Structure and motion from casual videos. In: Avidan, S., Brostow, G., Cissé, M., Farinella, G.M., Hassner, T. (eds.) Computer Vision – ECCV 2022. ECCV 2022. LNCS, vol. 13693, pp. 20–37. Springer, Cham (2022). https://doi.org/10.1007/978-3-031-19827-4_2

47. Zhou, K., et al.: Manydepth2: motion-aware self-supervised monocular depth estimation in dynamic scenes. IEEE Robot. Autom. Lett. (2025)

48. Zhou, T., Brown, M., Snavely, N., Lowe, D.G.: Unsupervised learning of depth and ego-motion from video. In: Proceedings of the IEEE Conference on Computer Vision and Pattern Recognition, pp. 1851–1858 (2017)

49. Zou, Y., Ji, P., Tran, Q.H., Huang, J.B., Chandraker, M.: Learning monocular visual odometry via self-supervised long-term modeling. In: Vedaldi, A., Bischof, H., Brox, T., Frahm, J.M. (eds.) Computer Vision – ECCV 2020. ECCV 2020. LNCS, vol. 12359, pp. 710–727. Springer, Cham (2020). https://doi.org/10.1007/978-3-030-58568-6_42

Combining Absolute and Semi-generalized Relative Poses for Visual Localization

Vojtech Panek[1,2]([✉]) [ID], Torsten Sattler[2] [ID], and Zuzana Kukelova[3] [ID]

[1] Faculty of Electrical Engineering, Czech Technical University (CTU) in Prague, Prague, Czechia
[2] Czech Institute of Informatics Robotics and Cybernetics, CTU in Prague, Prague, Czechia
vojtech.panek@cvut.cz
[3] Visual Recognition Group, Faculty of Electrical Engineering, CTU in Prague, Prague, Czechia

Abstract. Visual localization is the problem of estimating the camera pose of a given query image within a known scene. Most state-of-the-art localization approaches follow a structure-based paradigm and use 2D-3D matches between pixels in a query image and 3D points in the scene for pose estimation. These approaches assume an accurate 3D model of the scene, which might not always be available, especially if only relatively few images are available to compute the scene representation. In contrast, structure-less methods only use 2D-2D matches and do not require any 3D scene model. However, they are also less accurate than structure-based methods. Although some prior works proposed to combine structure-based and structure-less pose estimation strategies, their practical relevance has not been shown. We analyze combining structure-based and structure-less strategies while exploring how to select between poses obtained from 2D-2D and 2D-3D matches, respectively. We show that combining both strategies improves localization performance in multiple practically relevant scenarios. In particular, the combined strategy allows to gracefully handle degradations in 3D scene model quality.

Keywords: Visual localization · RANSAC

1 Introduction

Estimating the position and orientation from which a given image was taken in a known scene, known as visual localization, is an important part of applications such as augmented reality [33,34] and robotics [19,30]. Most state-of-the-art methods establish 2D-3D matches between pixels in a query image and 3D scene points [6,9,13,36,41,52]. The matches are then used for camera pose estimation,

---

Supplementary Information The online version contains supplementary material available at https://doi.org/10.1007/978-3-032-12840-9_33.

e.g., by applying a P3P solver [38] within RANSAC [16,28]. Given accurate 3D point positions, this approach leads to precise estimates.

An alternative to structure-based approaches are structure-less methods [5, 15,59,61,63]. They estimate the pose of a query image from 2D-2D matches between the query and multiple database images with known poses, *e.g.*, by semi-generalized relative pose estimation [5,61] or triangulation [15,59,63]. Such methods are typically less accurate [15], but are applicable even with an inaccurate 3D structure model or a small overlap between database images [61].

Rather than using either 2D-3D or 2D-2D matches, Camposeco *et al.* proposed to use both types of matches [10]. In each iteration, their proposed Hybrid RANSAC first randomly samples a minimal solver. Based on the solver, their method draws the required set of 2D-2D and 2D-3D correspondences, estimates the pose, and counts inliers. Then it updates the probability distribution that is used to select the solver. Their approach does not choose between a structure-based or a structure-less strategy a priori. Rather, it selects the appropriate pose estimation strategy per query image based on which approach performs best. Experiments with simulated 2D-2D matches showed promising results. MAD-Pose [58], developed concurrently with our work, uses Hybrid RANSAC [10] for relative pose estimation with monocular depth priors for the two images.

The contribution of [10] is two-fold: (1) they proposed multiple minimal solvers based on both 2D-2D and 2D-3D matches. (2) they proposed the Hybrid RANSAC framework, discussed above, that can use multiple solvers with different input sets. When selecting the best pose during Hybrid RANSAC, they simply added up the number of inliers for 2D-2D and 2D-3D matches. In contrast, [58] selects poses based on the sum of two robust cost functions. In this paper, we discuss multiple equally simple (and thus practically useful) pose selection strategies. We show that the simple approach from [10] for selecting the best camera pose (and thus selecting between different camera pose estimation strategies) does not work well in practice, whereas the strategy from [58] performs well. Our approach adaptively selects the best query pose among poses estimated with structure-based and structure-less methods without any prior knowledge about which solver should work better in a given scenario. In addition to selecting between different poses within a (Hybrid) RANSAC framework (as in [10]), we also investigate the selection of poses obtained by separate RANSACs for structure-based and structure-less methods. Experiments on different real-world datasets show that: (1) the choice of selection strategy has a significant impact on pose accuracy. (2) strategies that combine structure-based and structure-less pose estimation approaches are practically relevant. Especially if only a sparse set of database images is available, or the 3D geometry estimates are inaccurate, adaptive approaches can significantly improve performance.

In summary, this paper makes the following contributions: (1) we show that strategies adaptively selecting between structure-based and structure-less approaches are practically relevant. In particular, we show in which scenarios such strategies are useful. (2) we analyze how to select between these two approaches by selecting an appropriate pose estimate scoring function. We show that the choice of the function has a significant impact on the pose accuracy. (3) we evaluate a simple selection strategy for pairs of pose estimates made using structure-based and structure-less methods. (4) we will make our code publicly available.

2 Related Work

Structure-based methods form the leading, well-established branch of visual localization. They use 2D-3D matches between 2D pixel positions and 3D scene points for camera pose estimation, typically by applying an absolute pose solver [25,38] inside RANSAC [3,4,16,39]. There are multiple ways to establish the 2D-3D correspondences. SfM (Structure from Motion)-based methods [41] start with a set of reference images and build a sparse SfM point cloud where each point is triangulated from feature matches between database images. Each 3D point is associated with its corresponding image features. For a given query image, 2D-2D matches are established by extraction of local features [14,32,55,62] with a subsequent matching step [43] or directly with a detector-less matcher [51]. The 2D-2D matches are lifted to 2D-3D matches using the SfM point cloud. Image retrieval [1,18,22,40] can be used to pre-filter image pairs to avoid computationally demanding exhaustive matching. Alternatively to SfM point clouds, other explicit or implicit 3D models that capture the geometry and appearance of the scene, such as a mesh [36,37] or a NeRF [31], can be used to obtain 2D-3D matches. Scene coordinate regression [6–9,11–13,49,56] learns to directly predict corresponding 3D points for pixels in a query image. The pose accuracy of all these methods directly depends on the accuracy of the geometry. Accuracy tends to degrade if the 3D structure is estimated from only a few database images.

Structure-less approaches are based on estimating the pose of the query image relative to at least two database images (with known absolute poses) solely from 2D-2D matches. Unlike relative pose estimation between two images, since the relative pose is estimated *w.r.t.* to multiple database images, the scale of the translation can be recovered. Structure-less approaches are typically not used in practice because their accuracy usually does not reach the structure-based methods [15]. As the relative pose solvers [24,26,50,61] generally use more matches than the absolute pose solvers, they also need more RANSAC iterations. The main advantage (which we actively exploit in this paper) is their independence from any scene geometry model. We show that structure-less approaches more gracefully handle representations with less accurate scene geometry, thus creating a strong motivation for using such approaches in practice.

Adaptive approaches use both 2D-2D and 2D-3D matches for camera pose estimation. These methods are not deeply studied in the literature, and we are only aware of two such approaches [10,58] (described in Sect. 3). While [10] showed promising results, they did not evaluate their approach in a practical setting. The second approach [58] uses monocular depth priors and presents results on publicly available relative pose benchmarks. We build upon the previous works but focus on making adaptive approaches work in practice. In particular, we show the performance of adaptive approaches heavily depends on the scoring function used to choose between poses. We show that the scoring function used in [10] is not a good choice, while the scoring function from [58] performs well. We present an extensive evaluation on multiple localization datasets and show that selecting between poses after RANSAC, rather than within each RANSAC iteration, can boost performance in certain scenarios. In general, we showcase different practical scenarios where adaptive approaches excel.

3   Adaptive Pose Selection

This paper investigates whether we can automatically select between structure-based and structure-less approaches so that we get the best of both. *I.e.*, using the former when the 3D geometry is accurate (without explicitly measuring it) and the latter otherwise. To answer this question, we designed a simple pipeline that adaptively selects the strategy leading to better pose estimates.

A Simple Adaptive Pose Estimation Strategy. Given 2D-2D and 2D-3D matches, we run a RANSAC loop with two pose solvers: P3P [38] and E5+1 [61]. In each iteration, we draw two samples, one from the 2D-3D matches for the P3P solver and one from the 2D-2D matches for the E5+1 solver. The predicted poses are scored using both match types (using reprojection error for 2D-3D matches and Sampson error for 2D-2D matches). If a new best pose is found, the pose estimate is updated and refined using local optimization (LO) [28].

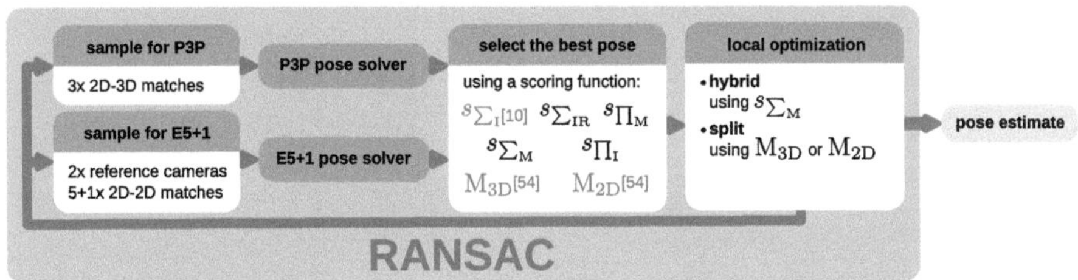

Fig. 1. A block diagram of our simple adaptive pose estimation strategy.

Our approach is a simplified version of [10], using only two solvers[1] and applying both in each iteration. This simplification is a deliberate choice. Combining 2D-3D and 2D-2D inliers evaluated using different errors is nontrivial. Thus, the main question we pose here is: How to define and refine the best pose using these two sources of data? Our simplified approach is sufficient to answer this question. The pose selection and optimization strategies described below can be applied directly in the Hybrid RANSAC from [10] if efficiency is of concern.

---

[1] In contrast to the other solvers used in [10], P3P and E5+1 have efficient and publicly available implementations and therefore seem to be the most practically relevant.

Camera Pose Scoring. Given a single type of matches, *e.g.*, only 2D-3D matches, the common strategy is to rate pose estimates based on the number of inliers I or based on minimizing a robust cost function. An example of the latter is the MSAC scoring function $M = \sum_i \min(e_i^2, t^2)$ [54], where e_i is the error of the i-th match *w.r.t.* the pose estimate and t is the threshold used to distinguish between inliers and outliers. For two types of matches, we obtain the numbers of inliers I_{3D} and I_{2D} for 2D-3D and 2D-2D matches, respectively. Similarly, we obtain MSAC scores M_{3D} and M_{2D} for 2D-3D and 2D-2D matches, respectively. As shown in Sect. 4, how we combine these scores has a significant impact on the overall pose accuracy. As such, whether our approach is able to adapt to the quality of the two sets of matches strongly depends on the pose scoring function.

The hybrid RANSAC approach from [10] simply *sums up the numbers of inliers* (denoted as $\sum_I$ in the following) to obtain a single score

$$s_{\sum_I} = I_{3D} + I_{2D} \ . \tag{1}$$

Typically, there are more 2D-2D than 2D-3D matches[2]. To avoid giving a greater weight to 2D-2D matches, we either *sum up the inlier ratios* $(\sum_{IR})$

$$s_{\sum_{IR}} = I_{3D}/N_{3D} + I_{2D}/N_{2D} \ , \tag{2}$$

(where N_{3D} and N_{2D} are the numbers of 2D-3D and 2D-2D matches), or we *multiply the numbers of inliers* $(\prod_I)$

$$s_{\prod_I} = I_{3D} \cdot I_{2D} \ . \tag{3}$$

Note that the product of inlier counts or inlier ratios leads to the same ordering as they both differ by a constant term $(1/(N_{3D} \cdot N_{2D}))$. Similarly, we can either *sum up the individual MSAC scores* $(\sum_M)$ similarly to [58]

$$s_{\sum_M} = M_{3D}/t_{3D}^2 + M_{2D}/t_{2D}^2 \ , \tag{4}$$

or *multiply the two MSAC scores* $(\prod_M)$,

$$s_{\prod_M} = M_{3D} \cdot M_{2D} \ , \tag{5}$$

or *use them individually* $(M_{3D}$, or $M_{2D})$. We normalize MSAC scores by the inlier thresholds t_{3D} and t_{2D}, to account for their different scales. The score used in [58] is similar to $s_{\sum_M}$, but contains two 2D-3D terms (one per depth map in query-reference pair). The multiplication-based scores ($s_{\prod_I}$ and $s_{\prod_M}$) emphasize poses good for both modalities (2D-2D and 2D-3D), similar to the logical "and" operator. *E.g.*, a pose with 50 2D-3D and 50 2D-2D inliers is preferred over a pose with 10 2D-3D and 100 2D-2D inliers. Note that scores based on the inlier numbers are maximized, while MSAC-based scores are minimized.

---

[2] *E.g.*, HLoc [41,43] method performs 2D-2D matching between a query and similar database images. It then uses an SfM model to determine which of the matching 2D pixels in the database images has a corresponding 3D point in the SfM model. Thus, not every 2D-2D match necessarily results in a 2D-3D match.

The scoring functions using both 2D and 3D information aim to select a pose that is consistent with both sets of matches. In some scenarios, 2D-3D matches can be unreliable, *e.g.*, when using noisy depth maps for the creation of 2D-3D matches from 2D-2D matches, and so finding a pose consistent with both sets of matches is not meaningful. For such cases, we consider the `Select` strategy, that selects between the best pose estimated from the 2D-2D and the best pose estimated from the 2D-3D matches. As 2D-3D matches might be unreliable, we score the poses using only 2D-2D matches.[3] Let I_{2D}^{P3P} and I_{2D}^{E5+1} be the number of 2D-2D inliers found by P3P respectively E5+1. We select the P3P pose if

$$I_{2D}^{P3P} > \alpha \cdot I_{2D}^{E5+1} \tag{6}$$

for a threshold α and E5+1 pose otherwise. Intuitively, we select the P3P pose if it is consistent with the 2D-2D inliers of the E5+1 pose, assuming that the 2D-3D matches are then reliable. The `Select` approach does not need to be used inside RANSAC. It is sufficient to run both P3P and E5+1 RANSAC in parallel and to select the more appropriate pose using the `Select` strategy afterwards.

Local Optimization. The goal of local optimization in RANSAC is to reduce the impact of measurement noise on pose accuracy [28]. Hybrid RANSAC [10] optimizes poses only based on 2D-3D matches. We investigate multiple ways how to locally optimize the pose hypotheses. The first option is to use a `hybrid` refinement (H), optimizing both 2D-2D and 2D-3D matches. A similar approach is used in [58]. The second option called `split` (denoted as S) optimizes only one of the scores, selected based on the pose solver, which generated the pose hypothesis that is being optimized. If the P3P solver generates the pose, the 2D-3D error is optimized. If the E5+1 solver generates the pose, the 2D-2D error is optimized. The intuition is that in the case of imprecise scene geometry, the E5+1 solver will generate the final pose estimate, which will not be skewed by the inaccurate 2D-3D matches during the local optimization. We also tested optimization based only on the 2D-2D MSAC error (denoted again M_{2D}) or the 2D-3D MSAC error (denoted M_{3D}). In all cases, local optimization is implemented as a non-linear refinement of the reprojection and Sampson error, respectively, using the implementation provided in PoseLib [27].

A Simple Hybrid Localization Approach. We use our pose estimation approach in a standard localization pipeline [36,41,43]: given a set of database images with known poses and intrinsics, we compute a geometric representation of the scene in an offline step. For a given query image, we use image retrieval to get a set of relevant database images and match features between the query and each retrieved image. For every resulting 2D-2D match, we use the geometric representation to identify whether there is a 3D point corresponding to the 2D position in the database image. This look-up, based on a sparse SfM point cloud of the scene [21,41,45] or dense depth maps [36], results in a set of 2D-3D matches. The 2D-3D and 2D-2D matches are then used for pose estimation.

---

[3] 2D-3D matches are obtained by "lifting" 2D-2D matches, *i.e.*, linking 2D-2D matches to corresponding 3D points. Even if the 3D points are inaccurate and the 2D-3D matches unreliable, it is reasonable to assume that the 2D-2D matches are reliable.

4   Experimental Evaluation

The focus of this paper is to answer the question of whether visual localization approaches that use both 2D-2D and 2D-3D matches are useful in practice. To this end, we pose several important practical questions: (A) Is traditional structure-based localization always outperforming structure-less localization in terms of precision? (B) Is it possible to design a simple and effective method that combines these two approaches, which, without additional knowledge of the scene geometry, takes advantage of both? (C) Are the two individual strategies performing differently for different types of scene representation? (D) In which use cases do adaptive approaches offer improved performance? To answer these questions, we evaluated different variants of the proposed adaptive scheme and compared them with structure-based and structure-less baselines.

4.1   Experimental Setup

Datasets. We evaluate on multiple publicly available datasets. The 7 Scenes dataset [17,49] (in the supp. mat.) captures small room-scale scenes, while the Gangnam Station [29] shows a large-scale indoor public facility. Database and query images were captured at (roughly) the same time for Cambridge Landmarks, 7 Scenes, and Gangnam Station, and thus depict the scenes under very similar conditions. In contrast, the Aachen [44,45,60] and Extended CMU Seasons [2,44] datasets contain query images taken under different conditions compared to the database images, *e.g.*, day-night and seasonal changes.

Methods. We evaluate the following methods: (1) P3P computes the camera pose from 2D-3D matches via P3P solver [38] within RANSAC with local optimization; (2) E5+1 computes the camera pose from 2D-2D matches via E5+1 solver [61] within RANSAC with local optimization; (3) "Oracle" selects the better (relative to ground truth[4]) of the poses estimated by P3P and E5+1 based on absolute error[5]; (4) HLoc [41,43] is a state-of-the-art structure-based method[6]; (5) Adaptive, described in Sect. 3, selects poses inside RANSAC based on both types of matches. Select, described in Sect. 3, selects either the P3P or E5+1 pose based on the number of 2D-2D inliers. All methods except Hloc are implemented in PoseLib (P3P, E5+1) or based on PoseLib (Adaptive, "Oracle", Select). We evaluate all scoring functions from Sect. 3 for the Adaptive approach: the sum of inliers ($s_{\sum_I}$) from [10], the individual MSAC scores (M_{3D}, M_{2D}) from [54] and all the remaining scores ($s_{\sum_{IR}}$, s_{Π_I}, $s_{\sum_M}$, s_{Π_M}) introduced in this paper.

---

[4] Note that "Oracle" is not an upper bound, as it selects only from the P3P and E5+1 poses using only either 2D-2D or 2D-3D matches. Better poses can potentially be obtained by taking both sets of matches into account. Still, "Oracle" has access to the ground truth camera poses, which are not available to any of the other methods.

[5] The absolute error is the greater of position (cm) and orientation (°) errors.

[6] Hloc and P3P differ in implementation. P3P is based on PoseLib [27]. HLoc is build on top of COLMAP [46–48] and implements covisibility clustering [42].

Evaluation Metric. We report the percentage of query images localized within certain error bounds (*e.g.*, ≤ 5 cm and ≤ 5°) [49]. We also report median position and orientation errors for the 7 Scenes datasets (in the supp. mat.).

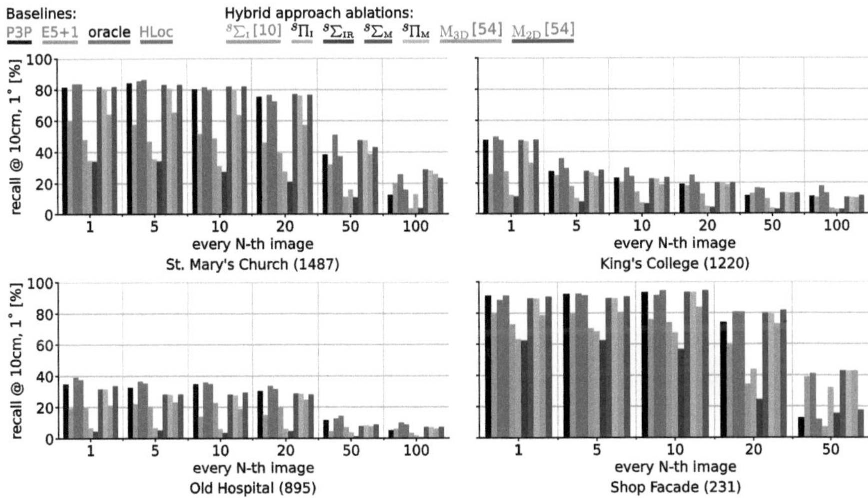

Fig. 2. Ablating scoring functions on the Cambridge Landmarks [23]. We report the localization recall within 10 cm and 1° from the ground truth. The scene is represented using SfM point cloud computed using every N-th database image. All the ablations use the **hybrid** local optimization strategy. Approaches and scoring functions already introduced in the literature are marked gray in the legend.

4.2   Ablation Study

We first assess the impact of scoring functions and local optimization strategies.

Ablating Scoring Functions. Fig. 2 shows the percentage of queries localized within 10 cm and 1 degree from their ground truth pose for the **Adaptive** approach when using different scoring functions and the hybrid refinement strategy. In addition, we report results for **P3P**, **E5+1**, **"Oracle"**, and **HLoc**. Methods that use 2D-3D matches represent the scene as a Structure-from-Motion (SfM) point cloud. 2D-2D matches are obtained by matching the SuperPoint [14] features with the SuperGlue [43] matcher between the query image and the database images found via NetVLAD-based [1] retrieval. The resulting 2D-2D matches are lifted to 2D-3D matches via the SfM model [41]. We report results for scene representations obtained using every N-th image from the database image sequences for varying N. Increasing N leads to fewer database images being used. This increases the distance between database images, making the matching between database images harder. The triangulation is performed from fewer images,

Table 1. Ablating scoring functions and local optimization (LO) strategies on the nighttime queries of the Aachen Day-Night v1.1 dataset [44,45,60], using every N-th of the 6,697 database images. Showing localization recalls (higher is better) at the pose error thresholds of $(0.25\,\mathrm{m}, 2°)/(0.5\,\mathrm{m}, 5°)/(5\,\mathrm{m}, 10°)$. We mark the best, second-, and third-best results per column. The $\sum_I$ score was introduced in [10] and the MSAC scoring (M_{3D}, M_{2D}) is from [54].

	Score	LO	N = 1	N = 5	N = 10	N = 20	N = 50
P3P	M_{3D}	M_{3D}	77.0 / 86.9 / 99.0	67.5 / 83.8 / 93.7	57.1 / 73.8 / 83.8	30.9 / 50.3 / 67.5	7.3 / 14.7 / 33.5
E5+1	M_{2D}	M_{2D}	69.1 / 86.4 / 96.3	62.3 / 75.4 / 90.1	48.2 / 63.9 / 81.2	27.2 / 45.0 / 66.5	15.7 / 25.1 / 39.8
Adaptive	$\sum_I$	H	52.9 / 72.3 / 91.1	26.2 / 39.3 / 71.2	19.4 / 30.4 / 59.2	8.4 / 11.5 / 34.0	1.6 / 4.2 / 12.6
		S	52.4 / 70.7 / 91.6	24.1 / 39.8 / 71.2	14.7 / 27.7 / 59.2	8.9 / 11.0 / 34.6	1.0 / 2.6 / 12.6
	Π_I	H	59.2 / 81.2 / 97.9	48.7 / 69.6 / 93.2	35.6 / 61.8 / 82.7	23.0 / 41.4 / 68.6	8.4 / 15.2 / 34.6
		S	59.7 / 80.6 / 97.9	47.6 / 69.1 / 91.6	35.6 / 61.8 / 82.7	19.9 / 38.2 / 69.1	5.8 / 14.1 / 35.6
	$\sum_{IR}$	H	55.5 / 80.1 / 97.9	44.5 / 71.2 / 93.7	30.9 / 59.2 / 86.4	16.8 / 40.8 / 71.2	5.8 / 13.6 / 42.9
		S	55.5 / 80.1 / 97.9	44.5 / 71.2 / 93.7	30.9 / 59.2 / 86.4	16.8 / 40.8 / 71.2	5.8 / 13.6 / 42.9
	$\sum_M$	H	78.5 / 89.0 / 99.0	68.6 / 83.8 / 93.7	58.6 / 73.8 / 86.9	39.3 / 56.5 / 71.7	16.2 / 28.8 / 48.2
		S	75.9 / 88.0 / 99.0	68.1 / 82.7 / 93.7	58.6 / 73.8 / 86.9	35.1 / 52.4 / 71.2	13.1 / 27.2 / 46.1
	Π_M	H	78.5 / 89.0 / 99.0	69.1 / 83.8 / 93.7	59.2 / 74.9 / 87.4	40.8 / 57.6 / 73.8	15.7 / 27.7 / 44.5
		S	75.4 / 88.0 / 99.0	67.5 / 84.3 / 93.7	60.2 / 75.4 / 86.9	36.1 / 56.0 / 72.3	13.6 / 24.1 / 45.0
	M_{3D}	M_{3D}	75.9 / 85.9 / 98.4	67.5 / 83.8 / 93.7	57.1 / 74.3 / 84.3	30.9 / 49.7 / 67.5	7.3 / 14.1 / 33.0
		H	78.0 / 88.0 / 99.0	69.6 / 84.3 / 93.7	57.1 / 73.8 / 84.3	35.6 / 53.9 / 67.5	9.9 / 16.8 / 33.5
		S	75.9 / 85.9 / 98.4	67.5 / 83.8 / 93.7	57.1 / 74.3 / 84.3	30.9 / 50.3 / 67.5	7.3 / 14.1 / 33.0
	M_{2D}	M_{2D}	66.5 / 85.3 / 96.9	51.3 / 75.9 / 90.1	40.3 / 62.8 / 84.3	25.7 / 41.4 / 68.1	12.0 / 27.2 / 42.4
		H	74.9 / 86.9 / 96.9	66.0 / 80.1 / 91.6	53.4 / 68.6 / 83.8	33.5 / 48.7 / 68.6	15.7 / 26.7 / 43.5
		S	69.6 / 86.4 / 96.9	61.8 / 79.1 / 92.1	50.3 / 66.0 / 83.8	31.4 / 44.0 / 69.1	13.1 / 24.6 / 43.5
Select	$\alpha = 0.7$		73.3 / 86.4 / 97.9	65.4 / 84.8 / 93.2	51.3 / 74.9 / 86.9	33.5 / 57.6 / 75.9	11.5 / 28.8 / 49.2
	$\alpha = 0.8$		73.3 / 86.9 / 97.9	65.4 / 84.8 / 93.2	51.3 / 74.9 / 86.9	33.5 / 56.5 / 74.9	12.0 / 29.3 / 49.2
	$\alpha = 0.9$		73.3 / 86.4 / 97.9	64.9 / 84.3 / 92.7	51.3 / 74.3 / 86.4	33.5 / 57.1 / 74.3	12.6 / 30.4 / 49.2
	$\alpha = 1.0$		57.6 / 78.0 / 96.9	56.5 / 79.6 / 90.1	48.2 / 68.6 / 82.7	29.8 / 52.9 / 71.7	13.6 / 26.7 / 47.6
HLoc			77.0 / 89.5 / 99.0	70.7 / 85.9 / 93.2	60.7 / 75.4 / 84.3	35.1 / 54.5 / 66.5	8.4 / 17.3 / 31.9

resulting in a smaller number of generated 3D points. Figure 2 shows results for Cambridge Landmarks and Table 1 for Aachen Day-Night v1.1 [44,45,60].

The results shown in Fig. 2 lead to multiple interesting observations: (**1**) For densely sampled scenes, (small N), structure-based approach (P3P) outperforms structure-less localization (E5+1). As the sparsity increases (larger N), the performance of P3P degrades faster than that of E5+1. For sparsely sampled scenes, *e.g.*, the Shop Facade N = 50[7] or Aachen N = 50, E5+1 can (significantly) outperform P3P, as well as the HLoc baseline. Thus, the answer to *question (A)* is that *structure-less approaches can outperform structure-based approaches*. (**2**) the choice of the score function has a significant impact on pose accuracy. Simply adding the numbers of 2D-2D and 2D-3D inliers, as done in [10], performs worse than using the MSAC scores. MSAC scores are known to select more accurate poses than inlier counting when using the same type of matches [28], *e.g.*, only 2D-2D matches. Combining MSAC scores (vis sum or product) also provides a better estimate of pose quality when using both types of matches, with both strategies perform similarly. Individual MSAC scores are falling behind combined MSAC scores. The M_{2D} score does not achieve the quality of the combined scores for densely sampled scenes, while M_{3D} falls behind for sparsely sampled scenes. (**3**) the **Adaptive** approach, using a combined MSAC-based score function, consistently performs similarly or better than both P3P and E5+1. In particular, the **Adaptive** approach achieves a similar accuracy as P3P for small values of N while performing similarly or better to E5+1 for large values of N. In addition, it is competitive with **Hloc** and the **"Oracle"** baseline which selects between P3P and

---

[7] For reference, the Shop Facade scene contains a total of only 231 database images.

E5+1 based on their distance from the ground-truth pose. As such, the answer to *question (B)* is that *it is possible to design a simple and effective method that combines the best of structure-based and structure-less strategies.*

Ablating Local Optimization Strategies. Table 1 evaluates the impact of refinement strategy on pose accuracy. In general, the `hybrid` strategy performs similarly or better than the `split` strategy, especially for higher values of N. This is not surprising, as the `hybrid` approach optimizes over both match types, while the `split` strategy only uses a single type of matches. We observed a similar behavior for the Cambridge Landmarks dataset (in the supp. mat.). The M_{3D} achieves very similar results to S, while M_{2D} achieves the lowest recalls.

Table 2. Experiments using 3D geometry from a monocular depth estimator or an MVS mesh of the Aachen Day-Night v1.1 dataset [44,45,60]. Note that E5+1 is independent on the geometry. Using the hybrid local optimization for the adaptive approach. Showing localization recalls (higher is better) at the pose error thresholds of $(0.25\,\text{m},\ 2°)/(0.5\,\text{m},\ 5°)/(5\,\text{m},\ 10°)$.

	RE thr.	in. thr.	rel. thr.	day Metric3D	day AC13 mesh	night Metric3D	night AC13 mesh
Adaptive-$\prod M$	-	-	-	52.9 / 78.8 / 97.9	87.3 / 94.7 / 98.5	42.9 / 71.7 / 97.4	72.3 / 88.0 / 97.9
	4.0	3/20	-	52.5 / 71.7 / 94.3	83.4 / 91.5 / 96.8	37.7 / 61.3 / 92.7	65.4 / 87.4 / 94.8
	4.0	3/20	0.8	68.8 / 81.3 / 96.0	84.1 / 92.5 / 97.2	53.4 / 72.8 / 93.7	67.0 / 86.4 / 96.3
	4.0	18/20	-	70.6 / 84.1 / 96.8	72.6 / 86.5 / 95.5	58.1 / 75.9 / 97.4	57.6 / 74.9 / 93.2
	2.0	3/20	-	55.2 / 72.5 / 94.5	82.9 / 91.6 / 96.8	40.8 / 58.1 / 91.1	64.9 / 86.9 / 94.8
	2.0	3/20	0.8	69.7 / 82.8 / 94.9	83.3 / 92.4 / 97.1	51.8 / 71.7 / 93.7	68.6 / 85.9 / 95.3
	2.0	18/20	-	69.7 / 83.7 / 97.0	66.1 / 82.4 / 94.2	60.2 / 77.5 / 95.8	57.1 / 74.3 / 91.1
Adaptive-$\sum M$	-	-	-	51.6 / 77.7 / 98.2	86.3 / 93.8 / 98.5	41.9 / 67.0 / 97.4	73.3 / 88.5 / 97.9
	4.0	3/20	-	60.7 / 81.6 / 97.6	83.7 / 91.7 / 97.9	48.7 / 73.8 / 96.9	66.0 / 88.0 / 97.9
	4.0	3/20	0.8	75.5 / 89.4 / 97.7	83.4 / 92.2 / 98.1	64.4 / 81.2 / 97.9	66.0 / 86.4 / 97.9
	4.0	18/20	-	78.3 / 90.3 / 97.8	76.8 / 90.0 / 97.8	62.8 / 83.2 / 97.9	64.4 / 81.7 / 97.9
	2.0	3/20	-	65.5 / 84.5 / 97.8	83.3 / 91.6 / 97.9	52.9 / 75.9 / 96.9	66.5 / 88.5 / 97.4
	2.0	3/20	0.8	79.0 / 91.0 / 97.8	82.3 / 91.7 / 98.1	63.4 / 83.2 / 97.9	67.0 / 86.4 / 97.9
	2.0	18/20	-	78.9 / 90.9 / 97.7	77.7 / 90.8 / 97.7	64.9 / 84.8 / 97.9	64.4 / 83.8 / 97.9
P3P	-	-	-	19.9 / 39.3 / 93.2	87.3 / 94.2 / 98.5	18.8 / 46.6 / 96.3	72.3 / 88.5 / 98.4
E5+1	-	-	-	78.5 / 90.7 / 97.8	78.5 / 90.7 / 97.8	66.0 / 85.3 / 97.9	66.0 / 85.3 / 97.9

Impact of the Scene Representation on Pose Accuracy. The experiments above used an SfM-based representation, where only a subset of all 2D-2D matches has a corresponding 2D-3D match, potentially biasing pose estimates to better fit the 2D-2D matches. In addition to an SfM-based representation, we also tested lifting 2D-3D correspondences from 2D-2D matches using depth maps from an MVS (Multi-View Stereo) mesh [36], NeRF [35,53] or generated using Metric3D [20,57] monocular metric depth estimator. In this case, nearly every 2D-2D match has a corresponding 2D-3D match. Results for the NeRF-based representation are shown in the supp. mat. We observe that in some scenes, E5+1 outperforms P3P due to inaccuracies in the estimated scene geometry. `Adaptive` approach with an MSAC-based scoring function typically offers the best of both pose estimation strategies (structure-based and structure-less).

The depth maps from mesh result in accurate 2D-3D matches, while the monocular depth maps are noisy and lack consistency between images, resulting in unreliable 2D-3D matches. The adaptive solver should ideally handle both. This experiment tackles a scenario different from the reduced set of reference images (Table 1) as the 3D points triangulated from the reduced reference set are sparser, but still accurate. Given the amount of noise in the monocular depth maps, we experimented with filtering inaccurate correspondences: Every 3D point is projected into all the retrieved reference images containing the corresponding 2D point, and we count the number of such images where the reprojection error is below a threshold (RE thr.). If the number of such inlier images is smaller than a threshold (in. thr.), the 3D point is not used. In addition to a hard inlier threshold, we also use a second threshold, which is on the fraction of the number of retrieved images observing the corresponding 2D point (rel. thr.).

We compare the scenarios with and without filtering in Table 2. Filtering can significantly improve the performance of Metric3D [20,57] depth maps, but can be detrimental if the geometry is accurate. While the `Adaptive` method with the sum or product of MSAC scores performs similarly on SfM representations in Table 1, the sum of scores combined with filtering better handles the Metric3D depths in Table 2. From the experiments, we conclude that *question (C) can be answered as: while the choice of structure-based and structure-less approaches depends on the scene representation, adaptive methods can handle different kinds of scene representation out of the box.* For details, please see the supp. mat.

Select Strategy. Table 3 shows that selecting from the two pose estimates can outperform `Adaptive` for the extreme cases where the geometry is either rather unreliable or very accurate. As can be seen in Table 1, when 2D-3D matches remain reliable (but there are fewer of them), there is naturally a benefit when using both matches for pose estimation/refinement. However, the gap is not large for values of α around 0.8. Again, this shows that the answer to *question B* is yes, as *the selection strategy is a simple alternative to the adaptive approach.*

Table 3. Experiments with `Select` method using 3D geometry from a monocular depth estimator or an MVS mesh of the Aachen Day-Night v1.1 dataset [44,45,60]. Note that `E5+1` is independent on the geometry. Showing localization recalls (higher is better) at the error thresholds of $(0.25\,\mathrm{m}, 2°)/(0.5\,\mathrm{m}, 5°)/(5\,\mathrm{m}, 10°)$. The `Adaptive` approach uses the filtering with (2.0 px, 3/20, 80%) parameters.

	α	day		night	
		Metric3D	AC13 mesh	Metric3D	AC13 mesh
Select	0.7	34.8 / 56.1 / 96.1	87.3 / 94.2 / 98.5	29.8 / 58.1 / 96.9	72.3 / 88.5 / 98.4
Select	0.8	41.3 / 62.9 / 97.2	87.3 / 94.2 / 98.5	34.0 / 63.9 / 97.4	71.7 / 88.0 / 97.9
Select	0.9	49.4 / 70.3 / 97.3	87.3 / 94.3 / 98.5	40.3 / 70.7 / 97.4	71.7 / 88.0 / 97.9
Select	0.95	54.4 / 75.5 / 97.5	87.0 / 94.1 / 98.4	47.6 / 78.5 / 97.4	71.7 / 88.0 / 97.9
Select	1.0	76.9 / 89.9 / 97.8	84.6 / 93.2 / 97.9	64.9 / 86.4 / 97.9	69.1 / 85.9 / 97.9
P3P	-	19.9 / 39.3 / 93.2	87.3 / 94.2 / 98.5	18.8 / 46.6 / 96.3	72.3 / 88.5 / 98.4
E5+1	-	78.5 / 90.7 / 97.8	78.5 / 90.7 / 97.8	66.0 / 85.3 / 97.9	66.0 / 85.3 / 97.9
Adaptive-Σ_{M}-H	-	79.0 / 91.0 / 97.8	82.3 / 91.7 / 98.1	63.4 / 83.2 / 97.9	67.0 / 86.4 / 97.9

4.3   Practical Use in Visual Localization

The following experiments aim to find scenarios in which adaptive approaches are especially preferable over structure-based and structure-less methods.

Sparse Scene Representations. Previous experiments showed that `Adaptive` excels in handling sparse scenes where only relatively few database images are used to build the scene representation. The same can be seen in Table 4 for the Extended CMU Seasons dataset. These results are interesting because a sparser set of database images typically results in more memory-efficient representations. In this context, adaptive approaches are an interesting direction to explore.

Table 4. Results on Extended CMU Seasons [2,44]. We report the localization recall within $(0.25\,\text{m},\ 2°)/(0.5\,\text{m},\ 5°)/(5\,\text{m},\ 10°)$ from the ground truth when using every database image (N = 1) or every 11th database image (N = 11) to build the SfM model. For the sparse case, the `Adaptive` approach clearly performs the best, while offering competitive performance when using all images.

	N	P3P	E5+1	Adaptive-Π_M -H
urban	1	95.7 / 99.0 / 99.6	71.9 / 87.2 / 96.9	95.7 / 98.9 / 99.6
	11	63.6 / 75.3 / 89.6	20.9 / 35.8 / 74.2	70.5 / 81.1 / 91.5
suburban	1	95.0 / 98.0 / 99.4	70.4 / 85.6 / 94.6	95.0 / 97.8 / 98.9
	11	50.3 / 69.3 / 90.9	13.0 / 25.7 / 65.9	58.0 / 76.2 / 92.8
park	1	90.7 / 94.4 / 96.3	54.6 / 68.0 / 78.5	89.5 / 93.2 / 94.5
	11	30.8 / 45.3 / 69.1	4.9 / 10.8 / 38.3	37.6 / 51.9 / 71.2

Challenging Indoor Scenes. Table 5 shows results on the Gangnam Station dataset [29] capturing a large indoor space with complex appearance (weakly textured surfaces, dynamic video screens, repetitive textures, *etc.*.). As can be seen, the adaptive approach consistently improves accuracy.

Table 5. Results on Gangnam Station [29] using an SfM model. We report localization recalls within $(0.1\,\text{m},\ 1°)/(0.25\,\text{m},\ 2°)/(1\,\text{m},\ 5°)$.

	B1	B2
P3P	40.4 / 56.6 / 63.9	35.7 / 48.3 / 52.1
E5+1	23.9 / 42.4 / 53.1	23.9 / 39.8 / 46.4
Adaptive-Π_M-H	41.4 / 58.1 / 65.6	37.6 / 51.0 / 54.6

Continuous Scene Representation Updates. The literature typically assumes a static scene representation that is never updated. We consider a simple approach to extend the scene representation with a newly localized query image: its pose, image-level descriptor, local features, and 2D-3D correspondences (if any) are stored. The following queries use both the original database images and all previously localized queries for retrieval and matching. This approach is much simpler and more efficient compared to updating the 3D structure of the scene, *e.g.*, via triangulation and bundle adjustment. Note that such an approach can be used together with a more expensive representation update: the latter is run infrequently, *e.g.*, at the end of each day, while the former is run in the meantime.

Table 6 shows the results with the continuous scene updates. Compared to the results obtained without updates (*cf.* Table 1) and `HLoc` without updates, the performance drops when using densely sampled database images. The drop is particularly noticeable for the E5+1 approach that is sensitive to the pose accuracy of the images in the scene representation. The P3P approach is less affected as it does not use the poses of the previously localized queries. For sparser representations (using every 20th or 50th image), the Adaptive strategy improves performance, also compared to the static case, suggesting that it can be used for densification of initially sparse representations.

Table 6. Localization with continuous scene updates on Aachen Day-Night v1.1 [44, 45, 60] nighttime queries, using SfM models triangulated from every N-th database image. The HLoc baseline uses a static scene.

	N=1	N=5	N=10	N=20	N=50
P3P	73.8 / 89.0 / 99.0	65.4 / 84.3 / 95.3	58.6 / 79.6 / 89.5	34.6 / 57.6 / 69.1	9.4 / 20.9 / 38.2
E5+1	38.7 / 65.4 / 95.8	40.3 / 61.8 / 88.5	37.7 / 64.4 / 82.2	28.3 / 52.9 / 79.1	23.0 / 42.4 / 64.4
Adaptive-Π_{M}-H	70.2 / 88.0 / 98.4	63.9 / 86.9 / 95.8	55.0 / 78.0 / 90.1	42.4 / 66.0 / 81.7	23.6 / 47.1 / 67.5
Adaptive-Σ_{M}-H	73.3 / 88.0 / 98.4	66.5 / 86.9 / 95.8	60.2 / 79.1 / 89.5	40.8 / 67.0 / 81.2	17.8 / 40.8 / 65.4
Select	65.4 / 84.8 / 97.9	57.6 / 82.2 / 91.6	47.1 / 72.3 / 86.4	34.6 / 59.2 / 79.1	20.4 / 38.7 / 61.3
HLoc [41, 43]	77.0 / 89.5 / 99.0	70.7 / 85.9 / 93.2	60.7 / 75.4 / 84.3	35.1 / 54.5 / 66.5	8.4 / 17.3 / 31.9

5   Conclusion

In this paper, we investigated whether adaptive selection between structure-based and structure-less camera pose estimation strategies is useful in practice. Our key observation is that the way we select the best camera pose among the poses estimated by both strategies has a significant impact on pose accuracy and thus whether or not an adaptive approach is practically useful. We have shown that adaptive approaches with an appropriate camera pose scoring function and local refinement strategy can offer the best of both worlds: high accuracy with accurate 3D scene geometry (from structure-based methods) and the robustness to inaccurate scene geometry (from structure-less methods). Our experiments show that adaptive approaches are especially useful when only a few database images are available, which is convenient when memory consumption is an issue. Our method is simple to implement, and we will release our code.

Acknowledgements. This work was supported by the Czech Science Foundation (GAČR) EXPRO Grant No. 23-07973X and JUNIOR STAR Grant No. 22-23183M, and the Grant Agency of the Czech Technical University in Prague (No. SGS23/121/OHK3/2T/13).

References

1. Arandjelović, R., Gronát, P., Torii, A., Pajdla, T., Sivic, J.: NetVLAD: CNN architecture for weakly supervised place recognition. In: 2016 IEEE Conference on Computer Vision and Pattern Recognition (CVPR), pp. 5297–5307 (2015)

2. Badino, H., Huber, D., Kanade, T.: The CMU Visual Localization Data Set (2011). http://3dvis.ri.cmu.edu/data-sets/localization

3. Baráth, D., Matas, J.: MAGSAC: marginalizing sample consensus. In: 2019 IEEE/CVF Conference on Computer Vision and Pattern Recognition (CVPR), pp. 10189–10197 (2018)

4. Baráth, D., Noskova, J., Ivashechkin, M., Matas, J.: MAGSAC++, a fast, reliable and accurate robust estimator. In: 2020 IEEE/CVF Conference on Computer Vision and Pattern Recognition (CVPR), pp. 1301–1309 (2019)

5. Bhayani, S., Sattler, T., Baráth, D., Beliansky, P., Heikkila, J., Kukelova, Z.: Calibrated and partially calibrated semi-generalized homographies. In: 2021 IEEE/CVF International Conference on Computer Vision (ICCV), pp. 5916–5925 (2021)

6. Brachmann, E., Cavallari, T., Prisacariu, V.A.: Accelerated coordinate encoding: learning to relocalize in minutes using RGB and poses. In: 2023 IEEE/CVF Conference on Computer Vision and Pattern Recognition (CVPR), pp. 5044–5053 (2023)

7. Brachmann, E., et al.: DSAC - differentiable RANSAC for camera localization. In: CVPR (2017)

8. Brachmann, E., Rother, C.: learning less is more - 6D camera localization via 3D surface regression. In: CVPR (2018)

9. Brachmann, E., Rother, C.: Visual camera re-localization from RGB and RGB-D images using DSAC. IEEE Trans. Pattern Anal. Mach. Intell. **44**, 5847–5865 (2020)

10. Camposeco, F., Cohen, A., Pollefeys, M., Sattler, T.: Hybrid camera pose estimation. In: 2018 IEEE/CVF Conference on Computer Vision and Pattern Recognition, pp. 136–144 (2018)

11. Cavallari, T., Bertinetto, L., Mukhoti, J., Torr, P., Golodetz, S.: Let's take this online: adapting scene coordinate regression network predictions for online RGB-D camera relocalisation. In: 3DV (2019)

12. Cavallari, T., Golodetz, S., Lord, N.A., Valentin, J., Di Stefano, L., Torr, P.H.S.: On-The-Fly adaptation of regression forests for online camera relocalisation. In: CVPR (2017)

13. Cavallari, T., et al.: Real-Time RGB-D camera pose estimation in novel scenes using a relocalisation cascade. TPAMI (2019)

14. DeTone, D., Malisiewicz, T., Rabinovich, A.: SuperPoint: self-supervised interest point detection and description. In: 2018 IEEE/CVF Conference on Computer Vision and Pattern Recognition Workshops (CVPRW), pp. 337–33712 (2017)

15. Dong, S., Liu, S., Guo, H., Chen, B.X., Pollefeys, M.: Lazy visual localization via motion averaging. ArXiv **abs/2307.09981** (2023)

16. Fischler, M.A., Bolles, R.C.: Random sample consensus: a paradigm for model fitting with applications to image analysis and automated cartography. Commun. ACM **24**, 381–395 (1981)

17. Glocker, B., Izadi, S., Shotton, J., Criminisi, A.: Real-time RGB-D camera relocalization. In: 2013 IEEE International Symposium on Mixed and Augmented Reality (ISMAR), pp. 173–179 (2013)

18. Gordo, A., Almazan, J., Revaud, J., Larlus, D.: End-to-end learning of deep visual representations for image retrieval. IJCV (2017)

19. Heng, L., et al.: Project AutoVision: localization and 3D scene perception for an autonomous vehicle with a multi-camera system. In: 2019 International Conference on Robotics and Automation (ICRA), pp. 4695–4702 (2018)

20. Hu, M., et al.: Metric3d v2: a versatile monocular geometric foundation model for zero-shot metric depth and surface normal estimation. IEEE Trans. Pattern Anal. Mach. Intell. **PP** (2024)
21. Irschara, A., Zach, C., Frahm, J.M., Bischof, H.: From structure-from-motion point clouds to fast location recognition. In: 2009 IEEE Conference on Computer Vision and Pattern Recognition, pp. 2599–2606 (2009)
22. Jégou, H., Douze, M., Schmid, C., Pérez, P.: Aggregating local descriptors into a compact image representation. In: 2010 IEEE Computer Society Conference on Computer Vision and Pattern Recognition, pp. 3304–3311 (2010)
23. Kendall, A., Grimes, M.K., Cipolla, R.: PoseNet: a convolutional network for Real-Time 6-DOF camera relocalization. In: 2015 IEEE International Conference on Computer Vision (ICCV), pp. 2938–2946 (2015)
24. Kukelova, Z., Bujnak, M., Pajdla, T.: Automatic generator of minimal problem solvers. In: European Conference on Computer Vision (2008)
25. Kukelova, Z., Heller, J., Fitzgibbon, A.W.: Efficient intersection of three quadrics and applications in computer vision. In: 2016 IEEE Conference on Computer Vision and Pattern Recognition (CVPR), pp. 1799–1808 (2016)
26. Larsson, V., Åström, K., Oskarsson, M.: Efficient solvers for minimal problems by syzygy-based reduction. In: 2017 IEEE Conference on Computer Vision and Pattern Recognition (CVPR), pp. 2383–2392 (2017)
27. Larsson, V.: Contributors: PoseLib - Minimal Solvers for Camera Pose Estimation (2020). https://github.com/vlarsson/PoseLib
28. Lebeda, K., Matas, J., Chum, O.: Fixing the locally optimized RANSAC. In: BMVC (2012)
29. Lee, D., et al.: Large-scale localization datasets in crowded indoor spaces. In: 2021 IEEE/CVF Conference on Computer Vision and Pattern Recognition (CVPR), pp. 3226–3235 (2021)
30. Lim, H., Sinha, S.N., Cohen, M.F., Uyttendaele, M.: Real-time image-based 6-DOF localization in large-scale environments. In: 2012 IEEE Conference on Computer Vision and Pattern Recognition, pp. 1043–1050 (2012)
31. Liu, J., Nie, Q., Liu, Y., Wang, C.: NeRF-Loc: visual localization with conditional neural radiance field. In: 2023 IEEE International Conference on Robotics and Automation (ICRA), pp. 9385–9392 (2023)
32. Lowe, D.G.: Distinctive image features from scale-invariant keypoints. Int. J. Comput. Vis. **60**, 91–110 (2004)
33. Lynen, S., Sattler, T., Bosse, M., Hesch, J.A., Pollefeys, M., Siegwart, R.Y.: Get out of my lab: large-scale, real-time visual-inertial localization. In: Robotics: Science and Systems (2015)
34. Middelberg, S., Sattler, T., Untzelmann, O., Kobbelt, L.P.: Scalable 6-DOF localization on mobile devices. In: European Conference on Computer Vision (2014)
35. Mildenhall, B., Srinivasan, P.P., Tancik, M., Barron, J.T., Ramamoorthi, R., Ng, R.: NeRF: representing scenes as neural radiance fields for view synthesis. Commun. ACM **65**, 99–106 (2020)
36. Panek, V., Kukelova, Z., Sattler, T.: MeshLoc: mesh-based visual localization. In: European Conference on Computer Vision (ECCV) (2022)
37. Panek, V., Kukelova, Z., Sattler, T.: Visual localization using imperfect 3D models from the internet. In: 2023 IEEE/CVF Conference on Computer Vision and Pattern Recognition (CVPR), pp. 13175–13186 (2023)
38. Persson, M., Nordberg, K.: Lambda twist: an accurate fast robust perspective three point (P3P) solver. In: ECCV (2018)

39. Raguram, R., Chum, O., Pollefeys, M., Matas, J., Frahm, J.M.: USAC: a universal framework for random sample consensus. IEEE Trans. Pattern Anal. Mach. Intell. **35**, 2022–2038 (2013)
40. Revaud, J., Almazan, J., Rezende, R., de Souza, C.: Learning with average precision: training image retrieval with a listwise loss. In: ICCV (2019)
41. Sarlin, P.E., Cadena, C., Siegwart, R., Dymczyk, M.: From coarse to fine: robust hierarchical localization at large scale. In: CVPR (2019)
42. Sarlin, P.E., Debraine, F., Dymczyk, M., Siegwart, R.Y., Cadena, C.: Leveraging deep visual descriptors for hierarchical efficient localization. In: Conference on Robot Learning (2018)
43. Sarlin, P.E., DeTone, D., Malisiewicz, T., Rabinovich, A.: SuperGlue: learning feature matching with graph neural networks. In: CVPR (2020)
44. Sattler, T., et al.: Benchmarking 6DOF outdoor visual localization in changing conditions. In: Conference on Computer Vision and Pattern Recognition (CVPR) (2018)
45. Sattler, T., Weyand, T., Leibe, B., Kobbelt, L.: Image retrieval for image-based localization revisited. In: British Machine Vision Conference (BMCV) (2012)
46. Schönberger, J.L., Frahm, J.M.: Structure-from-motion revisited. In: Conference on Computer Vision and Pattern Recognition (CVPR) (2016)
47. Schönberger, J.L., Price, T., Sattler, T., Frahm, J.M., Pollefeys, M.: A vote-and-verify strategy for fast spatial verification in image retrieval. In: Asian Conference on Computer Vision (ACCV) (2016)
48. Schönberger, J.L., Zheng, E., Frahm, J.-M., Pollefeys, M.: Pixelwise view selection for unstructured multi-view stereo. In: Leibe, B., Matas, J., Sebe, N., Welling, M. (eds.) ECCV 2016. LNCS, vol. 9907, pp. 501–518. Springer, Cham (2016). https://doi.org/10.1007/978-3-319-46487-9_31
49. Shotton, J., Glocker, B., Zach, C., Izadi, S., Criminisi, A., Fitzgibbon, A.W.: Scene coordinate regression forests for camera relocalization in RGB-D images. In: 2013 IEEE Conference on Computer Vision and Pattern Recognition, pp. 2930–2937 (2013)
50. Stewénius, H., Engels, C., Nistér, D.: Recent developments on direct relative orientation. ISPRS J. Photogramm. Remote Sens. **60**, 284–294 (2006)
51. Sun, J., Shen, Z., Wang, Y., Bao, H., Zhou, X.: LoFTR: detector-free local feature matching with transformers. In: 2021 IEEE/CVF Conference on Computer Vision and Pattern Recognition (CVPR), pp. 8918–8927 (2021)
52. Taira, H.: InLoc: indoor visual localization with dense matching and view synthesis. IEEE Trans. Pattern Anal. Mach. Intell. **43**, 1293–1307 (2019)
53. Tancik, M., et al.: Nerfstudio: a modular framework for neural radiance field development. In: ACM SIGGRAPH 2023 Conference Proceedings. SIGGRAPH '23 (2023)
54. Torr, P.H.S., Zisserman, A.: MLESAC: a new robust estimator with application to estimating image geometry. Comput. Vis. Image Underst. **78**, 138–156 (2000)
55. Tyszkiewicz, M.J., Fua, P., Trulls, E.: DISK: learning local features with policy gradient. ArXiv **abs/2006.13566** (2020)
56. Walch, F., Hazirbas, C., Leal-Taixé, L., Sattler, T., Hilsenbeck, S., Cremers, D.: Image-based localization using LSTMs for structured feature correlation. In: ICCV (2017)
57. Yin, W., et al.: Metric3d: towards zero-shot metric 3D prediction from a single image. In: ICCV (2023)
58. Yu, Y., Liu, S., Pautrat, R., Pollefeys, M., Larsson, V.: Relative pose estimation through affine corrections of monocular depth priors. In: CVPR (2025)

59. Zhang, W., Kosecka, J.: Image based localization in urban environments. In: Third International Symposium on 3D Data Processing, Visualization, and Transmission (3DPVT'06), pp. 33–40 (2006)
60. Zhang, Z., Sattler, T., Scaramuzza, D.: Reference pose generation for visual localization via learned features and view synthesis. arXiv **2005.05179** (2020)
61. Zheng, E., Wu, C.: Structure from motion using structure-less resection. In: ICCV (2015)
62. Zhou, Q., Sattler, T., Leal-Taixé, L.: Patch2Pix: epipolar-guided pixel-level correspondences. In: 2021 IEEE/CVF Conference on Computer Vision and Pattern Recognition (CVPR), pp. 4667–4676 (2020)
63. Zhou, Q., Sattler, T., Pollefeys, M., Leal-Taixé, L.: To learn or not to learn: visual localization from essential matrices. In: 2020 IEEE International Conference on Robotics and Automation (ICRA) (2020)

Graph-Based Roof Reconstruction with Synthetic Data Supervision from Misaligned Labels

Chaikal Amrullah$^{(\boxtimes)}$ and Ksenia Bittner

German Aerospace Center (DLR), 82234 Oberpfaffenhofen, Germany
{chaikal.armullah,ksenia.bittner}@dlr.de

Abstract. Graph-based deep learning provides an efficient, single-stage solution for reconstructing digital city models from Very-High Resolution (VHR) aerial or satellite imagery. However, these models are highly sensitive to label quality—particularly in detecting roof corners and identifying the relationships between points to form polygons.—making them vulnerable to the misaligned annotations often found in open-source datasets.

This study investigates the impact of annotation quality on reconstruction performance and proposes a mitigation strategy using generative synthetic datasets. Leveraging Stable Diffusion with ControlNet, we generate synthetic Red Green Blue (RGB)–label pairs conditioned on misaligned label masks. This process realigns the imagery to noisy annotations, producing spatially consistent training data. Texture control is introduced to enhance visual fidelity and support better feature learning.

We evaluate this approach using PolyRoof, a graph-based reconstruction model. While models trained solely on synthetic data achieve moderate performance, pretraining with synthetic datasets followed by fine-tuning with accurately labeled real data leads to significant gains.

When integrated into the training pipeline, synthetic pretraining improves reconstruction quality and can even outperform models trained exclusively on real labels. These improvements are observed across both quantitative metrics and qualitative visual results.

Overall, the findings indicate that synthetic data—when spatially aligned with noisy annotations and combined with transfer learning—serves as an effective pretraining resource. This can be followed by fine-tuning on real datasets as part of a dataset enrichment strategy aimed at addressing label quality issues in graph-based building reconstruction.

Chaikal Amrullah is currently funded by a DLR-DAAD Doctoral Research Fellowship (No. 57681552) to pursue his PhD studies.

Supplementary Information The online version contains supplementary material available at https://doi.org/10.1007/978-3-032-12840-9_34.

Keywords: Roof Reconstruction · Misaligned Label · Generative Synthetic Dataset · Graph Neural Network (GNN)

1 Introduction

1.1 Problem Statement

The growing demand for digital city management tools, such as Digital Twin (DT) [1], requires city models as pivotal aspect that are geometrically, semantically, and temporally detailed to support key applications like urban planning, disaster management, and energy analysis [9,13,16]. However, traditional data production methods face challenges in meeting these needs due to high costs, limited automation, and difficulties balancing detail with scalability.

Deep learning offers a promising solution, particularly for automating building reconstruction from aerial and satellite imagery [5,20,26,29,33]. Yet, these approaches remain heavily dependent on high-quality annotated datasets—something that is difficult to obtain at scale, especially for detail-rich, structurally accurate models.

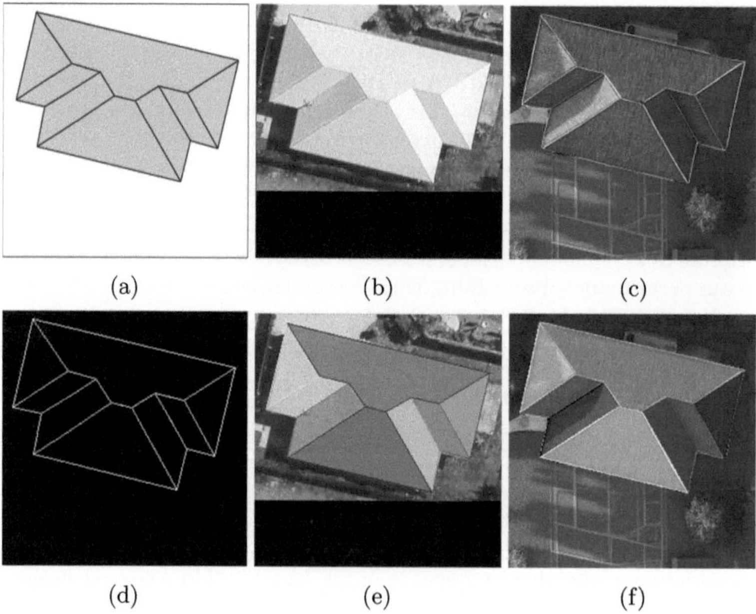

Fig. 1. Visualization of real and synthetic datasets with their corresponding building reconstruction predictions. The first row shows (a) the misaligned (translation) label, (b) real image, and (c) the generated synthetic image. The second row shows (d) the roof boundary mask, (e) the roof segment prediction on the real image, and (f) the roof prediction on the synthetic image.

To overcome limitations in data quality and diversity, synthetic datasets have emerged as a powerful alternative—offering perfect ground truth, large-scale variability, and the ability to simulate diverse building styles [19,23,27]. This paper investigates their use in enhancing graph-based roof reconstruction model for complex urban buildings. On the other hand, synthetic data is employed to tackle label misalignment, texture realism, and data scarcity, aiming to improve model accuracy, robustness, and generalization.

This study demonstrates that synthetic datasets, when used for pretraining and combined with real data during fine-tuning, can significantly enhance the accuracy and generalization of graph-based roof reconstruction models beyond what is achievable with real data alone.

1.2   Related Study

Providing digital city models for urban management requires careful consideration of geometric detail to meet the varying demands of applications such as planning, simulation, and analysis [3,16]. With this need for precision established, attention turns to how deep learning can address the challenges of reconstructing detailed building geometry.

Deep learning has become a leading approach, supporting tasks from footprint and roof extraction [5,6,18,32] to fine-grained geometric modeling [7,20,26,29,33]. While pixel-based methods are common, their reliance on raster-to-vector conversion adds complexity. In contrast, graph-based methods, like PolyRoof [2], offer a more direct solution, achieving higher point-level accuracy and better handling of complex geometries [7,15,33].

Despite these advantages, graph-based models are highly sensitive to label noise and misalignment, as they depend on accurate point and edge relationships [10–12]. Even small inconsistencies between imagery and annotations can degrade performance and generalization. This sensitivity underscores a broader limitation: the scarcity of high-quality labeled data for detailed building reconstruction.

To mitigate this, synthetic datasets have gained attraction as a scalable alternative. Traditional 3D-rendered datasets [19,23,27] help alleviate data scarcity, while recent advances in generative and diffusion models enable more realistic and flexible data generation [4,14,24,30,31]. These developments open new possibilities for producing rich training data, enhancing model robustness in geometry-focused tasks for digital city applications.

However, creating synthetic datasets through rendering is a well-established but time-consuming process, influenced by factors like scene complexity, lighting, object variability, and the need for precise annotations [8,23,25]. In contrast, generative deep learning models have recently shown promise in efficiently generating realistic data [31]. This study investigates their potential to address accuracy and availability challenges in graph-based building reconstruction.

2   Dataset

2.1   Real Dataset

This study evaluates both the fidelity of the generated synthetic dataset and the generalization capability of deep learning models trained on it. To support this evaluation, we utilize two publicly available real-world datasets introduced in the Roof Intuitive [22] and Holistic Edge Attention Transformer for Structured Reconstruction (HEAT) [7] studies. For simplicity, we refer to these as the Roof Intuitive and HEAT datasets, respectively (see labels and RGB samples in the first row of Fig. 1).

Both datasets contain VHR RGB imagery paired with detailed vector annotations of building geometries. The Roof Intuitive dataset has an estimated Ground Sampling Distance (GSD) of 0.1–0.2 m, while the HEAT dataset varies between 0.1–0.5 m due to differences in object framing and image capture height. Annotations define roof corner points as vertices in local image coordinates, with roof segments represented as closed loops formed by these vertex indices.

Using Principal Component Analysis (Principal Component Analysis (PCA)), we quantitatively highlight differences in building types and geometric complexity between the datasets based on their geometric properties (Fig. 2). Qualitatively, Roof Intuitive mainly includes suburban residential buildings, while HEAT is dominated by industrial structures. This imbalance in spatial distribution and architectural detail indicates differences in the characteristics of the two datasets, which can be used to assess the generalization capabilities of the reconstruction model from PolyRoof [2] across diverse urban environments.

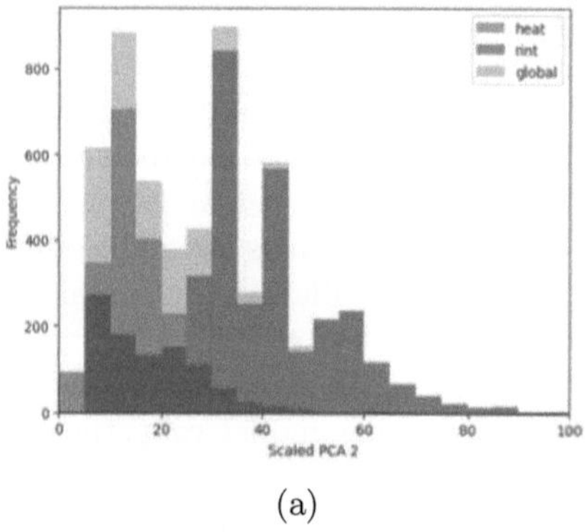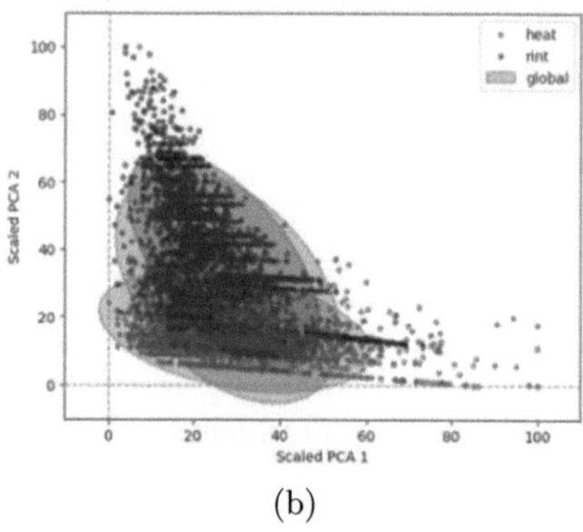

(a)   (b)

Fig. 2. Geometry complexity analysis of both datasets using PCA. The histogram (a) and scatter plot (b) illustrate the distribution of geometric characteristics in Roof Intuitive (blue) and HEAT (red), with green representing the combined data from both datasets. Axes are scaled based on the global value range across both datasets to enable consistent comparison. (Color figure online)

2.2 Misaligned Label Augmentation

In real dataset, while overall pixel-to-point accuracy is preserved, minor inconsistencies between the imagery and labels remain. Despite these small discrepancies, the datasets were chosen for their high geometric fidelity and are treated as correct-label baselines. To evaluate model robustness under more realistic noise conditions, we introduce misaligned labels through an augmentation process illustrated in Fig. 3.

Misalignment in this context refers to discrepancies between labeled roof edge segments and their corresponding features in the overlaid RGB image. Such errors commonly arise from imperfections in the data pipeline, including orthophoto rectification issues, extraction artifacts, or manual annotation inaccuracies. To simulate these conditions, we apply a series of controlled perturbations to the vector labels—such as translation (axis shifts), rotation (about the centroid), uniform scaling, and point-level noise that displaces individual vertices.

(a) Misaligned label in real dataset   (b) Misaligned label with augmentation

Fig. 3. Visualization of misaligned dataset between image and label.

While label snapping techniques can help realign annotations to the image, they often fall short when labels are highly detailed or when the imagery exhibits distortions like zigzag edges, void pixels, or stretched features. In these cases, snapping cannot reliably recover the precise alignment required for graph-based reconstruction, particularly when label segments are divided into multiple parts or have ambiguous edge definitions.

To address this limitation, synthetic datasets present a viable solution. By allowing for the controlled generation of image-label pairs with guaranteed alignment, they eliminate the noise and inconsistencies of real-world annotations—offering a degree of reliable foundation for training and evaluating spatially sensitive models.

2.3 Generating Synthetic Dataset

The generative synthetic dataset is created using a combination of text prompts and control masks. Text prompts (e.g., roof materials, time-of-day, environmental context) introduce visual diversity, while binary building masks—derived from the augmented, misaligned vector dataset—preserve geometric accuracy. These masks guide ControlNet in aligning generated images with the intended roof contours [31] (see Fig. 4). Image generation is performed via inference using pre-trained models from the public repositories black-forest-labs/FLUX.1-dev [17] and XLabs-AI/flux-controlnet-canny-v3 [28].

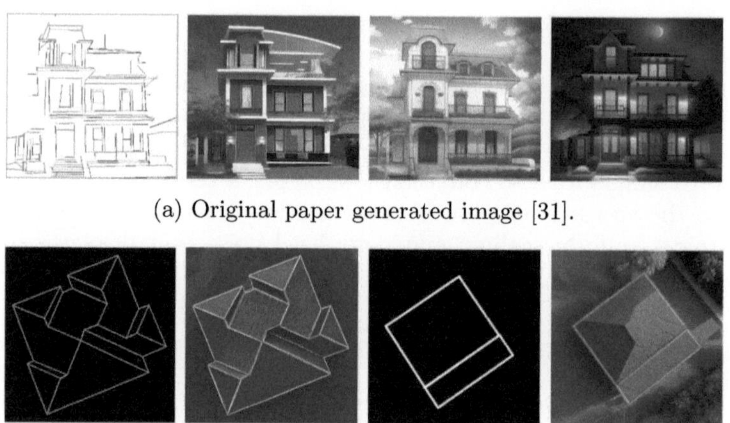

(a) Original paper generated image [31].

(b) Our generated synthetic image using Roof Intuitive [22] and HEAT [7] label.

Fig. 4. Generative synthetic image dataset examples.

To evaluate the fidelity of the synthetic imagery, we explore the use of the Structural Similarity Index (SSIM) (Eq. 1) as a texture control metric. SSIM scores are computed separately for buildings and backgrounds by comparing the synthetic images to the real RGB dataset. Mathematically, this can be expressed as:

$$\mathrm{SSIM}(real, synt) = \frac{(2\mu_{real}\mu_{synt} + C_1)(2\sigma_{real,synt} + C_2)}{(\mu_{real}^2 + \mu_{synt}^2 + C_1)(\sigma_{real}^2 + \sigma_{synt}^2 + C_2)}, \tag{1}$$

where $real$ and $synt$ are the two images being compared, μ_{real} and μ_{synt} are the average pixel intensities of $real$ and $synt$, σ_{real}^2 and σ_{synt}^2 are the variances of $real$ and $synt$, $\sigma_{real,synt}$ is the covariance between $real$ and $synt$. C_1 and C_2 are constants used to stabilize the division with weak denominator values.

This approach is designed to ensure both structural and textural consistency in building geometry, while allowing for controlled variability in the background between real and synthetic dataset images (see Fig. 4b). However, despite these constraints—such as the use of text captions, masks, and SSIM-based filtering—errors in dataset generation can still occur. For example, a roof intended to be flat is incorrectly generated with segmented structures.

3   Methodology

1. How Do Label Quality and Synthetic Data Stability Influence the Performance of the PolyRoof Model?

PolyRoof [2] is a graph-based building reconstruction model that integrates an attention-augmented R2AU-Net encoder [21], a GNN for edge inference, and a Geometry Product Loss to jointly optimize roof and building instance reconstruction. It leverages data augmentations—such as rotation, flipping, and dynamic range shifts—to simulate real-world variation while preserving label fidelity. Specialized losses, including Point Positional and Area Segmentation Loss, enhance geometric accuracy, especially in dense urban scenes.

Model performance is strongly influenced by label quality. Precise pixel-to-point alignment is essential for accurate vertex detection and edge connectivity. Even minor misalignments can degrade graph construction, leading to poor polygon reconstruction. High-fidelity labels enable the model to learn fine-grained spatial relationships, making them critical for robust training.

To mitigate issues with noisy or misaligned labels, synthetic datasets offer a viable alternative. Generated using text prompts and control masks based on the original annotations, models like ControlNet [31] produce RGB images aligned to the label masks, effectively correcting spatial mismatches. These synthetic image–label pairs simulate high-quality data conditions for training.

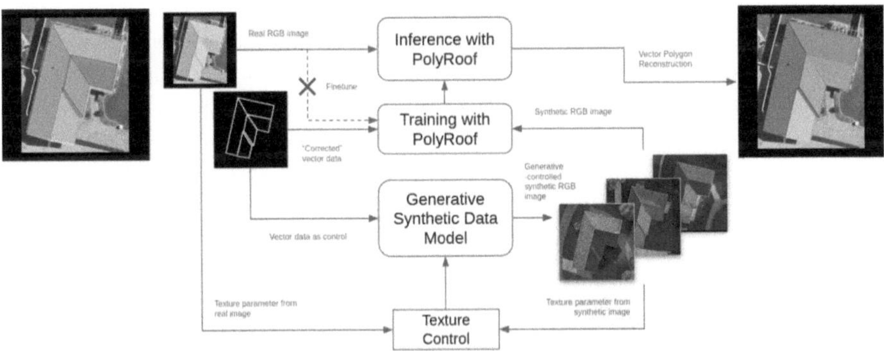

Fig. 5. Schematic overview of the process in which generative synthetic datasets are used to compensate for or "correct" misaligned labels during model training.

To assess the stability and reproducibility of this synthetic data pipeline, datasets are generated in triplicate under identical settings. A separate PolyRoof model is trained from scratch on each synthetic set and evaluated on both synthetic and real test data. Low variance in performance across runs indicates consistent generation and generalization. Higher variability may reflect sensitivity to generative factors such as prompt diversity or mask fidelity. This setup is illustrated in Fig. 5.

Both label accuracy and synthetic data consistency are pivotal to PolyRoof's performance. Where real-world annotations fall short, high-quality synthetic data provides a scalable, reproducible solution for maintaining model reliability and spatial precision.

2. How Does Texture Control in Synthetic Data and Pretraining Influence Model Performance?

Generative models like ControlNet enable the flexible creation of synthetic datasets by combining structural masks with text prompts to vary surrounding context, object presence, and lighting. While this enriches training diversity, such outputs can occasionally appear overly stylized, diverging from the realism expected in aerial imagery—potentially undermining their utility for precise spatial learning.

To counter this, we introduce texture control using the Structural Similarity Index (SSIM) to enforce realism, particularly at key structural regions like corners and edges. This step is crucial for graph-based reconstruction models such as PolyRoof, which depend on visual cues to accurately detect roof vertices and spatial relationships. Unrealistic or simplified textures can impair point detection, degrade edge inference, and ultimately lead to poor polygon reconstruction. Thus, maintaining texture fidelity is not just an aesthetic concern but a functional requirement for robust performance.

To further investigate model, we conduct a two-part experiment involving pretraining with synthetic data and fine-tuning with real data. In the first experiment, models are trained exclusively on synthetic datasets—generated across three reproducible runs with perfect label alignment and structural control—and then evaluated directly on real test data. This setup assesses the extent to which synthetic training alone can generalize to real-world conditions, especially in the presence of label misalignment in real data as shown also in Fig. 5.

In the second experiment, we use the best-performing synthetic model checkpoints from the first phase as pretrained weights. These are then fine-tuned on varying fractions (5%, 10%, 20%, 40%, 80%, and 100%) of real data with accurate labels. This allows us to evaluate how much clean real-world data is required to recover or exceed baseline performance, and to what extent synthetic pretraining can compensate for limited high-quality annotations.

Together, these experiments demonstrate that texture-controlled synthetic data enhances model learning, while strategic pretraining and fine-tuning can effectively mitigate the negative impacts of label misalignment—improving both reconstruction accuracy and model generalization.

3. How is the performance of the synthetic generative dataset evaluated in terms of its accuracy and detail in building model reconstruction?

To evaluate the synthetic dataset's performance, we use the same metrics from the original PolyRoof study [2] for direct baseline comparison. These include accuracy metrics—Point Position Accuracy and Line Distance Accuracy—and precision metrics—Building Instance F1-Score, Roof Segment Instance F1-Score, and Reconstruction Score. Metrics are computed only on reconstructions with an Intersection over Union (IoU) above 50%, ensuring meaningful structural alignment.

Point Position Accuracy is measured by Root Mean Square Error (RMSE) between predicted and ground truth roof corners, with lower values indicating better accuracy. Line Distance Accuracy combines Hausdorff and Fréchet Distances to capture maximum and sequential deviations in roof outlines. The Building and Roof Segment F1-Scores use IoU-based Precision and Recall to assess prediction alignment. The Reconstruction Score harmonizes these F1-Scores, highlighting both overall building shape and roof detail consistency.

$$\text{Reconstruction Score} = \frac{2 \cdot F1_{\text{Building}} \cdot F1_{\text{Roof}}}{F1_{\text{Building}} + F1_{\text{Roof}}} \tag{2}$$

The original PolyRoof study highlighted a limitation in evaluating high-Level of Detail (LoD) building models, particularly regarding discrepancies in the number of geometric elements. To address this, we introduce an additional metric to assess **prediction completeness**, capturing how well the predicted count of points, lines, and polygons matches the ground truth. For each component, the score is calculated as:

$$\text{Completeness Score} = \max\left(0, 1 - \frac{|\text{count}_{\text{pred}} - \text{count}_{\text{gt}}|}{\text{count}_{\text{gt}}}\right) \tag{3}$$

This formulation ensures that any over- or under-estimation reduces the score, while preserving a lower bound of 0 (no completeness) and an upper bound of 1 (perfect match), then this value is scaled in percentage form. It provides a direct measure of how well the structural richness of the ground truth is preserved in the prediction, making it especially useful for high-detail reconstruction tasks. This score balances the accuracy of the overall building shape with the finer details of individual roof segments, capturing the whole-and-part relationship through position accuracy, segmentation precision, and geometric completeness.

4   Result and Discussion

4.1   Baseline Experiment

The experiments begin by establishing a baseline using datasets with correctly aligned labels to evaluate the model's optimal performance. As shown in Table 1, the results on the Roof Intuitive dataset exhibit minor deviations from the original study. These discrepancies are likely due to differences in training configurations, such as hyperparameter choices, initialization schemes, or random seed variations. Performance differences between Roof Intuitive and HEAT can be attributed to variations in their geometric complexity distributions, as discussed in the original paper and illustrated in Fig. 2.

Table 1. Performance on real datasets with correct and misaligned labels. Misalignment (Mis-al) leads to NaN values, reflecting a collapse in vertex detection and connectivity.

Dataset	Label	Position		Area Segmentation			Count		
		Pt. Acc. (px ↓)	Line Dist. (px ↓)	Build. F1 (% ↑)	Roof F1 (% ↑)	Recon. Score (% ↑)	Point (% ↑)	Line (% ↑)	Poly. (% ↑)
Roof Intuitive	Correct	1.43	15.22	93.21	89.17	91.15	88.94	85.55	84.05
	Mis-al	NaN	NaN	NaN	NaN	NaN	NaN	NaN	NaN
HEAT	Correct	1.62	14.96	87.54	91.04	89.26	84.78	81.59	74.21
	Mis-al	NaN	NaN	NaN	NaN	NaN	NaN	NaN	NaN

To assess the impact of label misalignment, the model is subsequently trained on real images paired with deliberately misaligned, augmented labels. In this setting, no meaningful building reconstruction occurs, resulting in NaN or undefined performance metrics. These findings, also reported in Table 1, highlight the critical importance of accurate annotations. Because the model relies on precise localization of roof corner points, any spatial misalignment severely impairs vertex detection and connectivity, ultimately causing reconstruction to fail.

Finally, the dataset with correctly aligned real labels is compared against a synthetic dataset—also featuring aligned labels—to evaluate model performance across real and synthetic domains under consistent annotation quality.

4.2 Misaligned Synthetic Dataset with Texture Control

The next phase of experimentation evaluates the performance of generative synthetic datasets constructed using control masks derived from misaligned labels. This setup simulates a form of "label correction," in which real RGB images are spatially realigned to match the misaligned annotations, ensuring consistency between input and ground truth. The goal is to assess whether synthetic data generated under these corrected conditions can improve model performance despite originating from inaccurate labels. Additionally, the impact of texture control is examined to determine how texture conditioning influences the predictive quality of each synthetic replication as illustrate in Fig. 5.

The results, summarized in Table 2, show that alignment-corrected synthetic datasets significantly outperform misaligned real datasets, which often produce invalid or empty outputs. Although the synthetic data still under-perform compared to real data with accurate labels, the improvements observed confirm that synthetic generation based on misaligned annotations can effectively mitigate label errors. Furthermore, the low errors and standard deviations across multiple synthetic replications demonstrate the stability and reliability of the synthetic data generation process. Importantly, the inclusion of texture control leads to consistent performance gains across all metrics, suggesting that texture cues enhance reconstruction accuracy and improve model robustness.

Table 2. Average performance on generative synthetic misaligned labels datasets with texture control

Dataset	Label	Position		Area Segmentation			Count		
		Pt. Acc. (px ↓)	Line Dist. (px ↓)	Build. F1 (% ↑)	Roof F1 (% ↑)	Recon. Score (% ↑)	Point (% ↑)	Line (% ↑)	Poly. (% ↑)
Roof Intuitive	Correct	1.43	15.22	93.21	89.17	91.15	88.94	85.55	84.05
	No Ctrl.	1.92	19.15	38.64	**91.01**	54.25	54.06	46.30	47.38
	w. SSIM	**1.78**	**16.57**	**43.66**	90.99	**58.99**	**61.51**	**53.49**	**51.43**
HEAT	Correct	1.62	14.96	87.54	91.04	89.26	84.78	81.59	74.21
	No Ctrl.	2.14	17.11	20.23	**90.01**	33.03	30.23	28.21	29.60
	w. SSIM	**2.13**	**15.96**	**26.45**	89.72	**40.85**	**40.66**	**39.12**	**38.03**

Building on these insights, the final analysis examines the transferability of models pretrained on texture-controlled synthetic datasets. The models used in this process are the best-performing synthetic replications.

4.3 Synthetic Dataset Pretraining with Real Dataset Finetuning

Given the strong performance of texture-controlled synthetic models—especially compared to failures from misaligned real labels—we assess the transferability of the best pretrained models: SSIM-Control Synthetic 2 for Roof Intuitive and SSIM-Control Synthetic 3 for HEAT. While synthetic data enhances evaluation, it remains insufficient for reliable prediction alone, making fine-tuning with accurately labeled real data essential. The best results are presented in Table 3.

Table 3. Average performance on generative synthetic misaligned labels datasets with texture control

Dataset	Label	Position		Area Segmentation			Count		
		Pt. Acc. (px ↓)	Line Dist. (px ↓)	Build. F1 (% ↑)	Roof F1 (% ↑)	Recon. Score (% ↑)	Point (% ↑)	Line (% ↑)	Poly. (% ↑)
Roof Intuitive	Correct	1.43	15.22	93.21	89.17	91.15	88.94	85.55	84.05
	Ft. 20%	**1.40**	14.67	91.06	93.39	92.21	89.71	87.22	84.30
	Ft. 100%	1.42	**13.14**	**91.57**	**93.55**	**92.55**	**91.16**	**89.61**	**89.12**
HEAT	Correct	1.62	14.96	87.54	91.04	89.26	**84.78**	**81.59**	**74.21**
	Ft. 80%	1.55	16.77	90.65	91.22	90.94	78.90	74.05	64.65
	Ft. 100%	**1.53**	**13.88**	**91.83**	**91.34**	**91.58**	82.86	78.53	69.22

Across different real-data partitions, these pretrained checkpoints consistently performed well. Model accuracy steadily improves with more real data, even with as little as 5–10% of labeled samples. For Roof Intuitive, baseline performance is surpassed with only 20% real data, while HEAT requires at least

40%—reflecting domain shift due to differences in geometric complexity across two datasets. While both datasets eventually exceed their baselines in most metrics, completeness remains a challenging parameter. Roof Intuitive surpasses the baseline in completeness, while HEAT continues to face challenges in this aspect.

These findings reinforce that while synthetic data alone is insufficient, it serves as an effective pretraining and dataset enrichment strategy—substantially boosting reconstruction quality when combined with well-aligned real data.

4.4 Qualitative Result

Beyond quantitative improvements, qualitative gains are also evident. As shown in Fig. 6, which presents detail-oriented reconstructions of building roofs, the different polygon colors represent distinct roof segments. The combination of pretraining and fine-tuning consistently enhances reconstruction quality across various roof geometries. The model demonstrates an ability to accurately recover distinct roof segments and finer structural details, even across a wide range

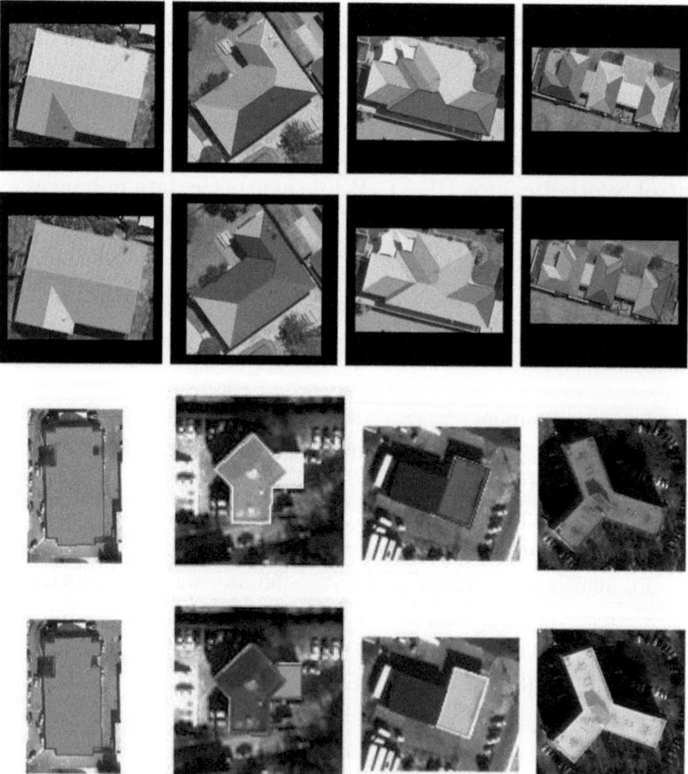

Fig. 6. Qualitative results of roof reconstruction from fine-tuned models. Top two rows show results from Roof Intuitive with 20% and 100% real data, while the bottom two rows show HEAT with 80% and 100% real data.

of complexity levels. Notably, polygon predictions improve in both datasets, highlighting the model's capacity to generalize structural priors learned during pretraining.

However, some inconsistencies remain. In certain cases, the model fails to reconstruct relatively simple structures—such as missing segments or incomplete outlines—despite successfully handling more complex roofs. Interestingly, fine-tuning with larger real-data partitions does not always yield better results than smaller subsets, suggesting that reconstruction performance depends not only on data volume but also on data quality and alignment.

5   Conclusion

Graph-based roof reconstruction models like PolyRoof perform well when trained on accurately labeled data but show a dramatic performance drop—with NaN value—when trained with misaligned annotations. To address this, synthetic datasets generated from misaligned labels using Stable Diffusion and ControlNet offer a reliable alternative. These datasets consistently preserved structure and precision, as demonstrated by stable reconstruction performance across three synthetic replications. However, models trained solely on synthetic data still fall short of those trained on perfectly aligned real-world labels. Incorporating texture control improved results further, but remained insufficient for direct real-world deployment.

Where synthetic datasets prove most valuable is in pretraining. Models initialized on synthetic data and fine-tuned with even small amounts of accurately labeled real data—such as those from public datasets—achieved significant performance gains. As the proportion of real data increased, performance steadily improved and, in some cases, exceeded that of models trained only on real data. Nonetheless, completeness metrics—particularly polygon count—remain relatively low, reflecting limitations in reconstructing certain roof geometries with specific structural complexities.

Overall, these findings highlight that while synthetic data alone cannot fully replace high-quality labels, it is a powerful pretraining and dataset enrichment strategy. When combined with even limited real data, it enhances model performance and robustness, offering a practical solution to challenges in label quality and data scarcity in roof reconstruction tasks using graph-based model.

References

1. Abdelrahman, M., Macatulad, E., Lei, B., Quintana, M., Miller, C., Biljecki, F.: What is a digital twin anyway? Deriving the definition for the built environment from over 15,000 scientific publications. arXiv preprint arXiv:2409.19005 (2024)
2. Amrullah, C., Panangian, D., Bittner, K.: Polyroof: precision roof polygonization in urban residential building with graph neural networks. In: 2025 Joint Urban Remote Sensing Event (JURSE), vol. CFP25RSD-ART, pp. 1–4 (2025). https://doi.org/10.1109/JURSE60372.2025.11075990

3. Biljecki, F., Ledoux, H., Stoter, J.: An improved lod specification for 3d building models. Comput. Environ. Urban Syst. **59**, 25–37 (2016)

4. Bird, J.J., Lotfi, A.: CIFAKE: image classification and explainable identification of ai-generated synthetic images. IEEE Access **12**, 15642–15650 (2024)

5. Bittner, K., Liebel, L., Körner, M., Reinartz, P.: Long-short skip connections in deep neural networks for dsm refinement. Int. Arch. Photogramm. Remote Sens. Spat. Inf. Sci. **43**(B2), 383–390 (2020)

6. Cai, B., Shao, Z., Huang, X., Zhou, X., Fang, S.: Deep learning-based building height mapping using sentinel-1 and sentinel-2 data. Int. J. Appl. Earth Obs. Geoinf. **122**, 103399 (2023)

7. Chen, J., Qian, Y., Furukawa, Y.: Heat: holistic edge attention transformer for structured reconstruction (2022). https://arxiv.org/abs/2111.15143

8. Dosovitskiy, A., Ros, G., Codevilla, F., Lopez, A., Koltun, V.: Carla: an open urban driving simulator. In: Conference on Robot Learning, pp. 1–16. PMLR (2017)

9. Fan, C., Zhang, C., Yahja, A., Mostafavi, A.: Disaster city digital twin: a vision for integrating artificial and human intelligence for disaster management. Int. J. Inf. Manag. **56**, 102049 (2021)

10. Georgousis, S., Kenning, M.P., Xie, X.: Graph deep learning: state of the art and challenges. IEEE Access **9**, 22106–22140 (2021)

11. Henry, C., Fraundorfer, F., Vig, E.: Aerial road segmentation in the presence of topological label noise. In: 2020 25th International Conference on Pattern Recognition (ICPR), pp. 2336–2343. IEEE (2021)

12. Jing, J., Gao, T., Zhang, W., Gao, Y., Sun, C.: Image feature information extraction for interest point detection: a comprehensive review. IEEE Trans. Pattern Anal. Mach. Intell. **45**(4), 4694–4712 (2022)

13. Khan, A.H., Omar, S., Mushtary, N., Verma, R., Kumar, D., Alam, S.: Digital twin and artificial intelligence incorporated with surrogate modeling for hybrid and sustainable energy systems. In: Fathi, M., Zio, E., Pardalos, P.M. (eds.) Handbook of Smart Energy Systems, LNCS, pp. 1–23. Springer, Cham (2022). https://doi.org/10.1007/978-3-030-72322-4_147-1

14. Koetzier, L.R., et al.: Generating synthetic data for medical imaging. Radiology **312**(3), e232471 (2024)

15. Kollem, S., Reddy, K.R.L., Rao, D.S.: A review of image denoising and segmentation methods based on medical images. Int. J. Mach. Learn. Comput. **9**(3), 288–295 (2019)

16. Kutzner, T., Chaturvedi, K., Kolbe, T.H.: Citygml 3.0: new functions open up new applications. PFG–J. Photogramm. Remote Sens. Geoinf. Sci. **88**(1), 43–61 (2020)

17. Labs, B.F.: Flux.1-dev (2023). https://huggingface.co/black-forest-labs/FLUX.1-dev. Accessed 13 Jan 2025

18. Meng, S., Soleimani-Babakamali, M.H., Taciroglu, E.: Automatic roof type classification through machine learning for regional wind risk assessment. arXiv preprint arXiv:2305.17315 (2023)

19. Qian, Y., Zhang, H., Furukawa, Y.: Roof-gan: learning to generate roof geometry and relations for residential houses. In: Proceedings of the IEEE/CVF Conference on Computer Vision and Pattern Recognition, pp. 2796–2805 (2021)

20. Qian, Z., et al.: Deep roof refiner: a detail-oriented deep learning network for refined delineation of roof structure lines using satellite imagery. Int. J. Appl. Earth Obs. Geoinf. **107**, 102680 (2022)

21. Qiang, Z., Songyu, C., Zhifang, W.: R2au-net: attention recurrent residual convolutional neural network for multimodal medical image segmentation. Secur. Com-

mun. Netw. **2021**, 1–10 (2021). https://doi.org/10.1155/2021/6625688, https://cir.nii.ac.jp/crid/1360580628164331648

22. Ren, J., et al.: Intuitive and efficient roof modeling for reconstruction and synthesis (2021). https://arxiv.org/abs/2109.07683

23. Reyes, M.F., d'Angelo, P., Fraundorfer, F.: Syntcities: a large synthetic remote sensing dataset for disparity estimation. IEEE J. Sel. Top. Appl. Earth Obs. Remote Sens. **15**, 10087–10098 (2022)

24. Rombach, R., Blattmann, A., Lorenz, D., Esser, P., Ommer, B.: High-resolution image synthesis with latent diffusion models. In: Proceedings of the IEEE/CVF Conference on Computer Vision and Pattern Recognition, pp. 10684–10695 (2022)

25. Schrotter, G., Hürzeler, C.: The digital twin of the city of Zurich for urban planning. PFG-J. Photogramm. Remote Sens. Geoinf. Sci. **88**(1), 99–112 (2020)

26. Schuegraf, P., Bittner, K.: Automatic building footprint extraction from multi-resolution remote sensing images using a hybrid fcn. ISPRS Int. J. Geo Inf. **8**(4), 191 (2019)

27. Schuegraf, P., Fuentes Reyes, M., Xu, Y., Bittner, K.: Roof3d: a real and synthetic data collection for individual building roof plane and building sections detection. ISPRS Ann. Photogramm. Remote Sens. Spat. Inf. Sci. **10**, 971–979 (2023)

28. XLabs-AI: flux-controlnet-canny-v3 (2023). https://huggingface.co/XLabs-AI/flux-controlnet-canny-v3. Accessed 13 Jan 2025

29. Xu, Y., Jubanski, J., Bittner, K., Siegert, F.: Roof plane parsing towards lod-2.2 building reconstruction based on joint learning using remote sensing images. Int. J. Appl. Earth Obs. Geoinf. **133**, 104096 (2024)

30. Yang, Z., Zhan, F., Liu, K., Xu, M., Lu, S.: AI-generated images as data source: the dawn of synthetic era. arXiv preprint arXiv:2310.01830 (2023)

31. Zhang, L., Rao, A., Agrawala, M.: Adding conditional control to text-to-image diffusion models. In: Proceedings of the IEEE/CVF International Conference on Computer Vision, pp. 3836–3847 (2023)

32. Zhou, W., Persello, C., Stein, A.: Building usage classification using a transformer-based multimodal deep learning method. In: 2023 Joint Urban Remote Sensing Event (JURSE), pp. 1–4. IEEE (2023)

33. Zorzi, S., Fraundorfer, F.: Re: polyworld-a graph neural network for polygonal scene parsing. In: Proceedings of the IEEE/CVF International Conference on Computer Vision, pp. 16762–16771 (2023)

SshELF: Single-Shot Hierarchical Extrapolation of Latent Features for 3D Reconstruction from Sparse-Views

Eyvaz Najafli[1,2], Marius Kästingschäfer[1,3(✉)], Sebastian Bernhard[1], Thomas Brox[3], and Andreas Geiger[2]

[1] Continental, Hanover, Germany
[2] University of Tübingen, Tübingen, Germany
[3] University of Freiburg, Freiburg, Germany
`marius.kaestingschaefer@continetal.de`

Abstract. Reconstructing unbounded outdoor scenes from sparse outward-facing views poses significant challenges due to minimal view overlap. Previous methods often lack cross-scene understanding and their primitive-centric formulations overload local features to compensate for missing global context, resulting in blurriness in unseen parts of the scene. We propose sshELF, a fast, single-shot pipeline for sparse-view 3D scene reconstruction via hierarchal extrapolation of latent features. Our key insights is that disentangling information extrapolation from primitive decoding allows efficient transfer of structural patterns across training scenes. Our method: (1) learns cross-scene priors to generate intermediate virtual views to extrapolate to unobserved regions, (2) offers a two-stage network design separating virtual view generation from 3D primitive decoding for efficient training and modular model design, and (3) integrates a pre-trained foundation model for joint inference of latent features and texture, improving scene understanding and generalization. sshELF can reconstruct 360° scenes from six sparse input views and achieves competitive results on synthetic and real-world datasets. We find that sshELF faithfully reconstructs occluded regions, supports real-time rendering, and provides rich latent features for downstream applications. Code will be made available.

Keywords: Feed-Forward 3D Reconstruction · Neural Rendering

1 Introduction

We consider reconstructing unbounded outdoor scenes from sparse outward-facing cameras with minimal overlap between adjacent views. This problem poses two fundamental challenges: (1) resolving distant object occlusions (areas hidden behind terrain or other vehicles) and ego-occlusions (regions obscured by the

---

E. Najafli and M. Kästingschäfer—Equal contribution.

© The Author(s), under exclusive license to Springer Nature Switzerland AG 2026
M. Keuper and F. Locatello (Eds.): DAGM GCPR 2025, LNCS 16125, pp. 550–567, 2026.
https://doi.org/10.1007/978-3-032-12840-9_35

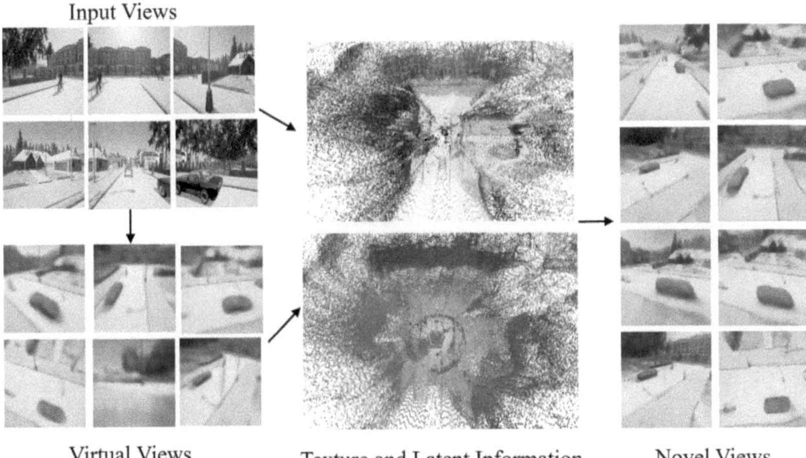

Fig. 1. Overview. Given a number of input images, sshELF first reconstructs several virtual views and only then predicts the 3D Gaussian primitives of the scene from which novel views are rendered. The colors of the latent information correspond to different object classes, such as purple for buildings and green for vegetation.

sensor platform itself), and (2) overcoming limited multi-view correspondence cues due to minimal overlap. In practical autonomous driving applications, this dual challenge becomes even more demanding since dense bird's-eye views or occupancy maps are required in real-time.

While traditional neural radiance fields (NeRFs) and 3D Gaussian Splatting have advanced novel view synthesis, their reliance on per-scene optimization and dense view coverage limits applicability in real-world scenarios with sparse, non-overlapping inputs [19,26]. Existing per-scene optimization methods are often tested on inward-facing datasets with high view overlap [10,31,57] or close-by novel views. In contrast, vehicle-mounted cameras are usually outward-facing with minimal camera overlap [2,4,34] and operate in large, unbounded outdoor environments. Recent feedforward approaches aim to generalize across scenes but struggle with large viewpoint changes [7,53], some lack support for multi-view aggregation necessary for 360-degree surround-view synthesis, [35], or aren't real-time renderable [13].

Although Vision transformers trained on large datasets for metric depth prediction can provide useful priors [3,18,51], the resulting depth maps, when combined with pixel information, are inadequate for generating complete 3D representations [14,22,50]. A key limitation is their inability to account for unobserved regions, including areas obscured by the sensor platform itself, such as the ground beneath the vehicle. As a result, subsequent reconstructions exhibit incomplete geometry in those regions. Furthermore, when reconstructing geometry from multiple depth maps simultaneously, multi-view scale inconsistency at the border regions leads to artifacts. Thus resulting in low-quality 3D reconstructions and inadequate novel views [22,35].

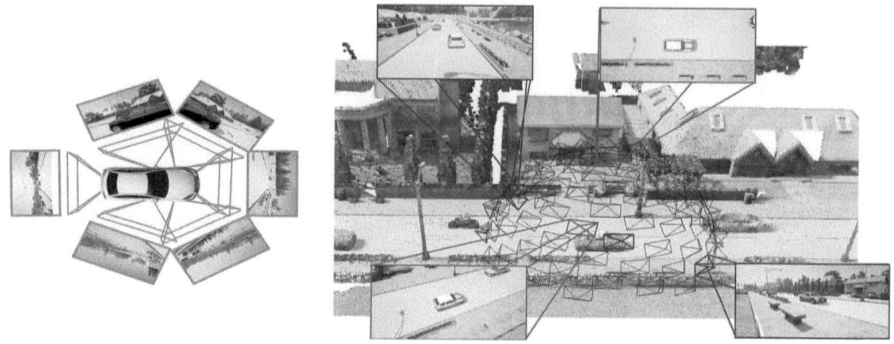

Fig. 2. Reference, Virtual and Novel Views. An example showing input views in green, a set of virtual views in red, and potential novel views in blue. Virtual view generation is key to enhancing representational capacity and extrapolating to unobserved scene areas.

Problem Statment. Our work tackles the problem of fast single-shot sparse-view 3D reconstruction for outdoor traffic scenes. We introduce **sshELF** an efficient, performant single-shot pipeline for sparse-view 3D reconstruction via hierarchical extrapolation of latent features. Our approach is based on three insighs:

First, existing models are constrained in their ability to infer unseen regions and views far from the input images since their representational capacity is limited [5,7]. By restricting the process only to the information present in the input images, without intermediate steps or representations, the models struggle to generalize to unobserved parts of the scene. Unlike previous methods, sshELF generates intermediate virtual views that help to reconstruct unseen regions. This way, our method is not restricted to the information in the given input images. In Fig. 2, we visualize example input, virtual, and novel views. Second, we decompose our network into a *backbone*, generating virtual views, and a *translator* that decodes the reference and virtual views into explicit Gaussian primitives. This separation enables the backbone to increase the information content while allowing the translator to lift higher-quality Gaussian primitives. The decomposition facilitates isolated training, reduces computational requirements, and increases the virtual view number and resolution. Third, large pre-trained foundation models such as DinoV2 [27] and near-metric depth estimation methods [49] are underutilized when used solely as input to the model [35]. We incorporate these directly into our architecture, and we train our backbone to output both texture and latent information for reference and virtual views. Leveraging intermediate latents enables effective multi-stage depth prediction. Additionally, extracting latents alongside Gaussian primitives supports downstream tasks such as semantic scene understanding. See Fig. 1 for an example latent clustering.

Overall, sshELF is a fast two-stage single-shot unbounded 3D scene reconstruction pipeline, particularly well suited for outward-facing cameras with little view overlap. The contributions of this paper can be summarized as follows: **(1) Reconstruct Occluded Regions**. Our method reconstructs occluded regions faithfully where other methods fail, as shown by competitive results on both synthetic and real-world data. **(2) High Speed and Visual Quality**. Our method can perform fast end-to-end 360° scene reconstruction and novel view synthesis from six unbounded surround vehicle views in 0.18 s. sshELF can render far-away viewpoints with high quality as measured on synthetic and real-world data. **(3) Optimal Utilization of Latent Information**. Since our method jointly predicts latent and texture information, as well as depth, we can leverage latent features to obtain insights into spatial semantics, occupancy, and geometry.

We perform an in-depth analysis to justify our architectural choices and compare our final model with multiple state-of-the-art approaches. The code will be made available.

2 Related Work

Iterative Driving Scene Reconstruction. Iterative driving scene reconstruction methods perform test-time per-scene fitting, making them infeasible for real-time applications. Iterative scene reconstruction methods can be classified into NeRF-based and 3D Gaussian-based approaches. NeRF-based approaches like Neural Scene Graph (NSG) [28] decompose a scene into static and dynamic objects [12,39,40,48]. These methods often require LiDAR data and take up to 30 min for training. Gaussian-based parameterizations enable real-time rendering but still require lengthy offline reconstruction. Many of them model backgrounds and objects separately, using bounding boxes and scene graphs [9,46,56,58]. To alleviate artifacts, per-scene reconstruction pipelines have been combined with diffusion-based priors [15,54] or by enforcing symmetry [20]. Most per-scene optimization methods rely on posed input images, though a few methods also jointly learn poses [8,24]. Despite being real-time renderable, offline reconstruction remains time-intensive and often LiDAR-dependent, limiting real-time applicability.

Few-View Reconstruction. Feedforward methods address the time limitations of iterative approaches. Early NeRF-based methods retrieve image features via view projection and aggregate the resulting features [6,42,53]. Some methods apply diffusion priors [1,36,45] but focus on small-scale scenes. A method focusing on single-shot prediction in driving scenarios is DistillNeRF [41], which distills single-shot priors from the per-scene optimization method EmerNeRF. Closest to our work are Neo360 [16], which is limited to inward-facing views, and 6Img-to-3D [13], which uses a slow triplane-based representation. Gaussian-based methods model scenes explicitly, enabling simpler single-shot parameterization. Recent works focus on single objects or small-scale scenes [37,47,52,59],

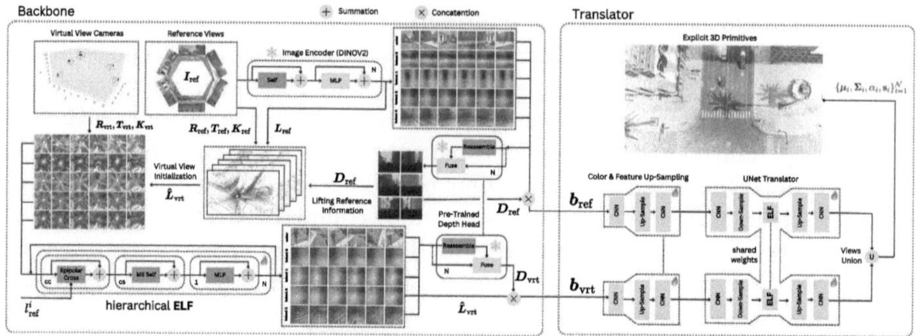

Fig. 3. Overview of sshELF. Given a few input images, sshELF first encodes them into latent features using a pre-trained DinoV2 (Sect. 3.1). As part of the *backbone*, the latent features, together with a pre-trained depth head, are used to initialize the virtual views, which are refined using hierarchical ELF blocks consisting of cross- and self-attention layers (Sect. 3.2). Reference and virtual views are then fed into the *translator* part to predict 3D Gaussian splats (Sect. 3.3). Not shown here is the rasterization part used for creating novel views (Sect. 3.4).

but require significant input views with overlap. Flash3D [35] uses depth prediction but fails to inpaint unseen regions. Methods like pixelSplat [5], latentSplat [44], and MVSplat [7] leverage cross-attention for image pairs, excelling in close-range novel view synthesis but struggling with large camera displacements. Concurrent work DrivingForward [38] reconstructs driving scenes from nuScenes but is limited to small viewpoint changes.

Many few-shot 3D reconstructions and novel view synthesis methods overload the 3D Gaussian predictor to inpaint occluded parts of the scene by predicting several Gaussians per ray. This causes blurriness in the unseen parts of the scene, which are far away from the input views. Unlike existing methods, our work utilizes intermediate representations to generate unobserved views and thus obtain a more complete scene reconstruction.

3   Method

We distinguish between reference, virtual, and novel views. Reference views describe the captured viewpoints fed as input into the architecture, and novel views describe the novel synthesized viewpoints. While previous work focuses on reference and novel views, we additionally introduce virtual views that define intermediate viewpoints between them, facilitating the inpainting of unobserved regions in the final reconstruction.

Given n_ref reference views containing RGB images $I_\text{ref} \in \mathbb{R}^{3 \times H \times W}$, their associated camera extrinsics $P_\text{ref} = [R_\text{ref}|T_\text{ref}] \in \mathbb{R}^{3 \times 4}$ and intrinsics $K_\text{ref} \in \mathbb{R}^{3 \times 3}$, sshELF generates consistent 3D geometry and synthesize n_nvs novel surround views $I_\text{nvs} \in \mathbb{R}^{3 \times H \times W}$. The method is visualized in Fig. 3. The number of reference, virtual, and novel views can be flexibly varied within our pipeline. The image encoder, backbone, translator, and rendering process are described in the following sections.

3.1   Image Encoder

Given images $\boldsymbol{I}_{\text{ref}}$, sshELF applies a pre-trained self-supervised vision transformer (ViT) [11] to obtain patch-wise latent features $\boldsymbol{L}_{\text{ref}} = \{\boldsymbol{l}^i_{\text{ref}} \mid i = 1,...,n_{\text{ref}}\} \in \mathbb{R}^{n_{\text{ref}} \times (d_E+3) \times (H/14) \times (W/14)}$, and a class token [CLS] $\{\boldsymbol{g}^i_{\text{ref}}\}^n_{i=1} \in \mathbb{R}^{d_E}$ containing aggregated global feature information. The model retrieves latent embeddings from the last n ViT blocks at various depths, each of which is a d_E dimensional vector. We use DINOv2 [27] since it is semantically rich and retains geometric information well. To optimally preserve texture information, the normalized and resized RGB tensor is concatenated with each of the n layer's patch embeddings, increasing the channel dimension of $\boldsymbol{l}^i_{\text{ref}}$ to $d_E + 3$.

3.2   Backbone: Generating Virtual Views

Given the intrinsics $\boldsymbol{K}_{\text{ref}}$ and extrinsic $\boldsymbol{P}_{\text{ref}}$ of the reference views, along with ground-truth image information and intrinsics $\boldsymbol{K}_{\text{vrt}}$ and extrinsic $\boldsymbol{P}_{\text{vrt}}$ of n_{vrt} virtual views, the task of the backbone is to construct latent and texture information for the virtual views. During cross-scene training we randomly sample the virtual views with probabilities proportional to the degree of overlap with the reference views to maximize the information content of occluded regions.

To initialize n_{vrt} virtual views, texture information from the reference views is projected into 3D and back-projected onto the virtual views using point cloud rendering [17]. To obtain the required depth maps $\boldsymbol{D}_i$, the latents $\boldsymbol{L}_{\text{ref}}$ without texture information obtained from the reference views are fed into a fine-tuned dense depth prediction transformer [30]. The resulting depth maps $\boldsymbol{D}_i$ can then be used to project pixel information from the reference views into 3D space by

$$\mathbf{M_i} = \begin{bmatrix} \mathbf{R}_{\text{ref}} & \mathbf{T}_{\text{ref}} \\ \mathbf{0}^\mathsf{T} & 1 \end{bmatrix}^{-1} \begin{bmatrix} \mathbf{K}_{\text{ref}} & \mathbf{0} \\ \mathbf{0}^\mathsf{T} & 1 \end{bmatrix}^{-1} \hat{\mathbf{m}}_\mathbf{i}, \tag{1}$$

where $\hat{\mathbf{m}}_\mathbf{i} = \begin{bmatrix} \mathbf{m_i} & 1 & 1/\boldsymbol{D}_i \end{bmatrix}^\mathsf{T}$ representing the pixel coordinate in image space and M_i representing the 3D point in world coordinates. In the next step, the feature information from the reference views is projected into 3D space to initialize the latent and texture information of the virtual views $\tilde{\boldsymbol{L}}_{\text{vrt}} = \{\boldsymbol{l}^i_{\text{vrt}} \mid i = 1,...,n\}$. The initialized virtual views are now more informative than randomly initialized ones since they contain approximate texture and latent information, but they still suffer from occlusions and other artifacts. To refine the virtual views, we hierarchically extrapolate the latent features via **ELF** blocks, each denoted as $\mathcal{E}(\cdot)$. Ground Truth reference view information, virtual view initializations, and the output from the previous blocks are fed as input to the corresponding ELF block. In each ELF block, a succession of cc cross-attention denoted as **CA** and cs self-attention denotes as **SA** operations are applied to transfer information between reference and virtual views, followed by an **MLP** layer:

$$\hat{l}^i_{\text{vrt}} = \hat{l}^{i-1}_{\text{vrt}} + \tilde{l}^i_{\text{vrt}} \tag{2}$$

$$C(\hat{l}^i_{\text{ref}}, \hat{l}^i_{\text{vrt}})_j + = \mathbf{CA}(C(\hat{l}^i_{\text{ref}}, \hat{l}^i_{\text{vrt}})_j) \quad \forall j \in \{1, \ldots, cc\} \tag{3}$$

$$C(\hat{l}^i_{\text{ref}}, \hat{l}^i_{\text{vrt}})_k + = \mathbf{SA}(C(\hat{l}^i_{\text{ref}}, \hat{l}^i_{\text{vrt}})_k) \quad \forall k \in \{1, \ldots, cs\} \tag{4}$$

$$C(\hat{l}^i_{\text{ref}}, \hat{l}^i_{\text{vrt}}) + = \mathbf{MLP}(C(\hat{l}^i_{\text{ref}}, \hat{l}^i_{\text{vrt}})), \tag{5}$$

where $C(\cdot, \cdot)$ concatenates two feature maps along the view dimension. The ELF block performs an inpainting-like refinement, addressing occlusions and enhancing texture. By predicting features for both virtual and reference views, we introduce a cycle-consistency constraint, ensuring that the ELF block preserves the reference features as close to the ground truth as possible while reconstructing virtual views. Following [44], we use epipolar geometry to inform and constrain the cross-attention computation described in Eq. (3). A sequence of CNN and MLP layers is applied on the output of Eq. 5 to infer the [CLS] token from the latent features.

In the final stage of the backbone, the resulting multi-stage latent codes for the virtual views are passed through a pre-trained depth head to obtain near-metric depth maps D_{vrt}. To achieve a complete scene reconstruction, we concatenate latent, texture, and depth predictions for the virtual views with the ground truth information from the reference views and feed them all as input to the translator.

3.3   Translator: Lifting to 3D

The translator transforms the features resulting from the backbone into 3D Gaussian primitives. The input consists of aggregated latent, color, and approximate depth information of both reference and virtual views.

$$C(\boldsymbol{b}_{\text{ref}}, \boldsymbol{b}_{\text{vrt}}) \in \mathbb{R}^{(n_{\text{ref}} + k_{\text{vrt}}) \times (d_E + 3 + 1) \times (h) \times (w)} \tag{6}$$

where $h \times w$ is the spatial dimension of the latent embeddings. We utilize a UNet-like architecture [32,33] to map from each view's backbone features to 3D Gaussian splats. The translator architecture $\mathcal{T}(\cdot)$ consists of two parts: an encoder and a decoder. The output of Eq. 6 is fed into the encoder, which is passed through a single layer of **ELF** block $\mathcal{E}$ to enforce multi-view consistency over reference and virtual views on the lowest layers in the UNet. The decoder then predicts splats per view whereby intermediate skip connections between the decoder and the encoder help to preserve fine-grained details. The resulting Gaussian splats are projected to ego vehicle coordinates, concatenated across spatial and views dimensions. The scene is now parameterized with the 3D Gaussian primitives

$$\{\boldsymbol{\mu}_i, \boldsymbol{\Sigma}_i, \alpha_i, \mathbf{s}_i\}_{i=1}^{(n_{\text{ref}} + n_{\text{vrt}}) \times N} \tag{7}$$

where $\boldsymbol{\mu}_i \in \mathbb{R}^3$ is the per pixel location of the Gaussians, $\boldsymbol{\Sigma}_i \in \mathbb{R}^{3 \times 3}$ is the covariance, $\alpha_i \in [0, 1)$ the opacity and $\mathbf{s}_i \in \mathbb{R}^{(l+1)^2}$ represents the coefficients for the spherical harmonics of degree l and N stands for the number of Gaussians generated per view. To ensure that the covariance matrix remains positive semi-definite, we predict a diagonal scaling matrix $\mathbf{S}$ and orthonormal rotation matrix $\mathbf{R}$ such that $\mathbf{\Sigma} = \mathbf{R}\mathbf{S}\mathbf{S}^\mathsf{T}\mathbf{R}^\mathsf{T}$, parameterized by the axis-scales $\mathbf{s} \in \mathbb{R}^3$ and $\mathbf{q} \in \mathbb{R}^4$ defining a normalized quaternion [19]. To alleviate local minima during the learning process of 3D primitives, we apply a probabilistic depth map prediction similar to pixelSplat [5].

3.4 Rendering Novel Views

Given extrinsics $\boldsymbol{P}_{\text{nvs}}$ and intrinsics $\boldsymbol{K}_{nvs}$, we render novel views $\hat{\boldsymbol{I}}_{\text{nvs}}$ using gaussian rasterization. To compute the unnormalized density of the ith 3D Gaussian the following function is applied

$$G_i(\mathbf{x}) = \exp\left(-\frac{1}{2}(\mathbf{x} - \boldsymbol{\mu}_i)^\mathsf{T}\mathbf{\Sigma}_i^{-1}(\mathbf{x} - \boldsymbol{\mu}_i)\right). \tag{8}$$

The color of the Gaussians $\boldsymbol{c} \in \mathbb{R}^3$ when viewed from direction $\boldsymbol{d} \in \mathbb{R}^3$ is computed by summing the spherical harmonics basis $\boldsymbol{c}(\boldsymbol{d}) = \sum_{i=1}^{n} s_i \mathcal{B}_i(\boldsymbol{d})$, here $\mathcal{B}_i$ is the ith spherical harmonics basis function. Finally, the pixel intensity $\boldsymbol{c}$ is computed from the $(n_{\text{ref}} + n_{\text{vrt}}) \times N$ ordered Gaussians using alpha compositing in the following way

$$\boldsymbol{c} = \sum_{i=1}^{n} c_i \alpha_i \prod_{j=1}^{i-1} (1 - \alpha_j) \tag{9}$$

The Gaussians can be rendered in real-time following [19]. The full architecture remains end-to-end differentiable; however, we train the backbone and the translator separately to be able to increase the number and resolution of inferred virtual views.

3.5 Training Objectives

During cross-scene training, the model is compelled to learn transferable structural priors, enabling generalization across different scenes. We assume the virtual views to be available for supervision, which can be sampled from the existing data in practice. This allows us to obtain the ground truth virtual view features by feeding them through the pre-trained ViT blocks to get $\{l^i_{\text{vrt}}\}_{i=1}^{n}$ for the training of the backbone. The translator can be trained separately with ground truth reference and virtual views.

Backbone Objectives. The backbone reconstructs virtual views consisting of latent features and texture information from reference views. An MSE loss between reconstructed features and ground truth features is applied at every stage of the backbone:

$$\mathcal{L}_{bb} = \lambda_1 \mathcal{L}_{\text{MSE}}\left(\hat{\boldsymbol{L}}_{\text{vrt}}, \boldsymbol{L}_{\text{vrt}}\right) + \lambda_2 \mathcal{L}_{\text{MSE}}\left(\hat{\boldsymbol{L}}_{\text{ref}}, \boldsymbol{L}_{\text{ref}}\right) \tag{10}$$

where λ_1, $\lambda_2 > 0$. The first part of the loss enforces the backbone to reconstruct intermediate and final latent features and low-resolution texture information of the virtual views. As an additional constraint, the second part of the loss enforces processed reference features to be similar to the ground truth reference features. This can be viewed as a cycle-consistency constraint whereby the information flowing from reference views to virtual views and then back should be maintained with minimal change.

Translator Objectives. The translator predicts the Gaussian primitives from which the novel views are rasterized. The translator is trained with:

$$\mathcal{L}_{tr} = \lambda_3 \mathcal{L}_{\mathrm{MSE}} \left(\hat{\boldsymbol{I}}_{\mathrm{nvs}}, \boldsymbol{I}_{\mathrm{nvs}} \right) + \lambda_4 \mathcal{L}_{\mathrm{MAE}} \left(\hat{\boldsymbol{D}}_{\mathrm{ref}}, \boldsymbol{D}_{\mathrm{nvs}} \right) \tag{11}$$

where $\lambda_3 > 0$, $\lambda_4 \geq 0$ and $\hat{\boldsymbol{D}}_{\mathrm{ref}}$ is the Z-buffer (also known as depth buffer) retrieved from the renderer, which provides a depth approximation [19]. This way, the error enforces texture and geometric correspondence where ground-truth depth maps are available; in the case of nuScenes, λ_4 is set to zero. When point cloud information is available, we also experimented with adding a Chamfer distance loss.

4   Experiments

A number of experiments are conducted to assess the capabilities of our method. We use synthetic and real-world driving data (described in Sect. 4.1) to test the performance of our method. Our quantitative and qualitative results (Sect. 4.2) show the visual quality and the high inference speed of our method.

4.1   Experimental Setup

Datasets. We evaluate on *SEED4D* [22], a synthetic dataset with 212k images from 2k driving scenes containing six outward-facing ego-vehicle images and 100 spherical supervision images per scene. We use Towns 1, 3–7, and 10 for training (1900 scenes) and Town 2 for testing (100 scenes). The ego-centric camera setup resembles the relative camera placement within the nuScene dataset, whereby the overlap between adjacent outward-looking views is minimal. We use the ego-vehicle images as reference views and sample virtual and novel views from the exocentric views. We additionally test on *nuScenes* [4] with six ego views (with 10% overlap [38]), using 700 scenes for training and 150 for testing. Since NuScenes does not contain exocentric views, we construct a multi-view evaluation setup by aggregating egocentric views captured across temporal sequences. In our framework, we utilize views with a temporal difference (TD) of zero (i.e., simultaneous captures from all vehicle-mounted cameras) as reference views. Novel view synthesis targets are then defined at TD = 2, 3, and 4 timesteps after the reference timestep, equivalent to 1 s, 1.5 s, and 2 s temporal offsets, respectively. Virtual views are placed between reference and novel views.

Evaluation Metrics. Performance is measured using the peak signal-to-noise ratio (PSNR), structural similarity index (SSIM) [43], and learned perceptual image patch similarity (LPIPS) [55]. We additionally compute the depth root mean square error (D-RMSE) where ground truth metric depth is available or the Chamfer distance when LiDAR data is accessible.

Baselines. We compare our method against a number of recent few-image novel-view-synthesis baselines. PixelNeRF [53] uses projected image feature for conditioning a neural radiance field. SplatterImage [37] predicts pixel-aligned 3D Gaussian primitives using a U-net. MVSplat [7] utilizes cross-attention, a cost volume, and a pre-trained depth model. 6Img-to-3D [13] uses self- and cross-attention for parameterizing a triplane together with image feature projection. PixelSplat [5] utilizes epipolar cross-attention and performs a probabilistic prediction of pixel-aligned Gaussians. For nuScenes we focus exclusively on the most recent real-time capable methods.

4.2 Results

SEED4D. As shown in Table 1, sshELF outperforms all previous methods in terms of PSNR, and ranks second in SSIM and D-RMSE. Other methods suffer from incomplete geometry, particularly in hidden or sensor-blocked regions. sshELF achieves a runtime of 0.182 s, demonstrating competitive performance. Notably, sshELF's end-to-end performance is more than 15x faster than the second-best model, 6Img-to-3D.

Table 1. SEED4D Results. Runtime comparison of scene-to-novel view inference, presented in both seconds and milliseconds to account for the large variations in execution time across different methods.

Methods	PSNR	SSIM	LPIPS	D-RMSE	Time
MVSplat	13.86	0.46	0.66	16.79	0.42ms
PixelNeRF	14.50	0.55	0.65	19.24	1.86s
SplatterImg.	17.79	0.58	0.57	11.05	32ms
pixelSplat	18.03	0.60	0.44	7.26	1.1ms
6Img-to-3D	18.68	0.73	0.45	6.23	2.85s
sshELF (Ours)	18.93	0.65	0.50	6.61	182ms

We visualize the qualitative performance of the different novel view synthesis methods on the SEED4D test set in Fig. 4.

NuScenes. Quantitative multi-timestep results in Table 2 demonstrate our method's superiority across visual and geometric metrics. The virtual view sampling in sshELF enables strategic allocation of scene representation capacity: by prioritizing reconstruction fidelity for distant viewpoints critical for wide-baseline

Fig. 4. Qualitative Novel View Synthesis Comparison on SEED4D Test Set. Comparison of large-baseline novel view synthesis under sparse observation conditions. Six ego-centric input frames (top row) with limited overlap serve as reference views. We evaluate each method's ability to reconstruct exo-centric with a large offset to the input views.

tasks, our method inherently trades off minor quality reductions in near-field regions. In contrast, methods like MVSplat [7] and PixelSplat [5], which reproject input pixels onto local planes, a design that limits scalability to far-view synthesis. This approach fails to model occlusions or parallax effects at larger distances as seen in Fig. 5 for MVSplat. Compared to the baselines, our method more accurately represents color information and reconstructs occluded regions with greater fidelity.

Table 2. nuScenes Results. Results are shown for temporal differences (TD) of 2, 3, and 4 in terms of PSNR, SSIM, LPIPS and Chamfer distance.

	Methods	PSNR↑	SSIM↑	LPIPS↓	Chamfer↓
TD2	MVSplat	16.624	0.436	0.553	646.11
	pixelSplat	18.031	0.459	0.495	1.191M
	sshELF (Ours)	19.133	0.645	0.634	51.67
TD3	MVSplat	16.551	0.448	0.575	2861.61
	pixelSplat	17.332	0.426	0.532	0.144M
	sshELF (Ours)	18.174	0.635	0.650	124.80
TD4	MVSplat	12.610	0.380	0.714	202.00
	pixelSplat	17.306	0.438	0.539	0.163M
	sshELF (Ours)	17.594	0.628	0.653	171.81

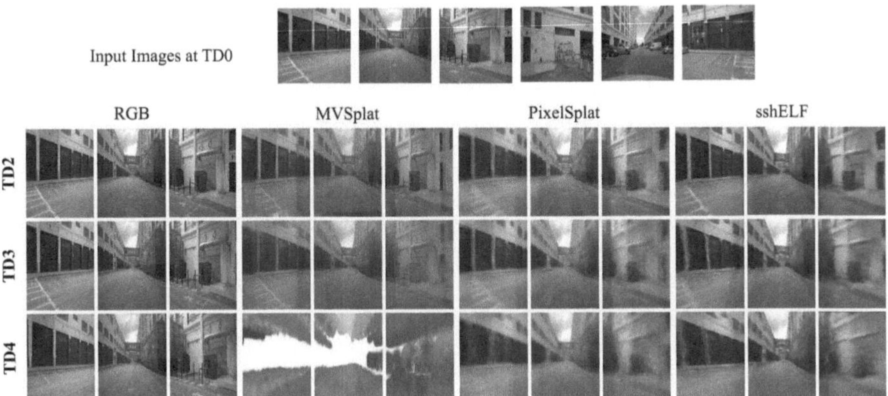

Fig. 5. Qualitative Novel View Synthesis Comparison on nuScenes Test Set. Visualization of multi-view synthesis results using six reference views captured at t = 0. We compare novel views reconstructed at temporal difference of TD = 2, 3, and 4 (1 s, 1.5 s, and 2 s, respectively).

5   Conclusion

This paper introduces sshELF, a fast 3D Gaussian-based framework for reconstructing unbounded driving scenes from sparse, outward-facing views. Our method overcomes the critical challenge of reconstructing unobserved regions, such as distant object occlusions and ego-occlusions, that existing approaches fail to resolve. Our key innovation lies in decoupling information extrapolation from primitive decoding, enabling cross-scene transfer of structural patterns while maintaining a modular, real-time capable pipeline.

Experiments on challenging synthetic and real-world datasets demonstrate that sshELF achieves competitive novel view synthesis results, even for heavily occluded regions. A current limitation is sensitivity to dynamic objects when aggregating multi-timestep data, which can introduce transient artifacts. Future work will focus on (1) temporal filtering to mask dynamic objects during training, and (2) exploring the downstream performance of the obtained latent features.

Acknowledgement. The research leading to these results is partially funded by the German Federal Ministry for Economic Affairs and Climate Action within the project "NXT GEN AI METHODS".

Appendix

A   Implementation Details

We implement sshELF using PyTorch [29], a memory-efficient attention mechanism [23] and the renderer implementation from the original 3DGS paper [19].

Each hierarchical ELF block consists of two (cc) epipolar-cross attention parts and one (cs) self-attention block. The total number of ELF blocks is four in the backbone and one in the translator.

During cross-scene training, we set the number of reference views to 6, the number of virtual views to 6, and the number of novel views to 2. For the SEED4D dataset, the input views have a resolution of 896×896, the resolution of the virtual views in the backbone is 64×64, the DINO features are obtained with an input resolution of 896×896, and novel views have a resolution of 256×256. When working with the nuScenes dataset, most values remain the same except for the rendering resolution of sshELF, which is increased to 896×896. The same resolutions are used for SplatterImage, pixelSplat, and MVSplat.

The translator is trained on ground truth reference and virtual views until convergence. Once the backbone is converged, the translator is fine-tuned with the estimated virtual views until convergence. We leverage the knowledge learned over the synthetic dataset and continue training on the nuScene dataset from the best model checkpoints for 100K steps. During the training of the backbone $\lambda_1 = 1000.0$, $\lambda_2 = 0.1$ and for the translator training $\lambda_3 = 100.0$ and $\lambda_4 = 0.001$. We use an Adam optimizer [21] and an intial learning rate of 1×10^{-5}, cosine annealing. The backbone is trained using an A40 GPU with 48 GB, and the translator using a V100 GPU with 32 GB.

B   Ablations and Analysis

Here we demonstrate the necessity of the different model components. The following questions are investigated:

<u>Question 1</u> Which ELF block architecture is best suited for reconstructing virtual views?

<u>Question 2</u>: How impactful is the size of the reconstructed views for the overall model performance?

<u>Question 3</u>: Does adding a Chamfer distance loss to the model loss improve the results?

Backbone Design (Q1). We experiment with varying the number of cross-attention and self-attention blocks within each ELF block. Performance is evaluated using PSNR, SSIM, and LPIPS metrics on reconstructed virtual views. Each resulting backbone is trained for 60K steps. The results obtained on the SEED4D dataset are summarized in Table 3.

Translator Design (Q2). We investigate the impact of input view resolution by varying the size of the views inputted into the translator. Additionally, we explore a different gradient propagation styles, as proposed in Depth Normalization Regularized Gaussians (DNG) [25]. Table 4, presents the training results for each configuration after 60K steps on the SEED4D dataset, highlighting the influence of these design choices.

Table 3. Backbone Performance. cc indicates the number of cross-attention blocks and cs the number of self-attention blocks.

ELF	PSNR ↑	SSIM↑	LPIPS↓
1 cc with 1 cs	16.3002	0.4049	0.6032
2 cc with 1 cs	16.5557	0.4184	0.5990
3 cc with 1 cs	16.4709	0.4022	0.6044
3 cc with 3 cs	16.2464	0.4053	0.5980
4 cc with 1 cs	16.3215	0.4017	0.5982

Table 4. Translator ablation. Our analysis reveals that DNG underperforms, while reconstruction quality improves with higher image resolution.

Resolution	PSNR ↑	SSIM↑	LPIPS↓
64 w/o DNG	17.8219	0.5970	0.6089
64 with DNG	17.9062	0.5947	0.6106
128 w/o DNG	17.9950	0.6116	0.6041
128 with DNG	15.2253	0.5437	0.6787
256 w/o DNG	18.1216	0.6137	0.6017
256 with DNG	14.8780	0.5318	0.6802

Chamfer Distance Loss (Q3). Since the nuScenes dataset includes LiDAR data, we compute the Chamfer distance and experiment with enforcing a Chamfer distance loss during training. While this loss improves alignment with the ground truth geometry, it results in a slight degradation of visual metrics. Detailed results are provided in Table 5.

Table 5. Chamfer Distance Loss. Results are shown for temporal differences (TD) of 2, 3, and 4 in terms of PSNR, SSIM, LPIPS, and Chamfer distance.

	Methods	PSNR↑	SSIM↑	LPIPS↓	Chamfer↓
TD2	Ours w C	18.980	0.645	0.641	10.89
	Ours w/o C	19.133	0.645	0.634	51.67
TD3	Ours w C	18.133	0.636	0.654	13.30
	Ours w/o C	18.174	0.635	0.650	124.80
TD4	Ours w C	17.557	0.628	0.658	13.51
	Ours w/o C	17.594	0.628	0.653	171.81

References

1. Anciukevičius, T., et al.: Renderdiffusion: image diffusion for 3D reconstruction, inpainting and generation. In: Proceedings of the IEEE/CVF Conference on Computer Vision and Pattern Recognition (CVPR), pp. 12608–12618 (2023)
2. Behley, J., et al.: Semantickitti: a dataset for semantic scene understanding of lidar sequences. In: 2019 IEEE/CVF International Conference on Computer Vision (ICCV), pp. 9296–9306 (2019). https://doi.org/10.1109/ICCV.2019.00939
3. Bhat, S.F., Birkl, R., Wofk, D., Wonka, P., Müller, M.: Zoedepth: zero-shot transfer by combining relative and metric depth. CoRR **abs/2302.12288** (2023)
4. Caesar, H., et al.: Nuscenes: a multimodal dataset for autonomous driving. In: CVPR (2020)
5. Charatan, D., Li, S.L., Tagliasacchi, A., Sitzmann, V.: Pixelsplat: 3D gaussian splats from image pairs for scalable generalizable 3D reconstruction. In: Proceedings of the IEEE/CVF Conference on Computer Vision and Pattern Recognition (CVPR), pp. 19457–19467 (2024)
6. Chen, A., et al.: Mvsnerf: fast generalizable radiance field reconstruction from multi-view stereo. In: Proceedings of the IEEE/CVF International Conference on Computer Vision, pp. 14124–14133 (2021)
7. Chen, Y., et al.: MVSplat: efficient 3D gaussian splatting from sparse multi-view images. In: Leonardis, A., Ricci, E., Roth, S., Russakovsky, O., Sattler, T., Varol, G. (eds.) Computer Vision – ECCV 2024. ECCV 2024. LNCS, vol. 15079, pp. 370–386. Springer, Cham (2025). https://doi.org/10.1007/978-3-031-72664-4_21
8. Chen, Y., Gu, C., Jiang, J., Zhu, X., Zhang, L.: Periodic vibration gaussian: dynamic urban scene reconstruction and real-time rendering. arXiv:2311.18561 (2023)
9. Chen, Z., et al.: Omnire: omni urban scene reconstruction. arXiv preprint arXiv:2408.16760 (2024)
10. Deitke, M., et al.: Objaverse: a universe of annotated 3d objects. In: 2023 IEEE/CVF Conference on Computer Vision and Pattern Recognition (CVPR), pp. 13142–13153. IEEE Computer Society, Los Alamitos, CA, USA (2023). https://doi.org/10.1109/CVPR52729.2023.01263
11. Dosovitskiy, A., et al.: An image is worth 16×16 words: transformers for image recognition at scale. ICLR (2021)
12. Fischer, T., Porzi, L., Rota Bulò, S., Pollefeys, M., Kontschieder, P.: Multi-level neural scene graphs for dynamic urban environments. In: Proceedings of the IEEE/CVF Conference on Computer Vision and Pattern Recognition (CVPR) (2024)
13. Gieruc, T., Kästingschäfer, M., Bernhard, S., Salzmann, M.: 6Img-to-3d: few-image large-scale outdoor driving scene reconstruction. arXiv preprint arXiv:2404.12378 (2024)
14. Guizilini, V., Vasiljevic, I., Ambrus, R., Shakhnarovich, G., Gaidon, A.: Full surround monodepth from multiple cameras. IEEE Robot. Autom. Lett. **7**(2), 5397–5404 (2022). https://doi.org/10.1109/LRA.2022.3150884
15. Hwang, S., Kim, M., Kang, T., Kang, J., Choo, J.: VEGS: view extrapolation of urban scenes in 3d gaussian splatting using learned priors. CoRR **abs/2407.02945** (2024). https://doi.org/10.48550/ARXIV.2407.02945
16. Irshad, M.Z., et al.: Neo 360: neural fields for sparse view synthesis of outdoor scenes. In: International Conference on Computer Vision (ICCV) (2023)

17. Johnson, J., et al.: Accelerating 3D deep learning with pytorch3d. In: SIGGRAPH Asia 2020 Courses. SA '20, Association for Computing Machinery, New York, NY, USA (2020). https://doi.org/10.1145/3415263.3419160

18. Ke, B., Obukhov, A., Huang, S., Metzger, N., Daudt, R.C., Schindler, K.: Repurposing diffusion-based image generators for monocular depth estimation. In: Proceedings of the IEEE/CVF Conference on Computer Vision and Pattern Recognition (CVPR) (2024)

19. Kerbl, B., Kopanas, G., Leimkühler, T., Drettakis, G.: 3D gaussian splatting for real-time radiance field rendering. ACM Trans. Graph. **42**(4) (2023)

20. Khan, M., et al.: Autosplat: constrained gaussian splatting for autonomous driving scene reconstruction. arXiv preprint arXiv:2407.02598 (2024)

21. Kingma, D.P., Ba, J.: Adam: a method for stochastic optimization. In: Bengio, Y., LeCun, Y. (eds.) 3rd International Conference on Learning Representations, ICLR 2015, San Diego, CA, USA, 7–9 May 2015, Conference Track Proceedings (2015)

22. Kästingschäfer, M., et al.: Seed4d: a synthetic ego–exo dynamic 4d data generator, driving dataset and benchmark. arXiv preprint arXiv:2412.00730 (2025). https://arxiv.org/abs/2412.00730

23. Lefaudeux, B., et al.: xFormers: a modular and hackable transformer modelling library (2022). https://github.com/facebookresearch/xformers

24. Li, H., et al.: VDG: vision-only dynamic gaussian for driving simulation. arXiv preprint (2024)

25. Li, J., et al.: Dngaussian: optimizing sparse-view 3d gaussian radiance fields with global-local depth normalization. arXiv preprint arXiv:2403.06912 (2024). https://arxiv.org/abs/2403.06912

26. Mildenhall, B., Srinivasan, P.P., Tancik, M., Barron, J.T., Ramamoorthi, R., Ng, R.: NeRF: representing scenes as neural radiance fields for view synthesis. In: Vedaldi, A., Bischof, H., Brox, T., Frahm, J.M. (eds.) Computer Vision – ECCV 2020. ECCV 2020. LNCS, vol. 12346, pp. 405–421. Springer, Cham (2020). https://doi.org/10.1007/978-3-030-58452-8_24

27. Oquab, M., et al.: Dinov2: learning robust visual features without supervision. arXiv preprint arXiv:2304.07193 (2023)

28. Ost, J., Mannan, F., Thuerey, N., Knodt, J., Heide, F.: Neural scene graphs for dynamic scenes. In: Proceedings of the IEEE/CVF Conference on Computer Vision and Pattern Recognition (CVPR), pp. 2856–2865 (2021)

29. Paszke, A., et al.: Pytorch: an imperative style, high-performance deep learning library. In: Advances in Neural Information Processing Systems, vol. 32, pp. 8024–8035. Curran Associates, Inc. (2019)

30. Ranftl, R., Bochkovskiy, A., Koltun, V.: Vision transformers for dense prediction. In: Proceedings of the IEEE/CVF International Conference on Computer Vision (ICCV), pp. 12179–12188 (2021)

31. Reizenstein, J., Shapovalov, R., Henzler, P., Sbordone, L., Labatut, P., Novotny, D.: Common objects in 3D: large-scale learning and evaluation of real-life 3d category reconstruction. In: 2021 IEEE/CVF International Conference on Computer Vision (ICCV), pp. 10881–10891. IEEE Computer Society, Los Alamitos, CA, USA (2021). https://doi.org/10.1109/ICCV48922.2021.01072

32. Ronneberger, O., Fischer, P., Brox, T.: U-net: convolutional networks for biomedical image segmentation. CoRR **abs/1505.04597** (2015)

33. Song, Y., Sohl-Dickstein, J., Kingma, D.P., Kumar, A., Ermon, S., Poole, B.: Score-based generative modeling through stochastic differential equations. In: International Conference on Learning Representations (2021)

34. Sun, P., et al.: Scalability in perception for autonomous driving: waymo open dataset. In: Proceedings of the IEEE/CVF Conference on Computer Vision and Pattern Recognition (CVPR) (2020)
35. Szymanowicz, S., et al.: Flash3d: feed-forward generalisable 3d scene reconstruction from a single image. arxiv (2024)
36. Szymanowicz, S., Rupprecht, C., Vedaldi, A.: Viewset diffusion: (0-)image-conditioned 3d generative models from 2d data. In: International Conference on Computer Vision (2023)
37. Szymanowicz, S., Rupprecht, C., Vedaldi, A.: Splatter image: ultra-fast single-view 3d reconstruction. In: The IEEE/CVF Conference on Computer Vision and Pattern Recognition (CVPR) (2024)
38. Tian, Q., Tan, X., Xie, Y., Ma, L.: Drivingforward: feed-forward 3d gaussian splatting for driving scene reconstruction from flexible surround-view input. arXiv preprint arXiv:2409.12753 (2024)
39. Tonderski, A., Lindström, C., Hess, G., Ljungbergh, W., Svensson, L., Petersson, C.: Neurad: neural rendering for autonomous driving. In: Proceedings of the IEEE/CVF Conference on Computer Vision and Pattern Recognition (CVPR), pp. 14895–14904 (2024)
40. Turki, H., Zhang, J.Y., Ferroni, F., Ramanan, D.: Suds: scalable urban dynascenes. In: Computer Vision Pattern Recognition (CVPR) (2023)
41. Wang, L., et al.: Distillnerf: perceiving 3d scenes from single-glance images by distilling neural fields and foundation model features. In: Conference on Neural Information Processing Systems (2024)
42. Wang, Q., et al.: Ibrnet: learning multi-view image-based rendering. In: CVPR (2021)
43. Wang, Z., Bovik, A.C., Sheikh, H.R., Simoncelli, E.P.: Image quality assessment: from error visibility to structural similarity. IEEE Trans. Image Process. **13**(4), 600–612 (2004)
44. Wewer, C., Raj, K., Ilg, E., Schiele, B., Lenssen, J.E.: LatentSplat: autoencoding variational gaussians for fast generalizable 3D reconstruction. In: Leonardis, A., Ricci, E., Roth, S., Russakovsky, O., Sattler, T., Varol, G. (eds.) Computer Vision – ECCV 2024. ECCV 2024. LNCS, vol. 15145, pp. 456–473. Springer, Cham (2025). https://doi.org/10.1007/978-3-031-73021-4_27
45. Wu, R., et al.: Reconfusion: 3d reconstruction with diffusion priors. In: Proceedings of the IEEE/CVF Conference on Computer Vision and Pattern Recognition (CVPR), pp. 21551–21561 (2024)
46. Yan, Y., et al.: Street gaussians: modeling dynamic urban scenes with gaussian splatting. In: ECCV (2024)
47. Yang, C., et al.: Gaussianobject: high-quality 3d object reconstruction from four views with gaussian splatting. ACM Trans. Graph. (2024)
48. Yang, J., et al.: Emernerf: emergent spatial-temporal scene decomposition via self-supervision. In: International Conference on Learning Representations (2024)
49. Yang, L., Kang, B., Huang, Z., Xu, X., Feng, J., Zhao, H.: Depth anything: unleashing the power of large-scale unlabeled data. In: IEEE/CVF Conference on Computer Vision and Pattern Recognition, CVPR 2024, Seattle, WA, USA, 16–22 June 2024, pp. 10371–10381. IEEE (2024). https://doi.org/10.1109/CVPR52733.2024.00987
50. Yang, Y., Wang, X., Li, D., Tian, L., Sirasao, A., Yang, X.: Towards scale-aware full surround monodepth with transformers. arXiv preprint arXiv:2407.10406 (2024)

51. Yin, W., et al.: Metric3d: towards zero-shot metric 3d prediction from a single image. In: Proceedings of the IEEE/CVF International Conference on Computer Vision, pp. 9043–9053 (2023)
52. Yinghao, X., et al.: GRM: large gaussian reconstruction model for efficient 3d reconstruction and generation. arXiv preprint arXiv:2403.14621 (2024)
53. Yu, A., Ye, V., Tancik, M., Kanazawa, A.: pixelNeRF: neural radiance fields from one or few images. In: CVPR (2021)
54. Yu, Z., et al.: SGD: street view synthesis with gaussian splatting and diffusion prior. ArXiv **abs/2403.20079** (2024)
55. Zhang, R., Isola, P., Efros, A.A., Shechtman, E., Wang, O.: The unreasonable effectiveness of deep features as a perceptual metric. In: 2018 IEEE/CVF Conference on Computer Vision and Pattern Recognition, pp. 586–595 (2018)
56. Zhou, H., et al.: Hugs: holistic urban 3d scene understanding via gaussian splatting. In: Proceedings of the IEEE/CVF Conference on Computer Vision and Pattern Recognition (CVPR), pp. 21336–21345 (2024)
57. Zhou, T., Tucker, R., Flynn, J., Fyffe, G., Snavely, N.: Stereo magnification: learning view synthesis using multiplane images. ACM Trans. Graph. (Proc. SIGGRAPH) **37** (2018)
58. Zhou, X., Lin, Z., Shan, X., Wang, Y., Sun, D., Yang, M.H.: Drivinggaussian: composite gaussian splatting for surrounding dynamic autonomous driving scenes. In: Proceedings of the IEEE/CVF Conference on Computer Vision and Pattern Recognition, pp. 21634–21643 (2024)
59. Zou, Z.X., et al.: Triplane meets gaussian splatting: fast and generalizable single-view 3d reconstruction with transformers. In: Proceedings of the IEEE/CVF Conference on Computer Vision and Pattern Recognition (CVPR), pp. 10324–10335 (2024)

Photogrammetry and Remote Sensing

NaT-ReX: Naturalness Assessment with Transformer-Based Reliable Explainability

Ahmed Emam[1](✉) [ID], Mohamed Farag[1] [ID], Marc Rußwurm[2] [ID], and Ribana Roscher[3] [ID]

[1] University of Bonn, Bonn, Germany
{aemam,mibra2}@uni-bonn.de
[2] Wageningen University, Wageningen, Netherlands
marc.russwurm@wur.nl
[3] Forschungszentrum Jülich GmbH, Jülich, Germany
r.roscher@fz-juelich.de

Abstract. Protected natural areas, minimally affected by modern human influence, are essential for ecological stability and processes such as water cycles and pollination. A continuous and efficient monitoring of these areas has become increasingly important, and machine learning and satellite imagery offer new opportunities for getting insights and assessing their naturalness. However, current approaches rely on predefined assumptions of naturalness or do not account for model uncertainty, limiting robustness and interpretability of the results. We propose NaT-ReX, a Transformer-based Reliable Explainability framework that integrates explainable machine learning with uncertainty quantification. NaT-ReX highlights areas that are reliably associated with naturalness while discounting regions with higher uncertainty. To support this, we introduce the ReX score, a novel metric to evaluate both pixel-wise relevance to naturalness and land cover classes based on their contributions to naturalness and the associated uncertainty. Our experiments on two satellite datasets—AnthroProtect and MapInWild—demonstrate both qualitative and quantitative insights. Our findings demonstrate that shrublands and wetlands contribute the most to naturalness, while open water and snow-dominated regions exhibit the lowest ReX scores due to higher uncertainty or lower semantic attribution. These findings align with both data-driven and expert-informed assessments of naturalness, highlighting the potential of NaT-ReX as an efficient and uncertainty-aware monitoring and analysis framework.

Keywords: Explainable Machine Learning (XAI) · Uncertainty Quantification · Naturalness · Wilderness

This work was supported by the Deutsche Forschungsgemeinschaft (DFG, German Research Foundation) under the following grants: RO 4839/5-1 and SCHM 3322/4-1 (project no. 458156377 – MapInWild), RO 4839/6-1 (project no. 459376902 – AID4Crops), and as part of the DFG's Excellence Strategy – EXC-2070 – 390732324 – PhenoRob.

M. Keuper and F. Locatello (Eds.): DAGM GCPR 2025, LNCS 16125, pp. 571–585, 2026.
https://doi.org/10.1007/978-3-032-12840-9_36

1   Introduction

Areas of minimal human influence play a critical role in preserving ecological stability, supporting biodiversity, and maintaining essential ecosystem services such as water cycles, pollination, and habitat provision [5,27]. In addition to their environmental importance, these regions offer cultural, recreational, and educational value, reinforcing the need for their protection and sustainable management [3].

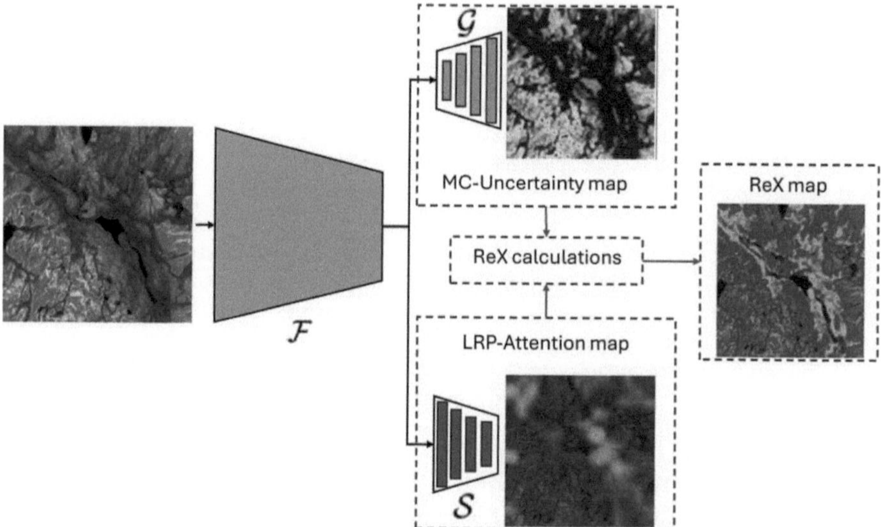

Fig. 1. Inference pipeline of the NaT-ReX framework. The input image is passed through the shared encoder $\mathcal{F}$, producing two outputs: an uncertainty map from the reconstruction head $\mathcal{G}$ using Monte Carlo Dropout, and an LRP attention map from the classification head $\mathcal{S}$ via attention rollout. These two outputs are integrated per pixel using the ReX formulation to generate the final ReX map, which highlights spatial contributions to the class **naturalness** while accounting for uncertainty.

It is essential to monitor and analyze these natural areas at scale. Satellite remote sensing provides a powerful means for doing so, offering high-resolution, multispectral observations across large and often inaccessible regions. Such imagery enables researchers to track land cover changes, vegetation dynamics, and other ecological indicators over time. However, characterizing naturalness from satellite data remains challenging. Human impact on ecosystems often occurs gradually, and the boundary between natural and anthropogenically influenced areas is not always clear. Traditional mapping approaches with rigid classifications may oversimplify the nuanced continuum between untouched and influenced states [14,30].

Machine learning (ML) offers a promising solution for modeling such complexity. Techniques like Convolutional Neural Networks (CNN) extract spatial features from multispectral or temporal satellite data [26]. These models can be adapted for monitoring tasks such as land cover classification, environmental change detection, or pattern recognition [21]. Many machine learning-based approaches for assessing naturalness are black-box models, meaning they do not reveal how predictions are made. This lack of transparency is problematic in environmental applications, where understanding the reasoning behind a prediction is essential. Explainability methods allow us to see which parts of the input the model relies on, helping to verify whether the model focuses on meaningful ecological features. Without such tools, there is a risk that models make decisions based on irrelevant or misleading patterns—a problem demonstrated in the so-called Clever Hans effect, where models learn shortcuts that do not generalize well [20]. In addition, these approaches do not address the uncertainty associated with models or data. As a result, they may produce insights while they are unsure, leading to decisions based on outputs that may be overconfident or unreliable [17]. This combination—lack of explainability and missing uncertainty estimates limits the trustworthiness and robustness of naturalness assessments, especially when applied to sensitive or policy-relevant tasks.

To address these gaps, we propose NaT-ReX (see Fig. 1) with the following key contributions: (1) a framework that integrates explainability, in the form of propagated relevance, and uncertainty for naturalness investigation, (2) the ReX score that quantifies naturalness as uncertainty-weighted relevance, and (3) a qualitative and quantitative analysis of naturalness at both the pixel and class levels.

2   Related Work

2.1   Naturalness Assessment

Efforts to assess naturalness have primarily focused on quantifying human influence to identify and protect minimally disturbed areas. Early work by Sanderson et al. (2002) [27] introduced the Human Influence Index (HII), which aggregates factors such as population density, land use, and road networks. The HII, based on data from the 1960s to 1990s at a $1\,km^2$ resolution, is widely used but limited by its coarse scale, lack of temporal adaptability, and reliance on static assumptions. Similarly, Winter et al. (2010) [32] proposed the Wilderness Quality Index for Europe, which incorporates terrain features but focuses mainly on forested ecosystems and does not produce spatially detailed outputs.

Ekim et al. [8,9] extended this line of work by introducing the Naturalness Index (NI), which improved spatial resolution and integrated multimodal inputs such as Sentinel-1/2 bands, nightlight intensity, and land cover maps. While technically robust, the NI is partially guided by predefined assumptions—for instance, it assigns lower naturalness to shrublands and sparsely vegetated areas based on predefined beliefs. Such assumptions, while reasonable in certain contexts, may limit the index's applicability in ecosystems where shrublands are strong indicators of naturalness and highlight the need for more data-driven approaches.

Recent developments in machine learning (ML) and Earth observation (EO) offer more flexible and data-driven alternatives. CNN-based frameworks [29,30], and generative approaches [14] have been used to analyze protected regions, revealing spatial patterns through activation-based methods. Building on this, Emam et al. (2024) [12] proposed the Confident Naturalness Explanation (CNE) framework, the first to combine explainability with uncertainty quantification for this task. The CNE score measures the confident contribution of specific patterns to naturalness.

Despite its novelty, CNE has key limitations: it flattens spatial input into 1D vectors for logistic regression, leading to a loss of spatial structure, and assigns scores only at the class level, not per patch. These research gaps emphasize the need for pixel-wise naturalness contributions, uncertainty-aware frameworks that avoid fixed assumptions and enable fine-grained naturalness assessments.

Table 1 summarizes the main contributions and limitations of these approaches.

2.2 Explainability and Uncertainty

Explainable machine learning (XAI) methods are commonly categorized into model-agnostic and model-specific approaches [2,18]. Model-agnostic techniques such as LIME [25] and SHAP [22] are adaptable to a wide range of models and offer local explanations of individual predictions. However, these methods can suffer from instability, high computational cost, and lack of spatial resolution when applied to high-dimensional inputs such as satellite imagery. Consequently, they are less suitable for spatially detailed and class-specific attribution in Earth observation tasks.

Model-specific explainability techniques, in contrast, exploit the structure of specific model architectures to provide more targeted and reliable explanations. A widely used method in convolutional neural networks (CNNs) is Grad-CAM [28], which generates class-specific saliency maps based on gradients flowing through convolutional layers. While effective for image-level classification, Grad-CAM often produces low-resolution heatmaps. Emam et al. [11] proposed a framework to compare models based on how well their explanations align with domain knowledge, evaluating different architectures and explainability methods.

In transformer-based models, particularly Vision Transformers (ViTs) [7], explainability presents unique challenges due to the absence of convolutional layers and the use of self-attention mechanisms. To address this, Chefer et al. [6] introduced a transformer-specific adaptation of Layer-wise Relevance Propagation (LRP) that propagates class-specific relevance scores through the attention layers. This method, known as LRP attention rollout, provides high-resolution attribution maps that maintain the spatial context of input patches and identify the most relevant regions contributing to a specific class. In our framework, we adopt LRP attention rollout to generate pixel-level relevance for the class **naturalness**, allowing spatially fine-grained interpretation of model decisions.

Table 1. Summary of Related Work in Naturalness Assessment

Publication	Key Features	Limitations
Sanderson et al. (2002) [27]	- Quantifies global human impact. - Uses factors such as population density, land use, and road access. - Broad-scale assessment.	- Low spatial and temporal resolution. - Relies on predefined assumptions. - Lacks detailed representation of ecological patterns.
Winter et al. (2010) [32]	- Emphasizes wilderness quality across Europe. - Uses terrain ruggedness and remoteness.	- Limited generalizability beyond study region. - No temporal or pixel-level resolution.
Ekim et al. (2021) [8]	- Provides higher spatial resolution (10 m). - Incorporates refined land cover and accessibility data. - Suitable for regional assessments.	- Relies on subjective assumptions of naturalness. - Potential misalignment with local domain knowledge. - Sensitive to cultural/regional interpretations.
Ekim (2024) [9]	- Incorporates multimodal inputs (Sentinel-1/2, nightlights, land cover). - Enhances the depth of naturalness assessment. - Builds upon the Naturalness Index (NI).	- Still relies on predefined assumptions. - May introduce bias due to cultural or regional subjectivity.
Stomberg et al. (2022, 2023) [29,30]	- Uses CNNs for pixel-level analysis of satellite data. - Highlights protected and impacted patterns in imagery.	- Occludes activations in a specific layer, leading to inconsistency when the layer changes. - Sensitive to size and placement of sliding occlusion window. - Focuses on identifying patterns but not full explanations.
Emam et al. (2024) [14]	- Uses adversarial generative training and activation maximization. - Produces high-resolution and interpretable heatmaps.	- High computational cost due to dual GAN networks and a regressor. - Lacks uncertainty quantification in data or architecture.
Emam et al. (2024) [12]	- Introduces the Confident Naturalness Explanation (CNE) score. - Combines relevance and uncertainty into a single metric. - Provides pixel-level uncertainty visualization. - Integrates domain knowledge for interpretability.	- Converts images to 1D vectors, losing spatial context. - Scores limited to land cover classes, not individual patches. - High computational cost due to Monte Carlo sampling.
NaT-ReX Framework	- Preserves spatial structure using a transformer-based encoder. - Uses LRP attention rollout to identify pixel-level contributions to naturalness. - Integrates pixel-level uncertainty via MC-Dropout.	- Requires multiple forward passes for Monte Carlo sampling, increasing inference time. - Captures only epistemic uncertainty. - May require better uncertainty methods for critical applications.

Complementary to explainability, uncertainty quantification (UQ) provides a measure of the model's confidence in its predictions, which is critical in sensitive domains like environmental monitoring and land use assessment. Among the many UQ techniques, Bayesian Neural Networks (BNNs) [17] offer a theoretically grounded framework for estimating uncertainty but are computationally intractable in large models. Scalable approximations such as Monte Carlo Dropout (MC-Dropout) [16] and deep ensembles [19] have been widely adopted to estimate epistemic uncertainty—the uncertainty due to limited data or model capacity.

In this work, we estimate uncertainty by applying MC-Dropout in the reconstruction head of the NaT-ReX framework. By performing multiple stochastic forward passes of the same input image, we compute the pixel-wise variance across reconstructions, which serves as a proxy for epistemic uncertainty. This allows us to quantify how confidently the model reconstructs each region of the input, providing an interpretable uncertainty map at high spatial resolution.

Recent work has begun to explore the integration of explainability and uncertainty to improve model reliability. For instance, Mehdiyev et al. [23] combined total predictive uncertainty with feature attribution for complex systems, and B-LRP [4] extended relevance propagation to Bayesian models to estimate explanation confidence. However, these approaches are either limited to CNNs or require computationally expensive Bayesian frameworks. In contrast, our NaT-ReX framework employs a transformer-based encoder with dual heads: one using LRP attention rollout for explainability, the other leveraging MC-Dropout-based reconstruction for pixel-wise uncertainty. This setup enables fine-grain, uncertainty-aware relevance scoring for naturalness assessment, offering uncertainty-aware, interpretable analysis of naturalness. Emam et al. [13] recently proposed the Confidence-Filtered Relevance (CFR) framework to analyze how model uncertainty influences the interpretability of relevance heatmaps. Their results show that with increasing uncertainty, the entropy of the relevance distribution grows, indicating less selective and more ambiguous attributions. This demonstrates that higher epistemic uncertainty reduces the clarity of explanations, reinforcing the need for uncertainty-aware interpretability in naturalness assessment.

3   Methodology

3.1   NaT-ReX Architecture and Training Strategy

NaT-ReX is built on a Vision Transformer (ViT-B/16) encoder [7] and includes two output heads trained jointly in a multitask setup: a classification head for predicting the class **naturalness** versus **non-naturalness** and a reconstruction head for image reconstruction. The use of a transformer encoder allows the model to capture long-range dependencies and global context, which are critical for scene-level understanding in naturalness assessment. See Fig. 2

The classification head is a fully connected layer that outputs a score for each class. During inference, we apply Layer-wise Relevance Propagation (LRP) to the naturalness score to identify the regions of the image that contributed most to the prediction. The reconstruction head transforms the encoder's output back into the original image layout. Tokens are reshaped into image patches and passed through three convolutional layers—two with ReLU activations—to improve reconstruction quality.

Training is performed end-to-end using a combined loss: a cross-entropy loss for the classification head and a mean squared error loss for the reconstruction head. This multitask formulation encourages the encoder to learn spatial features that support both attribution and uncertainty quantification in the inference stage.

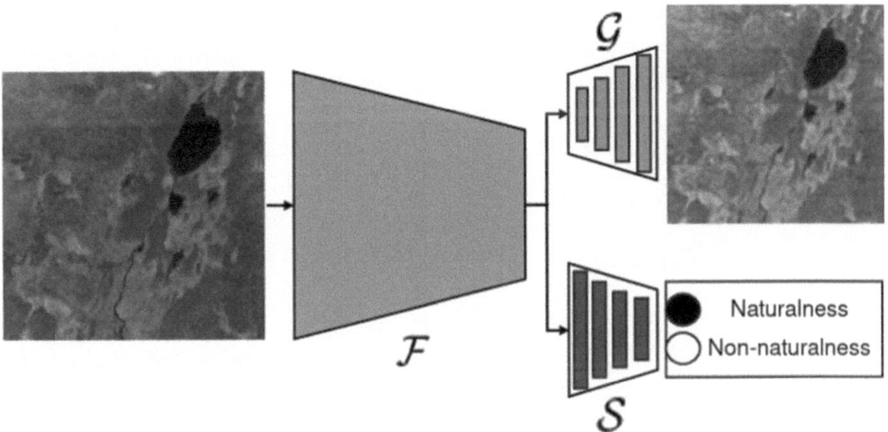

Fig. 2. Training architecture of the NaT-ReX framework. The input satellite image is processed by a Vision Transformer-based encoder $\mathcal{F}$, which feeds into two parallel heads: a reconstruction head $\mathcal{G}$ that learns to reconstruct the input image, and a classification head $\mathcal{S}$ that predicts **naturalness** versus **non-naturalness**. Both heads are trained simultaneously in a multi-task learning setup to optimize both classification and reconstruction objectives.

Classification Head: Relevance to Naturalness via LRP Attention Rollout. To generate class-specific relevance maps, we use the attention-based Layer-wise Relevance Propagation (LRP) method adapted for Vision Transformers by Chefer et al. [6]. This method propagates relevance scores from the classification output back through the attention layers. Unlike standard attention rollout [1], which produces unguided and less interpretable heatmaps, our approach highlights features that specifically contribute to the **naturalness** class. Figure 3 (bottom) highlights the image regions contributing to both the **naturalness** and **non-naturalness** classes.

Let $A^{(b)}$ denote the attention matrix in transformer block b, and $R^{(n_b)}$ the relevance at that layer's output. The adjusted attention map is defined as:

$$\bar{A}^{(b)} = I + \frac{1}{H} \sum_{h=1}^{H} \max\left(\nabla A_h^{(b)} \odot R_h^{(n_b)}, 0\right) \tag{1}$$

Equation 1 updates the attention in block b by averaging the gradient-based relevance across all attention heads, keeping only positive contributions. The identity matrix I ensures residual connections are preserved, allowing each token to retain part of its own relevance.

The final relevance map is computed as:

$$M = \bar{A}^{(1)} \cdot \bar{A}^{(2)} \cdot \ldots \cdot \bar{A}^{(B)} \tag{2}$$

Equation 2 accumulates relevance across all transformer blocks, effectively tracing how importance propagates from the model's output back to the input tokens. For a detailed derivation, we refer the reader to Chefer et al. [6].

Reconstruction Head: Uncertainty Quantification via MC-Dropout. To estimate epistemic uncertainty, we use Monte Carlo Dropout (MC-Dropout) in the reconstruction head. During inference, J stochastic forward passes are performed with dropout enabled, producing a set of slightly varied reconstructions.

Let $Y_{h,w,c,j}$ be the reconstructed pixel value at position (h, w, c) from the jth forward pass. The pixel-wise mean is:

$$\bar{Y}_{h,w,c} = \frac{1}{J} \sum_{j=1}^{J} Y_{h,w,c,j} \tag{3}$$

And the corresponding uncertainty estimate is the standard deviation:

$$S_{h,w,c} = \sqrt{\frac{1}{J} \sum_{j=1}^{J} \left(Y_{h,w,c,j} - \bar{Y}_{h,w,c}\right)^2} \tag{4}$$

The resulting uncertainty map $S \in \mathbb{R}^{H \times W \times C}$ reflects the model's epistemic uncertainty in reconstructing each pixel, with higher values indicating lower confidence.

ReX Score: Combining Naturalness, Relevancy, and Uncertainty. The ReX score R_n measures how confidently a pixel n contributes to the class "naturalness," combining its relevance and associated uncertainty:

$$R_n = \left[M_{\text{norm},n} \log\left(1 + \alpha \cdot \frac{1}{S_{\text{norm},n} + c}\right) \right]^{\beta} \tag{5}$$

Here, $M_{\text{norm},n}$ denotes the normalized LRP relevance for patch n, and $S_{\text{norm},n}$ represents the normalized pixel-wise uncertainty. The relevance map M_{norm} is normalized using min-max scaling based on the minimum and maximum relevance values across the image. The logarithmic term penalizes high uncertainty, ensuring that only patches with both high relevance and low uncertainty receive high ReX scores. The parameters are set as follows: $\alpha = 0.5$ (controls the impact of uncertainty), $c = 0.2$ (sets a floor to prevent division by near-zero), and $\beta = 0.8$ (adjusts the sharpness of the score distribution).

This formulation results in pixel-wise uncertainty-aware contribution to naturalness, improving the robustness and interpretability of naturalness assessments. Figure 1 illustrates the inference pipeline and score calculation.

4   Data, Experiments, and Results

4.1   Datasets

AnthroProtect [30] and MapInWild [10] contain Sentinel-2 images from both preserved and unpreserved areas. Each image is associated with a binary label indicating whether it represents an area of *naturalness* or *non-naturalness* area. In addition, each image is accompanied by a land cover segmentation map, derived from CORINE [15] for AnthroProtect and ESA WorldCover [33] for MapInWild. AnthroProtect includes 23,919 images of size 256×256 from Fennoscandia, covering protected regions as a proxy for naturalness. We used 80% of the data for training, 10% for validation, and 10% for testing. For consistency, we selected scenes from the Fennoscandia region in the MapInWild dataset as well, since it offers relatively homogeneous ecological conditions and a clearly defined concept of naturalness. Importantly, the MapInWild dataset was not used in any part of the training process and serves purely as an unseen test set to evaluate generalization. Following Sanderson et al. [27], naturalness is biome-dependent: in Fennoscandia, vegetated areas are primary indicators of naturalness, whereas in regions like North Africa or the Arabian Peninsula, deserts are dominant contributors.

4.2   Experimental Setup

The NaT-ReX framework was trained on the AnthroProtect dataset using a multitask learning strategy. The classification head, responsible for predicting naturalness versus non-naturalness, was trained for 10 epochs and achieved 100% accuracy on the training dataset and 98% on the test dataset. The reconstruction head, which is used for pixel-wise uncertainty estimation, was trained for 30 epochs with an effective batch size of 16 and reached a best reconstruction loss of 0.129 and 0.133 for the training and test datasets, respectively. Training was performed using a batch size of 64.

In the first experiment, we computed the ReX score for each image patch in the AnthroProtect dataset to analyze pixel-level contributions to naturalness and the associated uncertainty. These scores were correlated with the provided land cover segmentation masks to determine the average ReX score of each land cover class. For comparability, ReX values were normalized to the range [0, 1], assigning 1.0 to the class with the highest confident contribution to naturalness and 0.0 to the lowest. In a second experiment, we evaluated the generalizability of the trained NaT-ReX model on the unseen MapInWild dataset. We calculated ReX scores for each pixel and correlated them with the corresponding land cover classes to determine the average ReX score per class. This allowed us to assess the model's transferability and consistency across geographically and semantically distinct protected areas.

4.3   Results

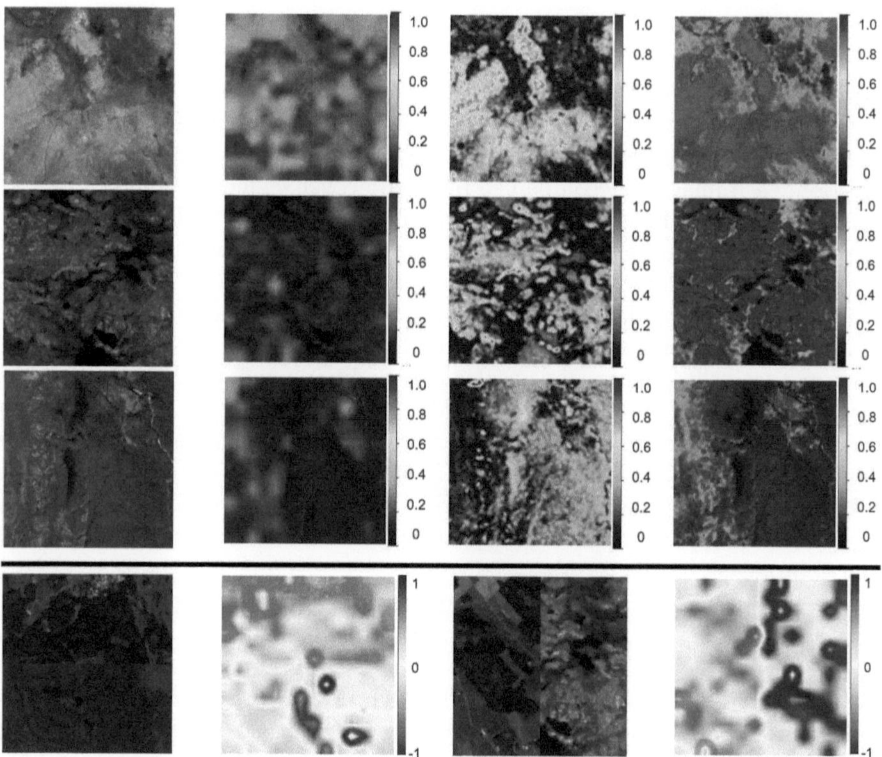

Fig. 3. Top: NaT-ReX visualizations showing the original input, LRP attention maps for *naturalness*, MC-Dropout uncertainty maps, and resulting ReX maps. Bottom: Cut-Mix visualizations used to evaluate class-specific relevance under mixed patch compositions. Column 1 and 3 shows CutMix images blending natural and urban regions. Columns 2 and 4 show LRP attention maps for **non-naturalness** in negative values and **naturalness** in positive values, respectively.

Qualitative Results. Figure 3 presents two subplots. The bottom subplot illustrates different relevance signals derived from the same input image when processed by the ReX approach. Features such as croplands and urban areas exhibit high relevance toward the **non-naturalness** class, while vegetated regions and wetlands show high relevance for the **naturalness** class. The top subplot displays the weighted relevance for the **naturalness** class, where relevance is weighted by uncertainty. Regions with both high relevance and high certainty retain strong ReX scores, whereas areas with low relevance and high uncertainty are suppressed, resulting in lower ReX scores.

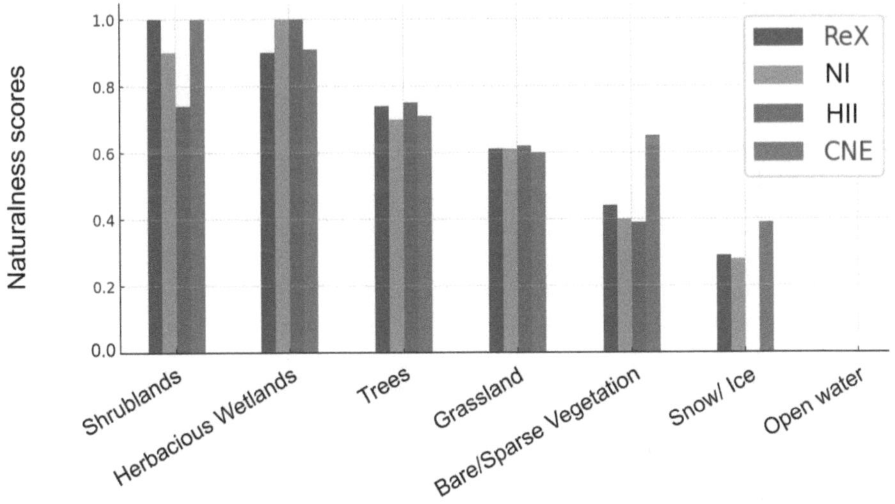

Fig. 4. Comparison of normalized naturalness-related indices across land cover classes. The indices include ReX (ours), which integrates relevance to naturalness and uncertainty; the Naturalness Index (NI) from Ekim et al. [8]; the Human influence index (HII) from Sanderson et al. [27], reversed to represent naturalness; and the Confident Naturalness Index (CNE) from Emam et al. [12], based on attribution scores filtered by model confidence. The plot highlights consistent patterns across indices, with shrubland, wetland, and forest classes ranked highest in naturalness, and water- and ice-related classes ranked lowest.

Quantitative Results. All ReX scores were normalized to [0, 1] for comparability across indices. Figure 4 presents a cross-index comparison of normalized naturalness scores across seven main land cover classes using four different indices: our ReX score, the Naturalness Index (NI) from Ekim et al. [8], the Human Influence Index (HII) from Sanderson et al. [27], and the Confident Naturalness Explanation (CNE) score from Emam et al. [12]. The illustration shows clear trends: *shrubland*, *trees*, and *wetland* classes receive consistently high naturalness scores across indices, while *snow and ice* and *open water* score the lowest. ReX exhibits strong Pearson correlations with the other numerical indices: $r = 0.96$ with NI, $r = 0.924$ with HII, and $r = 0.970$ with CNE, indicating high consistency while also preserving key distinctions.

Despite the general alignment, certain differences emerge. For example, CNE assigns higher naturalness to *bare/sparse vegetation* than other indices. This discrepancy stems from the fact that CNE transforms satellite images into 1D vectors before applying logistic regression, thus discarding spatial context and structure. Similarly, both NI and HII rely on predefined expert assumptions of what constitutes `naturalness`, whereas our ReX framework derives its scores in a fully data-driven manner, grounded in learned semantic relevance to the concept of naturalness and the model confidence.

4.4 Limitations of NaT-ReX

NaT-ReX currently relies on Monte Carlo Dropout to approximate epistemic uncertainty, which requires multiple forward passes and increased inference cost. MC-Dropout captures only epistemic uncertainty and not aleatoric uncertainty arising from noise or inherent data ambiguity. This limitation is especially relevant in real-world conservation applications, where more complete uncertainty modeling is needed. Future work could explore deep ensembles [31], deterministic uncertainty models [24] to improve robustness under distribution shift.

5 Conclusion

We presented NaT-ReX, a transformer-based framework for assessing naturalness in satellite imagery by integrating explainability and uncertainty estimation. At its core is the ReX score, which combines LRP-based attention maps with pixel-level uncertainty from Monte Carlo Dropout. This allows relevance to be modulated by model confidence, enabling more robust and interpretable spatial analysis. NaT-ReX preserves spatial structure, avoids reliance on subjective assumptions, and assigns patch-level relevance scores. It is trained end-to-end and generalizes well across datasets, as consistent results on AnthroProtect and MapInWild show. Land cover types such as *transitional woodland-shrub, shrubland*, and *peat bogs* receive high ReX scores, while *snow and ice, open water*, and *bare rock* are down-weighted due to higher uncertainty or lower relevance to naturalness. These results align with prior explainability and expert-based studies. By combining spatial relevance to naturalness with uncertainty, NaT-ReX enables more transparent and reliable assessments of natural areas, supporting naturalness monitoring efforts.

References

1. Abnar, S., Zuidema, W.: Quantifying attention flow in transformers. In: Proceedings of the 58th Annual Meeting of the Association for Computational Linguistics (ACL), pp. 4190–4197 (2020)
2. Adadi, A., Berrada, M.: Peeking inside the black-box: a survey on explainable artificial intelligence (XAI). IEEE Access **6**, 52138–52160 (2018). https://doi.org/10.1109/ACCESS.2018.2870052, https://ieeexplore.ieee.org/document/8466590. conference Name: IEEE Access
3. Anderson, E., Mammides, C.: The role of protected areas in mitigating human impact in the world's last wilderness areas. Ambio **49**(2), 434–441 (2020). https://doi.org/10.1007/s13280-019-01213-x
4. Bykov, K., Höhne, M.M.C., Müller, K.R., Nakajima, S., Kloft, M.: How Much Can I Trust You? – Quantifying Uncertainties in Explaining Neural Networks (2020). https://doi.org/10.48550/arXiv.2006.09000, http://arxiv.org/abs/2006.09000, arXiv:2006.09000 [cs]
5. Carruthers-Jones, J., et al.: High-resolution naturalness mapping can support conservation policy objectives across scales. Commun. Earth Environ. **6**(279) (2025). https://doi.org/10.1038/s43247-025-02160-0
6. Chefer, H., Gur, S., Wolf, L.: Transformer interpretability beyond attention visualization. In: 2021 IEEE/CVF Conference on Computer Vision and Pattern Recognition (CVPR), pp. 782–791. IEEE, Nashville, TN, USA (2021). https://doi.org/10.1109/CVPR46437.2021.00084, https://ieeexplore.ieee.org/document/9577970/
7. Dosovitskiy, A., et al.: An image is worth 16x16 words: transformers for image recognition at scale (2021). https://doi.org/10.48550/arXiv.2010.11929, http://arxiv.org/abs/2010.11929, arXiv:2010.11929
8. Ekim, B., Dong, Z., Rashkovetsky, D., Schmitt, M.: The naturalness index for the identification of natural areas on regional scale. Int. J. Appl. Earth Obs. Geoinf. **105**, 102622 (2021). https://doi.org/10.1016/j.jag.2021.102622, https://www.sciencedirect.com/science/article/pii/S0303243421003299
9. Ekim, B., Schmitt, M.: Multi-scale context fusion for pixel-level naturalness mapping using sentinel-2 imagery. In: IGARSS 2024 - 2024 IEEE International Geoscience and Remote Sensing Symposium, pp. 403–406 (2024). https://doi.org/10.1109/IGARSS53475.2024.10640622, https://ieeexplore.ieee.org/abstract/document/10640622. iSSN: 2153-7003
10. Ekim, B., Stomberg, T.T., Roscher, R., Schmitt, M.: MapInWild: a remote sensing dataset to address the question what makes nature wild (2022). https://doi.org/10.48550/arXiv.2212.02265, http://arxiv.org/abs/2212.02265
11. Emam, A., Farag, M., Kierdorf, J., Klingbeil, L., Rascher, U., Roscher, R.: A framework for enhanced decision support in digital agriculture using explainable machine learning. In: Del Bue, A., Canton, C., Pont-Tuset, J., Tommasi, T. (eds.) Computer Vision – ECCV 2024 Workshops, pp. 31–45. Springer, Cham (2025). https://doi.org/10.1007/978-3-031-91835-3_3
12. Emam, A., Farag, M., Roscher, R.: Confident naturalness explanation (CNE): a framework to explain and assess patterns forming naturalness. IEEE Geosci. Remote Sens. Lett. **21** (2024). https://doi.org/10.1109/LGRS.2024.3365196, https://ieeexplore.ieee.org/document/10433174. conference Name: IEEE Geoscience and Remote Sensing Letters
13. Emam, A., Roscher, R.: Confidence-Filtered Relevance (CFR): An Interpretable and Uncertainty-Aware Machine Learning Framework for Naturalness Assessment

in Satellite Imagery (2025). https://doi.org/10.48550/arXiv.2507.13034, http://arxiv.org/abs/2507.13034, arXiv:2507.13034 [cs]

14. Emam, A., Farag, M., Roscher, R.: Confident naturalness explanation (CNE): a framework to explain and assess patterns forming naturalness. IEEE Geosci. Remote Sens. Lett. **21** (2024). https://doi.org/10.1109/LGRS.2024.3365196, https://ieeexplore.ieee.org/document/10433174. conference Name: IEEE Geoscience and Remote Sensing Letters

15. European Environment Agency: CORINE Land Cover 2018, Europe, 6-yearly - version 2020_20u1, May 2020 (2019). https://doi.org/10.2909/71C95A07-E296-44FC-B22B-415F42ACFDF0, https://sdi.eea.europa.eu/catalogue/copernicus/api/records/71c95a07-e296-44fc-b22b-415f42acfdf0?language=all

16. Gal, Y., Ghahramani, Z.: Dropout as a Bayesian approximation: representing model uncertainty in deep learning. In: International Conference on Machine Learning (2015)

17. Gal, Y., Islam, R., Ghahramani, Z.: Deep Bayesian active learning with image data. In: Precup, D., Teh, Y.W. (eds.) Proceedings of the 34th International Conference on Machine Learning. Proceedings of Machine Learning Research, vol. 70, pp. 1183–1192. PMLR (2017). https://proceedings.mlr.press/v70/gal17a.html

18. Höhl, A., et al.: Opening the black-box: a systematic review on explainable AI in remote sensing (2024). http://arxiv.org/abs/2402.13791, arXiv:2402.13791

19. Lakshminarayanan, B., Pritzel, A., Blundell, C.: Simple and scalable predictive uncertainty estimation using deep ensembles. In: Proceedings of the 31st International Conference on Neural Information Processing Systems, pp. 6405–6416. NIPS 2017, Curran Associates Inc., Red Hook, NY, USA (2017)

20. Lapuschkin, S., Wäldchen, S., Binder, A., Montavon, G., Samek, W., Müller, K.R.: Unmasking clever Hans predictors and assessing what machines really learn. Nat. Commun. **10**(1), 1096 (2019)

21. Lary, D.J., Alavi, A.H., Gandomi, A.H., Walker, A.L.: Machine learning in geosciences and remote sensing. Geosci. Front. **7**(1), 3–10 (2016). https://doi.org/10.1016/j.gsf.2015.07.003, https://www.sciencedirect.com/science/article/pii/S1674987115000821

22. Lundberg, S.M., Lee, S.I.: A unified approach to interpreting model predictions. In: Advances in Neural Information Processing Systems. vol. 30. Curran Associates, Inc. (2017). https://proceedings.neurips.cc/paper_files/paper/2017/hash/8a20a8621978632d76c43dfd28b67767-Abstract.html

23. Mehdiyev, N., Majlatow, M., Fettke, P.: Quantifying and explaining machine learning uncertainty in predictive process monitoring: an operations research perspective. Ann. Oper. Res. (2024). https://doi.org/10.1007/s10479-024-05943-4

24. Mukhoti, J., Kirsch, A., van Amersfoort, J., Torr, P.H., Gal, Y.: Deep deterministic uncertainty: a new simple baseline. In: Proceedings of the IEEE/CVF Conference on Computer Vision and Pattern Recognition (CVPR), pp. 24384–24394 (2023)

25. Ribeiro, M., Singh, S., Guestrin, C.: "Why should i trust you?": Explaining the predictions of any classifier. In: DeNero, J., Finlayson, M., Reddy, S. (eds.) Proceedings of the 2016 Conference of the North American Chapter of the Association for Computational Linguistics: Demonstrations, pp. 97–101. Association for Computational Linguistics, San Diego (2016). https://doi.org/10.18653/v1/N16-3020, https://aclanthology.org/N16-3020

26. Ronneberger, O., Fischer, P., Brox, T.: U-net: convolutional networks for biomedical image segmentation (2015). https://doi.org/10.48550/arXiv.1505.04597, http://arxiv.org/abs/1505.04597

27. Sanderson, E.W., Jaiteh, M., Levy, M.A., Redford, K.H., Wannebo, A.V., Woolmer, G.: The Human footprint and the last of the wild: the human footprint is a global map of human influence on the land surface, which suggests that human beings are stewards of nature, whether we like it or not. BioScience **52**(10), 891–904 (2002). https://doi.org/10.1641/0006-3568(2002)052[0891:THFATL]2.0.CO;2
28. Selvaraju, R.R., Cogswell, M., Das, A., Vedantam, R., Parikh, D., Batra, D.: Grad-CAM: visual explanations from deep networks via gradient-based localization. In: 2017 IEEE International Conference on Computer Vision (ICCV), pp. 618–626 (2017). https://doi.org/10.1109/ICCV.2017.74, https://ieeexplore.ieee.org/document/8237336. iSSN: 2380-7504
29. Stomberg, T.T., Leonhardt, J., Weber, I., Roscher, R.: Recognizing protected and anthropogenic patterns in landscapes using interpretable machine learning and satellite imagery. Front. Artif. Intell. **6** (2023). https://doi.org/10.3389/frai.2023.1278118, https://www.frontiersin.org/journals/artificial-intelligence/articles/10.3389/frai.2023.1278118/full. publisher: Frontiers
30. Stomberg, T.T., Stone, T., Leonhardt, J., Weber, I., Roscher, R.: Exploring wilderness characteristics using explainable machine learning in satellite imagery (2022). https://doi.org/10.48550/arXiv.2203.00379, http://arxiv.org/abs/2203.00379
31. Wilson, A.G., Izmailov, P.: Bayesian deep learning and a probabilistic perspective of generalization. CoRR **abs/2002.08791** (2020). https://arxiv.org/abs/2002.08791
32. Winter, S., Fischer, H.S., Fischer, A.: Relative quantitative reference approach for naturalness assessments of forests. Forest Ecol. Manage. **259**(8), 1624–1632 (2010). https://doi.org/10.1016/j.foreco.2010.01.040, https://www.sciencedirect.com/science/article/pii/S0378112710000599
33. Zanaga, D., et al.: ESA WorldCover 10 m 2021 v200 (2022). https://doi.org/10.5281/zenodo.7254221, https://zenodo.org/records/7254221

Semantic Segmentation of Structural Damage: A Comparative Study of YOLO11 and Encoder-Decoder Networks

Lorenz Krefft[(✉)] and Ludwig Hoegner

Hochschule München University of Applied Sciences, Munich, Germany
`{lorenz.krefft,ludwig.hoegner}@hm.edu`

Abstract. This paper presents a comparative study of semantic segmentation methods for the automated detection of structural damage in images. The goal is to identify models that offer an optimal balance between accuracy and computational efficiency, enabling practical applications in areas such as building inspection and infrastructure maintenance. Using the DACL10k dataset, which contains approximately 8,000 annotated images with 19 damage classes (e.g. cracks, corrosion, spalling), we evaluate a YOLO11-based segmentation method against encoder-decoder architectures, specifically DeepLabV3+ and UNet++, combined with different encoders such as ResNet, EfficientNet, MobileNet and the Mix Vision Transformer. These architectures are evaluated using standard segmentation metrics, such as mean Intersection over Union (mIoU), Precision, Recall and F1 Score. Our results show that DeepLabV3+ in combination with a transformer-based encoder achieves the highest mIoU of 0.409, significantly outperforming the YOLO11 model (mIoU = 0.321). These findings emphasize the limitations of object detection models such as YOLO for pixel-level segmentation tasks and highlight the potential of attention-based architectures for accurate and efficient structural damage analysis.

Keywords: Semantic segmentation · YOLO11 · DeepLabV3+ · UNet++

1   Introduction

Ensuring the structural integrity of buildings requires regular and accurate inspections. In practice, such inspections are usually carried out manually through visual assessments. However, these procedures are time-consuming, costly and highly dependent on the experience and subjective judgment of the inspector [6,12]. Automated damage detection offers significant potential to improve efficiency and consistency in this area. Recent advances in artificial intelligence (AI) have created new opportunities for automated inspection

© The Author(s), under exclusive license to Springer Nature Switzerland AG 2026
M. Keuper and F. Locatello (Eds.): DAGM GCPR 2025, LNCS 16125, pp. 586–599, 2026.
https://doi.org/10.1007/978-3-032-12840-9_37

through object recognition, classification and semantic segmentation at the pixel level.

Previous studies, such as [15], have shown that image-based AI models can achieve high accuracy in detecting certain types of damage, such as cracks. Nevertheless, these approaches often reach their limits in challenging environments or with low-contrast images, highlighting the need for further research and improvement.

In previous works, a method for the detection and quantification of cracks on masonry surfaces was presented. The core of this approach was a neural network based on YOLO11, which was trained using the DACL10k dataset for semantic segmentation. The results showed the potential of the process, but still leave potential for improvement, particularly in terms of the model architecture.

This study analyzes the potential of alternative network architectures to improve the accuracy of image-based damage detection. The analysis focuses on two encoder-decoder architectures. The DeepLabV3+ and U-Net++ in combination with different encoders were used.

2   Related Work

The latest YOLO version 11 was introduced in 2024. It can be used to perform segmentation tasks in near real time. The main strengths of this latest version are the refined model architecture, which optimizes the recognition of small objects even in difficult environments. The improved ability of the model to extract features means that a wider range of patterns in images can be processed and recognized. In tests on the COCO dataset, the new YOLO version outperformed all previous models in terms of speed and accuracy [11]. Technically, YOLO is able to handle segmentation tasks. But YOLO's strengths are object detection. For this reason, there are also approaches that combine the strengths of YOLO's object detection with the strengths of DeepLabv3+'s segmentation. In studies by [21], the segmentation of plant leaves could be increased with this methodology compared to classical methods.

2.1   Decoder Architectures

Encoder-decoder networks are widely used for semantic segmentation tasks. In the context of concrete surface damage, DeepLabV3+ and U-Net++ have proven especially effective [7]. For example, [4] demonstrated the suitability of these architectures for crack segmentation, while [22] reported strong results using DeepLabV3+ in sewer damage detection.

DeepLabV3+ is a further development of its predecessor DeepLabV3. Compared to DeepLabV3, DeepLabV3+ has a simpler but effective decoder model, which improves the segmentation boundaries, especially along the object boundaries. In addition, DeepLabV3+ introduces an encoder-decoder architecture and uses Atrous Separable Convolutions in the context modules to increase efficiency and improve accuracy [3].

Similar to DeepLabV3+, U-Net++ is a further development of U-Net. U-Net focuses on medical image processing. In contrast to U-Net, U-Net++ follows an approach in which the skip connections between encoder and decoder have been re-designed. Skip connections combine the information from the decoder with that of the encoder. The architecture of U-Net++ relies on nested and dense skip connections. The aim of this redesign is to reduce the semantic gap between the feature maps of the decoder and encoder networks [23].

2.2 Encoder Architectures

Both model architectures are based on an encoder-decoder architecture. Four different encoders are evaluated in this study. A mix Vision Transformer (mit_b5), EfficientNet (efficientnet-b7), ResNet (resnet152) and MobileNet (mobilenet_v2).

Transformers, and in particular the Mix Vision Transformer (MiT), have gained attention for their ability to capture both global context and local detail. MiT generates hierarchical multi-scale features using efficient self-attention without requiring positional encoding, enabling resolution-independent segmentation [13, 19].

EfficientNet is another powerful encoder that offers a good balance between accuracy and model complexity. It is a Convolutional Neural Network (CNN) that efficiently scales depth, width and resolution through balanced compound scaling, enabling powerful and resource-efficient feature extraction for image segmentation tasks [1, 14].

ResNet has proven itself as an encoder and is widely used. It is also a CNN that uses residual units to efficiently train deep models and avoid the problem of vanishing gradients. The architecture consists of stacked layers with skip connections that pass the original input directly to later layers [9, 20].

MobileNet is an efficient network architecture based on depthwise separable convolutions. It processes spatial and channel features separately, which can significantly reduce computational costs and improve accuracy by learning spatial and cross-channel correlations separately [18]. This encoder is used to illustrate the possibility of using segmentation tasks on low-resource devices.

3 Dataset

The freely available DACL10k dataset [5] is used as the data basis. It includes 6,935 training and 975 validation images. The dataset is annotated for a multi-label segmentation task in 19 classes: Crack, Alligator Crack, Efflorescence, Rockpocket, Washouts/Concrete Corrosion, Hollow Areas, Cavity, Spalling, Restformwork, Wetspot, Rust, Graffiti, Weathering, Exposed Rebars, Bearing, Expansion Joint, Drainage, Protective Equipment and Joint Tape. The following graphic 1 provides an overview of the class instance distribution within the dataset.

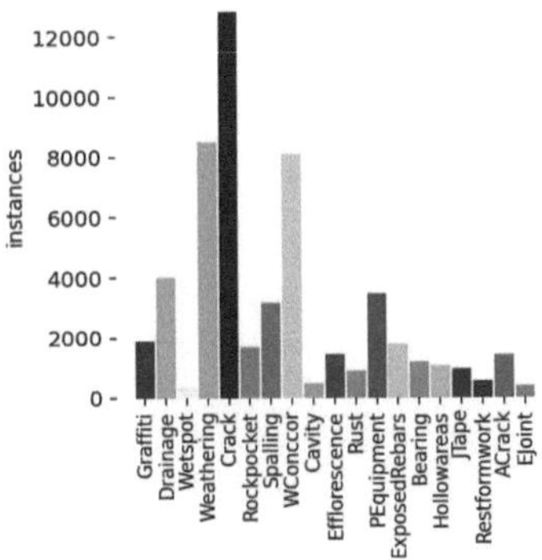

Fig. 1. Instances per class.

To compare the performance of different segmentation architectures, the validation subset of the DACL10k dataset is used. The mean intersection over union (mIoU) (1), F1 score (2) , precision (3) and recall (4) are used as evaluation metrics. The entire validation dataset is used to determine these metrics globally.

$$mIoU = \frac{TP}{TP + FN + FP} \tag{1}$$

$$F1 = \frac{2 \cdot TP}{2 \cdot TP + FN + FP} \tag{2}$$

$$Precision = \frac{TP}{TP + FP} \tag{3}$$

$$Recall = \frac{TP}{TP + FN} \tag{4}$$

where:

- TP: True Positive
- FP: False Positives
- FN: False Negatives

4   Training

All networks were trained on a local Ubuntu workstation equipped with two NVIDIA RTX A6000 GPUs providing a total of 96 GB of VRAM. For the YOLO11 model, the Ultralytics framework [10] was used, while the DeepLabV3+ and UNet++ models were implemented using PyTorch [16] and the Segmentation Models library [8].

4.1 YOLO11

Prior to training, a hyperparameter optimization was performed using 50% of the training dataset. The built-in tuning functionality of the Ultralytics framework was applied, which follows a mutation-based search strategy. Small adjustments are made to hyperparameters across iterations to converge towards an optimal configuration [10]. During hyperparameter tuning, training was conducted with an input resolution of 640 × 640 pixels, a batch size of 16, and a total of 300 epochs. However, training was terminated early at epoch 241, as no significant improvement in the fitness metric was observed. The fitness score is defined as a weighted combination of the standard detection metrics mAP50 and mAP50-95 (5).

$$Fitness = 0.1 \cdot mAP50 + 0.9 \cdot mAP50 - 95 \tag{5}$$

The following hyperparameters were selected during tuning:

- lr0 (initial learning rate): 0.01
- momentum: 0.937
- warmup_epochs: 3.0
- warmup_momentum: 0.8
- weight_decay: 0.0005
- Final learning rate: lrf = 0.01

In addition, loss weighting parameters were set as follows:

- box (bounding box regression loss weight): 7.5
- cls (classification loss weight): 0.5

A variety of data augmentation strategies were employed:

- **Geometric:** translate = 0.1, scale = 0.5, fliplr = 0.5
- **Color:** hsv_h = 0.015, hsv_s = 0.7, hsv_v = 0.4
- **Mosaic augmentation** (mosaic = 1.0)

A YOLO11m-seg model was trained with these hyperparameters. This model was also trained with a resolution of 640 × 640 pixels and a batch size of 16. In addition to these settings, the default settings from Ultralytics were used. A training for 300 epochs was set. This was stopped after epoch 188, as there was no evidence of increasing training success.

4.2 DeepLabV3+ and UNet++

Both the DeepLabV3+ and the UNet++ network were trained with an input resolution of 640 × 640 pixels, similar to the YOLO training. Each model was trained for 30 epochs using a multi-label classification setup. Pre-trained weights based on Imagenet were used for all encoder-decoder variations. The training configuration is described in detail below.

Data Augmentation

To improve the generalization capability, various augmentation techniques were used by using the albumentation library [2]. These include geometric transformations as well as photometric changes and image distortions. With geometric transformations such as HorizontalFlip and VerticalFlip, the images are mirrored horizontally or vertically in order to increase the model robustness against changes in position. RandomRotate90 also belongs to this category, where the image is randomly rotated by 90° to create more variations in position.

The Affine technique combines several geometric changes, including scaling, shifting and rotation, thus enabling a controlled distortion of the images. This creates slight changes to the images that are intended to improve model generalization.

The following operations affect the image brightness, contrast and image noise. With RandomBrightnessContrast, brightness and contrast are changed randomly, while GaussianBlur and GaussNoise make the image slightly blurred or noisy. These methods simulate different light or image conditions and make the model less sensitive to such disturbances.

RandomCrop randomly crops a section of the image. This helps the model to focus on different areas of the image instead of relying only on the center. Finally, ElasticTransform applies an elastic distortion that creates more complex, non-linear image deformations.

These augmentation strategies help the models to generalize better under varying image conditions and prevent them from overfitting.

Class Weights

As illustrated in Fig. 1, the DACL10k dataset exhibits a highly imbalanced class distribution. To address this, class-specific weights were introduced into the loss function. The relative frequency f_i of each class i is calculated as:

$$f_i = \frac{\text{Number of positive pixels of class } i}{\text{Total number of pixels for all classes}} \tag{6}$$

The corresponding class weight w_i is then defined as:

$$w_i = \frac{1}{f_i + \epsilon} \tag{7}$$

where $\epsilon = 10^{-6}$ is added to prevent division by zero. To avoid numerical instability, weights were capped at a maximum value of 5.

Loss Function

A composite loss function was used, combining Binary Cross-Entropy with Logits (BCEWithLogitsLoss) and the Jaccard Loss (IoU-based loss). Such hybridized loss combinations are more robust and accurate than pure BCE or Jaccard functions. This is especially the case with highly imbalanced datasets [17].

The two components are weighted according to Eq. (8).

$$\text{Loss} = 0.4 \cdot \text{BCEWithLogitsLoss} + 0.6 \cdot \text{JaccardLoss} \tag{8}$$

This combined approach allows simultaneous optimization of pixel classification (via BCE) and region-level segmentation performance (via Jaccard). Figures 2 and 3 show the training and validation loss curves for each encoder variant paired with DeepLabV3+ and U-Net++, respectively.

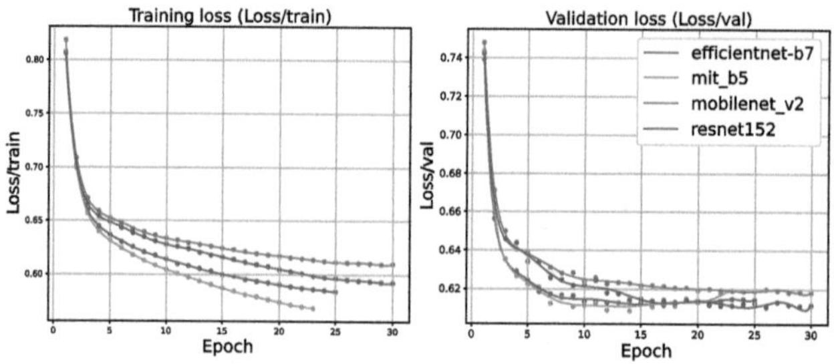

Fig. 2. Loss functions with DeepLabV3+ encoder.

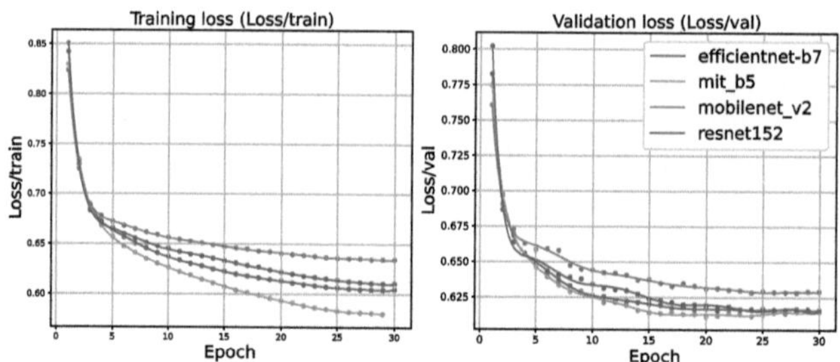

Fig. 3. Loss functions with U-Net++ encoder.

Optimizer and Learning Rate Scheduler

The optimizer used was AdamW, a variant of the classic Adam optimizer with an explicit weighting of weight decay. A weight decay of 10^{-4} was used.

A two-phase learning rate scheduler was employed:

- Warm-up phase over the first 4 epochs, linearly increasing the learning rate from $5{,}0 \cdot 10^{-5}$ to $1{,}25 \cdot 10^{-4}$
- Cosine annealing to gradually reduce the learning rate to a minimum of 10^{-6}

Early Stopping

To avoid overfitting, an early-stopping strategy was implemented that monitors the validation loss (Val/Loss). If there is no significant improvement ($< 10^{-4}$) over ten subsequent epochs, the training is automatically terminated. In addition, the mean intersection over union (mIoU) is calculated on the validation dataset after each epoch. The model with the highest mIoU so far is saved and used later for the final evaluation.

5   Results

5.1   YOLO

The YOLO11 network achieved the following performance on the validation set:

- **Precision:** 0.406
- **Recall:** 0.274
- **F1 Score:** 0.319
- **Mean Intersection over Union (mIoU):** 0.321
- **Model size (total parameters):** 22,400,000

This result highlights a key limitation. YOLO11 is capable of performing segmentation, its architecture is inherently optimized for bounding box-based object detection, not pixel-level segmentation.

5.2   DeepLabV3+

The best results were achieved using the DeepLabV3+ decoder in combination with the Mix Vision Transformer encoder (mit_b5). This configuration yielded:

- **Precision:** 0.579
- **Recall:** 0.660
- **F1 Score:** 0.611
- **Mean Intersection over Union (mIoU):** 0.409
- **Model size (total parameters):** 82,600,419

Figure 4 shows the mIoU progression across epochs for all tested encoders. The transformer-based encoder provided significant improvements over CNN-based backbones, particularly in capturing fine spatial details and contextual information. This confirms the benefit of attention-based architectures for complex segmentation tasks such as structural damage segmentation.

5.3   U-Net++

The best performance using the U-Net++ decoder was achieved with the Mix Vision Transformer encoder (mit_b5), resulting in:

- **Precision:** 0.552
- **Recall:** 0.647

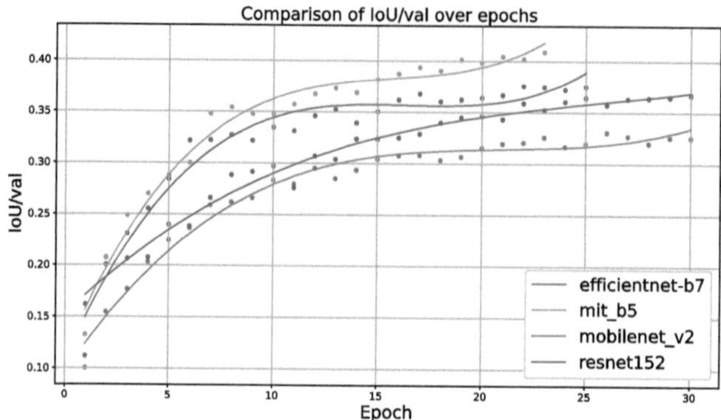

Fig. 4. Comparison of IoU on Validation Set Across Epochs for All Encoders (Decoder: **DeepLabV3+**)

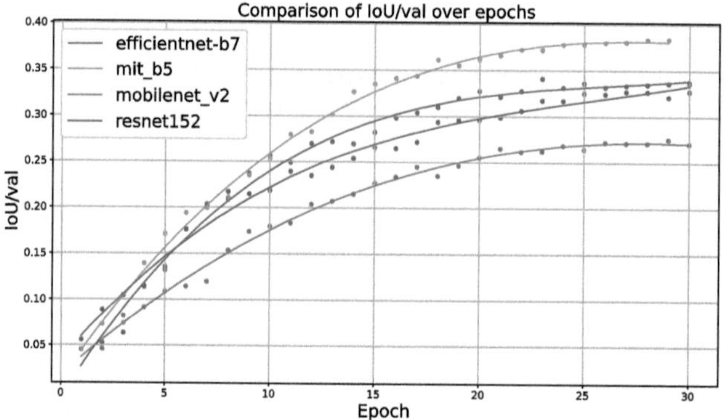

Fig. 5. Comparison of IoU on Validation Set Across Epochs for All Encoders (Decoder: **Unet++**)

- **F1 Score:** 0.595
- **Mean Intersection over Union (mIoU):** 0.384
- **Model size (total parameters):** 86,947,595

Figures 5 show the training progression in terms of mIoU across different encoders. While U-Net++ performed better than YOLO11, it did not match the segmentation quality of DeepLabV3+.

5.4   Summary

Figure 6 presents a qualitative comparison of segmentation results from the various network architectures. Four representative samples from the DACL10k validation set are shown. For each image, the original input, the corresponding ground truth, and the predicted masks generated by each model are displayed.

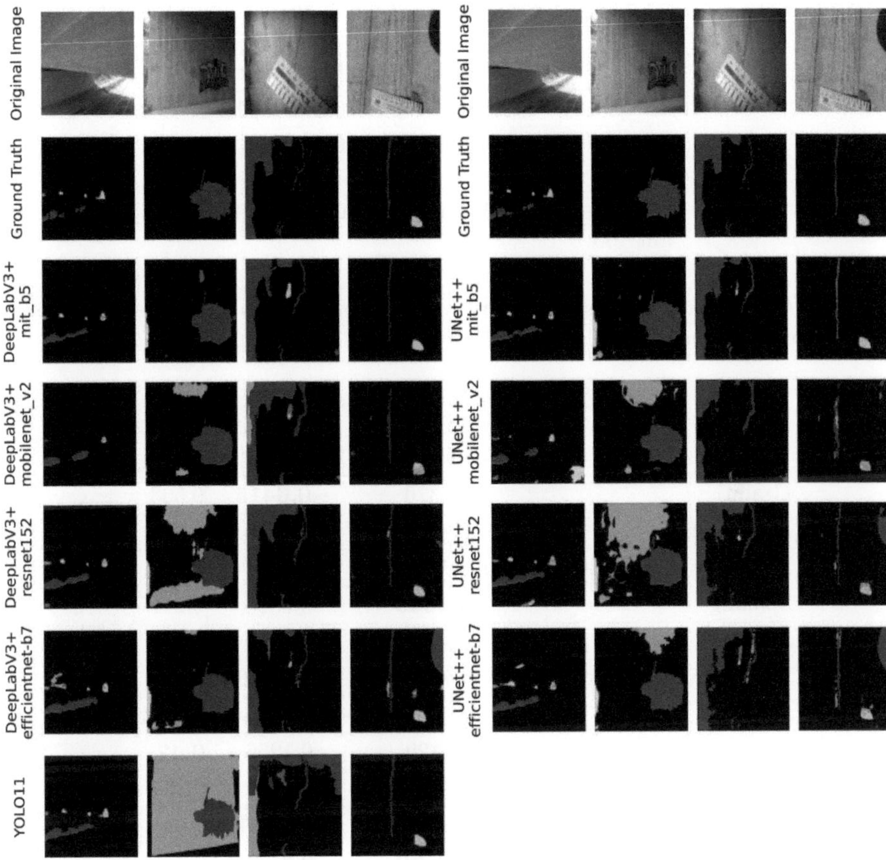

Fig. 6. A comparison of the different network architectures. The original image, the ground truth and the predictions of the networks

Table 1 shows that DeepLabV3+ in combination with the Mixed Vision Transvormer Encoder achieved the best results with an mIoU error of 0.409. These findings underline the limited suitability of YOLO11 for pixel-level segmentation tasks, particularly when compared to encoder-decoder architectures. While U-Net++ showed good generalization capabilities and recall, DeepLabV3+ with a transformer encoder consistently delivered the highest overall performance across all metrics.

In Table 2, the mIoU errors are analyzed class by class. Also here, the DeepLabV3+ network with Mixed Vision Transformer encoder performs better than the other networks.

Table 1. Comparison of the error metrics for the different network architectures.

	mIoU	Precision	Recall	F1
YOLO11	0.321	0.406	0.274	0.319
DeepLabV3+ mit_b5	**0.409**	**0.576**	**0.660**	**0.611**
UNet++ mit_b5	0.384	0.552	0.647	0.595

Table 2. Comparison of the mIoU errors for each damage class using the best encoder-decoder combination, as well as YOLO11.

	DeepLabV3+ mit_b5 [mIoU]	Unet++ mit_b5 [mIoU]	YOLO11 [mIoU]
Graffiti	0.6376	**0.6415**	0.503
Weathering	**0.4018**	0.3990	0.384
Washouts/Concrete Corrosion	**0.1193**	0.0921	0.045
Spalling	**0.4049**	0.3808	0.241
Rust	**0.4759**	0.4501	0.255
Protective Equipment	0.7130	**0.7446**	0.329
Crack	0.2659	0.2455	**0.308**
Cavity	0.1129	0.1256	**0.42**
Expansion Joint	**0.4719**	0.3989	0.267
Wetspot	0.2736	**0.2781**	0.09
Restformwork	**0.3569**	0.2149	0.1
Efflorescence	**0.3664**	0.3578	0.144
Exposed Rebars	**0.3916**	0.3809	0.086
Hollow Areas	0.5095	0.5048	**0.7**
Bearing	**0.6522**	**0.6522**	0.433
Joint Tape	0.3784	0.2720	**0.406**
Rockpocket	0.1481	0.1333	**0.729**
Drainage	**0.6304**	0.5749	0.32
Alligator Crack	**0.4588**	0.4403	0.332

6   Conclusion and Future Work

This study presented a comparative evaluation of semantic segmentation models for the detection of structural damage in civil infrastructure images. Among the examined methods, the encoder-decoder architecture DeepLabV3+ combined with a Mix Vision Transformer encoder achieved the best overall performance, with a mean IoU of 0.409 and an F1 score of 0.611. In contrast, the YOLO11-

based model demonstrated limitations in pixel-level segmentation, highlighting that its architecture is better suited for object detection tasks.

The results underline the potential of attention-based models for accurately segmenting fine-grained damage patterns, even in complex scenes. Although UNet++ showed strong recall, it fell short in terms of precision and overall segmentation quality compared to DeepLabV3+. Currently the DeepLabV3+ network in combination with a transformer-based encoder is able to detect damages in images. In order to quantify the identified damage in a more thorough context, such as the analysis of crack widths, subsequent optimizations will probably be required.

Future work could focus on:

- Extending the training dataset with more diverse examples.
- Incorporating segmentation strategies such as sliding window.
- Optimize loss functions and learning rate schedulers.
- Investigation of alternative transformer-based network architectures.

Acknowledgments. This work was supported by the NEMETSCHEK Innovationsstiftung.

Disclosure of Interests. The authors have no competing interests to declare that are relevant to the content of this article.

References

1. Abdelrahman, A., Viriri, S.: Efficientnet family u-net models for deep learning semantic segmentation of kidney tumors on CT images. Front. Comput. Sci. **5** (2023). https://doi.org/10.3389/fcomp.2023.1235622
2. Buslaev, A., Iglovikov, V.I., Khvedchenya, E., Parinov, A., Druzhinin, M., Kalinin, A.A.: Albumentations: fast and flexible image augmentations. Information **11**(2) (2020). https://doi.org/10.3390/info11020125, https://www.mdpi.com/2078-2489/11/2/125
3. Chen, L., Zhu, Y., Papandreou, G., Schroff, F., Adam, H.: Encoder-decoder with atrous separable convolution for semantic image segmentation. CoRR **abs/1802.02611** (2018). http://arxiv.org/abs/1802.02611
4. Eddy, L., Nagai, K., Hadinata, P.: Crack detection on concrete surfaces using deep encoder-decoder convolutional neural network: a comparison study between u-net and deeplabv3+. J. Civ. Eng. Forum **7**, 323–334 (2021). https://doi.org/10.22146/jcef.65288
5. Flotzinger, J., Rösch, P.J., Braml, T.: dacl10k: benchmark for semantic bridge damage segmentation. In: 2024 IEEE/CVF Winter Conference on Applications of Computer Vision (WACV), pp. 8611–8620 (2023)
6. Flotzinger, J., Rösch, P.J., Oswald, N., Braml, T.: Building inspection toolkit: unified evaluation and strong baselines for bridge damage recognition. In: 2022 IEEE International Conference on Image Processing (ICIP), pp. 1221–1225 (2022). https://doi.org/10.1109/ICIP46576.2022.9897743

7. Hadinata, P.N., Simanta, D., Eddy, L., Nagai, K.: Multiclass segmentation of concrete surface damages using u-net and deeplabv3+. Appl. Sci. **13**(4) (2023). https://doi.org/10.3390/app13042398, https://www.mdpi.com/2076-3417/13/4/2398

8. Iakubovskii, P.: Segmentation models pytorch (2019). https://github.com/qubvel/segmentation_models.pytorch

9. Isosalo, A., et al.: Evaluation of different convolutional neural network encoder-decoder architectures for breast mass segmentation. In: Medical Imaging (2022). https://api.semanticscholar.org/CorpusID:246977943

10. Jocher, G., Qiu, J., Chaurasia, A.: Ultralytics yolo. https://ultralytics.com, if you use this software, please cite it using the metadata from this file. Repository: https://github.com/ultralytics/ultralytics

11. Khanam, R., Hussain, M.: Yolov11: an overview of the key architectural enhancements. ArXiv (2024). https://doi.org/10.48550/arXiv.2410.17725

12. Lawin, F.J., Danelljan, M., Tosteberg, P., Bhat, G., Khan, F.S., Felsberg, M.: Deep projective 3D semantic segmentation. In: Felsberg, M., Heyden, A., Krüger, N. (eds.) CAIP 2017. LNCS, vol. 10424, pp. 95–107. Springer, Cham (2017). https://doi.org/10.1007/978-3-319-64689-3_8

13. Lima, J.G.P., Braz Junior, G., de Almeida, J.D.S., Matos, C.E.F.: Evaluation of encoder-decoder architectures for automatic skin lesion segmentation. In: Tucker, A., Henriques Abreu, P., Cardoso, J., Pereira Rodrigues, P., Riaño, D. (eds.) AIME 2021. LNCS (LNAI), vol. 12721, pp. 373–377. Springer, Cham (2021). https://doi.org/10.1007/978-3-030-77211-6_43

14. Mathews, M.R., Anzar, S., Kalesh Krishnan, R., Panthakkan, A.: Efficientnet for retinal blood vessel segmentation. In: 2020 3rd International Conference on Signal Processing and Information Security (ICSPIS), pp. 1–4 (2020). https://doi.org/10.1109/ICSPIS51252.2020.9340135

15. Mohan, A., Poobal, S.: Crack detection using image processing: a critical review and analysis. Alex. Eng. J. **57**(2), 787–798 (2018). https://doi.org/10.1016/j.aej.2017.01.020

16. Paszke, A., et al.: Pytorch: an imperative style, high-performance deep learning library. CoRR **abs/1912.01703** (2019), http://arxiv.org/abs/1912.01703

17. Polisi, X., Uka, A., Avdiu, D., Karras, D.: Efficient and accurate cell image segmentation through optimizer and loss function fine-tuning with quantization and pruning. Edelweiss Appl. Sci. Technol. **9**, 1675–1691 (2025). https://doi.org/10.55214/25768484.v9i3.5668

18. Siam, M., Gamal, M., Abdel-Razek, M., Yogamani, S., Jagersand, M.: Rtseg: real-time semantic segmentation comparative study. In: 2018 25th IEEE International Conference on Image Processing (ICIP), pp. 1603–1607 (2018). https://doi.org/10.1109/ICIP.2018.8451495

19. Xie, E., Wang, W., Yu, Z., Anandkumar, A., Álvarez, J.M., Luo, P.: Segformer: simple and efficient design for semantic segmentation with transformers. CoRR **abs/2105.15203** (2021). https://arxiv.org/abs/2105.15203

20. Xu, W., Fu, Y.L., Zhu, D.: Resnet and its application to medical image processing: research progress and challenges. Comput. Methods Programs Biomed. **240**, 107660 (2023). https://doi.org/10.1016/j.cmpb.2023.107660, https://www.sciencedirect.com/science/article/pii/S0169260723003255

21. Yang, T., Zhou, S., Xu, A., Ye, J., Yin, J.: An approach for plant leaf image segmentation based on yolov8 and the improved deeplabv3+. Plants **12**, 3438 (2023). https://doi.org/10.3390/plants12193438

22. Zhou, Q., Situ, Z., Teng, S., Liu, H., Chen, W., Chen, G.: Automatic sewer defect detection and severity quantification based on pixel-level semantic segmentation. Tunn. Undergr. Space Technol. **123**, 104403 (2022). https://doi.org/10.1016/j.tust.2022.104403
23. Zhou, Z., Siddiquee, M.M.R., Tajbakhsh, N., Liang, J.: Unet++: a nested u-net architecture for medical image segmentation. CoRR **abs/1807.10165** (2018). http://arxiv.org/abs/1807.10165

Can Multitask Learning Enhance Model Explainability?

Hiba Najjar[1,2(✉)] ⓘ, Bushra Alshbib[1], and Andreas Dengel[1,2] ⓘ

[1] Kaiserslautern-Landau University, Kaiserslautern, Germany
{hiba.najjar,andreas.dengel}@dfki.de, alshbib@rptu.de
[2] German Research Center for Artificial Intelligence, Kaiserslautern, Germany

Abstract. Remote sensing provides satellite data in diverse types and formats. The usage of multimodal learning networks exploits this diversity to improve model performance, except that the complexity of such networks comes at the expense of their interpretability. In this study, we explore how modalities can be leveraged through multitask learning to intrinsically explain model behavior. In particular, instead of additional inputs, we use certain modalities as additional targets to be predicted along with the main task. The success of this approach relies on the rich information content of satellite data, which remains as input modalities. We show how this modeling context provides numerous benefits: (1) in case of data scarcity, the additional modalities do not need to be collected for model inference at deployment, (2) the model performance remains comparable to the multimodal baseline performance, and in some cases achieves better scores, (3) prediction errors in the main task can be explained via the model behavior in the auxiliary task(s). We demonstrate the efficiency of our approach on three datasets, including segmentation, classification, and regression tasks. Code available as supplementary material and at git.opendfki.de/hiba.najjar/mtl_explainability/.

Keywords: Intrinsic interpretability · Multitask learning · Multimodal learning · Explaining model errors

1 Introduction

Multimodal learning is widely used across various fields, driven by the availability of data from diverse sources or sensors. Remote Sensing (RS) benefits

H. Najjar acknowledges support through a scholarship from the University of Kaiserslautern-Landau. The research results presented are part of a large collaborative project on agricultural yield predictions, which was partly funded through the ESA InCubed Programme (https://incubed.esa.int/) as part of the project AI4EO Solution Factory (https://www.ai4eo-solution-factory.de/.

Supplementary Information The online version contains supplementary material available at https://doi.org/10.1007/978-3-032-12840-9_38.

particularly from this field, as it provides a wide range of satellite images and satellite-derived products. In fact, it was shown that models fusing data from different modalities outperform their uni-modal counterparts both intuitively and provably [7]. To adjust to the multimodal setup, advanced modeling techniques are often implemented. However, these techniques often lead to increased model complexity, which comes at the expense of model interpretability [5,8].

In contrast, multitask learning aims at predicting multiple targets using a shared model, achieving in most cases smaller memory footprint, reduced number of calculations, and improved performance [3,10,11,13,16,18,28,35,36]. There are still certain scenarios in which single task networks might outperform multitask counterparts, due to the number of tasks, their types, and the accuracy of their annotated labels [23,29,34,35].

In this study, we investigate a specific approach to explaining model predictions in the context of multimodal learning by using the framework of multitask learning. By treating certain modalities as auxiliary tasks, we achieve two key objectives: first, we mitigate the model's dependence on these modalities during training, as such modalities are no longer required as inputs during deployment. Second, we provide insights into model behavior by analyzing prediction errors and accuracies across multiple tasks, in order to intrinsically interpret multimodal networks.

2   Related Work

2.1   Explainable Multimodal Networks

EXplainable AI (XAI) research line provides various techniques to tackle the interpretability of neural networks and achieves various objectives. A common goal of XAI is *Justification* [1], answering the question *"Why did the model make this prediction?"*. Feature attribution methods, for instance, measure the influence of each single (or group of) input feature(s) on the prediction [17,25,27,32]. Many such methods are model-agnostic, and can thus be readily applied to multimodal networks, but they are likely less accurate than intrinsic methods, which rely on the model's internal elements to explain its behavior. Another goal of XAI, less commonly addressed, is *Control*, consisting of understanding model errors, ultimately leading to improving its model reasoning and avoiding more errors [1]. In this manuscript, we aim at achieving this goal through an intrinsic technique which leverages multitask learning.

2.2   Explainability Through Multitask Learning

Among the few intrinsic methods in XAI based on multitask learning is **joint training**, which generates explanations by augmenting the original network with additional tasks to explicitly return textual, imagery or numerical explanations, along with the model's main decision [6,9,12,14,24,26,33]. Park et al. [24] introduce a framework for image classification tasks which generates textual and visual explanations as auxiliary tasks. Their main limitation is the necessity of an annotated explanation dataset, which should include text explanations and attention maps. Hendricks et al. [6] apply joint training to explain a classification task of bird species, by predicting the class label and a corresponding textual explanation. Although their proposed method relies on reinforcement learning, it requires textual annotations of the training dataset. Similarly, Rio et al. [26] also proposes a network which returns visual explanation to the classification task, yet relies as well on bounding boxes around the object to be classified, to learn the explanations in a weakly-supervised manner.

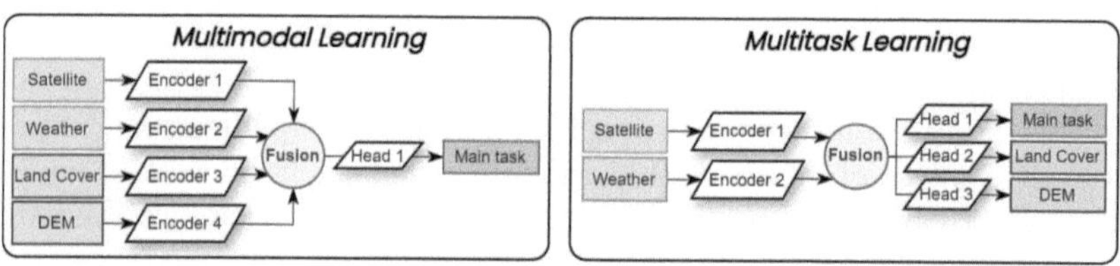

Fig. 1. Comparison of multimodal against multitask setups in a RS dataset. DEM refers to digital elevation maps.

Another line of explanation methods close to the joint training family are **semantic bottleneck networks**. Such models were introduced by Losch et al. [15] and consist of defining an intermediate *bottleneck* layer where latent features are enforced to align with semantic concepts. A study improved this method and proposed to place the semantic layer right before the final layer, enabling a linear mapping between the concepts and the predictions [19]. This approach was applied in different applications in remote sensing [11], healthcare [21], and autonomous driving [4].

While previous studies propose techniques to explicitly predict explanations for model predictions, they are often limited by the availability of annotations for the explanation task, in the form of semantic labels for the semantic bottleneck approach, or explicit sentences and scores for the joint training framework. In our work, we overcome this limitation by relying on available input modalities and turn them into explanatory auxiliary tasks. While this method does not provide explicit explanations, we explore how to extract insightful results from this framework to intrinsically explain model predictions and errors for three different tasks.

3   Methodology

3.1   Interpretability Through Multitask Learning

Additional modalities in multimodal datasets are typically incorporated as input data, yet not all of them may be essential for achieving the baseline model performance. In particular, satellite imagery inherently encodes a rich and diverse range of information about the Earth's surface. For instance, multispectral sensors capture spectral characteristics across multiple bands, while Synthetic Aperture Radar (SAR) sensors provide structural and textural details. Exploiting this characteristic of satellite data, we focus on RS multimodal datasets and explore the effect of shifting auxiliary modalities between input data and auxiliary tasks, as depicted in Fig. 1, analyzing its impact on both model performance and interpretability. To maintain a robust baseline, we ensure that satellite data remains an input modality in all multitask experiments, to avoid significant performance degradation. We evaluate our approach on the following three datasets.

3.2   Datasets

CropYield for Yield Prediction. The *CropYield* dataset contains approximately 500 crop yield maps of corn, soybean, and wheat fields located in Northern Argentina, covering crop seasons from 2017 to 2023. Since the dataset is processed on a pixel-wise basis, it contains more than 3.5 million input samples. The available modalities include satellite multispectral imagery, weather data, Digital Elevation Maps (DEM) properties, and crop type. Both satellite and weather data are temporal, spanning from seeding to harvesting dates each year. Yield maps, rasterized at a 10-meter resolution, are used as the main target (regression task). Further details are provided in Appendix A. Due to confidentiality restrictions, this dataset cannot be publicly released.

Benge for Land Cover Segmentation. *Benge* is an open-source multimodal dataset for Land Use and Land Cover (LULC) segmentation, extending the BigEarthNet dataset [22,30,31]. It contains SAR and multispectral satellite images, from Sentinel-1 and Sentinel-2 missions respectively, for 590,326 locations throughout Europe, complemented with elevation maps, environmental data, climate zone information, and seasonal encoding. Following the recommendations of [22], our experiments were initially conducted on a small subset of the dataset. Subsequently, the best-performing architectures were trained on the 0.2 split of the full dataset, in order to balance computational efficiency with comparable performance.

TreeSAT for Tree Identification. *TreeSAT* is an open-source dataset for tree species classification in Central Europe based on multi-sensor data from aerial imagery and satellite observations, including SAR and multispectral images [2]. The dataset contains labels of 15 tree genera (the main classification task), nine forest stand types, and three foliage types, corresponding to classification levels L3, L2, and L1, respectively. Additionally, it includes an approximation of tree age, which is treated as a continuous feature.

3.3   Experimental Setup

Modality Encoders. Given the diversity of the input data types, we adopt an intermediate fusion approach: each input modality is processed by a dedicated encoder, generating an intermediate representation, which is then fused across modalities before being passed to a task-specific head for the final predictions. This approach facilitates handling multiple input modalities despite differences in data type, spatial characteristics, and temporal resolutions. It has also often outperformed early and late fusion techniques in RS applications [20]. The architecture of the encoder is chosen based on the types of the input and the target: For imagery inputs, we either use a U-Net architecture in segmentation tasks or a convolutional network in other tasks. If the input image is small, such as in low-resolution satellite imagery, we flatten it and process it using a multi-layer perceptron (MLP). Time-series inputs are processed using Transformers, including positional encoding based on each timestamp. Tabular data are processed using MLPs, whether they include a single or multiple features. Finally, for categorical inputs, we use an MLP or an embedding layer.

Fusion Block. The intermediate representations generated by the modality encoders are combined at the fusion block through concatenation, optionally followed by convolutional layers: For regression and classification tasks, each encoder outputs a one-dimensional feature vector representing its respective modality. These vectors are simply concatenated at the fusion stage, with no additional processing. For segmentation tasks, modalities are encoded into a three-dimensional latent representation (i.e., channels × height × width). If the input is an image processed via a U-Net, this representation is obtained naturally. For tabular data encoded through a MLP, the one-dimensional output can be expanded into additional dimensions to align with the spatial structure of other representations. This alignment facilitates the concatenation along the channel dimension, followed by additional convolutional layers that preserve the spatial characteristics (height and width) of the fused representation.

Prediction Heads. Multiple prediction heads can branch out from the fusion block, each dedicated to a specific target: For segmentation tasks, the prediction head consists of convolutional layers, which preserve the spatial dimensions of the image. For regression and classification tasks, a MLP is used to return the appropriate number of output neurons for the task.

Loss and Metrics. The optimization loss for each task is defined based on its nature. For classification tasks, including semantic segmentation, the cross-entropy loss is used, whereas for regression tasks, including dense segmentation, we use the mean squared error (MSE) function. In the multitask learning scenario, the loss contributions of individual tasks are manually fine-tuned. For example, we evaluated strategies such as equally distributing the loss contribution across all tasks, or prioritizing the primary task by assigning it a higher weight (e.g., 60% or 80%) while maintaining a uniform distribution of weights across auxiliary tasks. To further evaluate and report performance, additional metrics are included. Mean absolute error (MAE) and coefficient of determination (R^2) are used for regression and dense segmentation tasks, the F1 score for classification tasks, and the intersection over union (IoU) for semantic segmentation tasks.

In Table 2 in Appendix A, we provide a summary of the encoder, prediction head, loss function, and evaluation metric used for each modality in each dataset.

4   Results

4.1   Multimodal vs. Multitask Modeling

In this section, we analyze the performance results of the different modeling setups, including baselines, which include the remotely sensed images (aerial and satellites) and temporal modalities, multimodal learning experiments (MML), which test different combinations of additional input modalities, and multitask learning experiments (MTL), which shifts some modalities from being additional input to auxiliary targets.

Starting with the CropYield dataset, Table 1 combines the results of the main experiments. Table 3 in Appendix B.1 contains more results, particularly extending the baseline experiments. In multimodal setups, performance comparable to the baseline is observed when including weather and DEM as additional inputs to the model, in Experiment **5**, while any other combination of auxiliary inputs yields a decline in the performance. Surprisingly, this includes Experiments **2, 4,** and **6**, where we provide the model with the crop label of each pixel sample. In contrast, forcing the model to predict this label improved its performance, particularly when including weather and DEM modalities as inputs, in Experiment **9**, and when including no additional input modality, in Experiment **7**. The latter even reached the highest overall R^2 score across all experiments. The model further reached a very high F1-score of 99.4% in the crop classification task, which brings a great benefit in practice, enabling the distinction of crop types along the accurate yield prediction. We assume that the performance gap in yield prediction between Experiments **2** and **7** is due to the shared representation of the multitask learning setup, in which the model is forced to learn representations related to the different crop labels, which positively influences the accuracy of the predicted yield. In the explainability analysis, we will focus on Experiment **7**, which predicts the yield and crop labels using the satellite data alone.

Moving to the Benge dataset, we present the results in Table 2. The complete table including model performance on auxiliary tasks is presented in Table 4 in Appendix B.2. In the baseline experiment, the model is trained on the multispectral and SAR satellite images alone, achieving the second best scores in the main task of LULC, with an accuracy of 87.94% and an IoU score of 0.388. In the multimodal Experiments (**2–8**), we evaluate different combinations of one or more additional input modalities, prioritizing elevation data due to its spatial dimension, which the remaining modalities lack. While all multimodal experiments yielded results comparable to the baseline, Experiment **7** including the elevation and weather data have slighlty outperformed it, achieving an accuracy of 87.95%. Similarly, Experiment **4**, which includes seasonal information, achieves a marginally higher IoU score of 0.389, also surpassing the baseline. In

Table 1. Modeling performance on the test set of the CropYield dataset. The best and second-best scores are highlighted in bold and underlined, respectively. Crop classification performance is given in micro F1 score.

Experiments		Modalities				Main task	Auxiliary tasks	
		Satellite	Crop label	Weather	DEM	Yield (R)	Crop cls. (F1)	DEM (MAE)
Baseline	1	Input				<u>0.81</u>	-	-
MML	2	Input	Input			0.77	-	-
	3	Input		Input		0.75	-	-
	4	Input	Input	Input		0.79	-	-
	5	Input		Input	Input	<u>0.81</u>	-	-
	6	Input	Input	Input	Input	0.79	-	-
MTL	7	Input	Output			**0.82**	<u>99.4</u>	-
	8	Input	Output	Input		0.77	**99.5**	-
	9	Input	Output	Input	Input	0.80	**99.5**	-
	10	Input	Output	Input	Output	0.75	99.3	**0.42**

Input | Output | cls.:classification.

the multitask setup, the LULC accuracies remain within a similar range, while IoU scores marginally declined. Notably, certain modality combinations reached improved accuracies when incorporated as auxiliary tasks rather than as input modalities, such as climate zone (in Experiments **3** and **10**) and the combination of all modalities (in Experiments **8** and **15**). Overall, we find that the additional input modalities do not contribute to improved model performance. However, our results remain consistent with the scores reported in [22]. Moreover, the multitask setup neither degrades nor enhances the primary task's performance, while its other benefits persist. In Sect. 4.2, we further investigate the explanatory capacity of each output modality, using Experiment **15** as a testbed.

TreeSAT dataset exhibits different patterns, as shown in the results displayed in Table 3. The baseline model, trained on the three imagery modalities (i.e. aerial imagery and two satellite images), achieves a micro F1-score of 74.3%, ranking second. Using the same best-performing model architecture, this represents a significant improvement compared to the 71.66% accuracy reported by Ahlswede et al. [2]. As shown in Table 3, the highest accuracy of 76.9% is reached by the multimodal experiment that includes the age as an additional input data. Tree type labels from levels 1 and 2 were not included as input features, as acquiring this data at inference time would be impractical in real-world scenarios. In contrast, age can, in some cases, be inferred from historical records and old maps which document events such as deforestation, wildfires, or planting. In the multitask experiments, the primary task's performance declines slightly but maintains F1-scores above 70%. Specifically, Experiment **4**, which predicts only the first level (L1), and Experiment **8**, which infers all modalities, yield the lowest L1 F1-scores of 70.3% and 70.4%, respectively. In contrast, including the second level (L2) in Experiment **3** achieved the same accuracy as the baseline model (74.3%) while also yielding accurate labels for the second level labels, reaching a

Table 2. Test set performance on the Benge dataset. The best and second-best scores are highlighted in bold and underlined, respectively. Climate zone classification performance is given in micro F1 score.

Experiment		Satellite	Elevation	Climate Zone	Season	Weather	LULC (Accuracy)	LULC (IoU)
		Modalities					**Main task**	
Baseline	1	→□					<u>87.94</u>	<u>0.388</u>
MML	2	→□	→□				87.91	0.386
	3	→□		→□			87.90	0.386
	4	→□			→□		87.91	**0.389**
	5	→□				→□	87.93	0.387
	6	→□	→□		→□		87.90	0.385
	7	→□	→□			→□	**87.95**	0.383
	8	→□	→□	→□	→□	→□	87.85	0.387
MTL	9	→□	□→				87.90	0.380
	10	→□		□→			87.93	0.379
	11	→□			□→		87.91	0.380
	12	→□				□→	87.91	0.381
	13	→□	□→		□→		87.91	0.377
	14	→□	□→			□→	87.89	0.377
	15	→□	□→	□→	□→	□→	87.89	0.373

micro F1-score of 78.2%. Overall, in the multitask experiments, L2 classification (with 9 classes) demonstrates high accuracy, L1 classification (with 3 classes) achieves significantly better scores, while age prediction (with normalized values) exhibits moderate performance. Experiment **7**, which reached the second performance in the main task among multitask experiments, will be explored in the explanatory analysis in the following section.

4.2 Model Explainability

CropYield . In the CropYield dataset, we evaluate the model performance in Experiment **7** across epochs, analyzing the relationship between yield relative error and crop prediction accuracy. In a preliminary analysis, we analyze crop-specific performance and include the results in Appendix C.1. Since a more significant correlation between correct crop classification and improved yield prediction was noticed in soybean fields, we further examine subfield-level performance of two soybean fields by analyzing a random sample of pixels. The results displayed in Fig. 2 show the yield prediction relative error for correctly and incorrectly classified pixels throughout the training. In both fields, the yield prediction relative error is generally higher for misclassified pixels (orange) compared to correctly classified ones (blue), with this effect appearing in early epochs for one field and persisting after the model reaches optimal performance (epoch 11) in another. These findings suggest that incorrect crop classification at the subfield level negatively impacts yield prediction. Additionally, Fig. 3 illustrates yield and crop type prediction maps at different epochs, from a field where

608   H. Najjar et al.

Table 3. Test set performance on the TreeSAT dataset. The best and second-best scores are highlighted in bold and underlined, respectively. *Images* refer to the aerial and two satellite images (from Sentinel-1 and Sentinel-2 missions). L3, L2, and L1 classification performance are given in micro F1 score.

Experiment	Modalities				Main task	Auxiliary tasks		
	Images	L2	L1	Age	L3 (F1)	L2 (F1)	L1 (F1)	Age (MAE)
Baseline 1	→□				<u>74.3</u>			
MML 2	→□			→□	**76.9**			
MTL 3	→□	□→			<u>74.3</u>	**78.2**		
4	→□		□→		70.3		<u>92.1</u>	
5	→□			□→	71.8			**0.52**
6	→□	□→	□→		71.1	76.6	**92.3**	
7	→□	□→		□→	72.2	<u>77.3</u>		**0.52**
8	→□	□→	□→	□→	70.4	75.5	<u>92.2</u>	<u>0.53</u>

we clearly notice that regions with crop misclassification correspond to areas with significant yield underestimation. More similar examples are included in Appendix C.1.

Benge . To investigate the explanatory potential of auxiliary tasks in the Benge dataset, we analyze Experiment **15** (see Table 2), which predicts all available modalities as auxiliary tasks. We first compute the Pearson correlation between the error of the main task, LULC classification, and the errors of the auxiliary tasks, on 10% of the test set. The results presented in Fig. 4 indicate a decreasing correlation for all task combinations during early training epochs. While the LULC-Season correlation exhibits fluctuations throughout training, these variations are less pronounced in the LULC-Weather and LULC-ClimateZone combinations. In contrast, the LULC-DEM correlation remains more stable, likely due to the similar spatial resolution of both tasks, as they each produce a single-channel image as output. This differs from the other auxiliary tasks, which predict tabular data. Although the correlations do not exceed 0.23, we verified that the p-values remain below 0.05. To further examine this correlation between LULC and DEM, we present in Fig. 5 a data sample where this relationship is clearly visible, with additional examples provided in Appendix C.2.

Through the examination of a group of samples, we extracted more insightful conclusions regarding the model behavior across tasks; we observed that prediction errors of LULC and DEM tend to correlate in regions where the model fails to accurately determine elevation, particularly along boundaries such as terrain edges or riverbanks. In these regions, land cover classification errors were more frequent. Conversely, when LULC misclassifications are scattered within a patch containing highly heterogeneous land cover, the correlation is weak. These areas typically feature stable terrain elevation, leading to DEM prediction errors that do not exhibit the same scattered distribution.

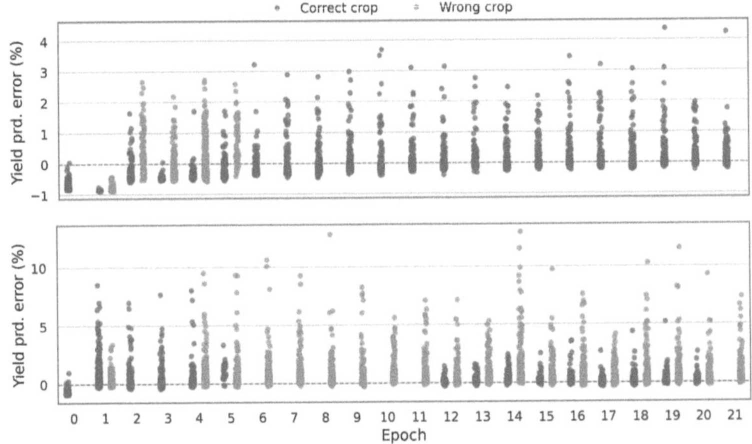

Fig. 2. Comparison of model performance on the tasks of yield prediction (measured in relative error) and crop prediction accuracy for the CropYield dataset across 21 learning epochs. Results correspond to two soybean fields. 300 correctly classified and another 300 misclassified pixels are displayed for each field.

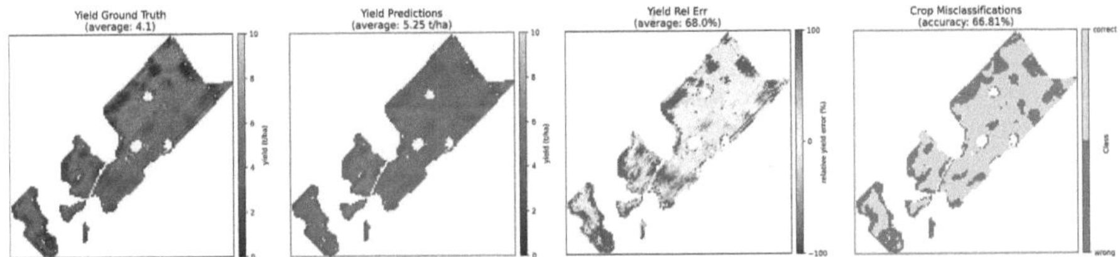

Fig. 3. CropYield model performance on a soybean field at epoch 16. From left to right: Target yield, predicted yield, relative yield error, and crop misclassifications. More in Appendix C.1

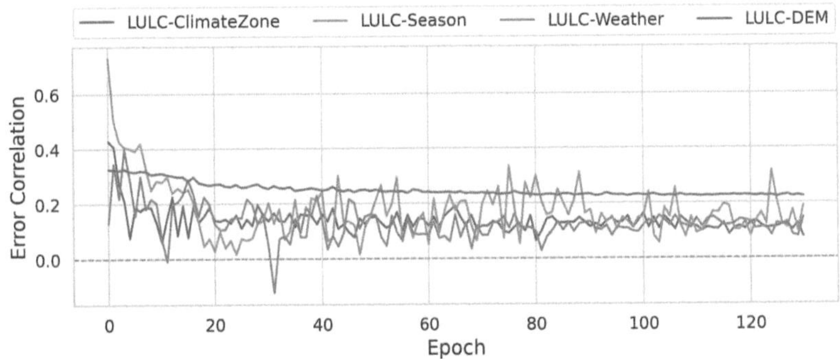

Fig. 4. Error correlation between the main Benge task (i.e. LULC) and auxiliary tasks.

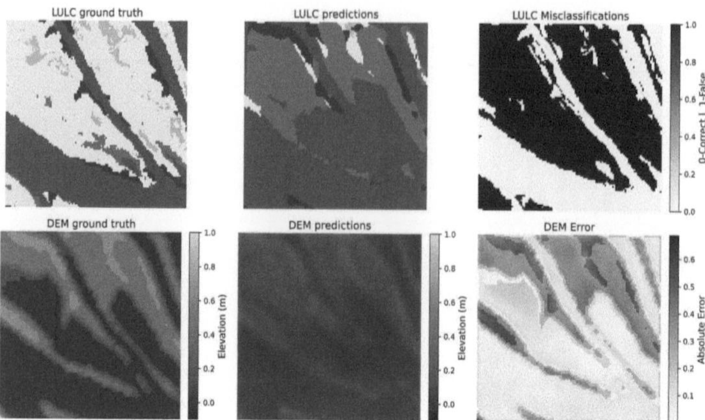

Fig. 5. Model predictions and errors, compared against the ground truths, on the LULC and DEM prediction tasks. The predictions are of the best epoch, on a random Benge dataset sample from the test set. More examples in Appendix C.2

TreeSAT . We investigate Experiment **7** in TreeSAT dataset, which predicts L2 and age alongside the main L3 label. We examine the combinations of L2 and L3 predictions in the test set throughout training, with results presented in Fig. 6.a. Here, 'C' denotes a correctly predicted label, while 'F' indicates a false prediction. The notation follows the order of L2 and L3 predictions; for instance, 'CF' means that L2 was correctly predicted, but L3 was not. The results reveal that the count of instances where one label is correct while the other is incorrect (i.e., CF and FC) remain relatively stable throughout training. In contrast, the number of samples where both labels are correct (CC) consistently increases, while instances where both labels are misclassified (FF) decrease correspondingly. This trend reveals an interesting pattern about the model behavior; it suggests that FF samples are more likely to be corrected into CC as training progresses, whereas instances in which only one label is initially correct (CF or FC) are less likely to be fully corrected later during the learning process. This hypothesis is verified and confirmed in Fig. 6.b.

Given the hierarchical nature of tree classes, we further examine how this structure influences the model's predictions. Figure 7 illustrates the distribution of L2-L3 prediction combinations and their adherence to the hierarchy at an early training epoch (epoch 7) and at the best-performing epoch (epoch 93). We add '-in' to the label of samples where the predicted L3 belongs to the predicted parent class L2 and '-out' to instances where it does not. The results indicate that when L3 is misclassified (i.e., in CF and FF cases), the proportion of instances where the predicted L3 remains within the predicted L2 class is consistently higher than those where it falls outside, regardless of whether L2 is correctly predicted. In other words, at both early training stages and the model's peak performance, CF-in is more frequent than CF-out, and FF-in is more frequent than FF-out. This suggests that the model has learned aspects of the hierarchical relationship

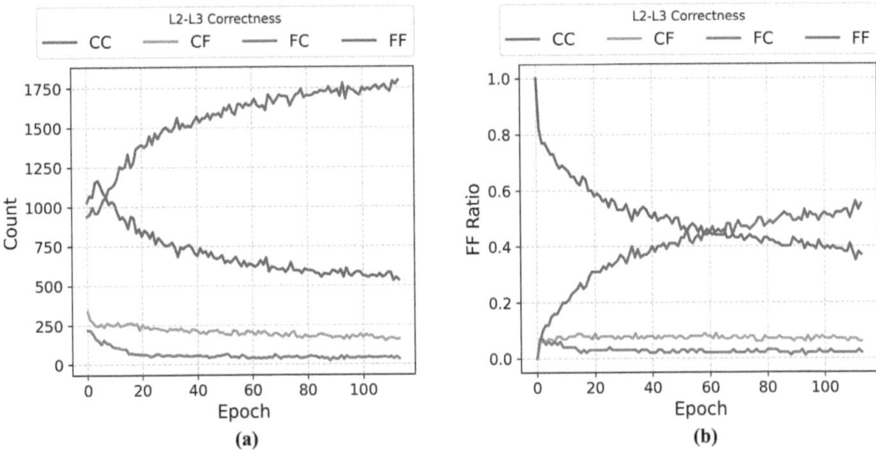

Fig. 6. (a) Count of combinations of correct or false classifications of L2 and L3 labels in the test set of TreeSAT dataset, throughout the training. (b) Categorisation ratio of the samples categorized as FF at epoch 0 throughout the training.

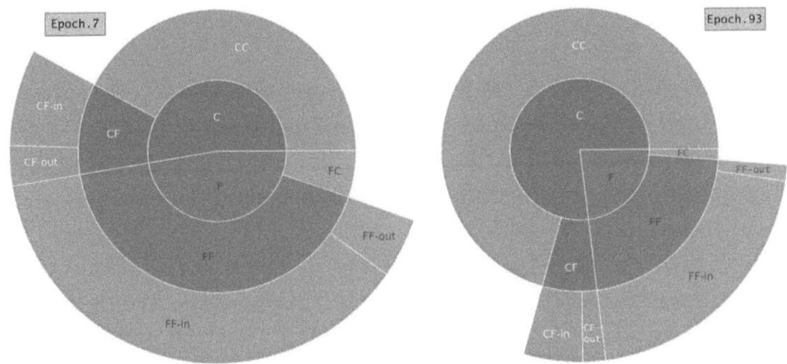

Fig. 7. Pie Chart of the distribution of combinations of correct or false classifications of L2 and L3 labels. The results are shown for the test set, inferred at epochs 7 and 93.

between L2 and L3 and tends to respect it even when misclassifying L3. Note that in CC cases the hierarchy is always maintained, whereas in FC cases it is always violated. Since the experiment explained here also predicts the age, we include an analysis of the correlation between this modality and different L2-L3 correctness combinations in Appendix C.3.

5   Discussion

While our findings demonstrate the potential of multitask learning for model interpretability, we would like to highlight certain limitations which are to be addressed in future work.

The correlation patterns identified through the analysis of error maps in Benge and CropYield were observed in a limited number of samples. However, the presented examples provide evidence of the tight interaction of the model behavior across multiple tasks, and leveraging these observations to correct model errors would enhance performance in both tasks. For instance, integrating interpretability insights as constraints within the loss function could enforce meaningful relationships between tasks. Using the hierarchical structure of labels in the TreeSAT dataset to refine predictions is one example. Another promising direction is to refine the selection of task weights in multitask learning. Automating this process using uncertainty estimation [10] or adaptive weighting based on loss improvement rates [13] could enhance the balance between tasks. We conducted initial experiments to test both approaches, but they were not more successful than the manual selection of weights, yet further experiments are needed. Finally, automating the neural architecture search could further optimize our approach, reducing reliance on manual expertise and improving model performance to align with findings from prior studies in which multitask learning outperformed single-task baselines [3, 10, 11, 13, 16, 18, 28].

6   Conclusion

In this work, we proposed a multitask learning framework to enhance model explainability in RS. We exploited the rich information content of satellite data to shift additional input modalities into auxiliary tasks. This approach not only maintained comparable performance to baseline models but also reduced the need for additional data at deployment. More importantly, it provided valuable explainability insights through the analysis of error correlations between the main and auxiliary tasks across three diverse RS datasets. We demonstrate how this analysis can improve understanding of model reasoning and inner workings. Further, focusing on a specific use case and conducting deeper analysis could yield even greater insights into the model behavior. Future work will integrate these insights into the data preparation and modeling pipeline to refine model reasoning and, consequently, enhance performance.

References

1. Adadi, A., Berrada, M.: Peeking inside the black-box: a survey on explainable artificial intelligence (XAI). IEEE Access **6**, 52138–52160 (2018)
2. Ahlswede, S., et al.: TreeSatAI benchmark archive: a multi-sensor, multi-label dataset for tree species classification in remote sensing. Earth Syst. Sci. Data Discuss. **2022**, 1–22 (2022)
3. Ding, D.Y., Simpson, C., Pfohl, S., Kale, D.C., Jung, K., Shah, N.H.: The effectiveness of multitask learning for phenotyping with electronic health records data. In: Pacific Symposium on Biocomputing. Pacific Symposium on Biocomputing, vol. 24, p. 18. NIH Public Access (2019)

4. Echterhoff, J., Yan, A., Han, K., Abdelraouf, A., Gupta, R., McAuley, J.: Driving through the concept gridlock: unraveling explainability bottlenecks in automated driving. In: Proceedings of the IEEE/CVF Winter Conference on Applications of Computer Vision, pp. 7346–7355 (2024)

5. Günther, A., Najjar, H., Dengel, A.: Explainable multi-modal learning in remote sensing: challenges and future directions. IEEE Geosci. Remote Sens. Lett. (2024)

6. Hendricks, L.A., Akata, Z., Rohrbach, M., Donahue, J., Schiele, B., Darrell, T.: Generating visual explanations. In: Leibe, B., Matas, J., Sebe, N., Welling, M. (eds.) ECCV 2016. LNCS, vol. 9908, pp. 3–19. Springer, Cham (2016). https://doi.org/10.1007/978-3-319-46493-0_1

7. Huang, Y., Du, C., Xue, Z., Chen, X., Zhao, H., Huang, L.: What makes multimodal learning better than single (provably). Adv. Neural. Inf. Process. Syst. **34**, 10944–10956 (2021)

8. Joshi, G., Walambe, R., Kotecha, K.: A review on explainability in multimodal deep neural nets. IEEE Access **9**, 59800–59821 (2021)

9. Kanehira, A., Harada, T.: Learning to explain with complemental examples. In: Proceedings of the IEEE/CVF Conference on Computer Vision and Pattern Recognition, pp. 8603–8611 (2019)

10. Kendall, A., Gal, Y., Cipolla, R.: Multi-task learning using uncertainty to weigh losses for scene geometry and semantics. In: Proceedings of the IEEE Conference on Computer Vision and Pattern Recognition, pp. 7482–7491 (2018)

11. Levering, A., Marcos, D., Tuia, D.: On the relation between landscape beauty and land cover: a case study in the UK at Sentinel-2 resolution with interpretable AI. ISPRS J. Photogramm. Remote. Sens. **177**, 194–203 (2021)

12. Liu, H., Yin, Q., Wang, W.Y.: Towards explainable NLP: a generative explanation framework for text classification. In: Proceedings of the 57th Annual Meeting of the Association for Computational Linguistics, pp. 5570–5581 (2019)

13. Liu, S., Johns, E., Davison, A.J.: End-to-end multi-task learning with attention. In: Proceedings of the IEEE/CVF Conference on Computer Vision and Pattern Recognition, pp. 1871–1880 (2019)

14. Liu, Y., Tuytelaars, T.: A deep multi-modal explanation model for zero-shot learning. IEEE Trans. Image Process. **29**, 4788–4803 (2020)

15. Losch, M., Fritz, M., Schiele, B.: Interpretability beyond classification output: semantic bottleneck networks. arXiv preprint arXiv:1907.10882 (2019)

16. Lu, J., Goswami, V., Rohrbach, M., Parikh, D., Lee, S.: 12-in-1: multi-task vision and language representation learning. In: Proceedings of the IEEE/CVF Conference on Computer Vision and Pattern Recognition, pp. 10437–10446 (2020)

17. Lundberg, S.M., Lee, S.I.: A unified approach to interpreting model predictions. In: Advances in Neural Information Processing Systems, vol. 30 (2017)

18. Maniscalco, A., et al.: Multimodal radiotherapy dose prediction using a multi-task deep learning model. Med. Phys. (2024)

19. Marcos, D., Lobry, S., Tuia, D.: Semantically interpretable activation maps: what-where-how explanations within CNNs. In: 2019 IEEE/CVF International Conference on Computer Vision Workshop (ICCVW), pp. 4207–4215. IEEE (2019)

20. Mena, F., Arenas, D., Nuske, M., Dengel, A.: Common practices and taxonomy in deep multi-view fusion for remote sensing applications. IEEE J. Sel. Top. Appl. Earth Obs. Remote Sens. (2024)

21. Mojab, N., Noroozi, V., Philip, S.Y., Hallak, J.A.: Deep multi-task learning for interpretable glaucoma detection. In: 2019 IEEE 20th International Conference on Information Reuse and Integration for Data Science (IRI), pp. 167–174. IEEE (2019)

22. Mommert, M., Kesseli, N., Hanna, J., Scheibenreif, L., Borth, D., Demir, B.: Benge: Extending BigEarthNet with geographical and environmental data. In: IGARSS 2023-2023 IEEE International Geoscience and Remote Sensing Symposium, pp. 1016–1019. IEEE (2023)

23. Narazani, M., Sarasua, I., Pölsterl, S., Lizarraga, A., Yakushev, I., Wachinger, C.: Is a pet all you need? a multi-modal study for alzheimer's disease using 3D CNNs. In: International Conference on Medical Image Computing and Computer-Assisted Intervention, pp. 66–76. Springer (2022)

24. Park, D.H., et al.: Multimodal explanations: Justifying decisions and pointing to the evidence. In: Proceedings of the IEEE Conference on Computer Vision and Pattern Recognition, pp. 8779–8788 (2018)

25. Ribeiro, M.T., Singh, S., Guestrin, C.: Why should I trust you? Explaining the predictions of any classifier. In: Proceedings of the 22nd ACM SIGKDD International Conference on Knowledge Discovery and Data Mining, pp. 1135–1144 (2016)

26. Rio-Torto, I., Fernandes, K., Teixeira, L.F.: Understanding the decisions of CNNs: an in-model approach. Pattern Recogn. Lett. **133**, 373–380 (2020)

27. Selvaraju, R.R., Cogswell, M., Das, A., Vedantam, R., Parikh, D., Batra, D.: Gradcam: Visual explanations from deep networks via gradient-based localization. In: Proceedings of the IEEE International Conference on Computer Vision, pp. 618–626 (2017)

28. Sener, O., Koltun, V.: Multi-task learning as multi-objective optimization. In: Advances in Neural Information Processing Systems, vol. 31 (2018)

29. Standley, T., Zamir, A., Chen, D., Guibas, L., Malik, J., Savarese, S.: Which tasks should be learned together in multi-task learning? In: International Conference on Machine Learning, pp. 9120–9132. PMLR (2020)

30. Sumbul, G., Charfuelan, M., Demir, B., Markl, V.: Bigearthnet: a large-scale benchmark archive for remote sensing image understanding. In: IGARSS 2019-2019 IEEE International Geoscience and Remote Sensing Symposium, pp. 5901–5904. IEEE (2019)

31. Sumbul, G., et al.: BigEarthNet-MM: a large-scale, multimodal, multilabel benchmark archive for remote sensing image classification and retrieval [software and data sets]. IEEE Geosci. Remote Sens. Mag. **9**(3), 174–180 (2021)

32. Sundararajan, M., Taly, A., Yan, Q.: Axiomatic attribution for deep networks. In: International Conference on Machine Learning, pp. 3319–3328. PMLR (2017)

33. Tang, Z., Surdeanu, M.: It takes two flints to make a fire: multitask learning of neural relation and explanation classifiers. Comput. Linguist. **49**(1), 117–156 (2023)

34. Thomason, J., Gordon, D., Bisk, Y.: Shifting the baseline: single modality performance on visual navigation & QA. In: Proceedings of the 2019 Conference of the North American Chapter of the Association for Computational Linguistics: Human Language Technologies, Volume 1 (Long and Short Papers), pp. 1977–1983 (2019)

35. Vandenhende, S., Georgoulis, S., Van Gansbeke, W., Proesmans, M., Dai, D., Van Gool, L.: Multi-task learning for dense prediction tasks: a survey. IEEE Trans. Pattern Anal. Mach. Intell. **44**(7), 3614–3633 (2021)

36. Zhang, Y., Yang, Q.: A survey on multi-task learning. IEEE Trans. Knowl. Data Eng. **34**(12), 5586–5609 (2021)

Out-of-Distribution Detection in LiDAR Semantic Segmentation Using Epistemic Uncertainty from Hierarchical GMMs

Hanieh Shojaei Miandashti$^{(\boxtimes)}$ and Claus Brenner

Institute of Cartography and Geo-informatics, Leibniz University Hannover,
30167 Hannover, Germany
{hanieh.shojaei,claus.brenner}@ikg.uni-hannover.de
https://www.ikg.uni-hannover.de/de/

Abstract. In addition to accurate scene understanding through precise semantic segmentation of LiDAR point clouds, detecting out-of-distribution (OOD) objects—instances not encountered during training—is essential to prevent the incorrect assignment of unknown objects to known classes. While supervised OOD detection methods depend on auxiliary OOD datasets, unsupervised methods avoid this requirement but typically rely on predictive entropy, the entropy of the predictive distribution obtained by averaging over an ensemble or multiple posterior weight samples. However, these methods often conflate epistemic (model) and aleatoric (data) uncertainties, misclassifying ambiguous in-distribution regions as OOD. To address this issue, we present an unsupervised OOD detection approach that employs epistemic uncertainty derived from hierarchical Bayesian modeling of Gaussian Mixture Model (GMM) parameters in the feature space of a deep neural network. Without requiring auxiliary data or additional training stages, our approach outperforms existing uncertainty-based methods on the SemanticKITTI dataset—achieving an 18% improvement in AUROC, 22% increase in AUPRC, and 36% reduction in FPR95 (from 76% to 40%), compared to the predictive entropy approach used in prior works.

Keywords: Out-of-distribution detection · Semantic segmentation · Uncertainty estimation · LiDAR scene understanding

1 Introduction

Recent advances in deep learning have substantially improved the accuracy of semantic segmentation for LiDAR point clouds, along with more reliable methods for estimating prediction uncertainty. These developments are critical for

This project is supported by the German Research Foundation (DFG), as part of the Research Training Group i.c.sens, GRK 2159, 'Integrity and Collaboration in Dynamic Sensor Networks'.

safety-critical applications such as autonomous driving, where accurate perception and awareness of uncertainty help mitigate decision-making risks. However, real-world environments often include OOD instances—inputs that differ significantly from the in-distribution (ID) data seen during training. Deep models tend to make overly confident yet incorrect predictions on such OOD inputs, misclassifying them as known classes. While uncertainty estimation captures the likelihood of error in predictions, OOD detection aims to determine whether an input belongs to the training distribution. Robust OOD detection is thus essential for identifying and excluding anomalous inputs, ultimately improving the safety and reliability of autonomous systems.

Existing research on OOD detection can be broadly categorized into two approaches: supervised methods that rely on auxiliary data and unsupervised methods that operate without requiring additional data. The limitations of supervised methods are discussed in Sect. 2.1, including their dependence on auxiliary datasets, which may be unavailable in certain applications. In contrast, our work focuses on unsupervised methods that identify OOD samples by estimating uncertainty, based on the intuition that highly uncertain predictions are indicative of OOD inputs. Recent Bayesian approaches, based on the entropy of the averaged decision (predictive entropy) from Monte Carlo dropout sampling [7] or deep ensembles [16], have been considered to compute uncertainty, which can be later used to detect OOD samples.

It has been argued by [15] that predictive entropy is an unreliable metric for OOD detection because it conflates two distinct types of uncertainty: epistemic uncertainty, caused by limited knowledge of model parameters, and aleatoric uncertainty, stemming from inherent data noise. While OOD samples are characterized by high epistemic uncertainty, ambiguous ID samples exhibit high aleatoric uncertainty, causing both cases to potentially yield high predictive entropy. This overlap reduces the effectiveness of predictive entropy for distinguishing OOD from ambiguous ID inputs. Consequently, predictive entropy is only a reliable OOD indicator when aleatoric uncertainty is negligible, an assumption rarely valid in practice.

To address this limitation, [15,25] have proposed explicitly isolating epistemic uncertainty from the total predictive uncertainty. A principled approach is to use the mutual information (MI) between the model parameters θ and the predicted label y, conditioned on the input x, as a measure of epistemic uncertainty:

$$\underbrace{\mathbb{I}[y; \theta \mid x]}_{\text{Epistemic Uncertainty (MI)}} = \underbrace{\mathcal{H}(p(y \mid x))}_{\text{Predictive Entropy}} - \underbrace{\mathbb{E}_\theta \left[\mathcal{H}(p(y \mid x, \theta))\right]}_{\text{Aleatoric Uncertainty}}.$$

Here, the first term represents the entropy of the marginal predictive distribution and captures the total uncertainty (predictive entropy) associated with the prediction. The predictive distribution for a given input x is obtained by marginalizing over the posterior distribution of the model parameters $p(\theta \mid \mathcal{D})$ where $\mathcal{D}$ denotes the training dataset, i.e., $p(y \mid x, \mathcal{D}) = \mathbb{E}_{\theta \sim p(\theta \mid \mathcal{D})}[p(y \mid x, \theta)]$. The second term quantifies the aleatoric uncertainty, the expected data uncertainty under fixed model parameters. This type of uncertainty is only defined for ID inputs, as it relies on class ambiguity captured within the training data distribution. For OOD inputs, where $p(x) \approx 0$, the conditional distribution $p(y \mid x) = \frac{p(x,y)}{p(x)}$ becomes ill-defined, rendering both aleatoric uncertainty and mutual information undefined. Therefore, in practical settings using deep ensembles or Monte Carlo Dropout (MC Dropout), predictive entropy remains the only accessible uncertainty estimate for OOD detection, although it must be interpreted cautiously, as it reflects both epistemic and aleatoric components. As such, predictive entropy serves only as an upper bound on epistemic uncertainty.

With this work, we focus on an unsupervised pixel-wise OOD detection based on the epistemic uncertainty derived from the hierarchical Bayesian uncertainty measurement from the GMM feature space of a deep model. Unlike purely discriminative models that directly learn decision boundaries between classes $p(y \mid \mathbf{x})$, [23] proposed employing GMMSeg [18], a generative classifier, to model class-specific Gaussian distributions in the feature space and model the uncertainty over the parameters of this GMM (mean and covariance). As a result, they propose epistemic uncertainty as the variability of the classification decisions made by the GMM samples in the feature space. This allows us to move beyond predictive entropy, which entangles aleatoric and epistemic components, and apply epistemic uncertainty for OOD detection.

It is noteworthy that, although this paper focuses on LiDAR data, the data is represented in the form of range-view images; thus, we refer to image elements as pixels rather than points. These pixels can subsequently be projected back into 3D space to reconstruct the original point cloud.

To summarize, we make two main claims: First, we demonstrate that epistemic uncertainty provides a sharper distinction between ID and OOD samples compared to predictive entropy, leading to improved OOD detection performance. Second, our method is fully unsupervised—it does not require auxiliary OOD data and avoids retraining the segmentation network, making it practical and efficient for real-world deployment.

2   Related Works

OOD detection, also known as novelty or anomaly detection, has been extensively studied in the context of classification tasks, which are image-level OOD detection [11,17,22,24]. However, in this section, we focus on OOD detection methods specifically developed for semantic segmentation, where the domain is pixel-level, rather than image-level OOD detection.

2.1   OOD Detection Using Outlier Exposure

Supervised OOD detection methods train models to distinguish ID from OOD samples using auxiliary datasets, a strategy known as outlier exposure [10]. Some adopt a separate discriminative model [2], while others integrate OOD detection into the segmentation network via multi-task learning [3]. Williams et al. [28] further extend this by combining contrastive loss with data augmentation for joint segmentation and OOD detection. Hornaue and Belagiannis [12] attach a decoder to a fixed backbone to generate heatmaps with low responses for ID inputs and high activations for OOD inputs.

Despite their advantages, supervised methods have notable limitations: they (1) depend on auxiliary data, which is often unavailable or difficult to obtain, particularly in LiDAR-based segmentation [13]; (2) make assumptions about the nature of potential anomalies that might not align with real-world cases [27]; (3) require retraining segmentation models as multi-task architectures, potentially degrading performance [26]; (4) their reliance on specific OOD training samples limits their ability to generalize to unseen or diverse types of OOD data, since even diverse auxiliary outliers during training may fail to cover the full range of real-world OOD instances [6].

2.2 OOD Detection Using Uncertainty Estimation

Assuming that OOD inputs should exhibit higher uncertainty (i.e., lower confidence) than ID data, early works employed softmax-based scores for OOD detection, with Maximum Softmax Probability (MSP) proposed as a baseline method [9]. However, softmax outputs not only conflate epistemic and aleatoric uncertainty [15], but also suffer from poor calibration, often tend to be overconfident [8,14,20], even for inputs far from the training distribution [21], which limits their effectiveness in distinguishing ID from OOD samples. To overcome these limitations, ODIN [19] introduced temperature scaling for confidence calibration and input perturbations to increase the separability between ID and OOD samples. Although ODIN improves detection performance without requiring model retraining, it does depend on access to OOD data for parameter tuning.

Bayesian methods offer a principled approach to uncertainty estimation by placing a prior over model parameters and marginalizing predictions over the resulting posterior. As exact inference is intractable in deep networks, approximations such as MC Dropout [7], which performs multiple forward passes with dropout enabled at inference time, and deep ensembles [16] consist of independently trained networks with different random initializations, are commonly used. However, in addition to the limitations of predictive entropy derived from these methods, as discussed in Sect. 1, deep ensembles also require multiple independent training runs, significantly increasing computational cost.

Our work belongs to the category of unsupervised OOD detection methods that do not require additional data, and it also addresses key limitations of deep ensembles and MC Dropout, specifically, the need for retraining to produce uncertainty estimation and reliance on predictive entropy for OOD detection.

3 Methodology

To advance beyond conventional discriminative approaches for LiDAR point cloud segmentation, we adopt a GMM semantic segmentation approach inspired by GMMSeg [18]. Unlike some methods that naively assume that features follow Gaussian distributions in the feature space [24], GMMSeg explicitly models each semantic class with a dedicated Gaussian distribution. As illustrated in the methodology framework (Fig. 1), our model encodes raw LiDAR point clouds into structured multi-channel image representations, which are then processed through a deep feature extractor to obtain a compact multi-dimensional feature space. Within this feature space, the joint distribution $p(\mathbf{z}, c)$ of pixel-wise features $\mathbf{z}$ and semantic class labels c is modeled using class-conditional Gaussian Mixture Models (GMMs). This generative component captures the underlying feature distributions for each semantic class, while a discriminative training objective employs cross-entropy loss on the posterior class probabilities $p(c \mid \mathbf{z})$ derived from the GMM responsibilities, ensuring the learned features are both semantically meaningful and well-structured. Building on the epistemic uncertainty modeling framework from [23], we further propose an unsupervised OOD detection employing epistemic uncertainty estimates derived from the GMM parameters, enabling robust identification of OOD inputs in LiDAR semantic segmentation.

3.1   Generative-Discriminative Framework Semantic Segmentation

Given the LiDAR point cloud projected into a range-view image and building on GMMSeg [18], we employ a deep neural network to extract pixel-wise feature representations $\mathbf{z} \in \mathbb{R}^D$. We model the pixel-wise data distribution (joint distribution) for each class $c \in \{1, \ldots, C\}$ in a D-dimensional feature space using a weighted mixture of M multivariate Gaussian components in each class as:

$$p(\mathbf{z} \mid c) = \sum_{k=1}^{K} \pi_k^{(c)} \mathcal{N}(\mathbf{z} \mid \boldsymbol{\mu}_k^{(c)}, \boldsymbol{\Sigma}_k^{(c)}),$$

where $\pi_k^{(c)}$, $\boldsymbol{\mu}_k^{(c)}$, and $\boldsymbol{\Sigma}_k^{(c)}$ denote the mixture weight, mean, and covariance of the k-th Gaussian component for class c, respectively. These parameters are estimated via the Expectation-Maximization (EM) algorithm during training. As [18] considered a uniform prior on the class mixture weights, i.e., $p(c) = \frac{1}{C}$, allows us to simplify the class posterior as:

$$p(c \mid \mathbf{z}) = \frac{p(\mathbf{z} \mid c)}{\sum_{c'} p(\mathbf{z} \mid c')}. \tag{1}$$

Simultaneously, the feature extractor is trained with the discriminative (cross-entropy) loss, i.e., maximizing the conditional likelihood $p(c \mid \mathbf{z})$, also referred to as responsibility value derived from GMM, promoting class separability in the learned feature space.

3.2   Bayesian Modeling of GMM Parameters

To capture epistemic uncertainty, following the approach in [23], we adopt a hierarchical Bayesian uncertainty modeling by placing conjugate priors over the

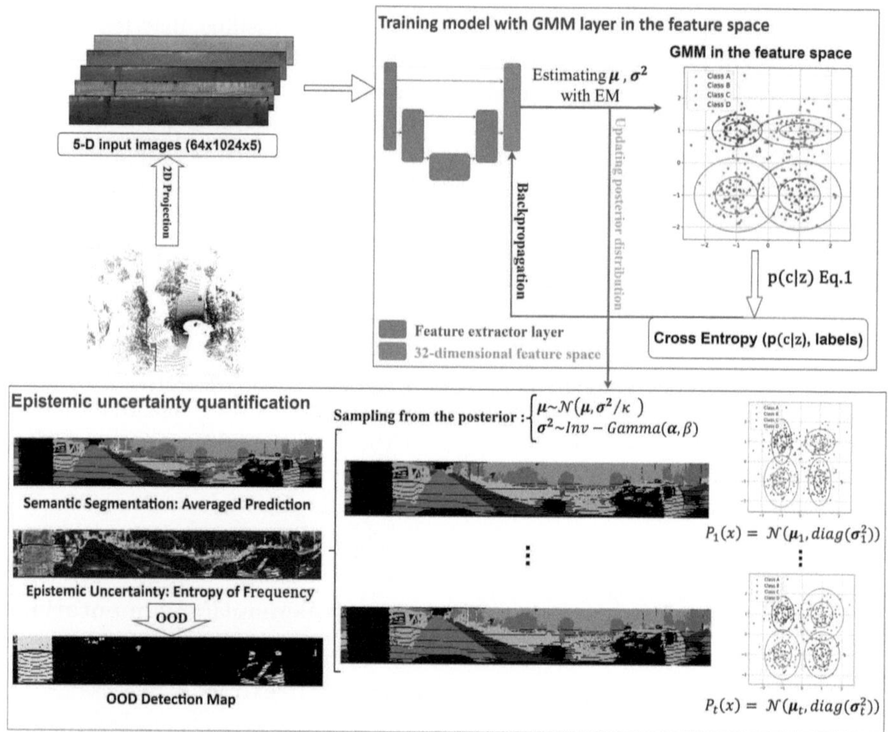

Fig. 1. Proposed epistemic uncertainty-based OOD detection. A deep neural network extracts a 32-dimensional feature space from 5D LiDAR input. Class-conditional GMMs model the feature distribution per class. During inference, epistemic uncertainty is quantified by aggregating multiple predictions obtained through sampling GMM parameters (mean and variance) from their posterior distributions. Pixels exhibiting higher epistemic uncertainty scores are considered more likely to represent OOD instances.

GMM parameters to model their uncertainty and updating them in a Bayesian manner to approximate the posterior distribution over the GMM parameters.

Following [18], each multivariate Gaussian distribution is modeled as D independent univariate Gaussians, where D is the dimensionality of the feature space. During training, the mean and variance of each Gaussian component are estimated from the training data. However, unlike standard GMMs that rely on point estimates, the Bayesian approach models these parameters as random variables. Specifically, the mean and variance of each component are treated as random variables, modeled by a Gaussian and an Inverse Gamma distribution, respectively.

To enable Bayesian inference, a Gaussian–Inverse Gamma prior is placed over these parameters, serving as a conjugate prior for the unknown Gaussian mean and variance. This formulation allows the model to compute a posterior distribution over the mean and variance for each component. At inference time, the mean $\mu_k^{(c)}$ and variance $\sigma^{2(c)}{}_k$ of each component are treated as random variables drawn from the learned posterior.

$$\mu_k^{(c)} \sim \mathcal{N}(\mu_0, \sigma^{2(c)}{}_k / \kappa_0), \quad \sigma^{2(c)}{}_k \sim \text{Inv-Gamma}(\alpha_0, \beta_0),$$

where μ_0, κ_0, α_0, and β_0 are hyperparameters of the prior distributions. During training, these priors are updated to posteriors based on the observed data as explained in [23], allowing for modeling the distribution over the parameters of the GMM.

3.3   Inference and Uncertainty Estimation

At inference time, we sample multiple sets of GMM parameters $(\mu_k^{(c)}, \sigma^{2(c)}{}_k)$ from their respective posterior distributions. For each sample, we compute the class-conditional density $p(\mathbf{z} \mid c)$ for a given feature vector $\mathbf{z} \in \mathbb{R}^d$. Given an ensemble of n GMMs, the predicted class for each sample is selected as the one with the highest density. The final prediction for each pixel is obtained by majority voting across the ensemble outputs.

To quantify uncertainty, we estimate the class-wise frequency distribution of the predicted labels y over all samples. We then compute the entropy of this empirical distribution $(\bar{p}_c = \frac{1}{n} \sum_{i=1}^{n} \mathbb{I}[y^{(i)} = c])$ as:

$$\mathcal{H}[y \mid \mathbf{z}] = - \sum_{c=1}^{C} \bar{p}_c \log \bar{p}_c,$$

where $\bar{p}_c$ denotes the relative frequency (i.e., empirical probability) of class c among the sampled predictions. This entropy reflects the degree of disagreement across sampled GMMs, capturing the epistemic uncertainty induced by variation in the GMM parameters. Higher entropy values indicate greater model uncertainty, which typically correlates with OOD regions.

3.4   OOD Detection via Epistemic Uncertainty

We use the computed epistemic uncertainty to detect OOD regions in the input data, based on the assumption that higher epistemic uncertainty indicates a greater likelihood of the sample being OOD. Pixels with entropy values exceeding a predefined percentile-based threshold are classified as OOD. Specifically, the threshold is set such that the top 5% of pixels with the highest epistemic uncertainty are labeled as OOD samples. Nonetheless, to ensure robustness, we also assess epistemic uncertainty using threshold-independent evaluation metrics, as detailed in the following Sect. (4).

4   Experiments

Experimental Setup and Dataset. We consider the GMM feature space using the 32-dimensional penultimate layer of a convolutional neural network, SalsaNext [5], and conduct experiments on the SemanticKITTI benchmark dataset [1], which provides 3D LiDAR semantic segmentation annotations for 19 semantic classes along with an outlier class which is excluded during training. For OOD detection, we use the outlier class, which includes diverse objects not belonging to the 19 standard classes, such as trash bins, placards, animals, and other uncommon street elements.

When projecting 3D point clouds into 2D range-view images, due to occlusion and limited field-of-view, some pixels correspond to no 3D points and are empty. It is noteworthy that these pixels are ignored during training and excluded from OOD evaluation to avoid confusion with true outliers.

Input images are represented as tensors of shape $64 \times 1024 \times 5$, where the five channels correspond to the x, y, z coordinates, intensity, and range. Forwarding into the network, the extracted features have a shape of $64 \times 1024 \times 32$, corresponding to the 32-dimensional feature space. For each semantic class, we model the distribution of features using a GMM with two components (a hyperparameter that can be tuned). As a result, the mean and variance parameters for each class are of shape 32×2, representing two Gaussian components across the 32 feature dimensions. Once the posterior distribution of Gaussian-Inverse Gamma is computed in the last training epoch, which allows the posterior to see the whole data once, we derive the entropy of the frequency of 20 sampled GMMs.

We employ epistemic uncertainty for OOD detection by framing it as a binary classification task, where pixels with the top 5% highest uncertainty values are identified as OOD. While access to OOD annotations allows for the determination of an optimal threshold, such labels are typically unavailable in real-world scenarios. Therefore, to simulate a more realistic deployment setting, we evaluate our method using an unsupervised percentile-based thresholding strategy, independent of ground-truth for OOD annotations during inference. It is important to note that this thresholding method is used solely for generating the OOD maps (Fig. 3), while quantitative evaluation is conducted using threshold-independent metrics (Table 1).

Evaluation Metrics. To evaluate OOD detection performance, we report standard metrics that are threshold-independent, including AUROC, AUPRC, and FPR95. While AUROC is widely used, AUPRC (also referred to as average precision) is more informative in the presence of class imbalance, as it focuses on precision and recall for OOD pixels [4]. Additionally, we report FPR95, which quantifies the false positive rate when the true positive rate for OOD pixels reaches 95%, offering a safety-relevant measure of detection reliability. Moreover, the accuracy of semantic segmentation is evaluated using the mean Intersection over Union (mIoU) metric.

Baselines. We compare our approach with existing OOD detection methods based on uncertainty estimation that do not rely on auxiliary data. Specifically, we consider Maximum Softmax Probability (MSP) [9] and ODIN [19] as representative single deterministic methods, and MC Dropout [7] and deep ensembles (DE) [16] as representative Bayesian neural network (BNN) approaches. Additionally, we include the original GMMSeg [18] baseline without the proposed hierarchical epistemic uncertainty estimation. For a fair comparison, all methods use SalsaNext [5] as the backbone architecture.

4.1   Quantitative Results

Evaluating the performance of our proposed method against established OOD detection baselines of MSP, ODIN, GMMSeg, MC Dropout, and DE, as shown in Table 1, highlights that generally our approach consistently outperforms all baselines across all OOD detection metrics.

Specifically, our method achieves the highest AUROC of 91.06%, substantially surpassing GMMSeg (87.62%) and DE (73.03%). In terms of AUPRC, our method reaches 37.67%, improving over the next best (GMMSeg, 26.14%) by over 11% points. Moreover, our method attains the lowest FPR95 of 40.14%, reflecting its effectiveness in reducing false positives among in-distribution pixels.

In addition to OOD detection performance, our method also yields the highest mIoU (57.71%) among all compared methods. This slight improvement in segmentation accuracy is attributed to the voting-based prediction strategy introduced through our uncertainty-aware framework.

To gain further insight into how epistemic uncertainty distinguishes OOD from ID samples, we compare the distributions of predictive entropy and epistemic uncertainty in Fig. 2, derived from DE and our proposed approach, respectively. While both methods show generally higher uncertainty values for OOD samples shown in gray color, Fig. 2a reveals that predictive entropy from DE produces a substantial overlap between ID and OOD distributions, particularly in the mid-to-high entropy range. In contrast, Fig. 2b demonstrates that our epistemic uncertainty estimates produce a clearer separation, with ID samples concentrated around low uncertainty values and OOD samples distributed more distinctly across higher values. This improved separation highlights the advantage of modeling epistemic uncertainty directly via hierarchical Bayesian inference in the GMM feature space, enabling more reliable OOD detection.

4.2   Qualitative Results

Figure 3 presents a qualitative comparison of OOD detection results between our proposed method (using epistemic uncertainty) and DE, across four representative LiDAR scenes. Each column corresponds to a different scene, while each row illustrates intermediate and final outputs, including semantic segmentation, OOD ground-truth (OODs are shown in yellow color), uncertainty maps, and detected OOD maps. The final row includes the corresponding RGB camera images for better interpretation of the scene content. OOD objects, such as

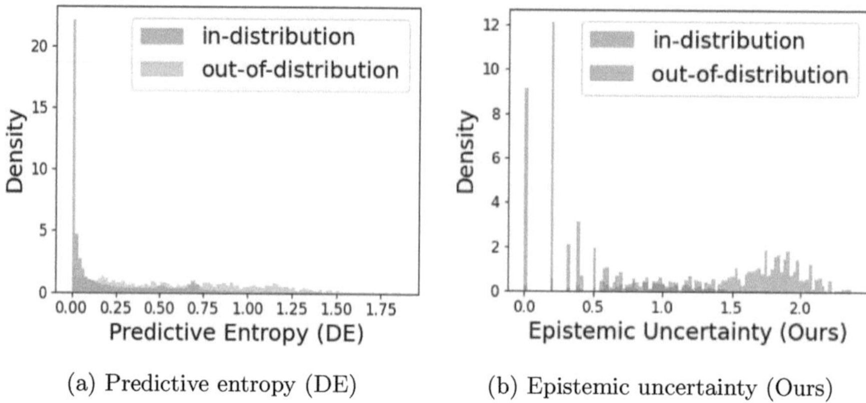

(a) Predictive entropy (DE)   (b) Epistemic uncertainty (Ours)

Fig. 2. Comparison of predictive entropy and epistemic uncertainty for OOD detection. The proposed epistemic uncertainty measure offers a more precise separation between ID and OOD samples.

Table 1. Comparison of OOD detection methods. Our approach achieves higher AUROC and AUPRC (AP), along with lower FPR95 compared to existing methods. Additionally, mIoU shows a slight improvement due to the voting-based prediction strategy in our approach. All metrics are represented in percentages.

Method	Uncertainty Type	↑AUROC	↑AUPRC(AP)	↓FPR95	↑mIoU
MSP	Deterministic Entropy	70.41	10.90	76.00	56.37
ODIN	Deterministic Entropy	73.74	12.45	75.54	56.37
MCDropout	Predictive Entropy	73.64	13.65	75.92	57.15
DE	Predictive Entropy	73.03	16.14	76.48	57.17
GMMSeg	Deterministic Entropy	87.62	26.14	48.84	57.60
Ours	Epistemic Uncertainty	**91.06**	**37.67**	**40.14**	**57.71**

placards, trash bins, and unknown structures, are highlighted with red dashed boxes across all images.

Overall, the detected OOD regions based on our epistemic uncertainty estimation (row 4) closely align with the ground-truth annotations (row 2). In particular, the epistemic uncertainty maps (row 3) show strong activations over truly unknown regions, while maintaining moderate uncertainty levels for misclassified ID samples. In contrast, predictive entropy maps from DE (row 5) suffer from over-activation due to their conflation of epistemic and aleatoric uncertainties. As a result, DE produces false positives in regions of high aleatoric uncertainty, especially along semantic boundaries, rather than reliably focusing on OOD objects.

In Fig. 3a, the placard is completely missed by OOD prediction from DE approach, while high predictive entropy arises along the sidewalk–vegetation border, leading to incorrect OOD detection. A similar misdetection occurs in

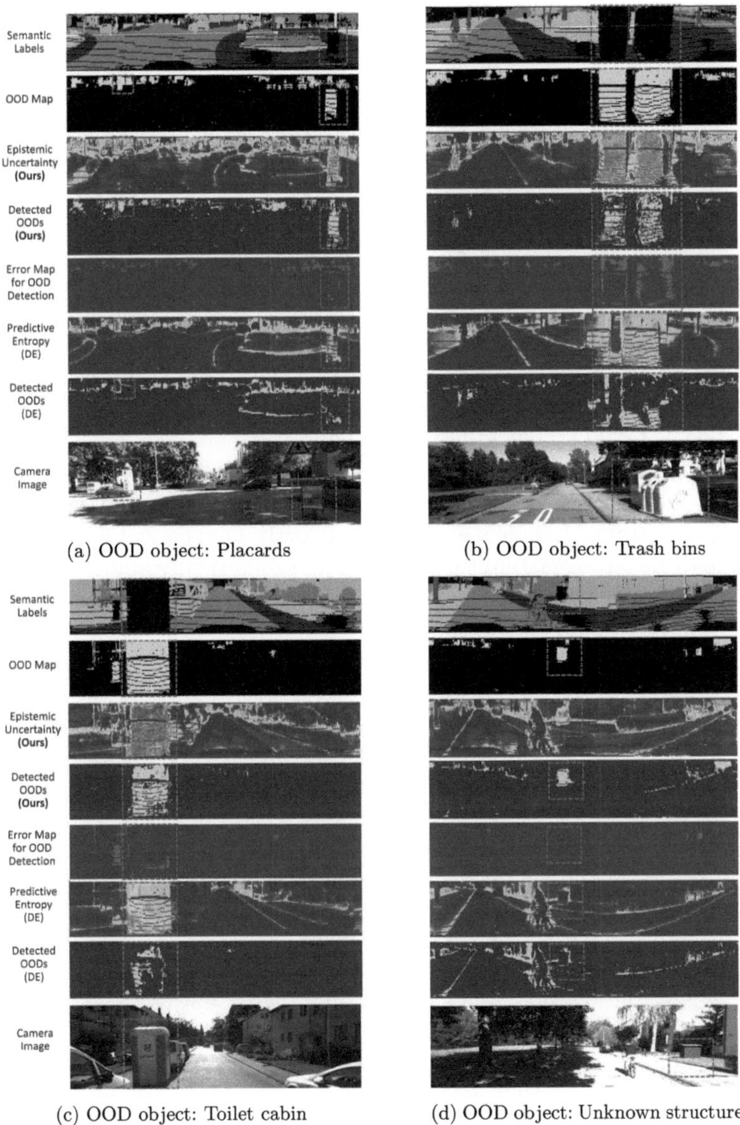

(a) OOD object: Placards

(b) OOD object: Trash bins

(c) OOD object: Toilet cabin

(d) OOD object: Unknown structure

Fig. 3. Qualitative comparison of OOD detection using epistemic uncertainty from our proposed approach versus predictive entropy from DE across four representative LiDAR scenes. From top to bottom, the rows depict: (1) Semantic predictions with class color coding: outlier , car , road , sidewalk , building , fence , vegetation , trunk , terrain , pole ; (2) OOD ground truth, where ID pixels are black and OOD pixels are yellow; (3) Epistemic uncertainty map from our method and (5) predictive entropy map from DE, visualized with a temperature scale from low to high uncertainty; (4) OOD detection results from our method and (7) DE, highlighting detected OOD regions in yellow; (5) Error map highlighting OOD objects not identified by our method, marked in red; (8) Camera image for visual reference.

Fig. 3d, where the boundary between the bicycle and street, as well as between terrain and road, is incorrectly identified as OOD. In these cases, the true OOD instances are either missed or partially detected.

In Fig. 3a, the placard is completely missed by OOD prediction from DE approach, while high predictive entropy arises along the sidewalk–vegetation border, leading to incorrect OOD detection. A similar misdetection occurs in Fig. 3d, where the boundary between the bicycle and street, as well as between terrain and road, is incorrectly identified as OOD. In these cases, the true OOD instances are either missed or partially detected. Figure 3b also highlights the limitations of the DE approach in comparison to ours. While our method accurately detects the trash bins as OOD samples, DE only partially identifies them.

Figure 3 reveals a minor shortcoming of our method: it assigns high epistemic uncertainty to misclassified ID objects in some cases. It reveals a few ID pixels misclassified as OOD by our approach, though these are significantly fewer than those misclassified by the DE method. This helps explain why, despite achieving the highest AUROC and AUPRC, our method's FPR@95 remains at 40.14%, indicating that some ID pixels are still incorrectly flagged as OOD. This is primarily due to elevated epistemic uncertainty in semantically ambiguous or poorly segmented regions. For instance, thin structures, or mislabeled ID instances (e.g., fences, poles, or dynamic objects like bicyclists) tend to receive high epistemic uncertainty scores. These cases can lead to false positive detections, particularly when the uncertainty threshold is too sensitive to subtle representation variations.

5   Conclusion

In this work, we introduce an unsupervised OOD detection method in LiDAR semantic segmentation by employing the epistemic uncertainty, estimated from GMMs in the feature space of a deep classifier. Our approach addresses key limitations of existing predictive entropy-based approaches, which often misidentify ambiguous ID samples as OOD. By employing epistemic uncertainty, we demonstrate improved discrimination between ID and OOD data. Experimental results on SemanticKITTI validate that our approach surpasses existing methods such as MSP, ODIN, MC Dropout, and deep ensembles, achieving the highest AUROC, highest AUPRC, lowest FPR95, and improved segmentation accuracy (mIoU). Despite these advancements, our approach still exhibits some false positives due to elevated uncertainty in complex boundary regions and misclassified objects. Future work will investigate strategies to reduce such ambiguity and refine the uncertainty threshold selection to further enhance real-world applicability.

References

1. Behley, J., et al.: Semantickitti: a dataset for semantic scene understanding of lidar sequences. In: Proceedings of the IEEE/CVF International Conference on Computer Vision, pp. 9297–9307 (2019)
2. Bevandić, P., Krešo, I., Oršić, M., Šegvić, S.: Discriminative out-of-distribution detection for semantic segmentation. arXiv preprint arXiv:1808.07703 (2018)
3. Bevandić, P., Krešo, I., Oršić, M., Šegvić, S.: Simultaneous semantic segmentation and outlier detection in presence of domain shift. In: Fink, G.A., Frintrop, S., Jiang, X. (eds.) DAGM GCPR 2019. LNCS, vol. 11824, pp. 33–47. Springer, Cham (2019). https://doi.org/10.1007/978-3-030-33676-9_3
4. Chawla, N.V., Japkowicz, N., Kotcz, A.: Special issue on learning from imbalanced data sets. ACM SIGKDD Explor. Newsl **6**(1), 1–6 (2004)
5. Cortinhal, T., Tzelepis, G., Erdal Aksoy, E.: SalsaNext: fast, uncertainty-aware semantic segmentation of LiDAR point clouds. In: Bebis, G., Yin, Z., Kim, E., Bender, J., Subr, K., Kwon, B.C., Zhao, J., Kalkofen, D., Baciu, G. (eds.) ISVC 2020. LNCS, vol. 12510, pp. 207–222. Springer, Cham (2020). https://doi.org/10.1007/978-3-030-64559-5_16
6. Di Biase, G., Blum, H., Siegwart, R., Cadena, C.: Pixel-wise anomaly detection in complex driving scenes. In: Proceedings of the IEEE/CVF Conference on Computer Vision and Pattern Recognition, pp. 16918–16927 (2021)
7. Gal, Y., Ghahramani, Z.: Dropout as a Bayesian approximation. arXiv preprint arXiv:1506.02157 (2015)
8. Guo, C., Pleiss, G., Sun, Y., Weinberger, K.Q.: On calibration of modern neural networks. In: International Conference on Machine Learning, pp. 1321–1330. PMLR (2017)
9. Hendrycks, D., Gimpel, K.: A baseline for detecting misclassified and out-of-distribution examples in neural networks. arXiv preprint arXiv:1610.02136 (2016)
10. Hendrycks, D., Mazeika, M., Dietterich, T.: Deep anomaly detection with outlier exposure. arXiv preprint arXiv:1812.04606 (2018)
11. Hendrycks, D., Mazeika, M., Kadavath, S., Song, D.: Using self-supervised learning can improve model robustness and uncertainty. In: Advances in Neural Information Processing Systems, vol. 32 (2019)
12. Hornauer, J., Belagiannis, V.: Heatmap-based out-of-distribution detection. In: Proceedings of the IEEE/CVF Winter Conference on Applications of Computer Vision, pp. 2603–2612 (2023)
13. Huang, C., et al.: Out-of-distribution detection for lidar-based 3d object detection. In: 2022 IEEE 25th International Conference on Intelligent Transportation Systems (ITSC), pp. 4265–4271. IEEE (2022)
14. Jiang, H., Kim, B., Guan, M., Gupta, M.: To trust or not to trust a classifier. In: Advances in Neural Information Processing Systems, vol. 31 (2018)
15. Kirsch, A., Mukhoti, J., van Amersfoort, J., Torr, P.H., Gal, Y.: On pitfalls in OOD detection: entropy considered harmful. In: Uncertainty & Robustness in Deep Learning Workshop. ICML (2021)
16. Lakshminarayanan, B., Pritzel, A., Blundell, C.: Simple and scalable predictive uncertainty estimation using deep ensembles. In: Advances in Neural Information Processing Systems, vol. 30 (2017)
17. Lee, K., Lee, K., Lee, H., Shin, J.: A simple unified framework for detecting out-of-distribution samples and adversarial attacks. In: Advances in Neural Information Processing Systems, vol. 31 (2018)

18. Liang, C., Wang, W., Miao, J., Yang, Y.: Gmmseg: Gaussian mixture based generative semantic segmentation models. Adv. Neural. Inf. Process. Syst. **35**, 31360–31375 (2022)
19. Liang, S., Li, Y., Srikant, R.: Enhancing the reliability of out-of-distribution image detection in neural networks. arXiv preprint arXiv:1706.02690 (2017)
20. Minderer, M., et al.: Revisiting the calibration of modern neural networks. Adv. Neural. Inf. Process. Syst. **34**, 15682–15694 (2021)
21. Nguyen, A., Yosinski, J., Clune, J.: Deep neural networks are easily fooled: high confidence predictions for unrecognizable images. In: Proceedings of the IEEE Conference on Computer Vision and Pattern Recognition, pp. 427–436 (2015)
22. Rezende, D., Mohamed, S.: Variational inference with normalizing flows. In: International Conference on Machine Learning, pp. 1530–1538. PMLR (2015)
23. Shojaei, H.: Hierarchical bayesian modeling of epistemic uncertainty in lidar semantic segmentation (2025). https://doi.org/10.5281/zenodo.15635087
24. Shojaei Miandashti, H., Zou, Q., Mehltretter, M.: Uncertainty estimation and out-of-distribution detection for lidar scene semantic segmentation. In: European Conference on Computer Vision, pp. 116–131. Springer (2024)
25. Smith, L., Gal, Y.: Understanding measures of uncertainty for adversarial example detection. arXiv preprint arXiv:1803.08533 (2018)
26. Vandenhende, S., Georgoulis, S., Van Gansbeke, W., Proesmans, M., Dai, D., Van Gool, L.: Multi-task learning for dense prediction tasks: a survey. IEEE Trans. Pattern Anal. Mach. Intell. **44**(7), 3614–3633 (2021)
27. Vojíř, T., Šochman, J., Matas, J.: Pixood: pixel-level out-of-distribution detection. In: European Conference on Computer Vision, pp. 93–109. Springer (2024)
28. Williams, D.S., Gadd, M., De Martini, D., Newman, P.: Fool me once: robust selective segmentation via out-of-distribution detection with contrastive learning. In: 2021 IEEE International Conference on Robotics and Automation (ICRA), pp. 9536–9542. IEEE (2021)

RadarSeq: A Temporal Vision Framework for User Churn Prediction via Radar Chart Sequences

Sina Najafi[1(✉)] ⓘ, M. Hadi Sepanj[2] ⓘ, and Fahimeh Jafari[1] ⓘ

[1] University of East London, London, UK
`{u2735128,F.Jafari}@uel.ac.uk`
[2] Systems Design Engineering Department, University of Waterloo, Waterloo, Canada
`mhsepanj@uwaterloo.ca`

Abstract. Predicting user churn—that is, when users stop participating—in non-subscription gig platforms such as food delivery or ride-hailing services, poses unique challenges due to the absence of explicit labels and the dynamic nature of user behavior. Existing methods often rely on aggregated behavioral snapshots or static visual representations, which obscure short-term temporal cues critical for early detection. In this work, we propose a temporally-aware computer vision framework that models user activity patterns as a sequence of radar chart images—circular plots that visually encode multivariate behavioral features at the daily level. By integrating a pretrained convolutional neural network (CNN) with a bidirectional LSTM, our architecture captures both spatial patterns within each day and temporal dynamics across time. Extensive experiments on a large real-world dataset demonstrate that our method outperforms classical models and Vision Transformer (ViT)-based radar chart baselines, yielding gains of +17.7 in F1 score, +29.4 in precision, and +16.1 in AUC. The framework's modular design and efficient deployment characteristics make it well-suited for large-scale churn modeling in dynamic gig-economy settings.

Keywords: Customer churn prediction · Temporal modeling · Computer vision · Radar charts · LSTM · Deep learning · Delivery · Courier churn

1 Introduction

Churn prediction is a long-standing problem in the fields of marketing analytics [11,28,35], operations [24,53,64], and customer lifecycle modeling [57,61,84]. The ability to identify disengaging users early enables companies to deploy personalized retention strategies and mitigate revenue loss [27,67]. In traditional subscription-based domains such as telecommunications, churn is clearly defined and easily labeled [5,42,48]. However, in non-subscription-based services [6,14,32] such as e-commerce [54,90] or gig platforms [37,59], churn is

© The Author(s), under exclusive license to Springer Nature Switzerland AG 2026
M. Keuper and F. Locatello (Eds.): DAGM GCPR 2025, LNCS 16125, pp. 629–646, 2026.
https://doi.org/10.1007/978-3-032-12840-9_40

often latent and can only be inferred retrospectively from behavioral inactivity [9,20,80]. This makes early detection both more difficult and more valuable.

On-demand delivery platforms [58,77,86] experience notably high churn rates, often exceeding 40% annually. For instance, Uber has reported that only 4% of newly recruited drivers remain active after one year [8,62], while similar trends are documented across platforms like DoorDash and Deliveroo [30,38]. This churn epidemic necessitates scalable predictive solutions. Based on operational insights, a courier inactive for 45 consecutive days is typically considered lost to competitors or other employment—thus providing a robust, real-world validated definition of churn [3,34].

From an economic perspective, courier retention is significantly more cost-effective than replacement. Industry estimates indicate that recruiting and onboarding a new courier can cost between $8,000 and $10,000 per individual [59]. These figures account for direct costs such as training and lost productivity, and often exclude secondary impacts like service disruptions and safety risks associated with inexperienced workers. In contrast, proactive churn prevention—e.g., offering targeted incentives or scheduling flexibility to at-risk couriers—can often retain them at a fraction of the cost. This return on investment is amplified when churn prediction models are used to focus retention efforts only where needed [44]. By reducing turnover, platforms not only lower operational expenses but also benefit from a more stable, experienced, and efficient workforce, directly enhancing long-term profitability and scalability [7].

A common strategy for churn modeling involves aggregating behavioral features—such as order frequency, transaction amounts, and recency—into static summary statistics [13,16,36], a simplification that our method explicitly avoids by modeling temporal behavior directly. Classical machine learning methods (e.g., logistic regression [46,82], random forests [41,72], and gradient boosting models [12,78]) have shown strong performance when trained on such feature sets [1,15]. However, these approaches discard fine-grained temporal patterns in user behavior, potentially missing early indicators of disengagement [99].

To overcome the limitations of tabular modeling, recent research has explored the visual encoding of behavior logs. Coolwijk et al. [18] introduced a Vision Transformer [25] (ViT)-based pipeline where aggregated customer features are converted into radar chart images, enabling the use of pre-trained image classification models for churn detection. While effective, this approach relies on a single static image per user, abstracting away the evolution of user behavior over time.

In this work, we argue that temporal structure is essential for early and accurate churn prediction. Rather than summarizing behavior, we propose to model it as a time-indexed visual sequence. Specifically, we transform each user's daily transaction profile into a radar chart image and model the sequence of images using a convolutional-recurrent architecture [22,76,93]. This preserves behavioral dynamics and enables temporal pattern recognition across multiple scales. Radar charts preserve spatial relationships between multi-dimensional data points, maintaining contextual dependencies and enabling visual feature learning via CNNs [43]. Unlike heatmaps or recurrence plots, radar charts offer consistent geometric encoding of features, enhancing interpretability and preserving domain semantics across time steps. Prior research supports their value in temporal feature retention and interpretability [23,68,97]. Our method represents the first known attempt to use radar chart imagery combined with CNN+LSTM [81] architectures for churn prediction, thus capturing complex spatio-temporal behavioral patterns. Our contributions are as follows:

- We introduce a novel vision-based framework for churn prediction that preserves the full temporal granularity of user behavior by generating daily radar chart images.
- We propose a hybrid CNN+LSTM architecture that learns both spatial patterns within daily behavior encodings and temporal dependencies across time.
- We conduct extensive experiments comparing our approach against traditional ML models and the ViT-based radar chart baseline. Our method achieves state-of-the-art performance on multiple metrics, including AUC [89], precision [79], and F1-score [92].

By combining visual representation learning [70,95] with temporal modeling [17,21,71], our method provides a generalizable framework for user behavior modeling in domains where churn is implicit and dynamically emerging, and these visual temporal sequences allow the application of spatial-temporal deep learning architectures.

Accurately predicting courier churn has direct economic implications for on-demand delivery platforms. Studies indicate that retaining existing couriers is up to five times more cost-effective than recruiting and onboarding new workers [10,19]. Effective churn prediction reduces recruitment expenditure, minimizes downtime in delivery operations, and enhances user satisfaction through consistent courier availability [74]. At scale, a modest 5–10% improvement in retention can lead to substantial savings in operational costs and platform incentives [23].

2   Background

User churn prediction remains a critical problem in e-commerce and gig platforms, where users do not explicitly unsubscribe but instead silently disengage [46]. Initial studies in churn modeling relied on structured tabular features [54] and classical machine learning models [75] such as logistic regression [33], decision trees [33], support vector machines (SVMs) [46], and ensemble methods including random forests [33], XGBoost [65], and CatBoost [13,40,42]. While interpretable and computationally efficient, these models typically depend on temporal aggregation—often through Recency-Frequency-Monetary (RFM) variables—which discards short-term behavioral fluctuations crucial for early churn detection [4].

To better capture user dynamics, deep learning models such as Long Short-Term Memory (LSTM) [55] networks and Gated Recurrent Units (GRUs) [98] have been explored for sequence modeling in churn prediction [48,51,96]. Transformers have further extended this capability via parallelized attention mechanisms [47] that model global dependencies [29,83,94]. Despite their success, these models are rarely combined with visual encoding techniques.

Recent efforts have introduced vision-based methods for behavioral modeling. Wang et al. [87] and Li et al. [49] proposed converting time-series data into image representations—such as Gramian Angular Fields [87] or radar plots—enabling the application of convolutional neural networks (CNNs) to discover spatial patterns. Coolwijk et al. [18] advanced this idea by transforming RFM features into radar chart images and applying a Vision Transformer (ViT) pretrained on ImageNet [18,26] for churn classification. Their pipeline, inspired by ChurnViT [66], clusters customers via k-means [52] to generate pseudo-churn labels. Although promising in recall and AUC, this approach presents several drawbacks:

- **Static Representation:** Each customer is encoded into a single radar chart summarizing their entire behavioral history, eliminating temporal continuity and masking changes in behavior over time.
- **No Sequential Modeling:** ViTs classify each image independently, making them less suited for temporal modeling tasks such as churn prediction.
- **Interpretability Challenges:** Radar charts with non-aligned features and attention-based decisions obscure transparency, especially when no temporal context is preserved.

In contrast, temporal models like LSTMs and temporal CNNs are well-suited for capturing sequential patterns in behavior [73,85]. However, their integration with visual encodings remains underexplored. Most prior work either uses raw tabular features or aggregates transactional logs into coarse temporal bins before classification [2], which compromises the temporal resolution of the user history.

Our proposed method addresses these limitations by transforming each day of the user behavior pattern into a radar chart image, preserving both visual and temporal information. These daily radar charts form an image sequence input to a hybrid CNN+LSTM model: the CNN encodes spatial feature patterns, and the LSTM captures temporal evolution. This design retains the interpretability of image-based models while enabling trajectory-level modeling of user behavior (Table 1).

Table 1. Comparison of churn prediction methods across key design dimensions

Model	Temporal	Visual	Input Type	Supervision
CatBoost	No	No	Tabular	Explicit
ChurnViT	No	Yes	Radar Img	Pseudo
Proposed CNN+LSTM	Yes	Yes	Radar Seq	Explicit

In doing so, our method generalizes the radar-ViT framework to a temporal regime. This integration of visual encoding and recurrent architectures enables early and accurate churn prediction, as demonstrated by our empirical improvements in F1-score, precision, and AUC. Our framework, therefore, surpasses both traditional ML and static vision-based approaches in performance while offering greater interpretability through spatial-temporal decomposition [91].

3   Methodology

We propose a temporally-aware, image-based churn prediction framework that processes each biker's behavioral timeline as a sequence of daily radar chart images. The core idea is to preserve behavioral dynamics over time while enabling visual representation learning through a hybrid CNN+LSTM architecture. Unlike prior approaches that compress user history into a single image for Vision Transformer classification [18], our method retains temporal structure and enables trajectory-level modeling.

3.1   Data Representation

Let each biker $c \in \mathcal{C}$ have a historical timeline of daily activities represented as a sequence of feature vectors:

$$\mathbf{x}_c = \left\{ \mathbf{x}_c^{(1)}, \mathbf{x}_c^{(2)}, \ldots, \mathbf{x}_c^{(T)} \right\}, \quad \mathbf{x}_c^{(t)} \in \mathbb{R}^d \tag{1}$$

where d is the number of behavioral features (e.g., earnings, trip count, ride duration, etc.) and T is the number of days in the sliding window. Each $\mathbf{x}_c^{(t)}$ is transformed into a radar chart image $\mathbf{I}_c^{(t)} \in \mathbb{R}^{H \times W}$, using a polar plot rendering function $\mathcal{R} : \mathbb{R}^d \to \mathbb{R}^{H \times W}$. We choose $(H, W) = (32, 32)$ for efficiency.

The resulting input is a spatiotemporal image sequence:

$$\mathbf{I}_c = \left\{ \mathbf{I}_c^{(1)}, \mathbf{I}_c^{(2)}, \ldots, \mathbf{I}_c^{(T)} \right\}, \quad \mathbf{I}_c^{(t)} \in \mathbb{R}^{H \times W} \tag{2}$$

Figure 1 shows an example of a daily radar chart image generated from a courier's behavioral feature vector.

3.2   Architecture Overview

Our model consists of three components:

1. A convolutional encoder $\mathcal{F}_{\text{CNN}}$ that maps each radar chart image to a high-dimensional embedding:

$$\mathbf{z}_c^{(t)} = \mathcal{F}_{\text{CNN}}(\mathbf{I}_c^{(t)}), \quad \mathbf{z}_c^{(t)} \in \mathbb{R}^p \tag{3}$$

2. A recurrent encoder $\mathcal{F}_{\text{LSTM}}$ that processes the temporal sequence $\{\mathbf{z}_c^{(1)}, \ldots, \mathbf{z}_c^{(T)}\}$ to produce a global representation:

$$\mathbf{h}_c = \mathcal{F}_{\text{LSTM}}\left(\{\mathbf{z}_c^{(t)}\}_{t=1}^{T} \right), \quad \mathbf{h}_c \in \mathbb{R}^h \tag{4}$$

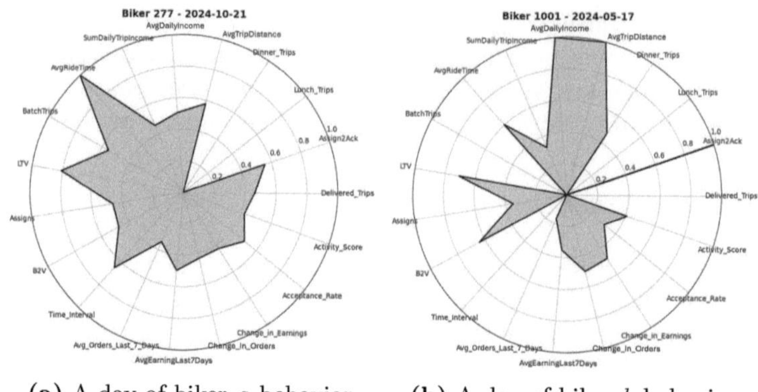

(a) A day of biker a behavior   **(b)** A day of biker b behavior

Fig. 1. Examples of radar chart images representing daily courier behavior. Each chart encodes multivariate features such as earnings, trip count, and idle time. Temporal differences in chart shapes reflect changes in behavioral patterns over time, which our CNN+LSTM model captures to predict churn.

3. A binary classifier $\mathcal{F}_{\text{clf}}$ that outputs a churn probability:

$$\hat{y}_c = \sigma(\mathbf{w}^\top \mathbf{h}_c + b) \tag{5}$$

where $\sigma(\cdot)$ denotes the sigmoid function. The model is optimized via the binary cross-entropy loss:

$$\mathcal{L}_{\text{BCE}} = -\sum_{c \in \mathcal{C}} [y_c \log \hat{y}_c + (1 - y_c) \log(1 - \hat{y}_c)] \tag{6}$$

Figure 2 illustrates the overall architecture of our proposed method.

3.3   CNN Encoder

We adopt a truncated MobileNetV2 backbone pretrained on ImageNet [69]. Each input image $\mathbf{I}_c^{(t)}$ is passed through the convolutional trunk up to the penultimate layer, producing a compact embedding $\mathbf{z}_c^{(t)} \in \mathbb{R}^{1280}$. No fine-tuning is applied initially to reduce overfitting, though experiments explore end-to-end training.

3.4   Temporal Modeling

The temporal encoder is a two-layer bidirectional LSTM [39] with hidden size $h = 128$. We fine-tune the entire CNN+BiLSTM architecture end-to-end [45], meaning the bidirectional LSTM is trained jointly with the CNN encoder, allowing gradient updates to flow through both components:

$$\mathbf{h}_c = \left[\overrightarrow{\mathbf{h}}_T \parallel \overleftarrow{\mathbf{h}}_1 \right] \in \mathbb{R}^{2h} \tag{7}$$

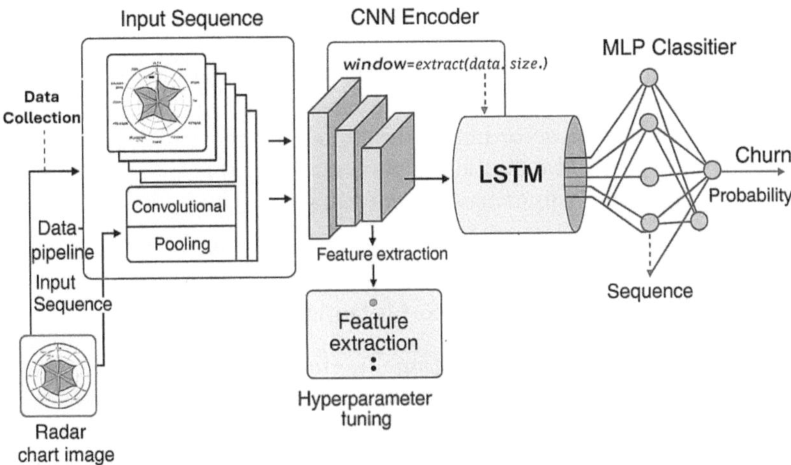

Fig. 2. Overview of our hybrid CNN+LSTM churn prediction framework. Daily behavioral vectors are transformed into radar chart images and fed into a CNN encoder to extract spatial features. A sliding window captures sequences of fixed temporal length with coarse and fine strides. CNN outputs are aggregated and processed by a bidirectional LSTM to model temporal dependencies. The resulting representation is passed to an MLP classifier that outputs churn probability. Dashed arrows represent preprocessing steps (e.g., windowing), hyperparameter tuning feedback loops.

where $\|$ denotes vector concatenation, and $\overrightarrow{h}_T$, $\overleftarrow{h}_1$ are the last hidden states in forward and backward directions, respectively.

3.5   Sliding Window Strategy

To account for variable-length histories, we employ a fixed-length windowing strategy with length $T = 50$ days, aligned to precede the 45-day churn threshold. For couriers with shorter histories, zero-padded white radar charts are prepended. For longer histories, overlapping sliding windows are generated using coarse (stride $= 5$) and fine (stride $= 1$) strategies to maximize temporal diversity while focusing on behavior leading up to potential churn events.

3.6   Training Details

We train the model using Adam optimizer with learning rate $\eta = 10^{-4}$. Mixed-precision training is employed via PyTorch AMP [56] for GPU efficiency. To accommodate memory constraints, we use gradient accumulation over 4 steps with a physical batch size of 256 sequences. The model is trained for 20 epochs with early stopping at epoch 13—when validation AUC failed to improve for 5 consecutive epochs. The checkpoint from epoch 8 (with the highest AUC) was retained for final evaluation.

3.7 Churn Label Generation

Since explicit churn labels are unavailable in non-subscription settings, we adopt a business-informed labeling strategy rather than clustering-based heuristics. Churn labels are assigned according to the 45-day inactivity definition introduced in Sect. 1. This real-world definition offers a more reliable supervision signal for training compared to unsupervised bootstrapping methods such as k-means on RFM features [18].

3.8 Hardware and Performance Optimization

We significantly optimized computational performance by reducing radar chart image resolution from 224×224 to 32×32 pixels, dramatically decreasing image processing overhead. Additionally, we employed offline batch resizing using Pillow-SIMD [60], reducing image input/output and transformation overhead by approximately 70–80%. Implementing mixed-precision inference and utilizing PyTorch's DataLoader `pin_memory` function further minimized GPU memory utilization by nearly 50% and substantially increased throughput. On an NVIDIA RTX 5000 Ada Generation GPU with 16 GB dedicated memory, these enhancements enabled efficient, end-to-end training and evaluation of approximately 100,000 sequences per epoch in under two hours, marking notable performance improvements compared to standard resolutions and non-optimized pipelines [56].

4 Experiments and Results

We evaluate our proposed temporal radar-sequence modeling framework against both traditional machine learning baselines and the Vision Transformer-based radar chart classification approach from [18]. Our experiments are designed to answer the following questions. Does preserving the temporal structure of daily user behavior improve churn prediction performance? How does the CNN+LSTM hybrid model compare to static image-level ViT classification? What are the contributions of visual encoding, temporal modeling, and pseudo-label quality?

We compare our CNN+LSTM radar-based pipeline against classical LSTM, Transformer, and Random Forest models. Consistent with prior literature, hybrid models demonstrate superior performance in capturing high-order dependencies across time and feature space [50,91,96].

These performance metrics are vital in churn modeling. Improved recall reduces the risk of overlooking actual churners, while higher precision minimizes the misclassification of active couriers. These trade-offs have direct implications on business KPIs, including retention costs and incentive allocation effectiveness [40,63,84].

4.1 Dataset and Setup

Our dataset comprises approximately 16,000 bikers with daily transactional logs, including features such as earnings, trip counts, ride durations, Biker to Vendor distance (B2V) ratios, and derived temporal gaps. Each biker is represented by a sequence of 50 radar chart images encoding daily behavior. Churn labels are assigned based on a 45-day inactivity threshold. This threshold is informed by empirical analysis of engagement patterns, where extended inactivity strongly correlates with long-term disengagement. This definition aligns with usage-based churn modeling practices commonly adopted in both subscription and non-subscription services, providing a clear and operationally relevant criterion for supervised learning.

Table 2. Feature-engineered behavioral metrics used in radar chart generation.

Feature	Description
Average Orders (7 Days)	Mean number of deliveries completed in the past week.
Average Earnings (7 Days)	Average daily income over the previous seven days.
Change in Orders	Week-over-week delta in delivery volume.
Acceptance Rate	Ratio of accepted orders to total order offers.
Activity Score	Composite score combining login, acceptance, and completion behavior.
Biker-to-Vendor Distance	Average geodesic distance between courier and vendor at assignment time.
Lunch and Delivered Trips	Number of deliveries during midday peak hours (11:00–14:00).
Assigns	Number of orders assigned to the courier.
Average Ride Time	Average duration from pickup to drop-off.
Batch Trips	Whether multiple deliveries were completed in a single dispatch.
Lifetime Value (LTV)	Total historical revenue generated by the courier.
Average Distance per Delivery	Typical travel distance per order.
Average Daily Trips	Mean number of trips per active day.
Average Daily Income	Average earnings per active day.

The full list of engineered behavioral features used to generate the radar charts is summarized in Table 2.

Splits: We divide the data into training (80%), validation (10%), and test (10%) sets at the user level to prevent identity leakage.

Preprocessing: Radar charts are rendered as 32×32 grayscale images without annotations. Data standardization and image generation are applied independently within each fold to ensure no information leakage.

4.2   Baselines and Evaluation Metrics

We compare against the following models: **CatBoost:** A gradient boosting model trained on aggregated features (e.g., mean, max, recency). **ChurnViT:** The Vision Transformer baseline from [18], using a single radar chart per user constructed from summary statistics. **CNN-Only:** Our radar sequence with MobileNetV2 applied independently to the final image, without temporal modeling. **CNN+MLP:** Mean-pooling CNN features across time, followed by a multi-layer perceptron.

Given the class imbalance, we emphasize the following metrics: **F1 Score:** Harmonic mean of precision and recall. **Precision and Recall:** Key for handling false positives and false negatives. **ROC-AUC:** Area under ROC and precision-recall curves. **MCC (Matthews Correlation Coefficient):** Provides a balanced evaluation across all classes (Table 3).

4.3   Quantitative Results

Table 3. Performance comparison on the test set. Dashes (—) indicate metrics not reported in the original baseline papers.

Model	F1	Precision	Recall	ROC-AUC	MCC
CatBoost	0.710	0.690	—	0.880	0.52
ChurnViT [18]	0.670	0.590	0.760	0.820	0.47
CNN-Only	0.702	0.754	0.658	0.881	0.50
CNN + MLP	0.778	0.816	0.743	0.912	0.57
Ours (CNN+LSTM)	**0.847**	**0.884**	**0.813**	**0.981**	**0.71**

Our method significantly outperforms all baselines. Compared to ChurnViT, we observe a +17.7 point gain in F1 score, +29.4 in precision, and +16.1 in ROC-AUC. These improvements result from learning behavioral transitions across time instead of relying on a static behavioral snapshot.

Figures 3 and 5 further validate the robustness of our model. The static matrix confirms balanced classification with minimal error, while the temporal plot shows that performance stabilizes within the first few epochs. The low variance in false predictions over time indicates effective generalization, even under class imbalance. These trends reinforce the model's reliability and explain its strong aggregate metrics across F1, precision, and ROC-AUC.

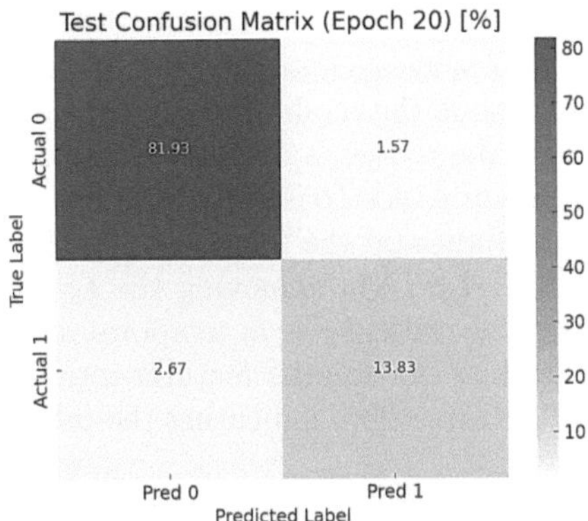

Fig. 3. Epoch 20's confusion matrix shows 81.93% true negatives and 13.83% true positives, with 1.57% false positives and 2.67% false negatives, reflecting strong precision and recall.

Fig. 4. UMAP of sequence embeddings. Blue: retained users; red: churners. Overlap highlights behavioral complexity and supports temporal over static modeling. (Color figure online)

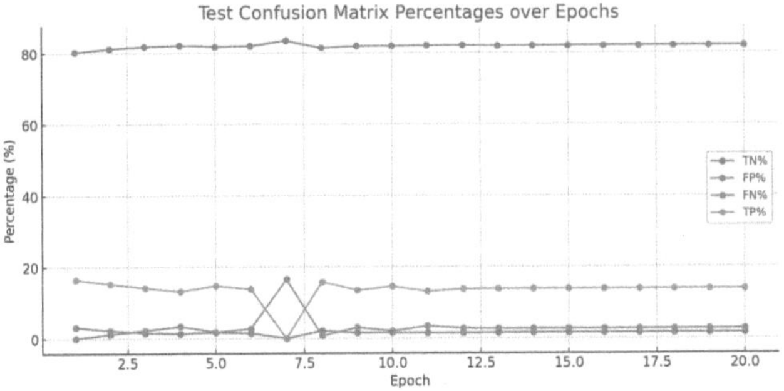

Fig. 5. Temporal evolution of confusion matrix components over 20 training epochs: TN% stays above 80%, TP% fluctuates early then stabilizes at 13–14%. FP% and FN% converge below 3%, highlighting robust convergence and learning stability.

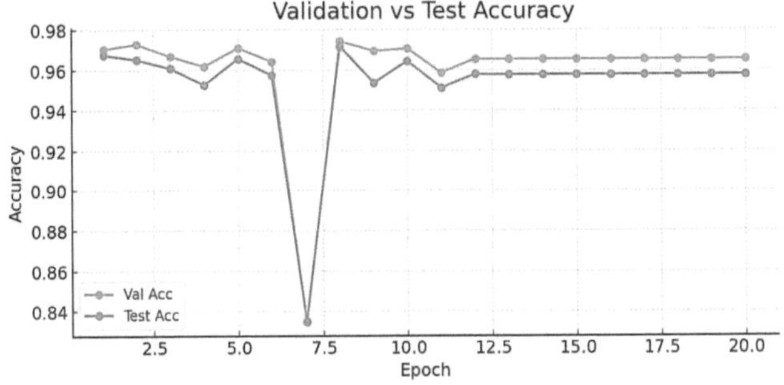

Fig. 6. Validation and test accuracy across epochs: curves stay closely aligned, with only a brief dip at epoch 7, and converge near 96%, demonstrating strong generalization, effective early stopping, and CNN+LSTM robustness.

As shown in Fig. 6, the model maintains high and stable accuracy across both validation and test sets. The brief dip at epoch 7 suggests a momentary instability, potentially due to noise or outlier batches, but the model rapidly recovers. The convergence of both curves confirms that the model is not overfitting and validates the choice of early stopping on validation AUC. To isolate the contribution of each component, we conduct ablation studies on the temporal modeling and image encoding: **CNN+MLP vs. CNN+LSTM:** Removing the LSTM results in a 6.9-point drop in AUC, confirming the critical role of temporal modeling. **Raw features vs. Radar images:** Feeding raw tabular features into the LSTM (bypassing radar encoding) reduces AUC to 0.901, indicating the added value of visual inductive bias.

Discussion: The key advantage of our approach lies in preserving temporal continuity. While ViT models interpret static summaries of user behavior, our model learns the unfolding process of disengagement. The use of pretrained CNN backbones ensures effective spatial feature extraction, while the radar chart encoding introduces useful priors absent in raw tabular data.

To further understand the structure of the learned representations, we visualize the LSTM-encoded sequences using UMAP (Fig. 4). The embedding shows that churners (in red) are distributed across the manifold without forming clearly separable clusters. This reinforces the observation that churn behavior is not linearly distinguishable and exhibits significant overlap with retained users. Consequently, the model's success relies not on static feature separability but on its ability to capture nuanced temporal dynamics across sequences.

- **Generalizability and Robustness:** Our modular design supports deployment across diverse geographic and operational contexts. Prior studies have emphasized cross-regional validation as crucial for robust churn modeling [31,88]. Future work includes expanding evaluation to international datasets to substantiate generalization performance.
- **Limitations:** While effective, our method depends on consistent daily data collection, which may limit applicability in platforms with sparse or irregular activity logs.
- **Broader Impact:** This work contributes to workforce sustainability in the gig economy. Early identification of at-risk couriers enables targeted interventions that improve retention, reduce income volatility, and promote operational fairness [23,74]. Sustained courier engagement also boosts platform reputation and logistical efficiency.

5   Conclusion

We proposed a temporally-aware vision framework for churn prediction using radar chart sequences. Combining CNN-based spatial encoding with LSTM-driven temporal modeling, our method surpasses traditional ML and ViT baselines in accuracy, F1, and AUC, offering scalability. Capturing behavioral dynamics via temporal visual sequences ensures robust churn prediction for gig economy platforms. Future work will explore hybrid multimodal representations (e.g., combining geolocation and radar sequences).

References

1. Ahmed, M.P., et al.: A comparative study of machine learning models for predicting customer churn in retail banking: insights from logistic regression, random forest, GBM, and SVM. J. Comput. Sci. Technol. Stud. **6**(4), 92–101 (2024)
2. Ahn, D., Lee, D., Hosanagar, K.: Modeling lengthy behavioral log data for customer churn management: a representation learning approach (2021). Available at SSRN 3969455
3. Al Salmi, A.Z., Khalifa, R.Z.: Analyzing the advertising language of talabat & hunger station food delivery apps using grice maxims of cooperative principles. Int. J. Res. Human. Soc. Stud. **10**(1), 31–42 (2023)
4. Aleksandrova, Y.: Application of machine learning for churn prediction based on transactional data (RFM analysis). In: 18 International Multidisciplinary Scientific Geoconference SGEM 2018: Conference Proceedings, vol. 18, pp. 125–132 (2018)
5. Al_Janabi, S., Razaq, F.: Intelligent big data analysis to design smart predictor for customer churn in telecommunication industry. In: Farhaoui, Y., Moussaid, L. (eds.) ICBDSDE 2018. SBD, vol. 53, pp. 246–272. Springer, Cham (2019). https://doi.org/10.1007/978-3-030-12048-1_26
6. Amsal, A.A., Albar, B.B., Yeni, Y.H.: Systematic literature review on customer switching behaviour from marketing and data science perspectives. AMAR (Andalas Manag. Rev.) **5**(2), 95–123 (2021)
7. Andersson, V.: Developing a systematic framework for churn mitigation in a b2b saas environment (2024)
8. Benner, C., Mason, S., Carré, F., Tilly, C.: Delivering insecurity: E-commerce and the future of work in food retail (2020)
9. Bernat, J., Koning, A., Fok, D.: Modelling customer lifetime value in a continuous, non-contractual time setting. Netherlands (2019)
10. Blattberg, R.C., Kim, B.D., Neslin, S.A.: Database marketing: analyzing and managing customers (2008)
11. Blattberg, R.C., Malthouse, E.C., Neslin, S.A.: Customer lifetime value: empirical generalizations and some conceptual questions. J. Interact. Mark. **23**(2), 157–168 (2009)
12. Bogaert, M., Delaere, L.: Ensemble methods in customer churn prediction: a comparative analysis of the state-of-the-art. Mathematics **11**(5), 1137 (2023)
13. Buckinx, W., Van den Poel, D.: Customer base analysis: partial defection of behaviourally loyal clients in a non-contractual FMCG retail setting. Eur. J. Oper. Res. **164**(1), 252–268 (2005)
14. Burez, J., Van den Poel, D.: Handling class imbalance in customer churn prediction. Expert Syst. Appl. **36**(3), 4626–4636 (2009)
15. Chang, V., Hall, K., Xu, Q.A., Amao, F.O., Ganatra, M.A., Benson, V.: Prediction of customer churn behavior in the telecommunication industry using machine learning models. Algorithms **17**(6), 231 (2024)
16. Chen, K., Hu, Y.H., Hsieh, Y.C.: Predicting customer churn from valuable b2b customers in the logistics industry: a case study. IseB **13**, 475–494 (2015)

17. Cheng, Z., et al.: Videollama 2: advancing spatial-temporal modeling and audio understanding in video-llms. arXiv preprint arXiv:2406.07476 (2024)
18. Coolwijk, S., Ziabari, S.S.M., Angileri, F.: Vision transformer approach to customer churn prediction radar chart image classification for non-subscription based e-commerce. In: International Conference on Information Integration and Web Intelligence, pp. 75–80. Springer (2025)
19. Dai, X., Wang, P.: Cost optimization in retention strategies. Inf. Process. Manage. (2021)
20. De, S., Prabu, P.: Predicting customer churn: a systematic literature review. J. Discrete Math. Sci. Cryptogr. **25**(7), 1965–1985 (2022)
21. Ding, L., Zhang, J., Guo, H., Zhang, K., Liu, B., Bruzzone, L.: Joint spatio-temporal modeling for semantic change detection in remote sensing images. IEEE Trans. Geosci. Remote Sens. (2024)
22. Donahue, J., et al.: Long-term recurrent convolutional networks for visual recognition and description. In: Proceedings of the IEEE Conference on Computer Vision and Pattern Recognition, pp. 2625–2634 (2015)
23. Dong, F., Lim, Y.: Worker satisfaction and retention in platform delivery. J. Labor Econ. (2023)
24. Donohue, K., Özer, Ö., Zheng, Y.: Behavioral operations: past, present, and future. Manuf. Serv. Oper. Manage. **22**(1), 191–202 (2020)
25. Dosovitskiy, A., Beyer, L., Kolesnikov, A., Weissenborn, D., Zhai, X.: Thomas unterthiner mostafa dehghani matthias minderer georg heigold sylvain gelly jakob uszkoreit and neil houlsby. an image isworth 16×16 words: transformers for image recognition atscale. In: International Conference on Learning Representations (2021)
26. Dosovitskiy, A., et al.: An image is worth 16x16 words: transformers for image recognition at scale. arXiv preprint arXiv:2010.11929 (2020)
27. East, R., Lomax, W., Narain, R.: Customer tenure, recommendation and switching. J. Consum. Satisfaction, Dissatisfaction Complaining Behav. **14**, 46–54 (2001)
28. Fader, P.S., Hardie, B.G., Shang, J.: Customer-base analysis in a discrete-time noncontractual setting. Mark. Sci. **29**(6), 1086–1108 (2010)
29. Fu, Z., et al.: Sagn: semantic adaptive graph network for skeleton-based human action recognition. In: Proceedings of the 29th ACM International Conference on Multimedia, pp. 197–205 (2021). https://doi.org/10.1145/3460426.3463633
30. Ganapathy, V.: Decoding customer engagement: a data-driven analysis of food delivery apps in Bangalore. In: Practical Strategies and Case Studies for Online Marketing 6.0, pp. 251–298. IGI Global Scientific Publishing (2025)
31. Gao, L., Tan, Z.: Generalizing churn predictors across regional delivery markets. Data Min. Knowl. Discov. (2023)
32. Gattermann-Itschert, T., Thonemann, U.W.: Proactive customer retention management in a non-contractual b2b setting based on churn prediction with random forests. Ind. Mark. Manage. **107**, 134–147 (2022)
33. Granov, A.: Customer loyalty, return and churn prediction through machine learning methods: for a Swedish fashion and e-commerce company (2021)
34. Guo, S., et al.: Seeking in ride-on-demand service: a reinforcement learning model with dynamic price prediction. IEEE Internet Things J. (2024)
35. Gupta, S.: Research note–channel structure with knowledge spillovers. Mark. Sci. **27**(2), 247–261 (2008)
36. Hadden, J., Tiwari, A., Roy, R., Ruta, D.: Computer assisted customer churn management: state-of-the-art and future trends. Comput. Oper. Res. **34**(10), 2902–2917 (2007)

37. Hall, J.V., Krueger, A.B.: An analysis of the labor market for uber's driver-partners in the united states. ILR Rev. **71**(3), 705–732 (2018)
38. Heing, B.: The Gig Economy. Greenhaven Publishing LLC (2020)
39. Hochreiter, S., Schmidhuber, J.: Long short-term memory. Neural Comput. **9**(8), 1735–1780 (1997)
40. Huang, B., Kechadi, M.T., Buckley, B.: Customer churn prediction in telecommunications. Expert Syst. Appl. **39**(1), 1414–1425 (2012)
41. Idris, A., Rizwan, M., Khan, A.: Churn prediction in telecom using random forest and PSO based data balancing in combination with various feature selection strategies. Comput. Electr. Eng. **38**(6), 1808–1819 (2012)
42. Imani, M.: Customer churn prediction in telecommunication industry: A (2024)
43. Jastrzebska, A.: Lagged encoding for image-based time series classification using convolutional neural networks. Stat. Anal. Data MinâĂŕ: ASA Data Sci. J. **13**(3), 245–260 (2020)
44. Katyayan, S.S., Singh, S.: Optimizing consumer retention strategies through data-driven insights in digital marketplaces. Int. J. Res. All Subj. Multi Lang. **13**(1), 153 (2025)
45. Khattak, A., Mehak, Z., Ahmad, H., Asghar, M.U., Asghar, M.Z., Khan, A.: Customer churn prediction using composite deep learning technique. Sci. Rep. **13**(1), 17294 (2023)
46. Khodabandehlou, S., Zivari Rahman, M.: Comparison of supervised machine learning techniques for customer churn prediction based on analysis of customer behavior. J. Syst. Inf. Technol. **19**(1/2), 65–93 (2017)
47. Kougioumtzidis, G., Poulkov, V.K., Lazaridis, P.I., Zaharis, Z.D.: Mobile network traffic prediction using temporal fusion transformer. IEEE Trans. Artif. Intell. (2025)
48. Krishnan, K.P., Kombaiya, A.K.: Customer churn prediction in telecom industry using DWHBI approaches and r programming. Turk. Online J. Qual. Inq. **12**(3) (2021)
49. Li, Z., Li, S., Yan, X.: Time series as images: vision transformer for irregularly sampled time series. Adv. Neural. Inf. Process. Syst. **36**, 49187–49204 (2023)
50. Liu, S., Wang, Y., Zhao, H.: Hybrid bilstm-cnn for churn prediction. Appl. Intell. (2024)
51. Liu, Y., Hou, J., Zhao, W.: Deep learning and user consumption trends classification and analysis based on shopping behavior. J. Org. End User Comput. (JOEUC) **36**(1), 1–23 (2024)
52. Lloyd, S.: Least squares quantization in PCM. IEEE Trans. Inf. Theory **28**(2), 129–137 (1982)
53. Lu, M., Shen, Z.J.M.: A review of robust operations management under model uncertainty. Prod. Oper. Manag. **30**(6), 1927–1943 (2021)
54. Matuszelański, K., Kopczewska, K.: Customer churn in retail e-commerce business: Spatial and machine learning approach. J. Theor. Appl. Electron. Commer. Res. **17**(1), 165–198 (2022)
55. Mena, G., Coussement, K., De Bock, K.W., De Caigny, A., Lessmann, S.: Exploiting time-varying RFM measures for customer churn prediction with deep neural networks. Ann. Oper. Res. **339**(1), 765–787 (2024)
56. Micikevicius, P., et al.: Mixed precision training. arXiv preprint arXiv:1710.03740 (2017)
57. Mozer, F., Bale, S., Phan, T.: Evidence of diffusion regions at a subsolar magnetopause crossing. Phys. Rev. Lett. **89**(1), 015002 (2002)

58. Mukhopadhyay, B.R., Chatwin, C.: Your driver is didi and minutes away from your pick-up point': understanding employee motivation in the gig economy of china. Int. J. Dev. Emerg. Econ. **8**(1), 1–16 (2020)
59. Muñoz, L.E., et al.: Customer churn detection and marketing retention strategies in the online food delivery business (2022)
60. Murray, A.C.: pillow-simd (2018). https://github.com/uploadcare/pillow-simd
61. Neslin, S.A., et al.: Challenges and opportunities in multichannel customer management. J. Serv. Res. **9**(2), 95–112 (2006)
62. Oblander, E.S., McCarthy, D.: How has COVID-19 impacted customer relationship dynamics at restaurant food delivery businesses. Mark. Sci. Inst. Work. Pap. Ser **23**(2139), 35 (2021)
63. Osbat, C., et al.: Measuring inflation with heterogeneous preferences, taste shifts and product innovation: methodological challenges and evidence from microdata. No. 323, ECB Occasional Paper (2023)
64. Paiva, R.G., Melo, Y.R., Cavalcante, C.A., Tenório, V.A., Do, P.: Developing data-driven o&m policy through sequential pattern mining: a case study. Comput. Ind. Eng. **193**, 110318 (2024)
65. Panimalar, S.A., Krishnakumar, A.: A review of churn prediction models using different machine learning and deep learning approaches in cloud environment. J. Current Sci. Technol. **13**(1), 136–161 (2023)
66. Rabbah, J., Ridouani, M., Hassouni, L.: New approach to telecom churn prediction based on transformers. In: The International Conference on Artificial Intelligence and Computer Vision, pp. 565–574. Springer, Cham (2023)
67. Reichheld, F.F., Sasser, W.E.: Zero defeofions: Quoliiy comes to services. Harv. Bus. Rev. **68**(5), 105–111 (1990)
68. Sacha, D., et al.: Visual interaction with dimensionality reduction: a structured literature analysis. IEEE Trans. Visual Comput. Graph. **23**(1), 241–250 (2016)
69. Sandler, M., Howard, A., Zhu, M., Zhmoginov, A., Chen, L.C.: Mobilenetv2: inverted residuals and linear bottlenecks. In: CVPR (2018)
70. Sepanj, M.H., Ghojogh, B., Fieguth, P.: Self-supervised learning using nonlinear dependence. arXiv preprint arXiv:2501.18875 (2025)
71. Sepanj, M.H., Moradi, S., Azimifar, Z., Fieguth, P.: Uncertainty-aware δ-glmb filtering for multi-target tracking. Big Data Cogn. Comput. **9**(4), 84 (2025)
72. Sharma, A., Patel, N., Gupta, R.: Enhancing predictive customer retention using machine learning algorithms: a comparative study of random forest, xgboost, and neural networks. Eur. Adv. AI J. **11**(8) (2022)
73. Sheil, H., Rana, O., Reilly, R.: Predicting purchasing intent: automatic feature learning using recurrent neural networks. arXiv preprint arXiv:1807.08207 (2018)
74. Silverman, B., Long, T.: The economic sustainability of gig economy platforms. J. Ind. Econ. (2022)
75. Sina Mirabdolbaghi, S.M., Amiri, B.: Model optimization analysis of customer churn prediction using machine learning algorithms with focus on feature reductions. Discret. Dyn. Nat. Soc. **2022**(1), 5134356 (2022)
76. Srivastava, N., Mansimov, E., Salakhudinov, R.: Unsupervised learning of video representations using LSTMs. In: International Conference on Machine Learning, pp. 843–852. PMLR (2015)
77. Sun, G., Kim, Y., Tan, Y., Parker, G.G.: Dinner at your doorstep: service innovation via the gig economy on food delivery platforms. Inf. Syst. Res. **35**(3), 1216–1234 (2024)

78. Sung, C., Higgins, C.Y., Zhang, B., Choe, Y.: Evaluating deep learning in churn prediction for everything-as-a-service in the cloud. In: 2017 International Joint Conference on Neural Networks (IJCNN), pp. 3664–3669. IEEE (2017)

79. Tatsunami, Y., Taki, M.: Sequencer: deep LSTM for image classification. Adv. Neural. Inf. Process. Syst. **35**, 38204–38217 (2022)

80. Torfs, E.: In vitro biological investigation of novel anti-tubercular compound classes and the development of improved research tools. University of Antwerp (2019)

81. Ullah, A., Ahmad, J., Muhammad, K., Sajjad, M., Baik, S.W.: Action recognition in video sequences using deep bi-directional LSTM with CNN features. IEEE Access **6**, 1155–1166 (2017)

82. Vafeiadis, T., Diamantaras, K.I., Sarigiannidis, G., Chatzisavvas, K.C.: A comparison of machine learning techniques for customer churn prediction. Simul. Model. Pract. Theory **55**, 1–9 (2015)

83. Vaswani, A., et al.: Attention is all you need. In: Advances in Neural Information Processing Systems, vol. 30 (2017)

84. Verbraken, T., Verbeke, W., Baesens, B.: A novel profit maximizing metric for measuring classification performance of customer churn prediction models. IEEE Trans. Knowl. Data Eng. **25**(5), 961–973 (2012)

85. Wang, C., Rao, C., Hu, F., Xiao, X., Goh, M.: Risk assessment of customer churn in telco using FCLCNN-LSTM model. Expert Syst. Appl. **248**, 123352 (2024)

86. Wang, L., Webster, S., Rabinovich, E.: Structural estimation of attrition in a last-mile delivery platform: the role of driver heterogeneity, compensation, and experience. Manuf. Serv. Oper. Manag. (2025)

87. Wang, Z., Oates, T.: Imaging time-series to improve classification and imputation. arXiv preprint arXiv:1506.00327 (2015)

88. Wei, X., Zhou, Y.: Cross-platform churn modeling: Challenges and insights. ACM Trans. Knowl. Discov. Data (2020)

89. Xie, G., Shangguan, A., Fei, R., Ji, W., Ma, W., Hei, X.: Motion trajectory prediction based on a CNN-LSTM sequential model. SCIENCE CHINA Inf. Sci. **63**, 1–21 (2020)

90. Yang, L., Niu, X., Wu, J.: Rf-lighgbm: a probabilistic ensemble way to predict customer repurchase behaviour in community e-commerce. arXiv preprint arXiv:2109.00724 (2021)

91. Yang, W., Chen, X., Hu, B.: CNN-LSTM hybrid for telecom churn. IEEE Access (2022)

92. Yang, X., Molchanov, P., Kautz, J.: Making convolutional networks recurrent for visual sequence learning. In: Proceedings of the IEEE Conference on Computer Vision and Pattern Recognition, pp. 6469–6478 (2018)

93. Yue-Hei Ng, J., Hausknecht, M., Vijayanarasimhan, S., Vinyals, O., Monga, R., Toderici, G.: Beyond short snippets: Deep networks for video classification. In: Proceedings of the IEEE Conference on Computer Vision and Pattern Recognition, pp. 4694–4702 (2015)

94. Zahin, M.A.: Multi-Headed Self-Attention Mechanism-Based Transformer Model for Predicting Bus Travel Times Across Multiple Bus Routes Using Heterogeneous Datasets. Master's thesis, University of Missouri-Columbia (2023)

95. Zhang, D., Yin, J., Zhu, X., Zhang, C.: Network representation learning: a survey. IEEE Trans. Big Data **6**(1), 3–28 (2018)

96. Zhang, L., Feng, D., Li, H.: Comparative study of deep models in customer attrition. Expert Syst. Appl. (2023)

97. Zhang, T., Liu, Y.: Explainable AI in churn prediction using shap. AI Open (2022)

98. Zhang, X., Guo, F., Chen, T., Pan, L., Beliakov, G., Wu, J.: A brief survey of machine learning and deep learning techniques for e-commerce research. J. Theor. Appl. Electron. Commer. Res. **18**(4), 2188–2216 (2023)
99. Zhang, Y., Bradlow, E.T., Small, D.S.: Predicting customer value using clumpiness: From RFM to RFMC. Mark. Sci. **34**(2), 195–208 (2015)

Author Index